1949 Lithium salts first used for bipolar disorder. *p. 221*

1951 Chlorpromazine, first antipsychotic drug, tested. *p. 372*

1951 Carl Rogers publishes *Client-Centered Therapy*. *p. 52*

1952 First edition of DSM published by the American Psychiatric Association. *p. 83*

1952 Sex-change operation performed on Christine Jorgensen. *p. 345*

1953 Samaritans, first suicide prevention center, founded in England. *p. 247*

1955 The Los Angeles Suicide Prevention Center founded. *p. 247*

1956 Family systems theory and therapy launched. *p. 56*

1958 Joseph Wolpe develops desensitization. *p. 46*

1961 Thomas Szasz publishes *The Myth of Mental Illness*. *p. 4*

1962 Albert Ellis proposes rational-emotive therapy. *pp. 48, 102*

1963 The Community Mental Health Act helps trigger deinstitutionalization in the United States. *p. 376*

1963 Antianxiety drug Valium introduced in the United States. *p. 105*

1964 U.S. Surgeon General warns that smoking can be dangerous to human health. *p. 290*

1965 Norepinephrine and serotonin theories of depression proposed. *p. 198*

1967 Aaron Beck publishes cognitive theory and therapy for depression. *pp. 209, 211*

1967 Methadone maintenance treatment begins. *p. 308*

1967 Holmes and Rahe develop Social Adjustment Rating Scale to measure life stress. *p. 152*

1969 Elisabeth Kübler Ross publishes *On Death and Dying*. *p. 451*

1970 Masters and Johnson publish *Human Sexual Inadequacy* and launch sex therapy. *p. 328*

1972 CAT scan introduced. *p. 77*

1973 DSM stops listing homosexuality as a mental disorder. *p. 374*

1973 David Rosenhan conducts study *On Being Sane in Insane Places*. *pp. 57, 367*

1975 Endorphins — natural opioids — discovered in human brain. *pp. 173, 287*

1975 U.S. Supreme Court declares that patients in institutions have right to adequate treatment. *p. 483*

1981 MRI first used as diagnostic tool. *p. 77*

1981 Researchers discover that Ritalin helps persons with ADHD. *p. 431*

1982 John Hinckley found not guilty by reason of insanity of the attempted murder of President Reagan. *p. 473*

1987 Antidepressant Prozac approved in the United States. *p.200*

1988 American Psychological Society founded. *p. 18*

1990 Dr. Jack Kevorkian performs his first assisted suicide. *p. 246*

1990 FDA approves first atypical antipsychotic drug, *clozapine*. *p. 374*

1994 DSM-IV published. *p. 83*

1995 APA task force begins search to identify empirically supported (evidence-based) treatments. *p. 87*

1998 Viagra goes on sale in the United States. *p. 336*

1999 Killing rampage at Columbine High School stirs public concern about dangerousness in children. *p. 483*

2000 DSM changes criteria for pedophilia, exhibitionism, voyeurism, frotteurism, and sexual sadism: behavior alone also warrants diagnosis. *p. 341*

2000 Scientists finish mapping (i.e., sequencing) the human genome — spelling out the chemical "letters" that make up human DNA. *p. 35*

2001 Around 1,600 mental health workers mobilize to help 57,000 victims in wake of 9/11 terrorist attacks. *p. 147*

2002 New Mexico grants prescription privileges to specially trained psychologists. *p. 486*

2003 First case of mad cow disease uncovered in the United States, raising concerns that some U.S. residents may contract the disease *vCJD*. *p. 463*

Fundamentals of
ABNORMAL
PSYCHOLOGY

Fundamentals of ABNORMAL PSYCHOLOGY

Fourth Edition

RONALD J. COMER

Princeton University

Worth Publishers

New York

Fundamentals of Abnormal Psychology, Fourth Edition

Publisher: Catherine Woods
Sponsoring Editor: Marge Byers
Associate Managing Editor: Tracey Kuehn
New Media and Supplements Editor: Danielle Pucci
Project Editor: Bradley Umbaugh
Assistant Editor: Danielle Storm
Marketing Manager: Katherine Nurre
Art Director and Text/Cover Designer: Babs Reingold
Cover Illustration: Wiktor Sadowski
Layout Design: Paul Lacy
Art Research and Photo Editor: Vikii Wong
Production Manager: Sarah Segal
Composition: Compset, Inc.
Manufacturing: RR Donnelley & Sons Company

We gratefully acknowledge the following for permission to reprint the artwork used in chapter opening pages and their full image in the table of contents: p. 0, A Beautiful Relationship (Les Belles Relations), 1967, René Magritte, Scheidweiler Collection, Brussels, Belgium/ Lauros-Giraudon Bridgeman Art Library, © 2003 C. Herscovici, Brussels/Artists Rights Society (ARS), New York; p. 30, Models of Psychology, 1999, Mieczyslaw Gôrowski; p. 66, Ecriteau, 1993, Ed Paschke, © Ed Paschke/SuperStock; p. 94, Anxiety, 2001, Jordan Islip; p. 132, Terror, 1978, Juan Genoves, Private Collection/Index/Bridgeman Art Library; p. 162, 1997, Ferruccio Sardella; p. 192, Anna Washington Derry (Detail), 1927, Laura Wheeler Waring, National Museum of American Art, Washington, DC/Art Resource; p. 226, 1993, Selcuk Demirel; p. 252, 2001, Marlena Zubcr; p. 278, 2001, Marlena Zuber; p. 314, Summer in the City, 1950, Edward Hopper, Private Collection/James Goodman Gallery/New York, USA/Bridgeman Art Library: p. 350, La Maisan de Verre, 1939, René Magritte, Ex-Edward James Foundation, Sussex, UK/Bridgeman Art Library, © 2003 C. Hcrscovici, Brussels/Artists Rights Society (ARS), New York; p. 384, 2001, Gianpaolo l'agni; p. 418, l.a Gallinu Ciega, Antonio Berni, © Elena Berni and José Antonio Berni, Fortabat Collection/Christie's Images; p. 448, 1998, Gerard DuBois; p. 470, Looking Back, 1984, Evelyn Williams, Private Collection/Bridgeman Art Library.

Credits for timeline photos, inside front cover (by date): Stone Age, John W. Verano; 1893, Sigmund Freud Copyrights/Everett Collection; 1901, W. H. Freeman & Company; 1963, Jcrry Cook/Photo Researchers; 1967, Leif Skoogfors/Woodfin Camp & Associates; 1987, © William Whitehurst/CORBIS; 2001, AP Photo/Ernesto Mora.

Library of Congress Cataloging-in-Publication Control Number: 2004101045
ISBN 0-7167-8625-7
EAN 9 780716 786252

Printed in the United States of America

Fourth printing

Worth Publishers
41 Madison Avenue
New York, NY 10010
(212) 576-9400

www.worthpublishers.com
Faculty Services: (800) 446-8923
Technical Support: (800) 936-6899

To Marge Byers
Wonderful sponsoring editor
and valued friend

about the author

Ronald J. Comer has been a professor in Princeton University's Department of Psychology for the past 30 years and has served as Director of Clinical Psychology Studies for most of that time. He is also currently the director of the department's undergraduate program.

Professor Comer has received the President's Award for Distinguished Teaching at the university. His course "Abnormal Psychology" is one of the university's most popular, and he has offered it almost every year since his arrival at Princeton.

He is also a practicing clinical psychologist and serves as a consultant to the Eden Institute for Persons with Autism and to hospitals and family practice residency programs throughout New Jersey. Additionally, he holds an adjunct position as Clinical Associate Professor of Family Medicine at the UMDNJ-Robert Wood Johnson Medical School.

In addition to writing *Fundamentals of Abnormal Psychology*, Professor Comer is the author of the textbook *Abnormal Psychology*, now in its fifth edition, and the co-author of *Case Studies in Abnormal Psychology*. He has also published a number of journal articles in clinical psychology, social psychology, and family medicine.

Professor Comer completed his undergraduate studies at the University of Pennsylvania and his graduate work at Clark University. He currently lives in Lawrenceville, New Jersey, with his wife, Marlene. From there, he can keep an eye on his New York–residing son, Greg, and his Philadelphia-residing son, Jon, and the Philadelphia sports teams with whom he grew up.

Contents in Brief

Abnormal Psychology in Science and Clinical Practice

Problems of Anxiety and Mood

Problems of the Mind and Body

Problems of the Psychosis and Cognitive Function

Life-Span Problems

Conclusion

Contents

CHAPTER   ③

Clinical Assessment, Diagnosis, and Treatment   67

CHAPTER   ④

Anxiety Disorders   95

CHAPTER ⑩

Substance-Related Disorders   279

CHAPTER ⑪

Sexual Disorders and Gender Identity Disorder   315

This is the fourth edition of my textbook *Fundamentals of Abnormal Psychology*. The completion of this book actually marks my ninth abnormal psychology textbook edition, counting both *Fundamentals* and my larger textbook, *Abnormal Psychology*, currently in its fifth edition. I am gratified by the success of these books and delighted that students continue to find them enlightening and enjoyable. But I am also humbled by this success and aware of the responsibilities that accompany it.

One of the key responsibilities and challenges faced by textbook authors as they move from edition to edition is that of "quality control." How can an author maintain and even enhance the quality of an abnormal psychology textbook over numerous editions? The answer to this question differs from author to author. For me, the answer entails five rules

1. Approach each edition with the same basic goals as the first edition— that is, to excite and capture students; to bring the field to life; to convey my passion for the field; and to demonstrate that behavior, including abnormal behavior, pervades our lives and our world.

2. Keep each edition current and fresh, being sure to include recent research and developments and repeatedly drawing upon examples from the world around us.

3. Incorporate new pedagogical techniques that will help students enjoy and process the material.

4. Keep listening to the feedback of my colleagues in this enterprise—the students and professors who have used my textbooks over the past 15 years.

5. Don't make changes just for the sake of change: retain those techniques that have proved effective previously.

Keeping these rules in mind, I believe I have produced a new edition of *Fundamentals of Abnormal Psychology* that will continue to excite readers and open the world of abnormal psychology to them. Let me describe what I believe is special about this fourth edition, although because I fear that such descriptions always come perilously close to self-aggrandizement, I offer my apologies at the top.

Changes and Features New to This Edition

The study of abnormal psychology continues to grow steadily. Similarly, the field of undergraduate education is in constant motion, with new pedagogical techniques and insights emerging each day. Such developments have spurred me to include a variety of important changes and new features in the current edition.

THOROUGH UPDATE I have presented recent theories, research, and events— including more than 1,000 new references from the years 2002–2004, as well as many new tables, illustrations, and photos.

NUMEROUS NEW BOXES A variety of new boxes have been added, covering topics such as the psychological impact of 9/11, postpartum psychosis, "Ecstasy," anxiety and sports performance, and direct-to-consumer medication advertising.

A NEW CHAPTER, "STRESS DISORDERS," combines posttraumatic stress disorder and psychophysiological (including immune system) disorders. The chapter examines the impact of stress on both psychological and physical dysfunction. It reflects the post–9/11 concern with stress and its impact, and the interest in prevention as well as treatment of stress disorders.

REORGANIZED CHAPTERS reflect current emphases in the field and offer a more straightforward table of contents. Changes include adding a chapter on stress disorder (5); combining the coverage of disorders of aging with the coverage of disorders of memory and cognition into one chapter (15); offering a single chapter on anxiety disorders (4); including a chapter on dissociative and somatoform disorders (6); and expanding the coverage of disorders emerging in childhood (14). Note that the total number of chapters remains at sixteen, and the book's length does not increase.

CRITICAL THINKING QUESTIONS are now assembled at the end of each chapter in a section called *Critical Thoughts*, helping students to consider, analyze, and apply the material they've just read.

Continuing Strengths

In this edition of *Fundamentals of Abnormal Psychology*, I have also been careful to retain the goals, themes, material, and techniques that have worked successfully and been embraced enthusiastically by past readers.

MODERATE IN LENGTH, SOLID IN CONTENT Even though *Fundamentals of Abnormal Psychology* is of moderate length, it offers probing coverage of its broad subject. It expands and challenges students' thinking rather than short-changing or underestimating their intellectual capacity.

BREADTH AND BALANCE The field's many theories, studies, disorders, and treatments are presented accurately, without bias toward any single approach. All major models—psychological, biological, and sociocultural—receive objective and up-to-date coverage.

INNOVATIVE DESIGN In an outstanding lecture, a variety of stimulating elements merge with the basic presentation to captivate the audience—anecdotes, interesting side points, provocative questions, slides, video, and the like. Shouldn't textbook discussions offer the same exciting blend? This edition of *Fundamentals of Abnormal Psychology* continues to offer a unique and accessible design—a single text column adjoined by a large margin space—that allows precise intersections between text discussions and carefully placed side points, such as fun facts, current events, historical notes, interesting trends, lists, and quotes.

INTEGRATION OF MODELS Discussions throughout the text, and particularly the *Crossroads* discussions, help students better understand where and how the various models work together, along with clarifying how the models differ.

HUMANITY The subject of abnormal psychology is people—very often people in great pain. I have therefore tried to write always with humanity and to impart this awareness to students. The book also speaks with a single voice, in clear and straightforward language—the main advantage of a single-author book.

INTEGRATED COVERAGE OF TREATMENT Discussions of treatment are presented throughout the book. In addition to a complete overview of treatment in the opening chapters, each of the pathology chapters includes a full discussion of relevant treatment approaches.

RICH CASE MATERIAL I integrate numerous clinical examples to bring theoretical and clinical issues to life.

CROSS-CULTURAL AND GENDER COVERAGE Issues raised by ethnic and gender differences, as well as related problems of bias, are given constant consideration, and, in fact, the sociocultural model is presented on an equal footing with the other models of psychological abnormality.

TOPICS OF SPECIAL INTEREST I devote full chapters to important subjects that are of special interest to college-age readers, such as eating disorders and suicide, and I also cover controversial issues that are currently being spotlighted by the news media, including the impact of managed care, direct-to-consumer advertising, the rise in Ritalin use, treatment over the Internet, and the right to commit suicide.

DSM-IV CHECKLISTS The discussion of each disorder is accompanied by a detailed checklist of the DSM-IV criteria used to diagnose the disorder.

MARGIN GLOSSARY Hundreds of key words are defined in the margins of pages on which the words appear. In addition, a traditional glossary is available at the back of the book.

"SUMMING UP" SECTIONS These sections appear at critical points throughout each chapter, providing readers with short periodic reviews of the text material.

"CROSSROADS" The concluding section in each chapter, *Crossroads*, brings together the principles and findings of the various models of abnormality. Each *Crossroads* section asks whether competing models can work together in a more integrated approach and also summarizes where the field now stands and where it may be going.

CHAPTER-ENDING "KEY TERMS" AND "QUICK QUIZ" SECTIONS These sections, keyed to appropriate pages in the chapter for easy reference, allow students to review and test their knowledge of chapter materials.

"CYBERSTUDY" Each chapter ends with a *CyberStudy* section—a guide for integrating the chapter material with videos and other features found on the Student CD-ROM.

STIMULATING ILLUSTRATIONS Chapters illustrate concepts, disorders, treatments, and applications with stunning photographs, diagrams, and graphs. All graphs and tables, many new to this edition, reflect the most up-to-date data available.

Supplements

The very enthusiastic response to the supplements accompanying previous editions has been gratifying. This edition is able to retain those supplements, revising and enhancing them, and to add a number of exciting new ones.

FOR PROFESSORS

REVISED AND ENHANCED: VIDEO SEGMENTS FOR ABNORMAL PSYCHOLOGY with Faculty Guide included, produced and edited by Ronald J. Comer. I have completely revised and enhanced this videotape series, which includes a full 100 clips that depict disorders, show historical footage, and illustrate clinical topics, pathologies, treatments, experiments, and dilemmas. The video series adds hours of new clips, while at the same time retaining many of the best clips from the past video series. Videos are available on DVD, VHS, or CD-ROM (in MPEG format). I have also written an accompanying guide that fully describes and discusses each video clip, so that professors can make informed decisions about the use of the clips in lectures.

POWERPOINT® SLIDES Available at www.worthpublishers.com/comer These PowerPoint® slides can be used directly or customized to fit a professor's needs. There are two pre-built, customizable slide sets for each chapter of the book—one featuring chapter text, the other featuring all chapter figures, tables and illustrations.

NEW ENHANCED POWERPOINT® presentation slides by Karen Clay Rhines, Seton Hall University, available at www.worthpublishers.com/comer. These customized slides focus on key text terms and themes, and feature tables, graphs, and illustrations from the book.

IMAGE AND LECTURE GALLERY Available at www.worthpublishers.com/ILG The Image and Lecture Gallery is a convenient way to access electronic versions of lecture materials. Registered users can browse, search, and download illustrations from Worth titles plus pre-built PowerPoint® presentation files for specific chapters, containing all chapter illustrations or all chapter section headings in text form. Users can also create personal folders on a personalized home page for easy organization of the materials.

TRANSPARENCIES Fifty full-color diagrams and graphs from the text are available for use in lectures. Additionally, there are many transparency masters of text tables and DSM-IV criteria listings available in the Instructor's Manual.

INSTRUCTOR'S RESOURCE MANUAL by Karen Clay Rhines, Seton Hall University. This comprehensive guide ties together the ancillary package for professors and teaching assistants. The *Manual* includes detailed chapter outlines, lists of principal learning objectives, and ideas for lectures and for launching class discussions. It also offers strategies for using the accompanying media, including the CD-ROM, the companion Web site, and transparencies, as well as detailing precise DSM-IV criteria for each of the disorders discussed in the text. In addition, Ann Brandt-Williams, Glendale Community College, has created crossword puzzles to accompany each text chapter—an inventive way to help students process text material.

ASSESSMENT TOOLS

PRINTED TEST BANK by Debra B. Hull, Wheeling Jesuit University, and John H. Hull, Bethany College. This comprehensive test bank offers more than 2,000 multiple-choice, fill-in-the-blank, and essay questions. Each question is graded according to difficulty, identified as factual or applied, and keyed to the page in the text where the source information appears.

DIPLOMA COMPUTERIZED TEST BANK Windows and Macintosh Dual-Platform CD-ROM. This CD-ROM guides professors step by step through the process of creating a test and allows them to add an unlimited number of questions, edit or scramble questions, format a test, and include pictures, equations, and multimedia links. The accompanying grade-book enables them to record students' grades throughout the course and includes the capacity to sort student records and view detailed analyses of test items, curve tests, generate reports, add weights to grades, and more. The CD-ROM provides the access point for Diploma Online Testing, as well as Blackboard- and WebCT-formatted versions of the *Test Bank* for *Fundamentals of Abnormal Psychology, Fourth Edition.*

ONLINE TESTING, powered by Diploma, at www.brownstone.net With Diploma, professors can create and administer secure exams over a network and over the Internet, with questions that incorporate multimedia and interactive exercises. The program also allows them to restrict tests to specific computers or time blocks and includes a suite of grade-book and result-analysis features.

ONLINE QUIZZING, POWERED BY QUESTIONMARK Access via the companion Web site at www.worthpublishers.com/comer Professors can easily and securely quiz students online using prewritten multiple-choice questions for each chapter. Students receive instant feedback and can take the quizzes multiple times. Professors can view results by quiz, student, or question, or can get weekly results via e-mail.

COURSE MANAGEMENT AIDS: ONLINE COURSE MATERIALS *[WebCT and Blackboard]* As a service for adopters using WebCT or Blackboard course management systems, we are able to provide the various resources for this textbook in the appropriate format for their system. Course outlines, pre-built quizzes, links, activities, and a whole array of materials are included, eliminating hours of work.

FOR STUDENTS

REVISED AND ENHANCED: *FUNDAMENTALS OF ABNORMAL PSYCHOLOGY* CD-ROM produced and edited by Ronald J. Comer. Upon request, this CD-ROM is free when packaged with the text. Tied directly to the CyberStudy sections in the text, this CD-ROM offers numerous intriguing videos running three to five minutes each, followed by thought-provoking questions. The CD-ROM also includes a series of practical, research, and decision-making exercises. Additionally, the CD-ROM contains multiple-choice practice test questions with built-in instructional feedback for every option.

STUDENT WORKBOOK by Carmen Wilson VanVoorhis, University of Wisconsin-La Crosse, and Katherine Nicolai, Rockhurst University. This student guide actively involves students in the text material, using a variety of engaging exercises. Each chapter includes a variety of practice tests and exercises, as well as key concepts, guided study questions, and section reviews.

CASE STUDIES IN ABNORMAL PSYCHOLOGY by Ethan E. Gorenstein, Behavioral Medicine Program, Columbia-Presbyterian Hospital, and Ronald J. Comer, *2001, Paper, 301 pages*. This casebook provides 20 case histories, each going beyond DSM-IV diagnoses to describe the individual's history and symptoms, a theoretical discussion of treatment, a specific treatment plan, and the actual treatment conducted. The casebook also provides 3 cases without diagnoses or treatment, so students can identify disorders and suggest appropriate therapies. In addition, Appendix E of the *Instructor's Resource Manual* offers case study evaluations by Ann Brandt-Williams, Glendale Community College. Each evaluation accompanies a specific case and can be assigned to students to assess their understanding as they work through the text.

THE *SCIENTIFIC AMERICAN* READER TO ACCOMPANY *FUNDAMENTALS OF ABNORMAL PSYCHOLOGY,* FOURTH EDITION. Edited by Ronald J. Comer. Upon request, this reader is free when packaged with the text. Drawn from *Scientific American*, this full-color collection of articles enhances coverage of important topics within the course. Keyed to specific chapters, the selections have been handpicked by me and provide a preview and discussion questions for each article.

SCIENTIFIC AMERICAN EXPLORES THE HIDDEN MIND: A COLLECTOR'S EDITION Upon request, this reader is free when packaged with the text. In this special edition, *Scientific American* provides a compilation of updated articles that explore and reveal the mysterious inner workings of our wondrous minds and brains.

IMPROVING THE MIND AND BRAIN: A *SCIENTIFIC AMERICAN* SPECIAL ISSUE
Upon request, this reader is free when packaged with the text. This new single-topic issue from *Scientific American* magazine features the latest findings from distinguished researchers in the field.

ABNORMAL PSYCHOLOGY COMPANION WEB SITE by Elaine Cassel, Marymount University and Lord Fairfax Community College, at www.worthpublishers.com/comer This Web site provides students with a virtual study guide, 24 hours a day, seven days a week. These resources are free and do not require any special access codes or passwords. The tools on the site include: chapter outlines, annotated Web links, online quizzes, interactive flashcards, case studies, research exercises, frequently asked questions about clinical psychology, and the Abnormal Psychology Forum, a link that features various teachers' insights into specific disorders and current topics in the diagnosis and treatment of disorders.

MAKING SENSE OF PSYCHOLOGY ON THE WEB (with Research Assistant, Hyper-Folio CD-ROM) Connie K. Varnhagen, University of Alberta. Useful for the novice researcher as well as for the experienced Internet user, this brief book helps students to become discriminating Web users and researchers. The guide includes a CD-ROM containing the award-winning Research Assistant HyperFolio, innovative software that enables students to clip bits and pieces of Web sites and other electronic resources (snippets of text, illustrations, video clips, audio clips, and more) and compile them into worksheets and an easily accessible electronic "filing cabinet."

Acknowledgments

I am enormously grateful to the many people who have contributed to writing and producing this book. I particularly thank Marlene Comer for her superb, never-ending work on every aspect of the manuscript, making astute editorial judgments and offering invaluable suggestions.

In addition, I am greatly indebted to Marion Kowalewski for her outstanding and tireless work on the manuscript and her constant good cheer; to Sharon Krause for her fine work on the references; and to Donna O'Leary, Karen Moss, Vera Sohl, Bernie VanUiter, and Carole Zaffarese for their wonderful help. And I sincerely appreciate the superb work of the book's research assistants, including Kenworthey Bilz, Lisa Pugh, Linda Chamberlin, Jon Comer, and Greg Comer.

Throughout four editions of *Fundamentals of Abnormal Psychology*, I have received valuable feedback from academicians and clinicians who have reviewed portions of the manuscript and commented on its clarity, accuracy, and completeness. Their collective knowledge, and their willingness to share it with me, have in large part shaped the fourth edition. I am of course indebted to those whose insights contributed to this new edition: Glenn M. Callaghan, San Jose State University; Timothy K. Daugherty, Winthrop University; William F. Flack, Jr., Bucknell University; Dale Fryxell, Chaminade University; Karla Klein Murdock, University of Massachusetts-Boston; and Ryan Newell, Oklahoma Christian Univeristy.

In the same vein, I wish to acknowledge and thank once again the reviewers of the previous editions of *Fundamentals of Abnormal Psychology*. Their contributions remain integral to the accuracy and soundness of this edition: They include: Kerm Almos, Capital University; Otto Berliner, Alfred State College; Dorothy M. Bianco, Rhode Island College; Connie R. Borowicz, Milwaukee School of Engineering; Catherine Campbell, University of Southern Mississippi; Katharine Cimini, Lycoming College; Steve Collins,

Rio Hondo Community College; John Conklin, Camosun College; Eric J. Cooley, Western Oregon University; Laurie M. Corey. Westchester Community College; Andrew L. Dickson, University of Southern Mississippi; Ellen Domm, Green River Community College; Linda E. Flickinger, St. Clair County Community College; Frank Goodkin, Castleton State College; Marjorie Hatch, Southern Methodist University; Debra B. Hull, Wheeling Jesuit University; Heidi M. Inderbitzen-Nolan, University of Nebraska-Lincoln; David Liebert, St. Petersburg Junior College; Mary Livingston, Louisiana Tech University; Marlene Moretti, Simon Fraser University; Shelly Nygard, Lakeland College; Sonia Jean Powell, Olive-Harvey College; Lynn P. Rehm, University of Houston; Ronald G. Ribble, University of Texas at San Antonio; Beth M. Rienzi, California State University—Bakersfield; Mary A, Rogers, Inver Hills Community College; Anita Rosenfield, Chaffey Community College; Katherine Elaine Royal, Middle Tennessee State University; Michael Simon, San Francisco State University; Charles Spirrison, Mississippi State University; Helen Taylor, Bellevue Community College; Irving F. Tucker, Shepherd College; MichaelW.Vasey, Ohio State University; Fred Whitford, Montana State University; and Amy R. Wolfson, College of the Holy Cross.

The authors of the book's supplements package have my thanks for doing splendid jobs with their respective supplements: Debra B. Hull, Wheeling Jesuit University, and John H. Hull, Bethany College (*Test Bank*); Karen Clay Rhines, Seton Hall University (*Instructor's Resource Manual*); Carmen Wilson VanVoorhis, University of Wisconsin-La Crosse, and Katherine M. Nicolai, Rockhurst University (*Student Workbook*); Elaine Cassel, Marymount University and Lord Fairfax Community College (*Web site*); and Ann Brandt-Williams, Glendale Community College (additional material in the *Instructor's Resource Manual*).

I also wish to extend my deep appreciation to the core team of professionals at Worth Publishers and W. H. Freeman and Company who have worked so closely with me to produce this edition. Although the author gets most of the credit, the production of a textbook represents a collaboration by more people than one can possibly imagine. Ultimately, the book's quality reflects the ability, judgment, and dedication of these people. In my case, I was blessed with a core team of extraordinary people—each extremely talented, each committed to excellence, each dedicated to the education of readers, each bound by a remarkable work ethic, and each a wonderful person. It is accurate to say that these people were my co-authors and co-teachers in this enterprise, and I am forever in their debt. They are, in alphabetical order: Marge Byers, sponsoring editor; Paul Lacy, page layout artist; Barbara Reingold, art director; Sarah Segal, production manager; Brad Umbaugh, project editor; Vikii Wong, photo editor; and Catherine Woods, publisher.

In addition to this core team, there are a number of other people at Worth and at Freeman to whom I am indebted. Elizabeth Widdicombe, president of Worth and Freeman, has continued to lead the companies courageously, to create a very supportive environment for my books, and to be a good friend. I am also indebted to Danielle Pucci, Worth media and supplements editor, who has so skillfully developed and guided the production of the extraordinary and innovative supplements package that accompanies the text. Still other professionals from Worth and Freeman to whom I am indebted are: Todd Elder, director of advertising; Tracey Kuehn, associate managing editor; Barbara Salazar, copy editor; Karen Osborne, proofreader; Ellen Brennan, subject indexer; Anthony Calcara, name indexer; Sharon Krause, referencer; Danielle Storm, assistant editor; Nancy Giraldo Walker, rights and permissions manager; and John Philp, for his work on the video and CD-ROM supplements.

Finally, not to be overlooked are the superb professionals at Worth and at Freeman who continuously work with remarkable energy, skill, and judgment to bring my books to the attention of professors across the world: Renee Altier, executive marketing manager; Kate Nurre, psychology marketing manager; Tom Kling, National Psychology Consultant; Tom Scotty, vice president, sales and operations; and the company's wonderful sales representatives. Thank you.

Like all previous editions, a project of this scope would not be possible without a loving and supportive family, and I am truly grateful to mine, particularly my wife, Marlene, and my sons, Greg and Jon, who make my life so rich and complete and joyful. Whenever one of my books or any task feels tiring and its challenges overwhelming, they are always there—caring, supportive, inspiring. I know how fortunate I am that they are at the center of my life.

Ron Comer
Princeton University
February 2004

Fundamentals of

ABNORMAL
PSYCHOLOGY

RENÉ MAGRITTE, 1967

Abnormal Psychology: Past and Present

Alexandra cries herself to sleep every night. She is certain that the future holds nothing but misery. Indeed, this is the only thing she does feel certain about. "I'm going to die and my daughters are going to die. We're doomed. The world is ugly. I now detest every moment of my life." She has great trouble sleeping. She is afraid to close her eyes, afraid that she will never wake up, and what will happen to her daughters then? When she does drift off to sleep, her dreams are nightmares filled with blood, dismembered bodies, thunder, decay, death, destruction.

One morning Alexandra even has trouble getting out of bed. The thought of facing another day frightens and overwhelms her. She wishes that she and her daughters were dead. "Get it over with. We'd all be better off." She feels paralyzed by her depression and anxiety, too tired to move and too afraid to leave her house. She decides to stay home and to keep her daughters with her. She makes sure that all shades of the apartment are drawn and that every conceivable entrance is secured. She is afraid of the world and afraid of life.

During the past year Brad has been hearing mysterious voices that tell him to quit his job, leave his family, and prepare for the coming invasion. These voices have brought tremendous confusion and emotional turmoil to Brad's life. He believes that they come from beings in distant parts of the universe who are somehow wired to him. Although it gives him a sense of purpose and specialness to be the chosen target of their communications, they also make him tense and anxious. He dreads the coming invasion. When he refuses an order, the voices insult and threaten him and turn his days into a waking nightmare.

Brad has put himself on a sparse diet against the possibility that his enemies may be contaminating his food. He has found a quiet apartment far from his old haunts where he has laid in a good stock of arms and ammunition. His family and friends have tried to reach out to Brad, to understand his problems, and to dissuade him from the disturbing course he is taking. Every day, however, he retreats further into his world of mysterious voices and imagined dangers.

Most of us would probably consider Alexandra's and Brad's emotions, thoughts, and behavior psychologically abnormal, the result of a state sometimes called *psychopathology, maladjustment, emotional disturbance,* or *mental illness.* These terms have been applied to the many problems that seem closely tied to the human brain or mind. Psychological abnormality affects the famous and the unknown, the rich and the poor. Actors, writers, politicians, and other public figures of the present and the past have struggled with it. Psychological problems can bring great suffering, but they can also be the source of inspiration and energy.

Because they are so common and so personal, these problems capture the interest of us all. Hundreds of novels, plays, films, and television programs have explored what many people see as the dark side of human nature, and self-help books flood the market. Mental health experts are popular guests on both television and radio, and some even have their own shows.

A Beautiful Mind *Psychological disorders are a popular subject in today's movies, novels, and television shows. The film* A Beautiful Mind, *for example, which portrayed the struggles against schizophrenia of Nobel Prize winner John Nash, received the Academy Award for best picture of the year in 2001.*

The field devoted to the scientific study of the problems we find so fascinating is usually called **abnormal psychology**. As in any science, workers in this field, called *clinical scientists*, gather information carefully so that they may describe, predict, and explain the phenomena they study. The knowledge that they acquire is then used by *clinical practitioners* to detect, assess, and treat abnormal patterns of functioning.

What Is Psychological Abnormality?

Although their general goals are similar to those of other scientific professionals, clinical scientists and practitioners face problems that make their work especially difficult. One problem is that psychological abnormality is very hard to define. Consider once again Alexandra and Brad. Why are we so ready to call their responses abnormal?

Although many definitions of abnormality have been proposed over the years, none have won total acceptance (Woolfolk, 2001). Still, most of the definitions do have some common features, often called "the four D's": deviance, distress, dysfunction, and danger. That is, patterns of psychological abnormality are typically *deviant* (different, extreme, unusual, perhaps even bizarre); *distressing* (unpleasant and upsetting to the person); *dysfunctional* (interfering with the person's ability to conduct daily activities in a constructive way); and possibly *dangerous*. This definition offers a useful starting point from which to explore the phenomena of psychological abnormality. As we shall see, however, it has key limitations.

Deviance

Abnormal psychological functioning is *deviant*, but deviant from what? Alexandra's and Brad's behaviors, thoughts, and emotions are different from those that are considered normal in our place and time. We do not expect people to cry themselves to sleep each night, wish themselves dead, or obey voices that no one else hears.

In short, behavior, thoughts, and emotions are those that differ markedly from a society's ideas about proper functioning. Each society establishes **norms**—stated and unstated rules for proper conduct. Behavior that breaks legal norms is called criminal. Behavior, thoughts, and emotions that break norms of psychological functioning are called abnormal.

Judgments of abnormality vary from society to society. A society's norms grow from its particular **culture**—its history, values, institutions, habits, skills, technology, and arts. Thus, a society that values competition and assertiveness may accept aggressive behavior, whereas one that emphasizes cooperation and gentleness may consider aggressive behavior unacceptable and even abnormal. A society's values may also change over time, causing its views of what is psychologically abnormal to change as well. In Western society, for example, a woman's participation in the business world was widely considered inappropriate and strange a hundred years ago. Today the same behavior is valued.

Judgments of abnormality depend on *specific circumstances* as well as on cultural norms. What if, for example, we were to learn that the fears and desperate unhappiness of Alexandra were in fact occurring in the days following the deadly terrorist attack on the World Trade Center on September 11, 2001—an attack that killed her husband as he was at work on the 94th floor of the North Tower and wrecked the family's nearby apartment, shattering the secure and happy life they had all once known? In the ensuing weeks, as the horror and losses settled in, as she came to the conclusion that her missing husband must indeed be dead, as she and her daughters moved from one temporary location to another, Alexandra stopped expecting anything except more of the same. In

Deviance and abnormality *Along the Niger River, men of the Wodaabe tribe put on elaborate makeup and costumes to attract women. In Western society, the same behavior would break behavioral norms and probably be judged abnormal.*

this light, Alexandra's reactions do not seem quite so inappropriate. If anything is abnormal here, it is her situation. Many human experiences produce intense reactions—large-scale catastrophes and disasters, rape, child abuse, war, terminal illness, chronic pain. Is there an "appropriate" way to react to such things? Should we ever call reactions to them abnormal?

Distress

Even functioning that is considered unusual does not necessarily qualify as abnormal. According to many clinical theorists, behavior, ideas, or emotions usually have to cause *distress* before they can be labeled abnormal. Consider the Ice Breakers, a group of people in Michigan who go swimming in lakes throughout the state every weekend from November through February. The colder the weather, the better they like it. One man, a member of the group for 17 years, says he loves the challenge. Man against nature. A 37-year-old lawyer believes that the weekly shock is good for her health. "It cleanses me," she says. "It perks me up and gives me strength." Another Ice Breaker likes the special bond the group members share. "When we get together, we know we've done something special, something no one else understands. I can't even tell most of the people I know that I'm an Ice Breaker."

A spiritual experience *In the Val d' Isère, France, students bury themselves in snow up to their necks. Far from experiencing distress or displaying abnormality, they are engaging in a Japanese practice designed to open their hearts and enlarge their spirits.*

Certainly these people are different from most of us, but is their behavior abnormal? Far from experiencing distress, they feel energized. Their positive feelings must cause us to hesitate before we decide that they are functioning abnormally.

Should we conclude, then, that feelings of distress must always be present before a person's functioning can be considered abnormal? Not necessarily. Some people who function abnormally continue to hold a positive frame of mind. Consider once again Brad, who hears mysterious voices. Brad does experience severe distress over the coming invasion and the life changes he feels forced to make. But what if, instead, he enjoyed listening to the voices, felt honored to be chosen, and looked forward to saving the world? Shouldn't we still consider his functioning abnormal?

Dysfunction

Abnormal behavior tends to be *dysfunctional*; that is, it interferes with daily functioning. It so distracts or confuses people that they cannot care for themselves properly, take part in ordinary social interactions, or work productively. Brad, for example, has quit his job, left his family, and prepared to withdraw from the productive life he once led.

Here again culture plays a role in the definition of abnormality. Our society holds that it is important to carry out daily activities in an effective manner. Thus Brad's behavior is likely to be regarded as abnormal and undesirable, whereas that of the Ice Breakers, who continue to perform well in their jobs and have fulfilling relationships, would probably be considered simply unusual.

Danger

Perhaps the ultimate in psychological dysfunctioning is behavior that becomes *dangerous* to oneself or others. Individuals whose behavior is consistently careless, hostile, or confused may be placing themselves or those around them at risk. Brad, for example, seems to be endangering himself by his diet and others by his buildup of arms and ammunition.

Although danger is often cited as a feature of abnormal psychological functioning, research suggests that it is actually the exception rather than the rule (Monahan, 2001, 1993, 1992). Most people struggling with anxiety, depression, and even bizarre thinking pose no immediate danger to themselves or to anyone else.

ABNORMAL PSYCHOLOGY The scientific study of abnormal behavior in order to describe, predict, explain, and change abnormal patterns of functioning.

NORMS A society's stated and unstated rules for proper conduct.

CULTURE A people's common history, values, institutions, habits, skills, technology, and arts.

The Elusive Nature of Abnormality

Efforts to define psychological abnormality typically raise as many questions as they answer. The major problem is that the concept depends on the norms and values of the society in question. Ultimately, a society selects general criteria for defining abnormality and then uses those criteria to judge particular cases.

One clinical theorist, Thomas Szasz (2000, 1997, 1970), places such emphasis on society's role that he finds the whole concept of mental illness to be invalid, a

A CLOSER LOOK

Marching to a Different Drummer: Eccentrics

❙ Gary Holloway, an environmental planner in San Francisco, keeps a veritable stable of hobbyhorses. He is also fascinated by Martin Van Buren. . . . He discovered that Van Buren was the only U.S. president not to have a society dedicated to his memory, so he promptly founded the Van Buren Fan Club. Holloway is a lifelong devotee of St. Francis of Assisi, and frequently dresses in the habit of a Franciscan monk. "It's comfortable, fun to wear, and I like the response I get when I wear it," he explains. "People always offer me a seat on the bus." ❙

(WEEKS & JAMES, 1995, pp. 29, 36–37)

*T*he dictionary defines an *eccentric* as a person who deviates from common behavior patterns or displays odd or whimsical behavior. But how can we separate a psychologically healthy person who has unusual habits from a person whose oddness is a symptom of psychopathology? For years, little research was done on eccentrics, but some recent studies and reviews seem to have started the ball rolling (Pickover, 1998; Weeks & James, 1995).

For example, the researcher David Weeks studied 1,000 eccentrics over a 10-year period, and estimated that as many as 1 in 5,000 persons may be "classic, full-time eccentrics." Men and women seem equally prone to such patterns. Weeks pinpointed 15 characteristics common to the eccentrics in his study: *nonconformity, creativity, strong curiosity, idealism, happy obsession with hobbies, lifelong awareness of being different, high intelligence, outspokenness, noncompetitiveness, unusual eating and living habits, disinterest in others' opinions or company, mischievous sense of humor, nonmarriage, eldest or only child, poor spelling skills.*

Weeks suggests that eccentrics do not typically suffer from mental disorders. Whereas the unusual behavior of persons with mental disorders is thrust upon them and usually causes them suffering, eccentricity is chosen freely and provides pleasure. In short, "eccentrics know they're different and glory in it" (Weeks & James, 1995, p. 14). Similarly, the thought processes of eccentrics are not severely disrupted and do not leave them dysfunctional.

In fact, Weeks found that eccentrics actually had fewer emotional problems than the general population. Perhaps being an "original" is good for mental health. The eccentrics in his study also seemed physically healthier than others, visiting a doctor only once every eight years on average. Weeks concludes that most eccentrics, despite their deviant behavior—perhaps even because of it—are happy, well-adjusted, and joyful people.

Famous Eccentrics

❖ **James Joyce** always carried a tiny pair of lady's bloomers, which he waved in the air to show approval.

❖ **Emily Dickinson** always wore white, never left her room, and hid her poems in tiny boxes.

❖ **Benjamin Franklin** took "air baths" for his health, sitting naked in front of an open window.

❖ **President John Quincy Adams** swam nude in the Potomac River each morning.

❖ **Alexander Graham Bell** covered the windows of his house to keep out the rays of the full moon. He also tried to teach his dog how to talk.

❖ The writer **D. H. Lawrence** enjoyed removing his clothes and climbing mulberry trees.

(ASIMOV, 1997; WEEKS & JAMES, 1995)

Gamma Liaison

Eccentricity takes a break
Gene Pool, a 37-year-old carpenter, journeys repeatedly around New York City wearing an outfit made of 500 empty cans. The reason? To make a statement about the need for recycling and to be noticed. Here he rests for a while on a city park bench.

myth of sorts. According to Szasz, the deviations that society calls abnormal are simply "problems in living," not signs of something wrong within the person. Societies, he is convinced, invent the concept of mental illness so that they can better control or change people whose unusual patterns of functioning upset or threaten the social order.

Even if we assume that psychological abnormality is an appropriate concept, we may be unable to apply its definition consistently. If a behavior—excessive use of alcohol among college students, say—is familiar enough, the society may fail to recognize that it is deviant, distressful, dysfunctional, and dangerous. Thousands of college students are so dependent on alcohol that it interferes with their personal and academic lives, causes them great discomfort, jeopardizes their health, and often endangers them and the people around them. Yet their problem often goes unnoticed, certainly undiagnosed, by college administrators, other students, and health professionals. Alcohol is so much a part of the college subculture that it is easy to overlook drinking behavior that has become abnormal.

Conversely, a society may have trouble separating an abnormality that needs intervention and an *eccentricity*, an unusual pattern that others have no right to interfere with. From time to time we see or hear about people who behave in ways we consider strange, such as a man who lives alone with two dozen cats and rarely talks to other people. The behavior of such people is deviant, and it may well be distressful and dysfunctional, yet many professionals think of it as eccentric rather than abnormal.

In short, while we may agree to define psychological abnormalities as patterns of functioning that are deviant, distressful, dysfunctional, and sometimes dangerous, we should be clear that these criteria are often vague. In turn, few of the current categories of abnormality that we will meet in this book are as clear-cut as they may seem, and most continue to be debated by clinicians.

> ## >>IN THEIR WORDS
> ### Mental Dysfunction
>
> "The only difference between me and a madman is that I am not mad."<<
>
> Salvador Dali
>
> -
>
> "Insanity: doing the same thing over and over again and expecting different results."<<
>
> Albert Einstein
>
> -
>
> "Insanity—a perfectly rational adjustment to an insane world."<<
>
> R. D. Laing
>
> -
>
> "The distance between insanity and genius is measured only by success."<<
>
> James Bond in *Tomorrow Never Dies*
>
> -
>
> "One of the symptoms of an approaching nervous breakdown is the belief that one's work is terribly important."<<
>
> Bertrand Russell

SUMMING UP

What Is Psychological Abnormality?

The field devoted to the scientific study of abnormal behavior is called abnormal psychology. Its goals are to understand and treat abnormal patterns of functioning. Abnormal functioning is generally considered to be deviant, distressful, dysfunctional, and dangerous. Behavior must also be considered in the context in which it occurs, however, and the concept of abnormality depends on the norms and values of the society in question.

What Is Treatment?

Once clinicians decide that a person is suffering from some form of psychological abnormality, they seek to treat it. **Treatment**, or *therapy*, is a procedure to help change abnormal behavior into more normal behavior; it, too, requires careful definition (Compas & Gotlib, 2002). For clinical scientists, the problem is closely related to defining abnormality. Consider the case of Bill:

February: He cannot leave the house; Bill knows that for a fact. Home is the only place where he feels safe—safe from humiliation, danger, even ruin. If he were to go to work, his co-workers would somehow reveal their contempt for him. A pointed remark, a quizzical look—that's all it would take for him to get the message. If he were to go shopping at the store, before long everyone would be staring at him. Surely others would see his dark mood and thoughts; he wouldn't be able to hide them. He dare not even go for a walk alone in the woods—his heart

TREATMENT A procedure designed to help change abnormal behavior into more normal behavior. Also called *therapy*.

>>BY THE NUMBERS
Treatment Effectiveness

85% Those with panic disorder who improve with leading treatments‹‹

65% Those with depression helped by leading treatments‹‹

70% Those with eating disorders who respond to leading treatments‹‹

0% with Alzheimer's disease who eventually overcome their disorder‹‹

would probably start racing again, bringing him to his knees and leaving him breathless, incoherent, and unable to get home. No, he's much better off staying in his room, trying to get through another evening of this curse called life.

July: Bill's life revolves around his circle of friends: Bob and Jack, whom he knows from the office, where he was recently promoted to director of customer relations, and Frank and Tim, his weekend tennis partners. The gang meets for dinner every week at someone's house, and they chat about life, politics, and their jobs. Particularly special in Bill's life is Janice. They go to movies, restaurants, and shows together. She thinks Bill's just terrific, and Bill finds himself beaming whenever she's around. Bill looks forward to work each day and his one-on-one dealings with customers. He is enjoying life and basking in the glow of his many activities and relationships.

Bill's thoughts, feelings, and behavior interfered with all aspects of his life in February. Yet most of his symptoms had disappeared by July. All sorts of factors may have contributed to Bill's improvement. Friends and family members may have offered support or advice. A new job or vacation may have lifted his spirits. Perhaps he changed his diet or started to exercise. Any or all of these things may have been useful to Bill, but they could not be considered treatment, or therapy. Those terms are usually reserved for special, systematic procedures for helping people overcome their psychological difficulties. According to the clinical theorist Jerome Frank, all forms of therapy have three key features:

1. A *sufferer* who seeks relief from the healer.
2. A trained, socially accepted *healer*, whose expertise is accepted by the sufferer and his or her social group.
3. A *series of contacts* between the healer and the sufferer, through which the healer, tries to produce certain changes in the sufferer's emotional state, attitudes, and behavior.

(Frank, 1973, pp. 2–3)

Despite this straightforward definition, clinical treatment is surrounded by conflict and confusion. Carl Rogers, a pioneer in the modern clinical field whom we will meet in Chapter 2, noted that "therapists are not in agreement as to their goals or aims. . . . They are not in agreement as to what constitutes a successful outcome of their work. They cannot agree as to what constitutes a failure. It seems as though the field is completely chaotic and divided."

Some clinicians view abnormality as an illness and so consider therapy a procedure that helps *cure* the illness. Others see abnormality as a problem in living and therapists as *teachers* of more useful behavior and thought. Clinicians even differ on what to call the person who receives therapy: those who see abnormality as an illness speak of the "patient," while those who view it as a problem in living refer to the "client." Because both terms are so common, this book will use them interchangeably.

Despite their differences, most clinicians do agree that large numbers of people need therapy of one kind or another. Later we shall see evidence that therapy is indeed often helpful.

>>PSYCH•LISTINGS
Famous Psych Lines from the Movies

"Take baby steps." (*What About Bob?* 1991)‹‹

"Rosebud." (*Citizen Kane*, 1941)‹‹

"I see dead people." (*The Sixth Sense*, 1999)‹‹

"Dave, my mind is going. . . . I can feel it." (*2001: A Space Odyssey*, 1968)‹‹

"Uh oh." (*Rain Man*, 1988)‹‹

"All right, Mr. DeMille, I'm ready for my close-up." (*Sunset Boulevard*, 1950)‹‹

"I forgot my mantra." (*Annie Hall*, 1977)‹‹

"I love the smell of napalm in the morning." (*Apocalypse Now*, 1979)‹‹

"Snakes, why does it always have to be snakes?" (*Raiders of the Lost Ark*, 1981)‹‹

SUMMING UP
What Is Treatment?

Therapy is a special, systematic process for helping people overcome their psychological difficulties. It may vary from problem to problem and therapist to therapist, but it typically includes a patient, a therapist, and a series of professional contacts.

How Was Abnormality Viewed and Treated in the Past?

In any given year as many as 30 percent of the adults and 20 percent of the children and adolescents in the United States display serious psychological disturbances and are in need of clinical treatment (Narrow et al., 2002; Kazdin, 2000). The rates in other countries are similarly high. Furthermore, most people have difficulty coping at various times in their lives and go through periods of extreme tension, dejection, or other forms of psychological discomfort.

It is tempting to conclude that something about the modern world is responsible for these many emotional problems—perhaps rapid technological change, the growing threats of terrorism, or a decline in religious, family, or other support systems (Schumaker, 2001). Although the special pressures of modern life probably do contribute to psychological dysfunctioning, they are hardly its primary cause. Every society, past and present, has witnessed psychological abnormality. Perhaps, then, the proper place to begin our examination of abnormal behavior and treatment is in the past.

As we look back, we can see how each society has struggled to understand and treat psychological problems, and we can observe that many present-day ideas and treatments have roots in the past. A look backward makes it clear that progress in the understanding and treatment of mental disorders has hardly been a steady movement forward. In fact, many of the inadequacies and controversies that mark the clinical field today are similar to those of the past. At the same time, looking back can help us to appreciate the wonder of recent breakthroughs and the importance of the journey that lies ahead.

Ancient Views and Treatments

Historians who have examined the unearthed bones, artwork, and other remnants of ancient societies have concluded that these societies probably regarded abnormal behavior as the work of evil spirits. People in prehistoric societies apparently believed that all events around and within them resulted from the actions of magical beings who controlled the world. In particular, they viewed the human body and mind as a battleground between external forces of good and evil. Abnormal behavior was typically interpreted as a victory by evil spirits, and the cure for such behavior was to force the demons from a victim's body.

This supernatural view of abnormality may have begun as far back as the Stone Age, a half-million years ago. Some skulls from that period recovered in Europe and South America show evidence of an operation called **trephination**, in which a stone instrument, or *trephine*, was used to cut away a circular section of the skull. Some historians have concluded that this operation was performed as a treatment for severe abnormal behavior—either hallucinations, in which people saw or heard things not actually present, or melancholia, characterized by extreme sadness and immobility. The purpose of opening the skull was to let out the evil spirits that were supposedly causing the problem (Selling, 1940).

Later societies also explained abnormal behavior by pointing to possession by demons. Egyptian, Chinese, and Hebrew writings, for example, all account for psychological problems this way. The Bible describes how an evil spirit from the Lord affected King Saul and how David pretended to be mad in order to convince his enemies that he was visited by divine forces.

The treatment for abnormality in these early societies was often **exorcism**. The idea was to coax the evil spirits to leave or to make the person's body an uncomfortable place for them to live in. A *shaman*, or priest, might recite prayers, plead with the evil spirits, insult them, perform magic, make loud noises, or have the person drink bitter liquids. If these techniques failed, the shaman performed a more extreme form of exorcism, such as whipping or starving the person.

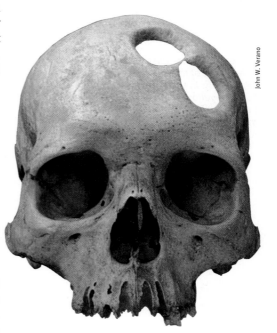

John W. Verano

Expelling evil spirits *The two holes in this skull recovered from ancient times indicate that the person underwent trephination, possibly for the purpose of releasing evil spirits and curing mental dysfunctioning.*

TREPHINATION An ancient operation in which a stone instrument was used to cut away a circular section of the skull, perhaps to treat abnormal behavior.

EXORCISM The practice in early societies of treating abnormality by coaxing evil spirits to leave the person's body.

Greek and Roman Views and Treatments

In the years from about 500 B.C. to A.D. 500, when the Greek and Roman civilizations thrived, philosophers and physicians often offered different explanations for abnormal behaviors. Hippocrates (460–377 B.C.), called the father of modern medicine, taught that illnesses had *natural* causes. He saw abnormal behavior as a disease caused by internal physical problems. Specifically, he believed that some form of brain disease was to blame, and that it resulted—like all other forms of disease, in his view—from an imbalance of four fluids, or **humors**, that flowed through the body: *yellow bile, black bile, blood,* and *phlegm*. An excess of yellow bile, for example, caused frenzied joy; an excess of black bile was the source of unshakable sadness.

Zentralbibliothek, Zurich

Humors in action *Hippocrates believed that imbalances of the four humors affected personality. In these depictions of two of the humors, yellow bile (left) drives a husband to beat his wife, and black bile (right) leaves a man melancholic and sends him to bed.*

Hippocrates' focus on internal causes for abnormal behavior was shared by the great Greek philosophers Plato (427–347 B.C.) and Aristotle (384–322 B.C.) and by influential Greek and Roman physicians. Correspondingly, many physicians treated mental disorders with a mixture of medical and psychological techniques, from bleeding and restraining patients to providing them with supportive and soothing atmosphere, music, massage, exercise, and baths.

Europe in the Middle Ages: Demonology Returns

The enlightened views of Greek and Roman physicians and scholars were not enough to shake ordinary people's belief in demons. And with the decline of Rome, demonological views and practices became popular once again. A growing distrust of science spread throughout Europe.

From A.D. 500 to 1350, the period known as the Middle Ages, the power of the clergy increased greatly throughout Europe. In those days the church rejected scientific forms of investigation, and it controlled all education. Religious beliefs, which were highly superstitious and demonological, came to dominate all aspects of life. Once again behavior was usually interpreted as a conflict between good and evil, God and the devil. Deviant behavior, particularly psychological dysfunctioning, was seen as evidence of Satan's influence. Although some scientists and physicians still insisted on medical explanations and treatments, their views carried little weight in this atmosphere.

The Middle Ages were a time of great stress and anxiety, of war, urban uprisings, and plagues. People blamed the devil for these troubles and feared being possessed by him. Abnormal behavior apparently increased greatly during this period. In addition, there were outbreaks of *mass madness*, in which large numbers of people apparently *shared delusions and hallucinations*. In one such disorder, *tarantism* (also known as *St. Vitus's dance*), groups of people would suddenly start to jump, dance, and go into convulsions (Sigerist, 1943). All were convinced that they had been bitten and possessed by a wolf spider, now called a tarantula. In another form of mass madness, *lycanthropy*, people thought they were possessed by wolves or other animals. They acted wolflike and imagined that fur was growing all over their bodies.

Not surprisingly, some of the earlier demonological treatments for psychological abnormality reemerged during the Middle Ages. Once again the cure was to rid the person's body of the devil that possessed it. Exorcisms were revived, and

THECURRENT SCENE

Exorcism Lives

*E*xorcism has a long history as a "treatment" for persons who behave abnormally; it was particularly favored during biblical times and again during the Middle Ages. But all that is a thing of the distant past, right? Well, not completely, it turns out (Rosik, 2003).

By the 1970s exorcism had all but disappeared from Western culture (Cuneo, 2000). Then in 1973, the enormously popular book and movie *The Exorcist* spurred a rash of books and movies on demonic possession, and public interest in this procedure increased dramatically. Since then, numerous evangelical ministers and charismatics have declared themselves exorcists and performed exorcisms on people with behavioral disturbances. In most such instances, the exorcist blesses the person who is thought to be possessed, recites passages from the Bible, and commands the evil spirits to leave the body (Fountain, 2000). Often a support group is present to pray for the person while he or she cries out and perhaps even thrashes on the floor, regurgitates, or flails about (Cuneo, 2000).

During the 1990s, the techniques used by some contemporary exorcists seemed to grow more extreme, at times dangerous. The media reported cases of death by exorcism; a New York mother accidentally smothered her teenage daughter during one procedure, and a Rhode Island man jammed steel crosses down his mother-in-law's throat (Fountain, 2000). In addition, a growing number of priests began to perform spiritual cleansing ceremonies not sanctioned by the Roman Catholic Church (Cuneo, 2000).

In order to regulate this growing field, both within and outside the church, and to ensure more acceptable procedures, the Roman Catholic Church in the United States has become more actively involved in exorcisms during the past decade. The number of full-time exorcists formally appointed by the church increased from 1 in 1990 to 10 in 2000 (Fountain, 2000). These officials have investigated and evaluated hundreds of cases in which individuals or their relatives or priests have sought exorcisms, determining in each case whether exorcism is appropriate. In 1999 the church issued a revised rite of exorcism for the first time since 1614, establishing rules to be followed in making such decisions and in the exorcisms themselves. For example, a church exorcism can take place only after the church-approved exorcist consults with physicians to rule out mental or physical disorders. Also, church exorcisms must be approved by a bishop.

As a result of such rules and procedures, only a small number of potential cases actually result in church-approved exorcisms (Fountain, 2000). Even a small number of exorcisms, however, is excessive in the eyes of many mental health professionals, who see this intervention as a misguided "treatment" for psychological dysfunctioning. Given exorcism's long history and deep roots, this debate is not likely to be settled in the near future.

Exorcism at the movies *In the remarkably popular horror movie* The Exorcist, *an exorcist offers prayers and administers holy water to try to force the devil to leave the body of a troubled teenage girl.*

clergymen, who generally were in charge of treatment during this period, would plead, chant, or pray to the devil or evil spirit. If these techniques did not work, they had others to try, such as starving, whipping, scaulding, or stretching the individual.

It was not until the Middle Ages drew to a close that demonology and its methods began to lose favor. Towns throughout Europe grew into cities, and government officials gained more power and took over nonreligious activities. Among their responsibilities, they began to run hospitals and direct the care of people suffering from mental disorders. Medical views of abnormality gained favor, and many people with psychological disturbances received treatment in medical hospitals, such as Trinity Hospital in England.

HUMORS According to Greek and Roman physicians, bodily chemicals that influence mental and physical functioning.

Bewitched or bewildered? *A great fear of witchcraft swept Europe even during the "enlightened" Renaissance. Tens of thousands of people, mostly women, were thought to have made a pact with the devil. Some appear to have had mental disorders, which caused them to act strangely (Zilboorg & Henry, 1941). This individual is being "dunked" repeatedly until she confesses to witchery.*

The Renaissance and the Rise of Asylums

During the early part of the Renaissance, a period of widespread cultural and scientific activity (about 1400–1700), demonological views of abnormality continued to decline. The German doctor Johann Weyer (1515–1588), the first physician to specialize in mental illness, believed that the mind was as susceptible to sickness as the body. He is now considered the founder of the modern study of mental dysfunction.

The care of people with mental disorders continued to improve in this atmosphere. In England such individuals might be kept at home while their families were helped financially by the local parish. Across Europe religious shrines were devoted to the humane and loving treatment of people with mental disorders. Perhaps the best known of these shrines was at Gheel in Belgium. Beginning in the fifteenth century, people came to it from all over the world for psychic healing. Local residents welcomed these pilgrims into their homes, and many stayed on to form the world's first "colony" of mental patients. Gheel was the forerunner of today's community mental health programs, and it continues to demonstrate that people with psychological disorders can respond to loving care and respectful treatment (Morton, 2002; Aring, 1975, 1974). Many patients still live in foster homes there, interacting with other residents, until they recover.

Unfortunately, these improvements in care began to disappear by the mid-sixteenth century. Government officials discovered that private homes and community residences could house only a small percentage of those with severe mental disorders and that medical hospitals were too few and too small. More and more, they converted hospitals and monasteries into **asylums**, institutions whose primary purpose was to care for people with mental illness. These institutions began with every intention of providing good care. Once the asylums started to overflow, however, they became prisons where patients were held in filthy conditions and treated with unspeakable cruelty.

In 1547, for example, Bethlehem Hospital was given to the city of London by Henry VIII for the sole purpose of confining the mentally ill. In this asylum

---

STEPPING BACK

Verbal Debuts

We use words like "abnormal" and "mental disorder" so often that it is easy to forget that there was a time not so long ago when these terms did not exist. When did these and similar words (including slang terms) make their debut in print as expressions of psychological dysfunctioning? The *Oxford English Dictionary* offers the following dates.

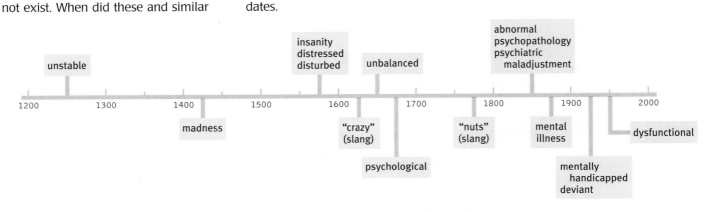

patients bound in chains cried out for all to hear. The hospital actually became a popular tourist attraction; people were eager to pay to look at the howling and gibbering inmates. The hospital's name, pronounced "Bedlam" by the local people, has come to mean a chaotic uproar.

The Nineteenth Century: Reform and Moral Treatment

As 1800 approached, the treatment of people with mental disorders began to improve once again. Historians usually point to La Bicêtre, an asylum in Paris for male patients, as the first site of asylum reform. In 1793, during the French Revolution, Philippe Pinel (1745–1826) was named the chief physician there. He argued that the patients were sick people whose illnesses should be treated with sympathy and kindness rather than chains and beatings. He allowed them to move freely about the hospital grounds; replaced the dark dungeons with sunny, well-ventilated rooms; and offered support and advice. Pinel's approach proved remarkably successful. Patients who had been shut away for decades improved greatly over a short period of time and were released. Pinel later brought similar reforms to a mental hospital in Paris for female patients, La Salpetrière.

Meanwhile an English Quaker named William Tuke (1732–1819) was bringing similar reforms to northern England. In 1796 he founded the York Retreat, a rural estate where about 30 mental patients lived as guests in quiet country houses and were treated with a combination of rest, talk, prayer, and manual work (Borthwick et al., 2001).

THE SPREAD OF MORAL TREATMENT The methods of Pinel and Tuke, called **moral treatment** because they emphasized moral guidance and humane and respectful techniques, caught on throughout Europe and the United States. Patients with psychological problems were increasingly perceived as potentially productive human beings whose mental functioning had broken down under stress. They were considered deserving of individual care, including discussions of their problems, useful activities, work, companionship, and quiet.

The person most responsible for the early spread of moral treatment in the United States was Benjamin Rush (1745–1813), an eminent physician at Pennsylvania Hospital. Limiting his practice to mental illness, Rush developed new, humane approaches to treatment (Whitaker, 2002). For example, he required that the hospital hire intelligent and sensitive attendants to work closely with patients, reading and talking to them and taking them on regular walks. He also suggested that it would be therapeutic for doctors to give small gifts to their patients now and then.

Rush's work was influential, but it was a Boston schoolteacher named Dorothea Dix (1802–1887) who made humane care a public concern in the United States. From 1841 to 1881, Dix went from state legislature to state legislature and to Congress speaking of the horrors she had observed at asylums throughout the country and calling for reform. Dix's campaign led to new laws and greater government funding to improve the treatment of people with mental disorders. Each state was made responsible for developing effective public mental hospitals. Dix personally helped establish 32 of these **state hospitals**, all intended to offer moral treatment (Bickman & Dokecki, 1989). Similar hospitals were established throughout Europe.

THE DECLINE OF MORAL TREATMENT By the 1850s, a number of mental hospitals throughout Europe and America reported success using moral approaches. By the end of that century, however, several factors led to

ASYLUM A type of institution that first became popular in the sixteenth century to provide care for persons with mental disorders. Most became virtual prisons.

MORAL TREATMENT A nineteenth-century approach to treating people with mental dysfunction that emphasized moral guidance and humane and respectful treatment.

STATE HOSPITALS State-run public mental institutions in the United States.

Dance in a madhouse *A popular feature of moral treatment was the "lunatic ball." Hospital officials would bring patients together to dance and enjoy themselves. One such ball is shown in this painting,* Dance in a Madhouse, *by George Bellows.*

George Wesley Bellow, *Dance in a Madhouse*, 1907. Photograph © 1997 The Art Institute of Chicago.

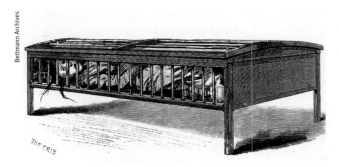

The "crib" *Outrageous devices and techniques, such as the "crib," were used in asylums, and some continued to be used even during the reforms of the nineteenth century.*

a reversal of the moral treatment movement (Bockoven, 1963). One factor was the speed with which the moral movement had spread. As mental hospitals multiplied, severe money and staffing shortages developed, and recovery rates declined. Another factor was the assumption behind moral treatment that all patients could be cured if treated with humanity and dignity. For some, this was indeed sufficient. Others, however, needed more effective treatments than any that had yet been developed. An additional factor contributing to the decline of moral treatment was the emergence of a new wave of prejudice against people with mental disorders. As more and more patients disappeared into large, distant mental hospitals, the public came to view them as strange and dangerous. In turn, people were less open-handed when it came to making donations or allocating government funds. Moreover, many of the patients entering public mental hospitals in the United States in the late nineteenth century were poor foreign immigrants, whom the public had little interest in helping.

By the early years of the twentieth century, the moral treatment movement had ground to a halt in both the United States and Europe. Public mental hospitals were providing only custodial care and ineffective medical treatments and were becoming more overcrowded every year. Long-term hospitalization became the rule once again.

The Early Twentieth Century: The Somatogenic and Psychogenic Perspectives

As the moral movement was declining in the late 1800s, two opposing perspectives emerged and began to compete for the attention of clinicians: the *somatogenic perspective*, the view that abnormal psychological functioning has physical causes, and the *psychogenic perspective*, the view that the chief causes of abnormal functioning are psychological. These perspectives came into full bloom during the twentieth century.

Back wards *Overcrowding, limited funding, and ineffective hospital treatments led to the creation of crowded, often appalling back wards in state hospitals across the United States, which continued well into the twentieth century.*

THE SOMATOGENIC PERSPECTIVE The **somatogenic perspective** has at least a 2,400-year history—remember Hippocrates' view that abnormal behavior resulted from brain disease and an imbalance of humors? Not until the late nineteenth century, however, did this perspective make a triumphant return and begin to gain wide acceptance.

Two factors were responsible for this rebirth. One was the work of an eminent German researcher, Emil Kraepelin (1856–1926). In 1883 Kraepelin published an influential textbook which argued that physical factors, such as fatigue, are responsible for mental dysfunction. In addition, as we shall see in Chapter 3, he also developed the first modern system for classifying abnormal behavior (Kihlstrom, 2002).

Biological discoveries also triggered the rise of the somatogenic perspective. One of the most important discoveries was that an organic disease, *syphilis*, led to *general paresis*, an irreversible disorder with both physical and mental symptoms, including paralysis and delusions of grandeur. In 1897 Richard von Krafft-Ebing (1840–1902), a German neurologist, injected matter from syphilis sores into patients suffering from general paresis and found that none of the patients developed symptoms of syphilis. Their immunity could have been caused only by an earlier case of syphilis. Since all patients with general paresis were now immune to syphilis, Krafft-Ebing theorized that syphilis had been the cause of their general paresis.

The work of Kraepelin and the new understanding of general paresis led many researchers and practitioners to suspect that phys-

Table 1-1

Eugenics and Mental Disorders

YEAR	EVENT
1896	Connecticut became the first state in the United States to prohibit persons with mental disorders from marrying.
1896–1933	Every state in the United States passed a law prohibiting marriage by persons with mental disorders.
1907	Indiana became the first state to pass a bill calling for people with mental disorders, as well as criminals and other "defectives," to undergo sterilization.
1927	The U.S. Supreme Court ruled that eugenic sterilization was constitutional.
1907–1945	Around 45,000 Americans were sterilized under eugenic sterilization laws; 21,000 of them were patients in state mental hospitals.
1929–1932	Denmark, Norway, Sweden, Finland, and Iceland passed eugenic sterilization laws.
1933	Germany passed a eugenic sterilization law, under which 375,000 people were sterilized by 1940.
1940	Nazi Germany begain to use "proper gases" to kill people with mental disorders; 70,000 or more people were killed in less than two years.

Source: Whitaker, 2002.

ical factors were responsible for many mental disorders, perhaps all of them. These theories and the possibility of quick and effective medical solutions for mental disorders were especially welcomed by those who worked in mental hospitals, where patient populations were now growing at an alarming rate.

Despite the general optimism, biological approaches yielded mostly disappointing results throughout the first half of the twentieth century. Although many medical treatments were developed for patients in mental hospitals during that time, most of the techniques did not work. Physicians tried tooth extraction, tonsillectomy, hydrotherapy (alternating hot and cold baths), and lobotomy, a surgical cutting of certain nerve fibers in the brain. Even worse, biological views and claims led, in some circles, to proposals for immoral solutions such as *eugenesis*, the selective elimination (through medical or other means) of individuals' ability to reproduce (see Table 1-1). Not until the 1950s, when a number of effective medications were finally discovered, did the somatogenic perspective truly begin to pay off for patients.

THE PSYCHOGENIC PERSPECTIVE The late nineteenth century also saw the emergence of the **psychogenic perspective**, the view that the chief causes of abnormal functioning are often psychological. This view, too, had a long history, but it did not gain much of a following until studies of hypnotism demonstrated its potential.

Hypnotism is a procedure that places people in a trancelike mental state during which they become extremely suggestible. It was used to help treat psychological disorders as far back as 1778, when an Austrian physician named Friedrich Anton Mesmer (1734–1815) started a clinic in Paris. His patients suffered from *hysterical disorders*, bodily ailments that had no apparent physical basis. Mesmer had his patients sit in a darkened room filled with music; then he appeared, dressed in a colorful costume, and touched the troubled area of each patient's body with a special rod. A surprising number of patients seemed to be helped by this treatment, called *mesmerism*. Their pain, numbness, or paralysis disappeared. Several scientists believed that Mesmer was inducing a trancelike state in his patients and that this

SOMATOGENIC PERSPECTIVE The view that abnormal psychological functioning has physical causes.

PSYCHOGENIC PERSPECTIVE The view that the chief causes of abnormal functioning are psychological.

The roots of psychogenic theory *The nineteenth century's leading neurologist, Jean Charcot, gives a clinical lecture in Paris on hypnotism and hysterical disorders.*

state was causing their symptoms to disappear. The treatment was so controversial, however, that eventually Mesmer was banished from Paris (Spiegal, 2002).

It was not until years after Mesmer had died that many researchers had the courage to investigate his procedure, later called hypnotism (from *hypnos*, the Greek word for "sleep"), and its effects on hysterical disorders. The experiments of two physicians practicing in the city of Nancy in France, Hippolyte-Marie Bernheim (1840–1919) and Ambroise-Auguste Liébault (1823–1904), showed that hysterical disorders could actually be produced in otherwise normal subjects while they were under hypnosis. That is, the physicians could make normal people experience deafness, paralysis, blindness, or numbness by means of hypnotic suggestion—and they could remove these artificial symptoms by the same means. Thus, they established that a *mental* process—hypnotic suggestion—could both cause and cure even a physical dysfunction. Influential scientists concluded that hysterical disorders were largely psychological in origin, and the psychogenic perspective rose in popularity.

Among those who studied the effects of hypnotism on hysterical disorders was Josef Breuer (1842–1925) of Vienna. This physician discovered that his patients sometimes awoke without their hysterical symptoms after speaking freely under hypnosis about past upsetting events. During the 1890s Breuer was joined in his work by another Viennese physician, Sigmund Freud (1856–1939). As we shall see in Chapter 2, Freud's work eventually led him to develop the theory of **psychoanalysis**, which holds that many forms of abnormal and normal psychological functioning are psychogenic. In particular, he believed that *unconscious* psychological processes are at the root of such functioning.

Freud also developed the *treatment* of psychoanalysis, a form of discussion in which clinicians help troubled people gain insight into their unconscious psychological processes. He believed that such insight, even without hypnotic procedures, would help the patients overcome their psychological problems.

Freud and his followers offered psychoanalytic treatment primarily to patients with psychological disorders who did not require hospitalization. These patients visited therapists in their offices for sessions of approximately an hour and then went about their daily activities—a format of treatment now known as *outpatient therapy*. By the early twentieth century, psychoanalytic theory and treatment were widely accepted throughout the Western world.

PSYCHOANALYSIS Either the theory or the treatment of abnormal mental functioning that emphasizes unconscious psychological forces as the cause of psychopathology.

PSYCHOTROPIC MEDICATIONS Drugs that mainly affect the brain and reduce many symptoms of mental dysfunctioning.

DEINSTITUTIONALIZATION The practice, begun in the 1960s, of releasing hundreds of thousands of patients from public mental hospitals.

SUMMING UP | **How Was Abnormality Viewed and Treated in the Past?**

The history of psychological disorders, stretching back to ancient times, provides us with many clues about the nature of psychological abnormality. There is evidence that Stone Age cultures used trephination, a primitive form of brain surgery, to treat abnormal behavior. People of early societies also sought to drive out evil spirits by exorcism.

Physicians of the Greek and Roman empires offered more enlightened explanations of mental disorders. Hippocrates believed that abnormal behavior was due to an imbalance of the four bodily fluids, or humors: black bile, yellow bile, blood, and phlegm.

Unfortunately, throughout history each period of enlightened thinking about psychological functioning has been followed by a period of backward thinking. For example, in the Middle Ages, Europeans returned to demonological explanations of abnormal behavior. The clergy was very influential and held that mental disorders were the work of the devil. Demonology declined once again as the Middle Ages drew to a close, and care of people with psychological disorders improved during the early part of the Renaissance. Certain religious shrines offered humane treatment. Unfortunately, this enlightened approach was short-lived, and by the middle of the sixteenth century, persons with mental disorders were being warehoused in asylums.

Care of people with mental disorders began to improve yet again in the nineteenth century. Moral treatment began in Europe and spread to the United States, where Dorothea Dix's national campaign helped lead to the establishment of state hospitals. Unfortunately, the moral treatment movement disintegrated in the latter part of the nineteenth century, and public mental hospitals again became warehouses where the inmates received minimal care.

The late nineteenth century saw the return of the somatogenic perspective, the view that abnormal psychological functioning is caused largely by physical factors. The same period saw the rise of the psychogenic perspective, the view that the chief causes of abnormal functioning are psychological. Sigmund Freud's psychogenic approach, psychoanalysis, eventually gained wide acceptance and influenced future generations of clinicians.

>>PSYCH•NOTES
Sigmund Freud

Freud's fee for one session of therapy was $20—$160 in today's dollars.<<
- -
For almost 40 years Freud treated patients 10 hours per day, five or six days per week.<<
- -
Freud's parents often favored the precociously intelligent Sigmund over his siblings—for example, by giving him his own room in which to study in peace.<<

(Gay, 1999; Asimov, 1997; Schwartz, 1993)

Current Trends

It would hardly be accurate to say that we now live in a period of great enlightenment or dependable treatment of mental disorders. In fact, some recent surveys found that 43 percent of respondents believe that people bring on such disorders themselves and 35 percent consider the disorders to be caused by sinful behavior (NMHA, 1999; Murray, 1993). Nevertheless, the past 50 years have brought major changes in the ways clinicians understand and treat mental disorders. There are more theories and types of treatment, more research studies, more information, and, perhaps for these reasons, more disagreements about abnormal functioning today than at any time in the past. In some ways the study and treatment of psychological disorders have come a long way, but in other respects clinical scientists and practitioners are still struggling to make a difference.

How Are People with Severe Disturbances Cared For?

In the 1950s researchers discovered a number of new **psychotropic medications**—drugs that primarily affect the brain and reduce many symptoms of mental dysfunctioning. They included the first *antipsychotic drugs*, to correct extremely confused and distorted thinking; *antidepressant drugs*, to lift the mood of depressed people; and *antianxiety drugs*, to reduce tension and worry.

When given these drugs, many patients who had spent years in mental hospitals began to show signs of improvement. Hospital administrators, encouraged by these results and pressured by a growing public outcry over the terrible conditions in public mental hospitals, began to discharge patients almost immediately.

Since the discovery of these medications, mental health professionals in most of the developed nations of the world have followed a policy of **deinstitutionalization**, releasing hundreds of thousands of patients from public mental hospitals. On any given day in 1955, close to 600,000 people lived in public mental institutions across the United States (see Figure 1-1). Today the daily patient population in the same kinds of hospitals is around 60,000 (Torrey, 2001).

In short, outpatient care has now become the primary mode of treatment for people with severe psychological disturbances as well as for those with more moderate problems. Today when very

FIGURE 1-1
The impact of deinstitutionalization *The number of patients (60,000) now hospitalized in public mental hospitals in the United States is a small fraction of the number hospitalized in 1955. (Adapted from Torrey, 2001; Lang, 1999.)*

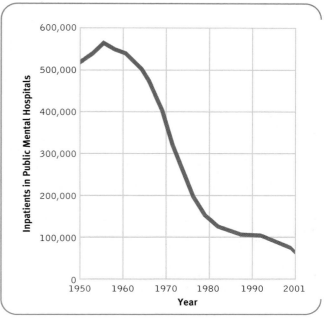

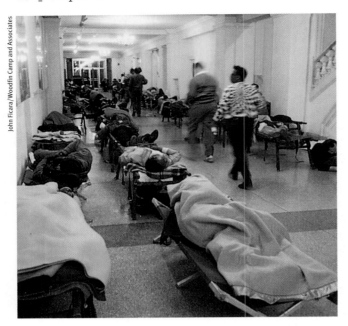

John Ficara/Woodfin Camp and Associates

Alternative treatment? *Tens of thousands of people with severe mental disorders are currently homeless. They receive no treatment and wind up on the streets or in public shelters, such as this shelter for the homeless in Washington, D.C.*

disturbed people do need institutionalization, they are usually given short-term hospitalization (NAPHS, 1999). Ideally, they are then given outpatient psychotherapy and medication in community programs and residences.

Chapters 2 and 12 will look more closely at this recent emphasis on community care for people with severe psychological disturbances—a philosophy called the *community mental health approach.* The approach has been helpful for many patients, but too few community programs are available to address current needs in the United States. As a result, hundreds of thousands of persons with severe disturbances fail to make lasting recoveries, and they shuffle back and forth between the mental hospital and the community. After release from the hospital, they at best receive minimal care and often wind up living in decrepit rooming houses or on the streets. In fact, only 40 percent of persons with severe psychological disturbances currently receive treatment of any kind (Wang, Demler, & Kessler, 2002). At least 100,000 individuals with such disturbances are homeless on any given day; another 135,000 or more are inmates of jails and prisons (Gilligan, 2001; Torrey, 2001). Their abandonment is truly a national disgrace.

How Are People with Less Severe Disturbances Treated?

The treatment picture for people with moderate psychological disturbances has been more positive than that for people with severe disorders. Since the 1950s, outpatient care has continued to be the preferred mode of treatment for them, and the number and types of facilities that offer such care have increased to meet the need (NAPHS, 1999).

Before the 1950s, almost all outpatient care took the form of *private psychotherapy,* an arrangement by which an individual directly pays a psychotherapist for counseling services. This tended to be an expensive form of treatment, available only to the wealthy. Since the 1950s, however, most health insurance plans have expanded coverage to include private psychotherapy, so that it is now also widely available to people with modest incomes. In addition, outpatient therapy is now offered in a number of less expensive settings, such as community mental health

Zigy Kaluzny/Stone

The availability of therapy *Private psychotherapy is now widely available in individual, group, and family formats.*

centers, crisis intervention centers, family service centers, and other social service agencies. The new settings have spurred a dramatic increase in the number of persons seeking outpatient care for psychological problems. Nationwide surveys suggest that one of every six adults and one of every five children over the age of 9 now receive some form of mental health service in the course of a year (DHHS, 1999).

Outpatient treatments are also becoming available for more and more kinds of problems. When Freud and his colleagues first began to practice, most of their patients suffered from anxiety or depression. These problems still dominate therapy today; almost half of all clients suffer from them. However, people with other kinds of disorders are also receiving therapy (Zarin et al., 1998; Narrow et al., 1993). In addition, at least 25 percent of clients enter therapy because of milder problems in living—problems with marital, family, job, social, or school relationships.

Yet another change in outpatient care since the 1950s has been the development of programs devoted exclusively to one kind of psychological problem. We now have, for example, suicide prevention centers, substance abuse programs, eating disorder programs, phobia clinics, and sexual dysfunction programs. Clinicians in these programs offer the kind of expertise that can come only by concentration in a single area.

A Growing Emphasis on Preventing Disorders and Promoting Mental Health

Although the community mental health approach has often failed to address the needs of people with severe disorders, it has given rise to an important principle of mental health care—**prevention** (Compas & Gotlib, 2002; Felner et al., 2000). Rather than wait for psychological disorders to occur, many of today's community programs try to correct the social conditions that give rise to psychological problems (poverty or violence in the community, for example) and to help individuals who are at risk for developing emotional problems (for example, teenage mothers or the children of people with severe psychological disorders).

Prevention programs have been further energized in the past few years by the field's growing interest in **positive psychology** (Lazarus, 2003; Seligman & Csikszentmihalyi, 2000). Positive psychology is the study and encouragement of positive feelings such as optimism and happiness; positive traits like hard work and wisdom; positive abilities such as social skills; and group-directed virtues, including generosity and tolerance.

In the clinical arena, positive psychology suggests that practitioners can help people best by promoting positive development and psychological wellness. Clinicians with this orientation may teach people coping skills that help protect them from stress and adversity and may encourage them to become more involved in meaningful activities and relationships (Compas & Gotlib, 2002). Promotion and prevention programs have been offered during pregnancy, unemployment, divorce, and other periods of stress and have targeted such problem areas as substance abuse, violence, disaster trauma, and depression.

The Growing Influence of Insurance Coverage

So many people now seek therapy that private insurance companies have changed their coverage for mental health patients. Today the leading form of coverage is the **managed care program**—a program in which the insurance company determines such issues as which therapists its clients may choose, the cost of sessions, and the number of sessions for which a client may be reimbursed (Feldman, 2003).

At least 75 percent of all privately insured persons in the United States are currently enrolled in managed care programs (Kiesler, 2000). The coverage for mental health treatment under such programs follows the same basic principles as coverage for medical treatment, including a limited list of practitioners for patients to choose from, preapproval of treatment by the insurance company, strict standards for judging whether problems and treatments qualify for reimbursement, and ongoing reviews and assessments. In the mental health realm, both therapists and clients typically dislike the managed care programs. They fear that the programs shorten therapy (often for the worse), unfairly favor treatments whose results are not always lasting (for example, drug therapy), pose special hardships for those with severe mental disorders, and put control of therapy into the hands of insurance companies rather than of therapists (Mowbray et al., 2002).

A special problem with insurance coverage—both managed care and other kinds of insurance programs—is that reimbursements for mental disorders tend to be lower than those for medical disorders. This places persons with psychological difficulties at a distinct disadvantage (Feldman et al., 2002). Recently the federal government and many states have passed so-called *parity laws* that direct insurance companies to offer equal coverage for mental and medical problems. It is not yet clear, however, whether these laws will actually lead to improved coverage or better treatment (Feldman et al., 2002).

PREVENTION Interventions aimed at deterring mental disorders before they can develop.

POSITIVE PSYCHOLOGY The study and enhancement of positive feelings, traits, and abilities.

MANAGED CARE PROGRAM A system of health care coverage in which the insurance company largely controls the nature, scope, and cost of medical or psychological services.

"I wish I could help you. The problem is that you're too sick for managed care."

What Are Today's Leading Theories and Professions?

One of the most important developments in the clinical field has been the growth of numerous theoretical perspectives (Compas & Gotlib, 2002). Before the 1950s, the *psychoanalytic* perspective, with its emphasis on unconscious psychological problems as the cause of abnormal behavior, was dominant. Then the discovery of effective psychotropic drugs inspired new respect for the somatogenic, or *biological*, view. As we shall see in Chapter 2, other influential perspectives that have come forth since the 1950s are the *behavioral, cognitive, humanistic-existential*, and *sociocultural* schools of thought. At present no single viewpoint dominates the clinical field as the psychoanalytic perspective once did. In fact, the perspectives often conflict with one another; yet, as we shall see, in some instances they complement each other and together provide more complete explanations and treatments for psychological disorders (Widiger & Sankis, 2000).

In addition, a variety of professionals now offer help to people with psychological problems (Compas & Gotlib, 2002). Before the 1950s, psychotherapy was offered only by *psychiatrists*, physicians who complete three to four additional years of training after medical school (a *residency*) in the treatment of abnormal mental functioning. After World War II, however, the demand for mental health services increased so rapidly that other professional groups stepped in to fill the need (Humphreys, 1996).

Among those other groups are *clinical psychologists*—professionals who earn a doctorate in clinical psychology by completing four to five years of graduate training in abnormal functioning along with a one-year internship at a mental hospital or mental health agency. Psychotherapy and related services are also provided by *counseling psychologists, educational and school psychologists, psychiatric nurses, marriage therapists, family therapists*, and—the largest group—*psychiatric social workers* (see Table 1-2). Each of these specialties has its own graduate training program. Theoretically, each conducts therapy in a different way, but in reality clinicians from the various specialties often use similar techniques. In fact, the individual differences within a professional group are sometimes greater than the general differences between groups.

One final important development in the study and treatment of mental disorders since World War II has been a growing appreciation of the need for effective research (Goodwin, 2002). As theories and forms of treatment have increased, *clinical researchers* have tried to determine which concepts best explain and predict abnormal behavior, which treatments are most effective, and what kinds of changes may be required. Today well-trained clinical researchers carry out studies in universities, medical schools, laboratories, mental hospitals, mental health centers, and other clinical settings throughout the world.

Table 1-2

Profiles of Mental Health Professionals

	DEGREE	BEGAN TO PRACTICE	CURRENT NUMBER	MEDIAN AGE	PERCENT MALE
Psychiatrists	M.D., D.O.	1840s	33,486	52	75
Psychologists	Ph.D., Psy.D., Ed.D.	Late 1940s	69,817	48	52
Social workers	M.S.W., D.S.W.	Early 1950s	188,792	47	23
Marriage and family therapists	Various	1940s	46,227	52	45

Source: Barber, 1999; Zarin et al., 1988; Peterson et al., 1996; Knowlton, 1995.

SUMMING UP

Current Trends

In the 1950s, researchers discovered new psychotropic medications, drugs that mainly affect the brain and reduce many symptoms of mental dysfunctioning. Their success led to a policy of deinstitutionalization, under which hundreds of thousands of patients were released from public mental hospitals. In addition, outpatient treatment became the main approach for most persons with mental disorders, both mild and severe.

Currently prevention programs are growing in number and influence. At the same time, insurance coverage—particularly managed care—now has a significant impact on the way treatment is conducted. In addition, a variety of perspectives and professionals have come to operate in the field of abnormal psychology, and many well-trained clinical researchers now investigate the field's theories and treatments.

NOMOTHETIC UNDERSTANDING A general understanding of the nature, causes, and treatments of abnormal psychological functioning in the form of laws or principles.

SCIENTIFIC METHOD The process of systematically gathering and evaluating information through careful observations to gain an understanding of a phenomenon.

What Do Clinical Researchers Do?

Research is the key to accuracy in all fields of study, and it is particularly important in abnormal psychology, because wrong beliefs in this field can lead to great suffering. However, clinical researchers, also called clinical scientists, face certain challenges that make their work very difficult. They must figure out ways to measure elusive concepts such as unconscious motives, private thoughts, mood change, and human potential (Kazdin, 2003), and they must be sure that the rights of their subjects, both human and animal, are not violated (Kapp, 2002). By examining the leading methods used by today's researchers, we can better understand their tasks and challenges and judge their findings.

Clinical researchers try to discover broad laws, or principles, of abnormal psychological functioning. They search for **nomothetic**, or general, **understanding** of the nature, causes, and treatments of abnormality. To gather such insights, they, like scientists in other fields, use the **scientific method**—that is, they collect and evaluate information through careful observations (Gould, 2002). These observations in turn enable them to pinpoint relationships between variables.

Simply stated, a *variable* is any characteristic or event that can vary, whether from time to time, from place to place, or from person to person. Age, sex, and race are human variables. So are eye color, occupation, and social status. Clinical researchers are interested in variables such as childhood upsets, present life experiences, moods, social functioning, and responses to treatment. They try to determine whether two or more such variables change together and whether a change in one variable causes a change in another. Will the death of a parent cause a child to become depressed? If so, will a given treatment reduce that depression?

Such questions cannot be answered by logic alone, because scientists, like all human beings, make frequent errors in thinking. Thus clinical researchers rely mainly on three methods of investigation: the *case study*, which typically focuses on one individual, and the *correlational method* and *experimental method*, approaches that usually observe many individuals. Each is best suited to certain circumstances and questions (Beutler et al., 1995). As a group, these methods allow scientists to form and test *hypotheses*, or hunches, that certain variables are related in certain ways—and to draw broad conclusions as to why.

"I'm a social scientist, Michael. That means I can't explain electricity or anything like that, but if you ever want to know about people I'm your man."

>> STEPPING BACK

Too Obvious to Research?

Each of the following statements was once accepted as gospel. Had their validity not been tested, had they been judged on the basis of conventional wisdom alone, and had new ideas not been proposed and investigated, human knowledge and progress would have been severely limited. What enabled thinkers to move beyond such misperceptions? The answer, quite simply, is *research*, the systematic search for facts through the use of careful observations and investigations.

"The brain is an organ of minor importance."
Aristotle, Greek philosopher, Fourth Century B.C.

"Woman may be said to be an inferior man."
Aristotle

"[Louis Pasteur's] theory of germs is a ridiculous fiction."
Pierre Pochet, Professor of Physiology, 1872

"Everything that can be invented has been invented."
Charles Duell, U.S. Patent Office, 1899

"The theory of relativity [is] worthless and misleading."
T. J. J. See, U.S. Government Observatory, 1924

"If excessive smoking actually plays a role in the production of lung cancer, it seems to be a minor one."
W. C. Heuper, National Cancer Institute, 1954

"Space travel is utter bilge."
Richard van der Riet Wooley, British Astronomer Royal, 1956

"There is no reason for any individual to have a computer in their home."
Ken Olson, Digital Equipment Corp., 1977

"The cloning of mammals . . . is biologically impossible."
James McGrath and Davor Solter, Genetic Researchers, 1984

"Reality TV will never succeed."
Television critic, 2001

>>PSYCH•LISTINGS

Top Autobiographies Recommended by Therapists

An Unquiet Mind (K. R. Jamison)<<

Nobody Nowhere: The Autobiography of an Autistic (D. Williams)<<

Darkness Visible: A Memoir of Madness (W. Styron)<<

Out of the Depths (A. T. Boisen)<<

Girl, Interrupted (S. Kaysen)<<

Too Much Anger, Too Many Tears: A Personal Triumph over Psychiatry (Gotkin and Gotkin)<<

Undercurrents: A Therapist's Reckoning with Depression (M. Manning)<<

Getting Better: Inside Alcoholics Anonymous (N. Robertson)<<

The Case Study

A **case study** is a detailed description of a person's life and psychological problems. It describes the person's background, present circumstances, and symptoms. It may also speculate about why the problems developed, and it may describe the person's treatment. One of the field's best-known case studies, called *The Three Faces of Eve*, describes a woman with multiple personality disorder. The case study focuses on the woman's three alternating personalities, each having a distinct set of memories, preferences, and personal habits (Thigpen & Cleckley, 1957).

Most clinicians take notes and keep records in the course of treating their patients, and some further organize their notes into a formal case study to be shared with other professionals. The clues offered by a case study may help a clinician better understand or treat the person under discussion (Stricker & Trierweiler, 1995). In addition, case studies may play a role that goes far beyond the individual clinical case (Goodwin, 2002).

HOW ARE CASE STUDIES HELPFUL? Case studies can be a *source of new ideas* about behavior and "open the way for discoveries" (Bolgar, 1965). For example, Freud's theory of psychoanalysis was based mainly on the cases he saw in private practice. In addition, a case study may offer *tentative support* for a theory. Freud used case studies in this way as well, regarding them as evidence for the accuracy of his ideas. Conversely, case studies may serve to *challenge a theory's assumptions* (Kratochwill, 1992).

Case studies may also show the value of *new therapeutic techniques* or unique applications of existing techniques. And, finally, case studies may offer opportunities to study *unusual problems* that do not occur often enough to permit a large number of observations (Goodwin, 2002). Investigators of problems such as multiple personality disorder once relied entirely on case studies for information.

WHAT ARE THE LIMITATIONS OF CASE STUDIES? Case studies, although useful in many ways, also have limitations. First, they are reported by *biased observers*;

that is, by therapists who have a personal stake in seeing their treatments succeed (Goodwin, 2002). They must choose what to include in a case study, and their choices may at times be self-serving. Case studies also rely on *subjective evidence*. Is a client's problem really caused by the events that the therapist or client says are responsible? After all, those are only a fraction of the events that may have contributed to the problem. Finally, case studies provide *little basis for generalization*. Events or treatments that seem important in one case may be of no help at all in efforts to understand or treat others.

The limitations of the case study are largely addressed by two other methods of investigation: the *correlational method* and the *experimental method*. They do not offer the richness of detail that makes case studies so interesting, but they do help investigators draw broad conclusions about abnormality in the population at large. Thus they are now the preferred methods of clinical investigation.

Three features of the correlational and experimental methods enable clinical investigators to gain general insights: (1) The researchers typically observe many individuals. (2) They apply procedures uniformly and can thus repeat, or *replicate*, their investigations. (3) They use *statistical tests* to analyze and validate the results of a study.

The Correlational Method

Correlation is the degree to which events or characteristics vary with each other. The **correlational method** is a research procedure used to determine this "co-relationship" between variables. This method can, for example, answer the question "Is there a correlation between the amount of stress in people's lives and the degree of depression they experience?" That is, as people keep experiencing stressful events, are they increasingly likely to become depressed?

To test this question, researchers have collected life stress scores (for example, the number of threatening events experienced during a certain period of time) and depression scores (for example, scores on a depression survey). Typically, they have found that these variables increase or decrease together (Monroe & Hasdjiyannakis, 2002). That is, the greater a particular person's life stress score, the higher his or her score on a depression survey. Correlations of this kind are said to have a positive *direction*, and the correlation is referred to as a *positive correlation*.

Alternatively, correlations can have a negative rather than a positive direction. In a *negative correlation*, as the value of one variable increases, the value of the other variable decreases. Researchers have found, for example, a negative correlation between depression and activity level. The greater one's depression, the lower the number of one's activities.

There is still a third possible relationship in a correlational study. The variables under study may be *unrelated*, meaning that there is no consistent relationship between them. As the measures of one variable increase, those of the other variable sometimes increase and sometimes decrease. Studies have found, for example, that depression and intelligence are unrelated.

In addition to knowing the direction of a correlation, researchers need to know its *magnitude*, or strength. That is, how closely do the two variables correspond? Does one *always* vary along with the other, or is their relationship less exact? When two variables are found to vary together very closely in subject after subject, the correlation is said to be high, or strong.

The direction and magnitude of a correlation are often calculated numerically and expressed by a statistical term called the *correlation coefficient*. The correlation coefficient can vary from +1.00, which indicates a perfect positive correlation between two variables, down to −1.00, which represents a perfect negative correlation. The *sign* of the coefficient (+ or −) signifies the direction of the correlation; the *number* represents its magnitude. The closer the coefficient is to 0, the weaker, or lower in magnitude, it is. Thus correlations of +.75 and −.75 are of equal magnitude and equally strong, whereas a correlation of +.25 is weaker than either.

The most fantastic personal story ever told!

Case study, Hollywood style *Case studies often find their way into the arts or media and capture the public's attention. Unfortunately, as this movie poster of* The Three Faces of Eve *illustrates, the studies may be trivialized or sensationalized in those venues.*

CASE STUDY A detailed account of a person's life and psychological problems.

CORRELATIONAL METHOD A research procedure used to determine how much events or characteristics vary along with each other.

Monika Graff/The Image Works

The impact of stress *On the day after the September 11, 2001, terrorist attacks on the World Trade Center, a New York City couple and their cat make their way out of downtown Manhattan. Researchers have found that the stress produced by these attacks was accompanied by a significant rise in the onset of psychological symptoms and disorders.*

Everyone's behavior is changeable, and many human responses can be measured only approximately. Most correlations found in psychological research, therefore, fall short of a perfect positive or negative correlation. One study of life stress and depression in 68 adults found a correlation of +.53 (Miller et al., 1976). Although hardly perfect, a correlation of this magnitude is considered large in psychological research.

WHEN CAN CORRELATIONS BE TRUSTED? Scientists must decide whether the correlation they find in a given group of subjects accurately reflects a real correlation in the general population. Could the observed correlation have occurred only by chance? They can test their conclusions by a *statistical analysis* of their data, using principles of probability. In essence, they ask how likely it is that the study's particular findings have occurred by chance. If the statistical analysis indicates that chance is unlikely to account for the correlation they found, researchers call the correlation *statistically significant* and conclude that their findings reflect a real correlation in the general population.

WHAT ARE THE MERITS OF THE CORRELATIONAL METHOD? The correlational method has certain advantages over the case study. Because researchers measure their variables, observe many subjects, and apply statistical analyses, they are in a better position to generalize their correlations to people beyond the ones they have studied. Researchers are also able to repeat correlational studies on new samples of subjects so that they can check the results of such studies.

Although correlational studies allow researchers to describe the relationship between two variables, they do not explain the relationship. When we look at the positive correlation found in many life stress studies, we may be tempted to conclude that increases in recent life stress cause people to feel more depressed. In fact, however, the two variables may be correlated for any one of three reasons: (1) Life stress may cause depression. (2) Depression may cause people to experience more life stress (for example, a depressive approach to life may cause people to mismanage their money or may interfere with social relationships). (3) Depression and life stress may each be caused by a third variable, such as poverty. Questions about causality call, as we shall see, for the use of the experimental method.

SPECIAL FORMS OF CORRELATIONAL RESEARCH *Epidemiological studies* and *longitudinal studies* are two kinds of correlational research used widely by clinical investigators. **Epidemiological studies** reveal the incidence and prevalence of a disorder in a particular population. *Incidence* is the number of new cases that emerge during a given period of time. **Prevalence** is the total number of cases in the population during a given time period; prevalence includes both existing and new cases.

Over the past 30 years clinical researchers throughout the United States have worked on the largest epidemiological study ever conducted, called the Epidemiologic Catchment Area Study. They have interviewed more than 20,000 people in five cities to determine the prevalence of many psychological disorders and the treatment programs used (Regier et al., 1993). Another large-scale epidemiological study in the United States, the National Comorbidity Survey, has questioned more than 8,000 individuals (Kessler & Walters, 2002). Both studies have been further compared with epidemiological studies in other countries, to see how rates of mental disorders and treatment programs vary around the world (Alegria et al., 2000).

Such epidemiological studies have helped researchers detect groups at risk for particular disorders. Women, it turns out, have a higher rate of anxiety disorders and depression than men, while men have a higher rate of alcoholism than women. Elderly people have a higher rate of suicide than younger people. And per-

Twins, correlation, and inheritance
Correlational studies of many pairs of twins have suggested a link between genetic factors and certain psychological disorders. Identical twins (who have identical genes) display a higher correlation for some disorders than do fraternal twins (whose genetic makeup is not identical).

sons in some non-Western countries (such as Taiwan) have a higher rate of mental disorders than those in Western countries.

In **longitudinal studies**, correlational studies of another kind, researchers observe the same subjects on many occasions over a long period of time. In one such study, investigators have observed the progress over the years of normally functioning children whose mothers or fathers suffered from schizophrenia (Schiffman et al., 2002, 2001; Mednick, 1971). The researchers have found, among other things, that the children of the parents with the most severe cases of schizophrenia were more likely to develop a psychological disorder and to commit crimes at later points in their development.

The Experimental Method

An **experiment** is a research procedure in which a variable is manipulated and the manipulation's effect on another variable is observed. The manipulated variable is called the **independent variable**, and the variable being observed is called the **dependent variable**.

One of the questions that clinical scientists most often ask is: "Does a particular therapy reduce the symptoms of a given disorder?" Because this question is about a causal relationship, it can be answered only by an experiment (see Table 1-3 on the next page). That is, experimenters must give therapy to people who are suffering from a disorder and then observe whether they improve. Here the therapy is the independent variable, and psychological improvement is the dependent variable.

As with correlational studies, investigators must then do a statistical analysis on the data and find out how likely it is that the observed differences are due to chance. Again, if the likelihood is very low, the deserved differences are called statistically significant, and the experimenter concludes with some confidence that they are due to the independent variable.

If the true cause of changes in the dependent variable cannot be separated from other possible causes, then an experiment gives us very little information. Thus, experimenters must try to eliminate all *confounds* from the study—variables other than the independent variable that may also be affecting the dependent variable. When there are confounds in an experiment, they, rather than the independent variable, may be causing the observed changes.

EPIDEMIOLOGICAL STUDY A study that measures the incidence and prevalence of a disorder in a given population.

PREVALENCE The total number of cases of a disorder occurring in a population over a specific period of time.

LONGITUDINAL STUDY A study that observes the same subjects on many occasions over a long period of time.

EXPERIMENT A research procedure in which a variable is manipulated and the effect of the manipulation is observed.

INDEPENDENT VARIABLE The variable in an experiment that is manipulated to determine whether it has an effect on another variable.

DEPENDENT VARIABLE The variable in an experiment that is expected to change as the independent variable is manipulated.

Table 1-3

Relative Strengths and Weaknesses of Research Methods

	PROVIDES INDIVIDUAL INFORMATION	PROVIDES GENERAL INFORMATION	PROVIDES CAUSAL INFORMATION	STATISTICAL ANALYSIS POSSIBLE	REPLICABLE
Case study	Yes	No	No	No	No
Correlational method	No	Yes	No	Yes	Yes
Experimental method	No	Yes	Yes	Yes	Yes

For example, situational variables, such as the location of the therapy office (say, a quiet country setting) or a soothing color scheme in the office, may have a therapeutic effect on participants in a therapy study. Or perhaps the participants are unusually motivated or have high expectations that the therapy will work, factors that thus account for their improvement. To guard against the influence of confounds, researchers include three important features in their experiments—a *control group*, *random assignment*, and a *blind design* (Goodwin, 2002).

THE CONTROL GROUP A **control group** is a group of subjects who are not exposed to the independent variable under investigation but whose experience is similar to that of the **experimental group**, the subjects who are exposed to the independent variable. By comparing the two groups, an experimenter can better determine the effect of the independent variable.

To study the effectiveness of therapy, for example, experimenters typically divide subjects into two groups. The experimental group may come into an office and receive the therapy for an hour, while the control group may simply come into the office for an hour. If the experimenters find later that the people in the experimental group improve more than the people in the control group, they may conclude that the therapy was effective, above and beyond the effects of time, the office setting, and any other confounds. To guard against confounds, experimenters try to provide all participants, both control and experimental, with experiences that are identical in every way—except for the independent variable.

RANDOM ASSIGNMENT Researchers must also watch out for differences in the makeup of the experimental and control groups, since those differences may also confound a study's results. In a therapy study, for example, it may happen that the experimenter has unintentionally put wealthier subjects in the experimental group and poorer subjects in the control group. This difference, rather than their therapy, could be the cause of the greater improvement later found among the experimental subjects. To reduce the effects of preexisting differences, experimenters typically use **random assignment**. This is the general term for any selection procedure that ensures that every subject in the experiment is as likely to be placed in one group as the other. We might, for example, try flipping a coin or picking names out of a hat.

BLIND DESIGN A final confound problem is *bias*. Participants may bias an experiment's results by trying to please or help the experimenter (Goodwin, 2002). In a therapy experiment, for example, those who receive the treatment, knowing the purpose of the study and knowing which group they are in, might actually work harder to feel better

Is laughter a good medicine? *Members of this laughter club in Bombay, India, practice therapeutic laughing, or Hasyayog, a relatively new group treatment based on the belief that laughing at least 15 minutes each day will drive away depression and other ills. As many as 400 kinds of therapy are currently used for psychological problems. An experimental design is needed to determine whether this or any other form of treatment actively causes clients to improve.*

Robert Nickelsberg/The Image Works

or fulfill the experimenter's expectations. If so, *subject bias* rather than therapy could be causing their improvement.

To avoid this bias, experimenters can prevent participants from finding out which group they are in. This strategy is called a **blind design** because subjects are blind as to their assigned group. In a therapy study, for example, control subjects could be given a *placebo*, something that looks or tastes like real therapy but has none of its key ingredients. This "imitation" therapy is called *placebo therapy*. If the experimental (true therapy) subjects then improve more than the control (placebo therapy) subjects, experimenters have more confidence that the true therapy has caused their improvement.

An experiment may also be confounded by *experimenter bias* (Kazdin, 2003; Margraf et al., 1991)—that is, experimenters may have expectations that they unintentionally transmit to their subjects. This bias is sometimes referred to as the *Rosenthal effect*, after the psychologist who first identified it (Rosenthal, 1966). Experimenters can eliminate their own bias by arranging to be blind themselves. In a drug therapy study, for example, an aide could make sure that the real medication and the placebo drug look identical. The experimenter could then administer treatment without knowing which participants were receiving true medications and which were receiving false medications. While the participants or the experimenter may be kept blind in an experiment, it is best that *both* be blind (a *double-blind* design). In fact, most medication experiments now use double-blind designs to test promising drugs.

ALTERNATIVE EXPERIMENTAL DESIGNS Clinical researchers must often settle for experimental designs that are less than ideal (Kazdin, 2003). The most common such variations are the *quasi-experimental design*, the *natural experiment*, the *analogue experiment*, and the *single-subject experiment*.

In **quasi-experiments**, or **mixed designs**, investigators do not randomly assign subjects to control and experimental groups but instead make use of groups that already exist in the world at large (Goodwin, 2002). For example, because investigators of child abuse cannot actually abuse a randomly chosen group of children, they must instead compare children who already have a history of abuse with children who do not. To make this comparison as valid as possible, they may further use *matched control subjects*. That is, they match the experimental subjects with control subjects who are similar in age, sex, race, socioeconomic status, type of neighborhood, or other important characteristics. For every abused child in the experimental group, they choose an unabused child with similar characteristics to be included in the control group (Kinard, 1982).

In **natural experiments** nature itself manipulates the independent variable, while the experimenter observes the effects. Natural experiments must be used for studying the psychological effects of unusual and unpredictable events such as floods, earthquakes, plane crashes, and fires. Because the subjects in such studies are selected by an accident of fate rather than by investigator design, natural experiments are actually a kind of quasi-experiment.

Experimenters often run **analogue experiments**. Here they produce abnormal-like behavior in laboratory subjects—either animals or human—and then conduct experiments on the subjects in the hope of shedding light on the real-life abnormality. For example, the investigator Martin Seligman has produced depression-like symptoms in laboratory subjects by repeatedly exposing them to negative events (shocks, loud noises, task failures) over which they have no control. In these "learned helplessness" studies, the participants seem to give up, lose their initiative, and become sad.

Finally, scientists sometimes do not have the luxury of experimenting on many subjects. They may, for example, be investigating a disorder so rare that few subjects are available. Experimentation is still possible, however, with a **single-subject experimental design**. Here a single subject

CONTROL GROUP In an experiment, a group of subjects who are not exposed to the independent variable.

EXPERIMENTAL GROUP In an experiment, the subjects who are exposed to the independent variable under investigation.

RANDOM ASSIGNMENT A selection procedure that ensures that subjects are randomly placed either in the control group or in the experimental group.

BLIND DESIGN An experiment in which subjects do not know whether they are in the experimental or the control condition.

QUASI-EXPERIMENT An experiment which makes use of control and experimental groups that already exist in the world at large. Also called a *mixed design*.

NATURAL EXPERIMENT An experiment in which nature, rather than an experimenter, manipulates an independent variable.

ANALOGUE EXPERIMENT A research method in which the experimenter produces abnormal-like behavior in laboratory subjects and then studies the subjects.

SINGLE-SUBJECT EXPERIMENT An experiment which measures a single subject both before and after the manipulation of an independent variable.

Natural experiments *A man surveys the damage wrought by a hurricane upon his home and belongings. Natural experiments conducted in the aftermath of such catastrophes have found that many survivors experience lingering feelings of anxiety and depression.*

THE CURRENT SCENE

Subjects Have Rights

For years researchers have learned about abnormal human behavior from experiments with animals. Animals have sometimes been shocked, prematurely separated from their parents, and starved. They have had their brains surgically changed and they have even been killed, or "sacrificed," so that researchers could autopsy them. Are such actions always ethically acceptable?

Animal rights activists say no (Cohen & Regan, 2001). They have called the undertakings cruel and unnecessary and have fought many forms of animal research with legal protests and demonstrations. Some have even harassed scientists and vandalized their labs. In turn, some researchers accuse the activists of caring more about animals than about human beings. In response to this controversy, a number of state courts, government agencies, and the American Psychological Association have issued rules and guidelines for animal research. Still, the battle goes on (Goodwin, 2002).

No less controversial are debates over the rights of human subjects in studies of abnormal behavior. Regulations were established in the 1970s to ensure that the rights of all human subjects, particularly those with psychological disorders, were protected in research. In the United States, the Department of Health and Human Services insisted, for example, that all human subjects be clearly informed about the nature of the study in which they were participating, including its foreseeable risks (Lemonick & Goldstein, 2002). Other countries set up similar procedures and guidelines.

These efforts have greatly improved the ethics of clinical research, but some serious problems remain (Kapp, 2002; Saks et al., 2002). In fact, the clinical field was rocked just a few years ago by a series of reports that revealed that during the 1980s and 1990s, many patients with severe mental disorders had been harmed or placed at risk in clinical studies (Kong, 1998). The studies in question typically involved antipsychotic drug treatments for patients with psychosis

(loss of contact with reality). It appears that many patients in these studies had agreed to receive drug treatments (or not to receive them) without fully understanding the risks involved. In addition, the drugs used in these studies left some of the subjects with more intense psychotic symptoms. Four types of studies were cited:

❖ **New Drug Studies** Patients are administered an experimental drug to see whether it reduces their symptoms. The new drug is being tested for effectiveness, safety, undesired effects, and dosage, meaning that the patients may be helped, unaffected, or damaged by the drug.

❖ **Placebo Studies** When a new drug is being tested on a group of experimental subjects, researchers may administer a *placebo drug* to a group of control subjects. The improvement of the experimental subjects is then compared with that of the placebo control subjects to determine the new drug's effectiveness. Unfortunately, in such studies, the placebo control subjects—often people with severe disorders—are receiving no treatment at all.

❖ **Symptom-Exacerbation Studies** Patients are given drugs designed to intensify their symptoms, so that researchers may learn more about the biology of their disorder. For example, people suffering from psychotic disorders have been given apomorphine, amphetamine, ketamine, and other drugs that lead to more delusions, hallucinations, and the like.

❖ **Medication-Withdrawal Studies** Researchers prematurely stop medications for patients who have been symptom-free while taking the medications. The researchers then follow the patients as they relapse, in the hope of learning more about how and when patients can be taken off particular medications.

Each of these kinds of studies seeks to increase understanding of certain disorders and to improve treatment. Yet at what risk? When does the benefit to many outweigh the suffering of a few? As the clinical community and the public have grown more aware of the risks involved in these studies, they have called for better safeguards to protect research subjects with mental disorders. In 1999, for example, the National Institute of Mental Health suspended some of its symptom-exacerbation studies. Moreover, the Office for Human Research Protection has recently undergone sweeping changes designed to make the agency more aggressive in its protection of human subjects (Lemonick & Goldstein, 2002). And Congress is currently preparing to introduce legislation that will protect the rights of human subjects in all studies, not just those receiving federal funding. Nevertheless, this important issue is far from being resolved.

is observed both before and after the manipulation of an independent variable.

For example, using a particular single-subject design, called an *ABAB,* or *reversal, design*, one researcher sought to determine whether the systematic use of rewards would reduce a teenage boy's habit of disrupting his special education class with loud talk (Deitz, 1977). He rewarded the boy, who suffered from mental retardation, with extra teacher time whenever he went 55 minutes without interrupting the class more than three times. In condition A, the student was observed prior to receiving any rewards, and he was found to disrupt the class frequently with loud talk. In condition B, the boy was given a series of teacher reward sessions (introduction of the independent variable); his loud talk was found to decrease dramatically, as expected. Then the rewards from the teacher were stopped (condition A again), and the student's loud talk increased once again. Apparently the independent variable had indeed been the cause of the improvement. To be still more confident about this conclusion, the researcher had the teacher apply reward sessions yet again (condition B again). Once again the boy's behavior improved.

Similar enough? *Chimpanzees and human beings share more than 90 percent of their genetic material, but their brains and bodies are very different, as are their perceptions and experiences. Thus, abnormal-like behavior produced in animal analogue experiments may differ from the human abnormality under investigation.*

What Are the Limits of Clinical Investigations?

We began this discussion by noting that clinical scientists look for general laws that will help them understand, prevent, and treat psychological disorders. As we have seen, however, various circumstances can interfere with their progress (Kazdin, 2003).

Each method of investigation that we have observed addresses some of the problems involved in studying human behavior, but no one approach overcomes them all. Thus, it is best to view each research method as part of a team of approaches that together may shed considerable light on abnormal human functioning. When more than one method has been used to investigate a disorder, it is important to ask whether all the results seem to point in the same direction. If they do, we are probably that much closer to understanding that disorder fully and treating it effectively. Conversely, if the various methods seem to produce conflicting results, we must admit that our knowledge in that particular area is still limited.

SUMMING UP

What Do Clinical Researchers Do?

Clinical researchers use the scientific method to uncover general principles of abnormal psychological functioning. They depend primarily on three methods of investigation: the case study, the correlational method, and the experimental method.

A case study is a detailed account of a person's life and psychological problems.

Correlational studies systematically observe the degree to which events or characteristics vary together. This method allows researchers to draw broad conclusions about abnormality in the population at large. Two widely used forms of the correlation method are epidemiological studies and longitudinal studies.

In experiments, researchers manipulate suspected causes to see whether expected effects will result. This method allows investigators to pinpoint the causes of various conditions or events. Clinical experimenters must often settle for experimental designs that are less than ideal, including quasi-experiments, natural experiments, analogue experiments, and single-subject experiments.

>>**PSYCH•LISTINGS**

Most Investigated Causal Questions in Clinical Research

Does factor X cause a disorder?‹‹

Is cause A more influential than cause B?‹‹

How do family communication and structure affect family members?‹‹

How does a disorder affect the quality of a person's life?‹‹

How does a person's disorder affect family members?‹‹

Does treatment X alleviate a disorder?‹‹

Is treatment A more helpful than treatment B?‹‹

Why does treatment X work?‹‹

Does greater therapist expertise lead to greater progress in treatment?‹‹

Can an intervention prevent abnormal functioning?‹‹

>>PSYCH•NOTES

Science and Scientists

The word "scientist" did not exist until it was coined by the nineteenth-century English scholar William Whewell.<<

An estimated 20 million people were subjects in medical or psychological studies in 2001.<<

(Shamoo, 2002; Asimov, 1997)

CROSSROADS:
A Work in Progress

Since ancient times, people have tried to explain, treat, and study abnormal behavior. By examining the way past societies responded to such behaviors we can better understand the roots of our present views and treatments. In addition, a look backward helps us appreciate just how far we have come—how humane our present views, how impressive our recent discoveries, and how important our current emphasis on research.

At the same time we must recognize the many problems in abnormal psychology today. The field has yet to agree on one definition of abnormality. It is currently made up of conflicting schools of thought and treatment whose members are often unimpressed by the claims and accomplishments of the others. Clinical practice is carried out by a variety of professionals trained in different ways. And current research methods each have flaws that limit our knowledge and use of clinical information.

As we proceed through the topics in this book and look at the nature, treatment, and study of abnormal functioning, we must keep in mind the field's current strengths and weaknesses, the progress that has been made, and the journey that lies ahead. Perhaps the most important lesson to be learned from our look at the history of this field is that our current understanding of abnormal behavior represents a work in progress. The clinical field stands at a *crossroads*, with some of the most important investigations, insights, and changes yet to come.

CRITICAL THOUGHTS

1. Why are movies and novels with themes of abnormal functioning so popular? Why do actresses and actors who portray characters with psychological disorders tend to receive more awards for their performances? *p. 1*

2. What behaviors might fit the criteria of deviant, distressful, dysfunctional, or dangerous, yet would not be considered abnormal by most people? *pp. 4–5*

3. Have episodes of mass madness occurred in recent times? How might the Internet, cable television, or other forms of modern technology pose a special danger in the emergence and spread of new forms of mass madness? *p. 8*

4. Even when there are credible, well-known research findings to the contrary, many people hold on to false beliefs about human behavior, particularly abnormal behavior. Why does research fail to change their views? *pp. 19–20, 27*

5. Why might sugar pills or other kinds of placebo treatments help some people feel better? *p. 25*

KEY TERMS

QUICK QUIZ

1. What features are common to abnormal psychological functioning? *pp. 2–3*

2. Name two past treatments that reflect a demonological view of abnormal behavior. *pp. 7–10*

3. Give examples of the somatogenic view of psychological abnormality from Hippocrates, the Renaissance, the nineteenth century, and the recent past. *pp. 8–16*

4. Discuss the rise and fall of moral treatment. *pp. 11–12*

5. Describe the role of hypnotism and hysterical disorders in the development of the psychogenic view. *pp. 13–14*

6. How did Sigmund Freud come to develop the theory and technique of psychoanalysis? *p. 14*

7. Describe the major changes in the treatment of people with mental disorders that have occurred since the 1950s. *pp. 15–18*

8. What are the advantages and disadvantages of the case study, correla-

tional method, and experimental method? *pp. 19–25*

9. What techniques do researchers include in experiments to guard against the influence of confounds? *pp. 23–25*

10. Describe four kinds of alternative experimental designs that researchers often use. *pp. 25–27*

CYBER STUDY

SEARCH THE *FUNDAMENTALS OF ABNORMAL PSYCHOLOGY* CD-ROM FOR

▲ Chapter 1 Video Case Enrichment
What did past hospital treatments for severe mental disorders look like?
How do researchers study and measure psychopathology?
Observe the power of bias and expectations in research.

▲ Chapter 1 Practical, Research, and Decision-Making Exercises
Comparing today's treatments to those of the past
Abnormality and the arts
Misusing anecdotal information

▲ Chapter 1 Practice Test and Feedback

LOG ON TO THE COMER WEB PAGE FOR

▲ Suggested Web links, exercises, FAQ page, additional Chapter 1 practice test questions
<www.worthpublishers.com/comer>

‹‹‹

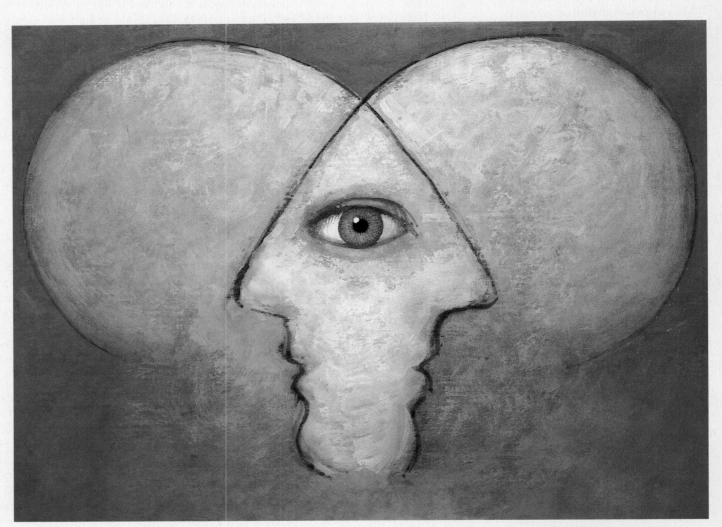

MIECZYSLAW GÓROWSKI, 1995

Models of Abnormality

Philip Berman, a 25-year-old single unemployed former copy editor for a large publishing house, . . . had been hospitalized after a suicide attempt in which he deeply gashed his wrist with a razor blade. He described [to the therapist] how he had sat on the bathroom floor and watched the blood drip into the bathtub for some time before he telephoned his father at work for help. He and his father went to the hospital emergency room to have the gash stitched, but he convinced himself and the hospital physician that he did not need hospitalization. The next day when his father suggested he needed help, he knocked his dinner to the floor and angrily stormed to his room. When he was calm again, he allowed his father to take him back to the hospital.

The immediate precipitant for his suicide attempt was that he had run into one of his former girlfriends with her new boyfriend. The patient stated that they had a drink together, but all the while he was with them he could not help thinking that "they were dying to run off and jump in bed." He experienced jealous rage, got up from the table, and walked out of the restaurant. He began to think about how he could "pay her back."

Mr. Berman had felt frequently depressed for brief periods during the previous several years. He was especially critical of himself for his limited social life and his inability to have managed to have sexual intercourse with a woman even once in his life. As he related this to the therapist, he lifted his eyes from the floor and with a sarcastic smirk said, "I'm a 25-year-old virgin. Go ahead, you can laugh now." He has had several girlfriends to date, whom he described as very attractive, but who he said had lost interest in him. On further questioning, however, it became apparent that Mr. Berman soon became very critical of them and demanded that they always meet his every need, often to their own detriment. The women then found the relationship very unrewarding and would soon find someone else.

During the past two years Mr. Berman had seen three psychiatrists briefly, one of whom had given him a drug, the name of which he could not remember, but that had precipitated some sort of unusual reaction for which he had to stay in a hospital overnight. . . . Concerning his hospitalization, the patient said that "It was a dump," that the staff refused to listen to what he had to say or to respond to his needs, and that they, in fact, treated all the patients "sadistically." The referring doctor corroborated that Mr. Berman was a difficult patient who demanded that he be treated as special, and yet was hostile to most staff members throughout his stay. After one angry exchange with an aide, he left the hospital without leave, and subsequently signed out against medical advice.

Mr. Berman is one of two children of a middle-class family. His father is 55 years old and employed in a managerial position for an insurance company. He perceives his father as weak and ineffectual, completely dominated by the patient's overbearing and cruel mother. He states that he hates his mother with "a passion I can barely control." He claims that his mother used to call him names like "pervert" and "sissy" when he was growing up, and that in an argument she once "kicked me in the balls." Together, he sees his parents as rich, powerful, and selfish, and, in turn, thinks that they see him as lazy, irresponsible, and a behavior problem. When his parents called the therapist to discuss their son's treatment, they stated that his problem began with the birth of his younger brother, Arnold, when Philip was 10 years old. After

Arnold's birth Philip apparently became an "ornery" child who cursed a lot and was difficult to discipline. Philip recalls this period only vaguely. He reports that his mother once was hospitalized for depression, but that now "she doesn't believe in psychiatry."

Mr. Berman had graduated from college with average grades. Since graduating he had worked at three different publishing houses, but at none of them for more than one year. He always found some justification for quitting. He usually sat around his house doing very little for two or three months after quitting a job, until his parents prodded him into getting a new one. He described innumerable interactions in his life with teachers, friends, and employers in which he felt offended or unfairly treated, . . . and frequent arguments that left him feeling bitter . . . and spent most of his time alone, "bored." He was unable to commit himself to any person, he held no strong convictions, and he felt no allegiance to any group.

The patient appeared as a very thin, bearded, and bespectacled young man with pale skin who maintained little eye contact with the therapist and who had an air of angry bitterness about him. Although he complained of depression, he denied other symptoms of the depressive syndrome. He seemed preoccupied with his rage at his parents, and seemed particularly invested in conveying a despicable image of himself. . . .

(Spitzer et al., 1983, pp. 59–61)

Philip Berman is clearly a troubled person, but how did he come to be that way? How do we explain and correct his many problems? To answer these questions, we must first look at the wide range of complaints we are trying to understand: Philip's depression and anger, his social failures, his lack of employment, his distrust of those around him, and the problems within his family. Then we must sort through all kinds of potential causes, internal and external, biological and interpersonal, past and present. Which is having the biggest impact on his behavior?

Although we may not realize it, we all use theoretical frameworks as we read about Philip. Over the course of our lives, each of us has developed a perspective that helps us make sense of the things other people say and do. In science, the perspectives used to explain events are known as **models**, or **paradigms**. Each model spells out the scientist's basic assumptions, gives order to the field under study, and sets guidelines for its investigation (Kuhn, 1962). It influences what the investigators observe as well as the questions they ask, the information they seek, and how they interpret this information (Sharf, 2000). To understand how a clinician explains or treats a specific set of symptoms, such as Philip's, we must know his or her preferred model of abnormal functioning.

Until recently, clinical scientists of a given place and time tended to agree on a single model of abnormality—a model greatly influenced by the beliefs of their culture. The demonological model that was used to explain abnormal functioning during the Middle Ages, for example, borrowed heavily from medieval society's concerns with religion, superstition, and warfare. Medieval practitioners would have seen the devil's guiding hand in Philip Berman's efforts to commit suicide and his feelings of depression, rage, jealousy, and hatred. Similarly, their treatments for him—from prayers to whippings—would have sought to drive foreign spirits from his body.

Today several models are used to explain and treat abnormal functioning. This variety has resulted from shifts in values and beliefs over the past half-century, as well as improvements in clinical research. At one end of the spectrum is the *biological model*, which sees physical processes as the key to human behavior. At the other end is the *sociocultural model*, which examines the effects of society and culture on individual behavior. In between are four models that focus on more psychological and personal aspects of human functioning: the *psychodynamic model* looks at people's unconscious internal events and conflicts; the *behavioral model*

>>PSYCH•NOTES

Brain Matters

A worm's brain has 23 neurons.
- -
An ostrich's brain is smaller than its eye.
- -
The average human brain weighs 3 pounds; the human liver weighs around 4 pounds.
- -
80 percent of the human brain is water.
- -
Messages travel to the brain at 224 miles per hour.
- -
One neuron may connect to as many as 25,000 others.
- -

(Ash, 1999; Jordon, 1998; Asimov, 1997; Roan, 1995)

emphasizes behavior and the ways in which it is learned; the *cognitive model* concentrates on the thinking that underlies behavior; and the *humanistic-existential model* stresses the role of values and choices.

Given their different assumptions and concepts, the models are sometimes in conflict. Those who follow one perspective often scoff at the "naive" interpretations, investigations, and treatment efforts of the others. Yet none of the models are complete in themselves. Each focuses mainly on one aspect of human functioning, and none can explain all aspects of abnormality.

MODEL A set of assumptions and concepts that helps scientists explain and interpret observations. Also called a *paradigm*.

NEURON A nerve cell.

The Biological Model

Philip Berman is a biological being. His thoughts and feelings are the results of biochemical and bioelectrical processes throughout his brain and body. Proponents of the *biological model* believe that a full understanding of his thoughts, emotions, and behavior must therefore include an understanding of their biological basis. Not surprisingly, they believe that the most effective treatments for Philip's problems will then be biological ones.

How Do Biological Theorists Explain Abnormal Behavior?

Adopting a medical perspective, biological theorists view abnormal behavior as an illness brought about by malfunctioning parts of the organism. Typically, they point to a malfunctioning brain as the cause of abnormal behavior (Andreasen, 2001).

BRAIN ANATOMY AND ABNORMAL BEHAVIOR The brain is made up of approximately 100 billion nerve cells, called **neurons**, and thousands of billions of support cells, called *glia* (from the Greek meaning "glue"). Within the brain large groups of neurons form distinct areas, or *brain regions*. To identify the regions of the brain more easily, let us imagine them as continents, countries, and states.

At the bottom of the brain is the "continent" known as the *hindbrain*, which is in turn made up of countrylike regions called the *medulla*, *pons*, and *cerebellum* (see Figure 2-1). In the middle of the brain is the "continent" called the *midbrain*. And at the top is the "continent" called the *forebrain*, which consists of countrylike regions called the *cerebrum* (the two cerebral hemispheres), the *thalamus*, and the *hypothalamus*, each in turn made up of statelike regions. The cerebrum, for instance, consists of the *cortex, corpus callosum, basal ganglia, hippocampus,* and *amygdala*. The neurons in each of these brain regions control important functions. The hippocampus helps control emotions and memory, for example. Clinical researchers have discovered connections between certain psychological disorders and problems in specific areas of the brain. One such disorder is *Huntington's disease*, a disorder marked by violent emotional outbursts, memory loss, suicidal thinking, involuntary body movements, and absurd beliefs. This disease has been traced to a loss of cells in the basal ganglia.

FIGURE 2-1 **The human brain** *A slice through the center of the brain reveals its major divisions and regions. Each region, composed of numerous neurons, is responsible for certain functions.*

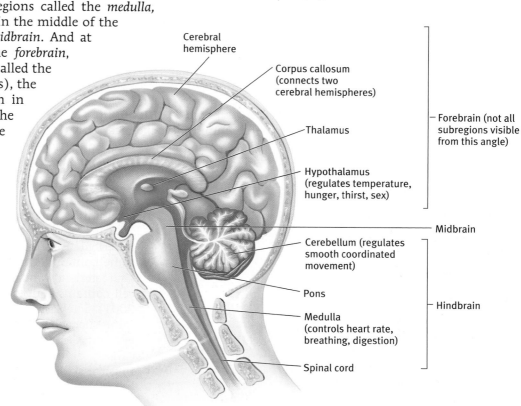

Cerebral hemisphere

Corpus callosum (connects two cerebral hemispheres)

Thalamus

Hypothalamus (regulates temperature, hunger, thirst, sex)

Forebrain (not all subregions visible from this angle)

Midbrain

Cerebellum (regulates smooth coordinated movement)

Pons

Hindbrain

Medulla (controls heart rate, breathing, digestion)

Spinal cord

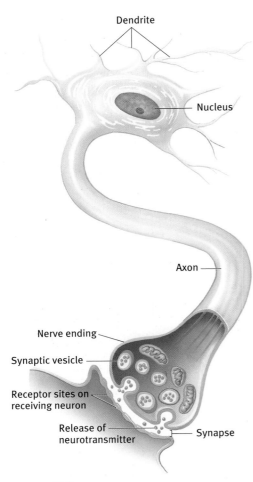

Dendrite

Nucleus

Axon

Nerve ending

Synaptic vesicle

Receptor sites on
receiving neuron

Release of
neurotransmitter

Synapse

FIGURE 2-2 **A typical neuron** *A message travels down the neuron's axon to the nerve ending, where neurotransmitters carry the message across the synaptic space to a receiving neuron. (Adapted from Bloom et al., 1985, p. 35.)*

Biological breakthrough *The Human Genome Project was completed in 2000. In this massive undertaking, scientists used the tools of molecular biology to produce a map, shown here, of all the genes in the human body.*

AP Photo/Ron Edmonds

BRAIN CHEMISTRY AND ABNORMAL BEHAVIOR Biological researchers have also learned that psychological disorders can be related to problems in the transmission of messages from neuron to neuron. Information spreads throughout the brain in the form of electrical impulses that travel from one neuron to one or more others. An impulse is first received by a neuron's *dendrites*, antenna-like extensions located at one end of the neuron. From there it travels down the neuron's *axon*, a long fiber extending from the neuron body. Finally, it is transmitted to other neurons through the *nerve endings*, at the far end of the neuron (see Figure 2-2).

But how do messages get from the nerve endings of one neuron to the dendrites of another? After all, the neurons do not actually touch each other. A tiny space, called the *synapse*, separates one neuron from the next, and the message must somehow move across that space. When an electrical impulse reaches a neuron's ending, the nerve ending is stimulated to release a chemical, called a **neurotransmitter**, that travels across the synaptic space to *receptors* on the dendrites of the adjacent neurons. Upon reception, some neurotransmitters tell the receiving neurons to "fire"; that is, to trigger their own electrical impulse. Other neurotransmitters tell receiving neurons to stop all firing. Obviously, neurotransmitters play a key role in moving information through the brain.

Researchers have identified dozens of neurotransmitters in the brain, and they have learned that each neuron uses only certain kinds (Andreasen, 2001). Studies indicate that abnormal activity by certain neurotransmitters can lead to specific mental disorders. Certain anxiety disorders, for example, have been linked to low activity of the neurotransmitter *gamma-aminobutyric acid (GABA)*, schizophrenia has been linked to excessive activity of the neurotransmitter *dopamine*, and depression has been linked to low activity of the neurotransmitters *serotonin* and *norepinephrine*. Perhaps low serotonin activity is responsible for Philip Berman's pattern of depression and rage.

In addition to focusing on neurons and neurotransmitters, researchers have learned that mental disorders are sometimes related to abnormal chemical activity in the body's *endocrine system*. Endocrine glands, located throughout the body, work along with neurons to control such vital activities as growth, reproduction, sexual activity, heart rate, body temperature, energy, and responses to stress. The glands release chemicals called **hormones** into the bloodstream, and these chemicals then propel body organs into action. During times of stress, for example, the *adrenal glands*, located on top of the kidneys, secrete the hormone *cortisol*. Abnormal secretions of this chemical have been tied to anxiety and mood disorders.

SOURCES OF BIOLOGICAL ABNORMALITIES Why do some people have brain structures or biochemical activities that differ from the norm? Three factors have received particular attention from clinical theorists in recent years—*genetics, evolution,* and *viral infections*.

GENETICS AND ABNORMAL BEHAVIOR Abnormalities in brain anatomy or chemistry are sometimes the result of genetic inheritance. Each cell in the human brain and body contains 23 pairs of *chromosomes*, with each chromosome in a pair inherited from one of the person's parents. Every chromosome contains numerous **genes**—segments that control the characteristics and traits a person inherits. Altogether, each cell contains between 30,000 and 40,000 genes (Andreasen, 2001). Scientists have known for years that genes help determine such physical characteristics as hair color, height, and eyesight. Genes can make people more prone to heart disease, cancer, or diabetes, and perhaps to possessing artistic or musical skill.

Studies also suggest that inheritance plays a part in mood disorders, schizophrenia, Alzheimer's disease, and other mental disorders. Yet, with few exceptions, researchers have not been able to identify the specific genes that are the culprits. Nor do they yet know the extent to which genetic factors contribute to various mental disorders. It appears that in most cases several genes combine to help produce our actions and reactions, both functional and dysfunctional.

EVOLUTION AND ABNORMAL BEHAVIOR Genes that contribute to mental disorders are typically viewed as unfortunate occurrences—almost mistakes of inheritance. The responsible gene may be a *mutation*, an abnormal form of the appropriate gene that emerges by accident. Or the problematic gene may be inherited by an individual after it has initially entered the family line as a mutation (Andreasen, 2001). According to some theorists, however, many of the genes that contribute to abnormal functioning are actually the result of normal *evolutionary* principles (Fábrega, 2002; Caporael, 2001).

In general, evolutionary theorists argue that human reactions and the genes responsible for them have survived over the course of time because they have helped individuals to thrive and adapt. Ancestors who had the ability to run fast, for example, or the craftiness to hide, were most able to escape their enemies and to reproduce. In turn, the genes responsible for effective walking, running, or problem solving were particularly likely to be passed on from generation to generation to the present day.

The evolutionary position with regard to abnormal functioning follows a similar logic. For example, according to evolutionary theorists, the capacity to experience fear was, and in many instances still is, adaptive. Fear alerted our ancestors to dangers, threats, and losses, so that they could avoid or escape potential problems. People who were particularly sensitive to danger—those with greater fear responses—were more likely to survive catastrophes, battles, and the like, and to reproduce, and so to pass on their intense fear genes. Of course, in today's world pressures are more numerous, subtle, and complex than they were in the past, condemning individuals who have inherited such fear genes to a near-endless stream of fear and arousal. That is, the very genes that helped their ancestors to survive and reproduce might now leave these individuals particularly prone to fear reactions and anxiety disorders.

VIRAL INFECTIONS AND ABNORMAL BEHAVIOR Another possible source of abnormal brain structure or biochemical dysfunctioning is *viral infections*. As we shall see in Chapter 12, for example, research suggests that schizophrenia, a disorder marked by delusions, hallucinations, or other departures from reality, may be related to a fetus's exposure to certain viruses before birth (de Messias et al., 2001; Torrey, 2001, 1991). Studies have found that the mothers of many individuals with this disorder contracted influenza or related viruses during their pregnancy. On the basis of this and related pieces of circumstantial evidence, some theorists believe that a damaging virus enters the brain in certain fetuses and remains dormant in these individuals until puberty or young adulthood. At that time, the virus may produce the symptoms of schizophrenia.

More than coincidence? *Studies of twins suggest that some aspects of behavior and personality are influenced by genetic factors. Many identical twins, like these musicians, are found to have similar tastes, behave in similar ways, and make similar life choices. Some even develop similar abnormal behaviors.*

Biological Treatments

Biological practitioners look for certain kinds of clues when they try to understand abnormal behavior. Does the person's family have a history of that behavior, and hence a possible genetic predisposition to it? (Philip Berman's case history mentions that his mother was once hospitalized for depression.) Is the behavior produced by events that could have had a physiological effect? (Philip was having a drink when he flew into a jealous rage at the restaurant.)

Once the clinicians have pinpointed physical sources of dysfunctioning, they are in a better position to choose a biological course of treatment. The three

NEUROTRANSMITTER A chemical that, released by one neuron, crosses the synaptic space to be received at receptors on the dendrites of neighboring neurons.

HORMONES The chemicals released by glands into the bloodstream.

GENE Chromosome segments that control the characteristics and traits we inherit.

Preclinical Phase (5 years)
New drug is developed and identified.
Drug is tested on animals, usually rats, to help determine its safety and efficacy.

Clinical Phase I: Safety Screening (1.5 years)
Investigators test drug on human subjects to determine its safety.
• Number of subjects: 10–100
• Typical cost: $10 million

Clinical Phase II: Preliminary Testing (2 years)
Investigators conduct studies with human subjects to determine how drug can best be evaluated and to obtain preliminary estimates of correct dosage and treatment procedures.
• Number of subjects: 50–500
• Typical cost: $20 million

Clinical Phase III: Final Testing (3.5 years)
Investigators conduct controlled studies to fully determine drug's efficacy and important side effects.
• Number of subjects: 300–30,000
• Typical cost: $45 million

Review by FDA (1.5 years)
Research is reviewed by FDA, and drug is approved or disapproved.

Postmarketing Surveillance (10 years)
Long after the drug is on the marketplace, testing continues and doctors' reports are gathered. Manufacturer must report any unexpected long-term effects and side effects.

FIGURE 2-3 **How does a new drug reach the marketplace?** *It takes an average of 14 years and tens of millions of dollars for a pharmaceutical company in the United States to bring a newly discovered drug to market. The company must carefully follow steps that are mandated by law. (Adapted from Lemonick & Goldstein, 2002; Andreasen, 2001; Zivin, 2000.)*

Worldwide phenomenon *The psychotropic drug revolution has spread throughout the world. Here a nurse gives medications to patients at Cambodia's largest mental health facility.*

leading kinds of biological treatments used today are *drug therapy, electroconvulsive therapy*, and *psychosurgery*. Drug therapy is by far the most common of these approaches; psychosurgery is infrequent.

In the 1950s, researchers discovered several effective **psychotropic medications**, drugs that mainly affect emotions and thought processes (see Figure 2-3). These drugs have greatly changed the outlook for a number of mental disorders and today are used widely, either alone or with other forms of therapy. However, the psychotropic drug revolution has also produced some major problems. Many people believe, for example, that the drugs are overused. Moreover, while drugs are effective in many cases, they do not help everyone.

Four major psychotropic drug groups are used in therapy: antianxiety, antidepressant, antibipolar, and antipsychotic drugs. *Antianxiety drugs,* also called *minor tranquilizers* or *anxiolytics,* help reduce tension and anxiety. *Antidepressant drugs* help improve the mood of people who are depressed. *Antibipolar drugs,* also called *mood stabilizers,* help steady the mood of those with a bipolar disorder, a condition marked by mood swings from mania to depression. And *antipsychotic drugs* help reduce the confusion, hallucinations, and delusions of *psychotic disorders*, disorders marked by a loss of contact with reality.

The second form of biological treatment, used primarily on depressed patients, is **electroconvulsive therapy (ECT)**. Two electrodes are attached to a patient's forehead and an electrical current of 65 to 140 volts is passed briefly through the brain. The current causes a brain seizure that lasts up to a few minutes. After seven to nine ECT sessions, spaced two or three days apart, many patients feel considerably less depressed. The treatment is used on tens of thousands of depressed persons annually, particularly those whose depression fails to respond to other treatments (Johnstone, 2000).

A third form of biological treatment is **psychosurgery**, brain surgery for mental disorders. It is thought to have roots as far back as trephining, the prehistoric practice of chipping a hole in the skull of a person who behaved strangely. Modern procedures are derived from a technique first developed in the late 1930s by a Portuguese neuropsychiatrist, Antonio de Egas Moniz. In that procedure, known as a *lobotomy*, a surgeon would cut the connections between the brain's frontal lobes and the lower centers of the brain. Today's psychosurgery procedures are considered experimental and are used only after certain severe disorders have continued for years without responding to any other form of treatment.

Assessing the Biological Model

Today the biological model enjoys considerable respect. Biological research constantly produces valuable new information. And biological treatments often bring great relief when other approaches have failed. At the same time, this model has its shortcomings. Some of its followers seem to expect that all human behavior can be explained in biological terms and treated with biological methods. This view can limit rather than enhance our understanding of abnormal functioning (Kosslyn et al., 2002). Our mental life is an interplay of biological and nonbiological factors, and it is important to understand that interplay rather than to focus on biological variables alone.

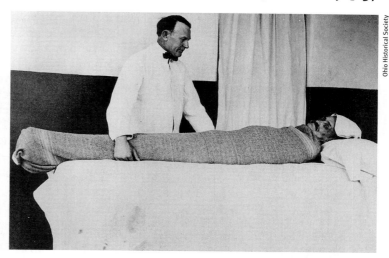

Not that long ago *Before effective psychotropic drugs were developed, clinicians in mental institutions used techniques such as the "wet pack," designed for calming excited patients.*

A second shortcoming is that much of the evidence for biological explanations is incomplete or inconclusive. Many brain studies, for example, are conducted on animals in whom symptoms of depression, anxiety, or some other abnormality have been produced by drugs, surgery, or experimental manipulation. Researchers can never be certain that the animals are experiencing the human disorder under investigation.

Finally, several of today's biological treatments are capable of producing significant undesirable effects. Antipsychotic drugs, for example, may produce movement problems such as severe shaking, bizarre-looking contractions of the face and body, and extreme restlessness. Clearly such costs must be addressed and weighed against the drug's benefits.

SUMMING UP

The Biological Model

Biological theorists look at the biological processes of human functioning. To explain abnormal behavior, they point to anatomical or biochemical problems in the brain and body. Such problems are sometimes the result of the genetic inheritance of abnormalities, normal evolution, or viral infections. Biological therapists use physical and chemical methods to help people overcome their psychological problems. The leading ones are drug therapy, electroconvulsive therapy, and, on rare occasions, psychosurgery.

The Psychodynamic Model

The *psychodynamic model* is the oldest and most famous of the modern psychological models. Psychodynamic theorists believe that a person's behavior, whether normal or abnormal, is determined largely by underlying psychological forces of which he or she is not consciously aware. These internal forces are described as *dynamic*—that is, they interact with one another; and their interaction gives rise to behavior, thoughts, and emotions. Abnormal symptoms are viewed as the result of *conflicts* between these forces.

Psychodynamic theorists would view Philip Berman as a person in conflict. They would want to explore his past experiences because, in their view, psychological conflicts are tied to early relationships and to traumatic experiences that occurred during childhood. Psychodynamic theories rest on the *deterministic* assumption that no symptom or behavior is "accidental": all behavior is determined by past experiences. Thus Philip's hatred for his mother, his memories of her as cruel and overbearing, the weakness and ineffectiveness of his father, and

PSYCHOTROPIC MEDICATIONS Drugs that primarily affect the brain and reduce many symptoms of mental dysfunctioning.

ELECTROCONVULSIVE THERAPY (ECT) A form of biological treatment, used primarily on depressed patients, in which a brain seizure is triggered as an electric current passes through electrodes attached to the patient's forehead.

PSYCHOSURGERY Brain surgery for mental disorders.

Freud and Freud *Anna Freud, the last of Sigmund Freud's six children, studied psychoanalysis with her father and then opened a practice next door to his. (They shared a waiting room.) Her work on defense mechanisms, other ego activities, and child development made her a major figure in her own right.*

ID According to Freud, the psychological force that produces instinctual needs, drives, and impulses.

EGO According to Freud, the psychological force that employs reason and operates in accordance with the reality principle.

EGO DEFENSE MECHANISMS Strategies developed by the ego to control unacceptable id impulses and to avoid or reduce the anxiety they arouse.

SUPEREGO According to Freud, the psychological force that represents a person's values and ideals.

FIXATION A condition in which the id, ego, and superego do not mature properly and are frozen at an early stage of development.

the birth of a younger brother when Philip was 10 may all be important to the understanding of his current problems.

The psychodynamic model was first formulated by the Viennese neurologist Sigmund Freud (1856–1939) at the turn of the twentieth century. After studying hypnosis, Freud developed the theory of *psychoanalysis* to explain both normal and abnormal psychological functioning; he also developed a corresponding method of treatment, a conversational approach also called psychoanalysis. During the early 1900s, Freud and several of his colleagues in the Vienna Psychoanalytic Society—including Carl Gustav Jung (1875–1961) and Alfred Adler (1870–1937)—became the most influential clinical theorists in the Western world.

How Did Freud Explain Normal and Abnormal Functioning?

Freud believed that three central forces shape the personality—instinctual needs, rational thinking, and moral standards. All these forces, he believed, operate at the *unconscious* level, unavailable to immediate awareness; and he believed them to be dynamic, or interactive. Freud called the forces the *id, ego*, and *superego*.

THE ID Freud used the term **id** to denote instinctual needs, drives, and impulses. The id operates in accordance with the *pleasure principle*; that is, it always seeks gratification. Freud also believed that all id instincts tend to be sexual, noting that from the very earliest stages of life a child's pleasure is obtained from nursing, defecating, masturbating, or engaging in other activities that he considered to have sexual links. He further suggested that a person's *libido*, or sexual energy, fuels the id.

THE EGO During our early years we come to recognize that our environment will not meet every instinctual need. Our mother, for example, is not always available to do our bidding. A part of the id separates off and becomes the **ego**. Like the id, the ego unconsciously seeks gratification, but it does so in accordance with the *reality principle*, the knowledge we acquire through experience that it can be unacceptable to express our id impulses outright. The ego, employing reason, guides us to know when we can and cannot express those impulses.

The ego develops basic strategies, called **ego defense mechanisms**, to control unacceptable id impulses and avoid or reduce the anxiety they arouse. The most basic defense mechanism, *repression*, prevents unacceptable impulses from ever reaching consciousness. There are many other ego defense mechanisms, and each of us tends to favor some over others (see Table 2-1).

THE SUPEREGO The **superego** grows from the ego, just as the ego grows out of the id. As we learn from our parents that many of our id impulses are unacceptable, we unconsciously adopt our parents' values. Judging ourselves by their standards, we feel good when we uphold their values; conversely, when we go against them, we feel guilty. In short, we develop a *conscience*.

According to Freud, these three parts of the personality—the id, the ego, and the superego—are often in some degree of conflict. A healthy personality is one in which an effective working relationship, an acceptable compromise, has formed among the three forces. If the id, ego, and superego are in excessive conflict, the person's behavior may show signs of dysfunction.

Freudians would therefore view Philip Berman as someone whose personality forces have a poor working relationship. His ego and superego are unable to control his id impulses, which lead him repeatedly to act in impulsive and often dangerous ways—suicide gestures, jealous rages, job resignations, outbursts of temper, frequent arguments.

DEVELOPMENTAL STAGES Freud proposed that at each stage of development, from infancy to maturity, new events and pressures challenge individuals and require adjustments in their id, ego, and superego. If the adjustments are successful, they lead to personal growth. If not, the person may become **fixated**, or

Table 2-1

Defense Mechanisms to the Rescue

DEFENSE	OPERATION	EXAMPLE
Repression	Person avoids anxiety by simply not allowing painful or dangerous thoughts to become conscious.	An executive's desire to run amok and attack his boss and colleagues at a board meeting is denied access to his awareness.
Denial	Person simply refuses to acknowledge the existence of an external source of anxiety.	You are not prepared for tomorrow's final exam, but you tell yourself that it's not actually an important exam and that there's no good reason not to go to a movie tonight.
Fantasy	Person imagines events as a means of satisfying unacceptable, anxiety-producing desires that would otherwise go unfulfilled.	An aggressive driver cuts in front of you and pulls into the last remaining parking space. You later fantasize about getting out of your car and beating the person to a pulp in front of admiring onlookers.
Projection	Person attributes own unacceptable impulses, motives, or desires to other individuals.	The executive who repressed his destructive desires may project his anger onto his boss and claim that it is actually the boss who is hostile.
Rationalization	Person creates a socially acceptable reason for an action that actually reflects unacceptable motives.	A student explains away poor grades by citing the importance of the "total experience" of going to college and claiming that too much emphasis on grades would actually interfere with a well-rounded education.
Reaction formation	Person adopts behavior that is the exact opposite of impulses he or she is afraid to acknowledge.	A man experiences homosexual feelings and responds by taking a strong antihomosexual stance.
Displacement	Person displaces hostility away from a dangerous object and onto a safer substitute.	After your parking spot was taken, you released your pent-up anger by starting a fight with your roommate.
Intellectualization (isolation)	Person represses emotional reactions in favor of overly logical response to a problem.	A woman who has been beaten and raped gives a detached, methodical description of the effects that such attacks may have on victims.
Undoing	Person tries to make up for unacceptable desires or acts, frequently through ritualistic behavior.	A woman who has aggressive feelings toward her husband dusts and straightens their wedding photograph every time such thoughts occur to her.
Regression	Person retreats from an upsetting conflict to an early developmental stage at which no one is expected to behave maturely or responsibly.	A boy who cannot cope with the anger he feels toward his rejecting mother regresses to infantile behavior, soiling his clothes and no longer taking care of his basic needs.
Overcompensation	Person tries to cover up a personal weakness by focusing on another, more desirable trait.	A very shy young woman overcompensates for her weak social skills by spending many hours in the gym trying to perfect her physical condition.
Sublimation	Person expresses sexual and aggressive energy in ways that are acceptable to society.	Athletes, artists, surgeons, and other highly dedicated and skilled people may be reaching their high levels of accomplishment by directing otherwise potentially harmful energies into their work.

entrapped, at an early stage of development. Then all subsequent development suffers, and the individual may well be headed for abnormal functioning in the future. Because parents are the key figures during one's early years of life, they are often seen as the cause of improper development.

Critical training *Freud believed that toilet training is a critical developmental experience. Children whose training is too harsh may become "fixated" at the anal stage and develop an "anal character"—stubborn, contrary, stingy, or controlling.*

Freud named each stage of development after the body area that he considered most important to the child at that time. For example, he referred to the first 18 months of life as the *oral* stage. During this stage, children fear that the mother who feeds and comforts them will disappear. Children whose mothers consistently fail to gratify their oral needs may become fixated at the oral stage and display an "oral character" throughout their lives, marked by extreme dependence or extreme mistrust. Such persons are particularly prone to develop depression. As we shall see in later chapters, Freud linked fixations at the other stages of development—*anal* (18 months to 3 years of age), *phallic* (3 to 5 years), *latency* (5 to 12 years), and *genital* (12 years to adulthood)—to yet other kinds of psychological dysfunction.

How Do Other Psychodynamic Explanations Differ from Freud's?

Personal and professional differences between Freud and his colleagues led to a split in the Vienna Psychoanalytic Society early in the twentieth century. Carl Jung, Alfred Adler, and others developed new theories. Although the new theories departed from Freud's ideas in important ways, each held on to Freud's belief that human functioning is shaped by interacting psychological forces. Thus all such theories, including Freud's, are referred to as *psychodynamic*.

Three of today's most influential psychodynamic theories are ego theory, self theory, and object relations theory. **Ego theorists** emphasize the role of the ego and consider it a more independent and powerful force than Freud did (Sharf, 2004). **Self theorists**, in contrast, give greatest attention to the role of the *self*—the unified personality—and believe that the basic human motive is to strengthen the wholeness of the self (Schore, 2002; Kohut, 1984, 1977). **Object relations theorists** propose that people are motivated mainly by a need to have relationships with others and that severe problems in the relationships between children and their caregivers may lead to abnormal development (Goodman, 2002; Kernberg, 2001, 1997).

Psychodynamic Therapies

Psychodynamic therapies range from Freudian psychoanalysis to modern therapies based on self theory or object relations theory. All seek to uncover past traumas and the inner conflicts that have resulted from them. All try to help clients resolve, or settle, those conflicts and to resume personal development.

According to most psychodynamic therapists, therapists must subtly and slowly guide the explorations so that the patients discover their underlying problems for themselves. To aid in the process, the therapists rely on such techniques as *free association, therapist interpretation, catharsis,* and *working through*.

FREE ASSOCIATION In psychodynamic therapies, the patient is responsible for starting and leading each discussion. The therapist tells the patient to describe any thought, feeling, or image that comes to mind, even if it seems unimportant. This practice is known as **free association**. The therapist expects that the patient's associations will eventually uncover unconscious events and underlying dynamics. Notice how free association helps this New Yorker to discover threatening impulses and conflicts within herself:

>>**Q & A**

Does the unconscious differ from the subconscious?

Yes. The unconscious consists of deep-seated thoughts, needs, or desires that are not organized into conscious awareness. Often they are thoughts that have been repressed because the person cannot accept them. The subconscious consists of thoughts and needs that lie much closer to conscious awareness. They are unnoticed, rather than repressed, and can be brought to the surface relatively easily (Padwa, 1996).<<

Patient: So I started walking, and walking, and decided to go behind the museum and walk through Central Park. So I walked and went through a back field and felt very excited and wonderful. I saw a park bench next to a clump of bushes and sat down. There was a rustle behind me and I got frightened. I thought of men concealing themselves in the bushes. I thought of the sex perverts I read about in Central Park. I wondered if there was someone behind me exposing himself. The idea is repulsive, but exciting too. I think of father now and feel excited. I think of an erect penis. This is connected with my father. There is something about this pushing in my mind. I don't know what it is, like on the border of my memory. (*Pause*)

Therapist: Mm-hmm. (*Pause*) On the border of your memory?

Patient: (*The patient breathes rapidly and seems to be under great tension*) As a little girl, I slept with my father. I get a funny feeling. I get a funny feeling over my skin, tingly-like. It's a strange feeling, like a blindness, like not seeing something. My mind blurs and spreads over anything I look at. I've had this feeling off and on since I walked in the park. My mind seems to blank off like I can't think or absorb anything.

(*Wolberg, 1967, p. 662*)

THERAPIST INTERPRETATION Psychodynamic therapists listen carefully as patients talk, looking for clues, drawing tentative conclusions, and sharing interpretations when they think the patient is ready to hear them. Interpretations of three phenomena are particularly important—*resistance, transference,* and *dreams.*

Patients are showing **resistance**, an unconscious refusal to participate fully in therapy, when they suddenly cannot free associate or when they change a subject to avoid a painful discussion. They demonstrate **transference** when they act and feel toward the therapist as they did or do toward important persons in their lives, especially their parents, siblings, and spouses. Consider again the woman who walked in Central Park. As she continues talking, the therapist helps her to explore her transference:

Patient: I get so excited by what is happening here. I feel I'm being held back by needing to be nice. I'd like to blast loose sometimes, but I don't dare.

Therapist: Because you fear my reaction?

Patient: The worst thing would be that you wouldn't like me. You wouldn't speak to me friendly; you wouldn't smile; you'd feel you can't treat me and discharge me from treatment. But I know this isn't so, I know it.

Therapist: Where do you think these attitudes come from?

Patient: When I was nine years old, I read a lot about great men in history. I'd quote them and be dramatic. I'd want a sword at my side; I'd dress like an Indian. Mother would scold me. Don't frown, don't talk so much. Sit on your hands, over and over again. I did all kinds of things. I was a naughty child. She told me I'd be hurt. Then at fourteen I fell off a horse and broke my back. I had to be in bed. Mother then told me on the day I went riding not to, that I'd get hurt because the ground was frozen. I was a stubborn, self-willed child. Then I went against her will and suffered an accident that changed my life, a fractured back. Her attitude was, "I told you so." I was put in a cast and kept in bed for months.

(*Wolberg, 1967, p. 662*)

Finally, many psychodynamic therapists try to help patients interpret their **dreams**. Freud (1924) called dreams the "royal road to the unconscious." He believed that repression and other defense mechanisms operate less completely during sleep and that dreams, correctly interpreted, can reveal unconscious instincts, needs, and wishes. Freud identified two kinds of dream content, manifest and latent. *Manifest content* is the consciously remembered dream; *latent content* is its symbolic meaning. To interpret a dream, therapists must translate its manifest content into its latent content.

EGO THEORY The psychodynamic theory that emphasizes the role of the ego and considers it an independent force.

SELF THEORY The psychodynamic theory that emphasizes the role of the self—our unified personality.

OBJECT RELATIONS THEORY The psychodynamic theory that views the desire for relationships as the key motivating force in human behavior.

FREE ASSOCIATION A psychodynamic technique in which the patient describes any thought, feeling, or image that comes to mind, even if it seems unimportant.

RESISTANCE An unconscious refusal to participate fully in therapy.

TRANSFERENCE According to psychodynamic theorists, a process that occurs during psychotherapy, in which patients act toward the therapist as they did or do toward important figures in their lives.

DREAM A series of ideas and images that form during sleep.

>>BY THE NUMBERS
Honoring the Mother–Child Relationship

74% Adult children who give a gift to their mother on Mother's Day<<

44% Adult children who visit their mother on Mother's Day<<

38% Adult children who call their mother on Mother's Day<<

95% Mothers who prefer personal contact or communication over a gift on Mother's Day<<

(Fetto, 2002)

A CLOSER LOOK

Perchance to Dream

All people dream; so do dogs, and maybe even fish. In fact, although they may not remember them, people average close to 1,500 dreams per year. Some claim that dreams reveal the future; others see them as inner journeys or alternate realities (Baruss, 2003). Sigmund Freud (1900) believed that we express and attempt to fulfill unsatisfied desires with our dreams. Biological theorists, on the other hand, view dreams as our cortex's effort to make sense of the random signals that come from various areas of the brain as we sleep (Solms, 2002; Titone, 2002).

According to surveys and studies, two-thirds of people's dreams involve unpleasant material, such as aggression, threats, rejection, confusion, or an inability to communicate (Van de Castle, 1993). Commonly, a dreamer is chased or attacked by a threatening figure, suggesting to some theorists that the dreamer is running from real-life fears, unpleasant issues, or distrusted persons.

Eighty percent of college students report having had dreams of falling. Such dreams are thought to occur when our sense of security is threatened or when we are in fear of losing control. Many people say falling dreams are the first ones they can remember, although people can have them at any stage of

The Nightmare by Johann Heinrich Füssli

life (Van de Castle, 1993; Cartwright & Lamberg, 1992).

Another common theme is public nudity. One study found that 43 percent of American college-age subjects reported having such dreams, compared to 18 percent of Japanese subjects (Vieira, 1993). Freud (1900) viewed dreams of nudity as an unconscious wish to exhibit oneself. Others argue that people who have these dreams may be afraid of being seen for who they really are (Van de Castle, 1993).

Dreams also may differ by gender. In a landmark study in 1951, the researcher Calvin Hall found that men dreamed twice as often about men as they did about women, whereas women dreamed about men and women in equal proportions. In addition, most male dreams took place outdoors, while female dreams were more often set in the home or elsewhere indoors. Men's sexual dreams were more likely to include women they did not know, whereas women dreamed more often about men they cared for. A later study in 1980 found no significant changes in these patterns (Van de Castle, 1993). However, more recent studies find that men's and women's dreams are becoming more similar, that women's dreams now take place outdoors more than they did in the past, and that women are now as likely as men to behave aggressively in their dreams (Krippner & Weinhold, 2002; Kramer, 2000, 1989).

CATHARSIS Insight must be an emotional as well as intellectual process. Psychodynamic therapists believe that patients must experience **catharsis**, a reliving of past repressed feelings, if they are to settle internal conflicts and overcome their problems.

WORKING THROUGH A single episode of interpretation and catharsis will not change a person. The patient and therapist must examine the same issues over and over in the course of many sessions, each time with greater clarity. This process, called **working through**, usually takes a long time, often years.

SHORT-TERM PSYCHODYNAMIC THERAPIES In several short versions of psychodynamic therapy, developed over the past few decades, patients choose a single problem—a *dynamic focus*—to work on, such as difficulty getting along with other people (Charman, 2004; Hoyt, 2003). The therapist and patient focus on this problem throughout the treatment and work only on the psychodynamic issues that relate to it (such as unresolved oral needs). Only a limited number of studies have tested the effectiveness of these short-term psychodynamic therapies,

CATHARSIS The reliving of past repressed feelings in order to settle internal conflicts and overcome problems.

WORKING THROUGH The psychoanalytic process of facing conflicts, reinterpreting feelings, and overcoming one's problems.

but their findings do suggest that the approaches are sometimes quite helpful to patients (Hoyt, 2003; Messer, 2001).

Assessing the Psychodynamic Model

Freud and his followers have helped change the way abnormal functioning is understood (Sharf, 2004; Nietzel et al., 1994). Largely because of their work, a wide range of theorists today look for answers and explanations outside biological processes. Psychodynamic theorists have also helped us to understand that abnormal functioning may be rooted in the same processes as normal functioning. Psychological conflict is a common experience; it leads to abnormal functioning only if the conflict becomes excessive.

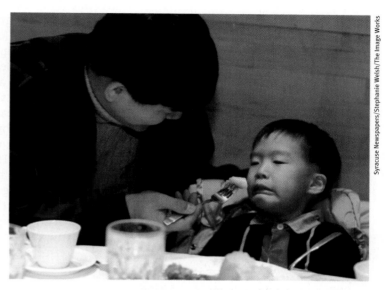

Freud and his many followers have also had a monumental impact on treatment (Kernberg, 2002). They were the first to apply theory and techniques systematically to treatment. They were also the first to demonstrate the potential of psychological, as opposed to biological, treatment, and their ideas have served as starting points for many other psychological treatments.

At the same time, the psychodynamic model has shortcomings. Its concepts are hard to define and to research. Because processes such as id drives, ego defenses, and fixation are abstract and supposedly operate at an unconscious level, there is no way of knowing for certain if they are occurring. Not surprisingly, then, psychodynamic explanations and treatments have received limited research support, and psychodynamic theorists have been forced to rely largely on evidence provided by individual case studies (Prochaska & Norcross, 2003). Nevertheless, 19 percent of today's clinical psychologists identify themselves as psychodynamic therapists (Prochaska & Norcross, 2003).

The father factor *Because mothers provided almost all infant care in his day, Freud looked largely to maternal influences for explanations of psychological developments and problems. Today, however, many fathers also actively care for their children, causing psychodynamic theorists to adjust their explanations.*

SUMMING UP

The Psychodynamic Model

Psychodynamic theorists believe that a person's behavior, whether normal or abnormal, results from underlying psychological forces. They consider psychological conflicts to be rooted in early parent–child relationships and traumatic experiences. The model was first developed by Sigmund Freud, who said that three dynamic forces—the id, ego, and superego—interact to produce thought, feeling, and behavior. Other psychodynamic theories include ego theory, self theory, and object relations theory. Psychodynamic therapists help people uncover past traumas and the inner conflicts that have resulted from them. They use a number of techniques, including free association and interpretations of psychological phenomena such as resistance, transference, and dreams.

"I think what Polly really want is approval."

GREGORY

© 2002 The New Yorker Collection from cartoonbank.com

The Behavioral Model

Like psychodynamic theorists, behavioral theorists believe that our actions are determined largely by our experiences in life. However, the *behavioral model* concentrates entirely on *behaviors*, the responses an organism makes to its environment. Behaviors can be external (going to work, say) or internal (having a feeling or thought). In turn, behavioral theorists base their explanations and treatments on *principles of learning*, the processes by which behaviors change in response to the environment.

Many learned behaviors help people to cope with daily challenges and to lead happy, productive lives. However, abnormal behaviors also can be learned. Behaviorists who try to explain Philip Berman's problems might view him as a man who has received improper training: he has learned behaviors that offend others and repeatedly work against him.

Whereas the psychodynamic model had its beginnings in the clinical work of physicians, the behavioral model began in laboratories where psychologists were running experiments on **conditioning**, simple forms of learning. The researchers manipulated *stimuli* and *rewards*, then observed how their manipulations affected their subjects' responses.

During the 1950s, many clinicians became frustrated with what they viewed as the vagueness and slowness of the psychodynamic model. Some of them began to apply the principles of learning to the study and treatment of psychological problems (Spiegler & Guevremont, 2003). Their efforts gave rise to the behavioral model of abnormality.

How Do Behaviorists Explain Abnormal Functioning?

Learning theorists have identified several forms of conditioning, and each may produce abnormal behavior as well as normal behavior. In **operant conditioning**, for example, humans and animals learn to behave in certain ways as a result of receiving *rewards*—any satisfying consequences—whenever they do so. In **modeling**, individuals learn responses simply by observing other individuals and repeating their behaviors.

In a third form of conditioning, **classical conditioning**, learning occurs by *temporal association*. When two events repeatedly occur close together in time, they become fused in a person's mind, and before long the person responds in the same way to both events. If one event produces a response of joy, the other brings joy as well; if one event brings feelings of relief, so does the other. A closer look at this form of conditioning illustrates how the behavioral model can account for abnormal functioning.

See and do *Modeling may account for some forms of abnormal behavior. A well-known study by Albert Bandura and his colleagues (1963) demonstrated that children learned to abuse a doll by observing an adult hit it. Children who had not been exposed to the adult model did not mistreat the doll.*

Ivan Pavlov (1849–1936), a famous Russian physiologist, first demonstrated classical conditioning with animal studies. He placed a bowl of meat powder before a dog, producing the natural response that all dogs have to meat: they start to salivate (see Figure 2-4). Next Pavlov added a step: just before presenting the dog with meat powder, he sounded a metronome. After several such pairings of metronome tone and presentation of meat powder, Pavlov noted that the dog began to salivate as soon as it heard the metronome. The dog had learned to salivate in response to a sound.

In the vocabulary of classical conditioning, the meat in this demonstration is an *unconditioned stimulus (US)*. It produces the *unconditioned response (UR)* of salivation; that is, a natural response with which the dog is born. The sound of the metronome is a *conditioned stimulus (CS)*, a previously neutral stimulus that comes to be linked with meat in the dog's mind. As such, it too produces a salivation response. When the salivation response is produced by the conditioned stimulus rather than by the unconditioned stimulus, it is called a *conditioned response (CR)*.

BEFORE CONDITIONING	AFTER CONDITIONING
CS: Tone → No response	CS: Tone → CR: Salivation
US: Meat → UR: Salivation	US: Meat → UR: Salivation

Classical conditioning explains many familiar behaviors. The romantic feelings a young man experiences when he smells his girlfriend's perfume, say, may represent a conditioned response. Initially this perfume may have had little emotional effect on him, but because the fragrance was present during several romantic encounters, it too came to elicit a romantic response.

Abnormal behaviors, too, can be acquired by classical conditioning. Consider a young boy who is repeatedly frightened by a neighbor's large German shepherd dog. Whenever the child walks past the neighbor's front yard, the dog barks loudly and lunges at him, stopped only by a rope tied to the porch. In this situation, the boy's parents are not surprised to discover that he develops a fear of dogs. They are stumped, however, by another intense fear the child displays, a fear of sand. They cannot understand why he cries whenever they take him to the beach and screams if sand even touches his skin.

Where did this fear of sand come from? Classical conditioning. It turns out that a big sandbox is set up in the neighbor's front yard for the dog to play in. Every time the dog barks and lunges at the boy, the sandbox is there too. After repeated pairings of this kind, the child comes to fear sand as much as he fears the dog.

FIGURE 2-4 **Working for Pavlov** *In Ivan Pavlov's experimental device, the dog's saliva was collected in a tube as it was secreted, and the amount was recorded on a revolving cylinder called a kymograph. The experimenter observed the dog through a one-way glass window.*

Behavioral Therapies

Behavioral therapy aims to identify the behaviors that are causing a person's problems and then tries to replace them with more appropriate ones, by applying the principles of classical conditioning, operant conditioning, or modeling. The therapist's attitude toward the client is that of teacher rather than healer. A person's early life matters only for the clues it can provide to current conditioning processes.

Classical conditioning treatments, for example, may be used to change abnormal reactions to particular stimuli. **Systematic desensitization** is one such method, often applied in cases of *phobia*—a specific and unreasonable fear. In this step-by-step procedure, clients learn to react calmly instead of with fear to the objects or situations they dread (Wolpe, 1997, 1995, 1990). First, they are taught the skill of relaxation over the course of several sessions. Next, they construct a *fear hierarchy*, a list of feared objects or situations, starting with those that are less feared and ending with the ones that are most dreaded. Here is the hierarchy developed by a man who was afraid of criticism, especially about his mental stability:

1. Friend on the street: "Hi, how are you?"
2. Friend on the street: "How are you feeling these days?"
3. Sister: "You've got to be careful so they don't put you in the hospital."
4. Wife: "You shouldn't drink beer while you are taking medicine."
5. Mother: "What's the matter, don't you feel good?"
6. Wife: "It's just you yourself, it's all in your head."
7. Service station attendant: "What are you shaking for?"
8. Neighbor borrows rake: "Is there something wrong with your leg? Your knees are shaking."
9. Friend on the job: "Is your blood pressure okay?"
10. Service station attendant: "You are pretty shaky, are you crazy or something?"

(Marquis & Morgan, 1969, p. 28)

CONDITIONING A simple form of learning.

OPERANT CONDITIONING A process of learning in which behavior that leads to satisfying consequences is likely to be repeated.

MODELING A process of learning in which an individual acquires responses by observing and imitating others.

CLASSICAL CONDITIONING A process of learning by temporal association in which two events that repeatedly occur close together in time become fused in a person's mind and produce the same response.

SYSTEMATIC DESENSITIZATION A behavioral treatment in which clients with phobias learn to react calmly instead of with intense fear to the objects or situations they dread.

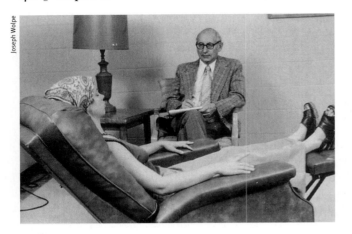

Desensitization *Joseph Wolpe, the psychiatrist who developed the behavioral treatment of systematic desensitization, first teaches a client to relax, then guides her to confront feared objects or situations, real or imagined, while she remains relaxed.*

Desensitization therapists next have their clients either imagine or actually confront each item on the hierarchy while in a state of relaxation. In step-by-step pairings of feared items and relaxation, clients move up the hierarchy until at last they can face every one of the items without experiencing fear. As we shall see in Chapter 4, research has shown systematic desensitization and other classical conditioning techniques to be effective in treating phobias (Compas & Gotlib, 2002).

Assessing the Behavioral Model

The number of behavioral clinicians has grown steadily since the 1950s, and the behavioral model has become a powerful force in the clinical field. Various behavioral theories have been proposed over the years, and many treatment techniques have been developed. Approximately 13 percent of today's clinical psychologists report that their approach is mainly behavioral (Prochaska & Norcross, 2003) (see Figure 2-5).

Perhaps the greatest appeal of the behavioral model is that it can be tested in the laboratory, whereas psychodynamic theories generally cannot. The behaviorists' basic concepts—stimulus, response, and reward—can be observed and measured. Experimenters have in fact successfully used the principles of learning to create clinical symptoms in laboratory subjects, suggesting that psychological disorders may indeed develop in the same way. In addition, research has found that behavioral treatments can be helpful to people with specific fears, compulsive behavior, social deficits, mental retardation, and other problems (Compas & Gotlib, 2002).

At the same time, research has also revealed weaknesses in the model. Certainly behavioral researchers have produced specific symptoms in subjects. But are these symptoms *ordinarily* acquired in this way? There is still no indisputable evidence that most people with psychological disorders are victims of improper conditioning. Similarly, behavioral therapies have limitations. The improvements noted in the therapist's office do not always extend to real life. Nor do they necessarily last without continued therapy.

Finally, some critics hold that the behavioral view is too simplistic, that its concepts fail to account for the complexity of human behavior. In 1977 the behaviorist Albert Bandura argued that in order to feel happy and function effectively people must develop a positive sense of *self-efficacy*. That is, they must have confidence that they can master and perform needed behaviors whenever necessary. Other behaviorists of the 1960s and 1970s similarly recognized that human beings engage in *cognitive behaviors*, such as anticipating or interpreting—ways of thinking that until then had been largely ignored in behavioral theory and

FIGURE 2-5 Theoretical orientations of today's clinical psychologists *In one survey, 27 percent of clinical psychologists labeled themselves as "eclectic," 24 percent considered themselves "cognitive," and 19 percent called their orientation "psychodynamic." (Adapted from Prochaska & Norcross, 2003; Norcross et al., 1997.)*

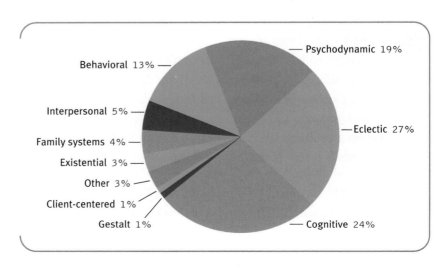

Psychodynamic 19%
Behavioral 13%
Interpersonal 5%
Family systems 4%
Existential 3%
Other 3%
Client-centered 1%
Gestalt 1%
Eclectic 27%
Cognitive 24%

THE CURRENT SCENE

Maternal Instincts

On an August day in 1996, a 3-year-old boy climbed over a barrier at the Brookfield Zoo in Illinois and fell 24 feet onto the cement floor of the gorilla compound. An 8-year-old 160-pound gorilla named Binti-Jua picked up the child and cradled his limp body in her arms. The child's mother, fearing the worst, screamed out, "The gorilla's got my baby!" But Binti protected the boy as if he were her own. She held off the other gorillas, rocked him gently, and carried him to the entrance of the gorilla area, where rescue workers were waiting. Within hours, the incident was seen on videotape replays around the world, and Binti was being hailed for her maternal instincts.

Robert Allison/Contact Press Images

When Binti was herself an infant, she had been removed from her mother, Lulu, who did not have enough milk. To make up for this loss, keepers at the zoo worked around the clock to nurture Binti; she was always being held in someone's arms. When Binti became pregnant at age 6, trainers were afraid that the early separation from her mother would leave her ill prepared to raise an infant of her own. So they gave her mothering lessons and taught her to nurse and carry around a stuffed doll.

Clinical theorists have had a field day interpreting the gorilla's nurturing care for the child, each within his or her preferred theory. Many *evolutionary theorists,* for example, view the behavior as an expression of the maternal instincts that have helped the gorilla's species to survive and evolve. Some *psychodynamic theorists* suggest that the gorilla was expressing feelings of attachment and bonding, already experienced with her own 17-month-old daughter. And *behaviorists* hold that the gorilla may have been imitating the nurturing behavior that she had observed in human models during her own infancy or enacting the parenting training that she had received during her pregnancy. While the clinical field tries frantically to sort out this issue, Binti-Jua, the heroic gorilla, has returned to her relatively quiet and predictable life at the zoo.

therapy. These individuals developed *cognitive-behavioral theories* that took cognitive behaviors into greater account (Goldiamond, 1965).

Cognitive-behavioral theorists bridge the behavioral model and the cognitive model, the view we turn to next. On the one hand, their explanations are based squarely on learning principles. They believe, for example, that cognitive processes are learned by classical conditioning, operant conditioning, and modeling. On the other hand, cognitive-behavioral theorists share with other kinds of cognitive theorists a belief that the ability to think is the most important aspect of human functioning (Compas & Gotlib, 2002).

Margaret Norton/AP Photo

Conditioning for fun and profit *Pet owners have discovered that they can teach animals a wide assortment of tricks by using the principles of conditioning. Only 3 percent of all dogs have learned to "sing," while 21 percent know how to sit, the most common dog trick (Pet Food Institute).*

SUMMING UP

The Behavioral Model

Behaviorists focus on behaviors and propose that they develop in accordance with the principles of learning. They hold that three types of conditioning—classical conditioning, operant conditioning, and modeling—account for all behavior, whether normal or dysfunctional. The goal of the behavioral therapies is to identify a person's problematic behaviors and replace them with more appropriate ones, using techniques based on one or more of the principles of learning. The classical conditioning approach of systematic desensitization, for example, has been effective in treating phobias.

"Stimulus, response! Stimulus, response! Don't you ever *think*?"

The Cognitive Model

Philip Berman, like the rest of us, has *cognitive* abilities—special intellectual capacities to think, remember, and anticipate. These abilities can certainly help him in life. Yet they can also work against him. As he thinks about his experiences, Philip may misinterpret experiences in ways that lead to poor decisions, maladaptive responses, and painful emotions.

In the early 1960s two clinicians, Albert Ellis (1962) and Aaron Beck (1967), proposed that cognitive processes are at the center of behavior, thought, and emotions and that we can best understand abnormal functioning by looking to cognition—a perspective known as the *cognitive model*. Ellis and Beck claimed that clinicians must ask questions about the assumptions and attitudes that color a client's perceptions, the thoughts running through that person's mind, and the conclusions they are leading to. Other theorists and therapists soon embraced and expanded their ideas and techniques.

How Do Cognitive Theorists Explain Abnormal Functioning?

To cognitive theorists, we are all artists. We reproduce and create the world in our minds as we try to understand the events going on around us. If we are effective artists, our cognitions tend to be accurate (they agree with the perceptions of others). If we are ineffective artists, we may create a cognitive inner world that is painful and harmful to ourselves.

Abnormal functioning can result from several kinds of cognitive problems. Some people may make *assumptions* and adopt *attitudes* that are disturbing and inaccurate (Brown & Beck, 2002; Dryden & Ellis, 2001). Philip Berman, for example, often seems to assume that his past history has locked him in his present situation. He believes that he was victimized by his parents and that he is now forever doomed by his past. He seems to approach all new experiences and relationships with expectations of failure and disaster.

Illogical thinking processes are another source of abnormal functioning, according to cognitive theorists. Beck (2002, 1991, 1967), for example, has found that some people consistently think in illogical ways and keep arriving at self-defeating conclusions. As we shall see in Chapter 7, he has identified a number of illogical thought processes regularly found in depression, such as *overgeneralization*, the drawing of broad negative conclusions on the basis of a single insignificant event. One depressed student couldn't remember the date of Columbus's third voyage to America during a history class. Overgeneralizing, she spent the rest of the day in despair over her general ignorance.

Cognitive Therapies

According to cognitive therapists, people with psychological disorders can overcome their problems by developing new, more functional ways of thinking. Because different forms of abnormality may involve different kinds of cognitive dysfunctioning, cognitive therapists have developed a number of strategies. Beck (2002, 1996, 1967), for example, has developed an approach that is widely used in cases of depression.

In Beck's approach, called simply **cognitive therapy**, therapists help clients recognize the negative thoughts, biased interpretations, and errors in logic that dominate their thinking and, according to Beck, cause them to feel depressed. Therapists also guide clients to challenge their dysfunctional thoughts, try out new interpretations, and ultimately apply the new ways of thinking in their daily lives. As we shall see in Chapter 7, people with depression who are treated with Beck's approach improve much more than those who receive no treatment (Hollon et al., 2002).

In the excerpt that follows, a cognitive therapist guides a 26-year-old graduate student who is experiencing depression to see the tie between the way she interprets

COGNITIVE THERAPY A therapy developed by Aaron Beck that helps people recognize and change their faulty thinking

her experiences and the way she feels and to begin questioning the accuracy of her interpretations:

> *Therapist:* How do you understand it?
> *Patient:* I get depressed when things go wrong. Like when I fail a test.
> *Therapist:* How can failing a test make you depressed?
> *Patient:* Well, if I fail I'll never get into law school.
> *Therapist:* So failing the test means a lot to you. But if failing a test could drive people into clinical depression, wouldn't you expect everyone who failed the test to have a depression? . . . Did everyone who failed get depressed enough to require treatment?
> *Patient:* No, but it depends on how important the test was to the person.
> *Therapist:* Right, and who decides the importance?
> *Patient:* I do.
> *Therapist:* And so, what we have to examine is your way of viewing the test (or the way that you think about the test) and how it affects your chances of getting into law school. Do you agree?
> *Patient:* Right. . . .
> *Therapist:* Now what did failing mean?
> *Patient:* (Tearful) That I couldn't get into law school.
> *Therapist:* And what does that mean to you?
> *Patient:* That I'm just not smart enough.
> *Therapist:* Anything else?
> *Patient:* That I can never be happy.
> *Therapist:* And how do these thoughts make you feel?
> *Patient:* Very unhappy.
> *Therapist:* So it is the meaning of failing a test that makes you very unhappy. In fact, believing that you can never be happy is a powerful factor in producing unhappiness. So, you get yourself into a trap—by definition, failure to get into law school equals "I can never be happy."
>
> *(Beck et al., 1979, pp. 145–146)*

Assessing the Cognitive Model

The cognitive model has had broad appeal. In addition to the behaviorists who now include cognitive concepts in their theories about learning, there are many clinicians who believe that thinking processes are in fact much more than conditioned reactions. Cognitive theory, research, and treatments have developed in so many interesting ways that the model is now viewed as separate from the behavioral school that gave birth to it.

Approximately 24 percent of today's clinical psychologists identify their approach as cognitive (Prochaska & Norcross, 2003). There are several reasons for the model's popularity. First, it focuses on a process unique to human beings—the process of human thought—and many theorists from varied backgrounds find themselves drawn to a model that sees this unique process as the primary cause of normal and abnormal behavior.

Cognitive theories also lend themselves to research. Investigators have found that people with psychological disorders often make the kinds of assumptions and errors in thinking the theorists claim (Brown & Beck, 2002; Whisman & McGarvey, 1995). Yet another reason for the popularity of this model is the impressive performance of cognitive therapies. They have proved very effective for treating depression, panic disorder, and sexual dysfunctions, for example (Barlow, 2001; DeRubeis et al., 2001).

A clinical pioneer *Aaron Beck proposes that many forms of abnormal behavior can be traced to cognitive factors, such as upsetting thoughts and illogical thinking.*

Leif Skoogfors/Woodfin Camp & Associates

THE CURRENT SCENE

Cybertherapy

In this age of the Internet, it is hardly surprising that thousands of therapists are setting up online services, inviting persons with problems to e-mail their questions and concerns (Heinlen et al., 2003; Castelnuovo et al., 2001). Such services, often called *e-therapy*, can cost as much as $2 per minute. They have raised concerns about confidentiality and the quality of care (Landau, 2001; Gorman, 1998). Many e-therapists do not even have advanced clinical training.

Similarly, there are now thousands of chat groups and "virtual" support groups available around the clock on the Internet for everything from depression to substance abuse, anxiety, and eating disorders (Moskowitz, 2001). These groups provide opportunities for people with similar problems to communicate with each other, freely trading advice and empathy (Bresnahan & Murray-Johnson, 2002; Landau, 2001). Of course, people who choose "chat group therapy" do not know who is on the other end of the computer connection or whether the advice they receive is at all appropriate. Distasteful or insulting messages are not uncommon (Ehrman, 1995).

Another new computer-age development is software programs that claim to offer help for emotional distress (Jacobs et al., 2001; Oldenburg, 1995). Advocates suggest that people may find it easier to reveal sensitive personal information to a computer than to a therapist. The computer offers them the freedom to express their thoughts and emotions without fear of being judged. Moreover, the computer therapist is always available, it can reach a large number of people, and its fees are modest. These are all attractive attributes in a therapist. Research indicates that some of these software programs are indeed helpful (Jacobs et al., 2001; Elias, 2000, 1995).

Computers may never substitute fully for the judgment of a trained therapist. Yet, as more complex and humanlike computer programs are developed, both computer and Internet services may indeed find a place as adjuncts to other forms of treatment.

"Please dear! I need my own cyberspace."

© 2002 The New Yorker Collection from cartoonbank.com

Nevertheless, the cognitive model, too, has its drawbacks (Holmes, 2002). First, although disturbed cognitive processes are found in many forms of abnormality, their precise role has yet to be determined. The cognitions seen in psychologically troubled people could well be a result rather than a cause of their difficulties. Second, although cognitive therapies are clearly of help to many people, they do not help everyone. Is it enough to change the cognitive habits of a person with a serious psychological dysfunction? Can such specific changes make a lasting difference in the way the person feels and behaves?

Furthermore, like the other models we have examined, the cognitive model is narrow in certain ways. Although cognition is a very special human dimension, it is still only one part of human functioning. Aren't human beings more than the sum total of their thoughts, emotions, and behaviors? Shouldn't explanations of human functioning also consider broader issues such as how people approach life, what value they get from it, and how they deal with the question of life's meaning? This is the position of the humanistic-existential perspective.

SUMMING UP | The Cognitive Model

According to the cognitive model, we must understand human thought to understand human behavior. When people display abnormal patterns of functioning, cognitive theorists point to cognitive problems, such as maladaptive assumptions and illogical thinking processes. Cognitive therapists try to help people recognize and change their faulty ideas and thinking processes. Among the most widely used cognitive treatments is Beck's cognitive therapy.

The Humanistic-Existential Model

Philip Berman is more than the sum of his psychological conflicts, learned behaviors, or cognitions. Being human, he also has the ability to pursue philosophical goals such as self-awareness, strong values, a sense of meaning in life, and freedom of choice. According to humanistic and existential theorists, Philip's problems can be understood only in the light of such complex goals (Bohart, 2003; Schneider, 2003). Humanistic and existential theorists are usually grouped together—in an approach known as the *humanistic-existential model*—because of their common focus on these broader dimensions of human existence. At the same time, there are important differences between them.

Humanists, the more optimistic of the two groups, believe that human beings are born with a natural tendency to be friendly, cooperative, and constructive. People, these theorists propose, are driven to **self-actualize**—that is, to fulfill this potential for goodness and growth. They can do so, however, only if they honestly recognize and accept their weaknesses as well as their strengths and establish satisfying personal values to live by. Humanists further suggest that self-actualization leads naturally to a concern for the welfare of others and to behavior that is loving, courageous, spontaneous, and independent (Maslow, 1970).

Existentialists agree that human beings must have an accurate awareness of themselves and live meaningful—they say "authentic"—lives in order to be psychologically well adjusted. These theorists do not believe, however, that people are naturally inclined to live positively. They believe that from birth we have total freedom, either to face up to our existence and give meaning to our lives or to shrink from that responsibility. Those who decide to "hide" from responsibility and choice will view themselves as helpless and weak and may live empty, inauthentic, and dysfunctional lives as a result.

The humanistic and existential views of abnormality both date back to the 1940s. At that time Carl Rogers (1902–1987), often considered the pioneer of the humanistic perspective, developed *client-centered therapy*, a warm and supportive approach that contrasted sharply with the psychodynamic techniques of the day. He also proposed a theory of personality that paid little attention to irrational instincts and conflicts.

The existential view of personality and abnormality appeared during this same period. Many of its principles came from the ideas of nineteenth-century European existential philosophers who held that human beings are constantly defining and so giving meaning to their existence through their actions (Walsh & McElwain, 2002). In the late 1950s a book titled *Existence* described a number of major existential ideas and treatment approaches and helped them gain recognition (May et al., 1958).

The humanistic and existential theories and their uplifting implications were extremely popular during the 1960s and 1970s, years of considerable soul-searching and social upheaval in Western society. They have since lost some of their popularity, but they continue to influence the ideas and work of many clinicians.

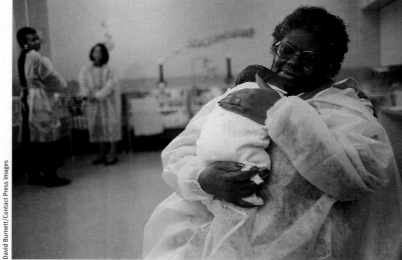

David Burnett/Contact Press Images

Actualizing the self *Humanists suggest that self-actualized people, such as this hospital volunteer who works with drug-addicted babies, show concern for the welfare of humanity. They are also thought to be highly creative, spontaneous, independent, and humorous.*

Rogers's Humanistic Theory and Therapy

According to Carl Rogers (2000, 1987, 1951), the road to dysfunction begins in infancy. We all have a basic need to receive *positive regard* from the important people in our lives (primarily our parents). Those who receive *unconditional* (nonjudgmental) *positive regard* early in life are likely to develop *unconditional self-regard*. That is, they come to recognize their worth as persons, even while recognizing that they are not perfect. Such people are in a good position to actualize their positive potential.

Unfortunately, some children are repeatedly made to feel that they are not worthy of positive regard. As a result, they acquire *conditions of worth*, standards

SELF-ACTUALIZATION The humanistic process by which people fulfill their potential for goodness and growth.

CLIENT-CENTERED THERAPY The humanistic therapy developed by Carl Rogers in which clinicians try to help clients by conveying acceptance, accurate empathy, and genuineness.

GESTALT THERAPY The humanistic therapy developed by Fritz Perls in which clinicians actively move clients toward self-recognition and self-acceptance by using techniques such as role-playing and self-discovery exercises.

that tell them they are lovable only when they conform to certain guidelines. In order to maintain positive self-regard, these people have to look at themselves very selectively, denying or distorting thoughts and actions that do not measure up to their conditions of worth. They thus acquire a distorted view of themselves and their experiences. They do not know what they are truly feeling, what they genuinely need, or what values and goals would be meaningful for them. Problems in functioning are then inevitable.

Rogers might view Philip Berman as a man who has gone astray. Rather than striving to fulfill his positive human potential, he drifts from job to job and relationship to relationship. In every interaction he is defending himself, trying to interpret events in ways he can live with, usually blaming his problems on other people. Nevertheless, his basic negative self-image continually reveals itself. Rogers would probably link this problem to the critical ways Philip was treated by his mother throughout his childhood.

Clinicians who practice Rogers's **client-centered therapy** try to create a supportive climate in which clients feel able to look at themselves honestly and acceptingly (Bohart, 2003; Rogers, 2000, 1992, 1957). The therapist must display three important qualities throughout the therapy—*unconditional positive regard* (full and warm acceptance of the client), *accurate empathy* (skillful listening and restatements), and *genuineness* (sincere communication). The following interaction shows the therapist using these three qualities to move the client toward greater self-awareness:

> *Client:* Yes, I know I shouldn't worry about it, but I do. Lots of things—money, people, clothes. In classes I feel that everyone's just waiting for a chance to jump on me.... When I meet somebody I wonder what he's actually thinking of me. Then later on I wonder how I match up to what he's come to think of me.
>
> *Therapist:* You feel that you're pretty responsive to the opinions of other people.
>
> *Client:* Yes, but it's things that shouldn't worry me.
>
> *Therapist:* You feel that it's the sort of thing that shouldn't be upsetting, but they do get you pretty much worried anyway.
>
> *Client:* Just some of them. Most of those things do worry me because they're true. The ones I told you, that is. But there are lots of little things that aren't true.... Things just seem to be piling up, piling up inside of me.... It's a feeling that things were crowding up and they were going to burst.
>
> *Therapist:* You feel that it's a sort of oppression with some frustration and that things are just unmanageable.
>
> *Client:* In a way, but some things just seem illogical. I'm afraid I'm not very clear here but that's the way it comes.
>
> *Therapist:* That's all right. You say just what you think.
>
> *(Snyder, 1947, pp. 2-24)*

In such an atmosphere, persons are expected to feel accepted by their therapists. They then may be able to look at themselves with honesty and acceptance—a process called *experiencing*. That is, they begin to value their own emotions, thoughts, and behaviors, and so they are freed from the insecurities and doubts that prevent self-actualization.

Client-centered therapy has not fared very well in research (Patterson, 2000; Greenberg et al., 1998, 1994). Although some studies show that people who receive this therapy improve more than control subjects, many other studies have failed to find any such advantage. All the same, Rogers's therapy has had a positive influence on clinical practice (Bozarth et al., 2002). It was one of the first major alternatives to psychodynamic therapy, and it helped open up the field to new approaches. Rogers also helped pave the way for psychologists to practice psychotherapy; it had previously been considered the territory of psychiatrists. And his commitment to clinical research helped promote the systematic study of treatment. Approximately 1 percent of today's clinical psychologists, 2 percent of social workers, and 4 percent of counseling psychologists report that they employ the client-centered approach (Prochasca & Norcross, 2003).

Gestalt Theory and Therapy

Gestalt therapy, another humanistic approach, was developed in the 1950s by a charismatic clinician named Frederick (Fritz) Perls (1893–1970). Gestalt therapists, like client-centered therapists, guide their clients toward self-recognition and self-acceptance (Bohart, 2003). But unlike client-centered therapists, they often try to achieve this goal by challenging and even frustrating their clients. Some of Perls's favorite techniques were skillful frustration, role-playing, and numerous rules and exercises.

In the technique of *skillful frustration*, gestalt therapists refuse to meet their clients' expectations or demands. This use of frustration is meant to help people see how often they try to manipulate others into meeting their needs. In the technique of *role-playing*, the therapists instruct clients to act out various roles. A person may be told to be another person, an object, an alternative self, or even a part of the body. Role-playing can become intense, as individuals are encouraged to fully express emotions. Many cry out, scream, kick, or pound. Through this experience they may come to "own" (accept) feelings that previously made them uncomfortable.

Perls also developed a list of *rules* to ensure that clients will look at themselves more closely. In some versions of gestalt therapy, for example, clients may be required to use "I" language rather than "it" language. They must say, "I am frightened" rather than "The situation is frightening." Yet another common rule requires clients to stay in the *here and now*. They have needs now, are hiding their needs now, and must observe them now.

Approximately 1 percent of clinical psychologists and other kinds of clinicians describe themselves as gestalt therapists (Prochaska & Norcross, 2003). Because they believe that subjective experiences and self-awareness cannot be measured objectively, controlled research has not often been done on the gestalt approach (Strumpfel & Goldman, 2002; Greenberg et al., 1998, 1994).

Techniques of gestalt therapy *Gestalt therapists may guide their clients to express their needs and feelings in their full intensity through role-playing, banging on pillows, and other exercises. In a gestalt therapy group, members may help each other to "get in touch" with their needs and feelings.*

Spiritual Views and Interventions

For most of the twentieth century, clinical scientists viewed religion as a negative—or at best neutral—factor in mental health (Richards & Bergin, 2004, 2000; Bergin & Richards, 2001). In the early 1900s, for example, Freud argued that religious beliefs were defense mechanisms, "born from man's need to make his helplessness tolerable" (1961, p. 23). Subsequently, clinical theorists proposed that people with strong religious beliefs were more suspicious, irrational, guilt-ridden, and unstable than others, and less able to cope with life's difficulties. Correspondingly, spiritual principles and issues were considered a taboo topic in most forms of therapy.

The division between the clinical field and religion now seems to be ending. During the past decade, many articles and books linking spiritual issues to clinical treatment have been published, and the ethical codes of psychologists, psychiatrists, and counselors now state that religion is a type of diversity that mental health professionals are obligated to respect (Richards & Bergin, 2004, 2000). Researchers have learned that spirituality can, in fact, be of psychological benefit to people. In particular, studies have examined the mental health of people who are devout and who view God as warm, caring, helpful, and dependable. Repeatedly, these persons are found to be less lonely, pessimistic, depressed, or anxious than people without any religious beliefs or those who view God as cold and unresponsive (Koenig, 2002; Bergin & Richards, 2001; Clay, 1996). Such

>>**BY THE NUMBERS**

Charitable Acts

$150 billion	Amount contributed to charity each year in the United States‹‹
57%	Percentage of charitable donations contributed to religious organizations‹‹
43%	Percentage of donations directed to education, human services, health, and the arts‹‹
75%	Percentage of incoming college freshmen who have done volunteer work in the past year‹‹

(Kate, 1998; Reese, 1998)

Human aftershocks *These Armenian citizens seek solace in church after a devastating earthquake. Strong religious beliefs and institutional and social ties can help reduce individual stress reactions after traumatic events such as natural disasters.*

individuals also seem to cope better with major life stresses—from illness to war—and to attempt suicide less often. In addition, they are less likely to abuse drugs.

In line with such findings, many therapists now make a point of focusing on spiritual issues when treating religious clients (Richards & Bergin, 2004; Worthington & Sandage, 2001). At the very least, they try to respect how religious beliefs and values are affecting their clients' psychological functioning and to include such beliefs in their therapy discussions. Some therapists further encourage clients to use their spiritual resources to help them cope with current stresses.

Existential Theories and Therapy

Like humanists, existentialists believe that psychological dysfunctioning is caused by self-deception; but existentialists are talking about a kind of self-deception in which people hide from life's responsibilities and fail to recognize that it is up to them to give meaning to their lives. According to existentialists, many people become overwhelmed by the pressures of present-day society and so look to others for guidance and authority. They overlook their personal freedom of choice and avoid responsibility for their lives and decisions (Schneider, 2003; May & Yalom, 1995, 1989). Such people are left with empty, inauthentic lives. Their dominant emotions are anxiety, frustration, boredom, alienation, and depression.

Existentialists might view Philip Berman as a man who feels overwhelmed by the forces of society. He sees his parents as "rich, powerful, and selfish," and he perceives teachers, acquaintances, and employers as abusive and oppressing. He fails to appreciate his choices in life and his capacity for finding meaning and direction. Quitting becomes a habit with him—he leaves job after job, ends every romantic relationship, and flees difficult situations.

In **existential therapy** people are encouraged to accept responsibility for their lives and for their problems. They are helped to recognize their freedom so that they may choose a different course and live with greater meaning (Schneider, 2003). For the most part, existential therapists care more about the *goals* of therapy than the use of specific techniques; methods vary greatly from clinician to clinician. At the same time, most do place great emphasis on the *relationship* between therapist and client and try to create an atmosphere of candor, hard work, and shared learning and growth.

> *Patient:* I don't know why I keep coming here. All I do is tell you the same thing over and over. I'm not getting anywhere.
> *Doctor:* I'm getting tired of hearing the same thing over and over, too.
> *Patient:* Maybe I'll stop coming.
> *Doctor:* It's certainly your choice.
> *Patient:* What do you think I should do?
> *Doctor:* What do you want to do?
> *Patient:* I want to get better.
> *Doctor:* I don't blame you.
> *Patient:* If you think I should stay, ok, I will.
> *Doctor:* You want me to tell you to stay?
> *Patient:* You know what's best; you're the doctor.
> *Doctor:* Do I act like a doctor?
>
> *(Keen, 1970, p. 200)*

Existential therapists do not believe that experimental methods can adequately test the effectiveness of their treatments (Walsh & McElwain, 2002; May & Yalom, 1995, 1989). To them, research dehumanizes individuals by reducing them to test measures. Not surprisingly, then, very little controlled research has been devoted to the effectiveness of this approach. Nevertheless, around 3 percent of today's therapists use an approach that is primarily existential (Prochaska & Norcross, 2003).

EXISTENTIAL THERAPY A therapy that encourages clients to accept responsibility for their lives and to live with greater meaning and values.

Assessing the Humanistic-Existential Model

The humanistic-existential model appeals to many people in and out of the clinical field. In recognizing the special challenges of human existence, humanistic and existential theorists tap into an aspect of psychological life that is typically missing from the other models (Seeman, 2002). Moreover, the factors that they say are critical to effective functioning—self-acceptance and personal values, meaning, and choice—are certainly lacking in many people with psychological disturbances.

The optimistic tone of the humanistic-existential model is also an attraction. Proponents of these principles offer great hope when they claim that despite past and present events, we can make our own choices, determine our own destiny, and accomplish much. Still another attractive feature of the model is its emphasis on health. Unlike clinicians from some of the other models who see individuals as patients with psychological illnesses, humanists and existentialists view them simply as people whose special potential has yet to be fulfilled.

At the same time, the humanistic-existential focus on abstract issues of human fulfillment gives rise to a major problem from a scientific point of view: such issues are difficult to research. In fact, with the notable exception of Rogers, who tried to carefully investigate his clinical methods, humanists and existentialists have traditionally rejected the use of empirical research. This anti-research position is just now beginning to change. Humanistic researchers have conducted several recent studies that use appropriate control groups and statistical analyses, and they have found that such therapies can be beneficial in some cases (Elliott, 2002). This newfound interest in humanistic research and the clinical field's growing concern with religious issues should lead to important insights about this model in the coming years.

SUMMING UP

The Humanistic-Existential Model

The humanistic-existential model focuses on distinctly human issues such as self-awareness, values, meaning, and choice.

Humanists believe that people are driven to self-actualize. When this drive is interfered with, abnormal behavior may result. One group of humanistic therapists, client-centered therapists, try to create a very supportive therapy climate in which people can look at themselves honestly and acceptingly, thus opening the door to self-actualization. Another group, gestalt therapists, use more active techniques to help people accept their needs. Recently the role of religion as an important factor in mental health has caught the attention of researchers and clinicians.

According to existentialists, abnormal behavior results from hiding from life's responsibilities. Existential therapists encourage people to accept responsibility for their lives, to recognize their freedom to choose a different course, and to choose to live with greater meaning.

The Sociocultural Model

Philip Berman is also a social being. He is surrounded by people and by institutions, he is a member of a family and a society, and he takes part in both social and professional relationships. Thus social forces are always operating upon Philip, setting rules and expectations that guide or pressure him, helping to shape his behavior, thoughts, and emotions.

According to the *sociocultural model*, abnormal behavior is best understood in light of the social and cultural forces that influence an individual. What are the norms of the society? What roles does the person play in the social environment? What kind of cultural background or family structure is the person a part of? And how do other people view and react to him or her?

How Do Sociocultural Theorists Explain Abnormal Functioning?

Because behavior is shaped by social forces, sociocultural theorists hold, we must examine a person's social and cultural surroundings if we are to understand abnormal behavior. Sociocultural explanations focus on *family structure and communication, cultural influences, social networks, societal conditions,* and *societal labels and roles.*

FAMILY STRUCTURE AND COMMUNICATION According to **family systems theory**, the family is a system of interacting parts—the family members—who relate to one another in consistent ways and follow rules unique to each family (Kaslow et al., 2003). Family systems theorists believe that the structure and communication patterns of some families actually force individual members to behave in a way that otherwise seems abnormal. If the members were to behave normally, they would severely strain the family's usual manner of operation and would actually increase their own and their family's turmoil.

Family systems theory holds that certain family systems are particularly likely to produce abnormal functioning in individual members. Some families, for example, have an *enmeshed* structure in which the members are grossly overinvolved in each other's activities, thoughts, and feelings. Children from this kind of family may have great difficulty becoming independent in life (Santiesteban et al., 2001). Some families display *disengagement,* which is marked by very rigid boundaries between the members. Children from these families may find it hard to function in a group or to give or request support (Corey, 2001).

In the sociocultural model, Philip Berman's angry and impulsive personal style might be seen as the product of a disturbed family structure. According to family systems theorists, the whole family—mother, father, Philip, and his brother Arnold—relate in such a way as to maintain Philip's behavior. Family theorists might be particularly interested in the conflict between Philip's mother and father and the imbalance between their parental roles. They might see Philip's behavior as both a reaction to and stimulus for his parents' behaviors. With Philip acting out the role of the misbehaving child, or scapegoat, his parents may have little time to question their own relationship.

Family systems theorists would also seek to clarify the precise nature of Philip's relationship with each parent. Is he enmeshed with his mother and/or disengaged from his father? They would look too at the rules governing the sibling relationship in the family, the relationship between the parents and Philip's brother, and the nature of parent–child relationships in previous generations of the family.

TV's favorite family *Unlike viewers in the 1950s, when problem-free families like the Nelsons (Ozzie and Harriet) ruled the airwaves, today's viewers prefer reality-based families, like the Osbournes, whose interactions and behaviors are occasionally complex, problematic, and perhaps dysfunctional.*

CULTURE "Culture" refers to the set of values, attitudes, beliefs, history, and behaviors shared by a group of people and communicated from one generation to the next (Matsumoto, 1994). During the past two decades, sociocultural researchers have greatly increased their focus on possible ties between culture and abnormal behavior. They have learned that some of the disorders we shall be coming across in this textbook—anorexia nervosa, for example—are much less common in non-Western countries (Cooper, 2001; Paris, 2001). It may be that key Western values—such as favoring a thin appearance —help set the stage for such disorders.

SOCIAL NETWORKS AND SUPPORTS Sociocultural theorists are also concerned with the social networks in which people operate, including their social and pro-

FAMILY SYSTEMS THEORY A theory that views the family as a system of interacting parts whose interactions exhibit consistent patterns and unstated rules.

The dysfunctional society *The pressures and uncertainty of living in a war-torn environment may contribute to the development of psychological problems. The environment's ongoing violence may leave some individuals feeling numb and confused. This child seemed hardly to notice the burning bombed truck behind him as he bicycled through Northern Ireland several years ago.*

fessional relationships. How well do they communicate with others? What kind of signals do they send to or receive from others? Researchers have often found ties between deficiencies in social networks and a person's functioning (Segrin, 2001; Paykel & Cooper, 1992). They have noted, for example, that people who are isolated and lack social support or intimacy in their lives are more likely to become depressed when under stress and to remain depressed longer than are people with supportive spouses or warm friendships.

SOCIETAL CONDITIONS Wide-ranging societal conditions may create special stresses and increase the likelihood of abnormal functioning in some members. Researchers have learned, for example, that psychological abnormality, especially severe psychological abnormality, is more common in the lower socioeconomic classes than in the higher ones (Draine et al., 2002). Perhaps the special pressures of lower-class life explain this relationship. That is, the higher rates of crime, unemployment, overcrowding, and homelessness; the inferior medical care; and the limited educational opportunities of lower-class life may place great stress on members of these groups.

Sociocultural researchers have noted that racial and sexual prejudice may also contribute to certain forms of abnormal functioning (Simons et al., 2002). Women in Western society receive diagnoses of anxiety and depressive disorders at least twice as often as men (Nolen-Hoeksema, 2002). Similarly, African Americans experience unusually high rates of anxiety disorders (Blazer et al., 1991). Hispanic persons, particularly young men, have higher rates of alcoholism than members of most other ethnic groups (Helzer, Burnman, & McEvoy, 1991). And Native Americans display exceptionally high alcoholism and suicide rates (Kinzie et al., 1992). Although many factors may combine to produce these differences, racial and sexual prejudice and the problems they pose may contribute to abnormal patterns of tension, unhappiness, low self-esteem, and escape (Winston, 2004; Prochaska & Norcross, 2003).

SOCIETAL LABELS AND ROLES Sociocultural theorists also believe that abnormal functioning is influenced greatly by the labels and roles assigned to troubled people (Link et al., 2001). When people stray from the norms of their society, the society calls them deviant and, in many cases, "mentally ill." Such labels tend to stick. Moreover, when people are viewed in particular ways, reacted to as "crazy," and perhaps even encouraged to act sick, they gradually learn to play the assigned role. Ultimately the label seems appropriate.

A famous study by the clinical investigator David Rosenhan (1973) supports this position. Eight normal people presented themselves at various mental hospitals,

>>LOOKING AROUND
Gender Issues in the Workplace

According to the Bureau of Labor Statistics, women today earn 76 cents for every $1 earned by a man.‹‹

Around 62 percent of young adult men believe that men and women are currently paid the same for similar work; only 30 percent of young adult women agree.‹‹

Around 42 percent of young adult women believe that women have to outperform men at work to get the same rewards; only 11 percent of young adult men agree.‹‹

(Yin, 2002)

CULTURE-SENSITIVE THERAPIES
Approaches that address the unique issues faced by members of minority groups.

GENDER-SENSITIVE THERAPIES
Approaches geared to the special pressures of being a woman in Western society. Also called *feminist therapies.*

GROUP THERAPY A therapy format in which a group of people with similar problems meet together with a therapist to work on those problems.

SELF-HELP GROUP A group made up of people with similar problems who help and support one another without the direct leadership of a clinician. Also called a *mutual help group.*

complaining that they had been hearing voices say the words "empty," "hollow," and "thud." On the basis of this complaint alone, each was diagnosed as having schizophrenia and admitted. As the sociocultural model would predict, the "pseudopatients" had a hard time convincing others that they were well once they had been given the diagnostic label. Their hospitalizations ranged from 7 to 52 days, even though they behaved normally as soon as they were admitted. In addition, the label kept influencing the way the staff viewed and dealt with them. For example, one pseudopatient who paced the corridor out of boredom was, in clinical notes, described as "nervous." Overall, the pseudopatients came to feel powerless, invisible, and bored.

Sociocultural Treatments

Sociocultural theories have helped spur the growth of several treatment approaches, including *culture-sensitive therapy, group therapy, family and couple therapy,* and *community treatment.* Therapists of any orientation may work with clients in these various formats, applying the techniques and principles of their preferred models. In such instances the therapy approach is not purely sociocultural. However, more and more of the clinicians who use these formats believe that psychological problems emerge in a social setting and are best treated in such a setting, and they include special sociocultural strategies in their work.

CULTURE-SENSITIVE THERAPY A number of recent studies have found that many members of ethnic and racial minority groups improve less in clinical treatment than members of majority groups (Sue, 2003; Lee & Sue, 2001). Similarly, studies conducted throughout the world have found that minority clients use mental health services less often than members of majority groups (Gaw, 2001). In some cases, cultural beliefs, a language barrier, or lack of information about available services may prevent minority individuals from seeking help; in other cases, such persons may not trust the establishment, relying instead on traditional remedies that are available in their immediate social environment.

Research also indicates that members of minority groups stop therapy sooner than persons from majority groups. In the United States, African Americans, Native Americans, Asian Americans, and Hispanic Americans all have higher therapy dropout rates than white Americans (Lee & Sue, 2001). Members of these groups may stop treatment because they do not feel they are benefiting from it or because ethnic and racial differences prevent the development of a strong rapport with their therapist (Whaley, 1998).

How can clinicians be more helpful to people from minority groups? A number of studies suggest that two features of treatment can increase a therapist's effectiveness with minority clients: (1) greater therapist sensitivity to cultural issues and (2) inclusion of cultural morals and models in treatment, especially in therapies for children and adolescents (Lee & Sue, 2001; Whaley, 1998). Given such findings, clinicians have developed **culture-sensitive therapies,** approaches that seek to address the unique issues faced by members of minority groups (Prochaska & Norcross, 2003; Sue, 2003; Lee & Sue, 2001). Similarly, some clinicians have developed therapies geared to the special pressures of being a woman in Western society, called **gender-sensitive** or **feminist therapies** (Sweeney, 2003).

GROUP THERAPY Thousands of therapists specialize in **group therapy**, a format in which a therapist meets with a group of clients who have similar problems. Indeed, one survey of clinical psychologists revealed that almost one-third of them devoted some portion of their practice to group therapy (Norcross et al., 1993). Typically, members of a therapy group meet together with a therapist and

Victims of hate *This memorial service for Matthew Shepard, brutally beaten to death in 1998 because of his gay orientation, is a powerful reminder of the prejudice, discrimination, and even danger that members of minority groups can confront in our society. Culture-sensitive therapies seek to address the special impact of such stressors upon individuals, as well as other psychological issues.*

Liss Steve/Corbis Sygma

THE CURRENT SCENE

Self-Help Groups: Too Much of a Good Thing?

Self-help groups are widely accepted in our society, by consumers and clinicians alike. One survey of mental health professionals revealed that almost 90 percent of all therapists in the United States often recommend such groups to their clients as a supplement to therapy (Clifford et al., 1998). Small wonder that the number, range, and appeal of such groups have grown rapidly over the past several decades. The self-help group movement and its impact on our society are brought to life in the following notice that was posted in a Colorado church in 1990 (Moskowitz, 2001), listing support groups that would be meeting at the church during the coming week:

Sunday	
12:00 noon	Cocaine Anonymous, main floor
5:30 p.m.	Survivors of Incest, main floor
6:00 p.m.	Al-Anon, 2nd floor
6:00 p.m.	Alcoholics Anonymous, basement
Monday	
5:30 p.m.	Debtors Anonymous, basement
6:30 p.m.	Codependents of Sex Addicts Anonymous, 2nd floor
7:00 p.m.	Adult Children of Alcoholics, 2nd floor
8:00 p.m.	Alcoholics Anonymous, basement
8:00 p.m.	Al-Anon, 2nd floor
8:00 p.m.	Alateen, basement
8:00 p.m.	Cocaine Anonymous, main floor
Tuesday	
8:00 p.m.	Survivors of Incest Anonymous, basement

Wednesday	
5:30 p.m.	Sex & Love Addicts Anonymous, basement
7:30 p.m.	Adult Children of Alcoholics, 2nd floor
8:00 p.m.	Cocaine Anonymous, main floor
Thursday	
7:00 p.m.	Codependents of Sex Addicts Anonymous, 2nd floor
7:00 p.m.	Women's Cocaine Anonymous, main floor
Friday	
5:30 p.m.	Sex & Love Addicts Anonymous, basement
5:45 p.m.	Adult Overeaters Anonymous, 2nd floor
7:30 p.m.	Codependents Anonymous, basement
7:30 p.m.	Adult Children of Alcoholics, 2nd floor
8:00 p.m.	Cocaine Anonymous, main floor
Saturday	
10:00 a.m.	Adult Children of Alcoholics, main floor
12:00 p.m.	Self-Abusers Anonymous, 2nd floor

discuss the problems of one or more of the people in the group. Together they develop important insights, build social skills, strengthen feelings of self-worth, and share useful information or advice (Dies, 2003; Yalom, 1995). Many groups are created with particular client populations in mind; for example, there are groups for people with alcoholism, for those who are physically handicapped, and for people who are divorced, abused, or bereaved (Corey & Corey, 2002).

Research suggests that group therapy is of help to many clients, often as helpful as individual therapy (Dies, 2003; McDermut et al., 2001). The group format has also been used for purposes that are educational rather than therapeutic, such as "consciousness raising" and spiritual inspiration.

A format similar to group therapy is the **self-help group** (or **mutual help group**). Here people who have similar problems (bereavement, substance abuse, illness, unemployment, divorce) come together to help and support one another without the direct leadership of a professional clinician (Wituk et al., 2002). According to estimates, there are now between 500,000 and 3 million such groups in the United States alone, attended each year by 3 to 4 percent of the population. Indeed, it is estimated that 25 million Americans will participate in self-help groups at some point in their lives (Davison et al., 2000). Self-help groups tend to offer more direct advice than is provided in group therapy and to encourage more exchange of information or "tips."

FAMILY THERAPY A therapy format in which the therapist meets with all members of a family and helps them to change in therapeutic ways.

COUPLE THERAPY A therapy format in which the therapist works with two people who share a long-term relationship. Also called *marital therapy.*

COMMUNITY MENTAL HEALTH TREATMENT A treatment approach that emphasizes community care.

FAMILY THERAPY **Family therapy** was first introduced in the 1950s. A therapist meets with all members of a family, points out problem behaviors and interactions, and helps the whole family to change (Cottrell & Boston, 2002; Minuchin, 1997). Here the entire family is viewed as the unit under treatment, even if only one of the members receives a clinical diagnosis. The following is a typical interaction between family members and a therapist:

Tommy sat motionless in a chair gazing out the window. He was fourteen and a bit small for his age. . . . Sissy was eleven. She was sitting on the couch between her Mom and Dad with a smile on her face. Across from them sat Ms. Fargo, the family therapist.

Ms. Fargo spoke. "Could you be a little more specific about the changes you have seen in Tommy and when they came about?"

Mrs. Davis answered first. "Well, I guess it was about two years ago. Tommy started getting in fights at school. When we talked to him at home he said it was none of our business. He became moody and disobedient. He wouldn't do anything that we wanted him to. He began to act mean to his sister and even hit her."

"What about the fights at school?" Ms. Fargo asked.

This time it was Mr. Davis who spoke first. "Ginny was more worried about them than I was. I used to fight a lot when I was in school and I think it is normal. . . . But I was very respectful to my parents, especially my Dad. If I ever got out of line he would smack me one."

"Have you ever had to hit Tommy?" Ms. Fargo inquired softly.

"Sure, a couple of times, but it didn't seem to do any good."

All at once Tommy seemed to be paying attention, his eyes riveted on his father. "Yeah, he hit me a lot, for no reason at all!"

"Now, that's not true, Thomas." Mrs. Davis had a scolding expression on her face. "If you behaved yourself a little better you wouldn't get hit. Ms. Fargo, I can't say that I am in favor of the hitting, but I understand sometimes how frustrating it may be for Bob."

"You don't know how frustrating it is for me, honey." Bob seemed upset. "You don't have to work all day at the office and then come home to contend with all of this. Sometimes I feel like I don't even want to come home."

Ginny gave him a hard stare. "You think things at home are easy all day? I could use some support from you. You think all you have to do is earn the money and I will do everything else. Well, I am not about to do that anymore." . . .

Mrs. Davis began to cry. "I just don't know what to do anymore. Things just seem so hopeless. Why can't people be nice in this family anymore? I don't think I am asking too much, am I?"

Ms. Fargo spoke thoughtfully. "I get the feeling that people in this family would like things to be different. Bob, I can see how frustrating it must be for you to work so hard and not be able to relax when you get home. And, Ginny, your job is not easy either. You have a lot to do at home and Bob can't be there to help because he has to earn a living. And you kids sound like you would like some things to be different too. It must be hard for you, Tommy, to be catching so much flack these days. I think this also makes it hard for you to have fun at home too, Sissy."

She looked at each person briefly and was sure to make eye contact. "There seems to be a lot going on. . . . I think we are going to need to understand a lot of things to see why this is happening. . . ."

(Sheras & Worchel, 1979, pp. 108–110)

Family therapists may follow any of the major theoretical models (Kaslow et al., 2003), but more and more of them are adopting the sociocultural principles of family systems theory. Today 4 percent of all clinical psychologists, 13 percent of social workers, and 1 percent of psychiatrists identify themselves mainly as *family systems therapists* (Prochaska & Norcross, 2003).

As we observed earlier, family systems theory holds that each family has its own rules, structure, and communication patterns that shape the individual members' behavior. In one family systems approach, *structural family therapy*, therapists try to change the family power structure, the role each person plays, and the alliances between members (Vetere, 2001; Minuchin, 1997, 1987, 1974). In another, *conjoint family therapy*, therapists try to help members change harmful patterns of communication (Innes, 2002; Satir, 1987, 1967, 1964).

Family therapies of various kinds are often helpful to individuals, although research has not yet clarified how helpful (Sexton & Alexander, 2002). Some studies have found that as many as 65 percent of individuals treated with family approaches improve, while other studies suggest much lower success rates. Nor has any one type of family therapy emerged as consistently more helpful than the others (Alexander et al., 2001; Diamond & Diamond, 2001).

COUPLE THERAPY In **couple therapy**, or **marital therapy**, the therapist works with two individuals who are in a long-term relationship. Often they are husband and wife, but the couple need not be married or even living together. Like family therapy, couple therapy often focuses on the structure and communication patterns occurring in the relationship (Gurman, 2003; Baucom et al., 2000, 1998). A couple approach may also be used when a child's psychological problems are traced to problems that may exist between the parents.

Although some degree of conflict exists in any long-term relationship, many adults in our society experience serious marital discord. The divorce rate in Canada, the United States, and Europe is now close to 50 percent of the marriage rate (NCHS, 2000, 1999). Many couples who live together without marrying apparently have similar levels of difficulty (Greeley, 1991).

Couple therapy, like family and group therapy, may follow the principles of any of the major therapy orientations. *Behavioral couple therapy*, for example, uses many techniques from the behavioral perspective (Gollan & Jacobson, 2001). Therapists help spouses recognize and change problem behaviors largely by teaching specific problem-solving and communication skills. A broader, more sociocultural version, called *integrative couple therapy*, further helps partners accept behaviors that they cannot change and embrace the whole relationship nevertheless (Wheeler, Christensen, & Jacobson, 2001). Partners are asked to see such behaviors as an understandable result of basic differences between them.

Couples treated by couple therapy seem to show greater improvement in their relationships than couples with similar problems who fail to receive treatment, but no one form of couple therapy stands out as superior to others (Gurman, 2003; Gollan & Jacobson, 2001; Gottman et al., 2001). Although two-thirds of treated couples experience improved marital functioning by the end of therapy, fewer than half of those who are treated achieve "distress-free" or "happy" relationships. Moreover, one-third of successfully treated couples may relapse within two years after therapy. Couples who are younger, well adjusted, and less rigid in their gender roles tend to have the best results.

COMMUNITY TREATMENT Following sociocultural principles, **community mental health treatment** programs allow clients, particularly those with severe psychological difficulties, to receive treatment in familiar surroundings as they try to recover. In 1963 President Kennedy called for such a "bold new approach" to the treatment of mental disorders—a community approach that would enable most people with psychological problems to receive services from nearby agencies rather than distant facilities or institutions. Congress passed the Community Mental Health Act soon after, launching the community mental health movement across

"I've been a cow all my life, honey. Don't ask me to change now."

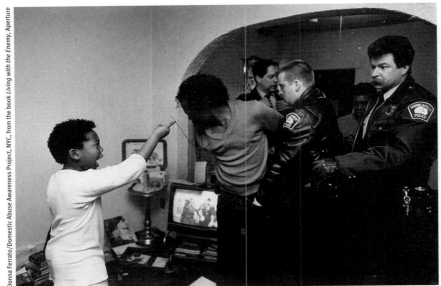

Donna Ferrato/Domestic Abuse Awareness Project, NYC, from the book *Living with the Enemy*, Aperture

Secondary prevention in action *Community mental health professionals sometimes work with police and other public servants, teaching them how to address the psychological needs of people who are under extreme stress and upset. This 8-year-old had to call the police when he saw his father attacking his mother with a knife. The child's rage, frustration, and emotional pain are apparent.*

the United States. A number of other countries have launched similar movements.

As we observed in Chapter 1, a key principle of community treatment is *prevention* (Felner et al., 2000). Here clinicians actively reach out to clients rather than wait for them to seek treatment. Research suggests that such efforts are often very successful (Oxley, 2000; Wolff, 2000). Community workers recognize three types of prevention, which they call *primary, secondary,* and *tertiary.*

Primary prevention consists of efforts to improve community attitudes and policies. Its goal is to prevent psychological disorders altogether. Community workers may lobby for better community recreational programs, consult with a local school board, or offer public workshops on stress reduction.

Secondary prevention consists of identifying and treating psychological disorders in the early stages, before they become serious. Community workers may work with schoolteachers, ministers, or police to help them recognize the early signs of psychological dysfunction and teach them how to help people find treatment (Newman et al., 1996).

The goal of *tertiary prevention* is to provide effective treatment as soon as it is needed so that moderate or severe disorders do not become long-term problems. Today community agencies across the United States do successfully offer tertiary care for millions of people with moderate psychological problems, but, as we observed in Chapter 1, they often fail to provide the services needed by hundreds of thousands with severe disturbances. One of the reasons for this failure is lack of funding, an issue that we shall return to in later chapters (Humphreys & Rappaport, 1993).

Assessing the Sociocultural Model

The sociocultural model has added greatly to the understanding and treatment of abnormal functioning. Today most clinicians take family, cultural, social, and societal issues into account, factors that were overlooked just 30 years ago. In addition, clinicians have become more aware of the impact of clinical and social labels. Finally, as we have just observed, sociocultural treatment formats sometimes succeed where traditional approaches have failed.

At the same time, the sociocultural model, like the other models, has certain problems. To begin with, sociocultural research findings are often difficult to interpret. Research may reveal a relationship between certain sociocultural factors and a particular disorder yet fail to establish that they are its *cause*. Studies show a link between family conflict and schizophrenia, for example, but that finding does not necessarily mean that family dysfunction causes schizophrenia. It is equally possible that family functioning is disrupted by the tension created by the schizophrenic behavior of a family member (Eakes, 1995).

Another limitation of the model is its inability to predict abnormality in specific individuals (Reynolds, 1998). For example, if societal conditions such as prejudice are key causes of anxiety and depression, why do only some of the people subjected to such forces experience psychological disorders? Are still other factors necessary for the development of the disorders?

Given these limitations, most clinicians view sociocultural explanations as operating in conjunction with biological or psychological explanations. They agree that sociocultural factors may create a climate favorable to the development of certain disorders. They believe, however, that biological or psychological conditions or both must also be present in order for the disorders to spring forth.

BIOPSYCHOSOCIAL THEORIES
Explanations that attribute the cause of abnormality to an interaction of genetic, biological, developmental, emotional, behavioral, cognitive, social, and societal influences.

The Sociocultural Model

The sociocultural model looks outward to the social forces that affect members of a society. Some sociocultural theorists focus on the family system, while others look at cultural background, social networks, societal conditions, or societal labels and roles. Sociocultural principles are on display in culture-sensitive, group, family, and couple therapies. Research indicates that these treatment approaches are useful for some problems and under some circumstances. In community treatment, therapists try to work with people in settings close to home, school, and work. Their goal is either primary, secondary, or tertiary prevention.

CROSSROADS:

Integration of the Models

Today's leading models vary widely (see Table 2-2). They look at behavior differently, begin with different assumptions, arrive at different conclusions, and apply different treatments. Yet none of the models have proved consistently superior. Each helps us appreciate a key aspect of human functioning, and each has important strengths as well as serious limitations.

With all their differences, the conclusions and techniques of the various models are often compatible (Friman et al., 1993). Certainly our understanding and treatment of abnormal behavior are more complete if we appreciate the biological, psychological, *and* sociocultural aspects of a person's problem rather than only one of them. Not surprisingly, then, a growing number of clinicians now favor explanations of abnormal behavior that consider more than one kind of cause at a time. These explanations, sometimes called **biopsychosocial theories**, state that abnormality results from the interaction of genetic, biological, developmental,

Table 2-2

Comparing the Models

	BIOLOGICAL	PSYCHODYNAMIC	BEHAVIORAL	COGNITIVE	HUMANISTIC	EXISTENTIAL	SOCIO-CULTURAL
Cause of dysfunction	Biological malfunction	Underlying conflicts	Maladaptive learning	Maladaptive thinking	Self-deceit	Avoidance of responsibility	Family or social stress
Research support	Strong	Modest	Strong	Strong	Weak	Weak	Moderate
Consumer designation	Patient	Patient	Client	Client	Patient or client	Patient or client	Client
Therapist role	Doctor	Interpreter	Teacher	Persuader	Observer	Collaborator	Social facilitator
Key therapist technique	Biological intervention	Free association and interpretation	Conditioning	Reasoning	Reflection	Varied	Social intervention
Therapy goal	Biological repair	Broad psychological change	Functional behaviors	Adaptive thinking	Self-actualization	Authentic life	Effective family or social system

>>Q & A
How do genetic defects differ from congenital defects?

The terms "genetic" and "congenital" both come from the Greek for "birth." Genetic defects are inherited, are determined at the moment of conception, and can be passed down to future generations. Congenital defects—defects with which a child is born—are not inherited; they develop after conception, during the gestation period (Johnsen, 1994).<<

emotional, behavioral, cognitive, social, cultural, and societal influences. A case of depression, for example, might best be explained by pointing collectively to an individual's inheritance of unfavorable genes, traumatic losses during childhood, negative ways of thinking, and social isolation.

Some biopsychosocial theorists favor a *diathesis-stress explanation* of how the various factors work together to cause abnormal functioning ("diathesis" means a predisposed tendency). According to this theory, people must first have a biological, psychological, or sociocultural predisposition to develop a disorder and must then be subjected to episodes of severe stress. In a case of depression, for example, we might find that unfavorable genes and related biochemical abnormalities predispose the individual to develop the disorder, while the loss of a loved one actually triggers its onset.

In a similar search for integration, many therapists are now combining treatment techniques from several models (Stricker & Gold, 2003). In fact, 27 percent of today's clinical psychologists, 34 percent of social workers, and 53 percent of psychiatrists describe their approach as "eclectic" or "integrative" (Prochaska & Norcross, 2003). Studies confirm that clinical problems often respond better to combined approaches than to any one therapy alone. For example, as we shall see, drug therapy combined with behavioral and cognitive approaches is sometimes the most effective treatment for severe social anxiety.

Given the recent rise in biopsychosocial theories and combination treatments, our look at abnormal behavior throughout this book will take a particular direction. As different disorders are presented, we will be interested in how today's models explain each disorder and how clinicians who endorse each model treat people with the disorder. Just as important, however, we will also be observing how the explanations and treatments may build upon and strengthen each other, and we will examine current efforts toward integration of the models.

CRITICAL THOUGHTS

1. What might the enormous popularity of psychotropic drugs suggest about the needs and coping styles of individuals today and about problem solving in our technological society? *pp. 35–37*

2. In *Paradise Lost* Milton wrote, "The mind . . . can make a heaven of hell, a hell of heaven." Which model(s) of abnormal functioning would agree with this statement? *pp. 37–55*

3. Twenty-one percent of Americans say they are regularly "bored out of their mind" (Kanner, 1999). How might humanistic-existential theorists explain the phenomenon of severe boredom and such reactions to it? *pp. 51–55*

4. Why might positive religious beliefs be linked to mental health? Why have so many clinicians been suspicious of religious beliefs for so long? *pp. 53–54*

5. In *Anna Karenina* the writer Leo Tolstoy wrote, "All happy families resemble one another; every unhappy family is unhappy in its own fashion." Would family systems theorists agree with Tolstoy? *p. 56*

6. What might be the advantages and disadvantages of self-help groups in comparison with professional treatment? *p. 59*

KEY TERMS

neuron p. 33
neurotransmitter p. 34
endocrine system p. 34
hormone p. 34
gene p. 34
evolution p. 35

psychotropic medication p. 36
electroconvulsive therapy (ECT) p. 36
psychosurgery p. 36
unconscious p. 38
id p. 38
ego p. 38

ego defense mechanism p. 38
superego p. 38
free association p. 40
resistance p. 41
transference p. 41
dream p. 41

conditioning p. 44
systematic desensitization p. 45
cognitive therapy p. 48
self-actualization p. 51
client-centered therapy p. 52

gestalt therapy p. 53
existential therapy p. 54
family systems theory p. 56
culture-sensitive therapy p. 58
group therapy p. 58

self-help group p. 59
family therapy p. 60
couple therapy p. 61
community mental health treatment p. 61
diathesis-stress explanation p. 64

QUICK QUIZ

1. What are the key regions of the brain, and how do messages travel throughout the brain? Describe the biological treatments for psychological disorders. *pp. 33–37*

2. Identify the model associated with learned responses (*p. 44*), values (*p. 51*), responsibility (*p. 54*), spirituality (*p. 53*), underlying conflicts (*p. 38*), and maladaptive assumptions (*p. 48*).

3. Identify the treatments that use unconditional positive regard (*p. 51*), free association (*p. 40*), classical conditioning (*p. 44*), skillful frustration (*p. 53*), and dream interpretation (*p. 41*).

4. What are the key principles of the psychodynamic, behavioral, cognitive, and humanistic-existential models? *pp. 37–55*

5. According to psychodynamic theorists, what roles do the id, ego, and superego play in the development of both normal and abnormal behavior? What are the key techniques used by psychodynamic therapists? *pp. 38–43*

6. What forms of conditioning do behaviorists rely on in their explanations and treatments of abnormal behaviors? *pp. 44–46*

7. What kinds of cognitive dysfunctioning can lead to abnormal behavior? *p. 48*

8. How do humanistic theories and therapies differ from existential ones? *pp. 51–54*

9. How might family factors, culture, social networks, societal conditions, and societal labels help produce abnormal behavior? *pp. 55–58*

10. What are the key features of culture-sensitive therapy, group therapy, family therapy, couple therapy, and community treatment? How effective are these various approaches? *pp. 58–62*

 CYBER STUDY

SEARCH THE *FUNDAMENTALS OF ABNORMAL PSYCHOLOGY* CD-ROM FOR

▲ **Chapter 2 Video Case Enrichment**
  Observe the biological, psychodynamic, and sociocultural models in operation. How do treatments vary?
  Are dreams the "royal road to the unconscious"?

▲ **Chapter 2 Practical, Research, and Decision-Making Exercises**
  Sorting out today's models: The lingering impact of past models
  Recognizing Freud's wide-ranging influence

▲ **Chapter 2 Practice Test and Feedback**

LOG ON TO THE COMER WEB PAGE FOR

▲ Suggested Web links, exercises, FAQ page, additional Chapter 2 practice test questions
  <www.worthpublishers.com/comer>

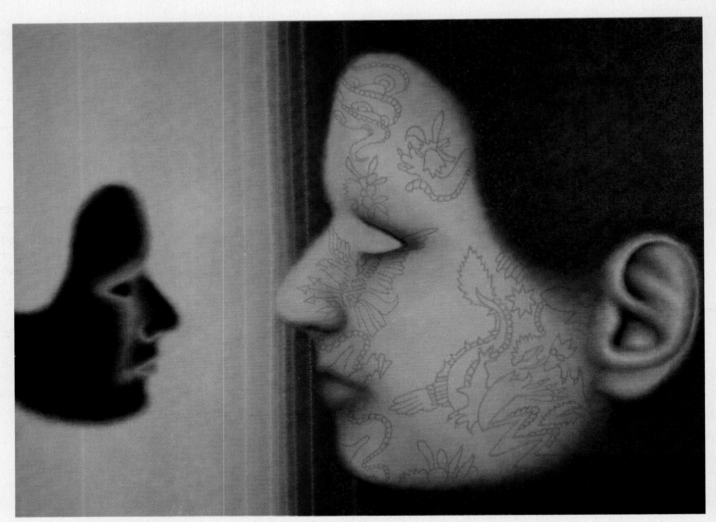

ED PASCHKE, 1993

Clinical Assessment, Diagnosis, and Treatment

Angela Savanti was 22 years old, lived at home with her mother, and was employed as a secretary in a large insurance company. She . . . had had passing periods of "the blues" before, but her present feelings of despondency were of much greater proportion. She was troubled by a severe depression and frequent crying spells, which had not lessened over the past two months. Angela found it hard to concentrate on her job, had great difficulty falling asleep at night, and had a poor appetite. . . . Her depression had begun after she and her boyfriend Jerry broke up two months previously.

(Leon, 1984, p. 109)

Her feelings of despondency led Angela Savanti to make an appointment with a therapist at a local counseling center. The first step the clinician took was to learn as much as possible about Angela and her disturbance. Who is she, what is her life like, and what precisely are her symptoms? The answers might help to reveal the causes and probable course of her present dysfunction and suggest what kinds of strategies would be most likely to help her. Treatment could then be tailored to Angela's needs and particular pattern of abnormal functioning.

In Chapters 1 and 2 we saw how researchers in abnormal psychology build a broad understanding of abnormal functioning. Clinical practitioners certainly apply that general information in their work, but their main focus when faced with a new client is to gather **idiographic**, or individual, information about their clients. To help persons overcome their problems, practitioners must fully understand them and their particular difficulties. In order to gather such individual information, clinicians use the procedures of *assessment* and *diagnosis*. Then they are in a position to offer *treatment*.

Clinical Assessment: How and Why Does the Client Behave Abnormally?

Assessment is simply the collecting of relevant information in an effort to reach a conclusion. It goes on in every realm of life. We make assessments when we decide what cereal to buy or which presidential candidate to vote for. College admissions officers, who have to select the "best" of the students applying to their college, depend on academic records, recommendations, achievement test scores, interviews, and application forms to help them decide. Employers, who have to predict which applicants are most likely to be effective workers, collect information from résumés, interviews, references, and perhaps on-the-job observations.

Clinical assessment is used to determine how and why a person is behaving abnormally and how that person may be helped. It also enables clinicians to evaluate people's progress after they have been in treatment for a

IDIOGRAPHIC UNDERSTANDING An understanding of the behavior of a particular individual.

ASSESSMENT The process of collecting and interpreting relevant information about a client or subject.

while and decide whether the treatment should be changed. The specific tools that are used to do an assessment depend on the clinician's theoretical orientation (Spiegler & Guevremont, 2003; Haynes & O'Brien, 2000). Psychodynamic clinicians, for example, use methods that assess a client's personality and probe for any unconscious conflicts he or she may be experiencing. Behavioral and cognitive clinicians are more likely to use assessment methods that reveal specific dysfunctional behaviors and cognitions.

The hundreds of clinical assessment techniques and tools that have been developed fall into three categories: *clinical interviews*, *tests*, and *observations*. To be useful, these tools must be *standardized* and have clear *reliability* and *validity*.

Characteristics of Assessment Tools

All clinicians must follow the same procedures when they use a particular technique of assessment. To **standardize** a technique is to set up common steps to be followed whenever it is administered. Similarly, clinicians must standardize the way they interpret the results of an assessment tool in order to be able to understand what a particular score means. They may standardize the scores of a test, for example, by first administering it to a group of subjects whose performance will then serve as a common standard, or norm, against which later individual scores can be measured. The group that initially takes the test must be typical of the larger population for whom the test is intended. If an aggressiveness test meant for the public at large were standardized on a group of marines, for example, the resulting "norm" might turn out to be misleadingly high.

Reliability refers to the *consistency* of assessment measures. A good assessment tool will always yield the same results in the same situation (Shrout, 2002; Wiens, Mueller, & Bryan, 2001). An assessment tool has high *test–retest reliability*, one kind of reliability, if it yields the same results every time it is given to the same people. If a woman's responses on a particular test indicate that she is generally a heavy drinker, the test should produce the same result when she takes it again a week later. To measure test–retest reliability, subjects are tested on two occasions and the two scores are correlated. The higher the correlation (see Chapter 1), the greater the test's reliability.

An assessment tool shows high *interrater* (or *interjudge*) *reliability*, another kind of reliability, if different judges independently agree on how to score and interpret it. True–false and multiple-choice tests yield consistent scores no matter who evaluates them, but other tests require that the evaluator make a judgment. Consider a test that requires the person to draw a copy of a picture, which a judge then rates for accuracy. Different judges may give different ratings to the same drawing.

Finally, an assessment tool must have **validity**: it must *accurately* measure what it is supposed to measure (Goodwin, 2002). Suppose a weight scale reads 12 pounds every time a 10-pound bag of sugar is placed on it. Although the scale is reliable because its readings are consistent, those readings are not valid, or accurate.

A given assessment tool may appear to be valid simply because it makes sense and seems reasonable. However, this sort of validity, called *face validity*, does not by itself mean that the instrument is trustworthy. A test for depression, for example, might include questions about how often a person cries. Because it makes sense that depressed people would cry, these test questions would have face validity. It turns out, however, that many people cry a great deal for reasons other than depression, and some extremely depressed people fail to cry at all. Thus an assessment tool should not be used unless it has high predictive or concurrent validity (Kamphaus & Frick, 2002).

Predictive validity is a tool's ability to predict future characteristics or behavior. Let us say that a test has been developed to identify elementary school children

The Palm Beach Post, photo by Mark Mirko

Oops! *These judges of a high school diving competition, actually coaches from the opposing teams, arrive at very different assessments of the same diver. The low interrater reliability may reflect evaluator bias or defects in the scoring procedure.*

who are likely to take up cigarette smoking in junior high school. The test gathers information about the children's parents—their personal characteristics, smoking habits, and attitudes toward smoking—and on that basis identifies high-risk children. To establish the test's predictive validity, we could administer it to a group of elementary school students, wait until they were in junior high school, and then check to see which children actually did become smokers.

Concurrent validity is the degree to which the measures gathered from one tool agree with measures gathered from other assessment techniques. Subjects' scores on a new anxiety test, for example, should correlate highly with their scores on other anxiety tests or with their behavior during clinical interviews.

"We're going to run some tests: blood work, a cat-scan, and the S.A.T.'s."

Clinical Interviews

Most of us feel that the best way to get to know people is to meet with them face to face. Under these circumstances, we can see them react to what we do and say, observe as well as listen as they answer, watch them observing us, and generally get a sense of who they are. A **clinical interview** is just such a face-to-face encounter (Sommers-Flanagan & Sommers-Flanagan, 2003). If during a clinical interview a man looks as happy as can be while describing his sadness over the recent death of his mother, the clinician may suspect that the man actually has conflicting emotions about this loss.

CONDUCTING THE INTERVIEW The interview is often the first contact between client and clinician. Clinicians use it to collect detailed information about the person's problems and feelings, lifestyle and relationships, and other personal history. They may also ask about the person's expectations of therapy and motives for seeking it. The clinician who worked with Angela Savanti began with a face-to-face interview:

Angela was dressed neatly when she appeared for her first interview. She was attractive, but her eyes were puffy and ringed with dark circles. She answered questions and related information about her life history in a slow, flat tone of voice, which had an impersonal quality to it. She sat stiffly in her chair. . . .

The client stated that the time period just before she and her boyfriend terminated their relationship had been one of extreme emotional turmoil. She was not sure whether she wanted to marry Jerry, and he began to demand that she decide either one way or the other. Mrs. Savanti [Angela's mother] did not seem to like Jerry and was very cold and aloof whenever he came to the house. Angela felt caught in the middle and unable to make a decision about her future. After several confrontations with Jerry over whether she would marry him or not, he told her he felt that she would never decide, so he was not going to see her anymore. . . .

Angela stated that her childhood was a very unhappy period. Her father was seldom home, and when he was present, her parents fought constantly. . . .

Angela recalled feeling very guilty when Mr. Savanti left. . . . She revealed that whenever she thought of her father, she always felt that she had been responsible in some way for his leaving the family. . . .

Angela described her mother as the "long-suffering type" who said that she had sacrificed her life to make her children happy, and the only thing she ever got in return was grief and unhappiness. . . . When Angela and [her sister] began dating, Mrs. Savanti . . . would make disparaging remarks about the boys they had been with and about men in general. . . .

Angela revealed that she had often been troubled with depressed moods. During high school, if she got a lower grade in a subject than she had expected,

STANDARDIZATION The process in which a test is administered to a large group of persons, whose performance then serves as a common standard or norm against which any individual's score can be measured.

RELIABILITY A measure of the consistency of test or research results.

VALIDITY The accuracy of a test's or study's results; that is, the extent to which the test or study actually measures or shows what it claims.

CLINICAL INTERVIEW A face-to-face encounter in which clinicians ask questions of clients, weigh their responses and reactions, and learn about them and their psychological problems.

>>LOOKING AROUND
Revealing Interview

During World War II, recruits were briefly interviewed and tested by clinicians to determine their fitness for military service. When the famous (and witty) pianist Oscar Levant was asked whether he thought he was capable of killing, he is alleged to have pondered the question for a moment and then replied, "I am not sure about strangers, but friends and family, definitely yes" (Bahrick, 1996).<<

her initial response was one of anger, followed by depression. She began to think that she was not smart enough to get good grades, and she blamed herself for studying too little. Angela also became despondent when she got into an argument with her mother or felt that she was being taken advantage of at work. . . .

The intensity and duration of the [mood change] that she experienced when she broke up with Jerry were much more severe. She was not sure why she was so depressed, but she began to feel it was an effort to walk around and go out to work. Talking with others became difficult. Angela found it hard to concentrate, and she began to forget things she was supposed to do. . . . She preferred to lie in bed rather than be with anyone, and she often cried when alone.

(Leon, 1984, pp. 110–115)

Beyond gathering basic background data of this kind, clinical interviewers give special attention to whatever topics they consider most important (Compas & Gotlib, 2002). Psychodynamic interviewers try to learn about the person's needs and memories of past events and relationships. Behavioral interviewers try to pinpoint information about the stimuli that trigger abnormal responses and their consequences. Cognitive interviewers try to discover assumptions and interpretations that influence the person. Humanistic clinicians ask about the person's self-evaluation, self-concept, and values. Biological clinicians look for signs of biochemical or brain dysfunction. And sociocultural interviewers ask about the family, social, and cultural environments.

Interviews can be either unstructured or structured (Kamphaus & Frick, 2002). In an *unstructured interview*, the clinician asks open-ended questions, perhaps as simple as "Would you tell me about yourself?" The lack of structure allows the interviewer to follow interesting leads and explore relevant topics that could not be anticipated before the interview.

In a *structured interview*, clinicians ask prepared questions. Sometimes they use a published *interview schedule*—a standard set of questions designed for all interviews. Many structured interviews include a **mental status exam**, a set of questions and observations that systematically evaluate the client's awareness,

ABNORMALITY AND THE ARTS

Assessing van Gogh

Vincent van Gogh led a tortured and unhappy life. In a legendary incident the artist cut off one of his ears. Later he was admitted to a mental institution, and ultimately he committed suicide. Van Gogh wrote a great deal about his pain and anguish, describing mental and physical torment and hallucinations. For years clinicians speculated that the artist suffered from a mood disorder, schizophrenia, or both. Recently, however, these assessments have been challenged (Blumer, 2002; Rosenfeld, 1998).

A Harvard neurologist, for example, has suggested that van Gogh in fact suffered from *Geschwind's syndrome*, technically known as *interictal personality disorder*, caused by brain seizure disorder, or epilepsy. Van Gogh displayed many of its symptoms, including excessive drawing (hypergraphia), hyperreligiosity, and aggression (Hochman, 2000; Trotter, 1985).

In contrast, medical specialists in Colorado have concluded that van Gogh suffered from an extreme form of *Menière's syndrome*, a disorder marked by an excessive buildup of fluid in the inner ear. The enormous pressure may produce nausea, dizziness, poor balance, pain, deafness, and constant buzzing or ringing sensations. Perhaps van Gogh cut off his ear in an effort to reduce the pain. And perhaps his other problems and pains arose from the severe secondary psychological problems that can accompany Menière's syndrome (Hochman, 2000; Scott, 1990).

Courtesy of the Fogg Art Museum, Harvard University Art Museums

Vincent van Gogh, a self-portrait

orientation with regard to time and place, attention span, memory, judgment and insight, thought content and processes, mood, and appearance (Robinson, 2000). A structured format ensures that clinicians will cover the same kinds of important issues in all their interviews and enables them to compare the responses of different individuals (Shear et al., 2001).

Although most clinical interviews have both unstructured and structured portions, many clinicians favor one kind over the other. Unstructured interviews typically appeal to psychodynamic and humanistic clinicians, while structured formats are widely used by behavioral and cognitive clinicians, who need to pinpoint behaviors, attitudes, or thinking processes that may underlie abnormal behavior (Fischer, 2002; Pope, 1983).

WHAT ARE THE LIMITATIONS OF CLINICAL INTERVIEWS? Although interviews offer valuable information about people, there are limits to what they can accomplish (Meyer et al., 2001). One problem is that they sometimes lack validity, or accuracy. Individuals may intentionally mislead in order to present themselves in a positive light or to avoid discussing embarrassing topics. Or people may be unable to give an accurate report in their interview. Individuals who suffer from depression, for example, take a pessimistic view of themselves and may describe themselves as poor workers or inadequate parents when that isn't the case at all.

Interviewers, too, may make mistakes in judgment that slant the information they gather. They usually rely too heavily on first impressions, for example, and give too much weight to unfavorable information about a client (Meehl, 1996, 1960). Interviewer biases, including gender, race, and age biases, may also influence the interviewers' interpretations of what a client says (Plante, 1999).

Interviews, particularly unstructured ones, may also lack reliability (Wood et al., 2002). People respond differently to different interviewers, providing less information to a cold interviewer than to a warm and supportive one (Eisenthal et al., 1983). Similarly, a clinician's race, sex, age, and appearance may influence a client's responses (Paurohit et al., 1982).

Because different clinicians can obtain different answers and draw different conclusions, even when they ask the same questions of the same person, some researchers believe that interviewing should be discarded as a tool of clinical assessment. As we shall see, however, the two other kinds of clinical assessment methods also have serious limitations.

Clinical Tests

Tests are devices for gathering information about a few aspects of a person's psychological functioning, from which broader information about the person can be inferred (Gregory, 2004). On the surface, it may look easy to design an effective test. Every month, magazines and newspapers present new tests that supposedly tell us about our personalities, our relationships, our sex lives, our reactions to stress, our ability to succeed. Such tests might sound convincing, but most of them fail to produce consistent, accurate information or clarify where we stand in comparison with others.

More than 500 clinical tests are currently in use throughout the United States. The ones that clinicians use most often are of six kinds: *projective tests, personality inventories, response inventories, psychophysiological tests, neurological and neuropsychological tests,* and *intelligence tests.*

PROJECTIVE TESTS **Projective tests** require subjects to interpret vague stimuli, such as inkblots or vague pictures, or follow open-ended instructions such as "Draw a person." Theoretically, when clues and instructions are so general, subjects will

THE FAR SIDE **BY GARY LARSON**

© 1982 FarWorks, Inc. All Rights Reserved/Dist. by Creators Syndicate

The Far Side® by Gary Larson © 1982 FarWorks, Inc. All Rights Reserved. Used with permission.

"So, Mr. Fenton ... let's begin with your mother."

The structured interview *In a structured interview, clinicians gather information by asking a set of standard questions regardless of the client's particular symptoms.*

MENTAL STATUS EXAM A set of interview questions and observations designed to reveal the degree and nature of a client's abnormal functioning.

TEST A device for gathering information about a few aspects of a person's psychological functioning from which broader information about the person can be inferred.

PROJECTIVE TEST A test consisting of ambiguous material that people interpret or respond to.

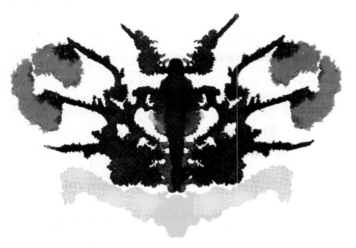

FIGURE 3-1 *An inkblot similar to those used in the Rorschach test*

"project" aspects of their personality into the task. Projective tests are used mainly by psychodynamic clinicians to help assess the unconscious drives and conflicts they believe to be at the root of abnormal functioning (McGowen, 2001). The most widely used projective tests are the *Rorschach test*, the *Thematic Apperception Test*, *sentence-completion tests*, and *drawings*.

RORSCHACH TEST In 1911 Hermann Rorschach, a Swiss psychiatrist, experimented with the use of inkblots in his clinical work. He made thousands of blots by dropping ink on paper and then folding the paper in half to create a symmetrical but wholly accidental design, such as the one shown in Figure 3-1. Rorschach found that everyone saw images in these blots. In addition, the images a viewer saw seemed to correspond in important ways with his or her psychological condition. People diagnosed with schizophrenia, for example, tended to see images that differed from those described by people suffering from depression.

Rorschach selected 10 inkblots and published them in 1921 with instructions for their use in assessment. This set was called the *Rorschach Psychodynamic Inkblot Test*. Rorschach died just eight months later, at the age of 37, but his work was continued by others, and his inkblots took their place among the most widely used projective tests of the twentieth century.

Clinicians administer the "Rorschach," as it is commonly called, by presenting one inkblot card at a time and asking respondents what they see, what the inkblot seems to be, or what it reminds them of. In the early years, Rorschach testers paid special attention to the *themes* and *images* that the inkblots brought to mind (Meyer, 2001; Weiner, 2000). Testers now also pay attention to the *style* of the responses: Do the subjects view the design as a whole or see specific details? Do they focus on the blots or on the white spaces between them? Do they use or do they ignore the shadings and colors in several of the cards?

FIGURE 3-2 *A picture used in the Thematic Apperception Test*

THEMATIC APPERCEPTION TEST The *Thematic Apperception Test* (TAT) is a pictorial projective test (Aranow et al., 2002; Morgan & Murray, 1935). People who take the TAT are commonly shown 30 black-and-white pictures of individuals in vague situations and are asked to make up a dramatic story about each card. They must tell what is happening in the picture, what led up to it, what the characters are feeling and thinking, and what the outcome of the situation will be.

Clinicians who use the TAT believe that people always identify with one of the characters on each card. The stories are thought to reflect the individuals' own circumstances, needs, and emotions. For example, a female client seems to be revealing her own feelings in this story about the TAT picture shown in Figure 3-2, one of the few TAT pictures permitted for display in textbooks:

> This is a woman who has been quite troubled by memories of a mother she was resentful toward. She has feelings of sorrow for the way she treated her mother, her memories of her mother plague her. These feelings seem to be increasing as she grows older and sees her children treating her the same way that she treated her mother.
>
> *(Aiken, 1985, p. 372)*

SENTENCE-COMPLETION TEST The sentence-completion test, first developed in the 1920s (Payne, 1928), asks people to complete a series of unfinished sentences, such as "I wish _____" or "My father _____." The test is considered a good springboard for discussion and a quick and easy way to pinpoint topics to explore.

DRAWINGS On the assumption that a drawing tells us something about its creator, clinicians often ask clients to draw human figures and talk about them. Evaluations of these drawings are based on the details and shape of the drawing, solidity of the pencil line, location of the drawing on the paper, size of the figures, features of the figures, use of background, and comments made by the respondent during the drawing task. In the *Draw-a-Person (DAP) Test*, the most popular of the drawing tests, subjects are first told to draw "a person" and then are instructed to draw another person of the opposite sex.

WHAT ARE THE MERITS OF PROJECTIVE TESTS? Until the 1950s, projective tests were the most common technique for assessing personality. In recent years, however, clinicians and researchers have relied on them largely to gain "supplementary" insights (Westen et al., 1999). One reason for this shift is that practitioners who follow the newer models have less use for the tests than psychodynamic clinicians do. Even more important, the tests have rarely shown much reliability or validity (Wood et al., 2002).

In reliability studies, different clinicians have tended to score the same person's projective test quite differently (Wood et al., 2002; Lilienfeld et al., 2000). Similarly, in validity studies, when clinicians try to describe a client's personality and feelings on the basis of responses to projective tests, their conclusions often fail to match the self-report of the client, the view of the psychotherapist, or the picture gathered from an extensive case history (Wood et al., 2002).

Another validity problem is that projective tests are sometimes biased against minority ethnic groups. For example, people are supposed to identify with the characters in the Thematic Apperception Test (TAT) when they make up stories about them, yet no members of minority groups are in the TAT pictures. In response to this problem, some clinicians have developed other TAT-like tests with African American or Hispanic figures (Costantino et al., 2001).

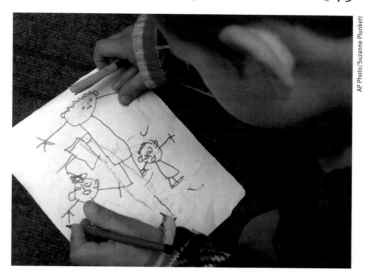

Drawing test *Drawing tests are commonly used to assess the functioning of children. A popular one is the Kinetic Family Drawing test, in which children draw their household members performing some activity ("kinetic" means "active").*

The art of assessment *Clinicians often view works of art as informal projective tests in which artists reveal their conflicts and mental stability. The sometimes bizarre cat portraits of the early-twentieth-century artist Louis Wain, for example, have been interpreted by some observers as reflections of the psychosis with which he struggled for many years.*

PERSONALITY INVENTORIES An alternative way to collect information about individuals is to ask them to assess themselves. The **personality inventory** asks respondents a wide range of questions about their behavior, beliefs, and feelings. In the typical personality inventory, individuals indicate whether or not each of a long list of statements applies to them. Clinicians then use the responses to draw conclusions about the person's personality and psychological functioning.

By far the most widely used personality inventory is the *Minnesota Multiphasic Personality Inventory (MMPI)* (Nichols, 2001; Butcher, 2000). Two adult versions

PERSONALITY INVENTORY A test designed to measure broad personality characteristics, consisting of statements about behaviors, beliefs, and feelings that people evaluate as characteristic or uncharacteristic of them.

are available—the original test, published in 1945, and the *MMPI-2*, a 1989 revision. A special version of the test for adolescents, the *MMPI-A*, is also used widely.

The original MMPI consists of 550 self-statements, to be labeled "true," "false," or "cannot say." The statements cover issues ranging from physical concerns to mood, sexual behaviors, and social behaviors. Altogether the statements make up 10 clinical scales, on each of which an individual can score from 0 to 120. When people score above 70 on a scale, their functioning on that scale is considered deviant. When the 10 scale scores are considered side by side, a pattern called the *profile* takes shape, indicating the person's general personality. The 10 scales on the MMPI are:

Hypochondriasis (HS) Items showing abnormal concern with bodily functions ("I have chest pains several times a week.")

Depression (D) Items showing extreme pessimism and hopelessness ("I often feel hopeless about the future.")

Conversion hysteria (Hy) Items suggesting that the person may use physical or mental symptoms as a way of unconsciously avoiding conflicts and responsibilities ("My heart frequently pounds so hard I can feel it.")

Psychopathic deviate (PD) Items showing a repeated and gross disregard for social customs and an emotional shallowness ("My activities and interests are often criticized by others.")

Masculinity-femininity (Mf) Items that are thought to separate male and female respondents ("I like to arrange flowers.")

Paranoia (Pa) Items that show abnormal suspiciousness and delusions of grandeur or persecution ("There are evil people trying to influence my mind.")

Psychasthenia (Pt) Items that show obsessions, compulsions, abnormal fears, and guilt and indecisiveness ("I save nearly everything I buy, even after I have no use for it.")

Schizophrenia (Sc) Items that show bizarre or unusual thoughts or behavior, including extreme withdrawal, delusions, or hallucinations ("Things around me do not seem real.")

Hypomania (Ma) Items that show emotional excitement, overactivity, and scattered ideas ("At times I feel very 'high' or very 'low' for no apparent reason.")

Social introversion (Si) Items that show shyness, little interest in people, and insecurity ("I am easily embarrassed.")

The MMPI-2, the newer version of the MMPI, contains 567 items—many identical to those in the original, some rewritten to reflect current language ("upset stomach," for instance, replaces "acid stomach"), and others that are new. To the original scales the MMPI-2 adds several new scales that cover issues such as eating problems and a tendency to abuse drugs. Before being adopted, the MMPI-2 was tested on a more diverse group of people than was the original test. Thus scores on the new test may be more accurate indicators of personality and abnormal functioning (Dorfman & Leonard, 2001).

The MMPI and other personality inventories have several advantages over projective tests (Wood et al., 2002). Because they are paper-and-pencil tests, they do not take much time to administer, and they are objectively scored. Most of them are standardized, so one person's scores can be compared with those of many others. Moreover, they often display greater test–retest reliability than projective tests. For example, people who take the MMPI a second time after a period of less than two weeks receive approximately the same scores (Graham, 2000).

Personality inventories also appear to have greater validity, or accuracy, than projective tests (Graham et al., 2002). However, they can hardly be considered *highly* valid. When clinicians have used these tests alone, they have not regularly been able to judge an individual's personality with accuracy (Johnson et al., 1996). One problem is that the personality traits that the tests seek to measure cannot be examined directly. How can we fully know a person's character, emotions, and needs from self-reports alone?

Despite their limited validity, personality inventories continue to be popular (Kamphaus & Frick, 2002). Research indicates that they can help clinicians learn about people's personal styles and disorders as long as they are used in combination with interviews or other assessment tools.

RESPONSE INVENTORIES Like personality inventories, **response inventories** ask people to provide detailed information about themselves, but these tests focus on only one specific area of functioning. For example, one such test may measure affect (emotion), another social skills, and still another cognitive processes. Clinicians can use them to determine the roles such factors play in a person's disorder.

Affective inventories measure the severity of such emotions as anxiety, depression, and anger (Beidel et al., 2000, 1995). In one of the most widely used affective inventories, the Beck Depression Inventory, shown in Table 3-1, people rate their level of sadness and its effect on their functioning. *Social skills inventories*, used particularly by behavioral and sociocultural clinicians, ask respondents to indicate how they would react in a variety of social situations (Wiggins & Trobst, 2002). *Cognitive inventories* reveal a person's typical thoughts and assumptions and can uncover counterproductive patterns of thinking (Glass & Merluzzi, 2000). They are, not surprisingly, often used by cognitive therapists and researchers.

Because response inventories collect information directly from the clients themselves, they have strong face validity. Thus both the number of these tests and the number of clinicians who use them have increased steadily in the past 25 years. However, these inventories do have major limitations. With the notable exceptions of the Beck Depression Inventory and a few others, only some of them have been subjected to careful standardization, reliability, and validity procedures (Kamphaus & Frick, 2002; Canals et al., 2001). Often they are created as a need arises, without being tested for accuracy and consistency.

RESPONSE INVENTORIES Tests designed to measure a person's responses in one specific area of functioning, such as affect, social skills, or cognitive processes.

>>**IN THEIR WORDS**

"If you don't ask the right questions, you don't get the right answers."<<

Edward Hodnett

"A prudent question is one half of wisdom."<<

Francis Bacon

Table 3-1

Sample Items from the Beck Depression Inventory

ITEMS		INVENTORY
Suicidal ideas	0	I don't have any thoughts of killing myself.
	1	I have thoughts of killing myself but I would not carry them out.
	2	I would like to kill myself.
	3	I would kill myself if I had the chance.
Work inhibition	0	I can work about as well as before.
	1	It takes extra effort to get started at doing something.
	2	I have to push myself very hard to do anything.
	3	I can't do any work at all.
Loss of libido	0	I have not noticed any recent change in my interest in sex.
	1	I am less interested in sex than I used to be.
	2	I am much less interested in sex now.
	3	I have lost interest in sex completely.

PSYCHOPHYSIOLOGICAL TESTS Clinicians may also use **psychophysiological tests**, which measure physiological responses as possible indicators of psychological problems (Allen, 2002). This practice began three decades ago after several studies suggested that states of anxiety are regularly accompanied by physiological changes, particularly increases in heart rate, body temperature, blood pressure, skin reactions (galvanic skin response), and muscle contraction. The measuring of physiological changes has since played a key role in the assessment of certain psychological disorders.

One psychophysiological test is the *polygraph*, popularly known as a *lie detector* (Kleiner, 2002). Electrodes attached to various parts of a person's body detect changes in breathing, perspiration, and heart rate while the individual answers questions. The clinician observes these functions while the subject answers yes to *control questions*—questions whose answers are known to be yes, such as "Are your parents both alive?" Then the clinician observes the same physiological functions while the person answers *test questions*, such as "Did you commit this robbery?" If breathing, perspiration, and heart rate suddenly increase, the subject is suspected of lying.

Like other kinds of clinical tests, psychophysiological tests have their drawbacks. Many require expensive equipment that must be carefully tuned and maintained. In addition, psychophysiological measurements can be inaccurate and unreliable. The laboratory equipment itself—impressive, unusual, and sometimes frightening—may arouse a subject's nervous system and thus change his or her physical responses. Physiological responses may also change when they are mea-

A CLOSER LOOK

The Truth, the Whole Truth, and Nothing but the Truth

*I*n movies, criminals being grilled by the police reveal their guilt by sweating, shaking, cursing, or twitching. When they are hooked up to a *polygraph* (a lie detector), the needles bounce all over the paper. This image has been with us since World War I, when some clinicians developed the theory that people who are telling lies display certain changes in their breathing, perspiration, and heart rate (Marston, 1917).

The danger of relying on polygraph tests is that there is no clear evidence that they work as well as we would like (Raskin & Houts, 2002; Steinbrook, 1992). The public did not pay much attention to this inconvenient fact until the mid-1980s, when the American Psychological Association officially reported that polygraphs were often inaccurate and the United States Congress voted to restrict their use in criminal prosecution and employment screening (Krapohl, 2002). Research clarifies that 8 out of 100 truths, on average, are called lies in polygraph testing (Raskin & Honts,

2002; MacLaren, 2001). Imagine, then, how many innocent people might be convicted of crimes if polygraph findings were taken as valid evidence in criminal trials.

Given such findings, polygraphs are less trusted and less popular today than they once were. For example, few courts now admit results from such tests as evidence of criminal guilt (Daniels, 2002).

Polygraph testing has by no means disappeared, however. The FBI uses it extensively in counterintelligence work; parole boards and probation offices routinely use it to help decide whether to release convicted sex offenders; and in public-sector hiring (such as for police officers), the use of polygraph screening may actually be on the increase (Krapohl, 2002).

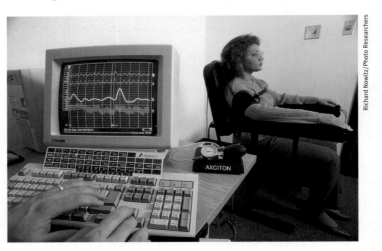

Polygraph, a test that lies?

The EEG *The electroencephalogram, used here to measure the brain waves of a 4-month-old being stimulated with toys, is only a gross indicator of the brain's activity.*

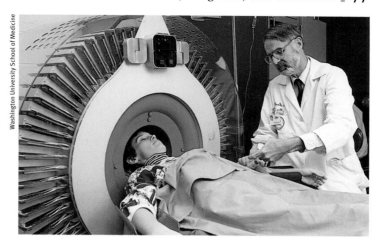

The PET scan *Elaborate neuroimaging tests such as positron emission tomography (PET) help detect abnormal brain activity that may be causing psychological problems.*

sured repeatedly in a single session. Galvanic skin responses, for example, often decrease during repeated testing.

NEUROLOGICAL AND NEUROPSYCHOLOGICAL TESTS Some problems in personality or behavior are caused primarily by damage to the brain or changes in brain activity. Head injury, brain tumors, brain malfunctions, alcoholism, infections, and other disorders can all cause such impairment. If a psychological dysfunction is to be treated effectively, it is important to know whether its primary cause is a physical abnormality in the brain.

A number of techniques may help pinpoint brain abnormalities. Some procedures, such as brain surgery, biopsy, and X ray, have been used for many years. More recently, scientists have developed a number of **neurological tests**, designed to measure brain structure and activity directly. One neurological test is the *electroencephalogram* (EEG), which records *brain waves*, the electrical activity taking place within the brain as a result of neurons firing. In this procedure, electrodes placed on the scalp send brain-wave impulses to a machine that records them.

Other neurological tests actually take "pictures" of brain structure or brain activity. These tests, called **neuroimaging techniques**, include *computerized axial tomography* (CAT scan or CT scan), in which X rays of the brain's structure are taken at different angles; *positron emission tomography* (PET scan), a computer-produced motion picture of chemical activity throughout the brain; and *magnetic resonance imaging* (MRI), a procedure that uses the magnetic property of certain atoms in the brain to create a detailed picture of the brain's structure and activity.

Though widely used, these various techniques are sometimes unable to detect subtle brain abnormalities. Clinicians have therefore developed less direct but sometimes more revealing **neuropsychological tests** that measure cognitive, perceptual, and motor performances on certain tasks and interpret abnormal performances as indicators of underlying brain problems (Sadock & Sadock, 2003). Brain damage is especially likely to affect visual perception, memory, and visual-motor coordination, and so neuropsychological tests focus particularly on these areas.

The *Bender Visual-Motor Gestalt Test* (Bender, 1938), one widely used neuropsychological test, consists of nine cards, each displaying a simple design (see Figure 3-3 on the next page). Patients look at the designs one at a time and copy each one on a piece of paper. Later they try to redraw the designs from memory. By the age of 12, most people can remember and redraw the designs accurately. Notable errors in accuracy are thought to reflect organic brain impairment. To

PSYCHOPHYSIOLOGICAL TEST A test that measures physical responses (such as heart rate and muscle tension) as possible indicators of psychological problems.

NEUROLOGICAL TEST A test that directly measures brain structure or activity.

NEUROIMAGING TECHNIQUES Neurological tests that provide images of brain structure or brain activity, including CT scans, PET scans, and MRIs.

NEUROPSYCHOLOGICAL TEST A test that detects brain impairment by measuring a person's cognitive, perceptual, and motor performances.

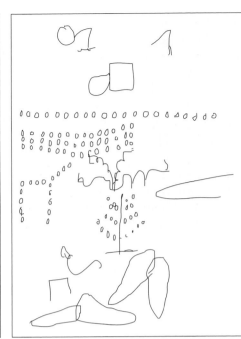

Original   Copy

FIGURE 3-3 The Bender Visual-Motor Gestalt Test *Individuals copy each of nine designs on a piece of paper, then produce them again from memory. Sizable errors in a drawing (as in the one on the right, which was done by a person with brain damage) may reflect organic brain dysfunction. (Adapted from Lacks, 1984, p. 33.)*

achieve greater precision and accuracy in their assessments of brain abnormalities, clinicians often use a **battery**, or series, of neuropsychological tests, each targeting a specific skill area (Reitan & Wolfson, 2001, 1996).

INTELLIGENCE TESTS An early definition of intelligence described it as "the capacity to judge well, to reason well, and to comprehend well" (Binet & Simon, 1916, p. 192). Because intelligence is an *inferred* quality rather than a specific physical process, it can be measured only indirectly. In 1905 the French psychologist Alfred Binet and his associate Theodore Simon produced an **intelligence test** consisting of a series of tasks requiring people to use various verbal and nonverbal skills. The general score derived from this and subsequent intelligence tests is termed an **intelligence quotient**, or **IQ**.

There are now more than 100 intelligence tests available, including the widely used *Wechsler Adult Intelligence Scale, Wechsler Intelligence Scale for Children*, and *Stanford-Binet Intelligence Scale*. As we shall see in Chapter 14, intelligence tests play a key role in the diagnosis of mental retardation, but they can also help clinicians identify other problems (Compas & Gotlib, 2002).

Intelligence tests are among the most carefully produced of all clinical tests. Because they have been standardized on large groups of subjects, clinicians have a good idea how each individual's score compares with the performance of the population at large. These tests have also shown very high reliability: people who repeat the same IQ test years later receive approximately the same score (Compas & Gotlib, 2002). Finally, the major IQ tests appear to have fairly high validity: children's IQ scores often correlate with their performance in school, for example (Sternberg et al., 2001).

Nevertheless, intelligence tests have some key shortcomings. Factors that have nothing to do with intelligence, such as low motivation and high anxiety, can greatly influence a performance (Gregory, 2004). In addition, IQ tests may contain cultural biases in their language or tasks that place people of one background at an advantage over those of another (Gopaul-McNicol & Armour-Thomas, 2002). Similarly, members of some minority groups may have little experience with this kind of test, or they may be uncomfortable with test examiners of a majority ethnic background. Either way, their performances may suffer.

The Wechsler Adult Intelligence Scale–Revised (WAIS-R) *This widely used intelligence test has 11 subtests, which cover such areas as factual information, memory, vocabulary, arithmetic, design, and eye–hand coordination.*

Travis Amos

Clinical Observations

In addition to interviewing and testing people, clinicians may systematically observe their behavior. In one technique, called **naturalistic observation**, clinicians observe clients in their everyday environments. In another, **analog observation**, they observe them in an artificial setting, such as a clinical office or laboratory. Finally, in **self-monitoring**, clients are instructed to observe themselves.

NATURALISTIC AND ANALOG OBSERVATIONS Naturalistic clinical observations usually take place in homes, schools, institutions such as hospitals and prisons, or community settings. Most of them focus on parent–child, sibling–child, or teacher–child interactions and on fearful, aggressive, or disruptive behavior (Kaplan, 1999). Often such observations are made by *participant observers*, key persons in the client's environment, and reported to the clinician (Spiegler & Guevremont, 2003).

When naturalistic observations are not practical, clinicians may resort to analog observations, often aided by special equipment such as a videotape recorder or one-way mirror (Haynes, 2001). Analog observations have often focused on children interacting with their parents, married couples attempting to settle a disagreement, speech-anxious people giving a speech, and fearful people approaching an object they find frightening.

Although much can be learned from actually witnessing behavior, clinical observations have certain disadvantages. For one thing, they are not always reliable (Banister et al., 1994). It is possible for various clinicians who observe the same person to focus on different aspects of behavior, assess the person differently, and arrive at different conclusions. Careful training of observers and the use of observer checklists can help reduce this problem (Kamphaus & Frick, 2002).

Similarly, observers may make errors that affect the validity, or accuracy, of their observations (Goodwin, 2002; Banister et al., 1994). The observer may suffer from *overload* and be unable to see or record all the important behaviors and events. Or the observer may experience *observer drift*, a steady decline in accuracy as a result of fatigue or of a gradual unintentional change in the standards used when an observation continues for a long period of time. Another possible problem is *observer bias*—the observer's judgments may be influenced by information and expectations he or she already has about the person.

A client's *reactivity* may also limit the validity of clinical observations; that is, his or her behavior may in fact be affected by the very presence of the observer

BATTERY A series of tests, each of which produces a different kind of data.

INTELLIGENCE TEST A test designed to measure a person's intellectual ability.

INTELLIGENCE QUOTIENT (IQ) A general score derived from intelligence tests that is considered to represent a person's overall level of intelligence.

NATURALISTIC OBSERVATION A method for observing behavior in which clinicians or researchers observe people in their everyday environments.

ANALOG OBSERVATION A method for observing behavior in which people are observed in artificial settings such as clinicians' offices or laboratories.

SELF-MONITORING A technique for observing behavior in which clients observe themselves.

Jeff Greenberg/Photo Edit

An ideal observation *Using a one-way mirror, a clinical observer is able to view the classroom behaviors of young children without distracting the children or influencing their behaviors in any way.*

>>**LOOKING AROUND**

The Power of Observation Everyday observations are more prone to error than clinical observations and often more damaging. Mistaken eyewitness testimony is the primary cause of the conviction of innocent people (Wells et al., 1998).<<

Believing Is Seeing Persons' beliefs often wrongly influence their observations and recollections. Most moviegoers recall seeing Bambi's mother die in the snow and a knife slash Janet Leigh in the shower in *Psycho*, and hearing Tarzan say, "Me Tarzan, you Jane," and Humphrey Bogart say, "Play it again, Sam," in *Casablanca*. Yet none of these events took place in their respective movies.<<

(Kamphaus & Frick, 2002). If schoolchildren are aware that someone special is watching them, for example, they may change their usual classroom behavior, perhaps in the hope of creating a good impression.

Finally, clinical observations may lack *cross-situational validity*. A child who behaves aggressively in school is not necessarily aggressive at home or with friends after school. Because behavior is often specific to particular situations, observations in one setting cannot always be applied to other settings (Haynes, 2001).

SELF-MONITORING As we saw earlier, personality and response inventories are tests in which persons report their own behaviors, feelings, or cognitions. In a related assessment procedure, *self-monitoring*, people observe themselves and record the frequency of certain behaviors, feelings, or thoughts as they occur over time (Compas & Gotlib, 2002). How frequently, for instance, does a drug user have an urge for drugs or a headache sufferer have a headache? Self-monitoring is especially useful in assessing behavior that occurs so infrequently it is unlikely to be seen during other kinds of observations. It is also useful for behaviors that occur so frequently that any other method of observing them in detail would be impossible—for example, smoking, drinking, or other drug use. Third, self-monitoring may be the only way to observe and measure private thoughts or perceptions (Hollon et al., 2002).

Like all other clinical assessment procedures, however, self-monitoring has drawbacks. Here too validity is often a problem (Barker et al., 1994). People do not always receive proper instruction in this form of observation, nor do they always try to record their observations accurately. Furthermore, when people monitor themselves, they may change their behaviors unintentionally (Plante, 1999). Smokers, for example, often smoke fewer cigarettes than usual when they are monitoring themselves, drug users take drugs less frequently, and teachers give more positive and fewer negative comments to their students.

SUMMING UP | **Clinical Assessment**

Clinical practitioners are interested primarily in gathering individual information about their clients. They seek an understanding of the specific nature and origins of a client's problems through assessment.

Most assessment methods fall into three general categories: clinical interviews, tests, and observations. The interview may be either unstructured or structured. Types of clinical tests include projective, personality, response, psychophysiological, neurological, neuropsychological, and intelligence tests. Types of observation include naturalistic observation, analog observation, and self-monitoring.

To be useful, assessment tools must be standardized, reliable, and valid. Each of the methods in current use falls short on at least some of these characteristics.

>>**Q & A**

What is a nervous breakdown?

The term nervous breakdown is used by laypersons, not clinicians. Most people use it to refer to a sudden psychological disturbance that incapacitates a person, perhaps requiring hospitalization. Some people use the term simply to connote the onset of any psychological disorder (Padwa, 1996).<<

Diagnosis: Does the Client's Syndrome Match a Known Disorder?

Clinicians use the information from interviews, tests, and observations to construct an integrated picture of the factors that are causing and maintaining a client's disturbance, a construction sometimes known as a *clinical picture*. The clinical pictures drawn by clinicians are also influenced by their theoretical orientation (Wood et al., 2002). The psychologist who worked with Angela Savanti held a cognitive-behavioral view of abnormality and so produced a picture that emphasized modeling and reinforcement principles and Angela's expectations, assumptions, and interpretations:

Angela was rarely reinforced for any of her accomplishments at school, but she gained her mother's negative attention for what Mrs. Savanti judged to be poor performance at school or at home. Mrs. Savanti repeatedly told her daughter that she was incompetent, and any mishaps that happened to her were her own fault. . . . When Mr. Savanti deserted the family, Angela's first response was that somehow she was responsible. From her mother's past behavior, Angela had learned to expect that in some way she would be blamed. At the time that Angela broke up with her boyfriend, she did not blame Jerry for his behavior, but interpreted this event as a failing solely on her part. As a result, her level of self-esteem was lowered still more.

The type of marital relationship that Angela saw her mother and father model remained her concept of what married life is like. She generalized from her observations of her parents' discordant interactions to an expectation of the type of behavior that she and Jerry would ultimately engage in. . . .

Angela's uncertainties intensified when she was deprived of the major source of gratification she had, her relationship with Jerry. Despite the fact that she was overwhelmed with doubts about whether to marry him or not, she had gained a great deal of pleasure through being with Jerry. Whatever feelings she had been able to express, she had shared with him and no one else. Angela labeled Jerry's termination of their relationship as proof that she was not worthy of another person's interest. She viewed her present unhappiness as likely to continue, and she attributed it to some failing on her part. As a result, she became quite depressed.

(Leon, 1984, pp. 123–125)

DIAGNOSIS A determination that a person's problems reflect a particular disorder.

With the assessment data and clinical picture in hand, clinicians are ready to make a **diagnosis**—that is, a determination that a person's psychological problems constitute a particular disorder (Scotti & Morris, 2001). When clinicians decide, through diagnosis, that a client's pattern of dysfunction reflects a particular disorder, they are saying that the pattern is basically the same as one that has been displayed by many other people, been investigated in a variety of studies, and perhaps responded to particular forms of treatment. They can then apply what is generally known about the disorder to the particular individual they are trying to help. They can, for example, better predict the future course of the person's problem and the treatments that are likely to be helpful (Compas & Gotlib, 2002).

Elizabeth Eckert, Middletown, NY. From L. Gamwell and N. Tomes, *Madness in America*, 1995, Cornell University Press

The power of labeling *When looking at this late-nineteenth-century photograph of a baseball team at the State Homeopathic Asylum for the Insane in Middletown, New York, most observers assume that the players are patients, so they "see" depression or confusion in the players' faces and posture. In fact, the players are members of the asylum staff.*

STEPPING BACK

Culture-Bound Abnormality

Red Bear sits up wild-eyed [and] stares at his young wife lying asleep on the far side of the wigwam, illuminated by the dying embers.

His troubles began several days before, when he came back from a hunting expedition empty-handed. Ashamed of his failure, he fell prey to a deep, lingering depression. Others in the village, noticing a change in Red Bear, watched him nervously, afraid that he was becoming bewitched by a windigo. Red Bear was frightened too. The signs of windigo were all there: depression, lack of appetite, nausea, sleeplessness and, now, the dream. Indeed, there could be no mistake.

He had dreamed of the windigo—the monster with a heart of ice—and the dream sealed his doom. Coldness gripped his own heart. The ice monster had entered his body and possessed him. He himself had become a windigo, and he could do nothing to avert his fate.

Suddenly, the form of Red Bear's sleeping wife begins to change. He no longer sees a woman, but a deer. His eyes flame. Silently, he draws his knife from under the blanket and moves stealthily toward the motionless figure. Saliva drips from the corners of his mouth, and a terrible hunger twists his intestines. A powerful desire to eat raw flesh consumes him.

With the body of the "deer" at his feet, Red Bear raises the knife high, preparing the strike. Unexpectedly, the deer screams and twists away. But the knife flashes down, again and again. Too late, Red Bear's kinsmen rush into the wigwam. With cries of outrage and horror, they drag him outside into the cold night air and swiftly kill him.

(LINDHOLM & LINDHOLM, 1981, P. 52)

Red Bear was suffering from *windigo*, a disorder once common among Algonquin Indian hunters. They believed in a supernatural monster that ate human beings and had the power to bewitch them and turn them into cannibals. Red Bear was among the few afflicted hunters who actually did kill and eat members of their households.

Windigo is but one of several unusual mental disorders discovered around the world, each unique to a particular culture, each apparently growing from that culture's pressures, history, institutions, and ideas (Gaw, 2001; Lindholm & Lindholm, 1981). Such disorders remind us that the classifications and diagnoses applied in one culture may not always be appropriate in another.

Susto, a disorder found among members of Indian tribes in Central and South America and Hispanic natives of the Andean highlands of Peru, Bolivia, and Colombia, is most likely to occur in infants and young children. The symptoms are extreme anxiety, excitability, and depression, along with loss of weight, weakness, and rapid heartbeat. The culture holds that this disorder is caused by contact with supernatural beings or with frightening strangers or by bad air from cemeteries and other supposedly dangerous places.

Persons afflicted with *amok*, a disorder found in Malaya, the Philippines, Java, and some parts of Africa, jump around violently, yell loudly, grab knives or other weapons, and attack any people and objects they encounter. This behavior is usually preceded by social withdrawal and some loss of contact with reality. The periods of violent behavior are followed by depression and by amnesia concerning the outburst. Within the culture, amok is thought to be caused by stress, severe shortage of sleep, alcohol consumption, and extreme heat.

Koro is a pattern of anxiety found in Southeast Asia in which a man suddenly becomes intensely fearful that his penis will withdraw into his abdomen and that he will die as a result. Cultural lore holds that the disorder is caused by an imbalance of "yin" and "yang," two natural forces believed to be the fundamental components of life. Accepted forms of treatment include having the individual keep a firm hold on his penis until the fear passes, often with the assistance of family members or friends, and clamping the penis to a wooden box.

Latah is a disorder found in Malaya. Certain circumstances (hearing someone say "snake" or being tickled, for example) trigger a fright reaction that is marked by repeating the words and acts of other people, uttering obscenities, and doing the opposite of what others ask.

Western values and abnormality
Anorexia nervosa and bulimia nervosa are eating disorders found largely in Western countries. Many clinicians believe that these are culture-bound disorders caused in part by Western society's overemphasis on thinness as the aesthetic ideal for women, a preoccupation on display throughout Western ads, magazines, movies, and the like.

Classification Systems

The principle behind diagnosis is straightforward. When certain symptoms regularly occur together—a cluster of symptoms is called a **syndrome**—and follow a particular course, clinicians agree that those symptoms make up a particular mental disorder. When people display this particular pattern of symptoms, diagnosticians assign them to that diagnostic category. A list of such categories, or disorders, with descriptions of the symptoms and guidelines for assigning individuals to the categories, is known as a **classification system**.

In 1883 Emil Kraepelin developed the first modern classification system for abnormal behavior (see Chapter 1). His categories have formed the foundation for the psychological part of the *International Classification of Diseases* (*ICD*), the classification system now used by the World Health Organization. They have also influenced the *Diagnostic and Statistical Manual of Mental Disorders* (*DSM*), a classification system developed by the American Psychiatric Association.

The DSM, like the ICD, has been changed over time. The current edition, **DSM-IV**, published in 1994, is the most widely used classification system in the United States (APA, 2000, 1994). The descriptions of mental disorders presented throughout this book follow its categories.

DSM-IV

DSM-IV lists approximately 400 mental disorders (see Figure 3-4). Each entry describes the criteria for diagnosing the disorder and its key clinical features. The system also describes related features, which are often but not always present. The classification system is further accompanied by text information (that is, background information) such as research indications; age, culture, and gender trends; and each disorder's prevalence and risk, course, complications, predisposing factors, and family patterns.

In 2000, the American Psychiatric Association published an update of the text information that accompanies DSM-IV. Because this update, called the "DSM-IV Text Revision" (DSM-IV-TR), continues to use DSM-IV's diagnostic categories and diagnostic criteria in almost all cases, DSM-IV technically remains the current edition of the DSM, although some writers choose to cite DSM-IV-TR as the current edition. Either way, the diagnostic categories and criteria are the same with but a few exceptions. The diagnostic criteria were changed for a few disorders (certain sexual disorders) in the 2000 text revision publication, as we shall observe in Chapter 11 (see pages 337 and 341).

DSM-IV requires clinicians to evaluate a client's condition on five separate *axes*, or branches of information, when making a diagnosis. First, they must decide whether the person is displaying one or more of the disorders found on *Axis I*, an extensive list of clinical syndromes that typically cause significant impairment. Some of the most frequently diagnosed disorders listed on this axis are the anxiety disorders and mood disorders—problems we shall discuss later:

Anxiety disorders People with anxiety disorders may experience general feelings of anxiety and worry (*generalized anxiety disorder*), anxiety centered on a specific situation or object (*phobias*), periods of panic (*panic disorder*), persistent thoughts or repetitive behaviors or both (*obsessive-compulsive disorder*), or lingering anxiety reactions to unusually traumatic events (*acute stress disorder* and *posttraumatic stress disorder*).

Mood disorders People with mood disorders feel extremely sad or elated for long periods of time. These disorders include *major depressive disorder* and *bipolar disorders* (in which episodes of mania alternate with episodes of depression).

SYNDROME A cluster of symptoms that usually occur together.

CLASSIFICATION SYSTEM A list of disorders, along with descriptions of symptoms and guidelines for making appropriate diagnoses.

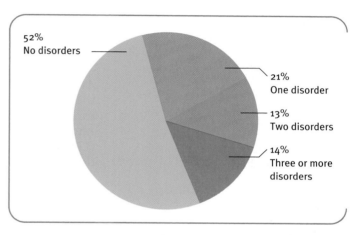

52% No disorders

21% One disorder

13% Two disorders

14% Three or more disorders

FIGURE 3-4 **How many people in the United States qualify for a DSM diagnosis during their lives?** *Almost half, according to one survey. Some of them even experience two or more disorders, an occurrence known as comorbidity. (Adapted from Kessler & Zhao, 1999; Kessler et al., 1994.)*

>>Q & A
   What happened to neurosis?

One of Freud's most famous concepts was neurosis, his term for any disorder in which a person's ego defense mechanisms repeatedly failed to reduce the anxiety aroused by unconscious conflicts. In some neurotic disorders the uncontrolled anxiety was apparent, while in others it was hidden. Because the DSM now defines disorders by symptoms and not causes, the term "neurosis" has been dropped from the diagnostic system. Disorders in which anxiety is particularly apparent are now categorized as anxiety disorders. The other former neurotic disorders are now labeled mood disorders, somatoform disorders, and dissociative disorders.<<

Next, diagnosticians must decide whether the person is displaying one of the disorders listed on *Axis II*, which includes long-standing problems that are frequently overlooked in the presence of the disorders on Axis I. There are only two groups of Axis II disorders: *mental retardation* and *personality disorders*. We will also examine these patterns in later chapters:

Mental retardation People with this disorder display significantly subaverage intellectual functioning and poor adaptive functioning by 18 years of age.

Personality disorders People with these disorders display a very rigid maladaptive pattern of inner experience and outward behavior that has continued for many years. People with *antisocial personality disorder*, for example, persistently disregard and violate the rights of others. People with *dependent personality disorder* are persistently dependent on others, clinging, obedient, and very afraid of separation.

Although people usually receive a diagnosis from *either* Axis I or Axis II, they may receive diagnoses from both axes. Angela Savanti would first receive a diagnosis of *major depressive disorder* from Axis I (a mood disorder). Let us suppose that the clinician judged that Angela also displayed a life history of dependent behavior. She might then also receive an Axis II diagnosis of *dependent personality disorder*.

The remaining axes of DSM-IV guide diagnosticians in reporting other factors. *Axis III* asks for information concerning relevant medical conditions from which the person is currently suffering. *Axis IV* asks about special psychosocial or environmental problems the person is facing, such as school or housing problems. And *Axis V* requires the diagnostician to make a *global assessment of functioning* (*GAF*), that is, to rate the person's psychological, social, and occupational functioning overall.

If Angela Savanti had diabetes, for example, the clinician might include that under Axis III information. Angela's recent breakup with her boyfriend would be noted on Axis IV. And because she seemed fairly dysfunctional at the time of diagnosis, Angela's GAF would probably be around 55 on Axis V, indicating a moderate level of dysfunction. The complete diagnosis for Angela Savanti would then be:

Axis I: Major depressive disorder

Axis II: Dependent personality disorder

Axis III: Diabetes

Axis IV: Problem related to the social environment (termination of engagement)

Axis V: GAF = 55 (current)

Are Classifications Reliable and Valid?

A classification system, like an assessment method, is judged by its reliability and validity. Here *reliability* means that different diagnosticians are likely to agree on the diagnosis when they use the system to diagnose the same client. Early versions of the DSM were at best moderately reliable (Malik & Beutler, 2002; Kirk & Kutchins, 1992). In the early 1960s, for example, four clinicians, each relying on DSM-I, independently interviewed 153 patients (Beck et al., 1962). Only 54 percent of their diagnoses were in agreement.

DSM-IV appears to have greater reliability than any of its predecessors (Reeb, 2000; Nathan & Lagenbucher, 1999). Its framers conducted extensive reviews of research to pinpoint which categories in past DSMs had been too vague and unreliable. In turn, they developed a number of new diagnostic criteria and categories, and then ran *field trials* to make sure that the new criteria and categories were in fact reliable (Malik & Beutler, 2002). Still, many clinicians worry that DSM-IV's reliability may not be as strong as its framers claim (Beutler & Malik, 2002).

The *validity* of a classification system is the accuracy of the information that its diagnostic categories provide. Categories are of most use to clinicians when

>>IN THEIR WORDS

"Love is a form of mental illness not yet recognized in any of the standard diagnostic manuals."<<

Stuart Sutherland, psychologist, 1989

The Battle over Premenstrual Dysphoric Disorder

Some categories of mental dysfunctioning are much more controversial than others, causing clinicians and the public alike to battle over their appropriateness. After long and heated discussions two decades ago, for example, DSM-III dropped homosexuality as a category of mental dysfunctioning, citing a lack of evidence for including it and a concern about the social implications of calling a sexual orientation abnormal.

One of the biggest controversies in the development of DSM-IV centered on the category *premenstrual dysphoric disorder* (PMDD) (Freeman, 2003; Rapkin, 2003). A DSM work group recommended in 1993 that PMDD be formally listed as a new kind of depressive disor-

der. The category was to be applied when a woman was regularly impaired by at least 5 of 11 symptoms during the week before her menses: sad or hopeless feelings; tense or anxious feelings; marked mood changes; frequent irritability or anger and increased interpersonal conflicts; decreased interest in her usual activities; lack of concentration; lack of energy; changes in appetite; insomnia or sleepiness; a subjective feeling of being overwhelmed or out of control; and physical symptoms such as swollen breasts, headaches, muscle pain, a "bloated" sensation, or weight gain.

This recommendation set off an uproar. Many clinicians (including some dissenting members of the work group),

several national organizations, interest groups, and the media warned that this diagnostic category would "pathologize" severe cases of *premenstrual syndrome,* or *PMS,* the premenstrual discomforts that are common and normal, and might cause women's behavior in general to be attributed largely to "raging hormones" (a stereotype that society is finally rejecting). They also argued that data were lacking to include the new category (Chase, 1993; DeAngelis, 1993).

The DSM solution? A compromise. PMDD is not currently listed as a formal category in DSM-IV, but the pattern is listed in the DSM appendix, with the suggestion that it be studied more thoroughly in the coming years.

they demonstrate *predictive validity*—that is, when they help predict future symptoms or events. A common symptom of major depressive disorder, for example, is either insomnia or excessive sleep. When clinicians give Angela Savanti a diagnosis of major depressive disorder, they expect that she may eventually develop sleep problems even if none are present now. In addition, they expect her to respond to treatments that are helpful to other depressed persons. The more often such predictions are accurate, the greater a category's predictive validity.

DSM-IV's framers tried to ensure the validity of this version of the DSM by again conducting extensive reviews of research and running many field studies. As a result, its criteria and categories appear to have stronger validity than those of earlier versions of the DSM (Reeb, 2000; Nathan & Lagenbucher, 1999). Yet, again, more research is needed to determine the precise strength of DSM-IV's validity (Beutler & Malik, 2002).

Can Diagnosis and Labeling Cause Harm?

Even with trustworthy assessment data and reliable and valid classification categories, clinicians will sometimes arrive at a wrong conclusion (Wood et al., 2002). Like all human beings, they are flawed information processors. Studies show that they are overly influenced by information gathered early in the assessment process (Meehl, 1996, 1960). They sometimes pay too much attention to certain sources of information, such as a parent's report about a child, and too little to others, such as the child's point of view (McCoy, 1976). Finally, their judgments can be influenced by any number of personal biases—gender, age, race, and socioeconomic status, to name just a few (Delahanti et al., 2001). Given the limitations of both assessment tools and assessors, it is small wonder that studies sometimes uncover shocking errors in diagnosis, especially in hospitals (Chen, Swann, & Burt, 1996).

Beyond the potential for misdiagnosis, the very act of classifying people can lead to unintended results. As we observed in Chapter 2, for example, many sociocultural theorists believe that diagnostic labels can become self-fulfilling prophecies. When people are diagnosed as mentally disturbed, they may be viewed

>>**LOOKING AROUND**

The Power of Diagnosis

People who are diagnosed with a mental disorder report having twice as much difficulty obtaining and keeping medical insurance as do people with any other condition, including diabetes and hypertension (Druss & Rosenheck, 1998).<<

and reacted to correspondingly. If others expect them to take on a sick role, they may begin to consider themselves sick as well and act that way. Furthermore, our society attaches a stigma to abnormality (Link et al., 2001). People labeled mentally ill may find it difficult to get a job, especially a position of responsibility, or to be welcomed into social relationships (Perlick et al., 2001). Once a label has been applied, it may stick for a long time.

Because of these problems, some clinicians would like to do away with diagnoses (Gurman & Messer, 2003). Others disagree. They believe we must simply work to increase what is known about psychological disorders and improve diagnostic techniques (Cunningham, 2000). They hold that classification and diagnosis are critical to understanding and treating people in distress.

SUMMING UP | **Diagnosis**

After collecting assessment information, clinicians form a clinical picture and decide on a diagnosis. The diagnosis is chosen from a classification system. The system used most widely in the United States is the *Diagnostic and Statistical Manual of Mental Disorders* (DSM). The most recent version of the DSM, known as DSM-IV, lists approximately 400 disorders and includes five axes. The reliability and validity of this edition continue to receive broad clinical review.

Even with trustworthy assessment data and reliable and valid classification categories, clinicians will not always arrive at the correct conclusion. Moreover, the prejudices that labels arouse may be damaging to the person who is diagnosed.

Treatment: How Might the Client Be Helped?

Over the course of 10 months, Angela Savanti was treated for depression and related symptoms. She improved considerably during that time, as the following report describes.

> Angela's depression eased as she began to make progress in therapy. A few months before the termination of treatment, she and Jerry resumed dating. Angela discussed with Jerry her greater comfort in expressing her feelings and her hope that Jerry would also become more expressive with her. They discussed the reasons why Angela was ambivalent about getting married, and they began to talk again about the possibility of marriage. Jerry, however, was not making demands for a decision by a certain date, and Angela felt that she was not as frightened about marriage as she previously had been. . . .
>
> Psychotherapy provided Angela with the opportunity to learn to express her feelings to the persons she was interacting with, and this was quite helpful to her. Most important, she was able to generalize from some of the learning experiences in therapy and modify her behavior in her renewed relationship with Jerry. Angela still had much progress to make in terms of changing the characteristic ways she interacted with others, but she had already made a number of important steps in a potentially happier direction.
>
> *(Leon, 1984, pp. 118, 125)*

Clearly, treatment helped Angela, and by its conclusion she was a happier, more functional person than the woman who had first sought help 10 months earlier. But how did her therapist decide on the treatment program that proved to be so helpful?

Treatment Decisions

Angela's therapist began, like all therapists, with assessment information and diagnostic decisions. Knowing the specific details and background of Angela's problem (idiographic information), and combining this with established information about the nature and treatment of depression (nomothetic information), the clinician could arrive at a treatment plan for her.

Yet therapists may also be influenced by other factors when they make treatment decisions. Their treatment plans typically reflect their theoretical orientations and how they have learned to conduct therapy (Maher, 2000). As therapists apply a favored model in case after case, they become more and more familiar with its principles and treatment techniques and tend to use them in work with still other clients.

Current research may also play a role. Most clinicians say that they value research as a guide to practice (Beutler et al., 1995). However, not all of them actually read research articles, so they cannot be directly influenced by them. In fact, according to surveys, today's therapists actually gather most of their information about the latest developments in the field from colleagues, professional newsletters, workshops, conferences, books, and the like (Goldfried & Wolfe, 1996; Beutler et al., 1995). Unfortunately, the accuracy and usefulness of these sources vary widely.

To help clinicians become more familiar with and apply research findings, there is currently a movement afoot in North America, the United Kingdom, and elsewhere called *empirically supported*, or *evidence-based*, *treatment* (Kazdin & Weisz, 2003; Chambless, 2002; Chambless & Ollendick, 2001). Proponents of this approach have formed task forces that seek to pinpoint those therapies that receive clear research support, develop corresponding treatment guidelines, and spread such information to clinicians.

But how much, in fact, do we currently know about treatment and treatment effectiveness? We turn to this question next.

The Effectiveness of Treatment

Altogether, as many as 400 forms of therapy are currently practiced in the clinical field (Prochaska & Norcross, 2003). Naturally, the most important question to ask about each of them is whether it does what it is supposed to do. Does a particular treatment really help people overcome their psychological problems? On the surface, the question may seem simple. In fact, it is one of the most difficult questions for clinical researchers to answer.

>>LOOKING AROUND

Treatment Delay Most individuals with mood, anxiety, or addictive disorders fail to contact a therapist until at least six years after the initial onset of their symptoms (Kessler et al., 1998).<<

College Counseling At least 8 percent of all college students seek psychotherapy at their college's counseling center. The percentage is higher at small, private colleges and at prestigious schools (Gallagher, 1998).<<

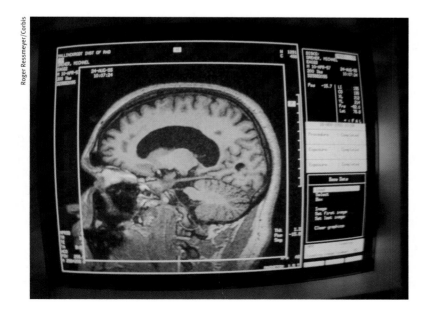

Crystal clear *More precise assessment leads to better treatment decisions. Thus most clinicians have welcomed the arrival of the MRI and other neuroimaging techniques. This MRI of a person's brain is so detailed that it looks more like a photograph than a computer-based image.*

STEPPING BACK

Oppression and Mental Health: The Politics of Labeling

Throughout history governments have applied the label of mental illness as a way of controlling or changing people whose views threaten the social order. This was a common practice in the former Soviet Union. There, political dissent was considered a symptom of abnormal mental functioning, and many dissidents were committed to mental hospitals.

In a more subtle process, a country's cultural values often influence the clinical assessments made by its practitioners. The historians Lynn Gamwell and Nancy Tomes (1995) have noted, for example, the widespread clinical belief in the nineteenth-century United States that freedom would drive such "primitive" people as Native Americans insane. Medical experts of that time went so far as to claim that the forcible movement of tribal groups onto reservations was in their best interest because it would save them from the madness that awaited them in free society. The medical officer who supervised the "removal" of the Cherokees from their homeland to Oklahoma was later pleased to report that during the whole time he oversaw the migration of 20,000 Cherokees (over 4,000 of whom died), he had not observed a single case of insanity.

Slave owners, too, liked to believe that slaves were psychologically comfortable with their situation and that those who tried to escape either were or would soon become insane. Secretary of State John Calhoun of South Carolina pointed to the 1840 census, conducted by his office, as evidence: it identified almost *no* insanity among slaves in the South but many cases among former slaves living in the North. Calhoun asserted: "Our nation must conclude that the abolition of slavery would be to the African a curse instead of a blessing."

The work of clinicians at that time lent support to this belief. One specialist claimed that several kinds of mental disorders were unique to African Americans, including *drapetomania* (from the Latin *drapeta*, "fugitive")—an obsessive desire for freedom that drove some slaves to try to flee. Any slave who tried to run away more than twice was considered insane.

Drapetomania is long forgotten, but cultural views continue to influence psychological assessments and categories. Many clinicians have argued that categories such as "homosexuality," "sexual frigidity," and "masochistic personality"— each an established clinical category during much of the twentieth century— show all too well the impact of cultural beliefs on clinical categorizations and diagnoses.

A ride for liberty *Eastman Johnson's 1862 painting,* A Ride for Liberty—The Fugitive Slaves, *demonstrates the courage and clear-mindedness slaves needed to escape, in stark contrast to the mental instability of which they were accused.*

The first problem is how to *define* "success" (Erwin, 2000; Strupp, 1996, 1989). If, as Angela's therapist suggests, she still has much progress to make at the conclusion of therapy, should her recovery be considered successful? The second problem is how to *measure* improvement (Luborsky et al., 2002, 1999). Should researchers give equal weight to the reports of clients, friends, relatives, therapists, and teachers? Should they use rating scales, inventories, therapy insights, observations, or some other measure?

Perhaps the biggest problem in determining the effectiveness of treatment is the *variety* and *complexity* of the treatments currently in use. People differ in their problems, personal styles, and motivations for therapy. Therapists differ in skill, experience, orientation, and personality. And therapies differ in theory, format, and setting. Because an individual's progress is influenced by all these factors and more, the findings of a particular study will not always apply to other clients and therapists.

Proper research procedures address some of these problems. By using control groups, random assignment, matched subjects, and the like, clinicians can draw certain conclusions about various therapies. Even in studies that are well designed, however, the complexity of treatment limits the conclusions that can be reached (Kazdin, 1994).

Despite these difficulties, the job of evaluating therapies must be done, and clinical researchers have plowed ahead with it. Investigators have, in fact, conducted thousands of *therapy outcome studies*, studies that measure the effects of various treatments. The studies typically ask one of three questions:

1. Is therapy in *general* effective?
2. Are *particular* therapies generally effective?
3. Are *particular* therapies effective for *particular* problems?

IS THERAPY GENERALLY EFFECTIVE? Studies suggest that therapy is often more helpful than no treatment or than placebos. A pioneering review examined 375 controlled studies, covering a total of almost 25,000 people seen in a wide assortment of therapies (Smith, Glass, & Miller, 1980; Smith & Glass, 1977). The reviewers combined the findings of these studies by using a special statistical technique called *meta-analysis*. They rated the level of improvement in each person treated and in each untreated control subject and measured the average difference between the two groups. According to this statistical analysis, the average person who received treatment was better off than 75 percent of the untreated control subjects (see Figure 3-5). Other meta-analyses have found similar relationships between treatment and improvement (Prochaska & Norcross, 2003).

Some clinicians have concerned themselves with an important related question: Can therapy be harmful? Freud himself believed that therapy had this potential (Kardiner, 1977), and a number of studies agree that more than 5 percent of patients actually seem to get worse because of therapy (Compas & Gotlib, 2002; Lambert & Bergin, 1994). Their symptoms may become more intense, or the individuals may develop new ones, such as a sense of failure, guilt, reduced self-concept, or hopelessness, because of their inability to profit from therapy (Lambert et al., 1986; Hadley & Strupp, 1976).

>>**Q & A**

What is the difference between treatment efficacy and treatment effectiveness?

Many writers use the terms "treatment efficacy" and "treatment effectiveness" interchangeably. Technically, however, efficacy research determines whether a treatment can work under ideal conditions (for example, with therapists who are given special training for the study), while effectiveness research examines whether a treatment works well in the real world (for example, as offered by practicing therapists) (Compas & Gotlib, 2002).<<

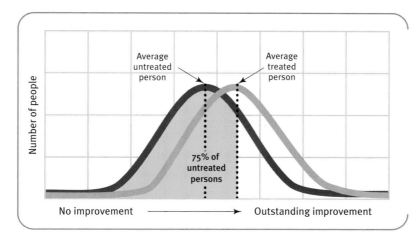

FIGURE 3-5 **Does therapy help?** *Combining subjects and results from hundreds of studies, investigators have determined that the average person who receives psychotherapy experiences greater improvement than do 75 percent of all untreated people with similar problems. (Adapted from Prochaska & Norcross, 2003; Lambert et al., 1993; Smith et al., 1980.)*

ARE PARTICULAR THERAPIES GENERALLY EFFECTIVE? The studies we have looked at so far have lumped all therapies together to consider their general effectiveness. Many researchers, however, consider it wrong to treat all therapies alike. One critic suggests that these studies are operating under a *uniformity myth*—a false belief that all therapies are equivalent despite differences in the therapists' training, experience, theoretical orientations, and personalities (Kiesler, 1995, 1966).

Thus, an alternative approach examines the effectiveness of *particular* therapies. Most research of this kind shows each of the major forms of therapy to be superior to no treatment or to placebo treatment (Prochaska & Norcross, 2003, 1999, 1994). A number of other studies have compared particular therapies with one another and found that no one form of therapy generally stands out over all others (Luborsky et al., 2002, 1975).

If different kinds of therapy have similar successes, might they have something in common? A **rapprochement movement** has tried to identify a set of common strategies that may run through the work of all effective therapists, regardless of the clinicians' particular orientation (Luborsky et al., 2002; Messer & Wampold, 2002). A survey of highly successful therapists suggests, for example, that most give feedback to patients, help patients focus on their own thoughts and behavior, pay attention to the way they and their patients are interacting, and try to promote self-mastery in their patients. In short, effective therapists of any type may practice more similarly than they preach (Korchin & Sands, 1983).

ARE PARTICULAR THERAPIES EFFECTIVE FOR PARTICULAR PROBLEMS? People with different disorders may respond differently to the various forms of therapy. Gordon Paul, an influential clinical theorist, said some years back that the most appropriate question regarding the effectiveness of therapy may be "*What* specific treatment, by *whom*, is most effective for *this* individual with *that* specific problem, and under *which* set of circumstances?" (Paul, 1967, p. 111). Researchers have investigated how effective particular therapies are at treating particular disorders, and they have often found sizable differences among the various therapies (Chambless, 2002). Behavioral therapies, for example, appear to be the most effective of all in treating phobias (McLean & Woody, 2001), whereas drug therapy is the single most effective treatment for schizophrenia (Breier, 2001).

As we observed previously, studies also show that some clinical problems may respond better to *combined* approaches (Kupfer & Frank, 2001). Drug therapy is sometimes combined with certain forms of psychotherapy, for example, to treat depression. In fact, it is now common for clients to be seen by two therapists—one of them a **psychopharmacologist**, a psychiatrist who primarily prescribes medications, and the other a psychologist, social worker, or other therapist who conducts psychotherapy.

Obviously, knowledge of how particular therapies fare with particular disorders can help therapists and clients alike make better decisions about treatment (Beutler, 2002, 2000, 1991) (see Figure 3-6). Thus this is a question to which we shall keep returning throughout the textbook.

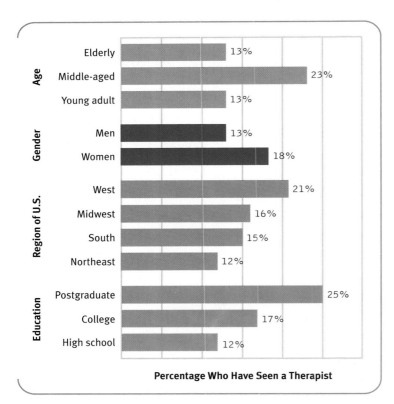

Percentage Who Have Seen a Therapist

FIGURE 3-6 Who seeks therapy? *According to surveys conducted in the United States, people who are middle-aged, female, from western states, and highly educated are the most likely to have been in therapy at some point in their lives. (Adapted from Fetto, 2002.)*

SUMMING UP

Treatment

The treatment decisions of therapists may be influenced by assessment information, the diagnosis, the clinician's theoretical orientation and familiarity with research, and the field's state of knowledge.

Determining the effectiveness of treatment is difficult. Nevertheless, therapy outcome studies have led to three general conclusions: (a) people in therapy are usually better off than people with similar problems who receive no treatment; (b) the various therapies do not appear to differ dramatically in their general effectiveness; (c) certain therapies or combinations of therapies do appear to be more effective than others for certain disorders.

RAPPROCHEMENT MOVEMENT An effort to identify a set of common strategies that run through the work of all effective therapists.

PSYCHOPHARMACOLOGIST A psychiatrist who primarily prescribes medications. Also known as a *pharmacotherapist*.

CROSSROADS:
Renewed Respect Collides with Economic Pressure

In Chapter 2 we observed that today's leading models of abnormal behavior often differ widely in their assumptions, conclusions, and treatments. It should not surprise us, then, that clinicians also differ considerably in their approaches to assessment and diagnosis. Yet when all is said and done, no assessment technique stands out as consistently superior to the rest. Each of the hundreds of available tools has major limitations, and each produces at best an incomplete picture of how a person is functioning and why.

In short, the present state of assessment and diagnosis argues against relying exclusively on any one approach. As a result, more and more clinicians now use *batteries* of assessment tools in their work (Meyer et al., 2003, 2001). Such batteries are already providing invaluable guidance in the assessment of Alzheimer's disease and certain other disorders that are particularly difficult to diagnose, as we shall see later.

Attitudes toward clinical assessment have shifted back and forth over the past several decades. Before the 1950s, assessment was a highly regarded part of clinical practice. As the number of clinical models grew during the 1960s and 1970s, however, followers of each model favored certain tools over others, and the practice of assessment became fragmented. Meanwhile, research began to reveal that a number of tools were inaccurate or inconsistent. In this atmosphere, many clinicians lost confidence in systematic assessment and diagnosis, and some came to approach these tasks casually.

Today respect for assessment and diagnosis is on the rise once again. One reason for the renewal of interest is the development of more precise diagnostic criteria, as presented in DSM-IV. Another is the drive by researchers for more rigorous tests to help them select appropriate subjects for clinical studies. Still another factor is the clinical field's growing awareness that certain disorders can be properly identified only after careful assessment procedures.

Along with heightened respect for assessment and diagnosis has come increased research. Every major kind of assessment tool—from projective tests to personality inventories—is now undergoing careful scrutiny. This work is helping many clinicians perform their work with more accuracy and consistency—welcome news for people with psychological problems.

Ironically, just as today's clinicians and researchers are rediscovering systematic assessment, powerful economic forces have emerged to work against the use of assessment tools. In particular, managed care insurance plans, which emphasize

>>PSYCH•LISTINGS
Famous Movie Clinicians

Dr. Crowe (*The Sixth Sense*, 1999)<<

Dr. McGuire (*Good Will Hunting*, 1997)<<

Dr. Lecter (*The Silence of the Lambs*, 1991; *Hannibal*, 2001; and *Red Dragon*, 2002)<<

Dr. Marvin (*What About Bob?*, 1991)<<

Dr. Sobel (*Analyze This*, 1999, and *Analyze That*, 2002)<<

Dr. Livingston (*Agnes of God*, 1985)<<

Dr. Berger (*Ordinary People*, 1980)<<

Dr. Dysart (*Equus*, 1977)<<

Nurse Ratched (*One Flew over the Cuckoo's Nest*, 1975)<<

Dr. Swinford (*David and Lisa*, 1962)<<

Dr. Petersen (*Spellbound*, 1945)<<

Dr. Murchison (*Spellbound*, 1945)<<

lower cost and shorter treatments, often refuse to provide coverage for extensive clinical testing or observations (Wood et al., 2002). Which of these forces will ultimately have a greater influence on clinical assessment and diagnosis—promising research or economic pressure? We shall find out in the coming years.

CRITICAL THOUGHTS

1. How would you grade the tests you take in school? That is, how reliable and valid are they? How about the tests you see in magazines? *pp. 68–69, 71*

2. Would people react to van Gogh's work differently if they thought of him as having had an ear disorder rather than a psychological disorder? Why do people find it fascinating to assess famous people, particularly those in the arts, long after their death? *p. 70*

3. How might IQ scores be misused by school officials, parents, or other individuals? Why do you think our society is so preoccupied with the concept of intelligence and with IQ scores? *p. 78*

4. Many people argue for a "people first" approach to clinical labeling. For example, they recommend using the phrase "a person with schizophrenia" rather than "a schizophrenic" (Foderaro, 1995). Why might this approach to labeling be preferable? *pp. 85–86*

5. How can persons make wise decisions about therapists and treatment approaches when they are seeking treatment? *pp. 86–90*

KEY TERMS

idiographic understanding p. 67
assessment p. 67
standardization p. 68
reliability p. 68
validity p. 68
clinical interview p. 69
mental status exam p. 70
test p. 71
projective test p. 71
Rorschach test p. 72
Thematic Appreciation Test (TAT) p. 72

personality inventory p. 73
MMPI p. 73
response inventories p. 75
psychophysiological test p. 76
neurological tests p. 77
EEG, CAT, PET, MRI p. 77
neuropsychological test p. 77
battery p. 78
intelligence test p. 78
intelligence quotient (IQ) p. 78
naturalistic observation p. 79

analog observation p. 79
self-monitoring p. 79
diagnosis p. 81
syndrome p. 83
classification system p. 83
DSM-IV p. 83
DSM-IV-TR p. 83
empirically supported treatment p. 87
therapy outcome study p. 89
rapprochement movement p. 90
psychopharmacololgist p. 90

QUICK QUIZ

1. What forms of reliability and validity should clinical assessment tools display? *pp. 68–69*

2. What are the strengths and weaknesses of structured and unstructured interviews? *pp. 70–71*

3. What are the strengths and weaknesses of projective tests, personality inventories, and other kinds of clinical tests? *pp. 71–78*

4. List and describe today's leading projective tests. *pp. 71–73*

5. What are the key features of the MMPI? *p. 75*

6. How do clinicians determine whether psychological problems are linked to brain damage? *pp. 76–78*

7. Describe the ways in which clinicians may make observations of clients' behaviors. *pp. 79–80*

8. What is the purpose of clinical diagnoses? *pp. 80–81*

9. Describe DSM-IV. What problems may accompany the use of classification systems and the process of clinical diagnosis? *pp. 83–86*

10. According to therapy outcome studies, how effective is therapy? *pp. 89–90*

SEARCH THE *FUNDAMENTALS OF ABNORMAL PSYCHOLOGY* CD-ROM FOR

▲ Chapter 3 Video Case Enrichment
  How do clinicians arrive at a diagnosis?
  See neuroimaging in action.
  What causes aggression and violence?

▲ Chapter 3 Practical, Research, and Decision-Making Exercises
  Assessing and labeling in everyday life
  Uncovering the effects of expectations on observations

▲ Chapter 3 Practice Test and Feedback

LOG ON TO THE COMER WEB PAGE FOR

▲ Suggested Web links, exercises, FAQ page, additional Chapter 3 practice test questions
  <www.worthpublishers.com/comer>

⟨⟨⟨

JORDAN ISLIP, 2001

Anxiety Disorders

Bob Donaldson was a 22-year-old carpenter referred to the psychiatric outpatient department of a community hospital. . . . During the initial interview Bob was visibly distressed. He appeared tense, worried, and frightened. He sat on the edge of his chair, tapping his foot and fidgeting with a pencil on the psychiatrist's desk. He sighed frequently, took deep breaths between sentences, and periodically exhaled audibly and changed his position as he attempted to relate his story:

> *Bob:* It's been an awful month. I can't seem to do anything. I don't know whether I'm coming or going. I'm afraid I'm going crazy or something.
> *Doctor:* What makes you think that?
> *Bob:* I can't concentrate. My boss tells me to do something and I start to do it, but before I've taken five steps I don't know what I started out to do. I get dizzy and I can feel my heart beating and everything looks like it's shimmering or far away from me or something—it's unbelievable.
> *Doctor:* What thoughts come to mind when you're feeling like this?
> *Bob:* I just think, "Oh, Christ, my heart is really beating, my head is swimming, my ears are ringing—I'm either going to die or go crazy."
> *Doctor:* What happens then?
> *Bob:* Well, it doesn't last more than a few seconds, I mean that intense feeling. I come back down to earth, but then I'm worrying what's the matter with me all the time, or checking my pulse to see how fast it's going, or feeling my palms to see if they're sweating.
> *Doctor:* Can others see what you're going through?
> *Bob:* You know, I doubt it. I hide it. I haven't been seeing my friends. You know, they say "Let's stop for a beer" or something after work and I give them some excuse—you know, like I have to do something around the house or with my car. I'm not with them when I'm with them anyway—I'm just sitting there worrying. My friend Pat said I was frowning all the time. So, anyway, I just go home and turn on the TV or pick up the sports page, but I can't really get into that either.

Bob went on to say that he had stopped playing softball because of fatigability and trouble concentrating. On several occasions during the past two weeks he was unable to go to work because he was "too nervous."

(Spitzer et al., 1983, pp. 11–12)

One does not need to be as troubled as Bob Donaldson to experience fear and anxiety. Think about a time when your breathing quickened, your muscles tensed, and your heart pounded with a sudden sense of dread. Was it when your car almost skidded off the road in the rain? When your professor announced a pop quiz? What about when the person you were in love with went out with someone else, or your boss suggested that your job performance ought to improve? Any time you face what seems to be a serious threat to your well-being, you may react with the state of immediate alarm known as **fear**. Sometimes you cannot pinpoint a specific cause for your alarm, but still you feel tense and edgy, as if you expected something

FEAR The central nervous system's physiological and emotional response to a serious threat to one's well-being.

FIGURE **4-1** **Does anxiety beget anxiety?**
People with one anxiety disorder usually experience another as well, either simultaneously or at another point in their lives. One study of persons with anxiety disorders found that 81 percent actually suffered from multiple disorders. (Adapted from Hunt & Andrews, 1995.)

unpleasant to happen. The vague sense of being in danger is usually termed **anxiety**, and it has the same features—the same increase in breathing, muscular tension, perspiration, and so forth—as fear (Barlow, 2002).

Although everyday experiences of fear and anxiety are not pleasant, they are often useful: they prepare us for action—for "fight or flight"—when danger threatens. They may lead us to drive more cautiously in a storm, keep up with our reading assignments, treat our dates more sensitively, and work harder at our jobs. Unfortunately, some people suffer such disabling fear and anxiety that they cannot lead normal lives. Their discomfort is too severe or too frequent; it lasts too long; or it is triggered too easily. These people are said to have an *anxiety disorder* or a related kind of disorder.

Anxiety disorders are the most common mental disorders in the United States. In any given year as many as 19 percent of the adult population suffer from one or another of the six anxiety disorders identified by DSM-IV. These disorders cost society at least $42 billion each year in health care expenses, lost wages, and lost productivity (Barlow, 2002; Greenberg et al., 1999).

People with *generalized anxiety disorder* experience general and persistent feelings of anxiety. People with *phobias* experience a persistent and irrational fear of a specific object, activity, or situation. Individuals with *panic disorder* have recurrent attacks of terror. Those with *obsessive-compulsive disorder* feel overrun by repeated thoughts that cause anxiety or by the need to perform repetitive actions to reduce anxiety. And those with *acute stress disorder* and *posttraumatic stress disorder* are tormented by fear and related symptoms well after a traumatic event (military combat, rape, torture) has ended. Most individuals with one anxiety disorder suffer from a second one as well (Roemer et al., 2002) (see Figure 4-1). Bob Donaldson, for example, experiences the excessive worry found in generalized anxiety disorder and the repeated attacks of terror that mark panic disorder.

In this chapter we shall look at generalized anxiety disorder, phobias, panic disorder, and obsessive-compulsive disorder. The other anxiety disorders—acute and posttraumatic stress disorders—will be examined in the next chapter when we consider the special effects that intense or ongoing stress have on both our psychological and physical functioning.

Generalized Anxiety Disorder

People with **generalized anxiety disorder** experience excessive anxiety under most circumstances and worry about practically anything. In fact, their problem is sometimes described as *free-floating anxiety*. Like the young carpenter Bob Donaldson, they typically feel restless, keyed up, or on edge; tire easily; have difficulty concentrating; suffer from muscle tension; and have sleep problems (see Table 4-1). The symptoms last at least six months. Nevertheless, most people with the disorder are able, with some difficulty, to carry on social relationships and job activities (Keller, 2002).

Generalized anxiety disorder is common in Western society. Surveys suggest that as many as 4 percent of the United States population and 3 percent of Britain's population have the symptoms of this disorder in any given year (Roemer et al., 2002; Kessler et al., 2001, 1999). It may emerge at any age, but usually it first appears in childhood or adolescence. Women diagnosed with the disorder outnumber men 2 to 1.

A variety of factors have been cited to explain the development of generalized anxiety disorder. Here we shall observe the views and treatments offered by the sociocultural, psychodynamic, humanistic,

Table 4-1

GENERALIZED ANXIETY DISORDER

1. Excessive or ongoing anxiety and worry, for at least six months, about numerous events or activities.
2. Difficulty controlling the worry.
3. At least three of the following symptoms: restlessness • easy fatigue • irritability • muscle tension • sleep disturbance.
4. Significant distress or impairment.

Based on APA, 2000, 1994.

cognitive, and biological models. The behavioral perspective will be examined when we turn to phobias later in the chapter because that model approaches generalized anxiety disorder and phobias in basically the same way.

The Sociocultural Perspective

According to sociocultural theorists, generalized anxiety disorder is most likely to develop in people who are faced with societal conditions that are truly dangerous. Studies have found that people in highly threatening environments are indeed more likely to develop the general feelings of tension, anxiety, and fatigue and the sleep disturbances found in this disorder (Kendler, Karkowski, & Prescott, 1998).

Take, for example, the psychological impact of living near the Three Mile Island nuclear power plant after the nuclear reactor accident of March 1979 (Baum, 1990; Bromet et al., 1984, 1982). In the months following the accident, local mothers of preschool children were found to display five times as many anxiety or depression disorders as mothers living elsewhere. Although the number of disorders decreased during the next year, the Three Mile Island mothers still displayed high levels of anxiety or depression a year later.

One of the most powerful forms of societal stress is poverty. Poor people are likely to live in run-down communities with high crime rates, have fewer educational and job opportunities, and run a greater risk for health problems. As sociocultural theorists would predict, such people also have a higher rate of generalized anxiety disorder. In the United States, the rate is twice as high among people with low incomes as among those with higher incomes (Blazer et al., 1991). As salaries and wages decrease, the rate of generalized anxiety disorder steadily increases.

Since race is closely tied to income and job opportunity in the United States (Belle, 1990), it is also tied to the prevalence of generalized anxiety disorder. In any given year, approximately 6 percent of all African Americans suffer from this disorder, compared to 3.5 percent of white Americans. African American women, perhaps the country's most socially stressed group, have the highest rate of all—6.6 percent.

Although poverty and other societal pressures may create a climate in which generalized anxiety disorder is more likely to develop, sociocultural variables are not the only factors at work. After all, most people in poor, war-torn, politically oppressed, or dangerous environments do not develop this anxiety disorder. Even if sociocultural factors play a broad role, theorists still must explain why some people develop the disorder and others do not. The psychodynamic, humanistic-existential, cognitive, and biological schools of thought have all tried to explain why and have offered corresponding treatments.

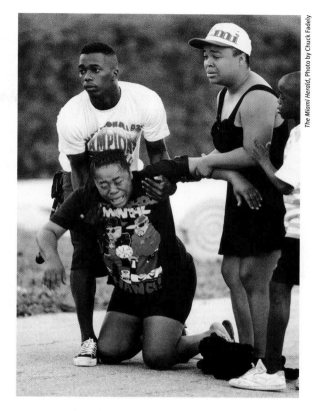

The Miami Herald, Photo by Chuck Fadely

The role of society *Upon learning that her son was a victim of a drive-by shooting, a woman collapses in the arms of relatives at the scene. People who live in dangerous environments experience greater anxiety and have a higher rate of generalized anxiety disorder than those residing in other settings.*

The Psychodynamic Perspective

Sigmund Freud (1933, 1917) believed that all children experience some degree of anxiety as part of growing up, and all use ego defense mechanisms to help control such anxiety (see pp. 38–39). Children experience *realistic anxiety* when they face actual danger; *neurotic anxiety* when they are repeatedly prevented, by parents or by circumstances, from expressing their id impulses; and *moral anxiety* when they are punished or threatened for expressing their id impulses. According to Freud, some children experience particularly high levels of such anxiety, or their defense mechanisms are particularly inadequate, and these individuals may, in turn, develop generalized anxiety disorder.

PSYCHODYNAMIC EXPLANATIONS: WHEN CHILDHOOD ANXIETY GOES UNRESOLVED According to Freud, some children are overrun by neurotic or moral anxiety, thus setting the stage for generalized anxiety disorder. Early developmental experiences may produce an unusually high level of anxiety in these children.

ANXIETY The central nervous system's physiological and emotional response to a vague sense of threat or danger.

GENERALIZED ANXIETY DISORDER A disorder marked by persistent and excessive feelings of anxiety and worry about numerous events and activities.

A CLOSER LOOK

Pressure and Sports: Does Anxiety Hinder Performance?

❚ I knew the stakes were high. . . . But I love pressure. The more competitive it gets, the better I do. Still, half an hour before the contest, my stomach was in knots. I wanted to puke. I didn't know if I could compete, I was so nervous. Then when I got the start, I got this amazing buzz of confidence. And I nailed my line. It was the best run of my life. ❚

—GUERLAIN CHICHERIT, WINNER OF THE 2001 WORLD FREESKIING CHAMPIONSHIPS (BEADRY, 2002)

Just about everyone has tasted the anxiety of competitive sports, from first-graders participating in their gym class's kickball game to elite runners facing the 5,000-kilometer race in the Olympics. When individuals perform well in such endeavors, we speak of their "competitive juices." In contrast, when they do poorly, they are often described as "choking." Clearly, anxiety plays a key role in sports performance, but what exactly is that role?

According to sports psychologists, competitive anxiety comes in two flavors. *Somatic anxiety* is physiological; it is characterized by physical arousal, such as shakiness, racing heartbeat, and sweating (Hardy et al., 1996). It is different from *cognitive anxiety*, which is characterized by psychological symptoms such as negative expectations about an upcoming performance. These two types of anxiety are often related, and experiencing one can trigger or intensify the other.

Interestingly, research suggests that somatic and cognitive anxiety tend to influence sports performance differently. Somatic anxiety actually improves performance up to a point; it makes athletes more alert and energetic—the result of "turning on" the brain and body. At a certain point, however, somatic anxiety can cause one's performance to deteriorate (Burton, 1988). If a person has too much adrenaline coursing through the veins, arousal can turn into distraction and shakiness.

Cognitive anxiety, in contrast, has little upside at all when it comes to competitive sports, according to most research (Burton, 1988). Cognitive anxiety is, at heart, a fear of the consequences of failure. The more important an event, the higher the level of cognitive anxiety. Thus, when coaches spend time emphasizing and reemphasizing the importance of an upcoming game to their players (Krane et al., 1994), or when they try to "psych up" their athletes before a meet by reminding them of the difficulty or dangers of the task ahead (Murphy & Woolfolk, 1987), they may be doing more harm than good.

According to sports psychologists, coaches should also pay attention to factors beyond somatic and cognitive anxiety. For one thing, individuals vary greatly in their general level of anxiety. Generally anxious athletes tend to focus on threatening elements during competition, while their less anxious teammates are more likely to ignore such threats deliberately (Hanton et al., 2003, 2002).

A recent longitudinal study in New Zealand suggests that differences in general levels of anxiety during childhood may help predict whether persons will later succeed in competitive sports (Hagan, 2002; Poulton & Milne, 2002). In the study, individuals who displayed little fear of anything between the ages of 5

Say that a boy is spanked every time he cries for milk as an infant, messes his pants as a 2-year-old, and explores his genitals as a toddler. He may eventually come to believe that his various id impulses are very dangerous, and he may experience overwhelming anxiety whenever he has such impulses.

Alternatively, a child's ego defense mechanisms may be too weak to cope with even normal levels of anxiety. Overprotected children, shielded by their parents from all frustrations and threats, have little opportunity to develop effective defense mechanisms. When they face the pressures of adult life, their defense mechanisms may be too weak to cope with the resulting anxieties.

Today's psychodynamic theorists often disagree with specific aspects of Freud's explanation for generalized anxiety disorder. Most continue to believe, however, that the disorder can be traced to inadequacies in the early relationships between children and their parents. Researchers have tested the psychodynamic explanations in various ways. In one strategy, they have tried to show that people with generalized anxiety disorder are particularly likely to use defense mechanisms. For example, one team of investigators examined the early therapy transcripts of patients with this diagnosis and found that the patients did indeed often react defensively. When asked by their therapists to discuss upsetting experiences, they would quickly forget (*repress*) what they had just been talking about, change the direction of the discussion, or deny having negative feelings (Luborsky, 1973).

In another line of research, investigators have studied people who as children suffered extreme punishment for id impulses. As psychodynamic theorists would

and 11 were three times more likely than their generally anxious peers to achieve later success in sports ranging from badminton and tennis to rugby and soccer.

The effects and experiences of competitive anxiety also depend on the type of sport in question. Athletes on *teams* typically experience less anxiety than those in *individual* sports (Simon & Martens, 1977). Moreover, athletes participating in explosive, or strength-based, sports such as track and field are more likely to be helped by somatic anxiety than are athletes in sports that depend primarily on fine motor skills, such as skeet shooting (Hanton, Jones, & Mullen, 2000). The athletes in the explosive sports also tend to experience less cognitive anxiety than those in the fine motor sports.

Not surprisingly, one of the strongest findings in this area of study is that athletes with more experience are better able to keep feelings of anxiety under control and harness its energy to competitive advantage (Gould et al., 1984). Experienced athletes have had more opportunities to evaluate their previous performances and to judge their own preparedness for competition. Besides, they have experienced somatic anxiety in the past and are more likely to have learned to cope with it and channel it positively (Jones et al., 1990). Indeed, for many experienced athletes bodily arousal becomes a familiar friend rather than a mysterious and dangerous stranger.

The agony of defeat *Few baseball fans will forget the anguished reaction of then Arizona Diamondbacks pitcher Byung-Hyun Kim on November 1, 2001, after he gave up a tying home run to the New York Yankees with two outs in the ninth inning during game five of the World Series. It was the second night in a row that Kim, normally one of baseball's top pitchers, had lost the lead in that manner.*

predict, these people have higher levels of anxiety later in life (Chiu, 1971). In cultures where children are regularly punished and threatened, for example, adults seem to have more fears and anxieties (Whiting et al., 1966). In addition, several studies have supported the psychodynamic claim that extreme protectiveness by parents may often lead to high levels of anxiety in their children (Jenkins, 1968; Eisenberg, 1958).

Although these studies are consistent with psychodynamic explanations, some scientists question whether they show what they claim to show. When people have difficulty talking about upsetting events early in therapy, for example, they are not necessarily repressing those events. They may be purposely focusing on the positive aspects of their lives, or they may be too embarrassed to share personal negative events until they develop trust in the therapist.

Another problem is that some research studies and clinical reports have actually contradicted the psychodynamic explanations. In one, 16 people with generalized anxiety disorder were interviewed about their upbringing (Raskin et al., 1982). They reported little of the excessive discipline or disturbed childhood environments that psychodynamic therapists might expect for people with this disorder.

PSYCHODYNAMIC THERAPIES Psychodynamic therapists use the same general techniques to treat all psychological problems: *free association* and the therapist's interpretations of *transference, resistance,* and *dreams. Freudian psychodynamic therapists* use these methods to help clients with generalized anxiety disorder become less afraid of their id impulses and more successful in controlling them. Other psychodynamic therapists, particularly *object relations therapists*, use them to help anxious patients identify and settle the childhood relationship problems that continue to produce anxiety in adulthood (Zerbe, 1990).

Controlled studies have typically found psychodynamic treatments to be of only modest help to persons with generalized anxiety disorder (Goisman et al., 1999). An exception to this trend is *short-term psychodynamic therapy* (see Chapter 2), which has in some cases significantly reduced the levels of anxiety, worry, and social difficulty of patients with this disorder (Crits-Christoph, 2002).

The Humanistic Perspective

Humanistic theorists propose that generalized anxiety disorder, like other psychological disorders, arises when people stop looking at themselves honestly and acceptingly. Repeated denials of their true thoughts, emotions, and behavior make these people extremely anxious and unable to fulfill their potential as human beings.

The humanistic view of why people develop this disorder is best illustrated by Carl Rogers's explanation. As we saw in Chapter 2, Rogers believed that children who fail to receive *unconditional positive regard* from others may become overly critical of themselves and develop harsh self-standards, what Rogers called *conditions of worth*. They try to meet these standards by repeatedly distorting and denying their true thoughts and experiences. Despite such efforts, however, threatening self-judgments keep breaking through and causing them intense anxiety. This onslaught of anxiety sets the stage for generalized anxiety disorder or some other form of psychological dysfunctioning.

Practitioners of Rogers's treatment approach, **client-centered therapy**, try to show unconditional positive regard for their clients and to empathize with them. The therapists hope that an atmosphere of genuine acceptance and caring will help clients feel secure enough to recognize their true needs, thoughts, and emotions. When clients eventually are honest and comfortable with themselves, their anxiety or other symptoms will subside. In the following excerpt, Rogers describes the progress made by a client with anxiety and related symptoms:

"Don't make me come over there."

No judgment allowed *According to* client-centered therapists, *individuals can overcome their psychological problems only if they feel accepted and understood by their therapists.*

> Therapy was an experiencing of herself, in all its aspects, in a safe relationship. At first it was her guilt and her concern over being responsible for the maladjustments of others. Then it was her hatred and bitterness toward life for having cheated and frustrated her in so many different areas, particularly the sexual, and then it was the experiencing of her own hurt, of the sorrow she felt for herself for having been so wounded. But along with these went the experiencing of self as having a capacity for wholeness . . . a self that cared about others. This last followed . . . the realization that the therapist cared, that it really mattered to him how therapy turned out for her, that he really valued her. She gradually became aware of the fact that, though she had searched in every corner of herself, there was nothing fundamentally bad, but rather, at heart she was positive and sound.
>
> *(Rogers, 1954, pp. 261–264)*

In spite of such optimistic case reports, controlled studies have failed to offer strong support for this approach. Although research does suggest that client-centered therapy is usually more helpful to anxious clients than no treatment, the approach is only sometimes superior to placebo therapy (Prochaska & Norcross, 2003; Grawe et al., 1998). In addition, researchers have found, at best, only limited support for Rogers's explanation of generalized anxiety disorder and other forms of abnormal behavior. Nor have other humanistic theories and treatment received much research support.

The Cognitive Perspective

Followers of the cognitive model suggest that psychological problems are often caused by dysfunctional ways of thinking. Given that excessive worry—a cognitive symptom—is a key characteristic of generalized anxiety disorder, it is not surprising that cognitive theorists have had much to say about the causes of and treatments for this particular disorder.

COGNITIVE EXPLANATIONS: MALADAPTIVE ASSUMPTIONS Several influential cognitive theories suggest that generalized anxiety disorder is caused by *maladaptive assumptions*. Albert Ellis, for example, believes that many people are guided by irrational beliefs that lead them to act and react in inappropriate ways (Ellis, 2002, 1977, 1962). Ellis calls these **basic irrational assumptions**, and he claims that people with generalized anxiety disorder often hold the following ones:

> "It is a dire necessity for an adult human being to be loved or approved of by virtually every significant other person in his community."
>
> "It is awful and catastrophic when things are not the way one would very much like them to be."
>
> "If something is or may be dangerous or fearsome, one should be terribly concerned about it and should keep dwelling on the possibility of its occurring."
>
> "One should be thoroughly competent, adequate, and achieving in all possible respects if one is to consider oneself worthwhile."
>
> *(Ellis, 1962)*

When people who make these assumptions are faced with a stressful event, such as an exam or a blind date, they are likely to interpret it as dangerous, to overreact, and to experience fear. As they apply the assumptions to more and more events, they may begin to develop generalized anxiety disorder (Warren, 1997).

Similarly, the cognitive theorist Aaron Beck holds that people with generalized anxiety disorder constantly hold unrealistic silent assumptions (for example, "A situation or a person is unsafe until proven to be safe" or "It is always best to assume the worst") that imply they are in imminent danger (Beck, 1997, 1976; Beck et al., 1985).

Researchers have found that people with generalized anxiety disorder do indeed hold maladaptive notions about dangerousness, as Ellis and Beck claim (Boegels & Zigterman, 2000). One study found that 32 participants with this disorder held overblown beliefs that they would come to harm (Beck et al., 1974). Each person reported upsetting assumptions and images regarding such issues as physical injury, illness, or death; psychological dysfunctioning; and rejection. Related studies have also found that people with generalized anxiety symptoms pay unusually close attention to threatening cues (Dalgleish et al., 2003; Atkins & Craske, 2001).

What kinds of people are likely to have exaggerated expectations of danger? Some cognitive theorists point to those whose lives have been filled with *unpredictable negative events*. These individuals become generally fearful of the unknown and always wait for the boom to drop (Roemer et al., 2002). To avoid being blindsided, they keep trying to predict negative events. They look everywhere for signs of danger, and they wind up seeing danger everywhere, thus setting up a life of anxiety. In support of this idea, studies have demonstrated that both animal and human subjects respond more fearfully to unpredictable negative events than to predictable ones and that people with generalized anxiety disorder worry much more about the future than others do (Barlow, 2002; Dugas et al., 2002). However, researchers have yet to determine whether people with this disorder have, in fact, experienced an unusual number of unpredictable negative events in life.

COGNITIVE THERAPIES Two kinds of cognitive approaches are commonly used in cases of generalized anxiety disorder. In one, based on the theories of Ellis and

CLIENT-CENTERED THERAPY The humanistic therapy developed by Carl Rogers in which clinicians try to help clients by being accepting, empathizing accurately, and conveying genuineness.

BASIC IRRATIONAL ASSUMPTIONS The inaccurate and inappropriate beliefs held by people with various psychological problems, according to Albert Ellis.

>>BY THE NUMBERS

Treating Pet Anxiety

5 million   Dogs with severe separation anxiety<<

33%   Owners who leave radio or television on when pet is alone<<

50%   Those who leave toys out<<

41%   Those who leave lights on<<

(Klein, 1998)

A CLOSER LOOK

Fears, Shmears: The Odds Are Usually on Our Side

People with anxiety disorders have many unreasonable fears, but millions of other people, too, worry about disaster every day. Most of the catastrophes they fear are not probable. Perhaps the ability to live by laws of *probability* rather than *possibility* is what separates the fearless from the fearful. What are the odds, then, that commonly feared events will happen? The range of probability is wide, but the odds are usually heavily in our favor.

A city resident will be a victim of a violent crime . . . 1 in 60

A suburbanite will be a victim of a violent crime . . . 1 in 1,000

A small-town resident will be a victim of a violent crime . . . 1 in 2,000

A child will suffer a high-chair injury this year . . . 1 in 6,000

The IRS will audit you this year . . . 1 in 100

You will be murdered this year . . . 1 in 12,000

You will be killed on your next bus ride . . . 1 in 500 million

You will be hit by a baseball at a major league game . . . 1 in 300,000

You will drown in the tub this year . . . 1 in 685,000

Your house will have a fire this year . . . 1 in 200

Your carton will contain a broken egg . . . 1 in 10

You will develop a tooth cavity . . . 1 in 6

You will contract AIDS from a blood transfusion . . . 1 in 100,000

You will die in a fall . . . 1 in 200,000

You will be attacked by a shark . . . 1 in 4 million

You will receive a diagnosis of cancer this year . . . 1 in 8,000

A woman will develop breast cancer during her lifetime . . . 1 in 9

A piano player will eventually develop lower back pain . . . 1 in 3

You will be killed on your next automobile outing . . . 1 in 4 million

Condom use will eventually fail to prevent pregnancy . . . 1 in 10

An IUD will eventually fail to prevent pregnancy . . . 1 in 10

Coitus interruptus will eventually fail to prevent pregnancy . . . 1 in 5

(ADAPTED FROM KRANTZ, 1992)

Jim Harrison/Stock Boston

Build with care
The chance of a construction worker's being injured at work during the year is 1 in 27.

Beck, therapists help clients change the maladaptive assumptions that are supposedly at the root of their disorders. In the other, therapists teach clients how to cope during stressful situations.

CHANGING MALADAPTIVE ASSUMPTIONS In Ellis's technique of **rational-emotive therapy**, practitioners point out the irrational assumptions held by clients, suggest more appropriate assumptions, and assign homework that gives the individuals practice at challenging old assumptions and applying new ones (Ellis, 2002, 2001). Research has been limited, but studies do suggest that this approach brings at least modest relief to persons suffering from anxiety (Cowan & Brunero, 1997). The approach is illustrated in the following discussion between Ellis and an anxious client who fears failure and disapproval at work, especially over a testing procedure that she has developed for her company:

Client: I'm so distraught these days that I can hardly concentrate on anything for more than a minute or two at a time. My mind just keeps wandering to that damn testing procedure I devised, and that they've put so much money into; and whether it's going to work well or be just a waste of all that time and money. . . .

Ellis: Point one is that you must admit that you are telling yourself something to start your worrying going, and you must begin to look, and I mean really look, for the specific nonsense with which you keep reindoctrinating yourself. . . . The false statement is: "If, because my testing procedure doesn't work and I am functioning inefficiently on my job, my co-workers do not want me or approve of me, then I shall be a worthless person." . . .

Client: But if I want to do what my firm also wants me to do, and I am useless to them, aren't I also useless to me?

Ellis: No—not unless you think you are. You are frustrated, of course, if you want to set up a good testing procedure and you can't. But need you be desperately unhappy because you are frustrated? And need you deem yourself completely unworthwhile because you can't do one of the main things you want to do in life?

(Ellis, 1962, pp. 160–165)

Beck's similar but more systematic approach, called, simply, *cognitive therapy*, is an adaptation of his influential and very effective treatment for depression (which is discussed in Chapter 7). Researchers have found that it and similar cognitive approaches often reduce generalized anxiety to more tolerable levels (Sanderson et al., 2002; Brown et al., 2001).

TEACHING CLIENTS TO COPE The clinical innovator Donald Meichenbaum (2003, 1997, 1993) has developed a cognitive technique for coping with stress called **self-instruction training**, or **stress inoculation training**. It teaches clients to rid themselves of the unpleasant thoughts that keep raising their anxiety during difficult situations (so-called *negative self-statements*) and replace them with *coping self-statements* instead.

In Meichenbaum's approach, people are taught coping self-statements that they can apply during four stages of a stressful situation—say, talking to their boss about a raise. First, they learn to say things to themselves that prepare them for the situation. Second, they learn self-statements that enable them to cope with the stressful situation as it is occurring—for instance, when they are actually in the boss's office. Third, they learn self-statements that will help them through the difficult moments when the situation seems to be going badly, as when the boss glares at them as they ask for more money. Finally, they learn to make self-congratulatory self-statements after they have coped effectively. Here are a few examples of the four kinds of self-statements:

Preparing for a Stressor
What is it you have to do?
Just think about what you can do about it. That's better than getting anxious.

Confronting and Handling a Stressor
Just psych yourself up—you can meet this challenge.
Relax: you're in control. Take a slow, deep breath.

Coping with the Feeling of Being Overwhelmed
When fear comes, just pause.
Keep the focus on the present. What is it you have to do?
You should expect your fear to rise.

Reinforcing Self-Statements
It worked! You did it.
Your damn ideas—that's the problem. When you control them, you control your fear.

RATIONAL-EMOTIVE THERAPY A cognitive therapy developed by Albert Ellis which helps clients to identify and change the irrational assumptions and thinking that help cause their psychological disorder.

SELF-INSTRUCTION TRAINING A cognitive treatment developed by Donald Meichenbaum which teaches clients to use coping self-statements at times of stress. Also known as *stress inoculation training*.

>>LAB•NOTES

Facing Fear Studies find that subjects with generally high levels of anxiety are more likely than calmer subjects to notice and remember pictures of threatening faces. Attention to happy or neutral faces is the same in both groups (Bradley et al., 1998).<<

Clocking Fear Researchers in Germany momentarily flashed pictures of snakes and spiders for subjects who were afraid of the creatures. The subjects began to experience physical fear reactions (autonomic arousal) just 300 microseconds after each picture's brief appearance (Globisch et al., 1999).<<

Fearful delights *Many people enjoy the feeling of fear as long as it occurs under controlled circumstances, as when they are safely watching the tension grow in the enormously popular* Blair Witch Project.

Self-instruction training has proved to be of modest help in cases of generalized anxiety disorder and moderately helpful to people whose anxiety is specifically linked to life change, test-taking, and performance anxiety (Rokke & Rehm, 2001; Meichenbaum, 1993, 1972). It has also been used with some success to help athletes compete better and to encourage people to behave less impulsively, control anger, and control pain (Spiegler & Guevremont, 2003). In view of its limited effectiveness in treating generalized and other anxiety disorders, Meichenbaum (1972) himself has suggested that this approach should be combined with other treatments. In fact, anxious people treated with a combination of self-instruction training and Ellis's rational-emotive therapy improve more than people treated by either approach alone (Glogower, Fremouw, & McCroskey, 1978).

The Biological Perspective

Biological theorists believe that generalized anxiety disorder is caused chiefly by biological factors. For years this claim was supported primarily by **family pedigree studies**, in which researchers determine how many and which relatives of a person with a disorder have the same disorder. If biological tendencies toward generalized anxiety disorder are inherited, people who are biologically related should have similar probabilities of developing this disorder. Studies have in fact found that blood relatives of persons with generalized anxiety disorder are more likely than nonrelatives to have the disorder, too (Hettema et al., 2001) (see Table 4-2). Approximately 15 percent of the relatives of people with the disorder display it themselves—much more than the 4 percent found in the general population. And the closer the relative (an identical twin, for example, as opposed to a fraternal twin or other sibling), the greater the likelihood that he or she will also have the disorder (APA, 2000).

Of course, investigators cannot have full confidence in biological interpretations of such studies. Because relatives are likely to share aspects of the same environment, their shared disorders may reflect similarities in environment and upbringing rather than similarities in biological makeup. The closer the relatives, the more similar their environmental experiences are likely to be. Because identical twins are more physically alike than fraternal twins, they may even experience more similarities in their upbringing.

BIOLOGICAL EXPLANATIONS: GABA INACTIVITY In recent decades important discoveries by brain researchers have offered clearer evidence that generalized anxiety disorder is related to biological factors, in particular to biochemical dysfunc-

Table 4-2

Anxiety Disorders Profile

	ONE-YEAR PREVALENCE (%)	FEMALE:MALE RATIO	TYPICAL AGE AT ONSET	PREVALENCE AMONG CLOSE RELATIVES	PERCENTAGE RECEIVING TREATMENT
Generalized anxiety disorder	4.0%	2:1	0–20 years	Elevated	27%
Specific phobias	9.0	2:1	Variable	Elevated	12%
Social phobias	8.0	3:2	10–20 years	Elevated	21%
Panic disorder	2.3	5:2	15–35 years	Elevated	54.4%
Obsessive-compulsive disorder	2.0	1:1	4–25 years	Elevated	41.3%

Source: Ingersoll & Burns, 2001; APA, 2000, 1994; Kessler et al., 1999, 1994; Regier et al., 1993; Blazer et al., 1991; Davidson et al., 1991; Eaton et al., 1991.

tion in the brain. One of the first such discoveries occurred in the 1950s, when researchers determined that **benzodiazepines**, the family of drugs that includes *diazepam* (Valium) and *alprazolam* (Xanax), provide relief from anxiety. At first, no one understood why benzodiazepines reduce anxiety. Eventually, however, the development of radioactive techniques enabled researchers to pinpoint the exact sites in the brain that are affected by benzodiazepines (Mohler & Okada, 1977). Apparently certain neurons have receptors that receive the benzodiazepines, just as a lock receives a key.

Investigators soon discovered that these benzodiazepine receptors ordinarily receive **gamma-aminobutyric acid (GABA)**, a common and important neurotransmitter in the brain (Grilly, 2002; Costa & Guidotti., 1996). As we observed in Chapter 2, neurotransmitters are chemicals that carry messages from one neuron to another. GABA carries *inhibitory* messages: when GABA is received at a receptor, it causes the neuron to stop firing.

On the basis of such findings, biological researchers eventually pieced together several scenarios of how fear reactions may occur. One of the leading ones begins with the notion that in normal fear reactions, key neurons throughout the brain fire more rapidly, triggering the firing of still more neurons and creating a general state of excitability throughout the brain and body. Perspiration, breathing, and muscle tension increase. This state is experienced as fear or anxiety. After neuron firing continues for a while, it triggers a feedback system—that is, brain and body activities that reduce the level of excitability. Some neurons throughout the brain release the neurotransmitter GABA, which then binds to GABA receptors on certain neurons and instructs those neurons to stop firing. The state of excitability ends, and the experience of fear or anxiety subsides (Sanders & Shekhar, 1995; Costa, 1985, 1983).

Some researchers believe that a problem in this feedback system can cause fear or anxiety to go unchecked (Lloyd et al., 1992). In fact, when investigators reduced GABA's ability to bind to GABA receptors, they found that animal subjects reacted with a rise in anxiety (Costa, 1985; Mohler et al., 1981). This finding suggests that people with generalized anxiety disorder may have ongoing problems in their anxiety feedback system. Perhaps their brain supplies of GABA are too low. Perhaps they have too few GABA receptors, or their GABA receptors do not readily capture the neurotransmitter.

This explanation is promising, but it has problems. One is that recent discoveries have complicated the picture (Barlow, 2002). It has been found, for example, that other neurotransmitters and receptors may also play important roles in anxiety and anxiety disorders—acting alone or in conjunction with GABA. Another problem is that much of the research on the biology of anxiety has been done on laboratory animals. When researchers produce fear responses in animals, they assume that the animals are experiencing something similar to human anxiety, but it is impossible to be certain (Kalin, 1993). The animals may be experiencing a high level of arousal that is quite different from human anxiety.

Finally, biological theorists are faced with the problem of establishing a causal relationship. Although studies do tie physiological functioning to generalized anxiety disorder, they do not establish that the physiological events *cause* the disorder. The biological responses of anxious persons may be the result, rather than the cause, of their anxiety disorders. Perhaps long-term anxiety eventually leads to poorer GABA reception, for example.

BIOLOGICAL TREATMENTS The leading biological approach to treating generalized anxiety disorder is to prescribe *antianxiety drugs,* known popularly as tranquilizers. Other biological interventions are *relaxation training*, in which people learn to relax the muscles throughout their bodies, and *biofeedback*, in which clients learn to control underlying biological processes voluntarily.

ANTIANXIETY DRUGS Before the 1950s, a family of drugs labeled *barbiturates* were the major biological treatment for anxiety disorders (Grilly, 2002). Because these drugs were used in low doses to calm people and in higher doses to help them fall

FAMILY PEDIGREE STUDY A research design in which investigators determine how many and which relatives of a person with a disorder have the same disorder.

BENZODIAZEPINES The most common group of antianxiety drugs, which include Valium and Xanax.

GABA The neurotransmitter gamma-aminobutyric acid, whose low activity has been linked to generalized anxiety disorder.

University of Wisconsin Primate Laboratory, Madison

Do monkeys experience anxiety? *Clinical researchers must be careful in interpreting the reactions of animal subjects. This infant monkey was considered "fearful" after being separated from its mother. But perhaps it was feeling depressed or experiencing a level of arousal that does not correspond to either fear or depression.*

Table 4-3

Drugs That Reduce Anxiety

CLASS/GENERIC NAME	TRADE NAME
Benzodiazepines	
Alprazolam	Xanax
Chlordiazepoxide	Librium
Clonazepam	Klonopin
Clorazepate	Tranxene
Diazepam	Valium
Halazepam	Paxipam
Lorazepam	Ativan
Oxazepam	Serax
Prazepam	Centrax
Azaspirones	
Buspirone	BuSpar
Beta blockers	
Propranolol	Inderal
Atenolol	Tenormin

asleep, they were generally known as **sedative-hypnotic drugs**. However, barbiturates created serious problems. They made people very drowsy, too high a dose could lead to death, and those who took them over a long period could become physically dependent on them. In the late 1940s, a drug called *meprobamate* was developed and later released as a new kind of sedative-hypnotic medication under the brand name Miltown (Cole & Yonkers, 1995). This drug was less dangerous and less addictive than barbiturates, but it still caused great drowsiness. Finally, in the late 1950s another group of antianxiety drugs called *benzodiazepines* were marketed (see Table 4-3). These drugs did not seem to produce as much tiredness as the others and were quickly embraced by both doctors and patients.

Only years later did investigators come to understand the reasons for the drugs' effectiveness. As we have observed, researchers eventually learned that there are specific neuron sites in the brain that receive benzodiazepines (Mohler & Okada, 1977) and that these same receptor sites ordinarily receive the neurotransmitter GABA. Apparently, when benzodiazepines bind to these neuron receptor sites, particularly those receptors known as *GABA-A receptors*, they increase the ability of GABA to bind to them as well, and so improve GABA's ability to stop neurons from firing and to reduce anxiety (Grilly, 2002).

Benzodiazepines are prescribed for generalized anxiety disorder more than for most other kinds of anxiety disorders (Keltner & Folks, 2001). Controlled studies show that they do sometimes provide temporary and modest relief (Rickels & Rynn, 2002). However, clinicians have come to realize the potential dangers of these drugs. First, when the medications are stopped, many persons' anxieties return as strong as ever. Second, we now know that people who take benzodiazepines in large doses for an extended time can become physically dependent on them. Third, the drugs can produce undesirable effects such as drowsiness, lack of coordination, memory loss, depression, and aggressive behavior. Finally, the drugs mix badly with certain other drugs or substances. For example, if people on benzodiazepines drink even small amounts of alcohol, their breathing can slow down dangerously, sometimes fatally (Gorman, 2002; Grilly, 2002).

In recent years, still other kinds of antianxiety drugs have become available for people with generalized anxiety disorder (Brawman-Mintzer, 2001). One of these drugs, *buspirone* (trade name BuSpar), has gained particular popularity. Binding to a different set of receptors in the brain, this drug is often just as effective as benzodiazepines yet is less likely to lead to physical dependence (Grilly, 2002).

RELAXATION TRAINING A nonchemical biological technique commonly used to treat generalized anxiety disorder is **relaxation training**. The notion behind this approach is that physical relaxation will lead to a state of psychological relaxation. In one version, therapists teach clients to identify individual muscle groups, tense them, release the tension, and ultimately relax the whole body. With continued practice, they can bring on a state of deep muscle relaxation at will, reducing their state of anxiety.

Research indicates that relaxation training is more effective than no treatment or placebo treatment in cases of generalized anxiety disorder (Gorman, 2002). The improvement it produces, however, tends to be modest (Butler et al., 1991), and other techniques that are known to relax people, such as *meditation*, often seem to be equally effective (Kabat-Zinn et al., 1992). Relaxation training is of greatest help to people with generalized anxiety disorder when it is combined with cognitive therapy or with biofeedback (Brown et al., 2001; Overholser & Nasser, 2000).

Modern relaxation *At the Brain Mind Gym, business executives receive pulsations of light and sound from goggles and headphones, which are meant to lull their brains into deep relaxation.*

Torin Boyd Photo, Tokyo, Japan

BIOFEEDBACK In **biofeedback**, therapists use electrical signals from the body to train people to control physiological processes such as heart rate or muscle tension. Clients are connected to a monitor that gives them continuous information about their bodily activities. By attending to the therapist's instructions and the signals from the monitor, they may gradually learn to control even seemingly involuntary physiological processes.

The most widely applied method of biofeedback for the treatment of anxiety uses a device called an **electromyograph** (**EMG**), which provides feedback about the level of muscular tension in the body. Electrodes are attached to the client's muscles—usually the forehead muscles—where they detect the minute electrical activity that accompanies muscle tension (see Figure 4-2). The device then converts electric potentials coming from the muscles into an image, such as lines on a screen, or into a tone whose pitch changes along with changes in muscle tension. Thus clients "see" or "hear" when their muscles are becoming more or less tense. Through repeated trial and error, the individuals become skilled at voluntarily reducing muscle tension and, theoretically, at reducing tension and anxiety in everyday stressful situations.

Research finds that in most cases, EMG biofeedback, like relaxation training, has only a modest effect on a person's anxiety level (Brown et al., 2001, 1992). As we shall see in the next chapter, this and other forms of biofeedback have had their greatest impact when they play adjunct roles in the treatment of certain medical problems, including headaches, back pain, gastrointestinal disorders, seizure disorders, and neuromuscular disorders (Sadock & Sadock, 2003; Andrasik, 2000).

FIGURE 4-2 **Biofeedback at work** *This biofeedback system is recording tension in the forehead muscle of an anxious person. The system receives, amplifies, converts, and displays information about the tension, allowing the client to "observe" it and to try to reduce his tension responses.*

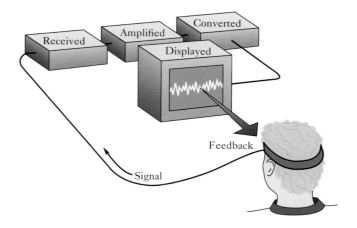

SUMMING UP
Generalized Anxiety Disorder

People with generalized anxiety disorder experience excessive anxiety and worry about a wide range of events and activities. The various explanations and treatments for this disorder have received only limited research support, although recent cognitive and biological approaches seem to be promising.

According to the sociocultural view, increases in societal dangers and pressures create a threatening climate in which cases of generalized anxiety disorder are more likely to develop.

In the original psychodynamic explanation, Freud said that this disorder may develop when individuals come to fear their various id impulses, or when their defense mechanisms break down, or both. Psychodynamic therapists use free association, interpretation, and related psychodynamic techniques to help people overcome this problem.

Carl Rogers, the leading humanistic theorist, believed that people with this disorder fail to receive unconditional positive regard from significant others during their childhood and so become overly critical of themselves. He treated such individuals with client-centered therapy.

Cognitive theorists believe that generalized anxiety disorder is caused by maladaptive assumptions and beliefs that lead people to view most life situations as dangerous. Cognitive therapists help their clients change such thinking, and they teach them how to cope during stressful situations.

Biological theorists hold that this disorder results from low activity of the neurotransmitter GABA. The most common biological treatment is antianxiety drugs, particularly benzodiazepines. Relaxation training and biofeedback are also applied in many cases.

SEDATIVE-HYPNOTIC DRUGS Drugs that calm people at lower doses and help them to fall asleep at higher doses.

RELAXATION TRAINING A treatment procedure that teaches clients to relax at will so they can calm themselves in stressful situations.

BIOFEEDBACK A treatment technique in which a client is given information about physiological reactions as they occur and learns to control the reactions voluntarily.

ELECTROMYOGRAPH (EMG) A device that provides feedback about the level of muscular tension in the body.

PHOBIA A persistent and unreasonable fear of a particular object, activity, or situation.

SPECIFIC PHOBIA A severe and persistent fear of a specific object or situation (other than agoraphobia and social phobia).

SOCIAL PHOBIA A severe and persistent fear of social or performance situations in which embarrassment may occur.

Phobias

A **phobia** (from the Greek for "fear") is a persistent and unreasonable fear of a particular object, activity, or situation. People with a phobia become fearful if they even think about the object or situation they dread, but they usually remain comfortable as long as they avoid the object or thoughts about it. Most are well aware that their fears are excessive and unreasonable.

We all have our areas of special fear, and it is normal for some things to upset us more than other things, perhaps even different things at different stages of our lives (Antony & Barlow, 2002). A survey of residents of a community in Burlington, Vermont, found that fears of crowds, death, injury, illness, and separation were more common among people in their 60s than in other age groups (Agras, Sylvester, & Oliveau, 1969). Among 20-year-olds, fears of snakes, heights, storms, enclosures, and social situations were much more common.

How do these common fears differ from phobias? DSM-IV indicates that a phobia is more intense and persistent and the desire to avoid the object or situation is greater (APA, 2000, 1994). People with phobias often feel so much distress that their fears may interfere dramatically with their lives.

Phobias are common in our society. Surveys suggest that 10 to 11 percent of the adults in the United States suffer from one in any given year, and more than 14 percent develop a phobia at some point in their lives (Magee et al., 1996; Regier et al., 1993). The disorder is more than twice as common in women as in men.

Most phobias technically fall under the category of **specific phobias**, DSM-IV's label for a marked and persistent fear of a specific object or situation. In addition, there are two broader kinds of phobias: **social phobia**, a fear of social or performance situations in which embarrassment may occur, and *agoraphobia*, a fear of venturing into public places, especially when one is alone. Because agoraphobia is usually, perhaps always, experienced in conjunction with panic attacks, unpredictable attacks of terror, we shall examine that phobia later within the discussion of panic disorders.

Specific Phobias

As we have observed, a specific phobia is a persistent fear of a specific object or situation (see Table 4-4). When sufferers are exposed to the object or situation, they typically experience immediate fear. Common specific phobias are intense fears of specific animals or insects, heights, enclosed spaces, thunderstorms, and blood. Here, for example, Marianne and Andrew talk about their phobic fears of spiders and of flying:

>>**PSYCH•LISTINGS**
Famous Movie Phobias

Snakes (*Raiders of the Lost Ark*)<<

Illness (*Hannah and Her Sisters*)<<

The outside world (*Copycat*)<<

Social situations (*Annie Hall*)<<

Flying (*Rain Man*)<<

Heights (*Vertigo*)<<

The color red (*Marnie*)<<

Enclosed spaces (*Body Double*)<<

Spiders (*Arachnophobia*)<<

Marianne Seeing a spider makes me rigid with fear, hot, trembling and dizzy. I have occasionally vomited and once fainted in order to escape from the situation. These symptoms last three or four days after seeing a spider. Realistic pictures can cause the same effect, especially if I inadvertently place my hand on one.

(Melville, 1978, p. 44)

Andrew We got on board, and then there was the take-off. There it was again, that horrible feeling as we gathered speed. It was creeping over me again, that old feeling of panic. I kept seeing everyone as puppets, all strapped to their seats with no control over their destinies, me included. Every time the plane did a variation of speed or route, my heart would leap and I would hurriedly ask what was happening. When the plane started to lose height, I was terrified that we were about to crash.

(Melville, 1978, p. 59)

Each year as many as 9 percent of the people in the United States have the symptoms of a specific phobia (APA, 2000; Kessler & Zhao, 1999). Eleven percent develop such phobias at some time during their lives, and many people have more than one at a time. Women with the disorder outnumber men by at least 2 to 1. For reasons that are not clear, the prevalence of specific phobias also differs among racial and ethnic minority groups. Hispanic Americans, for example, report twice as many of them as white Americans (Antony & Barlow, 2002).

The impact of a specific phobia on a person's life depends on what arouses the fear. People whose phobias center on dogs, insects, or water will keep encountering the objects they dread. Their efforts to avoid them must be elaborate and may greatly restrict their activities. People with snake phobias have a much easier time. As we saw in Table 4-2, the vast majority of people with a specific phobia—almost 90 percent of them—do not seek treatment. They try instead to avoid the objects they fear (Antony & Barlow, 2002).

Social Phobias

Many people worry about interacting with others or talking or performing in front of others. A number of entertainers, including Barbra Streisand and Carly Simon, have described major bouts of nervousness before going onstage. Social fears of this kind are inconvenient, but usually the people who have them manage to function adequately, some at a very high level.

People with a social phobia, by contrast, have severe, persistent, and unreasonable fears of social or performance situations in which embarrassment may occur (see Table 4-5). A social phobia may be *narrow*, such as a fear of talking in public or writing in front of others, or it may be *broader*, such as a general fear of functioning poorly in front of others (Turk, Heimberg, & Hope, 2001). In both forms, people repeatedly judge themselves as performing less adequately than they actually do (Rosser et al., 2003).

A social phobia can interfere greatly with one's life. A person who is unable to interact with others or speak in public may fail to perform important responsibilities. One who cannot eat in public may reject dinner invitations and other social opportunities. Since most people with this phobia keep their fears secret, their social reluctance is often misinterpreted as snobbery, lack of interest, or hostility.

As many as 8 percent of the population—around three women for every two men—experience a social phobia in any given year (Kessler & Zhao, 1999). More than 13 percent experience this problem at some point in their lives. The disorder often begins in late childhood or adolescence and continues into adulthood (APA, 2000).

Table 4-4

SPECIFIC PHOBIA

1. Marked and persistent fear of a specific object or situation that is excessive or unreasonable, lasting at least six months.
2. Immediate anxiety usually produced by exposure to the object.
3. Recognition that the fear is excessive or unreasonable.
4. Avoidance of the feared situation.
5. Significant distress or impairment.

Based on APA, 2000, 1994.

Table 4-5

SOCIAL PHOBIA

1. Marked and persistent fear of social or performance situations involving exposure to unfamiliar people or possible scrutiny by others, lasting at least six months. Concern about humiliating or embarrassing oneself.
2. Anxiety usually produced by exposure to the social situation.
3. Recognition that the fear is excessive or unreasonable.
4. Avoidance of feared situations.
5. Significant distress or impairment.

Based on APA, 2000, 1994.

"And what do you think will happen if you do get on the couch?"

Phobias, Familiar and Not So Familiar

Animals—zoophobia
Beards—pogonophobia
Being afraid—phobophobia
Blood—hematophobia
Books—bibliophobia
Churches—ecclesiaphobia
Corpses—necrophobia
Crossing a bridge—gephyrophobia
Crowds—ochlophobia
Darkness—achluophobia, nyctophobia
Demons or devils—demonophobia
Dogs—cynophobia
Dolls—pediophobia
Drugs—pharmacophobia
Enclosed spaces—claustrophobia
Eyes—ommatophobia
Feces—coprophobia
Fire—pyrophobia
Flood—antlophobia
Flowers—anthophobia
Flying—aerophobia
Fog—homichlophobia
Fur—doraphobia
Germs—spermophobia
Ghosts—phasmophobia
God—theophobia
Graves—taphophobia
Heat—thermophobia
Heights—acrophobia
Homosexuality—homophobia

Horses—hippophobia
Ice, frost—cryophobia
Insects—entomophobia
Machinery—mechanophobia
Marriage—gamophobia
Meat—carnophobia
Mice—musophobia
Mirrors—eisoptrophobia
Money—chrometrophobia
Night—nyctophobia
Noise or loud talking—phonophobia
Odors—osmophobia
Pleasure—hedonophobia

Poison—toxiphobia
Poverty—peniaphobia
Pregnancy—maieusiophobia
Railways—siderodromophobia
Rain—ombrophobia
Rivers—potamophobia
Robbers—harpaxophobia
Satan—Satanophobia
Sexual intercourse—coitophobia, cypridophobia
Shadows—sciophobia
Sleep—hypnophobia
Snakes—ophidiophobia
Snow—chionophobia
Speed—tachophobia
Spiders—arachnophobia
Stings—cnidophobia
Strangers—xenophobia
Sun—heliophobia
Surgery—ergasiophobia
Teeth—odontophobia
Travel—hodophobia
Trees—dendrophobia
Wasps—spheksophobia
Water—hydrophobia
Wind—anemophobia
Worms—helminthophobia
Wounds, injury—traumatophobia

Ophidiophobia *A fear of snakes is one of the most common specific phobias.*

Michael Melford

(MELVILLE, 1978, PP. 196–202)

What Causes Phobias?

Each of the models offers explanations for phobias. Evidence tends to support the behavioral explanations. Behaviorists believe that people with phobias first learn to fear certain objects, situations, or events through conditioning (Field & Davey, 2001). Once the fears are acquired, the individuals avoid the dreaded object or situation, permitting the fears to become all the more locked in.

HOW ARE FEARS LEARNED? Behaviorists propose **classical conditioning** as a common way of acquiring phobic reactions. Here, two events that occur close together in time become closely associated in a person's mind, and, as we saw in Chapter 2, the person then reacts similarly to both of them. If one event triggers a fear response, the other may also.

In the 1920s a clinician described the case of a young woman who apparently acquired a phobia of running water through classical conditioning (Bagby, 1922). As a child of 7 she went on a picnic with her mother and aunt and ran off by herself into the woods after lunch. While she was climbing over some large rocks, her feet were caught between two of them. The harder she tried to free herself, the more trapped she became. No one heard her screams, and she grew more and more terrified. In the language of behaviorists, the entrapment was eliciting a fear response.

Entrapment → Fear response

As she struggled to free her feet, the girl heard a waterfall nearby. The sound of the running water became linked in her mind to her terrifying battle with the rocks, and she developed a fear of running water as well.

Running water → Fear response

Eventually the aunt found the screaming child, freed her from the rocks, and comforted her; but the psychological damage had been done. From that day forward, the girl was terrified of running water. For years family members had to hold her down to bathe her. When she traveled on a train, friends had to cover the windows so that she would not have to look at any streams. The young woman had apparently acquired a phobia through classical conditioning.

In conditioning terms, the entrapment was an *unconditioned stimulus* (*US*) that understandably elicited an *unconditioned response* (*UR*) of fear. The running water represented a *conditioned stimulus* (*CS*), a formerly neutral stimulus that became associated with entrapment in the child's mind and came also to elicit a fear reaction. The newly acquired fear was a *conditioned response* (*CR*).

US: Entrapment → UR: Fear

CS: Running water → CR: Fear

Another way of acquiring a fear reaction is through **modeling**; that is, through observation and imitation (Bandura & Rosenthal, 1966). A person may observe that others are afraid of certain objects or events and develop fears of the same things. Consider a young boy whose mother is afraid of illnesses, doctors, and hospitals. If she frequently expresses those fears, before long the boy himself may fear illnesses, doctors, and hospitals.

Why should one upsetting experience develop into a long-term phobia? Shouldn't the trapped girl later have seen that running water would bring her no harm? Shouldn't the boy later see that illnesses are temporary and doctors and hospitals helpful? Behaviorists believe that after acquiring a fear response, people try to *avoid* what they fear. Whenever they find themselves near a fearsome object, they quickly move away. They may also plan ahead to ensure that such encounters will not occur. Remember that the girl had friends cover the windows on trains so that she could avoid looking at streams. People with phobias do not get close to the dreaded objects often enough to learn that they are really quite harmless.

Behaviorists also propose that specific learned fears will blossom into a generalized anxiety disorder when a person acquires a large number of them. This development is presumed to come about through **stimulus generalization**: responses to one stimulus are also produced by similar stimuli. The fear of running water acquired by the girl in the rocks could have generalized to such similar stimuli as milk being poured into a glass or even the sound of bubbly music. Perhaps a person experiences a series of upsetting events, each event produces one or more feared stimuli, and the person's reactions to each of these stimuli generalize to yet

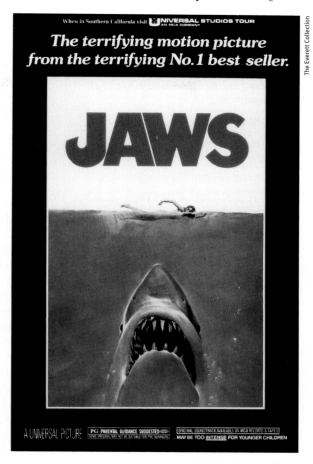

Viewer beware *When people observe others (models) cower from or do battle with a threatening object or situation, they themselves may develop a fear of the object. Steven Spielberg's film* Jaws *led to heightened fears of sharks around the world.*

CLASSICAL CONDITIONING A process of learning in which two events that repeatedly occur close together in time become tied together in a person's mind and so produce the same response.

MODELING A process of learning in which a person observes and then imitates others. Also, a therapy approach based on the same principle.

STIMULUS GENERALIZATION A phenomenon in which responses to one stimulus are also produced by similar stimuli.

other stimuli. That person may then build up a large number of fears and eventually develop generalized anxiety disorder.

HOW HAVE BEHAVIORAL EXPLANATIONS FARED IN RESEARCH? Some laboratory studies have found that animals and humans can indeed be taught to fear objects through classical conditioning (Miller, 1948; Mowrer, 1947, 1939). In one famous report, the psychologists John B. Watson and Rosalie Rayner (1920) described how they taught a baby boy called Little Albert to fear white rats. For weeks Albert was allowed to play with a white rat and appeared to enjoy doing so. One time when Albert reached for the rat, however, the experimenter struck a steel bar with a hammer, making a very loud noise that upset and frightened Albert. The next several times that Albert reached for the rat, the experimenter again made the loud noise. Albert acquired a fear and avoidance response to the rat. As Watson (1930) described it, "The instant the rat was shown, the baby began to cry . . . and . . . crawl away" (p. 161).

Research has also supported the behavioral position that fears can be learned through modeling. The psychologists Albert Bandura and Theodore Rosenthal (1966), for example, had human subjects observe a person apparently being shocked by electricity whenever a buzzer sounded. The victim was actually the experimenter's accomplice—in research terminology, a *confederate*—who pretended to experience pain by twitching and yelling whenever the buzzer went on. After the unsuspecting subjects had observed several such episodes, they themselves experienced a fear reaction whenever they heard the buzzer.

Although these studies support behaviorists' explanations of phobias, other research has called those explanations into question (Antony & Barlow, 2002). Some laboratory studies with children and adults have failed to condition fear reactions. In addition, although most case studies trace phobias to possible incidents of classical conditioning or modeling, quite a few fail to do so. So, although it appears that a phobia *can* be acquired by classical conditioning or modeling, researchers have not established that the disorder is *ordinarily* acquired in this way.

A BEHAVIORAL-EVOLUTIONARY EXPLANATION Some phobias are much more common than others (see Figure 4-3). Phobic reactions to animals, heights, and darkness are more common than phobic reactions to meat, grass, and houses. Theorists often account for these differences by proposing that human beings, as a species, have a predisposition to develop certain fears (Mineka & Ohman, 2002; Seligman, 1971). This idea is referred to as **preparedness** because human beings, theoretically, are "prepared" to acquire some phobias and not others. The following case description by I. M. Marks (1977) makes the point:

> A four-year-old girl was playing in the park. Thinking that she saw a snake, she ran to her parents' car and jumped inside, slamming the door behind her. Unfortunately, the girl's hand was caught by the closing car door, the results of which were severe pain and several visits to the doctor. Before this, she may have been afraid of snakes, but not phobic. After this experience, a phobia developed, not of cars or car doors, but of snakes. The snake phobia persisted into adulthood, at which time she sought treatment from me.
>
> (p. 192)

In a series of studies on preparedness, the psychologist Arne Ohman and his colleagues have conditioned different kinds of fears in human subjects (Ohman & Soares, 1993; Ohman et al., 1975). In one study they showed all subjects slides of faces, houses, snakes, and spiders. One group received electric shocks whenever they observed the slides of faces and houses, while the other group received shocks when they looked at snakes and spiders. Were subjects more prepared to fear snakes and spiders? Using skin reactions, called *galvanic skin responses (GSRs)*, as a measure of fear, the experimenters found that both groups learned to fear the intended objects after repeated shock pairings. But then they noted an interesting difference: after a short shock-free period, the persons who had learned to fear faces and houses stopped registering high GSRs in the presence of those objects, while the persons who had learned to fear snakes and spiders continued to show high GSRs in response to them for a long while. One interpretation is that animals and insects are stronger candidates for human phobias than faces or houses.

Researchers do not know whether human predispositions to fear are the result of evolutionary or environmental factors (Mineka & Ohman, 2002; Clum & Febbraro, 2001). Those who propose an *evolutionary* explanation argue that a tendency to fear has been transmitted genetically through the evolutionary process. Among our ancestors, the ones who more readily acquired a fear of animals, darkness, heights, and the like were more likely to survive long enough to reproduce. Proponents of an *environmental* explanation argue instead that experiences teach us early in life that certain objects are legitimate sources of fear, and this training predisposes many people to acquire corresponding phobias.

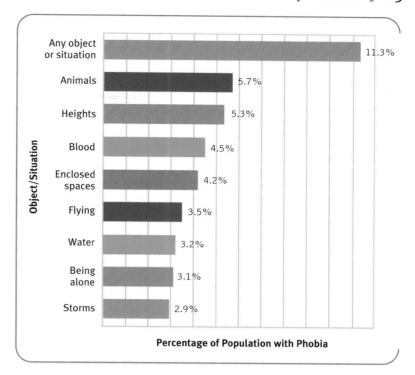

FIGURE 4-3 **How common are the specific phobias?** *Over the course of their lives, 11.3 percent of people in the United States develop a specific phobia. The most common ones are fears of certain animals and of heights. Most sufferers experience more than one specific phobia. (Adapted from Curtis et al., 1998.)*

How Are Phobias Treated?

Every theoretical model has its own approach to treating phobias, but behavioral techniques are more widely used than the rest, particularly for specific phobias. Research has shown them to be highly effective and to fare better than other approaches in most head-to-head comparisons. Thus we shall focus primarily on the behavioral interventions.

TREATMENTS FOR SPECIFIC PHOBIAS Specific phobias were among the first anxiety disorders to be treated successfully in clinical practice. The major behavioral approaches to treating them are *desensitization, flooding,* and *modeling.* Together, these approaches are called **exposure treatments** because in all of them individuals are exposed to the objects or situations they dread.

People treated by **systematic desensitization**, a technique developed by Joseph Wolpe (1997, 1987, 1969), learn to relax while gradually facing the objects or situations they fear. Since relaxation and fear are incompatible, the new relaxation response is thought to substitute for the fear response. Desensitization therapists first offer *relaxation training* to clients, teaching them how to bring on a state of deep muscle relaxation at will. In addition, the therapists help clients create a *fear hierarchy,* a list of feared objects or situations, ordered from mildly to extremely upsetting.

Then clients learn how to pair relaxation with the objects or situations they fear. While the client is in a state of relaxation, the therapist has the client face the event at the bottom of his or her hierarchy. This may be an actual confrontation, a process called *in vivo desensitization.* A person who fears heights, for example, may stand on a chair or climb a stepladder. Or the confrontation may be imagined, a process called *covert desensitization.* In this case, the person imagines the frightening event while the therapist describes it. The client moves through the entire list, pairing his or her relaxation responses with each feared item. Because the first item is only mildly frightening, it is usually only a short while before the person is able to relax totally in its presence. Over the course of several sessions, clients move up the ladder of their fears until they reach and overcome the one that frightens them most of all.

Another behavioral treatment for specific phobias is **flooding**. Flooding therapists believe that people will stop fearing things when they are exposed to them

PREPAREDNESS A predisposition to develop certain fears.

EXPOSURE TREATMENTS Behavioral treatments in which persons are exposed to the objects or situations they dread.

SYSTEMATIC DESENSITIZATION A behavioral treatment that uses relaxation training and a fear hierarchy to help clients with phobias react calmly to the objects or situations they dread.

FLOODING A treatment for phobias in which clients are exposed repeatedly and intensively to a feared object and made to see that it is actually harmless.

repeatedly and made to see that they are actually quite harmless. Clients are forced to face their feared objects or situations without relaxation training and without a gradual buildup. The flooding procedure, like desensitization, can be either in vivo or covert.

When flooding therapists guide clients in imagining feared objects or situations, they often exaggerate the description so that the clients experience intense emotional arousal. In the case of a woman with a snake phobia, the therapist had her imagine the following scene, among others:

> Close your eyes again. Picture the snake out in front of you, now make yourself pick it up. Reach down, pick it up, put it in your lap, feel it wiggling around in your lap, leave your hand on it, put your hand out and feel it wiggling around. Kind of explore its body with your fingers and hand. You don't like to do it, make yourself do it. Make yourself do it. Really grab onto the snake. Squeeze it a little bit, feel it. Feel it kind of start to wind around your hand. Let it. Leave your hand there, feel it touching your hand and winding around it, curling around your wrist.
>
> *(Hogan, 1968, p. 423)*

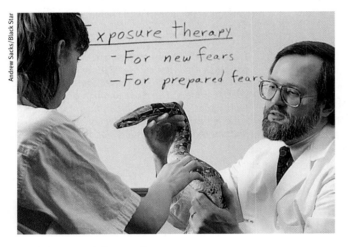

Participant modeling *In the exposure technique of participant modeling, a therapist treats a client with a snake phobia by first handling a snake himself, then encouraging the client to touch and handle it.*

In *modeling*, it is the therapist who confronts the feared object or situation while the fearful person observes (Bandura, 1977, 1971; Bandura et al., 1977). The behavioral therapist acts as a model to demonstrate that the person's fear is groundless. After several sessions many clients are able to approach the objects or situations calmly. In one version of modeling, *participant modeling*, the client is actively encouraged to join in with the therapist.

Clinical researchers have repeatedly found that each of the exposure treatments helps people with specific phobias (Barlow et al., 2002). The key to success in all these therapies appears to be *actual* contact with the feared object or situation (van Hout & Emmelkamp, 2002). In vivo desensitization is more effective than covert desensitization, in vivo flooding more effective than covert flooding, and participant modeling more helpful than strictly observational modeling (Spiegler & Guevremont, 2003).

TREATMENTS FOR SOCIAL PHOBIAS Only in recent years have clinicians been able to treat social phobias successfully (Heimberg, 2001). Their newfound success is due in part to the growing recognition that social phobias have two separate features that may feed upon each other: (1) people with the phobias may have overwhelming social fears, and (2) they may lack skill at starting conversations, communicating their needs, or meeting the needs of others. Armed with this insight, clinicians now treat social phobias by trying to reduce social fears, by providing training in social skills, or both.

HOW ARE SOCIAL FEARS REDUCED? Unlike specific phobias, which do not typically respond to psychotropic drugs, social fears are often reduced through medication (Schneier, 2001). Somewhat surprisingly, it is *antidepressant medications* that seem to be most helpful for this disorder, often more helpful than benzodiazepines or other kinds of antianxiety drugs (Rivas-Vazquez, 2001). At the same time, several types of psychotherapy have proved at least as effective as medication at reducing social fears. Moreover, people helped by these psychological treatments are apparently less likely to relapse than people treated with drugs alone (Turk et al., 2001). This finding suggests to some clinicians that the psychological approaches should always be included in the treatment of social fears.

One psychological approach is *exposure therapy* (Hofman & Barlow, 2002), the behavioral intervention so effective with specific phobias. Exposure therapists guide, encourage, and persuade clients with social fears to expose themselves to the dreaded social situations and to remain until their fears subside. Usually the exposure is gradual, and it often includes homework assignments that are carried out in social settings (Edelman & Chambless, 1995). In addition, group therapy offers an ideal setting for exposure treatments by allowing people to face social situations in an atmosphere of support and concern (Turk et al., 2001). In one group, for example, a man who was afraid that his hands would tremble in the presence of other people had to write on a blackboard in front of the group and serve tea to the other members (Emmelkamp, 1982).

Cognitive therapies have also been widely used to treat social fears, often in combination with behavioral techniques (Barlow et al., 2002). In the following discussion, Albert Ellis uses rational-emotive therapy to help a man who fears he will be rejected if he speaks up at gatherings. The discussion took place after the man had done a homework assignment in which he was to observe his self-defeating social expectations and force himself to say anything he had on his mind in social situations, no matter how stupid it might seem to him:

Sam Jones/Liaison

Conquering coasterphobia *Missing out on thousands of dollars each year because many persons are afraid of riding on roller coasters, some amusement parks offer behavioral programs to help customers overcome their fears. After "treatment," some clients are able to ride the rails with the best of them. For others, it's back to the relative calm of the Ferris wheel.*

After two weeks of this assignment, the patient came into his next session of therapy and reported: "I did what you told me to do. . . . [Every] time, just as you said, I found myself retreating from people, I said to myself: 'Now, even though you can't see it, there must be some sentences. What are they?' And I finally found them. And there were many of them! And they all seemed to say the same thing."

"What thing?"

"That I, uh, was going to be rejected. . . . [If] I related to them I was going to be rejected. And wouldn't that be perfectly awful if I was to be rejected. And there was no reason for me, uh, to take that, uh, sort of thing, and be rejected in that awful manner." . . .

"And did you do the second part of the homework assignment?"

"The forcing myself to speak up and express myself?"

"Yes, that part."

"That was worse. That was really hard. Much harder than I thought it would be. But I did it."

"And?"

"Oh, not bad at all. I spoke up several times; more than I've ever done before. Some people were very surprised. Phyllis was very surprised, too. But I spoke up." . . .

"And how did you feel after expressing yourself like that?"

"Remarkable! I don't remember when I last felt this way. I felt, uh, just remarkable—good, that is. It was really something to feel! But it was so hard. I almost didn't make it. And a couple of other times during the week I had to force myself again. But I did. And I was glad!"

(Ellis, 1962, pp. 202–203)

Studies show that rational-emotive therapy and similar cognitive approaches do help reduce social fears (Heimberg, 2001; Turk et al., 2001). And these reductions may persist for years. At the same time, research also suggests that cognitive therapy, like drug therapy and exposure therapy, does not typically overcome social phobias fully (Hofman & Barlow, 2002). It helps reduce social fear, but it does not consistently enable people to perform effectively in social settings. This is where social skills training has come to the forefront.

>>**LOOKING AROUND**

Sour Notes

Musical performers often experience enormous anxiety as a play date approaches (Steptoe, 2001). In fact, according to a survey of 1,600 professional musicians, 2 of every 10 orchestra musicians in Great Britain use psychotropic drugs to soothe their nerves (Hall, 1997). Overall, 22 percent of the musicians report long stretches of anxiety, and 28 percent experience depression. Around 40 percent have trouble sleeping through the night. Many hyperventilate.<<

How Are Social Skills Improved? In **social skills training**, therapists combine several behavioral techniques in order to help people improve their social skills. They usually model appropriate social behaviors and encourage the clients to try them out. The clients then role-play with the therapists, rehearsing their new behaviors until they become more effective. Throughout the process, therapists provide frank *feedback* and *reinforce* (praise) the clients for effective performances.

Reinforcement from other people with similar social difficulties is often more powerful than reinforcement from a therapist alone. In *social skills training groups* and *assertiveness training groups*, members try out and rehearse new social behavior with other group members. The group can also provide guidance on what is socially appropriate.

Social skills training has helped many people perform better in social situations (Spiegler & Guevremont, 2003). Some people, however, continue to experience uncomfortable levels of fear despite such treatments (Juster et al., 1996). In fact, research indicates that no single approach—drug therapy, exposure treatment, cognitive therapy, or social skills training—consistently causes social phobias to disappear (Wlazlo et al., 1990). Yet each is helpful, and when the approaches are combined, the results have been very encouraging (Barlow et al., 2002; Turk et al., 2001).

SUMMING UP

Phobias

A phobia is a severe, persistent, and unreasonable fear of a particular object, activity, or situation. There are three main categories of phobias: specific phobias, social phobias, and agoraphobia. Behavioral explanations of phobias, particularly specific phobias, are the most influential. Behaviorists believe that phobias are learned through classical conditioning or modeling, and then are maintained by avoidance behaviors.

Specific phobias have been treated most successfully by behavioral exposure techniques. The exposure may be gradual and relaxed (desensitization), intense (flooding), or vicarious (modeling).

Therapists who treat social phobias typically separate two features of this disorder: social fears and poor social skills. They try to reduce social fears by drug, exposure, group, or cognitive therapy, or a combination of these approaches. They may try to improve social skills by social skills training.

Panic Disorder

Sometimes an anxiety reaction takes the form of a smothering, nightmarish panic in which people lose control of their behavior and, in fact, are practically unaware of what they are doing. Anyone can react with panic when a real threat looms up suddenly. Some people, however, experience **panic attacks**—periodic short bouts of panic that occur suddenly, reach a peak within 10 minutes, and gradually pass.

The attacks feature at least four of the following symptoms of panic: palpitations of the heart, tingling in the hands or feet, shortness of breath, sweating, hot and cold flashes, trembling, chest pains, choking sensations, faintness, dizziness, and a feeling of unreality. Small wonder that during a panic attack many people fear they will die, go crazy, or lose control.

I was inside a very busy shopping precinct and all of a sudden it happened: in a matter of seconds I was like a mad woman. It was like a nightmare, only I was awake; everything went black and sweat poured out of me—my body, my hands and even my hair got wet through. All the blood seemed to drain out of me; I

SOCIAL SKILLS TRAINING A therapy approach that helps people learn or improve social skills and assertiveness through role-playing and rehearsing of desirable behaviors.

PANIC ATTACKS Periodic short bouts of panic that occur suddenly, reach a peak within minutes, and gradually pass.

PANIC DISORDER An anxiety disorder marked by recurrent and unpredictable panic attacks.

AGORAPHOBIA An anxiety disorder in which a person is afraid to be in places or situations from which escape might be difficult (or embarrassing) or help unavailable if paniclike symptoms were to occur.

went as white as a ghost. I felt as if I were going to collapse; it was as if I had no control over my limbs; my back and legs were very weak and I felt as though it were impossible to move. It was as if I had been taken over by some stronger force. I saw all the people looking at me—just faces, no bodies, all merged into one. My heart started pounding in my head and in my ears; I thought my heart was going to stop. I could see black and yellow lights. I could hear the voices of the people but from a long way off. I could not think of anything except the way I was feeling and that now I had to get out and run quickly or I would die. I must escape and get into the fresh air.

(Hawkrigg, 1975)

People with any of the anxiety disorders (or, for that matter, people without an anxiety disorder) may experience a panic attack when they are faced with something they dread. Some people, however, have panic attacks repeatedly and unexpectedly without apparent reason. They may be suffering from **panic disorder**. In addition to the panic attacks, people who are diagnosed with panic disorder experience dysfunctional changes in their thinking or behavior as a result of the attacks for a period of a month or more (see Table 4-6). For example, they may worry persistently about having another attack, have concerns about what such an attack means ("Am I losing my mind?"), or plan their behavior around the possibility of a future attack.

Panic disorder is often accompanied by **agoraphobia**, one of the three categories of phobia mentioned earlier. People with agoraphobia are afraid to leave the house and travel to public places or other locations where escape might be difficult or help unavailable should panic symptoms develop. The intensity of agoraphobia may fluctuate. In severe cases, people become virtual prisoners in their own homes. Their social life dwindles, and they cannot hold a job.

Until recently, clinicians failed to recognize the close link between agoraphobia and panic attacks. They now realize that panic attacks, or at least some panic-like symptoms, typically set the stage for agoraphobia (White & Barlow, 2002): after experiencing one or more unpredictable attacks, certain individuals become fearful of having new attacks in public places where help or escape might be difficult.

Not everyone with panic disorder develops agoraphobia, but many such persons do. Thus DSM-IV distinguishes *panic disorder without agoraphobia* from *panic disorder with agoraphobia*. Around 2.3 percent of all people in the United States suffer from one or the other of these patterns in a given year; 3.5 percent develop one of the patterns at some point in their lives (Carlbring et al., 2002; Kessler et al., 1994). Both kinds of panic disorder are likely to develop in late adolescence and early adulthood and are at least twice as common among women as among men (APA, 2000).

The Biological Perspective

In the 1960s, clinicians made the surprising discovery that persons with panic disorder were helped less by benzodiazepine drugs, the drugs useful in treating generalized anxiety disorder, than by certain *antidepressant drugs*, drugs that are usually used to reduce the symptoms of depression (Klein, 1964; Klein & Fink, 1962). This observation led to the first biological explanations and treatments for panic disorder.

WHAT BIOLOGICAL FACTORS CONTRIBUTE TO PANIC DISORDER? To understand the biology of panic disorder, researchers worked backward from their understanding of the antidepressant drugs that seemed to control it. They knew that

---

Table 4-6

PANIC DISORDER

1. Recurrent unexpected panic attacks.
2. A month or more of one of the following after at least one of the attacks.
   (a) Persistent concern about having additional attacks.
   (b) Worry about the implications or consequences of the attack.
   (c) Significant change in behavior related to the attacks.

Based on APA, 2000, 1994.

>>**IN THEIR WORDS**

Panic in the Real World

"They just kept pushin' forward and they would just walk right on top of you, just trample over ya like you were a piece of the ground. They wouldn't even help ya; people were just screamin' 'help me' and nobody cared."<<

Patron at The Who concert, Cincinnati, 1979, where 11 people were trampled to death (Johnson, 1987)

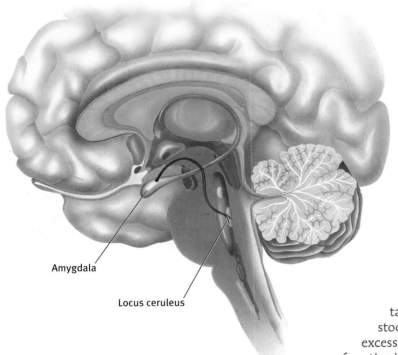

Amygdala

Locus ceruleus

FIGURE 4-4 **The biology of panic** *The locus ceruleus sends its major messages to the amygdala, a brain region known to trigger emotional reactions. Many neurons in the locus ceruleus use norepinephrine, a neurotransmitter implicated in panic disorder and in depression.*

many of the antidepressant drugs change the activity of **norepinephrine**, one of the neurotransmitters that carry messages from neuron to neuron in the brain. If the drugs also eliminated panic attacks, researchers wondered, might panic disorder be caused in the first place by abnormal norepinephrine activity?

Several studies have produced evidence that norepinephrine activity is indeed irregular in people who suffer from panic attacks (Gorman et al., 2000, 1995). For example, the **locus ceruleus** is a brain area rich in neurons that use norepinephrine. When this area is electrically stimulated in monkeys, the monkeys have a paniclike reaction, suggesting that panic reactions may be related to changes in norepinephrine activity in the locus ceruleus (Redmond, 1981, 1979, 1977) (see Figure 4-4). In another line of research, scientists have produced panic attacks in human beings by injecting them with chemicals known to affect the activity of norepinephrine (Bourin et al., 1995; Charney et al., 1990, 1987).

These findings strongly tie norepinephrine to panic attacks. Just what goes wrong, however, is still not fully understood. It is not clear, for example, whether the problem is excessive activity, deficient activity, or some other form of dysfunctioning involving norepinephrine. To complicate matters, there is growing evidence that other neurotransmitters also may have roles to play in panic disorder (Barlow, 2002; Gorman et al., 2000, 1995).

Furthermore, investigators do not know why some people have such biological abnormalities. One possibility is that a predisposition to develop panic disorder is inherited (Stein et al., 1999; Kendler et al., 1995; Torgersen, 1990, 1983). If a genetic factor is indeed at work, close relatives should have higher rates of panic disorder than more distant relatives. One study did find that among identical twins (twins who share all of their genes), if one twin had panic disorder, the other twin had the same disorder in 24 percent of cases. Among fraternal twins (who share only some of their genes), if one twin had panic disorder, the other twin had the same disorder in only 11 percent of cases (Kendler et al., 1993). Other twin studies, however, have not always found such clear trends (Stein & Uhde, 1995), leaving the issue of genetic predisposition open to debate.

DRUG THERAPIES In 1962 it was discovered that certain antidepressant drugs could prevent panic attacks or reduce their frequency. As we have seen, this finding was a surprise at first. Since then, however, studies across the world have repeatedly confirmed this observation (Keltner & Folks, 2001).

It appears that many of these antidepressant drugs restore proper activity of the neurotransmitter norepinephrine, particularly at neurons in the locus ceruleus (Gorman et al., 1995). They bring at least some improvement to 80 percent of patients who have panic disorder (Ballenger, 1998; Hirschfeld, 1992). Approximately 40 to 60 percent recover markedly or fully, and the improvements can last indefinitely, as long as the drugs are continued (McNally, 2001). In recent years *alprazolam* (Xanax) and other powerful benzodiazepine drugs have also proved very effective (Keltner & Folks, 2001).

Clinicians have also found the antidepressant drugs or powerful benzodiazepines to be helpful in most cases of panic disorder with agoraphobia (Clum & Febbraro, 2001). As the drugs eliminate or reduce a sufferer's panic attacks, he or she becomes confident enough to journey out into public places once again. Some people with this disorder, however, need a combination of medication and behavioral exposure treatment to fully overcome their agoraphobic fears (Antony & Swinson, 2000).

The Cognitive Perspective

Cognitive theorists have come to recognize that biological factors are but part of the cause of panic attacks. In their view, full panic reactions are experienced only by people who misinterpret certain physiological events that are occurring within their bodies. Cognitive treatments are aimed at changing such misinterpretations.

Joy turns to panic *Anyone is capable of experiencing panic in the face of a fast-moving and severe threat. Celebrations of soccer victories have led to several famous outbursts of panic in which thousands of fans have been injured or killed by stampeding crowds. Mindful of such tragedies, police now intervene at the earliest signs of loss of control or panic by crowd members, as we see here in the aftermath of the 2002 World Cup game in Saitama, Japan.*

THE COGNITIVE EXPLANATION: MISINTERPRETING BODILY SENSATIONS Cognitive theorists believe that panic-prone people may be very sensitive to their bodily sensations; when they unexpectedly experience certain sensations, they misinterpret them as signs of a medical catastrophe (McNally, 2001, 1999). Rather than understanding the probable cause of such sensations as "something I ate" or "a fight with the boss," the panic-prone grow more and more worried about losing control, fear the worst, lose all perspective, and rapidly plunge into panic. Moreover, they develop the belief that the "dangerous" sensations may return at any time and so set themselves up for future panic attacks.

Why might some people be prone to such misinterpretations? Clinicians have identified several possible factors (Stewart et al., 2001). Perhaps the individuals have poor coping skills or lack social support. Perhaps their childhoods were filled with unpredictable events, lack of control, chronic illnesses in the family, or parental overreactions to their children's bodily symptoms.

Whatever the precise causes, research suggests that panic-prone individuals have a high degree of what cognitive theorists have come to call **anxiety sensitivity**: they focus on their bodily sensations much of the time, are unable to assess them logically, and interpret them as potentially harmful (Schmidt & Bates, 2003; Muris et al., 2001). One study found that people who scored high on an anxiety sensitivity survey were five times more likely than other subjects to develop panic disorder (Maller & Reiss, 1992). Other studies have found that individuals with panic disorder are indeed more aware of and frightened by bodily sensations than other people (McNally, 2001).

According to cognitive theorists, people with high anxiety sensitivity are likely to experience and misinterpret certain kinds of sensations more than others. Many seem to "overbreathe," or hyperventilate, in stressful situations. Apparently the abnormal breathing makes them think they are in danger or even dying of suffocation, so they panic (Dratcu, 2000). Other commonly misinterpretted physical sensations are excitement, breathing discomfort, fullness in the abdomen, and acute anger (McNally, Hornic, & Donnell, 1995; Verburg et al., 1995). One person, on learning that her artwork had been accepted for exhibit at a gallery, became so excited that she experienced "palpitations of the heart." Misinterpreting them as a sign of a heart attack, she panicked.

In **biological challenge tests**, researchers produce hyperventilation or other biological sensations by administering drugs or by instructing subjects to breathe, exercise, or simply think in certain ways. As one might expect, people with panic disorder experience greater anxiety during these tests than people without the disorder, particularly when they believe that their bodily sensations are dangerous or out of control (Antony & Barlow, 2002).

COGNITIVE THERAPY Cognitive therapists try to correct people's misinterpretations of their body sensations (Craske & Barlow, 2001). The first step is to educate clients about the general nature of panic attacks, the actual causes of bodily sensations, and the tendency of clients to misinterpret their sensations. The next step is to teach clients to apply more accurate interpretations during stressful situations, thus short-circuiting the panic sequence at an early point. Therapists may

NOREPINEPHRINE A neurotransmitter whose abnormal activity is linked to panic disorder and depression.

LOCUS CERULEUS A small area of the brain that seems to be active in the regulation of emotions. Many of its neurons use norepinephrine.

ANXIETY SENSITIVITY A tendency to focus on one's bodily sensations, assess them illogically, and interpret them as harmful.

BIOLOGICAL CHALLENGE TEST A procedure used to produce panic in subjects or clients by having them exercise vigorously or perform some other potentially panic-inducing task in the presence of a researcher or therapist.

"*I'm sorry, I didn't hear what you said. I was listening to my body.*"

also teach clients to cope better with anxiety—for example, by applying relaxation and breathing techniques—and to distract themselves from their sensations, perhaps by striking up a conversation with someone.

Cognitive therapists may also use biological challenge procedures (called *interoceptive exposure* when applied in therapy) to produce panic sensations, so that clients can apply their new skills under watchful supervision. Individuals whose attacks are typically triggered by a rapid heart rate, for example, may be told to jump up and down for several minutes or to run up a flight of stairs. They can then practice interpreting the resulting sensations appropriately and not dwelling on them.

According to research, cognitive treatments often help people with panic disorder (Furukawa, 2003; Craske & Barlow, 2001; Stuart et al., 2000). In international studies, 85 percent of subjects given these treatments were free of panic for as long as two years or more, compared to only 13 percent of control subjects. As with drug therapy, cognitive treatments are only sometimes sufficient for persons whose panic disorders are accompanied by agoraphobia. For many such persons, therapists add exposure techniques to the cognitive treatment program—an addition that has produced high success rates.

Cognitive therapy has proved to be at least as helpful as antidepressant drugs or alprazolam in the treatment of panic disorder, sometimes more so (Barlow et al., 2000). In view of the effectiveness of both cognitive and drug treatments, many clinicians have tried combining them. It is not yet clear, however, whether or not this strategy is more effective than cognitive therapy alone (Loerch et al., 1999).

SUMMING UP

Panic Disorder

Panic attacks are periodic short bouts of panic that occur suddenly. Sufferers of panic disorder experience such attacks repeatedly and unexpectedly and without apparent reason. When panic disorder leads to agoraphobia, it is termed panic disorder with agoraphobia.

Some biological theorists believe that abnormal norepinephrine activity in the brain's locus ceruleus is the key to panic disorder. Biological therapists use certain antidepressant drugs or powerful benzodiazepines to treat people with this disorder. Patients whose panic disorder is accompanied by agoraphobia may need a combination of drug therapy and behavioral exposure treatment.

Cognitive theorists suggest that panic-prone people are very sensitive to their bodily sensations and misinterpret some of them as signs of medical catastrophe. Such persons have a high degree of anxiety sensitivity and also experience greater anxiety during biological challenge tests. Cognitive therapists teach patients to interpret their physical sensations more accurately and to cope better with anxiety. In cases of panic disorder with agoraphobia, practitioners may combine a cognitive approach with behavioral exposure techniques.

OBSESSION A persistent thought, idea, impulse, or image that is experienced repeatedly, feels intrusive, and causes anxiety.

COMPULSION A repetitive and rigid behavior or mental act that a person feels driven to perform in order to prevent or reduce anxiety.

OBSESSIVE-COMPULSIVE DISORDER A disorder in which a person has recurrent and unwanted thoughts, a need to perform repetitive and rigid actions, or both.

Obsessive-Compulsive Disorder

Obsessions are persistent thoughts, ideas, impulses, or images that seem to invade a person's consciousness. **Compulsions** are repeated and rigid behaviors or mental acts that people feel they must perform in order to prevent or reduce anxiety. As Figure 4-5 indicates, minor obsessions and compulsions are familiar to almost everyone (Sketekee & Barlow, 2002). We may find ourselves filled with thoughts about an upcoming performance or exam; worry that we forgot to turn

Table 4-7

OBSESSIVE-COMPULSIVE DISORDER

1. Recurrent obsessions or compulsions.
2. Past or present recognition that the obsessions or compulsions are excessive or unreasonable.
3. Significant distress or impairment, or disruption by symptoms for more than one hour a day.

Based on APA, 2000, 1994.

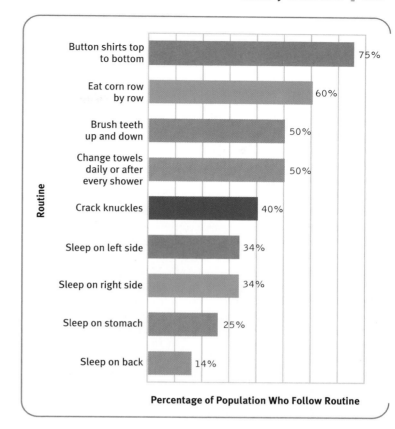

Percentage of Population Who Follow Routine

FIGURE 4-5 **Normal routines** *Most people find it comforting to follow set routines when they carry out everyday activities, and, in fact, 40 percent become irritated if they are forced to depart from their routines. (Adapted from Kanner, 1998, 1995.)*

off the stove or lock the door; or be haunted for days by the same song or melody. We may feel better when we avoid stepping on cracks, turn away from black cats, or arrange our closets in a particular manner.

Minor obsessions and compulsions can play a helpful role in life. Distracting tunes or little rituals often calm us during times of stress. A person who repeatedly hums a tune or taps his or her fingers during a test may be releasing tension and thus improving performance. Many people find it comforting to repeat religious or cultural rituals, such as touching a mezuzah, sprinkling holy water, or fingering rosary beads.

According to DSM-IV, a diagnosis of **obsessive-compulsive disorder** may be called for when obsessions or compulsions feel excessive or unreasonable, cause great distress, take up considerable time, or interfere with daily functions (see Table 4-7). Obsessive-compulsive disorder is classified as an anxiety disorder because the victims' obsessions cause great anxiety, while their compulsions are aimed at preventing or reducing anxiety. In addition, their anxiety rises if they try to resist their obsessions or compulsions.

Georgia, a woman with this disorder, observed: "I can't get to sleep unless I am sure everything in the house is in its proper place so that when I get up in the morning, the house is organized. I work like mad to set everything straight before I go to bed, but, when I get up in the morning, I can think of a thousand things that I ought to do. . . . I can't stand to know something needs doing and I haven't done it" (McNeil, 1967, pp. 26–28). Georgia's family was no less affected by her symptoms, as these comments by her husband indicate:

"Sometimes I think she never sleeps. I got up one night at 4 a.m. and there she was doing the laundry downstairs. . . . If I forget to leave my dirty shoes outside the back door she gives me a look like I had just crapped in the middle of an operating room. I stay out of the house a lot and I'm about half-stoned when I do have to be home. She even made us get rid of the dog because she said he was always filthy. When we used to have people over for supper she would jitterbug around everybody till they couldn't digest their food. I hated to call them up and ask them over because I could always hear them hem and haw and make up excuses not to come over. Even the kids are walking down the street nervous about getting dirt on them. I'm going out of my mind but you can't talk to her. She just blows up and spends twice as much time cleaning things. We have guys in to wash the walls so often I think the house is going to fall down from being scrubbed all the time."

(McNeil, 1967, pp. 26–27)

As many as 2 percent of the people in the United States and other countries throughout the world suffer from obsessive-compulsive disorder in any given year (Steketee & Barlow, 2002; Frost & Steketee, 2001). It is equally common in men and women and among people of different races and ethnic groups. The disorder usually begins by young adulthood and typically persists for many years, although its symptoms and their severity may fluctuate over time.

What Are the Features of Obsessions and Compulsions?

Obsessions are thoughts that feel both intrusive and foreign to the people who experience them. Attempts to ignore or resist these thoughts may arouse even more anxiety, and before long they come back more strongly than ever. Like Georgia, people with obsessions are quite aware that their thoughts are excessive.

Touch for luck *A University of Georgia football player touches a statue of the school mascot, a bulldog, before the homecoming game. Athletes often follow rituals that they believe will help them perform better on the field. Like compulsions, their superstitious behaviors may be reinforced by reductions in anxiety.*

Obsessions often take the form of obsessive *wishes* (for example, repeated wishes that one's spouse would die), *impulses* (repeated urges to yell out obscenities at work or in church), *images* (fleeting visions of forbidden sexual scenes), *ideas* (notions that germs are lurking everywhere), or *doubts* (concerns that one has made a wrong decision).

Certain basic themes run through the thoughts of most people troubled by obsessive thinking (APA, 2000, 1994). The most common theme appears to be dirt or contamination. Other common ones are violence and aggression, orderliness, religion, and sexuality.

Compulsions are similar to obsessions in many ways. For example, although compulsive behaviors are technically under voluntary control, the people who feel they must do them have little sense of choice in the matter. Most of these individuals recognize that their behavior is unreasonable, but they believe at the same time something terrible will happen if they don't perform the compulsions. After performing a compulsive act, they usually feel less anxious for a short while. For some people the compulsive acts develop further into detailed *rituals*. They must go through the ritual in exactly the same way every time, according to certain rules.

Like obsessions, compulsions take various forms. *Cleaning compulsions* are particularly common. Like Georgia, people with these compulsions feel compelled to keep cleaning themselves, their clothing, or their homes. The cleaning may follow ritualistic rules and be repeated dozens or hundreds of times a day. People with *checking compulsions* check the same items over and over—door locks, gas taps, important papers—to make sure that all is as it should be. Another common compulsion is the constant effort to seek *order* or *balance*. People with this compulsion keep placing certain items (clothing, books, foods) in perfect order in accordance with strict rules.

Ted is a 13-year-old referred to a Midwestern inpatient psychiatric research ward because of "senseless rituals and attention to minutiae." He can spend 3 hours centering the toilet paper roll on its holder or rearranging his bed and other objects in his room. When placing objects down, such as books or shoelaces after tying them, he picks them up and replaces them several times until they seem "straight." Although usually placid, he becomes abusive with family members who try to enter his room for fear they will move or break his objects. When he is at school, he worries that people may disturb his room. He sometimes has to be forced to interrupt his routine to attend meals. Last year he hid pieces of his clothing around the house because they wouldn't lie straight in his drawers. Moreover, he often repeats to himself, "This is perfect; you are perfect."

(Spitzer et al., 1983, p. 15)

Touching, *verbal*, and *counting* compulsions are also common. People with touching compulsions repeatedly touch or avoid touching certain items. Individuals with verbal rituals feel compelled to repeat expressions, phrases, or chants. And those with counting compulsions constantly count things they see around them.

Although some people with obsessive-compulsive disorder experience obsessions only or compulsions only, most of them experience both. In fact, compulsive acts are often a response to obsessive thoughts (Foa & Franklin, 2001). One study found that in most cases, compulsions seemed to represent a *yielding* to obsessive doubts, ideas, or urges (Akhtar et al., 1975). A woman who keeps doubting that her house is secure may yield to that obsessive doubt by repeatedly checking locks and gas jets. Or a man who obsessively fears contamination may yield to that fear by performing cleaning rituals. The study also found that compulsions sometimes serve to help *control* obsessions. A teenager describes how she tried to control her obsessive fears of contamination by performing counting and verbal rituals:

> *Patient:* If I heard the word, like, something that had to do with germs or disease, it would be considered something bad, and so I had things that would go through my mind that were sort of like "cross that out and it'll make it okay" to hear that word.
> *Interviewer:* What sort of things?
> *Patient:* Like numbers or words that seemed to be sort of like a protector.
> *Interviewer:* What numbers and what words were they?
> *Patient:* It started out to be the number 3 and multiples of 3 and then words like "soap and water," something like that; and then the multiples of 3 got really high, and they'd end up to be 124 or something like that. It got real bad then.
>
> *(Spitzer et al., 1981, p. 137)*

Many people with obsessive-compulsive disorder worry that they will act out their obsessions. A man with obsessive images of wounded loved ones may worry that he is but a step away from committing murder; or a woman with obsessive urges to yell out in church may worry that she will one day give in to them and embarrass herself. Most such concerns are unfounded. Although many obsessions lead to compulsive acts—particularly to cleaning and checking compulsions—they do not usually lead to violence or immoral conduct.

Obsessive-compulsive disorder was once among the least understood of the psychological disorders. In recent years, however, researchers have begun to learn more about it. The most influential explanations and treatments come from the psychodynamic, behavioral, cognitive, and biological models.

The Psychodynamic Perspective

As we have observed, psychodynamic theorists believe that an anxiety disorder develops when children come to fear their own id impulses and use ego defense mechanisms to lessen the resulting anxiety. What distinguishes obsessive-compulsive disorder from other anxiety disorders, in their view, is that here the battle between anxiety-provoking id impulses and anxiety-reducing defense mechanisms is not buried in the unconscious but is played out in dramatic thoughts and actions. The id impulses usually take the form of obsessive thoughts, and the ego defenses appear as counterthoughts or compulsive actions. A woman who keeps imagining her mother lying broken and bleeding, for example, may counter those thoughts with repeated safety checks throughout the house.

According to psychodynamic theorists, three defense mechanisms are particularly common in obsessive-compulsive disorder: *isolation*, *undoing*, and *reaction formation*. People who resort to **isolation** simply disown their unwanted thoughts and experience them as foreign intrusions. People who engage in **undoing** perform acts that are meant to cancel out their undesirable impulses. Those who

ISOLATION An ego defense mechanism in which people unconsciously isolate and disown undesirable and unwanted thoughts, experiencing them as foreign intrusions.

UNDOING An ego defense mechanism whereby a person unconsciously cancels out an unacceptable desire or act by performing another act.

wash their hands repeatedly, for example, may be symbolically undoing their unacceptable id impulses. People who develop a **reaction formation** take on a lifestyle that directly opposes their unacceptable impulses. A person may live a life of compulsive kindness and devotion to others in order to counter unacceptably aggressive impulses.

Sigmund Freud believed that during the *anal stage* of development (occurring at about 2 years of age) some children experience intense rage and shame that fuel the battle between id and ego. He theorized that children at this stage get pleasure from their bowel movements. When their parents try to toilet train them, the children must learn to delay their anal pleasure. If parents are premature or too harsh in their toilet training, the children may feel such rage that they develop *aggressive id impulses*—antisocial impulses that repeatedly seek expression. They may soil their clothes all the more frequently and become generally destructive, messy, or stubborn.

If parents handle the child's aggressiveness by further pressure and embarrassment, the child may also feel ashamed, guilty, and dirty. The aggressive impulses will now compete with a strong desire to control them; the child who wants to soil will also have a desire to retain. If this conflict between the id and the ego continues, it may eventually blossom into obsessive-compulsive disorder.

Not all psychodynamic theorists agree with Freud's explanation. Some believe, for example, that the aggressive impulses of people with this disorder are rooted in feelings of insecurity rather than poor toilet-training experiences (Erikson, 1963; Sullivan, 1953; Horney, 1937). Even these theorists, however, agree with Freud that people with the disorder have strong aggressive impulses and a competing need to control them. Overall, research has not clearly supported the various psychodynamic theories (Fitz, 1990).

When treating patients with obsessive-compulsive disorder, psychodynamic therapists try to help the individuals uncover and overcome their underlying conflicts and defenses, using the customary techniques of free association and therapist interpretation. Research has offered little evidence, however, that a traditional psychodynamic approach is of much help (Salzman, 1985, 1980). Thus some psychodynamic therapists now prefer to treat these patients with short-term psychodynamic therapies, which, as we observed in Chapter 2, are more direct and action-oriented than the classical techniques.

ABNORMALITY AND THE ARTS

Terror behind the Smile

Many of today's college students grew up watching *Double Dare* and *Family Double Dare*, two of the messiest game shows in television history. Young contestants were regularly splattered with goo and dunked in slime and muck (Summers, 1996). All the while, the host, Marc Summers, seemed to be having a great time, especially when the kids picked him up and threw him into the mess as well. In 1996, however, Summers revealed that his years on the show had been a personal nightmare because he had an obsessive-compulsive disorder.

Steve Labadessa/Outline

Summers says that his disorder dates back to the age of 8. He remembers cleaning his room for hours, removing and dusting every book in his bookcase. When he got the offer to host *Double Dare*, he couldn't turn down the career opportunity. But the price was high. After the shows, he would spend hours in the shower. "It was the most uncomfortable feeling in the world—a feeling of physical revulsion." Only later did Summers recognize his disorder and receive successful treatment for it. In 1999, he wrote a book titled *Everything in Its Place: My Trials and Triumphs with Obsessive-Compulsive Disorder*.

The Behavioral Perspective

Behaviorists have concentrated on explaining and treating compulsions rather than obsessions. They propose that people happen upon their compulsions quite randomly. In a fearful situation, they happen just coincidentally to wash their hands, say, or dress a certain way. When the threat lifts, they tie the improvement to that particular action. After repeated accidental associations, they believe that the action is bringing them good luck or actually changing the situation, and so they perform the same actions again and again in similar situations. The act becomes a key method of avoiding or reducing anxiety (Frost & Steketee, 2001).

The famous clinical scientist Stanley Rachman and his associates have shown that compulsions do appear to be rewarded by a reduction in anxiety. In one of their experiments, for example, 12 people with compulsive hand-washing rituals were placed in contact with objects that they considered contaminated (Hodgson & Rachman, 1972). As behaviorists would predict, the hand-washing rituals of these subjects seemed to lower their anxiety. Of course, although such investigations suggest that compulsions may eventually be rewarded by a reduction in anxiety, they do not show that compulsions are acquired in the first place as a result of such reductions.

If people keep performing compulsive behaviors in order to prevent bad outcomes and ensure positive outcomes, can't they be taught that such behaviors are not really serving this purpose? In a behavioral treatment called **exposure and response prevention**, first developed by the psychiatrist Victor Meyer (1966), clients are repeatedly exposed to objects or situations that produce anxiety, obsessive fears, and compulsive behaviors, but they are then instructed to resist performing the behaviors they feel so bound to perform. Because people find it very difficult to resist such behaviors, therapists may set an example first.

Many behavioral therapists now use exposure and response prevention, in both individual and group therapy formats. Some of them have people carry out *self-help* procedures at home (Emmelkamp, 1994). That is, they assign homework in exposure and response prevention, such as these assignments given to a woman with a cleaning compulsion:

- Do not mop the floor of your bathroom for a week. After this, clean it within three minutes, using an ordinary mop. Use this mop for other chores as well without cleaning it.

- Buy a fluffy mohair sweater and wear it for a week. When taking it off at night do not remove the bits of fluff. Do not clean your house for a week.

- You, your husband, and children all have to keep shoes on. Do not clean the house for a week.

- Drop a cookie on the contaminated floor, pick the cookie up and eat it.

- Leave the sheets and blankets on the floor and then put them on the beds. Do not change these for a week.

(Emmelkamp, 1982, pp. 299–300)

Eventually this woman was able to set up a reasonable routine for cleaning herself and her home.

Between 55 and 85 percent of clients with obsessive-compulsive disorder have been found to improve considerably with exposure and response prevention, improvements that often continue indefinitely (Kirkby, 2003; Foa & Franklin, 2001). The effectiveness of this approach suggests that people with this disorder are like the superstitious man in the old joke who keeps snapping his fingers to keep elephants away. When someone points out, "But there aren't any elephants around here," the

REACTION FORMATION An ego defense mechanism whereby a person suppresses an unacceptable desire by taking on a lifestyle that expresses the opposite desire.

EXPOSURE AND RESPONSE PREVENTION A behavioral treatment for obsessive-compulsive disorder that exposes clients to anxiety-arousing thoughts or situations and then prevents them from performing their compulsive acts.

Bob Daemmrich/The Image Works

Group work *Group therapy was once considered a lesser form of treatment, to be used mainly when individual psychotherapy was unavailable. However, many of today's therapists have found that group formats, with their special social opportunities and challenges, are often advantageous in the treatment of anxiety disorders such as social phobias, agoraphobia, and obsessive-compulsive disorder.*

man replies, "See? It works!" One review concludes, "With hindsight, it is possible to see that the obsessional individual has been snapping his fingers, and unless he stops (response prevention) and takes a look around at the same time (exposure), he isn't going to learn much of value about elephants" (Berk & Efran, 1983, p. 546).

At the same time, research has revealed certain limitations in exposure and response prevention. Few clients who receive the treatment overcome all their symptoms, and as many as one-quarter fail to improve at all (Frost & Steketee, 2001; Marks & Swinson, 1992). Also, the approach is of limited help to those who have obsessions but no compulsions (Hohagen et al., 1998; Jenike, 1992). And, finally, the favorable results have come mainly from studies of cleaning and checking compulsions. The effectiveness of this approach with other kinds of compulsions or with multiple compulsions is unclear (Ball et al., 1996).

The Cognitive Perspective

The cognitive explanation for obsessive-compulsive disorder begins by pointing out that everyone has repetitive, unwanted, and intrusive thoughts. Anyone might have thoughts of harming others or being contaminated by germs, for example, but most people dismiss or ignore them with ease (Baer, 2001). Those who develop this disorder, however, typically blame themselves for such thoughts and expect that somehow terrible things will happen (Salkovskis, 1999, 1989, 1985). To avoid such negative outcomes, they try to **neutralize** the thoughts—thinking or behaving in ways meant to put matters right or to make amends.

Neutralizing acts might include requesting special reassurance from others, deliberately thinking "good" thoughts, washing one's hands, or checking for possible sources of danger. When a neutralizing effort of some kind brings about a temporary reduction in discomfort, it is reinforced and will likely be repeated. Eventually the neutralizing thought or act is used so often that it becomes, by definition, an obsession or compulsion. At the same time, the individual becomes more and more convinced that his or her unpleasant intrusive thoughts are

Painful thoughts *Like the man in George Cruikshank's painting* The Blue Devils, *some people may find unwanted thoughts particularly threatening and debilitating. According to cognitive theorists, their reactions to intrusive thoughts may set the stage for obsessive-compulsive disorder.*

dangerous. As the person's fear of such thoughts increases, the thoughts begin to occur more frequently and they, too, become obsessions.

In support of this explanation, studies have found that people with obsessive-compulsive disorder experience intrusive thoughts more often than other people, resort to more elaborate neutralizing strategies than other people when they try to stop the unwanted thoughts, and experience reductions in anxiety after using neutralizing techniques (Sketekee & Barlow, 2002; Freeston et al., 1992).

Although everyone sometimes has undesired thoughts, only some people develop obsessive-compulsive disorder. Why do these individuals find such normal thoughts so disturbing to begin with? Researchers have found that this population tends (1) to be more depressed than other people (Frost & Steketee, 2001); (2) to have exceptionally high standards of conduct and morality (Rachman, 1993); (3) to believe that their intrusive negative thoughts are equivalent to actions and capable of causing harm to themselves or others (Wilson & Chambless, 1999); and (4) generally to believe that they should have perfect control over all their thoughts and behaviors (Frost & Steketee, 2001; Bouchard et al., 1999).

Cognitive therapists have developed approaches to obsessive-compulsive disorder that combine cognitive and behavioral techniques (Freeston et al., 1996). Therapists may use **habituation training**, for example, and have clients call forth their obsessive thoughts again and again. The clinicians expect that intense exposure to the thoughts will reduce their power to frighten or threaten, so that the thoughts produce less anxiety and trigger fewer new obsessive thoughts or compulsive acts (Salkovskis & Westbrook, 1989). In one version of habituation training, clients are simply instructed to summon obsessive thoughts or images to mind and hold them for a while. In another version, clients spend up to an hour once or twice a day listening to their own voices on tape stating their obsessive thoughts again and again. So far, support for habituation training and related cognitive-behavioral techniques has come mostly from case studies rather than empirical investigations (Ladouceur et al., 1995).

The Biological Perspective

Partly because obsessive-compulsive disorder was so difficult to explain in the past, researchers tried repeatedly to identify hidden biological factors that might contribute to it. Their efforts have come to fruition in recent years, and promising biological treatments have been developed as well.

BIOLOGICAL EXPLANATIONS Two lines of research now offer great promise for explaining the biology of obsessive-compulsive disorder. One points to abnormally low activity of the neurotransmitter *serotonin*, the other to abnormal functioning in key areas of the brain.

Serotonin, like GABA and norepinephrine, is a brain chemical that carries messages from neuron to neuron. The first clue to its role in obsessive-compulsive disorder was the surprising finding by clinical researchers that two antidepressant drugs, *clomipramine* and *fluoxetine* (Anafranil and Prozac), reduce obsessive and compulsive symptoms (Grilly, 2002; Rapoport, 1991, 1989). Since these particular drugs increase serotonin activity, some researchers concluded that the disorder is caused by low serotonin activity. In fact, only those antidepressant drugs that increase serotonin activity help in cases of obsessive-compulsive disorder; antidepressants that mainly affect other neurotransmitters typically have no effect on it (Jenike, 1992).

Another line of research has linked obsessive-compulsive disorder to abnormal brain functioning in specific regions of the brain: the **orbital region of the frontal cortex** (just above each eye) and the **caudate nuclei** (structures located within the brain region known as the *basal ganglia*). Together, these parts set up a brain circuit that converts sensory information into thoughts and actions. The circuit begins in the orbital region, where sexual, violent, and other primitive impulses normally arise. These impulses next move on to the caudate nuclei, which act as filters that send only the most powerful impulses on to the *thalamus*, the

NEUTRALIZING A person's attempt to eliminate unwanted thoughts by thinking or behaving in ways that put matters right internally, making up for the unacceptable thoughts.

HABITUATION TRAINING A therapeutic technique in which a therapist tries to call forth a client's obsessive thoughts again and again, with the expectation that the thoughts will eventually lose their power to frighten and thus to cause anxiety.

SEROTONIN A neurotransmitter whose abnormal activity is linked to depression, obsessive-compulsive disorder, and eating disorders.

ORBITAL FRONTAL CORTEX A region of the brain in which impulses involving excretion, sexuality, violence, and other primitive activities normally arise.

CAUDATE NUCLEI Structures in the brain, within the region known as the basal ganglia, that help convert sensory information into thoughts and actions.

>>**PSYCH•NOTES**
Obsessive Love

One team of researchers found that the serotonin activity of subjects who claimed to be newly in love was about as low as that of subjects with obsessive-compulsive disorder (Marazziti et al., 1999; Asimov, 1997).<<

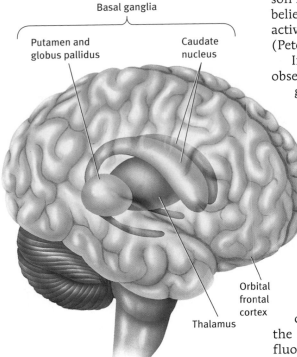

Basal ganglia

Putamen and globus pallidus

Caudate nucleus

Orbital frontal cortex

Thalamus

FIGURE 4-6 **The biology of obsessive-compulsive disorder** *A three-dimensional view of the brain shows the regions that have been linked to obsessive-compulsive disorder. These areas may be too active in people with the disorder. (Adapted from Rapoport, 1989, p. 85.)*

next stop on the circuit (see Figure 4-6). If impulses reach the thalamus, the person is driven to think further about them and perhaps to act. Many theorists now believe that either the orbital region or the caudate nuclei of some people are too active, leading to a constant eruption of troublesome thoughts and actions (Peterson et al., 1999).

In support of this theory, medical scientists have observed for years that obsessive-compulsive symptoms do sometimes arise or subside after the orbital region, caudate nuclei, or related brain areas are damaged by accident or illness (Berthier et al., 2001). Similarly, PET scans, which offer pictures of brain activity, have shown that the caudate nuclei and the orbital region of patients with obsessive-compulsive disorder are generally more active than those of control subjects (Baxter et al., 2001, 1990).

These biological variables may themselves be linked. It turns out that the neurotransmitter serotonin plays a very active role in the operation of the orbital region and the caudate nuclei; thus low serotonin activity might well interfere with the proper functioning of those brain parts.

BIOLOGICAL THERAPIES As we have seen, researchers have learned that certain antidepressant drugs are very useful in the treatment of obsessive-compulsive disorder (Kirkby, 2003). Not only do they increase brain serotonin activity, but they also produce more normal activity in the orbital region and caudate nuclei, the brain areas that have been implicated in the disorder (Baxter et al., 2001, 1992). Studies have found that clomipramine, fluoxetine, and fluvoxamine (Anafranil, Prozac, and Luvox) bring improvement to between 50 and 80 percent of those with obsessive-compulsive disorder (Grilly, 2002). The obsessions and compulsions do not usually disappear totally, but on average they are cut almost in half within eight weeks of treatment (DeVeaugh-Geiss et al., 1992). People who are treated with drugs alone, however, tend to relapse if the medication is stopped (Maina et al., 2001).

Thus the treatment of obsessive-compulsive disorder, like that of panic disorder, has improved greatly over the past decade. Once a very stubborn problem, obsessive-compulsive disorder is now helped by several forms of treatment, particularly exposure and response prevention and antidepressant drugs, often used in combination (Foster & Eisler, 2001). In fact, at least two studies suggest that the behavioral and biological approaches may ultimately have the same effect on the brain. In these investigations, both subjects who responded to exposure and response prevention and those who responded to antidepressant drugs showed marked reductions in activity in the caudate nuclei (Schwartz et al., 1996; Baxter et al., 1992).

SUMMING UP | Obsessive-Compulsive Disorder

People with obsessive-compulsive disorder experience obsessions or perform compulsions or both. Compulsions are often a response to obsessive thoughts.

According to the psychodynamic view, obsessive-compulsive disorder arises out of a battle between id impulses and ego defense mechanisms. Behaviorists, on the other hand, believe that compulsive behaviors develop through chance associations. The leading behavioral treatment combines prolonged exposure with response prevention.

Cognitive theorists believe that obsessive-compulsive disorder grows from a normal human tendency to have unwanted and unpleasant thoughts. The efforts of some people to understand, eliminate, or avoid such thoughts actually lead to obsessions and compulsions. Biological researchers have linked obsessive-compulsive disorder to low serotonin activity and abnormal functioning in the orbital region of the frontal cortex and in the caudate nuclei. Antidepressant drugs that raise serotonin activity are a useful form of treatment.

CROSSROADS:
Diathesis-Stress in Action

Clinicians and researchers have developed many ideas about generalized anxiety disorder, phobias, panic disorder, and obsessive-compulsive disorder. At times, however, the sheer quantity of concepts and findings makes it difficult to grasp what is and what is not really known about the disorders.

Overall, it is fair to say that clinicians know more about the causes of phobias, panic disorder, and obsessive-compulsive disorder than about generalized anxiety disorder, even though the latter problem has been studied the longest of all the anxiety disorders. It is worth noting that the insights about panic disorder and obsessive-compulsive disorder—once among the field's most puzzling patterns—did not unfold until clinical theorists took a look at the disorders from more than one perspective and integrated those views. Today's cognitive explanation of panic disorder, for example, builds squarely on the biological idea that the disorder begins with unusual physical sensations. Similarly, the cognitive explanation of obsessive-compulsive disorder takes its lead from the biological position that some persons are predisposed to experience more unwanted and intrusive thoughts than other persons.

It may be that a better understanding of generalized anxiety disorder awaits a similar integration of the various models. In fact, a growing number of theorists are already coming to believe that people develop generalized anxiety disorder only when biological, psychological, and sociocultural factors are all at work (Brown et al., 2001). Adopting a *diathesis-stress* perspective, these theorists suggest that individuals with the disorder typically have a biological vulnerability toward experiencing anxiety that is brought to the surface by psychological and sociocultural forces (Kazdin & Weisz, 1998). Genetic investigators have discovered that certain genes may determine whether a person reacts to life's stressors calmly or in a tense manner, and developmental researchers have found that even during the earliest stages of life some infants consistently become aroused when stimulated while other infants remain quiet (Barlow, 2002; Plomin et al., 1997; Kalin, 1993). Perhaps the easily aroused infants have inherited defects in GABA functioning or other biological limitations that predispose them to generalized anxiety disorder. If, over the course of their lives, these individuals also face intense societal pressures and learn to interpret the world as a dangerous place, they may be candidates for developing the disorder.

An integration of insights from the various models may also shed light on phobias. Several studies suggest, for example, that certain infants are born with a style of social inhibition or shyness that may increase their risk of developing a social phobia (Kagan & Snidman, 1999, 1991). Perhaps people must have both a genetic predisposition and unfortunate conditioning experiences if they are to develop particular phobias.

In the treatment realm, integration of the models is already on display for each of the anxiety disorders. Therapists have discovered, for example, that treatment is at least sometimes more effective when medications are combined with cognitive techniques to treat panic disorders and with behavioral techniques to treat obsessive-compulsive disorder. Similarly, cognitive techniques such as self-instruction training are often combined with relaxation training or biofeedback in the treatment of generalized anxiety disorder—a package known as a **stress management program**. And treatment programs for social phobias often include a combination of medications, exposure therapy, cognitive therapy, and social skills training. For the millions of people who suffer from these various disorders, such treatment combinations are a welcome development.

"Wait a minute—I know there's something we've forgotten to worry about."

©2002 The New Yorker Collection from cartoonbank.com.

STRESS MANAGEMENT PROGRAM An approach to treating generalized and other anxiety disorders that teaches clients techniques for reducing and controlling stress.

CRITICAL THOUGHTS

1. How might antianxiety drugs be given so as to take advantage of their helpful effects yet reduce their undesired effects? *pp. 105–106*

2. Today's human-subject review boards probably would not permit Watson and Rayner to conduct their conditioning study on Little Albert. What concerns might they raise about the procedure? Do these con-cerns outweigh the insights gained from this study? *p. 112*

3. Why do so many professional performers seem particularly prone to social anxiety? Wouldn't their repeated exposure to audiences lead to a reduction in fear? *pp. 109, 115*

4. Why might people whose childhoods were filled with unpre-dictable or uncontrollable events or by chronic family illnesses be inaccurate interpreters of their bodily sensations? *p. 119*

5. Can you think of instances when you instinctively tried a simple version of exposure and response prevention in order to stop behaving in certain ways? Were your efforts successful? *pp. 125–126*

KEY TERMS

fear *p. 95*
generalized anxiety disorder *p. 96*
unconditional positive regard *p. 100*
client-centered therapy *p. 100*
basic irrational assumptions *p. 101*
rational-emotive therapy *p. 102*
self-instruction training *p. 103*
family pedigree study *p. 104*
benzodiazepines *p. 105*
gamma-aminobutyric acid (GABA) *p. 105*
relaxation training *p. 106*

biofeedback *p. 107*
specific phobia *p. 108*
social phobia *p. 108*
agoraphobia *pp. 108, 117*
classical conditioning *p. 110*
modeling *p. 111*
preparedness *p. 112*
exposure treatments *p. 113*
systematic desensitization *p. 113*
fear hierarchy *p. 113*
social skills training *p. 116*

panic disorder *p. 117*
norepinephrine *p. 118*
locus ceruleus *p. 118*
anxiety sensitivity *p. 119*
biological challenge test *p. 119*
obsessive-compulsive disorder *p. 121*
exposure and response prevention *p. 125*
neutralizing *p. 126*
serotonin *p. 127*
orbital frontal cortex *p. 127*
caudate nuclei *p. 127*

QUICK QUIZ

1. What are the key principles in the sociocultural, psychodynamic, humanistic, cognitive, and biological explanations of generalized anxiety disorder? *pp. 97–107*

2. How effective have treatments been for generalized anxiety disorder? *pp. 99–107*

3. Define and compare the three kinds of phobias. *pp. 108–109, 117*

4. How do behaviorists explain phobias? What evidence exists for these explanations? *pp. 110–113*

5. Describe the three behavioral exposure techniques used to treat specific phobias. *pp. 113–114*

6. What are the two components of a social phobia, and how is each of them addressed in treatment? *pp. 114–116*

7. How do biological and cognitive theorists explain panic disorder? What are the leading biological and cognitive treatments for this disorder? *pp. 117–120*

8. Describe various types of obsessions and compulsions *pp. 122–123*

9. Which factors do psychodynamic, behavioral, cognitive, and biological theorists believe are at work in obsessive-compulsive disorder? *pp. 123–128*

10. Describe and compare the effectiveness of exposure and response prevention and antidepressant medications as treatments for obsessive-compulsive disorder. *pp. 125–126, 128*

SEARCH THE *FUNDAMENTALS OF ABNORMAL PSYCHOLOGY* CD-ROM FOR

▲ Chapter 4 Video Case Enrichment
  How does worrying affect psychological functioning?
  How disruptive are obsessions and compulsions?

▲ Chapter 4 Practical, Research, and Decision-Making Exercises
  Irrational assumptions in action
  Distinguishing bothersome fears from phobias
  Detecting superstitions and habits in everyday life

▲ Chapter 4 Practice Test and Feedback

LOG ON TO THE COMER WEB PAGE FOR

▲ Suggested Web links, exercises, FAQ page, additional Chapter 4 practice test questions
  <www.worthpublishers.com/comer>

<<<

JUAN GENOVES, 1978

Stress Disorders

Mark remembers his first "firefight" and encountering the VC [Viet Cong] for the first time. He lost all bladder and bowel control—in a matter of a few minutes. In his own words, "I was scared and literally shitless; I pissed all over myself, and shit all over myself too. Man, all hell broke loose. I tell you, I was so scared, I thought I would never make it out alive. I was convinced of that. Charlie had us pinned down and [was] hitting the shit out of us for hours. We had to call in the napalm and the bombing." During the first fight, Mark, an infantryman, experienced gruesome sights and strange sounds in battle. He witnessed headless bodies. "One guy said to me, 'Hey, Mark, new greenhorn boy, you saw that head go flying off that gook's shoulder. Isn't that something?' " Within 2 weeks Mark saw the head of a running comrade blown off his shoulders, the headless body moving for a few feet before falling to the ground. Mark, nauseous and vomiting for a long time, couldn't see himself surviving much longer: "I couldn't get that sight out of my head; it just kept on coming back to me in my dreams, nightmares. Like clockwork, I'd see R's head flying, and his headless body falling to the ground. I knew the guy. He was very good to me when I first got to the unit. Nobody else seemed to give a damn about me; he broke me in. It's like I would see his head and body, you know, man, wow!" Mark often found himself crying during his first weeks of combat. "I wanted to go home. I was so lonely, helpless, and really scared. But I knew I could not go home until my year was up."

(Brende & Parson, 1985, pp. 23–24)

Mark's reaction to the horror of combat is normal and understandable. During battle, soldiers often become highly anxious and depressed and physically ill. And for many the effects of such stress continue well beyond the combat experience itself.

But it is not just combat soldiers who are affected by stress. Nor does stress have to rise to the level of combat trauma to have a marked effect on psychological and physical functioning. Stress comes in all sizes and shapes, and we are all greatly affected by it.

We feel some degree of stress whenever we are faced with demands or opportunities that require us to change in some manner. The state of stress has two components: a *stressor*, the event that creates the demands, and a *stress response*, the person's reactions to the demands. The stressors of life may include annoying everyday hassles, such as rush-hour traffic; turning-point events, such as college graduation or marriage; long-term problems, such as poverty or poor health; or traumatic events, such as major accidents, assaults, or military combat. Our response to such stressors is influenced by the way we judge both the events and our capacity to react to them in an effective way (Pretzer et al., 2002; Lazarus & Folkman, 1984). People who sense that they have the ability and the resources to cope are more likely to take stressors in stride and to respond well.

When we view a stressor as threatening, a natural reaction is arousal and a sense of fear—a response frequently on display in Chapter 4. As we observed in that chapter, fear is actually a package of responses—*physical*, *emotional*, and *cognitive*. Physically, we perspire, our breathing quickens, our muscles tense, and our hearts beat faster. Turning pale, developing goose

AUTONOMIC NERVOUS SYSTEM (ANS) The network of nerve fibers that connect the central nervous system to all the other organs of the body.

ENDOCRINE SYSTEM The system of glands located throughout the body that help control important activities such as growth and sexual activity.

SYMPATHETIC NERVOUS SYSTEM The nerve fibers of the autonomic nervous system that quicken the heartbeat and produce other changes experienced as arousal and fear.

PARASYMPATHETIC NERVOUS SYSTEM The nerve fibers of the autonomic nervous system that help maintain normal organ functioning. They also slow organ functioning after stimulation and return other bodily processes to normal.

HYPOTHALAMIC-PITUITARY-ADRENAL (HPA) PATHWAY One route by which the brain and body produce arousal and fear. At times of stress, the hypothalamus signals the pituitary gland, which in turn signals the adrenal glands. Stress hormones are then released to various body organs.

CORTICOSTEROIDS A group of hormones, including cortisol, released by the adrenal glands at times of stress.

TRAIT ANXIETY The general level of anxiety that a person brings to the various events in his or her life.

bumps, and feeling nauseated are other physical reactions. Emotional responses to extreme threats include horror, dread, and even panic, while in the cognitive realm fear can disturb our ability to concentrate and change our view of the world. We may exaggerate the harm that actually threatens us or later remember things incorrectly.

Stress reactions, and the sense of fear they produce, are often at play in psychological disorders. People who experience a large number of stressful events are particularly vulnerable to the onset of the anxiety disorders that we examined in Chapter 4. Similarly, increases in stress have been linked to the onset of depression, schizophrenia, sexual dysfunctioning, and yet other psychological problems.

In addition, stress plays a more central role in certain psychological and physical disorders (Suinn, 2001). In such disorders, the features of stress become severe and debilitating, linger for a long time, and may make it impossible for the individual to live a normal life. The key psychological stress disorders are *acute stress disorder* and *posttraumatic stress disorder*. DSM-IV technically lists these patterns as anxiety disorders, but as we shall see, their features extend far beyond the symptoms of anxiety. The physical stress disorders are typically called *psychophysiological disorders*, problems that DSM-IV now lists under the heading *psychological factors affecting medical condition*. These psychological and physical stress disorders are the focus of this chapter. Before examining them, however, we need to understand just how the brain and body react to stress.

Stress and Arousal: The Fight-or-Flight Response

The features of arousal and fear are set in motion by the brain area called the *hypothalamus*. When our brain interprets a situation as dangerous, neurotransmitters in the hypothalamus are released, triggering the firing of neurons throughout the brain and the release of chemicals throughout the body. In particular, the hypothalamus activates two important systems—the *autonomic nervous system* and the *endocrine system*. The **autonomic nervous system** (**ANS**) is the extensive network of nerve fibers that connect the *central nervous system* (the brain and spinal cord) to all the other organs of the body. These fibers help control the *involuntary* activities of the organs—breathing, heartbeat, blood pressure, perspiration, and the like (see Figure 5-1). The **endocrine system** is the network of *glands* located throughout the body. (As we observed in Chapter 3, glands release *hormones* into the bloodstream and on to the various body organs.) The autonomic nervous system and the endocrine system often overlap in their responsibilities and activities. There are two pathways, or routes, by which these systems produce arousal and fear reactions—the *sympathetic nervous system* pathway and the *hypothalamic-pituitary-adrenal* pathway.

When we face a dangerous situation, the hypothalamus first excites the **sympathetic nervous system**, a special group of autonomic nervous system fibers that work to quicken our heartbeat and produce the other changes that we experience as fear or anxiety. These nerves may stimulate the organs of the body directly—for example, they may directly stimulate the heart and increase heart rate. The nerves may also affect the organs indirectly, by stimulating the *adrenal glands* (glands located on top of the kidneys), particularly an area of these glands called the *adrenal medulla*. When the adrenal medulla is stimulated, the chemicals *epinephrine* (*adrenaline*) and *norepinephrine* (*noradrenaline*) are released. We have already observed that these chemicals are important neurotransmitters when they operate in the brain (pp. 34, 117–118). When released from the adrenal medulla, however, they act as hormones and travel through the bloodstream to various organs and muscles, further producing arousal and fear.

Computer challenged *The modern world offers all kinds of opportunities for stress, both invited and uninvited. An audience watches as the human chess champion Gary Kasparov struggles against the computer champion Deep Blue.*

Adam Nadel/AP Photo

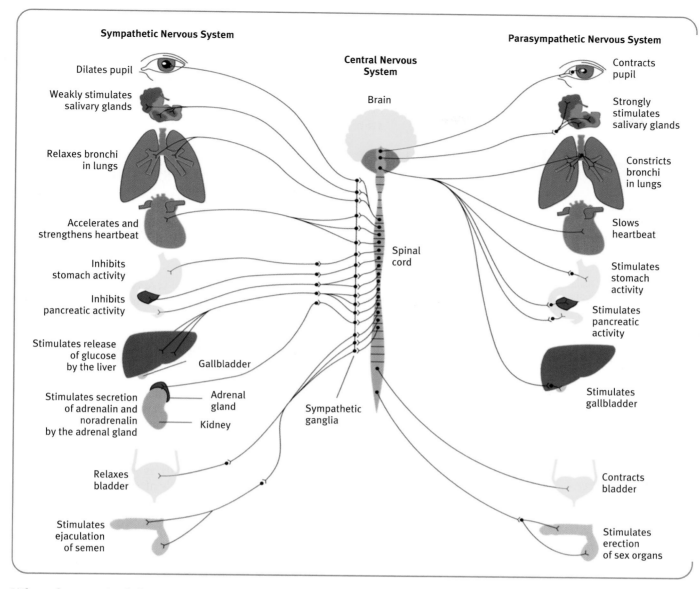

Sympathetic Nervous System

Dilates pupil

Weakly stimulates salivary glands

Relaxes bronchi in lungs

Accelerates and strengthens heartbeat

Inhibits stomach activity

Inhibits pancreatic activity

Stimulates release of glucose by the liver

Gallbladder

Stimulates secretion of adrenalin and noradrenalin by the adrenal gland

Adrenal gland

Kidney

Relaxes bladder

Stimulates ejaculation of semen

Central Nervous System

Brain

Spinal cord

Sympathetic ganglia

Parasympathetic Nervous System

Contracts pupil

Strongly stimulates salivary glands

Constricts bronchi in lungs

Slows heartbeat

Stimulates stomach activity

Stimulates pancreatic activity

Stimulates gallbladder

Contracts bladder

Stimulates erection of sex organs

When the perceived danger passes, a second group of autonomic nervous system fibers, called the **parasympathetic nervous system**, help return our heartbeat and other body processes to normal. Together the sympathetic and parasympathetic nervous systems help control our arousal and fear reactions.

The second pathway by which arousal and fear reactions are produced is the **hypothalamic-pituitary-adrenal (HPA) pathway** (see Figure 5-2 on the next page). When we are faced by stressors, the hypothalamus also signals the *pituitary gland*, which lies nearby, to release the *adrenocorticotropic hormone (ACTH)*, sometimes called the body's "major stress hormone." ACTH, in turn, stimulates yet another part of the adrenal glands, an area called the *adrenal cortex*, triggering the release of a group of stress hormones called **corticosteroids**, including the hormone *cortisol*. These corticosteroids travel to various body organs where they further produce arousal and fear reactions.

The reactions on display in these two pathways are collectively referred to as the *fight-or-flight* response, precisely because they arouse our body and prepare us for a response to danger. We all have particular patterns of autonomic and endocrine functioning and so particular ways of experiencing arousal and fear. Some people are almost always relaxed, while others typically feel some tension, even when no threat is apparent. A person's general level of arousal and anxiety is sometimes called **trait anxiety**, because it seems to be a general trait that each of us brings to the events in our lives (Spielberger, 1985, 1972, 1966). Psychologists have found that differences in trait anxiety appear soon after birth (Kagan & Snidman, 1999; Kalin, 1993).

FIGURE 5-1 **The autonomic nervous system (ANS)** *When the sympathetic division of the ANS is activated, it stimulates some organs and inhibits others. The result is a state of general arousal. In contrast, activation of the parasympathetic division leads to an overall calming effect.*

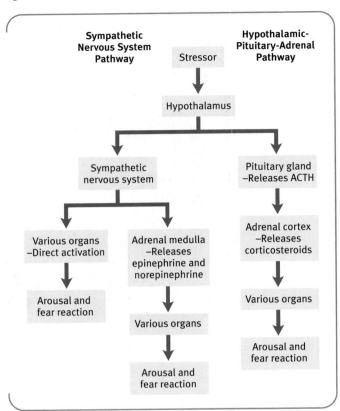

FIGURE 5-2 **Pathways of arousal and fear**
When we are confronted by a stressor, our bodies produce arousal and fear reactions through two pathways. In one, the hypothalamus sends a message to the sympathetic nervous system, which then activates key body organs, either directly or by causing the adrenal medulla to release epinephrine and norepinephrine into the bloodstream. In the other pathway, the hypothalamus sends a message to the pituitary gland, which then signals the adrenal cortex to release corticosteroids—the stress hormones—into the bloodstream.

SITUATION ANXIETY The various levels of anxiety produced in a person by different situations. Also called *state anxiety*.

ACUTE STRESS DISORDER An anxiety disorder in which fear and related symptoms are experienced soon after a traumatic event and last less than a month.

POSTTRAUMATIC STRESS DISORDER An anxiety disorder in which fear and related symptoms continue to be experienced long after a traumatic event.

People also differ in their sense of which situations are threatening (Turgeon & Chartrand, 2003). Walking through a forest may be fearsome for one person but relaxing for another. Flying in an airplane may arouse terror in some people and boredom in others. Such variations are called differences in **situation**, or **state**, **anxiety**.

The Psychological Stress Disorders: Acute and Posttraumatic Stress Disorders

At the beginning of this chapter we observed Mark's reaction to the stress of combat and noted that it is common for persons in such situations to become anxious and depressed. For some, however, such symptoms persist well after the situation is over. These people may be suffering from **acute stress disorder** or **posttraumatic stress disorder**, patterns that arise in reaction to a psychologically traumatic event. The event usually involves actual or threatened serious injury to the person or to a family member or friend. Unlike the anxiety disorders that we examined in Chapter 4, which typically are triggered by situations that most people would not find threatening, the situations that cause acute stress disorder or posttraumatic stress disorder—combat, rape, an earthquake, an airplane crash—would be traumatic for anyone.

If the symptoms begin within four weeks of the traumatic event and last for less than a month, DSM-IV assigns a diagnosis of *acute stress disorder* (APA, 2000, 1994). If the symptoms continue longer than a month, a diagnosis of *posttraumatic stress disorder* is given. The symptoms of posttraumatic stress disorder may begin either shortly after the traumatic event or months or years afterward. Many cases of acute stress disorder develop into posttraumatic stress disorder (Bremner, 2002). Aside from the differences in onset and how long they last, the symptoms of these two disorders are almost identical:

Reexperiencing the traumatic event People may be battered by recurring memories, dreams, or nightmares connected to the event. A few relive the event so vividly in their minds (flashbacks) that they think it is actually happening again.

Avoidance People will usually avoid activities that remind them of the traumatic event and will try to avoid related thoughts, feelings, or conversations.

Reduced responsiveness People feel detached from other people or lose interest in activities that once brought enjoyment. Some experience symptoms of *dissociation*, or psychological separation: they feel dazed, have trouble remembering things, or have a sense of derealization (feeling that the environment is unreal or strange.

Increased arousal, anxiety, and guilt People with these disorders may feel overly alert, be easily startled, develop sleep problems, and have trouble concentrating. They may feel extreme guilt because they survived the traumatic event while others did not. Some also feel guilty about what they may have had to do to survive.

We can see some of these symptoms in the recollections of a Vietnam combat veterans years after he returned home:

I can't get the memories out of my mind! The images come flooding back in vivid detail, triggered by the most inconsequential things, like a door slamming or the smell of stir-fried pork. Last night I went to bed, was having a good sleep for a change. Then in the early morning a storm-front passed through and there was a bolt of crackling thunder. I awoke instantly, frozen in fear. I am right back in Vietnam, in the middle of the monsoon season at my guard post. I am sure I'll get hit in the next volley and convinced I will die. My hands are freezing, yet sweat pours from my entire body. I feel each hair on the back of my neck standing on end. I can't catch my breath and my heart is pounding. I smell a damp sulfur smell.

(Davis, 1992)

The horror of combat *Soldiers often react to combat with severe anxiety or depression or both. These immediate responses to battle have at various times been called "shell shock," "combat fatigue," and most recently "acute stress disorder."*

What Triggers a Psychological Stress Disorder?

An acute or posttraumatic stress disorder can occur at any age, even in childhood (Fletcher, 2003), and can affect one's personal, family, social, or occupational life (Resick, 2001). People with these stress disorders may also experience depression or substance abuse. Some become suicidal (Kotler et al., 2001). Around 4 percent of people in the United States experience one of the stress disorders in any given year; 8 percent suffer from one of them during their lifetimes (Bremner, 2002; Kessler et al., 1994). Women are at least twice as likely as men to develop the disorders: around 20 percent of women who are exposed to a serious trauma may develop one, compared to 8 percent of men (Ursano et al., 1999; Kessler et al., 1995). While any traumatic event can trigger a stress disorder, some are particularly likely to do so. Among the most common are combat, disasters, and abuse and victimization.

COMBAT AND STRESS DISORDERS For years clinicians have recognized that many soldiers develop symptoms of severe anxiety and depression *during* combat (Bremner, 2002; Oei et al., 1990). It was called "shell shock" during World War I and "combat fatigue" during World War II and the Korean War (Figley, 1978). Not until after the Vietnam War, however, did clinicians learn that many soldiers also experience serious psychological symptoms *after* combat.

By the late 1970s, it became apparent that many Vietnam combat veterans were still experiencing war-related psychological problems (Williams, 1983). We now know that as many as 29 percent of all veterans, male and female, who served in Vietnam suffered an acute or posttraumatic stress disorder, while another 22 percent suffered from at least some stress symptoms (Weiss et al., 1992). In fact, 10 percent of the veterans of this war still experience posttraumatic stress symptoms, including flashbacks, night terrors, nightmares, and persistent images and thoughts.

DISASTERS AND STRESS DISORDERS Acute and posttraumatic stress disorders may also follow natural and accidental disasters such as earthquakes, floods, tornadoes, fires, airplane crashes, and serious car accidents (see Table 5-1). In fact, because they occur more often, civilian traumas have been the cause of stress disorders at least 10 times as often as combat traumas (Bremner, 2002). Studies have found, for example, that as many as one-third of victims—adult or child—of serious traffic accidents may develop posttraumatic stress disorder within a year of the accident (Blanchard & Hickling, 2004; Ursano et al., 1999).

Similarly, several studies found stress reactions among the survivors of

Table 5-1

Worst Natural Disasters of the Twentieth Century

DISASTER	YEAR	LOCATION	NUMBER KILLED
Flood	1926	Huang He River, China	3,700,000
Earthquake	1926	Tangshan, China	242,419
Volcanic eruption	1902	Mont-Pélée, Martinique	40,000
Landslide	1970	Yungay, Peru	17,500
Tidal wave	1960	Agadir, Morocco	12,000
Avalanche	1916	Italian Alps	10,000
Tornado	1989	Shaturia, Bangladesh	1,300

Adapted from Ash, 2001, 1999, 1998.

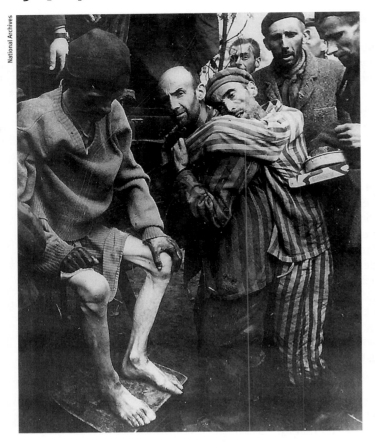

National Archives

Victimization and posttraumatic stress disorder
Many survivors of Nazi concentration camps faced a long road back to psychological health (Joffe et al., 2003). Because knowledge of posttraumatic stress disorder was nonexistent until recent years, most survivors had to find their way back without professional help.

Hurricane Andrew, the storm that ravaged Florida and other parts of the southeastern United States in 1992 (Vernberg et al., 1996). By a month after the storm the number of calls received by the domestic violence hot line in Miami and the number of women applying for police protection had doubled (Treaster, 1992). By six months after the storm it was apparent that many elementary-school-age children were also victims of posttraumatic stress disorder; their symptoms ranged from misbehavior in school to failing grades and problems with sleep (Fivush et al., 2004; Vernberg et al., 1996).

VICTIMIZATION AND STRESS DISORDERS People who have been abused, victimized, or terrorized often experience lingering stress symptoms. Research suggests that more than one-third of all victims of physical or sexual assault develop posttraumatic stress disorder (Jaycox & Foa, 2001). Similarly, as many as half of all civilians who are directly exposed to terrorism or torture may develop this disorder.

SEXUAL ASSAULT A common form of victimization in our society today is sexual assault. **Rape** is forced sexual intercourse or another sexual act committed against a nonconsenting person or intercourse with an underage person. Surveys suggest that in the United States more than 876,000 persons are victims of rape each year (NCVS, 1998). Most rapists are men and most victims are women. Around one in seven women is raped at some time during her life (Keane & Barlow, 2002). Surveys also suggest that most rape victims are young: 29 percent are under 11 years old, 32 percent are between the ages of 11 and 17, and 29 percent are between 18 and 29. More than 80 percent of the victims are raped by acquaintances or relatives (NCVS, 1998; Koss, 1992).

The psychological impact of rape on a victim is immediate and may last a long time (Koss & Kilpatrick, 2001). Rape victims typically experience enormous distress during the week after the assault. Stress continues to rise for the next 3 weeks, maintains a peak level for another month or so, and then starts to improve (Koss, 1993). In one study, 94 percent of rape victims fully qualified for a clinical diagnosis of acute stress disorder when they were observed around 12 days after the assault (Rothbaum et al., 1992). Although most rape victims improve psychologically within 3 or 4 months, the effects may persist for up to 18 months or longer. Victims typically continue to have higher than average levels of anxiety, suspiciousness, depression, self-esteem problems, self-blame, flashbacks, sleep problems, and sexual dysfunction (Thompson et al., 2003). The lingering psychological impact of rape is apparent in the following case description:

Mary Billings is a 33-year-old divorced nurse, referred to the Victim Clinic at Bedford Psychiatric Hospital for counseling by her supervisory head nurse. Mary had been raped two months ago. The assailant gained entry to her apartment while she was sleeping, and she awoke to find him on top of her. He was armed with a knife and threatened to kill her and her child (who was asleep in the next room) if she did not submit to his demands. He forced her to undress and repeatedly raped her vaginally over a period of 1 hour. He then admonished her that if she told anyone or reported the incident to the police he would return and assault her child.

After he left, she called her boyfriend, who came to her apartment right away. He helped her contact the Sex Crimes Unit of the Police Department, which is currently investigating the case. He then took her to a local hospital for a physical examination and collection of evidence for the police (traces of sperm, pubic hair samples, fingernail scrapings). She was given antibiotics as prophylaxis against venereal disease. Mary then returned home with a girlfriend who spent the remainder of the night with her.

Over the next few weeks Mary continued to be afraid of being alone and had her girlfriend move in with her. She became preoccupied with thoughts of what had happened to her and the possibility that it could happen again. Mary was frightened that the rapist might return to her apartment and therefore had additional locks installed on both the door and the windows. She was so upset and had such difficulty concentrating that she decided she could not yet return to work. When she did return to work several weeks later, she was still clearly upset, and her supervisor suggested that she might be helped by counseling.

During the clinic interview, Mary was coherent and spoke quite rationally in a hushed voice. She reported recurrent and intrusive thoughts about the sexual assault, to the extent that her concentration was impaired and she had difficulty doing chores such as making meals for herself and her daughter. She felt she was not able to be effective at work, still felt afraid to leave her home, to answer her phone, and had little interest in contacting friends or relatives.

. . . [Mary] talked in the same tone of voice whether discussing the assault or less emotionally charged topics, such as her work history. She was easily startled by an unexpected noise. She also was unable to fall asleep because she kept thinking about the assault. She had no desire to eat, and when she did attempt it, she felt nauseated. Mary was repelled by the thought of sex and stated that she did not want to have sex for a long time, although she was willing to be held and comforted by her boyfriend.

(Spitzer et al., 1983, pp. 20–21)

Although many rape victims are injured by their attacker or experience other physical problems as a result of their assault, only half receive the kind of formal medical care afforded Mary (Beebe, 1991; Koss et al., 1991). Between 4 and 30 percent of victims develop a sexually transmitted disease (Koss, 1993; Murphy, 1990) and 5 percent become pregnant (Beebe, 1991; Koss et al., 1991), yet surveys reveal that at least 60 percent of rape victims fail to receive pregnancy testing, preventive measures, or testing for exposure to HIV (National Victims Center, 1992).

Female victims of rape and other crimes are also much more likely than other women to suffer serious long-term health problems (Leserman et al., 1996; Koss & Heslet, 1992). Interviews with 390 women revealed that such victims had poorer physical well-being for at least five years after the crime and made twice as many visits to physicians.

As we shall see in Chapter 14, ongoing victimization and abuse in the family—specifically child and spouse abuse—may also lead to psychological stress disorders (Safren et al., 2002). Because these forms of abuse may occur over the long term and violate family trust, many victims develop other symptoms and disorders as well (Kemp et al., 1995).

TERRORISM People who are victims of terrorism or who live under the threat of terrorism often experience posttraumatic stress symptoms (Schlenger et al., 2002). Unfortunately, this source of traumatic stress is on the rise in our society. Few will ever forget the events of September 11, 2001, when hijacked airplanes crashed into and brought down the World Trade Center in New York City and partially destroyed the Pentagon in Washington, D.C., killing thousands of victims and rescue workers and forcing thousands more to desperately run, crawl, and even dig their way to safety. One of the many legacies of this infamous event is the lingering psychological effect that it has had on those people who were immediately affected and their family members, and on tens of millions of others who were traumatized simply by watching images of the disaster on their television sets as the day unfolded (Bremner, 2002). A number of recent studies clarify that stress reactions were common among victims and observers in the days and months following the terrorist attacks, and that these posttraumatic stress symptoms will, in many cases, linger for years.

>>**PSYCH•NOTES**
Victims of Violence

Gender Differences Rates of reported rape and other sexual assaults against women are 10 times higher than those against men (U.S. Department of Justice, 1995). Over 80 percent of male rapes are committed by other men (NCVS, 1998).<<

Violence Timetable In the United States, a violent crime is committed every 16 seconds, a rape every 5 minutes, a murder every 21 minutes (FBI Uniform Crime Report).<<

Rebound Effect In one study, rape victims suffering from posttraumatic stress disorder were instructed to deliberately suppress all thoughts about their sexual assault. This strategy not only failed to help them but led to a rise in rape-related thoughts (Shipherd & Beck, 1999).<<

Alain Keler/Sygma

Recovery from trauma *Many people eventually overcome the effects of traumatic stress. During a reunion, these concentration camp survivors proudly display their tattooed camp identification numbers as symbols of their triumph over their psychological wounds.*

Why Do People Develop a Psychological Stress Disorder?

Clearly, extraordinary trauma can cause a stress disorder. The stressful event alone, however, may not be completely to blame. Certainly, anyone who experiences an unusual trauma will be affected by it, but only some people develop a disorder (McNally, 2003, 2001). To understand the development of stress disorders more fully, researchers have looked to the survivors' biological processes, personalities, childhood experiences, and social support systems and to the severity of the traumas.

BIOLOGICAL AND GENETIC FACTORS Investigators have learned that traumatic events trigger physical changes in the brain and body that may lead to severe stress reactions and, in some cases, to stress disorders. They have, for example, found abnormal activity of the stress hormone *cortisol* and the neurotransmitter/hormone *norepinephrine* in the urine and blood of combat soldiers, rape victims, concentration camp survivors, and survivors of other severe stresses (Morris et al., 2004; Tobin, 2001). There is also some suspicion that once a stress disorder sets in, individuals experience further biochemical arousal and this continuing arousal may eventually damage brain regions that are needed to help control the body's stress reactions—thus further locking in the disorder (McNally, 2003; Bremner, 2002, 1999).

Perhaps people whose biochemical reactions to stress are particularly strong are more likely than others to develop acute and posttraumatic stress disorders (Kellner & Yehuda, 1999). But why would certain people be prone to such strong biological reactions? It may be that the propensity is inherited. One study of approximately 4,000 pairs of twins who had served in the Vietnam War found that if one twin developed stress symptoms after combat, an identical twin was more likely than a fraternal twin to develop the same problems (True & Lyons, 1999).

PERSONALITY Some studies suggest that people with certain personality profiles, attitudes, and coping styles are more likely to develop stress disorders (Everly & Lating, 2004; Ozer et al., 2003). In the aftermath of Hurricane Hugo in 1989, for example, children who had been highly anxious before the storm were more likely than other children to develop severe stress reactions (Lonigan et al., 1994). Similarly, the victims who are most likely to develop stress disorders after being raped are the ones who had psychological problems before their sexual assault or who were struggling with stressful life situations (Darvres-Bornoz et al., 1995). The same is true of war veterans who had psychological problems before they went into combat (Orsillo et al., 1996). Finally, people who generally view life's negative events as beyond their control tend to develop more severe stress symptoms after sexual or other kinds of criminal assaults than people who feel greater control over their lives (Bremner, 2002; Regehr et al., 1999).

CHILDHOOD EXPERIENCES A recent wave of studies have found that certain childhood experiences seem to leave some people at risk for later acute and posttraumatic stress disorders. People whose childhoods have been marked by poverty appear more likely to develop these disorders in the face of later trauma. So do people whose family members suffered from psychological disorders; who experienced assault, abuse, or catastrophe at an early age; or who were younger than 10 when their parents separated or divorced (Ozer et al., 2003; Bremner, 2002; Bremner et al., 1993).

SOCIAL SUPPORT It has been found that people whose social support systems are weak are also more likely to develop a stress disorder after a traumatic event (Ozer et al., 2003). Rape victims who feel loved, cared for, valued, and accepted by their friends and relatives recover more successfully. So do those treated with dignity and respect by the criminal justice system (Davis et al., 1991; Sales et al., 1984). In contrast, clinical reports have suggested that poor social support has contributed to the development of posttraumatic stress disorder in some combat veterans (Taft et al., 1999; Figley & Leventman, 1990).

SEVERITY OF TRAUMA As one might expect, the severity and nature of traumatic events help determine whether an individual will develop a stress disorder. Some events can override even a nurturing childhood, positive attitudes, and social support (Keane & Barlow, 2002). One study examined 253 Vietnam War prisoners five years after their release. Some 23 percent qualified for a clinical diagnosis, though all had been evaluated as well adjusted before their imprisonment (Ursano et al., 1981).

Generally, the more severe the trauma and the more direct one's exposure to it, the greater the likelihood of developing a stress disorder (Ozer et al., 2003; King et al., 1996). Among the Vietnam prisoners of war, for example, the men who had been imprisoned longest and treated most harshly had the highest percentage of disorders. Mutilation and severe physical injury in particular seem to increase the risk of stress reactions, as does witnessing the injury or death of other people. It is, as a survivor of trauma once said, "hard to be a survivor" (Kolff & Doan, 1985, p. 45).

How Do Clinicians Treat the Psychological Stress Disorders?

Treatment can make a major difference to a person with a stress disorder (Koenen et al., 2003; Suinn, 2001). One survey found that posttraumatic stress symptoms lasted an average of three years with treatment but five and a half years without it (Kessler & Zhao, 1999; Kessler et al., 1995). Today's treatment procedures for

Protection by personality *Millions reacted to the San Francisco earthquake of 1989 with dread and panic, but some laid-back individuals thrived on all the excitement. Their "hardy" personality styles may have helped to protect them from the development of stress disorders.*

>>**PSYCH•NOTES**

The Legacy of War

Postnuclear Trauma Major Claude Robert Eatherly was one of the pilots who dropped atom bombs on Hiroshima and Nagasaki in 1945. In subsequent years, feeling personally responsible for the nuclear devastation of the two cities, he made two suicide attempts and was hospitalized for psychological problems on several occasions (Hirsch et al., 1974).<<

- -

Returning Home One-quarter of the 1.5 million combat soldiers who returned from Vietnam were arrested within two years of their return (Williams, 1983).<<

- -

Bosnian Victims Studies indicate that between 18 and 50 percent of refugees from the wars in Bosnia and Kosovo developed a posttraumatic stress disorder (Favaro et al., 1999; Thulesius & Hakansson, 1999).<<

September 11, 2001: The Psychological Aftermath

Spencer Platt/Getty Images

O n September 11, 2001, the United States experienced the most catastrophic act of terrorism in history when four commercial airplanes were hijacked and three of them were crashed into the twin towers of the World Trade Center in New York City and the Pentagon in Washington, D.C. The attacks resulted in mass casualties and injuries, affecting not only the immediate victims and survivors but the entire nation, as millions witnessed the resulting death and destruction on television. Studies conducted since that fateful day have confirmed what psychologists knew all too well would happen—that in the aftermath of September 11, many individuals experienced immediate and long-term psychological and physical effects, ranging from brief stress reactions, such as shock, fear, and anger, to psychological disorders, such as posttraumatic stress disorder.

In a survey conducted the week after the terrorist attacks, 560 randomly selected adults across the United States were interviewed. Forty-four percent of them reported substantial stress symptoms; 90 percent reported at least some increase in stress (Schuster et al., 2001). Moreover, individuals closest to the disaster site experienced the greatest stress reactions: 61 percent of adults living within 100 miles of the World Trade Center had substantial stress symptoms, compared to 36 percent of those living over 1,000 miles from the site.

A later survey of close to 2,000 individuals revealed that many Americans were still feeling the psychological effects of September 11 five months after the terrorist attacks (Bossolo & Lichtenstein, 2002). Nearly 25 percent of Americans reported that they continued to feel more depressed or anxious since the time of the attacks, and 77 percent said that they were still trying to gain perspective on their lives and to repriori-

AP Photo/Suzanne Plunkett

During the first week

What percentage of the population had substantial stress reactions?

Adults	44%
Children	35
Women	50
Men	37
Nonwhite Americans	62
White Americans	41
Residents within 100 miles of attack	61
Residents beyond 1,000 miles of attack	36
Viewed TV for more than 13 hours on Sept. 11	58
Viewed TV for less than 7 hours on Sept. 11	39

(Schuster et al., 2001)

One month later

What percentage of the population developed posttraumatic stress disorder?

Adults who live in New York City	11%
Adults who live in Washington, D.C.	3
Adults who live in the United States	4
Adults who had watched TV for more than 12 hours on September 11	10
Adults who had watched TV for fewer than 7 hours on September 11	4
Adults whose relatives or friends were injured or killed on September 11	13
Adults who did not know persons injured or killed on September 11	4

(Schlenger et al., 2002)

AP Photo/Ernesto Mora

tize their goals. A related study indicated that people who had experienced a greater number of traumas in the past were more likely than others to develop stress symptoms and disorders in the aftermath of September 11 (Pugh, 2003).

Research focusing specifically on New Yorkers indicated that they were almost twice as likely as those living elsewhere to develop depressive, anxiety, or posttraumatic stress disorders (Bossolo & Lichtenstein, 2002). In addition, 40 percent of New York residents (twice the national average) reported extreme nervousness and anxiety at the sound of sirens or the sight of airplanes flying above.

Still other studies have been conducted, each looking at a particular aspect of the September 11 attack and its enormous psychological impact. Presented here are some key findings from these studies, each serving in its own way to build a more complete understanding of this trauma and its lingering effects.

One year later

What percentage of adults changed their attitudes and behaviors as a result of the attacks?

More accepting of psychotherapy	14%
Feel less safe in our homes	23
More distrustful of neighbors	11
Wrote or rewrote will	6
Purchased a house security system	4

(Fetto, 2002; Gardwyn, 2002)

How were New Yorkers changed by the attacks?

Consider life back to normal	65%
Feel uneasy about traveling by subway	36
Feel uneasy about entering skyscrapers	26
Concerned about another terrorist attack on city	70
Schoolchildren with posttraumatic stress disorder	11

(Connelly & Dutton, 2002; Lord, 2002)

What percentage of parents changed their approach to family life as a result of the attacks?

Consider family more of a priority	78%
Designate more family time to children	35
Call family members more often	30
Stricter about letting children go places alone	26
Worry more about children attending large-crowd events	26
Spend more money on gifts to family	19
Bought cell phone for family	15
Bought more life insurance	8

(Gardwyn, 2002)

How did children's attitudes change as a result of the attacks?

Think about attacks at least a few times a month	58%
Feel less safe traveling	46
Feel less safe in public places	35
Feel less safe at home	3
Feel less safe at school	16
Feel future bombings or other attacks are somewhat likely	51
Feel attacks have changed "the way I live my life"	27

(*Time* Poll, 2002)

>>**LOOKING AROUND**

Generation Gap **Over 74 percent of middle-aged persons in the United States and the United Kingdom believe that life is more stressful today than it was 50 years ago. Fewer than half of teenagers and young adults agree (Paul, 2002).<<**

The Pressures of Everyday Life **Almost one-third of surveyed adults report always feeling rushed, and more than half say they have felt considerable stress in the past two weeks (Americans' Use of Time Project for 1995).<<**

troubled survivors typically vary from trauma to trauma. Was it combat, sexual molestation, or a major accident? Yet all the programs share basic goals: they try to help survivors put an end to their stress reactions (see Table 5-2), gain perspective on their painful experiences, and return to constructive living. Programs for combat veterans who suffer from posttraumatic stress disorder illustrate how these issues may be addressed.

TREATMENT FOR COMBAT VETERANS Therapists have used a variety of techniques to reduce veterans' posttraumatic symptoms. Among the most common are *drug therapy, exposure techniques, insight therapy, family therapy,* and *group therapy*. Typically the approaches are combined, as no one of them successfully reduces all the symptoms.

Antianxiety drugs help control the tension that many veterans experience. In addition, antidepressant medications may reduce the occurrence of nightmares, panic attacks, flashbacks, and feelings of depression (Davidson et al., 2003; Gaffney, 2003).

Behavioral exposure techniques, too, have helped reduce specific symptoms, and they have often led to improvements in overall adjustment (Keane & Barlow, 2002). For example, flooding, along with relaxation training, helped rid a 31-year-old veteran of frightening flashbacks and nightmares (Fairbank & Keane, 1982). The therapist and the veteran first singled out combat scenes that the man had been reexperiencing frequently. The therapist then helped the veteran to imagine one of these scenes in great detail and urged him to hold on to the image until his anxiety stopped. After each of these flooding exercises, the therapist had the veteran switch to a positive image and led him through relaxation exercises.

Table 5-2

Initial Reactions to 1963 Kennedy Assassination and 2001 Terrorist Attacks (percent)

SYMPTOM	KENNEDY ASSASSINATION	TERRORIST ATTACKS
Felt anger	44%	65%
Felt very nervous and tense	68	51
Felt sort of dazed and numb	57	46
Cried	53	60
Had trouble getting to sleep	48	50
Didn't feel like eating	43	29
Felt more tired than usual	42	36
Kept forgetting things	34	19
Had rapid heartbeats	26	16
Had headaches	25	20
Had an upset stomach	22	35
Hands sweated, felt clammy	17	9
Felt dizzy at times	12	8
Felt ashamed that this could happen in the U.S.	50	22

(Smith & Rasinski, 2002)

A CLOSER LOOK

Adjustment Disorders: A Category of Compromise?

Some people react to a major stressor in their lives with extended and excessive feelings of anxiety, depressed mood, or antisocial behaviors. The symptoms do not quite add up to acute stress disorder or posttraumatic stress disorder, nor do they reflect an anxiety or mood disorder, but they do cause considerable distress or interfere with the person's life. Should we consider such reactions normal? No, says DSM-IV. Somewhere between effective coping strategies and stress or anxiety disorders lie the *adjustment disorders* (APA, 2000, 1994).

DSM-IV lists several types of adjustment disorders, including *adjustment disorder with anxiety* and *adjustment disorder with depressed mood*. People receive such diagnoses if they develop their symptoms within three months of the onset of a stressor. The symptoms may continue for as long as six months after the stressor subsides. If the stressor is long term, such as a medical condition, the adjustment disorder may last indefinitely.

Almost any kind of stressor may trigger an adjustment disorder. Common ones are the breakup of a relationship, marital problems, business difficulties, and living in a crime-ridden neighborhood. The disorder may also be triggered by developmental events such as going away to school, getting married, or retiring from a job.

Up to 30 percent of all people in outpatient therapy receive this diagnosis; it accounts for far more treatment claims submitted to insurance companies than any other (APA, 2000). However, some experts doubt that adjustment disorders are as common as this figure suggests. Rather, the diagnosis seems to be a favorite among clinicians—it can easily be applied to a range of problems yet is less stigmatizing than many other categories.

The Museum of Modern Art Film Stills Archive

A relatively new form of exposure therapy is *eye movement desensitization and reprocessing*, in which clients move their eyes in a rhythmic manner from side to side while flooding their minds with images of the objects and situations they ordinarily try to avoid. Case studies and controlled studies suggest that this treatment can sometimes be helpful to persons with posttraumatic stress disorder (Davidson & Parker, 2001; Jaycox & Foa, 2001).

Although drug therapy and exposure techniques bring some relief, most clinicians believe that veterans with posttraumatic stress disorder cannot fully recover with these approaches alone: they must also come to grips with their combat experiences and the impact those experiences continue to have (Marmar et al., 1993). Thus clinicians often try to help veterans bring out deep-seated feelings, accept what they have done and experienced, become less judgmental of themselves, and learn to trust other people once again (Resick & Calhoun, 2001; Shay & Munroe, 1999).

People who have a psychological stress disorder are sometimes helped in a couple or family therapy format (Glynn et al., 1995; Johnson, Feldman, & Lubin, 1995). The symptoms of posttraumatic stress disorder are particularly apparent to family members, who may be directly affected by the client's anxieties, depressive mood, or angry outbursts (Catherall, 1999). With the help and support of their family members, individuals may come to recognize their feelings, examine their impact on others, learn to communicate better, and improve their problem-solving skills.

Veterans may also benefit from **rap groups**, where they meet with others like themselves to share experiences and feelings, develop insights, and give mutual support (Ford & Stewart, 1999). One of the major issues rap groups deal with is *guilt*—guilt about things the members may have done to survive or about the very fact that they did survive while close friends died. These groups may also focus on the rage many combat veterans feel.

Today hundreds of small *Veteran Outreach Centers* across the country, as well as treatment programs in Veterans Administration hospitals and mental health clinics, specialize in rap groups (Ford & Stewart, 1999). These agencies also offer individual therapy, counseling for spouses and children, family therapy, and aid in seeking jobs, education, and benefits. Clinical reports suggest that these programs offer a necessary, sometimes life-saving treatment opportunity.

COMMUNITY THERAPY: THE SOCIOCULTURAL MODEL IN ACTION
People who are traumatized by disasters, victimization, or accidents may profit from many of the same treatments that are used to help survivors of combat. In addition, because their traumas occur in their own community, where mental health resources are close at hand, these individuals may profit from immediate community interventions. A case in point is the rapidly mobilized community care now offered by mental health professionals across the world to victims of large-scale disasters. These professionals typically receive special training in the delivery of emergency mental health services, called **critical incident stress debriefing**.

One of the largest such programs is the *Disaster Response Network (DRN)*, developed in 1991 by the American Psychological Association and the American Red Cross. The network is made up of more than 2,000 volunteer psychologists who offer free emergency mental health services at disaster sites throughout North America (Daw, 2002, 2001). They have been mobilized for such disasters as Hurricane Andrew in 1992, earthquakes in southern California, the 1995 Oklahoma City bombing, the 1999 shooting of 23 persons at Columbine High School in Colorado, and the 2001 World Trade Center attack.

The first aim of mental health professionals in disaster settings is to help survivors meet their basic needs as quickly as possible. During the Midwest flood of 1993, for example, professionals worked in shelters and service centers and rode in Red Cross emergency vehicles to deliver food and water along with counseling services. Some counselors joined flood victims in piling sandbags to protect their homes from further damage.

Once mental health volunteers become involved in the community, they may act more directly to help meet the psychological needs of the disaster victims. They often use a four-stage approach (Michaelson, 1993):

1. **Normalize people's responses to the disaster**. The counselors educate survivors about the symptoms they may be experiencing, such as sleep disturbances, difficulty concentrating, or feelings of grief, and they confirm that these are normal responses to a disaster.

2. **Encourage expressions of anxiety, anger, and frustration**. To reduce the anxiety, anger, and frustration that survivors often feel after a disaster, counselors help them talk about their experiences and their feelings.

3. **Teach self-helping skills**. Counselors train survivors to develop stress management and other self-help skills.

Charles H. Porter IV/Sygma

Everyone is affected *A fire captain cradles one-year-old Baylee Almon, a child killed in the bombing of the Oklahoma City federal building. This famous photograph reminds us that rescue workers are themselves subjected to enormous stress and trauma during disasters (Bryant & Harvey, 1995).*

RAP GROUP A group that meets to talk about and explore members' problems in an atmosphere of mutual support.

CRITICAL INCIDENT STRESS DEBRIEFING Training in how to help victims talk about their feelings and reactions to traumatic incidents.

A CLOSER LOOK

Disaster Counseling: The Other Side

Rapid-mobilization mental health programs for disaster victims are growing in number and popularity. Studies of these programs typically yield favorable results, and personal testimonials are supportive as well. At the same time, a number of clinical theorists question the effectiveness of these interventions (Stoil, 2001; Gist & Woodall, 1999).

An investigation conducted several years ago was among the first to raise concerns about the disaster mental health programs (Bisson & Deahl, 1994). Crisis counselors worked with 62 British soldiers whose job during the Gulf War was to handle and identify the bodies of individuals who had been killed. After receiving nine months of crisis counseling, half of the soldiers nevertheless displayed posttraumatic stress symptoms, a finding that led some theorists to conclude that disaster intervention programs do not really make much difference. Still worse, some clinicians now worry that the programs may encourage victims to dwell too long on the traumatic events that they have experienced. Moreover, certain clinicians are concerned that early disaster counseling may actually "suggest" problems to victims, thus helping to produce stress disorders in the first place (McClelland, 1998).

Finally, questions have been raised about the cultural differences that may exist between crisis counselors and disaster victims. When hundreds of clinicians were mobilized in New York City after the attacks of September 11, 2001, for example, many wound up working with residents of the Chinatown neighborhood, near the World Trade Center. It is not clear that the techniques of these counselors were fully appropriate for a population that prefers to speak Cantonese and whose culture is often uncomfortable with the kinds of openness that characterize Western therapy (Stoil, 2001).

The current clinical climate continues to favor disaster counseling, and such programs may indeed prove to be as helpful as many clinicians believe. However, the concerns that have been raised merit serious consideration. We are reminded here, as elsewhere, of the constant need for careful research in the field of abnormal psychology.

Paul Conner/AP Photo

Essential or excessive? *A relief worker comforts the family member of a victim of Egypt Air Flight 990, the plane that crashed off Nantucket Island in 1999 under mysterious circumstances, killing all 217 aboard.*

4. **Provide referrals**. The workers eventually may refer survivors to other professionals who can provide long-term counseling (Sleek, 1997). It is estimated that between 15 and 25 percent of survivors need this specialized assistance.

Relief workers, too, can become overwhelmed by the traumas they witness (Ursano et al., 1999). During the 1992 Los Angeles riots, for example, a key responsibility of many community mental health counselors was to help Red Cross workers vent and accept their own feelings as well as teach them about stress disorders and how to identify victims who needed further treatment.

Although this approach has detractors, most professionals believe that intervention at the community level is highly useful after a disaster. And sadly, our world seems to offer ever-increasing opportunities to test that belief. For example, during the weeks following the World Trade Center attack in 2001, 1,600 mental health workers were mobilized to counsel to more than 57,000 people (Pepe, 2002).

>>**PSYCH•NOTES**

Disaster's Aftermath

Around one-third of the adults who were inside or just outside the Oklahoma City federal building at the time of the 1995 bombing developed posttraumatic stress disorder (North et al., 1999).<<

PSYCHOPHYSIOLOGICAL DISORDERS Illnesses that result from an interaction of psychosocial and organic factors. Also known as *psychosomatic disorders*.

ULCER A lesion that forms in the wall of the stomach or of the duodenum.

ASTHMA A medical problem marked by narrowing of the trachea and bronchi, which results in shortness of breath, wheezing, coughing, and a choking sensation.

INSOMNIA Difficulty falling or staying asleep.

MUSCLE CONTRACTION HEADACHE A headache caused by the narrowing of muscles surrounding the skull. Also known as *tension headache*.

SUMMING UP

Stress and Psychological Stress Disorders

When we view a stressor as threatening, we often experience a stress response consisting of arousal and a sense of fear. The features of arousal and fear are set in motion by the hypothalamus, a brain area that activates the autonomic nervous system and the endocrine system through two pathways—the sympathetic nervous system pathway and the hypothalamic-pituitary-adrenal pathway.

People with acute stress disorder or posttraumatic stress disorder react with anxiety and related symptoms after a traumatic event, including reexperiencing the traumatic event. The symptoms of acute stress disorder last less than a month, while those of posttraumatic stress disorder may last for months or years.

In attempting to explain why some people develop a psychological stress disorder and others do not, researchers have focused on biological factors, personality, childhood experiences, social support, and the severity of the traumatic event. Treatments for these disorders include drug, exposure, insight, family, and group therapy. Rapidly mobilized community therapy can also be helpful after large-scale disasters.

The Physical Stress Disorders: Psychophysiological Disorders

As we have seen, stress can greatly affect our psychological functioning (see Figure 5-3). It can also have a great impact on our physical functioning, contributing in some cases to the development of medical problems (Dougall & Baum, 2001; Suinn, 2001). The idea that stress and related psychosocial factors may contribute to somatic illnesses has ancient roots, yet it had few supporters until about 75 years ago, when clinicians first identified a group of physical illnesses that seemed to result from an *interaction* of biological, psychological, and sociocultural factors (Dunbar, 1948; Bott, 1928). Early versions of the DSM labeled these illnesses **psychophysiological**, or **psychosomatic**, **disorders**, but DSM-IV labels them

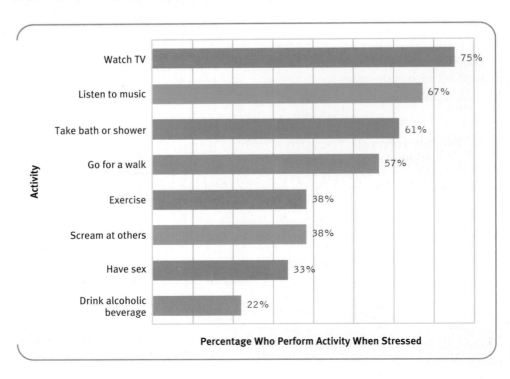

FIGURE 5-3 **What do people do to relieve stress?** *According to one large survey, most of us watch television or listen to music (Kanner, 1995).*

psychological factors affecting medical condition (see Table 5-3). We shall use the more familiar term "psychophysiological" in discussing them.

It is important to recognize that psychophysiological disorders bring about *actual* physical damage. They are different from "apparent" physical illnesses—*factitious disorders* or *somatoform disorders*—disorders that are accounted for entirely by factors such as hidden needs, repression, or reinforcement. We shall be examining those apparent physical disorders in the next chapter. Consistent with our current interest in stress and its direct role in certain psychological and physical disorders, we shall focus here only on psychophysiological disorders.

Traditional Psychophysiological Disorders

Before the 1970s, clinicians believed that only a limited number of illnesses were psychophysiological. The best known and most common of these disorders were ulcers, asthma, insomnia, chronic headaches, high blood pressure, and coronary heart disease. Recent research, however, has shown that many other physical illnesses—including bacterial and viral infections—may also be caused by an interaction of psychosocial and physical factors. We will look first at the traditional psychophysiological disorders and then at the newer illnesses in this category.

Ulcers are lesions (holes) that form in the wall of the stomach or of the duodenum, resulting in burning sensations or pain in the stomach, occasional vomiting, and stomach bleeding. This disorder is experienced by up to 10 percent of all people in the United States and is responsible for more than 6,000 deaths each year. Ulcers are often caused by an interaction of stress factors, such as environmental pressure or intense feelings of anger or anxiety, and physiological factors, such as bacterial infections (Carr, 2001).

Asthma causes the body's airways (the trachea and bronchi) to narrow periodically, making it hard for air to pass to and from the lungs. The resulting symptoms are shortness of breath, wheezing, coughing, and a terrifying choking sensation. Some 15 million people in the United States suffer from asthma, twice as many as 20 years ago (NCHS, 1999). Most victims are children or young teenagers at the time of the first attack (Melamed et al., 2001). Seventy percent of all cases appear to be caused by an interaction of stress factors, such as environmental pressures, troubled family relationships, or anxiety, and physiological factors, such as allergies to specific substances, a slow-acting sympathetic nervous system, or a weakened respiratory system (Melamed et al., 2001).

Insomnia, difficulty falling asleep or maintaining sleep, affects 35 percent of the population each year (Carr, 2001). Although many of us have temporary bouts of insomnia that last a few nights or so, a large number of people experience insomnia that lasts months or years. They feel as though they are almost constantly awake. Chronic insomniacs are often very sleepy during the day and may have difficulty functioning. Their problem may be caused by a combination of psychosocial factors, such as anxiety or depression, and physiological problems, such as an overactive arousal system or certain medical ailments (Espie, 2002; Hauri, 2000).

Chronic headaches are frequent intense aches of the head or neck that are not caused by another physical disorder. There are two types. **Muscle contraction**, or **tension**, **headaches** are marked by pain at the back or front of the head or the back of the neck. These occur when the muscles surrounding the skull tighten, narrowing the blood vessels. Approximately 40 million Americans suffer from

Table 5-3	DSM-IV Checklist

PSYCHOLOGICAL FACTORS AFFECTING GENERAL MEDICAL CONDITION

1. The presence of a general medical condition.
2. Psychological factors adversely affecting the general medical condition in one of the following ways:
   (a) Influencing the course of the general medical condition.
   (b) Interfering with the treatment of the general medical condition.
   (c) Posing additional health risks.
   (d) Stress-related physiological responses precipitating or exacerbating the general medical condition.

Based on APA, 2000, 1994.

Treating asthma *Children who suffer from asthma may use an aerochamber, or inhaler, to help them inhale helpful medications. The child pumps the medication into the device's plastic tube and then inhales it.*

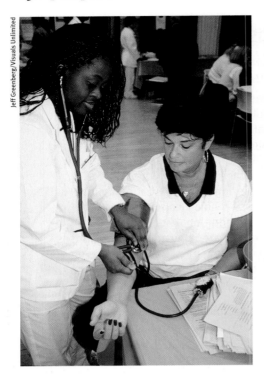

The silent killer *High blood pressure, a psychophysiological disorder with few outward signs, kills tens of thousands of people each year, prompting health care professionals to regularly provide free blood pressure checks in the workplace or other community settings.*

Risky business *A currency dealer shouts orders during trading at the Paris Stock Exchange. The stresses of working in high-pressure environments apparently increase one's risk of developing a medical illness, including coronary heart disease.*

such headaches. **Migraine headaches** are extremely severe, often near-paralyzing aches located on one side of the head. They are often preceded by a warning sensation called an *aura* and are sometimes accompanied by dizziness, nausea, or vomiting. Migraine headaches are thought by some medical theorists to develop in two phases: (1) blood vessels in the brain narrow, so that the flow of blood to parts of the brain is reduced, and (2) the same blood vessels later expand, so that blood flows through them rapidly, stimulating many neuron endings and causing pain. Migraines are suffered by about 23 million people in the United States.

Research suggests that chronic headaches are caused by an interaction of stress factors, such as environmental pressures or general feelings of helplessness, anger, anxiety, or depression (McGrath & Hillier, 2001), and physiological factors, such as abnormal activity of the neurotransmitter serotonin, vascular problems, or muscle weakness (Hargreaves & Shepheard, 1999).

Hypertension is a state of chronic high blood pressure. That is, the blood pumped through the body's arteries by the heart produces too much pressure against the artery walls. Hypertension has few outward symptoms, but it interferes with the proper functioning of the entire cardiovascular system, greatly increasing the likelihood of stroke, coronary heart disease, and kidney problems. It is estimated that 40 million people in the United States have hypertension, 14,000 die directly from it annually, and millions more perish because of illnesses caused by it (NCHS, 1999; Johnson et al., 1992). Around 10 percent of all cases are caused by physiological abnormalities alone; the rest result from a combination of psychosocial and physiological factors and are called *essential hypertension* (Carr, 2001). Some of the leading psychosocial causes of essential hypertension are constant environmental danger and general feelings of anger or depression (Gidron et al., 1999; Dubbert, 1995). Physiological causes include faulty *baroreceptors*—sensitive nerves in the blood vessels responsible for signaling the brain that blood pressure is becoming too high (Julius, 1992; Schwartz, 1977).

Coronary heart disease is caused by a blocking of the *coronary arteries*—the blood vessels that surround the heart and are responsible for carrying oxygen to the heart muscle. The term actually refers to several problems, including blockage of the coronary arteries and *myocardial infarction* (a "heart attack"). Together such problems are the leading cause of death in men over the age of 35 and of women over 40 in the United States, accounting for close to 1 million deaths each year, around 40 percent of all deaths in the nation (American Heart Association, 2003). The majority of all cases of coronary heart disease are related to an interaction of psychosocial factors, such as job stress or high levels of anger or depression, and physiological factors, such as a high level of cholesterol, obesity, hypertension, smoking, or lack of exercise (Williams, 2001).

Over the years, clinicians have identified a number of variables that may generally contribute to the development of psychophysiological disorders. It should not surprise us that several of these variables are the same as those that contribute to the onset of the psychological stress disorders—acute and posttraumatic stress disorders. The variables may be grouped as sociocultural, psychological, and biological factors.

SOCIOCULTURAL FACTORS The stressful demands placed on people by their culture or social group may set the stage for psychophysiological disorders. The stress may be wide-ranging, such as that produced by wars or natural disasters. After a 1979 nuclear accident at Three Mile Island in Pennsylvania, for example, people who lived near the nuclear plant experienced a high number of psychophysiological disorders, and they continued to do so for years (Schneiderman & Baum, 1992; Baum et al., 1983). Alternatively, local social conditions may produce persistent feelings of tension, such as living in a crime-ridden neighborhood or working in an unsatisfying job (Landsbergis et al., 1994). For example, hypertension is 50 percent more common among African Americans than among white Americans (Macera et al., 2001). Although physiological factors may largely explain this difference, some theorists believe that it is also linked to the dangerous environments in which so many African Americans live, the unsatisfying jobs at which so many must work, and the racial discrimination most face (Clark et al., 1999).

PSYCHOLOGICAL FACTORS According to many theorists, certain needs, attitudes, emotions, or coping styles may cause people to overreact repeatedly to stressors, and so increase their chances of developing psychophysiological disorders (Smith, 2001). Researchers have found, for example, that men with a *repressive coping style* (a reluctance to express discomfort, anger, or hostility) tend to experience a particularly sharp rise in blood pressure and heart rate when they are stressed (Coy, 1998).

Another personality style that may contribute to psychophysiological disorders is the **Type A personality style**, an idea introduced by two cardiologists, Meyer Friedman and Raymond Rosenman (1959). People with this style are said to be consistently angry, cynical, driven, impatient, competitive, and ambitious. They interact with the world in a way that, according to Friedman and Rosenman, produces continual stress and often leads to coronary heart disease. People with a **Type B personality style**, by contrast, are thought to be more relaxed, less aggressive, and less concerned about time. They are less likely to experience cardiovascular deterioration. In reality, of course, most people fall between these two extremes, tending toward one or the other but showing features of both.

"What do you mean, I have an ulcer? I give ulcers, I don't get them!"

The link between the Type A personality style and coronary heart disease has been supported by many studies. In one well-known investigation of more than 3,000 people, Friedman and Rosenman (1974) separated healthy men in their 40s and 50s into Type A and Type B categories and then followed their health over the next eight years. More than twice as many Type A men developed coronary heart disease. Later studies found that Type A functioning correlates similarly with heart disease in women (Haynes et al., 1980).

In recent studies the link found between the Type A personality style and heart disease has not been as strong as the earlier studies suggest. They do show, nevertheless, that some of the characteristics that supposedly make up the Type A style, particularly *hostility*, are very likely to be related to heart disease (Williams, 2001).

BIOLOGICAL FACTORS We saw earlier that one way in which the brain activates body organs is through the operation of the *autonomic nervous system (ANS)*, the network of nerve fibers that connect the central nervous system to the body's organs. Defects in this system are believed to contribute to the development of psychophysiological disorders (Hugdahl, 1995). If one's ANS is stimulated too easily, for example, it may overreact to situations that most people find only mildly stressful, eventually damaging certain organs and causing a psychophysiological disorder (Boyce et al., 1995).

Other more specific biological problems may also contribute to psychophysiological disorders. A person with a weak gastrointestinal system, for example, may be a prime candidate for an ulcer, whereas someone with a weak respiratory system may develop asthma readily. In a related vein, people may display favored biological reactions that raise their chances of developing psychophysiological disorders. Some individuals perspire in response to stress, others develop stomachaches, and still others experience a rise in blood pressure (Fahrenberg, Foerster, & Wilmers, 1995). Although such variations are perfectly normal, the repeated overuse of a single system may wear it down and eventually help cause a psychophysiological disorder. Some infants, for example, produce much more gastric

MIGRAINE HEADACHE An extremely severe headache that occurs on one side of the head, often preceded by a warning sensation and sometimes accompanied by dizziness, nausea, or vomiting.

HYPERTENSION Chronic high blood pressure.

CORONARY HEART DISEASE Illness of the heart caused by a blocking of the coronary arteries.

TYPE A PERSONALITY STYLE A personality pattern characterized by hostility, cynicism, drivenness, impatience, competitiveness, and ambition.

TYPE B PERSONALITY STYLE A personality pattern in which persons are more relaxed, less aggressive, and less concerned about time.

>>LOOKING AROUND
Stress and the Workplace

Unscheduled absences from work have risen 11 to 25 percent since 1995, with stress and personal matters cited as the fastest-growing causes (Shellenbarger, 1998).<<

In surveys, 35 percent of white Americans report being dissatisfied with their jobs, as compared with 44 percent of African Americans (Watson Wyatt Worldwide, 1995).<<

Almost two-thirds of workers say that their financial well-being is of more concern to them than their mortality (Yin, 2002).<<

Joyful stress *According to the Social Adjustment Rating Scale, even positive events such as pregnancy are stressful for everyone involved.*

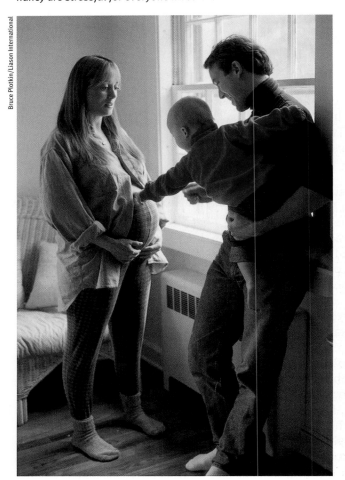

Bruce Plotkin/Liason International

acid under stress than other infants (Weiner, 1977; Mirsky, 1958). Perhaps, over the years, this physical reaction wears down the lining of the stomach or duodenum, leaving the individuals more vulnerable to ulcers.

Clearly, sociocultural, psychological, and biological variables combine to produce psychophysiological disorders. In fact, the interaction of psychosocial and physical factors is now considered the rule of bodily functioning, not the exception, and, as the years have passed, more and more illnesses have been added to the list of traditional psychophysiological disorders. Let us turn next to the "new" psychophysiological disorders.

New Psychophysiological Disorders

Since the 1960s, researchers have found many links between psychosocial stress and a wide range of physical illnesses. Let us look first at how these links were established and then at *psychoneuroimmunology*, a new area of study that ties stress and illness to the body's immune system.

ARE PHYSICAL ILLNESSES RELATED TO STRESS? In 1967 two researchers, Thomas Holmes and Richard Rahe, developed the *Social Adjustment Rating Scale*, which assigns numerical values to the stresses that most people experience at some time in their lives (see Table 5-4). Answers given by a large sample of subjects indicated that the most stressful event on the scale should be the death of a spouse, which receives a score of 100 *life change units* (*LCUs*). Lower on the scale is retirement (45 LCUs), and still lower is a minor violation of the law (11 LCUs). Even positive events, such as an outstanding personal achievement (28 LCUs), are somewhat stressful. This scale gave researchers a yardstick for measuring the total amount of stress a person faces over a period of time. If, for example, in the course of a year a businesswoman started a new business (39 LCUs), sent her son off to college (29 LCUs), moved to a new house (20 LCUs), and experienced the death of a close friend (37 LCUs), her stress score for the year would be 125 LCUs, a considerable amount of stress for such a period of time.

With the Social Adjustment Rating Scale in hand, the researchers were able to examine the relationship between life stress and the onset of illness. They found that the LCU scores of sick people during the year before they fell ill were much higher than those of healthy people (Holmes & Rahe, 1989, 1967). If a person's life changes totaled more than 300 LCUs over the course of a year, that person was particularly likely to develop a serious health problem.

The Social Adjustment Rating Scale has been updated and revised by various researchers over the years (Hobson et al., 1998; Miller & Rabe, 1997). Using either the original or the revised scale, studies have linked stresses of various kinds to a wide range of physical conditions, from trench mouth and upper respiratory infection to cancer (Cobb & Steptoe, 1998; Kiecolt-Glaser et al., 1991). Overall, the greater the amount of life stress, the greater the likelihood of illness. Researchers even have found a relationship between traumatic stress and death. Widows and widowers, for example, display an increased risk of death during their period of bereavement (Rees & Lutkin, 1967; Young et al., 1963).

One shortcoming of Holmes and Rahe's Social Adjustment Rating Scale is that it does not take into consideration the particular life stress reactions of specific populations. For example, in their development of the scale, the researchers sampled white Americans predominantly. Few of the subjects were African Americans. But since their ongoing life experiences often differ in significant ways, might not African Americans and white Americans differ in their stress reactions to various kinds of life events? One study indicates that indeed they do (Komaroff et al., 1989, 1986). Both white and

Table 5-4

Most Stressful Life Events

ADULTS: SOCIAL ADJUSTMENT RATING SCALE*

1. Death of spouse
2. Divorce
3. Marital separation
4. Jail term
5. Death of close family member
6. Personal injury or illness
7. Marriage
8. Fired at work
9. Marital reconciliation
10. Retirement
11. Change in health of family member
12. Pregnancy
13. Sex difficulties
14. Gain of new family member
15. Business readjustment
16. Change in financial state
17. Death of close friend
18. Change to different line of work
19. Change in number of arguments with spouse
20. Mortgage over $10,000
21. Foreclosure of mortgage or loan
22. Change in responsibilities at work

*Full scale has 43 items.
Source: Holmes & Rahe, 1967.

STUDENTS: UNDERGRADUATE STRESS QUESTIONNAIRE†

1. Death (family member or friend)
2. Had a lot of tests
3. It's finals week
4. Applying to graduate school
5. Victim of a crime
6. Assignments in all classes due the same day
7. Breaking up with boy-/girlfriend
8. Found out boy-/girlfriend cheated on you
9. Lots of deadlines to meet
10. Property stolen
11. You have a hard upcoming week
12. Went into a test unprepared
13. Lost something (especially wallet)
14. Death of a pet
15. Did worse than expected on test
16. Had an interview
17. Had projects, research papers due
18. Did badly on a test
19. Parents getting divorce
20. Dependent on other people
21. Having roommate conflicts
22. Car/bike broke down, flat tire, etc.

†Full scale has 83 items.
Source: Crandall et al., 1992.

African Americans rank death of a spouse as the single most stressful life event, but African Americans experience greater stress than white Americans from such events as a major personal injury or illness, a major change in work responsibilities, or a major change in living conditions. Similarly, studies have shown that women and men differ in their reactions to certain life changes on the scale (Miller & Rahe, 1997).

Finally, college students may face stressors that are different from those listed in the Social Adjustment Rating Scale. Instead of having marital difficulties, being fired, or applying for a job, a college student may have trouble with a roommate, fail a course, or apply to graduate school. When researchers developed special scales to measure life events more accurately in this population (see bottom half of Table 5-4), they found the expected relationships between stressful events and illness (Crandall et al., 1992).

PSYCHONEUROIMMUNOLOGY How do stressful events result in a viral or bacterial infection? An area of study called **psychoneuroimmunology** seeks to answer this question by examining the links among psychosocial stress, the immune system, and health (Kiecolt-Glaser et al., 2002).

The **immune system** is the body's network of activities and cells that identify and destroy **antigens**—foreign invaders, such as bacteria, viruses, fungi, and parasites—and cancer cells. Among the most important cells in the immune system are billions of **lymphocytes**, white blood cells that circulate through the lymph

PSYCHONEUROIMMUNOLOGY The study of the connections among stress, the body's immune system, and illness.

IMMUNE SYSTEM The body's network of activities and cells that identify and destroy antigens and cancer cells.

ANTIGEN A foreign invader of the body, such as a bacterium or virus.

LYMPHOCYTES White blood cells that circulate through the lymph system and bloodstream, helping the body identify and destroy antigens and cancer cells.

Killer T-cells at work *These killer T-cells surround a larger cancer cell and destroy it, thus helping to prevent the spread of cancer.*

Laboratory insights *Laboratory animals are widely used in research on the immune system. The destruction of the immune systems of these mice, which has caused their hair to fall out, enables researchers to produce and investigate invasions by various cells and viruses.*

system and the bloodstream. When stimulated by antigens, lymphocytes spring into action to help the body overcome the invaders.

One group of lymphocytes, called *helper T-cells*, identify antigens and then multiply and trigger the production of other kinds of immune cells. Another group, *natural killer T-cells*, seek out and destroy body cells that have already been infected by viruses, thus helping to stop the spread of a viral infection. A third group of lymphocytes, *B-cells*, produce *antibodies*, protein molecules that recognize and bind to antigens, mark them for destruction, and prevent them from causing infection.

Researchers now believe that stress can interfere with the activity of lymphocytes, slowing them down and thus increasing a person's susceptibility to viral and bacterial infections (Ader et al., 2001). In a landmark study, R. W. Bartrop and his colleagues (1977) in New South Wales, Australia, compared the immune systems of 26 people whose spouses had died eight weeks earlier with those of 26 matched control subjects whose spouses had not died. Blood samples revealed that lymphocyte functioning was much lower in the bereaved people than in the controls. Still other studies have shown slow immune functioning in persons who are exposed to long-term stress. For example, researchers have found poorer immune functioning among people who face the challenge of providing ongoing care for a relative with Alzheimer's disease (Kiecolt-Glaser et al., 2002, 1996, 1987).

These studies seem to be telling a remarkable story. During periods when healthy individuals happened to experience unusual levels of stress, they remained healthy on the surface, but their experiences apparently slowed their immune systems so that they became susceptible to illness. If stress affects our capacity to fight off illness, it is no wonder that researchers have repeatedly found a relationship between life stress and illnesses of various kinds. But why and when does stress interfere with the immune system? Several factors influence whether stress will result in a slowdown of the system, including *biochemical activity*, *behavioral changes*, *personality style*, and *degree of social support*.

BIOCHEMICAL ACTIVITY We observed earlier that abnormal activity of *norepinephrine* and of the *corticosteroids* may contribute to the development of acute and posttraumatic stress disorders. Similarly, these chemicals have been implicated in slowdowns of the immune system during prolonged periods of stress. Remember that stress leads to increased activity by the sympathetic nervous system, including an increase in the release of norepinephrine throughout the brain and body. It appears that, beyond supporting the activity of the sympathetic nervous system, this chemical eventually helps slow the functioning of the immune system (Lekander, 2002). During low stress or early stages of stress, norepinephrine travels to certain lymphocyte receptors and gives a message for the lymphocytes to increase their activity. As the stress continues or rises, however, the chemical travels to yet other receptors on the lymphocytes and gives them an *inhibitory message* to stop their activity. Thus, while the release of norepinephrine improves immune functioning at low levels of stress, it actually slows down immune functioning at higher levels.

Similarly, the corticosteroids—cortisol and other so-called stress hormones— contribute to poorer immune system functioning during periods of prolonged stress. Remember that when a person is under stress, the adrenal glands release these corticosteroids. At first the release of such hormones stimulates body organs to greater activity. After stress continues for 30 minutes or more, however, the stress hormones travel to certain receptor sites in the body and give *inhibitory messages*, which help calm down the overstressed body (Manuck et al., 1991). One such group of receptor sites is located on the lymphocytes. When the corticosteroids bind to these receptors, their inhibitory messages actually slow down the activity of the lymphocytes (Bellinger et al., 1994). Thus, again, the very chemicals that initially help people to deal with stress eventually serve to slow the immune system.

BEHAVIORAL CHANGES Stress may set in motion a series of behavioral changes that indirectly affect the immune system. Some people under stress may, for example, become anxious or depressed, perhaps even develop an anxiety or mood disorder (see Figure 5-4). As a result, they may sleep badly, eat poorly, exercise less, or smoke or drink more—behaviors known to slow down the immune system (Kiecolt-Glaser & Glaser, 2002, 1999, 1988; Cohen & Herbert, 1996).

PERSONALITY STYLE An individual's personality may also play a role in determining how much the immune system is slowed down by stress (Sarid et al., 2004). According to research, people who generally respond to life stress with optimism, constructive coping, and resilience—that is, people who welcome challenge and are willing to take control in their daily encounters—experience better immune system functioning and are better prepared to fight off illness (Taylor et al., 2000). Some studies find, for example, that people with "hardy" or resilient personalities remain healthy after stressful events, while those whose personalities are less hardy seem more susceptible to illness (Oulette & DiPlacido, 2001; Oulette, 1993). One study even discovered that men with a general sense of hopelessness die at above-average rates from heart disease and other causes (Everson et al., 1996). Similarly, a growing body of research suggests that people who are spiritual tend to be healthier than individuals without spiritual beliefs, and a few

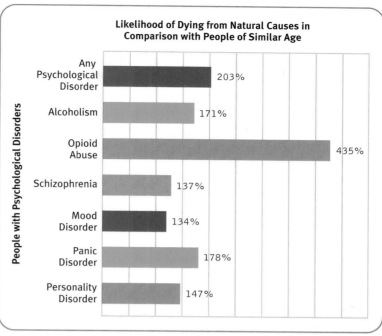

FIGURE 5-4 **Warning: psychological disorders may be dangerous to your health** *Psychological disorders are themselves a source of stress that can lead to medical problems. People with such disorders are twice as likely to die of natural causes (medical illnesses) as people in the same age group without psychological difficulties. (Adapted from Harris & Barraclough, 1998.)*

THE**CURRENT SCENE**

Working with Death

*O*ne of the least pleasant jobs in our society is that of tying up loose ends after a disaster or murder. Yet the work must be done, regardless of the toll it may take on the workers. It turns out that reactions to such responsibilities vary widely.

In 1993, 83 persons died in the fire at the Branch Davidian compound in Waco, Texas, when federal agents tried to end a 51-day standoff between the Branch Davidian sect and the FBI. Thirty-one dentists had to examine the dental remains of the dead. A study later revealed that these dentists went on to develop more psychological and physical symptoms of severe stress than did a control group of other dentists (McCarroll et al., 1996).

Vickie Lewis/People Weekly

Then there are Ray and Louise Barnes (see photo), who run a business called Crime Scene Clean-Up. They and their staffers are hired by police departments, funeral homes, and grieving families to clean up after homicides, suicides, and accidents. They use latex gloves, mops, respirators, and other tools of the trade to "scrub away the detritus of human disaster" (Howe & Nugent, 1996). While hardly indifferent to the grisly scenes, Ray Barnes says that he has grown somewhat used to them, and he and his wife have built a thriving business.

>>BY THE NUMBERS
Religion and Health

80 Years	Average life span of weekly church-goers
75 Years	Average life span of non-churchgoers
72%	Percentage of Americans who say they would welcome a conversation with their physician about faith
28%	Americans who think that religion and medicine should be separate

Kalb, 2003; Powell, 2003

studies have linked spirituality to better immune system functioning (Koenig & Cohen, 2002).

In related work, some studies have noted a relationship between certain personality characteristics and recovery from cancer (Hjerl et al., 2003). They have found that patients with certain forms of cancer who display a helpless coping style and who cannot easily express their feelings, particularly anger, tend to have less successful recoveries than patients who do express their emotions. Other studies, however, have found no relationship between personality and cancer outcome (Garssen & Goodkin, 1999; Holland, 1996).

SOCIAL SUPPORT Finally, people who have few social supports and feel lonely seem to display poorer immune functioning in the face of stress than people who do not feel lonely (Cohen, 2002; Kiecolt-Glaser et al., 2002, 1988, 1987). In one study, medical students were given the *UCLA Loneliness Scale* and then divided into "high" and "low" loneliness groups (Kiecolt-Glaser et al., 1984). The high-loneliness group showed lower lymphocyte responses during a final exam period.

Other studies have found that social support and affiliation may actually help protect people from stress, poor immune system functioning, and subsequent illness, or help speed up recovery from illness or surgery (Cohen, 2002; Kiecolt-Glaser et al., 2002, 1998, 1991). Similarly, some studies have suggested that patients with certain forms of cancer who receive social support in their personal lives or supportive therapy often have better immune system functioning and, in turn, more successful recoveries than patients without such supports (Spiegel & Fawzy, 2002).

SUMMING UP

Psychophysiological Disorders

Psychophysiological disorders are those in which psychosocial and physiological factors interact to cause a physical problem. Factors linked to these disorders are sociocultural factors, such as society-wide stressors; psychological factors, such as particular personality styles; and biological factors, such as defects in the autonomic nervous system.

For years clinical researchers singled out ulcers, asthma, insomnia, chronic headaches, hypertension, and coronary heart disease as the key psychophysiological disorders. Recently many other psychophysiological disorders have also been identified.

The field of psychoneuroimmunology has helped clarify the role of stress and the immune system in the onset of medical problems. Stress can slow lymphocyte and other immune system activity, thereby interfering with the system's ability to protect against illness. Factors that seem to affect immune functioning include norepinephrine and corticosteroid activity, behavioral changes, personality style, and social support.

In need of support *AIDS is a disease in which certain immune cells become infected by the human immunodeficiency virus (HIV) and, in turn, launch a full-scale attack on the immune system. Studies reveal that victims who receive positive social support are better able to fight off the disease than are those who are stigmatized and discriminated against by their social network (Nott & Vedhara, 1999; Schneiderman, 1999).*

Psychological Treatments for Physical Disorders

As clinicians have discovered that stress and related psychosocial factors may contribute to physical disorders, they have applied psychological treatments to more and more medical problems (Baum et al., 2001). The most common of these interventions are relaxation training, biofeedback, meditation, hypnosis, cognitive interventions, insight therapy, and support groups. The field of treatment that combines psychological and physical approaches to treat or prevent medical problems is known as *behavioral medicine*.

RELAXATION TRAINING As we saw in Chapter 4, people can be taught to relax their muscles at will, a process that sometimes reduces feelings of anxiety. Given the positive effects of relaxation on anxiety and the nervous system, clinicians believe that *relaxation training* can be of help in preventing or treating medical illnesses that are related to stress.

Relaxation training, often in combination with medication, has been widely used in the treatment of high blood pressure (Stetter & Kupper, 2002). It has also been of some help in treating headaches, insomnia, asthma, the undesirable effects of cancer treatments, pain after surgery, and certain vascular diseases (Stetter & Kupper, 2002; Powers et al., 2001).

BIOFEEDBACK As we also have seen in Chapter 4, patients given *biofeedback training* are connected to machinery that gives them continuous readings about their involuntary body activities. This information enables them gradually to gain control over those activities. Somewhat helpful in the treatment of anxiety disorders, the procedure has also been applied to a growing number of physical disorders.

In one study, *electromyograph* (*EMG*) feedback was used to treat 16 patients who were experiencing facial pain caused in part by tension in their jaw muscles (Dohrmann & Laskin, 1978). In an EMG procedure, electrodes are attached to a person's muscles so that the muscle contractions are detected and converted into a tone for the individual to hear (see p. 107). Changes in the pitch and volume of the tone indicate changes in muscle tension. After "listening" to EMG feedback repeatedly, the 16 patients in this study learned how to relax their jaw muscles at will and later reported a reduction in facial pain. In contrast, 8 control subjects, who were wired to similar equipment but not given biofeedback training, showed little improvement in muscle tension or pain.

EMG feedback has also been used successfully in the treatment of headaches and muscular disabilities caused by strokes or accidents. Still other forms of biofeedback training have been of some help in the treatment of heartbeat irregularities, asthma, migraine headaches, high blood pressure, stuttering, and pain from burns (Martin, 2002; Moss, 2002; Gatchel, 2001).

MEDITATION Although meditation has been practiced since ancient times, Western health care professionals have only recently become aware of its effectiveness in relieving physical distress. *Meditation* is a technique of turning one's concentration inward, achieving a slightly changed state of consciousness, and temporarily ignoring all stressors. In the most common approach, meditators go to a quiet place, assume a comfortable posture, utter or think a particular sound (called a *mantra*) to help focus their attention, and allow their minds to turn away from all outside thoughts and concerns (Dass & Levine, 2002).

Many people who meditate regularly report feeling more peaceful, engaged, and creative (Carrington, 1993, 1978). Meditation has been used to help manage pain in cancer patients (Goleman & Gurin, 1993) and to help treat high blood pressure, heart problems, asthma, skin disorders, diabetes, insomnia, and even viral infections (Andresen, 2000).

HYPNOSIS As we discussed in Chapter 1, individuals who undergo *hypnosis* are guided by a hypnotist into a sleeplike, suggestible state during which they can be directed to act in unusual ways, experience unusual sensations, remember seemingly forgotten events, or forget remembered events. With training some people are even able to induce

Relaxation, the hard way *Clinicians are always developing techniques to help people relax. A climber dangles from Alaska's Mount Barrile to demonstrate the use of "Tranquilite" sleep goggles, which are supposed to produce relaxation with blue light and a soothing "pink sound."*

Uniting the mind, body, and universe *The major league baseball player Barry Zito is known for doing yoga before games in which he pitches—a practice that combines the principles of meditation, hypnosis, and relaxation. Zito, one of baseball's most successful pitchers, performs this and related techniques in order to feel mentally and physically stronger during the game.*

Fighting HIV on all fronts *As part of his treatment at the Wellness Center in San Francisco, this man meditates and writes letters to his HIV virus.*

their own hypnotic state (*self-hypnosis*). Hypnosis is now used as an aid to psychotherapy and to help treat many physical conditions (Shenefelt, 2003; Barber, 1993, 1984).

Hypnosis seems to be particularly helpful in the control of pain (Kiecolt-Glaser et al., 1998). One case study describes a patient who underwent dental surgery under hypnotic suggestion: after a hypnotic state was induced, the dentist suggested to the patient that he was in a pleasant and relaxed setting listening to a friend describe his own success at undergoing similar dental surgery under hypnosis. The dentist then proceeded to perform a successful 25-minute operation (Gheorghiu & Orleanu, 1982). Although only some people are able to undergo surgery while anesthetized by hypnosis alone, hypnosis combined with chemical forms of anesthesia is apparently helpful to many patients (Fredericks, 2001). Beyond its use in the control of pain, hypnosis has been used successfully to help treat such problems as skin diseases, asthma, insomnia, high blood pressure, warts, and other forms of infection (Modin, 2002; Hornyak et al., 2000).

COGNITIVE INTERVENTIONS People with physical ailments have sometimes been taught new attitudes or cognitive responses toward their ailments as part of treatment (Kiecolt-Glaser et al., 2002, 1998; Compas et al., 1998). For example, *self-instruction training* has helped patients cope with severe pain, including pain from burns, arthritis, surgical procedures, headaches, back disorders, ulcers, multiple sclerosis, and cancer treatment (Meichenbaum, 1997, 1993, 1977, 1975). As we saw in Chapter 4, self-instruction therapists teach people to rid themselves of negative self-statements ("Oh, no, I can't take this pain") and to replace them with coping self-statements ("When pain comes, just pause; keep focusing on what you have to do").

INSIGHT THERAPY AND SUPPORT GROUPS If anxiety, depression, anger, and the like can contribute to a person's physical ills, therapy to reduce these negative emotions should help reduce the ills. In such cases, physicians may recommend insight therapy, support groups, or both to help patients overcome their medical difficulties (Dobkin & DaCosta, 2000). Research suggests that the discussion of past and present upsets may indeed help improve a person's health (Smyth & Pennebaker, 2001). In one study, asthma and arthritis patients who simply wrote down their thoughts and feelings about stressful events for a handful of days showed lasting improvements in their conditions. In addition, as we have seen, recovery from cancer and certain other illnesses is sometimes improved by participation in support groups (Spiegel & Fawzy, 2001).

COMBINATION APPROACHES Studies have found that the various psychological treatments for physical problems tend to be equal in effectiveness (Brauer, 1999). Relaxation and biofeedback training, for example, are equally helpful (and more helpful than placebos) in the treatment of high blood pressure, headaches, and asthma. Psychological interventions are, in fact, often of greatest help when they are combined with other psychological interventions and with medical treatments (Spiegler & Guevremont, 2002; Suinn, 2001). In one study, ulcer patients who were given relaxation, self-instruction, and assertiveness training along with medication were found to be less anxious and more comfortable, have fewer symptoms, and have a better long-term outcome than patients who received medication only (Brooks & Richardson, 1980). Combination interventions have also been helpful in changing Type A behavior patterns and reducing the risk of coronary heart disease among Type A people (Williams, 2001; Cohen et al., 1997).

>>LOOKING AROUND

Recovery from Illness

Surgical Risk People who experience more fear or stress before surgery tend to experience more pain and more complications after surgery and stay longer in the hospital (Kiecolt-Glaser et al., 1998).<<

Room with a View According to one hospital's records of individuals who underwent gallbladder surgery, those in rooms with a good view from their window had shorter hospitalizations and needed fewer pain medications than those in rooms without a good view (Ulrich, 1984).<<

Clearly, the treatment picture for physical illnesses has been changing dramatically. While medical treatments continue to dominate, the use of psychological approaches is on the rise. Today's medical practitioners are traveling a course far removed from that of their counterparts in centuries past.

SUMMING UP

Psychological Treatments for Physical Disorders

Behavioral medicine combines psychological and physical interventions to treat or prevent medical problems. Psychological approaches such as relaxation training, biofeedback training, meditation, hypnosis, cognitive techniques, insight therapy, and support groups are increasingly being included in the treatment of various medical problems.

CROSSROADS:

Expanding the Boundaries of Abnormal Psychology

The concept of stress is familiar to everyone, yet only in recent decades have clinical scientists and practitioners had much success in understanding and treating it and recognizing its enormous impact on our functioning; now that the importance and impact of stress have been identified, however, research efforts in this area are moving forward at near-lightning speed. What researchers once saw as a vague connection between stress and psychological dysfunctioning or between stress and physical illness is now understood as a complex interaction of many variables. Such factors as life changes, individual psychological and bodily reactions, social support, neurotransmitter and hormone activity, and slowing of the immune system are all recognized as contributors to psychological and physical stress disorders.

Insights into the treatment of the various stress disorders have been accumulating just as rapidly. In recent years clinicians have learned that a combination of approaches—from drug therapy to behavioral techniques to community interventions—are needed to help people overcome acute and posttraumatic stress disorders. Similarly, psychological approaches such as relaxation training and cognitive therapy are being applied to various physical ills, usually in combination with traditional medical treatments. Small wonder that many practitioners are convinced that such treatment combinations will eventually be the norm in treating the majority of physical ailments.

One of the most exciting aspects of these recent developments is the field's growing emphasis on the *interrelationship* of the social environment, the brain, and the rest of the body. Researchers have observed repeatedly that mental disorders are often best understood and treated when sociocultural, psychological, and biological factors are all taken into consideration. They now know that this interaction also helps explain medical problems. We are reminded that the brain is part of the body and that both are part of a social context. For better and for worse, the three are closely linked.

Another exciting aspect of this work on stress is the interest it has sparked in *illness prevention* and *health promotion* (Compas & Gotlib, 2002; Kaplan, 2000). If stress is indeed key to the development of both

"Under our holistic approach, Mr. Wyndot, we not only treat your symptoms, we also treat your dog."

>>**IN THEIR WORDS**

"As for me, except for the occasional heart attack, I feel as young as I ever did."<<

Robert Benchley

psychological and physical disorders, perhaps such disorders can be prevented by eliminating or reducing stress—for example, by helping people to cope better generally or by better preparing their bodies for stress's impact. With this notion in mind, illness prevention and health promotion programs are now being developed around the world. Clinical theorists have, for example, designed school-curriculum programs to help promote social competence in children (Weissberg, 2000) and teach children more optimistic ways of thinking (Gillham et al., 2000, 1995). And in the realm of acute and posttraumatic stress disorders, one team of clinical researchers has developed a program that immediately offers rape victims a combination of relaxation training, exposure techniques, cognitive interventions, and education about rape's impact, all before the onset of psychological or physical symptoms (Foa et al., 1995). Research indicates that women who receive such preventive measures do indeed develop fewer stress symptoms in the months following their attacks than do other rape victims.

CRITICAL THOUGHTS

1. What types of events in modern society might trigger acute and posttraumatic stress disorders? What kinds of factors might serve to relieve the stresses of modern society? *pp. 136–148*

2. Do you think the vivid images seen daily on television, in movies, in rock videos, and the like would make people more vulnerable to developing psychological stress disorders or less vulnerable? Why? *pp. 136–141*

3. How might physicians, police, the courts, and other agents better meet the psychological needs of rape victims? *pp. 138–139*

4. What jobs in our society might be particularly stressful and traumatizing? *pp. 151–152, 155*

5. Some observers fear that today there may be too much emphasis on psychosocial factors in explaining physical illness. What problems might result from an overemphasis on the role of psychosocial factors? *pp. 152–156*

KEY TERMS

stressor p. 133

hypothalamus p. 134

autonomic nervous system p. 134

endocrine system p. 134

sympathetic nervous system p. 134

epinephrine p. 134

norepinephrine p. 134

parasympathetic nervous system p. 135

hypothalamic-pituitary–adrenal pathway p. 135

corticosteroids p. 135

acute stress disorder p. 136

posttraumatic stress disorder p. 136

rape p. 138

critical incident stress debriefing p. 146

psychophysiological disorders p. 148

ulcer p. 149

asthma p. 149

insomnia p. 149

headaches pp. 149–150

hypertension p. 150

coronary heart disease p. 150

Type A personality style p. 151

Social Adjustment Rating Scale p. 152

psychoneuroimmuology p. 153

immune system p. 153

lymphocyte p. 153

behavioral medicine p. 156

relaxation training p. 157

biofeedback training p. 157

meditation p. 157

hypnosis p. 157

self-instruction training p. 158

QUICK QUIZ

1. What factors determine how people react to stressors in life? *pp. 133–136*

2. What factors seem to help influence whether a person will develop an acute stress disorder or posttraumatic stress disorder after experiencing a traumatic event? *pp. 137–141*

3. What treatment approaches have been used with people suffering from acute or posttraumatic stress disorders? *pp. 141–147*

4. What are the specific causes of ulcers, asthma, insomnia, headaches, hypertension, and coronary heart disease? *pp. 149–150*

5. What kinds of sociocultural, psychological, and biological factors appear to contribute to psychophysiological disorders? *pp. 150–152*

6. What kinds of links have been found between life stress and physical illnesses? What scale has helped researchers investigate this relationship? *pp. 152–153*

7. Describe the relationship among stress, the immune system, and physical illness. *pp. 153–156*

8. Explain the specific roles played by various types of lymphocytes. *pp. 153–154*

9. Discuss how immune system functioning at times of stress may be affected by a person's biochemical activity, behavioral changes, personality style, and social support. *pp. 154–156*

10. What psychological treatments have been used to help treat physical illnesses? To which specific illnesses has each been applied? *pp. 156–159*

CYBER STUDY

SEARCH THE *FUNDAMENTALS OF ABNORMAL PSYCHOLOGY* CD-ROM FOR

▲ Chapter 5 Video Case Enrichment
   How might stress and anxiety affect performance?
   Observe "fight-or-flight" reactions in operation.
   How do physical, psychological, and sociocultural factors affect health?

▲ Chapter 5 Practical, Research, and Decision-Making Exercises
   Stress, Coping, and Health

▲ Chapter 5 Practice Test and Feedback

LOG ON TO THE COMER WEB PAGE FOR

▲ Suggested Web links, exercises, FAQ page, additional Chapter 5 practice test questions
   <www.worthpublishers.com/comer>

‹‹‹

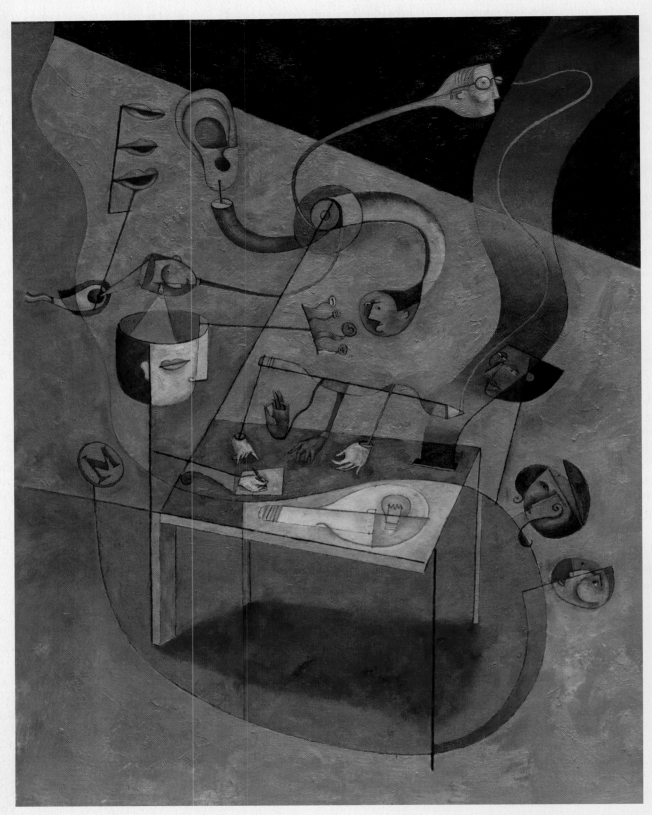

FERRUCCIO SARDELLA, 1997

Somatoform and Dissociative Disorders

Brian was spending Saturday sailing with his wife, Helen. The water was rough but well within what they considered safe limits. They were having a wonderful time and really didn't notice that the sky was getting darker, the wind blowing harder, and the sailboat becoming more difficult to control. After a few hours of sailing, they found themselves far from shore in the middle of a powerful and dangerous storm.

The storm intensified very quickly. Brian had trouble controlling the sailboat amidst the high winds and wild waves. He and Helen tried to put on the safety jackets they had neglected to wear earlier, but the boat turned over before they were finished. Brian, the better swimmer of the two, was able to swim back to the overturned sailboat, grab the side, and hold on for dear life, but Helen simply could not overcome the rough waves and reach the boat. As Brian watched in horror and disbelief, his wife disappeared from view.

After a time, the storm began to lose its strength. Brian managed to right the sailboat and sail back to shore. Finally he reached safety, but the personal consequences of this storm were just beginning. The next days were filled with pain and further horror: the Coast Guard finding Helen's body . . . conversations with friends . . . self-blame . . . grief . . . and more.

Compounding this horror, the accident had left Brian with a severe physical impairment—he could not walk properly. He first noticed this problem when he sailed the boat back to shore, right after the accident. As he tried to run from the sailboat to get help, he could hardly make his legs work. By the time he reached the nearby beach restaurant, all he could do was crawl. Two patrons had to lift him to a chair, and after he told his story and the authorities were alerted, he had to be taken to a hospital.

At first Brian and the hospital physician assumed that he must have been hurt during the accident. One by one, however, the hospital tests revealed nothing—no broken bones, no spinal damage, nothing. Nothing that could explain such severe impairment.

By the following morning, the weakness in his legs had become near paralysis. Because the physicians could not pin down the nature of his injuries, they decided to keep his activities to a minimum. He was not allowed to talk long with the police. Someone else had to inform Helen's parents of her death. He was not even permitted to attend Helen's funeral.

The mystery deepened over the following weeks. As Brian's paralysis continued, he became more and more withdrawn, unable to see more than a few friends and family members and unable to take care of the unpleasant tasks attached to Helen's death. He could not even bring himself to return to work or get on with his life. Almost from the beginning, Brian's paralysis had left him self-absorbed and drained of emotion, unable to look back and unable to move forward.

In Chapters 4 and 5, we have seen how stress and anxiety can negatively affect functioning. Indeed, anxiety is the key feature of disorders such as generalized anxiety disorder, phobias, panic disorder, and obsessive-compulsive

Annie Wells/© The New Press Democrat, Santa Rosa, CA

Deliverance from danger *As a creek's wild waters rage around her, a young woman is saved from drowning. Unfortunately, for some people deliverance from a life-threatening event, such as a boating accident, combat, flood, or tornado, is the beginning rather than the end of their trauma. Somatoform disorders (particularly conversion disorders) and dissociative disorders may emerge during or shortly after such stressful events.*

disorder. And stress can produce the lingering reactions seen in acute stress disorder, posttraumatic stress disorder, and psychophysiological disorders.

Two other kinds of disorders are commonly linked to stress and anxiety—somatoform disorders and dissociative disorders. *Somatoform disorders* are problems that appear to be medical, but are actually due to psychosocial factors. Unlike psychophysiological disorders, in which psychosocial factors interact with physical factors to produce genuine physical ailments, the somatoform disorders are psychological disorders masquerading as physical problems. Similarly, *dissociative disorders* are patterns that feature major losses or changes in memory and identity—losses that are due almost entirely to psychosocial factors rather than physical ones.

The somatoform and dissociative disorders have much in common (Brown, 2002). Both, for example, may occur in response to severe stress, and both have traditionally been viewed as forms of escape from stress. Because of such similarities, the two groups of disorders are commonly discussed together, as in this chapter. Moreover, theorists and clinicians often explain and treat the two groups of disorders in similar ways.

Somatoform Disorders

Think back to Brian, the young man whose tragic boating accident left him unable to walk. As medical test after test failed to explain his paralysis, physicians became convinced that the cause of his problem lay elsewhere.

When a physical ailment has no apparent medical cause, doctors may suspect a **somatoform disorder**, a pattern of physical complaints with largely psychosocial causes. People with such disorders do not consciously want or purposely produce their symptoms; like Brian, they almost always believe that their problems are genuinely medical (Lieb et al., 2000). In some somatoform disorders, known as *hysterical somatoform disorders*, there is an actual change in physical functioning. In others, the *preoccupation somatoform disorders*, people who are healthy mistakenly worry that there is something physically wrong with them.

What Are Hysterical Somatoform Disorders?

People with **hysterical somatoform disorders** suffer actual changes in their physical functioning. These somatoform disorders are often hard to distinguish from genuine medical problems (Hickie et al., 2000). In fact, it is always possible that a diagnosis of hysterical disorder is a mistake and that the patient's problem actually has an undetected organic cause (Cathebras, 2002). DSM-IV lists three hysterical somatoform disorders: *conversion disorder*, *somatization disorder*, and *pain disorder associated with psychological factors*.

CONVERSION DISORDER In **conversion disorder**, a psychosocial conflict or need is converted into dramatic physical symptoms that affect voluntary motor or sensory functioning (see Table 6-1). Brian, the man with the unexplained paralysis, would probably receive this particular diagnosis. The symptoms often seem neurological, such as paralysis, blindness, or loss of feeling (APA, 2000, 1994). One woman developed dizziness in apparent response to her unhappy marriage:

SOMATOFORM DISORDER A physical illness or ailment that is explained largely by psychosocial causes, in which the patient experiences no sense of wanting or guiding the symptoms.

HYSTERICAL SOMATOFORM DISORDERS Somatoform disorders in which people suffer actual changes in their physical functioning.

CONVERSION DISORDER A somatoform disorder in which a psychosocial need or conflict is converted into dramatic physical symptoms that affect voluntary motor or sensory function.

A 46-year-old married housewife . . . described being overcome with feelings of extreme dizziness, accompanied by slight nausea, four or five nights a week. During these attacks, the room around her would take on a "shimmering" appearance, and she would have the feeling that she was "floating" and unable to keep her balance. Inexplicably, the attacks almost always occurred at about 4:00 p.m. She usually had to lie down on the couch and often did not feel better until 7:00 or 8:00 p.m. After recovering, she generally spent the rest of the evening watching TV; and more often than not, she would fall asleep in the living room, not going to bed in the bedroom until 2:00 or 3:00 in the morning.

The patient had been pronounced physically fit by her internist, a neurologist, and an ear, nose, and throat specialist on more than one occasion. Hypoglycemia had been ruled out by glucose tolerance tests.

When asked about her marriage, the patient described her husband as a tyrant, frequently demanding and verbally abusive of her and their four children. She admitted that she dreaded his arrival home from work each day, knowing that he would comment that the house was a mess and the dinner, if prepared, not to his liking. Recently, since the onset of her attacks, when she was unable to make dinner he and the four kids would go to McDonald's or the local pizza parlor. After that, he would settle in to watch a ballgame in the bedroom, and their conversation was minimal. In spite of their troubles, the patient claimed that she loved her husband and needed him very much.

(Spitzer et al., 1981, pp. 92–93)

>>LOOKING AROUND

Time Out

Stretching the Truth Almost 60 percent of American adults have called in sick to work when they were perfectly healthy (Kanner, 1995).<<

- -

Gender Confusion In some cultures, fathers follow the custom of *couvade*: they feel ill and stay in bed before and during the deliveries of their children. They may even show some symptoms of pregnancy and experience the pangs of childbirth (Kahn & Fawcett, 1993).<<

Table 6-1 DSM-IV Checklist

CONVERSION DISORDER

1. One or more physical symptoms or deficits affecting voluntary motor or sensory function that suggest a neurological or other general medical condition.
2. Psychological factors judged to be associated with the symptom or deficit.
3. Symptom or deficit not intentionally produced or feigned.
4. Symptom or deficit not fully explained by a general medical condition or a substance.
5. Significant distress or impairment.

SOMATIZATION DISORDER

1. A history of many physical complaints, beginning before the age of 30, that occur over a period of several years and result in treatment being sought or in significant impairment.
2. Physical complaints over the period include all of the following:
   (a) Four different kinds of pain symptoms.
   (b) Two gastrointestinal symptoms.
   (c) One sexual symptom.
   (d) One neurological-type symptom.
3. Physical complaints not fully explained by a known general medical condition or a drug, or extending beyond the usual impact of such a condition.
4. Symptoms not intentionally produced or feigned.

PAIN DISORDER ASSOCIATED WITH PSYCHOLOGICAL FACTORS

1. Significant pain as the primary problem.
2. Psychological factors judged to have the major role in the onset, severity, exacerbation, or maintenance of the pain.
3. Symptom or deficit not intentionally produced or feigned.
4. Significant distress or impairment.

Based on APA, 2000, 1994.

Ulterior motives *Children often pretend to be sick in order to avoid school or other unpleasant situations. When individuals manufacture physical symptoms in order to achieve external gains of this kind, they are malingering, not displaying a somatoform disorder.*

SOMATIZATION DISORDER A somatoform disorder marked by numerous recurring physical ailments without an organic basis. Also known as *Briquet's syndrome.*

PAIN DISORDER ASSOCIATED WITH PSYCHOLOGICAL FACTORS A somatoform disorder marked by pain, with psychosocial factors playing a central role in the onset, severity, or continuation of the pain.

FACTITIOUS DISORDER An illness with no identifiable physical cause, in which the patient is believed to be intentionally producing or faking symptoms in order to assume a sick role.

Most conversion disorders begin between late childhood and young adulthood; they are diagnosed at least twice as often in women as in men (APA, 2000). They usually appear suddenly, at times of extreme stress, and last a matter of weeks. Some research suggests that people who develop this disorder are generally suggestible; many are highly susceptible to hypnotic procedures, for example (Roelofs et al., 2002). Conversion disorders are thought to be quite rare, occurring in at most 5 of every 1,000 persons.

SOMATIZATION DISORDER Sheila baffled medical specialists with the wide range of her symptoms:

> Sheila reported having abdominal pain since age 17, necessitating exploratory surgery that yielded no specific diagnosis. She had several pregnancies, each with severe nausea, vomiting, and abdominal pain; she ultimately had a hysterectomy for a "tipped uterus." Since age 40 she had experienced dizziness and "blackouts," which she eventually was told might be multiple sclerosis or a brain tumor. She continued to be bedridden for extended periods of time, with weakness, blurred vision, and difficulty urinating. At age 43 she was worked up for a hiatal hernia because of complaints of bloating and intolerance of a variety of foods. She also had additional hospitalizations for neurological, hypertensive, and renal workups, all of which failed to reveal a definitive diagnosis.
>
> *(Spitzer et al., 1981, pp. 185, 260)*

Like Sheila, people with **somatization disorder** have many long-lasting physical ailments that have little or no organic basis (see again Table 6-1). This hysterical pattern, first described by Pierre Briquet in 1859, is also known as **Briquet's syndrome**. To receive this diagnosis, a person must have a range of ailments, including several pain symptoms (such as headaches and chest pain), gastrointestinal symptoms (such as nausea and diarrhea), a sexual symptom (such as erectile or menstrual difficulties), and a neurological symptom (such as double vision or paralysis) (APA, 2000, 1994). People with somatization disorder usually go from doctor to doctor in search of relief (APA, 2000, 1994). They often describe their many symptoms in dramatic and exaggerated terms. Most also feel anxious and depressed (Holder-Perkins & Wise, 2001).

Between 0.2 and 2.0 percent of all women in the United States may experience a somatization disorder in any given year, compared to less than 0.2 percent of men (Ladwig et al., 2001; APA, 2000). The disorder often runs in families; 10 to 20 percent of the close female relatives of women with the disorder also develop it. It usually begins between adolescence and young adulthood (APA, 2000, 1994).

A somatization disorder lasts much longer than a conversion disorder, typically for many years (Simon & Gureje, 1999). The symptoms may fluctuate over time but rarely disappear completely without psychotherapy (Smith et al., 1995). Two-thirds of the people with this disorder in the United States receive treatment for their physical ailments from a medical or mental health professional in any given year (Regier et al., 1993).

PAIN DISORDER ASSOCIATED WITH PSYCHOLOGICAL FACTORS When psychosocial factors play a central role in the onset, severity, or continuation of pain, patients may receive a diagnosis of **pain disorder associated with psychological factors** (see again Table 6-1). Patients with a conversion or somatization disorder may also experience pain, but it is the key symptom in this disorder (Birket & Mortensen, 2002).

Mind over matter *The opposite of hysterical disorders—though again demonstrating the power of psychological processes—are instances in which people "ignore" pain or other physical symptoms. Despite a badly injured leg, Kerri Strug completes a near-perfect vault and landing, leading the United States gymnastics team to an Olympic gold medal in 1996.*

John Gaps III/AP Photo

Although the precise prevalence has not been determined, pain disorder associated with psychological factors appears to be fairly common (McGrady et al., 1999). The disorder may begin at any age, and women seem more likely than men to experience it (APA, 2000). Often it develops after an accident or during an illness that has caused genuine pain, which then takes on a life of its own. Laura, a 36-year-old woman, reported pains that went far beyond the usual symptoms of her tubercular disease, called sarcoidosis:

> Before the operation I would have little joint pains, nothing that really bothered me that much. After the operation I was having severe pains in my chest and in my ribs, and those were the type of problems I'd been having after the operation, that I didn't have before. . . . I'd go to an emergency room at night, 11:00, 12:00, 1:00 or so. I'd take the medicine, and the next day it stopped hurting, and I'd go back again. In the meantime this is when I went to the other doctors, to complain about the same thing, to find out what was wrong; and they could never find out what was wrong with me either. . . .
>
> . . . At certain points when I go out or my husband and I go out, we have to leave early because I start hurting. . . . A lot of times I just won't do things because my chest is hurting for one reason or another. . . . Two months ago when the doctor checked me and another doctor looked at the x-rays, he said he didn't see any signs of the sarcoid then and that they were doing a study now, on blood and various things, to see if it was connected to sarcoid. . . .
>
> *(Green, 1985, pp. 60–63)*

HYSTERICAL VS. MEDICAL SYMPTOMS Because hysterical somatoform disorders are so similar to "true" medical problems, physicians sometimes rely on oddities in the patient's medical picture to help distinguish the two (Roelofs et al., 2002). The symptoms of a hysterical disorder may, for example, be at odds with the way the nervous system is known to work (APA, 2000, 1994). In a conversion symptom called *glove anesthesia*, numbness begins sharply at the wrist and extends evenly right to the fingertips. As Figure 6-1 shows, real neurological damage is rarely as abrupt or equally distributed.

The physical effects of a hysterical disorder may also differ from those of the corresponding medical problem. For example, when paralysis from the waist down, or paraplegia, is caused by damage to the spinal cord, a person's leg muscles may *atrophy*, or waste away, unless physical therapy is applied. People whose paralysis is the result of a conversion disorder, in contrast, do not usually experience atrophy. Perhaps they exercise their muscles without being aware that they are doing so. Similarly, people with conversion blindness may have fewer accidents than people who are organically blind, an indication that they have at least some vision even if they are unaware of it.

HYSTERICAL VS. FACTITIOUS SYMPTOMS Hysterical somatoform disorders must also be distinguished from patterns in which individuals are faking medical symptoms (Ron, 2001). A patient may, for example, be *malingering*—intentionally faking illness to achieve some external gain, such as financial compensation or deferment from military service. Or a patient may intentionally produce or fake physical symptoms simply out of a wish to be a patient; that is, the motivation for assuming the sick role may be the role itself. Physicians would then decide that the patient is displaying a **factitious disorder**.

People with a factitious disorder often go to extremes to create the appearance of illness (Phillips, 2001). Many give themselves medications secretly. Some inject drugs to cause bleeding. High fevers are especially easy to create. In one study of patients with prolonged mysterious fever, more than 9 percent were eventually diagnosed with factitious disorder (Feldman, Ford, & Reinhold, 1994). People

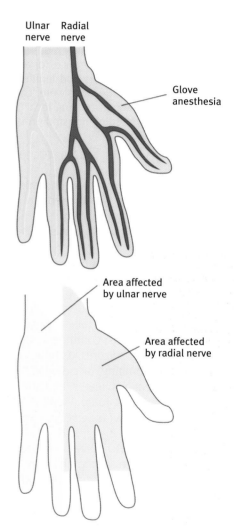

FIGURE 6-1 **Glove anesthesia** *In this conversion symptom the entire hand, extending from the fingertips to the wrist, becomes numb. Actual physical damage to the ulnar nerve, in contrast, causes anesthesia in the ring finger and little finger and beyond the wrist partway up the arm; and damage to the radial nerve causes loss of feeling only in parts of the ring, middle, and index fingers and the thumb and partway up the arm. (Adapted from Gray, 1959.)*

A CLOSER LOOK

Munchausen Syndrome by Proxy

❙ [Jennifer] had been hospitalized 200 times and undergone 40 operations. Physicians removed her gallbladder, her appendix and part of her intestines, and inserted tubes into her chest, stomach and intestines. [The 9-year-old from Florida] was befriended by the Florida Marlins and served as a poster child for health care reform, posing with Hillary Rodham Clinton at a White House rally. Then police notified her mother that she was under investigation for child abuse. Suddenly, Jennifer's condition improved dramatically. In the next nine months, she was hospitalized only once, for a viral infection. . . . Experts said Jennifer's numerous baffling infections were "consistent with someone smearing fecal matter" into her feeding line and urinary catheter. ❙

(KATEL & BECK, 1996)

Convalescent, **1994, by Frank Holl**

Christopher Wood Gallery, London, Bridgeman/Art Resource, NY

Cases like Jennifer's have horrified the public and called attention to *Munchausen syndrome by proxy* (Bentovin, 2001). This disorder is caused by a caregiver who uses various techniques to induce symptoms in a child—giving the child drugs, tampering with medications, contaminating a feeding tube, or even smothering the child, for example. The illness can take almost any form, but the most common symptoms are bleeding, seizures, asthma, comas, diarrhea, vomiting, "accidental" poisonings, infections, fevers, and sudden infant death syndrome (Plunkett & Southall, 2001; Libow & Schreier, 1998; Boros et al., 1995).

Between 6 and 30 percent of the victims of Munchausen syndrome by proxy die as a result of their symptoms, and 8 percent of those who survive are permanently disfigured or physically impaired (Mitchell, 2001; Von Burg & Hibbard,

1995). Psychological, educational, and physical development are also affected (Libow & Schreier, 1998; Libow, 1995). Jennifer missed so much school that at age 9 she could barely read or write.

The syndrome is very hard to diagnose (Sanders & Bursch, 2002) and may be more common than clinicians once thought. The parent (usually the mother) seems to be so devoted and caring that others sympathize with and admire her (Abdulhamid, 2002). Yet the physical problems disappear when child and parent are separated. In many cases siblings of the sick child have also been victimized (Skau & Mouridsen, 1995).

What kind of parent carefully inflicts pain and illness on her own child? The typical Munchausen mother is emotionally needy: she craves the attention and praise she receives for her devoted care of her sick child. She may have little social support outside the medical system. Many of these mothers are intelligent;

often they have a medical background of some kind—perhaps having worked formerly in a doctor's office. Typically they deny their actions, even in the face of clear evidence, and refuse to undergo therapy. In fact, to date, successful treatment has been uncommon (Bluglass, 2001; Ayoub et al., 2000).

Law enforcement authorities are reluctant to consider Munchausen syndrome by proxy a psychological disorder and instead approach it as a crime—a carefully planned form of child abuse (Taylor & Nicholls, 2001). They almost always require that the child be separated from the mother (Ayoub et al., 2000). At the same time, a parent who resorts to such actions is obviously experiencing serious psychological disturbance and greatly needs clinical help. Thus clinical researchers and practitioners must now work to develop clearer insights and more effective treatments for such parents and for their small victims.

with a factitious disorder often research their supposed ailments and are impressively knowledgeable about medicine (Sadock & Sadock, 2003).

Psychotherapists and physicians often become angry at people with a factitious disorder (Christison et al., 2002), feeling that these individuals are, among other issues, wasting their time. Yet people with this disorder, like most people with psychological disorders, feel they have no control over their problem, and they often experience great distress.

Munchausen syndrome is the extreme and long-term form of factitious disorder. It is named after Baron Munchausen, an eighteenth-century cavalry officer who journeyed from tavern to tavern in Europe telling fantastical tales about his supposed military adventures (Feldman et al., 1994). In a related disorder, **Munchausen syndrome by proxy**, parents make up or produce physical illnesses in their children, leading in some cases to repeated painful diagnostic tests, medication, and surgery.

What Are Preoccupation Somatoform Disorders?

Hypochondriasis and *body dysmorphic disorder* are **preoccupation somatoform disorders**. People with these problems misinterpret and overreact to bodily symptoms or features no matter what friends, relatives, and physicians may say. Although preoccupation disorders also cause great distress, their impact on one's life differs from that of hysterical disorders.

HYPOCHONDRIASIS People who suffer from **hypochondriasis** unrealistically interpret bodily symptoms as signs of a serious illness (see Table 6-2). Often their symptoms are merely normal bodily changes, such as occasional coughing, sores, or sweating. Although some patients recognize that their concerns are excessive, many do not.

Although hypochondriasis can begin at any age, it starts most often in early adulthood, among men and women in equal numbers (APA, 2000, 1994). Between 1 and 5 percent of all people experience the disorder (APA, 2000). As with pain disorder associated with psychological factors, physicians report seeing many cases. As many as 4.5 percent of all patients seen by primary care physicians may display hypochondriasis (Magarinos et al., 2002). For most patients, the symptoms rise and fall over the years.

BODY DYSMORPHIC DISORDER People who experience **body dysmorphic disorder**, also known as **dysmorphophobia**, become deeply concerned about some imagined or minor defect in their appearance (Buhlman et al., 2002) (see again Table 6-2). Most often they focus on wrinkles, spots on the skin, excessive facial hair, swelling of the face, or a misshapen nose, mouth, jaw, or eyebrow. Some worry about the appearance of their feet, hands, breasts, penis, or other body parts. Still others are concerned about bad odors coming from sweat, breath, genitals, or the rectum (Phillips & Castle, 2002). Here we see such a case:

> A woman of 35 had for 16 years been worried that her sweat smelled terrible. The fear began just before her marriage when she was sharing a bed with a close friend who said that someone at work smelled badly, and the patient felt that the remark was directed at her. For fear that she smelled, for 5 years she had not gone out anywhere except when accompanied by her husband or mother. She had not spoken to her neighbors for 3 years because she thought she had overheard them speak about her to some friends. She avoided cinemas, dances, shops, cafes, and private homes. . . . Her husband was not allowed to invite any friends home; she constantly sought reassurance from him about her smell. . . . Her husband bought all her new clothes as she was afraid to try on clothes in front of shop assistants. She used vast quantities of deodorant and always bathed and changed her clothes before going out, up to 4 times daily.
>
> *(Marks, 1987, p. 371)*

Table 6-2 DSM-IV Checklist

HYPOCHONDRIASIS

1. Preoccupation with fears or beliefs that one has a serious disease, based on misinterpretation of bodily symptoms, lasting at least six months.
2. Persistence of preoccupation despite appropriate medical evaluation and reassurance.
3. Absence of delusions.
4. Significant distress or impairment.

BODY DYSMORPHIC DISORDER

1. Preoccupation with an imagined or exaggerated defect in appearance.
2. Significant distress or impairment.

Based on APA, 2000, 1994.

MUNCHAUSEN SYNDROME The extreme and chronic form of factitious disorder.

MUNCHAUSEN SYNDROME BY PROXY A factitious disorder in which parents make up or produce illnesses in their children.

PREOCCUPATION SOMATOFORM DISORDERS Disorders in which people misinterpret and overreact to minor, even normal, bodily symptoms or features.

HYPOCHONDRIASIS A disorder in which people mistakenly fear that minor changes in their physical functioning indicate a serious disease.

BODY DYSMORPHIC DISORDER A disorder marked by excessive worry that some aspect of one's physical appearance is defective.

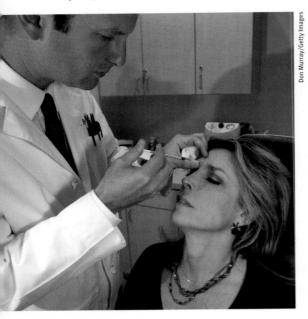

Frown lines disappear *A plastic surgeon injects Botox (Botulinum Toxin Type A) into the muscles between a patient's eyebrows, hoping to eliminate her so-called frown lines. A cautionary note: As many as 15 percent of people who seek help from cosmetic surgery or dermatologists are believed to have body dysmorphic disorder (APA, 2000).*

It is common in our society to worry about appearance. Many teenagers and young adults worry about acne, for instance. The concerns of people with body dysmorphic disorder, however, are extreme. Sufferers may be unable to look others in the eye, or they may go to great lengths to hide their "defects"—say, always wearing sunglasses to cover their supposedly misshapen eyes. Some seek plastic surgery. One study found that 30 percent of subjects with the disorder were housebound and 17 percent had attempted suicide (Phillips et al., 1993).

Most cases of the disorder begin during adolescence. Often, however, people don't reveal their concerns for many years. Up to 2 percent of people in the United States—4 percent of college students—may suffer from body dysmorphic disorder (Bohne et al., 2002). Clinical reports suggest that it may be equally common among men and women (APA, 2000).

What Causes Somatoform Disorders?

Theorists typically explain the preoccupation somatoform disorders much as they do anxiety disorders (Buhlman et al., 2002). Behaviorists, for example, believe that the fears found in hypochondriasis and body dysmorphic disorder have been acquired earlier in life through classical conditioning or modeling (Whitehead et al., 1994) (see Figure 6-2 and Table 6-3). Cognitive theorists suggest that people with the disorders are so sensitive to and threatened by bodily cues that they come to overinterpret them (Wilhelm & Neziroglu, 2002).

In contrast, the hysterical somatoform disorders—conversion, somatization, and pain disorders—are widely considered unique and in need of special explanations. The ancient Greeks believed that only women had hysterical disorders. The uterus of a sexually ungratified woman was supposed to wander throughout her body in search of fulfillment, producing a physical symptom wherever it lodged. Thus Hippocrates suggested marriage as the most effective treatment for such disorders. Today's leading explanations for hysterical somatoform disorders come from the psychodynamic, behavioral, and cognitive models. None have received

FIGURE 6-2 **"Mirror, mirror, on the wall . . ."** *People with body dysmorphic disorder are not the only ones who have concerns about their appearance. Surveys find that in our appearance-conscious society, large percentages of people regularly think about and try to change the way they look (Kimball, 1993; Poretz & Sinrod, 1991; Weiss, 1991; Simmon, 1990).*

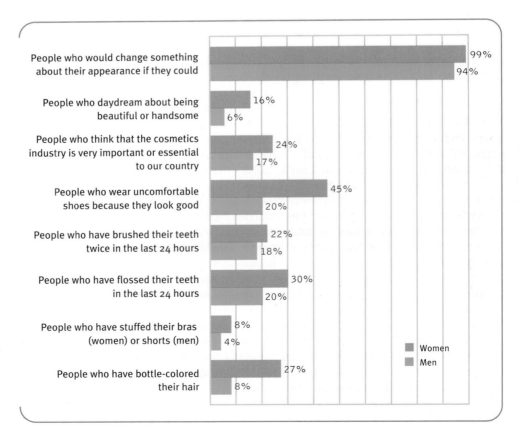

Table 6-3

When Did Body and Beauty Aids Make Their Debuts?

4000 B.C.	Egypt produces the first eye glitter, blue and black lipstick, rouge, and other cosmetics for women and men.
3000 B.C.	Fingernail paint originates in China. Creams, oils, and moisturizers are developed in Egypt. The art of wigmaking is developed in Egypt. Sumerians (in Mesopotamia) and Egyptians make the transition from incense to perfumes.
1500 B.C.	Assyria perfects the art of hair styling.
303 B.C.	The first professional barbers, formed into guilds, open shops in Rome.
A.D. 157	The Greek physician Galen develops the first cold cream.
1600–1700	Beauty patches (shaped like stars, crescent moons, hearts) are purchased throughout Europe to cover up scars left by smallpox.
1709	The Italian barber Jean-Baptiste Farina concocts an alcohol-based blend of fruits in Cologne, Germany—a product thereafter known by the name of the city.
1880	The Dutch immigrant Andrew Jergens forms a company to make prestigious toilet soap, called Jergens Lotion.
1886	The door-to-door salesman David McConnell launches Avon Calling in New York State.
1909	The French chemist Eugène Schueller develops the first safe commercial hair dye.

much research support, however, and the disorders are still poorly understood (Lautenbacher & Rollman, 1999; Kirmayer et al., 1994).

THE PSYCHODYNAMIC VIEW As we observed in Chapter 1, Freud's theory of psychoanalysis began with his efforts to explain hysterical symptoms. Indeed, he was one of the few clinicians of his day to treat patients with these symptoms seriously, as people with a genuine problem. After studying hypnosis in Paris, Freud became interested in the work of an older physician, Josef Breuer (1842–1925). Breuer had successfully used hypnosis to treat a woman he called Anna O., who suffered from hysterical deafness, disorganized speech, and paralysis. Critics have since questioned whether Anna's ailments were entirely hysterical and whether Breuer's treatment helped her as much as he claimed (Ellenberger, 1972). But on the basis of this and similar cases, Freud (1894) came to believe that hysterical disorders represented a *conversion* of underlying emotional conflicts into physical symptoms.

Observing that most of his patients with hysterical disorders were women, Freud centered his explanation of hysterical disorders on the needs of girls during their *phallic stage* (ages 3 through 5). At that time in life, he believed, all girls develop a pattern of desires called the *Electra complex*: each girl experiences sexual feelings for her father and at the same time recognizes that she must compete with her mother for his affection. However, aware of her mother's more powerful position and of cultural taboos, the child typically represses her sexual feelings and rejects these early desires for her father.

Freud believed that if a child's parents overreact to her sexual feelings—with strong punishments, for example—the Electra conflict will be unresolved and the

Electra complex goes awry *Freud argued that a hysterical disorder may result when parents overreact to their daughter's early displays of affection for her father. The child may go on to exhibit sexual repression in adulthood and convert sexual feelings into physical ailments.*

PRIMARY GAIN In psychodynamic theory, the gain achieved when hysterical symptoms keep internal conflicts out of awareness.

SECONDARY GAIN In psychodynamic theory, the gain achieved when hysterical symptoms elicit kindness from others or provide an excuse to avoid unpleasant activities.

PLACEBO A sham treatment that a patient believes to be genuine.

child may reexperience sexual anxiety throughout her life. Whenever events trigger sexual feelings, she may experience an unconscious need to hide them from both herself and others. Freud concluded that some women hide their sexual feelings by unconsciously converting them into physical symptoms.

Most of today's psychodynamic theorists take issue with Freud's explanation of hysterical disorders, particularly his notion that the disorders can always be traced to an unresolved Electra conflict (Hess, 1995; Scott, 1995). They continue to believe, however, that sufferers of these disorders have unconscious conflicts carried forth from childhood which arouse anxiety and that the individuals convert this anxiety into "more tolerable" physical symptoms (Kuechenhoff, 2002; Temple, 2002).

Psychodynamic theorists propose that two mechanisms are at work in hysterical somatoform disorders—primary gain and secondary gain (Colbach, 1987). People achieve **primary gain** when their hysterical symptoms keep their internal conflicts out of awareness. During an argument, for example, a man who has underlying fears about expressing anger may develop a conversion paralysis of the arm, thus preventing his feelings of rage from reaching consciousness. People achieve **secondary gain** when their hysterical symptoms further enable them to avoid unpleasant activities or to receive kindness or sympathy from others. When, for example, a conversion paralysis allows a soldier to avoid combat duty or conversion blindness prevents the breakup of a relationship, secondary gain may be operating. Similarly, the conversion paralysis of Brian, the man who lost his wife in the boating accident, seemed to help him avoid many painful duties after the accident, from telling his wife's parents of her death to attending her funeral and returning to work.

THE BEHAVIORAL VIEW Behavioral theorists propose that the physical symptoms of hysterical disorders bring *rewards* to sufferers (see Table 6-4). Perhaps the symptoms remove the individuals from an unpleasant relationship or bring attention from other people (Whitehead et al., 1994). In response to such rewards, the sufferers learn to display the symptoms more and more prominently. Behaviorists also hold that people who are familiar with an illness will more readily adopt its physical symptoms (Garralda, 1996). In fact, studies find that many sufferers develop their hysterical symptoms after they or their close relatives or friends have had similar medical problems (Stuart & Noyes, 1999). Clearly, the behavioral focus on rewards is similar to the psychodynamic idea of secondary gains.

Like the psychodynamic explanation, the behavioral view of hysterical disorders has received little research support. Even clinical case reports only occasionally support this position. In many cases the pain and upset that surround the disorders seem to outweigh any rewards the symptoms may bring.

THE COGNITIVE VIEW Some cognitive theorists propose that hysterical disorders are forms of *communication*, providing a means for people to express emotions that would otherwise be difficult to convey (Sundbom et al., 1999). Like their psychodynamic colleagues, these theorists hold that the emotions of patients with hysterical disorders are being converted into physical symptoms. They suggest, however, that the purpose of the conversion is not to defend against anxiety but to communicate extreme feelings—anger, fear, depression, guilt, jealousy—in a "physical language" that is familiar to and comfortable for the patient (Fry, 1993).

According to this view, people who find it particularly hard to recognize or express their emotions are candidates for a hysterical disorder. So are those who "know" the language of physical symptoms through firsthand experience with a genuine physical malady. Because children are less able to express their emotions verbally, they are particularly likely to develop physical symptoms as a form of

Table 6-4

Disorders That Have Physical Symptoms

DISORDER	VOLUNTARY CONTROL OF SYMPTOMS?	DO SYMPTOMS SERVE A GOAL?
Malingering	Yes	Yes
Factitious disorder	Yes	Yes
Somatoform disorder	No	Sometimes
Psychophysiological disorder	No	No
Physical illness	No	No

communication (Dhossche et al., 2002). Like the other explanations, however, this cognitive view has not been widely tested or supported by research.

A POSSIBLE ROLE FOR BIOLOGY Although hysterical somatoform disorders are, by definition, thought to result largely from psychosocial factors, the impact of biological processes should not be overlooked. To understand this point, consider first what researchers have learned about *placebos* and the *placebo effect*.

For centuries physicians have observed that patients suffering from many kinds of illnesses, from seasickness to angina, often find relief from **placebos**, substances that have no known medicinal value (Brody, 2000). Some reviews have raised questions about the actual number of patients helped by placebos (Hrobjartsson & Goltzsche, 2001), but it is generally agreed that such "pretend" treatments do bring help to many (Kirsch & Scoboria, 2001).

Why do placebos have a medicinal effect? Theorists used to believe that they operated in purely psychological ways—that the power of suggestion worked almost magically upon the body. Recently, however, researchers have found that a belief or expectation can trigger certain chemicals throughout the body into action, and these chemicals—hormones, lymphocytes, endorphins—then may produce a medicinal effect (Brody, 2000). Howard Brody, a leading theorist on the subject, compares the placebo effect to visiting a pharmacy:

> Our bodies are capable of producing many substances that can heal a wide variety of illnesses, and make us feel generally healthier and more energized. When the body simply secretes these substances on its own, we have what is often termed "spontaneous healing." Some of the time, our bodies seem slow to react, and a message from outside [a placebo] can serve as a wake-up call to our inner pharmacy. The placebo response can thus be seen as the reaction of our inner pharmacies to that wake-up call.
>
> (Brody, 2000, p. 61)

If placebos can "wake up" our inner pharmacies in this way, perhaps traumatic events and related concerns or needs are doing the same thing (although in a negative way) in cases of conversion disorder, somatization disorder, or pain disorder associated with psychological factors. That is, such events and reactions may, in fact, be triggering our inner pharmacies and setting in motion the bodily symptoms of hysterical somatoform disorders.

>>**PSYCH•NOTES**

The sense of having a "lump in the throat" when anxious is known in medical circles as globus hystericus.<<

"If this doesn't help you don't worry. It's a placebo."

THE CURRENT SCENE

Cultural Dysmorphophobia?

People almost everywhere want to be attractive, and they tend to worry about how they appear in the eyes of others. At the same time, these concerns take different forms in different cultures.

Whereas people in Western society worry in particular about their body size and facial features, women of the Padaung tribe in Burma focus on the length of their neck and wear heavy stacks of brass rings to try to extend it. Many of them seek desperately to achieve what their culture has taught them is the perfect neck size. Said one, "It is most beautiful when the neck is really long. The longer it is, the more beautiful it is. I will never take off my rings . . . I'll be buried in them" (Mydans, 1996).

Similarly, for centuries women of China, in response to the preferences and demands of men in that country, worried greatly about the size and appearance of their feet and practiced *foot binding* to stop the growth of these extremities (Wang Ping, 2000).

Steve McCurry/Magnum Photos

In this procedure, which began in the year 900 and was widely practiced until outlawed in 1911, young girls were instructed to tightly wrap a long bandage around their feet each day, forcing the four toes under the sole of the foot. The procedure, which was carried out for about two years, caused the feet to become narrower and smaller. Typically the practice led to serious medical problems and poor mobility, but it did produce the small feet that were considered attractive.

Western culture also falls victim to such cultural influences. Past decades have witnessed staggering increases in such procedures as rhinoplasty (reshaping of the nose), breast augmentation, and the new kid on the block, body piercing—all reminders that cultural values greatly influence each person's ideas and concerns about beauty, and in some cases may set the stage for body dysmorphic disorder.

How Are Somatoform Disorders Treated?

People with somatoform disorders usually seek psychotherapy only as a last resort (Asaad, 2000). They fully believe that their problems are medical and at first reject all suggestions to the contrary. When a physician tells them that their problems have no physical basis, they simply go to another physician. Eventually, however, many such patients do turn to psychotherapy.

Individuals with preoccupation somatoform disorders typically receive the kinds of treatment that are applied to anxiety disorders (Magarinos et al., 2002; Warwick & Salkovski, 2001). In one study, more than half of patients with body dysmorphic disorder improved considerably when treated with the particular *antidepressant drugs* that are also helpful in cases of obsessive-compulsive disorder (Albeertini & Phillips, 1999). In another study, 17 patients with body dysmorphic disorder were treated with *exposure and response prevention*—the behavioral approach that often helps persons with obsessive-compulsive disorder. Over the course of four weeks, the clients were repeatedly reminded of their perceived physical defects and prevented from doing anything (for example, checking their appearance) to help reduce their discomfort (Neziroglu et al., 1996). By the end of treatment, they were less concerned with their "defects" and spent less time checking their body parts, looking in the mirror, and avoiding social interactions. The effectiveness of such approaches, however, has yet to be tested widely (Looper & Kinmayer, 2002).

People with hysterical somatoform disorders are typically treated with approaches that emphasize either insight, suggestion, reinforcement, or confrontation. A commonly applied *insight* approach has been psychodynamic therapy, which tries to help people resolve their underlying anxiety-arousing conflicts, theoretically eliminating the need to convert anxiety into physical symptoms (Milrod, 2002). Therapists who employ *suggestion* offer emotional support to patients and tell them persuasively that their physical symptoms will soon disappear (Anooshian et al., 1999), or they suggest the same thing to them under hypnosis (Moene et al., 2002). Therapists who take a *reinforcement* approach arrange the removal of rewards for a client's "sick" behavior and an increase of rewards for healthy behaviors (Allen et al., 2001). Finally, therapists who take a *confrontational* approach attempt to force patients out of the sick role by straightforwardly telling them that their symptoms are without medical basis (Sjolie, 2002).

Researchers have not fully evaluated the effects of these various treatments on hysterical disorders (Moene et al., 2002). Case studies suggest, however, that conversion disorder and pain disorder respond better to treatment than does somatization disorder and that approaches using insight, suggestion, and reinforcement bring more lasting improvement than the confrontation strategy. Antidepressant medications have also been applied with some success to hysterical disorders, particularly in cases involving pain symptoms (Turkington et al., 2002).

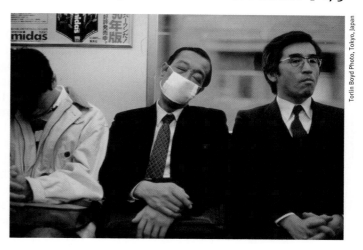

An extreme case of hypochondriasis? *Not necessarily. After a 1918 flu epidemic killed 20 million people, people in Japan started wearing a* masuku *to protect them from stray germs. Some, like this commuter, continue the tradition during cold and flu season.*

Torlin Boyd Photo, Tokyo, Japan

SUMMING UP
Somatoform Disorders

Patients with somatoform disorders have physical complaints whose causes are largely psychosocial. Nevertheless, the individuals genuinely believe that their illnesses are medical in origin.

Hysterical somatoform disorders involve an actual loss or change of physical functioning. They include conversion disorder, somatization disorder (or Briquet's syndrome), and pain disorder associated with psychological factors. Freud held that such disorders represent a conversion of underlying emotional conflicts into physical symptoms. According to behaviorists, the physical symptoms of these disorders bring rewards to the sufferer. Some cognitive theorists propose that the disorders are forms of communication. Biological factors may also be at work in these disorders, as we are reminded by recent studies of placebos. Treatments for hysterical disorders emphasize either insight, suggestion, reinforcement, or confrontation, or, in some cases, antidepressant medications.

People with preoccupation somatoform disorders worry greatly that something is wrong with them physically. In this category are hypochodriasis and body dysmorphic disorder. Theorists explain preoccupation somatoform disorders much as they do anxiety disorders. Treatment for the disorders includes medications, exposure and response prevention, and other treatments originally developed for anxiety disorders.

>>**LOOKING BACK**

Strictly a Coincidence?

On February 17, 1673, the French actor-playwright Molière collapsed onstage and died while performing in *Le Malade Imaginaire* (*The Hypochondriac*) (Ash, 1999).<<

Dissociative Disorders

Most of us experience a sense of wholeness and continuity as we interact with the world. We perceive ourselves as being more than a collection of isolated sensory experiences, feelings, and behaviors. In other words, we have an *identity*, a sense of who we are—and where we fit in our environment. Others recognize us and expect certain things of us. But more important, we recognize ourselves and have our own expectations, values, and goals.

Memory is a key to this sense of identity, the link between our past, present, and future. Our recall of past experiences, although not always precisely accurate, helps us react to present events and guides us in making decisions about the future. We recognize our friends and relatives, teachers and employers, and respond to them in appropriate ways. Without a memory, we would always be starting over; with it, life moves forward.

People sometimes experience a major disruption of their memory. They may, for example, lose their ability to remember new information they just learned or old information they once knew well. When such changes in memory lack a clear physical cause, they are called **dissociative disorders**. In such disorders, one part of the person's memory typically seems to be *dissociated*, or separated, from the rest.

There are several kinds of dissociative disorders. The primary symptom of *dissociative amnesia* is an inability to recall important personal events and information. A person with *dissociative fugue* not only forgets the past but also travels to a new location and may assume a new identity. Individuals with *multiple personality disorder (dissociative identity disorder)* have two or more separate identities that may not always have knowledge of each other's thoughts, feelings, and behavior.

Several memorable books and movies have portrayed dissociative disorders. Two of the best known are *The Three Faces of Eve* and *Sybil*, each about a woman with multiple personalities. The topic is so fascinating that most television drama series seem to include at least one case of dissociation every season, creating the impression that the disorders are very common. Many clinicians, however, believe that they are rare.

DSM-IV also lists *depersonalization disorder*, persistent feelings of being separated from one's own mental processes or body, as a dissociative disorder. People with this pattern feel as though they are observing themselves from the outside. Because memory problems are not the central feature of this disorder, it will not be discussed here.

As you read this chapter, keep in mind that dissociative symptoms are often found in cases of acute and posttraumatic stress disorders. Recall from Chapter 5, for example, that sufferers of those disorders may feel dazed or have trouble remembering things. When such symptoms occur as part of a stress disorder, they do not necessarily indicate a dissociative disorder—a pattern in which the dissociative symptoms dominate. On the other hand, it appears that people with one of these disorders are highly vulnerable to developing the other (Bremner, 2002).

Dissociative Amnesia

At the beginning of this chapter we met the unfortunate man named Brian. As you will recall, Brian developed a conversion disorder after a traumatic boating accident in which his wife was killed. To help us examine dissociative amnesia, let us now revisit that case, but change the reactions and symptoms that Brian develops in the aftermath of the traumatic event.

> Brian was spending Saturday sailing with his wife, Helen. The water was rough but well within what they considered safe limits. They were having a wonderful time and really didn't notice that the sky was getting darker, the wind blowing harder, and the sailboat becoming more difficult to control. After a few hours of sailing, they found themselves far from shore in the middle of a powerful and dangerous storm.
>
> The storm intensified very quickly. Brian had trouble controlling the sailboat amidst the high winds and wild waves. He and Helen tried to put on the safety jackets they had neglected to wear earlier, but the boat turned over before they were finished. Brian, the better swimmer of the two, was able to swim back to the overturned sailboat, grab the side, and hold on for dear life, but Helen simply could not overcome the rough waves and reach the boat. As Brian watched in horror and disbelief, his wife disappeared from view.

MEMORY The faculty for recalling past events and past learning.

DISSOCIATIVE DISORDERS Disorders marked by major changes in memory that do not have clear physical causes.

DISSOCIATIVE AMNESIA A dissociative disorder marked by an inability to recall important personal events and information.

After a time, the storm began to lose its strength. Brian managed to right the sailboat and sail back to shore. Finally he reached safety, but the personal consequences of this storm were just beginning. The next days were filled with pain and further horror: the Coast Guard finding Helen's body . . . conversations with friends . . . self-blame . . . grief . . . and more. On Wednesday, five days after that fateful afternoon, Brian collected himself and attended Helen's funeral and burial. It was the longest and most difficult day of his life. Most of the time, he felt as though he were in a trance.

Soon after awakening on Thursday morning, Brian realized that something was terribly wrong with him. Try though he might, he couldn't remember the events of the past few days. He remembered the accident, Helen's death, and the call from the Coast Guard after they had found her body. But just about everything else was gone, right up through the funeral. At first he had even thought that it was now Sunday, and that his discussions with family and friends and the funeral were all ahead of him. But the newspaper, the funeral guestbook, and a phone conversation with his brother soon convinced him that he had lost the past four days of his life.

In this revised scenario, Brian is reacting to his traumatic experience with symptoms of **dissociative amnesia**. People with this disorder are unable to recall important information, usually of an upsetting nature, about their lives (APA, 2000, 1994). The loss of memory is much more extensive than normal forgetting and is not caused by organic factors (see Table 6-5). Very often an episode of amnesia is directly triggered by a specific upsetting event (Kihlstrom, 2001).

Dissociative amnesia may be *localized*, *selective*, *generalized*, or *continuous*. Any of these kinds of amnesia can be triggered by a traumatic experience such as Brian's, but each represents a particular pattern of forgetting. Brian was suffering from *localized amnesia*, the most common type of dissociative amnesia, in which a person loses all memory of events that took place within a limited period of time, almost always beginning with some very disturbing occurrence. Recall that Brian awakened on the day after the funeral and could not recall any of the events of the past difficult days, beginning after the boating tragedy. He remembered everything that happened up to and including the accident. He could also recall everything from the morning after the funeral onward, but the days in between remained a total blank. The forgotten period is called the *amnestic episode*. During an amnestic episode, people may appear confused; in some cases they wander about aimlessly. They are already experiencing memory difficulties, but seem unaware of them. In the revised case, for example, Brian felt as though he were in a trance on the day of Helen's funeral.

People with *selective amnesia*, the second most common form of dissociative amnesia, remember some, but not all, events that occurred during a period of time. If Brian had selective amnesia, he might remember certain of his conversations with friends but perhaps not the funeral itself.

In some cases the loss of memory extends back to times long before the upsetting period. Brian might awaken after the funeral and find that, in addition to forgetting events of the past few days, he could not remember events that occurred earlier in his life. In this case, he would be experiencing *generalized amnesia*. In extreme cases, Brian might not even remember who he was and might fail to recognize relatives and friends.

In the forms of dissociative amnesia discussed so far, the period affected by the amnesia has an end. In *continuous amnesia*, however, forgetting continues into the present. Brian

Table 6-5 DSM-IV Checklist

DISSOCIATIVE AMNESIA

1. One or more episodes of inability to recall important personal information, usually of a traumatic or stressful nature, that is too extensive to be explained by ordinary forgetfulness.
2. Significant distress or impairment.

DISSOCIATIVE FUGUE

1. Sudden, unexpected travel away from home or one's customary place of work, with inability to recall one's past.
2. Confusion about personal identity, or the assumption of a new identity.
3. Significant distress or impairment.

DISSOCIATIVE IDENTITY DISORDER (MULTIPLE PERSONALITY DISORDER)

1. The presence of two or more distinct identities or personality states.
2. Control of the person's behavior recurrently taken by at least two of these identities or personality states.
3. An inability to recall important personal information that is too extensive to be explained by ordinary forgetfulness.

Based on APA, 2000, 1994.

Bettmann/Corbis

At risk *The stunned looks on the faces of these soldiers suggest confusion, shock, and exhaustion. Combat soldiers are particularly vulnerable to amnesia and other dissociative reactions.*

might forget new and ongoing experiences as well as what happened before and during the tragedy. Continuous forgetting of this kind is actually quite rare in cases of dissociative amnesia, but, as we shall see in Chapter 15, not in cases of organic amnesia.

All of these forms of dissociative amnesia are similar in that the amnesia interferes mostly with a person's memory of personal material. Memory for abstract or encyclopedic information usually remains. People with dissociative amnesia are as likely as anyone else to know the name of the president of the United States and how to write, read, or drive a car.

Clinicians do not know how common dissociative amnesia is, but they do know that many cases seem to begin during serious threats to health and safety, as in wartime and natural disasters (Witztum et al., 2002). Combat veterans often report memory gaps of hours or days, and some forget personal information, such as their names and addresses (Bremner, 2002; van der Hart et al., 1999). It appears that childhood abuse, particularly child sexual abuse, can also sometimes trigger dissociative amnesia; indeed, the 1990s witnessed an enormous number of reports in which adults claimed to suddenly recall long-repressed experiences of childhood abuse. In addition, dissociative amnesia may occur under more ordinary circumstances, such as the sudden loss of a loved one through rejection or death or guilt over behavior considered to be immoral (for example, an extramarital affair) (Koh et al., 2000; Loewenstein, 1991).

The personal impact of dissociative amnesia depends on how much is forgotten. Obviously, an amnestic episode of two years is more of a problem than one of two hours. Similarly, an amnestic episode during which a person's life changes in major ways causes more difficulties than one that is quiet.

Dissociative Fugue

People with a **dissociative fugue** not only forget their personal identities and details of their past lives but also flee to an entirely different location (see again Table 6-5). Some individuals travel but a short distance and make few social contacts in the new setting (APA, 2000, 1994). Their fugue may be brief—a matter of hours or days—and end suddenly. In other cases, however, the person may travel far from home, take a new name, and establish a new identity, new relationships, and even a new line of work. Such people may display new personality characteristics; often they are more outgoing (APA, 2000, 1994). This pattern is seen in the case of the Reverend Ansel Bourne:

DISSOCIATIVE FUGUE A dissociative disorder in which a person travels to a new location and may assume a new identity, simultaneously forgetting his or her past.

> On January 17, 1887, [the Reverend Ansel Bourne, of Greene, R.I.] drew 551 dollars from a bank in Providence with which to pay for a certain lot of land in Greene, paid certain bills, and got into a Pawtucket horsecar. This is the last incident which he remembers. He did not return home that day, and nothing was heard of him for two months. He was published in the papers as missing, and foul play being suspected, the police sought in vain his whereabouts. On the morning of March 14th, however, at Norristown, Pennsylvania, a man calling himself A. I. Brown who had rented a small shop six weeks previously, stocked it with stationery, confectionery, fruit and small articles, and carried on his quiet trade without seeming to any one unnatural or eccentric, woke up in a fright and called in the people of the house to tell him where he was. He said that his name was Ansel Bourne, that he was entirely ignorant of Norristown, that he knew nothing of shop-keeping, and that the last thing he remembered—it seemed only yesterday—was drawing the money from the bank, etc. in Providence. . . .

A CLOSER LOOK

Repressed Childhood Memories or False Memory Syndrome?

Throughout the 1990s, reports of *repressed childhood memory of abuse* attracted much public attention. Adults with this type of *dissociative amnesia* seemed to recover buried memories of sexual and physical abuse from their childhood. A woman might claim, for example, that her father had sexually molested her repeatedly between the ages of 5 and 7. Or a young man might remember that a family friend had made sexual advances on several occasions when he was very young. Often the repressed memories surfaced during therapy for another problem, perhaps for an eating disorder or depression.

Although the number of such claims currently seems to be declining, experts remain deeply split on this issue (McNally, 2003, 2001; Courtois, 2001). Some believe that recovered memories are just what they appear to be—horrible memories of abuse that have been buried for years in the person's mind (Leavitt, 2002, 2001). Other experts believe that the memories are actually illusions—false images created by a mind that is confused. In fact, an organization called the False Memory Syndrome Foundation assists people who claim to be falsely charged with abuse.

Opponents of the repressed memory concept suggest that the details of childhood sexual abuse are often remembered all too well, not completely wiped from memory (McNally, 2001; Loftus, 2000, 1993). They also point out that memory in general is hardly foolproof (Lindsay et al., 2004). Even when recalling events as dramatic as the Kennedy assassination, the explosion of the space shuttle *Challenger*, or the attacks on the World Trade Center, people give inaccurate accounts of where they were at the time of the event or who first told them about it. Moreover, false memories of various kinds can be created in the laboratory by tapping into subjects' imaginations (Thomas & Loftus, 2002). If memory in general is so flawed, questions certainly can be raised about the accuracy of recovered memories.

If the alleged recovery of childhood memories is not what it appears to be, what is it? According to opponents of the concept, it may be a powerful case of suggestibility (Loftus, 2003, 2001, 1997). These theorists hold that the attention paid to the phenomenon by both clinicians and the public has led some therapists to make the diagnosis without sufficient evidence (Frankel, 1993). The

therapists may actively search for signs of early sexual abuse in clients and even encourage clients to produce repressed memories (Ganaway, 1989). Certain therapists in fact use special memory recovery techniques, including hypnosis, regression therapy, journal writing, dream interpretation, and interpretation of bodily symptoms (Lindsay, 1996, 1994). Perhaps some clients respond to the techniques by unknowingly forming false memories of abuse (Nyman & Loftus, 2002). The apparent memories may then become increasingly familiar to them as a result of repeated therapy discussions of the alleged incidents. In short, recovered memories may actually be *iatrogenic*—unintentionally caused by the therapist.

Of course, repressed memories of childhood sexual abuse do not emerge only in clinical settings (Leavitt, 2002, 2001). Many individuals come forward on their own. Opponents of the repressed memory concept explain these cases by pointing to the many books, articles, and television shows that seem to validate repressed memories of childhood sexual abuse (Loftus, 1993). Several books even tell readers how to diagnose repression in themselves, often listing symptoms that are actually rather common—not clinical symptoms at all (Tavris, 1993). Readers with a number of these symptoms may begin a search for repressed memories of childhood abuse.

It is important to recognize that the experts who question the recovery of repressed childhood memories do not in any way deny the enormous problem of child sexual abuse (Chu, 2000; Knapp & Vande Creek, 2000; APA, 1996). In fact, proponents and opponents alike are greatly concerned that the public may take this debate to mean that clinicians have doubts about the scope of the problem of child sexual abuse. Whatever may be the final outcome of the repressed memory debate, the problem of childhood sexual abuse appears to be all too real and all too common.

Early recall *Research suggests that our memories of early childhood may be influenced by the reminiscences of family members, our dreams, television and movie plots, and our present self-image.*

He was very weak, having lost apparently over twenty pounds of flesh during his escapade, and had such a horror of the idea of the candy-store that he refused to set foot in it again.

(James, 1890, pp. 391–393)

Lost and found *Cheryl Ann Barnes is helped off a plane by her grandmother and stepmother upon arrival in Florida in 1996. The 17-year-old high school honor student had disappeared from her Florida home and was found one month later in a New York City hospital listed as Jane Doe, apparently suffering from fugue.*

Approximately 0.2 percent of the population experience dissociative fugue. Like dissociative amnesia, a fugue usually follows a severely stressful event (APA, 2000, 1994). Some adolescent runaways may be in a state of fugue (Loewenstein, 1991). Like cases of dissociative amnesia, fugues usually affect personal (episodic) memories from the past rather than encyclopedic or abstract knowledge (Kihlstrom, 2001; Kihlstrom et al., 1993).

Fugues tend to end suddenly. In some cases, as with Reverend Bourne, the person "awakens" in a strange place, surrounded by unfamiliar faces, and wonders how he or she got there. In other cases, the lack of personal history may arouse suspicion. Perhaps a traffic accident or legal problem leads police to discover the false identity; at other times friends search for and find the missing person. When people are found before their fugue has ended, therapists may find it necessary to ask them many questions about the details of their lives, repeatedly remind them who they are, and even begin psychotherapy before they recover their memories. As these people recover their past, some forget the events of the fugue period (APA, 2000, 1994).

The majority of people who experience dissociative fugue regain most or all of their memories and never have a recurrence. Since fugues are usually brief and totally reversible, individuals tend to experience few aftereffects (Keller & Shaywitz, 1986). People who have been away for months or years, however, often do have trouble adjusting to the changes that have occurred back at home during their flights. In addition, some people commit illegal or violent acts in their fugue state and later must face the consequences.

Dissociative Identity Disorder (Multiple Personality Disorder)

Multiple personality disorder is both dramatic and disabling, as we see in the case of Eric:

Dazed and bruised from a beating, Eric, 29, was discovered wandering around a Daytona Beach shopping mall on Feb. 9. . . . Transferred six weeks later to Daytona Beach's Human Resources Center, Eric began talking to doctors in two voices: the infantile rhythms of "young Eric," a dim and frightened child, and the measured tones of "older Eric," who told a tale of terror and child abuse. According to "older Eric," after his immigrant German parents died, a harsh stepfather and his mistress took Eric from his native South Carolina to a drug dealers' hideout in a Florida swamp. Eric said he was raped by several gang members and watched his stepfather murder two men.

One day in late March an alarmed counselor watched Eric's face twist into a violent snarl. Eric let loose an unearthly growl and spat out a stream of obscenities. "It sounded like something out of *The Exorcist*," says Malcolm Graham, the psychologist who directs the case at the center. "It was the most intense thing I've ever seen in a patient." That disclosure of a new personality, who insolently demanded to be called Mark, was the first indication that Graham had been dealing with a rare and serious emotional disorder: true multiple personality. . . .

Eric's other manifestations emerged over the next weeks: quiet, middle-aged Dwight; the hysterically blind and mute Jeffrey; Michael, an arrogant jock; the coquettish Tian, whom Eric considered a whore; and argumentative Phillip, the lawyer. "Phillip was always asking about Eric's rights," says Graham. "He was kind of obnoxious. Actually, Phillip was a pain."

To Graham's astonishment, Eric gradually unfurled 27 different personalities, including three females. . . . . They ranged in age from a fetus to a sordid old man who kept trying to persuade Eric to fight as a mercenary in Haiti. In one therapy session, reports Graham, Eric shifted personality nine times in an hour. "I felt I was losing control of the sessions," says the psychologist, who has eleven years of clinical experience. "Some personalities would not talk to me, and some of them were very insightful into my behavior as well as Eric's."

(*Time*, October 25, 1982, p. 70)

A person with **dissociative identity disorder**, or **multiple personality disorder**, develops two or more distinct personalities, often called **subpersonalities** (or **alternate personalities**), each with a unique set of memories, behaviors, thoughts, and emotions (see again Table 6-5). At any given time, one of the subpersonalities takes center stage and dominates the person's functioning. Usually one subpersonality, called the *primary*, or *host*, *personality*, appears more often than the others.

The transition from one subpersonality to another, called *switching*, is usually sudden and may be dramatic (APA, 2000, 1994). Eric, for example, twisted his face, growled, and yelled obscenities while changing personalities. Switching is usually triggered by a stressful event, although clinicians can also bring about the change with hypnotic suggestion (APA, 2000, 1994).

Cases of multiple personality disorder were first reported almost three centuries ago (Rieber, 2002). Many clinicians consider the disorder to be rare, but some reports suggest that it may be more common than was once thought (APA, 2000; Coons, 1998). Most cases are first diagnosed in late adolescence or early adulthood, but the symptoms usually begin in early childhood after episodes of abuse, typically before the age of 5 (Ross et al., 1991). In fact, studies suggest that as many as 97 percent of patients have been physically, often sexually, abused during their early years (Ross et al., 1991, 1990, 1989). Women receive this diagnosis at least three times as often as men (APA, 2000).

HOW DO SUBPERSONALITIES INTERACT? How subpersonalities relate to or recall one another varies from case to case. Generally, there are three kinds of relationships. In *mutually amnesic* relationships, the subpersonalities have no awareness of one another (Ellenberger, 1970). Conversely, in *mutually cognizant* patterns, each subpersonality is well aware of the rest. They may hear one another's voices and even talk among themselves. Some are on good terms, while others do not get along at all.

In *one-way amnesic* relationships, the most common relationship pattern, some subpersonalities are aware of others, but the awareness is not mutual. Those that are aware, called *co-conscious subpersonalities*, are "quiet observers" who watch the actions and thoughts of the other subpersonalities but do not interact with them. Sometimes while another subpersonality is present, the co-conscious personality makes itself known through indirect means, such as auditory hallucinations (perhaps a voice giving commands) or "automatic writing" (the current personality may find itself writing down words over which it has no control).

Investigators used to believe that most cases of multiple personality disorder involved two or three subpersonalities. Studies now suggest, however, that the average number of subpersonalities per patient is much higher—15 for women and 8 for men (APA, 2000; Ross et al., 1989). In fact, there have been cases in which 100 or more subpersonalities were observed (APA, 2000). Often the subpersonalities emerge in groups of two or three at a time.

In the case of "Eve White," made famous in the book and movie *The Three Faces of Eve*, a woman had three subpersonalities—Eve White, Eve Black, and Jane (Thigpen & Cleckley, 1957). Eve White, the primary personality, was quiet and serious; Eve Black was carefree and mischievous; and Jane was mature and intelligent. According to the book, these three subpersonalities eventually merged into Evelyn, a stable personality who was really an integration of the other three.

The book was wrong, however; this was not to be the end of Eve's dissociation. In an autobiography 20 years later, she revealed that altogether 22 subpersonalities had come forth during her life, including 9 subpersonalities after Evelyn. Usually they appeared in groups of three, and so the authors of *The Three Faces of Eve* apparently never knew about her previous or subsequent subpersonalities. She has now overcome her disorder, achieving a single, stable identity, and has been known as Chris Sizemore for over 25 years (Sizemore & Huber, 1988).

"I'm Eve" *In 1975 Chris Sizemore revealed that she had been the subject of the book and the film* The Three Faces of Eve. *A fully integrated personality for more than 25 years, Ms. Sizemore is now an accomplished author, artist, and mental health spokesperson.*

HOW DO SUBPERSONALITIES DIFFER? As in Chris Sizemore's case, subpersonalities often exhibit dramatically different characteristics. They may also have their own names and different *vital statistics, abilities and preferences,* and even *physiological responses.*

VITAL STATISTICS The subpersonalities may differ in features as basic as age, sex, race, and family history, as in the famous case of Sybil Dorsett. Sybil's multiple personality disorder has been described in fictional form (in the novel *Sybil*) but is based on a real case from the practice of the psychiatrist Cornelia Wilbur (Schreiber, 1973). Sybil displayed 17 subpersonalities, all with different identifying features. They included adults, a teenager, and a baby named Ruthie; two were male, named Mike and Sid. Sybil's subpersonalities each had particular images of themselves and of each other. The subpersonality named Vicky, for example, saw herself as an attractive blonde, while another, Peggy Lou, was described as a pixie with a pug nose. Mary was plump with dark hair, and Vanessa was a tall redhead with a willowy figure.

ABILITIES AND PREFERENCES Although memories of abstract or encyclopedic information are not usually affected by dissociative amnesia or fugue, they are often disturbed by multiple personality disorder. It is not uncommon for the different subpersonalities to have different abilities: one may be able to drive, speak a foreign language, or play a musical instrument, while the others cannot (Coons et al., 1988). Their handwriting can also differ (Coons, 1980). In addition, the subpersonalities usually have different tastes in food, friends, music, and literature. Chris Sizemore ("Eve") later pointed out, "If I had learned to sew as one personality and then tried to sew as another, I couldn't do it. Driving a car was the same. Some of my personalities couldn't drive" (1975, p. 4).

PHYSIOLOGICAL RESPONSES Researchers have discovered that subpersonalities may have physiological differences, such as differences in autonomic nervous system activity, blood pressure levels, and allergies (Putnam, Zahn, & Post, 1990). One study looked at the brain activities of different subpersonalities by measuring their *evoked potentials*—that is, brain-response patterns recorded on an electroencephalograph (Putnam, 1984). The brain pattern a person produces in response to a specific stimulus (such as a flashing light) is usually unique and consistent. However, when an evoked potential test was administered to four subpersonalities of each of 10 people with multiple personality disorder, the results were dramatic. The brain-activity pattern of each subpersonality was unique, showing the kinds of variations usually found in totally different people.

>>**LOOKING AROUND**
Profit Distributions

Chris Sizemore received almost no revenues from the 1957 book and movie *The Three Faces of Eve*. In contrast, profits from *Sybil* were shared by the patient, her psychiatrist, and the book's author. Moreover, when the psychiatrist Cornelia Wilbur died in 1992, she left $25,000 and all *Sybil* royalties to the former patient (Miller & Kantrowitz, 1999).<<

How Common Is Multiple Personality Disorder? As we have seen, multiple personality disorder has traditionally been thought of as rare. Some researchers even argue that many or all cases are **iatrogenic**—that is, unintentionally produced by practitioners (Lilienfeld & Lynn, 2003; Merskey, 1995, 1992). They believe that therapists create this disorder by subtly suggesting the existence of other personalities during therapy or by asking a patient to produce different personalities while under hypnosis. In addition, they believe, a therapist who is looking for multiple personalities may reinforce these patterns by displaying greater interest when a patient displays symptoms of dissociation.

These arguments seem to be supported by the fact that many cases of multiple personality disorder first come to attention while the person is already in treatment for a less serious problem (Allison, 1978). But such is not true of all cases; many other people seek treatment because they have noticed time lapses throughout their lives or because relatives and friends have observed their subpersonalities (Putnam, 2000, 1988, 1985).

The number of people diagnosed with multiple personality disorder has been increasing (Casey, 2001). Although the disorder is still uncommon, thousands of cases are now diagnosed in the United States and Canada alone (Merskey, 1995). Two factors may account for this increase. First, a growing number of today's clinicians believe that the disorder does exist and are willing to diagnose it (Pope et al., 2000, 1999). Second, diagnostic procedures tend to be more accurate today than in past years. For much of the twentieth century, schizophrenia was one of the clinical field's most commonly applied diagnoses (Rosenbaum, 1980). It was applied, often incorrectly, to a wide range of unusual behavioral patterns, perhaps including multiple personality disorder (Turkington & Harris, 2001). Under the stricter criteria of recent editions of the DSM, clinicians are now much more accurate in diagnosing schizophrenia, allowing more cases of multiple personality disorder to be recognized (Welburn et al., 2003; Spiegel, 1994). In addition, several diagnostic tests have been developed to help detect multiple personality disorder (Dell, 2002; Mann, 1995). Despite such changes, however, many clinicians continue to question the legitimacy of this category (Pope et al., 2000, 1999).

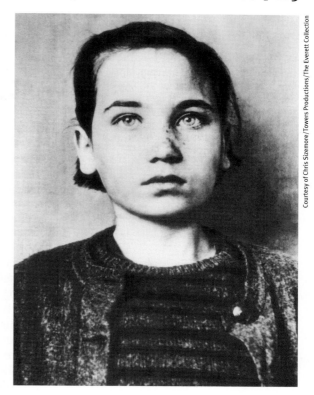

Early beginnings *Chris Sizemore's multiple personality disorder developed long before this photograph of her was taken at age 10. It emerged during her preschool years after she experienced several traumas (witnessing two deaths and a horrifying accident) within a three-month period.*

How Do Theorists Explain Dissociative Disorders?

A variety of theories have been proposed to explain dissociative disorders. Older explanations, such as those offered by psychodynamic and behavioral theorists, have not received much investigation. However, newer viewpoints, which combine cognitive, behavioral, and biological principles and highlight such factors as *state-dependent learning* and *self-hypnosis*, have begun to capture the interest of clinical scientists.

The Psychodynamic View Psychodynamic theorists believe that dissociative disorders are caused by *repression*, the most basic ego defense mechanism: people fight off anxiety by unconsciously preventing painful memories, thoughts, or impulses from reaching awareness. Everyone uses repression to a degree, but people with dissociative disorders are thought to repress their memories excessively (Brenner, 1999).

In the psychodynamic view, dissociative amnesia and fugue are single episodes of massive repression. In each of these disorders, a person unconsciously blocks the memory of an extremely upsetting event to avoid the pain of facing it (Turkington & Harris, 2001). Repressing may be the person's only protection from overwhelming anxiety.

In contrast, multiple personality disorder is thought to result from a *lifetime* of excessive repression. Psychodynamic theorists believe that continuous use of repression is motivated by very traumatic childhood events, particularly abusive parenting. Children who experience such traumas may come to fear the dangerous

IATROGENIC DISORDER A disorder that is unintentionally caused by a practitioner.

>>LOOKING BACK
Hidden Motives

In his book *The Psychopathology of Everyday Life*, Freud proposed that we all have a tendency to forget what is disagreeable. The forgetting of past events simply cannot be accidental or arbitrary, he argued. The experiences of childhood are too rich and powerful to merely slip away.<<

world they live in and take flight from it by pretending to be another person who is safely looking on from afar. Abused children may also come to fear the impulses that they believe are the reasons for their excessive punishments. Whenever they experience "bad" thoughts or impulses, they unconsciously try to disown and deny them by assigning them to other personalities.

Most of the support for the psychodynamic position is drawn from case histories, which report such brutal childhood experiences as beatings, cuttings, burnings with cigarettes, imprisonment in closets, rape, and extensive verbal abuse. Yet some individuals with multiple personality disorder do not seem to have experiences of abuse in their background (Bliss, 1980). Moreover, child abuse is far more common than multiple personality disorder. Why, then, do only a small fraction of abused children develop this disorder?

THE BEHAVIORAL VIEW Behaviorists believe that dissociation is a response learned through operant conditioning (Casey, 2001). People who experience a horrifying event may later find temporary relief when their minds drift to other subjects. For some, this momentary forgetting, leading to a drop in anxiety, increases the likelihood of future forgetting. In short, they are reinforced for the act of forgetting and learn—without being aware that they are learning—that such acts help them escape anxiety. Thus, like psychodynamic theorists, behaviorists see dissociation as escape behavior. But behaviorists believe that a reinforcement process rather than a hardworking unconscious is keeping the individuals unaware that they are using dissociation as a means of escape.

Like psychodynamic theorists, behaviorists have relied largely on case histories to support their view of dissociative disorders. Such descriptions do often support this view, but they are equally consistent with other kinds of explanations as well: a case that seems to show reinforcement of forgetting can usually also be interpreted as an instance of unconscious repression. In addition, the behavioral explanation fails to explain precisely how temporary and normal escapes from painful memories grow into a complex disorder or why more people do not develop dissociative disorders.

STATE-DEPENDENT LEARNING If people learn something when they are in a particular situation or state of mind, they are likely to remember it best when they are again in that same condition. If they are given a learning task while under the influence of alcohol, for example, their later recall of the information may be strongest under the influence of alcohol (Overton, 1966). Similarly, if they smoke cigarettes while learning, they may later have better recall when they are again smoking.

This link between state and recall is called **state-dependent learning**. It was initially observed in experimental animals who learned things while under the influence of certain drugs. Research with human subjects later showed that state-dependent learning can be associated with mood states as well: material learned during a happy mood is recalled best when the subject is again happy, and sad-state learning is recalled best during sad states (Eich, 1995; Bower, 1981) (see Figure 6-3).

What causes state-dependent learning? One possibility is that *arousal* levels are an important part of learning and memory. That is, a particular level of arousal will have a set of remembered events, thoughts, and skills attached to it. When a situation produces that particular level of arousal, the person is more likely to recall the memories linked to it.

Although people may remember certain events better in some arousal states than in others, most can recall events under a variety of states. However, perhaps people who are prone to develop dissociative disorders have state-to-memory links that are very rigid and narrow. Maybe each of their thoughts, memories, and skills is tied *exclusively* to a particular state of

FIGURE 6-3 **State-dependent learning** *In one study, subjects who learned a list of words while in a hypnotically induced happy state remembered the words better if they were in a happy mood when tested later than if they were in a sad mood. Conversely, subjects who learned the words when in a sad mood recalled them better if they were sad during testing than if they were happy (Bower, 1981).*

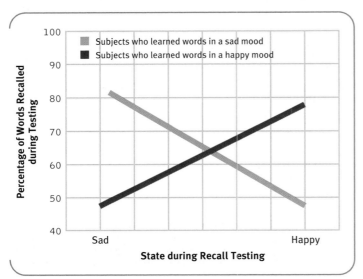

A CLOSER LOOK

Peculiarities of Memory

Usually memory problems must interfere greatly with a person's functioning before they are considered a sign of a disorder. Peculiarities of memory, on the other hand, fill our daily lives. Memory investigators have identified a number of these peculiarities—some familiar, some useful, some problematic, but none abnormal (Turkington & Harris, 2001; Noll & Turkington, 1994).

- **Absentmindedness** Often we fail to register information because our thoughts are focusing on other things. If we haven't absorbed the information in the first place, it is no surprise that later we can't recall it.

- **Déjà vu** Almost all of us have at some time had the strange sensation of recognizing a scene that we happen upon for the first time. We feel sure we have been there before.

- **Jamais vu** Sometimes we have the opposite experience: a situation or scene that is part of our daily life seems suddenly unfamiliar. "I knew it was my car, but I felt as if I'd never seen it before."

- **The tip-of-the-tongue phenomenon** To have something on the tip of the tongue is an acute "feeling of knowing": we are unable to recall some piece of information, but we know that we know it.

- **Eidetic images** Some people experience visual afterimages so vividly that they can describe a picture in detail after looking at it just once.

The images may be memories of pictures, events, fantasies, or dreams.

- **Memory while under anesthesia** Some anesthetized patients may process enough of what is said in their presence during surgery to affect their recovery. In such cases, the ability to understand language has continued under anesthesia, even though the patient cannot explicitly recall it.

- **Memory for music** Even as a small child, Mozart could memorize and reproduce a piece of music after having heard it only once. While no one yet has matched the genius of Mozart, many musicians can mentally hear whole pieces of music, so that they can rehearse anywhere, far from their instruments.

- **Visual memory** Most people recall visual information better than other kinds of information: they can easily bring to their mind the appearance of places, objects, faces, or the pages of a book. They almost never forget a face, yet they may well forget the name attached to it. Other people have stronger verbal memories: they remember sounds or words particularly well, and the memories that come to their minds are often puns or rhymes.

- **Prenatal memory** Some North American medicine men claim to remember parts of a prenatal existence, an ability they believe is lost to "common" people. Many practicing Buddhists also claim to remember past lives. A few—as did Buddha himself—claim to remember their very first existence.

© The New Yorker Collection 1998, Mick Stevens, from cartoonbank.com

arousal, so that they recall a given event from the past only when they experience an arousal state almost identical to the state in which the memory was acquired. When such people are calm, for example, they may forget what occurred during stressful times, thus laying the groundwork for dissociative amnesia or fugue. Similarly, in multiple personality disorder, different arousal levels may produce entirely different groups of memories, thoughts, and abilities—that is, different subpersonalities (Putnam, 1992). This could explain why personality transitions in multiple personality disorder tend to be sudden and stress-related.

STATE-DEPENDENT LEARNING Learning that becomes associated with the conditions under which it occurred, so that it is best remembered under the same conditions.

The Kobal Collection

Movie madness *One of the cinema's best-known fictional sufferers of multiple personality disorder, Norman Bates, is horrified to discover that his mother (actually his subpersonality) has stabbed a woman to death in the shower in the movie* Psycho.

SELF-HYPNOSIS As we first saw in Chapter 1, people who are *hypnotized* enter a sleeplike state in which they become very suggestible. While in this state, they can behave, perceive, and think in ways that would ordinarily seem impossible. They may, for example, become temporarily blind, deaf, or insensitive to pain. Hypnosis can also help people remember events that occurred and were forgotten years ago, a capability used by many psychotherapists. Conversely, it can make people forget facts, events, and even their personal identities—an effect called *hypnotic amnesia* (Barnier, 2002).

The parallels between hypnotic amnesia and dissociative disorders are striking (Bliss, 1980). Both are conditions in which people forget certain material for a period of time yet later remember it. And in both, the people forget without any insight into why they are forgetting or any awareness that something is being forgotten. These parallels have led some theorists to conclude that dissociative disorders may be a form of **self-hypnosis** in which people hypnotize themselves to forget unpleasant events (Casey, 2001; Bliss, 1985, 1980; Hilgard, 1977). Dissociative amnesia, for example, may occur in people who, consciously or unconsciously, hypnotize themselves into forgetting horrifying experiences that have recently occurred in their lives (Bryant et al., 2001). If the self-induced amnesia covers all memories of a person's past and identity, that person may undergo a dissociative fugue.

Self-hypnosis might also be used to explain multiple personality disorder. On the basis of several investigations, some theorists believe that multiple personality disorder often begins between the ages of 4 and 6, a time when children are generally very suggestible and excellent hypnotic subjects (Kluft, 2001, 1987; Bliss, 1985, 1980). These theorists argue that some children who experience abuse or other horrifying events manage to escape their threatening world by self-hypnosis, mentally separating themselves from their bodies and fulfilling their wish to become some other person or persons. One patient with multiple personality disorder observed, "I was in a trance often [during my childhood]. There was a little place where I could sit, close my eyes and imagine, until I felt very relaxed just like hypnosis" (Bliss, 1980, p. 1392).

How Are Dissociative Disorders Treated?

As we have seen, people with dissociative amnesia and fugue often recover on their own (Kihlstrom, 2001). Only sometimes do their memory problems linger and require treatment. In contrast, people with multiple personality disorder usually require treatment to regain their lost memories and develop an integrated personality. Treatments for dissociative amnesia and fugue tend to be more successful than those for multiple personality disorder, probably because the former disorders are less complex.

HOW DO THERAPISTS HELP PEOPLE WITH DISSOCIATIVE AMNESIA AND FUGUE?

The leading treatments for dissociative amnesia and fugue are *psychodynamic therapy*, *hypnotic therapy*, and *drug therapy*, although support for these interventions comes largely from case studies (Maldonado et al., 2002). Psychodynamic therapists ask patients with these disorders to free associate and search their unconscious in the hope of bringing forgotten experiences back to consciousness (Bartholomew, 2000; Loewenstein, 1991). The focus of psychodynamic therapy seems particularly well suited to the needs of people with these disorders. After all, the patients need to recover lost memories, and the general approach of psychodynamic therapists is to try to uncover memories—as well as other psychological processes—that have been repressed. Thus many theorists, including some who do not ordinarily favor psychodynamic approaches, believe that psychodynamic therapy may be the most appropriate treatment for these disorders.

SELF-HYPNOSIS The process of hypnotizing oneself, sometimes for the purpose of forgetting unpleasant events.

HYPNOTIC THERAPY A treatment in which the patient undergoes hypnosis and is then guided to recall forgotten events or perform other therapeutic activities. Also known as *hypnotherapy*.

Another common treatment for dissociative amnesia and fugue is **hypnotic therapy**, or **hypnotherapy** (see Table 6-6). Therapists hypnotize patients and then guide them to recall forgotten events (Degun-Mather, 2002). Given the possibility that dissociative amnesia and fugue may each be a form of self-hypnosis, hypnotherapy may be a particularly useful intervention. It has been applied both alone and in combination with other approaches.

Sometimes intravenous injections of barbiturates such as *sodium amobarbital* (Amytal) or *sodium pentobarbital* (Pentothal) are used to help patients with dissociative amnesia and fugue regain lost memories (Ruedrich et al., 1985). The drugs are often called "truth serums," but the key to their success is their ability to calm people and free their inhibitions, thus helping them to recall anxiety-producing events (Kluft, 1988; Perry & Jacobs, 1982). These drugs do not always work, however, and if used at all, they are likely to be combined with other treatment approaches (Spiegel, 1994).

HOW DO THERAPISTS HELP INDIVIDUALS WITH MULTIPLE PERSONALITY DISORDER? Unlike victims of amnesia and fugue, people with multiple personality disorder rarely recover without treatment (Spiegel, 1994). Like the disorder itself, treatment for this pattern is complex and difficult. Therapists usually try to help the clients (1) recognize fully the nature of their disorder, (2) recover the gaps in their memory, and (3) integrate their subpersonalities into one functional personality (Kihlstrom, 2001; Kluft, 2001, 2000, 1992, 1991).

Table 6-6

Myths about Hypnosis
Michael Nash (2001)

MYTH	REALITY
Hypnosis is all a matter of having a good imagination.	Ability to imagine vividly is unrelated to hypnotizability.
Relaxation is an important feature of hypnosis.	Hypnosis has been induced during vigorous exercise.
It's a matter of willful faking.	Physiological responses indicate that hypnotized subjects are not lying.
It is dangerous.	Standard hypnotic procedures are no more distressing than lectures.
It has something to do with a sleeplike state.	Hypnotized subjects are fully awake.
Responding to hypnosis is like responding to a placebo.	Placebo responsiveness and hypnotizability are not correlated.
People who are hypnotized lose control of themselves.	Subjects are perfectly capable of saying no or terminating hypnosis.
Hypnosis can enable people to "relive" the past.	Age-regressed adults behave like adults play-acting as children.
When hypnotized, people can remember more accurately.	Hypnosis may actually muddle the distinction between memory and fantasy and may artificially inflate confidence.
Hypnotized people can be led to do acts that conflict with their values.	Hypnotized subjects fully adhere to their usual moral standards.
Hypnotized people spontaneously forget what happened during the session.	Posthypnotic amnesia does not occur spontaneously.
Hypnosis can enable people to perform otherwise impossible feats of strength, endurance, learning, and sensory acuity.	Performance following hypnotic suggestions for increased muscle strength, learning, and sensory acuity does not exceed what can be accomplished by motivated subjects outside hypnosis.

Oscar Sosa/AP Photo

Faulty recall *A forensic clinician uses a hypnotic procedure to help a witness recall the details of a crime. Research reveals, however, that such procedures are as capable of creating false memories as they are of uncovering real memories. Thus recollections that initially emerge during hypnosis cannot be used as evidence in criminal cases.*

RECOGNIZING THE DISORDER Once a diagnosis of multiple personality disorder is made, therapists typically try to bond with the primary personality and with each of the subpersonalities (Kluft, 1999, 1992). As bonds are formed, therapists try to educate patients and help them to recognize fully the nature of their disorder (Krakauer, 2001; Allen, 1993). Some therapists actually introduce the subpersonalities to one another under hypnosis, and some have patients look at videotapes of their other personalities (Ross & Gahan, 1988; Sakheim et al., 1988). Many therapists have also found that group therapy helps to educate patients (Fine & Madden, 2000). Being with a group of people who all have multiple personality disorder helps relieve a person's feelings of isolation. Family therapy may also be used to help educate spouses and children about the disorder and to gather helpful information about the patient (Kluft, 2001, 2000; Porter et al., 1993).

RECOVERING MEMORIES To help patients recover the missing pieces of their past, therapists use many of the approaches applied in other dissociative disorders, including psychodynamic therapy, hypnotherapy, and drug treatment (Kluft, 2001, 1991, 1985). These techniques work slowly for patients with multiple personality disorder, as some subpersonalities may keep denying experiences that the others recall (Lyon, 1992). One of the subpersonalities may even assume a "protector" role, to prevent the primary personality from suffering the pain of recollecting traumatic experiences. Some patients become self-destructive and violent during this phase of treatment (Kelly, 1993).

INTEGRATING THE SUBPERSONALITIES The final goal of therapy is to merge the different subpersonalities into a single, integrated identity. Integration is a continuous process that occurs throughout treatment until patients "own" all of their behaviors, emotions, sensations, and knowledge. **Fusion** is the final merging of two or more subpersonalities. Many patients distrust this final treatment goal, and their subpersonalities are likely to see integration as a form of death (Kluft, 2001, 1999, 1991). As one subpersonality said, "There are too many advantages to being multiple. Maybe we're being sold a bill of goods by therapists" (Hale, 1983). Therapists have used a range of approaches to help merge subpersonalities, including psychodynamic, supportive, cognitive, and drug therapies (Goldman, 1995; Fichtner et al., 1990).

Once the subpersonalities are integrated, further therapy is typically needed to maintain the complete personality and to teach social and coping skills that may help prevent later dissociations (Kihlstrom, 2001). In case reports, some therapists note high success rates (Kluft, 2001, 1999, 1993, 1984), but others find that

FUSION The final merging of two or more subpersonalities in multiple personality disorder.

patients continue to resist final integration. A few therapists have in fact questioned the need for full integration.

SUMMING UP

Dissociative Disorders

People with dissociative disorders experience major changes in memory and identity that are not due to clear physical causes. Individuals with dissociative amnesia are suddenly unable to recall important personal information or past events in their lives. Those with dissociative fugue not only fail to remember their personal identities but also flee to a different location and may establish a new identity. In multiple personality disorder (dissociative identity disorder), people display two or more distinct subpersonalities. The number of people diagnosed with multiple personality disorder has increased in recent years.

The dissociative disorders are not well understood. Among the processes that have been cited to explain them are extreme repression, operant conditioning, state-dependent learning, and self-hypnosis. The latter two phenomena, in particular, have excited the interest of clinical scientists.

Dissociative amnesia and fugue may end on their own or may require treatment. Multiple personality disorder typically requires treatment. Approaches commonly used to help people with dissociative amnesia and fugue recover their lost memories are psychodynamic therapy, hypnotic therapy, and sodium amobarbital or sodium pentobarbital. Therapists who treat people with multiple personality disorder use the same approaches and, more generally, try to help clients recognize the full scope of their disorder, recover the gaps in their memories, and integrate their subpersonalities into one functional personality.

>>LOOKING AROUND

Major Impact Before the publication of *Sybil* in 1973, only 100 cases of multiple personality disorder had been published. Since then, an estimated 40,000 diagnoses have been made, most of them in North America (Acocella, 1999; Miller & Kantrowitz, 1999).<<

The Beginnings of Sybilization Several colleagues who worked closely with the author of *Sybil* and with the therapist claim that Sybil was actually highly hypnotizable, extremely suggestible, and eager to please her therapist, and that her disorder was in fact induced by the treatment techniques of hypnosis and sodium pentothal (Rieber, 2002, 1999; Miller & Kantrowitz, 1999).<<

CROSSROADS:
Disorders Rediscovered

Somatoform and dissociative disorders are among the clinical field's earliest identified psychological disorders. Indeed, as we observed in Chapter 1, they were key to the development of the psychogenic perspective. Despite this early impact, the clinical field stopped paying much attention to these disorders during the middle and latter parts of the twentieth century. The feeling among many clinical theorists was that the number of such cases was shrinking. And more than a few questioned the legitimacy of these diagnoses.

Much of that thinking has changed in the past two decades. The field's keen interest in the impact of stress upon health and physical illness has, by association, reawakened interest in somatoform disorders. Similarly, as we shall see in Chapter 15, the field has greatly intensified its efforts to understand and treat Alzheimer's disease in recent years, and that work has sparked a broad interest in the operation and wonder of memory, including an interest in dissociative disorders.

Over the past 20 years there has been an explosion of research seeking to help clinicians better recognize, understand, and treat unexplained physical and memory disorders. Although this research has yet to yield clear insights or highly effective treatments, it has already suggested that the disorders may be more common than clinical theorists had come to believe. Moreover, there is growing evidence that the disorders may be rooted in processes that are already well known from other areas of study, such as overattentiveness to bodily processes, cognitive misinterpretations, state-dependent learning, and self-hypnosis. Given this new wave of research enthusiasm, we may witness significant growth in our understanding and treatment of these disorders in the coming years.

>>Q & A

Why "a memory like an elephant's"?

The belief that elephants have long memories is based on the observation that the animals effortlessly find their way home even after traveling more than 30 miles to find water.<<

Researchers' growing interest in these disorders has been accompanied by intense public interest as well. Moreover, it has sparked a greater belief in somatoform and dissociative disorders among many clinicians. More and more therapists are now identifying patients with multiple personality disorder, for example, and they are trying to provide appropriate treatment.

With such heightened interest and work come new problems. Many of today's clinicians worry that the focus on somatoform and dissociative disorders may be swinging too far—that the current degree of interest in them may be creating a false impression of their prevalence or importance. Some clinicians note, for example, that physicians are often quick to assign the label "somatoform" to elusive medical problems such as chronic fatigue syndrome, Gulf War syndrome, and lupus—clearly a disservice to patients with such severe problems and to the progress of medical science. Similarly, a number of clinicians worry that at least some of the many legal defenses based on multiple personality disorder or other dissociative disorders are contrived or inaccurate. Of course, such possibilities serve to highlight even further the importance of continued investigations into all aspects of the disorders.

CRITICAL THOUGHTS

1. Why do the terms "hysteria" and "hysterical" currently have such negative connotations in our society, as in "mass hysteria" and "hysterical personality"? *pp. 164–169*

2. If parents who harm their children are clearly disturbed, as in cases of *Munchausen syndrome by proxy*, how should society react to them? Which is more appropriate—treatment or punishment? *pp. 168–169*

3. How might a culture help create individual cases of body dysmorphic disorder? Why do some people in a society carry a culture's aesthetic ideals to an extreme, while others stay within normal bounds? *p. 174*

4. Some accused criminals claim that they have multiple personality disorder and that their crimes were committed by one of their subpersonalities. If such claims are accurate, what would be an appropriate verdict? *pp. 180–183*

5. Therapists often use hypnosis to help *uncover* hidden memories and needs. But hypnotic therapists can also use this suggestive technique to *create* memories, desires, and the like. How can hypnotists know when they are uncovering a person's state of mind as opposed to creating it? *pp. 186–188*

KEY TERMS

somatoform disorder p. 164

hysterical somatoform disorders p. 164

conversion disorder p. 164

somatization disorder p. 166

pain disorder associated with psychological factors p. 166

malingering p. 167

factitious disorder p. 167

Munchausen syndrome p. 169

Munchausen syndrome by proxy p. 169

preoccupation somatoform disorders p. 169

hypochondriasis p. 169

body dysmorphic disorder p. 169

Electra complex p. 171

primary gain p. 172

secondary gain p. 172

placebo p. 173

memory p. 176

dissociative disorders p. 176

dissociative amnesia p. 177

amnestic episode p. 177

dissociative fugue p. 178

multiple personality disorder p. 181

subpersonalities p. 181

iatrogenic disorder p. 183

repression p. 183

state-dependent learning p. 184

hypnotic amnesia p. 186

self-hypnosis p. 186

hypnotic therapy p. 187

sodium amobarbitol p. 187

sodium pentobarbital p. 187

fusion p. 188

QUICK QUIZ

1. What are the symptoms of each of the hysterical somatoform disorders? How do practitioners distinguish hysterical disorders from "true" medical problems? *pp. 164–167*

2. How does a somatoform disorder differ from a factitious disorder? *pp. 168–169*

3. List the central features of each of the preoccupation somatoform disorders. *pp. 169–170*

4. What are the leading explanations and treatments for the somatoform disorders? How well does research support them? *pp. 170–175*

5. List and describe the different dissociative disorders. *pp. 175–181*

6. What are four kinds of dissociative amnesia? *pp. 177–178*

7. What are the different kinds of relationships that the subpersonalities may have in multiple personality disorder? *pp. 181–182*

8. Describe the psychodynamic, behavioral, state-dependent learning, and self-hypnosis explanations of dissociative disorders. How well is each supported by research? *pp. 183–186*

9. What approaches have been used to treat dissociative amnesia and dissociative fugue? *pp. 186–187*

10. What are the key features of treatment for multiple personality disorder? Is treatment successful? *pp. 187–189*

SEARCH THE *FUNDAMENTALS OF ABNORMAL PSYCHOLOGY* CD-ROM FOR

▲ Chapter 6 Video Case Enrichment
   When do somatoform symptoms impair functioning?
   Observe an individual with multiple personality disorder, and see "switches"
      from subpersonality to subpersonality.

▲ Chapter 6 Practical, Research, and Decision-Making Exercises
   The power of suggestion
   Manufacturing memories

▲ Chapter 6 Practice Test and Feedback

LOG ON TO THE COMER WEB PAGE FOR

▲ Suggested Web links, exercises, FAQ page, additional Chapter 6 practice test questions
   <www.worthpublishers.com/comer>

‹‹‹

LAURA WHEELER WARING, 1927

Mood Disorders

For . . . a six-month period, her irritability bordered on the irrational. She screamed in anger or sobbed in despair at every dirty dish left on the coffee table or on the bedroom floor. Each day the need to plan the dinner menu provoked agonizing indecision. How could all the virtues or, more likely, vices of hamburgers be accurately compared to those of spaghetti? . . . She had her whole family walking on eggs. She thought they would be better off if she were dead.

Beatrice could not cope with her job. As a branch manager of a large chain store, she had many decisions to make. Unable to make them herself, she would ask employees who were much less competent for advice, but then she could not decide whose advice to take. Each morning before going to work, she complained of nausea. . . .

Beatrice's husband . . . thought that she would improve if he made her life easier by taking over more housework, cooking, and child care. His attempt to help only made Beatrice feel more guilty and worthless. She wanted to make a contribution to her family. She wanted to do the chores "like normal people" did but broke down crying at the smallest impediment to a perfect job. . . . Months passed, and Beatrice's problem became more serious. Some days she was too upset to go to work. She stopped seeing her friends. She spent most of her time at home either yelling or crying.

(Lickey & Gordon, 1991, p. 181)

DEPRESSION A low, sad state marked by significant levels of sadness, lack of energy, low self-worth, guilt, or related symptoms.

MANIA A state or episode of euphoria or frenzied activity in which people may have an exaggerated belief that the world is theirs for the taking.

UNIPOLAR DEPRESSION Depression without a history of mania.

BIPOLAR DISORDER A disorder marked by alternating or intermixed periods of mania and depression.

Most people's moods come and go. Their feelings of joy or sadness are understandable reactions to daily events and do not affect their lives greatly. The moods of people with mood disorders, in contrast, tend to last a long time. As in Beatrice's case, the mood colors all of their interactions with the world and interferes with normal functioning.

Depression and mania are the key emotions in mood disorders. **Depression** is a low, sad state in which life seems dark and its challenges overwhelming. **Mania**, the opposite of depression, is a state of breathless euphoria, or at least frenzied energy, in which people may have an exaggerated belief that the world is theirs for the taking. Most people with a mood disorder suffer only from depression, a pattern called **unipolar depression**. They have no history of mania and return to a normal or nearly normal mood when their depression lifts. Others experience periods of mania that alternate with periods of depression, a pattern called **bipolar disorder**.

Mood disorders have always captured people's interest, in part because so many famous people have suffered from them. The Bible speaks of the severe depressions of Nebuchadnezzar, Saul, and Moses. Queen Victoria of England and Abraham Lincoln seem to have experienced recurring depressions. Mood disorders also have plagued such writers as Ernest Hemingway, Eugene O'Neill, Virginia Woolf, and Sylvia Plath. Their mood problems have been shared by millions, and today the economic costs (work loss, treatment, hospitalization) amount to more than $40 billion each year (Kessler, 2002; Wong & Licino, 2001). Of course, the human suffering that the disorders cause is beyond calculation.

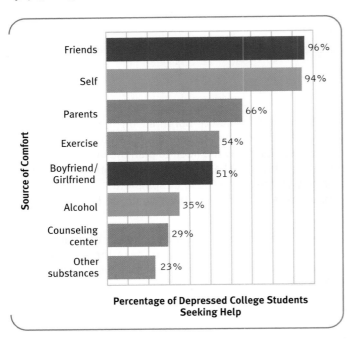

FIGURE 7-1 **Where do college students turn when they feel depressed?** *Typically they turn to friends and to themselves. Fewer than one-third go to a counseling center.* (Adapted from Oswalt & Finkelberg, 1995.)

Unipolar Depression

Whenever we feel particularly unhappy, we are likely to describe ourselves as "depressed." In all likelihood, we are merely responding to sad events, fatigue, or unhappy thoughts, and we are unlikely to think we need professional help (see Figure 7-1). This loose use of the term confuses a perfectly normal mood swing with a clinical syndrome. All of us experience dejection from time to time, but only some experience unipolar depression. Clinical depression brings severe and long-lasting psychological pain that may intensify as time goes by. Those who suffer from it may lose their will to carry out the simplest of life's activities; some even lose their will to live.

How Common Is Unipolar Depression?

Between 5 and 10 percent of adults in the United States suffer from a severe unipolar pattern of depression in any given year, while another 3 to 5 percent suffer from mild forms (Kessler, 2002; Regier et al., 1993). The rates are similar in Canada, England, and many other countries (Smith & Weissman, 1992). Around 17 percent of all adults in the world may experience an episode of severe unipolar depression at some point in their lives (Kessler, 2002; Angst, 1999, 1995).

In almost all countries, women are at least twice as likely as men to experience episodes of severe unipolar depression (Nolen-Hoeksema, 2002). As many as 26 percent of women may have an episode at some time in their lives, compared with 12 percent of men (APA, 1993). Among children, the prevalence is similar for girls and boys (Garber & Horowitz, 2002).

All of these rates hold steady across the various socioeconomic classes. Similarly, few differences in the prevalence of unipolar depression have been found among ethnic groups. In the United States, middle-aged white Americans have a somewhat higher rate than middle-aged African Americans, but the rates for younger and older adults are the same in both populations (Weissman et al., 1991). Approximately half of people with unipolar depression recover within six weeks and 90 percent recover within a year, some without treatment (Kessler, 2002; Kendler et al., 1997). However, most of them have at least one other episode of depression later in their lives (Boland & Keller, 2002).

What Are the Symptoms of Depression?

The picture of depression may differ from person to person. Earlier we saw how Beatrice's indecisiveness, uncontrollable sobbing, and feelings of despair, anger, and worthlessness brought her job and social life to a standstill. Other depressed people have symptoms that are less severe. They manage to function, although their depression typically robs them of much effectiveness or pleasure, as we see in the case of Derek:

Derek has probably suffered from depression all of his adult life but was unaware of it for many years. Derek called himself a night person, claiming that he could not think clearly until after noon even though he was often awake by 4:00 a.m. He tried to schedule his work as editorial writer for a small town newspaper so that it was compatible with his depressed mood at the beginning of the day. Therefore, he scheduled meetings for the mornings; talking with people got him moving. He saved writing and decision making for later in the day.

. . . Derek's private thoughts were rarely cheerful and self-confident. He felt that his marriage was a mere business partnership. He provided the money, and she provided a home and children. Derek and his wife rarely expressed affection for each other. Occasionally, he had images of his own violent death in a bicycle crash, in a plane crash, or in a murder by an unidentified assailant.

Derek felt that he was constantly on the edge of job failure. He was disappointed that his editorials had not attracted the attention of larger papers. He was certain that several of the younger people on the paper had better ideas and wrote more skillfully than he did. He scolded himself for a bad editorial that he had written ten years earlier. Although that particular piece had not been up to his usual standards, everyone else on the paper had forgotten it a week after it appeared. But ten years later, Derek was still ruminating over that one editorial. . . .

Derek brushed off his morning confusion as a lack of quick intelligence. He had no way to know that it was a symptom of depression. He never realized that his death images might be suicidal thinking. People do not talk about such things. For all Derek knew, everyone had similar thoughts.

(Lickey & Gordon, 1991, pp. 183–185)

As the cases of Beatrice and Derek indicate, depression has many symptoms other than sadness. The symptoms, which often feed upon one another, span five areas of functioning: emotional, motivational, behavioral, cognitive, and physical.

EMOTIONAL SYMPTOMS Most people who are depressed feel sad and dejected. They describe themselves as feeling "miserable," "empty," and "humiliated." They report getting little pleasure from anything, and they tend to lose their sense of humor. Some also experience anxiety, anger, or agitation (Noyes, 2001). This sea of misery may lead to crying spells.

MOTIVATIONAL SYMPTOMS Depressed people typically lose the desire to pursue their usual activities. Almost all report a lack of drive, initiative, and spontaneity. They may have to force themselves to go to work, talk with friends, eat meals, or have sex. One individual recalls, "I didn't want to do anything—just wanted to stay put and be let alone" (Kraines & Thetford, 1972, p. 20).

Suicide represents the ultimate escape from life's challenges. As we shall see in Chapter 8, many depressed people become uninterested in life or wish to die; others wish they could kill themselves, and some actually try. It has been estimated that between 6 and 15 percent of people who suffer from severe depression commit suicide (Stolberg et al., 2002; Rossow & Amundsen, 1995).

Triggers of depression *At a 1999 White House conference, Mike Wallace (CBS newsman) and Tipper Gore (wife of then–Vice President Al Gore) discuss their past bouts of depression. Wallace's episode was triggered by a lengthy civil trial, Gore's by her son's near-fatal accident.*

BEHAVIORAL SYMPTOMS Depressed people are usually less active and less productive. They spend more time alone and may stay in bed for long periods. One man recalls, "I'd awaken early, but I'd just lie there—what was the use of getting up to a miserable day?" (Kraines & Thetford, 1972, p. 21). Depressed people may also move and even speak more slowly (Joiner, 2002; Sobin & Sackeim, 1997).

COGNITIVE SYMPTOMS Depressed people hold extremely negative views of themselves. They consider themselves inadequate, undesirable, inferior, perhaps evil. They also blame themselves for nearly every unfortunate event, even things that have nothing to do with them, and they rarely credit themselves for positive achievements.

Another cognitive symptom of depression is pessimism. Sufferers are usually convinced that nothing will ever improve, and they feel helpless to change any aspect of their lives. Because they expect the worst, they are likely to procrastinate. Their sense of hopelessness and helplessness makes them especially prone to suicidal thinking.

People with depression frequently complain that their intellectual ability is poor. They feel confused, unable to remember things, easily distracted, and unable to solve even the smallest problems. In laboratory studies, depressed subjects do perform more poorly than nondepressed subjects on some tasks of memory, attention, and reasoning (Kalska et al., 1999; Hertel, 1998). It may be, however, that these difficulties reflect motivational problems rather than cognitive ones.

A CLOSER LOOK

Sadness at the Happiest of Times

Women usually expect the birth of a child to be a happy experience. But for 10 to 30 percent of new mothers, the weeks and months after childbirth bring clinical depression (O'Hara, 2003; Nonacs & Cohen, 1998). Postpartum depression typically begins within four weeks after the birth of a child (APA, 2000, 1994), and it is far more severe than simple "baby blues." It is also different from other postpartum syndromes such as *postpartum psychosis*, a problem that we shall observe in Chapter 12.

The "baby blues" are so common—as many as 80 percent of women experience them—that most researchers consider them normal. As new mothers try to cope with the wakeful nights, rattled emotions, and other stresses that accompany the arrival of a new baby, they may experience crying spells, fatigue, anxiety, insomnia, and sadness. These symptoms usually disappear within days or weeks (Najman et al., 2000; Horowitz et al., 1995).

In postpartum depression, however, depressive symptoms continue and may last up to a year (Terry et al., 1996). The symptoms include extreme sadness, despair, tearfulness, insomnia, anxiety, intrusive thoughts, compulsions, panic attacks, feelings of inability to cope, and suicidal thoughts. The mother–infant relationship and the health of the child may suffer as a result (O'Hara, 2003; Weinberg et al., 2001). Women who experience postpartum depression have a 25 to 50 percent chance of developing it again with a subsequent birth (Stevens et al., 2002; Wisner et al., 2001).

Many clinicians believe that the hormonal changes accompanying childbirth trigger postpartum depression (Parry, 1999). All women experience a kind of

Behind the smile *Singer Marie Osmond, performing here with her brother Donny, recently revealed that she suffered from postpartum depression after giving birth in 1999.*

hormone "withdrawal" after delivery, as estrogen and progesterone levels, which rise as much as 50 times above normal during pregnancy, now drop sharply to levels far below normal (Horowitz et al., 1995). Perhaps some women are particularly influenced by these dramatic hormone changes (Horowitz et al., 1995). Still other theorists suggest a genetic predisposition to postpartum depression (APA, 2000, 1994; Steiner & Tam, 1999).

At the same time, psychological and sociocultural factors may play important roles in the disorder. The birth of a baby brings enormous psychological and social change (Nicolson, 1999; Hopkins et al., 1984). A woman typically faces changes in her marital relationship, daily routines, and social roles. Sleep and relaxation are likely to decrease and financial pressures may increase. Perhaps she feels the added stress of giving up a career—or of trying to maintain one. This pileup of stress may heighten the risk of depression (Swendsen & Mazure, 2000; Terry et al., 1996).

Fortunately, treatment can make a big difference for most women with postpartum depression. Psychoeducation and self-help support groups have proved extremely helpful for many with the disorder (O'Hara, 2003; Stevens et al., 2002; Honikman, 1999). In addition, many respond well to the same approaches that are applied to other forms of depression—antidepressant medications, cognitive therapy, interpersonal psychotherapy, or a combination of these (O'Hara, 2003; Stuart et al., 2003; Stowe et al., 1995).

However, many women who would benefit from treatment do not seek help because they feel ashamed about being sad at a time that is supposed to be joyous or they are concerned about being judged harshly (APA, 1994). For them, and for the spouses and family members close to them, a large dose of education is in order (O'Hara, 2003). Even positive events can be stressful and upsetting if they also bring major change to one's life. Recognizing and addressing such upsets are in everyone's best interest.

PHYSICAL SYMPTOMS People who are depressed often have such physical ailments as headaches, indigestion, constipation, dizzy spells, and general pain (Fishbain, 2000). In fact, many depressions are misdiagnosed as medical problems at first (Simon & Katzelnick, 1997). Disturbances in appetite and sleep are particularly common (Ohayon & Roth, 2003). Most depressed people eat less, sleep less, and feel more fatigued than they did prior to the disorder. Some, however, eat and sleep excessively.

Diagnosing Unipolar Depression

According to DSM-IV, a *major depressive episode* is a period marked by at least five symptoms of depression and lasting for two weeks or more (see Table 7-1). In extreme cases, the episode may include psychotic symptoms, ones marked by a loss of contact with reality, such as *delusions*—bizarre ideas without foundation—or *hallucinations*—perceptions of things that are not actually present. A depressed man with psychotic symptoms may imagine that he can't eat "because my intestines are deteriorating and will soon stop working," or he may believe that he sees his dead wife.

People who experience a major depressive episode without having any history of mania receive a diagnosis of **major depressive disorder**. Individuals who display a longer-lasting but less disabling pattern of unipolar depression may receive a diagnosis of **dysthymic disorder**. When dysthymic disorder leads to major depressive disorder, the sequence is called *double depression* (Boland & Keller, 2002).

"Sometimes I don't read my mail."

Stress and Unipolar Depression

Episodes of unipolar depression often seem to be triggered by stressful events. In fact, researchers have found that depressed people experience a greater number of stressful life events during the month just before the onset of their disorder than do other people during the same period of time (Monroe & Hadjiyannakis, 2002). Of course, stressful life events also precede other psychological disorders, but depressed people report more such events than anybody else.

Table 7-1 DSM-IV Checklist

MAJOR DEPRESSIVE EPISODE

1. The presence of at least five of the following symptoms during the same two-week period: • depressed mood most of the day, nearly every day • markedly diminished interest or pleasure in almost all activities most of the day, nearly every day • significant weight loss or weight gain, or decrease or increase in appetite nearly every day • insomnia or hypersomnia nearly every day • psychomotor agitation or retardation nearly every day • fatigue or loss of energy nearly every day • feelings of worthlessness or excessive guilt nearly every day • reduced ability to think or concentrate, or indecisiveness, nearly every day • recurrent thoughts of death or suicide, a suicide attempt, or a specific plan for committing suicide.
2. Significant distress or impairment.

MAJOR DEPRESSIVE DISORDER

1. The presence of a major depressive episode.
2. No history of a manic or hypomanic episode.

Based on APA, 2000, 1994.

MAJOR DEPRESSIVE DISORDER A pattern of severe depression that is disabling and is not caused by such factors as drugs or a general medical condition.

DYSTHYMIC DISORDER A mood disorder that is similar to but longer-lasting and less disabling than a major depressive disorder.

ELECTROCONVULSIVE THERAPY (ECT)
A treatment for depression in which electrodes attached to a patient's head send an electrical current through the brain, causing a convulsion.

Some clinicians consider it important to distinguish a *reactive (exogenous) depression*, which follows clear-cut stressful events, from an *endogenous depression*, which seems to be a response to internal factors (Vetter et al., 2001). But can one ever know for certain whether a depression is reactive or not? Even if stressful events occurred before the onset of depression, that depression may not be reactive. The events could actually be a coincidence (Paykel et al., 1984). Thus, today's clinicians usually concentrate on recognizing both the situational and the internal aspects of any given case of unipolar depression.

The Biological Model of Unipolar Depression

Medical researchers have been aware for years that certain diseases and drugs produce mood changes. Could unipolar depression itself have biological causes? Evidence from genetic and biochemical studies suggests that often it does (Wallace, Schneider, & McGuffin, 2002).

GENETIC FACTORS Family pedigree studies and twin studies suggest that some people inherit a predisposition to unipolar depression; as we have observed, however, findings from such studies can also be interpreted in other ways. *Family pedigree studies* select people with unipolar depression, examine their relatives, and see whether depression also afflicts other members of the family. If a predisposition to unipolar depression is inherited, relatives should have a higher rate of depression than the population at large. Researchers have in fact found that as many as 20 percent of those relatives are depressed, compared with fewer than 10 percent of the general population (Harrington et al., 1993).

If a predisposition to unipolar depression is inherited, we would also expect to find a particularly large number of cases among the close relatives of depressed persons. *Twin studies* have supported this expectation (Wallace et al., 2002). One study looked at nearly 200 pairs of twins. When an identical twin had unipolar depression, there was a 46 percent chance that the other twin would have the same disorder. In contrast, when a fraternal twin had unipolar depression, the other twin had only a 20 percent chance of developing the disorder (McGuffin et al., 1996).

BIOCHEMICAL FACTORS As we have seen, neurotransmitters are the brain chemicals that carry messages from one nerve cell, or neuron, to another. Low activity of two such chemicals, *norepinephrine* and *serotonin*, has been strongly linked to unipolar depression. In the 1950s, several pieces of evidence began to point to this relationship. First, medical researchers discovered that certain medications for high blood pressure often caused depression (Ayd, 1956). As it turned out, some of these medications lowered norepinephrine activity and others lowered serotonin. A second piece of evidence was the discovery of the first truly effective antidepressant drugs. Although these drugs were discovered by accident, researchers soon learned that they relieve depression by increasing either norepinephrine or serotonin activity.

For years it was thought that low activity of *either* norepinephrine or serotonin was capable of producing depression, but researchers now believe that their relation to depression is more complicated than that (Delgado & Moreno, 2000). Investigations suggest that interactions between serotonin and norepinephrine activity, or between these neurotransmitters and yet other neurotransmitters in the brain, rather than the operation of one of the neurotransmitters alone, may account for unipolar depression (Thase et al., 2002).

Biological researchers have also learned that the body's *endocrine system* may play a role in unipolar depression. As we have seen, endocrine glands throughout the body release *hormones*, chemicals that in turn spur body organs into action (see Chapter 5). People

The importance of light *These children, who live 200 miles north of the Arctic Circle, receive a daily dose of ultraviolet light to compensate for the lack of midwinter sun. Similarly, people who suffer from* seasonal affective disorder *are often treated with* light therapy.

Mark S. Wexler, Chicago

with unipolar depression have been found to have abnormal levels of *cortisol*, one of the hormones released by the adrenal glands during times of stress (Holsboer, 2001). This relationship is not all that surprising, given that stressful events often seem to trigger depression. Still another hormone that has been tied to depression is *melatonin*, sometimes called the "Dracula hormone" because it is released only in the dark. People who experience a recurrence of depression each winter (a pattern called *seasonal affective disorder*) may secrete more melatonin during the winter season's long nights than other individuals do (Rosenthal & Blehar, 1989).

The biological explanations of unipolar depression have produced much enthusiasm, but research in this area has certain limitations. Some of it has relied on studies that create depression-like symptoms in laboratory animals. Researchers cannot be certain that these symptoms do in fact reflect the human disorder (Cox et al., 1999). Similarly, until recent years, technology was limited, and biological studies of human depression had to measure brain activity indirectly. As a result, investigators could never be certain of the biological events that were occuring in the brain. Current studies using newer technology, such as PET and MRI scans, are helping to clear up such uncertainties about brain activity.

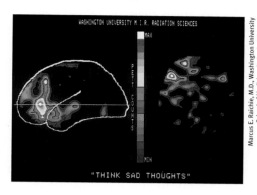

Sadness and the brain *A PET scan of a person thinking sad thoughts shows which areas of brain activity (shown in red, orange, and yellow) are related to such mood changes.*

WHAT ARE THE BIOLOGICAL TREATMENTS FOR UNIPOLAR DEPRESSION? Usually biological treatment means *antidepressant drugs*, but for severely depressed persons who do not respond to other forms of treatment, it sometimes means *electroconvulsive therapy*. Many people are surprised to learn that electroconvulsive therapy is, in fact, a highly effective approach for treating unipolar depression.

ELECTROCONVULSIVE THERAPY One of the most controversial forms of treatment for depression is **electroconvulsive therapy**, or **ECT**. In this procedure, two electrodes are attached to the patient's head, and an electric current of 65 to 140 volts is sent through the brain for half a second or less. The current causes a *brain seizure* that lasts from 25 seconds to a few minutes. After 6 to 12 such treatments, spaced over two to four weeks, most patients feel less depressed (Gitlin, 2002; Fink, 2001, 1992). In *bilateral ECT* one electrode is applied to each side of the forehead and a current passes through both sides of the brain. In *unilateral ECT* the electrodes are placed so that the current passes through only one side.

The discovery that electric shock can be therapeutic was made by accident. In the 1930s, clinical researchers mistakenly came to believe that brain seizures, or the convulsions (severe body spasms) that accompany them, could cure schizophrenia and other psychotic disorders, and so they searched for ways to produce seizures as a treatment for patients with psychosis. One early technique was to give the patients the drug *metrazol*. Another was to give them large doses of *insulin* (*insulin coma therapy*). These procedures produced the desired brain seizures, but each was quite dangerous and sometimes even caused death. Finally, an Italian psychiatrist named Ugo Cerletti discovered that he could produce seizures more safely by applying electric currents to patients' heads (Cerletti & Bini, 1938). ECT soon became popular and was tried out on various psychological problems, as new techniques so often are. Its effectiveness with severe depression in particular became apparent.

In the early years of ECT, broken bones and dislocations of the jaw or shoulders sometimes resulted from ECT's severe convulsions. Today's practitioners avoid this problem by giving patients strong *muscle relaxants* to minimize convulsions. They also use *anesthetics* to put patients to sleep during the procedure, reducing their terror (Gitlin, 2002).

Patients who receive ECT typically have difficulty remembering the events before and immediately after their treatments. In most cases, this memory loss clears up within a few months (Calev et al., 1995, 1991; Squire & Slater, 1983). Some patients, however, experience gaps in more distant memory, and this form of amnesia can be permanent (Fink, 2001; Squire, 1977).

ECT today *During ECT, patients are now given anesthetics to help them sleep, muscle relaxants to prevent severe jerks of the body and broken bones, and oxygen to guard against brain damage.*

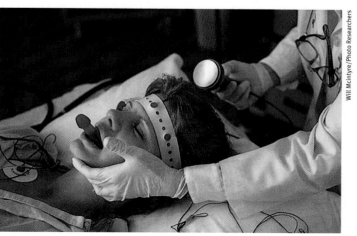

"And Remember to Ask Your Doctor about This Medication"

"Maybe you are suffering from depression" . . . "Ask your doctor about Zoloft" . . . "There is no need to suffer any longer." Anyone who watches television is familiar with phrases such as these. They are at the heart of *direct-to-consumer* (*DTC*) drug advertising—advertisements in which pharmaceutical companies appeal directly to consumers, coaxing them to ask their physicians to prescribe particular drugs for them. Research shows that consumers are, on average, familiar with 4 of every 10 drug ads (Wilkes et al., 2000). DTC drug ads on television are so commonplace that it is easy to forget they have been a major part of our viewing pleasure for only a few years. It was not until 1997, when the U.S. Food and Drug Administration (FDA) relaxed the rules of pharmaceutical advertising, that these ads really took off.

Antidepressants are among the leading drugs to receive DTC television advertising, along with oral antihistamines, cholesterol reducers, and anti-ulcer drugs (Pines, 1999). Sales of antidepressants are expected to reach $13 billion by the year 2005, and at least some of the success of these drugs is due to DTC ads.

Altogether, pharmaceutical companies now spend around $2 billion a year on American television advertising, around seven times the amount spent in 1997 (Fetto, 2002; Kaiser Family Foundation, 2001). In fact, 30 percent of adults say they have asked their doctors about specific medications that they saw advertised, and half of these individuals report that their doctors gave them a prescription for the advertised drug. With results like that, it is small wonder that the pharmaceutical companies are increasing their DTC budgets by at least 33 percent each year.

But how did we get here? Where did this tidal wave of advertising come from? And what's with those endless "side effects" that are blurted out so rapidly on each and every commercial? It's a long and complex story (Curtiss, 2002), but here are some of the key plot twists that helped set the stage for today's DTC television drug advertising.

1938: Food, Drug, and Cosmetic Act

Congress passed the *Food, Drug, and Cosmetic Act*, which gave the FDA control over the labels on prescriptions and over-the-counter drugs and over most related forms of drug advertising (Kessler & Pines, 1998).

1962: Kefauver-Harris Drug Amendments

In the spirit of consumer protection, Congress passed a law requiring that all pharmaceutical drugs be proved safe and effective (Wilkes et al., 2000). In addition, the law set up rules that companies were required to follow in their drug advertisements, including a detailed summary of the drug's contraindications, side effects, and effectiveness, and a "fair balance" coverage of risks and benefits.

1962–1981 Drug Ads for Physicians

For the next two decades, pharmaceutical companies targeted their ads to the *physicians* who were writing the prescriptions. As more and more *psychotropic* drugs were developed, psychiatrists were included among those targeted.

1981: First Pitch

The pharmaceutical drug industry proposed shifting the advertising of drugs directly to *consumers* instead of to physicians (Curtiss, 2002; Wilkes et al., 2000). Their argument was based on the notion that such advertising would protect consumers by directly educating them about available drugs.

1983–1985: First DTC Drug Ads

In 1983 the first direct-to-consumer drug ad appeared, and in 1985 the FDA decided to allow DTC drug ads as long as the ads met the previous physician-directed promotion standards. That is, each consumer-oriented ad also had to include a summary of the drug's side effects, contraindications, and effectiveness; avoid false advertising; and offer a fair balance in its information about effectiveness and risks (Curtiss, 2002; Ostrove, 2001; Pines, 1997).

1997: FDA Makes Television-Friendly Changes

Recognizing that its previous guidelines could not readily be applied to brief TV ads, which may run for only 30 seconds, the FDA changed its guidelines for DTC television drug ads. It passed a *Draft Guidance*, which ruled that DTC television advertisements must simply mention a drug's important risks and must indicate where consumers can get further information about the drug. The pharmaceutical company must also make available such information by providing a toll-free phone number and a Web site. In addition, it must refer consumers to a magazine ad or other printed material that contains more detailed information, and it must recommend that consumers speak with a doctor about the drug (Wilkes et al., 2000).

The old days
Before 1997, the vast majority of ads for psychotropic drugs appeared not on television but in physicians' journals and consumer magazines.

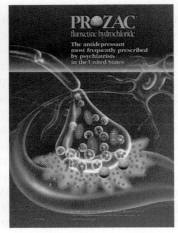

ECT is clearly effective in treating unipolar depression, although it has been difficult to determine why the procedure works so well. Studies find that between 60 and 70 percent of ECT patients improve (Fink, 2001). The procedure seems to be particularly effective in severe cases of depression that include delusions.

Although ECT is effective and ECT techniques have improved, its use has generally declined since the 1950s. It is estimated that more than 100,000 patients a year underwent ECT in the United States during the 1940s and 1950s. Today as few as 50,000 per year are believed to receive it (Cauchon, 1999). Two of the reasons for this decline are the memory loss caused by ECT and the frightening nature of the procedure. Another is the emergence of effective *antidepressant drugs*.

ANTIDEPRESSANT DRUGS Two kinds of drugs discovered in the 1950s reduce the symptoms of depression: *monoamine oxidase (MAO) inhibitors* and *tricyclics*. These drugs have recently been joined by a third group, the so-called *second-generation antidepressants* (see Table 7-2).

The effectiveness of **MAO inhibitors** as a treatment for unipolar depression was discovered accidentally. Physicians noted that *iproniazid*, a drug being tested on patients with tuberculosis, had an interesting effect: it seemed to make the patients happier (Sandler, 1990). It was found to have the same effect on depressed patients (Kline, 1958). What this and several related drugs had in common biochemically was that they slowed the body's production of the enzyme *monoamine oxidase (MAO)*. Thus they were called MAO inhibitors.

Normally, brain supplies of the enzyme MAO break down the neurotransmitter norepinephrine. MAO inhibitors block MAO from carrying out this activity and thereby stop the destruction of norepinephrine. The result is a rise in norepinephrine activity and, in turn, a reduction of depressive symptoms. Approximately half of depressed patients who take MAO inhibitors are helped by them (Thase et al., 1995). There is, however, a potential danger to taking MAO inhibitors. People who take them will experience a dangerous rise in blood pressure if they eat foods containing the chemical *tyramine* —including such common foods as cheeses, bananas, and certain wines. Thus people on MAO inhibitors must stick to a rigid diet.

The discovery of **tricyclics** in the 1950s was also accidental. Researchers who were looking for a new drug to combat schizophrenia ran some tests on a drug called *imipramine* (Kuhn, 1958). They discovered that imipramine was of no help in cases of schizophrenia, but it did relieve unipolar depression in many people. This drug and related ones became known as tricyclic antidepressants because they all share a three-ring molecular structure.

Literally hundreds of studies indicate that about 60 to 65 percent of depressed patients who take tricyclics are helped significantly by the drugs (Gitlin, 2002; Hirschfeld, 1999). If the patients stop taking these drugs immediately after obtaining relief, they run a high risk of relapsing within a year (Montgomery et al., 1993). If, however, they continue taking the drugs for five months or more after being free of depressive symptoms—a practice called "continuation therapy"—their chances of relapse decrease considerably (Kessler, 2002). As a result, clinicians often keep patients on the drugs indefinitely (Gitlin, 2002).

Most researchers have concluded that tricyclics reduce depression by acting on neurotransmitter "reuptake" mechanisms. We have seen that messages are carried from one neuron across the synaptic space to a receiving neuron by a neurotransmitter, a chemical released from the nerve ending of the sending neuron. However, there is a complication in this process. While the nerve ending is releasing the neurotransmitter, a pumplike

MAO INHIBITOR An antidepressant drug that prevents the action of the enzyme monoamine oxidase.

TRICYCLIC An antidepressant drug such as imipramine that has three rings in its molecular structure.

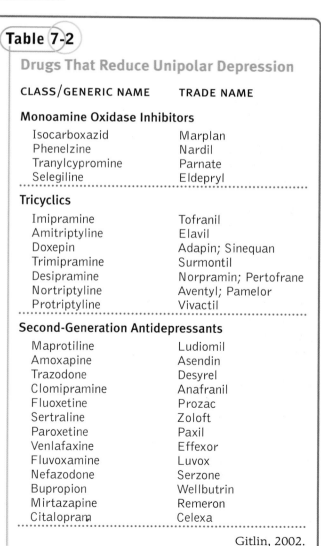

Table 7-2

Drugs That Reduce Unipolar Depression

CLASS/GENERIC NAME	TRADE NAME
Monoamine Oxidase Inhibitors	
Isocarboxazid	Marplan
Phenelzine	Nardil
Tranylcypromine	Parnate
Selegiline	Eldepryl
Tricyclics	
Imipramine	Tofranil
Amitriptyline	Elavil
Doxepin	Adapin; Sinequan
Trimipramine	Surmontil
Desipramine	Norpramin; Pertofrane
Nortriptyline	Aventyl; Pamelor
Protriptyline	Vivactil
Second-Generation Antidepressants	
Maprotiline	Ludiomil
Amoxapine	Asendin
Trazodone	Desyrel
Clomipramine	Anafranil
Fluoxetine	Prozac
Sertraline	Zoloft
Paroxetine	Paxil
Venlafaxine	Effexor
Fluvoxamine	Luvox
Nefazodone	Serzone
Bupropion	Wellbutrin
Mirtazapine	Remeron
Citalopram	Celexa

Gitlin, 2002.

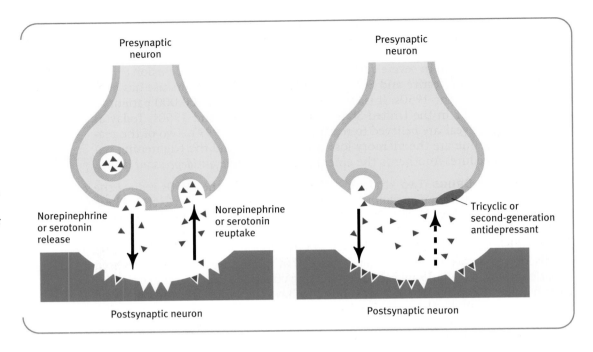

FIGURE 7-2 **Reuptake and antidepressants** *(Left) When a neuron releases norepinephrine or serotonin from its endings, a pumplike reuptake mechanism immediately starts to recapture the neurotransmitters before they are received by the postsynaptic (receptor) neuron. (Right) Tricyclic and most second-generation antidepressant drugs block this reuptake process, enabling more norepinephrine or serotonin to reach the postsynaptic neuron. (Adapted from Snyder, 1986, p. 106.)*

mechanism in the same ending is trying to recapture it. The purpose of this re-uptaken mechanism is to prevent the neurotransmitter from remaining in the synapse too long and repeatedly stimulating the receiving neuron. Perhaps this pumplike reuptake mechanism is too successful in some people, reducing norepinephrine or serotonin activity too much. The reduced activity of these neurotransmitters may, in turn, result in clinical depression. Apparently tricyclics block this reuptake process, thus increasing neurotransmitter activity (see Figure 7-2).

A third group of effective antidepressant drugs, structurally different from the MAO inhibitors and tricyclics, has been developed during the past few decades. Most of these second-generation antidepressants are labeled **selective serotonin reuptake inhibitors** (**SSRIs**) because they increase serotonin activity specifically, without affecting norepinephrine or other neurotransmitters. The SSRIs include *fluoxetine* (trade name Prozac) and *sertraline* (Zoloft). Newly developed *selective norepinephrine reuptake inhibitors* (which increase norepinephrine activity only) and *serotonin-norepinephrine reuptake inhibitors* (which increase both serotonin and norepinephrine activity) are also now available (Gitlin, 2002; Rivas-Vazquez, 2001).

In effectiveness the second-generation antidepressant drugs are about on a par with the tricyclics (Gitlin, 2002), yet their sales have skyrocketed. Prozac alone produced nearly $3 billion in sales in the year 2000. Clinicians often prefer the new antidepressants because it is harder to overdose on them than on the other kinds of antidepressants. In addition, they do not pose the dietary problems of the MAO inhibitors or produce some of the unpleasant effects of the tricyclics, such as dry mouth and constipation. At the same time, the new antidepressants can result in undesired effects of their own. Some people experience a reduction in their sex drive, for example (Gitlin, 2002).

Psychological Models of Unipolar Depression

The psychological models that have been most widely applied to unipolar depression are the psychodynamic, behavioral, and cognitive models. The psychodynamic explanation has not been strongly supported by research, and the behavioral view has

"Of course your daddy loves you. He's on Prozac—he loves everybody."

received only modest support. In contrast, cognitive explanations and treatments have received considerable research support and have gained a large following.

THE PSYCHODYNAMIC MODEL Sigmund Freud (1917) and his student Karl Abraham (1916, 1911) developed the first psychodynamic explanation and treatment for unipolar depression. Their emphasis on issues such as dependence and loss continues to influence today's psychodynamic clinicians.

PSYCHODYNAMIC EXPLANATIONS Freud and Abraham began by noting the similarity between clinical depression and grief in people who lose loved ones: constant weeping, loss of appetite, difficulty sleeping, loss of pleasure in life, and general withdrawal. According to the two theorists, a series of unconscious processes is set in motion when a loved one dies. Unable to accept the loss, mourners at first regress to the *oral stage* of development, the period of total dependency when infants cannot separate themselves from their parents. By regressing to this stage, the mourners merge their own identity with that of the person they have lost, and so symbolically regain the lost person. They direct all their feelings for the loved one, including sadness and anger, toward themselves.

For most mourners, this process is temporary. For some, however, grief worsens over time. They feel empty, they continue to avoid relationships, and their sense of loss increases. They become depressed. Freud and Abraham believed that two kinds of people are particularly likely to become clinically depressed in the face of loss: those whose parents failed to meet their needs during the oral stage and those whose parents gratified those needs excessively. People of either kind may devote their lives to others, desperately in search of love and approval (Bemporad, 1992). They are likely to feel a greater sense of loss when a loved one dies.

Of course, many people become depressed without losing a loved one. To explain why, Freud proposed the concept of **symbolic**, or **imagined**, **loss**, in which persons equate other kinds of events with the loss of a loved one. A college student might, for example, experience the failure of a calculus test as the loss of her parents, believing that they love her only when she excels academically.

Although many psychodynamic theorists have parted company with Freud and Abraham's theory of depression, it continues to influence current psychodynamic thinking. For example, *object relations theorists*, the psychodynamic theorists who emphasize relationships, propose that depression results when people's relationships leave them feeling unsafe and insecure (Kernberg, 1997, 1976). People whose parents pushed them toward either excessive dependence or

David Brauchli/AP/Wideworld Photos

Mass grief *The original psychodynamic explanation of depression took its lead from everyday experiences of grief. The deaths of Princess Diana, John F. Kennedy Jr., and the Columbine High School students each triggered mass grief reactions. Tens of thousands of people spontaneously came together to mourn these losses and built extemporaneous memorial sites with endless offerings of flowers, candles, notes, drawings, balloons, and other personal items, as at this site honoring Diana outside Kensington Palace in London.*

>>**LOOKING AROUND**
Spotting Depression

Family physicians recognize fewer than one-third of all cases of clinical depression that they encounter. Most of the undetected cases are mild (Coyne et al., 1995).<<

excessive self-reliance are more likely to become depressed when they later lose important relationships.

The following therapist description of a depressed middle-aged woman illustrates the psychodynamic concepts of dependence, loss of a loved one, and symbolic loss:

> Mrs. Marie Carls . . . had always felt very attached to her mother. As a matter of fact, they used to call her "Stamp" because she stuck to her mother as a stamp to a letter. She always tried to placate her volcanic mother, to please her in every possible way. . . .
>
> After marriage [to Julius], she continued her pattern of submission and compliance. Before her marriage she had difficulty in complying with a volcanic mother, and after her marriage she almost automatically assumed a submissive role. . . .
>
> When she was thirty years old . . . [she] and her husband invited Ignatius, who was single, to come and live with them. Ignatius and the patient soon discovered that they had an attraction for each other. They both tried to fight that feeling; but when Julius had to go to another city for a few days, the so-called infatuation became much more than that. There were a few physical contacts. . . . There was an intense spiritual affinity. . . . A few months later everybody had to leave the city. . . . Nothing was done to maintain contact. Two years later, approximately a year after the end of the war, Marie heard that Ignatius had married. She felt terribly alone and despondent. . . .
>
> Her suffering had become more acute as she realized that old age was approaching and she had lost all her chances. Ignatius remained as the memory of lost opportunities. . . . Her life of compliance and obedience had not permitted her to reach her goal. . . . When she became aware of these ideas, she felt even more depressed. . . . She felt that everything she had built in her life was false or based on a false premise.
>
> *(Arieti & Bemporad, 1978, pp. 275–284)*

Concern for Elián *Psychodynamic theorists hold that forced separations and other kinds of loss during early childhood may leave some individuals prone to develop depression. A recent case of widespread concern was that of Elián González, a 6-year-old rescued from waters off the coast of Florida in 1999 soon after a small boat carrying him, his mother, and 10 other refugees from Cuba had sunk, killing all except Elián. The child soon became the object of a six-month tug-of-war between his father in Cuba and relatives in Miami and between the governments of Cuba and the United States. Few will forget the child's violent separation by U.S. agents from his Miami family members so that he could be returned to Cuba.*

Studies have offered general support for the psychodynamic idea that losses suffered early in life may set the stage for later depression (Lara & Klein, 1999). When, for example, a depression scale was administered to 1,250 medical patients during visits to their family physicians, the patients whose fathers had died during their childhood scored higher on depression (Barnes & Prosen, 1985).

Related research supports the psychodynamic idea that people whose childhood needs were improperly met are particularly likely to become depressed after experiencing loss (Goodman, 2002; Parker, 1992, 1983). In some studies, depressed subjects have filled out a scale called the Parental Bonding Instrument, which indicates how much care and protection people feel they received as children. Many have identified their parents' child-rearing style as "affectionless control," consisting of a mixture of low care and high protection (Shah & Waller, 2000; Parker et al., 1995).

These studies offer some support for the psychodynamic view of unipolar depression, but this support has key problems. First, although the findings indicate that losses and inadequate parenting *sometimes* relate to depression, they do not establish that such factors are *typically* responsible for the disorder. In fact, it is estimated that less than 10 percent of all people who experience major losses in life actually become depressed (Paykel & Cooper, 1992; Paykel, 1982). Second, many findings are inconsistent. Though some studies find evidence of a relationship between childhood loss and later depression, others

AP Photos/Alan Diaz

THECURRENT SCENE

Happiness: More Common Than We Think

Judging from the evening news and the spread of self-help books, one would think that happiness was rare. But there's good news. Research indicates that people's lives are, in general, more upbeat than we think. In fact, most people around the world say they're happy—including most of those who are poor, unemployed, elderly, and disabled (Schimmack & Diener, 2003). Over 90 percent of people with quadriplegia say they're glad to be alive, and overall, people with spinal cord injuries report feeling only slightly less happy than other people (Diener & Diener, 1996). Men and women are equally likely to declare themselves satisfied or very happy. Wealthy people appear only slightly happier than those of modest means (Diener et al., 1993). Overall, only 1 person in 10 reports being "not too happy" (Myers, 2000; Myers & Diener, 1996).

Of course, some people are indeed happier than others. Particularly happy people seem to remain happy from decade to decade, regardless of job changes, moves, and family changes (Myers & Diener, 1996). Such people adjust to negative events and return to their usual cheerful state within a few months (Diener et al., 1992). Conversely,

unhappy people are not cheered in the long term even by positive events.

Some research indicates that happiness is dependent on personality characteristics and interpretive styles (Diener, 2000). Happy people are, for example, generally optimistic, outgoing, and tender-minded; they also tend to have several close friends, possess high self-esteem, and have a sense of control over their lives (Doyle & Youn, 2000). Some theorists also believe that people have a "happiness set point" to which they consistently return, despite life's ups and downs (Lucas et al., 2003). An in-

vestigation of 2,300 twins suggested to the researchers who conducted the study that as much as half of one's sense of happiness is related to genetic factors (Lykken & Tellegen, 1996).

A better understanding of the roots of happiness may emerge from the current flurry of research, perhaps providing useful solutions for those who are unhappy or even clinically depressed. In the meantime, we can take comfort in the knowledge that the human condition isn't quite so unhappy as news stories (and textbooks on abnormal psychology) may make it seem.

Myrleen Ferguson/Tony Stone Worldwide

do not (Parker, 1992; Owen, Lancee, & Freeman, 1986). Finally, certain features of the psychodynamic explanation are nearly impossible to test. Because symbolic loss is said to operate at an unconscious level, for example, it is difficult for researchers to determine if and when it is occurring.

WHAT ARE THE PSYCHODYNAMIC TREATMENTS FOR UNIPOLAR DEPRESSION?
Psychodynamic therapists use the same basic procedures with depressed clients as they use with others: they encourage the client to associate freely during therapy; suggest interpretations of the individual's associations, dreams, and displays of resistance and transference; and help the person review past events and feelings. Free association, for example, helped one man recall the early experiences of loss that, according to his therapist, had set the stage for his depression:

> Among his earliest memories, possibly the earliest of all, was the recollection of being wheeled in his baby cart under the elevated train structure and left there alone. Another memory that recurred vividly during the analysis was of an operation around the age of five. He was anesthetized and his mother left him with the doctor. He recalled how he had kicked and screamed, raging at her for leaving him.
>
> *(Lorand, 1968, pp. 325–326)*

>>LOOKING AROUND

The Insurance Factor

Insurance influences the type of treatment people receive for depression. Privately insured patients are more likely than Medicaid patients to receive psychotherapy. And among those on medications, the privately insured are more likely to receive second-generation antidepressants than the cheaper tricyclics (Melf et al., 1999).<<

Despite some successful case reports, researchers have found that long-term psychodynamic therapy is only occasionally helpful in cases of unipolar depression (APA, 1993; Prochaska, 1984). Two features of the approach may limit its effectiveness. First, depressed clients may be too passive and feel too weary to join fully in the subtle therapy discussions (Widloecher, 2001). Second, they may become discouraged and end treatment too early when this long-term approach is unable to provide the quick relief that they desperately seek. Generally, psychodynamic therapy seems to be of greatest help in cases of depression that clearly involve a history of childhood loss or trauma, a long-standing sense of emptiness, feelings of perfectionism, and extreme self-criticism (Blatt, 1999, 1995). Short-term psychodynamic therapies have performed better than the traditional approaches (Leichsenring, 2001; Jefferson & Greist, 1994).

THE BEHAVIORAL MODEL Behaviorists believe that unipolar depression results from significant changes in the number of rewards and punishments people receive in their lives, and they treat depressed people by helping them to build more favorable patterns of reinforcement. During the 1970s and 1980s, the clinical researcher Peter Lewinsohn developed one of the leading behavioral explanations and treatments (Lewinsohn et al., 1990, 1984).

Saying goodbye *As highlights of his glorious career appear on a screen, Wayne Gretsky announces his retirement from ice hockey. According to behaviorists, the reduction in rewards brought about by retirement places sports stars and other high achievers at risk for depression unless they can develop a healthy perspective about the change and add new sources of gratification to their lives.*

THE BEHAVIORAL EXPLANATION Lewinsohn suggested that the positive rewards in life dwindle for some persons, leading them to perform fewer and fewer constructive behaviors. The rewards of campus life, for example, disappear when a young woman graduates from college and takes a job; and an aging baseball player loses the rewards of high salary and praise when his skills deteriorate. Although many such people manage to fill their lives with other forms of gratification, some become particularly disheartened. The positive features of their lives decrease even more, and the decline in rewards leads them to perform still fewer constructive behaviors. In this manner, the individuals spiral toward depression.

In a series of studies, Lewinsohn and his colleagues found that the number of rewards people receive in life is indeed related to the presence or absence of depression. Not only did depressed subjects in his studies report fewer positive rewards than nondepressed subjects, but when their rewards began to increase, their mood improved as well (Lewinsohn et al., 1979). Similarly, more recent investigations have found a strong relationship between positive life events and feelings of life satisfaction and happiness (Lui, 1999).

Lewinsohn and other behaviorists further proposed that social rewards are particularly important in the downward spiral of depression (Peterson, 1993; Lewinsohn et al., 1984). This claim has been supported by research showing that depressed persons experience fewer social rewards than nondepressed persons and that as their mood improves, their social rewards increase. Although depressed people are sometimes the victims of social circumstances, it may also be that their dark mood and flat behaviors help produce a decline in social rewards (Joiner, 2002; Coyne, 2001).

WHAT ARE THE BEHAVIORAL TREATMENTS FOR UNIPOLAR DEPRESSION? In Lewinsohn's treatment approach to unipolar depression, therapists use a variety of strategies to help increase the positive behaviors of their clients (Lewinsohn et al., 1990, 1982). First, the therapist selects activities that the client considers pleasurable, such as going shopping or taking photographs, and encourages the client to set up a weekly schedule for engaging in them. Adding positive activities to a person's life is expected to lead to a better mood (Leenstra et al., 1995). Second, while reintroducing pleasurable events into a client's life, the therapist makes sure that the person's various behaviors are rewarded correctly. Behaviorists have argued that when people become depressed, their negative behaviors—crying, complaining, or self-criticism—keep others at a distance, reducing chances for rewarding experiences and interactions. To change this pattern, the therapist may try to ignore a client's depressive behaviors while praising or otherwise rewarding constructive statements and behavior, such as going to work. Finally, behavioral therapists may teach clients effective social skills (Segrin, 2000; Hersen et al., 1984). In group therapy programs, for example, members may work together to improve eye contact, facial expression, posture, and other behaviors that send social messages.

These behavioral techniques seem to be of only limited help when just one of them is applied. In one study, for example, depressed people who were instructed to increase their pleasant activities showed no more improvement than a control group who were told simply to keep track of their activities (Hammen & Glass, 1975). However, when two or more behavioral techniques are combined, much as Lewinsohn had envisioned, behavioral treatment does appear to reduce depressive symptoms, particularly if the depression is mild (Jacobson et al., 1996; Teri & Lewinsohn, 1986).

THE COGNITIVE MODEL Cognitive theorists believe that people with unipolar depression repeatedly view events in negative ways and that such perceptions eventually lead to their disorder. Not surprisingly, then, cognitive therapists focus largely on thinking processes rather than mood in their work with these individuals. The two most influential cognitive explanations are the theory of *learned helplessness* and the theory of *negative thinking*.

LEARNED HELPLESSNESS Feelings of helplessness fill this account of a young woman's depression:

Special companionship *Four-legged friends provide an important kind of social reward for millions of people. The companionship and warmth of dogs and other pets have been found to prevent loneliness and isolation and, in turn, to help alleviate or prevent depression.*

> Mary was 25 years old and had just begun her senior year in college. . . . Asked to recount how her life had been going recently, Mary began to weep. Sobbing, she said that for the last year or so she felt she was losing control of her life and that recent stresses (starting school again, friction with her boyfriend) had left her feeling worthless and frightened. Because of a gradual deterioration in her vision, she was now forced to wear glasses all day. "The glasses make me look terrible," she said, and "I don't look people in the eye much any more." Also, to her dismay, Mary had gained 20 pounds in the past year. She viewed herself as overweight and unattractive. At times she was convinced that with enough money to buy contact lenses and enough time to exercise she could cast off her depression; at other times she believed nothing would help. . . . Mary saw her life deteriorating in other spheres, as well. She felt overwhelmed by schoolwork and, for the first time in her life, was on academic probation. . . . In addition to her dissatisfaction with her appearance and her fears about her academic future, Mary complained of a lack of friends. Her social network consisted solely of her boyfriend, with whom she was living. Although there were times when she experienced this relationship as almost unbearably frustrating, she felt helpless to change it and was pessimistic about its permanence. . . .
>
> *(Spitzer et al., 1983, pp. 122–123)*

Mary feels that she is "losing control of her life." According to the psychologist Martin Seligman (1975), such feelings of helplessness are at the center of her depression. Since the mid-1960s Seligman has developed the **learned helplessness** theory of depression. It holds that people become depressed when they think (1) that they no longer have control over the reinforcements (the rewards and punishments) in their lives and (2) that they themselves are responsible for this helpless state.

LEARNED HELPLESSNESS The perception, based on past experiences, that one has no control over one's reinforcements.

FIGURE 7-3 Jumping to safety *Experimental animals learn to escape or avoid shocks that are administered on one side of a shuttle box by jumping to the other (safe) side.*

Seligman's theory first began to take shape when he was working with laboratory dogs. In one procedure, he strapped dogs into an apparatus called a hammock, in which they received shocks periodically no matter what they would do. The next day each dog was placed in a *shuttle box*, a box divided in half by a barrier over which the animal could jump to reach the other side (see Figure 7-3). Seligman applied shock to the dogs in the box, expecting that they, like other dogs in this situation, would soon learn to escape by jumping over the barrier. However, most of these dogs failed to learn anything in the shuttle box. After a flurry of activity, they simply "lay down and quietly whined" and accepted the shock.

Seligman decided that while receiving inescapable shocks in the hammock the day before, the dogs had learned that they had no control over unpleasant events (shocks) in their lives. That is, they had learned that they were helpless to do anything to change negative situations. Thus, when later they were placed in a new situation (the shuttle box) where they could in fact control their fate, they continued to believe that they were generally helpless. Seligman noted that the effects of learned helplessness greatly resemble the symptoms of human depression, and he proposed that people in fact become depressed after developing a general belief that they have no control over reinforcements in their lives.

In numerous human and animal studies, subjects who undergo helplessness training have displayed reactions similar to depressive symptoms. When, for example, human subjects are exposed to uncontrollable negative events, they later score higher than other subjects on a depressive mood survey (Miller & Seligman, 1975). Similarly, helplessness-trained animal subjects lose interest in sexual and social activities—a common symptom of human depression (Lindner, 1968). Finally, uncontrollable negative events result in lower norepinephrine and serotonin activity in rats (Wu et al., 1999). This, of course, is similar to the neurotransmitter activity found in the brains of people with unipolar depression.

The learned helplessness explanation of depression has been revised somewhat over the past two decades. According to a new version of the theory, when people view events as beyond their control, they ask themselves why this is so (Abramson et al., 2002, 1989, 1978). If they attribute their present lack of control to some *internal* cause that is both *global* and *stable* ("I am inadequate at everything and I always will be"), they may well feel helpless to prevent future negative outcomes and they may experience depression. If they make other kinds of *attributions*, this reaction is unlikely.

Consider a college student whose girlfriend breaks up with him. If he attributes this loss of control to an internal cause that is both global and stable—"It's my fault [internal], I ruin everything I touch [global], and I always will [stable]"—he then has reason to expect similar losses of control in the future and may generally experience a sense of helplessness. According to the learned helplessness view, he is a prime candidate for depression. If the student had instead attributed the breakup to causes that were more *specific* ("The way I've behaved the past couple of weeks blew this relationship"), *unstable* ("I don't know what got into me—I don't usually act like that"), or *external* ("She never did know what she wanted"), he might not expect to lose control again and would probably not experience helplessness and depression.

Hundreds of studies have supported the relationship between styles of attribution, helplessness, and depression (Kinderman & Bentall, 1997). In one, depressed persons were asked to fill out an Attributional Style Questionnaire both before and after successful therapy. Before therapy, their depression was accompanied by the internal/global/stable pattern of attribution. At the end of therapy and again one year later, their depression was improved and their attribution styles were less likely to be internal, global, and stable (Seligman et al., 1988).

Some theorists have refined the helplessness model yet again in recent years. They suggest that attributions are likely to cause depression only when they further produce a sense of *hopelessness* in an individual (Abramson et al., 2002, 1989). By taking this factor into consideration, clinicians are often able to predict depression with still greater precision (Robinson & Alloy, 2003).

Although the learned helplessness theory of unipolar depression has been very influential, it too has imperfections. First, much of the learned helplessness research relies on animal subjects. It is impossible to know whether the animals' symptoms do in fact reflect the clinical depression found in humans. Second, the attributional feature of the theory raises difficult questions. What about the dogs and rats who learn helplessness? Can animals make attributions, even implicitly?

NEGATIVE THINKING Like Seligman, Aaron Beck believes that negative thinking lies at the heart of depression. According to Beck (2002, 1991, 1967), *maladaptive attitudes*, a *cognitive triad*, *errors in thinking*, and *automatic thoughts* combine to produce the clinical disorder.

Beck believes that some people develop *maladaptive attitudes* as children, such as "My general worth is tied to every task I perform" or "If I fail, others will feel repelled by me." The attitudes result from their own experiences, their family relationships, and the judgments of the people around them (see Figure 7-4). Many failures are inevitable in a full, active life, so such attitudes are inaccurate and set the stage for all kinds of negative thoughts and reactions. Beck suggests that later in these people's lives, upsetting situations may trigger an extended round of negative thinking. That thinking typically takes three forms, which he calls the **cognitive triad**: the individuals repeatedly interpret (1) their *experiences*, (2) *themselves*, and (3) their *futures* in negative ways that lead them to feel depressed. The cognitive triad is at work in the thinking of this depressed person:

> I can't bear it. I can't stand the humiliating fact that I'm the only woman in the world who can't take care of her family, take her place as a real wife and mother, and be respected in her community. When I speak to my young son Billy, I know I can't let him down, but I feel so ill-equipped to take care of him; that's what frightens me. I don't know what to do or where to turn; the whole thing is too overwhelming. . . . I must be a laughing stock. It's more than I can do to go out and meet people and have the fact pointed up to me so clearly.
>
> *(Fieve, 1975)*

COGNITIVE TRIAD The three forms of negative thinking that Aaron Beck theorizes lead people to feel depressed. The triad consists of a negative view of one's experiences, oneself, and the future.

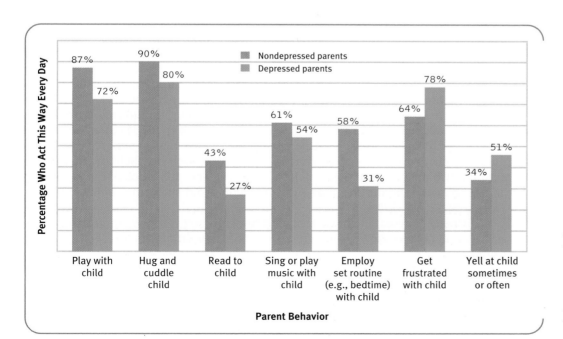

FIGURE 7-4 How depressed parents and their children interact *Depressed parents are less likely than nondepressed parents to play with, hug, read to, or sing to their young children each day or to employ the same routine each day. They are also more likely to get frustrated with their children on a daily basis. (Adapted from Princeton Survey Research Associates, 1996).*

PEANUTS reprinted by permission of United Features Syndicate, Inc.

Illogical thinking *Charlie Brown's feelings of depression are caused by errors in logic, such as arbitrary inferences.*

According to Beck, depressed people also make *errors in their thinking*. In one common error of logic, they draw *arbitrary inferences*—negative conclusions based on little evidence. A man walking through the park, for example, passes a woman who is looking at nearby flowers, and he concludes, "She's avoiding looking at me." Similarly, depressed people often *minimize* positive experiences or *magnify* negative ones. A college student receives an A on a difficult English exam, for example, but concludes that the grade reflects the professor's generosity rather than her own ability (minimization).

Finally, depressed people experience **automatic thoughts**, a steady train of unpleasant thoughts that keep suggesting to them that they are inadequate and that their situation is hopeless. Beck labels these thoughts "automatic" because they seem to just happen, as if by reflex. In the course of only a few hours, depressed people may be visited by hundreds of such thoughts: "I'm worthless. . . . I let everyone down. . . . Everyone hates me. . . . My responsibilities are overwhelming. . . . I've failed as a parent. . . . I'm stupid. . . . Everything is difficult for me. . . . Things will never change."

Many studies have produced evidence in support of Beck's explanation. Several of them confirm that depressed people hold maladaptive attitudes, and the more of these maladaptive attitudes they hold, the more depressed they tend to be (Whisman & McGarvey, 1995). Still other research has found the cognitive triad at work in depressed people (Ridout et al., 2003). In various studies, depressed subjects seem to recall unpleasant experiences more readily than positive ones, rate their performances on laboratory tests lower than nondepressed subjects do, and select pessimistic statements in storytelling tasks (for example, "I expect my plans will fail").

Beck's claims about errors in logic have also received research support (Cole & Turner, 1993). In one study, female subjects—some depressed, some not—were asked to read and interpret paragraphs about women in difficult situations. Depressed subjects made more errors in logic (such as arbitrary inference) in their interpretations than nondepressed women did (Hammen & Krantz, 1976).

Finally, research has supported Beck's claim that automatic thoughts are tied to depression. In several studies, nondepressed subjects who are tricked into reading negative automatic-thought-like statements about themselves become increasingly depressed (Bates et al., 1999; Strickland et al., 1975). In a related line of study, it has been found that people who generally make *ruminative responses* during their depressed moods—that is, repeatedly dwell on their mood without acting to change it—experience dejection longer and are more likely to develop clinical depression later in life than people who avoid such ruminations (Nolen-Hoeksema, 2002, 1998, 1995).

This body of research shows that negative thinking is indeed linked to depression, but it fails to show that such patterns of thought are the cause and core of unipolar depression. It could be that a central mood problem leads to thinking difficulties that then take a further toll on mood, behavior, and physiology (Scott, Winters, & Beevers, 2000).

COGNITIVE TREATMENT FOR UNIPOLAR DEPRESSION Beck has developed the leading form of **cognitive therapy** for unipolar depression. It is designed to help clients

>>**LOOKING AROUND**

Campus Depression

Common Experience In a survey of 300 college students, 90 percent considered themselves to have been at least mildly depressed since arriving at college. Half of the reported depressions lasted less than one month (Oswalt & Finkelbery, 1995).<<

Deconstructive Criticism College students who seek and receive negative feedback from their roommates feel more depressed than students who do not receive such feedback (Joiner, 1995).<<

recognize and change their maladaptive assumptions and negative thinking and thus to improve both their mood and their counterproductive behaviors (Beck, 2002, 1985, 1967). The approach is similar to Albert Ellis's rational-emotive therapy (discussed in Chapters 3 and 4), but it is tailored to the specific cognitive errors found in depression. Beck's approach follows four phases and usually requires fewer than 20 sessions.

Phase 1: Increasing activities and elevating mood Using behavioral techniques to set the stage for cognitive treatment, therapists first encourage individuals to become more active and confident. Clients spend time during each session preparing a detailed schedule of hourly activities for the coming week. As they become more active from week to week, their mood is expected to improve.

Phase 2: Challenging automatic thoughts Once people are more active and feeling some emotional relief, cognitive therapists begin to educate them about their negative automatic thoughts. The individuals learn to recognize and record automatic thoughts as they occur and they bring their lists to each session. Therapist and client then test the reality behind the thoughts, often concluding that they are groundless.

Phase 3: Identifying negative thinking and biases As people begin to recognize the flaws in their automatic thoughts, cognitive therapists show them how illogical thinking processes are contributing to these thoughts. The therapists also guide clients to recognize that almost all their interpretations of events have a negative bias and to change that style of interpretation.

Phase 4: Changing primary attitudes Therapists help clients change the maladaptive attitudes that set the stage for their depression in the first place. As part of the process, therapists often encourage clients to test their attitudes, as in the following therapy discussion:

> **Therapist:** On what do you base this belief that you can't be happy without a man?
> **Patient:** I was really depressed for a year and a half when I didn't have a man.
> **Therapist:** Is there another reason why you were depressed?
> **Patient:** As we discussed, I was looking at everything in a distorted way. But I still don't know if I could be happy if no one was interested in me.
> **Therapist:** I don't know either. Is there a way we could find out?
> **Patient:** Well, as an experiment, I could not go out on dates for a while and see how I feel.
> **Therapist:** I think that's a good idea. Although it has its flaws, the experimental method is still the best way currently available to discover the facts. You're fortunate in being able to run this type of experiment. Now, for the first time in your adult life you aren't attached to a man. If you find you can be happy without a man, this will greatly strengthen you and also make your future relationships all the better.
>
> *(Beck et al., 1979, pp. 253–254)*

Over the past three decades, literally hundreds of studies have shown that cognitive therapy helps with unipolar depression. Depressed people who receive this therapy improve much more than those who receive placebos or no treatment at all (Hollon et al., 2002; DeRubeis et al., 2001). Around 50 to 60 percent show a near-total elimination of their symptoms. In view of this strong research support, many therapists have adopted the cognitive approach, some offering it in a group therapy format (Petrocelli, 2002).

A Place for Laughter *Many comedians have histories of mood disorders. Drew Carey, for example, suffered from severe depression for much of his early life. He reports that he has been able to successfully overcome this mood disorder by developing a positive outlook—through reading psychology books, listening to tapes on positive thinking, and, of course, generating and communicating humorous thoughts.*

AUTOMATIC THOUGHTS Numerous unpleasant thoughts that help to cause or maintain depression, anxiety, or other forms of psychological dysfunction.

COGNITIVE THERAPY A therapy that helps people identify and change the maladaptive ways of thinking that be may contributing to their psychological disorders.

The Sociocultural Model of Unipolar Depression

Sociocultural theorists propose that unipolar depression is greatly influenced by the social structure in which people live. Their belief is supported by the finding, discussed earlier, that this disorder is often triggered by outside stressors. In addition, researchers have found ties between depression and factors such as culture, gender, race, and social support.

HOW ARE CULTURE AND DEPRESSION RELATED? On the one hand, depression is a worldwide phenomenon: persons in all countries and cultures are at risk for it. On the other hand, the precise picture of depression varies from culture to culture (Tsai & Chentsova-Dutton, 2002; Manson & Good, 1993). Depressed people in non-Western countries, for example, tend to be troubled by physical symptoms such as fatigue, weakness, sleep disturbances, and weight loss. Depression in these countries is less often marked by such psychological symptoms as self-blame and guilt. As these countries have become more Westernized, depression there has taken on the more psychological character it has in the West.

HOW DO GENDER AND RACE RELATE TO DEPRESSION? The rates of unipolar depression vary from subgroup to subgroup within a society. As we have already seen, the rate of depression is much higher among women than among men. One sociocultural theory holds that the special pressures and complexities of women's roles in society leave them particularly prone to depression.

Similarly, although few differences in the overall rate of unipolar depression have been found among white Americans, African Americans, and Hispanic Americans, researchers sometimes find striking differences when they look at specific ethnic populations living under special circumstances (Ayalon & Young, 2003). A study of one Native American village in the United States, for example, showed that the lifetime risk of developing depression was 37 percent among women, 19 percent among men, and 28 percent overall, much higher than the risk in the general United States population (Kinzie et al., 1992). High rates of this kind may be linked to the terrible social and economic pressures faced by the people who live on Native American reservations.

HOW DOES SOCIAL SUPPORT RELATE TO DEPRESSION? The availability of social support seems to influence the likelihood of depression (Monroe & Hadjiyannakis, 2002). As we see in Figure 7-5, across the United States, people who are separated or divorced display three times the depression rate of married or widowed persons and double the rate of people who have never been married. In some cases, the spouse's depression may contribute to a separation or divorce (Joiner, 2002), but often the interpersonal conflicts and low social support found in troubled relationships lead to depression (Beach & Jones, 2002; Wishman, 2001).

People whose lives are isolated and without intimacy seem particularly likely to become depressed at times of stress (Nezlek et al., 2000; Paykel & Cooper, 1992). Some highly publicized studies conducted in England a couple of decades ago showed that women who had three or more young children, lacked a close confidante, and had no outside employment were more likely than other women to become depressed after experiencing stressful events (Brown et al., 1995; Brown & Harris, 1978). Studies have also found that depressed people who lack social support remain depressed longer than those who have a supportive spouse or warm friendships (Moos & Cronkite, 1999).

WHAT ARE THE SOCIOCULTURAL TREATMENTS FOR UNIPOLAR DEPRESSION? The most effective sociocultural approaches to depression are *interpersonal psychotherapy* and *couple therapy*. The techniques used in these approaches often borrow

Non-Western depression *Depressed people in non-Western countries tend to have fewer cognitive symptoms, such as self-blame, and more physical symptoms, such as fatigue, weakness, and sleep disturbances.*

INTERPERSONAL PSYCHOTHERAPY (IPT) A treatment for unipolar depression that is based on the belief that clarifying and changing one's interpersonal problems will help lead to recovery.

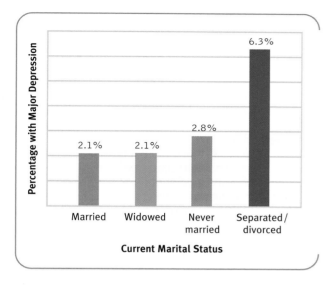

FIGURE 7-5 **Marital status and major depressive disorder** *Currently separated or divorced people are three times more likely to be depressed than people who currently are married. (Adapted from Weissman et al., 1991.)*

from the other models, but they are used in cases of depression to help persons overcome the social difficulties that may underlie their disorder.

INTERPERSONAL PSYCHOTHERAPY Developed during the 1980s by the clinical researchers Gerald Klerman and Myrna Weissman, **interpersonal psychotherapy (IPT)** holds that any of four interpersonal problem areas may lead to depression and must be addressed: interpersonal loss, interpersonal role dispute, interpersonal role transition, and interpersonal deficits (Weissman & Markowitz, 2002; Klerman & Weissman, 1992). Over the course of around 16 sessions, IPT therapists address these areas.

First, depressed persons may, as psychodynamic theorists suggest, be experiencing a grief reaction over an *interpersonal loss*, the loss of an important loved one. In such cases, IPT therapists encourage clients to explore their relationship with the lost person and express any feelings of anger they may discover. Eventually clients develop new ways of remembering the lost person and also seek new relationships.

Second, depressed people may find themselves in the midst of an *interpersonal role dispute*. Role disputes occur when two people have different expectations of their relationship and of the role each should play. IPT therapists help clients examine whatever role disputes they may be involved in and then develop ways of resolving them.

Depressed people may also be experiencing an *interpersonal role transition*, brought about by major life changes such as divorce or the birth of a child. They may feel overwhelmed by the role changes that accompany the life change. In such cases IPT therapists help them develop the social supports and skills the new roles require.

Finally, some depressed people display *interpersonal deficits*, such as extreme shyness or social awkwardness, which prevent them from having intimate relationships. IPT therapists may help such individuals recognize their deficits and teach them social

Role transition *A major life change such as marriage, the birth of a child, or divorce can present difficulties in role transition, one of the interpersonal problem areas addressed by IPT therapists in their work with depressed clients.*

A CLOSER LOOK

Depressing News for Women

Women in places as far apart as France, Sweden, Lebanon, New Zealand, and the United States are at least twice as likely as men to receive a diagnosis of unipolar depression (Nolen-Hoeksema, 2002; Pajer, 1995; Weissman & Olfson, 1995). Women also appear to be younger when depression strikes, to have more frequent and longer-lasting bouts, and to respond less successfully to treatment. Why the huge difference between the sexes? Several theories have been offered (Nolen-Hoeksema, 2002, 1995, 1990, 1987; Simonds, 2001).

The artifact theory One theory holds that women and men are equally prone to depression but that clinicians fail to detect depression in men. Perhaps men find it less socially acceptable to admit feeling depressed or to seek treatment. This explanation lacks consistent research support (Fennig et al., 1994). It turns out that women are actually no more willing or able than men to identify their depressive symptoms and seek treatment.

The hormone theory Another theory holds that hormone changes trigger depression in many women (Dunn & Steiner, 2000). A woman's biological life from her early teens to middle age is marked by frequent changes in hormone levels. Gender differences in rates of depression also span these same years (Weissman & Olfson, 1995). It is unlikely, however, that hormone changes alone are responsible for the high levels of depression in women. Important social and life events that occur at puberty, pregnancy, and menopause could likewise have an effect. Hormone explanations have also been criticized as sexist, since they imply that a woman's normal biology is flawed.

The quality-of-life theory Perhaps women in our society experience more stress than men (Hankin & Abramson, 2001; Stoppard, 2000). On average they face more poverty, more menial jobs, less adequate housing, and more discrimination than men—all factors that have been linked to depression (Maciejewski et al., 2001; Brems, 1995). And in many homes, women bear a disproportionate share of responsibility for child care and housework.

The societal pressure theory Almost from birth, females in Western society are taught to seek a low body weight and slender body shape—goals that are unreasonable, unhealthy, and often unattainable. The cultural standard for males is much more lenient. As girls approach adolescence, peer pressure may produce greater and greater dissatisfaction with their weight and body, increasing the likelihood of depression. Consistent with this theory, gender differences in depression do indeed first appear during adolescence (Galambos et al., 2004; Nolen-Hoeksema & Girgus, 1995) and persons with eating disorders often experience high levels of depression (Paxton & Diggens, 1997). However, it is not clear that eating and weight concerns actually cause depression; they may instead be the result of depression.

The lack-of-control theory According to this theory, women are more prone to depression because they feel less control over their lives. Studies have, in fact, confirmed that women are more prone to develop learned helplessness in the laboratory than men (Le Unes, Nation, & Turley, 1980). In addition, it has been found that victimization of any kind, from burglary to rape, often produces a general sense of helplessness and increases the symptoms of depression;

skills and assertiveness in order to improve their social effectiveness. In the following discussion, the therapist encourages a depressed man to recognize the effect his behavior has on others:

Client: (*After a long pause with eyes downcast, a sad facial expression, and slumped posture*) People always make fun of me. I guess I'm just the type of guy who really was meant to be a loner, damn it. (*Deep sigh*)

Therapist: Could you do that again for me?

Client: What?

Therapist: The sigh, only a bit deeper.

Client: Why? (*Pause*) Okay, but I don't see what . . . okay. (*Client sighs again and smiles*)

Therapist: Well, that time you smiled, but mostly when you sigh and look so sad I get the feeling that I better leave you alone in your misery, that I should walk on eggshells and not get too chummy or I might hurt you even more.

Client: (*A bit of anger in his voice*) Well, excuse me! I was only trying to tell you how I felt.

Therapist: I know you felt miserable, but I also got the message that you wanted to keep me at a distance, that I had no way to reach you.

Edvard Munch, *Melancholia, Laura*, Oslo kommunes kunstsamlinger Munch-Museet

Female melancholy *Edvard Munch's painting* Melancholy (Laura) *was inspired by his sister's bouts of severe depression.*

and women in our society are more likely than men to be victims, particularly of sexual assault and child abuse (Nolen-Hoeksema, 2002; Zuravin & Fontanella, 1999).

The self-blame theory Past research often indicated that women are more likely than men to blame their failures on lack of ability and to attribute their successes to luck—an attribution style that has also been linked to depression (Abramson et al., 2002; Wolfe & Russianoff, 1997). However, several more recent studies suggest that today's women and men may not differ as much as they used to in their levels of self-esteem and self-blame (Kling et al., 1999).

The rumination theory *Rumination* is the tendency to repeatedly focus on one's feelings when depressed and repeatedly consider the causes and consequences of that depression. "Why am I so down. . . . I won't be able to finish my work if I keep going like this. . . ." Research shows that people who tend to ruminate whenever they feel sad are more likely to become depressed and stay depressed longer. It turns out that women are more likely than men to ruminate when their moods darken, perhaps making them more vulnerable to the onset of clinical depression (Nolen-Hoeksema, 2002, 2000; Nolen-Hoeksema et al., 1999).

Each of these explanations for the gender difference in unipolar depression offers food for thought. Each has gathered just enough supporting evidence to make it interesting and just enough evidence to the contrary to raise questions about its usefulness. Thus, at present, the gender difference in depression remains one of the most talked-about but least understood phenomena in the clinical field.

> *Client:* (*Slowly*) I feel like a loner, I feel that even you don't care about me—making fun of me.
> *Therapist:* I wonder if other folks need to pass this test, too?
>
> *(Young & Beier, 1984, p. 270)*

Studies suggest that IPT and related interpersonal treatments for depression have a success rate similar to that of cognitive therapy (Weissman & Markowitz, 2002; Swartz, 1999). That is, symptoms almost totally disappear in 50 to 60 percent of clients who receive treatment. Not surprisingly, IPT is considered especially useful for depressed people who are struggling with social conflicts or undergoing changes in their careers or social roles (Weissman & Markowitz, 2002; APA, 1993).

COUPLE THERAPY As we have seen, depression can result from marital discord, and recovery from depression is often slower for people who do not receive support from their spouse (Bruce & Kim, 1992). In fact, as many as half of all depressed clients may be in a dysfunctional relationship. Thus it is not surprising that many cases of depression have been treated by **couple therapy**, the approach in which a therapist works with two people who share a long-term relationship.

Therapists who offer *behavioral marital therapy* help spouses change harmful marital behavior by teaching them specific communication and problem-solving

COUPLE THERAPY A therapy format in which the therapist works with two people who share a long-term relationship.

Patrick Johns/Corbis

Flower power *Recent research suggests that extracts from the common shrub* hypericum perforatum, *popularly known as St. John's wort, may be of help to 60 percent of people with mild to moderate depression. This herbal supplement, along with SAM-e, melatonin, and other so-called dietary supplements, are currently hot-selling treatments for depression.*

skills (see Chapter 2). When the depressed person's marriage is filled with conflict, this approach and similar ones may be as effective as individual cognitive therapy, interpersonal psychotherapy, or drug therapy in helping to reduce depression (Denton et al., 2003; Beach & Jones, 2002).

SUMMING UP | Unipolar Depression

People with unipolar depression, the most common pattern of mood disorder, suffer from depression only. The symptoms of depression span five areas of functioning: emotional, motivational, behavioral, cognitive, and physical. Women are at least twice as likely as men to experience severe unipolar depression.

According to the biological view, low activity of the neurotransmitters norepinephrine and serotonin helps cause depression. Hormonal factors may also be at work. These biological problems may be linked to genetic factors. Effective biological treatments for unipolar depression are antidepressant drugs (MAO inhibitors, tricyclics, and second-generation antidepressants) and electroconvulsive therapy (ECT).

According to the psychodynamic view, certain people who experience real or imagined losses may regress to an earlier stage of development, fuse with the person they have lost, and eventually become depressed. Psychodynamic therapists try to help persons with unipolar depression recognize and work through their losses and excessive dependence on others.

The behavioral view says that when people experience a large reduction in their positive rewards in life, they are more likely to become depressed. Behavioral therapists try to reintroduce clients to activities that they once found pleasurable, reward nondepressive behaviors, and teach effective social skills.

According to Seligman's learned helplessness theory, people become depressed when they believe that they have lost control over the reinforcements in their lives and when they attribute this loss to causes that are internal, global, and stable. According to Beck's cognitive theory, maladaptive attitudes, the cognitive triad, errors in thinking, and automatic thoughts help produce unipolar depression. Cognitive therapy for depression helps clients increase their activities, challenge their automatic thoughts, identify their negative thinking, and change their maladaptive attitudes.

Sociocultural theorists propose that unipolar depression is influenced by social factors. Supportive research finds that stressful events often seem to trigger unipolar depression; depression can vary by culture, gender, and race; and poor social support is linked to depression. Interpersonal psychotherapy addresses the interpersonal problem areas of depression. Couple therapy may also be of help when depression is tied to a troubled relationship.

Bipolar Disorders

People with a *bipolar disorder* experience both the lows of depression and the highs of mania. Many describe their life as an emotional roller coaster. They shift back and forth between extreme moods. This roller-coaster ride and its impact on relatives and friends are seen in the following case study:

> In his early school years he had been a remarkable student and had shown a gift for watercolor and oils. Later he had studied art in Paris and married an English girl he had met there. Eventually they had settled in London.
>
> Ten years later, when he was thirty-four years old, he had persuaded his wife and only son to accompany him to Honolulu, where, he assured them, he would

be considered famous. He felt he would be able to sell his paintings at many times the prices he could get in London. According to his wife, he had been in an accelerated state, but at that time the family had left, unsuspecting, believing with the patient in their imminent good fortune. When they arrived they found almost no one in the art world that he was supposed to know. There were no connections for sales and deals in Hawaii that he had anticipated. Settling down, the patient began to behave more peculiarly than ever. After enduring several months of the patient's exhilaration, overactivity, weight loss, constant talking, and unbelievably little sleep, the young wife and child began to fear for his sanity. None of his plans materialized. After five months in the Pacific, with finances growing thin, the patient's overactivity subsided and he fell into a depression.

During that period he refused to move, paint, or leave the house. He lost twenty pounds, became utterly dependent on his wife, and insisted on seeing none of the friends he had accumulated in his manic state. His despondency became so severe that several doctors came to the house and advised psychiatric hospitalization. He quickly agreed and received twelve electroshock treatments, which relieved his depressed state. Soon afterward he began to paint again and to sell his work modestly. Recognition began to come from galleries and critics in the Far East. Several reviews acclaimed his work as exceptionally brilliant.

This was the beginning of the lifelong career of his moodswing. In 1952, while still in Honolulu, he once again became severely depressed. . . . Four years later he returned to London in a high. . . . When this manic period subsided and he surveyed the wreckage of his life, an eight-month interval of normal mood followed, after which he again switched into a profound depression.

(Fieve, 1975, pp. 64–65)

What Are the Symptoms of Mania?

Unlike people sunk in the gloom of depression, those in a state of mania typically experience dramatic and inappropriate rises in mood (Torrey & Knable, 2002). The symptoms of mania span the same areas of functioning—*emotional, motivational, behavioral, cognitive,* and *physical*—as those of depression, but mania affects those areas in an opposite way (see Table 7-3 on the next page).

A person in the throes of mania has active, powerful emotions in search of an outlet. The mood of euphoric joy and well-being is out of all proportion to the actual happenings in the person's life. One person with mania explained, "I feel no sense of restriction or censorship whatsoever. I am afraid of nothing and no one" (Fieve, 1975, p. 68). Not every person with mania is a picture of happiness, however. Some instead become irritable and angry—especially when others get in the way of their exaggerated ambitions.

In the motivational realm, people with mania seem to want constant excitement, involvement, and companionship. They enthusiastically seek out new friends and old, new interests and old, and have little awareness that their social style is overwhelming, domineering, and excessive.

The behavior of people with mania is usually very active. They move quickly, as though there were not enough time to do everything they want to do. They may talk rapidly and loudly, their conversations filled with jokes and efforts to be clever or, conversely, with complaints and verbal outbursts. Flamboyance is not uncommon: dressing in flashy clothes, giving large sums of money to strangers, or even getting involved in dangerous activities.

In the cognitive realm, people with mania usually show poor judgment and planning, as if they feel too good or move too fast to consider possible pitfalls. Filled with optimism, they rarely listen when others try to slow them down, interrupt their buying sprees, or prevent them from investing money unwisely. They may also hold an inflated opinion of themselves, and sometimes their self-esteem approaches grandiosity. During severe episodes of mania, some have trouble remaining coherent or in touch with reality.

>>**IN THEIR WORDS**

"Manic depression is about buying a dozen bottles of Heinz ketchup and all bottles of Windex in stock at the Food Emporium on Broadway at 4:00 A.M."<<

Andy Behrman, sufferer of bipolar disorder, 2002

"Depression is terrifying, and elation, its non-identical twin sister, is even more terrifying—attractive as she may be for a moment."<<

Joshua Logan, film director, describing his bipolar disorder, 1973

"I took [lithium] faithfully and found that life was a much stabler and more predictable place than I had ever reckoned."<<

Kay Redfield Jamison, clinical researcher

BIPOLAR I DISORDER A type of bipolar disorder marked by full manic and major depressive episodes.

BIPOLAR II DISORDER A type of bipolar disorder marked by mildly manic (hypomanic) episodes and major depressive episodes.

CYCLOTHYMIC DISORDER A disorder marked by numerous periods of hypomanic symptoms and mild depressive symptoms.

Table 7-3 DSM-IV Checklist

MANIC EPISODE

1. A period of abnormally and persistently elevated, expansive, or irritable mood, lasting at least one week.
2. Persistence of at least three of the following: • inflated self-esteem or grandiosity • decreased need for sleep • more talkativeness than usual, or pressure to keep talking • flight of ideas or the experience that thoughts are racing • distractibility • increase in activity or psychomotor agitation • excessive involvement in pleasurable activities that have a high potential for painful consequences.
3. Significant distress or impairment.

BIPOLAR I DISORDER

1. The presence of a manic, hypomanic, or major depressive episode.
2. If currently in a hypomanic or major depressive episode, history of a manic episode.
3. Significant distress or impairment.

BIPOLAR II DISORDER

1. The presence of a hypomanic or major depressive episode.
2. If currently in a major depressive episode, history of a hypomanic episode. If currently in a hypomanic episode, history of a major depressive episode. No history of a manic episode.
3. Significant distress or impairment.

Based on APA, 2000, 1994.

Finally, in the physical realm, people with mania feel remarkably energetic. They typically get little sleep yet feel and act wide awake (Silverstone & Hunt, 1992). Even if they miss a night or two of sleep, their energy level may remain high.

Diagnosing Bipolar Disorders

People are considered to be in a full *manic episode* when for at least one week they display an abnormally high or irritable mood, along with at least three other symptoms of mania. The episode may even include psychotic features such as delusions or hallucinations. When the symptoms of mania are less severe (causing little impairment), the person is said to be experiencing a *hypomanic episode* (APA, 2000, 1994).

DSM-IV distinguishes two kinds of bipolar disorders—bipolar I and bipolar II. People with **bipolar I disorder** have full manic and major depressive episodes. Most of them experience an *alternation* of the episodes; for example, months of depression followed by months of mania. Some, however, have *mixed episodes*, in which they swing from manic to depressive symptoms and back again on the same day. In **bipolar II disorder**, hypomanic—that is, mildly manic—episodes alternate with major depressive episodes over the course of time (MacQueen & Young, 2001). Without treatment, the mood episodes tend to recur for people with either type of bipolar disorder.

Surveys from around the world indicate that between 1.0 and 1.5 percent of all adults suffer from a bipolar disorder at any given time. The disorders appear to be equally common in women and men and among all socioeconomic classes and ethnic groups (see Table 7-4). Onset usually occurs between the ages of 15 and 44 years. In most untreated cases of bipolar disorder, the manic and depressive episodes eventually subside, only to recur at a later time (APA, 2000, 1994).

>>LOOKING BACK
George Frideric Handel wrote his *Messiah* in less than a month during a manic episode (Roesch, 1991).<<

When a person experiences numerous periods of hypomanic symptoms and mild depressive symptoms, DSM-IV assigns a diagnosis of **cyclothymic disorder**. The symptoms of this milder form of bipolar disorder continue for two or more years, interrupted occasionally by normal moods that may last for only days or weeks. This disorder, like bipolar I and bipolar II disorders, usually begins in adolescence or early adulthood and is equally common among women and men. At least 0.4 percent of the population develops cyclothymic disorder (APA, 2000). In some cases, the milder symptoms eventually blossom into a bipolar I or II disorder.

What Causes Bipolar Disorders?

Throughout the first half of the twentieth century, the search for the cause of bipolar disorders made little progress. More recently, biological research has produced some promising clues. The biological insights have come from research into *neurotransmitter activity, ion activity,* and *genetic factors.*

NEUROTRANSMITTERS Could overactivity of norepinephrine be related to mania? This was the expectation of several clinicians back in the 1960s after investigators first found a relationship between low norepinephrine activity and unipolar depression (Schildkraut, 1965). One study did indeed find the norepinephrine activity of persons with mania to be higher than that of depressed or control subjects (Post et al., 1980, 1978). In another study patients with a bipolar disorder were given *reserpine,* the blood pressure drug known to reduce norepinephrine activity in the brain, and the manic symptoms of some subsided (Telner et al., 1986).

Because serotonin activity often parallels norepinephrine activity in unipolar depression, theorists at first expected that mania would also be related to high serotonin activity, but no such relationship has been found. Instead, research suggests that mania, like depression, may be linked to *low* serotonin activity (Sobczak et al., 2002). Perhaps low serotonin activity opens the door to a mood disorder and *permits* the activity of norepinephrine (or other neurotransmitters) to define the particular form the disorder will take. That is, low serotonin activity accompanied by low norepinephrine activity may lead to depression; low serotonin activity accompanied by high norepinephrine activity may lead to mania.

ION ACTIVITY On both sides of the cell membrane of each neuron sit positively charged *sodium ions.* The ions play a critical role in sending incoming messages down the neuron to the nerve endings. When the neuron is at rest, most of the

War of a different kind *While starring as Princess Leia, the invincible heroine in the* Star Wars *trilogy, from 1977 to 1983, the actress Carrie Fisher received a diagnosis of bipolar disorder. The disorder is now under control with the help of medication, and Fisher says, "I don't want peace [in my life], I just don't want war" (Epstein, 2001, p. 36).*

Table 7-4

Mood Disorders Profile

	ONE-YEAR PREVALENCE (%)	FEMALE: MALE RATIO	TYPICAL AGE AT ONSET (YEARS)	PREVALENCE AMONG FIRST-DEGREE RELATIVES	PERCENTAGE RECEIVING TREATMENT
Major depressive disorder	5–10	2:1	24–29	Elevated	49
Dysthymic disorder	2.5–5.4	Between 3:2 and 2:1	10–25	Elevated	37.8
Bipolar I disorder	0.7	1:1	15–44	Elevated	58.9
Bipolar II disorder	0.5	1:1	15–44	Elevated	58.9
Cyclothymic disorder	0.4	1:1	15–44	Elevated	Unknown

Source: APA, 2000, 1994; Kessler et al., 1994; Regier et al., 1993; Weissman et al., 1991.

ABNORMALITY AND THE ARTS

Abnormality and Creativity: A Delicate Balance

Up to a point, states of depression, mania, anxiety, and even confusion can be useful. This may be particularly true in the arts. The ancient Greeks believed that various forms of "divine madness" inspired creative acts, from poetry to performance (Ludwig, 1995). Even today many people expect "creative geniuses" to be psychologically disturbed. A popular image of the artist includes a glass of liquor, a cigarette, and a tormented expression. Classic examples include the poet Sylvia Plath, who experienced depression most of her life and eventually committed suicide, and the dancer Vaslav Nijinsky, who suffered from schizophrenia and spent many years in institutions. In fact, a number of studies indicate that artists and writers are somewhat more likely than others to suffer from mental disorders, particularly mood disorders (Jamison, 1995; Ludwig, 1995, 1994).

Why might creative people be prone to psychological disorders? Some may be predisposed to such disorders long before they begin their artistic careers; the careers may simply bring attention to their emotional struggles (Ludwig, 1995). Indeed, creative people often have a family history of psychological problems. A number also have experienced intense psychological trauma during childhood. The English novelist and essayist Virginia Woolf, for example, endured sexual abuse as a child.

Another reason for the creativity link may be that creative endeavors create emotional turmoil that is overwhelming. Truman Capote said that writing his fa-mous book *In Cold Blood* "killed" him psychologically. Before writing this account of the brutal murders of a family, he considered himself "a stable person. . . . Afterward something happened to me" (Ludwig, 1995).

Yet a third explanation for the link between creativity and psychological disorders is that the creative professions offer a welcome climate for those with psychological disturbances. In the worlds of poetry, painting, and acting, for example, emotional expression and personal turmoil are valued as sources of inspiration and success (Ludwig, 1995).

Much remains to be learned about the relationship between emotional turmoil and creativity, but work in this area has already clarified two important points. First, psychological disturbance is hardly a requirement for creativity. Many "creative geniuses" are, in fact, psychologically stable and happy throughout their entire lives. Second, *mild* psychological disturbances relate to creative achievement much more strongly than severe disturbances do. For example, the nineteenth-century composer Robert Schumann, who suffered from a bipolar disorder, produced 27 works during one mildly manic year but next to nothing during years when he was severely depressed and suicidal (Jamison, 1995). In fact, although some artists worry that their creativity would disappear if their psychological suffering were to stop, research suggests that successful treatment for severe psychological disorders more often than not improves the creative process (Jamison, 1995; Ludwig, 1995).

"Those? Oh, just a few souvenirs from my bipolar-disorder days."

sodium ions sit on the outer side of the membrane. When the neuron is stimulated by an incoming message at its receptor site, however, the sodium ions from the outer side of the membrane travel across to the inner side. This movement, in turn, starts a wave of electrochemical activity that continues down the length of the neuron and results in its "firing." Afterward, a flow of *potassium ions* from the inside to the outside of the neuron helps it to return to its original resting state (see Figure 7-6).

If brain messages are to be sent and received appropriately, the ions must travel properly back and forth between the outside and the inside of the neural mem-

LITHIUM A metallic element that occurs in nature as a mineral salt and is an effective treatment for bipolar disorders.

brane. Some theorists believe that improper transport of these ions may cause neurons to fire too easily (resulting in mania) or to stubbornly resist firing (resulting in depression) (El Mallakh & Huff, 2001). Not surprisingly, investigators have found membrane defects in the neurons of persons with bipolar disorders and have observed abnormal functioning in the proteins that help transport ions across a neuron's membrane (Wang et al., 1999; Meltzer, 1991).

GENETIC FACTORS   Many experts believe that people inherit a biological predisposition to develop bipolar disorders. Family pedigree studies support this idea. Identical twins of persons with a bipolar disorder have a 40 percent likelihood of developing the same disorder, and fraternal twins, siblings, and other close relatives of such persons have a 5 to 10 percent likelihood, compared to the 1 percent prevalence rate in the general population (Craddock & Jones, 1999; Gershon & Nurnberger, 1995).

Researchers have also conducted *genetic linkage* studies to identify possible patterns in the inheritance of bipolar disorders. They select large families that have had high rates of a disorder over several generations, observe the pattern of distribution of the disorder among family members, and determine whether it closely follows a predictable pattern of inheritance. Still other researchers have used techniques from *molecular biology* to examine possible genetic factors. These various undertakings have linked bipolar disorders to genes on chromosomes 1, 4, 6, 10, 11, 12, 13, 15, 18, 21, and 22 (Baron, 2002; Berrettini, 2000). Such wide-ranging findings may mean that the logic behind the various gene studies is flawed (Gershon, 2000) or that a number of genetic abnormalities combine to bring about bipolar disorders (Meltzer, 2000).

What Are the Treatments for Bipolar Disorders?

Until the past three decades, people with bipolar disorders were destined to spend their lives on an emotional roller coaster. Psychotherapists reported almost no success, and antidepressant drugs were of limited help (Prien et al., 1974). In fact, the drugs sometimes triggered a manic episode (Cusack, 2003; Bowden, 2001). ECT, too, only occasionally relieved either the depressive or the manic episodes of bipolar disorders (Jefferson & Greist, 1994).

LITHIUM THERAPY   The use of **lithium** has so dramatically changed this gloomy picture that many people view the silvery-white element—found in various simple mineral salts throughout the natural world—as a true miracle drug. Its effectiveness was first discovered in 1949 by the Australian psychiatrist John Cade.

Determining the correct lithium dosage for a given patient is a delicate process (Schou, 1997). Too low a dose will have little or no effect on the bipolar mood swings, but too high a dose can result in lithium *intoxication* (literally, poisoning), which can cause nausea, vomiting, sluggishness, tremors, dizziness, slurred speech, seizures, kidney dysfunction, and even death (Moncrieff, 1997). With the correct dose, however, lithium often produces a noticeable change. Some patients respond better to other drugs, such as the antiseizure drugs *carbamazepine* (*Tegretol*) and *valproate* (*Depakote*), or to a combination of such drugs (Cusack, 2002; Lennkh & Simhandl, 2000).

All manner of research has indicated that lithium is effective in treating manic episodes. More than 60 percent of patients with mania improve on this medication. In addition, most of them experience fewer new episodes as long as they continue taking lithium (Viguera et al., 2000). One study found that the risk of relapse is 28 times greater if patients stop taking lithium (Suppes et al., 1991). Thus, today's clinicians usually continue patients on some level of lithium even after their manic episodes subside (Cusack, 2003).

Lithium also helps those with a bipolar disorder overcome their depressive episodes, though to a lesser degree than it helps with manic episodes (Hlastala et al., 1997). In addition, continued doses of lithium apparently reduce the risk of

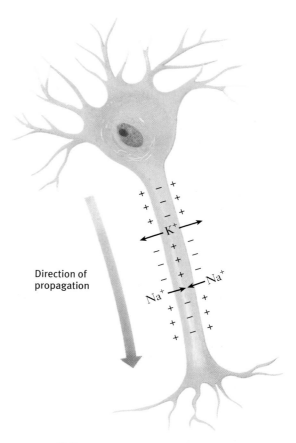

FIGURE 7-6   Ions and the firing of neurons *Neurons relay messages in the form of electrical impulses that travel down the axon toward the nerve endings. As an impulse travels along the axon, sodium ions (Na+), which had been resting on the outside of the neuron's membrane, flow to the inside, causing the impulse to continue down the axon. Once sodium ions flow in, potassium ions (K+) flow out, thus helping the membrane's electrical balance to return to its resting state, ready for the arrival of a new impulse. (Adapted from Snyder, 1986, p. 7.)*

Direction of propagation

>>**PSYCH•NOTES**

Taking the Lead

In 1998 *valproate* (Depakote) actually surpassed *lithium* to become the drug most prescribed for treating mania in bipolar disorders (UTMB, 1999).<<

"More lithium."

future depressive episodes, just as they seem to prevent the return of manic episodes (Baldessarini, Tondo, & Hennen, 1999).

Researchers do not fully understand how lithium operates. They suspect that it changes synaptic activity in neurons, but in a way different from that of antidepressant drugs (Ghaemi, Boiman, & Goodwin, 1999). The firing of a neuron actually consists of several phases that unfold at lightning speed. When a neurotransmitter binds to a receptor on the receiving neuron, a series of changes occur within the receiving neuron to set the stage for firing. The substances within the neuron that carry out those changes are often called **second messengers** because they relay the original message from the receptor site to the firing mechanism of the neuron. (The neurotransmitter itself is considered the first messenger.) Whereas antidepressant drugs affect a neuron's initial reception of neurotransmitters, lithium appears to affect a neuron's second messengers.

Different second-messenger systems are at work in different neurons (Andreasen, 2001). In one of the most important systems, chemicals called *phosphoinositides* are produced within certain neurons when neurotransmitters are received. Lithium apparently affects this particular messenger system (Manji et al., 1999). Lithium may in fact affect the activity of any neuron that uses this second-messenger system and in so doing may correct the biological abnormalities that lead to bipolar disorders.

ADJUNCTIVE PSYCHOTHERAPY Psychotherapy alone is rarely helpful for persons with bipolar disorders (Klerman et al., 1994). At the same time, clinicians have learned that lithium therapy alone is not always sufficient either. Thirty percent or more of patients with these disorders may not respond to lithium or a related drug, may not receive the proper dose, or may relapse while taking it (Kulhara et al., 1999; Solomon et al., 1995). In addition, a number of patients stop taking lithium on their own (Torrey & Knable, 2002).

In view of these problems, many clinicians now use individual, group, or family therapy as an *adjunct* to lithium treatment (George et al., 2000; Hammen et al., 2000). Most often, therapists use these formats to emphasize the importance of continuing to take one's medications and to help patients solve the special family, social, school, and occupational problems caused by their disorder. Few controlled studies have tested the effectiveness of such adjunctive therapy, but clinical reports suggest that it helps reduce hospitalization, improves social functioning, and increases clients' ability to obtain and hold a job (Colom et al., 2003; Scott, 1995).

SUMMING UP

Bipolar Disorders

In bipolar disorders, episodes of mania alternate or intermix with episodes of depression. These disorders are much less common than unipolar depression. They may take the form of bipolar I, bipolar II, or cyclothymic disorder.

Mania may be related to high norepinephrine activity along with a low level of serotonin activity. Researchers have also linked bipolar disorders to improper transport of ions back and forth between the outside and the inside of a neuron's membrane. Genetic studies suggest that people may inherit a predisposition to such biological abnormalities.

Lithium and other mood-stabilizing drugs may reduce and prevent both the manic and depressive episodes of bipolar disorders. It may be that lithium achieves its effect by acting on second messengers in key neurons. Patients tend to fare better when mood-stabilizing drugs are combined with psychotherapy.

SECOND MESSENGERS Chemical changes within a neuron just after the neuron receives a neurotransmitter message and just before it responds.

CROSSROADS:
Making Sense of All That Is Known

During the past 30 years, researchers and clinicians have made tremendous gains in the understanding and treatment of mood disorders. Unipolar depression, for example, has become one of the most treatable of all psychological disorders. Cognitive therapy, interpersonal psychotherapy, and antidepressant drugs are all helpful in cases of any severity; couple therapy is helpful in select cases; behavioral therapy helps in mild to moderate cases; and ECT is useful and effective in severe cases. During the same period of time, several factors have been closely tied to unipolar depression, including biological abnormalities, a reduction in positive reinforcements, negative ways of thinking, perceptions of helplessness, and sociocultural influences. Precisely how all of these factors relate to unipolar depression, however, is unclear (Meyer et al., 2003). Several relationships are possible:

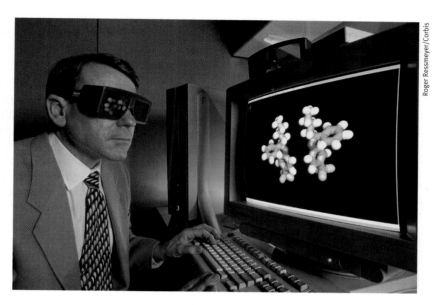

The antidepressant revolution *As we are reminded by this photo of a scientist studying the molecular structure of Prozac, antidepressant drugs are now a leading form of treatment for unipolar depression and will likely continue to be developed, studied, and prescribed in the years ahead.*

1. *One* of the factors may be the key cause of unipolar depression. If so, cognitive or biological factors are leading candidates, for factors in each of these categories have each been found sometimes to precede and predict depression.

2. *Different* factors may be capable of initiating unipolar depression in different persons. Some people may, for example, begin with low serotonin activity, which predisposes them to react helplessly in stressful situations, interpret events negatively, and enjoy fewer pleasures in life. Others may first suffer a severe loss, which triggers helplessness reactions, low serotonin activity, and reductions in positive rewards.

3. An *interaction* between two or more specific factors may be necessary to produce unipolar depression (Klocek et al., 1997). Perhaps people will become depressed only if they have low levels of serotonin activity, feel helpless, *and* repeatedly blame themselves for negative events.

4. The various factors may play *different roles* in unipolar depression. Some may cause the disorder, some may result from it, and some may keep it going.

As with unipolar depression, clinicians and researchers have learned much about bipolar disorders during the past 30 years. But bipolar disorders appear to be best explained by focusing largely on *one* kind of variable—biological factors. The evidence suggests that biological abnormalities, perhaps inherited and perhaps triggered by life stress, cause bipolar disorders. In addition, the choice of treatment for these disorders is narrow and simple—lithium or a related drug, perhaps combined with psychotherapy.

There is no question that investigations into and treatments for the mood disorders have been extremely fruitful. On the other hand, the sobering fact remains that as many as 40 percent of people with a mood disorder do not improve under treatment and must suffer their depression or mania until it runs its course. Now that clinical researchers have gathered so many important puzzle pieces, they must put the pieces together into a still more meaningful picture that will suggest even better ways to predict, prevent, and treat these disorders (Munoz et al., 2002).

>>LOOKING AROUND

Drugs on the Rise

Antidepressant medications are now the second most prescribed class of drugs, just behind drugs for high blood pressure (Express Scripts, 1999).<<

Currently 3 of the 12 most prescribed drugs of any kind in the United States are antidepressants (Gitlin, 2002).<<

CRITICAL THOUGHTS

1. Almost every day we experience ups and downs in mood. How can we distinguish the everyday blues from clinical depression? *pp. 193–198*

2. In one study, students who listened to a sad song became more depressed than those who listened to a happy song (Stratton & Zalanow, 1999, 1994). Yet the sad-song students reported "enjoying" their musical experience more than the happy-song students. What might be going on here? *pp. 193–198*

3. Some people argue that antidepressant drugs may act to curb useful behavior, destroy individuality, and blunt people's concerns about societal ills. Are such concerns justified? *pp. 201–202*

4. Friends and family members try, with limited success, to convince depressed people that their gloom-and-doom view of things is wrong. How does the successful cognitive approach to unipolar depression differ from such efforts at friendly persuasion? *pp. 210–211*

5. Many comedians report that they have grappled with depression. Is there something about performing that might improve their mood? Is there something about being depressed that might make them more skilled at thinking or acting funny? *p. 211*

6. If antidepressant drugs are highly effective, why would people seek out herbal supplements, such as St. John's wort, for depression? *p. 216*

KEY TERMS

depression p. 193
mania p. 193
unipolar depression p. 193
bipolar disorder p. 193
major depressive disorder p. 197
dysthymic disorder p. 197
reactive depression p. 198
endogenous depression p. 198
norepinephrine p. 198
serotonin p. 198
cortisol p. 199
melatonin p. 199

electroconvulsive therapy (ECT) p. 199
MAO inhibitors p. 201
tyramine p. 201
tricyclics p. 201
selective serotonin reuptake inhibitors (SSRIs) p. 202
symbolic loss p. 203
learned helplessness p. 207
attribution p. 208
cognitive triad p. 209
automatic thoughts p. 210
rumination p. 210

cognitive therapy p. 210
interpersonal psychotherapy (IPT) p. 213
couple therapy p. 215
hypomanic episode p. 218
bipolar I disorder p. 218
biopolar II disorder p. 218
cyclothymic disorder p. 219
sodium ion p. 219
lithium p. 221
carbamazepine (Tegretol) p. 221
valproate (Depakote) p. 221
second messengers p. 222

QUICK QUIZ

1. What are the key symptoms of depression and mania? *pp. 194–197, 217–218*

2. What is the difference between unipolar depression and bipolar disorder? *p. 193*

3. Describe the role of norepinephrine and serotonin in unipolar depression. *p. 198*

4. Describe Freud and Abraham's psychodynamic theory of depression and the evidence that supports it. *pp. 203–204*

5. How do behaviorists describe the role of rewards in depression? *p. 206*

6. How might learned helplessness in laboratory animals be related to human depression? *pp. 207–209*

7. What kinds of negative thinking may lead to mood problems? *pp. 209–210*

8. How do sociocultural theorists account for unipolar depression? *pp. 212–213*

9. What roles do biological and genetic factors seem to play in bipolar disorders? *pp. 219–221*

10. Discuss the leading treatments for unipolar depression and bipolar disorders. How effective are these various approaches? *pp. 199–202, 205–207, 210–216, 221–222*

SEARCH THE *FUNDAMENTALS OF ABNORMAL PSYCHOLOGY* CD-ROM FOR

▲ Chapter 7 Video Case Enrichment
   How do negative thoughts contribute to depression?
   Observe psychological and biological treatments for mood disorders at work.
   How has ECT changed over the years?

▲ Chapter 7 Practical, Research, and Decision-Making Exercises
   Observing the power of mood: Cheering oneself up
   Diagnosing mood disorders
   Creating depression in the laboratory
   Choosing the right treatment for depression

▲ Chapter 7 Practice Test and Feedback

LOG ON TO THE COMER WEB PAGE FOR

▲ Suggested Web links, exercises, FAQ page, additional Chapter 7 practice test questions
   <www.worthpublishers.com/comer>

‹‹‹

SELÇUK DEMIREL, 1993

Suicide

I had done all I could and I was still sinking. I sat many hours seeking answers, and all there was was a silent wind. The answer was in my head. It was all clear now: Die. . . .

The next day a friend offered to sell me a gun, a .357 magnum pistol. I bought it. My first thought was: What a mess this is going to make. That day I began to say goodbye to people: not actually saying it but expressing it silently.

Friends were around, but I didn't let them see what was wrong with me. I could not let them know lest they prevent it. My mind became locked on my target. My thoughts were: Soon it will all be over. I would obtain the peace I had so long sought. The will to survive and succeed had been crushed and defeated. I was like a general on a battlefield being encroached on by my enemy and its hordes: fear, hate, self-depreciation, desolation. I felt I had to have the upper hand, to control my environment, so I sought to die rather than surrender. . . .

I was only aware of myself and my plight. Death swallowed me long before I pulled the trigger. The world through my eyes seemed to die with me. It was like I was to push the final button to end this world. I committed myself to the arms of death. There comes a time when all things cease to shine, when the rays of hope are lost.

I placed the gun to my head. Then, I remember a tremendous explosion of lights like fireworks. Thus did the pain become glorious, an army rallied to the side of death to help destroy my life, which I could feel leaving my body with each rushing surge of blood. I was engulfed in total darkness.

(Shneidman, 1987, p. 56)

Salmon spawn and then die, after an exhausting upstream swim to their breeding ground. Lemmings rush to the sea and drown. But only humans knowingly take their own lives. The actions of salmon and lemmings are instinctual responses that may even help their species survive in the long run. Only in the human act of suicide do beings act for the specific purpose of putting an end to their lives.

Suicide has been recorded throughout history. The Old Testament described King Saul's suicide: "There Saul took a sword and fell on it." The ancient Chinese, Greeks, and Romans also provided examples. More recently, suicides by such famous individuals as the writer Ernest Hemingway, the actress Marilyn Monroe, and the rock star Kurt Cobain have both shocked and fascinated the public. Even more disturbing are mass suicides such as those of the Heaven's Gate cult in 1997.

Before you finish reading this page, someone in the United States will try to kill himself. At least 60 Americans will have taken their own lives by this time tomorrow. . . . Many of those who attempted will try again, a number with lethal success.

(Shneidman & Mandelkorn, 1983)

Today suicide ranks among the top 10 causes of death in the world. It has been estimated that 700,000 or more people may die by it each year,

Fatal attraction *A tiny male redback spider prepares to be eaten by his large female partner during copulation and even aids in his own death. While placing his intromittent organ into his partner, he also spins around and dangles his enticing abdomen in front of her mouth. The male may be shortsighted, but he is not intending to die. In fact, by keeping his partner busy eating him, he can deposit a maximum amount of sperm, thus increasing the chances of reproduction and the birth of an offspring with similar tendencies (Andrade, 1996).*

Table 8-1

Most Common Causes of Death in the United States

RANK	CAUSE	DEATHS PER YEAR	PERCENTAGE OF TOTAL DEATHS
1	Heart disease	733,834	31.6%
2	Cancer	544,278	23.4
3	Stroke	160,431	6.9
4	Lung diseases	106,146	4.6
5	Accident	93,874	4.0
6	Pneumonia and influenza	82,579	3.6
7	Diabetes	61,559	2.7
8	AIDS	32,655	1.4
9	**Suicide**	**30,862**	**1.3**
10	Liver disease	25,135	1.1

Source: Ash, 1999; U.S. National Center for Health Statistics.

31,000 in the United States alone (Stolberg et al., 2002; Clark & Goldney, 2000) (see Table 8-1). Millions of other people throughout the world—600,000 in the United States—make unsuccessful attempts to kill themselves; such attempts are called **parasuicides** (Welch, 2001). Actually, it is hard to obtain accurate figures on suicide, and many investigators believe that estimates are often low. For one thing, suicide can be difficult to distinguish from unintentional drug overdoses, automobile crashes, drownings, and other accidents (Wertheimer, 2001; Lester, 2000). Many apparent "accidents" were probably intentional. For another, suicide is frowned on in our society, causing relatives and friends to deny that loved ones have taken their own lives.

Suicide is not classified as a mental disorder by DSM-IV, but clinicians are aware of the key role that psychological dysfunctioning—a breakdown of coping skills, emotional turmoil, a distorted view of life—plays in this act. Although suicide is frequently linked to depression, around half of all suicides result from other mental disorders, such as schizophrenia or alcohol dependence, or involve no clear psychological disorder at all (Maris, 2001).

What Is Suicide?

Not every self-inflicted death is a suicide. A man who crashes his car into a tree after falling asleep at the steering wheel is not trying to kill himself. Thus Edwin Shneidman (2001, 1981, 1963), one of the most influential writers on this topic, defines **suicide** as an intentioned death—a self-inflicted death in which one makes an intentional, direct, and conscious effort to end one's life.

Intentioned deaths may take various forms. Consider the following examples. All three of these people intended to die, but their motives, concerns, and actions differed greatly.

PARASUICIDE A suicide attempt that does not result in death.

SUICIDE A self-inflicted death in which the person acts intentionally, directly, and consciously.

Dave was a successful man. By the age of 50 he had risen to the vice presidency of a small but profitable office machine firm. He had a devoted wife and two teenage sons who respected him. They lived in an upper-middle-class neighborhood, had a spacious house, and enjoyed a life of comfort.

In August of his fiftieth year, everything changed. Dave was fired. Just like that, after many years of loyal and effective service. The firm's profits were down and the president wanted to try new, fresher marketing approaches. He wanted to try a younger person in Dave's position.

Dave was shocked. The experience of rejection, loss, and emptiness was overwhelming. He looked for another position, but found only low-paying jobs for which he was overqualified. Each day as he looked for work Dave became more depressed, anxious, and desperate. He kept sinking, withdrew from others, and felt increasingly hopeless.

Six months after losing his job, Dave began to consider ending his life. The pain was too great, the humiliation unending. He hated the present and dreaded the future. Throughout February he went back and forth. On some days he was sure he wanted to die. On other days, an enjoyable evening or uplifting conversation might change his mind temporarily. On a Monday late in February he heard about a job possibility, and the anticipation of the next day's interview seemed to lift his spirits. But Tuesday's interview did not go well. It was clear to him that he would not be offered the job. He went home, took a recently purchased gun from his locked desk drawer, and shot himself.

Billy never truly recovered from his mother's death. He was only 7 years old and unprepared for such a loss. His father sent him to live with his grandparents for a time, to a new school with new kids and a new way of life. In Billy's mind, all these changes were for the worse. He missed the joy and laughter of the past. He missed his home, his father, and his friends. Most of all he missed his mother.

He did not really understand her death. His father said that she was in heaven now, at peace, happy. Billy's unhappiness and loneliness continued day after day and he began to put things together in his own way. He believed he would be happy again if he could join his mother. He felt she was waiting for him, waiting for him to come to her. These thoughts seemed so right to him; they brought him comfort and hope. One evening, shortly after saying good night to his grandparents, Billy climbed out of bed, went up the stairs to the roof of their apartment house, and jumped to his death. In his mind he was joining his mother in heaven.

Margaret and Bob had been going together for a year. It was Margaret's first serious relationship; it was her whole life. Thus when Bob told her that he no longer loved her and was leaving her for someone else, Margaret was shocked and shaken.

As the weeks went by, Margaret was filled with two competing feelings—depression and anger. Several times she called Bob, begged him to reconsider, and pleaded for a chance to win him back. At the same time, she hated him for putting her through such misery.

Margaret's friends became more and more worried about her. At first they sympathized with her pain, assuming it would soon lift. But as time went on, her depression and anger worsened, and Margaret began to act strangely. She started to drink heavily and to mix her drinks with all kinds of pills. She seemed to be flirting with danger.

One night Margaret went into her bathroom, reached for a bottle of sleeping pills, and swallowed a handful of them. She wanted to make her pain go away, and she wanted Bob to know just how much pain he had caused her. She continued swallowing pill after pill, crying and swearing as she gulped them down. When she began to feel drowsy, she decided to call her close friend Cindy. She was not sure why she was calling, perhaps to say good-bye, to explain her actions, or to make sure that Bob was told; or perhaps to be talked out of it. Cindy pleaded and reasoned with Margaret and tried to motivate her to live. Margaret was trying to listen, but she became less and less clear. Cindy hung up the phone and quickly called Margaret's neighbor and the police. When reached by her neighbor, Margaret was already in a coma. Seven hours later, while her friends and family waited for news in the hospital lounge, Margaret died.

Death darers? *A sky surfer tries to ride the perfect cloud over Sweden. Are thrill-seekers daredevils searching for new highs, as many of them claim, or are some actually death darers?*

While Margaret seemed to have mixed feelings about her death, Dave was clear in his wish to die. Whereas Billy viewed death as a trip to heaven, Dave saw it as an end to his existence. Such differences can be important in efforts to understand and treat suicidal persons. Accordingly, Shneidman has described four kinds of people who intentionally end their lives: the *death seeker, death initiator, death ignorer,* and *death darer.*

Death seekers clearly intend to end their lives at the time they attempt suicide. This singleness of purpose may last only a short time. It can change to confusion the very next hour or day, and then return again in short order. Dave, the middle-aged executive, was a death seeker. He had many misgivings about suicide and had mixed feelings about it for weeks, but on Tuesday night he was a death seeker—clear in his desire to die and acting in a manner that virtually guaranteed a fatal outcome.

Death initiators also clearly intend to end their lives, but they act out of a belief that the process of death is already under way and that they are simply quickening the process. Some expect that they will die in a matter of days or weeks. Many suicides among the elderly and very sick fall into this category. The robust novelist Ernest Hemingway was deeply concerned about his failing body—a concern that some observers believe was at the center of his suicide.

Death ignorers do not believe that their self-inflicted death will mean the end of their existence. They believe they are trading their present lives for a better or happier existence. Many child suicides, like Billy's, fall into this category, as do those of adult believers in a hereafter who commit suicide to reach another form of life. In 1997, for example, the world was shocked to learn that 39 members of an unusual cult named Heaven's Gate had committed suicide at an expensive house outside San Diego. It turned out that these members had acted out of the belief that their deaths would free their spirits and enable them to ascend to a "Higher Kingdom."

Death darers experience mixed feelings, or ambivalence, in their intent to die even at the moment of their attempt, and they show this ambivalence in the act itself. Although to some degree they wish to die, and they often do die, their risk-taking behavior does not guarantee death. The person who plays Russian roulette—that is, pulls the trigger of a revolver randomly loaded with one bullet—is a death darer. Many death darers are as interested in gaining attention, making someone feel guilty, or expressing anger as in dying per se. Margaret might be considered a death darer. Although her unhappiness and anger were great, she was not sure that she wanted to die. Even while taking pills, she called her friend, reported her actions, and listened to her friend's pleas.

When individuals play *indirect, covert, partial,* or *unconscious* roles in their own deaths, Shneidman (2001, 1993, 1981) classifies them in a suicide-like category called **subintentional death**. Seriously ill people who consistently mismanage their medicines may belong in this category. Although their deaths may represent a form of suicide, their true intent is unclear, and so these individuals are not included in the discussions of this chapter.

How Is Suicide Studied?

Suicide researchers face a major problem: their subjects are no longer alive. How can investigators draw accurate conclusions about the intentions, feelings, and circumstances of people who can no longer explain their actions? Two research methods attempt to deal with this problem, each with only partial success.

One strategy is *retrospective analysis*, a kind of psychological autopsy in which clinicians and researchers piece together data from the suicide victim's past (Houston, Hawton, & Sheppard, 2001). Relatives, friends, therapists, or physicians may remember past statements, conversations, and behavior that shed light on a suicide. Retrospective information may also be provided by the suicide notes that some victims leave behind (Leenaars et al., 2001). However, such sources of

DEATH SEEKER A person who clearly intends to end his or her life at the time of a suicide attempt.

DEATH INITIATOR A person who attempts suicide believing that the process of death is already under way and that he or she is simply hastening the process.

DEATH IGNORER A person who attempts suicide without recognizing the finality of death.

DEATH DARER A person who is ambivalent about the wish to die even as he or she attempts suicide.

SUBINTENTIONAL DEATH A death in which the victim plays an indirect, hidden, partial, or unconscious role.

❮ ABNORMALITY AND THE ARTS ❯

Suicide in the Family

On July 1, 1996, the model and actress Margaux Hemingway killed herself by taking an overdose of barbiturates. She was the fifth person in four generations of her family to commit suicide. Her death came almost 35 years to the day after the suicide of her famous grandfather, the novelist Ernest Hemingway, by shotgun. Severely depressed about his progressive physical illness, he had failed to respond to two series of electroconvulsive treatments.

Margaux Hemingway had suffered from severe depression, alcoholism, and bulimia nervosa. She had had a successful modeling and acting career in the 1970s, but in later years her work consisted primarily of infomercials and low-budget movies. According to friends, she had tried for years to handle her anguish and setbacks with grace. "I was taught it was Hemingwayesque to take your blows and walk stoically through them."

Famous cases such as this remind us that suicide sometimes runs in families. One study found that 11 percent of the subjects who committed suicide had a close relative who had done the same, compared to none of the control subjects, people who died of natural causes (Maris, 2001). But, as with other family-linked disorders, we cannot be certain whether genetic factors, environmental factors, or both produce family patterns of suicide. Indeed,

for members of celebrity families, the family name itself may add considerable stress to their lives. Just as Margaux Hemingway believed that she had to be "Hemingwayesque," members of celebrity families may feel trapped by the instant recognition and high expectations that go along with their family name.

Marc C. Biggins/Gamma Liaison

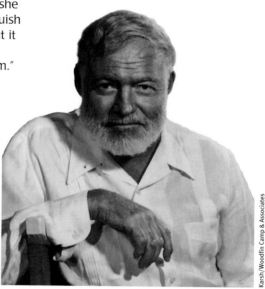

Karsh/Woodfin Camp & Associates

information are not always available. Around half of all suicide victims have never been in psychotherapy (Stolberg et al., 2002), and less than one-third leave notes (Maris, 2001; Black, 1993).

Because of these limitations, many researchers also use a second strategy—*studying people who survive their suicide attempts.* It is estimated that there are 8 to 20 nonfatal suicide attempts for every fatal suicide (Maris, 2001). However, it may be that people who survive suicide differ in important ways from those who do not (Cutler et al., 2001; Diekstra et al., 1995). Many of them may not really have wanted to die, for example. Nevertheless, suicide researchers have found it useful to study survivors of suicide; and this chapter will consider those who attempt suicide and those who commit suicide as more or less alike.

Patterns and Statistics

Suicide happens within a larger social setting, and researchers have gathered many statistics regarding the social contexts in which such deaths take place. They have found, for example, that suicide rates vary from country to country (Lester, 2000; Schmidtke et al., 1999). Russia, Hungary, Germany, Austria, Finland, Denmark, China, and Japan have very high rates, more than 20 suicides annually per 100,000 persons; conversely, Egypt, Mexico, Greece, and Spain have relatively low rates, fewer than 5 per 100,000. The United States and Canada fall in between, each with a suicide rate of around 12 per 100,000 persons, and England has a rate of 9 per 100,000.

»LOOKING AROUND

The China Profile

China's 300,000 annual suicides, 10 times the United States' toll, represent 40 percent of all suicides in the world. China is the only country in which female suicides are more common than male suicides, accounting for half of suicides by women worldwide (Kaplan, 1999; Phillips et al., 1999; Schmidtke et al., 1999).《

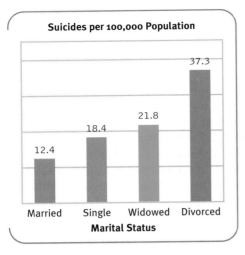

Suicides per 100,000 Population

37.3

21.8

18.4

12.4

| Married | Single | Widowed | Divorced |

Marital Status

FIGURE **8-1** **Suicide and marital status**
Approximately 37 of every 100,000 persons commit suicide, more than three times the rate of married persons. (Adapted from McIntosh, 1991, p. 64.)

Religious affiliation and beliefs may help account for these national differences (Brown, 2002). For example, countries that are largely Catholic, Jewish, or Muslim tend to have low suicide rates. Perhaps in these countries, strict prohibitions against suicide and a strong religious tradition discourage many people from committing suicide. Yet there are exceptions to this rule. Austria, a largely Roman Catholic country, has one of the highest suicide rates in the world.

Research is beginning to suggest that religious affiliation may not help prevent suicide as much as the degree of an individual's *devoutness*. Regardless of their particular persuasion, very religious people seem less likely to commit suicide (Jahangir, ur-Rehman, & Jan, 1998). Similarly, it seems that people who hold a greater respect for life are less prone to consider self-destruction (Lee, 1985).

The suicide rates of men and women also differ. Three times as many women attempt suicide as men, yet men succeed at more than three times the rate of women (Maris, 2001; Moscicki, 1999). Around the world 19 of every 100,000 men kill themselves each year; the suicide rate for women, which has been increasing in recent years, is 5 per 100,000 (Schmidtke et al., 1999).

One reason for these differing rates appears to be the different methods used by men and women. Men tend to use more violent methods, such as shooting, stabbing, or hanging themselves, whereas women use less violent methods, such as drug overdose. Guns are used in nearly two-thirds of the male suicides in the United States, compared to 40 percent of the female suicides (Maris, 2001; Canetto & Lester, 1995).

Suicide is also related to social support and marital status (Palmer, 2001) (see Figure 8-1). In one study, only half of the subjects who had committed suicide were found to have close friends (Maris, 2001). Fewer still had close relationships with parents and other family members. In a related vein, research has revealed that divorced persons have a higher suicide rate than married or cohabitating individuals (Stolberg et al., 2002).

Finally, in the United States at least, suicide rates seem to vary according to race (Wasserman & Stack, 2000) (see Figure 8-2). The suicide rate of white Americans, 12 per 100,000 persons, is almost twice as high as that of African Americans and members of other racial groups (Stolberg et al., 2002; Stillion & McDowell, 1996). A major exception to this pattern is the very high suicide rate of Native Americans, which overall is one and a half times the national average (DeAngelis, 2001). Although the extreme poverty of many Native Americans may partly explain such trends, studies show that such factors as alcohol use, modeling, and the availability of guns may also play a role (Berman & Jobes, 1995, 1991; Young, 1991). Studies of Native Americans in Canada yield similar results (Strickland, 1997; Bagley, 1991).

Some of these statistics on suicide have been questioned in recent years. One analysis suggests that the actual rate of suicide may be 15 percent higher for African Americans and 6 percent higher for women than usually reported (Phillips & Ruth, 1993). People in these groups are more likely than others to use methods of suicide that can be mistaken for causes of accidental death, such as poisoning, drug overdose, single-car crashes, and pedestrian accidents.

SUMMING UP

What Is Suicide?

Suicide is a self-inflicted death in which one makes an intentional, direct, and conscious effort to end one's life. Four kinds of people who intentionally end their lives have been described: the death seeker, the death initiator, the death ignorer, and the death darer. Two major strategies are used in the study of suicide: retrospective analysis and the study of people who survive suicide attempts.

Suicide ranks among the top 10 causes of death in Western society. Rates vary from country to country. One reason seems to be differences in religious affiliation, beliefs, or degree of devoutness. Suicide rates also vary according to race, gender, social support, and marital status.

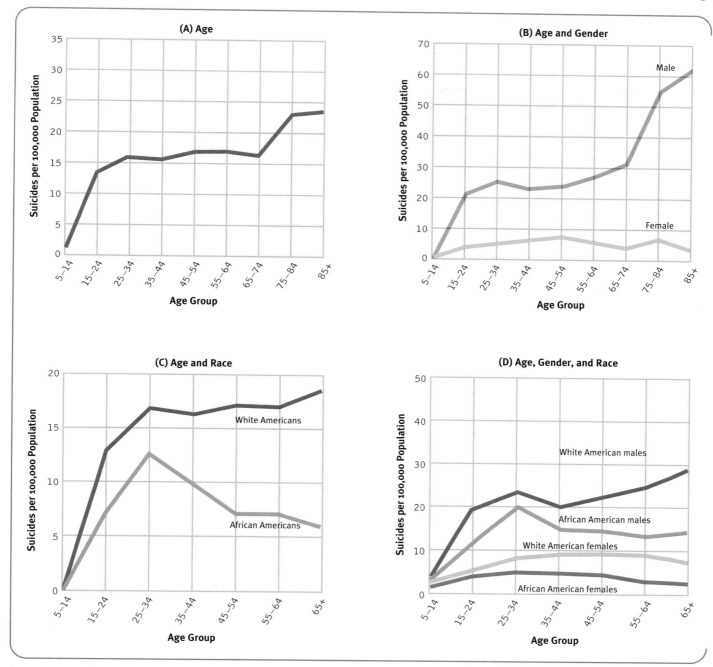

FIGURE 8-2 **Current U.S. suicide rates**
(A) People over the age of 65 are more likely to commit suicide than those in any other age group; (B) males commit suicide at higher rates than females; (C) white Americans commit suicide at higher rates than African Americans; (D) elderly white American men have the highest risk of suicide. (Adapted from Stillion & McDowell, 1996; U.S. Census, 1994, 1990; McIntosh, 1991, pp. 62–63.)

What Triggers a Suicide?

Suicidal acts may be connected to recent events or current conditions in a person's life. Although such factors may not be the basic motivation for the suicide, they can trigger it. Common triggering factors include *stressful events, mood and thought changes, alcohol and other drug use, mental disorders,* and *modeling.*

Stressful Events and Situations

Researchers have counted more stressful events in the recent lives of suicide attempters than in the lives of matched control subjects (Hendin et al., 2001). Common forms of *immediate stress* seen in cases of suicide are the loss of a loved one through death, divorce, or rejection (Jacobs et al., 1999); loss of a job (Maris, 2001); and the stress associated with hurricanes or other disasters, even among

>>LOOKING BACK

The Impact of Internment The suicide rate among the 110,000 Japanese Americans who were interned in "relocation centers" during World War II rose to double that of the national population (Jensen, 1998).<<

Political Integration and Disintegration After the reunification of Germany, East Germany's suicide rate dropped by one-third and West Germany's by one-quarter (Schmidtke et al., 1999). In contrast, suicide rates increased in the nations formed after the breakup of the Soviet Union in 1991 (Lester, 1998).<<

very young children (Cytryn & McKnew, 1996). People may also attempt suicide in response to long-term rather than recent stress. Three *long-term stressors* are particularly common—serious illness, an abusive environment, and occupational stress.

SERIOUS ILLNESS People whose illnesses cause them great pain or severe disability may try to commit suicide, believing that death is unavoidable and imminent (Hendin, 2002, 1999). They may also believe that the suffering and problems caused by their illnesses are more than they can endure. One study found that 37 percent of the subjects who died by suicide had been in poor physical health (Conwell et al., 1990); other studies tell a similar story (Maris, 2001). Illness-linked suicides have become more common, and controversial, in recent years (Leenaars et al., 2001). Although physicians can now keep seriously ill people alive much longer, they often fail to extend the quality and comfort of the patients' lives (Werth, 1995).

ABUSIVE ENVIRONMENT Victims of an abusive or repressive environment from which they have little hope of escape sometimes commit suicide. For example, prisoners of war, inmates of concentration camps, abused spouses, abused children, and prison inmates have tried to end their lives (Stolberg et al., 2002; Lester, 2000) (see Figure 8-3). Like those who have serious illnesses, these people may have felt that they could endure no more suffering and believed that there was no hope for improvement in their condition.

OCCUPATIONAL STRESS Some jobs create feelings of tension or dissatisfaction that may precipitate suicide attempts. Research has found particularly high suicide rates among psychiatrists and psychologists, physicians, nurses, dentists, lawyers, farmers, and unskilled laborers (Aasland et al., 2001; Wertheimer, 2001; Lester, 2000). Such findings do not necessarily mean that occupational pressures directly cause suicidal actions. Perhaps unskilled workers are responding to financial insecurity rather than job stress when they attempt suicide (Wasserman & Stack, 2000). Similarly, rather than reacting to the emotional strain of their work, suicidal psychiatrists and psychologists may have long-standing emotional problems that stimulated their career interest in the first place (Johnson, 1991).

Mood and Thought Changes

Many suicide attempts are preceded by a change in mood. The change may not be severe enough to call for a diagnosis of a mental disorder, but it does represent a significant shift from the person's past mood. The most common change is an increase in sadness (Hendin et al., 2001; Kienhorst et al., 1993). Also common are rises in feelings of anxiety, tension, frustration, anger, or shame. In fact, Shneidman (2001, 1993) suggests that the key to suicide is "psychache," a feeling of psychological pain that seems intolerable to the person.

Suicide attempts may also be preceded by shifts in patterns of thinking. Individuals may become preoccupied with their problems, lose perspective, and see suicide as the only effective solution to their difficulties (Shneidman, 2001, 1999, 1987). They often develop a sense of **hopelessness**—a pessimistic belief that their present circumstances, problems, or mood will not change (Brent, 2001). Some clinicians believe that a feeling of hopelessness is the single most likely indicator of suicidal intent, and they take special care to look for signs of hopelessness when they assess the risk of suicide (Hewitt et al., 1997).

Many people who attempt suicide fall victim to **dichotomous thinking**, viewing problems and solutions in rigid either/or terms (Shneidman, 2001, 1993;

FIGURE 8-3 **Suicide in prisons**
Approximately 107 of every 100,000 inmates in U.S. jails commit suicide each year, many times the national prevalence. Most such suicides occur during the first day of incarceration. (Adapted from Bonner, 1990; Hayes & Rowan, 1988.)

Weishaar, 2000). Indeed, Shneidman has said that the "four-letter word" in suicide is "only," as in "suicide was the only thing I could do" (Maris, 2001). In the following statement a woman who survived her leap from a building describes her dichotomous thinking at the time. She saw death as the only alternative to her pain:

> I was so desperate. I felt, my God, I couldn't face this thing. Everything was like a terrible whirlpool of confusion. And I thought to myself: There's only one thing to do. I just have to lose consciousness. That's the only way to get away from it. The only way to lose consciousness, I thought, was to jump off something good and high. . . .
>
> *(Shneidman, 1987, p. 56)*

HOPELESSNESS A pessimistic belief that one's present circumstances, problems, or mood will not change.

DICHOTOMOUS THINKING Viewing problems and solutions in rigid either/or terms.

Alcohol and Other Drug Use

Studies indicate that as many as 60 percent of the people who attempt suicide drink alcohol just before the act (Lester, 2000; Suokas & Lonnqvist, 1995). Autopsies reveal that about one-fourth of these people are legally intoxicated (Flavin et al., 1990). In such cases, it may be that the use of alcohol lowers the individuals' fears of committing suicide, releases underlying aggressive feelings, or impairs their judgment and problem-solving ability. Research shows that the use of other kinds of drugs may have a similar tie to suicide, particularly in teenagers and young adults (Lester, 2000; Rich et al., 1998). A high level of heroin, for example, was found in the blood of Kurt Cobain at the time of his suicide in 1994 (Colburn, 1996).

Mental Disorders

Although people who attempt suicide may be troubled or anxious, they do not necessarily have a psychological disorder as defined in DSM-IV. Nevertheless, the majority of all suicide attempters do display such a disorder (Stolberg et al., 2002; Maris, 2001). In fact, research suggests that as many as half of all suicide victims had been experienceing severe depression, 20 percent chronic alcoholism, and 10 percent schizophrenia. Correspondingly, as many as 15 percent of people with each of these disorders try to kill themselves. People who are both depressed and dependent on alcohol seem particularly prone to suicidal impulses (Cornelius et al., 1995).

As we observed in Chapter 7, people with major depressive disorder often experience suicidal thoughts (Nemeroff et al., 2001). One program in Sweden was able to reduce the community suicide rate by teaching physicians how to recognize and treat depression at an early stage (Rihmer, Rutz, & Pihlgren, 1995). Even when depressed people are showing improvements in mood, however, they may remain high suicide risks. In fact, among those who are severely depressed, the risk of suicide may actually increase as their mood improves and they have more energy to act on their suicidal wishes.

Severe depression also may play a key role in suicide attempts by persons with serious physical illnesses (Chochinov & Schwartz, 2002). A study of 44 patients with terminal illnesses revealed that fewer than one-quarter of them had thoughts of suicide or wished for an early death and that those who did were all suffering from major depressive disorder (Brown et al., 1986).

A number of the people who drink alcohol or use drugs just before a suicide attempt actually have a long history of abusing such substances (Preuss et al., 2003; Rossow & Lauritzen, 2001). The basis for the link

Words of despair *The influential English novelist and essayist Virginia Woolf (1882–1941) suffered major episodes of depression and mania at the ages of 13, 22, 28, and 30, and less severe mood swings throughout the rest of her life. She took her own life by drowning at the age of 59 during a depressive episode, fearing that she was "going mad again."*

Corbis

THE CURRENT SCENE

"I'm All Traveled Out"

On October 5, 1998, Margaret Mary Ray knelt down in front of an oncoming 105-car coal train in Hotchkiss, Colorado, and brought her life to an immediate end. Ms. Ray, 46, had suffered from schizophrenia for years, holding delusions that she was in intimate relationships with famous people and even stalking them in their residences. Like a number of other people with schizophrenia, she eventually grew weary and hopeless about the chances that her disorder would ever improve. In a suicide note sent to her mother, she said, "I'm all traveled out. . . . I choose a painless and instantaneous way to end my life. . . ."

One difference between Ms. Ray and most other people with schizophrenia is that millions of people knew something about her dysfunction. She gained notoriety during her last decade as the woman who believed that she was romantically involved with the television comedian David Letterman, repeatedly breaking into his home, sleeping on his tennis court, and on one occasion stealing his car. Her delusion first came to light in 1988 when she was arrested while driving Letterman's car at the entrance to the Lincoln Tunnel in New York City. When she was unable to pay the toll, she identified herself as Letterman's wife and her son as his son. Over the next decade, she was arrested repeatedly for trespassing and was forced to spend a total of 10 months in prison and 14 months in a state hospital. Newspaper accounts usually described her exploits in a lighthearted way, and readers generally considered her to be a strange and comical character.

Not until Ms. Ray killed herself did most people become aware of just how disturbed she was. In fact, two of her three brothers had also suffered from schizophrenia and killed themselves years earlier. Her adult life consisted of sudden trips across the country, strange ideas, and impulsive and erratic behavior that extended well beyond her focus on Letterman. Her surviving brother remembers times when she spoke in sentences that made no sense and warm days when she wore three layers of clothing (Bruni, 1998). Medications often

A weary Margaret Ray faces charges of stalking in 1997.

seemed to help her, but she usually stopped taking them outside of prison or the state hospital.

Letterman himself recognized the seriousness of Ms. Ray's problem and grappled with how best to handle things. He rarely talked about her, never mentioned her name on the air, and often declined to press charges against her. After her death, he recalled that she had sent him many letters between her uninvited house visits, and it had been apparent in each letter whether she was taking her medications (Bruni, 1998). "When she was on them, it was like hearing from your aunt. When she was off them, it was like hearing from your aunt on Neptune." On the day after her death, he observed, "This is a sad end to a confused life."

between substance-related disorders and suicide is not clear. Perhaps the tragic lifestyle of many persons with these disorders or their sense of being hopelessly trapped by a substance leads to suicidal thinking. Alternatively, a third factor—psychological pain, for instance, or desperation—may cause both substance abuse and suicidal thinking (Frances & Franklin, 1988). Such people may be caught in a downward spiral: they are driven toward substance use by psychological pain or loss, only to find themselves caught in a pattern of substance abuse that aggravates rather than solves their problems (Maris, 2001; Downey, 1991).

People with schizophrenia, as we shall see in Chapter 12, may hear voices that are not actually present (hallucinations) or hold beliefs that are clearly false and perhaps bizarre (delusions). There is a popular notion that when such persons kill themselves, they must be responding to an imagined voice commanding them to do so or to a delusion that suicide is a grand and noble gesture. Research indicates, however, that suicides by people with schizophrenia more often reflect feelings of *demoralization* or the like (Kim et al., 2003; Reid, 1998). For example, many young and unemployed sufferers who have had relapses over several years come to believe that the disorder will forever disrupt their lives. Still others seem to be disheartened by their unfortunate, sometimes dreadful, living conditions. Suicide is the leading cause of premature death in this population (Raymont, 2001; Tsuang et al., 1999).

Modeling: The Contagion of Suicide

It is not unusual for people, particularly teenagers, to try to commit suicide after observing or reading about someone else who has done so (Hanson et al., 2002; Wertheimer, 2001). Perhaps these people have been struggling with major problems and the other person's suicide seems to reveal a possible solution; or they have been thinking about suicide and the other person's suicide seems to give them permission or finally persuades them to act. Either way, one suicidal act apparently serves as a *model* for another. Suicides by celebrities, other highly publicized suicides, and suicides by co-workers are particularly common triggers.

CELEBRITIES When the researcher Steven Stack (1987) analyzed U.S. suicide data spanning 1948 to 1983, he found that suicides by entertainers and political figures are regularly followed by unusual increases in the number of suicides across the nation. During the week after the suicide of Marilyn Monroe in 1963, for example, the national suicide rate rose 12 percent (Phillips, 1974).

OTHER HIGHLY PUBLICIZED CASES Suicides with bizarre or unusual aspects often receive special coverage by the news media (Wertheimer, 2001). Such highly publicized accounts may lead to similar suicides (Gould, 2001). During the year after a widely publicized, politically motivated suicide by self-burning in England, for example, 82 other people set themselves on fire, with equally fatal results (Ashton & Donnan, 1981). Inquest reports revealed that most of those people had histories of emotional problems and that none of the suicides had the political motivation of the publicized suicide. The imitators seemed to be responding to their own problems in a manner triggered by the suicide they had observed or read about.

Some clinicians argue that more responsible reporting could reduce this frightening impact of highly publicized suicides (Gould, 2001; Wertheimer et al., 2001). A careful approach to reporting was seen in the media's coverage of the suicide of Kurt Cobain. MTV's repeated theme on the evening of the suicide was "Don't do it!" In fact, thousands of young people called MTV and other radio and television stations in the hours after Cobain's death, upset, frightened, and in some cases suicidal. Some of the stations responded by posting the phone numbers of suicide prevention centers, presenting interviews with suicide experts, and offering counseling services and advice directly to callers. Perhaps because of such efforts, the usual rate of suicide both in Seattle, Cobain's hometown, and elsewhere held steady during the weeks that followed (Colburn, 1996).

CO-WORKERS The word-of-mouth publicity that follows suicides in a school, workplace, or small community may trigger suicide attempts. The suicide of a recruit at a U.S. Navy training school, for example, was followed within two weeks by another and also by an attempted suicide at the school. To head off what threatened to become a suicide epidemic, the school began a program of staff

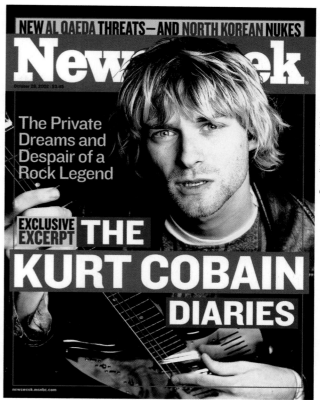

Retrospective analysis *Efforts to find the reasons behind rock star Kurt Cobain's suicide have continued since the day of his death in 1994. This search was given new energy in 2002 with the publication of his personal diaries—800 pages written over several years—which include Cobain's descriptions of his thoughts and concerns, bouts with depression, and drug addiction.*

>>**LOOKING AROUND**
Copycat Suicides

In 1999 a character in the popular British medical television show *Casualty* intentionally killed himself by overdosing on a drug. During the two weeks after the episode was aired, the number of attempted suicides in England rose 17 percent, most of them involving the same method (O'Connor et al., 1999).<<

Multiple risks *People who experience multiple suicide factors are at particular risk for self-destruction (Wunderlich et al., 1998). The actor Herve Villechaize (right) killed himself after losing his lucrative role in the television series* Fantasy Island *and also developing a chronic, painful medical condition.*

education on suicide and group therapy sessions for recruits who had been close to the suicide victims (Grigg, 1988). The kinds of post-suicide programs put into action by this school and by MTV in the aftermath of Kurt Cobain's death are often referred to by clinicians as *postvention.*

> **SUMMING UP** | **What Triggers a Suicide?**
>
> Many suicidal acts are triggered by the current events or conditions in a person's life. The act may be triggered by a recent stressor, such as loss of a loved one or of a job, or by a long-term stressor, such as serious illness, an abusive environment, or job stress. It may also be preceded by a change in mood or thought, particularly an increase in one's sense of hopelessness. In addition, the use of alcohol or other substances, a mental disorder, or news of another's suicide may precede a suicide attempt.

What Are the Underlying Causes of Suicide?

Most people faced with difficult situations never try to kill themselves. In an effort to understand why some people are more prone to suicide than others, theorists have proposed more basic explanations for self-destructive action than the immediate triggers considered in the previous section. The leading theories come from the psychodynamic, sociocultural, and biological perspectives. As a group, however, these explanations have received limited research support and fail to address the full range of suicidal acts. Thus the clinical field currently lacks a satisfactory understanding of suicide.

The Psychodynamic View

Many psychodynamic theorists believe that suicide results from depression and from anger at others that is redirected toward oneself. This theory was first stated by Wilhelm Stekel at a meeting in Vienna in 1910, when he proclaimed that "no one kills himself who has not wanted to kill another or at least wished the death of another" (Shneidman, 1979). Agreeing with this notion, the famous psychodynamic theorist Karl Menninger later called suicide "murder in the 180th degree."

As we saw in Chapter 7, Freud (1917) and Abraham (1916, 1911) proposed that when people experience the real or symbolic loss of a loved one, they unconsciously incorporate the lost person into their own identity and feel toward themselves as they had felt toward the other. For a short while, negative feelings toward the lost loved one are experienced as self-hatred. Anger toward the loved one may turn into intense anger against oneself and finally into depression. Suicide is thought to be an extreme expression of this self-hatred. The following description of a suicidal patient demonstrates how such forces may operate:

> A 27-year-old conscientious and responsible woman took a knife to her wrists to punish herself for being tyrannical, unreliable, self-centered, and abusive. She was perplexed and frightened by this uncharacteristic self-destructive episode and was enormously relieved when her therapist pointed out that her invective described her recently deceased father much better than it did herself.
>
> *(Gill, 1982, p. 15)*

In support of Freud's view, researchers have often found a relationship between childhood losses—real or symbolic—and later suicidal behaviors (Read et al., 2001;

>>PSYCH•NOTES

The Heavy Metal Link

Research finds that fans of heavy metal rock consider suicide more acceptable than do people who are not fans (Stack, 1998). But this attitude does not seem to result from the music or the lifestyle it espouses. Rather, heavy metal fans tend to be low in religiosity, and low religiosity relates to greater acceptability of suicide. Those fans who are religious rate suicide just as unacceptable as nonfans do.<<

Kaslow et al., 1998). One study of 200 family histories found that the early loss of a parent was much more common among suicide attempters (48 percent) than among nonsuicidal control subjects (24 percent) (Adam et al., 1982). Common forms of loss were death of the father and divorce or separation of the parents.

Late in his career, Freud proposed that human beings have a basic "death instinct." He called this instinct *Thanatos*, and said that it opposes the "life instinct." According to Freud, while most people learn to redirect their death instinct, by aiming it toward others, suicidal people, caught in a web of self-anger, direct it squarely upon themselves.

Sociological findings are consistent with this explanation of suicide. National suicide rates have been found to drop in times of war (Maris, 2001), when, one could argue, people are encouraged to direct their self-destructive energy against "the enemy." In addition, societies with high rates of homicide tend to have low rates of suicide, and vice versa (Somasundaram & Rajadurai, 1995). However, research has failed to establish that suicidal people are in fact overrun by feelings of anger. Although hostility is an important element in some suicides, several studies find that other emotional states are even more common (Castrogiovanni et al., 1998).

By the end of his career, Freud himself expressed dissatisfaction with his theory of suicide. Other psychodynamic theorists have also challenged his ideas over the years, yet themes of loss and self-directed aggression generally remain at the center of today's psychodynamic explanations (Maltsberger, 1999).

The Sociocultural View

Toward the end of the nineteenth century, Emile Durkheim (1897), a sociologist, developed a broad theory of suicidal behavior. Today this theory continues to be influential. According to Durkheim, the probability of suicide is determined by how attached a person is to such social groups as the family, religious institutions, and community. The more thoroughly a person belongs, the lower the risk of suicide. Conversely, people who have poor relationships with their society are at greater risk of killing themselves. He defined several categories of suicide, including *egoistic*, *altruistic*, and *anomic* suicide.

Egoistic suicides are committed by people over whom society has little or no control. These people are not concerned with the norms or rules of society, nor are they part of the social fabric. According to Durkheim, this kind of suicide is more likely in people who are isolated, alienated, and nonreligious. The larger the number of such people living in a society, the higher that society's suicide rate.

Altruistic suicides, in contrast, are committed by people who are so well integrated into their society that they intentionally sacrifice their lives for its well-being. Soldiers who threw themselves on top of a live grenade to save others, Japanese kamikaze pilots who gave their lives in air attacks, and Buddhist monks and nuns who protested the Vietnam War by setting themselves on fire—all were committing altruistic suicide. According to Durkheim, societies that encourage altruistic deaths and deaths to preserve one's honor (as Far Eastern societies do) are likely to have higher suicide rates.

Anomic suicides, another category proposed by Durkheim, are those committed by people whose social environment fails to provide stable structures, such as family and religion, to support and give meaning to life. Such a societal condition, called *anomie* (literally, "without law"), leaves individuals without a sense of belonging. Unlike egoistic suicides, which are the acts of persons who reject their society, anomic suicides are the acts of persons who have been let down by a disorganized, inadequate, often decaying society.

Durkheim argued that when societies go through periods of anomie, their suicide rates increase. Historical trends support this claim. Periods of economic

EGOISTIC SUICIDE Suicide committed by people over whom society has little or no control, people who are not inhibited by the norms or rules of society.

ALTRUISTIC SUICIDE Suicide committed by people who intentionally sacrifice their lives for the well-being of society.

ANOMIC SUICIDE Suicide committed by individuals whose social environment fails to provide stability, thus leaving them without a sense of belonging.

John Kaplan/Media Alliance

In the service of others *According to Emile Durkheim, people who intentionally sacrifice their lives for others are committing altruistic suicide. Betsy Smith, a heart transplant recipient who was warned that she would probably die if she did not terminate her pregnancy, elected to have the baby and died giving birth.*

A CLOSER LOOK

Suicide Notes

Bill: I am sorry for causing you so much trouble. I really didn't want to and if you would have told me at the first time the truth probably both of us would be very happy now. Bill I am sorry but I can't take the life any more, I don't think there is any goodness in the world. I love you very very much and I want you to be as happy in your life as I wanted to make you. Tell your parents I am very sorry and please if you can do it don't ever let my parents know what happened.

Please, don't hate me Bill, I love you.

Mary

(LEENAARS, 1991)

Many suicides go undetected or unconfirmed because the only people who could tell us the truth are gone from the world. Many other people who commit suicide, however—an estimated 12 to 33 percent—leave notes that reveal their intentions and psychological state only hours or minutes before they died (Maris, 2001; Lester, 2000).

Each suicide note is a personal document, unique to the writer and the circumstances (Leenaars, 1989). Some are barely a single sentence; others run several pages. People who leave notes clearly wish to send a powerful message to those they leave behind (Leenaars, 1989), whether it be "a cry for help, an epitaph, or a last will and testament" (Frederick, 1969, p. 17). Most suicide notes are addressed to specific individuals.

Clinical researchers have tried to improve their understanding of suicide by studying differences between genuine and fake suicide notes, the age and sex of note writers, the grammar of notes, the type and frequency of words used, conscious and unconscious contents, handwriting, and emotional, cognitive, and motivational themes (Wertheimer, 2001; Lester & Linn, 1998; Leenaars, 1989). One important finding is that suicide notes vary significantly with age (Lester, 1998). Younger persons express more hostility toward themselves and cite more interpersonal problems in their notes; those between 40 and 49 report being unable to cope with life; those between 50 and 59 tend not to cite a reason for their suicide; and those over 60 are motivated by such problems as illness, pain, disability, and loneliness (Lester, 1998).

A number of studies have also been conducted on writings that are similar to suicide notes. For example, one team of investigators compared poems by nine poets who committed suicide to those written by nine poets who did not commit suicide (Pennebaker & Stirman, 2001). The poets who committed suicide used more first-person self-references in their works, such as "I" and "me," as well as more words associated with death. In addition, the poets who committed suicide used fewer communication terms (such as "talk" and "listen") in the poems

Suicide note left by Paul Bern to his wife, the famed actress Jean Harlow, in 1932.

they had written close to the time of their suicides, while the nonsuicidal poets actually increased their use of such words during this same period of time. Thus, it may be that people who are thinking about suicide tend to use language in distinct ways—ways that may eventually help clinicians identify a person's risk for suicide.

Clearly, suicide notes are "not the royal road to an easy understanding of suicidal phenomena" (Shneidman, 1973, p. 380), but in combination with other sources they can point clinicians and researchers in the right direction (Black, 1995).

depression may bring about some degree of anomie in a country, and national suicide rates tend to rise during such times (Maris, 2001). Periods of population change and increased immigration, too, tend to bring about a state of anomie, and again suicide rates rise (Burvill, 1998; Ferrada et al., 1995).

A major change in an individual's immediate surroundings, rather than general societal problems, can also lead to anomic suicide. People who suddenly inherit a great deal of money, for example, may go through a period of anomie as their relationships with social, economic, and occupational structures are changed. Thus Durkheim predicted that societies with greater opportunities for change in individual wealth or status would have higher suicide rates, and this prediction, too, is supported by research (Cutright & Fernquist, 2001; Lester, 2000, 1985).

Although today's sociocultural theorists do not always embrace Durkheim's particular ideas, most agree that social structure and cultural stress often play major roles in suicide (Hassan, 1998). In fact, the sociocultural view pervades the study of suicide. We saw its impact earlier when we observed the many studies linking suicide to broad factors such as religious affiliation, marital status, gender, race, and societal stress. We will also see it when we consider the ties between suicide and age.

Despite the influence of sociocultural theories, they cannot by themselves explain why some people who experience particular societal pressures commit suicide whereas the majority do not. Durkheim himself concluded that the final explanation probably lies in the interaction between societal and individual factors.

The Biological View

For years biological researchers relied largely on family pedigree studies to support their position that biological factors contribute to suicidal behavior. They have repeatedly found higher rates of suicide among the parents and close relatives of suicidal people than among those of nonsuicidal people (Maris, 2001; Brent et al., 1998, 1996). Such findings may suggest that genetic, and so biological, factors are at work.

Studies of twins also have supported this view of suicide. Researchers who studied twins born in Denmark between 1870 and 1920, for example, located 19 identical pairs and 58 fraternal pairs in which at least one twin had committed suicide (Juel-Nielsen & Videbech, 1970). In four of the identical pairs the other twin also committed suicide (21 percent), while none of the other twins among the fraternal pairs had done so.

As with all family and twin research, there are nonbiological interpretations for these findings as well (Maris, 2001). Psychodynamic clinicians might argue that children whose close relatives commit suicide are prone to depression and suicide because they have lost a loved one at a critical stage of development. Behavioral theorists might emphasize the modeling role played by parents or close relatives who attempt suicide.

In the past two decades, laboratory research has offered more direct support for a biological view of suicide. The activity level of the neurotransmitter *serotonin* has often been found to be low in people who commit suicide (Oquendo et al., 2003; Mann et al., 2001, 1999). An early hint of this relationship came from a study by the psychiatric researcher Marie Asberg and her colleagues (1976). They studied 68 depressed patients and found that 20 of the patients had particularly low levels of serotonin activity. It turned out that 40 percent of the low-serotonin people attempted suicide, compared with 15 percent of the higher-serotonin subjects. The researchers interpreted this to mean that low serotonin activity may be "a predictor of suicidal acts." Later studies found that suicide attempters with low serotonin activity are 10 times more likely to make a repeat attempt and succeed than are suicide attempters with higher serotonin activity (Roy, 1992). Studies that have examined the autopsied brains of suicide victims point in the same direction (Mann & Arango, 1999; Stanley et al., 1986, 1982).

At first glance, these and related studies may appear to tell us only that depressed people often attempt suicide. After all, depression is itself related to low serotonin activity. On the other hand, there is evidence of low serotonin activity even among suicidal subjects who have no history of depression (Van Praag, 1983; Brown et al., 1982). That is, low serotonin activity seems also to have a role in suicide separate from depression.

How, then, might low serotonin activity increase the likelihood of suicidal behavior? One possibility is that it contributes to aggressive behavior. It has been found, for example, that serotonin activity is lower in aggressive men than in nonaggressive men and that serotonin activity is often low in those who commit such aggressive acts as arson and murder (Stanley et al., 2000; Bourgeois, 1991).

Murder-suicide *The lives of comedic actor Phil Hartman and his wife, Brynne, ended in 1998 when she shot him and then herself. Around 3.5 percent of suicides occur in the context of murder-suicide, usually involving spouses or lovers who have been in conflict (Stollberg et al., 2002; Nock & Marzuk, 1999).*

> **>> BY THE NUMBERS**
> Murder-Suicides
>
> **3.5%** Percentage of suicides in which someone else—a spouse, intimate friend, or relative—is murdered at the same time<<
>
> **5%** Individuals who attempt suicide soon after committing a homicide<<
>
> **20%** Persons who attempt suicide soon after killing a child<<
>
> (Stollberg et al., 2002)

Such findings suggest that low serotonin activity helps produce aggressive feelings and perhaps impulsive behavior (Mann et al., 2001). In people who are clinically depressed, low serotonin activity may produce aggressive tendencies that cause them to be particularly vulnerable to suicidal acts. Even in the absence of a depressive disorder, however, people with low serotonin activity may develop such aggressive feelings that they, too, are dangerous to themselves or to others.

SUMMING UP | What Are the Underlying Causes of Suicide?

The leading explanations for suicide come from the psychodynamic, sociocultural, and biological models. Each has received only limited support. Psychodynamic theorists believe that suicide usually results from depression and self-directed anger. Emile Durkheim's sociocultural theory defines three categories of suicide based on the person's relationship with society: egoistic, altruistic, and anomic suicides. And biological theorists suggest that the activity of the neurotransmitter serotonin is particularly low in individuals who commit suicide.

Is Suicide Linked to Age?

The likelihood of committing suicide generally increases with age, although people of all ages may try to kill themselves. Recently clinicians have paid particular attention to self-destructive behavior in three age groups: *children*, *adolescents*, and the *elderly*. Although the features and theories of suicide discussed throughout this chapter apply to all age groups, each group faces unique problems that may play key roles in the suicidal acts of its members.

Children

Although suicide is infrequent among children, it has been increasing over the past several decades (Pfeffer, 2000). Approximately 500 children under 14 years of age in the United States now commit suicide each year—around 0.9 per 100,000 in this age group, nearly 8 times the rate of 1950 (Goldman & Beardslee, 1999; Stillion & McDowell, 1996). Boys outnumber girls by as much as 5 to 1. In addition, it has been estimated that one of every 100 children tries to harm him- or herself, and many thousands of children are hospitalized each year for deliberately self-destructive acts, such as stabbing, cutting, burning, overdosing, or jumping from high places.

Researchers have found that suicide attempts by the very young are commonly preceded by such behavioral patterns as running away from home, accident-proneness, acting out, temper tantrums, self-criticism, social withdrawal and loneliness, extreme sensitivity to criticism by others, low tolerance of frustration, dark fantasies and daydreams, marked personality change, and overwhelming interest in death and suicide (Cytryn & McKnew, 1996; McGuire, 1982). Studies have further linked child suicides to the recent or upcoming loss of a loved one, family stress and parent unemployment, abuse by parents, and a clinical level of depression (Pfeffer, 2000; Goldman & Beardsley, 1999).

Most people find it hard to believe that children fully understand the meaning of a suicidal act. They argue that because a child's thinking is so limited, children who attempt suicide fall into Shneidman's category of "death ignorers," like Billy, who sought to join his mother in heaven (Fasko & Fasko, 1991). Many child suicides, however, appear to be based on a clear understanding of death and on a clear wish to die (Carlson et al., 1994; Pfeffer, 1993, 1986). In addition, suicidal thinking among even normal children is apparently more common than most people once believed (Kovacs et al., 1993; Pfeffer et al., 1984). Clinical interviews with schoolchildren have revealed that between 6 and 33 percent have thought about suicide (Culp, Clyman, & Culp, 1995; Jacobsen et al., 1994).

Adolescents

> Dear Mom, Dad, and everyone else,
>
> I'm sorry for what I've done, but I loved you all and I always will, for eternity. Please, please, please don't blame it on yourselves. It was all my fault and not yours or anyone else's. If I didn't do this now, I would have done it later anyway. We all die some day, I just died sooner.
>
> Love,
>
> John
>
> *(Berman, 1986)*

The suicide of John, age 17, was not an unusual occurrence. Suicidal actions become much more common after the age of 14 than at any earlier age. According to official records, over 2,000 teenagers, or 11 of every 100,000, commit suicide in the United States each year, although some clinicians believe the actual rate to be up to three times higher than this (Madge & Harvey, 1999). In addition, as many as 500,000 teenagers may make attempts (Popenhagen & Qualkley, 1998). Because fatal illnesses are uncommon among the young, suicide has become the third leading cause of death in this age group, after accidents and homicides. Furthermore, as many as half of all teenagers have thought about killing themselves (Goldman & Beardsley, 1999).

Although young white Americans are more prone to suicide than young African Americans, the rates of the two groups are becoming closer (Willis et al., 2002). The white American rate was 157 percent greater than the African American rate in 1980; today it is only 42 percent greater. This trend may reflect increasingly similar pressures on young African Americans and young white Americans—competition for grades and college opportunities, for example, is now intense for both groups. The growing suicide rate for young African Americans may also be linked to rising unemployment among them, the many anxieties of inner-city life, and the rage felt by many young African Americans over racial inequities in our society (Willis et al., 2002; Burr et al., 1999).

About half of teenage suicides, like those of people in other age groups, have been tied to clinical depression, low self-esteem, and feelings of hopelessness, but many teenagers who try to kill themselves also appear to struggle with anger and impulsiveness (Sheras, 2001) or to have serious alcohol or drug problems (Maris, 2001). In addition, some have deficiencies in their ability to sort out and solve problems (Brent, 2001).

Teenagers who consider or attempt suicide are often under great stress. They may experience long-term pressures such as poor (or missing) relationships with parents, family conflict, inadequate peer relationships, and social isolation (Houston et al., 2001; Sourander et al., 2001). Alternatively, their actions also may be triggered by more immediate stress, such as a parent's unemployment or medical illness, financial setbacks for the family, or problems with a boyfriend or girlfriend (Fergusson et al., 2000). Stress at school seems to be a particularly

Difficult years *The angst, confusion, conflict, and impulsivity that typically characterize adolescence provide fertile ground for the growth of suicidal thoughts and attempts.*

Jeff Isaac Greenberg/Photo Researchers

Dealing with the pain *To help address the trauma experienced by many young fans of celebrities who have recently taken their own lives, "postvention" approaches are often employed, including counseling sessions in schools and special media programs. In the days following the suicide of Nirvana's Kurt Cobain, a candlelight vigil in Seattle was attended by 5,000 people, including these two fans.*

common problem for teenagers who attempt suicide (Ho et al., 1995). Some have trouble keeping up at school, while others may be high achievers who feel pressured to be perfect and to stay at the top of the class (Delisle, 1986; Leroux, 1986).

Some theorists believe that the period of adolescence itself produces a stressful climate in which suicidal actions are more likely (Goldman & Beardsley, 1999). Adolescence is a period of rapid growth, and it is often marked by conflicts, depressed feelings, tensions, and difficulties at home and school. Adolescents tend to react to events more sensitively, angrily, dramatically, and impulsively than individuals in other age groups; thus the likelihood of suicidal acts during times of stress is increased (Taylor & Stansfeld, 1984). Finally, the suggestibility of adolescents and their eagerness to imitate others, including others who attempt suicide, may set the stage for suicidal action (Hazell & Lewin, 1993). One study found that 93 percent of adolescent suicide attempters had known someone who had attempted suicide (Conrad, 1992).

Far more teenagers attempt suicide than actually kill themselves—the ratio may be as high as 200 to 1. The unusually large number of unsuccessful suicides may mean that teenagers are less certain than older persons who make such attempts. While some do indeed wish to die, many may simply want to make others understand how desperate they are, get help, or teach others a lesson (Leenaars et al., 2001; Boergers et al., 1998). Up to half of teenage attempters make new suicide attempts in the future, and as many as 14 percent eventually die by suicide (Diekstra et al., 1995; Diekstra, 1989).

In countries around the world, the suicide rate for adolescents is not only high but increasing (Hawton et al., 2000). Overall, it has more than doubled in the past two decades, as has the rate for young adults (DeAngelis, 2001; McIntosh, 1996, 1991). Several theories, most pointing to societal changes, have been proposed to explain the dramatic rises in these two age groups. First, as the number and proportion of teenagers and young adults in the general population keep rising, the competition for jobs, college positions, and academic and athletic honors intensifies for them, leading increasingly to shattered dreams and ambitions (Holinger & Offer, 1993, 1991, 1982). Other explanations point to weakening ties in the family (which may produce feelings of alienation and rejection in many of today's young people) and to the increased availability of alcohol and other drugs and the pressure to use them among teenagers and young adults (Brent, 2001; Cutler et al., 2001).

The mass media coverage of suicide attempts by teenagers and young adults may also contribute to the rise in the suicide rate among the young (Grossman & Kruesi, 2000). The detailed descriptions of teenage suicide that the media and the arts have offered in recent years may serve as models for young people who are contemplating suicide (Wertheimer, 2001). Within days of the highly publicized suicides of four adolescents in one New Jersey town in 1987, dozens of teenagers across the United States took similar actions (at least 12 of them fatal)—two in the same garage just one week later. Similarly, a study conducted in 1986 found that the rate of adolescent suicide rose about 7 percent in New York City during the week following a television film on suicide, in contrast to a 0.5 percent increase in the adult suicide rate during the same week (Maris, 2001).

The Elderly

In Western society the elderly are more likely to commit suicide than people in any other age group. About 19 of every 100,000 persons over the age of 65 in the United States commit suicide (McIntosh, 1995, 1992). Elderly persons commit over 19 percent of all suicides in the United States, yet they account for only 12 percent of the total population (Conwell & Duberstein, 2001).

Many factors contribute to this high suicide rate (Pearson, 2000). As people grow older, all too often they become ill, lose close friends and relatives, lose control over their lives, and lose status in our society. Such experiences may result in feelings of hopelessness, loneliness, or depression among aged persons and so increase the likelihood that they will attempt suicide. In one study, 44 percent of elderly people who committed suicide gave some indication that their act was prompted by the fear of being placed in a nursing home (Loebel et al., 1991). Also, the suicide rate of elderly people who have recently lost a spouse is relatively high (Duberstein, Conwell, & Cox, 1998).

Elderly persons are typically more determined than younger persons in their decision to die and they give fewer warnings, so their success rate is much higher (DeLeo et al., 2001; Clark, 1999). Apparently one of every four elderly persons who attempts suicide succeeds. Given the determined thinking of aged persons and their physical decline, some people argue that older persons who want to die should be allowed to carry out their wishes. However, clinical depression appears to play an important role in as many as 60 percent of suicides by the elderly, suggesting that more elderly people who are suicidal should be receiving treatment for their depressive disorders (Conwell & Duberstein, 2001; Harwood et al., 2001).

The suicide rate among the elderly in the United States is lower in some minority groups (Kettl, 1998). Although Native Americans have the highest overall suicide rate, for example, the rate among elderly Native Americans is relatively low (NIH, 1999; McIntosh & Santos, 1982). The aged are held in high esteem by Native Americans and looked to for the wisdom and experience they have acquired over the years, and this may help account for their low suicide rate. Such high regard is in sharp contrast to the loss of status often experienced by elderly white Americans (Butler, 1975).

Similarly, the suicide rate is only one-third as high among elderly African Americans as among elderly white Americans (McIntosh, 1992). One reason for this low suicide rate may be the pressures faced by African Americans: "only the strongest survive" (Seiden, 1981). Those who reach an advanced age have overcome great adversity and often feel proud of what they have accomplished. Because reaching old age is not in itself a form of success for white Americans, their attitude toward aging is more negative.

The power of respect *Elderly persons are held in high esteem in many traditional societies because of the store of knowledge they have accumulated. Perhaps not so coincidentally, suicides among the elderly seem to be less common in these cultures than in those of many modern industrialized nations.*

SUMMING UP

Is Suicide Linked to Age?

The likelihood of suicide varies with age. It is uncommon among children, although it has been increasing in that group during the past several decades. Suicide by adolescents, a more common occurrence, is also on the increase. In particular, suicide attempts by this age group are numerous. Adolescent suicide has been linked to clinical depression, anger, impulsiveness, major stress, and adolescent life itself. The rising suicide rate among adolescents and young adults may be related to the growing number and proportion of young people in the general population, the weakening of family ties, the increased availability and use of drugs among the young, and the broad media coverage of suicide attempts by the young.

In Western society the elderly are more likely to commit suicide than people in any other age group. The loss of health, friends, control, and status may produce feelings of hopelessness, loneliness, or depression in this age group.

>>PSYCH•NOTES

Lingering Impact of Child Abuse

Adults who were sexually or physically abused in childhood harm themselves, think about suicide, and attempt suicide more than do adults without this history (Read et al., 2001; Dinwiddie et al., 2000).<<

The Right to Commit Suicide

In the fall of 1989, a Michigan doctor, Jack Kevorkian, built a "suicide device." A person using it could, at the touch of a button, change a saline solution being fed intravenously into the arm to one containing chemicals that would bring unconsciousness and a swift death. The following June, under the doctor's supervision, Mrs. J. Adkins took her life. She left a note explaining: "This is a decision taken in a normal state of mind and is fully considered. I have Alzheimer's disease and I do not want to let it progress any further. I do not want to put my family or myself through the agony of this terrible disease." Mrs. Adkins believed that she had a right to choose death. Michigan authorities promptly prohibited further use of Kevorkian's device, but the physician continued to assist in the suicides of medically ill persons throughout the 1990s until his conviction in 1999 for second-degree murder in one case.

(ADAPTED FROM BELKIN, 1990; MALCOLM, 1990)

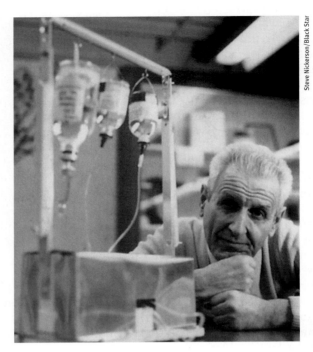

Dr. Jack Kevorkian and his suicide device.

Do individuals have a right to commit suicide, or does society have the right to stop them? Dr. Kevorkian's court battles have made many people ask just that.

The ancient Greeks valued physical and mental well-being in life and dignity in death. Therefore, individuals with a grave illness or mental anguish were permitted to commit suicide. Citizens could obtain official permission from the Senate to take their own lives, and judges were allowed to give them hemlock (Humphry & Wickett, 1986).

Western traditions, in contrast, discourage suicide, on the basis of belief in the "sanctity of life" (Eser, 1981). We speak of "committing" suicide, as though it were a criminal act (Wertheimer, 2001; Barrington, 1980), and we allow the state to use force, including involuntary commitment to a mental hospital, to prevent it. But times and attitudes are changing. Today the ideas of a "right to suicide" and "rational suicide" are receiving more support from the public, psychotherapists, and physicians (Leenaars et al., 2001). In fact, surveys suggest that half of today's physicians believe that

suicide can be rational in some circumstances (Ganzini et al., 2000; Duberstein et al., 1995).

Public support for a right to suicide seems strongest in connection with great pain and terminal illness (Werth, 2000, 1999, 1996). Studies show that about half or more of all Americans believe that terminally ill persons should be free to take their lives or to seek a physician's assistance to do so (Duberstein et al., 1995). In line with this belief, the state of Oregon in 1997 passed the "Death with Dignity" Act, allowing a doctor to assist a suicide (by administering a lethal dose of drugs) if two physicians determine that the patient has less than six months to live and is not basing the decision to die on depression or another mental disorder. Other states are currently considering similar laws.

Critics of this law and of the right to suicide movement point out that the suicidal acts of patients with severe or fatal illnesses do indeed often spring largely from psychological distress (Foley & Hendin, 2002; Akechi et al., 2001). A number of studies suggest that half or more of severely ill patients who are suicidal may be clinically depressed (Chochinov & Schwartz, 2002). Thus, in some cases, it may be more beneficial to help individuals come to terms with a fa-

tal illness than to offer them a license to end their lives.

Some clinicians also worry that the right to suicide could be experienced more as a "duty to die" than as the ultimate freedom (Foley & Hendin, 2003; Brock, 2001). Elderly people might feel selfish in expecting relatives to support and care for them when suicide is a socially approved alternative (Sherlock, 1983). Moreover, as care for the terminally ill grows ever more costly, might suicide be subtly encouraged among the poor and disadvantaged? Could assisted suicide become a form of medical cost control (Brock, 2001)? In the Netherlands, where physician-assisted suicide and euthanasia were approved by law in 2001 after years of informal acceptance, euthanasia is clearly on the increase. Around 2.6 percent of all deaths in that country are now the result of physician-assisted suicide and voluntary euthanasia (Hendin, 2002). In fact, almost 1 percent of deaths are the result of involuntary euthanasia.

How are these issues to be resolved? Understanding and preventing suicide remain challenges for the future, and so do questions about whether and when we should stand back and do nothing. Whatever one's position on this issue, it is a matter of life and death.

Steve Nickerson/Black Star

Treatment and Suicide

Treatment of suicidal people falls into two major categories: *treatment after suicide has been attempted* and *suicide prevention*. While treatment may also be beneficial to relatives and friends, whose feelings of loss, guilt, and anger after a suicide fatality or attempt can be intense (Wertheimer, 2001; Provini et al., 2000), the discussion here is limited to the treatment afforded suicidal people themselves.

What Treatments Are Used after Suicide Attempts?

After a suicide attempt, most victims need medical care. Some are left with severe injuries, brain damage, or other medical problems. Once the physical damage is treated, psychotherapy or drug therapy may begin, on either an inpatient or outpatient basis.

Unfortunately, even after trying to kill themselves, many suicidal people fail to receive systematic psychotherapy (Beautrais et al., 2000). In a random survey of several hundred teenagers, 9 percent were found to have made at least one suicide attempt, and of those only half had received later psychological treatment (Harkavy & Asnis, 1985). Similarly, in another study, one-third of adolescent attempters reported that they had not received any help after trying to end their lives (Larsson & Ivarsson, 1998). In some cases, health care professionals are at fault. In others, the person who has attempted suicide refuses follow-up therapy (Piacentini et al., 1995).

The goals of therapy are to keep people alive, help them achieve a nonsuicidal state of mind, and guide them to develop better ways of handling stress (Shneidman, 2001, 1999, 1993). Various therapies have been employed, including drug, psychodynamic, cognitive, group, and family therapies (Hawton, 2001; Rudd et al., 2001). Treatment appears to help. Studies have found that 30 percent of suicide attempters who do not receive treatment try again, compared with 16 percent of patients in treatment (Nordstrom et al., 1995; Allard et al., 1991). It is not clear, however, whether any one approach is more effective than the others (Canetto, 1995).

What Is Suicide Prevention?

During the past 35 years, emphasis around the world has shifted from suicide treatment to suicide prevention (Palmer, 2002). In some respects this change is most appropriate: the last opportunity to keep many potential suicide victims alive comes before the first attempt.

The first **suicide prevention program** in the United States was founded in Los Angeles in 1955; the first in England, called the *Samaritans*, was started in 1953. There are now hundreds of suicide prevention centers in the United States and in England. In addition, many of today's mental health centers, hospital emergency rooms, pastoral counseling centers, and poison control centers include suicide prevention programs among their services (Dorwart & Ostacher, 1999).

There are also hundreds of *suicide hot lines* in the United States, 24-hour-a-day telephone services. Callers reach a counselor, typically a *paraprofessional*, a person trained in counseling but without a formal degree, who provides services under the supervision of a mental health professional (Neimeyer & Bonnelle, 1997).

Suicide prevention programs and hot lines respond to suicidal people as individuals *in crisis*—that is, under great stress, unable to cope, feeling threatened or hurt, and interpreting their situations as unchangeable. Thus the programs offer **crisis intervention**: they try to help suicidal people see their situations more accurately, make better decisions, act more constructively, and overcome their crises (Frankish, 1994). Because crises can occur at any time, the centers advertise their hot lines and also welcome people who walk in without appointments.

Although specific features vary from center to center, the general approach used by the Los Angeles Suicide Prevention Center reflects the goals and techniques of

---

SUICIDE PREVENTION PROGRAM A program that tries to identify people who are at risk of killing themselves and to offer them crisis intervention.

CRISIS INTERVENTION A treatment approach that tries to help people in a psychological crisis to view their situation more accurately, make better decisions, act more constructively, and overcome the crisis.

≫BY THE NUMBERS
Doctor Visits

83% Percentage of suicide victims who had seen a family doctor in the previous year, typically for vague physical symptoms≪

66% Those who had visited a doctor in the previous month≪

40% Those who had seen a doctor in the previous week≪

20% Those who had visited a doctor within the past day≪

(Pirkis & Burgess, 1998; Hirschfeld & Russell, 1997)

many such organizations (Jacobs, 1999; Litman, 1995). During the initial contact, the counselor has several tasks (Shneidman & Farberow, 1968):

Establishing a positive relationship As callers must trust counselors in order to confide in them and follow their suggestions, counselors try to set a positive and comfortable tone for the discussion. They give the message that they are listening, understanding, interested, nonjudgmental, and available.

Understanding and clarifying the problem Counselors first try to understand the full scope of the caller's crisis and then help the person see the crisis in clear and constructive terms. In particular, they try to help callers see the central issues and the short-term nature of their crises and recognize the alternatives to suicide.

Assessing suicide potential Crisis workers at the Los Angeles Suicide Prevention Center fill out a questionnaire, often called a *lethality scale*, to estimate the caller's potential for suicide. It helps them determine the degree of stress the caller is under, relevant personality characteristics, how detailed the suicide plan is, the severity of symptoms, and the coping resources available to the caller.

Assessing and mobilizing the caller's resources Although they may view themselves as ineffective and helpless, people who are suicidal usually have many strengths and resources, including relatives and friends. It is the counselor's job to recognize, point out, and mobilize those resources.

Formulating a plan Together the crisis worker and caller develop a plan of action. In essence, they are agreeing on a way out of the crisis, an alternative to suicidal action. Most plans include a series of follow-up counseling sessions over the next few days or weeks, either in person at the center or by phone. Each plan also requires the caller to take certain actions and make certain changes in his or her personal life. Counselors usually negotiate a *no-suicide contract* with the caller—a promise not to attempt suicide, or at least a promise to reestablish contact if the caller again considers suicide. Although such contracts are popular, their usefulness been called into question in recent years (Miller et al., 1998). In addition, if callers are in the midst of a suicide attempt, counselors will try to find out their whereabouts and get medical help to them immediately.

Although crisis intervention appears to be sufficient treatment for some suicidal people, longer-term therapy is needed for most (Stolberg et al., 2002; Rudd, 2000). If the crisis intervention center does not offer this kind of therapy, the counselors will refer the clients elsewhere.

As the suicide prevention movement spread during the 1960s, many clinicians came to believe that crisis intervention techniques should also be applied to problems other than suicide. Crisis intervention has emerged during the past three decades as a respected form of treatment for such wide-ranging problems as teenage confusion, drug and alcohol abuse, rape victimization, and spouse abuse.

Do Suicide Prevention Programs Work?

It is difficult for researchers to measure the effectiveness of suicide prevention programs (Reisch, Schlatter, & Tschacher, 1999; Goldney, 1998). There are many kinds of programs, each with its own procedures and serving populations that vary in number, age, and the like. Communities with high suicide risk factors, such as a high elderly population or economic problems, may continue to have higher suicide rates than other communities regardless of the effectiveness of their local prevention centers.

Do suicide prevention centers reduce the number of suicides in a community? Clinical researchers do not know (Dorwart & Ostacher, 1999; Canetto, 1995). Studies comparing local suicide rates before and after the establishment of community prevention centers have yielded different findings. Some find a decline in a

Mass suicide *In 1997 the world was shocked to learn of the bizarre beliefs held by the Heaven's Gate cult when 39 of its members committed suicide in a suburban San Diego house. Influenced by the cult's leader, Marshall Herff Applewhite (above), the members believed that their bodies were "containers" for higher heavenly spirits and that their deaths would free them to fly to a higher kingdom on a UFO.*

≫PSYCH•LISTINGS

Famous Mass Suicides

AD 72–73 960 Jews commit suicide at Masada‹‹

1978 911 cult members die in Jonestown, Guyana (some were murdered)‹‹

1994 48 Swiss suicides-murders take place in the Order of the Solar Tradition‹‹

1997 39 members of the Heaven's Gate cult commit suicide in San Diego, California‹‹

(Maris, 2001)

community's suicide rates, others no change, and still others an increase (Lester, 1997, 1991, 1974; Dew et al., 1987). Of course, even an increase may represent a positive impact, if it is lower than the larger society's overall increase in suicidal behavior.

Do suicidal people contact prevention centers? Apparently only a small percentage do. Moreover, the typical caller to an urban prevention center appears to be young, African American, and female, whereas the greatest number of suicides are committed by older white men (Maris, 2001; Canetto, 1995; Lester, 2000, 1989, 1972). A key problem is that people who are suicidal do not necessarily admit or talk about their feelings in discussions with others, even with professionals (Stolberg et al., 2002).

Prevention programs do seem to reduce the number of suicides among those high-risk people who do call. One study identified 8,000 high-risk individuals who contacted the Los Angeles Suicide Prevention Center (Farberow & Litman, 1970). Approximately 2 percent of these callers later committed suicide, compared to the 6 percent suicide rate usually found in similar high-risk groups. Clearly, centers need to be more visible and available to people who are thinking of suicide. The growing number of advertisements and announcements in newspapers and on television, radio, and billboards indicates a movement in this direction.

Several theorists have called for more effective public education about suicide as the ultimate form of prevention, and at least some *suicide education* programs—most of them concentrating on teachers and students—have begun to emerge (Kalafat & Ryerson, 1999; Mauk & Sharpnack, 1998). The curriculum for such programs has been the subject of much debate (Dorwart & Ostacher, 1999), but clinicians typically agree with the goals behind them and, more generally, with Shneidman when he states:

> The primary prevention of suicide lies in education. The route is through teaching one another and . . . the public that suicide can happen to anyone, that there are verbal and behavioral clues that can be looked for . . ., and that help is available. . . .
> In the last analysis, the prevention of suicide is everybody's business.
>
> *(Shneidman, 1985, p. 238)*

Working with suicide *An individual breaks free from police and falls from a bridge in New York City. The scene reminds us that many kinds of professionals face suicidal behavior. Police departments typically provide special crisis intervention training so that officers can develop the skills to address suicidal individuals.*

Rob Sollett/Staten Island Advance

SUMMING UP

Treatment and Suicide

Treatment may follow a suicide attempt. In such cases, therapists seek to help the person achieve a nonsuicidal state of mind and develop better ways of handling stress and solving problems.

Over the past 35 years, emphasis has shifted to suicide prevention. Suicide prevention programs include 24-hour-a-day hot lines and walk-in centers staffed largely by paraprofessionals who follow a crisis interventiion model. Beyond the initial assessment and intervention, most suicidal people also need longer-term therapy. In a still broader attempt at prevention, suicide education programs for the public are on the increase.

>>PSYCH•NOTES

Clinical Encounters

Suicide is the most common clinical emergency encountered in mental health practice (Stolberg et al., 2002; Beutler et al., 2000).<<

- -

Suicidal behavior or thinking is the most common reason for admission to a mental hospital. Around two-thirds of patients who are admitted have aroused concern that they will harm themselves (Jacobson, 1999).<<

- -

Half of all psychiatrists and 20 percent of all psychologists lose a patient to suicide at some point in their career (Bongar et al., 1992).<<

CROSSROADS:
Psychological and Biological Insights Lag Behind

>>**PSYCH•NOTES**

Suicide Trends

Holiday Effects Studies in Europe indicate that suicide rates tend to drop before Christmas and Easter but then increase after those holidays (Jessen et al., 1999).<<

Most Common Killings More suicides (31,000) than homicides (23,000) are committed in the United States each year.<<

Once a mysterious and hidden problem, hardly acknowledged by the public and barely investigated by professionals, suicide today is the focus of much attention. During the past 30 years in particular, investigators have learned a great deal about this life-or-death problem.

In contrast to most other problems covered in this textbook, suicide has received much more examination from the sociocultural model than from any other (Aldridge, 1998). Sociocultural theorists have, for example, highlighted the importance of societal change and stress, national and religious affiliation, marital status, gender, race, and the mass media. The insights and information gathered by psychological and biological researchers have been more limited.

Although sociocultural factors certainly shed light on the general background and triggers of suicide, they typically leave us unable to predict that a given person will attempt suicide. When all is said and done, clinicians do not yet fully understand why some people kill themselves while others in similar circumstances manage to find better ways of dealing with their problems. Psychological and biological insights must catch up to the sociocultural insights if clinicians are truly to explain and understand suicide.

Treatments for suicide also pose some difficult problems. Clinicians have yet to develop clearly successful therapies for suicidal persons. Although suicide prevention programs certainly show the clinical field's commitment to helping people who are suicidal, it is not yet clear how much such programs actually reduce the overall risk or rate of suicide.

At the same time, the growth in the amount of research on suicide offers great promise. And perhaps most promising of all, clinicians are now enlisting the public in the fight against this problem. They are calling for broader public education about suicide—programs aimed at both young and old. It is reasonable to expect that the current commitment will lead to a better understanding of suicide and to more successful interventions. Such goals are of importance to everyone. Although suicide itself is typically a lonely and desperate act, the impact of such acts is very broad indeed.

CRITICAL THOUGHTS

1. As we observed in the case of Margaux Hemingway and Ernest Hemingway, suicide sometimes runs in families. Why might this be the case? *p. 231*

2. Suicide rates vary widely from country to country. What factors besides religion might help account for the differences? *pp. 231–232*

3. Often people view the suicide of an elderly or chronically sick person as less tragic than that of a young or healthy person. Why might they think this way, and is their reasoning valid? *pp. 234, 244–246*

4. Why do people tend to overlook or dismiss the psychological pain of people with bizarre ideas or erratic behaviors, such as those of Margaret Ray? How might such oversights contribute to the suffering or symptoms of such individuals? *p. 236*

5. A person's wish to die is often ambivalent. In addition, most people who think about suicide do not act. How, then, should clinicians decide whether to hospitalize a person who is considering suicide or even one who has made an attempt? *pp. 247–249*

KEY TERMS

parasuicide p. 228

suicide p. 228

death seeker p. 230

death initiator p. 230

death ignorer p. 230

death darer p. 230

subintentional death p. 230

retrospective analysis p. 230

hopelessness p. 234

dichotomous thinking p. 234

postvention p. 238

Thanatos p. 239

egoistic suicide p. 239

altruistic suicide p. 239

anomic suicide p. 239

serotonin p. 241

suicide prevention program p. 247

suicide hot line p. 247

paraprofessional p. 247

crisis intervention p. 247

suicide education progam p. 249

QUICK QUIZ

1. Define suicide and subintentional death. Describe four kinds of people who attempt suicide. *pp. 228–230*

2. What techniques do researchers use to study suicide? *pp. 230–231*

3. How do statistics on suicide vary by country, religion, gender, marital status, and race? *pp. 231–232*

4. What kinds of immediate and long-term stressors have been linked to suicide? *pp. 233–234*

5. What other conditions or events may help trigger suicidal acts? *pp. 234–238*

6. How do psychodynamic, sociocultural, and biological theorists explain suicide, and how well supported are their theories? *pp. 238–242*

7. Compare the risk, rate, and causes of suicide among children, adolescents, and elderly persons. *pp. 242–245*

8. How do theorists explain the increase in suicide attempts by adolescents and young adults? *pp. 243–244*

9. Describe the nature and goals of treatment given to people after they have attempted suicide. Do such people often receive this treatment? *p. 247*

10. Describe the principles of suicide prevention programs. What procedures are employed by counselors in these programs? How effective are the programs? *pp. 247–249*

CYBER STUDY

SEARCH THE *FUNDAMENTALS OF ABNORMAL PSYCHOLOGY* CD-ROM FOR

▲ Chapter 8 Video Case Enrichment
   Observe the behaviors, thought processes, and feelings of suicidal persons.
   What are the reactions of family members after an individual's suicide?
   What roles might weapon availability or other variables play in suicide?

▲ Chapter 8 Practical, Research, and Decision-Making Exercises
   Suicidal risk and intervention

▲ Chapter 8 Practice Test and Feedback

LOG ON TO THE COMER WEB PAGE FOR

▲ Suggested Web links, exercises, FAQ page, additional Chapter 8 practice test questions
   <www.worthpublishers.com/comer>

‹‹‹

MARLENA ZUBER, 2001

Eating Disorders

Janet Caldwell was . . . five feet, two inches tall and weighed 62 pounds. . . . Janet began dieting at the age of 12 when she weighed 115 pounds and was chided by her family and friends for being "pudgy." She continued to restrict her food intake over a two-year period, and as she grew thinner, her parents became increasingly more concerned about her eating behavior. . . .

Janet . . . felt that her weight problem began at the time of puberty. She said that her family and friends had supported her efforts to achieve a ten-pound weight loss when she first began dieting at age 12. Janet did not go on any special kind of diet. Instead, she restricted her food intake at meals, generally cut down on carbohydrates and protein intake, tended to eat a lot of salads, and completely stopped snacking between meals. At first, she was quite pleased with her progressive weight reduction, and she was able to ignore her feelings of hunger by remembering the weight loss goal she had set for herself. However, each time she lost the number of pounds she had set for her goal she decided to lose just a few more pounds. Therefore she continued to set new weight goals for herself. In this manner, her weight dropped from 115 pounds to 88 pounds during the first year of her weight loss regimen.

Janet felt that, in her second year of dieting, her weight loss had continued beyond her control. . . . She became convinced that there was something inside of her that would not let her gain weight. . . . Janet commented that although there had been occasions over the past few years when she had been fairly "down" or unhappy, she still felt driven to keep on dieting. As a result, she frequently went for walks, ran errands for her family, and spent a great deal of time cleaning her room and keeping it in a meticulously neat and unaltered arrangement.

When Janet's weight loss continued beyond the first year, her parents insisted that she see their family physician, and Mrs. Caldwell accompanied Janet to her appointment. Their family practitioner was quite alarmed at Janet's appearance and prescribed a high-calorie diet. Janet said that . . . she often responded to her parents' entreaties that she eat by telling them that she indeed had eaten but they had not seen her do so. She often listed foods that she said she had consumed which in fact she had flushed down the toilet. She estimated that she only was eating about 300 calories a day.

(Leon, 1984, pp. 179–184)

It has not always done so, but Western society today equates thinness with health and beauty (see Figure 9-1 on the next page). In fact, in the United States thinness has become a national obsession. Most of us are as preoccupied with how much we eat as with the taste and nutritional value of our food. Thus it is not surprising that during the past three decades we have also witnessed an increase in two eating disorders that have at their core a profound fear of gaining weight. Sufferers of *anorexia nervosa*, like Janet Caldwell, are convinced that they need to be extremely thin, and they lose so much weight that they may starve themselves to death. People with *bulimia nervosa* go on frequent eating binges, during which they uncontrollably consume large quantities of food, then force themselves to vomit or take other extreme steps to keep from gaining weight.

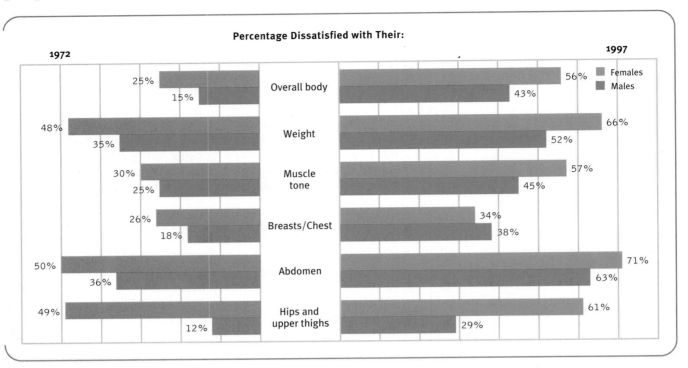

Percentage Dissatisfied with Their:

1972 / 1997

Females / Males

	1972 Females	1972 Males	1997 Females	1997 Males
Overall body	25%	15%	56%	43%
Weight	48%	35%	66%	52%
Muscle tone	30%	25%	57%	45%
Breasts/Chest	26%	18%	34%	38%
Abdomen	50%	36%	71%	63%
Hips and upper thighs	49%	12%	61%	29%

FIGURE 9-1 **Body dissatisfaction on the rise**
According to surveys on body image, people in our society are much more dissatisfied with their bodies now than they were a generation ago. Women are still more dissatisfied than men, but today's men are more dissatisfied with their bodies than the men of a generation past. (Adapted from Garner et al., 1997, p. 42; Rodin, 1992, p. 57.)

ANOREXIA NERVOSA A disorder marked by the pursuit of extreme thinness and by extreme loss of weight.

The news media have published many reports about anorexic or bulimic behavior. One reason for the surge in public interest is the frightening medical effects that can result. The death in 1983 of Karen Carpenter, a popular singer and entertainer, from medical problems related to anorexia nervosa serves as a reminder. Another reason for concern is the disproportionate prevalence of these disorders among adolescent girls and young women.

Anorexia Nervosa

Janet Caldwell, 14 years old and in the eighth grade, displays many symptoms of **anorexia nervosa**: she refuses to maintain more than 85 percent of her normal body weight, intensely fears becoming overweight, has a distorted view of her weight and shape, and has stopped menstruating (see Table 9-1 on page 256).

Like Janet, at least half of the people with anorexia nervosa reduce their weight by restricting their intake of food, a pattern called *restricting-type anorexia nervosa*. At first they tend to cut out sweets and fattening snacks and then, increasingly, other foods (APA, 2000, 1994). Eventually people with this kind of anorexia nervosa show almost no variability in diet. Others, however, lose weight by forcing themselves to vomit after meals or by abusing laxatives or diuretics, and they may even engage in eating binges, a pattern called *binge-eating/purging-type anorexia nervosa*, which we shall observe in more detail when we turn to bulimia nervosa (APA, 2000, 1994).

Approximately 90 to 95 percent of all cases of anorexia nervosa occur in females. Although the disorder can appear at any age, the peak age of onset is between 14 and 18 years (APA, 2000). Around 0.5 percent of all females in Western countries develop the disorder in their lifetime, and many more display at least some of its symptoms. It seems to be on the increase in North America, Europe, and Japan.

Typically the disorder begins after a person who is slightly overweight or of normal weight has been on a diet. The escalation toward anorexia nervosa may follow a stressful event such as separation of parents, a move away from home, or an experience of personal failure (Wilson et al., 2003; Gowers et al., 1996).

STEPPING BACK

We've Only Just Begun

Given the hard-living, substance-abusing, risk-taking image cultivated by many pop music artists, we are no longer shocked to read about the untimely death of one of them, from Elvis Presley, Jimi Hendrix, or Sid Vicious to Kurt Cobain, Tupac Shakur, or Notorious B.I.G. The 1983 death of Karen Carpenter, from the effects of anorexia nervosa, in contrast, stunned the country. Karen, the 32-year-old velvet-voiced lead singer of the soft-rock brother-and-sister duo The Carpenters, did not drink, take drugs, drive fast cars, or tear up the roadside on a motorcycle. She never appeared in the pages of the tabloids. Until her late 20s—well into her fame—she even continued to live at home with her parents and brother, Richard, in suburban Downey, California. Indeed, she and Richard were icons of unrebellious, quiet, youthful virtue.

The pressure to maintain this wholesome image may have contributed to Karen's destruction. After reading an early concert review describing her as "chubby," Karen began a downward spiral into anorexia nervosa. Always a dutiful family member and content to let others make all the decisions for their group, Karen seemed to have little control over her fame. One friend and fellow sufferer later said about Karen's eating disorder, "When you start denying yourself food, and begin feeling you have control over a life that has been pretty much controlled for you, it's exhilarating" (O'Neill, as cited in Levin, 1983).

For nine years Karen starved herself, abused laxatives and thyroid pills, and purged by repeatedly swallowing drugs that induce vomiting. Her weight dropped from a high of 140 pounds at the beginning of her singing career to a devastating low of 80 pounds. Ironically, in the last year of her life, it looked as though she had gotten a handle on her disorder. She had increased her weight to an almost-normal 108 pounds after a year of therapy. Yet on a visit home to her parents' house in California, on February 4, 1983, she collapsed. Paramedics could not revive her, and she died an hour later of cardiac arrest. Traces of a vomiting-inducing drug were found in her bloodstream.

Until Karen's death, the public knew little about anorexia nervosa, and what it knew did not sound serious—more like the latest celebrity fad diet than a dangerous, potentially fatal condition. But that lighthearted view changed dramatically with her death, as scores of articles in newspapers and magazines detailed not only the tragically short life of Karen Carpenter but also the disease that killed her. Anorexia nervosa was no longer something to be taken casually.

Although most victims recover, between 2 and 6 percent of them become so seriously ill that they die, usually from medical problems brought about by starvation or from suicide (Nielsen et al., 1998; Slade, 1995).

The Clinical Picture

Becoming thin is the key goal for people with anorexia nervosa, but fear provides their motivation (Russell, 1995). People with this disorder are afraid of becoming obese, of giving in to their growing desire to eat, and more generally of losing control over the size and shape of their bodies. In addition, despite their focus on thinness and the severe restrictions they may place on their food intake, people with anorexia are *preoccupied with food*. They may spend considerable time thinking and even reading about food and planning their limited meals (King, Polivy, & Herman, 1991). Many report that their dreams are filled with images of food and eating (Frayn, 1991; Levitan, 1981).

Laboratory starvation *Thirty-six conscientious objectors who were put on a semistarvation diet for six months developed many of the symptoms seen in anorexia nervosa and bulimia nervosa (Keys et al., 1950).*

Table **9-1** DSM-IV Checklist

ANOREXIA NERVOSA

1. Refusal to maintain body weight above a minimally normal weight for age and height.
2. Intense fear of gaining weight, even though underweight.
3. Disturbed body perception, undue influence of weight or shape on self-evaluation, or denial of the seriousness of the current low weight.
4. In postmenarcheal females, amenorrhea.

Based on APA, 2000, 1994.

This preoccupation with food may in fact be a result of food deprivation rather than its cause. In a famous "starvation study" conducted in the late 1940s, 36 normal-weight conscientious objectors were put on a semistarvation diet for six months (Keys et al., 1950). Like people with anorexia nervosa, the volunteers became preoccupied with food and eating. They spent hours each day planning their small meals, talked more about food than about any other topic, studied cookbooks and recipes, mixed food in odd combinations, and dawdled over their meals. Many also had vivid dreams about food.

Persons with anorexia nervosa also *think in distorted ways*. They usually have a low opinion of their body shape, for example, and consider themselves unattractive (Kaye et al., 2002). In addition, they are likely to overestimate their actual proportions. While most women in Western society overestimate their body size, the estimates of those with anorexia nervosa are particularly high. A 23-year-old patient said:

I look in a full-length mirror at least four or five times daily and I really cannot see myself as too thin. Sometimes after several days of strict dieting, I feel that my shape is tolerable, but most of the time, odd as it may seem, I look in the mirror and believe that I am too fat.

(Bruch, 1973)

This tendency to overestimate body size has been tested in the laboratory (Rushford & Ostermeyer, 1997). In a popular assessment technique, subjects look at a photograph of themselves through an adjustable lens. They are asked to adjust the lens until the image that they see matches their actual body size. The image can be made to vary from 20 percent thinner to 20 percent larger than actual appearance. In one study, more than half of the subjects with anorexia nervosa were found to overestimate their body size, stopping the lens when the image was larger than they actually were.

The distorted thinking of anorexia nervosa also takes the form of certain maladaptive attitudes and misperceptions (Wilson et al., 2003; Garner & Bemis, 1985, 1982). Sufferers tend to hold such beliefs as "I must be perfect in every way"; "I will become a better person if I deprive myself"; and "I can avoid guilt by not eating."

People with anorexia nervosa also display certain *psychological problems*, such as at least mild depression and anxiety and low self-esteem (O'Brien & Vincent, 2003; Flament et al., 2001). Some also experience insomnia or other sleep disturbances. A number grapple with substance abuse. And many display obsessive-compulsive patterns. They may set rigid rules for food preparation or even cut food into specific shapes. Broader obsessive-compulsive patterns are common as well (Milos et al., 2002; Shafran, 2002). In one study, people with anorexia nervosa and others with obsessive-compulsive disorder scored equally high for obsessiveness and compulsiveness (Bastiani et al., 1996). Finally, persons with anorexia nervosa tend to be perfectionistic, a characteristic that typically precedes the onset of the disorder (Shafran, Cooper, & Fairburn, 2002).

Medical Problems

The starvation habits of anorexia nervosa cause medical problems (Vestergaard et al., 2002; Mickley, 2001). Women develop **amenorrhea**, the absence of menstrual cycles. Other problems include lowered body temperature, low blood pressure, body swelling, reduced bone mineral density, and slow heart rate. Metabolic and electrolyte imbalances also may occur and can lead to death by heart failure or circulatory collapse (Froelich et al., 2001). The poor nutrition of people with anorexia nervosa may also cause their skin to become rough, dry, and cracked; nails to become brittle; and hands and feet to be cold and blue. Some people lose hair from the scalp and some grow *lanugo* (the fine, silky hair that covers some newborns) on their trunk, extremities, and face.

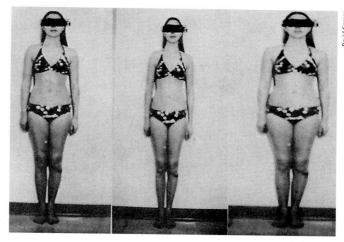

David Garner

Seeing is deceiving *In one research technique, people look at photographs of themselves through a special lens and adjust the lens until they see what they believe is their actual image. A subject may change her actual image (left) from 20 percent thinner (middle) to 20 percent larger (right).*

SUMMING UP
Anorexia Nervosa

Rates of eating disorders have increased dramatically as thinness has become a national obsession. People with anorexia nervosa pursue extreme thinness and lose dangerous amounts of weight. They may follow a pattern of restricting-type anorexia nervosa or binge-eating/purging-type anorexia nervosa.

The central features of anorexia nervosa are a drive for thinness, fear of weight, preoccupation with food, cognitive disturbances, psychological problems, and medical problems, including amenorrhea.

Bulimia Nervosa

People with **bulimia nervosa**—a disorder also known as **binge-purge syndrome**—engage in repeated episodes of uncontrollable overeating, or **binges**. A binge occurs over a limited period of time, often an hour, during which the person eats much more food than most people would eat during a similar time span (APA, 2000, 1994). In addition, people with this disorder repeatedly perform inappropriate *compensatory behaviors*, such as forcing themselves to vomit; misusing laxatives, diuretics, or enemas; fasting; or exercising excessively (see Table 9-2 on the next page). A married woman with bulimia nervosa, since recovered, describes a morning during her disorder:

> Today I am going to be really good and that means eating certain predetermined portions of food and not taking one more bite than I think I am allowed. I am very careful to see that I don't take more than Doug does. I judge by his body. I can feel the tension building. I wish Doug would hurry up and leave so I can get going!
>
> As soon as he shuts the door, I try to get involved with one of the myriad of responsibilities on the list. I hate them all! I just want to crawl into a hole. I don't

AMENORRHEA The cessation of menstrual cycles.

BULIMIA NERVOSA A disorder marked by frequent eating binges that are followed by forced vomiting or other extreme compensatory behaviors to avoid gaining weight. Also known as *binge-purge syndrome*.

BINGE An episode of uncontrollable eating during which a person ingests a very large quantity of food.

want to do anything. I'd rather eat. I am alone, I am nervous, I am no good, I always do everything wrong anyway, I am not in control, I can't make it through the day, I just know it. It has been the same for so long.

I remember the starchy cereal I ate for breakfast. I am into the bathroom and onto the scale. It measures the same, BUT I DON'T WANT TO STAY THE SAME! I want to be thinner! I look in the mirror, I think my thighs are ugly and deformed looking. I see a lumpy, clumsy, pear-shaped wimp. There is always something wrong with what I see. I feel frustrated trapped in this body and I don't know what to do about it.

I float to the refrigerator knowing exactly what is there. I begin with last night's brownies. I always begin with the sweets. At first I try to make it look like nothing is missing, but my appetite is huge and I resolve to make another batch of brownies. I know there is half of a bag of cookies in the bathroom, thrown out the night before, and I polish them off immediately. I take some milk so my vomiting will be smoother. I like the full feeling I get after downing a big glass. I get out six pieces of bread and toast one side in the broiler, turn them over and load them with patties of butter and put them under the broiler again till they are bubbling. I take all six pieces on a plate to the television and go back for a bowl of cereal and a banana to have along with them. Before the last toast is finished, I am already preparing the next batch of six more pieces. Maybe another brownie or five, and a couple of large bowlfuls of ice cream, yogurt or cottage cheese. My stomach is stretched into a huge ball below my ribcage. I know I'll have to go into the bathroom soon, but I want to postpone it. I am in never-never land. I am waiting, feeling the pressure, pacing the floor in and out of the rooms. Time is passing. Time is passing. It is getting to be time.

I wander aimlessly through each of the rooms again tidying, making the whole house neat and put back together. I finally make the turn into the bathroom. I brace my feet, pull my hair back and stick my finger down my throat, stroking twice, and get up a huge pile of food. Three times, four and another pile of food. I can see everything come back. I am glad to see those brownies because they are SO fattening. The rhythm of the emptying is broken and my head is beginning to hurt. I stand up feeling dizzy, empty and weak. The whole episode has taken about an hour.

(Hall, 1980, pp. 5–6)

Table 9-2 DSM-IV Checklist

BULIMIA NERVOSA

1. Recurrent episodes of binge eating.
2. Recurrent inappropriate compensatory behavior in order to prevent weight gain.
3. Symptoms continuing, on average, at least twice a week for three months.
4. Undue influence of weight or shape on self-evaluation.

Based on APA, 2000, 1994.

Like anorexia nervosa, bulimia nervosa usually occurs in females, again in 90 to 95 percent of the cases. It begins in adolescence or young adulthood (most often between 15 and 21 years of age) and often lasts for several years, with periodic letup. The weight of people with bulimia nervosa usually stays within a normal range, although it may fluctuate markedly within that range (APA, 2000, 1994). Some people with this disorder, however, become seriously underweight and may eventually qualify for a diagnosis of anorexia nervosa instead (see Figure 9-2). Clinicians have also observed that certain people, a number of them overweight, display a pattern of binge eating without vomiting or other inappropriate compensatory behaviors. This pattern, often called *binge-eating disorder,* is not yet listed in the DSM (Wilson et al., 2003). Around 2 percent of the population and 8 percent of severely overweight people are thought to have this disorder (De Angelis, 2002).

Many teenagers and young adults go on occasional eating binges or experiment with vomiting or laxatives after they hear about these behaviors from their friends or the media (Pyle, 1999). In one study, half of the college students surveyed reported periodic binges, 6 percent had tried vomiting, and 8 percent had experimented with laxatives at least once (Mitchell et al., 1982). Only some of these individuals, however, qualify for a diagnosis of bulimia nervosa. Surveys in several countries suggest that as many as 3 percent of women develop the full syndrome (Helgeson, 2002; APA, 2000; Foreyt et al., 1996).

Eating for sport *Many people go on occasional eating binges, particularly teenagers and young adults. In fact, sometimes binges are officially endorsed, as we see in this photo from the World Pizza Eating Championships in New York City. However, individuals are considered to have an eating disorder only when the binges recur, the pattern endures, and the issues of weight or shape dominate self-evaluation.*

Binges

People with bulimia nervosa may have 2 to 40 binge episodes per week, although the number is usually closer to 10 (Mizes, 1995, 1993). In most cases, the binges are carried out in secret. The person eats massive amounts of food very rapidly, with minimal chewing—usually sweet, high-calorie foods with a soft texture, such as ice cream, cookies, doughnuts, and sandwiches. The food is hardly tasted or thought about. Binge-eaters commonly consume more than 1,500 calories (often more than 3,000) during an episode (Agras, 1995).

Binges are usually preceded by feelings of great tension (Crowther et al., 2001). The person feels irritable, "unreal," and powerless to control an overwhelming need to eat "forbidden" foods. During the binge, the person feels unable to stop eating. Although the binge itself may be experienced as pleasurable in the sense that it relieves the unbearable tension, it is followed by feelings of extreme self-blame, shame, guilt, and depression, as well as fears of gaining weight and being discovered (Hayaki et al., 2002; Serpell & Treasure, 2002).

Compensatory Behaviors

After a binge, people with bulimia nervosa try to compensate for and undo its effects. Many resort to vomiting. But vomiting actually fails to prevent the absorption of half of the calories taken in during a binge. Furthermore, repeated vomiting affects one's general ability to feel full; thus it leads to greater hunger and more frequent and intense binges (Wooley & Wooley, 1985). The use of laxatives or diuretics largely fails to undo the caloric effects of bingeing (Garner et al., 1985).

Vomiting and other compensatory behaviors may temporarily relieve the uncomfortable physical feelings of fullness or reduce the feelings of anxiety and self-disgust attached to binge eating (Wilson et al., 2003). Over time, however, a cycle develops in which purging allows more bingeing, and bingeing requires more purging. The cycle eventually causes people with this disorder to feel powerless and disgusted with themselves (Hayaki et al., 2002). Most recognize fully that

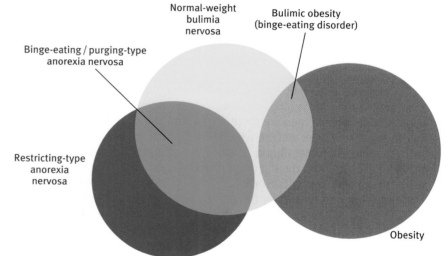

FIGURE 9-2 **Overlapping patterns** *Some people with anorexia nervosa binge and purge their way to weight loss, and some obese persons binge-eat. However, most people with bulimia nervosa are not obese, and most overweight people do not repeatedly binge-eat. (Adapted from APA, 2000, 1994; Garner & Fairburn, 1988; Russell, 1979.)*

A CLOSER LOOK

Not for Women Only

The number of young men with eating disorders appears to be on the rise, and more men are now seeking treatment for these disorders (Rob & Dadson, 2002). Nevertheless, males account for only 5 to 10 percent of all cases of eating disorders. The reasons for this striking gender difference are not entirely clear (Smolak & Murnen, 2001).

One possible explanation is that men and women are subject to different sociocultural pressures. For example, a survey of college men found that the majority selected "muscular, strong and broad shoulders" to describe the ideal male body and "thin, slim, slightly underweight" to describe the ideal female body (Kearney-Cooke & Steichen-Ash, 1990). A second reason for the different rates of eating disorders may be the different methods of weight loss favored by men and women. According to some clinical observations, men are more likely to use exercise to lose weight, whereas women more often diet (Braun, 1996; Mickalide, 1990). And dieting often precedes the onset of eating disorders.

Perhaps a third reason for the difference in reported cases is that eating disorders in men may be underdiagnosed. Some men do not want to admit that they have what many consider a "female problem."

Why do men develop eating disorders? For some the disorder is linked to the *requirements and pressures of a job or sport* (Thompson & Sherman, 1993). In fact, such factors are more likely to trigger eating disorders in men than in women. According to one study, 37 percent of males with eating disorders had jobs or played sports for which weight control was important, compared to 13 percent of women (Braun, 1996). The highest rates have been found among jockeys, wrestlers, distance runners, body builders, and swimmers. Jockeys commonly spend hours before a race in a sauna, shedding up to seven pounds of weight, and may restrict their food intake, abuse laxatives and diuretics, and force vomiting (King & Mezey, 1987).

Similarly, male wrestlers in high school and college commonly restrict their food for up to three days before a match in order to "make weight." Some lose up to five pounds of water weight by practicing or running in several layers of warm or rubber clothing before weighing in for a match (Thompson & Sherman, 1993).

Whereas most women with eating disorders are obsessed with thinness at all times, wrestlers and jockeys with such disorders are usually preoccupied with weight reduction only during their active season. After "making weight," many wrestlers go on eating and drinking binges in order to gain strength for the upcoming match, only to return to a weight-loss strategy after the match in preparation for the next weigh-in. A cycle of losing and regaining weight each season changes metabolic activity and jeopardizes the person's health and future efforts at weight control (Mickalide, 1990; Steen et al., 1988).

Beyond job or sport pressures, *body image* appears to be a strong predictor of eating disorders in men, just as it is in women. Some men who develop eating disorders report that they want a "lean, toned, thin" shape similar to the ideal female body, rather than the muscular, broad-shouldered shape of the typical male ideal (Kearney-Cooke & Steichen-Ash, 1990). However, those who aspire to the typical male ideal are also at risk. A study of 548 males—both young and old—revealed that 43 percent of them were dissatisfied with their bodies to some degree, with many of them expressing a desire to increase their muscle mass, especially in their abdomen and chest (Gorman & Kearney-Cooke, 1997). The most dissatisfied men were those in their 30s and 50s; the least dissatisfied were men in their 20s.

Given such concerns, it may not be surprising that a new kind of eating disorder has been emerging, found almost

The weigh-in *Although this jockey does not have an eating disorder, his prerace weigh-in illustrates the weight standards and pressures to which such athletes are subjected.*

exclusively among men, called *reverse anorexia nervosa* or *muscle dysmorphobia*. This disorder is displayed by men who are very muscular but still see themselves as scrawny and small and therefore continue to strive for a perfect body through extreme measures such as excessive weight lifting or the abuse of steroids (Robb & Dadson, 2002; Olivardia et al., 2000). Individuals with muscle dysmorphobia typically experience shame about their body image, and many have a history of depression, anxiety, or self-destructive compulsive behavior.

As the number of males with eating disturbances increases, researchers are increasing their efforts to understand both the similarities and the differences between males and females with these disorders. Since eating disturbances cause problems for both men and women, investigators must uncover the important factors that operate across the gender divide.

they have an eating disorder. The woman we met earlier recalls how the pattern of bingeing, purging, and self-disgust took hold while she was a teenager in boarding school:

> Every bite that went into my mouth was a naughty and selfish indulgence, and I became more and more disgusted with myself. . . .
>
> The first time I stuck my fingers down my throat was during the last week of school. I saw a girl come out of the bathroom with her face all red and her eyes puffy. She had always talked about her weight and how she should be dieting even though her body was really shapely. I knew instantly what she had just done and I had to try it. . . .
>
> I began with breakfasts which were served buffet-style on the main floor of the dorm. I learned which foods I could eat that would come back up easily. When I woke in the morning, I had to make the decision whether to stuff myself for half an hour and throw up before class, or whether to try and make it through the whole day without overeating. . . . I always thought people noticed when I took huge portions at mealtimes, but I figured they assumed that because I was an athlete, I burned it off. . . . Once a binge was under way, I did not stop until my stomach looked pregnant and I felt like I could not swallow one more time.
>
> That year was the first of my nine years of obsessive eating and throwing up. . . . I didn't want to tell anyone what I was doing, and I didn't want to stop. . . . [Though] being in love or other distractions occasionally lessened the cravings, I always returned to the food.
>
> *(Hall, 1980, pp. 9–12)*

As with anorexia nervosa, a bulimic pattern typically begins during or after a period of intense dieting, often one that has been successful and earned praise from family members and friends (Helgeson, 2002). Research has found that normal subjects placed on very strict diets also develop a tendency to binge. Some of the subjects in the conscientious objector "starvation study," for example, later binged when they were allowed to return to regular eating, and a number of them continued to be hungry even after large meals (Keys et al., 1950). A more recent study examined the binge-eating behavior of subjects at the end of a very low-calorie weight-loss program (Telch & Agras, 1993). Immediately after the program, 62 percent of the subjects, who had not previously been binge eaters, reported binge-eating episodes, although their binges did decrease during the three months after treatment stopped.

Bulimia Nervosa vs. Anorexia Nervosa

Bulimia nervosa is similar to anorexia nervosa in many ways. Both disorders typically begin after a period of dieting by people who are fearful of becoming obese; driven to become thin; preoccupied with food, weight, and appearance; and struggling with feelings of depression, anxiety, and the need to be perfect (Fairburn et al., 2003; Lehoux et al., 2000). Individuals with either of the disorders have a heightened risk of self-harm or attempts at suicide (Favaro & Santonastaso, 2002; Sansone & Levitt, 2002). Substance abuse may accompany either disorder, perhaps beginning with the excessive use of diet pills (O'Brien & Vincent, 2003). People with either disorder believe that they weigh too much and look too heavy regardless of their actual weight or appearance (Kaye et al., 2002). And both disorders are marked by disturbed attitudes toward eating (Walker et al., 2002).

Yet the two disorders also differ in important ways. Although people with either disorder worry about the opinions of others, those with bulimia nervosa tend to be more concerned about pleasing others, being attractive to others, and having intimate relationships (Striegel-Moore, Silberstein, & Rodin, 1993; Muuss, 1986). They also tend to be more sexually experienced and active than people with anorexia nervosa. On the positive side, individuals with bulimia nervosa display

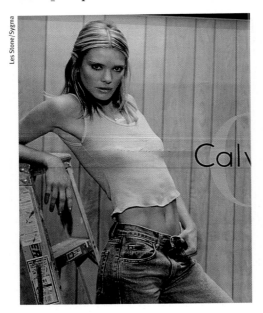

Harmful advertising *When Calvin Klein posed young teenagers in sexually suggestive clothing ads in 1995, the public protested and the ads were halted. However, what some researchers consider even more damaging—the use of very thin young models who influence the body ideals and dietary habits of millions of teenage girls—continued uninterrupted.*

fewer of the obsessive qualities that drive people with restricting-type anorexia nervosa to control their caloric intake so rigidly (Halmi, 1995; Andersen, 1985). On the negative side, they are more likely to have long histories of mood swings, become easily frustrated or bored, and have trouble coping effectively or controlling their impulses (Claes et al., 2002; APA, 2000). Individuals with bulimia nervosa also tend to be ruled by strong emotions and may change friends and relationships frequently. And more than one-third of them display the characteristics of a personality disorder, which we shall examine more closely in Chapter 13 (O'Brien & Vincent, 2003; Matsunaga et al., 2000).

Another difference is the nature of the medical complications that accompany the two disorders (Mickley, 2001). Only half of women with bulimia nervosa are amenorrheic or have very irregular menstrual periods, compared to almost all of those with anorexia nervosa (Crow et al., 2002). On the other hand, repeated vomiting bathes teeth and gums in hydrochloric acid, leading some women with bulimia nervosa to experience serious dental problems, such as breakdown of enamel and even loss of teeth (Helgeson, 2002; Casper, 1995). Moreover, frequent vomiting or chronic diarrhea (from the use of laxatives) can cause dangerous potassium deficiencies, which may lead to weakness, intestinal disorders, kidney disease, or heart damage (Turner et al., 2000; Halmi et al., 1994).

SUMMING UP

Bulimia Nervosa

Individuals with bulimia nervosa go on frequent eating binges and then force themselves to vomit or perform other inappropriate compensatory behaviors. The binges often occur in response to increasing tension and are followed by feelings of self-blame, shame, guilt, and depression.

Compensatory behavior is at first reinforced by the temporary relief from uncomfortable feelings of fullness or the reduction of feelings of anxiety and self-disgust attached to bingeing. Over time, however, people come to feel generally powerless, disgusted with themselves, and guilty.

People with bulimia nervosa may experience mood swings or have difficulty controlling their impulses. Some display a personality disorder. Around half are amenorrheic, a number develop dental problems, and some develop a potassium deficiency.

What Causes Eating Disorders?

Most of today's theorists and researchers use a **multidimensional risk perspective** to explain eating disorders. That is, they identify several key factors that place individuals at risk for the disorders (Lask, 2000; Lyon et al., 1997). The more of these factors that are present, the greater the likelihood that a person will develop an eating disorder. The factors cited most often include sociocultural conditions (societal and family pressures), psychological problems (ego, cognitive, and mood disturbances), and biological factors.

Societal Pressures

Many theorists believe that the current Western standards of female attractiveness have contributed to increases in eating disorders (Jambor, 2001). These standards have changed throughout history, with a noticeable shift toward preference for a thin female frame in recent decades. One study that tracked the height, weight, and age of contestants in the Miss America Pageant from 1959 through 1978 found an average decline of 0.28 pound per year among the contestants and

MULTIDIMENSIONAL RISK PERSPECTIVE A theory that identifies several kinds of risk factors that are thought to combine to help cause a disorder. The more factors present, the greater the risk of developing the disorder.

0.37 pound per year among winners (Garner et al., 1980). The researchers also examined data on all *Playboy* magazine centerfold models over the same time period and found that the average weight, bust, and hip measurements of these women had decreased steadily. More recent studies of Miss America contestants and *Playboy* centerfolds indicate that these trends have continued (Rubinstein & Caballero, 2000; Wiseman et al., 1992).

Because thinness is especially valued in the subcultures of fashion models, actors, dancers, and certain athletes, members of these groups are likely to be particularly concerned about their weight (Taylor & Ste-Marie, 2001). As sociocultural theorists would predict, studies have found that people in these professions are more prone than others to eating disorders (Golden, 2002; Thompson & Sherman, 1999). In fact, many famous young women in these fields have publicly acknowledged grossly disordered eating patterns in recent years. One survey of 1,443 athletes at 10 colleges around the United States revealed that more than 9 percent of female college athletes suffer from an eating disorder and another 50 percent admit to eating behaviors that put them at risk for such disorders (Johnson, 1995). A full 20 percent of the gymnasts surveyed had an eating disorder (see Figure 9-3).

Attitudes toward thinness may also help explain economic and racial differences in the rates of eating disorders. In the past, white American women in the upper socioeconomic classes expressed more concern about thinness and dieting than did African American women or white American women of the lower socioeconomic classes (Margo, 1985; Stunkard, 1975). Correspondingly, eating disorders were more common among white American women high on the socioeconomic scale (Foreyt et al., 1996; Rosen et al., 1991). In more recent years, however, dieting and preoccupation with thinness have increased in all classes and minority groups, as has the prevalence of eating disorders (Mulholland & Mintz, 2001; Striegel-Moore & Smolak, 2000).

Unfair game *As we are reminded by one of the key characters in the highly successful* Austin Powers *films, overweight people in Western society are typically treated with insensitivity. They are the targets of humor in magazines, books, television shows, and movies.*

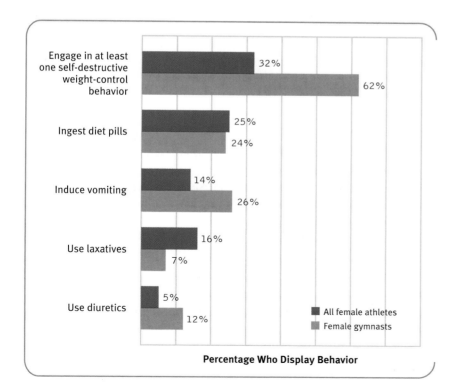

Percentage Who Display Behavior

Behavior	All female athletes	Female gymnasts
Engage in at least one self-destructive weight-control behavior	32%	62%
Ingest diet pills	25%	24%
Induce vomiting	14%	26%
Use laxatives	16%	7%
Use diuretics	5%	12%

FIGURE 9-3 **Dangerous shortcuts** *According to surveys, in sports ranging from field hockey to gymnastics, many female athletes engage in one or more self-destructive behaviors to control their weight (Taylor & Ste-Marie, 2001). One study found that close to two-thirds of female college gymnasts engage in at least one such behavior. (Adapted from Rosen & Hough, 1988; Rosen et al., 1986.)*

Body Image: A Matter of Race?

In the popular 1995 movie *Clueless*, Cher and Dionne, wealthy teenage friends of different races, have similar tastes, beliefs, and values about everything from boys to schoolwork. In particular, they have the same kinds of eating habits and beauty ideals, and they are even similar in weight and physical form. But does the story of these young women reflect the realities of white and African American females in our society?

In the early 1990s, the answer to this question appeared to be a resounding no. Most studies conducted up to the time of the movie's release indicated that the eating behaviors, values, and goals of young African American women were considerably healthier than those of young white American women (Lovejoy, 2001; Cash & Henry, 1995; Parker et al., 1995). However, it turns out that the movie and the later television show of the same name were in fact clued in to changes occurring in the United States. Most studies conducted *since* 1995 suggest that African American women, as well as women of other minority groups, are becoming more and more like white American women in their worries about weight and appearance, their inclination to diet, and their vulnerability to eating disorders.

Let's look first at the situation before 1995 and then at the clinical picture that has been unfolding since then.

Pre-1995

A widely publicized 1995 study at the University of Arizona offered findings consistent with other research in the early 1990s (Parker et al., 1995). The study found that the eating behaviors and attitudes of young African American women were more positive than those of young white American women. It found, specifically, that nearly 90 percent of the white respondents were dissatisfied with their weight and body shape, compared to around 70 percent of the African American teens.

The study also suggested that white and African American adolescent girls had very different ideals of beauty. The white teens, asked to define the "perfect

Courtesy of Everett Collection

Fact or fiction? *In the movie* Clueless, *best friends Dionne and Cher think, act, dress, and look alike and hold identical values and concerns. Here they talk to each other on cell phones while walking side by side.*

Cultural differences may also help explain the striking gender gap for eating disorders. Our society's emphasis on a thin appearance is aimed at women much more than men (Nichter & Nichter, 1991). Some theorists believe that this double standard has made women much more inclined to diet and more prone to eating disorders (Rand & Kuldau, 1991).

Western society not only glorifies thinness but creates a climate of prejudice against overweight people. Whereas slurs based on ethnicity, race, and gender are considered unacceptable, cruel jokes about obesity are standard fare on television and in movies, books, and magazines. Research indicates that the prejudice against obese people is deep-rooted (Tiggeman & Wilson-Barrett, 1998). Prospective parents who were shown pictures of a chubby child and a medium-weight or thin child rated the former as less friendly, energetic, intelligent, and desirable than the latter. In another study, preschool children who were given a choice between a chubby and a thin rag doll chose the thin one, although they could not say why. It is small wonder that as many as half of elementary school

girl," described a girl of 5′7″ weighing between 100 and 110 pounds—proportions that mirror those of so-called supermodels. Attaining a perfect weight, many said, was the key to being "totally happy," and they indicated that thinness was a requirement for popularity.

In contrast, the African American respondents tended to emphasize personality traits over physical characteristics when they described the ideal girl. They defined the "perfect" African American girl as smart, fun, easy to talk to, not conceited, and funny; she did not necessarily need to be "pretty," as long as she was well groomed. The body dimensions the African American teens described were more attainable for the typical girl; they favored fuller hips, for example. In addition, two-thirds of them defined beauty as "the right attitude." Given such definitions of beauty, it was not surprising that the African American subjects were less likely than the white American respondents to diet for extended periods.

Post-1995

Unfortunately, research conducted over the past decade suggests that body image concerns, dysfunctional eating patterns, and eating disorders are on the upswing among young African American women as well as among women of other minority groups. Here are some of the most striking findings:

Surveys conducted by *Essence*, the largest-circulation African American magazine, and by several teams of researchers have found that African American women today have about the same risk for developing eating disorders as white American women, along with similar attitudes regarding body image, weight, and eating (Mulhollan & Mintz, 2001; Pumariega et al., 1994). In the *Essence* survey, 65 percent of African American respondents reported dieting behavior, 39 percent said that food controlled their lives, 19 percent avoided eating when hungry, 17 percent used laxatives, and 4 percent vomited to lose weight.

African American women may be at particular risk for binge eating. In one study, African American women reported more bingeing than did white American women when they tried to lose weight through extreme methods (Striegel-Moore et al., 2000). Many African American subjects also reported using overeating to fill an emotional void in their lives, to cope with hardships such as racism, and to deal with fear and anger in their daily lives.

In a study of more than 2,000 girls aged 9 to 10 years, 40 percent of the respondents—African American and white American subjects in equal measure—reported wanting to lose weight (Schreiber et al., 1996).

Studies indicate that Hispanic women also engage in disordered eating behav-

iors and express body dissatisfaction at rates similar to those of white women (Chamorro & Flores-Ortiz, 2000; Striegel-Moore et al., 2000). Moreover, one study found that Hispanic subjects who were dissatisfied with their weight displayed more severe binge-eating behavior than white American or African American subjects with similar concerns (Fitzgibbon et al., 1998).

Eating disorders also appear to be on the increase among young Asian American women and young women in several Asian countries (Efron, 1997). Indeed, a study in Taiwan surveyed 843 schoolgirls, aged 10 to 14 years, and found that 8 percent were severely underweight and 10 percent were somewhat underweight (Wong & Huang, 2000). Around 65 percent of the underweight girls nevertheless wished they were thinner.

One study of 235 women from different racial and ethnic backgrounds found that 58 percent of the Hispanic subjects, 56 percent of the African Americans, 46 percent of the white Americans, and 43 percent of the Asian Americans were dissatisfied with their body image and were currently trying to lose weight (Dittrich, 1997).

Clearly the "protections" of race or culture that once seemed to operate in the realms of weight control and eating disorders no longer apply.

girls have tried to lose weight and 61 percent of middle school girls are currently dieting (Shisslak et al., 1998; Hunnicut & Newman, 1993).

Family Environment

Families may play an important role in the development of eating disorders. Research suggests that as many as half of the families of people with eating disorders have a long history of emphasizing thinness, physical appearance, and dieting (Moorhead et al., 2003; Haworth-Hoeppner, 2000). In fact, the mothers in these families are more likely to diet themselves and to be generally perfectionistic than are the mothers in other families (Woodside et al., 2002; Pike & Rodin, 1991). Abnormal interactions and communication patterns within a family may also set the stage for an eating disorder. Family systems theorists argue that the families of people who develop eating disorders are often dysfunctional to begin with and that the eating disorder of one member is a reflection of the

Like mother, like daughter? *Mother–daughter relationships have sometimes been pointed to as a key factor in the development of eating disorders. Researchers have found, for example, that many mothers of young women with eating disorders place particular emphasis on physical appearance, diet frequently, and are perfectionistic. Accordingly, treatments for eating disorders often include family education and family therapy.*

larger problem (Rowa et al., 2001; Dalzell, 2000). The influential family theorist Salvador Minuchin, for example, believes that what he calls an **enmeshed family pattern** often leads to eating disorders (Minuchin, Rosman, & Baker, 1978).

In an enmeshed system, family members are overinvolved in each other's affairs and overconcerned with the details of each other's lives. On the positive side, enmeshed families can be affectionate and loyal. On the negative side, they can be clinging and foster dependency. Parents are too involved in the lives of their children, allowing little room for individuality and independence. Minuchin argues that adolescence poses a special problem for these families. The teenager's normal push for independence threatens the family's apparent harmony and closeness. In response, the family may subtly force the child to take on a "sick" role—to develop an eating disorder or some other illness. The child's disorder enables the family to maintain its appearance of harmony. A sick child needs her family, and family members can rally to protect her. Some case studies have supported such family systems explanations, but systematic research fails to show that particular family patterns consistently set the stage for the development of eating disorders (Wilson et al., 2003, 1996). In fact, the families of people with either anorexia nervosa or bulimia nervosa vary widely (Eisler, 1995).

Ego Deficiencies and Cognitive Disturbances

Hilde Bruch, a pioneer in the study and treatment of eating disorders, developed a theory built on both psychodynamic and cognitive notions. She argued that disturbed mother–child interactions lead to serious *ego deficiencies* in the child (including a poor sense of independence and control) and to severe *cognitive disturbances* that jointly help produce disordered eating patterns (Bruch, 1991, 1983, 1962).

According to Bruch, parents may respond to their children either effectively or ineffectively. *Effective parents* accurately attend to their children's biological and emotional needs, giving them food when they are crying from hunger and comfort when they are crying out of fear. *Ineffective parents*, by contrast, fail to attend to their children's needs, deciding that their children are hungry, cold, or tired without correctly interpreting the children's actual condition. They may feed the children at times of anxiety rather than hunger, or comfort them at times of tiredness rather than anxiety. Children who receive such parenting may grow up confused and unaware of their own internal needs, not knowing for themselves when they are hungry or full and unable to identify their own emotions.

Unable to rely on internal signals, these children turn instead to external guides, such as their parents. They seem to be "model children," but they fail to develop genuine self-reliance and "experience themselves as not being in control of their behavior, needs, and impulses, as not owning their own bodies" (Bruch, 1973, p. 55). Adolescence increases their basic desire to establish independence, yet they feel unable to do so. To overcome their sense of helplessness, they seek excessive control over their body size and shape and over their eating habits. Helen, an 18-year-old, describes her experience:

> There is a peculiar contradiction—everybody thinks you're doing so well and everybody thinks you're great, but your real problem is that you think that you are not good enough. You are afraid of not living up to what you think you are expected to do. You have one great fear, namely that of being ordinary, or average, or common—just not good enough. This peculiar dieting begins with such anxiety. You want to prove that you have control, that you can do it. The peculiar part of it is that it makes you feel good about yourself, makes you feel "I can accomplish something." It makes you feel "I can do something nobody else can do."
>
> *(Bruch, 1978, p. 128)*

ENMESHED FAMILY PATTERN A family system in which members are overinvolved with each other's affairs and overconcerned about each other's welfare.

Clinical reports and research have provided some support for Bruch's theory. Clinicians have observed that the parents of teenagers with eating disorders do tend to define their children's needs rather than allow the children to define their own needs (Hart & Kenny, 1995; Steiner et al., 1991). When Bruch interviewed the mothers of 51 children with anorexia nervosa, many proudly recalled that they had always "anticipated" their young child's needs, never permitting the child to "feel hungry" (Bruch, 1973).

Research has also supported Bruch's belief that people with eating disorders perceive internal cues, including emotional cues, inaccurately (Espina et al., 2002; Fukunishi, 1998). When subjects with bulimia nervosa are anxious or upset, for example, many of them mistakenly think they are also hungry (see Figure 9-4), and they respond as they might respond to hunger—by eating (Rebert, Stanton, & Schwartz, 1991). Finally, studies support Bruch's argument that people with eating disorders rely excessively on the opinions, wishes, and views of others. They are more likely than other people to worry about how others view them, to seek approval, to be conforming, and to feel a lack of control over their lives (Button & Warren, 2001; Walters & Kendler, 1995).

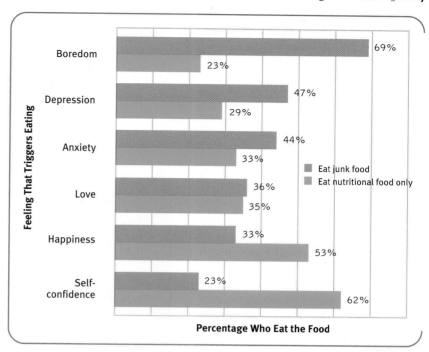

FIGURE **9-4**   **When do people seek junk food?** *Apparently, when they feel bad. People who eat junk food when they are feeling bad outnumber those who eat nutritional food under similar circumstances. In contrast, more people seek nutritional food when they are feeling good. (Adapted from Lyman, 1982.)*

Mood Disorders

Many people with eating disorders, particularly those with bulimia nervosa, experience symptoms of depression (Le Grange & Lock, 2002; Serpell & Treasure, 2002). This finding has led some theorists to suggest that mood disorders set the stage for eating disorders (Zaider et al., 2002; Hsu et al., 1992).

Their claim is supported by four kinds of evidence. First, many more people with an eating disorder qualify for a clinical diagnosis of major depressive disorder than do people in the general population (Brewerton et al., 1995). Second, the close relatives of people with eating disorders seem to have a higher rate of mood disorders than do close relatives of people without such disorders (Moorhead et al., 2003; APA, 2000). Third, as we shall see, many people with eating disorders, particularly bulimia nervosa, have low activity of the neurotransmitter serotonin, similar to the serotonin abnormalities found in depressed people. And finally, people with eating disorders are often helped by some of the same antidepressant drugs that reduce depression.

Although such findings suggest that depression may help cause eating disorders, other explanations are possible (Stice & Bearman, 2001; Wade et al., 2000). For example, the pressure and pain of having an eating disorder may *cause* a mood disorder. Whatever the correct interpretation, many people struggling with eating disorders also suffer from depression, among other psychological problems.

Biological Factors

Recent research has suggested that certain genes may leave some persons particularly susceptible to anorexia nervosa (Grice et al., 2002; Vink et al., 2002). Consistent with this idea, relatives of people with eating disorders are up to six times more likely than other individuals to develop the disorders themselves (Strober et al., 2001, 2000; Gorwood et al., 1998). Moreover, if one identical twin has bulimia nervosa, the other twin also develops the disorder in 23 percent of cases; in contrast, the rate for fraternal twins, who are genetically less similar, is 9 percent (Walters & Kendler, 1995; Kendler et al., 1991). Although such family

Obesity: To Lose or Not to Lose

By medical standards, one-third of adults in the United States weigh at least 20 percent more than people of their height typically do (Stice, 2002). In fact, despite the public's focus on thinness, obesity has become increasingly common in the United States (Stice, 2002). Being overweight is not a mental disorder, nor in most cases is it the result of abnormal psychological processes. Nevertheless, it causes great anguish, and not just because of its physical effects. The media, people on the streets, and even many health professionals treat obesity as shameful. Obese people are often the unrecognized victims of discrimination in efforts to gain admission to college, jobs, and promotions (Rothblum, 1992).

Mounting evidence indicates that overweight persons are not to be sneered at as weak and that obesity results from multiple factors. First, genetic and biological factors seem to play large roles. Researchers have found that children of obese biological parents are more likely to be obese than children whose biological parents are not obese, whether or not the people who raise those children are obese (Stunkard et al.,

1986). Other researchers have identified several genes that seem to be linked to obesity (Nagle et al., 1999; Halaas et al., 1995). And still others have identified chemicals in the body, including a hormone called *leptin* and a protein called

glucagon-like peptide-1 (GLP-1), that apparently act as natural appetite suppressants (Costa et al., 2002; Tartaglia et al., 1995). Suspicion is growing that the brain receptors for these chemicals may be defective in overweight persons.

Will Hart/PhotoEdit

Singled out *As we are reminded by these junior high school students in gym class, children approach puberty with a wide range of body sizes and metabolism rates. Yet those who are overweight typically will be held personally responsible for their size and targeted for scorn.*

and twin findings do not rule out environmental explanations, they have encouraged biological researchers to look further still for specific biological causes.

One factor that has interested investigators is the possible role of *serotonin*. Several researcher teams have found a link between eating disorders and the genes responsible for the production of this neurotransmitter (Enoch et al., 1998), and still others have measured low serotonin activity in many people with eating disorders (Carrasco et al., 2000). Thus some theorists believe that abnormal serotonin activity—a condition to which certain persons may be predisposed—causes the body to crave and binge on high-carbohydrate foods (Kaye et al., 2002, 2000; Wurtman, 1987).

Other biological researchers explain eating disorders by pointing to the **hypothalamus**, a part of the brain that controls many bodily functions (Tataranni et al., 1999; Leibowitz & Hoebel, 1998). Researchers have located two separate areas in the hypothalamus that help control eating. One, the *lateral hypothalamus (LH)*, produces hunger when it is activated. When the LH of a laboratory animal is stimulated electrically, the animal eats, even if it has been fed recently. In contrast, another area, the *ventromedial hypothalamus (VMH)*, reduces hunger when it is activated. When the VMH is electrically stimulated, laboratory animals stop eating (Duggan & Booth, 1986).

These different areas of the hypothalamus are apparently activated by chemicals from the brain and body, depending on whether the person is eating or fasting. One such brain chemical is *glucagon-like peptide-1 (GLP-1)*, a natural appetite

HYPOTHALAMUS A part of the brain that helps regulate various bodily functions, including eating and hunger.

WEIGHT SET POINT The weight level that a person is predisposed to maintain, controlled in part by the hypothalamus.

Environment also plays a causal role in obesity. Studies have shown that people eat more when they are in the company of others, particularly if the other people are eating (Logue, 1991). In addition, research finds that people in low socioeconomic environments are more likely to be obese than those of high socioeconomic background (Ernst & Harlan, 1991).

Health Risk?

Do mildly to moderately obese people have a greater risk of coronary disease, cancer, or other disease? Investigations into this question have produced conflicting results (Bender et al., 1999; Lean, Han, & Seidell, 1999). One long-term study found that while moderately overweight subjects had a 30 percent higher risk of early death, underweight subjects had a low likelihood of dying at an early age as long as their thinness could not be attributed to smoking or illness (Manson et al., 1995). However, another study found that the mortality rate of underweight subjects was as high as that of overweight subjects regardless of smoking behavior or illness (Troiano et al., 1996). These findings suggest that the jury is still out on this issue.

Does Dieting Work?

There are scores of diets and diet pills. There is almost no evidence, however, that any diet yet devised can ensure long-term weight loss in most cases (Wilson, 1994). In fact, long-term studies reveal a *rebound* effect, an eventual gain in weight by obese people who have lost weight on very low-calorie diets. Research also suggests that the feelings of failure that accompany diet rebounds may lead to dysfunctional eating patterns, including binge eating (Venditti et al., 1996).

Efforts are now under way to develop new kinds of drugs that will operate directly on the genes, hormones, and proteins that have been linked to obesity (Carek & Dickerson, 1999; Greenberg et al., 1999). Theoretically, these drugs will counteract the bodily reactions that undermine efforts at dieting. Whether such interventions can provide safe and permanent weight loss remains to be seen.

What Is the Proper Goal?

Some researchers argue that attempts to reduce obesity should focus less on weight loss and more on improving general health and attitudes (Painot et al., 2001; Rosen et al., 1995). If poor eating habits can be corrected, if a poor self-concept and distorted body image can be improved, and if overweight people can be educated about the myths and truths regarding obesity, perhaps everyone will be better off.

Most experts agree that extreme obesity is indeed a clear health hazard and that weight loss is advisable in such cases. For these individuals, the most promising path to long-term weight loss may be to set realistic, attainable goals rather than unrealistic ideals (Brownell & O'Neil, 1993; Brownell & Wadden, 1992). As for people who are mildly or even moderately overweight, a growing number of experts now suggest that perhaps they should be left alone or, at the very least, encouraged to set more modest and realistic goals. In addition, it is critical that the public overcome its prejudice against people who are overweight and come to appreciate that obesity is, at worst, a problem that requires treatment, and perhaps simply another version of the normal human condition.

---

suppressant. When a team of researchers collected and injected GLP-1 into the brains of rats, the chemical traveled to the hypothalamus and caused the rats to reduce their food intake almost entirely even though they had not eaten for 24 hours (Turton et al., 1996). Conversely, when "full" rats were injected with a substance that blocked the reception of GLP-1 in the hypothalamus, they more than doubled their food intake.

Some researchers believe that the LH and VMH and chemicals such as GLP-1, working together, comprise a "weight thermostat" in the body, responsible for keeping an individual at a particular weight level called the **weight set point** (Garner et al., 1985; Keesey & Corbett, 1983). Genetic inheritance and early eating practices seem to determine each person's weight set point. When a person's weight falls below his or her particular set point, the LH is activated and seeks to restore the lost weight by producing hunger and lowering the body's *metabolic rate*, the rate at which the body expends energy. When a person's weight rises above his or her set point, the VMH is activated, and it seeks to remove the excess weight by reducing hunger and increasing the body's metabolic rate.

According to the weight set point theory, when people diet and fall to a weight below their weight set point, their brain starts trying to restore the lost weight. Hypothalamic activity produces a preoccupation with food and a desire to binge. It also triggers bodily changes that make it harder to lose weight and easier to gain weight, however little is eaten (Spalter et al., 1993; Hill & Robinson, 1991). Once the brain and body begin conspiring to raise weight in this way, dieters actually

Laboratory obesity *By electrically stimulating parts of a rodent's hypothalamus, researchers can induce overeating and massive weight gain.*

Richard Howard © 1991 *Discover*

>>PSYCH•NOTES
Special Factor?

Although some clinicians claim that eating disorders are frequently the result of experiences of sexual abuse, research clarifies that the disorders are only sometimes linked to such experiences. Moreover, the elevated rate of sexual abuse is no higher among people with eating disorders than among people with mood, anxiety, and other psychological disorders (Welch & Fairburn, 1996, 1994; Pope & Hudson, 1992).<<

enter into a battle against themselves. Some people apparently manage to shut down the inner "thermostat" and control their eating almost completely. These people move toward restricting-type anorexia nervosa. For others, the battle spirals toward a binge-purge pattern (Pinel et al., 2000).

SUMMING UP | What Causes Eating Disorders?

Most theorists now apply a multidimensional risk perspective to explain eating disorders, identifying several key contributing factors. These factors include society's emphasis on thinness and bias against obesity; family environment, including, perhaps, an enmeshed family pattern; ego and cognitive disturbances, including a poor sense of independence and control; a mood disorder; and biological factors, such as activity of the hypothalamus, biochemical activity, and the body's weight set point.

How Are Eating Disorders Treated?

Today's treatments for eating disorders have two goals. The first to correct as quickly as possible the dangerous eating pattern. The second is to address the broader psychological and situational factors that have led to and now maintain the eating problem. Family and friends can also play an important role in helping to overcome the disorder (Sherman & Thompson, 1990).

Treatments for Anorexia Nervosa

The immediate aims of treatment for anorexia nervosa are to help individuals regain their lost weight, recover from malnourishment, and eat normally again. Therapists must then help them to make psychological and perhaps family changes to lock in those gains.

HOW ARE PROPER WEIGHT AND NORMAL EATING RESTORED? A variety of treatment methods are used to help patients with anorexia nervosa gain weight quickly and return to health within weeks. In the past, treatment almost always took place in a hospital, but now it is often offered in outpatient settings (Gowers et al., 2000; Pyle, 1999).

In life-threatening cases, clinicians may need to force *tube and intravenous feedings* on a patient who refuses to eat. Unfortunately, this use of such force may breed distrust in the patient (Robb et al., 2002; Treasure et al., 1995). In contrast, behavioral weight-restoration approaches have clinicians use *rewards* whenever patients eat properly or gain weight and offer no rewards when they eat improperly or fail to gain weight (Tacon & Caldera, 2001; Griffiths et al., 1998).

Perhaps the most popular weight-restoration technique of recent years has been a combination of *supportive nursing care* and a high-calorie diet (Roloff, 2001; Treasure et al., 1995). Here nurses gradually increase a patient's diet over the course of several weeks to more than 2,500 calories a day. The nurses educate patients about the program, track their progress, provide encouragement, and help them recognize that their weight gain is under control and will not lead to obesity. Studies find that patients in nursing-care programs usually gain the necessary weight over 8 to 12 weeks.

HOW ARE LASTING CHANGES ACHIEVED? Clinical researchers have found that people with anorexia nervosa must overcome their underlying psychological problems in order to achieve lasting improvement. Therapists typically provide both therapy and education to achieve this broader goal, using a combination of individual, group, and family approaches (King, 2001; Hindmarch, 2000).

>>BY THE NUMBERS
Mealtime

2,712 Average number of daily calories consumed by people across the world<<

3,603 Average number of daily calories consumed by people in the United States<<

821 billion Amount spent on food by Americans in 2000<<

111 billion Amount spent on "fast food" in 2000<<

(Gardyn, 2002; Ash, 1998)

BUILDING INDEPENDENCE AND SELF-AWARENESS One focus of treatment is to help patients with anorexia nervosa recognize their need for independence and teach them more appropriate ways to execise control (Dare & Crowther, 1995; Robin et al., 1995). Therapists may also teach patients to better identify and trust their internal sensations and feelings (Kaplan & Garfinkel, 1999). In the following session, a therapist tries to help a 15-year-old client recognize and share her feelings:

> *Patient:* I don't talk about my feelings; I never did.
> *Therapist:* Do you think I'll respond like others?
> *Patient:* What do you mean?
> *Therapist:* I think you may be afraid that I won't pay close attention to what you feel inside, or that I'll tell you not to feel the way you do—that it's foolish to feel frightened, to feel fat, to doubt yourself, considering how well you do in school, how you're appreciated by teachers, how pretty you are.
> *Patient:* (*Looking somewhat tense and agitated*) Well, I was always told to be polite and respect other people, just like a stupid, faceless doll. (*Affecting a vacant, doll-like pose*)
> *Therapist:* Do I give you the impression that it would be disrespectful for you to share your feelings, whatever they may be?
> *Patient:* Not really; I don't know.
> *Therapist:* I can't, and won't, tell you that this is easy for you to do. . . . But I can promise you that you are free to speak your mind, and that I won't turn away.
>
> (*Strober & Yager, 1985, pp. 368–369*)

CORRECTING DISTURBED COGNITIONS Another focus of treatment is to help people with anorexia nervosa change their attitudes about eating and weight (Garner & Magana, 2002; Christie, 2000) (see Table 9-3 on the next page). Using cognitive approaches, therapists may guide clients to identify, challenge, and change maladaptive assumptions, such as "I must always be perfect" or "My weight and shape determine my value" (Lask & Bryant-Waugh, 2000; Freeman, 1995). Therapists may also educate clients about the body distortions typical of anorexia nervosa and help them see that their own assessments of their size are incorrect (Wegner & Wegner, 2001; Mitchell & Peterson, 1997).

CHANGING FAMILY INTERACTIONS Family therapy is often part of the treatment program for anorexia nervosa (Lock, 2002; Lock & Le Grange, 2001). As in other family therapy situations, the therapist typically meets with the family as a whole, points out troublesome family patterns, and helps the members make appropriate changes. In particular, family therapists may try to help the person with anorexia nervosa separate her feelings and needs from those of other family members. Although the role of family in the development of anorexia nervosa is not yet clear, research strongly suggests that family therapy (or at least parent counseling) can be helpful in the treatment of this disorder (Eisler et al., 2000; Dare & Eisler, 1997, 1995).

> *Mother:* I think I know what [Susan] is going through: all the doubt and insecurity of growing up and establishing her own identity. (*Turning to the patient, with tears*) If you just place trust in yourself, with the support of those around you who care, everything will turn out for the better.
> *Therapist:* Are you making yourself available to her? Should she turn to you, rely on you for guidance and emotional support?
> *Mother:* Well, that's what parents are for.
> *Therapist:* (*Turning to patient*) What do you think?

> **Susan:** (*To mother*) I can't keep depending on you, Mom, or everyone else. That's what I've been doing, and it gave me anorexia. . . .
>
> **Therapist:** Do you think your mom would prefer that there be no secrets between her and the kids—an open door, so to speak?
>
> **Older sister:** Sometimes I do.
>
> **Therapist:** (*To patient and younger sister*) How about you two?
>
> **Susan:** Yeah. Sometimes it's like whatever I feel, she has to feel.
>
> **Younger sister:** Yeah.
>
> *(Strober & Yager, 1985, pp. 381–382)*

WHAT IS THE AFTERMATH OF ANOREXIA NERVOSA? The use of combined treatment approaches has greatly improved the outlook for people with anorexia nervosa, although the road to recovery can be difficult. The course and outcome of this disorder vary from person to person, but researchers have noted certain trends.

On the positive side, weight is often quickly restored once treatment begins, and treatment gains may continue for years. In one study, 83 percent of patients continued to show improvement when they were interviewed several years or more after their initial recovery: around 33 percent were fully recovered and 50 percent partially improved (Herzog et al., 1999; Treasure et al., 1995). Other studies have found that most individuals perform effectively at their jobs and express job satisfaction years after their recovery (Fombonne, 1995; Theander, 1970).

Another positive note is that most females with anorexia nervosa menstruate again when they regain their weight (Fombonne, 1995; Crisp, 1981), and other

---

Table 9-3

Sample Items from the Eating Disorder Inventory II

For each item, decide if the item is true about you ALWAYS (A), USUALLY (U), OFTEN (O), SOMETIMES (S), RARELY (R), or NEVER (N). Circle the letter that corresponds to your rating.

A	U	O	S	R	N	I think that my stomach is too big.
A	U	O	S	R	N	I eat when I am upset.
A	U	O	S	R	N	I stuff myself with food.
A	U	O	S	R	N	I think about dieting.
A	U	O	S	R	N	I think that my thighs are too large.
A	U	O	S	R	N	I feel extremely guilty after overeating.
A	U	O	S	R	N	I am terrified of gaining weight.
A	U	O	S	R	N	I get confused about what emotion I am feeling.
A	U	O	S	R	N	I have gone on eating binges where I felt that I could not stop.
A	U	O	S	R	N	I get confused as to whether or not I am hungry.
A	U	O	S	R	N	I think my hips are too big.
A	U	O	S	R	N	If I gain a pound, I worry that I will keep gaining.
A	U	O	S	R	N	I have the thought of trying to vomit in order to lose weight.
A	U	O	S	R	N	I think my buttocks are too large.
A	U	O	S	R	N	I eat or drink in secrecy.
A	U	O	S	R	N	I would like to be in total control of my bodily urges.

Source: Garner, Olmsted, & Polivy, 1991, 1984.

medical improvements follow (Iketani et al., 1995). Also encouraging is that the death rate from anorexia nervosa seems to be falling (Neumarker, 1997; Treasure & Szmukler, 1995). Earlier diagnosis and safer and faster weight-restoration techniques may account for this trend. Deaths that do occur are usually caused by suicide, starvation, infection, gastrointestinal problems, or electrolyte imbalance (Nielsen et al., 1998; Treasure & Szmukler, 1995).

On the negative side, close to 20 percent of persons with anorexia nervosa remain seriously troubled for years (Steinhausen, 2002; APA, 2000). Furthermore, recovery, when it does occur, is not always permanent. Anorexic behavior recurs in at least one-third of recovered patients, usually triggered by new stresses, such as marriage, pregnancy, or a major relocation (Fennig et al., 2002; Lay et al., 2002). Even years later, many recovered individuals continue to express concerns about their weight and appearance. Some continue to restrict their diets to a degree, experience anxiety when they eat with other people, or hold some distorted ideas about food, eating, and weight (Fichter & Pirke, 1995; Pirke et al., 1992).

About half of those who have suffered from anorexia nervosa continue to experience certain emotional problems—particularly depression, social anxiety, and obsessiveness—years after treatment. Such problems are particularly common in those who have not succeeded in reaching a fully normal weight (Steinhausen, 2002; Halmi, 1995).

The more weight persons have lost and the more time that has passed before they entered treatment, the poorer the recovery rate (Finfgeld, 2002). Individuals who had psychological or sexual problems before the onset of the disorder tend to have a poorer recovery rate than those without such a history (Finfgeld, 2002; Lewis & Chatoor, 1994). Teenagers seem to have a better recovery rate than older patients (APA, 2000; Steinhausen et al., 2000). Females have a better recovery rate than males.

Daily record *A teenager with anorexia nervosa writes in her journal as part of an inpatient treatment program. The writing helps her identify the fears, emotions, and needs that have contributed to her disorder.*

Treatments for Bulimia Nervosa

Treatment programs for bulimia nervosa are often offered in eating disorder clinics. Such programs share the immediate goal of helping clients to eliminate their binge-purge patterns and establish good eating habits and the more general goal of eliminating the underlying causes of bulimic patterns. The programs emphasize education as much as therapy (Davis et al., 1997; Button, 1993). Like programs for anorexia nervosa, they often combine several treatment strategies, including individual insight therapy, behavioral therapy, antidepressant drug therapy, and group therapy (Narash et al., 2002; King, 2001; Tobin, 2000).

INDIVIDUAL INSIGHT THERAPY The insight approach that is now receiving the most attention in cases of bulimia nervosa is *cognitive therapy*, which tries to help clients recognize and change their maladaptive attitudes toward food, eating, weight, and shape (Mitchell et al., 2002; Wilson et al., 2002). Cognitive therapists typically teach the individuals to identify and challenge the negative thoughts that regularly precede their urge to binge—"I have no self-control," "I might as well give up," "I look fat" (Mitchell & Peterson, 1997; Fairburn, 1985). They may also guide clients to recognize, question, and eventually change their perfectionistic standards, sense of helplessness, and low self-concept. Cognitive therapy seems to help as many as 65 percent of patients to stop bingeing and purging (Mitchell et al., 2002).

Because of its effectiveness in the treatment of bulimia nervosa, cognitive therapy is often tried first, before other individual insight therapies are considered. If clients do not respond to the cognitive approach, approaches with promising but less impressive track records may then be tried. A common alternative is *interpersonal psychotherapy*, the treatment that seeks to improve interpersonal functioning (Mitchell et al., 2002; Wegner & Wegner, 2001). A number of clinicians also suggest *self-help groups* for clients or *self-care manuals*, which describe education and treatment strategies for sufferers (Palmer et al., 2002; Garvin et al.,

>>**LAB•NOTES**

Upsetting Ads Immediately after looking at ads in fashion magazines and the models in those ads, undergraduate female subjects showed a greater rise in depression and hostility than did women exposed to ads without pictures of people (Pinhas et al., 1999).<<

- -

Forbidden Fruit (and Crackers) In one study, preschool children showed no special interest in fruit bars and Goldfish crackers until the foods were placed in a "no-no" jar. Once the foods had been given taboo status, the children made more positive comments about them, requested them more, tried to obtain them, and grabbed more of them when they were available (Fisher & Birch, 1999).<<

And She Lived Happily Ever After?

In May 1996 Alicia Machado, a 19-year-old woman from Venezuela, was crowned Miss Universe. Then her problems began. During the first eight months of her reign, her weight rose from 118 to 160 pounds, angering pageant officials and sparking rumors that she was about to be relieved of her crown. The "problem" received broad newspaper and television coverage and much ridicule on talk radio programs around the world.

Ms. Machado explained, "I was a normal girl, but my life has had big changes. I travel to many countries, eat different foods." Nevertheless, in response to all the pressure, she undertook a special diet and an extensive

Marcus/Sipa Press

exercise program to lose at least some of the weight she had gained. Her trainer claimed that a weight of 118 pounds was too low for her frame and explained that she had originally attained it by taking diet pills.

In the meantime, the whole episode served to demonstrate once again the powerful role of society in defining female beauty, acceptable weight, and "proper" eating. Ironically, many of the individuals who harshly criticized Ms. Machado or made fun of her—that is, the female critics—are themselves victims of the demanding and unrealistic standards of Western cultures that drive so many individuals toward dysfunctional patterns of eating.

2001). *Psychodynamic therapy* has also been used in cases of bulimia nervosa, but only a few research studies have tested and supported its effectiveness (Valbak, 2001; Yager, 1985).

BEHAVIORAL THERAPY Behavioral techniques are often applied in cases of bulimia nervosa, particularly as a supplement to cognitive therapy (Mizes & Bonifazi, 2002; Tacon & Caldera, 2001). Clients may, for example, be asked to keep diaries of their eating behaviors, changes in sensations of hunger and fullness, and the rise and fall of other feelings (Latner & Wilson, 2002). This helps them to observe their eating patterns more objectively and recognize the emotions that trigger their desire to binge.

Some behaviorists use the technique of *exposure and response prevention* to help break the binge-purge cycle. As we saw in Chapter 4, this approach consists of exposing people to situations that would ordinarily raise anxiety and then preventing them from performing their usual compulsive responses until they learn that the situations are actually harmless and their compulsive acts unnecessary. For bulimia nervosa, the therapists require clients to eat particular kinds and amounts of food and then prevent them from vomiting, to show that eating can be a harmless and even constructive activity that needs no undoing (Spiegler & Guevremont, 2003; Rosen & Leitenberg, 1985, 1982). Typically the therapist sits with the client during the eating of forbidden foods and stays until the urge to purge has passed. Studies find that this treatment often helps reduce eating-related anxieties, bingeing, and vomiting (Bulik et al., 1998).

ANTIDEPRESSANT MEDICATIONS During the past decade, antidepressant drugs such as *fluoxetine*, or Prozac, have been used to help treat bulimia nervosa (Mitchell, 2001; Walsh et al., 1997). According to research, the drugs may help as many as 40 percent of patients, reducing their binges by an average of 67 percent and vomiting by 56 percent. Once again, drug therapy seems to work best in combination with other forms of therapy. Alternatively, some therapists wait to see whether cognitive therapy or another insight approach is effective before trying antidepressants (Mitchell et al., 2002; Wilson et al., 2002).

GROUP THERAPY Finally, bulimia nervosa programs now often include group therapy to give clients an opportunity to share their concerns and experiences with one another (Riess, 2002; Pyle, 1999). Group members learn that their dis-

>>LOOKING AROUND
Worldly Concerns

Eating disorders are now on the increase in a number of countries around the world, including those in South America, Asia, Africa, and Eastern Europe (Simpson, 2002; Nasser et al., 2001). In such countries these increases have less to do with a fear of gaining weight than with sweeping changes in the social and political status of women.<<

order is not unique or shameful, and they receive support from one another, along with honest feedback and insights (Manley & Needham, 1995). In the group they can also work directly on underlying fears of displeasing others or being criticized. Research suggests that group therapy is at least somewhat helpful in as many as 75 percent of bulimia nervosa cases, particularly when it is combined with individual insight therapy (Valbak, 2001; McKisack & Waller, 1997).

WHAT IS THE AFTERMATH OF BULIMIA NERVOSA? Left untreated, bulimia nervosa can last for years, sometimes improving temporarily but then returning (APA, 2000). Treatment, however, produces immediate, significant improvement in approximately 40 percent of clients: they stop or greatly reduce their bingeing and purging, eat properly, and maintain a normal weight. Another 40 percent show a moderate response—at least some decrease in bingeing and purging. As many as 20 percent show little immediate improvement (Keel & Mitchell, 1997; Button, 1993). Follow-up studies suggest that by 10 years after treatment, 89 percent of persons with bulimia nervosa have recovered either fully (70 percent) or partially (19 percent) (Herzog et al., 1999; Keel et al., 1999). Those with partial recoveries continue to have recurrent binges or purges.

Relapse can be a problem even among people who respond successfully to treatment (Herzog et al., 1999; Keel & Mitchell, 1997). As with anorexia nervosa, relapses are usually triggered by a new life stress, such as an upcoming exam, job change, marriage, or divorce (Abraham & Llewellyn-Jones, 1985). One study found that close to one-third of persons who had recovered from bulimia nervosa relapsed within two years of treatment, usually within six months (Olmsted, Kaplan, & Rockert, 1994). Relapse is more likely among persons who had longer histories of bulimia nervosa before treatment, had vomited more frequently during their disorder, had histories of substance abuse, and continue to distrust others after treatment (Keel et al., 2000, 1999; Olmsted et al., 1994).

Research also indicates that treatment helps many, but not all, people with bulimia nervosa attain lasting improvements in their overall psychological and social functioning (Stein et al., 2002; Keel et al., 2000). Follow-up studies find former patients to be less depressed than they had been at the time of diagnosis (Halmi, 1995). Approximately one-third of former patients interact in healthier ways at work, at home, and in social settings, while another third interact effectively in two of these areas (Hsu & Holder, 1986).

Changing times Seated Bather, *by Pierre-Auguste Renoir (1841–1919), shows that the aesthetically ideal woman of the past was considerably larger than today's ideal.*

SUMMING UP
How Are Eating Disorders Treated?

The first step in treating anorexia nervosa is to increase calorie intake and quickly restore the person's weight, using a strategy such as supportive nursing care. The second step is to deal with the underlying psychological and family problems, using both therapy and education. About 83 percent of people who receive successful treatment for anorexia nervosa continue to show full or partial improvements years later. However, some of them relapse along the way, many continue to worry about their weight and appearance, and half continue to experience some emotional or family problems. Most menstruate again when they regain weight.

Treatments for bulimia nervosa focus first on stopping the binge-purge pattern and then on addressing the underlying causes of the disorder. Often several treatment strategies are combined, including individual insight therapy, behavioral therapy, antidepressant medications, and group therapy. Approximately 89 percent of those who receive treatment eventually improve either fully or partially. While relapse can be a problem along the way, treatment leads to lasting improvements in psychological and social functioning for many individuals.

>>LOOKING AROUND
Children's Playthings

Barbie In the 1990s clinical researchers noted that the doll Barbie had unattainable proportions. A 5′2″ 125-pound woman who aspired to Barbie's size would have to grow to be 7′2″, add 5 inches to her chest and 3.2 inches to the length of her neck, and lose 6 inches from her waist (Brownell & Napolitano, 1995).<<

GI Joe Male action figures, such as GI Joe and Luke Skywalker, have acquired the physiques of body builders in recent years, with sharp muscle definition in the chest, shoulders, and abdominals (Pope et al., 1999). If GI Joe were a real man, he would have larger biceps than any body builder in history, with a 5′10″ frame and 29-inch biceps, a 32-inch waist, and a 55-inch chest.<<

CROSSROADS:
A Standard for Integrating Perspectives

We have observed throughout this book that it is often useful to consider sociocultural, psychological, and biological factors jointly when one tries to explain or treat various forms of abnormal functioning. Nowhere is the argument for combining these perspectives more powerful than in the case of eating disorders.

According to the multidimensional risk perspective, embraced by many theorists, varied factors act together to encourage the development of eating disorders. One case may be the result of societal pressures, independence problems, the changes of adolescence, and hypothalamic overactivity, while another case may result from family pressures, depression, and the effects of dieting. No wonder that the most helpful treatment programs for eating disorders often combine sociocultural, psychological, and biological approaches. When the multidimensional risk perspective is applied to eating disorders, it demonstrates that scientists and practitioners who follow very different models can work together productively in an atmosphere of mutual respect.

Today's many investigations of eating disorders keep revealing new surprises that force clinicians to adjust their theories and treatment programs. For example, in recent times researchers have learned that people with bulimia nervosa sometimes feel strangely positive about their symptoms (Serpell & Treasure, 2002). A recovered patient said, "I still miss my bulimia as I would an old friend who has died" (Cauwels, 1983, p. 173). Only when feelings like these are understood will treatment become fully effective—another reason why the cooperative efforts of different kinds of theorists, clinicians, and researchers are so important.

While clinicians and researchers seek more answers about eating disorders, clients themselves have begun to take an active role. A number of patient-run organizations now provide information, education, and support through national telephone hot lines, Web sites, professional referrals, newsletters, workshops, and conferences. The National Anorexic Aid Society, the American Anorexia and Bulimia Association, the National Association of Anorexia Nervosa and Associated Disorders, and Anorexia Nervosa and Related Eating Disorders, Inc., help fight the feelings of isolation and shame experienced by people with eating disorders. They show countless sufferers that they are hardly alone or powerless.

Yvonne Hemsey/Liaison

A new look for Barbie *Partly in response to clinical concerns, the manufacturer of Barbie recently changed the proportions of the doll with whom so many women grew up.*

CRITICAL THOUGHTS

1. Many, perhaps most, women in Western society feel as if they are dieting or between diets their entire adult lives. Is it possible to be a woman in this society and not struggle with at least some issues of eating and appearance? *pp. 253–254, 262–265*

2. Who is responsible for the standards of weight and appearance that affect so many women? *pp. 262–265*

3. The most successful of today's fashion models, often referred to as supermodels, have a celebrity status that was not given to models in the past. Why do you think the fame and status of models have risen in this way? *pp. 262–265*

4. What does the 1996 Miss Universe flap suggest about the role of societal factors in the development of eating problems? Why do you think so many people held such strong, often critical opinions about Miss Universe's weight? *p. 274*

5. Relapse is a problem for some people who recover from anorexia nervosa and bulimia nervosa. Why might people remain vulnerable even after recovery? How might they and their therapists reduce the chances of relapse? *pp. 273, 275*

KEY TERMS

anorexia nervosa p. 254

restricting-type anorexia nervosa p. 254

amenorrhea p. 257

bulimia nervosa p. 257

binge p. 257

compensatory behavior pp. 257, 259

binge-eating disorder p. 258

multidimensional risk perspective p. 262

enmeshed family pattern p. 266

effective parents p. 266

hypothalamus p. 268

lateral hypothalamus (LH) p. 268

ventromedial hypothalamus (VMH) p. 268

weight set point p. 269

supportive nursing care p. 270

QUICK QUIZ

1. What are the symptoms and main features of anorexia nervosa? *pp. 254–257*

2. What are the symptoms and main features of bulimia nervosa? *pp. 257–261*

3. How are people with anorexia nervosa similar to those with bulimia nervosa? How are they different? *pp. 261–262*

4. Theorists usually apply a multidimensional risk perspective to explain the eating disorders. What does this mean? *p. 262*

5. What evidence suggests that sociocultural pressures and factors may set the stage for eating disorders? *pp. 262–265*

6. According to Hilde Bruch, how might parents' failure to attend appropriately to their baby's internal needs and emotions contribute to the later development of an eating disorder? *pp. 266–267*

7. How might a person's hypothalamus and weight set point contribute to the development of an eating disorder? *pp. 268–270*

8. When clinicians treat people with anorexia nervosa, what are their short-term and long-term goals? What approaches do they use to achieve them? *pp. 270–272*

9. How well do people with anorexia nervosa recover from their disorder? What factors affect a person's recovery? What risks and problems may linger after recovery? *pp. 272–273*

10. What are the key goals and approaches used in the treatment of bulimia nervosa? How successful are they? What factors affect a person's recovery? What risks and problems may linger after recovery? *pp. 273–275*

 CYBER STUDY

SEARCH THE *FUNDAMENTALS OF ABNORMAL PSYCHOLOGY* CD-ROM FOR

▲ Chapter 9 Video Case Enrichment
  Witness the feelings behind bingeing and purging.
  How does an eating disorder begin?
  How do individuals feel toward their eating disorders?

▲ Chapter 9 Practical, Research, and Decision-Making Exercises
  Attitudes toward eating, food, and weight
  Body image and eating: Tracing the media's role

▲ Chapter 9 Practice Test and Feedback

LOG ON TO THE COMER WEB PAGE FOR

▲ Suggested Web links, exercises, FAQ page, additional Chapter 9 practice test questions
  <www.worthpublishers.com/comer>

‹‹‹

MARLENA ZUBER, 2001

Substance-Related Disorders

"I am Duncan. I am an alcoholic." The audience settled deeper into their chairs at these familiar words. Another chronicle of death and rebirth would shortly begin [at] Alcoholics Anonymous. . . .

. . . "I must have been just past my 15th birthday when I had that first drink that everybody talks about. And like so many of them . . . it was like a miracle. With a little beer in my gut, the world was transformed. I wasn't a weakling anymore, I could lick almost anybody on the block. And girls? Well, you can imagine how a couple of beers made me feel, like I could have any girl I wanted. . . .

"Though it's obvious to me now that my drinking even then, in high school, and after I got to college, was a problem, I didn't think so at the time. After all, everybody was drinking and getting drunk and acting stupid, and I didn't really think I was different. . . . I guess the fact that I hadn't really had any blackouts and that I could go for days without having to drink reassured me that things hadn't gotten out of control. And that's the way it went, until I found myself drinking even more—and more often—and suffering more from my drinking, along about my third year of college.

. . . "My roommate, a friend from high school, started bugging me about my drinking. It wasn't even that I'd have to sleep it off the whole next day and miss class, it was that he had begun to hear other friends talking about me, about the fool I'd made of myself at parties. He saw how shaky I was the morning after, and he saw how different I was when I'd been drinking a lot— almost out of my head was the way he put it. And he could count the bottles that I'd leave around the room, and he knew what the drinking and carousing was doing to my grades. . . . [P]artly because I really cared about my room-mate and didn't want to lose him as a friend, I did cut down on my drinking by half or more. I only drank on weekends—and then only at night. . . . And that got me through the rest of college and, actually, through law school as well. . . .

"Shortly after getting my law degree, I married my first wife, and . . . for the first time since I started, my drinking was no problem at all. I would go for weeks at a time without touching a drop. . . .

"My marriage started to go bad after our second son, our third child, was born. I was very much career-and-success oriented, and I had little time to spend at home with my family. . . . My traveling had increased a lot, there were stimulating people on those trips, and, let's face it, there were some pretty exciting women available, too. So home got to be little else but a nag-ging, boring wife and children I wasn't very interested in. My drinking had got-ten bad again, too, with being on the road so much, having to do a lot of entertaining at lunch when I wasn't away, and trying to soften the hassles at home. I guess I was putting down close to a gallon of very good scotch a week, with one thing or another.

"And as that went on, the drinking began to affect both my marriage and my career. With enough booze in me and under the pressures of guilt over my fail-ure to carry out my responsibilities to my wife and children, I sometimes got

>>IN THEIR WORDS

"Wine is the most healthful and most hygienic of beverages."<<

Louis Pasteur

"There is a devil in every berry of the grape."<<

The Koran

kind of rough physically with them. I would break furniture, throw things around, then rush out and drive off in the car. I had a couple of wrecks, lost my license for two years because of one of them. Worst of all was when I tried to stop. By then I was totally hooked, so every time I tried to stop drinking, I'd experience withdrawal in all its horrors . . . with the vomiting and the 'shakes' and being unable to sit still or to lie down. And that would go on for days at a time. . . .

"Then, about four years ago, with my life in ruins, my wife given up on me and the kids with her, out of a job, and way down on my luck, [Alcoholics Anonymous] and I found each other. . . . I've been dry now for a little over two years, and with luck and support, I may stay sober. . . ."

(Spitzer et al., 1983, pp. 87–89)

Human beings enjoy a remarkable variety of foods and drinks. Every substance on earth probably has been tried by someone, somewhere, at some time. We also have discovered substances that have interesting effects—both medical and pleasurable—on our brains and the rest of our bodies. We may swallow an aspirin to quiet a headache, an antibiotic to fight an infection, or a tranquilizer to calm us down. We may drink coffee to get going in the morning or wine to relax with friends. We may smoke cigarettes to soothe our nerves. However, many of the substances we consume can harm us or disrupt our behavior or mood. The misuse of such substances has become one of society's biggest problems; it has been estimated that the cost of drug misuse is a staggering $414 billion each year in the United States alone (RWJF, 2001).

A *drug* is defined as any substance other than food that affects our bodies or minds. It need not be a medicine or be illegal. The term "substance" is now frequently used in place of "drug," in part because many people fail to see that such substances as alcohol, tobacco, and caffeine are drugs, too. When a person ingests a substance—whether it be alcohol, cocaine, marijuana, or some form of medication—trillions of powerful molecules surge through the bloodstream and into the brain (Nash, 1997). Once there, the molecules set off a series of biochemical events that disturb the normal operation of the brain and body. Not surprisingly, then, substance misuse may lead to various kinds of abnormal functioning.

Drugs may cause *temporary* changes in behavior, emotion, or thought. As Duncan found out, for example, an excessive amount of alcohol may lead to *intoxication* (literally, "poisoning"), a temporary state of poor judgment, mood changes, irritability, slurred speech, and poor coordination. Drugs such as LSD may produce a particular form of intoxication, sometimes called *hallucinosis*, consisting of perceptual distortions and hallucinations.

Some substances can also lead to *long-term problems*. People who regularly ingest them may develop maladaptive patterns of behavior and changes in their body's physical responses (APA, 2000). In one such pattern, called **substance abuse**, they rely on the drug excessively and chronically and in so doing damage their family and social relationships, function poorly at work, or put themselves and others in danger. A more advanced pattern, **substance dependence**, is also known as **addiction**. In this pattern, people not only abuse the drug but also center their lives on it and perhaps acquire a physical dependence on it, marked by a **tolerance** for it, withdrawal symptoms, or both (see Table 10-1). When people develop tolerance, they need increasing doses of a drug in order to keep getting the desired effect. **Withdrawal** consists of unpleasant and even dangerous symptoms—cramps, anxiety attacks, sweating, nausea—that occur when individuals suddenly stop taking or cut back on the drug.

Duncan, who described his problems to fellow members at an Alcoholics Anonymous meeting, was caught in a pattern of alcohol dependence. When he was a college student and later a lawyer, alcohol damaged his family, social, academic, and work life. He also built up a tolerance for the substance over time and experienced withdrawal symptoms such as vomiting and shaking when he tried to

SUBSTANCE ABUSE A pattern of behavior in which people rely on a drug excessively and regularly, bringing damage to their relationships, functioning poorly at work, or putting themselves or others in danger.

SUBSTANCE DEPENDENCE A pattern of behavior in which people organize their lives around a drug, possibly building a tolerance to it or experiencing withdrawal symptoms when they stop taking it, or both. Also called *addiction*.

TOLERANCE The adjustment that the brain and the body make to the regular use of certain drugs so that ever larger doses are needed to achieve the earlier effects.

WITHDRAWAL Unpleasant, sometimes dangerous reactions that may occur when people who use a drug regularly stop taking or reduce their dosage of the drug.

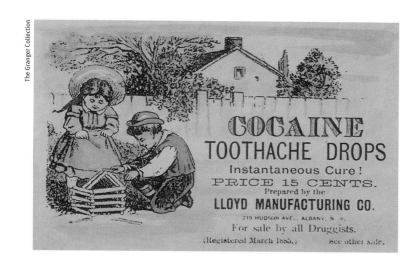

Wonder drug *Drugs often go through periods of broad acceptance before their dangers are discovered. Cocaine, for example, was legal in the United States until 1914 and was an ingredient in over-the-counter medicines, such as Cocaine Toothache Drops. This 1885 ad shows that it was used to treat children as well as adults. Cocaine was also part of Coca-Cola's formula until 1903.*

stop using it. In any given year, 7.3 percent of all adults in the United States display a pattern of substance abuse or dependence (NHSDA, 2002). Only 20 percent of them receive treatment.

Many drugs are available in our society, and new ones are introduced almost every day. Some are found in nature, others derived from natural substances, and still others produced in the laboratory. Some, such as antianxiety drugs and barbiturates, require a physician's prescription for legal use. Others, such as alcohol and nicotine, are legally available to adults. Still others, such as heroin, are illegal under all circumstances. In 1962 only 4 million people in the United States had ever used marijuana, cocaine, heroin, or another illegal substance; today the number has climbed to more than 94 million (NHSDA, 2002). In fact, 28 million people have used illegal substances within the past year, and 16 million are using one currently. More than one-quarter of all high school seniors have used an illegal drug within the past month (Johnston, O'Malley, & Bachman, 2002).

The substances people misuse fall into several categories: *depressants*, such as alcohol and opioids, which slow the central nervous system; *stimulants* of the central nervous system, such as cocaine and amphetamines; *hallucinogens*, such as LSD, which cause delusions, hallucinations, and other powerful changes in sensory perception; and *cannabis* substances, such as marijuana, which cause a mixture of hallucinogenic, depressant, and stimulant effects. Many people take more than one of these substances at a time, a practice known as *polydrug* use. In this chapter we shall look at some of the most problematic substances and the abnormal patterns they may produce. After first examining the substances separately, we shall consider the causes and treatments of substance-related disorders together as a group.

Table 10-1 DSM-IV Checklist

SUBSTANCE ABUSE

1. A maladaptive pattern of substance use leading to significant impairment or distress
2. At least one of the following features occurring within one year:
   (a) Recurrent substance use, resulting in failure to fulfill major role obligations at work, school, or home
   (b) Recurrent substance use in situations in which it is physically hazardous
   (c) Recurrent substance-related legal problems
   (d) Substance use that continues despite its causing or increasing persistent social or interpersonal problems

SUBSTANCE DEPENDENCE

1. A maladaptive pattern of substance use leading to significant impairment or distress
2. At least three of the following:
   (a) Tolerance
   (b) Withdrawal
   (c) Substance often taken in larger amounts over a longer period than was intended
   (d) Persistent desire for substance or unsuccessful efforts to control substance use
   (e) Considerable time spent trying to obtain, use, or recover from the substance
   (f) Substance use in place of important activities
   (g) Substance use that continues despite its causing or increasing persistent physical or psychological problems

Based on APA, 2000, 1994.

Depressants

Depressants slow the activity of the central nervous system. They reduce tension and inhibitions and may interfere with a person's judgment, motor activity, and concentration. The three most widely used groups of depressants are *alcohol, sedative-hypnotic drugs,* and *opioids*.

Alcohol

Two-thirds of the people in the United States at least from time to time drink beverages that contain **alcohol** (CDC, 2002). Purchases of beer, wine, and liquor amount to tens of billions of dollars each year in the United States alone. Nearly 6 percent of persons over 11 years of age are heavy drinkers, having at least five drinks on at least five occasions each month (NCHS, 2002). Among heavy drinkers, males outnumber females by more than three to one, around 9 percent to 3 percent.

All alcoholic beverages contain *ethyl alcohol*, a chemical that is quickly absorbed into the blood through the lining of the stomach and the intestine. The ethyl alcohol immediately begins to take effect as it is carried in the bloodstream to the central nervous system (the brain and spinal cord), where it acts to depress, or slow, functioning by binding to various neurons. One important group of neurons to which ethyl alcohol binds are those that normally receive the neurotransmitter GABA. As we observed in Chapter 4, GABA carries an *inhibitory* message —a message to stop firing—when it is received at certain neurons. When alcohol binds to receptors on those neurons, it apparently helps GABA to shut down the neurons, thus helping to relax the drinker (Harvey et al., 2002; Heinz et al., 2001).

At first ethyl alcohol slows down the areas of the brain that control judgment and inhibition; people become looser, more talkative, and often more friendly. As their inner control breaks down, they may feel relaxed, confident, and happy. When more alcohol is absorbed, it slows down additional areas in the central nervous system, leaving the drinkers less able to make sound judgments, their speech less careful and less clear, and their memory weaker. Many people become highly emotional and perhaps loud and aggressive.

Motor difficulties increase as drinking continues, and reaction times slow. People may be unsteady when they stand or walk and clumsy in performing even simple activities. They may drop things, bump into doors and furniture, and misjudge distances. Their vision becomes blurred, particularly side vision, and they have trouble hearing. As a result, people who have drunk too much alcohol may have great difficulty driving or solving simple problems.

The extent of the effect of ethyl alcohol is determined by its *concentration*, or proportion, in the blood. Thus a given amount of alcohol will have less effect on a large person than on a small one (see Table 10-2). Gender also affects the concentration of alcohol in the blood. Women have less of the stomach enzyme *alcohol dehydrogenase*, which breaks down alcohol in the stomach before it enters the blood. So women become more intoxicated than men on equal doses of alcohol.

Levels of impairment are closely related to the concentration of ethyl alcohol in the blood. When the alcohol concentration reaches 0.06 percent of the blood volume, a person usually feels relaxed and comfortable. By the time it reaches 0.09 percent, however, the drinker crosses the line into intoxication. If the level goes as high as 0.55 percent, death will probably result. Most people, however, lose consciousness before they can drink enough to reach this level.

The effects of alcohol subside only when the alcohol concentration in the blood falls. Most of the alcohol is broken down, or *metabolized*, by the liver into carbon dioxide and water, which can be exhaled and excreted. The average rate of this breakdown of alcohol is 13 percent of an ounce per hour, but different people's livers work at different speeds; thus rates of "sobering up" vary. Despite popular belief, only time and metabolism can make a person sober. Drinking black coffee, splashing cold water on one's face, or "pulling oneself together" cannot hurry the process.

Table 10-2

Relationships between Sex, Weight, Oral Alcohol Consumption, and Blood Alcohol Level

ABSOLUTE ALCOHOL (OZ.)	BEVERAGE INTAKE*	BLOOD ALCOHOL LEVEL (PERCENT)					
		FEMALE (100 LB.)	MALE (100 LB.)	FEMALE (150 LB.)	MALE (150 LB.)	FEMALE (200 LB.)	MALE (200 LB.)
1/2	1 oz. spirits[†] 1 glass wine 1 can beer	0.045	0.037	0.03	0.025	0.022	0.019
1	2 oz. spirits 2 glasses wine 2 cans beer	0.090	0.075	0.06	0.050	0.045	0.037
2	4 oz. spirits 4 glasses wine 4 cans beer	0.180	0.150	0.12	0.100	0.090	0.070
3	6 oz. spirits 6 glasses wine 6 cans beer	0.270	0.220	0.18	0.150	0.130	0.110
4	8 oz. spirits 8 glasses wine 8 cans beer	0.360	0.300	0.24	0.200	0.180	0.150
5	10 oz. spirits 10 glasses wine 10 cans beer	0.450	0.370	0.30	0.250	0.220	0.180

*In 1 hour.
[†]100-proof spirits.

Source: Ray & Ksir, 1993, p. 194.

ALCOHOL ABUSE AND DEPENDENCE Though legal, alcohol is actually one of the most dangerous of recreational drugs, and its reach extends across the life span. In fact, around 10 percent of elementary school students admit to some alcohol use, while nearly 50 percent of high school seniors drink alcohol each month (most to the point of intoxication) and 3.6 percent report drinking every day (Johnston et al., 2002; NIDA, 1995) (see Figure 10-1 on the next page). Similarly, alcohol misuse is a major problem on college campuses (Schulenberg et al., 2001).

Surveys indicate that over a one-year period, 5.9 percent of all adults in the United States fall into a long-term pattern of alcohol abuse or dependence, either of which is known in popular terms as *alcoholism* (NHSDA, 2002). Between 13 and 18 percent of the nation's adults display one of the patterns at some time in their lives, with men outnumbering women by at least 2 to 1 (NHSDA, 2002; Kessler & Zhao, 1999; Regier et al., 1993). Many teenagers also experience alcohol abuse or dependence (Johnston et al., 2002).

The prevalence of alcoholism in a given year is around 7 percent for both white Americans and African Americans and 9 percent for Hispanic Americans (APA, 2000; Anthony et al., 1995; Helzer et al., 1991). Generally, Asians in the United States and elsewhere have lower rates of alcoholism than do people from other cultures. As many as one-half of Asians have a deficiency of alcohol dehydrogenase, the chemical responsible for breaking down alcohol, so they react quite negatively to even a modest intake of alcohol. Such reactions in turn prevent extended use (Wall et al., 2001; APA, 2000).

ALCOHOL ABUSE Generally speaking, people who abuse alcohol drink large amounts regularly and rely on it to enable them to do things that would otherwise make

>>**LOOKING BACK**

Fighting Black Death

A popular theory in the mid-1300s was that strong drinks of alcohol offered protection from the Black Death, the bubonic plague that was sweeping Europe. This mistaken belief led to a plague of drunkenness as widespread as the plague of contagion (Asimov, 1997).<<

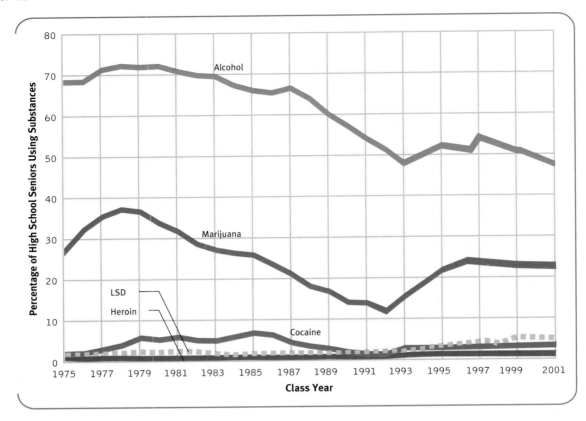

FIGURE 10-1 **Teenagers and substance use** *The overall percentage of high school seniors who admitted to using substances illicitly at least once within the previous 30 days rose in the 1970s, declined in the 1980s, rose again in the early 1990s, and has been declining slightly since 1997 (Johnston et al., 2002). In addition to the drugs shown in this figure, other drugs used by high school seniors within the past month include MDMA, or Ecstasy (2.8 percent), inhalants (1.7 percent), and steroids (1.3 percent).*

them anxious. Eventually the drinking interferes with their social behavior and ability to think and work. They may have frequent arguments with family members or friends, miss work repeatedly, and even lose their jobs (Schmidt et al., 2000).

Individually, however, people vary in their patterns of alcohol abuse. Some drink large amounts of alcohol every day and keep drinking until intoxicated. Others go on periodic binges of heavy drinking that can last weeks or months. They may remain intoxicated for days and later be unable to remember anything about the period. Still others may limit their excessive drinking to weekends or evenings, or both. The actor Dick Van Dyke commented:

> I didn't miss work ever because of drinking. And I never drank at work. Never drank during the day—only at home and only in the evenings. . . . I never craved a drink during the day. I was never a morning drinker—I didn't want one then. The idea made me as sick as it would make anyone else. But evening drinking is a form of alcoholism, just like periodic drinking is a form of alcoholism. . . .
>
> *(HEW, 1976, p. 76)*

ALCOHOL DEPENDENCE For many people, the pattern of alcohol misuse includes dependence. Their bodies build up a tolerance for alcohol and they need to drink ever greater amounts to feel its effects. They also experience withdrawal when they stop drinking. Within hours their hands, tongue, and eyelids begin to shake; they feel weak and nauseated; they sweat and vomit; their heart beats rapidly; and their blood pressure rises. They may also become anxious, depressed, unable to sleep, or irritable (APA, 2000).

A small percentage of people who are dependent on alcohol experience a particularly dramatic withdrawal reaction called **delirium tremens** ("**the DTs**"). It consists of terrifying visual hallucinations that begin within three days after they stop or reduce their drinking. Some people see small, frightening animals chasing or crawling on them or objects dancing about in front of their eyes. Like most other alcohol withdrawal symptoms, the DTs usually run their course in two to three days. However, people who experience severe withdrawal reactions such as this may also have seizures, lose consciousness, suffer a stroke, or even die. Today certain medical procedures can help prevent or reduce such extreme reactions (D'Onofrio et al., 1999).

WHAT IS THE PERSONAL AND SOCIAL IMPACT OF ALCOHOLISM? Alcoholism destroys millions of families, social relationships, and careers. Medical treatment, lost productivity, and losses due to deaths from alcoholism cost society as much as $148 billion annually (NIDA, 1998). The disorder also plays a role in more than one-third of all suicides, homicides, assaults, rapes, and accidental deaths, including 41 percent of all fatal automobile accidents in the United States (NHSDA, 2002; McClelland & Teplin, 2001; Mustaine & Tewksbury, 1998). Altogether, intoxicated drivers are responsible for 19,000 deaths each year (CDC, 2002). One of every ten adults has driven while intoxicated at least once in the past year (NHSDA, 2002).

Alcoholism has serious effects on the 30 million children of persons with this disorder. Home life for these children is likely to include much conflict and perhaps sexual or other forms of abuse. In turn, the children themselves have higher rates of psychological problems such as anxiety, depression, phobias, conduct disorder, attention-deficit disorder, and substance-related disorders during their lifetimes (Hall & Webster, 2002; Mylant et al., 2002). Many have low self-esteem, poor communication skills, poor sociability, and marital problems (Watt, 2002; Lewis-Harter, 2000).

Long-term excessive drinking can also seriously damage one's physical health. It so overworks the liver that people may develop an irreversible condition called *cirrhosis*, in which the liver becomes scarred and dysfunctional. Cirrhosis is the twelfth most frequent cause of death in the United States, accounting for some 26,000 deaths each year (CDC, 2002). Alcohol abuse and dependence may also damage the heart and lower the immune system's ability to fight off cancer and bacterial infections and to resist the onset of AIDS after infection (NIAAA, 1992).

Long-term excessive drinking also causes major nutritional problems. Alcohol makes people feel full and lowers their desire for food, yet it has no nutritional value. As a result, chronic drinkers become malnourished, weak, and prone to disease. Their vitamin and mineral deficiencies may also cause problems. An alcohol-related deficiency of vitamin B (thiamine), for example, may lead to **Korsakoff's syndrome**, a disease marked by extreme confusion, memory loss, and other neurological symptoms (Heap et al., 2002). People with Korsakoff's syndrome cannot remember the past or learn new information and may make up for their memory losses by *confabulating*—reciting made-up events to fill in the gaps.

Finally, women who drink during pregnancy place their fetuses at risk. Excessive alcohol use during pregnancy may cause a baby to be born with **fetal alcohol syndrome**, a pattern of abnormalities that can include mental retardation, hyperactivity, head and face deformities, heart defects, and slow growth (Hankin, 2002; Zevenbergen & Ferraro, 2001). It has been estimated that in the overall population 1 to 2 of every 1,000 babies are born with this syndrome (May & Gossage, 2001; Ray & Ksir, 1993). The rate may increase to as many as 29 of every 1,000 babies of women who are problem drinkers. In addition, heavy drinking early in pregnancy often leads to a miscarriage.

DELIRIUM TREMENS (DTs) A dramatic withdrawal reaction experienced by some people who are alcohol-dependent. It consists of confusion, clouded consciousness, and terrifying visual hallucinations.

KORSAKOFF'S SYNDROME An alcohol-related disorder marked by extreme confusion, memory impairment, and other neurological symptoms.

FETAL ALCOHOL SYNDROME A cluster of problems in a child, including low birth weight, irregularities in the head and face, and intellectual deficits, caused by excessive alcohol intake by the mother during pregnancy.

Kevin & Betty Collins/Visuals Unlimited

Spreading the word *Educating the public with billboard, television, and radio ads about the dangers of alcohol has helped reduce the number of alcohol-related automobile deaths by over 25 percent in recent years (CDC, 1997).*

College Binge Drinking: An Extracurricular Crisis

*D*rinking large amounts of alcohol in a short time, or *binge drinking*, is a serious problem on college campuses (Vicary & Karshin, 2002). Studies show that as many as 40 percent of college students binge-drink at times, around half of them at least six times per month (Wechsler et al., 2000, 1997, 1994; Bennett et al., 1999). These are higher rates than those displayed by people of the same age who are not in college. In many circles, alcohol use is an accepted part of college life (Schulenberg et al., 2001). Are we as a society taking the issue too lightly? Consider some of the following statistics:

⁺ Alcohol is a factor in nearly 40 percent of academic problems and 28 percent of all college dropouts (Anderson, 1994).

⁺ Although 84 percent of incoming freshmen consider heavy alcohol use to be a problem on campus, 68 percent drink during their first semester, at least half of them during their first week on campus (Harvard School of Public Health, 1995).

⁺ Alcohol affects not only those who drink but also those who do not, with approximately 600,000 students each year physically or emotionally traumatized or sexually assaulted by a student drinker (Higson et al., 2002).

⁺ Binge drinking has been linked to severe health problems and serious injury, auto crashes, unplanned and unprotected sex, aggressive behaviors, and various psychological problems (Wechsler et al., 1995; Wechsler & Isaac, 1992). Binge

drinking among college students has been associated with an estimated 1,400 student deaths, 500,000 injuries, and 70,000 cases of sexual assault, including date rape, every year (Wechsler et al., 2000)

⁺ There was a 31 percent increase in the number of female binge drinkers in colleges from 1993 to 2001.

These findings have led some educators to describe binge drinking as "the No. 1 public health hazard" for full-time college students, and many researchers and clinicians have turned their attention to it. Henry Wechsler and his colleagues (1995) at the Harvard School of Public Health mailed a questionnaire about drinking patterns to students at 140 college campuses around the United States and received close to 18,000 replies. According to the responses, people most likely to binge-drink were those who lived in a fraternity or sorority house, pursued a party-centered lifestyle, and engaged in high-risk behaviors such as smoking marijuana, having multiple sex partners, and smoking cigarettes. The study also

found that students who were binge drinkers in high school were more likely to binge-drink in college.

Efforts to change such patterns have begun to make a difference. For example, some universities now provide substance-free dorms: 36 percent of the residents in such dorms were binge drinkers, according to one study, compared to 75 percent of those who lived in a fraternity or sorority (Wechsler et al., 2002).

The results of studies on binge drinking are often based on self-administered questionnaires, and subjects' responses may be biased. Perhaps binge drinkers are more (or less) likely than nondrinkers to respond to such questionnaires. Still, the implications are clear: college drinking, certainly binge drinking, may be more common and more harmful than was previously believed. At the very least, it is a problem whose research time has come.

Andrew Lichtenstein/Corbis Sygma

Testing the limits *Binge drinking, similar to this display at a college campus party, has led to a number of deaths in recent years.*

Sedative-Hypnotic Drugs

Sedative-hypnotic drugs produce feelings of relaxation and drowsiness. At low dosages, the drugs have a calming or sedative effect. At higher dosages, they are sleep inducers, or hypnotics. The sedative-hypnotic drugs include *barbiturates* and *benzodiazepines.*

BARBITURATES First discovered in Germany more than 100 years ago, **barbiturates** were widely prescribed in the first half of the twentieth century to fight anxiety and to help people sleep. Although still prescribed by some physicians, these drugs have been largely replaced today by benzodiazepines, which are generally safer drugs. Barbiturates can cause many problems, not the least of which are abuse and dependence. Several thousand deaths a year are caused by accidental or suicidal overdoses.

Barbiturates are usually taken in pill or capsule form. In low doses they reduce a person's level of excitement in the same way that alcohol does, by attaching to receptors on the neurons that receive the inhibitory neurotransmitter GABA and by helping GABA operate at those neurons (Mazarakis & Nestoros, 2001; Frey et al., 1995). People can get intoxicated from large doses of barbiturates, just as they do from alcohol. At too high a dose, the drugs can halt breathing, lower blood pressure, and lead to coma and death.

Repeated use of barbiturates can quickly result in a pattern of abuse. Users may spend much of the day intoxicated, irritable, and unable to do their work. Dependence can also result. The user organizes his or her life around the drug and needs increasing amounts of it to calm down or fall asleep. A great danger of barbiturate dependence is that the lethal dose of the drug remains the same even while the body is building up a tolerance for its sedating effects (Landry, 1994; Gold, 1986). Once the prescribed dose stops reducing anxiety or inducing sleep, the user is all too likely to increase it without medical supervision and eventually may take a dose that proves fatal. Those caught in a pattern of barbiturate dependence may also experience withdrawal symptoms such as nausea, anxiety, and sleep problems. Barbiturate withdrawal is particularly dangerous, for it can cause convulsions.

BENZODIAZEPINES Chapter 4 described **benzodiazepines**, the antianxiety drugs developed in the 1950s, as the most popular sedative-hypnotic drugs available. Xanax and Valium are just two of the dozens of these compounds in clinical use. Like alcohol and barbiturates, they calm people by binding to receptors on the neurons that receive GABA and by increasing GABA's activity at those neurons (Nutt & Malizia, 2001). These drugs, however, relieve anxiety without making people as drowsy as other kinds of sedative-hypnotics. They are also less likely to slow a person's breathing, so they are less likely to cause death in the event of an overdose (Nishino et al., 1995).

When benzodiazepines were first discovered, they seemed so safe and effective that physicians prescribed them generously, and their use spread. Eventually it became clear that in high enough doses the drugs can cause intoxication and lead to abuse or dependence. As many as 1 percent of the adults in the United States abuse or become physically dependent on these antianxiety drugs at some point in their lives (APA, 2000; Anthony et al., 1995) and thus become subject to some of the same dangers that researchers have identified in barbiturate misuse.

Opioids

Opioids include opium—taken from the sap of the opium poppy—and the drugs derived from it, such as heroin, morphine, and codeine. **Opium** itself has been in use for thousands of years. In the past it was used widely in the treatment of medical disorders because of its ability to reduce both physical and emotional pain. Eventually, however, physicians discovered that the drug was physically addictive.

In 1804 a new substance, **morphine**, was derived from opium. Named after Morpheus, the Greek god of sleep, this drug relieved pain even better than opium did and initially was considered safe. However, wide use eventually revealed that it, too, could lead to addiction. So many wounded soldiers in the United States received morphine injections during the Civil War that morphine dependence became known as "soldiers' disease."

In 1898 morphine was converted into yet another new pain reliever, **heroin**. For several years heroin was viewed as a wonder drug and was used as a cough medicine and for other medical purposes. Eventually, however, physicians learned that heroin is even more addictive than the other opioids. By 1917 the

SEDATIVE-HYPNOTIC DRUG A drug used in low doses to reduce anxiety and in higher doses to help people sleep.

BARBITURATES Addictive sedative-hypnotic drugs used to reduce anxiety or to help people fall asleep.

BENZODIAZEPINES The most common group of antianxiety drugs, which includes Valium and Xanax.

OPIOID Opium or any of the drugs derived from opium, including morphine, heroin, and codeine.

OPIUM A highly addictive substance made from the sap of the opium poppy.

MORPHINE A highly addictive substance derived from opium that is particularly effective in relieving pain.

HEROIN One of the most addictive substances derived from opium, illegal in the United States under all circumstances.

>>**PSYCH•NOTES**
Opioids in Action

How Potent Is Heroin? When heroin is injected intravenously, 68 percent of it is absorbed in the brain, compared to less than 5 percent of injected morphine (Sporer, 1999).<<

Delicate Balance The drug quinine is often added to heroin to counteract potential infections. While quinine does have this effect, too much of it can be lethal. Many deaths attributed to heroin may actually have been caused by a quinine-induced flooding of the lungs.<<

Purer blend *In the past, heroin was usually injected. However, heroin, derived from poppies such as those cultivated in this field in Mexico, is purer today than it was in the 1980s (65 percent pure vs. 5 percent), so that users can heighten the impact of the drug considerably by snorting or smoking it.*

U.S. Congress had concluded that all drugs derived from opium were addictive (see Table 10-3), and it passed a law making opioids illegal except for medical purposes.

Still other drugs have been derived from opium, and *synthetic* (laboratory-blended) opioids such as *methadone* have also been developed. All these opioid drugs—natural and synthetic—are known collectively as *narcotics*. Each drug has a different strength, speed of action, and tolerance level. Morphine and *codeine* are medical narcotics usually prescribed to relieve pain. Heroin is illegal in the United States under all circumstances.

Narcotics are smoked, inhaled, snorted, injected by needle just beneath the skin ("skin popped"), or injected directly into the bloodstream ("mainlined"). Injection seems to be the most common method of narcotic use, although the other techniques have been used increasingly in recent years (NHSDA, 1998). An injection quickly brings on a *rush*—a spasm of warmth and ecstasy that is sometimes compared with orgasm. The brief spasm is followed by several hours of a pleasant feeling called a *high* or *nod*. During a high, the drug user feels relaxed, happy, and unconcerned about food, sex, or other bodily needs.

Opioids create these effects by depressing the central nervous system, particularly the centers that help control emotion. The drugs attach to brain receptor sites that ordinarily receive **endorphins**—neurotransmitters that help relieve pain and reduce emotional tension (Doweiko, 1999; Snyder, 1991, 1986). When neurons at these receptor sites receive opioids, they produce pleasurable and calming feelings just as they would do if they were receiving endorphins. In addition to reducing pain and tension, opioids cause nausea, narrowing of the pupils ("pinpoint pupils"), and constipation.

HEROIN ABUSE AND DEPENDENCE Heroin use exemplifies the kinds of problems posed by opioids. After taking heroin repeatedly for just a few weeks, users may become caught in a pattern of abuse: the drug interferes significantly with their

Table 10-3

Risks and Consequences of Drug Misuse

	INTOXICATION POTENTIAL	DEPENDENCY POTENTIAL	RISK OF ORGAN DAMAGE OR DEATH	RISK OF SEVERE SOCIAL OR ECONOMIC CONSEQUENCES	RISK OF SEVERE OR LONG-LASTING MENTAL AND BEHAVIORAL CHANGE
Opioids	High	High	Low	High	Low to moderate
Sedative-hypnotics Barbiturates	Moderate	Moderate to high	Moderate to high	Moderate to high	Low
Benzodiazepines	Moderate	Low	Low	Low	Low
Stimulants (cocaine, amphetamines)	High	High	Moderate	Low to moderate	Moderate to high
Alcohol	High	Moderate	High	High	High
Cannabis	High	Low to moderate	Low	Low to moderate	Low
Mixed drug classes	High	High	High	High	High

Source: APA, 2000, 1994; Gold, 1986, p. 28.

Rodolfo Vatierra/Corbis Sygma

social and occupational functioning. In most cases, heroin abuse leads to a pattern of dependence as well, and users soon center their lives on the substance, build a tolerance for it, and experience a withdrawal reaction when they stop taking it. At first the withdrawal symptoms are anxiety, restlessness, sweating, and rapid breathing; later they include severe twitching, aches, fever, vomiting, diarrhea, loss of appetite, high blood pressure, and weight loss of up to 15 pounds (due to loss of bodily fluids). These symptoms usually peak by the third day, gradually subside, and disappear by the eighth day. A person in withdrawal can either wait out the symptoms or end withdrawal by taking heroin again.

People who are dependent on heroin soon need the drug just to avoid going into withdrawal, and they must continually increase their doses in order to achieve even that relief. The temporary high becomes less strong and less important. The individuals may spend much of their time planning their next dose, in many cases turning to criminal activities, such as theft and prostitution, to support the expensive "habit."

Surveys suggest that close to 1 percent of adults in the United States become addicted to heroin or other opioids at some time in their lives (APA, 2000, 1994). The rate of addiction dropped considerably during the 1980s, rose in the early 1990s, and now seems to be falling once again (Johnston et al., 2002). The number of persons currently addicted to these drugs is estimated to be less than 150,000 (NHSDA, 2002, 1998; Morral et al., 2000). The actual number may be even higher, however, given the reluctance of many people to admit an illegal activity.

WHAT ARE THE DANGERS OF HEROIN ABUSE? The most immediate danger of heroin use is an overdose, which closes down the respiratory center in the brain, almost paralyzing breathing and in many cases causing death. Death is particularly likely during sleep, when a person is unable to fight this effect by consciously working to breathe. People who resume heroin use after having avoided it for some time often make the fatal mistake of taking the same dose they had built up to before. Because their bodies have been without heroin for a while, however, they can no longer tolerate this high level. Each year approximately 2 percent of persons dependent on heroin and other opioids die under the drug's influence, usually from an overdose (APA, 2000; Sporer, 1999).

Users run other risks as well. Often pushers mix heroin with a cheaper drug or even a deadly substance such as cyanide or battery acid. In addition, dirty needles and other unsterile equipment spread infections such as AIDS, hepatitis, and skin abscesses (Ferrando, 2001). In some areas of the United States the HIV infection rate among persons dependent on heroin is reported to be as high as 60 percent (APA, 2000, 1994).

ENDORPHINS Neurotransmitters that help relieve pain and reduce emotional tension. They are sometimes referred to as the body's own opioids.

Tony O'Brien/Picture Group

Injecting heroin *Opioids may be taken by mouth, inhaled, snorted, injected just beneath the surface of the skin, or, as here, injected intravenously. Users who share needles to inject themselves risk developing AIDS or hepatitis.*

SUMMING UP

Depressants

Depressants—including alcohol, sedative-hypnotic drugs, and opioids—are substances that slow the activity of the central nervous system. Long-term and high use of these substances can lead to a pattern of abuse or dependence.

Alcoholic beverages contain ethyl alcohol, which is carried by the blood to the central nervous system, depressing its function. Among other actions, alcohol increases the activity of the neurotransmitter GABA at key sites in the brain. The sedative-hypnotic drugs, which produce feelings of relaxation and drowsiness, include barbiturates and benzodiazepines. These drugs also increase the activity of GABA.

Opioids include opium and drugs derived from it, such as morphine and heroin, as well as laboratory-made opioids. They all reduce tension and pain and produce other effects. Opioids operate by binding to neurons that ordinarily receive endorphins.

A CLOSER LOOK

Tobacco, Nicotine, and Addiction

Almost one-quarter of all Americans over the age of 12 regularly smoke tobacco (NCHS, 2002). Surveys also suggest that nearly 30 percent of all high school seniors have smoked within the past month, more than half of them on a regular basis (Johnston et al., 2002). At the same time, 430,000 persons in the United States die each year as a result of smoking (Carpenter, 2001). Smoking is directly tied to high blood pressure, coronary heart disease, lung disease, cancer, strokes, and other deadly medical problems (NCHS, 2002). Nonsmokers who inhale cigarette smoke from their environment have a higher risk of lung cancer and other diseases (Report of the Surgeon General, 1987). And pregnant women who smoke are more likely than nonsmokers to deliver premature and underweight babies (NCHS, 2002).

Research suggests that smoking may actually increase stress levels (Parrott, 2000, 1999), and most smokers know that smoking is unhealthy, so why do they continue to smoke? Because *nicotine*, the active substance in tobacco and a *stimulant* of the central nervous system, is as addictive as heroin, perhaps even more so (Report of the Surgeon General, 1988). Regular smokers develop a tolerance for nicotine and must smoke more and more in order to achieve the same results. When they try to stop smoking, they experience withdrawal symptoms—irritability, increased appetite, sleep disturbances, slower metabolism, cognitive difficulties, and a powerful desire to smoke (APA, 2000). Nicotine acts on the same neurotransmitters and reward center in the brain as amphetamines and cocaine (McGehee et al., 1995). Inhaling a puff of cigarette smoke delivers a dose of nicotine to the brain faster than it could be delivered by injection into the bloodstream.

The declining acceptability of smoking in our society has created a market for products and techniques to help people kick the habit. Most of these meth-

An early start *An Albanian boy in Kosovo is already acquainted with the powers of nicotine.*

Michele McDonald, Arlington, Massachusetts

ods do not work very well. Self-help kits, commercial programs, and support groups are of limited help. Smokers who do quit permanently tend to be successful only after several failed attempts (Spanier et al., 1996).

One fairly successful behavioral treatment for nicotine addiction is *aversion therapy*. In one version of this approach, known as *rapid smoking*, the smoker sits in a closed room and puffs quickly on a cigarette, as often as once every six seconds, until he or she begins to feel ill and cannot take another puff. The feelings of illness become associated with smoking, and the smoker develops an aversion to cigarettes (Spiegler & Guevremont, 2003).

Several biological treatments have also been developed. A common one is the use of *nicotine gum*, which contains a high level of nicotine that is released as the smoker chews. Theoretically, people who obtain nicotine by chewing will no longer feel a need to smoke (Moss, 1999). A similar approach is the *nicotine patch*, which is attached to the skin like a Band-Aid. Its nicotine is absorbed through the skin throughout the day, supposedly easing withdrawal and re-

ducing the smoker's need for nicotine. Studies find that both nicotine gum and the nicotine patch help people to abstain from smoking (O'Brien & McKay, 2002; Shiffman et al., 2002). Combining the two techniques has also shown promise. *Nicotine nasal spray*, a relatively new biological approach, delivers nicotine much more rapidly than other methods (Perkins et al., 1996). It can be used several times an hour, whenever the urge to smoke arises. Finally, the antidepressant drug *bupropion* (brand names Zyban and Wellbutrin) has demonstrated some success as a treatment for cigarette smoking (Jorenby et al., 1999).

The more one smokes, the harder it is to quit. On the positive side, however, former smokers' risk of disease and death decreases steadily the longer they continue to avoid smoking (Goldstein, 1994; Jaffe, 1985). This assurance may be a powerful motivator for many smokers, and, in fact, around 45 percent of regular smokers want to stop and are eventually able to stop permanently (Wellner, 2001; APA, 2000). In the meantime, more than 1,000 people die of smoking-related diseases each day.

Stimulants

Stimulants are substances that increase the activity of the central nervous system, resulting in increased blood pressure and heart rate, greater alertness, and speeded-up behavior and thinking. Among the most troublesome stimulants are *cocaine* and *amphetamines*, whose effects on people are very similar. When users report different effects, it is often because they have ingested different amounts of the drugs. Two other widely used and legal stimulants are *caffeine* and *nicotine*.

COCAINE An addictive stimulant obtained from the coca plant. It is the most powerful natural stimulant known.

Cocaine

Cocaine—the central active ingredient of the coca plant, found in South America—is the most powerful natural stimulant now known. The drug was first separated from the plant in 1865. Native people of South America, however, have chewed the leaves of the plant since prehistoric times for the energy and alertness the drug offers. Processed cocaine is an odorless, white, fluffy powder. For recreational use, it is most often snorted so that it is absorbed through the mucous membrane of the nose. Some users prefer the more powerful effects of injecting cocaine intravenously or smoking it in a pipe or cigarette.

For years people believed that cocaine posed few problems aside from intoxication and, on occasion, temporary psychosis. Only later did researchers come to appreciate its many dangers. Their insights came after society witnessed a dramatic increase in the drug's popularity and in problems related to its use. In the early 1960s an estimated 10,000 persons in the United States had tried cocaine. Today 28 million people have tried it, and 1.7 million—most of them teenagers or young adults—are using it currently (NHSDA, 2002). In fact, nearly 5 percent of all high school seniors have used cocaine within the past year (Johnston et al., 2002). Altogether, close to 3 percent of the population become dependent on cocaine at some point in their lives (Anthony et al., 1995).

Cocaine brings on a euphoric rush of well-being and confidence. Given a high enough dose, this rush can be almost orgasmic, like the one produced by heroin. At first cocaine stimulates the higher centers of the central nervous system, making users feel excited, energetic, talkative, and even euphoric. As more is taken, it stimulates other centers of the central nervous system, producing a faster pulse, higher blood pressure, faster and deeper breathing, and further arousal and wakefulness.

Cocaine apparently produces these effects largely by increasing supplies of the neurotransmitter *dopamine* at key neurons throughout the brain (Maurice et al., 2002) (see Figure 10-2). Excessive amounts of dopamine travel to receiving neurons throughout the central nervous system and overstimulate them. In addition, cocaine appears to increase the activity of the neurotransmitters *norepinephrine* and *serotonin* in some areas of the brain (Quiñones-Jenab, 2001; Volkow et al., 1999, 1997).

High doses of the drug produce *cocaine intoxication*, whose symptoms are poor muscle coordination, grandiosity, bad judgment, anger, aggression, compulsive behavior, anxiety, and confusion. Some people experience hallucinations or delusions, or both, a condition known as *cocaine-induced psychotic disorder* (APA, 2000).

> A young man described how, after free-basing, he went to his closet to get his clothes, but his suit asked him, "What do you want?" Afraid, he walked toward the door, which told him, "Get back!" Retreating, he then heard the sofa say, "If you sit on me, I'll kick your ass." With a sense of impending doom, intense anxiety, and momentary panic, the young man ran to the hospital where he received help.
>
> *(Allen, 1985, pp. 19–20)*

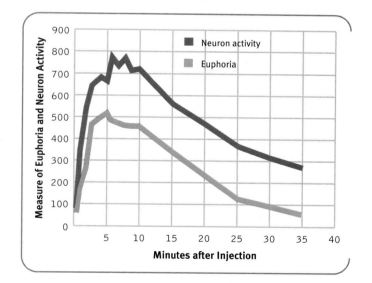

FIGURE 10-2 **Biochemical euphoria** *The subjective experiences of euphoria after a cocaine injection closely parallel cocaine's action at dopamine-using neurons. The peak experience of euphoria seems to occur around the same time as the peak of neuron activity (Fowler et al., 1994, p. 110; Cook et al., 1985).*

As the stimulant effects of cocaine subside, the user experiences a depression-like letdown, popularly called *crashing*, a pattern that may also include headaches, dizziness, and fainting (Doweiko, 2002). For occasional users, the aftereffects usually disappear within 24 hours, but they may last longer for people who have taken a particularly high dose. These individuals may sink into a stupor, deep sleep, or, in some cases, coma (Coambs & McAndrews, 1994).

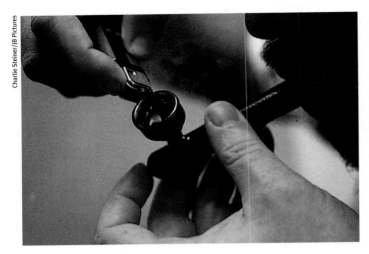

Smoking crack *Crack, a powerful form of free-base cocaine, is produced by boiling cocaine down into crystalline balls and is smoked with a special crack pipe.*

COCAINE ABUSE AND DEPENDENCE Regular use of cocaine may lead to a pattern of abuse in which the person remains under its effects much of each day and functions poorly in social relationships and at work. Regular drug use may also cause problems in short-term memory or attention (Rosselli & Ardila, 1996). Dependence may also develop, so that cocaine dominates the person's life, higher doses are needed to gain the desired effects, and stopping it results in depression, fatigue, sleep problems, irritability, and anxiety (APA, 2000). These withdrawal symptoms may last for weeks or even months after drug use has ended.

In the past, cocaine use and impact were limited by the drug's high cost. Moreover, cocaine was usually snorted, a form of ingestion that has less powerful effects than either smoking or injection. Since 1984, however, the availability of newer, more powerful, and sometimes cheaper forms of cocaine has produced an enormous increase in abuse and dependence. Currently, one user in five falls into a pattern of abuse or dependence. Many people now ingest cocaine by **free-basing**, a technique in which the pure cocaine basic alkaloid is chemically separated, or "freed," from processed cocaine, vaporized by heat from a flame, and inhaled through a pipe.

Millions more people use **crack**, a powerful form of free-base cocaine that has been boiled down into crystalline balls. It is smoked with a special pipe and makes a crackling sound as it is inhaled (hence the name). Crack is sold in small quantities at a fairly low cost, a practice that has resulted in crack epidemics among people who previously could not have afforded cocaine, primarily those in poor urban areas. Approximately 2 percent of high school seniors report having used crack within the past year, up from 1.5 percent in 1993, yet down from a peak of 2.7 percent just a few years ago (Johnston et al., 2002).

WHAT ARE THE DANGERS OF COCAINE? Aside from cocaine's harmful effects on behavior, the drug poses serious physical dangers. Its growing use in powerful forms has caused the annual number of cocaine-related emergency room incidents in the United States to multiply 44 times since 1982, from around 4,000 cases to 175,000 (NCHS, 2002; DAWN, 1998). In addition, cocaine use has been linked to as many as 20 percent of all suicides by persons under 61 years of age (Marzuk et al., 1992).

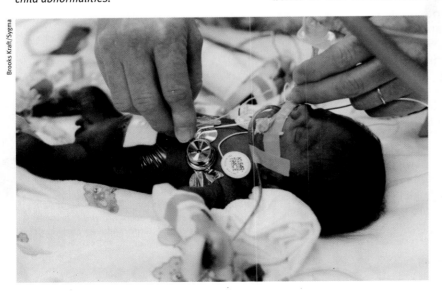

Prenatal concerns *This baby, born prematurely to a woman dependent on cocaine, lived only a few months. The use of cocaine, alcohol, or other drugs during pregnancy greatly increases the risk of miscarriage, premature birth, and child abnormalities.*

The greatest danger of cocaine use is an overdose. Excessive doses have a strong effect on the respiratory center of the brain, at first stimulating it and then depressing it, to the point where breathing may stop. Cocaine can also produce major, even fatal, heart irregularities (Doweiko, 2002; Mittleman et al., 1999) or brain seizures that bring breathing or heart functioning to a sudden stop. In addition, pregnant women who use cocaine run the risk of having a miscarriage (Ness et al., 1999) and of having children with abnormalities in immune functioning, attention and learning, thyroid size, and dopamine and serotonin activity in the brain (Adler, 1992).

Amphetamines

The **amphetamines** are stimulant drugs that are manufactured in the laboratory. Some common examples are amphetamine (Benzedrine), dextroamphetamine (Dexedrine), and methamphetamine (Methedrine). First produced in the 1930s to help treat asthma, these drugs soon became popular among people trying to lose weight; athletes seeking an extra burst of energy; soldiers, truck drivers, and pilots trying to stay awake; and students studying for exams through the night. Physicians now know the drugs are far too dangerous to be used so casually (Liu et al., 2002), and they prescribe them much less freely.

Amphetamines are most often taken in pill or capsule form, although some people inject the drugs intravenously for a quicker, more powerful effect. Others take the drugs in such forms as "ice" and "crank," counterparts of free-base cocaine and crack, respectively. Like cocaine, amphetamines increase energy and alertness and lower appetite when taken in small doses; produce a rush, intoxication, and psychosis in high doses; and cause an emotional letdown as they leave the body. Also like cocaine, amphetamines stimulate the central nervous system by increasing the release of the neurotransmitters dopamine, norepinephrine, and serotonin throughout the brain, although the brain actions of amphetamines differ somewhat from those of cocaine (Doweiko, 2002, 1999).

Tolerance to amphetamines builds very quickly, so users are at great risk of becoming dependent (Liu et al., 2002). People who start using the drug to reduce their appetite and weight, for example, may soon find they are as hungry as ever and increase their dose in response. Athletes who use amphetamines to increase their energy may also find before long that larger and larger amounts of the drug are needed. So-called speed freaks, who pop pills all day for days at a time, have built a tolerance so high that they now take as much as 200 times their first amphetamine dose. When people who depend on the drug stop taking it, they plunge into a deep depression and extended sleep identical to the withdrawal from cocaine. Around 1.5 to 2 percent of the population in the United States become dependent on amphetamines at some point in their lives (APA, 2000; Anthony et al., 1995).

FREE-BASE A technique for ingesting cocaine in which the pure cocaine basic alkaloid is chemically separated from processed cocaine, vaporized by heat from a flame, and inhaled with a pipe.

CRACK A powerful, ready-to-smoke free-base cocaine.

AMPHETAMINE A stimulant drug that is manufactured in the laboratory.

SUMMING UP
Stimulants

Stimulants are substances that increase the activity of the central nervous system. They may lead to intoxication, abuse, and dependence, including a withdrawal pattern marked by depression, fatigue, and irritability. Cocaine and amphetamines produce their effects by increasing the activity of dopamine, norepinephrine, and serotonin in the brain.

≫LOOKING AROUND
Wake-Up Call

Caffeine is the world's most widely used stimulant.‹‹

Around 75 percent of all caffeine is consumed in the form of coffee.‹‹

Many people who suddenly stop their usual intake of caffeine — even if the usual intake is low— experience withdrawal symptoms (headaches, depression, anxiety, fatigue).‹‹

Paton & Beer, 2001; APA, 2000; Chou, 1992; Silverman, 1992

"Nowadays, Hal is ninety-nine per cent caffeine-free."

Hallucinogens, Cannabis, and Combinations of Substances

Other kinds of substances may also cause problems for their users and for society. *Hallucinogens* produce delusions, hallucinations, and other sensory changes. *Cannabis substances* produce sensory changes, but they also have depressant and stimulant effects, and so they are considered apart from hallucinogens in DSM-IV. And many individuals take *combinations of substances*.

Hallucinogens

Hallucinogens are substances that cause powerful changes in sensory perception, from strengthening a person's normal perceptions to producing illusions and hallucinations. They produce sensations so out of the ordinary that they are sometimes called "trips." The trips may be exciting or frightening, depending on how a person's mind interacts with the drugs. Also called **psychedelic drugs**, the hallucinogens include LSD, mescaline, psilocybin, and MDMA (Ecstasy). Many of these substances come from plants or animals; others are laboratory-produced.

THE CURRENT SCENE

X Marks the (Wrong) Spot

You probably know of the drug MDMA (*3,4-methylenedioxy methamphetamine*) by its common street name, *Ecstasy*. It is also known as X, Adam, hug, beans, and love drug. This laboratory-produced drug is technically a *stimulant*, similar to amphetamines, but it also produces hallucinogenic effects and so is often considered a *hallucinogen drug*. MDMA was developed as far back as 1910, but only in the past two decades has it gained life as a "club drug"—the drug of choice for all-night techno-dance parties known as "raves." Today, in the United States alone, consumers collectively take hundreds of thousands of doses of MDMA weekly (Holland, 2001).

What is Ecstasy's attraction? As a stimulant and hallucinogen, it helps to raise the mood of many partygoers and provides them with an energy boost that enables them to keep dancing and partying. However, it also turns out to be a dangerous drug, particularly when taken repeatedly, and so in 1985 the federal government banned its use (Murray, 2001). However, as with many drugs, this taboo status seemed only to make it more attractive to many consumers. Altogether, 8 million Americans have tried it at least once in their lifetimes (NHSDA, 2002). More than 9 percent of all high school seniors have used it within the past year, double the number who used it five years ago (Johnston et al., 2002); and nearly 3 percent of seniors have used it within the past month. Use of the drug is even more widespread among 18- to 25-year-olds (NHSDA, 2002).

What Are the Dangers of Using Ecstasy?

The mood and energy lift produced by MDMA comes at a high price. The problems that the drug may cause include the following:

❖ Immediate psychological problems such as confusion, depression, sleep difficulties, severe anxiety, and paranoid thinking. These symptoms may also continue for weeks after taking MDMA (NIDA, 2002).

❖ Significant impairment of memory and other cognitive skills (Reneman et al., 2000).

❖ Physical symptoms such as muscle tension, nausea, blurred vision, faintness, and chills or sweating (NIDA, 2002). MDMA also causes many people to clench and grind their teeth for hours at a time (Milosevic et al., 1999; Redfearn, Agrawal, & Mair, 1998).

❖ Increases in heart rate and blood pressure, which place people with heart disease at special risk (NIDA, 2002).

❖ Reduced sweat production. At a hot, crowded dance party, taking Ecstasy can even cause heat stroke, or *hyperthermia* (Pedersen & Blessing, 2001). Users generally try to fix this problem by drinking lots of water, but since the body cannot sweat under the drug's influence, the excess fluid intake can result in an equally dangerous condition known as *hyponatremia*, or "water intoxication" (Braback & Humble, 2001; Holmes et al., 1999).

❖ Potential liver damage (De Carlis et al., 2001; Garbino et al., 2001). This may happen when users take MDMA in combination with other drugs that are broken down by the same liver enzyme, such as the cheaper compound *DXM*, which is commonly mixed in with Ecstasy by pushers (Malberg & Bonson, 2001).

How Does MDMA Operate in the Brain?

MDMA works by causing the neurotransmitter *serotonin*, and to a lesser extent *dopamine*, to be released all at once throughout the brain, at first increasing

LSD (**lysergic acid diethylamide**), one of the most famous and most powerful hallucinogens, was derived by the Swiss chemist Albert Hoffman in 1938 from a group of naturally occurring drugs called *ergot alkaloids*. During the 1960s, a decade of social rebellion and experimentation, millions of persons turned to the drug as a way of expanding their experience. Within two hours of being swallowed, LSD brings on a state of *hallucinogen intoxication*, sometimes called *hallucinosis*, marked by a general strengthening of perceptions, particularly visual perceptions, along with psychological and physical changes. People may focus on small details—the pores of the skin, for example, or individual blades of grass. Colors may seem enhanced or take on a shade of purple. Illusions may be experienced in which objects seem distorted and may appear to move, breathe, or change shape. A person under the influence of LSD may also hallucinate—seeing people, objects, or forms that are not actually present.

Hallucinosis may also cause one to hear sounds more clearly, feel tingling or numbness in the limbs, or confuse the sensations of hot and cold. Some people have been badly burned after touching flames that felt cool to them under the influence of LSD. The drug may also cause different senses to cross, an effect called *synesthesia*. Colors, for example, may be "heard" or "felt."

HALLUCINOGEN A substance that causes powerful changes primarily in sensory perception, including strengthening perceptions and producing illusions and hallucinations. Also called *psychedelic drug*.

LSD (LYSERGIC ACID DIETHYLAMIDE) A hallucinogenic drug derived from ergot alkaloids.

and then depleting a person's overall supply of the neurotransmitters (Malberg & Bonson, 2001). MDMA also interferes with the body's ability to produce new supplies of serotonin, reducing the availability of the neurotransmitter still further. With chronic use, the brain eventually produces less and less serotonin and shuts down the neuron receptors to which it normally binds (Baggot & Mendelson, 2001).

Ecstasy's impact on these neurotransmitters accounts for its various psychological effects. High levels of serotonin, such as those produced after one first ingests MDMA, produce feelings of well-being, sociability, and even euphoria. Remember, though, that MDMA also increases levels of dopamine. As we shall observe in Chapter 12, very high levels of that neurotransmitter can produce paranoid—even psychotic—thinking (Jansen, 2001).

Conversely, abnormally low serotonin levels are associated with depression and anxiety (Jansen, 2001). This is why "coming down" off a dose of Ecstasy often produces those psychological symptoms (Malberg & Bonson, 2001). Moreover, because repeated use of Ecstasy leads to long-term serotonin deficits, the depression and anxiety may be long-lasting. Finally, serotonin is

linked to our ability to concentrate; thus the repeated use of Ecstasy may produce problems in memory and learning (Heffernan et al., 2001; Rodgers, 2000).

End of the Honeymoon?

The dangers of MDMA do not yet seem to outweigh its pleasures in the minds of some individuals. In fact, use of the drug is now expanding to many social settings beyond raves, dance clubs, and

college scenes (NIDA, 2002). Clearly, the honeymoon for this drug is not yet over. In turn, MDMA emergency room visits are on the rise, as are the number of deaths caused by the drug, for reasons ranging from kidney failure (the result of heat stroke) to liver failure to a heart attack. Like other dangerous drugs over the years, it will eventually lose its popularity, but obviously not before it has taken a considerable toll.

Houston Scott/Corbis Sygma

Feeling the effects *Shortly after taking MDMA, this couple manifests a shift in mood, energy, and behavior. Although this drug can feel pleasurable and energizing, often it produces undesired immediate effects, including confusion, depression, anxiety, sleep difficulties, and paranoid thinking.*

Inspired art *Psychedelic art seemed all-pervasive in the 1960s. Displayed on advertisements, clothing, record albums, and book covers, it was inspired by the kinds of images and sensations produced by psychedelic drugs such as LSD.*

LSD can also induce strong emotions, from joy to anxiety or depression. The perception of time may slow dramatically. Long-forgotten thoughts and feelings may return. Physical symptoms can include sweating, palpitations, blurred vision, tremors, and poor coordination. All these effects take place while the user is fully awake and alert, and they wear off in about six hours.

It seems that LSD produces these symptoms primarily by binding to some of the neurons that normally receive the neurotransmitter *serotonin*, changing the neurotransmitter's activity at those sites (Goodman, 2002; Jacobs, 1994, 1984). These neurons ordinarily help the brain send visual information and control emotions (as we observed in Chapter 7); thus LSD's activity there produces various visual and emotional symptoms.

More than 12 percent of all persons in the United States have used LSD or another hallucinogen at some point in their lives (NHSDA, 2002). Around 2 percent have used such drugs within the past year. Although people do not usually develop tolerance to LSD or have withdrawal symptoms when they stop taking it, the drug poses dangers for both one-time and long-term users. It is so powerful that any dose, no matter how small, is likely to produce enormous perceptual, emotional, and behavioral reactions. Sometimes the reactions are extremely unpleasant—an experience called a "bad trip." Reports of LSD users who injure themselves or others usually involve a reaction of this kind:

> A 21-year-old woman was admitted to the hospital along with her lover. He had had a number of LSD experiences and had convinced her to take it to make her less constrained sexually. About half an hour after ingestion of approximately 200 microgm., she noticed that the bricks in the wall began to go in and out and that light affected her strangely. She became frightened when she realized that she was unable to distinguish her body from the chair she was sitting on or from her lover's body. Her fear became more marked after she thought that she would not get back into herself. At the time of admission she was hyperactive and laughed inappropriately. Her stream of talk was illogical and affect labile. Two days later, this reaction had ceased.
>
> *(Frosch, Robbins, & Stern, 1965)*

Another danger is the long-term effect that LSD may have. Some users eventually develop psychosis or a mood or anxiety disorder. About one-quarter of users have **flashbacks**—a recurrence of the sensory and emotional changes after the LSD has left the body (Lerner et al., 2002; APA, 2000). Flashbacks may occur days or even months after the last LSD experience. Although they typically become less severe and disappear within several months, some people report flashbacks a year or more after taking the drug.

Cannabis

Cannabis sativa, the hemp plant, grows in warm climates throughout the world. The drugs produced from varieties of hemp are, as a group, called **cannabis**. The most powerful of them is *hashish*; the weaker ones include the best-known form of cannabis, **marijuana**, a mixture derived from the buds, crushed leaves, and flowering tops of hemp plants. Of the several hundred active chemicals in cannabis, **tetrahydrocannabinol** (**THC**) appears to be the one most responsible for its effects. The greater the THC content, the more powerful the cannabis.

When smoked, cannabis produces a mixture of hallucinogenic, depressant, and stimulant effects. At low doses, the smoker typically has feelings of joy and relaxation and may become either quiet or talkative. Some smokers, however, be-

FLASHBACK LSD-induced sensory and emotional changes that recur long after the drug has left the body.

CANNABIS DRUGS Drugs produced from the varieties of the hemp plant *Cannabis sativa*. They cause a mixture of hallucinogenic, depressant, and stimulant effects.

MARIJUANA One of the cannabis drugs, derived from the buds, leaves, and flowering tops of the hemp plant *Cannabis sativa*.

TETRAHYDROCANNABINOL (THC) The main active ingredient of cannabis substances.

come anxious, suspicious, or irritated, especially if they have been in a bad mood or are smoking in an upsetting environment. Many smokers report sharpened perceptions and fascination with the intensified sounds and sights around them. Time seems to slow down, and distances and sizes seem greater than they actually are. This overall "high" is technically called *cannabis intoxication*. Physical changes include reddening of the eyes, fast heartbeat, increases in blood pressure and appetite, dryness in the mouth, and dizziness. Some people become drowsy and may fall asleep.

In high doses, cannabis produces odd visual experiences, changes in body image, and hallucinations (Mathew et al., 1993). Smokers may become confused or impulsive. Some worry that other people are trying to hurt them. Most of the effects of cannabis last three to six hours. The changes in mood, however, may continue longer (Chait, Fishman, & Schuster, 1985).

MARIJUANA ABUSE AND DEPENDENCE   Until the early 1970s, the use of marijuana, the weak form of cannabis, rarely led to a pattern of abuse or dependence. Today, however, many people, including large numbers of high school students, are caught in a pattern of marijuana abuse, getting high on marijuana regularly and finding their social and occupational or academic lives greatly affected. Many regular users also become physically dependent on marijuana (Johns, 2001). They develop a tolerance for it and may experience flulike symptoms, restlessness, and irritability when they stop smoking (Smith, 2002; Kouri & Pope, 2000). Around 1.5 percent of all persons in the United States have displayed marijuana abuse or dependence in the past year; between 4 and 5 percent fall into one of these patterns at some point in their lives (NHSDA, 2002; APA, 2000; Anthony et al., 1995).

Why have patterns of marijuana abuse and dependence increased in the last three decades? Mainly because the drug has changed (NIDA, 2002). The marijuana widely available in the United States today is 2 to 10 times more powerful than that used in the early 1970s (see Figure 10-3). The THC content of today's marijuana is as high as 10 to 15 percent, compared to 1 to 5 percent in the late 1960s (APA, 2000). Marijuana is now grown in places with a hot, dry climate, which increases the THC content.

IS MARIJUANA DANGEROUS?   As the strength and use of marijuana have increased, researchers have discovered that smoking it may pose certain dangers. It occasionally causes panic reactions similar to the ones caused by hallucinogens, and some smokers may fear they are losing their minds (APA, 2000; Ray & Ksir, 1993). Typically such reactions end in three to six hours, along with marijuana's other effects.

Because marijuana can interfere with the performance of complex sensorimotor tasks (Ashton, 2001; Volkow et al., 1995) and with cognitive functioning (NIDA, 2002; Quiroga, 2001), it has caused many automobile accidents. Furthermore, people on a marijuana high often fail to remember information, especially anything that has been recently learned, no matter how hard they try to concentrate; thus heavy marijuana smokers are at a serious disadvantage at school or work (NIDA, 2002).

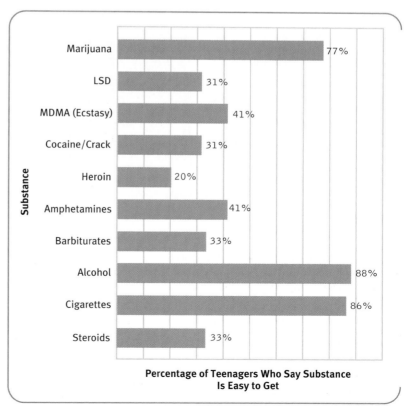

The source of marijuana *Marijuana is made from the leaves of the hemp plant,* Cannabis sativa. *The plant is an annual herb, reaches a height of between 3 and 15 feet, and is grown in a wide range of altitudes, climates, and soils.*

FIGURE 10-3   **How easy is it for teenagers to acquire substances?** *According to the vast majority of surveyed tenth graders, it is very easy in the case of cigarettes, alcohol, and marijuana. In addition, at least one-third of the students say it is easy to get Ecstasy, amphetamines, steroids, and barbiturates (Johnston et al., 2002).*

Percentage of Teenagers Who Say Substance Is Easy to Get

Substance	Percentage
Marijuana	77%
LSD	31%
MDMA (Ecstasy)	41%
Cocaine/Crack	31%
Heroin	20%
Amphetamines	41%
Barbiturates	33%
Alcohol	88%
Cigarettes	86%
Steroids	33%

>>**Q & A**

Do animals get high?

Animals sometimes do use substances to get high or relieve stress. Llamas in Peru get frisky eating coca leaves (which contain cocaine). Grasshoppers that eat wild marijuana leaves jump unusually high. Elephants seek out fermented ripe fruit (Siegel, 1990).<<

There are indications that regular marijuana smoking may also lead to long-term problems. It may, for example, contribute to lung disease. Studies show that marijuana smoking reduces the ability to expel air from the lungs even more than tobacco smoking does (NIDA, 2002; Nahas et al., 1999). In addition, marijuana smoke contains more tar and benzopyrene than tobacco smoke. Both of these substances have been linked to cancer (Ray & Ksir, 1993). Another concern is the effect of regular marijuana smoking on human reproduction. Studies since the late 1970s have discovered lower sperm counts in men who are chronic smokers of marijuana, and abnormal ovulation has been found in female smokers (Nahas et al., 1999).

Efforts to educate the public about the growing dangers of regular repeated marijuana use appeared to have paid off throughout the 1980s. The percentage of high school seniors who smoked the substance on a daily basis decreased from 11 percent in 1978 to 2 percent in 1992 (Johnston et al., 1993). Furthermore, in 1992 about 77 percent of high school seniors believed that regular marijuana smoking poses a serious health risk, a much higher percentage than that in earlier years. However, marijuana use among the young jumped up again during the 1990s. Today nearly 6 percent of high school seniors smoke marijuana daily, and fewer than 60 percent believe that regular use can be harmful (Johnston et al., 2002).

CANNABIS AND SOCIETY: A ROCKY RELATIONSHIP For centuries cannabis played a respected role in medicine. It was recommended as a surgical anesthetic by Chinese physicians 2,000 years ago and was used in other lands to treat cholera, malaria, coughs, insomnia, and rheumatism. When cannabis entered the United States in the early twentieth century, mainly in the form of marijuana, it was likewise used for various medical purposes. Soon, however, more effective medicines replaced it, and the favorable view of cannabis began to change. Marijuana began to be used as a recreational drug, and its illegal distribution became a law enforcement problem. Authorities assumed it was highly dangerous and outlawed the "killer weed."

But marijuana didn't go away. During the 1960s, a time of disillusionment, protest, and self-exploration, young people discovered the pleasures of getting high from smoking marijuana. By the end of the 1970s, 16 million people reported using it at least once, and 11 percent of the population were recent users.

In the 1980s researchers developed precise techniques for measuring THC and for extracting pure THC from cannabis; they also developed laboratory forms of THC. These inventions opened the door to new medical applications for cannabis (Mack & Joy, 2001; Watson et al., 2000), such as its use in treating glaucoma, a severe eye disease. Cannabis was also found to help patients with chronic pain or asthma, to reduce the nausea and vomiting of cancer patients in chemotherapy, and to improve the appetites of AIDS patients and so combat weight loss in people with that disorder.

Medicinal use *Suffering from severe arthritis and an eye condition similar to glaucoma, this woman puffs on a pipe filled with marijuana several times a day. It apparently eases her pain and helps clear her vision.*

In light of these findings, several interest groups campaigned during the late 1980s for the *medical legalization* of marijuana, which operates on the brain and body more quickly than the THC capsules developed in the laboratory. In 1992, however, the Drug Enforcement Administration opposed this measure and the Food and Drug Administration stopped reviewing requests for the "compassionate use" of marijuana (Karel, 1992). They held that prescriptions for pure THC served all needed medical functions.

Advocates of the medical use of marijuana challenged the government position again during the elections of 1996. Voter referendums, which have the force of law, were passed in California and Arizona, giving physicians the right to prescribe marijuana for "seriously ill" or "terminally ill" patients. Voters in a number of other states followed suit in subsequent years. But the federal government responded by threatening to revoke the prescription-writing privilege of any physician who prescribed marijuana and even to prosecute such physicians. In turn the *New England Journal of Medicine*, one of the world's most prestigious medical publications, published an editorial in 1997 favoring the medical use of marijuana. Unfazed, the federal government continued to fight and punish the production and distribution of marijuana for medical purposes. In 2003, a shift began to occur in this position by the federal government when the Supreme Court decided to let stand a federal circuit court's ruling that physicians in California and Oregon cannot be punished for generally advising patients on the medical use of marijuana. This ruling did not, however, apply to other states and the matter is far from settled.

The Canadian government has taken a different tack. In 2003 Canada's health minister announced an interim policy allowing eligible medical sufferers to buy marijuana from the government until that country's *medical marijuana research program* reaches a clear conclusion regarding this complex issue.

Combinations of Substances

Because people often take more than one drug at a time, a pattern called *polysubstance use*, researchers have studied the ways in which drugs interact with one another. When different drugs are in the body at the same time, they may multiply, or potentiate, each other's effects. The combined impact, called a **synergistic effect**, is often greater than the sum of the effects of each drug taken alone: a small dose of one drug mixed with a small dose of another can produce an enormous change in body chemistry.

One kind of synergistic effect occurs when two or more drugs have *similar actions*. For instance, alcohol, benzodiazepines, barbiturates, and opioids—all depressants—may severely depress the central nervous system when mixed (Miller & Gold, 1990). Combining them, even in small doses, can lead to extreme intoxication, coma, and even death (Nishino et al., 1995). A young man may have just a few alcoholic drinks at a party, for example, and shortly afterward take a moderate dose of barbiturates to help him fall asleep. He believes he has acted with restraint and good judgment—yet he may never wake up.

A different kind of synergistic effect results when drugs have *opposite*, or *antagonistic*, *actions*. Stimulant drugs, for example, interfere with the liver's usual disposal of barbiturates and alcohol. Thus people who combine barbiturates or alcohol with cocaine or amphetamines may build up toxic, even lethal, levels of the depressant drugs in their systems. Students who take amphetamines to help them study late into the night and then take barbiturates to help them fall asleep are unknowingly placing themselves in serious danger.

SYNERGISTIC EFFECT In pharmacology, an increase of effects that occurs when more than one substance is acting on the body at the same time.

Déjà vu *Polysubstance use, particularly a mixture of cocaine and opioids, proved fatal for John Belushi (left) and Chris Farley (right), each a featured actor on the television show* Saturday Night Live. *Farley had often stated his admiration for Belushi's talent and lifestyle.*

Each year tens of thousands of people are admitted to hospitals with a multiple-drug emergency, and several thousand of them die (DAWN, 2002). Sometimes the cause is carelessness or ignorance. Often, however, people use multiple drugs precisely because they enjoy the synergistic effects (Leri et al., 2003). In fact, **polysubstance-related disorders** are becoming as common as individual substance-related disorders in the United States, Canada, and Europe (Schuckit et al., 2001; Hoffman et al., 2000). As many as 90 percent of persons who use one illegal drug are also using another to some extent (Cornish et al., 1995).

Fans still mourn the deaths of many celebrities who have been the victims of polysubstance use. Elvis Presley's delicate balancing act of stimulants and depressants eventually killed him. Janis Joplin's mixtures of wine and heroin were ultimately fatal. And John Belushi's and Chris Farley's liking for the combined effect of cocaine and opioids ("speedballs") also ended in tragedy.

SUMMING UP | **Hallucinogens, Cannabis, and Combinations of Substances**

Hallucinogens, such as LSD, cause powerful changes primarily in sensory perception. Perceptions are intensified and illusions and hallucinations can occur. LSD apparently causes such effects by disturbing the release of the neurotransmitter serotonin.

The main ingredient of *Cannabis sativa*, a hemp plant, is tetrahydrocannabinol (THC). Marijuana, the most popular form of cannabis, is more powerful today than it was in years past. It can cause intoxication, and regular use can lead to abuse and dependence. The use of this substance for medical purposes continues to be debated.

Many people take more than one drug at a time, and the drugs interact. The use of two or more drugs at the same time has become increasingly common. Similarly, polysubstance-related disorders have also become a major problem.

What Causes Substance-Related Disorders?

Clinical theorists have developed sociocultural, psychological, and biological explanations for why people abuse or become dependent on various substances. No single explanation, however, has gained broad support. Like so many other disorders, excessive and chronic drug use is increasingly viewed as the result of a combination of these factors.

The Sociocultural View

A number of sociocultural theorists propose that people are most likely to develop patterns of substance abuse or dependence when they live under stressful socioeconomic conditions. In fact, studies have found that regions with higher levels of unemployment have higher rates of alcoholism. Similarly, lower socioeconomic classes have substance abuse rates that are higher than those of the other classes (Khan, Murray, & Barnes, 2002; Dohrenwend, 2000).

Other sociocultural theorists propose that substance abuse and dependence are more likely to appear in families and social environments where substance use is valued, or at least accepted. Researchers have, in fact, found that problem drinking is more common among teenagers whose parents and peers drink, as well as among teenagers whose family environments are stressful and unsupportive (Lieb et al., 2002; Wills et al., 1996). Moreover, lower rates of alcohol abuse are found among Jews and Protestants, groups in which drinking is typically acceptable only as long as it remains within clear limits, whereas alcoholism rates are higher among the Irish and Eastern Europeans, who do not, on average, draw as clear a line (Ledoux et al., 2002; Vaillant & Milofsky, 1982).

ABNORMALITY AND THE ARTS

Chasing Highs Wherever They May Lead

*J*onathan Melvoin, a backup keyboard player for the rock group Smashing Pumpkins, died of a heroin overdose in July 1996. Word soon spread that the brand of heroin he had taken was Red Rum, a strain smuggled in from Colombia. Its name—"murder" spelled backward—comes from the Stephen King novel *The Shining*.

Within hours the demand for Red Rum rose dramatically on the streets of Manhattan's Lower East Side. "It's kind of sick," a narcotics officer said when interviewed by the *New York Times*. "But when people die from something or nearly die, all of a sudden there's this rush to get it."

Smashing aftermath *The Smashing Pumpkins, posing here for a studio photo a year before the Melvoin incident, fired the band's drummer after learning that he had been using drugs with the keyboardist Melvoin.*

The Psychodynamic View

Psychodynamic theorists believe that people who abuse substances have powerful *dependency* needs that can be traced to their early years (Stetter, 2000; Shedler & Block, 1990). They claim that when parents fail to satisfy a young child's need for nurturance, the child is likely to grow up depending excessively on others for help and comfort, trying to find the nurturance that was lacking during the early years. If this search for outside support includes experimentation with a drug, the person may well develop a dependent relationship with the substance.

Some psychodynamic theorists also believe that certain people respond to their early deprivations by developing a *substance abuse personality* that leaves them particularly prone to drug abuse. Personality inventories and patient interviews have in fact indicated that people who abuse or depend on drugs tend to be more dependent, antisocial, impulsive, novelty-seeking, and depressive than other people (Coffey et al., 2003; Cox et al., 2001; Finn et al., 2000). These findings are correlational, however, and do not clarify whether such personality traits lead to drug use or whether drug use causes people to be dependent, impulsive, and the like.

In an effort to determine causation, one study measured the personality traits of a large group of nonalcoholic young men and then kept track of each man's development (Jones, 1971, 1968). Years later, the traits of the men who developed alcohol problems in middle age were compared with the traits of those who did not. The men who developed alcohol problems had been more impulsive as teenagers and continued to be so in middle age, a finding suggesting that impulsive men are indeed more prone to develop alcohol problems. Similarly, in one laboratory investigation, "impulsive" rats—those that generally had trouble delaying their rewards—were found to drink more alcohol when offered it than other rats (Poulos et al., 1995).

A major weakness of this line of argument is the wide range of personality traits that have been tied to substance abuse and dependence. In fact, different studies point to different "key" traits. Inasmuch as some people with a drug addiction appear to be dependent, others impulsive, and still others antisocial, researchers cannot presently conclude that any one personality trait or group of traits stands out in substance-related disorders (Chassin et al., 2001; Rozin & Stoess, 1993).

>>PSYCH•NOTES

Freud's Folly

Early in his career, Sigmund Freud was a staunch advocate of cocaine use. He proclaimed, "Cocaine brings about an exhilaration and lasting euphoria . . . an increase in self-control and . . . more vitality and capacity for work. . . . In other words, you are simply normal" (Freud, 1885).<<

Steven Rubin/The Image Works

Common substance, uncommon danger *A 13-year-old boy sniffs glue as he lies dazed near a garbage heap. In the United States, at least 6 percent of all people have tried to get high by inhaling the hydrocarbons found in common substances such as glue, gasoline, paint thinner, cleaners, and spray-can propellants (APA, 2000). Such behavior may lead to inhalant abuse or dependence and poses a number of serious medical dangers.*

The Behavioral and Cognitive Views

According to behaviorists, *operant conditioning* may play a key role in substance abuse. They argue that the temporary reduction of tension or raising of spirits produced by a drug has a rewarding effect, thus increasing the likelihood that the user will seek this reaction again (Rutledge & Sher, 2001). Similarly, the rewarding effects of a substance may eventually lead users to try higher dosages or more powerful methods of ingestion (see Table 10-4). Cognitive theorists further argue that such rewards eventually produce an *expectancy* that substances will be rewarding, and this expectation helps motivate individuals to increase drug use at times of tension (Chassin et al., 2001).

In support of these views, studies have found that many subjects do in fact drink more alcohol or seek heroin when they feel tense (Ham et al., 2002; Cooper,

Table 10-4

Methods of Taking Substances

METHOD	ROUTE	TIME TO REACH BRAIN
Inhaling	Drug in vapor form is inhaled through mouth and lungs into circulatory system.	7 seconds
Snorting	Drug in powdered form is snorted into the nose. Some of the drug lands on the nasal mucous membranes, is absorbed by blood vessels, and enters the bloodstream.	4 minutes
Injection	Drug in liquid form directly enters the body through a needle. Injection may be intravenous or intramuscular (subcutaneous).	20 seconds (intravenous); 4 minutes (intramuscular)
Oral ingestion	Drug in solid or liquid form passes through esophagus and stomach and finally to the small intestines. It is absorbed by blood vessels in the intestines.	30 minutes
Other routes	Drugs can be absorbed through areas that contain mucous membranes. Drugs can be placed under the tongue, inserted anally and vaginally, and administered as eyedrops.	Variable

Source: Landry, 1994, p. 24.

1994). In one study, as subjects worked on a difficult anagram task, a confederate planted by the researchers unfairly criticized and belittled them (Marlatt et al., 1975). The subjects were then asked to participate in an "alcohol taste task," supposedly to compare and rate alcoholic beverages. The subjects who had been harassed drank more alcohol during the taste task than did the control subjects who had not been criticized.

In a manner of speaking, the behavioral and cognitive theorists are arguing that many people take drugs to "medicate" themselves when they feel tense. If so, one would expect higher rates of drug abuse among people who suffer from anxiety, depression, or intense anger. In fact, substance abuse and dependence do appear to be fairly common among people with mood disorders (McDowell & Clodfelter, 2001; Swendsen & Merikangas, 2000). One study of 835 clinically depressed patients found that more than one-fourth abused drugs during episodes of depression (Hasin et al., 1985). Similarly, higher-than-usual rates of drug abuse have been found among people with posttraumatic stress disorder, eating disorders, schizophrenia, antisocial personality disorder, histories of being abused, and other psychological problems (Brown et al., 2003; Brooner et al., 1997; Yama et al., 1993).

A number of behaviorists have proposed that *classical conditioning* may also play a role in substance abuse and dependence (Drobes, Saladin, & Tiffany, 2001). Objects present at the time drugs are taken may act as classically conditioned stimuli and come to produce some of the same pleasure brought on by the drugs themselves. Just the sight of a hypodermic needle or a regular supplier, for example, has been known to comfort people who abuse heroin or amphetamines and to relieve their withdrawal symptoms. In a similar manner, objects that are present during withdrawal distress may produce withdrawal-like symptoms. One man who had formerly been dependent on heroin experienced nausea and other withdrawal symptoms when he returned to the neighborhood where he had gone through withdrawal in the past—a reaction that led him to start taking heroin again (O'Brien et al., 1975). Although classical conditioning may in fact be at work in particular cases of drug abuse and dependence, it has not received widespread research support as a key factor in such patterns (Drobes et al., 2001).

The Biological View

In recent years researchers have come to suspect that drug misuse may have biological causes. Studies on genetic predisposition and specific biochemical processes have provided some support for these suspicions.

GENETIC PREDISPOSITION   For years breeding experiments have been conducted to see whether certain animals are genetically predisposed to become dependent on drugs (Li, 2000; Kurtz et al., 1996). In several studies, for example, investigators have first identified animals that prefer alcohol to other beverages and then mated them to one another. Generally, the offspring of these animals have been found to also display an unusual preference for alcohol (Melo et al., 1996).

Similarly, some research with human twins has suggested that people may inherit a predisposition to abuse substances (Tsuang et al., 2001; Kendler et al., 1994, 1992). One classic study found an alcohol abuse *concordance* rate of 54 percent in a group of identical twins; that is, if one identical twin abused alcohol, the other twin also abused alcohol in 54 percent of the cases. In contrast, a group of fraternal twins had a concordance rate of only 28 percent (Kaij, 1960). As we have observed, however, such findings do not rule out other interpretations (Walters, 2002). For one thing, the parenting received by two identical twins may be more similar than that received by two fraternal twins.

A stronger indication that genetics may play a role in substance abuse and dependence comes from studies of alcoholism rates in people adopted shortly after birth (Walters, 2002; Cadoret, 1995; Goldstein, 1994). These studies have compared adoptees whose biological parents are dependent on alcohol with adoptees whose biological parents are not. By adulthood, the individuals whose biological

Addicted to chocolate? *Recent studies suggest that a craving for chocolate may be more than just a state of mind. Apparently some chemicals in chocolate may bind to the same neuron receptors that receive cannabis substances (di Tomaso, Beltramo, & Piomelli, 1996). At the same time, however, a person would have to eat 25 pounds of chocolate in one sitting to experience a cannabis-like effect. Then again, for chocolate lovers . . .*

parents are dependent on alcohol typically show higher rates of alcohol abuse than those with nonalcoholic biological parents.

Genetic linkage strategies and *molecular biology* techniques provide more direct evidence in support of a genetic explanation (Crabbe, 2002, 2001). One line of investigation has found an abnormal form of the so-called *dopamine-2 (D2) receptor gene* in a majority of subjects with alcohol dependence and half of subjects with cocaine dependence, but in less than 20 percent of nondependent subjects (Connor et al., 2002; Finckh, 2001; Blum & Noble, 1993). Other studies have tied still other genes to substance-related disorders (Cook & Gurling, 2001).

BIOCHEMICAL FACTORS Over the past few decades, investigators have pieced together a general biological understanding of drug tolerance and withdrawal symptoms (Wise, 1996). As we have seen, when a particular drug is ingested, it increases the activity of certain neurotransmitters whose normal purpose is to calm, reduce pain, lift mood, or increase alertness. When a person keeps on taking the drug, the brain apparently makes an adjustment and reduces its own production of the neurotransmitters. Because the drug is increasing neurotransmitter activity or efficiency, action by the brain is less necessary. As drug intake increases, the body's production of the neurotransmitters continues to decrease, leaving the person in need of more and more of the drug to achieve its effects. In this way, drug takers build tolerance for a drug, becoming more and more reliant on it rather than on their own biological processes to feel comfortable or alert. If they suddenly stop taking the drug, their supply of neurotransmitters will be low for a time, producing the symptoms of withdrawal. Withdrawal continues until the brain resumes its normal production of the necessary neurotransmitters.

Which neurotransmitters are affected depends on the drug used. Repeated and excessive use of alcohol or benzodiazepines may lower the brain's production of the neurotransmitter GABA; regular use of opioids may reduce the brain's production of endorphins; and regular use of cocaine or amphetamines may lower the brain's production of dopamine (Volkow et al., 1999). In addition, researchers have identified neurotransmitters called *anandamides* (from the Sanskrit word for "bliss") that operate much like THC; excessive use of marijuana may reduce the production of these neurotransmitters (Johns, 2001; Biegon & Kerman, 1995).

Peter Serling, New York, NY

One more for the road *During the 1990s many people believed that inhaling oxygen might energize them and reduce their stress levels, leading to the opening of "oxygen bars" across North America and Asia. Patrons would hook up to oxygen tanks and inhale nearly pure oxygen. This activity does not appear to be dangerous, but it did not prove to be particularly uplifting either. Most such bars have closed.*

This theory helps explain why people who regularly take substances experience tolerance and withdrawal reactions. But why are drugs so rewarding, and why do certain people turn to them in the first place? A number of brain-imaging studies suggest that many, perhaps all, drugs eventually activate a single **reward center**, or "pleasure pathway," in the brain (Kelley & Berridge, 2002; Volkow & Fowler, 2000). A key neurotransmitter in this pleasure pathway appears to be *dopamine*. When dopamine is activated there, a person experiences pleasure. Music may activate dopamine in the reward center. So may a hug or a word of praise. And so may drugs.

Certain drugs apparently stimulate the reward center directly. Remember that cocaine, amphetamines, and caffeine directly increase dopamine activity. Other drugs seem to stimulate it in roundabout ways. The biochemical reactions triggered by alcohol, opioids, and marijuana probably set in motion a series of chemical events that eventually lead to increased dopamine activity in the reward center.

A number of theorists suspect that people who abuse drugs suffer from a **reward-deficiency syndrome**: their reward center is not readily activated by the usual events in their lives (Blum et al., 2000; Nash, 1997), so they turn to drugs to stimulate this pleasure pathway, particularly at times of stress. Abnormal genes, such as the abnormal D2 receptor gene, have been cited as a possible cause of this syndrome (Finckh, 2001; Lawford et al., 1997).

SUMMING UP

What Causes Substance-Related Disorders?

Several explanations for substance abuse and dependence have been offered. Together these theories are beginning to shed light on the disorders.

According to the sociocultural view, the people most likely to abuse drugs are those living in stressful socioeconomic conditions or whose families value or accept drug use. In the psychodynamic view, people who turn to substance abuse have excessive dependency needs traceable to the early stages of life. Some psychodynamic theorists also believe that certain people have a substance abuse personality that makes them prone to drug use. Behaviorists propose that drug use is reinforced by the reduction in tension and raised spirits that it may bring about. According to cognitive theorists, such reductions may also lead to an expectancy that drugs will be comforting and helpful.

The biological explanations are supported by twin, adoptee, genetic linkage, and molecular biology studies, suggesting that people may inherit a predisposition to substance dependence. Researchers have also learned that drug tolerance and withdrawal symptoms may be caused by cutbacks in the brain's production of particular neurotransmitters during excessive and chronic drug use. Finally, biological studies suggest that many, perhaps all, drugs may ultimately lead to increased dopamine activity in the brain's reward center.

>>LOOKING AROUND

Songs of Substance

Substance use—illegal, legal, and medical—is a popular theme in music, particularly that favored by teenagers and young adults. Hit groups include Morphine, Xanax 25, and Halcion. Hit songs have ranged from the Velvet Underground's "Heroin" and "Sweet Jane" and Eric Clapton's "Cocaine" to Cyprus Hill's "I Wanna Get High" and "Insane in the Brain," Nirvana's "Lithium," Lil-Kim's "Drugs," and Jimmy Buffet's "Margaritaville."<<

How Are Substance-Related Disorders Treated?

Many approaches have been used to treat substance-related disorders, including psychodynamic, behavioral, cognitive-behavioral, biological, and sociocultural therapies. Although these treatments sometimes meet with great success, more often they are only moderately helpful (Prendergast et al., 2002; Miller et al., 2001). Today the treatments are typically used in combination (Galanter & Brooks, 2001) on both an outpatient and an inpatient basis (Rychtarik et al., 2000).

Psychodynamic Therapies

Psychodynamic therapists first guide patients with substance-related disorders to uncover and resolve the underlying needs and conflicts that they believe have led to the disorders. The therapists then try to help the individuals change their substance-related styles of living (Stetter, 2000; Hopper, 1995). Although often applied, this approach has not been found to be particularly effective in cases of substance-related disorders (Cornish et al., 1995; Holder et al., 1991). It may be that drug abuse or dependence, regardless of its causes, eventually becomes a stubborn independent problem that must be the direct target of treatment if people are to become drug-free. Psychodynamic therapy tends to be of greater help when it is combined with other approaches in a multidimensional treatment program (Galanter & Brooks, 2001; Carroll & Rounsaville, 1995).

Behavioral Therapies

A widely used behavioral treatment for substance-related disorders is **aversion therapy**, an approach based on the principles of classical conditioning. Individuals are repeatedly presented with an unpleasant stimulus (for example, an electric shock) at the very moment that they are taking a drug. After repeated pairings, they are expected to react negatively to the substance itself and to lose their craving for it.

Aversion therapy has been applied to alcohol abuse and dependence more than to other substance-related disorders. In one version of this therapy, drinking behavior is paired with drug-induced nausea and vomiting (Owen-Howard, 2001;

REWARD CENTER A dopamine-rich pathway in the brain that produces feelings of pleasure when activated.

REWARD-DEFICIENCY SYNDROME A condition, suspected to be present in some individuals, in which the brain's reward center is not readily activated by the usual events in their lives.

AVERSION THERAPY A treatment in which clients are repeatedly presented with unpleasant stimuli while performing undesirable behaviors such as taking a drug.

Welsh & Liberto, 2001). Another version, *covert sensitization*, requires people with alcoholism to imagine extremely upsetting, repulsive, or frightening scenes while they are drinking (Cautela, 2000; Kassel et al., 1999). The pairing of the imagined scenes with liquor is expected to produce negative responses to liquor itself. Here are the kinds of scenes therapists may guide a client to imagine:

> I'd like you to vividly imagine that you are tasting the (beer, whiskey, etc.). See yourself tasting it, capture the exact taste, colour and consistency. Use all of your senses. After you've tasted the drink you notice that there is something small and white floating in the glass—it stands out. You bend closer to examine it more carefully, your nose is right over the glass now and the smell fills your nostrils as you remember exactly what the drink tastes like. Now you can see what's in the glass. There are several maggots floating on the surface. As you watch, revolted, one manages to get a grip on the glass and, undulating, creeps up the glass. There are even more of the repulsive creatures in the glass than you first thought. You realize that you have swallowed some of them and you're very aware of the taste in your mouth. You feel very sick and wish you'd never reached for the glass and had the drink at all.
>
> *(Clarke & Saunders, 1988, pp. 143–144)*

A behavioral approach that has been effective in the short-term treatment of people who abuse cocaine and some other drugs is *contingency management*, which makes incentives (such as program privileges) contingent on the submission of drug-free urine specimens (Katz et al., 2001; Petry, 2000). In one study, 68 percent of cocaine abusers who completed a six-month contingency training program achieved at least eight weeks of continuous abstinence (Higgins et al., 1993).

Behavioral interventions for substance abuse and dependence have usually had only limited success when they are the sole form of treatment (Carroll & Rounsaville, 1995). A major problem is that the approaches can be effective only when individuals are motivated to continue with them despite their unpleasantness or demands. Generally, behavioral treatments work best in combination with either biological or cognitive approaches (Kassel et al., 1999; Whorley, 1996).

Cognitive-Behavioral Therapies

Two popular approaches combine cognitive and behavioral techniques to help people gain *control* over their substance-related behaviors. In one, **behavioral self-control training** (**BSCT**), applied to alcoholism in particular, therapists first have clients keep track of their own drinking behavior (Miller et al., 1992; Miller, 1983). Writing down the times, locations, emotions, bodily changes, and other circumstances of their drinking, they become more aware of the situations that place them at risk for excessive drinking. They are then taught coping strategies to use when such situations arise. They learn, for example, to set limits on their drinking, to recognize when the limits are being approached, to control their rate of drinking (perhaps by spacing their drinks or by sipping them rather than gulping), and to practice relaxation techniques, assertiveness skills, and other coping behaviors in situations in which they would otherwise be drinking. Approximately 70 percent of the people who complete this training apparently show some improvement, particularly those who are young and not physically dependent on alcohol (Walters, 2000; Hester, 1995).

In a related cognitive-behavioral approach, **relapse-prevention training**, heavy drinkers are assigned many of the same tasks as clients in BSCT (Spiegler & Guevremont, 2003; Parks & Marlatt, 2000, 1999). They are also taught to plan ahead of time how many drinks are appropriate, what to drink, and under what circumstances. The approach sometimes lowers the frequency of intoxication (Foxhall, 2001). Like BSCT, it seems most effective for people who abuse alcohol but are not physically dependent on it (Meyer et al., 1989). The approach has also been used, with some success, in the treatment of marijuana and cocaine abuse (Foxhall, 2001; Carroll & Rounsaville, 1995).

Biological Treatments

Biological approaches may be used to help people withdraw from substances, abstain from them, or simply maintain their level of use without further increases (Welsh & Liberto, 2001). As with the other forms of treatment, biological approaches alone rarely bring long-term improvement, but they can be helpful when combined with other approaches.

DETOXIFICATION **Detoxification** is systematic and medically supervised withdrawal from a drug. Some detoxification programs are offered on an outpatient basis (Allan, Smith, & Mellin, 2002, 2000). Others are located in hospitals and clinics and may also offer individual and group therapy, a "full-service" institutional approach that has become popular. One detoxification approach is to have clients withdraw gradually from the substance, taking smaller and smaller doses until they are off the drug completely (Wright & Thompson, 2002). A second detoxification strategy is to give clients other drugs that reduce the symptoms of withdrawal (Malcolm et al., 2002; Schuckit, 1999). Antianxiety drugs, for example, are sometimes used to reduce severe alcohol withdrawal reactions such as delirium tremens and seizures. Detoxification programs seem to help motivated people withdraw from drugs (Zhao et al., 2001; Allan et al., 2000). However, relapse rates tend to be high for those who fail to receive a follow-up form of treatment—psychological, biological, or sociocultural—after successful detoxification.

ANTAGONIST DRUGS After successfully stopping a drug, people must avoid falling back into a pattern of abuse or dependence. As an aid to resisting temptation, some people with substance-related disorders are given **antagonist drugs**, which block or change the effects of the addictive drug (Welsh & Liberto, 2001). *Disulfiram (Antabuse)*, for example, is often given to people who are trying to stay away from alcohol. By itself a low dose of this drug seems to have few negative effects, but a person who drinks alcohol while taking disulfiram will experience intense nausea, vomiting, blushing, faster heart rate, dizziness, and perhaps fainting. People taking disulfiram are less likely to drink alcohol because they know the terrible reaction that awaits them should they have even one drink. Disulfiram has proved helpful, but again only with people who are motivated to take it as prescribed (Cornish et al., 1995).

BEHAVIORAL SELF-CONTROL TRAINING (BSCT) A cognitive-behavioral approach to treating alcohol abuse and dependence in which clients are taught to keep track of their drinking behavior and to apply coping strategies in situations that typically trigger excessive drinking.

RELAPSE-PREVENTION TRAINING An approach to treating alcohol abuse that is similar to BSCT and also has clients plan ahead for risky situations and reactions.

DETOXIFICATION Systematic and medically supervised withdrawal from a drug.

ANTAGONIST DRUGS Drugs that block or change the effects of an addictive drug.

Patrick Davison / *The Dallas Morning News*

Forced detoxification *Abstinence does not always take place in a planned, medically supervised, voluntary manner. This sufferer of alcoholism begins to experience symptoms of withdrawal soon after being imprisoned for public intoxication.*

METHADONE MAINTENANCE PROGRAM
An approach to treating heroin dependence in which clients are given legally and medically supervised doses of a substitute drug, methadone.

Narcotic antagonists are sometimes used to treat people who are dependent on opioids (Kirchmayer et al., 2002). These drugs attach to *endorphin* receptor sites throughout the brain and make it impossible for the opioids to have their usual effect. Without the rush or high, continued drug use becomes pointless. Although narcotic antagonists have been helpful—particularly in emergencies, to rescue people from an overdose of opioids—some clinicians consider them too dangerous for regular treatment of opioid dependence. These antagonists must be given very carefully because of their ability to throw a person with an addiction into severe withdrawal (Roozen et al., 2002; Ling et al., 2001). In recent years, so-called *partial antagonists*, narcotic antagonists that produce less severe withdrawal symptoms, have been developed (Amass et al., 2000).

Recent studies indicate that narcotic antagonists may also be useful in the treatment of alcohol and cocaine dependence (Kiefer et al., 2003; O'Brien & McKay, 2002). In some studies, for example, the narcotic antagonist *naltrexone* has helped reduce cravings for alcohol (O'Malley et al., 2000, 1996, 1992). Why should narcotic antagonists, which operate at the brain's endorphin receptors, help with alcoholism, which has been tied largely to activity at GABA sites? The answer may lie in the reward center of the brain (Gianoulakis, 2001). If various drugs eventually stimulate the same pleasure pathway, it seems reasonable that antagonists for one drug may, in a roundabout way, affect the impact of other drugs as well.

DRUG MAINTENANCE THERAPY A drug-related lifestyle may be a greater problem than the drug's direct effects. Much of the damage caused by heroin addiction, for example, comes from overdoses, unsterile needles, and an accompanying life of crime. Thus clinicians were very enthusiastic when **methadone maintenance programs** were developed in the 1960s to treat heroin addiction (Dole & Nyswander, 1967, 1965). In these programs, people with an addiction are given the laboratory opioid *methadone* as a substitute for heroin. Although they then become dependent on methadone, their new addiction is maintained under safe medical supervision. Unlike heroin, methadone can be taken by mouth, thus eliminating the dangers of needles, and needs to be taken only once a day.

At first, methadone programs seemed very effective, and many of them were set up throughout the United States, Canada, and England (Payte, 1989). These programs became less popular during the 1980s, however, because of the dangers of methadone itself. Many clinicians and clients came to believe that substituting one addiction for another is not an acceptable "solution" for substance dependence (Cornish et al., 1995). In fact, methadone is sometimes harder to withdraw from than heroin, because the withdrawal symptoms can last nearly twice as long (Backmund et al., 2001; Kleber, 1981). Moreover, pregnant women maintained on methadone have the added concern of the drug's effect on their fetus (DeCubas & Field, 1993).

Despite such concerns, maintenance treatment with methadone (or with *buprenorphine*, a newly developed substitute drug) has again sparked interest among clinicians in recent years, partly because of new research support (Gossop et al., 2001; Ritter, 2001) and partly because of the rapid spread of the HIV virus among intravenous drug abusers and their sex partners and children (Cornish et al., 1995). More than one-quarter of AIDS cases reported in the early 1990s were directly tied to drug abuse, and intravenous drug abuse is the indirect cause in 60 percent of childhood AIDS cases (Brown, 1993; NIDA, 1991). Not only is methadone treatment safer than street opioid use, but many methadone programs now include AIDS education and other health instructions in their services (Sorensen & Copeland, 2000). Research suggests that methadone maintenance programs are most effective when they are combined with education, psychotherapy, family therapy, and employment counseling (O'Brien & McKay, 2002; Woody et al., 1998). Today

Is legalization the answer? *While clinicians try to identify and treat the effects of substance use and misuse, a number of groups are lobbying for the legalization of certain drugs. At a recent protest in England calling for the decriminalization of marijuana, this woman wears a necklace of cannibis leaves.*

more than 900 methadone clinics across the United States dispense the drug to as many as 160,000 patients at an average cost of $13 a day (ONDCP, 2002, 2000; Marks, 1998).

Sociocultural Therapies

As we have seen, sociocultural theorists believe that psychological problems emerge in a social setting and are best treated in a social context. Three sociocultural approaches have been applied to substance-related disorders: (1) *self-help programs*; (2) *culture-* and *gender-sensitive programs*: and (3) *community prevention programs*.

SELF-HELP AND RESIDENTIAL TREATMENT PROGRAMS Many people who abuse drugs have organized among themselves to help one another recover without professional assistance. The drug self-help movement dates back to 1935, when two

---

A CLOSER LOOK

Controlled Drug Use vs. Abstinence

Is total abstinence the only cure for drug abuse and dependence, or can people with substance-related disorders learn to keep drug use under control? This issue has been debated for years, especially when the drug in question is alcohol (King & Tucker, 2000).

Some cognitive-behavioral theorists believe that people can continue to drink in moderation if they learn to set appropriate drinking limits. They argue that demanding strict abstinence of people may in fact cause them to lose self-control entirely if they have a single drink (Marlatt et al., 2001; Peele, 1989; Heather et al., 1982). In contrast, those who view alcoholism as a disease take the AA position of "Once an alcoholic, always an alcoholic," and argue that people with alcoholism are in fact more likely to relapse when they believe that they can safely take one drink (Pendery et al., 1982). This misguided belief, they hold, will sooner or later open the door to alcohol once again and lead back to uncontrollable drinking.

Feelings run so strongly that the people on one side have at times challenged the motives and honesty of those on the other (Sobell & Sobell, 1984, 1973; Pendery et al., 1982). Research indicates, however, that both controlled drinking and abstinence may be useful treatment goals, depending on the individual's personality and on the nature of the particular drinking problem. Studies suggest, for example, that abstinence is a more appropriate goal for people who have a long-standing dependence on alcohol, while controlled drinking can be helpful to younger drinkers whose pattern does not include physical dependence. The latter individuals may in fact need to be taught a nonabusive form of drinking (Foxhall, 2001; Peele, 1992; Marlatt, 1985). Studies also suggest that abstinence is appropriate for people who believe that abstinence is the only answer for them (Rosenberg, 1993). These individuals are indeed more likely to relapse after having just one drink.

Generally speaking, both abstinence and controlled drinking are extremely difficult for persons with alcoholism to achieve. Although treatment may help them to improve for a while, many of them relapse (Allsop et al., 2000). Such statistics serve as a harsh reminder that substance abuse and dependence remain among society's most disabling problems.

Changing an image *Many kinds of persons in many kinds of places practice abstinence to help them overcome and control problems with alcohol or other substances. Here sober bikers get together at the Dry Gulch, a favorite spot in St. Paul, Minnesota.*

ALCOHOLICS ANONYMOUS (AA) A self-help organization that provides support and guidance for persons who abuse alcohol or are dependent on it.

RESIDENTIAL TREATMENT CENTER A place where people formerly dependent on drugs live, work, and socialize in a drug-free environment. Also called a *therapeutic community*.

Ohio men suffering from alcoholism met to discuss alternative treatment possibilities. The first discussion led to others and to the eventual formation of a self-help group whose members discussed alcohol-related problems, traded ideas, and provided support. The organization became known as **Alcoholics Anonymous (AA)**.

Today AA has more than 2 million members in 100,000 groups across the United States and 150 other countries (AA World Services, 2003). It offers peer support along with moral and spiritual guidelines to help people overcome alcoholism. Different members apparently find different aspects of AA helpful. For some it is the peer support (Galanter et al., 1990); for others it is the spiritual dimension (Swora, 2001). Meetings take place regularly, and members are available to help each other 24 hours a day.

By offering guidelines for living, the organization helps members abstain "one day at a time," urging them to accept as "fact" the idea that they are powerless over alcohol and that they must stop drinking entirely and permanently if they are to live normal lives. Related self-help organizations, *Al-Anon* and *Alateen*, offer support for people who live with and care about persons with alcoholism. Self-help programs such as *Narcotics Anonymous* and *Cocaine Anonymous* have been developed for other substance-related disorders.

Many self-help programs have expanded into **residential treatment centers**, or **therapeutic communities**—such as *Daytop Village* and *Phoenix House*—where people formerly dependent on drugs live, work, and socialize in a drug-free environment while undergoing individual, group, and family therapies and making a transition back to community life (Landry, 1994).

The evidence that keeps self-help and residential treatment programs going comes largely in the form of individual testimonials. Many tens of thousands of persons have revealed that they are members of these programs and credit them with turning their lives around (Gleick, 1995). Studies of the programs have also had favorable findings (Tonigan, 2001; Timko et al., 2000), but their numbers have been limited (Watson et al., 1997).

CULTURE- AND GENDER-SENSITIVE PROGRAMS Many persons who abuse substances live in a poor and perhaps violent setting. A growing number of today's treatment programs try to be sensitive to the special sociocultural pressures and problems faced by drug abusers who are poor, homeless, or members of minority groups (Straussner, 2001). Therapists who are sensitive to their clients' life challenges can do more to address the stresses that often lead to relapse.

Similarly, therapists have become more aware that women often require treatment methods different from those designed for men (Knowlton, 1998; Lisansky-Gomberg, 1993). Women and men have different physical and psychological reactions to drugs, for example (Hamilton, 1991). In addition, treatment of women who abuse substances may be complicated by the impact of sexual abuse, the possibility that they may become pregnant while taking drugs, the stresses of raising children, and the fear of criminal prosecution for abusing drugs during pregnancy (Thompson & Kingree, 1998; Cornish et al., 1995). Thus many women with such disorders feel more comfortable seeking help at gender-sensitive clinics or residential programs; some such programs also allow children to live with their recovering mothers (Clark, 2001).

COMMUNITY PREVENTION PROGRAMS Perhaps the most effective approach to substance-related disorders is to prevent them (Gottfredson & Wilson, 2003). The first drug-prevention efforts were conducted in schools. Today prevention programs are also offered in workplaces, activity centers, and other community settings, and even through the media (Bennett & Lehman, 2003; St. Pierre, 2001). Some prevention programs argue for total abstinence from drugs, while others teach responsible use. Some seek to interrupt drug use; others try to delay the age at which people first experiment with drugs. Programs may also differ in whether they offer drug education, teach alternatives to drug use, try to change

>>**LOOKING AROUND**

Drugs and the Law

Each year over 1.4 million arrests are made in the United States for driving under the influence of alcohol or opioids, involving one of every 123 drivers (Uniform Crime Reports, 1997).<<

In 60 percent of the 500 child passenger deaths linked to alcohol in 1996, it was the driver of the child's own car who was alcohol-impaired (CDC, 1997).<<

Fifty-seven percent of state prisoners and 45 percent of federal prisoners in the United States report using illicit drugs in the month before committing their offense (Bureau of Justice Statistics, 1999).<<

More than 800,000 teenagers are arrested and formally processed by juvenile courts each year. Around half of them test positive for marijuana (Crowley et al., 1998).<<

the psychological state of the potential user, seek to change relationships with peers, or combine these techniques.

Prevention programs may focus on the *individual* (for example, by providing education about unpleasant drug effects), the *family* (by teaching parenting skills), the *peer group* (by teaching resistance to peer pressure), the *school* (by setting up firm enforcement of drug policies), or the *community* at large (by public service announcements such as the "Just say no" campaign several years ago). The most effective prevention efforts focus on several of these areas to provide a consistent message about drug abuse in all areas of individuals' lives (Smith, 2001; Wagenaar et al., 2000). Some prevention programs have even been developed for preschool children (Hall & Zigler, 1997).

Marc R. Wood, Marinette, Wisconsin

Before it begins *Community prevention programs for substance-related disorders often target very young children. Here children pledge abstinence from drug use on Red Ribbon Day by releasing balloons.*

SUMMING UP

How Are Substance-Related Disorders Treated?

Treatments for substance abuse and dependence vary widely. Usually several approaches are combined. Psychodynamic therapies try to help clients become aware of and correct the underlying needs and conflicts that may have led to their use of drugs. A common behavioral technique is aversion therapy, in which an unpleasant stimulus is paired with the drug that the person is abusing. Cognitive and behavioral techniques have been combined in such forms as behavioral self-control training (BSCT) and relapse-prevention training. Biological treatments include detoxification, antagonist drugs, and drug maintenance therapy. Sociocultural treatments approach substance-related disorders in a social context by means of self-help groups (for example, Alcoholics Anonymous), culture- and gender-sensitive treatments, and community prevention programs.

CROSSROADS:
New Wrinkles to a Familiar Story

In some respects the story of the misuse of drugs is the same today as it was in the past. Substance use is still rampant, often creating damaging psychological disorders. New drugs keep emerging, and the public goes through periods of believing, naively, that they are "safe." Only gradually do people learn that these drugs, too, pose dangers. And treatments for substance-related disorders continue to have only limited effect.

Yet there are important new wrinkles in this familiar story. Researchers have begun to develop a clearer understanding of how drugs act on the brain and body. In treatment, self-help groups and rehabilitation programs are flourishing. And preventive education to make people aware of the dangers of drug misuse is also expanding and seems to be having an effect. One reason for these improvements is that investigators and clinicians have stopped working in isolation and are instead looking for intersections between their own work and that from other models. The same kind of integrated efforts that have helped with other psychological disorders are bringing new promise and hope to the study and treatment of substance-related disorders.

Perhaps the most important insight to be gained from these integrated efforts is that several of the models were already on the right track. Social pressures, personality characteristics, rewards, and genetic predispositions all seem to play roles in substance-related disorders, and in fact to operate together. For example, some people may inherit a malfunction of the biological reward center and so may need special doses of external stimulation—say, intense relationships, an abundance of certain foods, or drugs—to stimulate their reward center. Their pursuit of external rewards may take on the character of an addictive personality (Ebstein & Kotler,

>>**PSYCH•NOTES**

Spontaneous Remission

Between 20 and 30 percent of all people with substance-related disorders apparently recover within 10 years without treatment (Schuckit, 1999).<<

2002). Such individuals may be especially prone to experimenting with drugs, particularly when their social group makes the drugs available or when they are faced with intense social and personal stress.

Just as each model has identified important factors in the development of substance-related disorders, each has made important contributions to treatment. As we have seen, the various forms of treatment seem to work best when they are combined with approaches from the other models, making integrated treatment the most productive approach.

These recent developments are encouraging. At the same time, however, enormous and increasing levels of drug use continue. New drugs and drug combinations are discovered almost daily, and with them come new problems, new questions, and the need for new research and new treatments. Perhaps the most valuable lesson is an old one: there is no free lunch. The pleasures derived from these substances come with high psychological and biological costs, some not yet even known.

CRITICAL THOUGHTS

1. Different ethnic, religious, and national groups have different rates of alcohol abuse. What social factors might help explain this observation? Can we be certain that biological factors are not involved? *pp. 300–304*

2. What effects might the use of drugs by some rock performers have on teenagers? Who has the greater impact on the drug behaviors of teenagers: rock performers who speak out against drugs or rock performers who praise drugs? *pp. 301, 299–300*

3. Only one-third of the $15 billion the U.S. government spends on drug abuse goes to prevention and treatment. Does the focus on the criminalization of drugs add to the stigma of drug abuse and, in turn, make effective treatment more difficult (Nash, 1997)? *pp. 303, 305–311*

4. In 1995, the popular talk show host Oprah Winfrey revealed, with great emotion, that she had been physically dependent on cocaine in the mid-1970s. What impact might admissions like Winfrey's have on people's willingness to seek treatment for substance abuse? *pp. 305–311*

5. Society has periodically tried treatment programs that offer legal, medically supervised doses of heroin (in Great Britain) or of a heroin substitute (in the United States) to combat heroin dependence. What might be the virtues of such a treatment approach? Why has the effectiveness of such programs been limited? *pp. 308–309*

KEY TERMS

intoxication p. 280

hallucinosis p. 280

substance abuse p. 280

substance dependence p. 280

tolerance p. 280

withdrawal p. 280

alcohol p. 282

delirium tremens (DTs) p. 284

cirrhosis p. 285

Korsakoff's syndrome p. 285

fetal alcohol syndrome p. 285

sedative-hypnotic drug p. 286

opioid p. 287

endorphins p. 288

cocaine p. 291

free-basing p. 292

crack p. 292

amphetamine p. 293

hallucinogen p. 294

flashback p. 296

cannabis drugs p. 296

marijuana p. 296

tetrahydrocannabinol (THC) p. 296

polysubstance use p. 299

synergistic effect p. 299

substance-abuse personality p. 302

dopamine-2 (D2) receptor gene p. 304

reward center p. 304

aversion therapy p. 305

contingency management p. 306

behavioral self-control training p. 306

relapse-prevention training p. 306

detoxification p. 307

antagonist drug p. 307

disulfiram (Antabuse) p. 307

narcotic antagonist p. 308

methadone maintenance program p. 308

self-help program p. 309

Alcoholics Anonymous (AA) p. 310

residential treatment center p. 310

culture- and gender-sensitive programs p. 310

community prevention program p. 310

QUICK QUIZ

1. How does alcohol act on the brain and body? What are the problems and dangers of alcohol misuse? *pp. 282–286*

2. Describe the features and problems of the misuse of barbiturates and benzodiazepines. *pp. 286–287*

3. Compare the various opioids (opium, heroin, morphine, and codeine). What problems may result from their use, particularly from the use of heroin? *pp. 287–289*

4. List and compare two kinds of stimulant drugs. Describe their biological actions and the problems caused by each of them. *pp. 290–293*

5. Why has cocaine use become a major problem in recent years? *p. 288*

6. What are the effects of hallucinogens, particularly LSD? *pp. 294–296*

7. What are the effects of marijuana and other cannabis substances? Why is marijuana a greater danger today than it was twenty-five years ago? *pp. 296–299*

8. What special problems does poly-substance use pose? *pp. 299–300*

9. Describe the leading explanations for substance-related disorders. How well supported are these explanations? *pp. 300–305*

10. What are the leading treatments for substance-related disorders? How effective are they? *pp. 305–311*

CYBER STUDY

SEARCH THE *FUNDAMENTALS OF ABNORMAL PSYCHOLOGY* CD-ROM FOR

▲ Chapter 10 Video Case Enrichment
Why do some people develop substance-related disorders?
How does substance abuse affect personal, family, and occupational functioning?
What triggers a user's cravings?

▲ Chapter 10 Practical, Research, and Decision-Making Exercises
Abstinence versus moderation
The impact of peers in substance use and misuse

▲ Chapter 10 Practice Test and Feedback

LOG ON TO THE COMER WEB PAGE FOR

▲ Suggested Web links, exercises, FAQ page, additional Chapter 10 practice test questions
<www.worthpublishers.com/comer>

‹‹‹

EDWARD HOPPER, 1950

Sexual Disorders and Gender Identity Disorder

Robert, a 57-year-old man, came to sex therapy with his wife because of his inability to get erections. He had not had a problem with erections until six months earlier, when they attempted to have sex after an evening out, during which he had had several drinks. They attributed his failure to get an erection to his being "a little drunk," but he found himself worrying over the next few days that he was perhaps becoming impotent. When they next attempted intercourse, he found himself unable to get involved in what they were doing because he was so intent on watching himself to see if he would get an erection. Once again he did not, and they were both very upset. His failure to get an erection continued over the next few months. Robert's wife was very upset and . . . frustrated, accusing him of having an affair, or of no longer finding her attractive. Robert wondered if he was getting too old, or if his medication for high blood pressure, which he had been taking for about a year, might be interfering with erection. . . . When they came for sex therapy, they had not attempted any sexual activity for over two months.

(LoPiccolo, 1992, p. 492)

Sexual behavior is a major focus of both our private thoughts and public discussions. Sexual feelings are a crucial part of our development and daily functioning, sexual activity is tied to the satisfaction of our basic needs, and sexual performance is linked to our self-esteem. Most people are fascinated by the abnormal sexual behavior of others and worry about the normality of their own sexuality.

Experts recognize two general categories of sexual disorders: sexual dysfunctions and paraphilias. People with *sexual dysfunctions* experience problems with their sexual responses. Robert, for example, had a dysfunction known as erectile disorder, a repeated failure to attain or maintain an erection during sexual activity. People with *paraphilias* have repeated and intense sexual urges or fantasies in response to objects or situations that society deems inappropriate, and they may behave inappropriately as well. They may be aroused by the thought of sexual activity with a child, for example, or of exposing their genitals to strangers, and they may act on those urges. In addition to the sexual disorders, DSM-IV includes a diagnosis called *gender identity disorder*, a sex-related disorder in which people persistently feel that they have been assigned to the wrong sex and in fact identify with the other gender.

Sexual Dysfunctions

Sexual dysfunctions, disorders in which people cannot respond normally in key areas of sexual functioning, make it difficult or impossible to enjoy sexual intercourse. A large study suggests that as many as 31 percent of men and 43 percent of women in the United States suffer from such a dysfunction during their lives (Heiman, 2002; Laumann et al., 1999, 1994). Sexual

SEXUAL DYSFUNCTION A disorder marked by a persistent inability to function normally in some area of the human sexual response cycle.

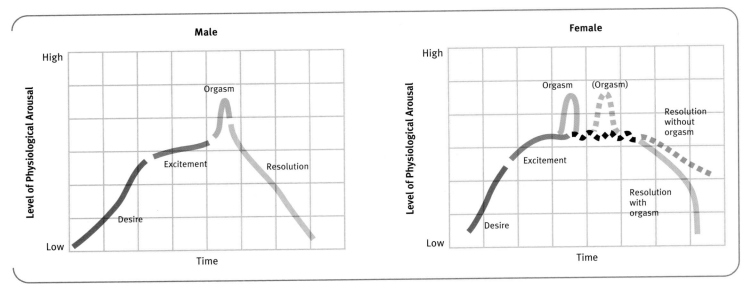

FIGURE 11-1 **The normal sexual response cycle** *Researchers have found a similar sequence of phases in both males and females. Sometimes, however, women do not experience orgasm; in that case, the resolution phase is less sudden. And sometimes women experience two or more orgasms in succession before the resolution phase. (Adapted from Kaplan, 1974; Masters & Johnson, 1970, 1966.)*

dysfunctions are typically very distressing, and they often lead to sexual frustration, guilt, loss of self-esteem, and interpersonal problems (Basson et al., 2001). Often these dysfunctions are interrelated, so that many patients with one experience another as well. Sexual dysfunctioning will be described here for heterosexual couples, the majority of couples seen in therapy. Homosexual couples have the same dysfunctions, however, and therapists use the same basic techniques to treat them (LoPiccolo, 1995).

The human sexual response can be described as a *cycle* with four phases: *desire*, *excitement*, *orgasm*, and *resolution* (see Figure 11-1). Sexual dysfunctions affect one or more of the first three phases. Resolution consists simply of the relaxation and reduction in arousal that follow orgasm. Some people struggle with a sexual dysfunction their whole lives; in other cases, normal sexual functioning preceded the dysfunction. In some cases the dysfunction is present during all sexual situations; in others it is tied to particular situations (APA, 1994).

Disorders of Desire

The **desire phase** of the sexual response cycle consists of an urge to have sex, sexual fantasies, and sexual attraction to others (see Figure 11-2). Two dysfunctions— *hypoactive sexual desire* and *sexual aversion*—affect the desire phase. A client named Ms. Bryarton experiences both of these disorders:

> Mr. and Ms. [Bryarton] have been married for 14 years and have three children, ages 8 through 12. They [complain that Ms. Bryarton] has never enjoyed [sex] since they have been married.
>
> Before their marriage, although they had intercourse only twice, Ms. Bryarton had been highly aroused by kissing and petting and felt she used her attractiveness to "seduce" her husband into marriage. She did, however, feel intense guilt about their two episodes of premarital intercourse; during their honeymoon, she began to think of sex as a chore that could not be pleasing. Although she periodically passively complied with intercourse, she had almost no spontaneous desire for sex. She never masturbated, had never reached orgasm, thought of all variations such as oral sex as completely repulsive, and was preoccupied with a fantasy of how disapproving her family would be if she ever engaged in any of these activities.
>
> Ms. Bryarton is almost totally certain that no woman she respects in any older generation has enjoyed sex, and that despite the "new vogue" of sexuality, only sleazy, crude women let themselves act like "animals." These beliefs have

DESIRE PHASE The phase of the sexual response cycle consisting of an urge to have sex, sexual fantasies, and sexual attraction to others.

HYPOACTIVE SEXUAL DESIRE DISORDER A disorder marked by a lack of interest in sex and hence a low level of sexual activity.

SEXUAL AVERSION DISORDER A disorder characterized by an aversion to and avoidance of genital sexual interplay.

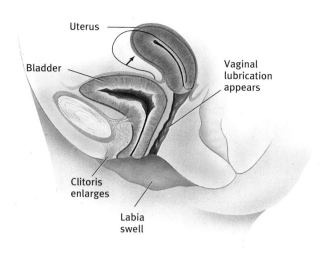

Uterus

Bladder

Vaginal lubrication appears

Clitoris enlarges

Labia swell

Desire

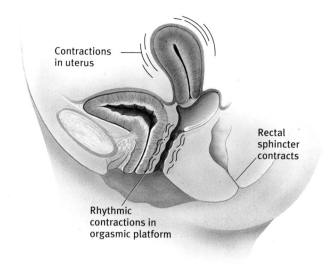

Contractions in uterus

Rectal sphincter contracts

Rhythmic contractions in orgasmic platform

Orgasm

FIGURE 11-2 **Normal female sexual anatomy** *Changes in the female anatomy occur during the different phases of the sexual response cycle. (Adapted from Hyde, 1990, p. 200.)*

led to a pattern of regular, but infrequent, sex that at best is accommodating and gives little or no pleasure to her or her husband. Whenever Ms. Bryarton comes close to having a feeling of sexual arousal, numerous negative thoughts come into her mind, such as "What am I, a tramp?" "If I like this, he'll just want it more often." Or "How could I look myself in the mirror after something like this?" These thoughts almost inevitably are accompanied by a cold feeling and an insensitivity to sensual pleasure. As a result, sex is invariably an unhappy experience. Almost any excuse, such as fatigue or being busy, is sufficient for her to rationalize avoiding intercourse.

Yet, intellectually Ms. Bryarton wonders, "Is something wrong with me?"

Spitzer et al., 1994, p. 251)

Hypoactive sexual desire is a lack of interest in sex and, in turn, a low level of sexual activity (see Table 11-1). Nevertheless, when people with hypoactive sexual desire do have sex, their physical responses may be normal and they may enjoy the experience. While our culture portrays men as wanting all the sex they can get, hypoactive sexual desire may be found in as many as 16 percent of men, and the number seeking therapy has increased during the past decade (Heiman, 2002; Laumann et al., 1999). It may also be found in 33 percent of women. A number of people experience normal sexual interest and arousal but choose, as a matter of lifestyle, not to engage in sexual relations. These individuals are not diagnosed as having hypoactive sexual desire.

DSM-IV defines hypoactive sexual desire as "deficient or absent sexual fantasies and desire for sexual activity," but it does not specify what a "deficient" level is. In fact, this criterion is difficult to define (Bach, Wineze, & Barlow, 2001; LoPiccolo, 1995). Age, number of years married, education, social class, race, and other factors may all influence the frequency of sex. In one survey, 93 happily married couples were asked to report how often they desire sexual encounters. Almost all of them said that they desire sex at least once every two weeks, and around 85 percent reported a desire rate of several times a week or more. On the basis of this survey, sexual desire would be considered hypoactive only when a person desires sex less frequently than once every two weeks.

People with **sexual aversion** find sex distinctly unpleasant or repulsive. Sexual advances may sicken, disgust, or frighten them. Some people are repelled by a particular aspect of sex,

---

Table 11-1 DSM-IV Checklist

HYPOACTIVE SEXUAL DESIRE DISORDER

1. Persistent or recurrent deficiency of sexual fantasies and desire for sexual activity.
2. Significant distress or interpersonal difficulty.

SEXUAL AVERSION DISORDER

1. Persistent or recurrent extreme aversion to, and avoidance of, almost all genital contact with a sexual partner.
2. Significant distress or interpersonal difficulty.

Based on APA, 2000, 1994.

such as penetration of the vagina; others experience a general aversion to all sexual stimuli, including kissing or touching. Aversion to sex seems to be quite rare in men and more common in women (Heiman, 2002).

A person's sex drive is determined by a combination of biological, psychological, and sociocultural factors, and any of them may reduce sexual desire (Williams & Leiblum, 2002). Most cases of low sexual desire or sexual aversion are caused primarily by sociocultural and psychological factors, but biological conditions can also lower sex drive significantly (Kresin, 1993).

BIOLOGICAL CAUSES A number of hormones interact to produce sexual desire and behavior, and abnormalities in their activity can lower the sex drive (Davis, 2001; Rosen & Leiblum, 1995). In both men and women, a high level of the hormone prolactin, a low level of the male sex hormone testosterone, and either a high or low level of the female sex hormone estrogen can lead to low sex drive. Low sex drive has been linked to the high levels of estrogen contained in some birth control pills, for example. Conversely, it has also been tied to the low level of estrogen found in many postmenopausal women or women who have recently given birth. Long-term physical illness can also lower the sex drive (Kalayjian & Morrell, 2000). The low drive may be a direct result of the illness or an indirect result due to stress, pain, or depression brought on by the illness.

Sex drive can be lowered by some pain medications, certain psychotropic drugs, and a number of illegal drugs such as cocaine, marijuana, amphetamines, and heroin (Stahl, 2001; Segraves, 1995). Low levels of alcohol may raise the sex drive by lowering a person's inhibitions, yet high levels will reduce it (Roehrich & Kinder, 1991).

PSYCHOLOGICAL CAUSES A general increase in anxiety or anger may reduce sexual desire in both men and women (Westheimer & Lopater, 2002; Beck & Bozman, 1996). Frequently, as cognitive theorists have noted, people with hypoactive sexual desire and sexual aversion have particular attitudes, fears, or memories that contribute to their dysfunction, such as a belief that sex is immoral or dangerous (LoPiccolo, 1995). Other people are so afraid of losing control over their sexual urges that they try to resist them completely. And still others fear pregnancy.

Certain psychological disorders may also lead to hypoactive sexual desire and sexual aversion. Even a mild level of depression can interfere with sexual desire, and some people with obsessive-compulsive symptoms find contact with another person's body fluids and odors to be highly unpleasant (Pesce, Seidman, & Roose, 2002; LoPiccolo, 1995).

SOCIOCULTURAL CAUSES The attitudes, fears, and psychological disorders that contribute to hypoactive sexual desire and sexual aversion occur within a social context, and thus certain sociocultural factors have also been linked to these dysfunctions. Many sufferers are feeling situational pressures—divorce, a death in the family, job stress, infertility difficulties, having a baby (Burns, 1995; Letourneau & O'Donohue, 1993). Others may be having problems in their relationships. People who are in an unhappy relationship, have lost affection for their partner, or feel powerless and dominated by their partner can lose interest in sex (Metz & Epstein, 2002; Westheimer & Lopater, 2002). Even in basically happy relationships, if one partner is a very unskilled, unenthusiastic lover, the other can begin to lose interest in sex. And sometimes partners differ in their needs for closeness. The one who needs more personal space may develop hypoactive sexual desire as a way of keeping distance (LoPiccolo, 1997, 1995).

Cultural standards can also set the stage for hypoactive sexual desire and sexual aversion. Some men adopt our culture's double standard and thus cannot feel sexual desire for a woman they love and respect. More generally, because our society equates sexual attractiveness with

Myth breakers *Few television shows have gone farther to challenge old myths about female sexuality than the comedy series* Sex and the City. *Although most sex theorists acknowledge this show's role in helping to change women's (and men's) misconceptions about female sexuality, some worry that at times it creates a few myths of its own that may be hard for women to identify with or live up to.*

Courtesy of the Everett Collection

THE CURRENT SCENE

Lifetime Patterns of Sexual Behavior

Sexual dysfunctions are, by definition, different from the usual patterns of sexual functioning. But in the sexual realm, what is "the usual"? In the mid-1980s, clinicians found their efforts to prevent the spread of AIDS hindered by a lack of available data and began to conduct large surveys on sexual behavior. Collectively, the studies provide a wealth of useful, sometimes eye-opening information about sexual patterns in the "normal" populations of North America (Brown & Ceniceros, 2001; Laumann et al., 1999, 1994; Seidman & Rieder, 1995; Janus & Janus, 1993).

Teenagers

More than 90 percent of boys masturbate by the end of adolescence, compared to 50 percent of girls. For the vast majority of them, masturbation began by age 14. Males report masturbating an average of one to two times a week, females once a month.

Around 20 percent of teenagers have heterosexual intercourse by the age of 15, and 80 percent by age 19. Today's teenagers are having intercourse younger than those of past generations. Most teens who are sexually experienced engage in only one sexual relationship at a time. Over the course of their teen years, however, most have at least two sex partners.

Extended periods without sex are still common, even for teenagers in a relationship. Half of sexually experienced adolescent girls have intercourse once a month or less. Sexually experienced teenage boys spend an average of six months of the year without intercourse.

Condom use by teenagers has increased somewhat during the past decade, partly because of warnings about AIDS. However, at most half of teenagers report having used a condom the last time they had sex. Less than a third of teenagers use condoms consistently and appropriately.

Early interest *Sexual curiosity and feelings typically begin well before the teenage years. Children may first discover such feelings in unexpected places and may be confused and anxious about them for a while.*

Frank Siteman/Stock Boston

Early Adulthood (Ages 18–24)

More than 80 percent of unmarried young adults have intercourse in a given year. Of those who are sexually active, around a third have intercourse two or three times a month and another third engage in it two or three times a week. Masturbation remains common in young adulthood: close to 60 percent of men masturbate, a third of them at least once a week, and 36 percent of women masturbate, a tenth of them at least once a week.

Mid-Adulthood (Ages 25–59)

From the age of 25 to 59, sexual relationships last longer and are more monogamous. More than 90 percent of people in this age range have sexual intercourse in a given year. Half of the unmarried men have two or more partners in a given year, compared to a quarter of the unmarried women.

Among sexually active adults, close to 60 percent of men have intercourse up to three times a week and around 60 percent of women once or twice a week. Middle-aged adults are still masturbating. Half of all middle-aged men masturbate at least monthly. Half of all women between 25 and 50 masturbate at least monthly, but only a third of those between 51 and 64 do so.

Old Age (Over Age 60)

More and more people stop having intercourse as the years go by—a total of 10 percent in their 40s, 15 percent in their 50s, 30 percent in their 60s, and 45 percent in their 70s. The decline in men's sexual activity usually comes gradually as they advance in age and their health fails. Sexual activity is more likely to drop off sharply for elderly women, commonly because of the death or illness of a partner. Elderly women also seem to lose interest in sex before elderly men do. Half of the women in their 60s report limited sexual interest, compared to fewer than 10 percent of the men.

Among elderly persons who remain sexually active, those in their 60s have intercourse an average of four times a month, those in their 70s two or three times a month. Around 70 percent of elderly men and 50 percent of elderly women continue to have sexual fantasies. Around half of men and a fourth of women continue to masturbate into their 90s.

Clearly sexual interests and behaviors remain an important part of life for large numbers of people, even as they grow older and as their sexual responses change to some degree.

youthfulness, many aging men and women lose interest in sex as their self-image or their attraction to their partner diminishes with age (LoPiccolo, 1995).

The trauma of sexual molestation or assault is especially likely to produce the fears, attitudes, and memories found in these sexual dysfunctions. Sexual aversion is very common in victims of sexual abuse and may persist for years, even decades (Heiman, 2002; Jackson et al., 1990). In extreme cases, individuals may experience vivid flashbacks of the assault during adult sexual activity.

Disorders of Excitement

The **excitement phase** of the sexual response cycle is marked by changes in the pelvic region, general physical arousal, and increases in heart rate, muscle tension, blood pressure, and rate of breathing. In men, blood pools in the pelvis and leads to erection of the penis; in women, this phase produces swelling of the clitoris and labia, as well as lubrication of the vagina. Dysfunctions affecting the excitement phase are *female sexual arousal disorder* (once referred to as "frigidity") and *male erectile disorder* (once called "impotence").

FEMALE SEXUAL AROUSAL DISORDER Women with a **sexual arousal disorder** are persistently unable to attain or maintain proper lubrication or genital swelling during sexual activity (see Table 11-2). Understandably, many of them also experience an orgasmic disorder or other sexual dysfunction. In fact, this disorder is rarely diagnosed alone (Heiman, 2002). Studies vary widely in their estimates of its prevalence, but most agree that more than 10 percent of women experience it (Laumann et al., 1999, 1994; Rosen et al., 1993). Because lack of sexual arousal in women is so often tied to an orgasmic disorder, researchers usually study and explain the two problems together. Correspondingly, we shall examine the causes of these problems together when we look at female orgasmic disorder.

> ### Table 11-2 DSM-IV Checklist
>
> **FEMALE SEXUAL AROUSAL DISORDER**
> 1. Persistent or recurrent inability to attain, or to maintain until completion of the sexual activity, adequate lubrication or swelling response of sexual excitement.
> 2. Significant distress or interpersonal difficulty.
>
> **MALE ERECTILE DISORDER**
> 1. Persistent or recurrent inability to attain, or to maintain until completion of the sexual activity, an adequate erection.
> 2. Significant distress or interpersonal difficulty.
>
> Based on APA, 2000, 1994.

MALE ERECTILE DISORDER Men with **erectile disorder** persistently fail to attain or maintain an adequate erection during sexual activity. This problem occurs in about 10 percent of the general male population, including Robert, the man whose difficulties opened this chapter (Heiman, 2002; Laumann et al., 1999). Carlos Domera also has erectile disorder:

Carlos Domera is a 30-year-old dress manufacturer who came to the United States from Argentina at age 22. He is married to an American woman, Phyllis, also age 30. They have no children. Mr. Domera's problem was that he had been unable to have sexual intercourse for over a year due to his inability to achieve or maintain an erection. He had avoided all sexual contact with his wife for the prior five months, except for two brief attempts at lovemaking which ended when he failed to maintain his erection.

The couple separated a month ago by mutual agreement due to the tension that surrounded their sexual problem and their inability to feel comfortable with each other. Both professed love and concern for the other, but had serious doubts regarding their ability to resolve the sexual problem. . . .

Mr. Domera conformed to the stereotype of the "macho Latin lover," believing that he "should always have erections easily and be able to make love at any time." Since he couldn't "perform" sexually, he felt humiliated and inadequate, and he dealt with this by avoiding not only sex, but any expression of affection for his wife.

Ms. Domera felt "he is not trying; perhaps he doesn't love me, and I can't live with no sex, no affection, and his bad moods." She had requested the separation temporarily, and he readily agreed. However, they had recently been seeing each other twice a week. . . .

During the evaluation he reported that the onset of his erectile difficulties was concurrent with a tense period in his business. After several "failures" to complete intercourse, he concluded he was "useless as a husband" and therefore a "total failure." The anxiety of attempting lovemaking was too much for him to deal with.

He reluctantly admitted that he was occasionally able to masturbate alone to a full, firm erection and reach a satisfying orgasm. However, he felt ashamed and guilty about this, from both childhood masturbatory guilt and a feeling that he was "cheating" his wife. It was also noted that he had occasional firm erections upon awakening in the morning. Other than the antidepressant, the patient was taking no drugs, and he was not using much alcohol. There was no evidence of physical illness.

(Spitzer et al., 1983, pp. 105–106)

EXCITEMENT PHASE The phase of the sexual response cycle marked by changes in the pelvic region, general physical arousal, and increases in heart rate, muscle tension, blood pressure, and rate of breathing.

FEMALE SEXUAL AROUSAL DISORDER A female dysfunction marked by a persistent inability to attain sexual excitement, including adequate lubrication or genital swelling, during sexual activity.

MALE ERECTILE DISORDER A dysfunction in which a man repeatedly fails to attain or maintain an erection during sexual activity.

NOCTURNAL PENILE TUMESCENCE (NPT) Erection during sleep.

Unlike Mr. Domera, most men with an erectile disorder are over the age of 50, largely because so many cases are associated with ailments or diseases of older adults (Seidman & Rieder, 1995). The disorder is experienced by 5 to 9 percent of all men who are 40 years old and increases to at least 15 percent at age 60 (Laumann et al., 1999; Feldman et al., 1994). Moreover, according to surveys, half of all adult men experience erectile difficulty during intercourse at least some of the time.

Most cases of erectile disorder result from an interaction of biological, psychological, and sociocultural factors. One study found that only 10 of 63 cases of this disorder were caused by purely psychosocial factors, and only 5 were the result of physical impairment alone (LoPiccolo, 1991).

BIOLOGICAL CAUSES The same hormonal imbalances that can cause hypoactive sexual desire can also produce erectile disorder. More commonly, however, vascular problems—problems with the body's blood vessels—are involved (Bach et al., 2001; Althof & Seftel, 1995). An erection occurs when the chambers in the penis fill with blood, so any condition that reduces blood flow into the penis, such as heart disease or clogging of the arteries, may lead to the disorder (Stahl, 2001; LoPiccolo, 1997). It can also be caused by damage to the nervous system as a result of diabetes, spinal cord injuries, multiple sclerosis, kidney failure, or treatment with an artificial kidney machine (Frohman, 2002; Leiblum & Segraves, 1995). In addition, as is the case with hypoactive sexual desire, the use of certain medications and various forms of substance abuse, from alcohol abuse to cigarette smoking, may interfere with erections (Westheimer & Lopater, 2002; Segraves, 1998).

Medical procedures, including ultrasound recordings and blood tests, have been developed for diagnosing biological causes of erectile disorder. Measuring **nocturnal penile tumescence** (**NPT**), or erections during sleep, is particularly useful in assessing whether physical factors are responsible (Westheimer & Lopater, 2002; Althof & Seftel, 1995). Men typically have erections during *rapid eye movement (REM) sleep*, the phase of sleep in which dreaming takes place. A healthy man is likely to have two to five REM periods each night, and perhaps two to three hours of erections. Abnormal or absent nightly erections usually (but not always) indicate some physical basis for erectile failure. As a rough screening device, a patient may be instructed to fasten a simple "snap gauge" band around his penis before going to sleep and then check it the next morning. A broken band indicates that erection has occurred during the night. An unbroken band indicates a lack of nighttime erections and suggests that the person's general erectile problem may have a physical basis (Mohr & Beutler, 1990).

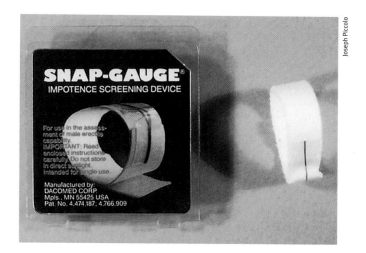

Joseph Piccolo

Psychological or organic? *The snap gauge, worn around the penis at night, is a fabric band with three plastic filaments. If the filaments are broken in the morning, the man knows that he has experienced normal erections during REM sleep and that erectile failures during intercourse are probably due to psychological factors.*

PERFORMANCE ANXIETY The fear of performing inadequately and a related tension experienced during sex.

SPECTATOR ROLE A state of mind that some people experience during sex, focusing on their sexual performance to such an extent that their performance and their enjoyment are reduced.

ORGASM PHASE The phase of the sexual response cycle during which an individual's sexual pleasure peaks and sexual tension is released as muscles in the pelvic region contract rhythmically.

PREMATURE EJACULATION A dysfunction in which a man reaches orgasm and ejaculates before, on, or shortly after penetration and before he wishes to.

MALE ORGASMIC DISORDER A male dysfunction characterized by a repeated inability to reach orgasm or long delays in reaching orgasm after normal sexual excitement.

PSYCHOLOGICAL CAUSES Any of the psychological causes of hypoactive sexual desire can also interfere with arousal and lead to erectile disorder. As many as 90 percent of all men with severe depression, for example, experience some degree of erectile dysfunction (Seidman, 2002; Leiblum & Segraves, 1995).

One well-supported psychological explanation for erectile disorder is a cognitive theory developed by William Masters and Virginia Johnson (1970). The explanation emphasizes **performance anxiety** and the **spectator role**. Once a man begins to experience erectile problems, for whatever reason, he becomes fearful about failing to have an erection and worries during each sexual encounter. Instead of relaxing and enjoying the sensations of sexual pleasure, he remains distanced from the activity, watching himself and focusing on the goal of reaching erection. Instead of being an aroused participant, he becomes a judge and spectator. Whatever the initial reason for the erectile dysfunction, the resulting spectator role becomes the reason for the ongoing problem. In this vicious cycle, the original cause of the erectile failure becomes less important than fear of failure.

SOCIOCULTURAL CAUSES Each of the sociocultural factors that contribute to hypoactive sexual desire has also been tied to erectile disorder. Men who have lost their jobs and are under financial stress, for example, are more likely to develop erectile difficulties than other men (Morokoff & Gillilland, 1993). Marital stress, too, has been tied to this dysfunction (Metz & Epstein, 2002). Two relationship patterns in particular may contribute to it (LoPiccolo, 1991). In one, the wife provides too little physical stimulation for her aging husband, who, because of normal aging changes, now requires more intense, direct, and lengthy physical stimulation of the penis for erection to occur. In the second relationship pattern, a couple believes that only intercourse can give the wife an orgasm. This idea increases the pressure on the man to have an erection and makes him more prone to erectile dysfunction. If the wife reaches orgasm manually or orally during their sexual encounter, his pressure to perform is reduced.

Disorders of Orgasm

During the **orgasm phase** of the sexual response cycle, an individual's sexual pleasure peaks and sexual tension is released as the muscles in the pelvic region contract, or draw together, rhythmically (see Figure 11-3). The man's semen is ejaculated, and the outer third of the woman's vaginal wall contracts. Dysfunctions of this phase of the sexual response cycle are *premature ejaculation, male orgasmic disorder,* and *female orgasmic disorder.*

FIGURE 11-3 **Normal male sexual anatomy** *Changes in the male anatomy occur during the different phases of the sexual response cycle. (Adapted from Hyde, 1990, p. 199.)*

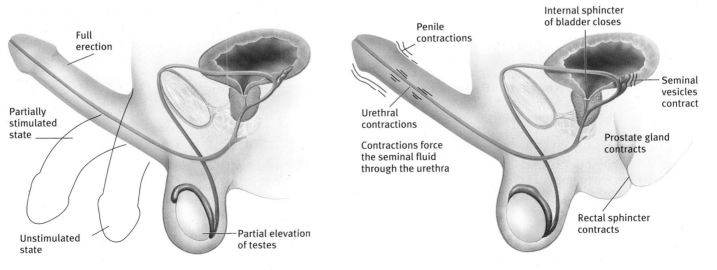

Desire

Orgasm

PREMATURE EJACULATION Eddie is typical of many men in his experience of premature ejaculation:

> Eddie, a 20-year-old student, sought treatment after his girlfriend ended their relationship because his premature ejaculation left her sexually frustrated. Eddie had had only one previous sexual relationship, during his senior year in high school. With two friends he would drive to a neighboring town and find a certain prostitute. After picking her up, they would drive to a deserted area and take turns having sex with her, while the others waited outside the car. Both the prostitute and his friends urged him to hurry up because they feared discovery by the police, and besides, in the winter it was cold. When Eddie began his sexual relationship with his girlfriend, his entire sexual history consisted of this rapid intercourse, with virtually no foreplay. He found caressing his girlfriend's breasts and genitals and her touching of his penis to be so arousing that he sometimes ejaculated before complete entry of the penis, or after at most only a minute or so of intercourse.
>
> *(LoPiccolo, 1995, p. 495)*

A man suffering from **premature ejaculation** persistently reaches orgasm and ejaculates with very little sexual stimulation before, on, or shortly after penetration, and before he wishes to (see Table 11-3). Around 29 percent of men in the United States experience premature ejaculation at some time (Heiman, 2002; Laumann et al., 1999, 1994). The typical length of intercourse in our society has increased over the past several decades, in turn increasing the distress of men who suffer from premature ejaculation, typically men under the age of 30 (Bancroft, 1989).

Psychological, particularly behavioral, explanations of premature ejaculation have received more research support than other kinds of explanations. The dysfunction seems to be typical of young, sexually inexperienced men such as Eddie, who simply have not learned to slow down, control their arousal, and extend the pleasurable process of making love (Brown & Ceniceros, 2001; Metz & Pryor, 2000). In fact, premature ejaculation is very common when a young man has his first sexual encounter. With continued sexual experience, most men gain greater control over their sexual responses. Men of any age who have sex only occasionally are also prone to ejaculate prematurely (LoPiccolo, 1985).

Clinicians have also suggested that premature ejaculation may be related to anxiety, hurried masturbation experiences during adolescence (in fear of being "caught" by parents), or poor recognition of one's own sexual arousal (Westheimer & Lopater, 2002; Dunn et al., 1999). However, these theories have only sometimes received clear research support.

Table 11-3 DSM-IV Checklist

PREMATURE EJACULATION

1. Persistent or recurrent ejaculation with minimal sexual stimulation before, on, or shortly after penetration and before the person wishes it.
2. Significant distress or interpersonal difficulty.

MALE ORGASMIC DISORDER

1. Persistent or recurrent delay in, or absence of, orgasm following a normal sexual excitement phase during sexual activity.
2. Significant distress or interpersonal difficulty.

FEMALE ORGASMIC DISORDER

1. Persistent or recurrent delay in, or absence of, orgasm following a normal sexual excitement phase during sexual activity.
2. Significant distress or interpersonal difficulty.

Based on APA, 2000, 1994.

MALE ORGASMIC DISORDER A man with **male orgasmic disorder** repeatedly cannot reach orgasm or is very delayed in reaching orgasm after normal sexual excitement. The disorder occurs in 8 percent of the male population (Heiman, 2002; Laumann et al., 1999) and is typically a source of great frustration and upset, as in the case of John:

> John, a 38-year-old sales representative, had been married for 9 years. At the insistence of his 32-year-old wife, the couple sought counseling for their sexual problem—his inability to ejaculate during intercourse. During the early years of

the marriage, his wife had experienced difficulty reaching orgasm until he learned to delay his ejaculation for a long period of time. To do this, he used mental distraction techniques and regularly smoked marijuana before making love. Initially, John felt very satisfied that he could make love for longer and longer periods of time without ejaculation and regarded his ability as a sign of masculinity.

About 3 years prior to seeking counseling, after the birth of their only child, John found that he was losing his erection before he was able to ejaculate. His wife suggested different intercourse positions, but the harder he tried, the more difficulty he had in reaching orgasm. Because of his frustration, the couple began to avoid sex altogether. John experienced increasing performance anxiety with each successive failure, and an increasing sense of helplessness in the face of his problem.

(Rosen & Rosen, 1981, pp. 317–318)

A low testosterone level, certain neurological diseases, and some head or spinal cord injuries can interfere with ejaculation (Stahl, 2001; LoPiccolo, 1997, 1995, 1985). Drugs that slow down the sympathetic nervous system (such as alcohol, some medications for high blood pressure, certain psychotropic medications) can also affect ejaculation (Altman, 2001; Segraves, 1998, 1995, 1993). For example, *fluoxetine*, or Prozac, and other serotonin-enhancing antidepressants appear to interfere with ejaculation in as many as 40 percent of men who take it (Clayton et al., 2002; Pesce et al., 2002).

A leading psychological cause of male orgasmic disorder appears to be performance anxiety and the spectator role, the cognitive factors also involved in male erectile disorder. Once a man begins to focus on reaching orgasm, he may stop being an aroused participant in his sexual activity and instead become an unaroused, self-critical, and fearful observer (Wiederman, 2001). Finally, male orgasmic disorder may develop out of hypoactive sexual desire (Rosen & Leiblum, 1995). A man who engages in sex largely because of pressure from his partner, without any real desire for it, simply may not get aroused enough to reach orgasm.

FEMALE ORGASMIC DISORDER Stephanie and Bill, married for three years, came for sex therapy because of her lack of orgasm.

Stephanie had never had an orgasm in any way, but because of Bill's concern, she had been faking orgasm during intercourse until recently. Finally she told him the truth, and they sought therapy together. Stephanie had been raised by a strictly religious family. She could not recall ever seeing her parents kiss or show physical affection for each other. She was severely punished on one occasion when her mother found her looking at her own genitals, at about age 7. Stephanie received no sex education from her parents, and when she began to menstruate, her mother told her only that this meant that she could become pregnant, so she mustn't ever kiss a boy or let a boy touch her. Her mother restricted her dating severely, with repeated warnings that "boys only want one thing." While her parents were rather critical and demanding of her (asking her why she got one B among otherwise straight A's on her report card, for example), they were loving parents and their approval was very important to her.

(LoPiccolo, 1995, p. 496)

FEMALE ORGASMIC DISORDER A dysfunction in which a woman rarely has an orgasm or repeatedly experiences a very delayed one.

Women with **female orgasmic disorder** rarely reach orgasm or generally experience a very delayed one. Around 24 percent of women apparently have this problem—including more than a third of postmenopausal women (Heiman, 2002; Rosen & Leiblum, 1995). Studies indicate that 10 percent or more of women today have never had an orgasm, either alone or during intercourse, and at least another 10 percent rarely have orgasms (LoPiccolo, 1995). At the same time, half of all women experience orgasm in intercourse at least fairly regularly (LoPiccolo & Stock, 1987). Women who are more sexually assertive (Hurlbert, 1991) and more comfortable with masturbation (Kelly et al., 1990) tend to have orgasms more regularly. Female orgasmic disorder appears to be more common among single women than among women who are married or cohabiting (Laumann et al., 1999, 1994).

Most clinicians agree that orgasm during intercourse is not mandatory for normal sexual functioning. Many women instead reach orgasm with their partners by direct stimulation of the clitoris (LoPiccolo, 1995). Although early psychoanalytic theory considered a lack of orgasm during intercourse to be pathological, evidence suggests that women who rely on stimulation of the clitoris for orgasm are entirely normal and healthy (Stock, 1993).

As we observed earlier, female orgasmic disorder typically is linked to female sexual arousal disorder, and the two tend to be studied, explained, and treated together (APA, 1995). Once again, biological, psychological, and sociocultural factors may combine to produce these disorders (Williams & Leiblum, 2002).

BIOLOGICAL CAUSES A variety of physiological conditions can affect a woman's arousal and orgasm. Diabetes can damage the nervous system in ways that interfere with arousal, lubrication of the vagina, and orgasm. Lack of orgasm has sometimes been linked to multiple sclerosis and other neurological diseases, to the same drugs and medications that may interfere with ejaculation in men, and to postmenopausal changes in skin sensitivity and in the structure of the clitoris and of the vaginal walls (Clayton et al., 2002; Frohman, 2002; Stahl, 2001).

PSYCHOLOGICAL CAUSES The psychological causes of hypoactive sexual desire and sexual aversion may also lead to the female arousal and orgasmic disorders (Heiman, 2000). In addition, as psychodynamic theorists might predict, memories of childhood traumas and relationships have sometimes been linked to these disorders. In one large study, memories of an unhappy childhood or loss of a parent during childhood were tied to lack of orgasm in adulthood (Raboch & Raboch, 1992). In another, childhood memories of a positive relationship with one's mother, affection between the parents, the mother's positive personality, and the mother's expression of positive emotions were all predictors of orgasm (Heiman et al., 1986).

SOCIOCULTURAL CAUSES For years many clinicians have believed that female arousal and orgasmic disorders may result from society's repeated message to women that they should hold back and deny their sexuality, a message that has often led to "less permissive" sexual attitudes and behavior among women than among men (see Figure 11-4 on the next page). In fact, many women with female arousal and orgasmic disorders report that they had a strict religious upbringing, were punished for childhood masturbation, received no preparation for the onset of menstruation, were restricted in their dating as teenagers, and were told that "nice girls don't" (LoPiccolo, 1997; Masters & Johnson, 1970).

A sexually restrictive history, however, is just as common among women who function well in sexual encounters (LoPiccolo, 1997; LoPiccolo & Stock, 1987). In addition, cultural messages about female sexuality have been more positive in recent years, while the rate of female arousal and orgasmic disorders remains the same. Why, then, do some women and not others develop sexual arousal and orgasmic dysfunctions? Researchers suggest that unusually stressful events, traumas, or relationships may help produce the fears, memories, and attitudes that are often found in these dysfunctions (Westheimer & Lopater, 2002). For example, more than

> **>>LOOKING BACK**
> **Nightly Visits**
>
> Orgasms can sometimes occur during sleep. Ancient Babylonians said that such nocturnal orgasms were caused by a "maid of the night" who visited men in their sleep and a "little night man" who visited women (Kahn & Fawcett, 1993).<<

"The region of insanity" *Medical authorities described "excessive passion" in Victorian women as dangerous and as a possible cause of insanity (Gamwell & Tomes, 1995). This illustration from a nineteenth-century medical textbook even labels a woman's reproductive organs as her "region of insanity."*

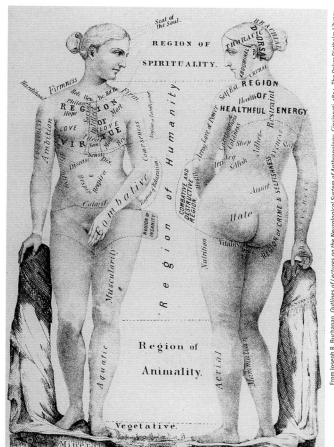

From Joseph R. Buchanan, *Outlines of Lectures on the Neurological System of Anthropology*, Cincinnati, 1854. The Oskar Diethelm Library, Department of Psychiatry, Cornell University Medical College and The New York Hospital, New York

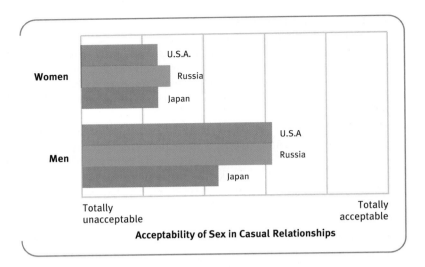

FIGURE 11-4 Is sex in a casual relationship acceptable? *Men and women around the globe have different opinions on this issue. On a scale ranging from "totally unacceptable" to "totally acceptable," college women in the United States, Russia, and Japan rated casual sex as "unacceptable" on average, whereas the ratings by men in those countries ranged from "fairly acceptable" to "quite acceptable" (Sprecher & Hatfield, 1996). Both men and women in the various countries typically considered sex among engaged or pre-engaged couples to be "quite acceptable."*

half of women molested as children or raped as adults have arousal and orgasm dysfunctions (Browne & Finklehor, 1986).

Research has also related orgasmic behavior to certain qualities in a woman's intimate relationships (Metz & Epstein, 2002). One study found that the likelihood of reaching orgasm was tied to how much emotional involvement each subject had during her first experience of intercourse and how long that relationship lasted, the pleasure the woman obtained during the experience, her current attraction to her partner's body, and her marital happiness (Heiman et al., 1986). Interestingly, the same study found that erotic fantasies during sex with their current partner were much more common in orgasmic than in nonorgasmic women.

Disorders of Sexual Pain

Two sexual dysfunctions do not fit neatly into a specific phase of the sexual response cycle. These are the sexual pain disorders, *vaginismus* and *dyspareunia*, each marked by enormous physical discomfort when sexual activity is attempted.

VAGINISMUS In **vaginismus**, involuntary contractions of the muscles around the outer third of the vagina prevent entry of the penis (see Table 11-4). Severe cases can prevent a couple from ever having intercourse. Perhaps 20 percent of women occasionally experience pain during intercourse, but vaginismus probably occurs in less than 1 percent of all women (LoPiccolo, 1995).

Most clinicians agree with the cognitive-behavioral position that vaginismus is usually a learned fear response, set off by a woman's expectation that intercourse will be painful and damaging. A variety of factors apparently can set the stage for this fear, including anxiety and ignorance about intercourse, exaggerated stories about how painful and bloody the first occasion of intercourse is for women, trauma caused by an unskilled lover who forces his penis into the vagina before the woman is aroused and lubricated, and, of course, the trauma of childhood sexual abuse or adult rape (Westheimer & Lopater, 2002; LoPiccolo, 1995).

Some women experience painful intercourse because of an infection of the vagina or urinary tract, a gynecological disease such as herpes simplex, or the physical effects of menopause. In such cases vaginismus can be overcome only if the women receive medical treatment for these conditions (LoPiccolo, 1995).

Table 11-4 DSM-IV Checklist

VAGINISMUS

1. Recurrent or persistent involuntary spasm of the muscles of the outer third of the vagina that interferes with sexual intercourse.
2. Significant distress or interpersonal difficulty.

DYSPAREUNIA

1. Recurrent or persistent genital pain associated with sexual intercourse in either a male or female.
2. Significant distress or interpersonal difficulty.

Based on APA, 2000, 1994.

Many women who have vaginismus also have other sexual dysfunctions (Reissing et al., 2003; Heiman, 2002). Some, however, enjoy sex greatly, have a strong sex drive, and reach orgasm with stimulation of the clitoris. They just fear penetration of the vagina.

DYSPAREUNIA A person with **dyspareunia** (from Latin words meaning "painful mating") experiences severe pain in the genitals during sexual activity. Surveys suggest that 14 percent of women and 3 percent of men suffer from this problem to some degree (Heiman, 2002; Laumann et al., 1999). Sufferers typically enjoy sex and get aroused but find their sex lives very limited by the pain that accompanies what used to be a positive event.

Dyspareunia in women usually has a physical cause (LoPiccolo, 1995). Among the most common is an injury during childbirth. Similarly, the scar left by an episiotomy (a cut often made to enlarge the vaginal entrance and ease delivery) can cause pain. Dyspareunia has also been tied to collision of the penis with remaining parts of the hymen; infection of the vagina; wiry pubic hair that rubs against the labia during intercourse; pelvic diseases; tumors; cysts; and allergic reactions to the chemicals in vaginal douches and contraceptive creams, the rubber in condoms or diaphragms, or the protein in semen (Brown & Ceniceros, 2001; LoPiccolo & Stock, 1987).

Although relationship problems or the psychological aftereffects of sexual abuse may contribute to this disorder, psychosocial factors alone are rarely responsible for it (Binik et al., 2002; Pukall et al., 2000). In cases that are truly psychogenic, the woman is in fact likely to be suffering from hypoactive sexual desire (Steege & Ling, 1993). That is, penetration into an unaroused, unlubricated vagina is painful.

VAGINISMUS A condition marked by involuntary contractions of the muscles around the outer third of the vagina, preventing entry of the penis.

DYSPAREUNIA A disorder in which a person experiences severe pain in the genitals during sexual activity.

SUMMING UP

Sexual Dysfunctions

Sexual dysfunctions make it difficult or impossible for a person to have or enjoy sexual intercourse. Disorders of the desire phase of the sexual response cycle are hypoactive sexual desire disorder and sexual aversion disorder. Biological causes for these disorders include abnormal hormone levels, certain drugs, and some medical illnesses. Psychological and sociocultural causes include specific fears, situational pressures, relationship problems, and the trauma of having been sexually molested or assaulted.

Disorders of the excitement phase are female sexual arousal disorder and male erectile disorder. Biological causes of male erectile disorder include abnormal hormone levels, vascular problems, medical conditions, and certain medications. Psychological and sociocultural causes include the combination of performance anxiety and the spectator role, situational pressures such as job loss, and relationship problems.

Premature ejaculation, a disorder of the orgasm phase of the sexual response cycle, has been related to behavioral causes, such as inappropriate early learning and inexperience. Male orgasmic disorder, another orgasm disorder, can have biological causes such as low testosterone levels, neurological diseases, and certain drugs, and psychological causes such as performance anxiety and the spectator role. The dysfunction may also develop from hypoactive sexual desire.

Female orgasmic disorder has, along with female sexual arousal disorder, been tied to biological causes such as medical diseases and changes that occur after menopause, psychological causes such as memories of childhood traumas, and sociocultural causes such as relationship problems.

In vaginismus, one of the sexual pain disorders, involuntary contractions of the muscles around the outer third of the vagina prevent entry of the penis. In dyspareunia, the person experiences severe pain in the genitals during sexual activity. Dyspareunia usually occurs in women and typically has a physical cause such as injury resulting from childbirth.

>>**BY THE NUMBERS**
First Sexual Encounters

36% Percentage of men in 1990 whose first sexual encounter was with a new acquaintance<<

67% Men in 1980 whose first sexual encounter was with a new acquaintance<<

12% Women in 1990 whose first sexual encounter was with a new acquaintance<<

33% Women in 1980 whose first sexual encounter was with a new acquaintance<<

(Netting, 1992)

Treatments for Sexual Dysfunctions

The last 35 years have brought major changes in the treatment of sexual dysfunctions. For the first half of the twentieth century, the leading approach was long-term psychodynamic therapy. Clinicians assumed that sexual dysfunctioning was caused by failure to move properly through the psychosexual stages of development, and they used techniques of free association and therapist interpretations to help clients gain insight about themselves and their problems. Although it was expected that broad personality changes would lead to improvement in sexual functioning, psychodynamic therapy was typically unsuccessful (Bergler, 1951).

In the 1950s and 1960s, behavioral therapists offered new treatments for sexual dysfunctions. Usually they tried to reduce the fears that they believed were causing the dysfunctions by applying such procedures as relaxation training and systematic desensitization (Lazarus, 1965; Wolpe, 1958). These approaches had some success, but they failed to work in cases where the key problems included misinformation, negative attitudes, and lack of effective sexual technique (LoPiccolo, 1995).

A revolution in the treatment of sexual dysfunctions occurred with the publication of William Masters and Virginia Johnson's landmark book *Human Sexual Inadequacy* in 1970. The *sex therapy* program they introduced has evolved into a complex approach, which now includes techniques from the various models, particularly cognitive, behavioral, couple, and family systems therapies (Bach et al., 2001; Leiblum & Rosen, 2000). In recent years, biological interventions, particularly drug therapies, have often been added to the treatment arsenal (Segraves & Althof, 2002).

What Are the General Features of Sex Therapy?

Modern sex therapy is short-term and instructive, typically lasting 15 to 20 sessions. It centers on specific sexual problems rather than on broad personality issues (Westheimer & Lopater, 2002; LoPiccolo, 1997, 1995). Carlos Domera, the Argentine man with an erectile disorder whom we met earlier, responded successfully to the multiple techniques of modern sex therapy:

At the end of the evaluation session the psychiatrist reassured the couple that Mr. Domera had a "reversible psychological" sexual problem that was due to several factors, including his depression, but also more currently his anxiety and embarrassment, his high standards, and some cultural and relationship difficulties that made communication awkward and relaxation nearly impossible. The couple was advised that a brief trial of therapy, focused directly on the sexual problem, would very likely produce significant improvement within ten to fourteen sessions. They were assured that the problem was almost certainly not physical in origin, but rather psychogenic, and that therefore the prognosis was excellent.

Mr. Domera was shocked and skeptical, but the couple agreed to commence the therapy on a weekly basis, and they were given a typical first "assignment" to do at home: a caressing massage exercise to try together with specific instructions not to attempt genital stimulation or intercourse at all, even if an erection might occur.

Not surprisingly, during the second session Mr. Domera reported with a cautious smile that they had "cheated" and had had intercourse "against the rules." This was their first successful intercourse in more than a year. Their success and happiness were acknowledged by the therapist, but they were cautioned strongly that rapid initial improvement often occurs, only to be followed by increased performance anxiety in subsequent weeks and a return of the initial problem. They were humorously chastised and encouraged to try again to have sexual contact involving caressing and non-demand light genital stimulation, without an expectation of erection or orgasm, and to avoid intercourse.

During the second and fourth weeks Mr. Domera did not achieve erections during the love play, and the therapy sessions dealt with helping him to accept himself with or without erections and to learn to enjoy sensual contact without intercourse. His wife helped him to believe genuinely that he could please her with manual or oral stimulation and that, although she enjoyed intercourse, she enjoyed these other stimulations as much, as long as he was relaxed.

Mr. Domera struggled with his cultural image of what a "man" does, but he had to admit that his wife seemed pleased and that he, too, was enjoying the nonintercourse caressing techniques. He was encouraged to view his new love-making skills as a "success" and to recognize that in many ways he was becoming a better lover than many husbands, because he was listening to his wife and responding to her requests.

By the fifth week the patient was attempting intercourse successfully with relaxed confidence, and by the ninth session he was responding regularly with erections. If they both agreed, they would either have intercourse or choose another sexual technique to achieve orgasm. Treatment was terminated after ten sessions.

(Spitzer et al., 1983, pp. 106–107)

As Mr. Domera's treatment indicates, modern sex therapy includes a variety of principles and techniques. The following ones are applied in almost all cases, regardless of the dysfunction:

1. **Assessment and conceptualization of the problem**. Patients are initially given a medical examination and are interviewed concerning their "sex history" (see Figure 11-5 on next page). The therapist's focus during the interview is on gathering information about past life events and, in particular, current factors that are contributing to the dysfunction (Bach et al., 2001). Sometimes proper assessment requires a team of specialists, perhaps including a psychologist, urologist, and neurologist.

2. **Mutual responsibility**. Therapists stress the principle of *mutual responsibility*. Both partners in the relationship share the sexual problem, regardless of who has the actual dysfunction, and treatment will be more successful when both are in therapy (Bach et al., 2001).

3. **Education about sexuality**. Many patients who suffer from sexual dysfunctions know very little about the physiology and techniques of sexual activity (Westheimer & Lopater, 2002). Thus sex therapists may discuss these topics and offer educational materials, including instructional books and videotapes.

4. **Attitude change**. Therapists help patients examine and change any beliefs about sexuality that are preventing sexual arousal and pleasure (Bach et al., 2001; Rosen, Leiblum, & Spector, 1994). Some of these

>>IN THEIR WORDS

"When [masturbation] is discovered, it must in young children be put a stop to by such means as tying the hands, strapping the knees together with a pad between them, or some mechanical plan."<<

Cradle to School, a Book for Mothers, 1902

"If [a woman] . . . is normally developed mentally and well-bred, her sexual desire is small. If this were not so, the whole world would become a brothel and marriage and a family impossible."<<

Health and Longevity, 1909

© 2000, Robert Mankoff, from cartoonbank.com.

"You're wasting your time. I'm asexual."

mistaken beliefs are widely shared in our society and can result from past traumatic events, family attitudes, or cultural ideas.

5. **Elimination of performance anxiety and the spectator role**. Therapists often teach couples *sensate focus*, or *nondemand pleasuring*, a series of sensual tasks, sometimes called "petting" exercises, in which the partners focus on the sexual pleasure that can be achieved by exploring and caressing each other's body at home, without demands to have intercourse or reach orgasm—demands that may be interfering with arousal. Couples are told at first to resist intercourse at home and to limit their sexual activity to kissing, hugging, and sensual massage of various parts of the body, but not of the breasts or genitals. Over time, they learn how to give and receive greater sexual pleasure and they build back up to the activity of sexual intercourse.

6. **Increasing sexual and general communication skills**. Couples are told to use their sensate-focus sessions at home to try sexual positions in which the person being caressed can guide the other's hands and control the speed, pressure, and location of the caressing. Couples are also taught to give instructions in a nonthreatening, informative manner ("It feels better over here, with a little less pressure"), rather than a threatening uninformative manner ("The way you're touching me doesn't turn me on"). Moreover, couples are often given broader training in how best to communicate with each other (Bach et al., 2001).

7. **Changing destructive lifestyles and marital interactions**. A therapist may encourage a couple to change their lifestyle or take other steps to improve a situation that is having a destructive effect on their relationship—to distance themselves from interfering in-laws, for example, or to change a job that is too demanding. Similarly, if the couple's general relationship is in conflict, the therapist will try to help them improve it (Metz & Epstein, 2002).

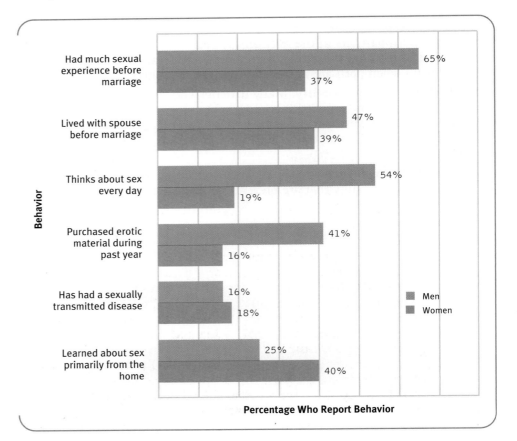

FIGURE 11-5 Sexual behavior and gender
According to questionnaires, men are much more likely than women to think about sex on a daily basis and to have purchased sexual material, such as erotic magazines, within the past year. Women are more likely to have learned about sex from the home. (Adapted from Michael et al., 1994; Janus & Janus, 1993.)

8. **Addressing physical and medical factors**. When sexual dysfunctions are caused by a medical problem, such as disease, injury, medication, or substance abuse, therapists try to address that problem (Winton, 2000). If antidepressant medications are causing a man's erectile disorder, for example, the clinician may lower the dosage of the medication, change the time of day when the drug is taken, or prescribe a different antidepressant (Segraves, 1998, 1995).

What Techniques Are Applied to Particular Dysfunctions?

In addition to the general components of sex therapy, specific techniques can help in each of the sexual dysfunctions.

HYPOACTIVE SEXUAL DESIRE AND SEXUAL AVERSION Hypoactive sexual desire and sexual aversion are among the most difficult dysfunctions to treat (Westheimer & Lopater, 2002; LoPiccolo, 1997, 1995). Thus therapists typically apply a combination of techniques. In a technique called *affectual awareness*, patients visualize sexual scenes in order to discover any feelings of anxiety, vulnerability, and other negative emotions they may have concerning sex. In another technique, patients receive cognitive *self-instruction training* to help them change their negative reactions to sex. That is, they learn to replace negative statements during sex with "coping statements," such as "I can allow myself to enjoy sex; it doesn't mean I'll lose control."

Therapists may also use behavioral approaches to help increase a patient's sex drive. They may instruct clients to keep a "desire diary" in which they record sexual thoughts and feelings, to read books and view films with erotic content, and to fantasize about sex. Pleasurable shared activities such as dancing and walking together are also encouraged (LoPiccolo, 1997, 1995).

For sexual aversion that has resulted from sexual assault or childhood molestation, additional techniques may be needed. A patient may be encouraged to remember, talk, and think about the assault until the memories no longer arouse fear or tension. Or the individual may be instructed to have a mock dialogue with the molester, in order to express lingering feelings of rage and powerlessness (LoPiccolo, 1997, 1995).

These and related approaches apparently help many women and men with hypoactive sexual desire and aversion disorders eventually to have intercourse more than once a week (Heiman, 2002; Hurlbert, 1993). However, only a few controlled studies have been conducted. Finally, biological interventions, such as hormone treatments, have been used, particularly among women whose problems arose after removal of their ovaries or later in life; these interventions have received some research support (Davis, 2000, 1998; Shifren et al., 2000).

ERECTILE DISORDER Treatments for erectile disorder focus on reducing a man's performance anxiety or increasing his stimulation or both (Segraves & Althof, 2002; Rosen, 2000). During sensate-focus exercises, the couple may be instructed to try the *tease technique*: the partner keeps caressing the man, but if the man gets an erection, the partner stops caressing him until he loses it. This exercise reduces pressure on the man to perform and at the same time teaches the couple that erections occur naturally in response to stimulation, as long as the partners do not keep focusing on performance. In another technique, the couple may be instructed to use manual or oral sex to try to achieve the woman's orgasm, again reducing pressure on the man to perform (LoPiccolo, 1997, 1995).

Biological approaches, applied particularly when erectile disorder has biological causes, gained great momentum with the development in 1998 of *sildenafil* (trade name Viagra) (Perelman, 2002). This drug increases blood flow to the penis within one hour of ingestion; the increased blood flow enables the user to attain an erection during sexual activity. Sildenafil appears to be safe except for men with certain coronary heart diseases and cardiovascular diseases, particularly

»LOOKING BACK

The term birth control was coined in 1914 by the Irish-American nurse Margaret Sanger, often called the mother of planned parenthood.«

The condom has been traced back to the Earl of Condom, the personal physician to England's King Charles II, in the mid-1600s. He designed the condom to protect the king from syphilis.«

The first truly effective intrauterine device (IUD) was designed in 1928 by the German physician Ernst Frafenberg.«

The first oral contraceptive ("the pill"), developed by the chemist Gregory Pincus, was approved for use in the United States in 1960.«

(Panati, 1987)

»LOOKING BACK

A Social Phenomenon

Viagra, the enormously popular drug for erectile problems, was discovered by accident. Testing it as a possible heart medication, researchers found that the drug increased blood flow more effectively to subjects' penises than to their hearts (Handy, 1998).«

Physicians wrote 120,000 prescriptions for Viagra during its first month on the market in 1998, making it the fastest-selling new prescription drug in history (Adler, 1998).«

those who are taking nitroglycerin and other heart medications (Bach et al., 2001; Speakman & Kloner, 1999).

Most of the other biological approaches for erectile disorder have been around for years (Frohman, 2002; Heiman, 2002). These include gel suppositories, injections of drugs into the penis, and a *vacuum erection device* (VED), a hollow cylinder that is placed over the penis. Here a man uses a hand pump to pump air out of the cylinder, drawing blood into his penis and producing an erection. In another biological approach, surgeons may implant a *penile prosthesis*—a semirigid rod made of rubber and wire—to produce an artificial erection. However, because Viagra is easy to take and helpful to more than half of patients, drug therapy is the approach now receiving the most attention (Bach et al., 2001). In fact, a number of other drugs for erectile disorder are currently in development (Rowland & Burnett, 2000).

MALE ORGASMIC DISORDER Like treatment for male erectile disorder, therapies for male orgasmic disorder include techniques to reduce performance anxiety and increase stimulation (Segraves & Althof, 2002). In one technique, a man may be instructed to masturbate to orgasm in the presence of his partner or to masturbate just short of orgasm before inserting his penis for intercourse (Marshall, 1997). This increases the likelihood that he will ejaculate during intercourse. He then is instructed to insert his penis at ever earlier stages of masturbation.

When male orgasmic disorder is caused by physical factors such as neurological damage or injury, treatment may include a drug to increase arousal of the sympathetic nervous system (Murphy & Lipshultz, 1988). However, few studies have systematically tested the effectiveness of such treatments (Rosen & Leiblum, 1995).

A CLOSER LOOK

Sex-Role Myths

Myths of Male Sexuality

❖ A real man isn't into stuff like feelings and communicating.

❖ A man is always interested in and ready for sex.

❖ Sex is centered on a hard penis and what is done with it.

❖ A man should be able to make the earth move for his partner.

❖ Men don't have to listen to women in sex.

❖ Bigger is better.

❖ Men should be able to last all night during sex.

❖ Women typically dislike or disapprove of men who are unable to have an erection.

❖ If a man can't have an erection, he must not really love his partner.

❖ If a man knows that he might not be able to get an erection, it's unfair for him to start sexual activity with a partner.

❖ Focusing more intensely on one's erection—trying harder—is the best way to get an erection.

Myths of Female Sexuality

❖ Sex is only for women under 30.

❖ Normal women have an orgasm every time they have sex.

❖ All women can have multiple orgasms.

❖ Pregnancy and delivery reduce women's sexual responsiveness.

❖ A woman's sex life ends with menopause.

❖ A sexually responsive woman can always be aroused by her partner.

❖ Nice women aren't aroused by erotic books or films.

❖ Women are "frigid" if they don't like the more exotic forms of sex.

❖ If a woman can't have an orgasm quickly and easily, there's something wrong with her.

❖ Feminine women don't initiate sex or become unrestrained during sex.

❖ Contraception is a woman's responsibility, and she's just making up excuses if she says contraception issues are inhibiting her sexually.

Myths of Male and Female Sexuality

❖ All touching is sexual or should lead to sex.

❖ Sex equals intercourse.

❖ Good sex requires orgasm.

❖ It isn't romantic if a person asks the partner what he or she enjoys.

❖ Too much masturbation is bad.

❖ Someone with a sex partner does not masturbate.

❖ Fantasizing about someone else during sex means a person is not happy with the person he or she is in a relationship with.

(BACH ET AL., 2001, P. 585)

PREMATURE EJACULATION Premature ejaculation has been treated successfully for years by behavioral procedures (Heiman, 2002; Masters & Johnson, 1970). In the *stop-start*, or *pause*, procedure, the penis is manually stimulated until the man is highly aroused. The couple then pauses until his arousal subsides, after which the stimulation is resumed. This sequence is repeated several times before stimulation is carried through to ejaculation, so the man ultimately experiences much more total time of stimulation than he has ever experienced before (LoPiccolo, 1995). Eventually the couple progresses to putting the penis in the vagina, making sure to withdraw it and to pause whenever the man becomes too highly aroused. According to clinical reports, after two or three months many couples can enjoy prolonged intercourse without any need for pauses (LoPiccolo, 1997, 1995).

Some clinicians treat premature ejaculation with *fluoxetine* (Prozac) and other serotonin-enhancing antidepressant drugs (Brown & Ceniceros, 2001). Because these drugs often reduce sexual arousal or orgasm, the reasoning goes, they may be helpful to men who experience premature ejaculation. Although some studies have reported positive results (Althof, 1995; Althof et al., 1994), researchers have yet to examine the long-term impact of these drugs on men with premature ejaculation. Nor have they determined whether such drugs may be combined effectively with psychological and interpersonal techniques (Rosen & Leiblum, 1995).

FEMALE AROUSAL AND ORGASMIC DISORDERS Specific treatment techniques for female arousal and orgasmic dysfunctions include self-exploration, enhancement of body awareness, and directed masturbation training (Heiman, 2002, 2000; LoPiccolo, 1997). These procedures are especially useful for women who have never had an orgasm under any circumstances. Hormone therapy is also being used increasingly (Davis, 2000, 1998; Warnock et al., 1999).

In **directed masturbation training**, a woman is taught step by step how to masturbate effectively and eventually to reach orgasm during sexual interactions. The training includes use of diagrams and reading material, private self-stimulation, erotic material and fantasies, "orgasm triggers" such as holding her breath or thrusting her pelvis, sensate focus with her partner, and sexual positioning that produces stimulation of the clitoris during intercourse. This training program appears to be highly effective: over 90 percent of women learn to have an orgasm during masturbation, about 80 percent during caressing by their partners, and about 30 percent during intercourse (LoPiccolo, 1997; Heiman & LoPiccolo, 1988).

As we observed earlier, a lack of orgasm during intercourse is not necessarily a sexual dysfunction, provided the woman enjoys intercourse and can reach orgasm through caressing, either by her partner or by herself. For this reason some therapists believe that the wisest course is simply to educate women whose only concern is lack of orgasm during intercourse, informing them that they are quite normal.

VAGINISMUS Specific treatment for vaginismus, involuntary contractions of the muscles around the vagina, takes two approaches. First, a woman may practice tightening and relaxing her vaginal muscles until she gains more voluntary control over them (LoPiccolo, 1995; Rosen & Leiblum, 1995). Second, she may receive gradual behavioral exposure treatment to help her overcome her fear of penetration, beginning by inserting increasingly large dilators in her vagina at home and at her own pace and eventually ending with the insertion of her partner's penis (Heiman, 2002). Over 75 percent of the women treated for vaginismus eventually have pain-free intercourse (Heinman, 2002; Beck, 1993). Many women with this problem, however, report that they received ineffective or inaccurate forms of treatment when they first sought help from their physicians (Ogden & Ward, 1995).

CALLAHAN

"When I touch him he rolls into a ball."

DIRECTED MASTURBATION TRAINING A sex therapy approach that teaches women with female arousal or orgasmic disorders how to masturbate effectively and eventually to reach orgasm during sexual interactions.

A CLOSER LOOK

Homosexuality and the Clinical Field

Homosexuality is not new; it has always existed in all cultures, as has the controversy that surrounds it. While most cultures do not openly advocate homosexuality, over the course of history few have condemned it as fiercely as Western culture does today (Minton, 2002). Nevertheless, research shows that a society's acceptance or rejection of people who engage in homosexual behavior does not affect the rate of the behavior.

Before 1973, the DSM listed homosexuality as a sexual disorder. Protests by gay activist groups and many psychotherapists eventually led to its elimination from the diagnostic manual as a sexual disorder (Minton, 2002). Most clinicians in the Western world now view homosexuality as a variant of normal sexual behavior, not a disorder (King & Bartlett, 1999).

Despite the growing acceptance of homosexuality by the clinical field, many people in Western society continue to hold antihomosexual attitudes and to spread myths about the lifestyles of homosexual persons (Kirby, 2000; Parker & Bhugra, 2000). Contrary to these myths, research has shown that homosexual persons do not suffer from gender confusion; they are not more prone to psychopathology than others; and there is not an identifiable "homosexual personality."

Psychologists do continue to debate one issue: whether homosexual people choose their lifestyle or whether it is a natural part of their physiological makeup. This debate has been fueled by findings pro and con (Minton, 2002; Dawood et al., 2000; Pillard & Bailey, 1995; LeVay & Hamer, 1994). In the early 1990s, for example, two influential genetic linkage studies concluded that homosexuality may in some instances be passed on by the mother's genes (Hu et al., 1995; Hamer et al., 1993), although more recent research has failed to support this particular conclusion (Rice et al., 1999). In addition, two studies found that when one identical twin was homosexual, his twin was also homosexual in more than 50 percent of the cases sampled. The number dropped to less than 20 percent when the siblings were fraternal twins or nontwins and to under 10 percent when the siblings were adopted and biologically unrelated (Bailey et al., 1997, 1993, 1991). Although environmental factors also have a major impact on homosexuality—otherwise all persons with a homosexual identical twin would be homosexual—genetics may well play a key role in it.

Homosexuality continues to be a lifestyle that many people adopt, whether because of environmental or genetic factors. Now that most psychologists agree that homosexuality is not a disorder, a key issue remains: How will society react to a significant proportion of its population that typically differs from the rest in but one way—their sexual orientation? So far, Western society cannot claim to have dealt very effectively or fairly with this question, but at least a trend toward understanding and equality seems to be emerging. Research suggests that through education and exposure, people of different sexual orientations can indeed learn to accept and work with one another (Beaty, 1999; Herek & Capitanio, 1993).

Mark Richards/PhotoEdit

Familiarity fosters acceptance *Although prejudice certainly remains, surveys indicate that the heterosexual public is growing more comfortable with displays of affection by homosexual couples—an important step toward the acceptance of differences in sexual orientation.*

DYSPAREUNIA We saw earlier that the most common cause of dyspareunia, genital pain during intercourse, is physical, such as pain-causing scars or tears. When the cause is known, a couple can learn intercourse positions that avoid putting pressure on the injured area. A medical intervention may also be tried, but it must still be combined with other sex therapy techniques to overcome the years of sexual anxiety and lack of arousal (Binik et al., 2002, 2000; Leiblum, 1996).

Because many cases of dyspareunia are in fact caused by undiagnosed physical problems, it is very important that clients receive expert gynecological exams (Reid & Lininger, 1993).

A new message *Over the past several decades, Western society has increasingly viewed female sexual arousal and expression as normal and healthful and has sent this message to women through novels, movies, television shows, and magazines. This Diet Coke ad in which two women openly ogle a sexy construction worker was one of the most discussed television commercials of the 1990s.*

What Are the Current Trends in Sex Therapy?

Sex therapists have now moved well beyond the approach first developed by Masters and Johnson (Bach et al., 2001; Rosen & Leiblum, 1995). For example, today's sex therapists regularly treat partners who are living together but not married. They also treat sexual dysfunctions that arise from psychological disorders such as depression, mania, schizophrenia, and certain personality disorders (Rowlands, 1995). In addition, sex therapists no longer screen out clients with severe marital discord, the elderly, the medically ill, or the physically handicapped (Schover, 2000; Dupont, 1995) or clients with a homosexual orientation or those who have no long-term sex partner (Stravynski et al., 1997). Sex therapists are also paying more attention to excessive sexuality, sometimes called *sexual addiction* (Kafka, 2000).

Many sex therapists currently worry about the sharp increase in the use of drugs and other medical interventions for sexual dysfunctions, particularly for hypoactive sexual desire and male erectile disorder. Their concern is that therapists will increasingly choose the biological interventions rather than integrating biological, psychological, and sociocultural interventions (Heiman, 2002; Leiblum, 2002). In fact, a narrow approach of any kind probably cannot fully address the complex factors that cause most sexual problems. It took sex therapists years to recognize the considerable advantages of an integrated approach to sexual dysfunctions. The development of new medical interventions should not lead to its abandonment.

SUMMING UP

Treatments for Sexual Dysfunctions

In the 1970s the work of William Masters and Virginia Johnson led to the development of sex therapy. Today sex therapy combines a variety of cognitive, behavioral, couple, and family systems therapies. It generally includes features such as careful assessment, education, acceptance of mutual responsibility, attitude changes, sensate-focus exercises, improvements in communication, and couple therapy. In addition, specific techniques have been developed for each of the sexual dysfunctions. The use of biological treatments for sexual dysfunctions is also increasing.

≫LOOKING AROUND

Sexual Census The World Health Organization estimates that around 115 million acts of sexual intercourse occur each day.≪

Unequal Distribution Sex is not distributed equally. Half of all sexual activity in the United States is engaged in by 15 percent of adults (General Social Survey, 1998).≪

Sexual Duration In a survey of people in the United States, respondents estimated that their average sexual experience lasts 39 minutes, including foreplay (Kanner, 1995).≪

THE**CURRENT SCENE**

Viagra vs. the Pill: Sexism in Health Care?

Many of us believe that we live in an enlightened world, where sexism is declining and where health care and benefits are available to men and women in equal measure. Periodically, however, such illusions are shattered. The responses of government agencies and insurance companies to the discovery and marketing of Viagra in 1998 may be a case in point.

Consider, first, the nation of Japan. In early 1999, just six months after Viagra's sensational introduction in the United States, the drug was approved for use among men in Japan (Martin, 2000). In contrast, low-dose contraceptives—"the pill"—were not approved for use among women in that country until June 1999—a full 40 years after their invention elsewhere! Many observers believe that birth control pills would still be unavailable to women in Japan had Viagra not led the way by receiving its quick approval.

Has the United States been able to avoid such an apparent double standard in its health care system? Not really. Before Viagra was introduced, insurance companies were not required to reimburse women for the cost of prescription contraceptives. As a result, women had to pay 68 percent more out-of-pocket expenses for health care than did men, largely because of uncovered reproductive health care costs (Hayden, 1998). Some legislators had sought to correct this problem by requiring contraceptive coverage in health insurance plans, but their efforts failed in state after state for more than a decade.

In contrast, when Viagra was introduced in 1998, many insurance companies readily agreed to cover the new drug and many states included Viagra as part of Medicaid coverage. As the public outcry grew over the contrast between coverage of Viagra for men and lack of coverage of oral contraceptives for women, laws across the country finally began to change. In fact, by the end of 1998, nine states required prescription contraceptive coverage (Hayden, 1998). Today 21 states require such coverage by private insurance companies and 35 states require it for state employees (NARAL, 2001). Moreover, Congress is considering a law that would require all insurers in the nation to reimburse women for the cost of oral contraceptives.

In the meantime, wishful thinkers express hope that generous private donors will help foot the bill for oral contraceptives as some donors have done for Viagra. Immediately after Viagra's approval, one noted philanthropist donated $1 million to provide this drug to the needy. In explaining his action, he said, "I saw an article saying that at $10 apiece, a lot of impotent men wouldn't be able to afford it. So I said [to my wife], . . . 'let's help,' and by Tuesday we had it done" (Carlson, 1998).

Bettmann/Corbis

Tom Lyle/Medichrome/The Stock Shop

Paraphilias

Paraphilias are disorders in which individuals repeatedly have intense sexual urges or fantasies or display sexual behaviors that involve nonhuman objects, children, nonconsenting adults, or the experience of suffering or humiliation. Many people with a paraphilia can become aroused only when a paraphilic stimulus is present, fantasized about, or acted out. Others need the stimulus only during times of stress or under other special circumstances.

According to DSM-IV, a diagnosis of paraphilia should be applied only when the urges, fantasies, or behaviors last at least six months (see Table 11-5). For most paraphilias, the urges, fantasies, or behaviors must also cause great distress or interfere with one's social life or job performance in order for a diagnosis to be applied (APA, 2000). For certain paraphilias, however, the DSM-IV Text Revision in 2000 has clarified that performance of the sexual behavior indicates a disorder even if the individual experiences no distress or impairment (Hilliard & Spitzer, 2002; APA, 2000). People who initiate sexual contact with children, for example, warrant a diagnosis of pedophilia regardless of how distressed the individuals may or may not be over their behavior.

Some people with one kind of paraphilia display others as well (McAnulty et al., 2001; Abel & Osborn, 1992). Relatively few people receive a formal diagnosis of paraphilia, but the large market in paraphilic pornography leads clinicians to suspect that the patterns may be quite common (APA, 2000). People whose paraphilias involve children or nonconsenting adults often come to the attention of clinicians when they get into legal trouble.

Although theorists have proposed various explanations for paraphilias, there is little formal evidence to support them (Weiss, 2001; Bradford, 1999). Moreover, none of the many treatments applied to paraphilias have received much research or proved clearly effective (Maletzky, 2002; Bradford, 1999, 1995). Psychological and sociocultural treatments for paraphilias have been available the longest, but today's professionals are also using biological interventions. Some clinicians administer drugs called *antiandrogens* that lower the production of testosterone, the male sex hormone, and reduce sex drive (Krueger & Kaplan, 2002; Raymond et al., 2001). Although such drugs do indeed reduce paraphilic patterns, several of them disrupt normal sexual feelings and behavior as well. Thus the drugs tend to be applied primarily when the paraphilias are of danger either to the individuals themselves or to other people. Clinicians have also become interested in the possible use of serotonin-enhancing antidepressant medications to treat persons with paraphilias, hoping that the drugs will reduce these compulsion-like sexual behaviors just as they help reduce other kinds of compulsions.

Fetishism

Key features of **fetishism** are recurrent intense sexual urges, sexually arousing fantasies, or behaviors that involve the use of a nonliving object, often to the exclusion of all other stimuli. Usually the disorder begins in adolescence. Almost anything can be a fetish; women's underwear, shoes, and boots are particularly common (APA, 2000, 1994). Some people with fetishism commit thievery in order to collect as many of the desired objects as possible. The objects may be touched, smelled, worn, or used in some other way while the person masturbates, or the individual may ask a partner to wear the object when they have sex. Several of these features are seen in the following case:

> A 32-year-old, single male . . . related that although he was somewhat sexually attracted by women, he was far more attracted by "their panties."
>
> To the best of the patient's memory, sexual excitement began at about age 7, when he came upon a pornographic magazine and felt stimulated by pictures of partially nude women wearing "panties." His first ejaculation occurred at 13 via masturbation to fantasies of women wearing panties. He masturbated into his older sister's panties, which he had stolen without her knowledge. Subsequently he stole panties from her friends and from other women he met socially. He found pretexts to "wander" into the bedrooms of women during social occasions, and would quickly rummage through their possessions until he found a pair of panties to his satisfaction. He later used these to masturbate into, and

---

Table 11-5 DSM-IV Checklist

PARAPHILIA

1. Over a period of at least six months, recurrent, intense sexually arousing fantasies, sexual urges, or behaviors involving certain inappropriate stimuli or situations (nonhuman objects; the suffering or humiliation of oneself or one's partner; or children or other non-consenting persons).

2. Significant distress or impairment over the fantasies, urges, or behaviors. (In some paraphilias—pedophilia, exhibitionism, voyeurism, frotteurism, and sexual sadism—the performance of paraphilic behaviors indicates a disorder, even in the absence of distress or impairment.)

Based on APA, 2000.

PARAPHILIAS Disorders characterized by recurrent and intense sexual urges, fantasies, or behaviors involving nonhuman objects, children, nonconsenting adults, or experiences of suffering or humiliation.

FETISHISM A paraphilia consisting of recurrent and intense sexual urges, fantasies, or behaviors that involve the use of a nonliving object, often to the exclusion of all other stimuli.

Researchers have not been able to pinpoint the causes of fetishism. Psychodynamic theorists view fetishes as defense mechanisms that help people avoid the anxiety produced by normal sexual contact. Psychodynamic treatment for this problem, however, has met with little success (LoPiccolo, 1992).

Behaviorists propose that fetishes are acquired through classical conditioning (Doctor & Neff, 2001). In one behavioral study, male subjects were shown a series of slides of nude women along with slides of boots (Rachman, 1966). After many trials, the subjects became aroused by the boot photos alone. If early sexual experiences similarly occur in the presence of particular objects, perhaps the stage is set for development of fetishes.

Behaviorists have sometimes treated fetishism with *aversion therapy* (Krueger & Kaplan, 2002). In one study, an electric shock was administered to the arms or legs of subjects with fetishes while they imagined their objects of desire (Marks & Gelder, 1967). After two weeks of therapy all subjects in the study showed at least some improvement. In another aversion technique, *covert sensitization*, people with fetishism are guided to imagine the pleasurable object and repeatedly to pair this image with an *imagined* aversive stimulus until the object of sexual pleasure is no longer desired.

Another behavioral treatment for fetishism is **masturbatory satiation** (Krueger & Kaplan, 2002; Quinsey & Earls, 1990). In this method, the client masturbates to orgasm while fantasizing about a sexually appropriate object, then switches to fantasizing in detail about fetishistic objects while masturbating again and continues the fetishistic fantasy for an hour. The procedure is meant to produce a feeling of boredom, which in turn becomes linked to the fetishistic object.

Yet another behavioral approach to fetishism, also used for other paraphilias, is **orgasmic reorientation**, which teaches individuals to respond to more appropriate sources of sexual stimulation. People are shown conventional stimuli while they are responding to unconventional objects. A person with a shoe fetish, for example, may be instructed to obtain an erection from pictures of shoes and then to begin masturbating to a picture of a nude woman. If he starts to lose the erection, he must return to the pictures of shoes until he is masturbating effectively, then change back to the picture of the nude woman. When orgasm approaches, he must direct all attention to the conventional stimulus.

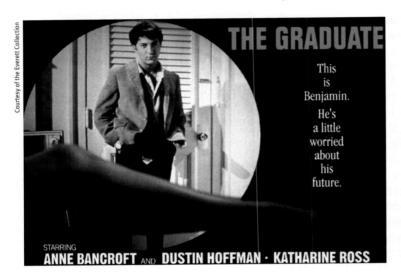

Courtesy of the Everett Collection

Mrs. Robinson's stockings *The 1967 film* The Graduate *helped define a generation by focusing on the personal confusion, apathy, and sexual adventures of a young man in search of meaning. Marketers decided to promote this film by using a fetishistic-like photo of Mrs. Robinson putting on her stockings under Benjamin's watchful eye, a scene forever identified with the movie.*

Transvestic Fetishism

Transvestic fetishism, also known as **transvestism** or **cross-dressing**, is a repeated need or desire to dress in clothes of the opposite sex in order to achieve sexual arousal. In the following passage, a 42-year-old married father describes his pattern:

I have been told that when I dress in drag, at times I look like Whistler's Mother [laughs], especially when I haven't shaved closely. I usually am good at detail, and I make sure when I dress as a woman that I have my nails done just so, and that my colors match. Honestly, it's hard to pin a date on when I began cross dressing. . . . If pressed, I would have to say it began when I was about 10 years of age, fooling around with and putting on my mom's clothes. . . . I was always careful to put everything back in its exact place, and in 18 years of doing this in her home, my mother never, I mean never, suspected, or questioned me about putting on her clothes. I belong to a transvestite support group . . . , a group for men who cross dress. Some of the group are homosexuals, but most are not. A true transvestite—and I am one, so I know—is not homosexual. We don't discriminate against them in the group at all; hey, we have enough trouble getting acceptance as normal people and not just a bunch of weirdos ourselves. They are a bunch of nice guys . . . , really. Most of them are like me.

Most of [the men in the group] have told their families about their dressing inclinations, but those that are married are a mixed lot; some wives know and some don't, they just suspect. I believe in honesty, and told my wife about this before we were married. We're separated now, but I don't think it's because of my cross dressing. . . . I have been asked many times why I cross dress, and it's hard to explain, other than it makes me feel good. There is something deep down that it gratifies. Some of my friends, when I was growing up, suggested psychotherapy, but I don't regard this as a problem. If it bothers someone else, then they have the problem. . . . I function perfectly well sexually with my wife, though it took her some time to be comfortable with me wearing feminine underwear; yes, sometimes I wear it while making love, it just makes it more exciting.

(Janus & Janus, 1993, p. 121)

MASTURBATORY SATIATION A behavioral treatment in which a client masturbates for a very long period of time while fantasizing in detail about a paraphilic object. The procedure is expected to produce a feeling of boredom, which in turn becomes linked to the object.

ORGASMIC REORIENTATION A procedure for treating certain paraphilias by teaching clients to respond to new, more appropriate sources of sexual stimulation.

TRANSVESTIC FETISHISM A paraphilia consisting of repeated and intense sexual urges, fantasies, or behaviors that involve dressing in clothes of the opposite sex. Also known as *transvestism* or *cross-dressing*.

Like this man, the typical person with transvestism, almost always a heterosexual male, begins cross-dressing in childhood or adolescence (Doctor & Neff, 2001; Bradley, 1995). He is the picture of characteristic masculinity in everyday life and is usually alone when he cross-dresses. A small percentage of such men cross-dress to visit bars or social clubs. Some wear a single item of women's clothing, such as underwear or hosiery, under their masculine clothes. Others wear makeup and dress fully as women. Some married men with transvestism involve their wives in their cross-dressing behavior (Kolodny et al., 1979). The disorder is often confused with *gender identity disorder* (*transsexualism*), but, as we shall see, they are two separate patterns.

The development of transvestic fetishism sometimes seems to follow the behavioral principles of operant conditioning. In such cases, parents or other adults may have openly encouraged the individuals to cross-dress as children or even rewarded them for this behavior. In one case, a woman was delighted to discover

Peter Yates/Picture Group

A group approach *"Crossroads" is a self-help group for men with transvestic fetishism, a recurrent need to dress in women's clothing as a means to achieve sexual arousal.*

Playful context *Dressing in clothes of the opposite sex does not necessarily convey a paraphilia. Here members of Harvard University's Hasty Pudding Theatricals Club, known for staging musicals in which male undergraduates dress like women, flank actor Samuel L. Jackson, the 1999 recipient of their Man of the Year award. Jackson's outfit is meant to spoof his famous "hamburger royal with cheese" discussion in the movie* Pulp Fiction.

that her young nephew enjoyed dressing in girls' clothes. She had always wanted a niece, and she proceeded to buy him dresses and jewelry and sometimes dressed him as a girl and took him out shopping.

Exhibitionism

A person with **exhibitionism** has recurrent urges to expose his genitals to another person, almost always a member of the opposite sex, or has sexually arousing fantasies of doing so. He may also carry out those urges but rarely attempts to initiate sexual activity with the person to whom he exposes himself (APA, 2000, 1994; Maletzky, 2000). More often, he wants to provoke shock or surprise. Sometimes an exhibitionist will expose himself in a particular neighborhood at particular hours. Around half of all women report having seen or had direct contact with an exhibitionist, or so-called flasher (Doctor & Neff, 2001). The urge to exhibit typically becomes stronger when the person has free time or is under significant stress.

Generally the disorder begins before age 18 and is most common in males (APA, 2000, 1994). Persons with exhibitionism are typically immature in their dealings with the opposite sex and have difficulty in interpersonal relationships. Around 30 percent of them are married and another 30 percent divorced or separated; their sexual relations with their wives are not usually satisfactory (Doctor & Neff, 2001). Many have doubts or fears about their masculinity, and some seem to have a strong bond to a possessive mother.

As with other paraphilias, treatment generally includes aversion therapy and masturbatory satiation, possibly combined with orgasmic reorientation, social skills training, or psychodynamic therapy (Krueger & Kaplan, 2002; Maletzky 2002, 2000). Clinicians have also reported some success with hypnotherapy (Epstein, 1983; Polk, 1983).

Voyeurism

A person who engages in **voyeurism** has recurrent and intense urges to secretly observe unsuspecting people as they undress or to spy on couples having intercourse. The person may also masturbate during the act of observing or when thinking about it afterward but does not generally seek to have sex with the person being spied on. This disorder usually begins before the age of 15 and tends to persist (APA, 2000, 1994).

The vulnerability of the people being observed and the probability that they would feel humiliated if they knew they were under observation are often part of the individual's enjoyment. In addition, the risk of being discovered often adds to the excitement.

Voyeurism, like exhibitionism, can play a role in normal sexuality, but in such cases it is engaged in with the consent or understanding of the partner. The clinical disorder of voyeurism is marked by the repeated invasion of other people's privacy. Some people with voyeurism are unable to have normal sexual relations; others, however, have a normal sex life apart from their voyeurism.

Many psychodynamic clinicians propose that people with voyeurism are seeking by their actions to gain power over others, possibly because they feel inadequate or are sexually or socially shy. Others have explained voyeurism as an attempt to reduce fears of castration, originally produced by the sight of an adult's genitals. Theoretically, people with voyeurism are repeating the behavior that produced the original fright, to reassure themselves that there is nothing to fear (Fenichel, 1945). Behaviorists explain the disorder as a learned behavior that can be traced to a chance and secret observation of a sexually arousing scene. If such observations are repeated on several occasions while the onlooker masturbates, a voyeuristic pattern may develop.

Frotteurism

A person who develops **frotteurism** has repeated and intense sexual urges to touch and rub against a nonconsenting person or has sexually arousing fantasies of doing so. The person may also act on the urges. Frottage (from French *frotter*, "to rub") is usually committed in a crowded place, such as a subway or a busy sidewalk (Horley, 2001; Krueger & Kaplan, 2000). The person, almost always a male, may rub his genitals against the victim's thighs or buttocks or fondle her genital area or breasts with his hands. Typically he fantasizes during the act that he is having a caring relationship with the victim. This paraphilia usually begins in the teenage years or earlier, often after the person observes others committing an act of frottage. After the person reaches the age of about 25, the acts gradually decrease and often disappear (APA, 2000, 1994).

Pedophilia

A person with **pedophilia** gains sexual gratification by watching, touching, or engaging in sexual acts with prepubescent children, usually 13 years old or younger. Some people with this disorder are satisfied by child pornography (Linz & Imrich, 2001) or seemingly innocent material such as children's underwear ads; others are driven to actually watching, fondling, or engaging in sexual intercourse with children (Howitt, 1995). Some people with pedophilia are attracted only to children; others are attracted to adults as well (APA, 2000, 1994). Both boys and girls can be pedophilia victims, but there is evidence suggesting that two-thirds of them are girls (Doctor & Neff, 2001; Koss & Heslet, 1992).

People with pedophilia usually develop their disorder during adolescence. Some were themselves sexually abused as children, and many were neglected, excessively punished, or deprived of genuinely close relationships during their childhood (Sawle & Kear, 2001; Berlin, 2000; Howitt, 1995). It is not unusual for

EXHIBITIONISM A paraphilia in which persons have repeated sexually arousing urges or fantasies about exposing their genitals to another person, and may act upon those urges.

VOYEURISM A paraphilia in which a person has repeated and intense sexual desires to observe unsuspecting people in secret as they undress or to spy on couples having intercourse, and may act upon these desires.

FROTTEURISM A paraphilia consisting of repeated and intense sexual urges, fantasies, or behaviors that involve touching and rubbing against a nonconsenting person.

PEDOPHILIA A paraphilia in which a person has repeated and intense sexual urges or fantasies about watching, touching, or engaging in sexual acts with prepubescent children, and may carry out these urges or fantasies.

STEPPING BACK

Serving the Public Good

As clinical practitioners and researchers conduct their work, should they consider the potential impact of their decisions on society? Many people, including a large number of clinicians, believe that the answer to this question is a resounding yes. Two clashes between the clinical field and the public interest in the 1990s—each centering on the disorder of *pedophilia*—brought this issue to life.

In 1994, the newly published DSM-IV ruled that people should receive a diagnosis of pedophilia only if their recurrent fantasies, urges, or behaviors involving sexual activity with children cause them significant distress or impairment in social, occupational, or other spheres of functioning. Critics worried that this criterion seemed to suggest that pedophilic behavior is acceptable, even normal, as

long as it causes no distress or impairment. Even the U.S. Congress condemned the DSM-IV definition.

In response to these criticisms, the American Psychiatric Association clarified its position in 1997, stating, "An adult who engages in sexual activity with a child is performing a criminal and immoral act which never can be considered moral or socially acceptable behavior." In 2000 the association went further still and changed the DSM criteria for pedophilia in the DSM-IV Text Revision, so that the disorder is now diagnosed if persons act on their sexual urges, regardless of whether they experience distress or impairment (APA, 2000). Similarly, acting on one's recurrent sexual urges or fantasies warrants a diagnosis in cases of exhibitionism, voyeurism, frotteurism, and sexual sadism.

Another clash between the clinical field and public sensibilities occurred in 1998 when a review article in the prestigious journal *Psychological Bulletin* concluded that the effects of child sexual abuse are not as long-lasting as usually believed. The study set off a firestorm, with critics arguing that the conclusion runs counter to evidence from a number of studies. Furthermore, many people worried that the article's conclusions could be used to legitimize pedophilia. After a groundswell of criticism, the American Psychological Association, publisher of the journal, acknowledged in 1999 that it should have given more thought to how the study would be received, and said that in the future it will more carefully weigh the potential consequences of research publications (Fowler, 1999).

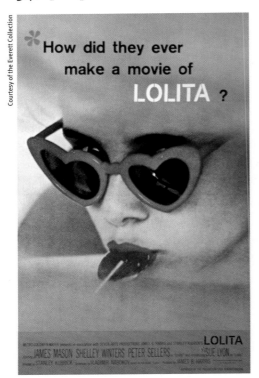

Courtesy of the Everett Collection

Pedophilia and the arts *This movie poster for the 1962 film* Lolita *posed a question that was, in fact, on the minds of many people, who worried that the film about a man's sexual interest in a 12-year-old girl might glamorize and trivialize the very serious problem of pedophilia. Initially, the 1955 novel by Vladimir Nabokov was available in the United States only in a contraband French edition, despite considerable critical acclaim. The 1962 movie enjoyed modest commercial success. A 1997 remake of the film was a commercial failure.*

SEXUAL MASOCHISM A paraphilia characterized by repeated and intense sexual urges, fantasies, or behaviors that involve being humiliated, beaten, bound, or otherwise made to suffer.

SEXUAL SADISM A paraphilia characterized by repeated and intense sexual urges, fantasies, or behaviors that involve inflicting suffering on others.

them to be married and to have sexual difficulties or other frustrations in life that lead them to seek an area in which they can be masters. Often these people are immature: their social and sexual skills may be underdeveloped, and thoughts of normal sexual relationships fill them with anxiety (Doctor & Neff, 2001). Some people with pedophilia also exhibit distorted thinking, such as "It's all right to have sex with children as long as they agree" (Abel et al., 2001, 1984). Studies have found that most men with this disorder also display at least one additional psychological disorder such as an anxiety or mood disorder, substance-related disorder, or personality disorder (Cohen & Galynker, 2002; Raymond et al., 1999). In recent years, some theorists have proposed that pedophilia may be related to a biochemical or brain structure abnormality (Maes et al., 2001), but a clear biological factor has yet to emerge in research.

Most pedophilic offenders are imprisoned or forced into treatment if they are caught (Stone et al., 2000). After all, they are committing child sexual abuse when they take any steps toward sexual contact with a child. Treatments include those already mentioned for other paraphilias, such as aversion therapy, masturbatory satiation, orgasmic reorientation, and antiandrogen drugs (Krueger & Kaplan 2002; LoPiccolo, 1992). There is also a cognitive-behavioral treatment for pedophilia: *relapse-prevention training*, modeled after the relapse-prevention programs used in the treatment of substance dependence (Maletzky, 2002; Fisher, Beech, & Browne, 2000) (see pages 306–307). In this approach, clients identify the kinds of situations that typically trigger their pedophilic fantasies and actions (such as depressed mood or distorted thinking). They then learn strategies for avoiding the situations or coping with them more effectively. Relapse-prevention training has sometimes been of help in pedophilia and in certain other paraphilias (Pithers & Cumming, 1989).

Sexual Masochism

A person with **sexual masochism** is intensely sexually aroused by the act or thought of being humiliated, beaten, bound, or otherwise made to suffer. Many people have fantasies of being forced into sexual acts against their will, but only those who are very upset or impaired by the fantasies receive this diagnosis. Some people with the disorder act on the masochistic urges by themselves, perhaps tying, sticking pins into, or even cutting themselves. Others have their sexual partners restrain, tie up, blindfold, spank, paddle, whip, beat, electrically shock, "pin and pierce," or humiliate them (APA, 2000, 1994).

An industry of products and services has arisen to meet the desires of people with sexual masochism. Here a 34-year-old woman describes her work as the operator of a sadomasochism house:

I get people here who have been all over looking for the right kind of pain they feel they deserve. Don't ask me why they want pain, I'm not a psychologist; but when they have found us, they usually don't go elsewhere. It may take some of the other girls an hour or even two hours to make these guys feel like they've had their treatment—I can achieve that in about 20 minutes. . . . Remember, these are businessmen, and they are not only buying my time, but they have to get back to work, so time is important.

Among the things I do, that work really quickly and well, are: I put clothespins on their nipples, or pins in their [testicles]. Some of them need to see their own blood to be able to get off. . . .

. . . All the time that a torture scene is going on, there is constant dialogue. . . . I scream at the guy, and tell him what a no-good rotten bastard he is, how this is even too good for him, that he knows he deserves worse, and I begin to list his sins. It works every time. Hey, I'm not nuts, I know what I'm doing. I act very tough and hard, but I'm really a very sensitive woman. But you have to watch out for a guy's health . . . you must not kill him, or have him get a heart attack. . . . I know of other places that have had guys die there. I've never lost a customer to death, though they may have wished for it during my "treatment." Remember, these are repeat customers. I have a clientele and a reputation that I value.

(Janus & Janus, 1993, p. 115)

In one form of sexual masochism, *hypoxyphilia*, people strangle or smother themselves (or ask their partner to strangle them) in order to heighten their sexual pleasure. There have, in fact, been a disturbing number of clinical reports of *autoerotic asphyxia*, in which individuals, usually males and as young as 10 years old, may accidentally produce a fatal lack of oxygen by hanging, suffocating, or strangling themselves while masturbating. There is some debate as to whether the practice should be characterized as sexual masochism, but it is at least sometimes accompanied by other acts of bondage (Blanchard & Hucker, 1991).

Most masochistic sexual fantasies begin in childhood. However, the person does not act out the urges until later, usually by early adulthood. The disorder typically continues for many years. Some people practice more and more dangerous acts over time or during times of particular stress (Santtila et al., 2002; APA, 2000, 1994).

In many cases sexual masochism seems to have developed through the behavioral process of classical conditioning. One case study tells of a teenage boy with a broken arm who was caressed and held close by an attractive nurse as the physician set his fracture without anesthesia (Gebhard, 1965). The powerful combination of pain and sexual arousal he felt then may have been the cause of his later masochistic urges and acts.

Sexual Sadism

A person with **sexual sadism**, usually male, is intensely sexually aroused by the thought or act of inflicting suffering on others by dominating, restraining, blindfolding, cutting, strangling, mutilating, or even killing the victim (Marshall & Kennedy, 2003). The label is derived from the name of the famous Marquis de Sade (1740–1814), who tortured others in order to satisfy his sexual desires. People who fantasize about sadism typically imagine that they have total control over a sexual victim who is terrified by the sadistic act. Many carry out sadistic acts with a consenting partner, often a person with sexual masochism. Some, however, act out their urges on nonconsenting victims. A number of rapists and sexual murderers, for example, display sexual sadism (Dickey et al., 2002). In all cases, the real or fantasized victim's suffering is the key to arousal.

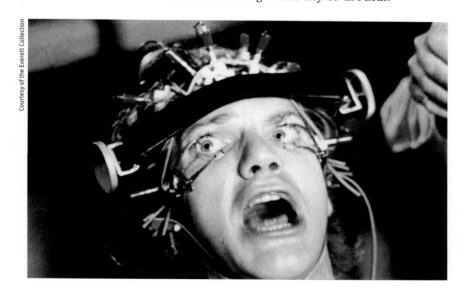

Courtesy of the Everett Collection

Cinematic introduction *In one of filmdom's most famous scenes, Alex, the sexually sadistic character in* A Clockwork Orange, *is forced to observe violent images while he experiences painful stomach spasms. Public attitudes toward aversion therapy were greatly influenced by this 1971 portrayal of the treatment approach.*

>>LOOKING AROUND
Sex and the Law

According to a Supreme Court decision in the 1997 case of *Kansas v. Hendricks*, convicted sex offenders may be removed from prison prior to release and committed to a mental hospital if a court judges them likely to engage in further "predatory acts of sexual violence" as the result of a "mental abnormality" or "personality disorder." They must then remain institutionalized until their disorder and sexual dangerousness are rectified.<<

In 1996 the California state legislature passed the first law in the United States allowing state judges to order antiandrogen drug treatments, often referred to as "chemical castration," for repeat sex crime offenders, such as men who repeatedly commit pedophiliac acts or rape.<<

The majority of arrests for sexual offenses involve acts of exhibitionism, pedophilia, or voyeurism (APA, 2000).<<

Fantasies of sexual sadism, like those of sexual masochism, may first appear in childhood or adolescence (Johnson & Becker, 1997); the sadistic acts, when they occur, develop by early adulthood (APA, 2000, 1994). The pattern is long-term. Sadistic acts sometimes stay at the same level of cruelty, but often they become more and more severe over the years (Santtila et al., 2002). Obviously, people with severe forms of the disorder may be highly dangerous to others.

Some behaviorists believe that classical conditioning is at work in sexual sadism. While inflicting pain, perhaps unintentionally, on an animal or person, a teenager may feel intense emotions and sexual arousal. The association between inflicting pain and being aroused sexually sets the stage for a pattern of sexual sadism. Behaviorists also propose that the disorder may result from modeling, when adolescents observe others achieving sexual satisfaction by inflicting pain. The many sexual magazines, books, and videotapes in our society make such models readily available (Seto, Maric, & Barbaree, 2001; Lebegue, 1991).

Psychodynamic and cognitive theorists view people with sexual sadism as having underlying feelings of sexual inadequacy; they inflict pain in order to gain a sense of power, which in turn increases their sexual arousal (Rathbone, 2001). In contrast, certain biological studies have found signs of possible abnormalities in the endocrine systems of persons with sadism (Langevin et al., 1988). None of these explanations, however, has been thoroughly investigated.

Sexual sadism has been treated by aversion therapy. The public's view of and distaste for this procedure have been influenced by Anthony Burgess's novel (later a movie) *A Clockwork Orange*, which describes simultaneous presentations of sadistic images and drug-induced stomach spasms to a sadistic young man until he is conditioned to feel nausea at the sight of such images. It is not clear that aversion therapy is helpful in cases of sexual sadism. However, relapse-prevention training, used in some criminal cases, seems to be of value (Maletzky, 2001; Pithers & Cumming, 1989).

A Word of Caution

The definitions of the paraphilias, like those of sexual dysfunctions, are strongly influenced by the norms of the particular society in which they occur (Leiblum, 2001; APA, 2000). Some clinicians argue that except when people are hurt by them, many paraphilic behaviors should not be considered disorders at all. We need to be very careful about applying these labels to others or to ourselves. Keep in mind that for years clinical professionals considered homosexuality a paraphilia, and their judgment was used to justify laws and even police actions against homosexual persons (Kirby, 2000). Only when the gay rights movement helped change society's understanding of and attitudes toward homosexuality did clinicians stop considering it a disorder. In the meantime, the clinical field had unintentionally contributed to the persecution, anxiety, and humiliation of millions of people because of personal sexual behavior that differed from the conventional norms.

>>LOOKING AROUND
Dangerous Interactions

A study of Internet chat rooms for children and teens estimated that two-thirds of the visitors were actually adults pretending to be children and seeking to engage in sex talk or to acquire or trade pornographic material (Lamb, 1998).<<

SUMMING UP

Paraphilias

Paraphilias are disorders marked by recurrent and intense sexual urges, fantasies, or behaviors involving either nonhuman objects, children, nonconsenting adults, or experiences of suffering or humiliation. The disorders are found primarily in men. The paraphilias include fetishism, transvestic fetishism (transvestism), exhibitionism, voyeurism, frotteurism, pedophilia, sexual masochism, and sexual sadism. Although various explanations have been proposed for these disorders, research has revealed little about their causes. A range of treatments have been tried, including aversion therapy, masturbatory satiation, orgasmic reorientation, and relapse-prevention training.

Gender Identity Disorder

One of the most fascinating disorders related to sexuality is **gender identity disorder**, or **transsexualism**, a disorder in which people persistently feel that a vast mistake has been made—they have been assigned to the wrong sex (see Table 11-6). Such persons would like to get rid of their primary and secondary sex characteristics—many of them find their own genitals repulsive—and acquire the characteristics of the other sex (APA, 2000, 1994). Men with gender identity disorder outnumber women by around 2 to 1. People with the problem often experience anxiety or depression and may have thoughts of suicide (Doctor & Neff, 2001; Bradley, 1995). Reactions of this kind are likely related to the confusion and pain brought on by the disorder itself, but they may also be tied to the prejudice typically experienced by individuals who display this pattern (Lombardi et al., 2001).

People with gender identity disorder usually feel uncomfortable wearing the clothes of their own sex and dress instead in clothes of the opposite sex. Their condition is not, however, transvestic fetishism (transvestism). People with that paraphilia cross-dress in order to become sexually aroused; persons with transsexualism have much deeper reasons for cross-dressing, reasons of gender identity. In addition to engaging in cross-dressing, individuals with transsexualism often take up roles and activities that are traditionally associated with the other sex (Brown et al., 1996; Bradley, 1995).

Sometimes gender identity disorder emerges in children (Griffiths, 2002; Wren, 2002). Like adults with this disorder, they feel uncomfortable about their assigned sex and yearn to be members of the opposite sex. This childhood pattern usually disappears by adolescence or adulthood, but in some cases it develops into adult gender identity disorder (Cohen-Kettenis, 2001; Bradley, 1995). Thus adults with this disorder may have had a childhood gender identity disorder, but most children with the disorder do not become transsexual adults. Some adults with gender identity disorder do not develop any symptoms until mid-adulthood.

Various theories have been proposed to explain this disorder (Doctor & Neff, 2001; Zucker, 2000), but research to test the ideas has been limited and generally weak. Some clinicians suspect that biological factors play a key role in the disorder. There is indeed evidence that the disorder sometimes runs in families (Green, 2000). Moreover, one biological study has received considerable attention (Zhou et al., 1995). Dutch investigators autopsied the brains of six people who had changed their sex from male to female. They found that a cluster of cells in the hypothalamus called the *bed nucleus of stria terminalis* (BST) was only half as large in these subjects as it was in a control group of normal men. Normally, a woman's BST is much smaller than a man's, so in effect the subjects with gender

GENDER IDENTITY DISORDER A disorder in which a person persistently feels extremely uncomfortable about his or her assigned sex and strongly wishes to be a member of the opposite sex. Also known as *transsexualism*.

>>**LOOKING AROUND**
Landmark Case

The first sex-change operation took place in 1931, but the procedure did not gain acceptance in the medical world until 1952, when an operation converted an ex-soldier named George Jorgensen into a woman, renamed Christine Jorgensen. This transformation made headlines around the world.<<

Table 11-6 DSM-IV Checklist

GENDER IDENTITY DISORDER

1. Strong and persistent cross-gender identification (for example, a stated desire to be the other sex, frequent passing as the other sex, desire to live or be treated as the other sex, or the conviction that one has the typical feelings and reactions of the other sex).
2. Persistent discomfort with one's sex or a sense of inappropriateness in the gender role of that sex (for example, preoccupation with getting rid of primary and secondary sex characteristics or belief that one was born the wrong sex).
3. Significant distress or impairment.

Based on APA, 2000, 1994.

(l.) Bettmann Archives (r.) David Levenson/Rex USA Ltd.

James and Jan *Feeling like a woman trapped in a man's body, the British writer James Morris (left) underwent sex-change surgery, described in his 1974 autobiography,* Conundrum. *Today Jan Morris (right) is a successful author and seems comfortable with her change of gender.*

identity disorder were found to have a female-sized BST. Scientists do not know for certain what the BST does in humans, but they know that it helps control sexual behavior in male rats. Although other interpretations of these findings are possible, it may well be that men who develop gender identity disorder have a key biological difference that leaves them very uncomfortable with their assigned sex characteristics.

Some adults with this disorder change their sexual characteristics by means of *hormone treatments* (Hepp et al., 2002; Bradley, 1995). Physicians prescribe the female sex hormone *estrogen* for male patients, causing breast development, loss of body and facial hair, and change in body fat distribution. Similar treatments with the male sex hormone *testosterone* are given to women with gender identity disorder.

Hormone therapy and psychotherapy enable many persons with this disorder to lead a satisfactory existence in the gender role that they believe represents their true identity. For others, however, this is not enough, and their dissatisfaction leads them to undergo one of the most controversial practices in medicine: **sex-change surgery** (Hepp et al., 2002; Liedl, 1999). This surgery is preceded by one to two years of hormone therapy. The operation itself involves, for men, amputation of the penis, creation of an artificial vagina, and face-changing plastic surgery. For women, surgery may include bilateral mastectomy and hysterectomy. The procedure for creating a functioning penis, called phalloplasty, is performed in some cases, but it is not yet perfected (Doctor & Neff, 2001). Doctors have, however, developed a silicone prosthesis that gives the patient the appearance of having male genitals. Studies in Europe suggest that one of every 30,000 men and one of every 100,000 women seek sex-change surgery (APA, 2000). In the United States, more than 6,000 persons are estimated to have undergone this surgical procedure (Doctor & Neff, 2001).

Clinicians have heatedly debated whether surgery is an appropriate treatment for gender identity disorder. Some consider it a humane solution, perhaps the most satisfying one to people with the disorder (Cohen-Kettenis & Gooren, 1999; Cohen-Kettenis & van Goozen, 1997). Others argue that transsexual surgery is a "drastic nonsolution" for a largely psychological problem. The long-term psychological outcome of surgical sex reassignment is not clear. Some people seem to function well for years after such treatments (Lewins, 2002; Michel et al., 2002), but others experience psychological difficulties. Without any form of treatment, gender identity disorder among adults is usually long-term, but some cases of recovery without intervention have reportedly occurred (Marks et al., 2000).

SEX-CHANGE SURGERY A surgical procedure that changes a person's sex organs and features, and, in turn, sexual identity.

SUMMING UP

Gender Identity Disorder

People with gender identity disorder persistently feel that they have been assigned to the wrong sex and would like to acquire the physical characteristics of the other sex. Its causes are not well understood. Hormone treatments and psychotherapy have been used to help some people adopt the gender role they believe to be right for them. Sex-change operations have also been performed, but the appropriateness of surgery as a form of "treatment" has been hotly debated.

CROSSROADS:

A Private Topic Draws Public Attention

For all the public interest in sexual disorders, clinical theorists and practitioners have only recently begun to understand their nature and how to treat them. As a result of research done over the past few decades, people with sexual dysfunctions are no longer doomed to a lifetime of sexual frustration. At the same time, however, insights into the causes and treatments of the other kinds of sexual disorders—paraphilias and gender identity disorder—remain limited.

Studies of sexual dysfunctions have pointed to many psychological, sociocultural, and biological causes. Often, as we have seen with so many disorders, the various causes may *interact* to produce a particular dysfunction, as in erectile disorder and female orgasmic disorder. For some dysfunctions, however, one cause alone is dominant, and integrated explanations may be inaccurate and unproductive. Premature ejaculation, for example, appears to have largely psychological causes, while dyspareunia usually has a physical cause.

Recent work has also yielded important progress in the treatment of sexual dysfunctions, and people with such problems are now often helped greatly by therapy. Sex therapy today is usually a complex program tailored to the particular problems of an individual or couple. Techniques from the various models may be combined, although in some instances the particular problem calls primarily for one approach (Bach et al., 2001).

> **>>IN THEIR WORDS**
>
> "Some nights he said that he was tired, and some nights she said that she wanted to read, and other nights no one said anything."<<
>
> Joan Didion, *Play It as It Lays*

Bettmann/Corbis

Does pornography lead to sexual misconduct? *In 1979, before the growth of the video sex industry, these women in New York City marched down 42nd Street to protest the proliferation of X-rated movie theaters in that area of the city. The concerns behind such rallies are that pornography offends many people's values, degrades women, and, in excess, may contribute to paraphilias and sexual misconduct. Today's clinicians acknowledge such concerns, but most are careful to clarify that, in moderation, exposure to sexually explicit material can often play a constructive role in fulfilling sexual needs and fantasies.*

One of the most important insights to emerge from all this work is that *education* about sexual dysfunctions can be as important as therapy. Sexual myths are still taken so seriously that they often lead to feelings of shame, self-hatred, isolation, and hopelessness—feelings that themselves contribute to sexual difficulty. Even a modest amount of education can help persons who are in treatment.

In fact, most people can benefit from a more accurate understanding of sexual functioning. Public education about sexual functioning—through books, television and radio, school programs, group presentations, and the like—has become a major clinical focus. It is important that these efforts continue and even increase in the coming years.

CRITICAL THOUGHTS

1. Many people feel that sex is private and refuse to participate in surveys of sexual behavior, and those who do participate tend to be more liberal, sexually experienced, and unconventional than the norm. What problems might this cause for sex researchers? *pp. 316–327*

2. Some theorists suggest that recent increases in the number of men receiving treatment for hypoactive sexual desire disorder may be linked to the impact of the women's movement (LoPiccolo, 1995). If this is the case, what factors might account for it? *pp. 317–320*

3. Performance anxiety and the spectator role may be contributing factors in certain sexual dysfunctions. Are there other areas of dysfunction in life that might also be explained by performance anxiety and the spectator role? *pp. 322, 324*

4. A key technique in sex therapy is to have a couple explore and caress each other's body (sensate focus) while resisting orgasm or intercourse. Why might people become more aroused during sexual caressing if they are prohibited from reaching orgasm or having intercourse? *p. 330*

5. Sex is one of the topics most commonly searched for on the Internet. Why might it be such a popular search topic? Is the availability of sex chat groups and other sexual material on the Internet psychologically healthy or damaging? *pp. 347–348, 315–347*

KEY TERMS

sexual dysfunction p. 315
desire phase p. 316
hypoactive sexual desire p. 317
sexual aversion disorder p. 317
excitement phase p. 320
female sexual arousal disorder p. 320
male erectile disorder p. 320
nocturnal penile tumescence p. 321
performance anxiety p. 322
spectator role p. 322
orgasm phase p. 322
premature ejaculation p. 323

male orgasmic disorder p. 323
female orgasmic disorder p. 324
vaginismus p. 326
dyspareunia p. 327
sex therapy p. 328
sensate focus p. 330
sildenafil (Viagra) p. 331
directed masturbation training p. 333
paraphilia p. 336
fetishism p. 337
aversion therapy p. 338
masturbatory satiation p. 338

orgasmic reorientation p. 338
transvestic fetishism p. 339
exhibitionism p. 340
voyeurism p. 340
frotteurism p. 341
pedophilia p. 341
relapse-prevention training p. 342
sexual masochism p. 342
sexual sadism p. 343
gender identity disorder p. 345
hormone treatments p. 345
sex-change surgery p. 345

QUICK QUIZ

1. What sexual dysfunctions are associated with the desire phase of the sexual response cycle? How common are they, and what causes them? *pp. 316–320*

2. What are the symptoms and prevalence of female sexual arousal disorder and male erectile disorder? To which phase of the sexual response cycle are they related? *pp. 320–321*

3. What are the possible causes of male erectile disorder? *pp. 321–322*

4. Which sexual dysfunctions seem to involve performance anxiety and the spectator role? *pp. 322, 324*

5. What are the symptoms, rates, and leading causes of premature ejaculation, male orgasmic disorder, and female orgasmic disorder? To which phase of the sexual response cycle are they related? *pp. 323–326*

6. Identify, describe, and explain the sexual pain disorders. *pp. 326–327*

7. What are the general features of modern sex therapy? What particular techniques are further used to treat specific sexual dysfunctions? *pp. 328–335*

8. List, describe, and explain the leading paraphilias. *pp. 336–344*

9. Describe the treatment techniques of aversion therapy, masturbatory satiation, orgasmic reorientation, and relapse-prevention training. Which paraphilias have they been used to treat, and how successful are they? *pp. 338–344*

10. Distinguish transvestism from gender identity disorder (transsexualism). What are the leading treatments for gender identity disorder? *pp. 345–346, 338–340*

CYBER STUDY

SEARCH THE *FUNDAMENTALS OF ABNORMAL PSYCHOLOGY* CD-ROM FOR

▲ Chapter 11 Video Case Enrichment
  How does stress affect sexual functioning?
  Are sexual beliefs and practices really changing?
  What choices are confronted by people with gender identity disorder?

▲ Chapter 11 Practical, Research, and Decision-Making Exercises
  Examining biases and myths about sex
  Uncovering sexual disorders in the media and the arts

▲ Chapter 11 Practice Test and Feedback

LOG ON TO THE COMER WEB PAGE FOR

▲ Suggested Web links, exercises, FAQ page, additional Chapter 11 practice test questions
  <www.worthpublishers.com/comer>

‹‹‹

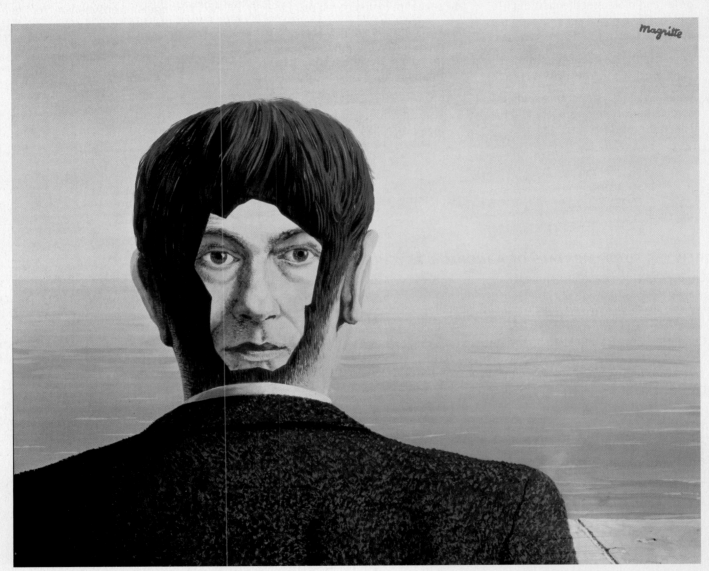

RENÉ MAGRITTE, 1939

Schizophrenia

> What . . . does schizophrenia mean to me? It means fatigue and confusion, it means trying to separate every experience into the real and the unreal and sometimes not being aware of where the edges overlap. It means trying to think straight when there is a maze of experiences getting in the way, and when thoughts are continually being sucked out of your head so that you become embarrassed to speak at meetings. It means feeling sometimes that you are inside your head and visualizing yourself walking over your brain, or watching another girl wearing your clothes and carrying out actions as you think them. It means knowing that you are continually "watched," that you can never succeed in life because the laws are all against you and knowing that your ultimate destruction is never far away.
>
> *(Rollin, 1980, p. 162)*

Does it surprise you to see such a clear firsthand description of how it feels to suffer from **schizophrenia**? People who have this disorder, though they previously functioned well or at least acceptably, deteriorate into an isolated wilderness of unusual perceptions, odd thoughts, disturbed emotions, and motor abnormalities. They experience **psychosis**, a loss of contact with reality. Their ability to perceive and respond to the environment becomes so disturbed that they may not be able to function at home, with friends, in school, or at work. They may have hallucinations (false sensory perceptions) or delusions (false beliefs), or they may withdraw into a private world. Taking LSD or abusing amphetamines or cocaine may produce psychosis (see Chapter 10). So may injuries to the brain and certain neurological diseases. Most commonly, however, psychosis appears in the form of schizophrenia.

Approximately one of every 100 people in the world suffers from schizophrenia during his or her lifetime (APA, 2000). An estimated 2.5 million with this disorder are currently living in the United States (Bichsel, 2001; McGuire, 2000). Its financial cost is enormous—according to some estimates, more than $100 billion annually, including the costs of hospitalization, lost wages, and disability benefits (Keltner & Folks, 2001; Black & Andreasen, 1994). The emotional cost is even greater. In addition, sufferers have an increased risk of suicide and of physical—often fatal—illness (Kim et al., 2003; Davidson, 2002). As we discussed in Chapter 8, it is estimated that up to 15 percent of persons with the disorder commit suicide.

Although schizophrenia appears in all socioeconomic groups, it is found more frequently in the lower levels (see Figure 12-1 on the next page), leading some theorists to believe that the stress of poverty is itself a cause of the disorder. However, it could be that schizophrenia causes its victims to fall from a higher to a lower socioeconomic level or to remain poor because they are unable to function effectively (Munk & Mortensen, 1992). This is sometimes called the *downward drift* theory.

Equal numbers of men and women receive a diagnosis of schizophrenia. In men, however, the disorder often begins earlier and may be more severe (Usall et al., 2002; Moriarty et al., 2001). Almost 3 percent of all those who are divorced or separated suffer from schizophrenia sometime during their lives, compared to 1 percent of married people and 2 percent of people who

SCHIZOPHRENIA A psychotic disorder in which personal, social, and occupational functioning deteriorate as a result of strange perceptions, disturbed thought processes, unusual emotions, and motor abnormalities.

PSYCHOSIS A state in which a person loses contact with reality in key ways.

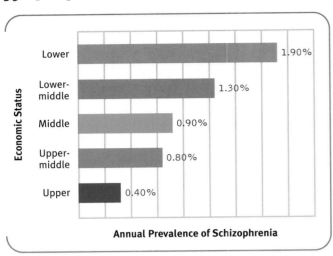

FIGURE 12-1 **Socioeconomic class and schizophrenia** *Poor people in the United States are more likely than wealthy people to experience schizophrenia. (Adapted from Keith et al., 1991.)*

remain single (Keith et al., 1991). Again, however, it is not clear whether marital problems are a cause or a result.

As many as 2.1 percent of African Americans receive a diagnosis of schizophrenia, compared with 1.4 percent of white Americans (Keith et al., 1991). According to census findings, however, African Americans are also more likely to be poor and to experience marital separation. When these factors are controlled for, the rates of schizophrenia are equal for the two racial groups.

People today, like those of the past, show great interest in schizophrenia, flocking to plays and movies that feature the disorder. Yet, as we shall see, all too many people with schizophrenia are neglected in our country, their needs almost entirely ignored. Although effective treatments have been developed, most sufferers live without adequate care and without nearly fulfilling their potential as human beings (Torrey, 2001).

The Clinical Picture of Schizophrenia

The symptoms of schizophrenia vary greatly, and so do its triggers, course, and responsiveness to treatment (APA, 2000). In fact, a number of clinicians believe that schizophrenia is actually a group of separate disorders that happen to have some features in common. To see the variety of forms schizophrenia may take, consider two people who were diagnosed as suffering from it. The cases are taken from the files of Silvano Arieti (1974), a famous theorist on the disorder.

> **LAURA, 40 YEARS OLD**
> Laura's desire was to become independent and leave home [in Austria] as soon as possible. . . . She became a professional dancer at the age of 20 . . . and was booked for vaudeville theaters in many European countries. . . .
>
> It was during one of her tours in Germany that Laura met her husband. . . . They were married and went to live in a small provincial town in France where the husband's business was. . . . She spent a year in that town and was very unhappy. . . . [Finally] Laura and her husband decided to emigrate to the United States. . . .
>
> They had no children, and Laura . . . showed interest in pets. She had a dog to whom she was very devoted. The dog became sick and partially paralyzed, and veterinarians felt that there was no hope of recovery. . . . Finally [her husband] broached the problem to his wife, asking her "Should the dog be destroyed or not?" From that time on Laura became restless, agitated, and depressed. . . .
>
> . . . Later Laura started to complain about the neighbors. A woman who lived on the floor beneath them was knocking on the wall to irritate her. According to the husband, this woman had really knocked on the wall a few times; he had heard the noises. However, Laura became more and more concerned about it. She would wake up in the middle of the night under the impression that she was hearing noises from the apartment downstairs. She would become upset and angry at the neighbors. . . . Later she became more disturbed. She started to feel that the neighbors were now recording everything she said; maybe they had hidden wires in the apartment. She started to feel "funny" sensations. There were many strange things happening, which she did not know how to explain; people were looking at her in a funny way in the street; in the butcher shop, the butcher had purposely served her last, although she was in the middle of the line. During the next few days she felt that people were planning to harm either her or her husband. . . . In the evening when she looked at television, it became obvious to her that the programs referred to her life. Often the people on the programs were just repeating what she had thought. They were stealing her ideas. She wanted to go to the police and report them.
>
> *(Arieti, 1974, pp. 165–168)*

>>PSYCH•NOTES
The Wrong Split

Despite popular misconceptions, people with schizophrenia do not display a "split" or multiple personality. That pattern is indicative of a dissociative disorder.<<

RICHARD, 23 YEARS OLD

In high school, Richard was an average student. After graduation from high school, he was drafted into the army. . . . Richard remembered [the] period . . . after his discharge from the army . . . as one of the worst in his life. . . . Any, even remote, anticipation of disappointment was able to provoke attacks of anxiety in him. . . .

Approximately two years after his return to civilian life, Richard left his job because he became overwhelmed by these feelings of lack of confidence in himself, and he refused to go look for another one. He stayed home most of the day. His mother would nag him that he was too lazy and unwilling to do anything. He became slower and slower in dressing and undressing and taking care of himself. When he went out of the house, he felt compelled "to give interpretations" to everything he looked at. He did not know what to do outside the house, where to go, where to turn. If he saw a red light at a crossing, he would interpret it as a message that he should not go in that direction. If he saw an arrow, he would follow the arrow, interpreting it as a sign sent by God that he should go in that direction. Feeling lost and horrified, he would go home and stay there, afraid to go out because going out meant making decisions or choices that he felt unable to make. He reached the point where he stayed home most of the time. But even at home, he was tortured by his symptoms. He could not act; any motion that he felt like making seemed to him an insurmountable obstacle, because he did not know whether he should make it or not. He was increasingly afraid of doing the wrong thing. Such fears prevented him from dressing, undressing, eating, and so forth. He felt paralyzed and lay motionless in bed. He gradually became worse, was completely motionless, and had to be hospitalized. . . .

Being undecided, he felt blocked, and often would remain mute and motionless, like a statue, even for days.

(Arieti, 1974, pp. 153–155)

POSITIVE SYMPTOMS Symptoms of schizophrenia that seem to be excesses of or bizarre additions to normal thoughts, emotions, or behaviors.

DELUSION A strange false belief firmly held despite evidence to the contrary.

What Are the Symptoms of Schizophrenia?

Laura and Richard both deteriorated from a normal level of functioning to become ineffective in dealing with the world. Each experienced some of the symptoms found in schizophrenia. The symptoms can be grouped into three categories: *positive symptoms* (excesses of thought, emotion, and behavior), *negative symptoms* (deficits of thought, emotion, and behavior), and *psychomotor symptoms* (Andreasen, 2001).

POSITIVE SYMPTOMS **Positive symptoms** are "pathological excesses," or bizarre additions, to a person's behavior. *Delusions, disorganized thinking and speech, heightened perceptions* and *hallucinations,* and *inappropriate affect* are the ones most often found in schizophrenia.

DELUSIONS Many people with schizophrenia develop **delusions**, ideas that they believe wholeheartedly but that have no basis in fact. Some people hold a single delusion that dominates their lives and behavior, whereas others have many delusions. *Delusions of persecution* are the most common in schizophrenia (APA, 2000). People with such delusions believe they are being plotted or discriminated against, spied on, slandered, threatened, attacked, or deliberately victimized. Laura believed that her neighbors were trying to irritate her and that other people were trying to harm her and her husband.

People with schizophrenia may also experience *delusions of reference:* they attach special and personal meaning to the actions of others or to various objects or events. Richard, for example, interpreted arrows on street signs as indicators of the direction he should take. People who experience *delusions of grandeur* believe themselves to be great inventors, religious saviors, or other specially empowered persons. And those with

Delusions of grandeur *In 1892, an artist who was a patient at a mental hospital claimed credit for this painting,* Self-Portrait as Christ. *Although few people with schizophrenia have his artistic skill, a number display similar delusions of grandeur.*

THE CURRENT SCENE

Relationships of the Mind

While playing in a professional tennis tournament in 1993, Monica Seles was stabbed by a 38-year-old man from Germany. The attacker was obsessed with another tennis star, Steffi Graf, and believed that it was his responsibility to help Graf's career by striking down her rival. Seles did not return to professional tennis for two years.

In 1989 the actress Rebecca Shaeffer of the television show *My Sister Sam* was shot and killed outside her West Hollywood apartment by a fan. He had closely followed Shaeffer's career for months, and eventually he journeyed to her apartment building. When she failed to greet him warmly, he took her rebuff as a sign of arrogance and shot her.

Stalking is a growing problem in today's world (Pathe, 2002). At least 200,000 people are victimized by stalkers in the United States each year (Corwin, 1993). As many as 1 in 12 women and 1 in 50 men are stalked during their lifetimes (Abrams & Robinson, 1998; Klein, 1998). The majority of victims experience substantial stress; indeed, many develop posttraumatic stress symptoms (Kamphuis & Emmelkamp, 2001).

Stalking occurs in various forms and has a range of causes (Kropp et al., 2002). However, many stalkers suffer from *erotomanic delusions*, beliefs without any basis whatsoever that they are loved by someone who may actually be a casual acquaintance or a complete stranger (Silva et al., 2000; Anderson, 1993). Some people with such delusions, like Shaeffer's and Graf's pursuers, develop fantasies in which they feel driven to protect, harm, or even kill the object of their desire (Menzies et al., 1995).

©Apple Corps/Camera Press/Retna Ltd., USA

The price of fame? *When the Beatles were enjoying worldwide success and fame, few could envision that John Lennon (second from left) would be shot dead in 1980 and that George Harrison (far right) would nearly be stabbed to death in 1999, each by a fan with erotomanic delusions.*

>> **LOOKING AROUND**

Neologisms in Literature

In *Alice in Wonderland*, Lewis Carroll often combined two legitimate words to form a nonsensical word. Some such words are now part of the English language ("chortle," "galumph"). <<

delusions of control believe their feelings, thoughts, and actions are being controlled by other people.

DISORGANIZED THINKING AND SPEECH People with schizophrenia may not be able to think logically and may speak in peculiar ways. These **formal thought disorders** can cause the sufferer great confusion and make communication extremely difficult. Often they take the form of positive symptoms (pathological excesses), as in *loose associations*, *neologisms*, *perseveration*, and *clang*.

People who have **loose associations**, or **derailment**, the most common formal thought disorder, rapidly shift from one topic to another, believing that their incoherent statements make sense. One man with schizophrenia, asked about his itchy arms, responded:

> The problem is insects. My brother used to collect insects. He's now a man 5 foot 10 inches. You know, 10 is my favorite number. I also like to dance, draw, and watch television.

Some people with schizophrenia use *neologisms*, made-up words that typically have meaning only to the person using them. One individual stated, for example,

"I am here from a foreign university . . . and you have to have a *'plausity'* of all acts of amendment to go through for the children's code . . . it is an *'amorition'* law . . . the children have to have this *'accentuative'* law . . ." (Vetter, 1969, p. 189). Others may display the formal thought disorder of *perseveration*, in which they repeat their words and statements again and again. Finally, some use *clang*, or rhyme, to think or express themselves. When asked how he was feeling, one man replied, "Well, hell, it's well to tell." Another described the weather as "So hot, you know it runs on a cot." Research suggests that some disorganized speech or thinking may appear long before a full pattern of schizophrenia unfolds (Torrey, 2001; Amminger et al., 1999).

HEIGHTENED PERCEPTIONS AND HALLUCINATIONS

The perceptions and attention of some people with schizophrenia seem to intensify. The persons may feel that their senses are being flooded by all the sights and sounds that surround them, making it almost impossible for them to attend to anything important:

Inner torment *Like this young woman, people with schizophrenia often appear to be trying to fight off the strange thoughts and perceptions that pervade their minds.*

> Everything seems to grip my attention. . . . I am speaking to you just now, but I can hear noises going on next door and in the corridor. I find it difficult to shut these out, and it makes it more difficult for me to concentrate on what I am saying to you.
>
> *(McGhie and Chapman, 1961)*

Laboratory studies have repeatedly found problems of perception and attention among people with schizophrenia (Gold & Thaker, 2002; Gold et al., 2002). Such problems may develop years before the onset of the actual disorder (Sabin et al., 2001; Cornblatt & Keilp, 1994). The difficulties in perception and attention may also contribute to memory impairment, another feature found among many individuals with the disorder (Hartman et al., 2003; Venneri et al., 2002).

Another kind of perceptual problem found in cases of schizophrenia is **hallucinations**, perceptions that occur in the absence of external stimuli. Hallucinations can involve any of the senses; however, auditory hallucinations are by far the most common kind in schizophrenia. The individuals hear sounds or voices that seem to come from outside their heads. The voices may talk directly to the hallucinatory, perhaps giving commands or warning of dangers, or they may be experienced as overheard:

> The voices . . . were mostly heard in my head, though I often heard them in the air, or in different parts of the room. Every voice was different, and each beautiful, and generally, speaking or singing in a different tone and measure, and resembling those of relations or friends. There appeared to be many in my head, I should say upwards of fourteen. I divide them, as they styled themselves, or one another, into voices of contrition and voices of joy and honour.
>
> *("Perceval's Narrative," in Bateson, 1974)*

Research suggests that people with auditory hallucinations actually produce the nerve signals of sound in their brains, "hear" them, and then believe that external sources are responsible (Javitt & Coyle, 2004; Keefe et al., 2002). One study measured blood flow in *Broca's area*, the region of the brain that helps people

FORMAL THOUGHT DISORDER A disturbance in the production and organization of thought.

LOOSE ASSOCIATIONS A common thinking disturbance in schizophrenia, characterized by rapid shifts from one topic of conversation to another. Also known as *derailment*.

HALLUCINATION The experiencing of sights, sounds, or other perceptions in the absence of external stimuli.

A Beautiful Mind: Movies vs. Reality

As we have observed, mental disorders and the people who experience them are popular subjects throughout the arts, including, of course, the cinema. One of the most successful such movies in recent years was *A Beautiful Mind*, based on the true story of John Forbes Nash. As the movie reveals, Nash is a brilliant mathematician who developed schizophrenia early in his academic and research career and struggled with the disorder for 35 years, unable to hold an academic position or function independently for most of those years. Nevertheless, in 1994 he was awarded the Nobel Prize in economics for his earlier doctoral work on game theory, a mathematical model of conflict resolution. For his doctoral thesis in 1951, Nash had altered this theory in key ways, and while he was later struggling with schizophrenia, his revised theory went on to greatly influence the field of economics—thus his Nobel Prize in that field.

The movie is true to the spirit of Nash's battle against and ultimate triumph over schizophrenia. Similarly, it does capture the essence of Nash's relationship with his wife, Alicia, whose loving devotion, support, and patience have, by everyone's account, been key to his improvement and later accomplishments. At the same time, the movie takes certain liberties with the facts of Nash's life and struggle. Because this film has been so popular and influential—it has provided millions of people with their primary education on schizophrenia—it may be useful to correct some of the movie's misrepresentations, each done in the spirit of artistic license:

The mathematician *John Forbes Nash gazes out the window of his house in Princeton, New Jersey, shortly after winning the Nobel Prize.*

The actor *Portraying Nash in the movie* A Beautiful Mind, *Russell Crowe uses a window at Princeton University to work out a complex mathematical problem.*

produce speech (McGuire et al., 1996, 1995, 1993). The researchers found more blood flow in Broca's area while patients were experiencing auditory hallucinations. A related study instructed six men with schizophrenia to press a button whenever they experienced an auditory hallucination (Silbersweig et al., 1995). PET scans revealed increased activity near the surfaces of their brains, in the tissues of the brain's hearing center, when they pressed the button.

Hallucinations and delusional ideas often occur together. A woman who hears voices issuing commands, for example, may have the delusion that the commands are being placed in her head by someone else. A man with delusions of persecution may hallucinate the smell of poison in his bedroom or the taste of poison in his coffee. Might one symptom cause the other? Whichever comes first, the hallucination and delusion eventually feed into each other:

> I thought the voices I heard were being transmitted through the walls of my apartment and through the washer and dryer and that these machines were talking and telling me things. I felt that the government agencies had planted transmitters and receivers in my apartment so that I could hear what they were saying and they could hear what I was saying.
>
> (Anonymous, 1996, p. 183)

Movie	Reality
❖ Nash's hallucinations and delusions begin in 1948, when he is a 20-year-old graduate student at Princeton University.	❖ His symptoms first appeared in 1958, when he was 30 years old, teaching and conducting research at MIT. In that same year *Fortune* magazine had named him one of the country's leading mathematicians (Wallace, 2002).
❖ Nash regularly interacts with a high-spirited roommate at Princeton and with a secretive federal agent at MIT, each of whom is but a visual hallucination.	❖ In his battle with schizophrenia, Nash experienced only auditory hallucinations (voices), never visual ones.
❖ Nash is hospitalized on one occasion for his psychotic symptoms.	❖ He was committed to mental hospitals several times throughout the course of his disorder.
❖ Nash meets his wife at MIT in 1952, when Alicia, a physics major, takes his calculus course. They marry in 1957 and remain married to the present day.	❖ After Nash's disorder worsened and his accusations against her intensified, an exasperated and frightened Alicia divorced him in 1963. She remained devoted to him, however. After his mother died in 1970, Alicia agreed to reunite with him, and they have continued to be together since then. They remarried in 2001 (Nasar, 2002).
❖ Although Nash stops taking antipsychotic drugs for years, he returns to them by the movie's end, saying that he has been helped by new (atypical) antipsychotic drugs.	❖ Nash refused to take any more medications in 1970, and he reports that he has not taken any such drugs since then (Duncan, 2001).
❖ Nash has one child, a son named John Charles Nash, born to him and Alicia.	❖ Nash also has an older son named John David Stier, born to him and a woman with whom Nash had a relationship before his marriage to Alicia. Nash currently has close relationships with both sons.
❖ Nash's son, John Charles Nash, is depicted as a healthy child, free of psychological disorders.	❖ Like his father, John Charles Nash went on to develop schizophrenia. Despite this disorder, the son, too, has earned a PhD in mathematics.

INAPPROPRIATE AFFECT Many people with schizophrenia display **inappropriate affect**, emotions that are unsuited to the situation. They may smile when making a serious statement or on being told terrible news, or they may become upset in situations that should make them happy. They may also undergo inappropriate shifts in mood. During a tender conversation with his wife, for example, a man with schizophrenia suddenly started yelling obscenities at her and complaining about her.

In at least some cases, these emotions may be merely a response to other features of the disorder. Consider a woman with schizophrenia who smiles when told of her husband's terminal illness. She may not actually be happy about the news; in fact, she may not be understanding or even hearing it. She could, for example, be responding instead to another of the many stimuli flooding her senses, perhaps a joke coming from an auditory hallucination.

NEGATIVE SYMPTOMS **Negative symptoms** are those that seem to be "pathological deficits," characteristics that are lacking in an individual. *Poverty of speech*, *blunted and flat affect*, *loss of volition*, and *social withdrawal* are commonly found in schizophrenia. Such deficits greatly affect one's life and activities.

POVERTY OF SPEECH People with schizophrenia often display **alogia**, or poverty of speech, a reduction in speech or speech content. Some people with this symptom

INAPPROPRIATE AFFECT Display of emotions that are unsuited to the situation; a symptom of schizophrenia.

NEGATIVE SYMPTOMS Symptoms of schizophrenia that seem to be deficits in normal thought, emotions, or behaviors.

ALOGIA A decrease in speech or speech content; a symptom of schizophrenia. Also known as *poverty of speech*.

FLAT AFFECT A marked lack of expressed emotions; a symptom of schizophrenia.

AVOLITION A symptom of schizophrenia marked by apathy and an inability to start or complete a course of action.

CATATONIA A pattern of extreme psychomotor symptoms found in some forms of schizophrenia, which may include catatonic stupor, rigidity, or posturing.

think and say very little. Others say quite a bit but still manage to convey little meaning.

BLUNTED AND FLAT AFFECT Many people with schizophrenia have a *blunted* affect—they show less anger, sadness, joy, and other feelings than most people. And some show almost no emotions at all, a condition known as **flat affect**. Their faces are still, their eye contact poor, and their voices monotonous. It may be that people with such limitations continue to feel emotion but cannot express it as others do. One study had subjects view very emotional film clips. Subjects with schizophrenia showed less facial expression than the others; however, they reported feeling just as much positive and negative emotion and in fact displayed greater skin arousal (Kring & Neale, 1996).

LOSS OF VOLITION Many people with schizophrenia experience **avolition**, or apathy, feeling drained of energy and of interest in normal goals and unable to start or follow through on a course of action (Lysaker & Bell, 1995). This problem is particularly common in people who have had schizophrenia for many years, as if they have been worn down by it. The avolition and indecisiveness of Richard, the young man whose case was presented earlier, made eating, dressing, and undressing impossible ordeals.

SOCIAL WITHDRAWAL People with schizophrenia may withdraw from their social environment and attend only to their own ideas and fantasies. Because their ideas are illogical and confused, the withdrawal has the effect of distancing them still further from reality (Venneri et al., 2002). The social withdrawal seems also to lead to a breakdown of social skills, including the ability to recognize other people's needs accurately (Corrigan & Penn, 2001; Trumbetta & Mueser, 2001).

PSYCHOMOTOR SYMPTOMS People with schizophrenia sometimes experience *psychomotor symptoms*; for example, awkward movements or repeated grimaces and odd gestures. These unusual gestures often seem to have a private purpose—perhaps magical.

The psychomotor symptoms of schizophrenia may take certain extreme forms, collectively called **catatonia** (Manschreck, 2003). People in a catatonic stupor stop responding to their environment, remaining motionless and silent for long stretches of time. Recall how Richard would lie motionless and mute in bed for days. People who display catatonic rigidity maintain a rigid, upright posture for hours and resist efforts to be moved. Still others exhibit catatonic posturing, assuming awkward, bizarre positions for long periods of time. Finally, people may display catatonic excitement, a different form of catatonia in which they move excitedly, sometimes with wild waving of arms and legs.

A catatonic pose *These patients, photographed in the early 1900s, display features of catatonia, including catatonic posturing, in which they assume bizarre positions for long periods of time.*

What Is the Course of Schizophrenia?

Schizophrenia usually first appears between the person's late teens and mid-30s (APA, 2000). Although its course varies widely from case to case, many sufferers seem to go through three phases—prodromal, active, and residual. During the *prodromal phase*, symptoms are not yet obvious, but persons are beginning to deteriorate. They may withdraw socially, speak in vague or odd ways, develop strange ideas, or express little emotion. During the *active phase*, symptoms become apparent. Sometimes this phase is triggered by stress in the person's life. For Laura, the middle-aged woman described earlier, the immediate trigger was the loss of her cherished dog. Finally, many people with schizophrenia eventually enter a *residual phase*, in which they return to a prodromal-like level of functioning. The striking symptoms of the active phase lessen, but some negative symptoms, such as blunted emotions, may remain (Andreasen, 2001). Although one-quarter or more

A CLOSER LOOK

Howling for Attention

I It's when I was bitten by a rabid dog. . . . When I'm emotionally upset, I feel as if I am turning into something else: my fingers go numb, as if I had pins and needles right in the middle of my hand; I can no longer control myself. . . . I get the feeling I'm becoming a wolf. I look at myself in the mirror and I witness my transformation. It's no longer my face; it changes completely. I stare, my pupils dilate, and I feel as if hairs are growing all over my body, as if my teeth are getting longer. . . . I feel as if my skin is no longer mine. I

(BENEZECH, DEWITTE, & BOURGEOIS, 1989)

Lycanthropy, the delusion of being an animal, is a rare psychological syndrome. The word "lycanthropy" comes from the Greek *lykos,* "wolf," and *anthropos,* "man." Accounts have been found all over the world of people who take on the characteristics and behavior of wolves or other animals. Belief in these tales has persisted for centuries. In the Middle Ages, lycanthropy was thought to be the result of demonic possession (Lehmann, 1985). Today it is commonly thought to be caused by mental disorders, including schizophrenia, severe mood disorders, and certain forms of brain damage.

Mention of lycanthropy continues to produce an image of a werewolf baring its fangs at a terrified villager on a fog-shrouded moor. The legend was that the former had been bitten by another werewolf in an unbroken chain that passes on the legacy. But there are now more reasonable explanations for this type of behavior. One explanation is that some people afflicted with lycanthropy actually suffer from *congenital generalized hypertrichosis,* an extremely rare disease marked by excessive amounts of hair on the face and upper body (Maugh, 1995). Others may suffer from *porphyria,* an inherited blood disease whose victims sprout extra facial hair and are sensitive to sunlight. Still another current explanation ties lycanthropy to a disturbance in the activity of the temporal lobe of the brain, which is close to areas of the brain that may be responsible for visual hallucinations.

Despite such possibilities, beliefs in werewolves as supernatural beings are

Crying wolf? *In the film* An American Werewolf in London, *a possessed man watches in terror as his hand stretches into the forepaw of a wolf.*

likely to continue for the foreseeable future. Tales of demonic possession are more alluring than histories of congenital disease or temporal lobe abnormalities. Nor are publishers or movie producers likely to say good-bye to such good friends. Old explanations of lycanthropy may be flawed scientifically, but the profits they produce are far from a delusion.

---

of patients recover completely from schizophrenia (Torrey, 2001; McGuire, 2000), the majority continue to have at least some residual problems for the rest of their lives.

Each of these phases may last for days or for years. A fuller recovery from schizophrenia is more likely in persons who functioned quite well before the disorder (had good *premorbid functioning*) or whose disorder was first triggered by stress, came on abruptly, or developed during middle age (Mamounas et al., 2001).

Diagnosing Schizophrenia

DSM-IV calls for a diagnosis of schizophrenia only after symptoms of the disorder continue for six months or more. In addition, people suspected of having this disorder must show a deterioration in their work, social relations, and ability to care for themselves (see Table 12-1 on the next page). The DSM distinguishes five types of schizophrenia: disorganized, catatonic, paranoid, undifferentiated, and residual.

The central symptoms of *disorganized type of schizophrenia* are confusion, incoherence, and flat or inappropriate affect. Attention and perception problems, extreme social withdrawal, and odd mannerisms or grimaces are common. So is

Table 12-1 DSM-IV Checklist

SCHIZOPHRENIA

1. At least two of the following symptoms, each present for a significant portion of time during a one-month period:
   a. Delusions.
   b. Hallucinations.
   c. Disorganized speech.
   d. Grossly disorganized or catatonic behavior.
   e. Negative symptoms.
2. Functioning markedly below the level achieved prior to onset.
3. Continuous signs of the disturbance for at least six months, at least one month of which includes symptoms in full and active form (as opposed to attentuated form).

Based on APA, 2000, 1994.

flat or inappropriate affect. In contrast, the central feature of *catatonic type of schizophrenia* is a psychomotor disturbance of some sort. Some of the people in this category spend their time in a catatonic stupor, others in the throes of catatonic excitement. Richard, the unemployed young man who became mute and statuelike, might receive a diagnosis of this type of schizophrenia.

People with *paranoid type of schizophrenia* have an organized system of delusions and auditory hallucinations that may guide their lives. Laura would receive this diagnosis. She believed people were out to get her (delusions of persecution) and that people on television were stealing her ideas (delusions of reference). In addition, she heard noises from the apartment downstairs and felt "funny sensations" that confirmed her beliefs.

When people with this disorder do not fall neatly into one of the other categories, they are diagnosed with *undifferentiated type of schizophrenia*. Because this category is somewhat vague, it has been assigned to a wide assortment of unusual patterns over the years. Many clinicians believe that it is in fact overused.

When the symptoms of schizophrenia lessen in strength and number yet remain in a residual form, the patient's diagnosis is usually changed to *residual type of schizophrenia*. As we observed earlier, people with this pattern may continue to display blunted or inappropriate emotions, as well as social withdrawal, eccentric behavior, and some illogical thinking.

Apart from these DSM-IV categories, many researchers believe that a distinction between so-called Type I and Type II schizophrenia helps predict the course of the disorder. People with **Type I schizophrenia** are dominated by positive symptoms, such as delusions, hallucinations, and certain formal thought disorders (Crow, 1995, 1985, 1982, 1980). Those with **Type II schizophrenia** display negative symptoms, such as flat affect, poverty of speech, and loss of volition. Type I patients generally have a better adjustment prior to the disorder, later onset of symptoms, and greater likelihood of improvement. In addition, the positive symptoms of Type I schizophrenia seem to be closely linked to *biochemical* abnormalities in the brain, while the negative symptoms of Type II schizophrenia have been tied to *structural* abnormalities in the brain.

TYPE I SCHIZOPHRENIA A type of schizophrenia characterized mainly by positive symptoms, such as delusions, hallucinations, and certain formal thought disorders.

TYPE II SCHIZOPHRENIA A type of schizophrenia characterized mainly by negative symptoms, such as flat affect, poverty of speech, and loss of volition.

SUMMING UP

The Clinical Picture of Schizophrenia

Schizophrenia is a disorder in which functioning deteriorates as a result of disturbed thought processes, distorted perceptions, unusual emotions, and motor abnormalities. Approximately 1 percent of the world's population suffers from this disorder. Its symptoms fall into three groupings. Positive symptoms include delusions, certain formal thought disorders, hallucinations and other disturbances in perception and attention, and inappropriate affect. Negative symptoms include poverty of speech, flat affect, loss of volition, and social withdrawal. The disorder may also include psychomotor symptoms. Schizophrenia usually emerges during late adolescence or early adulthood and tends to progress through three phases: prodromal, active, and residual.

DSM-IV identifies five types of schizophrenia: disorganized, catatonic, paranoid, undifferentiated, and residual. In addition, clinicians have distinguished between Type I schizophrenia and Type II schizophrenia.

How Do Theorists Explain Schizophrenia?

As with many other kinds of disorders, biological, psychological, and sociocultural theorists have each proposed explanations for schizophrenia. So far, the biological explanations have received by far the most research support. This is not to say that psychological and sociocultural factors play no role in the disorder. Rather, a *diathesis-stress* relationship may be at work: people with a biological predisposition will develop schizophrenia only if certain kinds of events or stressors are also present (Gottesman & Reilly, 2003; Schiffman et al., 2001).

Biological Views

Perhaps the most enlightening research on schizophrenia during the past several decades has come from genetic and biological studies. This work has revealed the key roles of inheritance and brain activity in the development of the disorder and has opened the door to important changes in its treatment.

GENETIC FACTORS Following the principles of the diathesis-stress perspective, genetic researchers believe that some people inherit a biological predisposition to schizophrenia and develop the disorder later when they face extreme stress, usually during late adolescence or early adulthood (Javitt & Coyle, 2004; Tsuang et al., 2001). The genetic view has been supported by studies of (1) relatives of people with schizophrenia, (2) twins with this disorder, (3) people with schizophrenia who are adopted, and (4) genetic linkage and molecular biology.

ARE RELATIVES VULNERABLE? Family pedigree studies have found repeatedly that schizophrenia is more common among relatives of people with the disorder (Gottesman & Reilly, 2003; Maier et al., 2002; Kendler et al., 1994, 1993). And the more closely related the relatives are to the person with schizophrenia, the greater their likelihood of developing the disorder (see Figure 12-2).

IS AN IDENTICAL TWIN AT GREATER RISK THAN A FRATERNAL TWIN? Twins, who are among the closest of relatives, have received particular study by schizophrenia researchers. If both members of a pair of twins have a particular trait, they are said to be *concordant* for that trait. If genetic factors are at work in schizophrenia, identical twins (who share all genes) should have a higher concordance rate for this disorder than fraternal twins (who share only some genes). This expectation has been supported consistently by research (Javitt & Coyle, 2004; Tsuang, 2000; Gottesman, 1991). Studies have found that if one identical twin develops schizophrenia, there is a 48 percent chance that the other twin will do so as well. If the twins are fraternal, on the other hand, the second twin has around a 17 percent chance of developing the disorder.

ARE THE BIOLOGICAL RELATIVES OF AN ADOPTEE VULNERABLE? Adoption studies look at adults with schizophrenia who were adopted as infants and compare them with both their biological and their adoptive relatives. Because they were reared apart from their biological relatives, similar symptoms in those relatives would indicate genetic influences. Conversely, similarities to their adoptive relatives would suggest environmental influences. Repeatedly, researchers have found that the biological relatives of adoptees with schizophrenia are more likely to experience schizophrenia or a

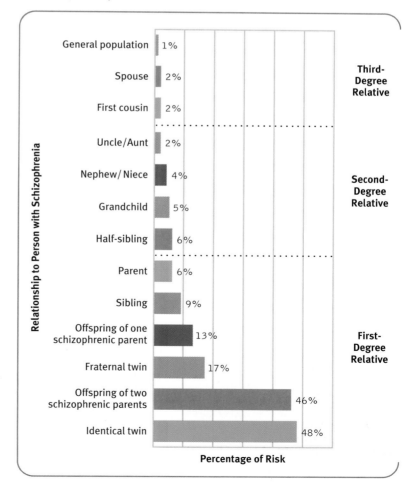

FIGURE 12-2 **Family links** *People who are biologically related to individuals with schizophrenia have a heightened risk of developing the disorder during their lifetimes. The closer the biological relationship (that is, the more similar the genetic makeup), the greater the risk of developing the disorder. (Adapted from Gottesman, 1991, p. 96.)*

Table 12-2

An Array of Psychotic Disorders

DISORDER	KEY FEATURES	LIFETIME DURATION	PREVALENCE
Schizophrenia	Various psychotic symptoms such as delusions, hallucinations, disorganized speech, flat or inappropriate affect, and catatonia	6 months or more	1.0%
Brief psychotic disorder	Various psychotic symptoms such as delusions, hallucinations, disorganized speech, flat or inappropriate affect, and catatonia	Less than 1 month	Unknown
Schizophreniform disorder	Various psychotic symptoms such as delusions, hallucinations, disorganized speech, flat or inappropriate affect, and catatonia	1 to 5 months	0.2%
Schizoaffective disorder	Marked symptoms of both schizophrenia and a mood disorder	6 months or more	Unknown
Delusional disorder	Persistent delusions that are not bizarre and not due to schizophrenia; persecutory, jealous, grandiose, and somatic delusions are common.	1 month or more	0.1%
Shared psychotic disorder	Person adopts delusions that are held by another individual, such as a parent or sibling; Also known as *folie à deux*	No minimum length	Unknown
Psychotic disorder due to a general medical condition	Hallucinations or delusions caused by a medical illness or brain damage	No minimum length	Unknown
Substance-induced psychotic disorder	Hallucinations or delusions caused directly by a substance, such as an abused drug	No minimum length	Unknown

related disorder (see Table 12-2) than their adoptive relatives (Janicak et al., 2001; Kety, 1988, 1968).

WHAT DO GENETIC LINKAGE AND MOLECULAR BIOLOGY STUDIES SUGGEST? As with bipolar disorders (see Chapter 7), researchers have run studies of *genetic linkage* and *molecular biology* to pinpoint the possible genetic factors in schizophrenia (Owen & O'Donovan, 2003). In one approach, they select large families in which schizophrenia is very common, take blood and DNA samples from all members of the families, and then compare gene fragments from members with and without schizophrenia. Applying this procedure to families from around the world, various studies have identified possible gene defects on chromosomes 1, 5, 6, 8, 9, 10, 11, 13, 18, 19, and 22, each of which may predispose individuals to develop schizophrenia (Badner & Gershon, 2002; Kendler et al., 2000; Pulver, 2000).

These varied findings may indicate that some of the suspected gene sites are cases of mistaken identity and do not actually contribute to schizophrenia. Alternatively, it may be that different kinds of schizophrenia are linked to different genes. Or perhaps, like a number of other disorders, schizophrenia is caused by a combination of gene defects (Javitt & Coyle, 2004; Joober et al., 2002).

How might genetic factors lead to the development of schizophrenia? Research has pointed to two kinds of biological abnormalities that could conceivably be inherited—*biochemical abnormalities* and *abnormal brain structure.*

BIOCHEMICAL ABNORMALITIES We have seen that the brain is made up of neurons whose impulses (or "messages") are carried from one to another by neurotransmitters. After an impulse arrives at a receiving neuron, it travels down the body

>>**PSYCH•NOTES**

Public Opinion Today two-thirds of people surveyed believe that genetic inheritance is a cause of schizophrenia and depression (NAMI, 1996).<<

Genetic Foundation More than half of the estimated 100,000 genes in human DNA seem to be dedicated to building and maintaining the nervous system (Cuticchia, 2000; Nash, 1997).<<

of that neuron until it reaches the nerve ending. The nerve ending then releases neurotransmitters that travel to and attach to receptors on yet another neuron, thus relaying the message to the next "station" by causing that neuron to fire.

Over the past three decades, researchers have developed a **dopamine hypothesis** to explain their findings on schizophrenia: certain neurons that use the neurotransmitter dopamine fire too often and transmit too many messages, thus producing the symptoms of the disorder (Grilly, 2002). This hypothesis has undergone adjustments in recent years, but it is still the foundation for present biochemical explanations of schizophrenia. The chain of events leading to this hypothesis began with the accidental discovery of **antipsychotic drugs**, medications that help remove the symptoms of schizophrenia. The first group of antipsychotic medications, the **phenothiazines**, were discovered in the 1950s by researchers who were looking for better *antihistamine* drugs to combat allergies. Although phenothiazines failed as antihistamines, their effectiveness in reducing schizophrenic symptoms became obvious, and clinicians began to prescribe them widely.

Researchers soon learned that these early antipsychotic drugs often produce troublesome muscular tremors, symptoms that are identical to the central symptom of *Parkinson's disease*, a disabling neurological illness. This undesired reaction to antipsychotic drugs gave researchers their first important clue to the biology of schizophrenia. Scientists already knew that people who suffer from Parkinson's disease have abnormally low levels of the neurotransmitter dopamine in some areas of the brain and that lack of dopamine is the reason for their uncontrollable shaking. If antipsychotic drugs produce Parkinsonian symptoms in persons with schizophrenia while removing their psychotic symptoms, perhaps the drugs reduce dopamine activity. And, scientists reasoned further, if lowering dopamine activity helps remove the symptoms of schizophrenia, perhaps schizophrenia is related to excessive dopamine activity in the first place.

Since the 1960s, research has supported and helped clarify the dopamine hypothesis. It has been found, for example, that some people with Parkinson's disease develop schizophrenic symptoms if they take too much L-dopa, a medication that raises dopamine levels in patients with that disease (Grilly, 2002; Carey et al., 1995). The L-dopa apparently raises the dopamine activity so much that it produces psychosis. Support has also come from research on *amphetamines*, drugs that, as we saw in Chapter 10, stimulate the central nervous system by increasing dopamine activity in the brain. Clinical investigators have observed that people who take high doses of amphetamines may develop *amphetamine psychosis*—a syndrome very similar to schizophrenia (Janowsky et al., 2001, 1973).

Investigators have located areas of the brain that are rich in dopamine receptors and have found that phenothiazines and other antipsychotic drugs bind to many of these receptors (Burt et al., 1977; Creese et al., 1977). Apparently the drugs are *dopamine antagonists*—drugs that bind to dopamine receptors, prevent dopamine from binding there, and so prevent the neurons from firing (Iversen, 1975). Researchers have identified five kinds of dopamine receptors in the brain—called the D-1, D-2, D-3, D-4, and D-5 receptors—and have found that phenothiazines bind most strongly to the *D-2 receptors* (Grilly, 2002).

These and related findings suggest that in schizophrenia, messages traveling from dopamine-sending neurons to dopamine receptors on other neurons, particularly to the D-2 receptors, may be transmitted too easily or too often. This theory is appealing because certain dopamine neurons are known to play a key role in guiding attention (Cohen et al., 1988). People whose attention is severely disturbed by excessive dopamine activity might well be expected to suffer from the problems of attention, perception, and thought found in schizophrenia.

Though enlightening, the dopamine hypothesis has certain problems. The greatest challenge to it has come with the recent discovery of a new group of antipsychotic drugs, referred to as **atypical antipsychotics**, which are often more

DOPAMINE HYPOTHESIS The theory that schizophrenia results from excessive activity of the neurotransmitter dopamine.

ANTIPSYCHOTIC DRUGS Drugs that help correct grossly confused or distorted thinking.

PHENOTHIAZINES A group of antihistamine drugs that became the first group of effective antipsychotic medications.

ATYPICAL ANTIPSYCHOTIC DRUGS A new group of antipsychotic drugs whose biological action is different from that of the traditional antipsychotic drugs.

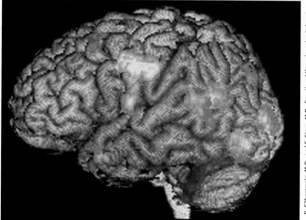

The human brain during hallucinations *This PET scan, taken at the moment a subject was experiencing auditory and visual hallucinations, shows heightened activity (yellow-orange) in hearing-related tissues at the brain's surface (Silbersweig et al., 1995). Conversely, the front of the brain, which is responsible for determining the source of sounds and other sensations, was quiet during the hallucinations. Thus a person who is hallucinating seems to hear sounds produced by his or her own brain, but the brain cannot recognize that the sounds are actually coming from within.*

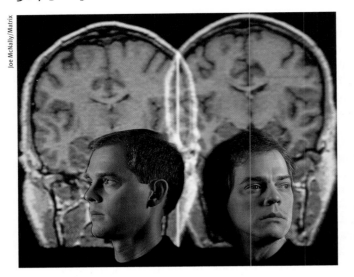

Not-so-identical twins *The man on the left is normal, while his identical twin, on the right, has schizophrenia. Magnetic resonance imaging (MRI), shown in the background, reveals that the brain of the twin with schizophrenia is smaller overall than his brother's and has larger ventricles, indicated by the dark butterfly-shaped spaces.*

effective than the traditional ones. The new drugs bind not only to D-2 dopamine receptors, like the traditional drugs, but also to many D-1 receptors and to receptors for other neurotransmitters such as *serotonin*. Thus, it may be that schizophrenia is related to abnormal activity or interactions of both dopamine and serotonin and perhaps other neurotransmitters as well, rather than to abnormal dopamine activity alone (Javitt & Coyle, 2004; Meltzer, 2002).

ABNORMAL BRAIN STRUCTURE During the past decade, researchers also have linked schizophrenia, particularly Type II schizophrenia, to abnormalities in brain structure. Using CAT and MRI scanning techniques, they have found, for example, that many people with schizophrenia have *enlarged ventricles*—the brain cavities that contain cerebrospinal fluid (Cahn et al., 2002; Torrey, 2002, 2001; Lieberman et al., 2001). Furthermore, patients who have enlarged ventricles tend to display Type II rather than Type I schizophrenia; that is, more negative symptoms, fewer positive symptoms, a poorer social adjustment prior to the disorder, and greater cognitive disturbances (Bornstein et al., 1992).

It may be that enlarged ventricles are actually a sign that nearby parts of the brain have not developed properly or have been damaged, and perhaps these problems are the ones that help produce schizophrenia, at least Type II schizophrenia. In fact, studies suggest that some patients with this disorder also have smaller temporal lobes and frontal lobes than other people, smaller amounts of cortical gray matter, and, perhaps most important, abnormal blood flow in certain areas of the brain (Kasai et al., 2003; Weinberger, 2002). Still other studies have linked schizophrenia to problems in the hippocampus, amygdala, and thalamus, among other brain areas (Spaniel et al., 2003; Seidman et al., 2002).

VIRAL PROBLEMS What might cause the biochemical and structural abnormalities found in many cases of schizophrenia? Various studies have pointed to genetic factors, poor nutrition, fetal development, birth complications, immune reactions,

The brain bank *At St. Elizabeths Hospital in Washington, DC, E. Fuller Torrey holds the brain of a person who had schizophrenia. Under Torrey's direction, more than 100 such brains have been gathered at the hospital brain bank, where they sit frozen in bucket-sized plastic tubs, available for study by researchers around the world.*

THE**CURRENT SCENE**

Postpartum Psychosis: The Case of Andrea Yates

On the morning of June 20, 2001, the nation's television viewers watched in horror as officials escorted 36-year-old Andrea Yates to a police car. Just minutes before, she had called police and explained that she had drowned her five children in the bathtub because "they weren't developing correctly" and because she "realized [she had not been] a good mother to them." Homicide sergeant Eric Mehl recalled how she twice recounted the order in which the children had died: first 3-year-old Paul, then 2-year-old Luke, followed by 5-year-old John and 6-month-old Mary. She then described how she had had to drag 7-year-old Noah to the bathroom and how he had come up twice as he fought for air. Later she told doctors she wanted her hair shaved so she could see the number 666—the mark of the Antichrist—on her scalp (Roche, 2002).

In Chapter 7 we observed that as many as 80 percent of mothers experience "baby blues" soon after giving birth, while between 10 and 30 percent display the clinical syndrome of *postpartum depression*. Yet another postpartum disorder that has become all too familiar to the public in recent times, by way of cases such as that of Andrea Yates, is *postpartum psychosis*.

Postpartum psychosis affects about one in 1,000 mothers who have recently given birth. Within days or at most a few months of childbirth, the woman develops signs of losing touch with reality, such as delusions (for example, she may become convinced that her baby is the devil); hallucinations (perhaps hearing voices); extreme anxiety, confusion, and disorientation; disturbed sleep; and illogical or chaotic thoughts (for example, thoughts about killing herself or her child) (Nonacs, 2002).

Women with a history of bipolar disorder, schizophrenia, or depression are particularly vulnerable to the disorder (Nonacs, 2002). In addition, women who have previously experienced postpartum depression or postpartum psychosis have an increased likelihood of developing this disorder after subsequent births

(Ruta & Cohen, 1998). Andrea Yates, for example, had developed signs of postpartum depression (and perhaps postpartum psychosis) and attempted suicide after the birth of her fourth child. At that time, however, she appeared to respond well to a combination of medications, including antipsychotic drugs, and so she and her husband later decided to conceive a fifth child. Although they were warned that she was at risk for serious postpartum symptoms once again, they believed that the same combination of medications would help if the symptoms were to recur (King, 2002).

After the birth of her fifth child, the symptoms did in fact recur, along with features of psychosis. Yates again attempted suicide. Although she was hospitalized twice and treated with a variety of medications, her condition failed to improve as medications were added and withdrawn. Six months after giving birth to Mary, her fifth child, she drowned all five of her children.

Most clinicians who are knowledgeable about this rare disorder agree that Yates was indeed a victim of postpartum psychosis. Although only a fraction of women with the disorder actually harm their children, the Yates case reminds us that such an outcome is indeed possible

(Dobson & Sales, 2000). The case also reminds us that early detection and intervention are critical.

Could more have been done for this woman as her disorder was progressing? Obviously. And, in fact, fingers have been pointed at her husband, her doctors, her insurers, and others who failed to appreciate or respond properly to the severity of her disorder, failed to make long-term hospitalization available to her, offered her little in the way of treatment options, allowed her to be alone at home with her children while her stress built up and her symptoms continued, and failed to dissuade her from having a fifth child.

On March 13, 2002, a Texas jury found Andrea Yates guilty of murdering her children and she was sentenced to life in prison. She had pleaded *not guilty by reason of insanity* during her trial, but the jury concluded that despite her profound disorder (which even the prosecutors had acknowledged), she did know right from wrong. The jury reached its verdict after 3 hours and 40 minutes of deliberation. The verdict itself stirred debate throughout the United States, but clinicians and the public alike were united in the belief that, at the very least, the mental health system had tragically failed this woman and her five children.

Courtesy of Yates Family/Getty Images

Family tragedy *In this undated photograph, Andrea Yates poses with her husband and four of the five children she later drowned.*

>>PSYCH•NOTES

Rapid Growth At birth, neurons in the human brain form more than 50 trillion synapses or connections. That number increases twentyfold to more than 1,000 trillion in the first months of life (Begley, 1997).

Brain Size The human brain is approximately one-quarter its final size at birth; the rest of the body is one-twentieth (Swerdlow, 1995).<<

and toxins (Andreasen, 2001; McNeil & Cantor-Graae, 2001). In addition, some investigators suggest that the brain abnormalities may result from exposure to *viruses* before birth. Perhaps the viruses enter the fetus's brain and remain quiet until puberty or young adulthood, when, activated by changes in hormones or by another viral infection, they may help to bring about schizophrenic symptoms (Gherardelli et al., 2002; Torrey, 2001, 1991).

Circumstantial evidence for the viral theory comes from the unusually large number of people with schizophrenia born during the winter (Torrey, 2001, 1991). The winter birth rate among people with schizophrenia is around 8 percent higher than among other persons. This finding could be due to an increase in fetal or infant exposure to viruses at that time of year. More direct evidence comes from studies showing that mothers of persons with schizophrenia were more often exposed to the influenza virus during pregnancy (particularly during the second trimester) than mothers of people without schizophrenia (de Messias et al., 2001; Torrey et al., 1994). And, finally, studies have found antibodies to *pestiviruses*, a particular group of viruses usually found in animals, in the blood of 40 percent of subjects with schizophrenia (Yolken et al., 2000; 1993; Torrey et al., 1994). The presence of such antibodies suggests that the subjects were at some time exposed to pestiviruses.

Together, the biochemical, brain structure, and viral findings are beginning to shed much light on the mysteries of schizophrenia. At the same time, it is important to recognize that many people who have these biological abnormalities never develop schizophrenia. Why not? Possibly, as we noted earlier, because biological factors merely set the stage for schizophrenia, while key psychological and sociocultural factors must be present for the disorder to appear.

Psychological Views

When schizophrenia investigators began to identify genetic and biological factors during the 1950s and 1960s, many clinicians abandoned the psychological and sociocultural theories of the disorder. Currently, however, psychological and sociocultural factors are once again considered important pieces of the schizophrenia puzzle. The leading psychological theories have come from the psychodynamic and cognitive perspectives.

THE PSYCHODYNAMIC EXPLANATION Freud (1924, 1915, 1914) believed that schizophrenia develops from two psychological processes: (1) *regression* to a pre-ego stage and (2) efforts to *reestablish* ego control. He proposed that when their world is extremely harsh or withholding—for example, when parents are cold or unnurturing—people who develop schizophrenia regress to the earliest point in their development, to the pre-ego state of *primary narcissism*, in which they recognize and meet only their own needs. Their near-total regression leads to self-centered symptoms such as neologisms, loose associations, and delusions of grandeur. Once people regress to such an infantile state, Freud continued, they then try to reestablish ego control and contact with reality. Their efforts give rise to yet other schizophrenic symptoms. Auditory hallucinations, for example, may be an individual's attempt to substitute for a lost sense of reality.

Years later, the noted psychodynamic clinician Frieda Fromm-Reichmann (1948) elaborated on Freud's notion that cold or unnurturing parents may set schizophrenia in motion. She described the mothers of people who develop this disorder as cold, domineering, and uninterested in their children's needs. According to Fromm-Reichmann, these mothers may appear to be self-sacrificing but are actually using their children to meet their own needs. At once overprotective and rejecting, they confuse their children and set the stage for schizophrenic functioning. She called them **schizophrenogenic** (schizophrenia-causing) **mothers**.

"And only you can hear this whistle?"

Fromm-Reichmann's theory, like Freud's, has received little research support (Willick, 2001). The majority of people with schizophrenia do not appear to have mothers who fit the schizophrenogenic description. Most of today's psychodynamic theorists have, in fact, rejected the views of Freud and Fromm-Reichmann. Although the theorists may retain some of the early notions (Spielrein, 1995), more and more of them believe that biological abnormalities leave certain persons particularly prone to extreme regression or other unconscious acts that may contribute to schizophrenia (Willick et al., 1998).

THE COGNITIVE VIEW A leading cognitive explanation of schizophrenia agrees with the biological view that during hallucinations and related perceptual difficulties the brains of people with schizophrenia are actually producing strange and unreal sensations—sensations triggered by biological factors. According to the cognitive explanation, however, further features of the disorder emerge when the individuals attempt to understand their unusual experiences. When first confronted by voices, visions, or other troubling sensations, these people turn to friends and relatives. Naturally, the friends and relatives deny the reality of the sensations, and eventually the sufferers conclude that the others are trying to hide the truth. They begin to reject all feedback and may develop beliefs (delusions) that they are being persecuted (Garety, 1991; Maher, 1974).

Researchers have established that people with schizophrenia do indeed experience sensory and perceptual problems. As we saw earlier, many of them have hallucinations, for example, and most have trouble keeping their attention focused (APA, 2000; Elkins & Cromwell, 1994). But researchers have yet to provide clear, direct support for the cognitive notion that misinterpretations of such sensory problems actually produce a syndrome of schizophrenia.

Sociocultural Views

Sociocultural theorists, believing that people with mental disorders are victims of social forces, claim that *social labeling* and *family dysfunctioning* contribute to the development of schizophrenia. Although societal and family forces are considered important in the development of this disorder, research has not yet clarified what the precise causal relationships might be.

SOCIAL LABELING Many sociocultural theorists believe that the features of schizophrenia are influenced by the diagnosis itself (Modrow, 1992). In their opinion, society assigns the label "schizophrenic" to people who fail to follow certain norms of behavior. Once the label is assigned, justified or not, it becomes a self-fulfilling prophecy that leads to the development of many schizophrenic symptoms.

We have already seen the very real dangers of diagnostic labeling. In the famous Rosenhan (1973) study, discussed in Chapter 2, eight normal people presented themselves at various mental hospitals, complaining that they had been hearing voices utter the words "empty," "hollow," and "thud." They were quickly diagnosed as schizophrenic, and all eight were hospitalized. Although the pseudopatients then dropped all symptoms and behaved normally, they had great difficulty getting rid of the label and gaining release from the hospital. They also reported that staff members treated them and other patients as though they were invisible. "A nurse unbuttoned her uniform to adjust her brassiere in the presence of an entire ward of viewing men. One did not have the sense that she was being seductive. Rather, she didn't notice us." In addition, the pseudopatients described feeling powerless, bored, tired, and uninterested. The investigation demonstrates that the label "schizophrenic" can itself have a negative effect not just on how people are viewed but on how they themselves feel and behave.

FAMILY DYSFUNCTIONING A number of studies suggest that schizophrenia, like certain other mental disorders, is often linked to *family stress*

SCHIZOPHRENOGENIC MOTHER A type of mother—supposedly cold, domineering, and uninterested in the needs of others—who was once thought to cause schizophrenia in her child.

No, it's not "the King" *But surveys indicate that as many as one of every eight Americans believes that Elvis Presley is still alive—a belief that has led to numerous Elvis sightings at 7-Eleven stores around the country and encouraged an army of Elvis impersonators. Clinicians stop short of calling such beliefs delusions, however, noting that the Elvis loyalists do not hold on to their beliefs with a high degree of conviction. Most can be persuaded that Elvis has indeed "left the building."*

David Graham/Black Star

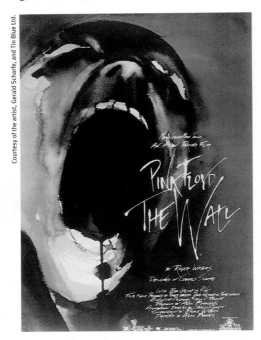

Courtesy of the artist, Gerald Scharfe, and Tin Blue Ltd.

"Is there anybody out there?" *Schizophrenia is a popular subject throughout the arts, where it is often depicted in positive terms. Pink Floyd's hugely popular album and movie* The Wall, *for example, follows the lead of certain sociocultural theorists and portrays the disorder as a constructive inward search undertaken by some persons in order to cure themselves of confusion and unhappiness caused by society.*

(Boye et al., 2002; Schiffman et al., 2002, 2001). Parents of people with this disorder often (1) display more conflict, (2) have greater difficulty communicating with one another, and (3) are more critical of and overinvolved with their children than other parents.

Family theorists have long recognized that some families are high in **expressed emotion**—that is, members frequently express criticism, disapproval, and hostility toward each other and intrude on one another's privacy (Hooley & Hiller, 2000). Individuals who are trying to recover from schizophrenia are almost four times more likely to relapse if they live with such a family than if they live with one low in expressed emotion (Linszen et al., 1997; Brown et al., 1962). Do such findings mean that family dysfunctioning helps cause and maintain schizophrenia? Not necessarily. It is also the case that individuals with schizophrenia greatly disrupt family life. In so doing, they themselves may help produce the family problems that clinicians and researchers continue to observe (Chou et al., 2002; Wuerker et al., 2002).

Although the sociocultural causes of schizophrenia, like the psychological causes, have yet to be fully understood, many clinicians currently believe that such factors play an important role in the disorder. As we have noted, most hold a diathesis-stress view of schizophrenia, believing that biological factors set up a predisposition to the disorder but that certain kinds of personal, family, or social stress may be needed for the syndrome to spring to life.

SUMMING UP | **How Do Theorists Explain Schizophrenia?**

The biological explanations of schizophrenia point to genetic, biochemical, brain structure, and viral causes. The leading biochemical explanation holds that the brains of people with Type I schizophrenia experience excessive dopamine activity. The leading brain structure explanation holds that certain brain structures are abnormal in the brains of people with Type II schizophrenia, as indicated by the enlarged ventricles and abnormal blood flow found in certain parts of their brains.

The leading psychological explanations for schizophrenia come from the psychodynamic and cognitive models. In influential psychodynamic explanations, Freud held that schizophrenia involves regression to a state of primary narcissism and efforts to restore ego control, and Fromm-Reichmann proposed that schizophrenogenic mothers help produce the disorder. Neither theory has received research support. Cognitive theorists hold that when people with schizophrenia try to understand their strange biological sensations, they develop delusional thinking.

One sociocultural explanation holds that society expects persons who are labeled as having schizophrenia to behave in certain ways and that these expectations actually lead to further symptoms. Another sociocultural view points to family dysfunctioning as a cause of schizophrenia. Research has not yet pinpointed the specific roles of such factors.

Most clinical theorists now agree that schizophrenia can probably be traced to a combination of biological, psychological, and sociocultural factors. However, the biological factors have been more precisely identified.

>>LAB•NOTES

A Rose by Any Other Name?

A study asked subjects to evaluate an individual based strictly on his label—a "schizophrenic," "person with schizophrenia," "person with severe mental illness," or "consumer of mental health services." Subjects had less negative reactions to the individual labeled a "consumer" and believed that he had fewer symptoms, was likely to improve, and was less responsible for his disorder (Penn & Nowlin-Drummond, 2001).<<

How Is Schizophrenia Treated?

They call us insane—and in reality they are as inconsistent as we are, as flighty and changeable. This one in particular. One day he derides and ridicules me unmercifully; the next he talks to me sadly and this morning his eyes misted over with tears as he told me of the fate ahead. Damn him and all of his wisdom!

> He has dinned into my ears a monotonous dirge—"Too Egotistical—too Egotistical—too Egotistical. Learn to think differently."—And how can I do it? How—how—can I do it? How the hell can I do it? I have tried to follow his suggestions but have not learned to think a bit differently. It was all wasted effort. Where has it got me?
>
> *(Jefferson, 1948)*

EXPRESSED EMOTION The general level of criticism, disapproval, and hostility expressed in a family. People recovering from schizophrenia are considered more likely to relapse if their families rate high in expressed emotion.

STATE HOSPITALS Public mental hospitals in the United States, run by the individual states.

With these words, Lara Jefferson, a young woman with schizophrenia, described her treatment experience in the 1940s. Her pain and frustration were typical of those experienced by hundreds of thousands of similar patients during that period of time. In fact, for much of human history, persons with schizophrenia were considered beyond help. The disorder is still extremely difficult to treat, but clinicians are much more successful today than they were in the past. Much of the credit goes to *antipsychotic drugs*, medications that help many people with schizophrenia think clearly and profit from therapies that previously would have had little effect on them. A look at how treatment has changed over the years will help us understand the nature, problems, and promise of today's approaches.

Institutional Care in the Past

For more than half of the twentieth century, most people with schizophrenia were *institutionalized* in a public mental hospital. Because patients with this disorder failed to respond to traditional therapies, the primary goals of these establishments were to restrain them and give them food, shelter, and clothing. Patients rarely saw therapists and were generally neglected. Many were abused. Oddly enough, this state of affairs unfolded in an atmosphere of good intentions.

As we saw in Chapter 1, the move toward institutionalization in hospitals began in 1793, when the French physician Philippe Pinel "unchained the insane" at La Bicêtre asylum and began the practice of "moral treatment." For the first time in centuries, patients with severe disturbances were viewed as human beings who should be cared for with sympathy and kindness. As Pinel's ideas spread throughout Europe and the United States, they led to the creation of large mental hospitals rather than asylums to care for those with severe mental disorders (Goshen, 1967).

These new mental hospitals were meant to protect patients from the stresses of daily life and offer them a healthful psychological environment in which they could work closely with therapists (Grob, 1966). States throughout the United States were even required by law to establish public mental institutions, **state hospitals**, for patients who could not afford private ones.

Eventually, however, the state hospital system faced serious problems. Between 1845 and 1955 nearly 300 state hospitals opened in the United States, and the number of hospitalized patients on any given day rose from 2,000 in 1845 to nearly 600,000 in 1955. During this expansion, wards became overcrowded, admissions kept rising, and state funding was unable to keep up.

The priorities of the public mental hospitals, and the quality of care they provided, changed over those 110 years. In the face of overcrowding and understaffing, the emphasis shifted from giving humanitarian care to keeping order. In a throwback to the asylum period, difficult patients were restrained and punished; individual attention disappeared. Patients were transferred to *back wards*, or chronic wards, if they failed to improve quickly (Bloom, 1984). Most of the patients on

Overcrowded conditions *A night nurse sits in the ward of a public mental hospital in 1956 darning socks while the patients sleep. The beds in the ward are crammed close together, leaving no personal space of any kind for the patients.*

Hulton Getty/Liaison Agency

STEPPING BACK

Lobotomy: How Could It Happen?

In 1949 a *New York Times* article reported on a medical procedure that appeared to offer hope to sufferers of severe mental disorders:

I Hypochondriacs no longer thought they were going to die, would-be suicides found life acceptable, sufferers from persecution complex forgot the machinations of imaginary conspirators. Prefrontal lobotomy, as the operation is called, was made possible by the localization of fears, hates, and instincts [in the prefrontal cortex of the brain]. It is fitting, then, that the Nobel Prize in medicine should be shared by Hess and Moniz. Surgeons now think no more of operations on the brain than they do of removing an appendix. I

We now know that the *lobotomy* was hardly a miracle treatment. Far from "curing" people with mental disorders, the procedure left thousands upon thousands extremely withdrawn, subdued, and even stuporous. The first lobotomy was performed by the Portuguese neuropsychiatrist Egas Moniz in 1935 (Tierney, 2000). His particular procedure, called a *prefrontal leukotomy*, consisted of drilling two holes in either side of the skull and inserting an instrument resembling an icepick into the brain tissue to cut or destroy nerve fibers. Moniz believed that severe abnormal thinking could be changed by cutting the nerve pathways that carried such thoughts from one part of the brain to another. In the 1940s Walter Freeman and his surgical partner, James Watts, developed a second kind of psychosurgery called the *transorbital lobotomy*, in which the surgeon inserted a needle into the brain through the eye socket and rotated it in order to destroy the brain tissue.

Why was the lobotomy so enthusiastically accepted by the medical community in the 1940s and 1950s? The

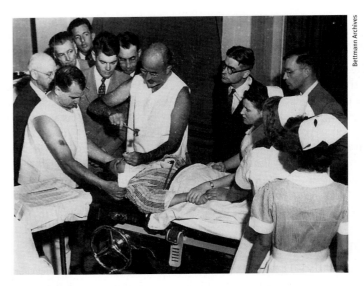

Lessons in psychosurgery *The neuropsychiatrist Walter Freeman performs a lobotomy in 1949 before a group of interested onlookers by inserting a needle through a patient's eye socket into the brain.*

neuroscientist Elliot Valenstein (1986) points first to the extreme overcrowding in mental hospitals at the time. This crowding was making it difficult to maintain decent standards in the hospitals. Valenstein also points to the personalities of the inventors of the procedure as important factors. Although they were gifted and dedicated physicians, Valenstein also believes that their professional ambitions led them to move too quickly and boldly in applying the procedure. Indeed, in 1949 Moniz was awarded the Nobel Prize for his work.

The prestige and diplomatic skills of Moniz and Freeman were so great and the field of neurology was so small that their procedures drew little criticism. Physicians may also have been misled by the seemingly positive findings of early studies of the lobotomy, which, as it turned out, were not based on sound methodology (Swayze, 1995; Valenstein, 1986). By the 1950s, better studies revealed that in addition to having a fatal-

ity rate of 1.5 to 6 percent, lobotomies could cause serious problems such as brain seizures, huge weight gain, loss of motor coordination, partial paralysis, incontinence, endocrine malfunctions, and very poor intellectual and emotional responsiveness. Finally, the discovery of effective antipsychotic drugs put an end to this inhumane treatment for mental disorders (Tierney, 2000).

Today's psychosurgical procedures are greatly refined and hardly resemble the lobotomies of 50 years back. Moreover, such procedures are considered experimental and used only as a last resort in the most severe cases of obsessive-compulsive disorder and depression (Kim et al., 2003; Weingarten & Cummings, 2001). Even so, many professionals believe that any kind of surgery that destroys brain tissue is inappropriate and perhaps unethical, and that it keeps alive one of the clinical field's most shameful efforts at cure (Bejerot, 2003).

these wards suffered from schizophrenia (Hafner & an der Heiden, 1988). The back wards were in fact human warehouses filled with hopelessness. Staff members relied on straitjackets and handcuffs to deal with difficult patients. More "advanced" forms of treatment included medical approaches such as lobotomy.

Institutional Care Takes a Turn for the Better

In the 1950s, clinicians developed two institutional approaches that finally brought some hope to patients who had lived in institutions for years: *milieu therapy*, based on humanistic principles, and the *token economy program*, based on behavioral principles. These approaches particularly helped improve the personal care and self-image of patients, problem areas that had been worsened by institutionalization. The approaches were soon adopted by many institutions and are now standard features of institutional care.

MILIEU THERAPY The principle behind **milieu therapy** is that institutions can help patients by creating a social climate, or milieu, that builds productive activities, self-respect, and individual responsibility. In such settings, patients are often given the right to run their own lives and make their own decisions. They may take part in institutional government and work with staff members to set up rules and decide penalities. The atmosphere is one of mutual respect, support, and openness. Patients may also take on special projects, jobs, and recreational activities. In short, their daily schedule is designed to resemble life outside the hospital.

Milieu-style programs have since been set up in institutions throughout the Western world. The programs vary from setting to setting, but at a minimum staff members try to encourage interactions (especially group interactions) between patients and staff, to keep patients active, and to raise patients' expectations of what they can accomplish.

Research over the years has shown that patients with schizophrenia in milieu hospital programs often improve and that they leave the hospital at higher rates than patients in programs offering primarily custodial care (Paul & Lentz, 1977; Cumming & Cumming, 1962). Many of these persons remain impaired, however, and must live in sheltered settings after their release. Despite such limitations, milieu therapy continues to be practiced in many institutions, often combined with other hospital approaches (Dobson et al., 1995).

THE TOKEN ECONOMY In the 1950s, behaviorists discovered that the systematic application of *operant conditioning* techniques on hospital wards could help change the behaviors of patients with schizophrenia (Ayllon, 1963; Ayllon & Michael, 1959). Programs that applied such techniques were named **token economy programs**.

In token economies patients are rewarded when they behave acceptably and are not rewarded when they behave unacceptably. The immediate rewards for acceptable behavior are often tokens that can later be exchanged for food, cigarettes, hospital privileges, and other desirable items, thus creating a "token economy." Acceptable behaviors likely to be targeted include caring for oneself and for one's possessions (making the bed, getting dressed), going to a work program, speaking normally, following ward rules, and showing self-control.

Researchers have found that token economies do help reduce psychotic and related behaviors (Kopelowicz et al., 2002; Emmelkamp, 1994). In one very successful program, Gordon Paul and Robert Lentz (1977) set up a hospital token economy for 28 patients with long-term schizophrenia, most of whom improved greatly. After four and a half years, 98 percent of the subjects had been released, mostly to sheltered-care facilities, compared with 71 percent of patients treated in a milieu program and 45 percent of patients who received custodial care only.

Despite the effectiveness of token economies, some clinicians have raised ethical and legal concerns about them. If token economy programs are to be effective, administrators need to control the important rewards in a patient's life, perhaps including such basic ones as food and a comfortable bed. But aren't there some things in life to which all human beings are entitled? Court decisions have ruled that patients do indeed have certain basic rights that clinicians cannot violate,

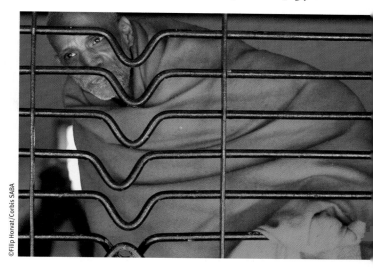

Incarceration posing as treatment *A mixture of clinical enlightenment and judicial decisions has led mental hospitals throughout the United States to place greater emphasis on treatment and patients' rights than they did in past times. However, patient restraint and confinement are still the primary "interventions" in many mental hospitals around the world. In this hospital in India, for example, patients are kept locked behind bars, much like criminals who have committed offenses against society.*

MILIEU THERAPY A humanistic approach to institutional treatment based on the belief that institutions can help patients recover by creating a climate that promotes self-respect, responsible behavior, and meaningful activity.

TOKEN ECONOMY PROGRAM A behavioral program in which a person's desirable behaviors are reinforced systematically throughout the day by the awarding of tokens that can be exchanged for goods or privileges.

regardless of the positive goals of a treatment program. They have a right to food, storage space, and furniture, as well as freedom of movement (Emmelkamp, 1994).

Still other clinicians have questioned the quality of the improvements made under token economy programs. Are behaviorists changing a patient's psychotic thoughts and perceptions or simply improving the patient's ability to *imitate* normal behavior? This question is raised by the case of a middle-aged man named John, who had the delusion that he was the U.S. government. Whenever he spoke, he spoke as the government. "We are happy to see you. . . . We need people like you in our service. . . . We are carrying out our activities in John's body." When John's hospital ward was made into a token economy, the staff members targeted his delusional statements and required him to identify himself properly to earn tokens. After a few months on the token economy program, John stopped referring to himself as the government. When asked his name, he would say, "John." Although staff members were understandably pleased with his improvement, John himself had a different view of the situation. In a private discussion he said:

> We're tired of it. Every damn time we want a cigarette, we have to go through their bullshit. "What's your name? . . . Who wants the cigarette? . . . Where is the government?" Today, we were desperate for a smoke and went to Simpson, the damn nurse, and she made us do her bidding. "Tell me your name if you want a cigarette. What's your name?" Of course, we said, "John." We needed the cigarettes. If we told her the truth, no cigarettes. But we don't have time for this nonsense. We've got business to do, international business, laws to change, people to recruit. And these people keep playing their games.
>
> *(Comer, 1973)*

Critics of the behavioral approach would argue that John was still delusional and therefore as psychotic as before. Behaviorists, however, would argue that at the very least, John's judgment about the effects of his behavior had improved.

Token economy programs are no longer as popular as they once were, but they are still used in many mental hospitals, usually along with medication. The approach has also been applied to other clinical problems, including mental retardation, delinquency, and hyperactivity, as well as in other fields, such as education and business (Spiegler & Guevremont, 2003).

Antipsychotic Drugs

Milieu therapy and token economy programs helped improve the gloomy outlook for patients with schizophrenia, but it was the discovery of *antipsychotic drugs* in the 1950s that truly revolutionized treatment for this disorder. These drugs eliminate many of its symptoms and today are almost always a part of treatment.

As we have observed, the discovery of antipsychotic medications dates back to the 1940s, when researchers were developing the first *antihistamine drugs* to treat allergies. The French surgeon Henri Laborit soon discovered that one group of antihistamines, *phenothiazines*, could also be used to help calm patients about to undergo surgery. Laborit suspected that the drugs might also have a calming effect on persons with severe psychological disorders. One of the phenothiazines, *chlorpromazine*, was eventually tested on six patients with psychotic symptoms and found to reduce their symptoms sharply. In 1954, it was approved for sale in the United States as an antipsychotic drug under the trade name Thorazine.

Since the discovery of the phenothiazines, other kinds of antipsychotic drugs have also been developed (see Table 12-3 on page 374). The ones developed throughout the 1960s, 1970s, and 1980s are now referred to as *conventional* antipsychotic drugs in order to distinguish them from the *atypical* antipsychotics that have been developed in recent years. The conventional drugs are also known as **neuroleptic drugs** because they often produce undesired movement effects similar to the symptoms of neurological diseases. As we saw earlier, the drugs reduce

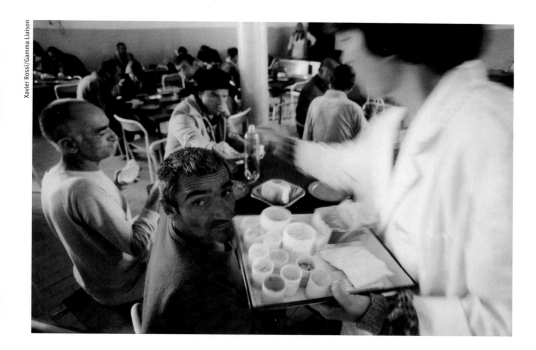

The drug revolution *Since the 1950s medications have become the center of treatment for patients hospitalized with schizophrenia and other severe mental disorders. The medications have resulted in shorter hospitalizations that last weeks rather than years.*

the symptoms of schizophrenia at least in part by blocking excessive activity of the neurotransmitter dopamine, particularly at the brain's dopamine D-2 receptors (Grilly, 2002).

How Effective Are Antipsychotic Drugs? Research has repeatedly shown that antipsychotic drugs reduce symptoms in the majority of patients with schizophrenia (Grilly, 2002). Moreover, in direct comparisons the drugs appear to be a more effective treatment for this disorder than any of the other approaches used alone, such as psychotherapy, milieu therapy, or electroconvulsive therapy (May, Tuma, & Dixon, 1981; May & Tuma, 1964). In most cases, the drugs produce the maximum level of improvement within the first six months of treatment (Szymanski et al., 1996); however, symptoms may return if patients stop taking the drugs too soon (Rzewuska, 2002).

Although antipsychotic drugs are now widely accepted, patients often dislike the powerful effects of the drugs—both intended and unintended—and some refuse to take them (Olfson et al., 2000). But like this man, they are typically helped by the medications.

> In my case it was necessary to come to terms with a specified drug program. I am a legalized addict. My dose: 100 milligrams of Thorazine and 60 milligrams of Stelazine daily. I don't feel this dope at all, but I have been told it is strong enough to flatten a normal person. It keeps me—as the doctors agree—sane and in good spirits. Without the brain candy, as I call it, I would go—zoom—right back into the bin. I've made the institution scene enough already to be familiar with what it's like and to know I don't want to go back.
>
> *(Snow, 1976)*

The Unwanted Effects of Conventional Antipsychotic Drugs In addition to reducing psychotic symptoms, the conventional antipsychotic drugs sometimes produce disturbing movement problems (Grilly, 2002). These effects are called **extrapyramidal effects** because they appear to be caused by the drugs' impact on the extrapyramidal areas of the brain, areas that help control motor activity.

The most common extrapyramidal effects are *Parkinsonian symptoms*, reactions that closely resemble the features of the neurological disorder Parkinson's

NEUROLEPTIC DRUGS Conventional antipsychotic drugs, so called because they often produce undesired effects similar to the symptoms of neurological disorders.

EXTRAPYRAMIDAL EFFECTS Unwanted movements, such as severe shaking, bizarre-looking grimaces, twisting of the body, and extreme restlessness, sometimes produced by conventional antipsychotic drugs.

Table 12-3

Antipsychotic Drugs

CLASS/GENERIC NAME	TRADE NAME
Conventional antipsychotics	
Chlorpromazine	Thorazine
Triflupromazine	Vesprin
Thioridazine	Mellaril
Mesoridazine besylate	Serentil
Piperacetazine	Quide
Trifluoperazine	Stelazine
Fluphenazine	Prolixin, Permitil
Perphenazine	Trilafon
Acetophenazine maleate	Tindal
Chlorprothixene	Taractan
Thiothixene	Navane
Haloperidol	Haldol
Loxapine	Loxitane
Molindone hydrochloride	Moban, Lidone
Pimozide	Orap
Atypical antipsychotics	
Risperidone	Risperdal
Clozapine	Clozaril
Olanzapine	Zyprexa
Quetiapine	Seroquel
Zipasidone	Zeldox

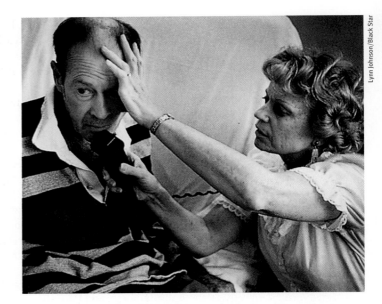

Unwanted effects *This man has a severe case of Parkinson's disease, a disorder caused by low dopamine activity, and his muscle tremors prevent him from shaving himself. The conventional antipsychotic drugs often produce similar Parkinsonian symptoms.*

disease. Patients may have severe muscle tremors and muscle rigidity; they may shake, move slowly, shuffle their feet, and show little facial expression (Janicak et al., 2001; APA, 2000). Some also display bizarre movements of the face, neck, tongue, and back, and a number experience great restlessness and discomfort in their limbs. In most cases, the symptoms can be reversed if an anti-Parkinsonian drug is taken along with the conventional antipsychotic drug (Grilly, 2002).

Whereas most of the undesired drug effects appear within days or weeks, a reaction called **tardive dyskinesia** (meaning "late-appearing movement disorder") does not usually unfold until after a person has taken conventional antipsychotic drugs for more than a year. This syndrome may include involuntary writhing or ticlike movements of the tongue, mouth, face, or whole body; involuntary chewing, sucking, and lip smacking; and jerky movements of the arms, legs, or entire body. It is believed that as many as 20 percent of the people who take the conventional drugs for an extended time develop tardive dyskinesia to some degree, and the longer the drugs are taken, the greater the risk becomes (Grilly, 2002; APA, 2000). Patients over 45 years of age seem to be at greater risk (Jeste et al., 1996). Tardive dyskinesia can be difficult, sometimes impossible, to eliminate. The longer patients are on the conventional antipsychotic drugs, the less likely it is that their tardive dyskinesia will disappear, even when the drugs are stopped.

Today clinicians are more knowledgeable and more cautious about prescribing conventional antipsychotic drugs than they were in the past. Previously, when patients did not improve with such a drug, their clinicians would keep increasing the dose (Kane, 1992); today a clinician will typically stop the drug (Coryell et al., 1998). Similarly, today's clinicians try to prescribe the lowest effective dose for each patient and to gradually reduce or stop medication weeks or months after the patient begins functioning normally (Torrey, 2001; Gilbert et al., 1995). However, it turns out that many patients cannot function without these medications (Tsuruta et al., 2003; Lerner et al., 1995).

TARDIVE DYSKINESIA Extrapyramidal effects that appear in some patients after they have taken conventional antipsychotic drugs for an extended time.

NEW ANTIPSYCHOTIC DRUGS New antipsychotic drugs have been developed in recent years (Alvarez et al., 2003; Meltzer, 2002). The most effective and widely used of these new drugs are *clozapine* (trade name Clozaril), *risperidone* (Risperdal), *olanzapine* (Zyprexa), *quetiapine* (Seroquel), and *ziprasidone* (Zeldox). The drugs are called *atypical* because their biological operation differs from that of the conventional antipsychotic medications. In fact, they appear to be more effective than the conventional drugs, helping as many as 85 percent of persons with schizophrenia, compared with the 65 percent helped by most of the conventional drugs (Citrome et al., 2002; Chakos et al., 2001). It is particularly promising that the new drugs also help patients who experience primarily negative symptoms (Type II schizophrenia)—people who do not respond well to the conventional drugs (Grilly, 2002; Lieberman et al., 1996). Another major benefit of the atypical antipsychotic drugs is that they cause fewer extrapyramidal symptoms and do not seem to produce tardive dyskinesia (Csernansky & Schuchart 2002; Kane, 2001). Given such advantages, it is not surprising that over half of all medicated patients with schizophrenia now take the atypical drugs (Torrey, 2001).

>>PSYCH•NOTES

Improper Dosage Recent interviews with over 700 people suffering from schizophrenia revealed that 39 percent of them were receiving too low a dosage of antipsychotic medication, 32 percent too high a dosage, and only 29 percent an appropriate dosage (PORT, 1998).<<

- -

Racial Difference Atypical antipsychotic drugs are more expensive than conventional antipsychotics. In turn, white Americans with schizophrenia are more likely to be prescribed the atypical drugs than are African Americans, a difference that may relate to the lower incomes and weaker insurance coverage plans typically available to African Americans (Mark et al., 2002).<<

Psychotherapy

Before the discovery of antipsychotic drugs, psychotherapy was not really an option for people with schizophrenia. Most were simply too far removed from reality to profit from it. Today, however, psychotherapy is successful in many cases of schizophrenia (Herz & Marder, 2002; Pilling et al., 2002). By helping to relieve thought and perceptual disturbances, the antipsychotic drugs allow people with schizophrenia to learn about their disorder, participate actively in therapy, think more clearly, and make changes in their behavior (Lublin, 2002; Svensson et al., 2000). The most helpful forms of psychotherapy include *insight therapy* and two broader sociocultural therapies—*family therapy* and *social therapy* (Pilling et al., 2002). Often these approaches are combined.

INSIGHT THERAPY A variety of insight therapies, from cognitive to psychodynamic, may be used in cases of schizophrenia (Johns et al., 2002; Pilling et al., 2002; Tarrier & Haddock, 2002). Such approaches may be offered in individual or group formats. Studies suggest that the particular orientations of insight therapists are often less important than their levels of experience with schizophrenia (Karon & Vandenbos, 1996). In addition, the therapists who are most successful tend to be those who take an active role, setting limits, expressing opinions, challenging patients' statements, providing guidance, displaying empathy, and gaining trust (Fox, 2000; Whitehorn & Betz, 1975).

FAMILY THERAPY Around 25 percent of persons who are recovering from schizophrenia live with family members: parents, siblings, spouses, or children (Torrey, 2001). Such situations create special pressures, so that even if family stress was not a factor in the onset of the disorder, a patient's recovery may be greatly affected by the behavior and reactions of the relatives at home. As we observed earlier, those living with relatives who display high levels of *expressed emotion*—that is, relatives who are very critical, emotionally overinvolved, and hostile—often have a higher relapse rate than those living with more positive and supportive relatives (Janicak et al., 2001).

For their part, family members may be greatly affected by the social withdrawal and unusual behaviors of a relative with schizophrenia (Boye et al., 2002; Creer & Wing, 1974). One individual complained, "In the evening you go into the sitting room and it's in darkness. You turn on the light and there he is just sitting there, staring in front of him."

© 1998 Sidney Harris

"I'M GLAD YOU CAME TO ME. VISIONS OF GHOSTS OF CHRISTMAS PAST, PRESENT AND FUTURE ARE CLEARLY DELUSIONS BASED ON UNDERLYING PSYCHOLOGICAL CONFLICTS."

DEINSTITUTIONALIZATION The discharge of large numbers of patients from long-term institutional care so that they might be treated in community programs.

COMMUNITY MENTAL HEALTH CENTER A treatment facility that provides medication, psychotherapy, and emergency inpatient care for psychological problems and coordinates treatment in the community.

AFTERCARE A program of posthospitalization care and treatment in the community.

DAY CENTER A program that offers hospital-like treatment during the day only. Also known as a *day hospital*.

HALFWAY HOUSE A residence for people with schizophrenia or other severe problems who cannot live alone or with their families, often staffed by paraprofessionals. Also known as a *group home* or *crisis house*.

To address such issues, clinicians now commonly include family therapy in their treatment of schizophrenia, providing family members with guidance, training, practical advice, education about the disorder, and emotional support and empathy (Bichsel, 2001; Pitschel et al., 2001). In family therapy, relatives develop more realistic expectations and become more tolerant, less guilt-ridden, and more willing to try new patterns of communication. Family therapy also helps the person with schizophrenia cope with the pressures of family life, make better use of family members, and avoid troublesome interactions. Research has found that family therapy—particularly when it is combined with drug therapy—helps reduce tensions within the family and so helps relapse rates go down (Falloon, 2002; Pilling et al., 2002).

The families of persons with schizophrenia may also turn to *family support groups* and *family psychoeducational programs* for assistance, encouragement, and advice (Chou et al., 2002; Johnson, 2002). In such programs, family members meet with others in the same situation to share their thoughts and emotions, provide mutual support, and learn about schizophrenia.

SOCIAL THERAPY Many clinicians believe that the treatment of people with schizophrenia should include techniques that address social and personal difficulties in the clients' lives. These clinicians offer practical advice; work with clients on problem solving, decision making, and social skills; make sure that the clients are taking their medications properly; and may even help them find work, financial assistance, and proper housing (Pratt & Mueser, 2002; McGuire, 2000). Research finds that this approach, called *social therapy* or *personal therapy*, does indeed help keep people out of the hospital (Hogarty, 2002; Hogarty et al., 1986, 1974).

The Community Approach

The broadest approach for the treatment of schizophrenia is the *community approach*. In 1963, partly in response to the terrible conditions in public mental institutions, the U.S. government ordered that patients be released and treated in the community. Congress passed the Community Mental Health Act, which provided that patients with psychological disorders were to receive a range of mental health services—outpatient therapy, inpatient treatment, emergency care, preventive care, and aftercare—in their communities rather than being transported to institutions far from home. The act was aimed at a variety of psychological disorders, but patients with schizophrenia, especially those who had been institutionalized for years, were affected most. Other countries around the world put similar community treatment programs into action shortly thereafter (Hafner & an der Heiden, 1988).

Thus began four decades of **deinstitutionalization**, an exodus of hundreds of thousands of patients with schizophrenia and other long-term mental disorders from state institutions into the community. On a given day in 1955 close to 600,000 patients were living in state institutions; today only around 60,000 patients reside in those settings (Torrey, 2001). Clinicians have learned that patients recovering from schizophrenia can profit greatly from community programs. As we shall see, however, the actual quality of community care for these people has been inadequate throughout the United States. The result is a "revolving door" syndrome: many patients have been released to the community, readmitted to an institution within months, released a second time, admitted yet again, and so on, over and over (Torrey, 2001).

Helping to meet the need *Because formal community services fall short for so many people with schizophrenia, the contributions of volunteers become especially important. Here a young man with schizophrenia tries a mountain bike while his volunteer friend of 12 years looks on. The volunteer was enlisted by Compeer Inc., an organization in Rochester, New York, dedicated to befriending community residents who have psychological disorders.*

David Duprey/AP Photo

WHAT ARE THE FEATURES OF EFFECTIVE COMMUNITY CARE?

People recovering from schizophrenia need medication, psychotherapy, help in handling daily pressures and responsibilities, guidance in making decisions, training in social skills, residential supervision, and vocational counseling—a combination of services sometimes called *assertive community treatment*. Those whose communities help them meet these needs make greater progress than people living in other communities (Zygmunt et al., 2002; McGuire, 2000). Some of the key features of effective community care programs are (1) coordination of patient services, (2) short-term hospitalization, (3) partial hospitalization, (4) supervised residencies, and (5) occupational training.

COORDINATED SERVICES When the Community Mental Health Act was first passed, it was expected that community care would center on a **community mental health center**, a treatment facility that would supply medication, psychotherapy, and inpatient emergency care to people with severe disturbances, as well as coordinate the services offered by other community agencies. When community mental health centers are available and do in fact provide these services, patients with schizophrenia often make considerable progress (Fenton et al., 2002; Scott & Dixon, 1995). Coordination of services is particularly important for the so-called *mentally ill chemical abusers* (*MICAs*), patients with both schizophrenia *and* a substance-related disorder. It is estimated that as many as half of all patients with schizophrenia also abuse alcohol or other drugs at some time during their disorder (Javitt & Coyle, 2004; Blanchard et al., 2000).

SHORT-TERM HOSPITALIZATION When people develop symptoms of schizophrenia, today's clinicians first try to treat them on an outpatient basis, usually with a combination of antipsychotic medication and psychotherapy (Marder, 1996). If this approach fails, *short-term hospitalization* that lasts a few weeks (rather than months or years) may be tried (Fenton et al., 2002). Soon after the patients improve, they are released for **aftercare**, a general term for follow-up care and treatment in the community.

PARTIAL HOSPITALIZATION People's needs may fall between full hospitalization and outpatient therapy, and so some communities offer **day centers**, or **day hospitals**, all-day programs in which patients return to their homes for the night. The day centers offer patients daily supervised activities, therapy, and programs to improve social skills. People recovering from schizophrenia in day centers often do better than those who spend extended periods in a hospital or in traditional outpatient therapy (Mayahara & Ito, 2002; Yoshimasu et al., 2002).

Another kind of institution that has become popular is the *semihospital*, or *residential crisis center*. Semihospitals are houses or other structures in the community that provide 24-hour nursing care for people with severe mental disorders (Torrey, 2001). Many individuals who would otherwise be cared for in state hospitals are now being transferred to these virtual hospitals (Fenton et al., 2002).

SUPERVISED RESIDENCES Many people do not require hospitalization but, at the same time, are unable to live alone or with their families. **Halfway houses**, also known as **crisis houses** or **group homes**, often serve these individuals well. Such residences may shelter between one and two dozen people. The live-in staff usually are *paraprofessionals*—lay people who receive training and ongoing supervision from outside mental health professionals. The houses are usually run with a *milieu therapy* philosophy that emphasizes mutual support, resident responsibility, and self-government. Research indicates that halfway houses help many people recovering from schizophrenia adjust to community life and avoid rehospitalization

From *The Power to Heal: Ancient Arts & Modern Medicine*, RX Media Group © Claus Meyer/Black Star

Art that heals *Art and other creative activities can be therapeutic for people with schizophrenia and other severe mental disorders. More than 250,000 pieces of patient-produced art are on display at the Museum of the Unconscious in Rio de Janeiro, Brazil, where supervisors work closely with patients every day. One of the museum's most famous and talented patients, Fernando Diniz, poses with some of his extraordinary artwork.*

(Hansson et al., 2002; McGuire, 2000). Here is how one woman described living in a halfway house after 10 hospitalizations in 12 years:

> The halfway house changed my life. First of all, I discovered that some of the staff members had once been clients in the program! That one single fact offered me hope. For the first time, I saw proof that a program could help someone, that it was possible to regain control over one's life and become independent. The house was democratically run; all residents had one vote and the staff members, outnumbered 5 to 22, could not make rules or even discharge a client from the program without majority sentiment. There was a house bill of rights that was strictly observed by all. We helped one another and gave support. When residents were in a crisis, no staff member hustled them off or increased their medication to calm them down. Residents could cry, be comforted and hugged until a solution could be found, or until they accepted that it was okay to feel bad. . . . Choices were real, and failure and success were accepted equally.
>
> *(Lovejoy, 1982, pp. 605–609)*

OCCUPATIONAL TRAINING Paid employment provides income, independence, self-respect, and the stimulation of working with others. It also brings companionship and order to one's daily life. For these reasons, occupational training and placement are important services for people with schizophrenia (Gaal et al., 2002; Bell et al., 1996).

Many people recovering from this disorder receive occupational training in a **sheltered workshop**—a supervised workplace for employees who are not ready for competitive or complicated jobs. For some, the sheltered workshop becomes a permanent workplace. For others, it is an important step toward better-paying and more demanding employment or a return to a previous job (Bustillo et al., 2001). In the United States, occupational training is not consistently available to people with severe mental disorders (Torrey, 2001; Drake et al., 1996). Some studies find that fewer than 15 percent of such people are competitively employed (Blyler, 2003).

HOW HAS COMMUNITY TREATMENT FAILED? There is no doubt that effective community programs can help people with schizophrenia recover (Bebbington et al., 2002). However, fewer than half of all the people who need them receive appropriate community mental health services (McGuire, 2000; PORT, 1998). In fact, in any given year, 40 to 60 percent of all people with schizophrenia and other severe mental disorders receive no treatment at all (Wang et al., 2002; Torrey, 2001). Two factors are primarily responsible: *poor coordination* of services and *shortage* of services.

POOR COORDINATION OF SERVICES The various mental health agencies in a community often fail to communicate with one another (Leshner et al., 1992). There may be an opening at a nearby halfway house, for example, and the therapist at the community mental health center may not know about it. In addition, even within a community agency a patient may not have continuing contacts with the same staff members. Still another problem is poor communication between state hospitals and community mental health centers (Torrey, 2001, 1997; Leshner et al., 1992). Sometimes community agencies are not even informed when patients are discharged from the hospital.

It is not surprising, then, that a growing number of community therapists have become **case managers** for people with schizophrenia. Like the social therapists described earlier, they offer therapy and advice, teach problem-solving and social skills, and ensure that medications are being taken properly. In addition, they try to coordinate available community services, guide clients through the community system, and, perhaps most important, help protect clients' legal

SHELTERED WORKSHOP A supervised workplace for people who are not yet ready for competitive jobs.

CASE MANAGER A community therapist who offers a full range of services for people with schizophrenia or other severe disorders, including therapy, advice, medication, guidance, and protection of patients' rights.

rights. Many professionals now believe that effective case management is the key to success for a community program (Zygmunt et al., 2002; Dozier, 1996).

SHORTAGE OF SERVICES The number of community programs available to people with schizophrenia falls woefully short. The roughly 800 community mental health centers now operating in the United States are only one-third of the number projected in the early 1960s. Halfway houses and sheltered workshops are in similarly short supply.

Also disturbing, the community mental health centers that do exist generally fail to provide adequate services for people with severe disorders. They tend to devote their efforts and money to people with less disabling problems, such as anxiety disorders or problems in social adjustment. Only a fraction of the patients treated by community mental health centers suffer from schizophrenia (Torrey, 2001).

Why is there such a shortage of services for people with schizophrenia? First, it appears that most mental health professionals simply prefer to work with people whose problems are less severe and shorter-term (Torrey, 2001; Lee et al., 1993). Second, neighborhood residents often object to the presence of community programs for patients recovering from schizophrenia (Cowan, 2002; Leshner et al., 1992). But perhaps the primary reason for the shortage of community care is economic. On the one hand, more public funds are available for people with psychological disorders now than in the past. On the other hand, rather little of this new money is going to community treatment programs for people with severe disorders. Much of it goes to monthly income payments such as social security disability income, to services for persons with mental disorders in nursing homes and general hospitals, and to community services for people who are less disturbed (Torrey, 2001; Stein, 1993). Today the financial burden of providing community treatment for persons with long-term severe disorders often falls on local governments and nonprofit organizations rather than the federal or state government, and local resources cannot always meet this challenge.

WHAT ARE THE CONSEQUENCES OF INADEQUATE COMMUNITY TREATMENT? What happens to persons with schizophrenia whose communities do not provide the services they need and whose families cannot afford private treatment (see Figure 12-3)? As we have observed, a large number receive no treatment at all; many others spend a short time in a state hospital or semihospital and are then discharged prematurely, often without adequate follow-up treatment (Torrey, 2001).

Many of the people with schizophrenia return to their families and receive medication and perhaps emotional and financial support, but little else in the way

>>LAB•NOTES
Public View

As part of an anti-stigma initiative, the World Psychiatric Association recently surveyed 1,200 subjects in order to assess public attitudes toward people with schizophrenia. Respondents rated "loss of mind" as more disabling than any other handicap. The majority also stated the belief that treatment does aid patients with schizophrenia and indicated a willingness to pay higher taxes to improve such treatment programs. At the same time, many expressed the belief that this disorder is linked to dangerousness (Thompson et al., 2002).<<

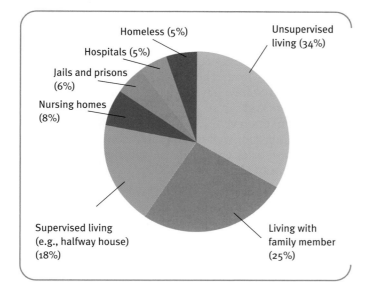

FIGURE 12-3 **Where do people with schizophrenia live?** *More than one-third live in unsupervised residences, 6 percent in jails, and 5 percent on the streets or in homeless shelters (Torrey, 2001).*

Society's forgotten people *Tens of thousands of homeless people in the United States suffer from schizophrenia or another severe mental disorder. The deinstitutionalization movement, failures in community treatment, and changing insurance priorities have left these individuals untreated and uncared for.*

of treatment. Around 8 percent enter an alternative institution such as a nursing home or rest home, where they receive only custodial care and medication (Torrey, 2001; Smyer, 1989). As many as 18 percent are placed in privately run residences where supervision is provided by untrained individuals—foster homes (small or large), boardinghouses, and similar facilities (Torrey, 2001). Another 31 percent of people with schizophrenia live in totally unsupervised settings. Some of these individuals are equal to the challenge of living alone, support themselves effectively, and maintain nicely furnished apartments. But many cannot really function independently and wind up in rundown single-room-occupancy hotels (SROs) or rooming houses, often located in inner-city neighborhoods (Torrey, 2001). They may live in conditions that are substandard and unsafe. Thus it is sometimes said that people with schizophrenia are now "dumped" in the community, just as they were once "warehoused" in institutions.

Finally, a great number of people with schizophrenia have become homeless (Javitt & Coyle, 2004). There are between 250,000 and 550,000 homeless people in the United States, and approximately one-third have a severe mental disorder, commonly schizophrenia (Torrey, 2001). Many such persons have been released from hospitals. Others are young adults who were never hospitalized in the first place. Another 135,000 or more people with severe mental disorders end up in prisons because their disorders have led them to break the law (Perez et al., 2003). Certainly deinstitutionalization and the community mental health movement have failed these individuals, and many report actually feeling relieved if they are able to return to hospital life (Drake & Wallach, 1992).

THE PROMISE OF COMMUNITY TREATMENT Despite these very serious problems, proper community care has shown great potential for assisting in the recovery from schizophrenia and other severe disorders, and clinicians and many government officials continue to press to make it more available. In recent years government and professional agencies have created task forces whose purpose is to find more effective ways for the federal government, states, and local organizations to meet the needs of people with such disorders (Knowlton, 1997; Leshner et al., 1992).

Another important development has been the formation of *national interest groups* in countries around the world that push for better community treatment (Johnson, 2002; Torrey, 2001). In the United States, for example, the *National Alliance for the Mentally Ill* began in 1979 with 300 members and has expanded to more than 220,000 members in 1,200 chapters (NAMI, 2002). Made up largely of relatives of people with severe mental disorders, this group has become a powerful lobbying force in state legislatures and has pressured community mental health centers to treat more persons with schizophrenia and other severe disorders.

Today community care is a major feature of treatment for people recovering from schizophrenia in countries around the world (Dencker & Dencker, 1995; Fog, 1995). Some countries, learning from the mistakes of deinstitutionalization in the United States, have organized their own community programs better and as a result have had more success with them (Honkonen et al., 2003; Perris, 1988). Both in the United States and abroad, well-coordinated community treatment is seen as an important part of the solution to the problem of schizophrenia (Melle et al., 2000).

Lobbying for better care *In a creative form of protest, members of the Florida Alliance for the Mentally Ill chained together figures without faces in 1997 and placed them outside the state capitol building. The members were reminding state legislators about the needs of the tens of thousands of faceless patients who are held captive by their disorders.*

SUMMING UP

How Is Schizophrenia Treated?

For more than half of the twentieth century, the main treatment for schizophrenia was institutionalization and custodial care. In the 1950s two in-hospital approaches were developed, milieu therapy and token economy programs. They often brought some improvement.

The discovery of antipsychotic drugs in the 1950s revolutionized the treatment of schizophrenia. Today they are almost always a part of treatment. Theorists believe that the first generation of antipsychotic drugs operate by reducing excessive dopamine activity in the brain. However, these "conventional" antipsychotic drugs can also produce dramatic unwanted effects, particularly movement abnormalities. One such effect, tardive dyskinesia, may develop after people have taken the drugs for an extended time. Recently "atypical" antipsychotic drugs have been developed, which seem to be more effective than the conventional drugs and to cause fewer unwanted effects.

Today psychotherapy is often used successfully in combination with antipsychotic drugs. Helpful forms include insight therapy, family therapy, and social therapy.

A community approach to the treatment of schizophrenia began in the 1960s, when a policy of deinstitutionalization in the United States brought about a mass exodus of hundreds of thousands of patients from state institutions into the community. Among the key elements of effective community care programs are coordination of patient services by a community mental health center, short-term hospitalization (followed by aftercare), day centers, halfway houses, and occupational training. However, the quality and funding of community care for people with schizophrenia have been inadequate throughout the United States, often resulting in a "revolving door" syndrome. One result is that many people with schizophrenia are now homeless or in jail.

CROSSROADS:
An Important Lesson

Schizophrenia—a bizarre and frightening disorder—was studied intensively throughout the twentieth century. Only since the discovery of antipsychotic drugs, however, have clinicians acquired any practical insight into its causes. As with most other psychological disorders, clinical theorists now believe that schizophrenia is probably caused by a combination of factors. At the same time, researchers have been far more successful in identifying the biological influences than the psychological and sociocultural ones. While biological investigations have closed in on specific genes, abnormalities in brain biochemistry and structure, and even viral infections, most of the psychological and sociocultural research has been able to cite only general factors, such as the roles of family conflict and diagnostic labeling. Clearly, researchers must identify psychological and sociocultural factors with greater precision if we are to gain a full understanding of the disorder.

The treatment picture for schizophrenia has also improved in recent decades. After years of frustration and failure, clinicians now have an arsenal of weapons to use against the disdorder—medication, institutional programs, psychotherapy, and community programs. It has become very clear that antipsychotic medications open the door for recovery, but in most cases other kinds of treatment are also needed to help the recovery process along. The various approaches must be combined in a way that meets each individual's specific needs.

Working with schizophrenia has taught clinicians an important lesson: no matter how compelling the evidence for biological causation may be, a strictly biological approach to the treatment of psychological disorders is a mistake more often than not (McCabe et al., 1999). Largely on the basis of pharmacological discoveries, hundreds of thousands of patients with schizophrenia and other severe mental disorders were released to their communities beginning in the 1960s. Little attention was paid to the psychological and sociocultural needs of these individuals, and many of them have been trapped in their pathology ever since. Clinicians must remember this lesson, especially in today's climate, when managed care and government priorities often promote medication as the sole treatment for psychological problems.

When Emil Kraepelin described schizophrenia at the end of the nineteenth century, he estimated that only 13 percent of its victims ever improved. Today, even with shortages in community care, many more such individuals show improvement (Torrey, 2001; McGuire, 2000). Certainly the clinical field has advanced considerably since Kraepelin's day, yet it still has far to go (Kane, 2001). It is unacceptable that the majority of people with this disorder receive few or none of the effective community interventions that have been developed, worse still that tens of thousands have become homeless. It is now up to clinicial professionals, along with public officials, to address the needs of all people with schizophrenia.

CRITICAL THOUGHTS

1. Some experts believe that erotomanic delusions are more common today than they were in the past. Why might this be? Do high-profile celebrity cases heighten or lower the probability that other cases of erotomanic delusions and stalking will emerge? *p. 354*

2. The psychodynamic explanations of schizophrenia reflect a long-standing tradition in the clinical field and in society of pointing to parents as key causes of mental disorders, even in cases where evidence is lacking.

Why are parents and family life so likely to be blamed? *pp. 366–367*

3. Rosenhan's pseudopatient study is one of the most controversial in the clinical field. What kinds of ethical, legal, and therapeutic concerns does it raise? *p. 367*

4. Why have people with schizophrenia been the victims of mistreatment (lobotomy or deinstitutionalization, for example) more often than people with other disorders? *pp. 368–381*

5. Should pharmaceutical companies have so much control over the cost and distribution of critical breakthrough drugs, such as antipsychotic drugs, that could improve millions of lives? *pp. 372–375*

6. The public often perceives people with schizophrenia as dangerous and violent even though most persons with this disorder are far from dangerous. Why does the public hold such a perception, and how can it be changed? *pp. 379–381, 354*

KEY TERMS

schizophrenia p. 351

psychosis p. 351

positive symptom p. 353

delusion p. 353

formal thought disorder p. 354

loose associations p. 354

hallucination p. 355

inappropriate affect p. 357

negative symptoms p. 357

alogia p. 357

flat affect p. 358

avolition p. 358

psychomotor symptom p. 358

catatonia p. 358

Type I schizophrenia p. 360

Type II schizophrenia p. 360

diathesis-stress relationship p. 361

dopamine hypothesis p. 363

Parkinson's disease p. 363

schizophrenogenic mother p. 366

expressed emotion p. 368

milieu therapy p. 371

token economy program p. 371

conventional antipsychotic drugs p. 372

atypical antipsychotic drugs p. 372, 375

extrapyramidal effects p. 373

tardive dyskinesia p. 374

deinstitutionalization p. 376

assertive community treatment p. 377

community mental health center p. 377

mentally ill chemical abuser (MICA) p. 377

aftercare p. 377

day center p. 377

halfway house p. 377

sheltered workshop p. 378

case manager p. 378

QUICK QUIZ

1. What is schizophrenia, and how prevalent is it? What is its relation to socioeconomic class, gender, and race? *pp. 351–352*

2. What are the positive, negative, and psychomotor symptoms of schizophrenia? *pp. 353–358*

3. What are the five types of schizophrenia identified by DSM-IV? What are the differences between Type I and Type II schizophrenia? *pp. 359–360*

4. Describe the genetic, biochemical, brain structure, and viral explanations of schizophrenia, and discuss how they have been supported in research. *pp. 361–366*

5. What are the key features of the psychodynamic, cognitive, social labeling, and family explanations of schizophrenia? *pp. 366–368*

6. Describe institutional care for people with schizophrenia over the course of the twentieth century. How effective are the token economy and milieu treatment programs? *pp. 369–372*

7. How do antipsychotic drugs operate on the brain, and how effective are they in the treatment of schizophrenia? What are the unwanted effects of these drugs? *pp. 372–375*

8. What kinds of psychotherapy seem to help people with schizophrenia? *pp. 375–376*

9. What is deinstitutionalization? What features of community care seem critical for helping people with schizophrenia? *pp. 376–378*

10. How and why has the community mental health approach been inadequate for people with schizophrenia? *pp. 378–381*

CYBER STUDY

SEARCH THE *FUNDAMENTALS OF ABNORMAL PSYCHOLOGY* CD-ROM FOR

▲ Chapter 12 Video Case Enrichment
How do hallucinations and delusions affect behavior?
How are relatives affected by a family member's psychosis?
Observe people before and after antipsychotic drug treatment

▲ Chapter 12 Practical, Research, and Decision-Making Exercises
Taking a "rational path to madness"
Distinguishing schizophrenia from substance-induced psychosis
Uncovering attitudes and biases toward severe mental disorders
Protecting the rights of people with severe mental disorders
Diagnosing psychotic disorders

▲ Chapter 12 Practice Test and Feedback

LOG ON TO THE COMER WEB PAGE FOR

▲ Suggested Web links, exercises, FAQ page, additional Chapter 12 practice test questions
<www.worthpublishers.com/comer>

‹‹‹

GIANPAOLO PAGNI, 2001

Personality Disorders

PERSONALITY A unique and long-term pattern of inner experience and outward behavior that leads to consistent reactions across various situations.

PERSONALITY DISORDER A very rigid pattern of inner experience and outward behavior that differs from the expectations of one's culture and leads to dysfunction.

While interviewing for the job of editor, Frederick said, "This may sound self-serving, but I am extraordinarily gifted. I am certain that I will do great things in this position, that I and the newspaper will soon set the standard for journalism in this city." The committee was impressed. Certainly, Frederick's credentials were strong, but even more important, his self-confidence and boldness had wowed them.

A year later, many of the same individuals were describing Frederick differently—arrogant, self-serving, cold, ego-maniacal, draining. He had performed well as editor (though not as spectacularly as he seemed to think), but that performance could not outweigh his impossible personality. Colleagues below and above him had grown weary of his manipulations, his emotional outbursts, his refusal ever to take the blame, his nonstop boasting, and his grandiose plans. Once again Frederick had outworn his welcome.

To be sure, Frederick had great charm, and he knew how to make others feel important, when it served his purpose. Thus he always had his share of friends and admirers. But in reality they were just passing through, until Frederick would tire of them or feel betrayed by their lack of enthusiasm for one of his self-serving interpretations or grand plans. Or until they simply could take Frederick no longer.

Bright and successful though he was, Frederick always felt entitled to more than he was receiving—to higher grades at school, greater compensation at work, more attention from girlfriends. If criticized even slightly, he reacted with fury, and was certain that the critic was jealous of his superior intelligence, skill, or looks. At first glance, Frederick seemed to have a lot going for him socially. Typically, he could be found in the midst of a deep, meaningful romantic relationship—one in which he might be tender, attentive, and seemingly devoted to his partner. But Frederick would always tire of his partner within a few weeks or months and would turn cold or even mean. Often he started affairs with other women while still involved with the current partner. The breakups—usually unpleasant and sometimes ugly—rarely brought sadness or remorse to him, and he would almost never think about his former partner again. He always had himself.

Each of us has a **personality**—a unique and long-term pattern of inner experience and outward behavior. We tend to react in our own predictable and consistent ways. These consistencies, often called *personality traits*, may be the result of inherited characteristics, learned responses, or a combination of the two. Yet our personalities are also flexible. We learn from experience. As we interact with our surroundings, we try out various responses to see which are more effective. This is a flexibility that people who suffer from a personality disorder usually do not have.

A **personality disorder** is a very rigid pattern of inner experience and outward behavior. The pattern is seen in most of the person's interactions, continues for years, and differs from the experiences and behaviors usually expected of people (see Table 13-1 on the next page). Frederick seems to display such a disorder. For most of his life, his narcissism, grandiosity, outbursts, and insensitivity to others have been excessive and have dominated his functioning. The rigid traits of people with personality disorders often

Table 13-1 **DSM-IV Checklist**

Personality Disorder

1. An enduring pattern of inner experience and behavior that deviates markedly from the expectations of the individual's culture, with at least two of the following areas affected:• cognition • affectivity • interpersonal functioning • impulse control.
2. Pattern is inflexible and pervasive across a broad range of personal and social situations.
3. Pattern is stable and long-lasting, and its onset can be traced back at least to adolescence or early adulthood.
4. Significant distress or impairment

Based on APA, 2000, 1994.

lead to psychological pain for the individual and social or occupational problems (Haslam et al., 2002). The disorders may also bring pain to others. Witness the turmoil experienced by Frederick's co-workers and girlfriends.

Personality disorders typically become recognizable in adolescence or early adulthood, although some start during childhood (APA, 2000, 1994). These are among the most difficult psychological disorders to treat. Many sufferers are not even aware of their personality problems and fail to trace their difficulties to their rigid style of thinking and behaving. It has been estimated that between 9 and 13 percent of all adults may have a personality disorder (Samuels et al., 2002; Mattia & Zimmerman, 2001).

As we saw in Chapter 3, DSM-IV separates Axis II disorders, disorders of long standing that usually begin well before adulthood and continue into adult life, from the Axis I disorders, more acute disorders that often begin as a noticeable change in a person's usual behavior and are, in many cases, of limited duration. The personality disorders are Axis II disorders; these patterns are not typically marked by changes in intensity or periods of clear improvement.

It is common for a person with a personality disorder to also suffer from an acute (Axis I) disorder, a relationship called *comorbidity* (Brieger et al., 2003, 2002). Perhaps personality disorders predispose people to develop certain Axis I disorders. For example, people with avoidant personality disorder, who fearfully shy away from all relationships, may be prone to develop a social phobia. Or certain Axis I disorders may set the stage for a personality disorder. Or perhaps some biological factor creates a predisposition to both (Koenigsberg et al., 2002, 1999). Whatever the reason for the relationship, research indicates that the presence of a personality disorder complicates a person's chances for a successful recovery from psychological problems (Tyrer & Simmonds, 2003; Mulder, 2002).

DSM-IV identifies 10 personality disorders and separates them into three groups, called *clusters* (APA, 2000, 1994). One group, marked by odd behavior, consists of the *paranoid*, *schizoid*, and *schizotypal* personality disorders. A second group features dramatic behavior and consists of the *antisocial*, *borderline*, *histrionic*, and *narcissistic* personality disorders. The final cluster features a high degree of anxiety and includes the *avoidant*, *dependent*, and *obsessive-compulsive* personality disorders.

The various personality disorders overlap so much that it can be difficult to distinguish one from the other (Gunderson & Ronningstam, 2001) (see Figure 13-1). In fact, diagnosticians sometimes determine that particular individuals have more than one personality disorder (Grilo et al., 2002). In addition, clinicians often disagree as to the correct diagnosis for people with personality disorders. This lack of agreement has raised serious questions about the *validity*

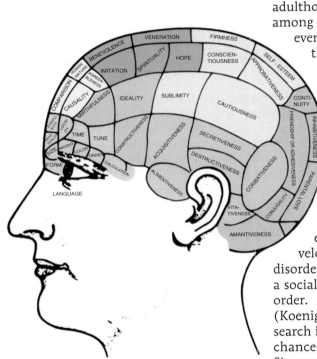

Early notions of personality *Scientists have long suspected that biological factors help account for personality and personality disorders. In the theory of* phrenology, *Franz Joseph Gall (1758–1828) held that the brain consists of distinct portions, each responsible for some aspect of personality. Phrenologists tried to assess personality by feeling bumps and indentations on a person's head.*

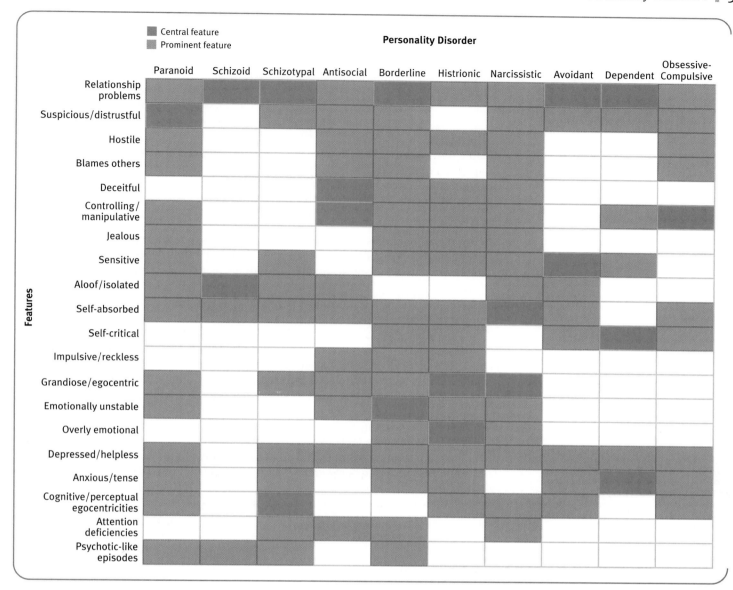

FIGURE 13-1 **Prominent and central features of DSM-IV's 10 personality disorders** *The symptoms of the various disorders often overlap greatly, leading to frequent misdiagnosis or to multiple diagnoses for a given client.*

(accuracy) and *reliability* (consistency) of the present DSM categories, a concern that we shall return to later in the chapter.

Finally, diagnoses of personality disorder can easily be overdone. We may catch glimpses of ourselves or of people we know in the descriptions of these disorders, and we may be tempted to conclude that we or they have a personality disorder. In the vast majority of instances, such interpretations are incorrect. We all display personality traits. Only occasionally are they so inflexible, maladaptive, and distressful that they can be considered disorders.

"Odd" Personality Disorders

The cluster of *"odd" personality disorders* consists of the *paranoid*, *schizoid*, and *schizotypal* personality disorders. People with these disorders typically display odd or eccentric behaviors that are similar to but not as extensive as those seen in schizophrenia, including extreme suspiciousness, social withdrawal, and peculiar ways of thinking and perceiving things. Such behaviors often leave the person isolated. Some clinicians believe that these personality disorders are actually related to schizophrenia, and they call them *schizophrenia-spectrum disorders*. In support of this idea, people with these personality disorders often qualify for an additional

PARANOID PERSONALITY DISORDER A personality disorder marked by a pattern of distrust and suspiciousness of others.

SCHIZOID PERSONALITY DISORDER A personality disorder characterized by persistent avoidance of social relationships and little expression of emotion.

diagnosis of schizophrenia or have close relatives with schizophrenia (Keown et al., 2002; APA, 2000, 1994).

Clinicians have learned much about the symptoms of the odd personality disorders but have not been so successful in determining their causes or how to treat them. In fact, people with these disorders rarely seek treatment (Fabrega et al., 1991).

Paranoid Personality Disorder

People with **paranoid personality disorder** deeply distrust other people and are suspicious of their motives (APA, 2000, 1994). Because they believe that everyone intends them harm, they avoid close relationships. Their trust in their own ideas and abilities can be excessive, though, as we see in the case of Charles:

> Charles, an only child of poorly educated parents, had been recognized as a "child genius" in early school years. He received a Ph.D. degree at 24, and subsequently held several responsible positions as a research physicist in an industrial firm.
>
> His haughty arrogance and narcissism often resulted in conflicts with his superiors; it was felt that he spent too much time working on his own "harebrained" schemes and not enough on company projects. Charles . . . began to feel that both his superiors and his subordinates were "making fun of him" and not taking him seriously. To remedy this attack upon his status, Charles began to work on a scheme that would "revolutionize the industry," a new thermodynamic principle which, when applied to his company's major product, would prove extremely efficient and economical. After several months . . . he presented his plans to the company president. Brilliant though it was, the plan overlooked certain obvious simple facts of logic and economy.
>
> Upon learning of its rejection, Charles withdrew to his home where he became obsessed with "new ideas," proposing them in intricate schematics and formulas to a number of government officials and industrialists. These resulted in new rebuffs which led to further efforts at self inflation.
>
> *(Millon, 1969, pp. 329–330)*

Partners at risk *It is estimated that spouse abuse occurs in 2 to 4 million homes in the United States each year. There is no one personality profile among men who batter their spouses, but at least some seem to manifest the symptoms of a personality disorder, such as the delusional jealousy of paranoid disorder or the antisocial, narcissistic, dependent, or controlling characteristics found in other personality disorders. A number of them also seem to manifest an intermittent explosive disorder (see p. 401).*

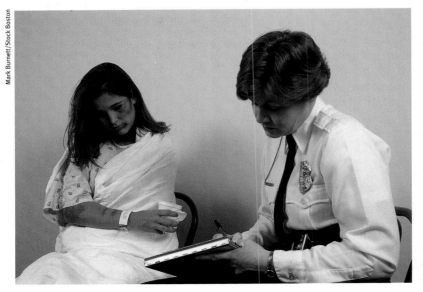

Mark Burnett/Stock Boston

Ever on guard and cautious, and seeing threats everywhere, people like Charles continually expect to be the targets of some trickery (see Figure 13-2). They find "hidden" meanings in everything, which are usually belittling or threatening. In a study that required individuals to role-play, subjects with paranoia were more likely than control subjects to read hostile intentions into the actions of others. In addition, they more often chose anger as the appropriate role-play response (Turkat et al., 1990).

Quick to challenge the loyalty or trustworthiness of those around them, people with paranoid personality disorder remain cold and distant. A woman might avoid confiding in anyone, for example, for fear of being hurt; or a husband might, without any justification, persist in questioning his wife's faithfulness. Although inaccurate, their suspicions are not usually *delusional*; the ideas are not so bizarre or so firmly held as to clearly remove the individuals from reality (Fenigstein, 1996).

People with this disorder are critical of weakness and fault in others, particularly at work. They are unable to recognize their own mistakes, however, and are extremely sensitive to criticism. They often blame others for the things that go wrong in their lives, and they repeatedly bear grudges. Between 0.5 and 3 percent of adults are believed to experience this disorder, apparently more men than women (Mattia & Zimmerman, 2001; APA, 2000, 1994).

HOW DO THEORISTS EXPLAIN PARANOID PERSONALITY DISORDER? The proposed explanations of paranoid personality disorder, like those of most other personality disorders, have received little systematic research. Psychodynamic theories, the oldest of the explanations for this disorder, trace the pattern to early interactions with demanding parents, particularly distant, rigid fathers and overcontrolling, rejecting mothers (Sperry, 2003). (We shall see that psychodynamic explanations for almost all the personality disorders begin the same way—with repeated mistreatment during childhood and lack of love.) According to one psychodynamic view, some individuals come to view their environment as unfriendly as a result of their parents' unreasonable demands. They must always be on the alert because they cannot trust others, and they are likely to develop feelings of extreme anger. They also project these feelings onto others and, as a result, feel increasingly persecuted (Garfield & Havens, 1991). Similarly, some cognitive theorists suggest that people with paranoid personality disorder generally hold maladaptive assumptions such as "People are evil" and "People will attack you if given the chance" (Beck et al., 2004, 2001).

Biological theorists propose that paranoid personality disorder has genetic causes (Jang & Vernon, 2001). A study that looked at self-reports of suspiciousness in 3,810 Australian twin pairs found that if one twin was excessively suspicious, the other had an increased likelihood of also being suspicious (Kendler et al., 1987). Once again, however, such similarities between twins might also be the result of common environmental experiences.

TREATMENTS FOR PARANOID PERSONALITY DISORDER
People with paranoid personality disorder do not typically see themselves as needing help, and few come to treatment willingly (Millon, 1999). Furthermore, many who are in treatment view the role of patient as inferior and distrust their therapists (Fenigstein, 1996). Thus it is not surprising that therapy for this disorder, as for most other personality disorders, has limited effect and moves very slowly (Piper & Joyce, 2001).

Object relations therapists, the psychodynamic therapists who give center stage to relationships, try to see past the patient's anger and work on what they view as his or her deep wish for a satisfying relationship (Auchincloss & Weiss, 1992). Behavioral and cognitive therapists, for their part, try to help these individuals control their anxiety and improve their skills at solving interpersonal problems. Cognitive therapists also try to guide the clients to develop more realistic interpretations of other people's words and actions and to become more aware of other people's points of view (Beck et al., 2004; Freeman, 2002). Drug therapy is of limited help (Koenigsberg et al., 2002).

Schizoid Personality Disorder

People with **schizoid personality disorder** persistently avoid and are removed from social relationships and show little in the way of emotion (APA, 2000, 1994). Like people with paranoid personality disorder, these individuals do not have close ties with others. The reason they avoid social contact, however, has nothing to do with paranoia—it is that they genuinely prefer to be alone. Take Roy:

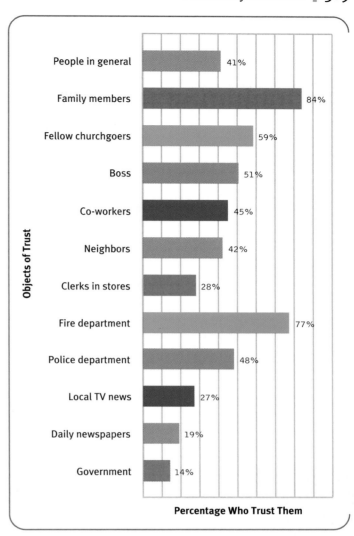

FIGURE 13-2 **Whom do you trust?** *Although distrust and suspiciousness are the hallmarks of paranoid personality disorder, even persons without this disorder are surprisingly untrusting. In a recent survey of a broad sample of society, only 41 percent of respondents said that they generally trust people. Most do trust their family members and local fire department; however, few trust clerks in stores, daily newspapers, or the government. (Adapted from* Pew Research Center for the People and the Press, 1997.)

>>IN THEIR WORDS

"The deepest principle of human nature is the craving to be appreciated."<<

William James

Roy was a successful sanitation engineer involved in the planning and mainte-nance of water resources for a large city; his job called for considerable foresight and independent judgment but little supervisory responsibility. In general, he was appraised as an undistinguished but competent and reliable employee. There were few demands of an interpersonal nature made of him, and he was viewed by most of his colleagues as reticent and shy and by others as cold and aloof.

Difficulties centered about his relationship with his wife. At her urging they sought marital counseling for, as she put it, "he is unwilling to join in family ac-tivities, he fails to take an interest in the children, he lacks affection and is disin-terested in sex."

The pattern of social indifference, flatness of affect and personal isolation which characterized much of Roy's behavior was of little consequence to those with whom a deeper or more intimate relationship was not called for; with his immediate family, however, these traits took their toll.

(Millon, 1969, p. 224)

People like Roy, often described as "loners," make no effort to start or keep friendships, take little interest in having sexual relationships, and even seem in-different to their families. They seek out jobs that require little or no contact with others. When necessary, they can form work relations to a degree, but they prefer to keep to themselves. Many live by themselves as well. Not surprisingly, their so-cial skills tend to be weak. If they marry, their lack of interest in intimacy may create marital or family problems, as it did for Roy.

People with schizoid personality disorder focus mainly on themselves and are generally unaffected by praise or criticism. They rarely show any feelings, express-ing neither joy nor anger. They seem to have no need for attention or acceptance; are typically viewed as cold, humorless, or dull; and generally suc-ceed in being ignored. This disorder is estimated to be present in fewer than 1 percent of the population (Mattia & Zimmerman, 2001). It is slightly more likely to occur in men than in women, and men may also be more limited by it (APA, 2000).

Joel Gordon, New York, NY

Alone, either way *Different personality disorders often yield similar behaviors. People with either schizoid or avoidant personality disorder spend much of their time alone. The former, however, truly want to be alone, whereas the latter yearn for but fear social relationships.*

HOW DO THEORISTS EXPLAIN SCHIZOID PERSONALITY DISORDER? Many psychodynamic theorists, particularly object relations theorists, propose that schizoid personality disorder has its roots in an unsatisfied need for human contact (Carstairs, 1992; Horner, 1991, 1975). The parents of people with this disor-der, like those of people with paranoid personality disorder, are be-lieved to have been unaccepting or even abusive of their children. Whereas individuals with paranoid symptoms react to such par-enting chiefly with distrust, those with schizoid personality disor-der are left unable to give or receive love. They cope by avoiding all relationships (Sperry, 2003).

Cognitive theorists propose, not surprisingly, that people with schizoid personality disorder suffer from deficiencies in their thinking and per-ceptual skills. Their thoughts tend to be vague and empty, and they have trouble scanning the environment to arrive at accurate perceptions (Beck & Freeman, 1990). Unable to pick up emotional signals from others, they simply cannot re-spond to emotions. As this theory might predict, children with schizoid personal-ity disorder develop language skills very slowly, whatever their level of intelligence (Wolff, 1991).

TREATMENTS FOR SCHIZOID PERSONALITY DISORDER Their social withdrawal prevents most people with schizoid personality disorder from entering therapy un-less some other disorder, such as alcoholism, makes treatment necessary. These clients are likely to remain distant from the therapist, seem not to care about their treatment, and make limited progress at best (Millon, 1999; Quality Assurance Project, 1990).

Cognitive therapists have sometimes been able to help people with this disorder experience more positive feelings and more satisfying social interactions (Beck et al., 2004; Freeman, 2002). Their techniques include presenting clients with lists of emotions to think about or having them write down and remember pleasurable experiences. Behavioral therapists have sometimes had success teaching social skills to such clients, using role-playing, exposure techniques, and homework assignments as tools (Piper & Joyce, 2001). Group therapy is apparently useful when it offers a safe setting for social contact, although people with this disorder may resist any pressure to take part (Piper & Joyce, 2001). As with paranoid personality disorder, drug therapy has offered only limited help (Koenigsberg et al., 2002).

Schizotypal Personality Disorder

People with **schizotypal personality disorder** display a range of interpersonal problems marked by extreme discomfort in close relationships, very odd patterns of thinking and perceiving, and behavioral eccentricities (APA, 2000, 1994). Anxious around others, they seek isolation and have few close friends. Many feel intensely lonely. The disorder is more severe than the paranoid and schizoid personality disorders, as we see in the case of Harold:

> Harold was the fourth of seven children. . . . "Duckie," as Harold was known, had always been a withdrawn, frightened and "stupid" youngster. The nickname "Duckie" represented a peculiar waddle in his walk; it was used by others as a term of derogation and ridicule. Harold rarely played with his sibs or neighborhood children; he was teased unmercifully because of his "walk" and his fear of pranksters. Harold was a favorite neighborhood scapegoat; he was intimidated even by the most innocuous glance in his direction. . . .
>
> Harold's family was surprised when he performed well in the first few years of schooling. He began to falter, however, upon entrance to junior high school. At about the age of 14, his schoolwork became extremely poor, he refused to go to classes and he complained of a variety of vague, physical pains. By age 15 he had totally withdrawn from school, remaining home in the basement room that he shared with two younger brothers. Everyone in his family began to speak of him as "being touched." He thought about "funny religious things that didn't make sense"; he also began to draw "strange things" and talk to himself. When he was 16, he once ran out of the house screaming "I'm gone, I'm gone, I'm gone . . . ," saying that his "body went to heaven" and that he had to run outside to recover it; rather interestingly, this event occurred shortly after his father had been committed by the courts to a state mental hospital. By age 17, Harold was ruminating all day, often talking aloud in a meaningless jargon; he refused to come to the family table for meals.
>
> *(Millon, 1969, pp. 347–348)*

As with Harold, the thoughts and behaviors of people with schizotypal personality disorder can be noticeably disturbed. These symptoms may include *ideas of reference*—beliefs that unrelated events pertain to them in some important way—and *bodily illusions*, such as sensing an external "force" or presence. A number of people with this disorder see themselves as having special extrasensory abilities, and some believe that they have magical control over others. Examples of schizotypal eccentricities include repeatedly arranging cans in a special alignment, organizing closets extensively, or wearing an odd assortment of clothing. The emotions of these individuals may be inappropriate, flat, or humorless.

People with this personality disorder often have great difficulty keeping their attention focused (Lenzenwerger et al., 1991). Correspondingly, their conversation

SCHIZOTYPAL PERSONALITY DISORDER
A personality disorder characterized by extreme discomfort in close relationships, odd forms of thinking and perceiving, and behavioral eccentricities.

>>LOOKING AROUND
A Common Belief

People who think that they have extrasensory abilities are not necessarily suffering from schizotypal personality disorder. In fact, according to one large survey, half of all people believe in ESP (Kanner, 1995).<<

Personality and the Brain: The Case of Phineas Gage

Most people are aware that damage to particular regions in the brain can lead to problems in movement, memory, or language, and even to the loss of particular senses such as vision or hearing. However, clinical scientists have come to appreciate that damage to the brain from strokes, injury, or tumors can also bring about major changes in personality. The tragic story of Phineas Gage provided science with history's most memorable evidence of this fact.

In mid-September 1848, 25-year-old Gage was laying tracks for a railroad, a hazardous but common occupation in those years. The smart, careful, and friendly Gage was liked by the men he supervised, and the company that wrote the paychecks called him "the most efficient and capable" employee they had. But that was all to change in a few seconds' time, when a rock-blasting mishap hurled a three-foot-long tamping iron under Gage's left cheek and straight through the top of his skull, piercing a one-and-a-half-inch hole through his brain's frontal lobes (Damasio, 1994).

Miraculously, Gage's body survived. But you could say that Gage himself, at least as others had known him, did not. From an even-tempered, responsible, and likable young man, Gage turned "fitful, irreverent, indulging at times in the grossest profanity which was not previously his custom, manifesting but little deference for his fellows, impatient of re-straint or advice when it conflicts with his desires, at times pertinaciously obstinate, yet capricious and vacillating, devising many plans of future operation which are no sooner arranged than they are abandoned" (Harlow, 1868, as cited in Damasio, 1994). Beyond being blind in one eye, Gage suffered no lasting physical or mental defects. He remained nimble, alert, and able to speak and think. The wound in his head laid waste to his personality alone.

After the accident, Gage could not keep his job, as he no longer had the motivation to perform up to expectations. His newly unpleasant behavior drove friends away and destroyed the possibility of finding a romantic partner with whom to share his life. Gage moved from job to job, including a stint in a circus sideshow in New York City. This once-promising and ambitious young man eventually ended up a penniless ward of his mother and sister. He died of a brain seizure at the age of 38 (Damasio, 1994).

What, exactly, was the critical injury suffered by Gage? Why did his personality change so profoundly? In his book *Descartes' Error* (1994), the neuroscientist Antonio Damasio speculates that the destruction of Gage's temporal lobe resulted in his inability to experience appropriate emotion. Imagine being unable to experience shame at saying rude things to your host at a dinner, or anger at being duped by a con man, or fear at walking through a dangerous area of town at midnight. Imagine being unable to feel affection for a spouse or child or pleasure at engaging in one activity versus another. All of these failures of emotion would leave you socially helpless, indecisive, and unable to behave consistently in ways designed to further your own interests. You would be, in any sense of the word, perfectly unreasonable. In short, you might be much like Phineas Gage.

Gage was far from the last person to lose this critical faculty. Damasio (1994) documents a number of such patients who display startling results in tests of their emotional capacities. When shown emotion-arousing pictures that raise the galvanic skin responses (GSR) of most people, frontally damaged patients register no GSR reaction at all. When performing "gambling" tasks in certain studies, control subjects adopt low-risk strategies, while frontally damaged patients engage in high-risk and bankrupting tactics. Most telling, when gamblers in such studies are hooked to a polygraph, the GSRs of control subjects increase (signaling increasing dread and nervousness) throughout the task, while those of patients remain constant.

If the ability to *feel* appropriately has such a profound impact on a person's personality and successes, then we shouldn't be surprised to hear that scientists in the relatively new and sometimes controversial field of *evolutionary psychology* have argued persuasively that emotions are adaptive, indeed critical to an organism's survival. This goes even for those darker emotions we normally view as counterproductive, such as jealousy (Buss, 2000) and vengefulness (Cosmides & Tooby, 2000). Such emotions, although unpleasant, may help us to navigate dangers and respond to social threats that a completely dispassionate, cool-headed person might miss.

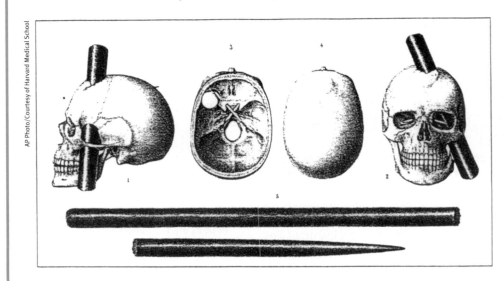

AP Photo/Courtesy of Harvard Medical School

Collateral damage *An 1850s' artist offered these drawings of the injury suffered by Phineas Gage when a three-foot tamping iron penetrated his brain. Although the holes in Gage's head eventually healed, his previous personality did not survive.*

tends to be vague and to move in various directions, even sprinkled with loose associations (Caplan et al., 1990). They often drift aimlessly and lead an idle, unproductive life (Skodol et al., 2002). They are likely to choose undemanding jobs in which they can work below their capacity and are not required to interact with other people. It has been estimated that 2 to 4 percent of all people—slightly more males than females—may have a schizotypal personality disorder (Mattia & Zimmerman, 2001; APA, 2000).

HOW DO THEORISTS EXPLAIN SCHIZOTYPAL PERSONALITY DISORDER? Because the symptoms of this personality disorder so often resemble those of schizophrenia, researchers have suggested that similar factors may be at work in both disorders (Raine et al., 1997). They have in fact found that schizotypal symptoms, like schizophrenic patterns, are often linked to family conflicts and to psychological disorders in parents (Asarnow et al., 1991). They have also learned that defects in attention and short-term memory may be at work in schizotypal personality disorder, just as they often are in schizophrenia (Butler et al., 2003; Roitman et al., 2000, 1997). Finally, researchers have begun to link this personality disorder to some of the same biological factors found in schizophrenia, such as high activity of the neurotransmitter dopamine, enlarged brain ventricles, smaller temporal lobes, and loss of gray matter (Cocarro, 2001; Downhill et al., 2001). As we saw in Chapter 12, there are indications that these biological factors may have a genetic base.

TREATMENTS FOR SCHIZOTYPAL PERSONALITY DISORDER Therapy is as difficult in cases of schizotypal personality disorder as it is in cases of paranoid and schizoid personality disorders. Most therapists agree on the need to help these clients "reconnect" with the world and recognize the limits of their thinking and their powers. The therapists may thus try to set clear limits—for example, by requiring punctuality—and work on helping the clients recognize where their views end and those of the therapist begin (Stone, 1989). Other therapy goals are to increase positive social contacts, ease loneliness, reduce overstimulation, and help the individuals become more aware of their personal feelings (Sperry, 2003; Piper & Joyce, 2001).

Cognitive therapists further try to teach clients to look at their unusual thoughts or perceptions objectively and to ignore the inappropriate ones (Beck et al., 2004; Freeman, 2002). A therapist may keep track of a person's odd or magical predictions, for example, and later point out their inaccuracy. When a client is speaking and begins to drift, the therapist might ask the individual to sum up what he or she is trying to say. On occasion, specific behavioral methods, such as speech lessons, social skills training, and tips on appropriate dress and manners, have helped clients learn to blend in better and be more comfortable around others (Liebowitz et al., 1986).

Antipsychotic drugs have been given to people with schizotypal personality disorder, again because of the disorder's similarity to schizophrenia (Markovitz, 2001). In low doses the drugs appear to have helped some people, usually by reducing certain of their thought problems (Koenigsberg et al., 2002; Coccaro, 2001).

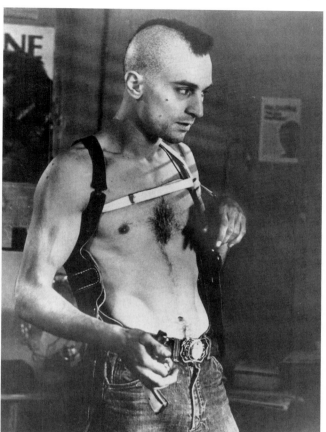

The Kobal Collection

Taxi Driver *Some of film's most memorable characters have displayed personality disorders. Travis Bickle, of* Taxi Driver *fame, seemed to manifest the symptoms of schizotypal personality disorder, including social discomfort and a reduced capacity for interpersonal relationships. He also displayed self-referential interpretations of various events, cognitive distortions, a highly suspicious nature, grandiosity, emotional flatness, and temporary psychotic episodes.*

SUMMING UP ⌐ **"Odd" Personality Disorders**

A personality disorder is a rigid pattern of inner experience and outward behavior. Such patterns are wide-ranging and long-lasting, differ markedly from the ones usually expected of people, and lead to dysfunctioning. Explanations for most of the personality disorders have received only limited research support. DSM-IV distinguishes 10 personality disorders and separates them into three groups, or clusters.

ANTISOCIAL PERSONALITY DISORDER A personality disorder marked by a general pattern of disregard for and violation of other people's rights.

Three of the personality disorders are marked by the kinds of odd or eccentric behavior often seen in the Axis I disorder schizophrenia. People with paranoid personality disorder display a broad pattern of distrust and suspiciousness. Those with schizoid personality disorder generally avoid social relationships and show little emotional expression. Individuals with schizotypal personality disorder display a range of interpersonal problems marked by extreme discomfort in close relationships, very odd forms of thinking and behavior, and behavioral eccentricities. People with these three kinds of disorders usually are resistant to treatment, and treatment gains tend to be modest at best.

"Dramatic" Personality Disorders

The cluster of *"dramatic" personality disorders* includes the *antisocial*, *borderline*, *histrionic*, and *narcissistic* personality disorders. The behaviors of people with these problems are so dramatic, emotional, or erratic that it is almost impossible for them to have relationships that are truly giving and satisfying.

These personality disorders are more commonly diagnosed than the others. However, only the antisocial and borderline personality disorders have received much study, partly because they create so many problems for other people. The causes of the disorders, like those of the odd personality disorders, are not well understood. Treatments range from ineffective to moderately effective.

Antisocial Personality Disorder

Sometimes described as *"psychopaths"* or *"sociopaths,"* people with **antisocial personality disorder** persistently disregard and violate others' rights (APA, 2000, 1994). Aside from substance-related disorders, this is the disorder most closely linked to adult criminal behavior. Most people with antisocial personality disorder have displayed some patterns of misbehavior before they were 15, including truancy, running away, physical cruelty to animals or people, destroying property, and setting fires.

Robert Hare (1993), a leading researcher of antisocial personality disorder, recalls an early professional encounter with a prison inmate named Ray:

In the early 1960s, I found myself employed as the sole psychologist at the British Columbia Penitentiary. . . . I wasn't in my office for more than an hour when my first "client" arrived. He was a tall, slim, dark-haired man in his thirties. The air around him seemed to buzz, and the eye contact he made with me was so direct and intense that I wondered if I had ever really looked anybody in the eye before. That stare was unrelenting—he didn't indulge in the brief glances away that most people use to soften the force of their gaze.

Without waiting for an introduction, the inmate—I'll call him Ray—opened the conversation: "Hey, Doc, how's it going? Look, I've got a problem. I need your help. I'd really like to talk to you about this."

Eager to begin work as a genuine psychotherapist, I asked him to tell me about it. In response, he pulled out a knife and waved it in front of my nose, all the while smiling and maintaining that intense eye contact.

Once he determined that I wasn't going to push the button, he explained that he intended to use the knife not on me but on another inmate who had been making overtures to his "protégé," a prison term for the more passive member of a homosexual pairing. Just why he was telling me this was not immediately clear, but I soon suspected that he was checking me out, trying to determine what sort of a prison employee I was. . . .

From that first meeting on, Ray managed to make my eight-month stint at the prison miserable. His constant demands on my time and his attempts to

>>LOOKING BACK
Previous Identity
Antisocial personality disorder was referred to as "moral insanity" during the nineteenth century.<<

manipulate me into doing things for him were unending. On one occasion, he convinced me that he would make a good cook . . . and I supported his request for a transfer from the machine shop (where he had apparently made the knife). What I didn't consider was that the kitchen was a source of sugar, potatoes, fruit, and other ingredients that could be turned into alcohol. Several months after I had recommended the transfer, there was a mighty eruption below the floorboards directly under the warden's table. When the commotion died down, we found an elaborate system for distilling alcohol below the floor. Something had gone wrong and one of the pots had exploded. There was nothing unusual about the presence of a still in a maximum-security prison, but the audacity of placing one under the warden's seat shook up a lot of people. When it was discovered that Ray was the brains behind the bootleg operation, he spent some time in solitary confinement.

Once out of "the hole," Ray appeared in my office as if nothing had happened and asked for a transfer from the kitchen to the auto shop—he really felt he had a knack, he saw the need to prepare himself for the outside world, if he only had the time to practice he could have his own body shop on the outside. . . . I was still feeling the sting of having arranged the first transfer, but eventually he wore me down.

Soon afterward I decided to leave the prison to pursue a Ph.D. in psychology, and about a month before I left Ray almost persuaded me to ask my father, a roofing contractor, to offer him a job as part of an application for parole.

Ray had an incredible ability to con not just me but everybody. He could talk, and lie, with a smoothness and a directness that sometimes momentarily disarmed even the most experienced and cynical of the prison staff. When I met him he had a long criminal record behind him (and, as it turned out, ahead of him); about half his adult life had been spent in prison, and many of his crimes had been violent. . . . He lied endlessly, lazily, about everything, and it disturbed him not a whit whenever I pointed out something in his file that contradicted one of his lies. He would simply change the subject and spin off in a different direction. Finally convinced that he might not make the perfect job candidate in my father's firm, I turned down Ray's request—and was shaken by his nastiness at my refusal.

Before I left the prison for the university, I took advantage of the prison policy of letting staff have their cars repaired in the institution's auto shop—where Ray still worked, thanks (he would have said no thanks) to me. The car received a beautiful paint job and the motor and drivetrain were reconditioned.

With all our possessions on top of the car and our baby in a plywood bed in the backseat, my wife and I headed for Ontario. The first problems appeared soon after we left Vancouver, when the motor seemed a bit rough. Later, when we encountered some moderate inclines, the radiator boiled over. A garage mechanic discovered ball bearings in the carburetor's float chamber; he also pointed out where one of the hoses to the radiator had clearly been tampered with. These problems were repaired easily enough, but the next one, which arose while we were going down a long hill, was more serious. The brake pedal became very spongy and then simply dropped to the floor—no brakes, and it was a long hill. Fortunately, we made it to a service station, where we found that the brake line had been cut so that a slow leak would occur. Perhaps it was a coincidence that Ray was working in the auto shop when the car was being tuned up, but I had no doubt that the prison "telegraph" had informed him of the owner of the car.

(Hare, 1993)

Bettmann/Corbis

Antisocial and homicidal *Charles Manson, who directed his followers to kill nine people in 1969, fits many of the criteria of antisocial personality disorder, including disregard for and violation of others' rights, disregard for truth, and lack of remorse. In a recent interview Manson bragged, "I was crazy when crazy meant something."*

Like Ray, people with antisocial personality disorder lie repeatedly (Seto et al., 1997). Many cannot work consistently at a job; they are absent frequently and are likely to quit their jobs altogether. Usually they are also careless with money and frequently fail to pay their debts. They are often impulsive, taking action without thinking of the consequences (Lykken, 1995). Correspondingly, they may be irritable, aggressive, and quick to start fights (Vaillant, 1994). Many travel from place to place.

Recklessness is another common trait: people with antisocial personality disorder have little regard for their own safety or for that of others, even their children. They are self-centered as well, and likely to have trouble maintaining close relationships (Birtchnell, 1996). Usually they develop a knack for gaining personal profit at the expense of other people. Because the pain or damage they cause seldom concerns them, clinicians commonly say that they lack a moral conscience. They think of their victims as weak and deserving of being conned or robbed.

Surveys indicate that up to 3.5 percent of people in the United States meet the criteria for antisocial personality disorder (Sperry, 2003; Mattia & Zimmerman, 2001). White Americans are somewhat more likely than African Americans to receive the diagnosis (Robins et al., 1991), and the disorder is as much as four times more common among men than women (Anderson et al., 2001; Kessler & Zhao, 1999).

Because people with this disorder are often arrested, researchers frequently look for people with antisocial patterns in prison populations (Fazel & Danesh, 2002; Rotter et al., 2002). Among men in urban jails, the antisocial personality pattern has been strongly linked to past arrests for crimes of violence (Abram & Teplin, 1990) (see Figure 13-3). For many people with this disorder, criminal behavior declines after the age of 40; some, however, continue their criminal activities throughout their lives (Hurt & Oltmanns, 2002).

Studies and clinical observations also indicate higher rates of alcoholism and other substance-related disorders among people with antisocial personality disorder than in the rest of the population (Myers, Stewart, & Brown, 1998). Perhaps intoxication and substance abuse help trigger the development of antisocial personality disorder by loosening a person's inhibitions. Perhaps this personality disorder somehow makes a person more prone to abuse substances. Or perhaps antisocial personality disorder and substance abuse both have the same cause, such as a deep-seated need to take risks. Interestingly, drug users with the personality disorder often cite the recreational aspects of drug use as their reason for starting and continuing it (Mirin & Weiss, 1991).

HOW DO THEORISTS EXPLAIN ANTISOCIAL PERSONALITY DISORDER? Explanations of antisocial personality disorder come from the psychodynamic, behavioral, and biological models. As with many other personality disorders, psychodynamic theorists propose that this one, too, begins with an absence of parental love during infancy, leading to a lack of basic trust (Sperry, 2003). In this view, some children—the ones who develop antisocial personality disorder—respond to the early inadequacies by becoming emotionally distant, and they bond with others through the use of power and destructiveness. In support of the psychodynamic explanation, researchers have found that people with this disorder are more likely than others to have had significant stress in their childhoods, particularly in such forms as family poverty, family violence, and parental conflict or divorce (Paris, 2001; Farrington, 1991).

Many behavioral theorists have suggested that antisocial symptoms may be learned through *modeling*, or imitation. As evidence, they point to the higher rate of antisocial personality disorder found among the parents of people with this disorder (Paris, 2001). Other behaviorists have suggested that some parents un-

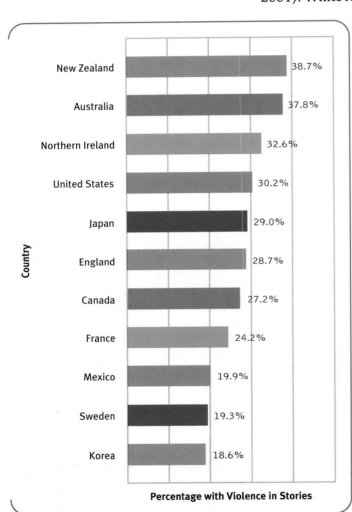

FIGURE 13-3 **Are some cultures more antisocial than others?** *In a cross-cultural study, teenagers were asked to write stories describing how imaginary characters would respond to various conflicts. About one-third of the respondents from New Zealand, Australia, Northern Ireland, and the United States described violent responses, compared to less than one-fifth of the subjects from Korea, Sweden, and Mexico. (Adapted from Archer & McDaniel, 1995.)*

Figure bars (Percentage with Violence in Stories):
New Zealand 38.7%
Australia 37.8%
Northern Ireland 32.6%
United States 30.2%
Japan 29.0%
England 28.7%
Canada 27.2%
France 24.2%
Mexico 19.9%
Sweden 19.3%
Korea 18.6%

intentionally teach antisocial behavior by regularly rewarding a child's aggressive behavior (Capaldi & Patterson, 1994; Patterson, 1986, 1982). When the child misbehaves or becomes violent in reaction to the parents' requests or orders, for example, the parents may give in to restore peace. Without meaning to, they may be teaching the child to be stubborn and perhaps even violent.

Finally, a number of studies suggest that biological factors may play an important role in antisocial personality disorder (Dolan et al., 2002). Research reveals that people with this disorder often experience less anxiety than other people, and so may lack a key ingredient for learning (Zuckerman, 1996; Lykken, 1995). This would help explain why they have so much trouble learning from negative life experiences or tuning in to the emotions of others. Several studies have found that subjects with antisocial personality disorder are less able than control subjects to learn laboratory tasks, such as finding their way out of a maze, when the key reinforcements are punishments such as shock or loss of money (Lykken, 1995, 1957; Newman et al., 1992, 1987). When experimenters make the punishments very apparent or force subjects to pay attention to them, learning improves; left to their own devices, however, subjects with this disorder are not influenced much by punishments. Perhaps they simply do not react as anxiously as other people to negative events.

Why should people with antisocial personality disorder experience less anxiety than other people? The answer may lie in the biological realm (Dolan et al., 2002; Raine et al., 2000). Subjects with the disorder often respond to warnings or expectations of stress with low brain and bodily arousal, such as slow autonomic arousal and slow EEG waves (Dinn & Harris, 2000; Patrick et al., 1993, 1990). Perhaps because of the low arousal, the individuals easily tune out threatening or emotional situations, and so are unaffected by them.

It could also be argued that because of their physical underarousal, people with this disorder will be more likely than other people to take risks and seek thrills. That is, they may be drawn to antisocial activity precisely because it meets an underlying biological need for more excitement and arousal. In support of this idea, as we observed earlier, antisocial personality disorder often goes hand in hand with sensation-seeking behavior (Hasselbrock & Hasselbrock, 1992).

TREATMENTS FOR ANTISOCIAL PERSONALITY DISORDER Approximately one-quarter of all people with antisocial personality disorder receive treatment for it (Regier et al., 1993), yet treatment is typically ineffective (Mannuzza & Klein, 1991). A major obstacle is the individuals' lack of conscience or desire to change (Millon, 1999). Most of those in therapy have been forced to participate by an employer, their school, or the law, or else they come to the attention of therapists when they also develop another psychological disorder (Fulwiler & Pope, 1987). Not surprisingly, one study found that 70 percent of these patients left treatment prematurely (Gabbard & Coyne, 1987).

Some cognitive therapists try to guide clients with antisocial personality disorder to think about moral issues and about the needs of other people (Beck et al., 2004; Freeman, 2002). In a similar vein, a number of hospitals and prisons have tried to create a therapeutic community for people with this disorder, a structured environment that teaches responsibility toward others (Piper & Joyce, 2001; Reid & Burke, 1989). Still another popular approach uses physically challenging wilderness programs to build self-confidence, self-esteem, and commitment to others in a group. Some patients seem to profit from such programs. Generally, however, most of today's treatment approaches have little or no impact on people with antisocial personality disorder.

Courtesy of Everett Collection

Mixed verdict *Crime boss Tony Soprano of the popular television series* The Sopranos *displays many symptoms of sociopathy, including his persistent disregard for and violation of others' rights, repeated lying, self-centeredness, and lack of conscience after cheating, robbing, or even killing other people. Nevertheless, clinicians point out that this character also possesses several qualities uncharacteristic of the personality disorder, such as genuine concern for and close personal relationships with his children and friends, bouts of overwhelming anxiety, and a capacity to persevere in and profit from long-term therapy.*

ABNORMALITY AND THE ARTS

When Life Imitates Art

Oliver Stone's 1994 movie *Natural Born Killers* tells the tale of two sociopathic thrill seekers, Mickey and Mallory, who grow world-famous as they travel the countryside committing brutal murders. Stone meant it to be a satire on our culture's appetite for violence, but the film itself inspired more copycat killings than any other movie ever made (Shnayerson, 1996). Numerous young people went on similar killing sprees, citing *Natural Born Killers* as their inspiration.

The copycat phenomenon is not new (Bushman & Anderson, 2001). When Stanley Kubrick's film *A Clockwork Orange* was released in 1971, critics praised its powerful social statement. But when some British youths copied the actions of the movie's gang leader and raped a woman to the tune of "Singin' in the Rain," Kubrick had the film banned in Britain (Shnayerson, 1996).

Must individuals already be antisocial in order to be influenced by films such as these, or do the films confuse people who are not antisocial by glorifying criminal and violent behavior? Should filmmakers and writers consider the possible psychological influence of their work on suggestible individuals before they undertake such projects? These are but a few of the important questions that are raised by the copycat phenomenon. Clinical, legal, and political figures have readily offered answers to such questions, but in fact the phenomenon is far from being understood.

W. B. Productions Ltd/Photofest

Borderline Personality Disorder

People with **borderline personality disorder** display great instability, including major shifts in mood, an unstable self-image, and impulsivity. These characteristics combine to make their relationships very unstable as well (APA, 2000, 1994). Some of Ellen Farber's difficulties are typical:

> Ellen Farber, a 35-year-old, single insurance company executive, came to a psychiatric emergency room of a university hospital with complaints of depression and the thought of driving her car off a cliff. . . . Ms. Farber appeared to be in considerable distress. She reported a 6-month period of increasingly persistent dysphoria and lack of energy and pleasure. Feeling as if she were "made of lead," Ms. Farber had recently been spending 15–20 hours a day in her bed. She also reported daily episodes of binge eating, when she would consume "anything I can find," including entire chocolate cakes or boxes of cookies. She reported problems with intermittent binge eating since adolescence, but these had recently increased in frequency. . . .
>
> She attributed her increasing symptoms to financial difficulties. Ms. Farber had been fired from her job two weeks before coming to the emergency room. She claimed it was because she "owed a small amount of money." When asked to be more specific, she reported owing $150,000 to her former employers and another $100,000 to various local banks. . . . From age 30 to age 33, she had used her employer's credit cards to finance weekly "buying binges," accumulating the $150,000 debt. [To relieve feelings of distress,] every few days she would impulsively buy expensive jewelry, watches, or multiple pairs of the same shoes. . . .
>
> In addition to lifelong feelings of emptiness, Ms. Farber described chronic uncertainty about what she wanted to do in life and with whom she wanted to be friends. She had many brief, intense relationships with both men and women,

BORDERLINE PERSONALITY DISORDER A personality disorder characterized by repeated instability in interpersonal relationships, self-image, and mood and by impulsive behavior.

but her quick temper led to frequent arguments and even physical fights. Although she had always thought of her childhood as happy and carefree, when she became depressed, she began to recall [being abused verbally and physically by her mother].

(Spitzer et al., 1994, pp. 395–397)

Like Ellen Farber, people with borderline personality disorder swing in and out of very depressive, anxious, and irritable states that last anywhere from a few hours to a few days or more (see Table 13-2). Their emotions seem to be always in conflict with the world around them. They are prone to bouts of anger, which sometimes result in physical aggression and violence. Just as often, however, they direct their impulsive anger inward and inflict bodily harm on themselves. Many seem troubled by deep feelings of emptiness (Koenigsberg et al., 2002, 1999).

Many of the patients who come to mental health emergency rooms are individuals with borderline personality disorder who have intentionally hurt themselves. Their impulsive, self-destructive activities may range from alcohol and substance abuse to delinquency, unsafe sex, reckless driving, and cutting themselves (Trull et al., 2003, 2000; Lavan & Johnson, 2002). Suicidal threats and actions are also common. Studies suggest that 70 percent of people with this disorder attempt suicide at least once in their lives; around 6 to 9 percent actually commit suicide (Davis et al., 1999). Many, like Ellen, try to hurt themselves as a way of dealing with their general feelings of emptiness, boredom, and identity confusion. A common pattern is for people with the disorder to enter clinical treatment by way of the emergency room, after a suicide attempt or episode of self-mutilation (Lambert, 2003).

Table 13-2

Comparison of Personality Disorders

	DSM-IV CLUSTER	SIMILAR DISORDERS ON AXIS I	RESPONSIVENESS TO TREATMENT
Paranoid	Odd	Schizophrenia; delusional disorder	Modest
Schizoid	Odd	Schizophrenia; delusional disorder	Modest
Schizotypal	Odd	Schizophrenia; delusional disorder	Modest
Antisocial	Dramatic	Conduct disorder	Poor
Borderline	Dramatic	Mood disorders	Moderate
Histrionic	Dramatic	Somatoform disorders; mood disorders	Modest
Narcissistic	Dramatic	Cyclothymic disorder (mild bipolar disorder)	Poor
Avoidant	Anxious	Social phobia	Moderate
Dependent	Anxious	Separation anxiety disorder; dysthymic disorder (mild depressive disorder)	Moderate
Obsessive-compulsive	Anxious	Obsessive-compulsive anxiety disorder	Moderate

Changing a personality *In 1974 the newspaper heiress Patty Hearst was kidnapped by a terrorist group called the Symbionese Liberation Army. After being locked in a closet for months and experiencing other tortures, the young woman willingly participated with the group in various antisocial activities. Had Hearst's personality been changed? Would anyone subjected to such tortures have undergone a shift in values and behaviors? A jury ruled in 1976 that Hearst, shown here during a bank robbery, had acted with free will, and sentenced her to seven years in prison for grand theft. She was released after two years when President Jimmy Carter commuted her sentence.*

People with borderline personality disorder often form intense, conflict-ridden relationships with people who do not necessarily share their feelings (Modestin & Villiger, 1989). They often violate the boundaries of relationships (Skodol et al., 2002) and may become furious when their expectations are not met; yet they remain very attached to the relationships, paralyzed by a fear of being left alone (Bender et al., 2001). Sometimes they cut themselves or carry out other self-destructive acts to prevent partners from leaving.

Around 1.5 percent of the general population are thought to suffer from borderline personality disorder (Sperry, 2003; APA, 2000). Close to 75 percent of the patients who receive this diagnosis are women. The course of the disorder varies from person to person. In the most common pattern, the instability and risk of suicide reach a peak during young adulthood and then gradually lessen with advancing age (Hurt & Oltmanns, 2002; APA, 2000).

How Do Theorists Explain Borderline Personality Disorder?

Because a fear of abandonment tortures so many people with borderline personality disorder, psychodynamic theorists have looked once again to early parental relationships to explain the disorder (Gunderson, 2001, 1996). Object relations theorists, for example, propose that an early lack of acceptance by parents may lead to a loss of self-esteem, increased dependence, and an inability to cope with separation (Bartholomew et al., 2001; Richman & Sokolove, 1992). Research has found that the early childhoods of people with the disorder are often consistent with this view. In many cases, the parents of such individuals neglected or rejected them, verbally abused them, or otherwise behaved inappropriately (Guttman, 2002; Johnson et al., 2001). Similarly, their childhoods were often marked by multiple parent substitutes, divorce, death, or traumas such as physical or sexual abuse (Yen et al., 2002). In fact, some theorists believe that the disorder may be an extended form of posttraumatic stress disorder, triggered by early horrors (Shea et al., 2000).

Some features of borderline personality disorder have also been linked to biological abnormalities. Sufferers who are particularly impulsive —those who attempt suicide or are very aggressive toward others—apparently have lower brain serotonin activity (Norra et al., 2003). In accord with such biological findings, close relatives of those with borderline personality disorder are five times more likely than the general population to have the disorder (Torgersen, 2000, 1984; Kendler et al., 1991).

Finally, some sociocultural theorists suggest that cases of borderline personality disorder are particularly likely to emerge in cultures that change rapidly. As a culture loses its stability, they argue, it inevitably leaves many of its members with problems of identity, a sense of emptiness, high anxiety, and fears of abandonment (Paris, 1991). Family units may come apart, leaving people with little sense of belonging. Changes of this kind in society today may explain growing reports of the disorder.

Treatments for Borderline Personality Disorder

It appears that psychotherapy can eventually lead to some degree of improvement for people with borderline personality disorder (Sperry, 2003; Gunderson, 2001). It is not easy, however, for a therapist to strike a balance between empathizing with the patient's dependency and anger and challenging his or her way of thinking (Goin, 2001).

Psychodynamic therapy has been somewhat effective when it focuses on the patient's central relationship disturbance, poor sense of self, and deep loneliness and emptiness (Gabbard, 2001; Piper & Joyce, 2001). During the past decade this treatment has often been combined with cognitive-behavioral interventions designed to help people recognize and address the perspectives of others (Linehan et al., 2001; Linehan, 1993, 1992). For example, the therapist may model alternative ways of interpreting and reacting to situations and also arrange for clients to

Gambling and Other Impulse Problems

Impulsivity is a symptom of many psychological disorders, including the antisocial and borderline personality disorders (Looper & Paris, 2000). DSM-IV also lists several disorders of which impulsivity, rather than personality, is the main feature. People with these *impulse-control disorders* fail to resist an impulse, drive, or temptation to perform an act that is harmful to themselves or others (APA, 2000, 1994). Usually they experience growing tension before the act and relief when they give in to the impulse. Some, but not all, feel regret or guilt afterward. The impulse-control disorders include pyromania, kleptomania, intermittent explosive disorder, trichotillomania, and pathological gambling.

Cliff Schiappa/AP Photo

+ *Pyromania* is the deliberate and repeated setting of fires to achieve intense pleasure or relief from tension. It is different from *arson*, the setting of fires for revenge or financial gain.

+ *Kleptomania* is a recurrent failure to resist the impulse to steal. People with this disorder often have more than enough money to pay for the articles they steal.

+ Individuals with *intermittent explosive disorder* have periodic aggressive outbursts in which they may seriously attack people and destroy property. Their explosiveness far exceeds any provocation.

+ People with *trichotillomania* repeatedly pluck hair from various parts of their bodies, particularly the scalp, eyebrows, and eyelashes (Pelissier & O'Connor, 2004; McElroy et al., 1994).

+ The most common of the impulse-control disorders is *pathological gambling*, persistent and repeated gambling behavior that disrupts one's life at home or at work (APA, 2000, 1994).

It is estimated that as many as 3.4 percent of adults and 3 to 8 percent of teenagers and college students suffer from pathological gambling (APA, 2000; Sadock & Sadock, 2003). Clinicians are careful, however, to distinguish between pathological and social gambling (Kaminer et al., 2002). Pathological gambling is defined less by the amount of time or money spent in gambling than by the addictive and impulsive nature of the behavior (Petry, 2001). People with

this disorder cannot walk away from a bet and are restless and irritable if gambling is denied them. Repeated losses of money lead to more gambling in an effort to win the money back, and the gambling continues even in the face of financial, social, and health problems.

A great deal of attention has been directed in recent years toward the treatment of pathological gambling. Treatments that combine cognitive, behavioral, and other approaches and that help build coping skills tend to be the most effective (Echeburúa et al., 1996; Bujold et al., 1994). People who join self-help support groups, such as Gamblers Anonymous, a network patterned after Alcoholics Anonymous, seem to have a higher recovery rate, perhaps in part because they have admitted that they have a problem and are seeking to conquer it.

Recently journalists and others have asked whether the "medicalization" of gambling has the effect of somehow excusing a pattern of irresponsible, often illegal behavior (Castellani, 2000; Vatz & Weinberg, 1993). However, several studies seem to suggest that pathological gambling and other impulse-control disorders are complex problems that often involve a variety of causes, including even biochemical factors (Blanco et al., 2000).

receive social skills training. This combination treatment, called *dialectical behavioral therapy*, has received growing research support and is now considered the treatment of choice in many clinical circles (Crits-Christoph & Barber, 2002). Group therapy has also been of help to some people with borderline personality disorder (Sperry, 2003; MacKenzie, 2001). It offers them an opportunity to form close attachments to a number of persons rather than focusing all their emotions and hopes on just one or two "chosen" relationships.

Finally, antidepressant, antibipolar, antianxiety, and antipsychotic drugs have helped some individuals to calm their emotional and aggressive storms (Fava et al., 2002; Markovitz, 2001). Given the high risk of suicide attempts by these patients, however, their use of drugs on an outpatient basis is controversial. Some individuals have benefited from a combination of drug therapy and psychotherapy (Livesley, 2000; Stone, 2000).

Histrionic Personality Disorder

People with **histrionic personality disorder**, once called **hysterical personality disorder**, are extremely emotional—they are typically described as "emotionally charged"—and continually seek to be the center of attention (APA, 2000, 1994). Their exaggerated, rapidly changing moods can complicate life considerably, as we see in the case of Suzanne:

> Suzanne, an attractive and vivacious woman, sought therapy in the hope that she might prevent the disintegration of her third marriage. The problem she faced was a recurrent one, her tendency to become "bored" with her husband and increasingly interested in going out with other men. She was on the brink of "another affair" and decided that before "giving way to her impulses again" she had "better stop and take a good look" at herself. . . .
>
> Suzanne was quite popular during her adolescent years. . . . Rather than going on to college, Suzanne attended art school where she met and married a fellow student—a "handsome, wealthy ne'er-do-well." Both she and her husband began "sleeping around" by the end of the first year, and she "wasn't certain" that her husband was the father of her daughter. A divorce took place several months after the birth of this child.
>
> Soon thereafter she met and married a man in his forties who gave both Suzanne and her daughter a "comfortable home, and scads of attention and love." It was a "good life" for the four years that the marriage lasted. . . . In the third year of this marriage she became attracted to a young man, a fellow dancing student. The affair was brief, but was followed by a quick succession of several others. Her husband learned of her exploits, but accepted her regrets and assurances that they would not continue. They did continue, and the marriage was terminated after a stormy court settlement.
>
> Suzanne "knocked about" on her own for the next two years until she met her present husband, a talented writer who "knew the scoop" about her past. . . . She had no inclination to venture afield for the next three years. She enjoyed the titillation of "playing games" with other men, but she remained loyal to her husband, even though he was away on reportorial assignments for periods of one or two months. The last trip, however, brought forth the "old urge" to start an affair. It was at this point that she sought therapy.
>
> *(Millon, 1969, p. 251)*

People with histrionic personality disorder are always "on stage," using theatrical gestures and mannerisms and the most grandiose language to describe ordinary everyday events. They keep changing themselves to attract and impress an audience, and in their pursuit they change not only their surface characteristics—according to the latest fads—but also their opinions and beliefs. In fact, their speech is actually scanty in detail and substance, and they seem to lack a sense of who they really are.

Approval and praise are the life's blood of these individuals; they must have others present to witness their exaggerated emotional states. Vain, self-centered, demanding, and unable to delay gratification for long, they overreact to any minor event that gets in the way of their quest for attention. Some make suicide attempts, often to manipulate others (Lambert, 2003; APA, 2000).

People with this disorder may draw attention to themselves by exaggerating their physical illnesses or fatigues. They may also behave very provocatively and try to achieve their goals through sexual seduction. Most obsess over how they look and how others will perceive them, often wearing bright, eye-catching clothes. They exaggerate the depth of their relationships, considering themselves to be the intimate friends of people who see them as no more than casual acquaintances. Often they become involved with romantic partners who may be exciting but who do not treat them well.

This disorder was once believed to be more common in women than in men, and clinicians long described the "hysterical wife" (Anderson et al., 2001; Char, 1985). Research, however, has revealed gender bias in past diagnoses. When evaluating case studies of people with a mixture of histrionic and antisocial traits, clinicians in several studies gave a diagnosis of histrionic personality disorder to women more than to men (Ford & Widiger, 1989; Hamilton et al., 1986). The latest statistics suggest that around 2 percent of adults have this personality disorder, with males and females equally affected (Mattia & Zimmerman, 2001; APA, 2000).

HOW DO THEORISTS EXPLAIN HISTRIONIC PERSONALITY DISORDER? The psychodynamic perspective was originally developed to help explain cases of hysteria (see Chapter 6), so it is no surprise that these theorists continue to have a strong interest in histrionic personality disorder today. Most psychodynamic theorists believe that as children, people with this disorder experienced unhealthy relationships in which cold and controlling parents left them feeling unloved and afraid of abandonment (Bender et al., 2001; Gunderson, 1988). To defend against deep-seated fears of loss, the individuals learned to behave dramatically, inventing crises that would require other people to act protectively (Kuriansky, 1988).

Cognitive explanations look instead at the lack of substance and extreme suggestibility found in people with this disorder. These theories see the individuals as becoming less and less interested in knowing about the world at large because they are so self-focused and emotional. With no detailed memories of what they never learned, they must rely on hunches or on other people to provide them with direction in life (Hollander, 1988). Some cognitive theorists also propose that people with this disorder hold a general assumption that they are helpless to care for themselves, and so they constantly seek out others who will meet their needs (Beck et al., 2004).

Finally, sociocultural theorists believe that histrionic personality disorder is produced in part by society's norms and expectations. Until recently, our society encouraged girls to hold on to childhood and dependency as they grew up. The vain and dramatic behavior of the histrionic person may actually be an exaggeration of femininity as our culture once defined it (Beck et al., 2004; Sprock, 2000).

TREATMENTS FOR HISTRIONIC PERSONALITY DISORDER Unlike people with most other personality disorders, those with histrionic personality disorder often seek out treatment on their own (Nestadt et al., 1990). Working with them can be very difficult, however, because of the demands, tantrums, and seductiveness they are likely to display (Phillips & Gunderson, 1994). Another problem is that these individuals may pretend to have important insights or to experience change during treatment, merely to please the therapist. To head off such problems, therapists must remain objective and maintain strict professional boundaries (Sperry, 2003; Gabbard, 1990).

Cognitive therapists have tried to help people with this disorder to change their belief that they are helpless and also to develop better, more precise ways of

HISTRIONIC PERSONALITY DISORDER A personality disorder characterized by a pattern of excessive emotionality and attention seeking. Once called *hysterical personality disorder*.

Transient hysterical symptoms *Typical of many rock fans in the 1960s, these young women at a Beatles concert express themselves with exaggerated and theatrical emotionality and an inability to restrain themselves. Similarly, many fans in the 1960s were known to develop mysterious physical symptoms during live music performances, such as fainting, tremors, or even convulsions. Small wonder that the press of that period regularly described concertgoers as "hysterical" and "histrionic"—the same labels now applied to personality disorders and somatoform disorders that are marked by such behaviors and symptoms.*

thinking and solving problems. Psychodynamic therapy and group therapy have also been applied (Beck et al., 2004; Freeman, 2002). In all these approaches, therapists ultimately aim to help the clients recognize their excessive dependency, find inner satisfaction, and become more independent (Chodoff, 1989). Clinical case reports suggest that each of the approaches can be useful. Drug therapy is less successful, however, except for relieving the depressive symptoms experienced by some patients (Fava et al., 2002; Koenigsberg et al., 2002).

Narcissistic Personality Disorder

People with **narcissistic personality disorder** are generally grandiose, need much admiration, and feel no empathy with others (APA, 2000, 1994). Convinced of their own great success, power, or beauty, they expect constant attention and admiration from those around them. Frederick, the man whom we met at the beginning of this chapter, was one such person. So is Steven, a 30-year-old artist, married, with one child:

> Steven came to the attention of a therapist when his wife insisted that they seek marital counseling. According to her, Steve was "selfish, ungiving and preoccupied with his work." Everything at home had to "revolve about him, his comfort, moods and desires, no one else's." She claimed that he contributed nothing to the marriage, except a rather meager income. He shirked all "normal" responsibilities and kept "throwing chores in her lap," and she was "getting fed up with being the chief cook and bottlewasher, tired of being his mother and sleep-in maid."
>
> On the positive side, Steven's wife felt that he was basically a "gentle and good-natured guy with talent and intelligence." But this wasn't enough. She wanted a husband, someone with whom she could share things. In contrast, he wanted, according to her, "a mother, not a wife"; he didn't want "to grow up, he didn't know how to give affection, only to take it when he felt like it, nothing more, nothing less."
>
> Steve presented a picture of an affable, self-satisfied and somewhat disdainful young man. He was employed as a commercial artist, but looked forward to his evenings and weekends when he could turn his attention to serious painting. He claimed that he had to devote all of his spare time and energies to "fulfill himself," to achieve expression in his creative work. . . .
>
> His relationships with his present co-workers and social acquaintances were pleasant and satisfying, but he did admit that most people viewed him as a "bit self-centered, cold and snobbish." He recognized that he did not know how to share his thoughts and feelings with others, that he was much more interested in himself than in them and that perhaps he always had "preferred the pleasure" of his own company to that of others.
>
> *(Millon, 1969, pp. 261–262)*

People with narcissistic personality disorder exaggerate their achievements and talents, expecting others to recognize them as superior, and often appear arrogant. They are very choosy about their friends and associates, believing that their problems are unique and can be appreciated only by other "special," high-status people. Because of their charm, they often make favorable first impressions. Yet they can rarely maintain long-term relationships.

Like Steven, people with narcissistic personality disorder are seldom interested in the feelings of others. Many take advantage of others to achieve their own ends, perhaps partly out of envy; at the same time they believe others envy them (Sperry, 2003; Wink, 1996). Though grandiose, some of these individuals react to criticism or frustration with bouts of rage or humiliation. Others may react with cold indifference. And still others become extremely pessimistic and filled with depression. Periods of zest may alternate with periods of disappointment (Wink, 1996).

NARCISSISTIC PERSONALITY DISORDER A personality disorder marked by a broad pattern of grandiosity, need for admiration, and lack of empathy.

Less than 1 percent of adults display narcissistic personality disorder, up to 75 percent of them men (Mattia & Zimmerman, 2001; APA, 2000). Narcissistic-type behaviors and thoughts are common and normal among teenagers and do not usually lead to adult narcissism (APA, 1994).

HOW DO THEORISTS EXPLAIN NARCISSISTIC PERSONALITY DISORDER? Psychodynamic theorists more than others have theorized about narcissistic personality disorder, and, again, they propose that the problem begins with cold, rejecting parents. They argue that some people with this background spend their lives defending against feeling unsatisfied, rejected, unworthy, and wary of the world (Wink, 1996). They do so by repeatedly telling themselves that they are actually perfect and desirable, and also by seeking admiration from others (Vaillant, 1994). Object relations theorists, the psychodynamic theorists who emphasize relationships, further interpret the grandiose self-image as a way for these people to convince themselves that they are totally self-sufficient and without need of warm relationships with their parents or anyone else (Kernberg, 1989). In support of the psychodynamic theories, research has found that children who are abused or who lose parents through adoption, divorce, or death are at particular risk for the later development of narcissistic personality disorder (Kernberg, 1989). Studies also reveal that people with this disorder do indeed believe that other persons are basically unavailable to them (Bender et al., 2001).

A number of behavioral and cognitive theorists propose that narcissistic personality disorder may develop when people are treated too *positively* rather than too negatively in early life. They hold that certain individuals acquire a superior attitude when their "admiring or doting parents" teach them to "overvalue their self worth" (Sperry, 2003; Millon, 1987). In support of this explanation, firstborn and only children, who are often viewed by their parents as having special talents or intelligence, score higher than other children on measures of narcissism (Curtis & Cowell, 1993).

Finally, many sociocultural theorists see a link between narcissistic personality disorder and "eras of narcissism" in society (Cooper & Ronningstam, 1992). They suggest that family values and social ideals in certain societies periodically break down, thus producing generations of youth who are self-centered and materialistic and have short attention spans. Western cultures in particular, which encourage self-expression, individualism, and competitiveness, are considered likely to produce such generations of narcissism.

TREATMENTS FOR NARCISSISTIC PERSONALITY DISORDER Narcissistic personality disorder is one of the most difficult personality patterns to treat (Lawrence,

>>Q & A

What is the difference between an egoist and an egotist?

An egoist is a person concerned primarily with his or her own interests. An egotist has an inflated sense of self-worth. A boastful egotist is not necessarily a self-absorbed egoist.**<<**

"Call it vanity, call it narcissism, call it egomania. I love you."

©The New Yorker Collection 1986, Edward Koren, from cartoonbank.com

Just a stage *Like this teenager, many adolescents are preoccupied with their own appearance, feelings, and needs, and many crave attention and seem convinced of their own importance or beauty. Psychologists caution, however, that such self-involvement and near-grandiosity are common and normal parts of development and do not necessarily predict later narcissism.*

1987). The clients who consult therapists usually do so because of a related disorder, most commonly depression (Piper & Joyce, 2001; Millon, 1999). Once in treatment, the individuals may try to manipulate the therapist into supporting their sense of superiority. Some also seem to project their grandiose attitudes onto their therapists and develop a love-hate stance toward them (Uchoa, 1985).

Psychodynamic therapists seek to help people with this disorder recognize their basic insecurities and defenses (Adler, 2000). Cognitive therapists, focusing on the self-centered thinking of such clients, try to redirect the clients' focus onto the opinions of others, teach them to interpret criticism more rationally, increase their ability to empathize, and change their all-or-nothing style of thinking (Beck et al., 2004; Freeman, 2002;). None of the approaches have had much success, however.

> ### SUMMING UP
> ## "Dramatic" Personality Disorders
>
> Four of the personality disorders are marked by highly dramatic, emotional, or erratic behavior. People with antisocial personality disorder display a pattern of disregard for and violation of the rights of others. No known treatment is particularly effective. People with borderline personality disorder display a pattern of instability in interpersonal relationships, self-image, and mood, along with extreme impulsivity. Treatment apparently can be helpful and lead to some improvement. People with histrionic personality disorder display a pattern of extreme emotionality and attention seeking. Clinical case reports suggest that treatment is helpful on occasion. Finally, people with narcissistic personality disorder display a pattern of grandiosity, need for admiration, and lack of empathy. It is one of the most difficult disorders to treat.

"Anxious" Personality Disorders

The cluster of *"anxious" personality disorders* includes the *avoidant*, *dependent*, and *obsessive-compulsive* personality disorders. People with these patterns typically display anxious and fearful behavior. Although many of the symptoms of these disorders are similar to those of the anxiety and depressive disorders, researchers have not found direct links between this cluster and those Axis I disorders (Weston & Siever, 1993). As with most of the other personality disorders, research support for the various explanations is very limited. At the same time, treatments for these disorders appear to be modestly to moderately helpful—considerably better than for other personality disorders.

Avoidant Personality Disorder

People with **avoidant personality disorder** are very uncomfortable and restained in social situations, overwhelmed by feelings of inadequacy, and extremely sensitive to negative evaluation (APA, 2000, 1994). They are so fearful of being rejected that they give no one an opportunity to reject them—or to accept them either:

> James was a bookkeeper for nine years, having obtained his position upon graduation from high school. He spoke of himself as a shy, fearful and quiet boy ever since early childhood. . . .
>
> James was characterized by his supervisor as a loner, a peculiar young man who did his work quietly and efficiently. They noted that he ate alone in the company cafeteria and never joined in coffee breaks or in the "horsing around" at the office. . . .

As far as his social life was concerned, James had neither dated nor gone to a party in five years. . . . He now spent most of his free time reading, watching TV, daydreaming and fixing things around the house.

James experienced great distress when new employees were assigned to his office section. Some 40 people worked regularly in this office and job turnover resulted in replacement of four or five people a year. . . . In recent months, a clique formed in his office. Although James very much wanted to be a member of this "in-group," he feared attempting to join them because "he had nothing to offer them" and thought he would be rejected. In a short period of time, he, along with two or three others, became the object of jokes and taunting by the leaders of the clique. After a few weeks of "being kidded," he began to miss work, failed to complete his accounts on time, found himself unsure of what he was doing and made a disproportionate number of errors. . . .

(Millon, 1969, pp. 231–232)

AVOIDANT PERSONALITY DISORDER A personality disorder characterized by consistent discomfort and restraint in social situations, overwhelming feelings of inadequacy, and extreme sensitivity to negative evaluation.

People like James actively avoid occasions for social contact. At the center of this withdrawal lies not so much poor social skills as a dread of criticism, disapproval, or rejection. They are timid in social situations, afraid of saying something foolish or of embarrassing themselves by blushing or acting nervous. Even in intimate relationships they express themselves very carefully, afraid of being shamed or ridiculed.

People with this disorder believe themselves to be unappealing or inferior to others. They exaggerate the potential difficulties of new situations, so they seldom take risks or try out new activities. They usually have few or no close friends, though they actually yearn for intimate relationships, and frequently feel depressed and lonely. As a substitute, some develop an inner world of fantasy and imagination (Millon, 1990).

Avoidant personality disorder is similar to a *social phobia* (see Chapter 4), and many people with one of these disorders also experience the other (Markovitz, 2001). The similarities include a fear of humiliation and low confidence. A key difference between the two conditions is that people with a social phobia mainly fear social *circumstances*, while people with the personality disorder tend to fear close social *relationships* (Turner et al., 1986).

Between 1 and 2 percent of adults have avoidant personality disorder, men as frequently as women (Mattia & Zimmerman, 2001; APA, 2000). Many children and teenagers are also painfully shy and avoid other people, but this is usually just a normal part of their development.

Just a stage, Take 2 *Many children and teenagers are painfully shy, withdrawn, easily embarrassed, and uncomfortable with people other than their parents, siblings, or close friends. Once again, however, such reactions are common and normal during childhood and do not, by themselves, indicate an avoidant or dependent personality disorder.*

HOW DO THEORISTS EXPLAIN AVOIDANT PERSONALITY DISORDER? Theorists often assume that avoidant personality disorder has the same causes as anxiety disorders—such as early traumas, conditioned fears, upsetting beliefs, or biochemical abnormalities. However, research has not yet tied the personality disorder directly to the anxiety disorders (Weston & Siever, 1993). In the meantime, psychodynamic and cognitive explanations are the most popular among clinicians.

Psychodynamic theorists focus mainly on the general sense of shame felt by people with avoidant personality disorder. Some trace the shame to childhood experiences such as early bowel and bladder accidents (Gabbard, 1990). If parents repeatedly punish or ridicule a child for having such accidents, the child may develop a negative self-image. This may lead to the individual's feeling unlovable throughout life and distrusting the love of others (Liebowitz et al., 1986). Similarly, cognitive theorists believe that harsh criticism and rejection in early childhood may lead certain people to assume that others in their environment will always judge them negatively. These individuals come to expect rejection, misinterpret the reactions of others to fit that expectation, discount positive feedback, and generally fear social involvements—setting the stage for avoidant personality disorder (Beck et al., 2004, 2001). In several studies, subjects with this disorder were asked to recall their childhood, and their descriptions supported both the psychodynamic and cognitive theories (Grilo & Masheb, 2002; Meyer & Carver, 2000). They remembered, for example, feeling rejected and isolated, receiving little encouragement from their parents, and experiencing few displays of parental love or pride.

TREATMENTS FOR AVOIDANT PERSONALITY DISORDER People with avoidant personality disorder come to therapy in the hope of finding acceptance and affection. Keeping them in treatment can be a challenge, however, for many of them soon begin to avoid the sessions (Millon, 1999; Beck & Freeman, 1990). Often they distrust the therapist's sincerity and start to fear his or her rejection. Thus, as with several of the other personality disorders, a key task of the therapist is to gain the individual's trust.

Beyond building trust, therapists tend to treat people with avoidant personality disorder much as they treat people with social phobias and other anxiety disorders (Markovitz, 2001; Reich, 2000). Such approaches have had at least modest success (Crits-Christoph & Barber, 2002). Psychodynamic therapists try to help clients recognize and overcome the unconscious conflicts that may be operating (Sperry, 2003). Cognitive therapists help them change their distressing beliefs and thoughts and improve their self-image (Beck et al., 2004; Freeman, 2002). Behavioral therapists provide social skills training as well as exposure treatments that require people to gradually increase their social contacts (Crits-Christoph & Barber, 2002; Stanley et al., 2002). Group therapy may also be applied to provide practice in social interactions (Piper & Joyce, 2001). Antianxiety and antidepressant drugs are sometimes useful in reducing the social anxiety of people with the disorder, although the symptoms may return when medication is stopped (Fava et al., 2002; Koenigsberg et al., 2002).

Dependent Personality Disorder

People with **dependent personality disorder** have a persistent, excessive need to be taken care of (APA, 2000, 1994). As a result, they are clinging and obedient, fearing separation from their parent, spouse, or other close relationship. They rely on others so much that they cannot make the smallest decision for themselves. Mr. G. is a case in point.

DEPENDENT PERSONALITY DISORDER A personality disorder characterized by a pattern of clinging and obedience, fear of separation, and an ongoing need to be taken care of.

Mr. G.['s] . . . place of employment for the past 15 years had recently closed and he had been without work for several weeks. He appeared less dejected about the loss of his job than about his wife's increasing displeasure with his decision to "stay at home until something came up." She thought he "must be sick" and insisted that he see a doctor. . . .

> Mr. G. was born in Europe, the oldest child and only son of a family of six children. . . . His mother kept a careful watch over him, prevented him from engaging in undue exertions and limited his responsibilities; in effect, she precluded his developing many of the ordinary physical skills and competencies that most youngsters learn in the course of growth. . . .
>
> A marriage was arranged by his parents. His wife was a sturdy woman who worked as a seamstress, took care of his home, and bore . . . four children. Mr. G. performed a variety of odds-and-ends jobs in his father's tailoring shop. His mother saw to it, however, that he did no "hard or dirty work," just helping about and "overlooking" the other employees. As a consequence, Mr. G. learned none of the skills of the tailoring trade.
>
> Shortly before the outbreak of World War II, Mr. G. came to visit two of his sisters who previously had emigrated to the United States; when hostilities erupted in Europe he was unable to return home. All members of his family, with the exception of a young son, perished in the war.
>
> During the ensuing years, he obtained employment at a garment factory owned by his brothers-in-law. Again he served as a helper, not as a skilled workman. Although he bore the brunt of essentially good-humored teasing by his co-workers throughout these years, he maintained a friendly and helpful attitude, pleasing them by getting sandwiches, coffee and cigarettes at their beck and call.
>
> He married again to a hard-working, motherly type woman who provided the greater portion of the family income. Shortly thereafter, the son of his first wife emigrated to this country. Although the son was only 19 at the time, he soon found himself guiding his father's affairs, rather than the other way around.
>
> *(Millon, 1969, p. 242)*

It is normal and healthy to depend on others, but those with dependent personality disorder constantly need assistance with even the simplest matters and demonstrate extreme feelings of inadequacy and helplessness. Afraid that they cannot care for themselves, they cling desperately to friends or relatives.

We observed earlier that people with avoidant personality disorder have difficulty *starting up* relationships. In contrast, people with dependent personality disorder have difficulty with *separation*. The individuals feel completely helpless and devastated when a close relationship ends, and they quickly seek out another relationship to fill the void. Many cling to relationships with partners who physically or psychologically abuse them.

Lacking confidence in their own ability and judgment, people with this disorder seldom disagree with others and allow even important decisions to be made for them. They may depend on a parent or spouse to decide where to live, what job to have, and which neighbors to befriend (APA, 2000, 1994; Overholser, 1996). Because they so fear rejection, they are overly sensitive to disapproval and keep trying to meet other people's wishes and expectations, even if it means volunteering for unpleasant or demeaning tasks.

Many people with dependent personality disorder feel distressed, lonely, and sad; often they dislike themselves. Thus they are at risk for depressive, anxiety, and eating disorders (Godt, 2002; Skodol et al., 1999). Their fear of separation and their feelings of helplessness may leave them particularly prone to suicidal thoughts, especially when they believe that a relationship is about to end (Kiev, 1989).

Studies suggest that over 2 percent of the population experience dependent personality disorder (Mattia & Zimmerman, 2001). For years clinicians have believed that more women than men display this pattern (Anderson et al., 2001), but some research suggests that the disorder is just as common in men (APA, 2000; Reich, 1990).

HOW DO THEORISTS EXPLAIN DEPENDENT PERSONALITY DISORDER? Psychodynamic explanations for this personality disorder are very similar to those for

>>LOOKING BACK

Character Ingestion

As late as the Victorian era, many English parents believed babies absorbed personality and moral uprightness as they took in milk. Thus, if a mother could not nurse, it was important to find a wetnurse of good character (Asimov, 1997).<<

THE**CURRENT SCENE**

Internet Dependence: A New Kind of Problem

The computer age has apparently brought with it a new psychological problem—an uncontrollable need to be online (Davis, 2001; Orzack, 1998). Some clinicians consider it a kind of *substance-related disorder*. Others think it has the qualities of an *impulse-control disorder*. And many note that the pattern resembles *dependent personality disorder*, except that in this new pattern the individual is excessively dependent on a cyberbeing and on numerous fellow users, ever seeking their company, guidance, and reassurance, and fearful of separation.

For some people, the Internet has become a black hole. Sufferers spend up to 60 hours a week surfing the Net, participating in chat groups, posting messages and receiving responses in news groups, e-mailing acquaintances, or playing complex computer games (Black et al., 1999; Young, 1999, 1998, 1996). A number describe their need to be online as an obsession for which they have unintentionally sacrificed their jobs, education, friends, and even spouses.

One study of 18,000 Internet users found that as many as 16 percent of respondents were overly dependent on it (Greenfield, 1999). Another found that one-quarter of employees spend more than 20 percent of their workday surfing on non-work-related Web sites (Hayday, 2002). In still other research, the investigator Kimberly S. Young (1999, 1998, 1996) classified subjects as dependent on the Internet if they met four or more of the following criteria over a 12-month period:

1. Felt preoccupied with the Internet
2. Needed to spend increasing amounts of time on the Internet to achieve satisfaction

"Daddy and I wish you'd spend less time with your computer and more time watching T.V."

3. Were unable to control their Internet use
4. Felt restless or irritable when they tried to cut down or stop Internet use
5. Used the Internet as a way of escaping from problems or of improving their mood
6. Lied to family members or friends to conceal the extent of their involvement with the Internet
7. Risked the loss of a significant relationship, job, or educational or career opportunity because of the Internet
8. Kept returning to the Internet even after spending an excessive amount of money on online fees
9. Went through withdrawal when offline
10. Stayed online longer than they originally intended

Not surprisingly, the availability of counseling programs and workshops for Internet dependence is on the increase, particularly on college campuses. Among the most popular treatment approaches are support groups similar to Alcoholics Anonymous—some of them, ironically, operating on the Internet. One such group has attracted many subscribers; the individuals who sign up admit to the problem, provide support for each other, and swap methods for reducing their use of the Internet (Murray, 1996). This sounds to some clinicians "like having an Alcoholics Anonymous meeting in a bar" (Orzack, 1996). Others point out, however, that many dependent Internet users cannot tear themselves away from their computers long enough to visit a traditional treatment center (Belluck, 1996).

depression. Freudian theorists argue, for example, that conflicts during the oral stage of development set the stage for a lifelong need for nurturance, thus heightening the likelihood of a dependent personality disorder (Greenberg & Bornstein, 1988). Similarly, object relations theorists say that early parental loss or rejection may prevent normal experiences of *attachment* and *separation*, leaving some children with fears of abandonment that persist throughout their lives. Still other psychodynamic theorists suggest that, to the contrary, many parents of people with this disorder were overinvolved and overprotective, thus increasing their children's dependency, insecurity, and separation anxiety (Sperry, 2003).

Behaviorists propose that parents of people with dependent personality disorder unintentionally rewarded their children's clinging and "loyal" behavior, while at the same time punishing acts of independence, perhaps through the withdrawal of love. Alternatively, some parents' own dependent behaviors may have served as models for their children.

Finally, cognitive theorists identify two maladaptive attitudes as helping to produce and maintain this disorder: (1) "I am inadequate and helpless to deal with the world," and (2) "I must find a person to provide protection so I can cope" (Beck et al., 2004, 2001). Dichotomous (black-and-white) thinking may also play a key role: "If I am to be dependent, I must be completely helpless," or "If I am to be independent, I must be alone." Such thinking prevents sufferers from making efforts to be independent.

TREATMENTS FOR DEPENDENT PERSONALITY DISORDER In therapy, people with this personality disorder usually place all responsibility for their treatment and well-being on the clinician (Beck, 1997; Perry, 1989). Thus a key task of therapy is to help patients accept responsibility for themselves. Because the domineering behaviors of a spouse or parent may feed into a patient's symptoms, some clinicians propose couple or family therapy as well, or even separate therapy for the partner or parent (Millon, 1999).

Treatment for dependent personality disorder can be at least modestly helpful. Psychodynamic therapy for this pattern focuses on many of the same issues as therapy for depressed people, including the *transference* of dependency needs onto the therapist (Sperry, 2003; Gabbard, 2001). Behavioral therapists often provide assertiveness training to help clients better express their own wishes in relationships. Cognitive therapists try to help clients challenge and change their assumptions of incompetence and helplessness (Beck et al., 2004; Freeman, 2002). Antidepressant drug therapy has been helpful for persons whose personality disorder is accompanied by depression (Fava et al., 2002).

Finally, as with avoidant personality disorder, a group therapy format can be helpful because it provides opportunities for the client to receive support from a

Dysfunctional toons *As the messages and technology found in film animation have become more complex over time, so have the personality problems of animated characters. (Left) Troubled characters of the past were usually defined by a single undesirable personality trait, as demonstrated by Snow White's friend Grumpy, second from left. (Right) Today's characters have clusters of problematic traits. For example, some critics suggest that the* South Park *kids display enduring grumpiness (especially Cartman, second from left); disrespect for authority, irreverence, and self-absorption; disregard for the feelings of others; general lack of conscience; and a tendency to get into trouble.*

number of peers rather than from a single dominant person (Sperry, 2003; Azima, 1993). In addition, group members may serve as models for one another as they practice better ways to express feelings and solve problems.

Obsessive-Compulsive Personality Disorder

People with **obsessive-compulsive personality disorder** are so focused on order, perfection, and control that they lose all flexibility, openness, and efficiency. Their concern for doing everything "right" impairs their productivity, as in the case of Wayne:

Wayne was advised to seek assistance from a therapist following several months of relatively sleepless nights and a growing immobility and indecisiveness at his job. When first seen, he reported feelings of extreme self-doubt and guilt and prolonged periods of tension and diffuse anxiety. It was established early in therapy that he always had experienced these symptoms. They were now merely more pronounced than before.

The precipitant for this sudden increase in discomfort was a forthcoming change in his academic post. New administrative officers had assumed authority at the college, and he was asked to resign his deanship to return to regular departmental instruction. In the early sessions, Wayne spoke largely of his fear of facing classroom students again, wondered if he could organize his material well, and doubted that he could keep classes disciplined and interested in his lectures. It was his preoccupation with these matters that he believed was preventing him from concentrating and completing his present responsibilities.

At no time did Wayne express anger toward the new college officials for the "demotion" he was asked to accept. He repeatedly voiced his "complete confidence" in the "rationality of their decision." Yet, when face-to-face with them, he observed that he stuttered and was extremely tremulous.

Wayne was the second of two sons, younger than his brother by three years. His father was a successful engineer, and his mother a high school teacher. Both were "efficient, orderly and strict" parents. Life at home was "extremely well planned," with "daily and weekly schedules of responsibilities posted" and "vacations arranged a year or two in advance." Nothing apparently was left to chance. . . . Wayne adopted the "good boy" image. Unable to challenge his brother either physically, intellectually or socially, he became a "paragon of virtue." By being punctilious, scrupulous, methodical and orderly, he could avoid antagonizing his perfectionistic parents, and would, at times, obtain preferred treatment from them. He obeyed their advice, took their guidance as gospel and hesitated making any decision before gaining their approval. Although he recalled "fighting" with his brother before he was six or seven, he "restrained his anger from that time on and never upset his parents again."

(Millon, 1969, pp. 278–279)

In Wayne's concern with rules and order and doing things right, he has trouble seeing the larger picture. When faced with a task, he and others who have obsessive-compulsive personality disorder may become so focused on organization and details that they fail to grasp the point of the activity. As a result, their work is often behind schedule (some seem unable to finish any job), and they may neglect leisure activities and friendships.

People with this personality disorder set unreasonably high standards for themselves and others. They can never be satisfied with their performance, but they typically refuse to seek help or to work with a team, convinced that others are too careless or incompetent to do the job right. Because they are so afraid of making mistakes, they may be reluctant to make decisions.

These individuals also tend to be rigid and stubborn, particularly in their morals, ethics, and values. They live by a strict personal code and use it as a yard-

OBSESSIVE-COMPULSIVE PERSONALITY DISORDER A personality disorder marked by such an intense focus on orderliness, perfectionism, and control that the individual loses flexibility, openness, and efficiency.

stick for measuring others. They may have trouble expressing much affection, and their relationships are sometimes stiff and superficial. In addition, they are often stingy with their time or money. Some cannot even throw away objects that are worn out or useless (Sperry, 2003; APA, 2000, 1994).

Between 2 and 5 percent of the population are believed to display obsessive-compulsive personality disorder, with white, educated, married, and employed individuals receiving the diagnosis most often (Mattia & Zimmerman, 2001; APA, 2000). Men are twice as likely as women to display the disorder.

Many clinicians believe that obsessive-compulsive personality disorder and obsessive-compulsive disorder (the anxiety disorder) are closely related. Certainly, the two disorders share a number of features. Moreover, many people who suffer from the anxiety disorder qualify for the personality disorder diagnosis as well (APA, 2000). However, other personality disorders (avoidant, histrionic, schizotypal, and dependent) may be even more common among those with the anxiety disorder (Steketee, 1990). In fact, researchers have not found a specific link between obsessive-compulsive personality disorder and the obsessive-compulsive anxiety disorder (Mavissakalian et al., 1990).

HOW DO THEORISTS EXPLAIN OBSESSIVE-COMPULSIVE PERSONALITY DISORDER? Most explanations of obsessive-compulsive personality disorder borrow heavily from those of obsessive-compulsive anxiety disorder, despite the doubts concerning a direct link between the two disorders. As with so many of the personality disorders, psychodynamic explanations dominate and research evidence is limited.

Freudian theorists suggest that people with obsessive-compulsive personality disorder are *anal regressive*. That is, because of overly harsh toilet training during the anal stage, they become filled with anger, and they remain *fixated* at this stage. To keep their anger under control, they persistently resist both their anger and their instincts to have bowel movements. In turn, they become extremely orderly and restrained; many become passionate collectors. Other psychodynamic theorists suggest that any early struggles with parents over control and independence may ignite the aggressive impulses at the root of this personality disorder (Kuriansky, 1988; Mollinger, 1980).

Cognitive theorists have little to say about the origins of obsessive-compulsive personality disorder, but they propose that illogical thinking helps keep it going (Beck et al., 2004, 2001). They point, for example, to dichotomous (black-and-white) thinking, which may produce rigidity and perfectionism. Similarly, they note that people with this disorder tend to misread or exaggerate the potential outcomes of mistakes or errors.

TREATMENTS FOR OBSESSIVE-COMPULSIVE PERSONALITY DISORDER People with obsessive-compulsive personality disorder do not usually believe there is anything wrong with them. They therefore are not likely to seek treatment unless they are also suffering from another disorder, most frequently anxiety or depression, or unless someone close to them insists that they get treatment (Beck & Freeman, 1990). Whereas drug therapy and behavioral therapy have been highly effective for people with obsessive-compulsive anxiety disorder, individuals with the personality disorder often appear to respond better to psychodynamic or cognitive therapy (Gabbard, 2001; Primac, 1993). Psychodynamic therapists typically try to help them recognize, experience, and accept their underlying feelings and insecurities, and perhaps to take risks and accept their personal limitations (Sperry, 2003; Salzman, 1989). Cognitive therapists focus on helping clients to change their dichotomous thinking, perfectionism, indecisiveness, procrastination, and chronic worrying (Beck et al., 2004).

Laura Dwight/Corbis

Toilet rage *According to Freud, toilet training often produces rage in a child. If parents are too harsh in their approach, the child may become fixated at the anal stage and prone to obsessive-compulsive functioning later in life.*

SUMMING UP

"Anxious" Personality Disorders

Three of the personality disorders are marked by the kinds of symptoms found in the Axis I anxiety and depressive disorders. People with avoidant personality disorder are consistently uncomfortable and restrained in social situations, overwhelmed by feelings of inadequacy, and extremely sensitive to negative evaluation. People with dependent personality disorder have a persistent need to be taken care of, are clinging and obedient, and fear separation. Individuals with obsessive-compulsive personality disorder are so focused on order, perfection, and control that they lose their flexibility, openness, and efficiency. A variety of treatment strategies have been used for people with these disorders and apparently have been modestly to moderately helpful.

It appears that the ten personality disorders listed in DSM IV are commonly misdiagnosed, an indication of serious problems in the validity and reliability of the categories.

PASSIVE-AGGRESSIVE PERSONALITY DISORDER A category of personality disorder listed in past versions of the DSM, marked by a pattern of negative attitudes and resistance to the demands of others.

What Problems Are Posed by the DSM Categories?

Most of today's clinicians believe that personality disorders are important and troubling patterns, yet these disorders are particularly hard to diagnose and easy to misdiagnose. These difficulties indicate serious problems with the *validity* (accuracy) and *reliability* (consistency) of the DSM categories (Jablensky, 2002).

One problem is that some of the criteria used to diagnose personality disorders cannot be observed directly. To separate paranoid from schizoid personality disorder, for example, clinicians must ask not only whether people avoid forming close relationships but also *why*. In other words, the diagnoses often rely heavily on the impressions of the individual clinician. A related problem is that clinicians differ widely in their judgments about when a normal personality style crosses the line and deserves to be called a disorder (Clark, 2002). Some even believe that it is wrong ever to think of personality styles as mental disorders, however troublesome they may be (Kendell, 2002).

The similarity of personality disorders within a cluster, or even between clusters, poses yet another problem (Grilo et al., 2002). Within the "anxious" cluster, for example, there is considerable overlap between the symptoms of avoidant personality disorder and those of dependent personality disorder. When clinicians see similar feelings of inadequacy, fear of disapproval, and the like, is it reasonable to consider them separate disorders (Bornstein, 1998; Livesley et al., 1994)? Also, the many borderline traits ("dramatic" cluster) found among some people with dependent personality disorder ("anxious" cluster) may indicate that these two disorders are but different versions of one basic pattern (Dolan et al., 1995; Flick et al., 1993).

Another problem is that people with quite different personalities may be given the same personality disorder diagnosis. Individuals must meet a certain number of criteria from DSM-IV to receive a given diagnosis, but no single feature is necessary for any diagnosis (Millon, 2002, 1999; Costello, 1996).

Partly because of these problems, diagnosticians keep changing the criteria used to assess each of the personality disorders. In fact, the diagnostic categories themselves have changed more than once, and they will no doubt change again. For example, DSM-IV dropped a past category, **passive-aggressive personality disorder**, a pattern of negative attitudes and resistance to the demands of others, because research failed to show that this was more than a single trait. The pattern is now being studied more carefully and may be included once again in future editions of the DSM.

Given these problems, some theorists believe that the personality disorders actually differ more in *degree* than in type of dysfunction and have proposed that the disorders be organized by the severity of certain key traits rather than by the presence or absence of specific traits (Costa & Widiger, 2002). It is not yet clear where such arguments will lead, but at the very least, the growing debate indicates once again that most clinicians believe personality disorders to be important categories in the understanding and treatment of human behavior.

CROSSROADS:
Disorders of Personality Are Rediscovered

During the first half of the twentieth century, clinicians believed deeply in the unique, enduring patterns we call personality, and they tried to define important personality traits. They then discovered how readily people can be shaped by the situations in which they find themselves, and a backlash developed. The concept of personality seemed to lose legitimacy, and for a while it became almost an obscene word in some circles. The clinical category of personality disorders experienced a similar rejection. When psychodynamic and humanistic theorists dominated the clinical field, personality disorders were considered useful clinical categories (Millon et al., 2000). But their popularity declined as other models grew in influence.

During the past two decades, serious interest in personality and personality disorders has rebounded (Millon, 2002). In case after case, clinicians have concluded that rigid personality traits do seem to pose special problems, and they have developed new objective tests and interview guides to assess these disorders, setting in motion a wave of systematic research (Widiger, 2002; Clark & Harrison, 2001). So far, only the antisocial and, to a lesser extent, borderline personality disorders have received much study. As other personality disorders attract research attention as well, however, clinicians should be better able to answer some pressing questions: How common are the various personality disorders? How useful are the present categories? How are the disorders related? And what treatments are most effective?

One of the most important questions is, Why do people develop these patterns? As we have seen, psychological, as opposed to biological and sociocultural, theories have offered the most suggestions so far, but these proposed explanations are not very precise, and they do not have strong research support. Given the current enthusiasm for biological explanations, genetic and biological factors are likely to receive more study in the coming years, helping researchers determine their possible interaction with psychological causes. And one would hope that sociocultural factors will be studied as well. As we have seen, sociocultural theorists have only occasionally offered explanations for personality disorders. However, sociocultural factors may well play an important role in these disorders and should be examined more carefully, especially since, by definition, each of the patterns diagnosed as a personality disorder differs markedly from the expectations of a person's culture.

The future will likely bring major changes to the explanations and treatments for personality disorders, and the categories of personality disorders will probably undergo change as well. Such changes, however, are now more likely to be based on research than on clinical intuitions and impressions. For the many people caught in the web of rigid and maladaptive personality traits, these changes should make an important, and overdue, difference.

Michio Hoshino/Minden Pictures

Personality au naturel *As suggested by the varied reactions of these polar bears to events at Canada's Hudson Bay, human beings are not the only creatures who demonstrate differences in personality, mood, and lifestyle. Natural data of this kind have led many theorists to suspect that inborn, biological factors contribute to personality differences and personality disorders.*

CRITICAL THOUGHTS

1. It is common for people outside the clinical field to mistakenly diagnose mental disorders in themselves, relatives, or acquaintances, and the personality disorders are among the most favored of their diagnoses. Why do you think these disorders are particularly subject to such efforts at amateur psychology? *pp. 385–415*

2. Do you agree that antisocial personality disorder should be a diagnostic category in DSM-IV, or do you believe that such a classification wrongly attaches a clinical label to a personality pattern that is offensive and sometimes criminal? Can research help clarify this issue? *pp. 394–398*

3. What might be the difference between "normal" lying and "pathological" lying? Why do people often admire someone who deceives—a flatterer, an art forger, a jewel thief? *pp. 394–397*

4. Some people believe that the past 15 years have witnessed an increase in narcissistic behavior and thinking in Western society. What features of Western society during this span of time (for example, child-rearing philosophies, advertising campaigns, sports heroes, book topics, television programming, and movies) may be contributing to a rise in narcissistic behavior? *p. 405*

5. Invent a way of organizing and defining personality disorders that improves upon the present diagnostic system. How would the current DSM categories fit into your new scheme? *pp. 414–415*

KEY TERMS

personality p. 385
personality traits p. 385
personality disorder p. 385
"odd" personality disorders p. 387
paranoid personality disorder p. 388
schizoid personality disorder p. 389
schizotypal personality disorder p. 391

"dramatic" personality disorders p. 394
antisocial personality disorder p. 394
borderline personality disorder p. 398
dialectical behavioral therapy p. 401
histrionic personality disorder p. 402
narcissistic personality disorder p. 404
"anxious" personality disorders p. 406

avoidant personality disorder p. 406
social phobia p. 407
dependent personality disorder p. 408
obsessive-compulsive personality disorder p. 412
anal regressive p. 413
passive-aggressive personality disorder p. 414

QUICK QUIZ

1. What is a personality disorder, and why are personality disorders listed on Axis II in DSM-IV? *pp. 385–387*

2. Describe the social relationship problems caused by each of the personality disorders. *pp. 387–413*

3. What are the three "odd" personality disorders, and what are the symptoms of each? *pp. 387–394*

4. What explanations and treatments have been applied to the paranoid, schizoid, and schizotypal personality disorders? *pp. 387–394*

5. What are the "dramatic" personality disorders, and what are the symptoms of each? *pp. 394–406*

6. How have theorists explained antisocial personality disorder? How effectively have clinicians treated this disorder? *pp. 396–397*

7. What are the leading explanations and treatments for the borderline, histrionic, and narcissistic personality disorders? How strongly does research support these explanations and treatments? *pp. 398–406*

8. Which Axis I disorders do each of the personality disorders listed in DSM-IV resemble? *p. 399*

9. What are the leading explanations for the avoidant, dependent, and obsessive-compulsive personality disorders, and to what extent are they supported by research? How are the disorders treated, and how effective are the treatments? *pp. 406–413*

10. What kinds of problems have clinicians run into when diagnosing personality disorders? What are the causes of these problems, and what solution has been proposed? *pp. 414–415*

CYBER STUDY

SEARCH THE *FUNDAMENTALS OF ABNORMAL PSYCHOLOGY* CD-ROM FOR

▲ Chapter 13 Video Case Enrichment
  How do clinicians assess antisocial personality disorder?
  How does antisocial personality disorder relate to criminal behavior?
  Can traditional treatments change people with antisocial personality disorder?

▲ Chapter 13 Practical, Research, and Decision-Making Exercises
  Distrust, narcissism, and anger in society
  Classifying personality problems in alternative ways

▲ Chapter 13 Practice Test and Feedback

LOG ON TO THE COMER WEB PAGE FOR

▲ Suggested Web links, exercises, FAQ page, additional Chapter 13 practice test questions
  <www.worthpublishers.com/comer>

<<<

ANTONIO BERNI

Disorders of Childhood and Adolescence

Billy, a 7-year-old . . . child, was brought to a mental health clinic by his mother because "he is unhappy and always complaining about feeling sick." . . . His mother describes Billy as a child who has never been very happy and never wanted to play with other children. From the time he started nursery school, he has complained about stomachaches, headaches, and various other physical problems. . . . Because of Billy's frequent somatic complaints, it is hard to get him off to school in the morning. . . . When he does go to school, he often is unable to do the work, which makes him feel hopeless about his situation. . . .

Although Billy's mother acknowledges that he has never been really happy, in the last 6 months, she feels, he has become much more depressed. He frequently lies around the house, saying that he is too tired to do anything. He has no interest or enjoyment in playing. His appetite has diminished. He has trouble falling asleep at night and often wakes up in the middle of the night or early in the morning. Three weeks ago, he talked, for the first time, about wanting to die. . . .

(Spitzer et al., 1994)

In the past year, Eddie [age 9] had been suspended twice for hyperactive and impulsive behavior. Most recently, he had climbed onto the overhead lights of the classroom and caused an uproar when he could not get himself down. . . . Even when he is seated, his rapid foot and hand movements are disruptive to the other children. Eddie has almost no friends and does not play games with his classmates due to his impulsivity and overly active behavior. After school, he likes to play with his dog or ride his bike alone.

Eddie's mother reports that he has been excessively active since he was a toddler. At the age of three, Eddie would awaken at 4:30 a.m. each day and go downstairs without any supervision. Sometimes he would "demolish" the kitchen or living room. . . . For first and second grade, he attended a special behavioral program. For third grade, he was allowed to attend a regular education class, with pull-out services for help with his behavior.

(Spitzer et al., 1994)

Billy and Eddie are both displaying psychological disorders that disrupt their family ties, school performances, and social relationships. Billy, who may qualify for a diagnosis of major depressive disorder, struggles constantly with sadness, along with stomachaches and other physical ailments. Eddie, on the other hand, cannot concentrate and is overly active and impulsive—difficulties that add up to attention-deficit/hyperactivity disorder (ADHD).

Abnormal functioning can occur at any time in life. Some patterns of abnormality, however, are more likely to emerge during particular periods—during childhood, for example, or, at the other end of the spectrum, during old age. In this chapter we shall focus on disorders that have their onset during childhood or early adolescence—disorders such as Billy's depression and Eddie's ADHD. In the next chapter, we shall turn to problems that are more common among the elderly.

>>BY THE NUMBERS
Teenage Concerns

59% Percentage of today's teens who worry about being victims of violence<<

58% Teens who worry about getting sexually transmitted diseases<<

54% Teens who worry about being able to afford college<<

43% Teens who worry about finding good jobs in the future<<

(Begley, 2000)

Childhood and Adolescence

People often think of childhood as a carefree and happy time—yet it can also be frightening and upsetting. In fact, children of all cultures typically experience at least some emotional and behavioral problems as they encounter new people and situations (Crijnen et al., 1999). Surveys reveal that *worry* is a common experience: close to half of all children in the United States have multiple fears, particularly concerning school, health, and personal safety (Ollendick, King, & Muris, 2002; Silverman et al., 1995). Bed-wetting, nightmares, temper tantrums, and restlessness are other problems experienced by many children.

Adolescence can also be a difficult period (Prinstein & LaGreca, 2002). Physical and sexual changes, social and academic pressures, personal doubts, and temptations cause many teenagers to feel anxious, confused, and depressed (Lerner, 2002; McNamara, 2000). Today's teens, although generally happy and optimistic and often spiritual, tend to feel less trusting, more sensitive, and more isolated from their families than adolescents of decades past (Begley, 2000).

Along with these common psychological difficulties, around one-fifth of all children and adolescents in North America also experience a diagnosable psychological disorder (Phares, 2003). Indeed, news reports of teenage suicides, school shootings, and other tragedies remind us daily of the extremes that psychological suffering and disturbances can reach in children and adolescents (see Table 14-1). Boys with psychological disorders outnumber girls, even though most of the

Table 14-1

SCHOOL VIOLENCE: SOME FACTS AND FIGURES

- Urban (inner-city) school shootings have a longer history than shootings in rural and suburban schools.
- Urban school shootings have most commonly been rooted in such issues as poverty, the drug trade, and gang rivalries. They often resemble and may even extend from violence as it occurs in surrounding urban communities.
- Suburban and rural school shootings have most often resembled the "rampage" shootings that occur in workplaces or public places.
- From 1992 to 2003, there were 17 multiple-victim shootings in rural and suburban U.S. schools.
- Multiple-victim school shootings have also occurred in other countries in recent years, such as in Germany and Bosnia-Herzegovina.
- In most of the suburban and rural school shootings, the shooters have previously told other students of their intentions or offered strong hints.
- In most of the suburban and rural school shootings, the shooters have planned the attacks days or weeks in advance.
- Although research has not yielded a consistent psychological profile of a school shooter, many suburban and rural school shooters have experienced extreme depression or desperation, experienced growing disillusionment, had suicidal thoughts, felt persecuted or bullied, sought revenge for real or imagined grievances, or experienced significant life changes or stress.
- Twenty-eight percent of public high school teachers in the United States have been verbally abused, 15 percent threatened, and 3 percent attacked.
- Twenty percent of urban students report that threats involving a weapon or assault in school represent a major problem for them.

Sources: *Infoplease*, 2003; Bowman, 2002; Elliot et al., 2002; Potier, 2002; Dedman, 2000.

adult psychological disorders are more common among women. Some disorders of children—childhood anxiety disorders, childhood depression, and disruptive disorders—are similar to patterns found among adults. Other childhood disorders—elimination disorders, for example—usually disappear or change form by adulthood. There are also disorders that begin during childhood and then persist in stable form into adult life, such as mental retardation and autism, the former an extensive disturbance in intellect, the latter marked by a lack of responsiveness to the environment.

Childhood Anxiety Disorders

As in adults, the anxiety disorders experienced by children and adolescents include specific phobias, social phobias, generalized anxiety disorder, and obsessive-compulsive disorder (Albano et al., 2003; Oest & Treffers, 2001). However, one form of anxiety in children, **separation anxiety disorder**, is different enough from the adult disorders to be listed as a separate category in DSM-IV. Children with this disorder feel extreme anxiety, often panic, whenever they are separated from home or a parent. Carrie, a 9-year-old girl, was referred to a local mental health center by her school counselor when she seemed to become extremely anxious at school for no apparent reason.

> She initially reported feeling sick to her stomach and later became quite concerned over being unable to get her breath. She stated that she was too nervous to stay at school and that she wanted her mother to come get her and take her home. . . . The counselor indicated that a similar incident occurred the next day with Carrie ending up going home again. She had not returned to school since. . . .
>
> At the time of the intake evaluation the mother indicated that she felt Carrie was just too nervous to go to school. She stated that she had encouraged her daughter to go to school on numerous occasions but that she seemed afraid to go and appeared to feel bad, so she had not forced her. . . . When asked if Carrie went places by herself, the mother stated that Carrie didn't like to do that and that the two of them typically did most everything together. The mother went on to note that Carrie really seemed to want to have her (the mother) around all the time and tended to become upset whenever the two of them were separated.
>
> *(Schwartz & Johnson, 1985, p. 188)*

Children like Carrie have great trouble traveling away from their family, and they often refuse to visit friends' houses, go on errands, or attend camp or school.

SEPARATION ANXIETY DISORDER A childhood disorder marked by excessive anxiety, even panic, whenever the child is separated from home or a parent.

Duck and cover *Childhood anxieties can be caused by society's repeated warnings of possible catastrophes. These schoolchildren in Japan dive for cover during an earthquake drill.*

Many cannot even stay alone in a room and cling to their parent around the house. Some also have temper tantrums, cry, or plead to keep their parents from leaving them. The children may fear that they will get lost when separated from their parents or that parents will meet with an accident or illness (APA, 2000, 1994). It has been estimated that about 4 percent of children and young adolescents suffer from separation anxiety disorder, somewhat more girls than boys (Masi et al., 2001; APA, 2000). In many cases it is triggered by a stressful event such as the death of a parent or pet, moving to a new home, or a change of schools (Phares, 2003). The symptoms last at least four weeks, usually much longer, but they may rise and fall over the course of childhood and adolescence.

As in Carrie's case, a separation anxiety disorder sometimes takes the form of a **school phobia**, or **school refusal**, a common problem in which children fear going to school and often stay home for a long period (Heyne et al., 2002). Many cases of school phobia, however, have causes other than separation fears, such as social or academic concerns, depression, and fears of specific objects or persons at school.

Childhood anxiety disorders are generally explained in much the same way as the adult anxiety disorders (see Chapter 4), with biological, behavioral, and cognitive factors pointed to most often (Phares, 2003). However, the special features of childhood can also play an important role (Walkup & Ginsburg, 2002). For example, since children have had fewer experiences than adults, their world is often new and scary. They may be frightened by common events, such as the beginning of school, or by special upsets, such as moving to a new house or becoming seriously ill (Tweed et al., 1989). Special features of their world can also frighten children and set the stage for anxiety disorders. Today's children, for example, are repeatedly warned, both at home and at school, about the dangers of child abduction and of drugs. They are bombarded by violent images in television shows, movies, and news programs. Even fairy tales and nursery rhymes contain frightening images that upset many children.

Because they are highly dependent on their parents for support and guidance, children may also be greatly affected by parental inadequacies (Mufson et al., 2002). If, for example, parents typically react to events with high levels of anxiety or overprotect their child, the child may be more likely to develop anxiety problems (Barrett & Short, 2003; Barrett et al., 1996). Similarly, if parents repeatedly reject, disappoint, avoid, or abuse their children, the world comes to seem an unpleasant and anxious place for them.

Psychodynamic, behavioral, cognitive, family, and group therapies, separately or in combination, have been used to treat anxiety disorders in children and adolescents, often with success (Rapee, 2003; Albano & Kendall, 2002). Clinicians have

SCHOOL PHOBIA A pattern in which children fear going to school and often stay home. Also known as *school refusal.*

A CLOSER LOOK

Child Abuse

I What I remember most about my mother was that she was always beating me. She'd beat me with her high-heeled shoes, with my father's belt, with a potato masher. When I was eight, she black and blued my legs so badly, I told her I'd go to the police. She said, "Go, they'll just put you into the darkest prison." So I stayed. When my breasts started growing at 13, she beat me across the chest until I fainted. Then she'd hug me and ask forgiveness. . . . Most kids have nightmares about being taken away from their parents. I would sit on our front porch crooning softly of going far, far away to find another mother. **I**

(*TIME*, SEPTEMBER 5, 1983, P. 20)

A problem that affects all too many children and has an enormous impact on their psychological development is *child abuse*, the nonaccidental use of excessive physical or psychological force by an adult on a child, often with the intention of hurting or destroying the child. At least 5 percent, and perhaps as many as 26 percent, of children in the United States are physically abused each year (Phares, 2003). Surveys suggest that one of every 10 children is the victim of severe violence, such as being kicked, bitten, hit, beaten, or threatened with a knife or a gun. In fact, some observers believe that physical abuse and neglect are the leading causes of death among young children.

Overall, girls and boys are physically abused at approximately the same rate. However, boys are at greatest risk when they are under the age of 12, while the risk for girls is highest when they are older than 12 (Azar et al., 1998). Although child abuse occurs in all socioeconomic groups, it is apparently more common among the poor (Phares, 2003; Gallup, 1995).

Abusers are usually the child's parents. Clinical investigators have learned that abusive parents often have poor impulse control and low self-esteem. Many have been abused themselves as children and have had poor role models (Bowen, 2000). In some cases, they are experiencing the stress of marital conflict or family unemployment (Whipple et al., 1991).

Studies suggest that the victims of child abuse may suffer both immediate and long-term psychological effects. Research has revealed, for example, that abused children have more performance and behavior problems in school. Long-term negative effects include lack of social acceptance, more medical and psychological disorders, more abuse of alcohol and other substances, more arrests during adolescence and adulthood, a greater risk of becoming criminally violent, a higher unemployment rate, and a higher suicide rate (Safren et al., 2002; Molnar et al., 2001; Widom, 2001, 1991, 1989). Finally, as many as one-third of abuse victims grow up to be abusive, neglectful, or inadequate parents themselves (Heyman & Slep, 2002; Clarke et al., 1999).

Two forms of child abuse have received special attention of late: psychological and sexual abuse. *Psychological abuse* may include severe rejection, excessive discipline, scapegoating and ridicule, isolation, and refusal to provide help for a child with psychological problems. *Child sexual abuse*, the use of a child for gratification of adult sexual desires, may occur outside of or within the home (Bal et al., 2004). In 25 percent of cases, the child is younger than 7 (Wurtele & Schmitt, 1992). Surveys suggest that at least 13 percent of women were forced into sexual contact with an adult male during their childhood, many of them with their father or stepfather (Hill, 2003; Phares, 2003). At least 4 percent of men were also sexually abused during childhood (Romano & DeLuca, 2001). Child sexual abuse appears to be equally common across all socioeconomic classes, races, and ethnic groups (Azar et al., 1998).

A variety of therapies have been used in cases of child abuse, including groups

Honoré Daumier's *Fatherly Discipline*

sponsored by Parents Anonymous, which help parents to develop insight into their behavior, provide training on alternatives to abuse, and teach parenting skills (Azar & Siegal, 1990; Wolfe et al., 1988). Still other treatments help parents deal more effectively with the stresses that often trigger the abuse, such as unemployment, marital conflict, and feelings of depression.

Research suggests that the psychological needs of the child victims should be addressed as early as possible (Gray et al., 2000; Roesler & McKenzie, 1994). Clinicians and educators have launched *early detection programs* that aim to (1) educate all children about child abuse; (2) teach them skills for avoiding or escaping from abusive situations; (3) encourage children to tell another adult if they are abused; and (4) assure them that abuse is never their own fault (Godenzi & DePuy, 2001; Finkelhor et al., 1995). These programs seem to increase the likelihood that children will report abuse, reduce their tendency to blame themselves for it, and increase their feelings of control (Goodman-Brown et al., 2003; MacIntyre & Carr, 1999).

Honoré Daumier, Fatherly Discipline, 1851. The Art Institute of Chicago, Arthur Heun Fund, 1952.

Constructive play *Therapists may use play therapy to assess the functioning of children, to help them express their feelings and thoughts, and to help them better understand themselves and others.*

How could you? *Childhood anxiety or depression may be the result of developmental upsets, such as the increasingly common experience of having to share a parent's affection with a new stepparent. The face of this boy after his mother's remarriage says it all.*

also used drug therapy in some cases, but this approach has only recently begun to receive much research attention (Walkup et al., 2002). Because children typically have difficulty recognizing and understanding their feelings and motives, many therapists, particularly psychodynamic therapists, use **play therapy** as part of treatment (Russ, 2004; Hall et al., 2002). In this approach, the children play with toys, draw, and make up stories, and in so doing reveal the conflicts in their lives and their related feelings. The therapists then introduce more play and fantasy to help the children address their conflicts and change their emotions and behavior.

Childhood Depression

Children, like adults, may develop depression, as did Billy, the boy we observed at the beginning of this chapter. Bobby has similar symptoms:

> In observing Bobby in the playroom it was obvious that his activity level was well below that expected for a child of 10. He showed a lack of interest in the toys that were available to him, and the interviewer was unable to get him interested in any play activity for more than a few minutes. In questioning him about home and school, Bobby indicated that he didn't like school because he didn't have any friends, and he wasn't good at playing games like baseball and soccer like the other kids were, stating "I'm not really very good at anything." . . . When asked what he would wish for if he could have any three wishes granted he indicated, "I would wish that I was the type of boy my mother and father want, I would wish that I could have friends, and I would wish that I wouldn't feel sad so much."
>
> In speaking with the parents, the mother reported that she and her husband had become increasingly concerned about their son during the past year. She indicated that he always seemed to look sad and cried a lot for no apparent reason and that he appeared to have lost interest in most of the things that he used to enjoy doing. The mother confirmed Bobby's statements that he had no friends, indicating that he had become more and more of a loner during the past 6 to 9 months. She stated that his schoolwork had also suffered in that he is unable to concentrate on school assignments and seems to have "just lost interest." The mother notes, however, that her greatest concern is that he has recently spoken more and more frequently about "killing himself," saying that the parents would be better off if he wasn't around.
>
> *(Schwartz & Johnson, 1985, p. 214)*

Between 2 and 4 percent of children under 17 years of age experience major depressive disorder; the rate for teenagers alone is about 7 percent (Phares, 2003; Kazdin, 1994). The symptoms in young sufferers are likely to include physical discomfort (for example, stomachaches or headaches), irritability, and social withdrawal (APA, 2000, 1994). There appears to be no difference in the rates of depression in boys and girls before the age of 11, but by the age of 16, girls are twice as likely as boys to be depressed (Hankin & Abramson, 2001, 1999).

Explanations of childhood depression are similar to those of adult depression. Theorists have pointed, for example, to factors such as loss, learned helplessness, negative cognitions, and low serotonin or norepinephrine activity (Garber & Horowitz, 2002; Lewinsohn & Essau, 2002). Also, like adult depression, many cases of childhood depression seem to be triggered by a negative life event, major change, rejection, or ongoing abuse.

Like depression among adults, childhood depression often is helped by cognitive therapy or interpersonal approaches such as social skills training (Weersing & Brent, 2003; Weisz et al., 2003).

In addition, family therapy can be effective. Antidepressant medications have not proved consistently useful in cases involving children, but they do seem to help some depressed adolescents.

Disruptive Behavior Disorders

Children often break rules or misbehave. If they consistently display extreme hostility and defiance, however, they may qualify for a diagnosis of **oppositional defiant disorder** or conduct disorder. Those with oppositional defiant disorder argue repeatedly with adults, lose their temper, and feel great anger and resentment. They often ignore adult rules and requests, try to annoy other people, and blame others for their own mistakes and problems. Between 2 and 16 percent of children display this pattern (APA, 2000). The disorder is more common in boys than in girls before puberty but equal in the two sexes after puberty.

Children with **conduct disorder**, a more severe problem, repeatedly violate the basic rights of others. They are often aggressive and may in fact be physically cruel to people or animals, deliberately destroy other people's property, skip school, or run away from home (see Table 14-2). Many steal from, threaten, or harm their victims, committing such crimes as shoplifting, forgery, breaking into buildings or cars, mugging, and armed robbery. As they get older, their acts of physical violence may include rape or, in rare cases, homicide (APA, 2000, 1994).

Conduct disorder usually begins between 7 and 15 years of age (APA, 2000). Between 1 and 10 percent of children display this pattern, more boys than girls. Children with a mild conduct disorder may improve over time, but severe cases frequently continue into adulthood and may develop into antisocial personality disorder or other psychological problems (Phares, 2003; Myers et al., 1998).

Cases of conduct disorder have been linked to genetic and biological factors, drug abuse, poverty, traumatic events, and exposure to violent peers or community

PLAY THERAPY An approach to treating childhood disorders that helps children express their conflicts and feelings indirectly by drawing, playing with toys, and making up stories.

OPPOSITIONAL DEFIANT DISORDER A childhood disorder in which children argue repeatedly with adults, lose their temper, and swear, feeling intense anger and resentment.

CONDUCT DISORDER A childhood disorder in which the child repeatedly violates the basic rights of others, displaying aggression and sometimes destroying others' property, stealing, or running away from home.

Table 14-2 DSM-IV Checklist

CONDUCT DISORDER

1. A repetitive and persistent pattern of behavior in which the basic rights of others or major age-appropriate societal norms or rules are violated, with at least three of the following present in the past twelve months (and at least one in the past six months):
   a. Frequent bullying or threatening of others.
   b. Frequent provoking of physical fights.
   c. Using dangerous weapons.
   d. Physical cruelty to people.
   e. Physical cruelty to animals.
   f. Stealing while confronting a victim.
   g. Forcing someone into sexual activity.
   h. Fire-setting.
   i. Deliberately destroying others' property.
   j. Breaking into a house, building, or car.
   k. Frequent manipulation of others.
   l. Stealing items of nontrivial value without confronting a victim.
   m. Frequent staying out beyond curfews, beginning before the age of 13.
   n. Running away from home overnight at least twice.
   o. Frequent truancy from school, beginning before the age of 13.

2. Significant impairment.

Based on APA, 2000, 1994.

violence (Webster-Stratton & Reid, 2003). However, they have most often been tied to troubled parent–child relationships, inadequate parenting, family conflict, marital conflict, and family hostility (Phares, 2003; Biederman et al., 2001). Children whose parents reject them, leave them, coerce them, or fail to provide

THE CURRENT SCENE

Bullying: A Growing Crisis?

Does bullying qualify as a national crisis? Even to pose the question sounds a bit silly, conjuring up images of the schoolyard thug from the *Calvin and Hobbes* comic strip or Bart's nemesis on *The Simpsons*. But many sober voices say that bullying is no laughing matter and warn that if society continues to overlook this problem, it will place its citizens, particularly its children, at considerable risk (Rigby, 2002).

Recently the Secret Service released a report examining the dozens of school shootings that have taken place across the United States since 1997. It found that bullying was a factor in two-thirds of them (Crisp, 2001). In some cases, the shooters had been bullies; much more often, they had been the *victims* of bullying. A survey released by the Kaiser Family Foundation and Nickelodeon asked a national sample of children aged 8 to 15 what issues in school concerned them most, and all age groups pointed to teasing and bullying as "big problems" that ranked higher than racism, AIDS, and peer pressure to try sex or alcohol (Cukan, 2001). Reports such as these have elevated bullying from a narrow concern that is best dealt with by students themselves (or perhaps by the teachers and parents of those directly involved) to a widespread problem that requires the attention of school-level programs and statewide policies.

For instance, in the wake of shooting disasters such as that at Columbine High School in Littleton, Colorado (where 2 students murdered 12 of their peers and a teacher and injured dozens of others before committing suicide), many schools have put "zero tolerance" programs in place. These rules require immediate suspension of pupils who bring any weapon into the school—or indeed any object at all that could be used in a

threatening way. A growing number of schools, too, have started programs—with names like "Taking the Bully by the Horns"—that teach children how to deal level-headedly with their tormenters and when to ask a teacher for help (Rahey & Craig, 2002).

While acknowledging the important role of bullying in the recent wave of school shootings, some experts worry that the public, school officials, and policymakers are focusing on this issue so intensely that more subtle and perhaps more significant factors are being ignored by clinicians and researchers. Why has the public centered so much attention on bullying as it tries to sort out school shootings and other unthinkable acts by schoolchildren? Perhaps, some experts argue, because bullying offers a quick explanation and a ready focus for intervention and change. After all, teachers and administrators have been observing and dealing with bullies since the first little red schoolhouse appeared on the prairie. As Charles Ewing, a law

professor, psychologist, and expert on homicides by children, puts it, "It's not rocket science to figure out who these unhappy kids are" (Cukan, 2001).

At the same time, the commonplace nature of bullying that makes it seem so familiar and treatable might actually make it a difficult problem to address. One study has found that a full 30 percent of American students are involved in moderate or frequent bullying—11 percent have been victims, 13 percent have been bullies, and 6 percent have been both (Tanner, 2001). Other studies have reported even higher rates (Haynie et al., 2001). How easy can it be for clinicians to identify which children will turn dangerously violent if indeed one-third of all children have experienced bullying? How can we rid ourselves of a problem as widespread as this? As one commentator said, "Short of raising kids in isolation chambers . . . bullying behaviors can never be eliminated entirely from the sustained hazing ritual known as growing up" (Angier, 2001).

SW Productions/Photodisc

Unthinkable *A surveillance camera shows the 1993 abduction of 2-year-old James Bulger from a shopping mall in England. The child holds the hand of one of his abductors—two 10-year-old boys who were later convicted of his torture and murder. The legal case stirred the emotions of people around the world and clarified that some children are indeed capable of extreme antisocial behavior.*

consistent discipline and supervision are apparently more likely to develop a conduct disorder. Similarly, children seem more prone to this disorder when their parents are antisocial, display excessive anger, or have substance-related, mood, or schizophrenic disorders (Wozniak et al., 2001; Kendall, 2000).

Because disruptive behavior patterns become more locked in with age, treatments for conduct disorder are generally most effective with children younger than 13 (Roach & Gross, 2002; Burnette & Murray, 1996). Given the importance of family factors in this disorder, therapists often use family interventions. In the most successful of these approaches, (1) parents are taught more effective ways to deal with their children (for example, they are taught to be consistent about rewarding appropriate behaviors), and (2) parents and children meet together in behavior-oriented family therapy (Kazdin, 2003, 2002; Frick & McCoy, 2001).

Sociocultural approaches such as residential treatment in the community, programs at school, and group therapy have also helped some children improve (Chamberlain & Smith, 2003; Henggeler & Lee, 2003). Individual approaches are sometimes effective as well, particularly those that teach the child how to cope with anger (Kazdin, 2002). And recently drug therapy has been tried to help control aggressive outbursts in these children (Gerardin et al., 2002). Institutionalization in so-called *juvenile training centers* has not met with much success (Tate et al., 1995). In fact, such institutions frequently serve to strengthen delinquent behavior rather than resocialize young offenders (see Figure 14-1).

It may be that the greatest hope for reducing the problem of conduct disorder lies in *prevention* programs that begin in early childhood (Webster-Stratton & Reid, 2003; LeMarquand et al., 2001). These programs try to change unfavorable social conditions before a conduct disorder is able to develop. The programs may offer training opportunities for young people, recreational facilities, and health care, and may try to ease the stresses of poverty and improve parents' child-rearing skills. All approaches work best when they educate and involve the family.

FIGURE 14-1 Teenage crime *Although teenagers make up only 14 percent of the total population, they commit around 30 percent of all violent crimes and 34 percent of all murders. They are also the victims of 33 percent of all violent crimes. (Adapted from Levesque, 2002; Benson, 1996; FBI Uniform Crime Reports, 1996; National Crime Victimization Survey, 1996, 1993.)*

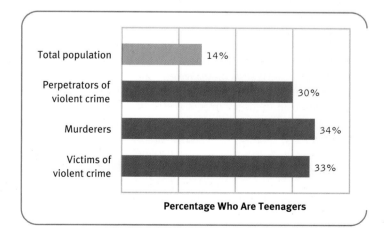

	Percentage Who Are Teenagers
Total population	14%
Perpetrators of violent crime	30%
Murderers	34%
Victims of violent crime	33%

Attention-Deficit/Hyperactivity Disorder

Children who display **attention-deficit/hyperactivity disorder (ADHD)** have great difficulty attending to tasks or behave overactively and impulsively, or both (see Table 14-3). The disorder often appears before the child starts school, as with Eddie, one of the boys we met at the beginning of this chapter (Phillips et al., 2002). Steven is another child whose symptoms began very early in life:

> Steven's mother cannot remember a time when her son was not into something or in trouble. As a baby he was incredibly active, so active in fact that he nearly rocked his crib apart. All the bolts and screws became loose and had to be tightened periodically. Steven was also always into forbidden places, going through the medicine cabinet or under the kitchen sink. He once swallowed some washing detergent and had to be taken to the emergency room. As a matter of fact, Steven had many more accidents and was more clumsy than his older brother and younger sister. . . . He always seemed to be moving fast. His mother recalls that Steven progressed from the crawling stage to a running stage with very little walking in between.
>
> Trouble really started to develop for Steven when he entered kindergarten. Since his entry into school, his life has been miserable and so has the teacher's. Steven does not seem capable of attending to assigned tasks and following instructions. He would rather be talking to a neighbor or wandering around the room without the teacher's permission. When he is seated and the teacher is keeping an eye on him to make sure that he works, Steven's body still seems to be in motion. He is either tapping his pencil, fidgeting, or staring out the window and daydreaming. Steven hates kindergarten and has few long-term friends; indeed, school rules and demands appear to be impossible challenges for him. The effects of this mismatch are now showing in Steven's schoolwork and attitude. He has fallen behind academically and has real difficulty mastering new concepts; he no longer follows directions from the teacher and has started to talk back.
>
> *(Gelfand, Jenson, & Drew, 1982, p. 256)*

Behavioral intervention *Educational and treatment programs for children with ADHD use behavioral principles that clearly spell out target behaviors and program rewards and systematically reinforce appropriate behaviors by the children.*

The symptoms of ADHD often feed into one another. Children who have trouble focusing attention may keep turning from task to task until they end up trying to run in several directions at once. Similarly, constantly moving children may find it hard to attend to tasks or show good judgment. Often one of these symptoms stands out much more than the other. About half of the children with ADHD also have learning or communication problems, many perform poorly in school, a number have difficulty interacting with other children, and about 80 percent misbehave, often quite seriously (Silver, 2004; Waldman et al., 2001). It is also common for the children to have mood or anxiety problems (Busch et al., 2002; Rowland et al., 2002).

Around 5 percent of schoolchildren display ADHD, as many as 90 percent of them boys. The disorder usually persists throughout childhood (Pennington, 2002). Many children show a marked lessening of symptoms as they move into mid-adolescence, but at least half continue to have problems (Silver, 2004; Barkley, 2002, 1998). Around one-third of affected children have ADHD as adults, although the symptoms of restlessness and overactivity are not usually as clear in adulthood (Goldstein & Ellison, 2002; Faraone, 2000).

Table 14-3 **DSM-IV Checklist**

ATTENTION-DEFICIT/HYPERACTIVITY DISORDER

1. Either of the following groups:
   A. At least six of the following symptoms of *inattention*, persisting for at least six months to a degree that is maladaptive and inconsistent with development level:
      a. Frequent failure to give close attention to details, or making careless mistakes.
      b. Frequent difficulty in sustaining attention.
      c. Frequent failure to listen when spoken to directly.
      d. Frequent failure to follow through on instructions and failure to finish work.
      e. Difficulty organizing tasks and activities.
      f. Avoidance of, dislike of, and reluctance to engage in tasks that require sustained mental effort.
      g. Frequent loss of items necessary for tasks or activities.
      h. Easy distraction by irrelevant stimuli.
      i. Forgetfulness in daily activities.
   B. At least six of the following symptoms of *hyperactivity-impulsivity*, persisting for at least six months to a degree that is maladaptive and inconsistent with developmental level:
      a. Fidgeting with hands or feet, or squirming in seat.
      b. Frequent wandering from seat in classroom or similar situation.
      c. Frequent running about or climbing excessively in situations in which it is inappropriate.
      d. Frequent difficulty playing or engaging in leisure activities quietly.
      e. Frequent "on the go" activity or acting as if "driven by a motor."
      f. Frequent excessive talking.
      g. Frequent blurting out of answers before questions have been completed.
      h. Frequent difficulty awaiting turn.
      i. Frequent interrupting of or intruding on others.
2. The presence of some symptoms before the age of 7.
3. Impairment from the symptoms in at least two settings.
4. Significant impairment.

Based on APA, 2000, 1994.

Those whose parents have had ADHD are more likely than others to develop it, and the disorder is also displayed by around one-fourth of the close relatives of people with the disorder (APA, 2000, 1994; Whalen & Henker, 1998).

Today's clinicians generally consider ADHD to have several interacting causes, including biological causes (abnormalities in certain regions of the brain have been implicated most often), high levels of stress, and family dysfunction (Barkley, 2002, 1998; Kirley et al., 2002). Each of these causes has received some research support. Sociocultural theorists further point out that ADHD symptoms and a diagnosis of ADHD may themselves create interpersonal problems and produce additional symptoms in the child. That is, children who are hyperactive tend to be viewed negatively by their peers and by their parents, and they often view themselves negatively as well (Busch et al., 2002; McCormick, 2000). Two other explanations have received wide press coverage: one is that ADHD is caused by sugar or food additives, and the other is that it results from environmental toxins such as lead. However, neither of these beliefs has been supported by research (Phares, 2003; Whalen & Henker, 1998).

>>**IN THEIR WORDS**

"It is an illusion that youth is happy, an illusion of those who have lost it."<<

W. Somerset Maugham,
Of Human Bondage, 1915

"Children nowadays are tyrants. They contradict their parents, gobble their food, and tyrannize their teachers."<<

Socrates, 425 B.C.

A CLOSER LOOK

Ritalin: Chemical Straightjacket or Miracle Drug?

When Tom was born, he acted like a "crack baby," his mother, Ann, says. "He responded violently to even the slightest touch, and he never slept." Shortly after Tom turned two, the local day care center asked Ann to withdraw him. They deemed his behavior "just too aberrant," she remembers. Tom's doctors ran a battery of tests to screen for brain damage, but they found no physical explanation for his lack of self-control. In fact, his IQ was high—even though he performed poorly in school. Eventually, Tom was diagnosed with attention-deficit/hyperactivity disorder (ADHD). . . . The psychiatrist told Ann that in terms of severity, Tom was 15 on a scale of one to 10. As therapy, this doctor prescribed methylphenidate, a drug better known by its brand name, Ritalin.

(LEUTWYLER, 1996, P. 13)

Like Tom, millions of children and adults with ADHD are treated with *methylphenidate*, or *Ritalin*, a stimulant drug that has actually been available for decades. As researchers have confirmed Ritalin's quieting effect on individuals with ADHD and its ability to help them focus and solve complex tasks, use of the drug has increased enormously—according to some estimates, as much as a fivefold increase since 1990 alone (DEA, 2000; Robison et al., 1999) (see accompanying figure). This increase in use also extends to preschoolers (Zito et al., 2000). As many as 12 percent of all American boys may take Ritalin for ADHD, and the number of girls taking it is growing. Around 8.5 tons of Ritalin are produced each year, and 90 percent of it is used in the United States (DEA, 2000; Diller, 1999). In recent years, certain other stimulant drugs have also been found to be helpful in cases of ADHD, and their use has increased correspondingly.

Many clinicians and parents, however, have questioned the need for and safety of Ritalin. During the late 1980s, several lawsuits were filed against physicians, schools, and even the American Psychiatric Association, claiming misuse of Ritalin (Safer, 1994). Most of the suits were dismissed, yet the media blitz they produced has affected public perceptions (Safer & Kragner, 1992). At the same time, Ritalin has become a popular recreational drug among teenagers; some snort it to get high, and a number become dependent on it. This development has further raised public concerns about the drug.

Extensive investigations conducted during the 1990s indicate that ADHD may in fact be overdiagnosed in the United States and that many children who receive Ritalin have been inaccurately diagnosed (DEA, 2000; UNINCB, 1996). ADHD can be reliably diagnosed only after a battery of observations, interviews, psychological tests, and physical exams (Silver, 2004; Buttross, 2000). Yet studies have found that fewer than half of children who receive this diagnosis from pediatricians or family physicians undergo psychological or educational testing to support the conclusion (Hoagwood et al., 2000; Leutwyler, 1996).

On the positive side, Ritalin is apparently very helpful to children and adults who do suffer from ADHD (Pennington, 2002). Parent training and behavioral programs are also effective in many cases, but not in all. Furthermore, the behavioral programs are often more likely to be effective in combination with Ritalin (Pelham et al., 2000, 1998; Klassen et al., 1999). When children with ADHD are taken off the drug, many fare badly (Safer & Krager, 1992).

There is heated disagreement about the most effective treatment for ADHD (Phares, 2003; Hoagwood et al., 2000). The most common approach has been the use of stimulant drugs, such as **methylphenidate** (**Ritalin**). These drugs have a quieting effect on most children with ADHD and sometimes increase their ability to solve problems, perform academically, and control aggression (Barkley, 2002, 1998; Brown & LaRosa, 2002). However, some clinicians worry about the possible long-term effects of the drugs. Behavioral therapy is also applied widely. Here parents and teachers learn how to reward attentiveness or self-control in their children or students. Such operant conditioning treatments have often been helpful, especially when combined with drug therapy (Barkley, 2002, 1998).

Elimination Disorders

Children with elimination disorders repeatedly urinate or pass feces in their clothes, in bed, or on the floor. They already have reached an age at which they are expected to control these bodily functions, and their symptoms are not caused by physical illness.

Studies to date suggest that Ritalin is safe for most people with ADHD (Pennington, 2002). Its undesired effects are usually no worse than insomnia, stomachaches, headaches, or loss of appetite. In a small number of cases, however, it may cause facial tics or psychotic symptoms (Cherland & Fitzpatrick, 1999). And Ritalin can affect the growth of some children, thus requiring "drug holidays" during the summer to prevent this effect.

Although Ritalin does not typically appear to have long-term effects (Vinson, 1994), more studies are needed to clarify this (Bennett et al., 1999). Similarly, research is needed on the long-term effects of the other stimulant drugs that are increasingly being applied in cases of ADHD.

The question, then, is what to do about a drug that is helpful for many people but almost certainly overused and even abused in some cases. The solution recommended by growing numbers of clinicians is better control of its use. Clearly, researchers must continue to study this and related drugs, and pediatricians and others who work with children must be better trained in the

assessment of ADHD, must be required to conduct broader testing before diagnosing ADHD, and must stay aware of helpful treatments other than Ritalin.

Only under these circumstances will drugs such as Ritalin fulfill their potential as a truly useful treatment for a serious problem.

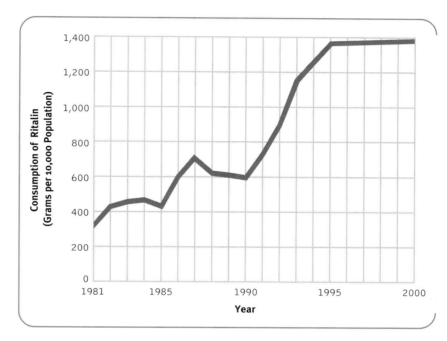

The rise of Ritalin *The use of Ritalin has been increasing since the early 1980s, when researchers discovered that it helped people with ADHD. Sales more than doubled during the 1990s alone. (Adapted from Drug Enforcement Administration, 2000, 1996.)*

ENURESIS **Enuresis** is repeated involuntary (or in some cases intentional) bedwetting or wetting of one's clothes. It typically occurs at night during sleep but may also occur during the day. Children must be at least 5 years of age to receive this diagnosis (see Table 14-4 on the next page). The problem may be brought on by a stressful event, such as hospitalization or entrance into school. The prevalence of enuresis decreases with age. As many as 10 percent of children who are 5 years old suffer from this disorder, compared to 3 to 5 percent of 10-year-olds and 1 percent of 15-year-olds (APA, 2000). Those with enuresis typically have a close relative (parent, sibling) who has had or will have the same disorder (APA, 2000).

Research has not favored one explanation for enuresis over the others. Psychodynamic theorists explain it as a symptom of broader anxiety and underlying conflicts (Olmos de Paz, 1990). Family theorists point to disturbed family interactions (Fletcher, 2000). Behaviorists often view it as the result of improper toilet training. And biological theorists suspect that the physical structure of the urinary system develops more slowly in certain children (Mikkelsen, 2001; Erickson, 1992).

Most cases of enuresis correct themselves even without treatment. However, therapy, particularly behavioral therapy, can speed up the process (Spiegler &

METHYLPHENIDATE A stimulant drug, known better by the trade name Ritalin, commonly used to treat ADHD.

ENURESIS A childhood disorder marked by repeated bed-wetting or wetting of one's clothes.

Table 14-4 DSM-IV Checklist

ENURESIS

1. Repeated voiding of urine into bed or clothes.
2. Behavior occurring twice a week for at least three consecutive months, or producing significant distress or impairment.
3. A chronological age of at least 5 (or equivalent developmental level).

ENCOPRESIS

1. Repeated passage of feces into inappropriate places (e.g., clothing or floor).
2. Behavior occurring at least once a month for at least three months.
3. A chronological age of at least 4 (or equivalent developmental level).

Based on APA, 2000, 1994.

Guevremont, 2003; Murphy & Carr, 2000). In a widely used classical conditioning approach, the *bell-and-battery technique*, a bell and a battery are wired to a pad consisting of two metallic foil sheets, and the entire apparatus is placed under the child at bedtime (Houts, 2003; Mowrer & Mowrer, 1938). A single drop of urine sets off the bell, awakening the child as soon as he or she starts to wet. Thus the bell (unconditioned stimulus) paired with the sensation of a full bladder (conditioned stimulus) produces the response of waking. Eventually, a full bladder alone awakens the child.

ENCOPRESIS **Encopresis**, repeatedly defecating into one's clothing, is less common than enuresis and less well researched. This problem seldom occurs at night during sleep (Levine, 1975). It is usually involuntary, starts after the age of 4, and affects about 1 percent of 5-year-olds (see Table 14-5 on page 434). The disorder is more common in boys than in girls (APA, 2000).

Encopresis causes social problems, shame, and embarrassment (Cox et al., 2002). Children who suffer from it will usually try to hide their condition and to avoid situations, such as camp or school, in which they might embarrass themselves (APA, 2000, 1994; Ross, 1981). Cases may stem from stress, constipation, or improper toilet training. The most common and successful treatments are behavioral and medical approaches or combinations of the two (McGrath et al., 2000; Murphy & Carr, 2000). Family therapy has also been helpful (Wells & Hinkle, 1990).

SUMMING UP | Disorders of Childhood and Adolescence

Emotional and behavioral problems are common in childhood and adolescence, but in addition, one-fifth of all children and adolescents in the United States experience a diagnosable psychological disorder. For example, many children experience an anxiety disorder (such as separation anxiety disorder) or depression.

Children with disruptive behavior disorders exceed the normal breaking of rules and act very aggressively. In one such disorder, oppositional defiant disorder, they argue repeatedly with adults, lose their temper, and feel intense anger and resentment. In conduct disorder, a more severe pattern, they repeatedly violate the basic rights of others, are often violent and cruel, and may deliberately destroy property, steal, and run away.

Children who display attention-deficit/hyperactivity disorder (ADHD) attend poorly to tasks or behave overactively and impulsively, or both. Ritalin and other stimulant drugs and behavioral programs are often effective treatments. Children with an elimination disorder—enuresis or encopresis—repeatedly urinate or pass feces in inappropriate places. The behavioral bell-and-battery technique is an effective treatment for enuresis.

ENCOPRESIS A childhood disorder characterized by repeated defecating in inappropriate places, such as one's clothing.

AUTISTIC DISORDER A long-term disorder marked by extreme unresponsiveness to others, poor communication skills, and highly repetitive and rigid behavior. Also known as *autism*.

Long-Term Disorders That Begin in Childhood

Most childhood disorders change or subside as the person ages. Two of the disorders that emerge during childhood, however, are likely to continue in stable form throughout a person's life: *autism* and *mental retardation*. Although it was not always so, clinicians have developed a range of interventions that can make a major difference in the lives of people with these problems.

Autism

A child named Mark presents a typical picture of autism:

> In retrospect [Susan, Mark's mother] can recall some things that appeared odd to her. For example, she remembers that . . . Mark never seemed to anticipate being picked up when she approached. In addition, despite Mark's attachment to a pacifier (he would complain if it were mislaid), he showed little interest in toys. In fact, Mark seemed to lack interest in anything. He rarely pointed to things and seemed oblivious to sounds. . . . Mark spent much of his time repetitively tapping on tables, seeming to be lost in his own world.
>
> After his second birthday, Mark's behavior began to trouble his parents. . . . Mark, they said, would "look through" people or past them, but rarely at them. He could say a few words but didn't seem to understand speech. In fact, he did not even respond to his own name. Mark's time was occupied examining familiar objects, which he would hold in front of his eyes while he twisted and turned them. Particularly troublesome were Mark's odd movements—he would jump, flap his arms, twist his hands and fingers, and perform all sorts of facial grimaces, particularly when he was excited—and what Robert [Mark's father] described as Mark's rigidity. Mark would line things up in rows and scream if they were disturbed. He insisted on keeping objects in their place and would become upset whenever Susan attempted to rearrange the living room furniture. . . .
>
> Slowly, beginning at age five, Mark began to improve. . . .
>
> *(Wing, 1976)*

>>IN THEIR WORDS
"No two people with autism are the same. Its precise form of expression is different in every case."<<

Oliver Sacks, 2000

Mark was displaying **autistic disorder**, also called **autism**, a pattern first identified by the American psychiatrist Leo Kanner in 1943. Individuals with this disorder are extremely unresponsive to others, uncommunicative, repetitive, and rigid. Their symptoms appear early in life, before 3 years of age. Autism affects only 5 of every 10,000 children (Phares, 2003; APA, 2000). Approximately 80 percent of them are boys. As many as 90 percent of individuals with autism remain severely disabled into adulthood and are unable to lead independent lives (APA, 2000; Werry, 1996). Moreover, even the highest-functioning adults with autism typically have problems in social interactions and communication and have limited interests and activities.

Several other disorders are similar to autism but differ to some degree in symptoms or time of onset (Kabot et al., 2003). Properly speaking, these different disorders are categorized as *pervasive developmental disorders,* but most clinicians refer to them in general as "autism," and this chapter will do the same.

WHAT ARE THE FEATURES OF AUTISM? The individual's *lack of responsiveness,* including extreme aloofness and lack of interest in other people, has long been considered the central feature of autism. Like Mark, children with this disorder typically do not reach for their parents during infancy. Instead they may arch their backs when they are held and appear not to recognize or care about those around them.

Language and communication problems take various forms in autism. Approximately half of all sufferers fail to speak or develop language skills (Dawson & Castelloe, 1992). Those who do talk may show peculiarities in their speech. One of the most common speech problems is *echolalia,* the exact echoing of phrases spoken by others. The individuals repeat the words with the same inflection, but with no sign of understanding. Some even repeat a

Autistic acts *This autistic child is comforted by standing on her chair and watching television close up, and she often repeats this behavior. People with autism often interact with objects and people in unusual ways that seem to fascinate, stimulate, comfort, or reassure them.*

Vicki Cronis, Norfolk, Virginia

Table 14-5

Comparison of Childhood Disorders

DISORDER	USUAL AGE OF IDENTIFICATION	PREVALENCE AMONG ALL CHILDREN	GENDER WITH GREATER PREVALENCE	ELEVATED FAMILY HISTORY	RECOVERY BY ADULTHOOD
Separation anxiety disorder	Before 12 years	4%	Females	Yes	Often
Conduct disorder	7–15 years	1–10%	Males	Yes	Often
ADHD	Before 12 years	5%	Males	Yes	Often
Enuresis	5–8 years	5%	Males	Yes	Usually
Encopresis	After 4 years	1%	Males	Unclear	Usually
Learning disorders	6–9 years	5%	Males	Yes	Often
Autism	0–3 years	0.05%	Males	Yes	Sometimes
Mental retardation	Before 10 years	1%	Males	Unclear	Sometimes

sentence days after they have heard it (delayed echolalia). People with autism may also display other speech oddities, such as *pronominal reversal*, or confusion of pronouns—the use of "you" instead of "I." When Mark was hungry, he would say, "Do you want dinner?" In addition, individuals may have problems naming objects, using abstract language, employing a proper tone when speaking, speaking spontaneously, or understanding speech.

Autism is also marked by *limited imaginative play* and *very repetitive and rigid behavior*. Affected children may be unable to play in a varied, spontaneous way or to include others in their play. Typically they become very upset at minor changes of objects, persons, or routine, and resist any efforts to change their repetitive behaviors. Mark, for example, lined things up and screamed if they were disturbed. Similarly, children with autism may react with tantrums if a parent wears an unfamiliar pair of glasses, a chair is moved to a different part of the room, or a word in a song is changed. Kanner (1943) labeled such reactions a *preservation of sameness*. Furthermore, many sufferers become strongly attached to particular objects—plastic lids, rubber bands, buttons, water. They may collect these objects, carry them, or play with them constantly. Some are fascinated by movement and may watch spinning objects, such as fans, for hours.

The *motor movements* of people with this disorder may also be unusual. Mark would jump, flap his arms, twist his hands and fingers, and make faces. These acts are called *self-stimulatory behaviors*. Some individuals perform *self-injurious behaviors*, such as repeatedly lunging into or banging their head against a wall, pulling their hair, or biting themselves.

These symptoms suggest a very disturbed and contradictory pattern of reactions to stimuli (Wing, 1976; Wing & Wing, 1971). Sometimes the individuals seem *overstimulated* by sights and sounds and to be trying to block them out, while at other times they seem *understimulated* and to be performing self-stimulatory actions. They may fail to react to loud noises, for example, yet turn around when they hear soda being poured. Similarly, they may fail to recognize that they have reached the edge of a dangerous high place, yet immediately spot a small object that is out of position in their room.

WHAT CAUSES AUTISM? A variety of explanations have been offered for autism. This is one disorder for which sociocultural explanations have probably been overemphasized and initially led investigators in the wrong direction. More recent work in the psychological and biological spheres has persuaded clinical theorists that cognitive limitations and brain abnormalities are the primary causes of autism.

SOCIOCULTURAL CAUSES At first, theorists thought that family dysfunction and social stress were the primary causes of autism. When he first identified autism, for example, Leo Kanner (1954, 1943) argued that *particular personality charac-teristics of the parents* created an unfavorable climate for development and contributed to the child's disorder. He saw these parents as very intelligent yet cold—"refrigerator parents." These claims had enormous influence on the public and on the self-image of the parents themselves, but research has totally failed to support a picture of rigid, cold, rejecting, or disturbed parents (Roazen, 1992).

Similarly, some other clinicians have proposed that a high degree of *social and environmental stress* is a key factor in autism. Once again, however, research has not supported this notion. Investigators who have compared children with autism to children without the disorder have found no differences in the rate of parental death, divorce, separation, financial problems, or environmental stimulation (Cox et al., 1975).

PSYCHOLOGICAL CAUSES According to some theorists, people with autism have a central perceptual or cognitive disturbance that makes normal communication and interactions impossible. One influential explanation holds that individuals with this disorder fail to develop a **theory of mind**—an awareness that other people base their behaviors on their own beliefs, intentions, and other mental states, not on information that they have no way of knowing (Frith, 2000; Happé, 1997, 1995; Leslie, 1997).

By 3 to 5 years of age, most children can take the perspective of another person into account and use it to anticipate what the person will do. In a way, they learn to read others' minds. Let us say, for example, that we watch Jessica place a marble in a container and then we observe Frank move the marble to a nearby room while Jessica is taking a nap. We know that later Jessica will search first in the container for the marble, because she is not aware that Frank moved it. We know that because we take Jessica's perspective into account. A normal child would also anticipate Jessica's search correctly. A person with autism would not. He or she would expect Jessica to look in the nearby room, because that is where the marble actually is. Jessica's own mental processes would be unimportant to the person.

Studies show that people with autism do have this kind of "mindblindness," although they are not necessarily the only kinds of individuals with this limitation (Dahlgren et al., 2003; Wellman et al., 2001). They thus have great difficulty taking part in make-believe play, using language in ways that include the perspectives of others, developing relationships, or participating in interactions. Why do people with autism have this and other cognitive limitations? Some theorists believe that they suffered early biological problems that prevented proper cognitive development.

BIOLOGICAL CAUSES For years researchers have tried to determine what biological abnormalities might cause theory-of-mind deficits and the other symptoms of autism. They have not yet developed a clear biological explanation, but they have uncovered some promising leads (Volkmar, 2001; Rodier, 2000). First, examinations of the relatives of people with autism keep suggesting a *genetic factor* in this disorder. The prevalence of autism among their siblings, for example, is as high as 8 per 100 (Piven et al., 1997), a rate up to 200 times higher than the general population's. Moreover, identical twins of people with autism display the highest risk of all (Treffert, 1999). In addition, chromosomal abnormalities have been discovered in around 10 percent of people with the disorder (Sudhalter et al., 1990).

THEORY OF MIND Awareness that other people base their behaviors on their own beliefs, intentions, and other mental states, not on information they have no way of knowing.

Randy Olson, from *Power to Heal*

Animal connection *Children with autism are often unresponsive to other people. Yet many of them interact warmly with animals. Regular sessions of stroking and touching this dolphin have helped this young teenager overcome his autistic fear of touch and behave more spontaneously.*

A CLOSER LOOK

A Special Kind of Talent

Most people are familiar with the savant syndrome, thanks to Dustin Hoffman's portrayal of a man with autism in the movie *Rain Man* (right). The savant skills that Hoffman portrayed—counting 246 toothpicks in the instant after they fall to the floor, memorizing the phone book through the G's, and doing numerical calculations at lightning speed—were based on the astounding talents of certain real-life people who are otherwise limited by autism or mental retardation.

A *savant* (French for "learned" or "clever") is a person with a major mental disorder or intellectual handicap who has some spectacular ability, some area of exceptional brilliance. Often these abilities are remarkable only in light of the handicap, but sometimes they are remarkable by any standard (Henley, 2003; Yewchuk, 1999).

A common savant skill is calendar calculating, the ability to calculate what day of the week a date will fall on, such as New Year's Day in 2050 (Heavey, 2003). A common musical skill such individuals may possess is the ability to play a piece of classical music flawlessly from memory after hearing it only once. Other individuals can paint exact replicas of scenes they saw years ago (Hou et al., 2000).

Some theorists believe that savant skills do indeed represent special forms of cognitive functioning;

others propose that the skills are merely a positive side to certain cognitive deficits (Scheuffgen et al., 2000; Miller, 1999). Special memorization skills, for example, may be made possible by the very narrow and intense focus often found in cases of autism.

Some studies have also linked autism to *prenatal difficulties* or *birth complications* (Rodier, 2000; Simon, 2000). The chances of developing the disorder are higher when the mother had *rubella* (German measles) during pregnancy, was exposed to toxic chemicals before or during pregnancy, or had complications during labor or delivery. In 1998 one team of investigators proposed that a *postnatal event*—the vaccine for measles, mumps, and rubella—might produce autism in some children, alarming many parents of toddlers. However, subsequent research has failed to find a link between the vaccine and the disorder (Taylor et al., 1999).

Finally, researchers have identified specific *biological abnormalities* that may contribute to autism. Some recent studies have pointed to the **cerebellum**, for example (Pierce & Courchesne, 2002, 2001; Carper & Courchesne, 2000). Brain scans and autopsies reveal abnormal development in this brain area occurring early in the life of people with autism. Scientists have long known that the cerebellum coordinates movement in the body, but they now suspect that it also helps control a person's ability to shift attention rapidly. It may be that people whose cerebellum develops abnormally will have great difficulty adjusting their level of attention, following verbal and facial cues, and making sense of social information, all key features of autism.

Many researchers believe that autism may in fact have multiple biological causes (Mueller & Courchesne, 2000). Perhaps all relevant biological factors (genetic, prenatal, birth, and postnatal) eventually lead to a common problem in the brain—a "final common pathway," such as neurotransmitter abnormalities, that produces the cognitive problems and other features of the disorder.

HOW IS AUTISM TREATED? Treatment can help people with autism adapt better to their environment, although no treatment yet known totally reverses the autistic pattern. Treatments of particular help are *behavioral therapy, communication training, parent training,* and *community integration.* In addition, psychotropic drugs and certain vitamins have sometimes helped when combined with other approaches (Volkmar, 2001; Tsai, 1999).

BEHAVIORAL THERAPY Behavioral approaches have been used in cases of autism for more than 30 years to teach new, appropriate behaviors, including speech, social skills, classroom skills, and self-help skills, while reducing negative, dysfunctional ones. Most often, the therapists use modeling and operant conditioning. In modeling, they demonstrate a desired behavior and guide people with the disorder to imitate it. In operant conditioning, they reinforce such behaviors, first by shaping them—breaking them down so they can be learned step by step—and then rewarding each step clearly and consistently (Lovaas, 2003, 1987; Erba, 2000). With careful planning and application, these procedures often produce new, more functional behaviors.

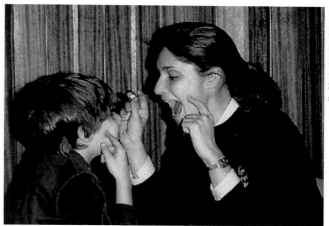

Learning to speak *Behaviorists have had success teaching many children with autism to speak. The therapist systematically models how to position the mouth and how to make appropriate sounds, and then rewards the child's accurate imitations.*

A long-term study compared the progress of two groups of children with autism (McEachin et al., 1993; Lovaas, 1987). Nineteen received intensive behavioral treatments, and 19 served as a control group. The treatment began when the children were 3 years old and continued until they were 7. By the age of 7, the behavioral group was doing better in school and scoring higher on intelligence tests than the control group. Many were able to go to school in regular classrooms. The gains continued into the subjects' teenage years. In light of such findings, many clinicians now consider early behavioral programs to be the preferred treatment for autism (Harris, 2000, 1995).

Therapies for people with autism, particularly the behavioral therapies, are ideally applied in school while they are young. The children attend special classes, often at special schools, where education and therapy can be combined. Specially trained teachers help the children improve their skills, behaviors, and interactions with the world. Higher-functioning persons with this disorder may spend at least part of their school day in normal classrooms, developing social and academic skills in the company of nonautistic students (Smith et al., 2002).

COMMUNICATION TRAINING Even when given intensive behavioral treatment, half of the people with autism remain speechless. As a result, many therapists also teach other forms of communication, including *sign language* and *simultaneous communication*, a method combining sign language and speech. They may also turn to **augmentative communication systems**, such as "communication boards" or computers that use pictures, symbols, or written words to represent objects or needs. A child may point to a picture of a fork to give the message "I am hungry," for example, or point to a radio for "I want music."

PARENT TRAINING Today's treatment programs involve parents in a variety of ways. Behavioral programs, for example, often train parents so that they can apply behavioral techniques at home (Erba, 2000; Love et al., 1990). Instruction manuals for parents and home visits by teachers and other professionals are often included in such programs. In addition, individual therapy and support groups are becoming more available to help parents deal with their own emotions and needs. A number of parent associations and lobbies also offer support and practical help.

COMMUNITY INTEGRATION Many of today's school-based and home-based programs for autism teach self-help, self-management, and living, social, and work skills as early as possible, to help the children function better in their communities (Koegel et al., 1992). In addition, greater numbers of carefully run *group homes* and *sheltered workshops* are now available for teenagers and young adults with autism (Van Bourgondien & Schopler, 1990). These and related programs help the individuals become a part of their community; they also reduce the concerns of aging parents whose children will always need supervision (Pfeiffer & Nelson, 1992).

CEREBELLUM An area of the brain that coordinates movement in the body and perhaps helps control a person's ability to shift attention rapidly.

AUGMENTATIVE COMMUNICATION SYSTEM A method for enhancing the communication skills of individuals with autism, mental retardation, or cerebral palsy by teaching them to point to pictures, symbols, letters, or words on a communication board or computer.

MENTAL RETARDATION A disorder marked by intellectual functioning and adaptive behavior that are well below average. Also known as *developmental disability*.

INTELLIGENCE QUOTIENT (IQ) A score derived from intelligence tests that theoretically represents a person's overall intellectual capacity.

Mental Retardation

Ed Murphy, aged 26, can tell us what it's like to be diagnosed as retarded:

> What is retardation? It's hard to say. I guess it's having problems thinking. Some people think that you can tell if a person is retarded by looking at them. If you think that way you don't give people the benefit of the doubt. You judge a person by how they look or how they talk or what the tests show, but you can never really tell what is inside the person.
>
> *(Bogdan & Taylor, 1976, p. 51)*

For much of his life Ed was labeled mentally retarded and was educated and cared for in special institutions. During his adult years, clinicians discovered that Ed's intellectual ability was in fact higher than had been assumed. In the meantime, however, he had lived the childhood and adolescence of a person labeled retarded, and his statement reveals the kinds of difficulties often faced by people with this disorder.

The term "mental retardation" has been applied to a varied population, including children in institutional wards who rock back and forth, young people who work in special job programs, and men and women who raise and support their families by working at undemanding jobs. In recent years, the term *developmental disability* has replaced the label "mental retardation" in many clinical settings (Phares, 2003). Approximately one of every 100 persons receives this diagnosis (APA, 2000). Around three-fifths of them are male and the vast majority are considered *mildly* retarded.

According to DSM-IV, people should receive a diagnosis of **mental retardation** when they display general *intellectual functioning* that is well below average, in combination with poor *adaptive behavior* (APA, 2000, 1994). That is, in addition to having a low IQ (a score of 70 or below), a person with mental retardation has great difficulty in areas such as communication, home living, self-direction, work, or safety. The symptoms must also appear before the age of 18 (see Table 14-6). Although these DSM-IV criteria may seem straightforward, they are in fact hard to apply.

ASSESSING INTELLIGENCE Educators and clinicians administer intelligence tests to measure intellectual functioning (see Chapter 3). These tests consist of a variety of questions and tasks that rely on different aspects of intelligence, such as knowledge, reasoning, and judgment. An individual's overall test score, or **intelligence quotient** (IQ), is thought to indicate general intellectual ability.

Many theorists have questioned whether IQ tests are indeed valid. Do they actually measure what they are supposed to measure? The correlation between IQ and school performance is rather high—around .50—indicating that many children with lower IQs do, as one might expect, perform poorly in school, while many of those with higher IQs perform better (Sternberg et al., 2001). At the same time, the correlation also suggests that the relationship is far from perfect. That is, a particular child's school performance is often higher or lower than his or her IQ might predict. Correlations between IQ and job performance or social effectiveness, other areas that might be expected to reflect intellectual ability, are even lower (Neisser et al., 1996).

Intelligence tests also appear to be socioculturally biased, as we observed in Chapter 3 (Gopaul-McNicol & Armour-Thomas, 2002; Neisser et al., 1996). Children reared in households at the middle and upper socioeconomic levels tend to have an advantage on the tests because they are regularly exposed to the kinds of language and

Table 14-6 DSM-IV Checklist

MENTAL RETARDATION

1. Significantly subaverage intellectual functioning: an IQ of approximately 70 or below on an individually administered IQ test.
2. Concurrent deficits or impairments in present adaptive functioning in at least two of the following areas:
   a. Communication.
   b. Self-care.
   c. Home living.
   d. Social/interpersonal skills.
   e. Use of community resources.
   f. Self-direction.
   g. Functional academic skills.
   h. Work.
   i. Leisure.
   j. Health.
   k. Safety.
3. Onset before the age of 18.

Based on APA, 2000, 1994.

Reading and 'Riting and 'Rithmetic

Over 20 percent of children, boys more often than girls, develop slowly and function poorly compared to their peers in an area such as learning, communication, or coordination (APA, 2000). The children do not suffer from mental retardation, and in fact they are often very bright, yet their problems may interfere with school performance, daily living, and in some cases social interactions (Geisthardt & Munsch, 1996). According to DSM-IV, these children may be suffering from a learning disorder, a communication disorder, or a developmental coordination disorder.

The skill in arithmetic, written expression, or reading of children with *learning disorders* is well below their intellectual capacity (APA, 2000, 1994). For example, children with *reading disorder*, also known as *dyslexia*, have great difficulty recognizing words and comprehending as they read. They typically read slowly and haltingly and may omit, distort, or substitute words as they go.

Children with *communication disorders* have severe difficulty pronouncing words, speaking fluently, or comprehending or expressing language. Those with *expressive language disorder*, for example, may struggle at learning new words, limit their speech to short simple sentences, or show a general lag in language development.

Finally, children with *developmental coordination disorder* perform coordinated motor activities at a level well below that of others their age (APA, 2000, 1994). Younger children with this disorder are clumsy and are slow to master

Will & Deni McIntyre/Science Source/Photo Researchers

Dyslexic impairment *A student with dyslexia has trouble copying words. His mistakes reflect the difficulties he experiences when reading.*

skills such as tying shoelaces, buttoning shirts, and zipping pants. Older children with the disorder may have great difficulty assembling puzzles, building models, playing ball, and printing or writing.

Studies have linked these various developmental disorders to genetic defects, birth injuries, lead poisoning, inappropriate diet, sensory or perceptual dysfunction, and poor teaching (Grigorenko, 2001; Lovett, 2000). Research on each of these factors has been limited, however, and the precise causes of the disorders remain unclear.

Some of the disorders respond to special treatment approaches (Pless & Carlsson, 2000; Merzenich et al., 1996). Reading therapy, for example, is very helpful in mild cases of reading disorder. Furthermore, learning, communication,

and developmental coordination disorders often disappear before adulthood, even without any treatment (APA, 2000).

The inclusion of learning, communication, and coordination problems in the DSM is controversial. Many clinicians view them as strictly educational or social problems, best addressed at school or at home. The framers of DSM-IV reasoned, however, that the additional problems created by these disorders and the frequent links to other psychological problems justify their clinical classifications (Mishna, 1996). Of special concern are studies that have found an increased risk of depression in adolescents with certain of these problems, particularly the learning disorders (Huntington & Bender, 1993).

thinking that the tests measure. The tests rarely measure the "street sense" needed for survival by people who live in poor, crime-ridden areas—a kind of know-how that certainly requires intellectual skills. Similarly, members of cultural minorities and people for whom English is a second language often appear to be at a disadvantage in taking these tests.

If IQ tests do not always measure intelligence accurately and objectively, then the diagnosis of mental retardation also may be biased (Wilson, 1992). That is, some people may receive the diagnosis partly because of cultural differences, discomfort with the testing situation, or the bias of a tester.

MILD RETARDATION A level of mental retardation (IQ between 50 and 70) at which people can benefit from education and can support themselves as adults.

MODERATE RETARDATION A level of mental retardation (IQ between 35 and 49) at which people can learn to care for themselves and can benefit from vocational training.

SEVERE RETARDATION A level of mental retardation (IQ between 20 and 34) at which individuals require careful supervision and can learn to perform basic work in structured and sheltered settings.

PROFOUND RETARDATION A level of mental retardation (IQ below 20) at which individuals need a very structured environment with close supervision.

ASSESSING ADAPTIVE FUNCTIONING Diagnosticians cannot rely solely on a cut-off IQ score of 70 to determine whether a person suffers from mental retardation. Some people with a low IQ are quite capable of managing their lives and functioning independently, while others are not. The cases of Brian and Jeffrey show the range of adaptive abilities.

> **Brian** comes from a lower-income family. He always has functioned adequately at home and in his community. He dresses and feeds himself and even takes care of himself each day until his mother returns home from work. He also plays well with his friends. At school, however, Brian refuses to participate or do his homework. He seems ineffective, at times lost, in the classroom. Referred to a school psychologist by his teacher, he received an IQ score of 60.

> **Jeffrey** comes from an upper-middle-class home. He was always slow to develop, and sat up, stood, and talked late. During his infancy and toddler years, he was put in a special stimulation program and given special help and attention at home. Still Jeffrey has trouble dressing himself today and cannot be left alone in the backyard lest he hurt himself or wander off into the street. Schoolwork is very difficult for him. The teacher must work slowly and provide individual instruction for him. Tested at age 6, Jeffrey received an IQ score of 60.

Brian seems well adapted to his environment outside of school. However, Jeffrey's limitations are widespread. In addition to his low IQ score, Jeffrey has difficulty meeting challenges at home and elsewhere. Thus a diagnosis of mental retardation may be more appropriate for Jeffrey than for Brian.

Several scales have been developed to assess adaptive behavior (Leland, 1991; Britton & Eaves, 1986). Here again, however, some people function better in their lives than the scales predict, while others fall short. Thus to properly diagnose mental retardation, clinicians should observe the functioning of each individual in his or her everyday environment, taking both the person's background and the community's standards into account. Even then, such judgments can be subjective, and clinicians are not always familiar with the standards of a particular culture or community.

WHAT ARE THE CHARACTERISTICS OF MENTAL RETARDATION? The most consistent sign of mental retardation is that the person learns very slowly (Hodapp & Dykens, 2003; Kail, 1992). Other areas of difficulty are attention, short-term memory, planning, and language. Those who are institutionalized with mental retardation are particularly likely to have these limitations. It may be that the unstimulating environment and minimal interactions with staff in many institutions contribute to such difficulties.

DSM-IV describes four levels of mental retardation: mild (IQ 50–70), moderate (IQ 35–49), severe (IQ 20–34), and profound (IQ below 20). In contrast, the American Association of Mental Retardation (1992) prefers to distinguish different kinds of mental retardation according to the level of support the person needs—intermittent, limited, extensive, or pervasive.

Getting a head start *Studies suggest that IQ scores and school performances of children from poor neighborhoods can be improved by enriching their daily environments at a young age through programs such as Head Start, thus revealing the powerful effect of the environment on IQ scores and intellectual performance.*

MILD RETARDATION Some 85 percent of all people with mental retardation fall into the category of **mild retardation** (IQ 50–70) (APA, 2000). They are sometimes called "educably retarded" because they can benefit from schooling and can support themselves as adults. Still, they typically need assistance when they are under stress. Their jobs tend to be unskilled or semiskilled. Mild mental retardation is not usually recognized until a child enters school and is assessed there. Interestingly, the intellectual performance of individuals in this category often seems to improve with age; some even seem to leave the label behind when they leave school, and they go on to function well in the community.

Research has linked mild mental retardation mainly to sociocultural and psychological causes, particularly poor and unstimulating environments, inadequate parent–child interactions, and insufficient learning experiences during a child's early years (Ratter & O'Connor, 2004; Stromme & Magnus, 2000). These relationships have been observed in studies comparing deprived and enriched environments (see Figure 14-2). In fact, some community programs have sent workers into the homes of young children with low IQ scores to help enrich the environment there, and their interventions have often improved the children's functioning. When continued, programs of this kind also help improve the individual's later performance in school and adulthood (Campbell et al., 2002; Ramey et al., 2002).

Although these factors seem to be the leading causes of mild mental retardation, at least some biological factors also may be operating. Studies suggest, for example, that a mother's moderate drinking, drug use, or malnutrition during pregnancy may lower her child's intellectual potential (Neisser et al., 1996; Stein et al., 1972). Similarly, malnourishment during a child's early years may hurt his or her intellectual development, although this effect can usually be reversed at least partly if a child's diet is improved before too much time goes by (Neisser et al., 1996).

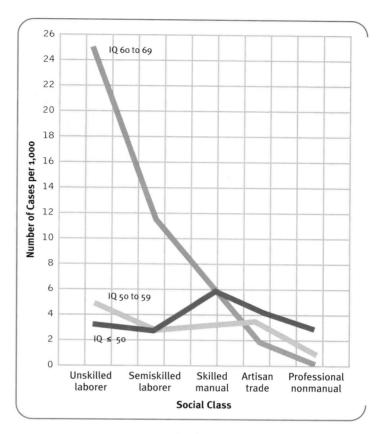

FIGURE 14-2 **Mental retardation and socioeconomic class** *The prevalence of mild mental retardation is much higher in the lower socioeconomic classes than in the upper classes. In contrast, the forms of mental retardation that result in greater impairment are evenly distributed. (Adapted from Popper, 1988; Birch et al., 1970.)*

MODERATE, SEVERE, AND PROFOUND RETARDATION Approximately 10 percent of persons with mental retardation function at a level of **moderate retardation** (IQ 35–49). They can learn to care for themselves and can benefit from vocational training, and many can work in unskilled or semiskilled jobs, usually under supervision. Most persons with moderate retardation also function well in the community if they have supervision (APA, 2000, 1994).

Approximately 4 percent of people with mental retardation display **severe retardation** (IQ 20–34). They usually require careful supervision, profit somewhat from vocational training, and can perform only basic work tasks in structured and sheltered settings. Their understanding of communication is usually better than their speech. Most are able to function well in the community if they live in group homes, in community nursing homes, or with their families (APA, 2000, 1994).

Around 1 percent of all people with mental retardation fall into the category of **profound retardation** (IQ below 20). With training they may learn or improve basic skills such as walking, some talking, and feeding themselves. They need a very structured environment, with close supervision and considerable help, including a one-to-one relationship with a caregiver, in order to develop to the fullest (APA, 2000, 1994). Severe and profound levels of mental retardation often appear as part of larger syndromes that include severe physical handicaps. In many cases these physical problems are even more limiting than an individual's low intellectual functioning.

WHAT ARE THE CAUSES OF MODERATE, SEVERE, AND PROFOUND MENTAL RETARDATION? The primary causes of moderate, severe, and profound retardation are biological, although people who function at these levels are also greatly affected by their family and social environment (Hodapp & Dykens, 2003; Bruce et al., 1996). Sometimes genetic factors are at the root of these biological problems, in the form of chromosomal or metabolic disorders. In fact, researchers have identified 1,000 genetic causes of mental retardation, although few of them have undergone much study (Dykens & Hodapp, 2001; Azar, 1995). Other

Brian Davies/The Appeal Democrat

Reaching higher *Until the 1970s, clinicians were pessimistic about the potential of people with Down syndrome. Today these people are viewed as individuals who can learn and accomplish many things in their lives. Derek Finstad, a 16-year-old with this disorder, celebrates with his football teammates after the team's 56–0 season-opening victory.*

DOWN SYNDROME A form of mental retardation caused by an abnormality in the 21st chromosome.

FETAL ALCOHOL SYNDROME A group of problems in a child, including lower intellectual functioning, low birth weight, and irregularities in the hands and face, that result from excessive alcohol intake by the mother during pregnancy.

STATE SCHOOL A state-supported institution for people with mental retardation.

NORMALIZATION The principle that institutions and community residences should expose people with mental retardation to living conditions and opportunities similar to those found in the rest of society.

biological causes of these kinds of mental retardation come from unfavorable conditions that occur before, during, or after birth.

CHROMOSOMAL CAUSES The most common of the chromosomal disorders leading to mental retardation is **Down syndrome**, named after Langdon Down, the British physician who first identified it. Fewer than 1 of every 1,000 live births result in Down syndrome, but this rate increases greatly when the mother's age is over 35. Many older expectant mothers are now encouraged to undergo *amniocentesis* (testing of the amniotic fluid that surrounds the fetus) during the fourth month of pregnancy to identify Down syndrome and other chromosomal abnormalities.

Individuals with Down syndrome may have a small head, flat face, slanted eyes, high cheekbones, and, in some cases, protruding tongue. The latter may affect their ability to pronounce words clearly. They are often very affectionate with family members but in general display the same range of personality characteristics as people in the general population (Carr, 1994).

Several types of chromosomal abnormalities may cause Down syndrome, but the most common type (94 percent of cases) is *trisomy 21*, in which the individual has three twenty-first chromosomes instead of two (Pueschel & Thuline, 1991). Most people with Down syndrome range in IQ from 35 to 55. The individuals appear to age early, and many even show signs of dementia as they approach 40 (Lawlor et al., 2001; Zigman et al., 1995). Studies suggest that Down syndrome and early dementia often occur together because the genes that produce them are located close to each other on chromosome 21 (Selkoe, 1991).

Fragile X syndrome is the second most common chromosomal cause of mental retardation. Children born with a fragile X chromosome (that is, an X chromosome with a genetic abnormality that leaves it prone to breakage and loss) generally have mild to moderate degrees of intellectual dysfunctioning, language impairment, and, in some cases, behavioral problems (Eliez & Feinstein, 2001).

METABOLIC CAUSES In metabolic disorders, the body's breakdown or production of chemicals is disturbed. The metabolic disorders that affect intelligence and development are typically caused by the pairing of two defective *recessive genes*, one from each parent. Although one such recessive gene would have no influence if it were paired with a normal gene, its pairing with another defective gene leads to major problems for the child.

The most common metabolic disorder to cause mental retardation is *phenylketonuria (PKU)*, which strikes 1 of every 17,000 children. Babies with PKU appear normal at birth but cannot break down the amino acid *phenylalanine*. The chemical builds up and is converted into substances that poison the system, causing severe retardation and several other symptoms. Today infants can be screened for PKU, and if started on a special diet before 3 months of age, they may develop normal intelligence.

Children with *Tay-Sachs disease*, another metabolic disorder resulting from a pairing of recessive genes, progressively lose their mental functioning, vision, and motor ability over the course of two to four years, and eventually die. One of every 30 persons of Eastern European Jewish ancestry carries the recessive gene responsible for this disorder, so that one of every 900 Jewish couples is at risk for having a child with Tay-Sachs disease.

PRENATAL AND BIRTH-RELATED CAUSES As a fetus develops, major physical problems in the pregnant mother can threaten the child's prospects for a normal life (Neisser et al., 1996). When a pregnant woman has too little iodine in her diet, for example, her child may develop *cretinism*, marked by an abnormal thyroid gland, slow development, mental retardation, and a dwarflike appearance. The disorder is rare today because the salt in most diets now contains extra iodine. Also, any infant born with this disorder may quickly be given thyroid extract to bring about a normal development.

Other prenatal problems may also cause mental retardation. As we observed in Chapter 10, children whose mothers drink too much alcohol during pregnancy may be born with **fetal alcohol syndrome**, a group of very serious problems that includes lower intellectual functioning. In fact, a generally safe level of alcohol consumption during pregnancy has not been established by research. In addition, certain maternal infections during pregnancy—*rubella* (German measles) and *syphilis*, for example—may cause childhood problems that include mental retardation.

Birth complications can also lead to mental retardation. A prolonged period without oxygen (*anoxia*) during or after delivery can cause brain damage and retardation in a baby (Erickson, 1992). Similarly, although premature birth does not necessarily lead to long-term problems for children, researchers have found that a birth weight of less than 3.5 pounds may sometimes result in retardation (Neisser et al., 1996).

CHILDHOOD PROBLEMS After birth, particularly up to age 6, certain injuries and accidents can affect intellectual functioning and in some cases lead to mental retardation. Poisonings, serious head injuries caused by accident or abuse, excessive exposure to X rays, and excessive use of certain drugs pose special dangers. For example, a serious case of *lead poisoning*, from eating lead-based paints or inhaling high levels of automobile fumes, can cause retardation in children. Mercury, radiation, nitrite, and pesticide poisoning may do the same. In addition, certain infections, such as *meningitis* and *encephalitis*, can lead to mental retardation if they are not diagnosed and treated in time (Baroff & Olley, 1999; Berney, 1993).

Environmental danger *Children such as this toddler who scrape and eat lead-based paint chips may experience lead poisoning, which can cause mental retardation.*

INTERVENTIONS FOR PEOPLE WITH MENTAL RETARDATION The quality of life attained by people with mental retardation depends largely on sociocultural factors: where they live and with whom, how they are educated, and the growth opportunities available at home and in the community. Thus intervention programs for these individuals try to provide comfortable and stimulating residences, social and economic opportunities, and a proper education. Once these needs are met, psychological or biological treatments are also of help in some cases.

WHAT IS THE PROPER RESIDENCE? Until recent decades, parents of children with mental retardation would send them to live in public institutions—**state schools**—as early as possible. These overcrowded institutions provided basic care, but residents were neglected, often abused, and isolated from society.

During the 1960s and 1970s, the public became more aware of these sorry conditions, and, as part of the broader *deinstitutionalization* movement (see Chapter 12), demanded that many people with mental retardation be released from the state schools (Beyer, 1991). In many cases, the releases occurred without adequate preparation or supervision. Like deinstitutionalized people suffering from schizophrenia, the individuals were virtually dumped into the community. Often they failed to adjust and had to be institutionalized once again.

Since that time, reforms have led to the creation of small institutions and other community residences (group homes, halfway houses, local branches of larger institutions, and independent residences) that teach self-sufficiency, devote more staff time to patient care, and offer educational and medical services. Many of these settings follow the principles of **normalization** first started in Denmark

>>**IN THEIR WORDS**
"The IQ test was invented to predict academic performance, nothing else. If we wanted something that would predict life success, we'd have to invent another test completely."<<

Robert Zajonc, psychologist, 1984

Artistic development *Clinicians have come to recognize that people with mental retardation can benefit from instruction in the arts as well as academic and vocational training. Individuals enrolled in this creative arts course at the center of the Association for Retarded Persons develop greater self-confidence and better communication skills along with improved artistic ability.*

and Sweden—they attempt to provide normal living conditions, flexible routines, and common developmental experiences, including opportunities for self-determination, sexual fulfillment, and economic freedom (Hodapp & Dykens, 2003).

Today the vast majority of children with mental retardation live at home rather than in an institution (Erickson, 1992). As they approach adulthood and as their parents age, however, the family may become less able to provide the kinds of assistance and experiences these individuals require (Krauss et al., 1992), and a community residence becomes an appropriate alternative for some. Most people with mental retardation, including almost all with mild mental retardation, now spend their adult lives either in the family home or in a community residence (Blacher & Baker, 1994, 1992).

WHICH EDUCATIONAL PROGRAMS WORK BEST? Because early intervention seems to offer such great promise, educational programs for individuals with mental retardation may begin during the earliest years. The appropriate education depends on the individual's degree of retardation (Patton et al., 2000). Educators hotly debate whether *special classes* or *mainstreaming* is most effective once the children enter school (Hodapp & Dykens, 2003; Freeman & Alkin, 2000). In **special education**, children with mental retardation are grouped together in a separate, specially designed educational program. **Mainstreaming**, in contrast, places them in regular classes with nonretarded students. Neither approach seems consistently superior (Gottlieb et al., 1991; Gottlieb, 1981). It may well be that mainstreaming is better for some areas of learning and for some children, special classes for others.

Many teachers use operant conditioning principles to improve the self-help, communication, social, and academic skills of individuals with mental retardation (Erickson, 1992). They break learning tasks down into small steps, giving positive rewards as each step is accomplished. In addition, many institutions, schools, and private homes have set up *token economy programs*—the operant conditioning programs that have also been used to treat institutionalized patients suffering from schizophrenia (Spiegler & Guevremont, 2003).

WHEN IS THERAPY NEEDED? Like anyone else, people with mental retardation sometimes experience emotional and behavioral problems. At least 10 percent of them have a diagnosable psychological disorder other than mental retardation (McBrien, 2003; Stromme & Diseth, 2000). Furthermore, some suffer from low self-esteem, interpersonal problems, and difficulties adjusting to community life. These problems are helped to some degree by either individual or group therapy (Rush & Frances, 2000). In addition, large numbers of people with retardation are given psychotropic medications (Matson et al., 2000). Many clinicians suggest, however, that too often the medications are used simply for the purpose of making the individuals easier to manage.

HOW CAN OPPORTUNITIES FOR PERSONAL, SOCIAL, AND OCCUPATIONAL GROWTH BE INCREASED? People need to feel effective and competent in order to move forward in life. Those with mental retardation are most likely to achieve these feelings if their communities allow them to grow and to make many of their own choices (Wehmeyer, 1992). Denmark and Sweden, where the normalization movement began, are again leaders in this area, developing youth clubs that encourage those with mental retardation to take risks and function independently (Perske, 1972).

Socializing, sex, and marriage are difficult issues for people with mental retardation and their families, but with proper training and practice, the individuals

SPECIAL EDUCATION An approach to educating children with mental retardation in which they are grouped together and given a separate, specially designed education.

MAINSTREAMING The placement of children with mental retardation in regular school classes.

SHELTERED WORKSHOP A protected and supervised workplace that offers job opportunities and training at a pace and level tailored to people with various psychological disabilities.

can usually learn to use contraceptives and carry out responsible family planning (Lumley & Scotti, 2001; Dowdney & Skuse, 1993). The National Association for Retarded Citizens offers guidance in these matters, and some clinicians have developed *dating skills programs* (Valenti-Hein et al., 1994).

Some states restrict marriage for people with mental retardation (Levesque, 1996). These laws are rarely enforced, however, and in fact between one-quarter and half of all people with mild mental retardation eventually marry (Grinspoon et al., 1986). Contrary to popular myths, the marriages can be very successful. Moreover, although some individuals may be incapable of raising children, many are quite able to do so, either on their own or with special help and community services (Levesque, 1996; Bakken et al., 1993).

Finally, adults with mental retardation—whatever the severity—need the personal and financial rewards that come with holding a job (Kiernan, 2000; AAMR, 1992). Many work in **sheltered workshops**, protected and supervised workplaces that train them at a pace and level tailored to their abilities. After training in the workshops, many with mild or moderate retardation move on to hold regular jobs (Moore et al., 2000).

Although training programs for people with mental retardation have improved greatly in quality over the past 35 years, there are too few of them. Consequently, most of these individuals fail to receive a complete range of educational and occupational training services. Additional programs are required so that more people with mental retardation may achieve their full potential, as workers and as human beings.

Normal needs *The social and sexual needs of people with mental retardation are normal, and many, such as this engaged couple, demonstrate considerable ability to express intimacy.*

SUMMING UP
Long-Term Disorders That Begin in Childhood

Autism and mental retardation are problems that emerge early and typically continue throughout a person's life. People with autism are very unresponsive to others, have poor communication skills, and behave in a very rigid and repetitive manner. They display perseveration of sameness, strong attachments to objects, self-stimulatory behaviors, and self-injurious behaviors. The leading explanations of this disorder point to cognitive deficits, such as failure to develop a theory of mind, and biological abnormalities, such as abnormal development of the cerebellum. Although no treatment totally reverses the autistic pattern, significant help is available in the form of behavioral treatments, communication training, treatment and training for parents, and community integration.

People with mental retardation are well below average in intelligence and adaptive ability. Mild retardation, by far the most common level of mental retardation, has been linked mainly to environmental factors such as understimulation, inadequate parent–child interactions, and insufficient early learning experiences. Moderate, severe, and profound mental retardation are caused primarily by biological factors, although individuals who function at these levels are also enormously affected by their family and social environment. The leading biological causes are chromosomal abnormalities, metabolic disorders, prenatal problems, birth complications, and childhood injuries or diseases.

Today intervention programs for people with mental retardation emphasize the importance of a comfortable and stimulating residence, either the family home or a small institution or group home that follows the principles of normalization. Other important interventions include proper education, therapy for psychological problems, and programs offering training in socializing, sex, marriage, parenting, and occupational skills.

>>BY THE NUMBERS
Residential Shift

200,000 — Number of people with mental retardation who lived in large state institutions in 1967‹‹

60,000 — People with mental retardation currently living in state institutions‹‹

(Lakin et al., 1999, 1996)

Undesirable effects? *A 4-year-old flexes his muscles in front of the Red Ranger during a Power Rangers Rocket Tour. Some child theorists worry that the fantasy heroes or heroines to which children are regularly exposed in cartoons, toys, video games, or movies may predispose them to aggressive behavior, overactivity, or other problematic patterns. Others argue that superhero play is actually a healthy activity.*

CROSSROADS: Clinicians Discover Childhood and Adolescence

Early in the twentieth century, mental health professionals virtually ignored children (Phares, 2003). At best, they viewed them as small adults and treated their psychological disorders as they would adult problems (Peterson & Roberts, 1991). Today the problems and special needs of young people have caught the attention of researchers and clinicians. Although all of the leading models have been used to help explain and treat these problems, the sociocultural perspective—especially the family perspective—is considered to play a special role.

Because children and adolescents have limited control over their lives, they are greatly affected by the attitudes and reactions of family members. Clinicians must therefore deal with those attitudes and reactions as they try to address the problems of the young. Treatments for conduct disorder, ADHD, mental retardation, and other problems of childhood and adolescence typically fall short unless clinicians educate and work with the family as well.

At the same time, clinicians who work with children and adolescents have learned that a narrow focus on any one model can lead to problems. For years autism was explained solely by family factors, an explanation that misled theorists and therapists alike, and added to the pain of parents already devastated by their child's disorder. Similarly, in the past, the sociocultural model often led professionals wrongly to accept anxiety among young children and depression among teenagers as inevitable, given the many new experiences faced by the former and the latter group's preoccupation with peer approval.

The increased clinical focus on the young has also been accompanied by increased attention to their human and legal rights. More and more, clinicians have called on government agencies to protect the rights and safety of this often powerless group. In doing so, they hope to fuel the fight against child abuse and neglect, sexual abuse, malnourishment, and fetal alcohol syndrome.

As the problems and, at times, mistreatment of young people receive greater attention, the special needs of these individuals are becoming more visible. Thus the study and treatment of psychological disorders among children and adolescents are likely to continue at a rapid pace. Now that clinicians and public officials have "discovered" this population, they are not likely to underestimate their needs and importance again.

CRITICAL THOUGHTS

1. Although boys with psychological disorders outnumber girls, adult women with such disorders outnumber adult men. How might this age-related shift in prevalence rates reflect the special pressures felt by women in Western society? What other explanations might there be for the shift? *pp. 419–432*

2. What psychological effects might bullying have on its victims? Why do many individuals seem able to overcome the trauma of being bullied, while others do not? *p. 426*

3. Clinicians sometimes use punishment to help eliminate the self-injurious behaviors of children with autism. The children may be squirted in the face with water, pinched, or, in extreme cases, shocked whenever they act to hurt themselves. Who should make the decision about whether to use punishments in given cases? *p. 437*

4. In past times, a child with a learning, communication, or coordination disorder might simply be called a "weak" reader, "clumsy," or the like. What are the advantages and disadvantages to the child of affixing clinical names to the patterns? Should these patterns be listed in DSM-IV as psychological disorders? *p. 439*

5. What might be the merits and flaws of special classes versus mainstreaming for people with mental retardation? *p. 444*

KEY TERMS

separation anxiety disorder p. 421

school phobia p. 422

play therapy p. 424

oppositional defiant disorder p. 425

conduct disorder p. 425

attention-deficit/hyperactivity disorder (ADHD) p. 428

methylphenidate (Ritalin) p. 430

enuresis p. 431

encopresis p. 432

autistic disorder p. 433

self-stimulatory behavior p. 434

self-injurious behavior p. 434

theory of mind p. 435

cerebellum p. 436

augmentative communication system p. 437

group home p. 437

mental retardation p. 438

intelligence quotient (IQ) p. 438

mild retardation p. 440

moderate retardation p. 441

severe retardation p. 441

profound retardation p. 441

Down syndrome p. 442

fragile X syndrome p. 442

recessive genes p. 442

phenylketonuria (PKU) p. 442

fetal alcohol syndrome p. 443

lead poisoning p. 443

state school p. 443

deinstitutionalization p. 443

normalization p. 443

special education p. 444

mainstreaming p. 444

token economy program p. 444

sheltered workshop p. 445

QUICK QUIZ

1. How do anxiety disorders and depression in childhood compare with adult versions of these disorders? What are separation anxiety disorder and school phobia? *pp. 421–425*

2. What are the prevalence rates and gender ratios for the various childhood disorders? *pp. 434, 421–445*

3. Describe oppositional defiant disorder and conduct disorders. What factors help cause conduct disorders, and how are these disorders treated? *pp. 425–427*

4. What are the symptoms of attention-deficit/hyperactivity disorder? What are the current treatments for it, and how effective are they? *pp. 428–431*

5. What are enuresis and encopresis? How are these disorders treated? *pp. 430–432*

6. What are the symptoms and possible causes of autism? *pp. 432–436*

7. What are the overall goals of treatment for autism, and which interventions have been most helpful for individuals with this disorder? *pp. 436–437*

8. Describe the different levels of mental retardation. *pp. 440–441*

9. What are the causes of mild mental retardation? What are the causes of moderate, severe, and profound mental retardation? *pp. 440–443*

10. What kinds of residences, educational programs, treatments, and community programs are helpful to persons with mental retardation? *pp. 443–445*

 CYBER STUDY

SEARCH THE *FUNDAMENTALS OF ABNORMAL PSYCHOLOGY* CD-ROM FOR

▲ Chapter 14 Video Case Enrichment
  How do children experience stranger and separation anxiety?
  Observe interventions for autism.
  Witness savant skills.

▲ Chapter 14 Practical, Research, and Decision-Making Exercises
  The impact of childhood disorders on the family
  Diagnosing autism: Distinguishing childhood disorders

▲ Chapter 14 Practice Test and Feedback

LOG ON TO THE COMER WEB PAGE FOR

▲ Suggested Web links, exercises, FAQ page, additional Chapter 14 practice test questions
  <www.worthpublishers.com/comer>

GERARD DUBOIS, 1998

Disorders of Aging and Cognition

Harry appeared to be in perfect health at age 58. . . . He worked in the municipal water treatment plant of a small city, and it was at work that the first overt signs of Harry's mental illness appeared. While responding to a minor emergency, he became confused about the correct order in which to pull the levers that controlled the flow of fluids. As a result, several thousand gallons of raw sewage were discharged into a river. Harry had been an efficient and diligent worker, so after puzzled questioning, his error was attributed to the flu and overlooked.

Several weeks later, Harry came home with a baking dish his wife had asked him to buy, having forgotten that he had brought home the identical dish two nights before. Later that week, on two successive nights, he went to pick up his daughter at her job in a restaurant, apparently forgetting that she had changed shifts and was now working days. A month after that, he quite uncharacteristically argued with a clerk at the phone company; he was trying to pay a bill that he had already paid three days before. . . .

Months passed and Harry's wife was beside herself. She could see that his problem was worsening. Not only had she been unable to get effective help, but Harry himself was becoming resentful and sometimes suspicious of her attempts. He now insisted there was nothing wrong with him, and she would catch him narrowly watching her every movement. . . . Sometimes he became angry—sudden little storms without apparent cause. . . . More difficult for his wife was Harry's repetitiveness in conversation: He often repeated stories from the past and sometimes repeated isolated phrases and sentences from more recent exchanges. There was no context and little continuity to his choice of subjects. . . .

Two years after Harry had first allowed the sewage to escape, he was clearly a changed man. Most of the time he seemed preoccupied; he usually had a vacant smile on his face, and what little he said was so vague that it lacked meaning. . . . Gradually his wife took over getting him up, toileted, and dressed each morning. . . .

Harry's condition continued to worsen slowly. When his wife's school was in session, his daughter would stay with him some days, and neighbors were able to offer some help. But occasionally he would still manage to wander away. On those occasions he greeted everyone he met—old friends and strangers alike—with "Hi, it's so nice." That was the extent of his conversation, although he might repeat "nice, nice, nice" over and over again. . . . When Harry left a coffee pot on a unit of the electric stove until it melted, his wife, desperate for help, took him to see another doctor. Again Harry was found to be in good health. [However] the doctor ordered a CAT scan [and eventually concluded] that Harry had "Pick-Alzheimer disease" and that there was no known cause and no effective treatment. . . .

Because Harry was a veteran . . . [he qualified for] hospitalization in a regional veterans' hospital about 400 miles away from his home. . . . Desperate, five years after the accident at work, [his wife] accepted with gratitude [this] hospitalization. . . .

GEROPSYCHOLOGY The field of psychology concerned with the mental health of elderly people.

At the hospital the nursing staff sat Harry up in a chair each day and, aided by volunteers, made sure he ate enough. Still, he lost weight and became weaker. He would weep when his wife came to see him, but he did not talk, and he gave no other sign that he recognized her. After a year, even the weeping stopped. Harry's wife could no longer bear to visit. Harry lived on until just after his sixty-fifth birthday, when he choked on a piece of bread, developed pneumonia as a consequence, and soon died.

(Heston, 1992, pp. 87–90)

Harry suffered from a form of *Alzheimer's disease*. This term is familiar to almost everyone in our society. It seems as if each decade is marked by a disease that everyone dreads—a diagnosis no one wants to hear because it feels like a death sentence. Cancer used to be such a diagnosis, then AIDS. But medical science has made remarkable strides with those diseases, and patients who now develop them have reason for hope and expectations of improvement. Alzheimer's disease, on the other hand, remains incurable and almost untreatable, although, as we shall see later, researchers are currently making enormous progress toward understanding it and reversing, or at least slowing, its march.

What makes Alzheimer's disease particularly frightening is that it not only means eventual physical death, but also, as in Harry's case, a slow psychological death—a progressive *dementia*, or deterioration of one's memory and related cognitive faculties. There are dozens of causes of dementia; however, Alzheimer's disease is the most common one.

Although dementia is currently the most publicized and feared psychological problem among the elderly, it is hardly the only one. Indeed, a variety of psychological disorders are tied closely to later life. As with childhood disorders, some of the disorders of old age are caused mainly by pressures that are particularly likely to appear at that time of life, others by unique personal issues, and still others—like dementia—by biological abnormalities.

Old Age and Stress

Old age is usually defined in our society as the years past age 65. By this account, more than 35 million people in the United States are "old," representing around 13 percent of the total population; this is an 11-fold increase since 1900 (Dietch, 2001; Fisher, Zeiss, & Carstensen, 2001) (see Figure 15-1). Older women outnumber older men by 3 to 2.

Like childhood, old age brings special pressures, unique upsets, and major biological changes. People become more prone to illness and injury as they age, and they are likely to experience the stress of loss—the loss of spouses, friends, and adult children, and the loss of former activities and roles. Many lose their sense of purpose after they retire. Even favored pets and possessions are sometimes lost (Gallagher-Thompson & Thompson, 1995).

The stresses of elderly people need not necessarily result in psychological problems (Schultz & Heckhausen, 1996). In fact, some older persons use the changes that come with aging as opportunities for learning and growth. For others, however, the stresses of old age do lead to psychological difficulties (Banerjee & Macdonald, 1996). Studies indicate that as many as half of elderly people would benefit from mental health services, yet fewer than 20 percent actually receive them. **Geropsychology**, the field of psychology dedicated to

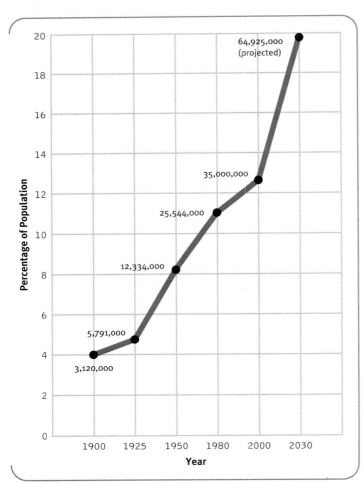

FIGURE 15-1 **On the rise** *The population of people aged 65 and older in the United States increased 11-fold during the twentieth century. The percentage of elderly people in the population increased from 4 percent in 1900 to 12.5 percent in 2000 and is expected to be 20 percent in 2030 (U.S. Census, 2000; Hobbs, 1997; AARP, 1990).*

the mental health of elderly people, has developed almost entirely within the last 30 years (Dittman, 2004), and at present fewer than 4 percent of all clinicians work primarily with elderly persons (Birren & Schroots, 2001, 2000).

The psychological problems of elderly persons may be divided into two groups. One group consists of disorders that may be common among people in all age groups but are often connected to the process of aging when they occur in an elderly person. These include depressive, anxiety, and substance-related disorders (Devanand, 2002). The other group consists of disorders of cognition, such as delirium and dementia, that result from biological abnormalities. As in Harry's case, these biological abnormalities are most often tied to aging, but they can sometimes occur in younger individuals as well.

Depression in Later Life

Depression is one of the most common mental health problems of older adults. The features of depression are the same for elderly people as for younger people, including feelings of extreme sadness and emptiness; low self-esteem, guilt, and pessimism; and loss of appetite and sleep disturbances. Depression is particularly common among those who have recently experienced a trauma, such as the loss of a spouse or close friend or the development of a serious physical illness.

Depression among the elderly *Old age may be accompanied by the loss of good health, of close relatives and friends, and of control over one's life. Clinical theorists link such losses to the high rate of depression found among the elderly. Yet depression is not inevitable as people age.*

[Oscar] was an 83-year-old married man with an episode of major depressive disorder. . . . He said that about one and one-half years prior to beginning treatment, his brother had died. In the following months, two friends whom he had known since childhood died. Following these losses, he . . . grew more and more pessimistic. Reluctantly, he acknowledged, "I even thought about ending my life." . . . .

During . . . treatment, [Oscar] discussed his relationship with his brother. He discussed how distraught he was to watch his brother's physical deterioration from an extended illness. He described the scene at his brother's deathbed and the moment "when he took his final breath." He experienced guilt over the failure to carry out his brother's funeral services in a manner he felt his brother would have wanted. . . . Later in therapy, he also reviewed different facets of his past relationships with his two deceased friends. He expressed sadness that the long years had ended. . . . [Oscar's] life had been organized around visits to his brother's home and outings with his friends. . . . [While] his wife had encouraged him to visit with other friends and family, it became harder and harder to do so as he became more depressed.

(Hinrichsen, 1999, p. 433)

Overall, as many as 20 percent of people experience depression at some point during old age (Blazer, 2002). The rate is highest in older women. This rate among the elderly is about the same as that among younger adults—even lower, according to some studies. However, it climbs much higher among aged persons who live in nursing homes (Fisher et al., 2001).

Several studies suggest that depression raises an elderly person's chances of developing significant medical problems (Powers et al., 2002). For example, older depressed people with high blood pressure are almost three times as likely to suffer a stroke as older nondepressed people with the same condition. Similarly, elderly people who are depressed recover more slowly and less completely from heart attacks, hip fractures, pneumonia, and other infections and illnesses. Small wonder that among the elderly in nursing homes, increases in clinical depression are tied to increases in the death rate (Fisher et al., 2001; Parmelee et al., 1991).

>>**PSYCH•NOTES**

Diagnostic Confusion

One out of 10 people who seem to have dementia may actually be suffering from depression (Janzing, 2003; Backmon, 1998; Noll & Turkington, 1994).<<

Sleep and Sleep Disorders among the Old and Not So Old

Sleep is affected by both physical and psychosocial factors. Sleep deprivation for 100 hours or more leads to hallucinations, paranoia, and bizarre behavior. When people remain awake for over 200 hours, they frequently experience periods of "microsleep," naps lasting two to three seconds. The body simply refuses to be entirely deprived of sleep for long.

To learn more about sleep, researchers bring people into the laboratory and record their activities as they sleep, using various types of recording devices. One important discovery has been that eyes move rapidly about 25 percent of the time a person is asleep (Aserinsky & Kleitman, 1953), a phenomenon known as *rapid eye movement*, or *REM*. REM sleep is often called "paradoxical sleep" because it resembles both deep sleep and wakefulness. Despite small movements and muscle twitches, the body is immobilized, almost paralyzed. At the same time, the eyes are darting back and forth, blood flow to the brain increases, and brain-wave activity is almost identical to that of an awake and alert person. Eighty percent of subjects who are awakened from REM sleep report that they were dreaming.

DSM-IV identifies a number of sleep disorders. The *dyssomnias* (insomnia, hypersomnia, breathing-related sleep disorder, narcolepsy, and circadian rhythm sleep disorder) involve disturbances in the amount, quality, or timing of sleep. The *parasomnias* (nightmare disorder, sleep terror disorder, and sleepwalking disorder) involve abnormal events that occur during sleep.

The most common of these disorders is *insomnia*, a dyssomnia in which people repeatedly have great difficulty falling asleep or maintaining sleep. More than 20 percent of the entire population experience this pattern each year (APA, 2000). People with insomnia feel as though they are almost constantly awake. Often they are very sleepy during the day and have difficulty functioning effectively. The problem may be caused by factors such as anxiety or depression, medical ailments, pain, or medication effects (Sadock & Sadock, 2003; Hauri, 2000).

Sleep Disorders among the Elderly

Insomnia is more common among older persons than younger ones (Cartwright, 2001). Around 40 percent of the popula-

©Ellen Senisi/The Image Works

As we observed in Chapter 8, elderly persons are also more likely to commit suicide than younger ones, and often their suicides are related to depression. The overall rate of suicide in the United States is 12 per 100,000 persons; among the elderly it is close to 20 per 100,000. Among 80- to 85-year-olds in particular, it is 27 per 100,000; and among white American men over the age of 85, it is 65 per 100,000 (CDC, 2001; Fisher et al., 2001).

Like younger adults, older individuals who are depressed may be helped by cognitive therapy, interpersonal therapy, antidepressant medications, or a combination of these approaches (Coon & Thompson, 2003; Powers et al., 2002). Both individual and group therapy formats have been used. More than half of elderly patients with depression improve with these various treatments. At the same time, it is sometimes difficult to use antidepressant drugs effectively and safely with older persons because the body breaks the drugs down differently in later life. Electroconvulsive therapy, applied with certain modifications, has also been used for elderly people who are severely depressed and unhelped by other approaches (Blazer, 2002).

tion over 65 years of age experience at least some measure of insomnia (Mellinger et al., 1985). Elderly people may be particularly prone to this problem because so many of them have medical ailments, experience pain, take medications, or grapple with depression and anxiety—each a known contributor to insomnia.

Another sleep disorder commonly found among the elderly is *breathing-related sleep disorder*, a respiratory problem in which persons are periodically deprived of oxygen to the brain while they sleep, so that they frequently wake up. *Sleep apnea*, the most common form of this disorder, may occur in more than 10 percent of the elderly population; it is less common in younger age groups (APA, 2000, 1994). Its victims, typically overweight men who are heavy snorers, actually stop breathing for up to 30 seconds or more as they sleep. Hundreds of episodes may occur nightly, without the victim's awareness.

Sleep Disorders throughout the Life Span

As we have observed, insomnia and breathing-related sleep disorder are particularly common among older persons, although they are found in younger persons as well. Other sleep disorders are just as common—in a few cases more common—among the other age groups.

In contrast to insomnia, *hypersomnia* is a sleep disorder marked by a heightened need for sleep and excessive sleepiness. Sufferers may need extra hours of sleep each night and may need to sleep during the daytime as well (APA, 2000, 1994).

Narcolepsy, a disorder marked by repeated sudden bouts of REM sleep during waking hours, afflicts more than 135,000 people in the United States. Although narcolepsy is a biological disorder, the bouts of REM sleep are often triggered by strong emotions. Sufferers may suddenly fall into REM sleep in the midst of an argument or during an exciting part of a football game.

People with *circadian rhythm sleep disorder* experience excessive sleepiness or insomnia as a result of a mismatch between their own sleep-wake pattern and the sleep-wake schedule of most other people in their environment. Often the disorder takes the form of falling asleep late and awakening late. This dyssomnia can result from night-shift work, frequent changes in work shifts, or repeated episodes of jet lag.

Nightmare disorder is the most common of the parasomnias. Although most people experience nightmares from time to time, in this disorder nightmares become frequent and cause such great distress that the individual must receive treatment. Such nightmares often increase under stress.

Persons with *sleep terror disorder* awaken suddenly during the first third of their evening sleep, screaming in extreme fear and agitation. They are in a state of panic, are often incoherent, and have a heart rate to match. Sleep terrors most often appear in children and disappear during adolescence.

People with a *sleepwalking disorder*—usually children—repeatedly leave their beds and walk around, without being conscious of the episode or remembering it later. The episodes occur in the first third of the individuals' nightly sleep. Those who are awakened while sleepwalking are confused for several moments. If allowed to continue sleepwalking, they eventually return to bed. Sleepwalkers usually manage to avoid obstacles, climb stairs, and perform complex activities, in a seemingly emotionless state. Accidents do happen, however: tripping, bumping into furniture, and even falling out of windows have all been reported. Sleepwalking usually disappears by age 15 (APA, 2000, 1994).

Anxiety Disorders in Later Life

Anxiety is also common among elderly people (Wetherell & Gatz, 2001; Fuentes & Cox, 2000). At any given time, around 6 percent of elderly men and 11 percent of elderly women in the United States experience at least one of the anxiety disorders (Fisher et al., 2001). Surveys indicate that generalized anxiety disorder is particularly common, experienced by up to 7 percent of all elderly persons (Flint, 1994). The prevalence of anxiety also increases throughout old age. For example, individuals over 85 years of age report higher rates of anxiety than those between 65 and 84 years. In fact, all of these numbers may be low, as anxiety in the elderly tends to be underreported (Dada et al., 2001). Both the elderly individual and the clinician may interpret physical symptoms of anxiety, such as heart palpitations and sweating, as symptoms of a medical condition.

There are many things about aging that may heighten the anxiety levels of certain individuals. Declining health, for example, has often been pointed to, and in fact, older persons who experience major medical illnesses or injuries report

>>**IN THEIR WORDS**

"I am an old man and have known many troubles, but most of them never happened."<<

Mark Twain

Racing to mental health *Gerontologists propose that elderly people need to pursue pleasurable and personally meaningful activities in order to thrive psychologically. The elderly men above compete in a race in the Senior Olympics. The elderly gentleman on the right is also interested in racing; at a horse race at Saratoga Springs he shades his face with the program that lists the day's post parade statistics. Which of these two activities might clinical theorists have more confidence in as a key to successful psychological functioning during old age?*

more anxiety than those who are healthy or injury-free (Fisher et al., 2001). Researchers have not, however, systematically tied anxiety disorders among the elderly to specific events or losses in their lives. Nor have they been able to pinpoint why certain individuals become anxious during old age while others who face similar circumstances remain more or less calm.

Older adults with anxiety disorders have been treated with psychotherapy of various kinds, particularly cognitive therapy (Mohlman et al., 2003; Stanley et al., 2003). Many also receive benzodiazepines or other antianxiety medications; those with obsessive-compulsive disorder or panic disorder may be treated with serotonin-enhancing antidepressant drugs such as fluoxetine (Prozac), just as younger sufferers are (Calamari & Cassiday, 1999). Again, however, all such drugs must be used cautiously with older people.

Substance Abuse in Later Life

Although alcohol abuse and other forms of substance abuse are problems for many older persons, the prevalence of such patterns actually appears to decline after age 60, perhaps because of declining health or reduced financial status (Oslin & Holden, 2002; Stewart & Oslin, 2001). The majority of older adults do not misuse alcohol or other substances despite the fact that aging can sometimes be a time of considerable stress and that in our society alcohol and drugs are widely turned to in times of stress. At the same time, accurate data about the rate of substance abuse among older adults are difficult to gather because many elderly persons do not suspect or admit that they have such a problem (Gallagher-Thompson & Thompson, 1995).

Surveys find that 4 to 6 percent of older people, particularly men, have alcohol-related disorders in a given year (Adams & Cox, 1997). Men under 30 are four times as likely as men over 60 to display an alcohol-related behavioral problem, such as repeated falling, spells of dizziness or blacking out, secretive drinking, or social withdrawal. Older patients who are institutionalized, however, do display high rates of problem drinking. For example, alcohol problems among older persons admitted to general and mental hospitals range from 15 percent to 49 percent,

>>BY THE NUMBERS
Prescription Drugs and the Elderly

25% Percentage of all prescribed drugs that are taken by elderly people<<

13% Percentage of the total population who are elderly<<

(Blazer, 2002)

and estimates of alcohol-related problems among patients in nursing homes range from 26 percent to 60 percent (Klein & Jess, 2002; Gallagher-Thompson & Thompson, 1995).

Researchers often distinguish between older problem drinkers who have had alcohol-related problems for many years, perhaps since their 20s, and those who do not start the pattern until their 50s or 60s. The latter group typically begins abusive drinking as a reaction to the negative events and pressures of growing older, such as the death of a spouse or unwanted retirement. Alcohol abuse and dependence in elderly people are treated much as in younger adults (see Chapter 10), with such approaches as detoxification, Antabuse, Alcoholics Anonymous (AA), and cognitive-behavioral therapy (Gurnack et al., 2002; Dupree & Schonfeld, 1999).

A leading kind of substance problem in the elderly is the misuse of prescription drugs (Graham et al., 1996). Most often it is unintentional. Older people typically receive twice as many prescriptions as younger persons, and one-quarter or more take at least three drugs daily (Blazer, 2002; Patterson et al., 1999). Thus their risk of confusing medications or skipping doses is high (Salzman et al., 1995). Today's physicians and pharmacists often try to simplify medications, educate older patients about their prescriptions, clarify directions, and teach them to watch for undesired effects (Gallagher-Thompson & Thompson, 1995). On the other hand, physicians themselves are sometimes to blame in cases of prescription drug misuse, perhaps overprescribing medications for elderly patients or unwisely mixing certain medicines (Wolfe et al., 1999).

Psychotic Disorders in Later Life

Elderly people have a higher rate of psychotic symptoms than younger persons (Fisher et al., 2001). Among aged people, these symptoms are usually due to underlying medical conditions such as delirium and dementia, the disorders of cognition that we shall be turning to in the next section. However, some elderly persons suffer from *schizophrenia* or *delusional disorder*.

Dreary setting *Most aging persons fear that poor health will eventually force them to live in a nursing home, separated from their families, friends, and homes. An additional concern is that many of today's nursing homes are unstimulating settings in which residents may be neglected, mistreated, and overmedicated. Such conditions heighten the risk of various problems, from depression and anxiety to delirium and dementia.*

Actually, schizophrenia is less common in older persons than in younger ones. In fact, many persons with schizophrenia find that their symptoms lessen in later life (Fisher et al., 2001). Improvement can occur in people who have displayed schizophrenia for 30 or more years, particularly in such areas as social skills and work capacity, as we are reminded by the remarkable late-life improvement of the Nobel Prize recipient John Nash (see pp. 356–357).

It is uncommon for new cases of schizophrenia to emerge late in life. Thus some of the elderly people with schizophrenia have been receiving antipsychotic drugs and related treatments for many years and are continuing to do so in old age. In contrast, others have been untreated for years and continue to be untreated as elderly persons, winding up in nursing homes, in run-down apartments, homeless, or in jail.

Another kind of psychotic disorder found among the elderly is *delusional disorder*, in which individuals develop beliefs that are false but not bizarre. This disorder is rare in most age groups—around 3 of every 10,000 persons—but its prevalence appears to increase in the elderly (Fisher et al., 2001; APA, 2000, 1994). Older persons with a delusional disorder may develop deeply held suspicions of persecution; they believe that other persons—often family members, doctors, or friends—are conspiring against, cheating, spying on, or slandering them. They may become irritable, angry, or depressed, or pursue legal action because of such ideas (APA, 2000). It is not clear why this disorder increases among elderly people, but some clinicians suggest that the rise is related to the deficiencies in hearing, social isolation, greater stress, or heightened poverty experienced by many elderly persons (Fisher et al., 2001; APA, 2000, 1994).

SUMMING UP Disorders of Later Life

The problems of elderly people are often linked to the losses and other stresses and changes that accompany advancing age. As many as half of the elderly would benefit from mental health services, yet fewer than 20 percent receive them. Depression is a common mental health problem among this age group. Older people may also suffer from anxiety disorders. Between 4 and 6 percent exhibit alcohol-related problems in any given year, and many others misuse prescription drugs. In addition, some elderly persons display psychotic disorders such as schizophrenia or delusional disorder.

Disorders of Cognition

Most of us worry from time to time that we are losing our memory and other mental abilities. We rush out the door without our keys; we meet a familiar person and cannot remember her name; or in the middle of an important test our mind goes blank. Actually such mishaps are a common and quite normal feature of stress or of aging. As people move through middle age, these memory difficulties and lapses of attention increase, and they may occur regularly by the age of 60 or 70. Sometimes, however, people experience memory and other cognitive changes that are far more extensive.

In Chapter 6 we observed that problems in memory and related cognitive processes can occur without biological causes, in the form of *dissociative disorders*. More often, however, cognitive problems do have organic roots, particularly when they appear late in life. The leading cognitive disorders among elderly persons are *delirium* and *dementia*.

Delirium

Delirium is a clouding of consciousness. As the person's awareness of the environment becomes less clear, he or she has great difficulty concentrating, focusing attention, and thinking sequentially, which leads to misinterpretations, illusions, and, on occasion, hallucinations (APA, 2000, 1994). Sufferers may believe that it is morning in the middle of the night or that they are home when actually they are in a hospital room.

This state of massive confusion typically develops over a short period of time, usually hours or days. Delirium apparently affects more than 2 million people in the United States each year (Clary & Krishnan, 2001). It may occur in any age group, including children, but is most common in elderly persons. In fact, when elderly people enter a hospital to be treated for a general medical condition, one in 10 of them shows the symptoms of delirium (APA, 2000, 1994). At least another 10 percent develop delirium during their stay in the hospital (APA, 2000; Inouye et al., 1999; Inouye, 1998).

Fever, certain diseases and infections, poor nutrition, head injuries, strokes, and stress (including the trauma of surgery) may all cause delirium (Schneider et al., 2002; Brust & Caplan, 2001; Sarhill et al., 2001). So may intoxication by certain substances, such as prescription drugs. Partly because older people face so many of these problems, they are more likely than younger ones to experience delirium. If a clinician accurately identifies delirium, it can often be easy to correct—by treating the underlying infection, for example, or changing the patient's drug prescription. However, delirium is not always recognized for what it is (Monette et al., 2001; Inouye, 1999, 1998). One study on a medical ward found that admission doctors detected only one of 15 consecutive cases of delirium (Cameron et al., 1987). Incorrect diagnosis of this kind may contribute to a high death rate for older people with delirium (Coulson & Almeida, 2002; Kelly et al., 2001).

DELIRIUM A rapidly developing clouding of consciousness; the person has great difficulty concentrating, focusing attention, and following an orderly sequence of thought.

DEMENTIA A syndrome marked by severe problems in memory and in at least one other cognitive function.

ALZHEIMER'S DISEASE The most common form of dementia, usually occurring after the age of 65.

Dementia

People with **dementia** experience significant memory losses along with losses in other cognitive functions such as abstract thinking or language (APA, 2000, 1994). Those with certain forms of dementia may also undergo personality changes—they may begin to behave inappropriately, for example—and their symptoms may worsen steadily.

At any given time, around 3 percent of the world's adult population are suffering from dementia (Muir, 1997). Its occurrence is closely related to age (see Figure 15-2). Among people 65 years of age, the prevalence is around 1 to 2 percent, increasing to between 25 and 50 percent for those over the age of 85 (APA, 2000; Cowley, 2000; De Leon et al., 1996).

Altogether, 4 million persons in the United States experience some form of dementia (Katzman, 2001; St. George-Hyslop, 2000). More than 70 forms have been identified (Noll & Turkington, 1994). Like delirium, dementia is sometimes the result of nutritional or other problems that can be corrected. Most forms of dementia, however, are caused by brain diseases or injuries, such as Alzheimer's disease or stroke, which are currently difficult or impossible to correct.

ALZHEIMER'S DISEASE **Alzheimer's disease** is named after Alois Alzheimer, the German physician who formally identified it in 1907. Dr. Alzheimer first became aware of the syndrome in 1901 when a new patient, Auguste D., was placed under his care:

> On November 25, 1901, a . . . woman with no personal or family history of mental illness was admitted to a psychiatric hospital in Frankfurt, Germany, by her husband, who could no longer ignore or hide quirks and lapses that had overtaken her in recent months. First, there were unexplainable bursts of anger, and then a strange series of memory problems. She became increasingly unable to locate things in her own home and began to make surprising mistakes in the kitchen. By the time she arrived at [the mental hospital], her condition was as severe as it was curious. The attending doctor, senior physician Alois Alzheimer, began the new file with these notes. . . .
>
> > She sits on the bed with a helpless expression.
> > "What is your name?"
> > *Auguste.*
> > "Last name?"
> > *Auguste.*
> > "What is your husband's name?"
> > *Auguste, I think.*
> > "How long have you been here?"
> > (She seems to be trying to remember.)
> > *Three weeks.*
>
> It was her second day in the hospital. Dr. Alzheimer, a thirty-seven-year-old neuropathologist and clinician . . . , observed in his new patient a remarkable cluster of symptoms: severe disorientation, reduced comprehension, aphasia (language impairment), paranoia, hallucinations, and a short-term memory so incapacitated that when he spoke her full name, *Frau Auguste D____*, and asked her to write it down, the patient got only as far as "Frau" before needing the doctor to repeat the rest.
>
> > He spoke her name again. She wrote "Augu" and again stopped.
> > When Alzheimer prompted her a third time, she was able to write her entire first name and the initial "D" before finally giving up, telling the doctor, "I have lost myself."
>
> Her condition did not improve. It became apparent that there was nothing that anyone at this or any other hospital could do for Frau D. except to insure her safety and try to keep her as clean and comfortable as possible for the rest of her days. Over the next four and a half years, she became increasingly disoriented, delusional, and incoherent. She was often hostile.

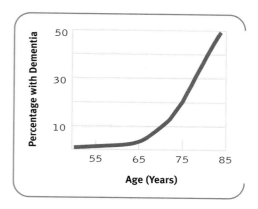

FIGURE 15-2 **Dementia and age** *The occurrence of dementia is closely related to age. Fewer than 1 percent of all 60-year-olds have dementia, compared to as many as 50 percent of those who are 85. After 60, the prevalence of dementia doubles every six years up to age 85 or so, then the increase tapers off. (Adapted from Cowley, 2000; Alzheimer's Association, 1997; Ritchie et al., 1992.)*

"Her gestures showed a complete helplessness," Alzheimer later noted in a published report. "She was disoriented as to time and place. From time to time she would state that she did not understand anything, that she felt confused and totally lost. . . . Often she would scream for hours and hours in a horrible voice."

By November 1904, three and a half years into her illness, Auguste D. was bedridden, incontinent, and largely immobile. . . . Notes from October 1905 indicate that she had become permanently curled up in a fetal position with her knees drawn up to her chest, muttering but unable to speak, and requiring assistance to be fed.

(Shenk, 2001, pp. 12–14)

Alzheimer's disease is the most common form of dementia, accounting for at least half of the cases (Muir, 1997). This gradually progressive disease sometimes appears in middle age, but most often it occurs after the age of 65, and its prevalence increases greatly among people in their late 70s and early 80s (see Table 15-1 on page 460).

A CLOSER LOOK

Amnestic Disorders: Forgetting to Remember

People who suffer from dementia experience both severe memory problems and other cognitive impairments. In contrast, those with *amnestic disorders*, another group of disorders caused by brain diseases or injuries, have memory problems only. Amnestic disorders are just as likely to occur in younger people as among the elderly.

Retrograde amnesia is an inability to remember events from the past. *Anterograde amnesia* is an ongoing inability to form new memories. People with amnestic disorders sometimes suffer from retrograde amnesia, depending on the particular disorder, but they almost always experience anterograde amnesia.

In anterograde amnesia, it is as though information from short-term memory can no longer cross over into long-term memory. Not surprisingly, it is often the result of damage to the brain's *temporal lobes* or *diencephalon*, areas largely responsible for transforming short-term memory into long-term memory. In severe forms of anterograde amnesia, new acquaintances are forgotten almost immediately, and problems solved one day must be tackled again the next. The person may not remember anything that has happened since his or her problem first began. Nevertheless,

sufferers may continue to possess all of their earlier verbal skills and many problem-solving abilities, and their IQ is not changed. The best known of the amnestic disorders are *Korsakoff's syndrome* and disorders resulting from *head injuries* or *brain surgery*.

Korsakoff's Syndrome

Fred, a 69-year-old man, was admitted to a mental hospital in a state of confusion, the result of *Korsakoff's syndrome*, an amnestic disorder that causes its victims to keep forgetting newly learned information (anterograde amnesia):

Fred . . . had a history of many years of heavy drinking, although he denied drinking during the past several years. When seen in the admitting ward, the patient was neatly dressed, but there was some deterioration of his personal habits. Although pleasant and sociable with the interviewer and ward personnel, he was definitely confused. He wandered about the ward, investigating objects and trying on other people's clothing. He talked freely, though his speech tended to be rambling and at times incoherent. Most of his spontaneous conversation centered on himself, and there were a number of hypochondriacal complaints. Fred was disoriented for time and place, although he was able to give his name. He could not give

his correct address, said his age was 91, and was unable to name the day, the month, or the year. He did not know where he was, although he said he was sent here by his landlord because he had been drinking. He admitted that he had been arrested for fighting and drinking, but he said that he had never had an attack of delirium tremens. [Fred] showed the characteristic symptom picture of Korsakoff's syndrome, with disorientation, confusion, and a strong tendency toward confabulation. When asked where he was, he said he was in a brewery. He gave the name of the brewery, but when asked the same question a few minutes later, he named another brewery. Similarly, he said that he knew the examiner, called him by an incorrect name, and a little later changed the name again. When leaving the examining room, he used still another name when he said politely, "Goodbye, Mr. Wolf!"

(KISKER, 1977, P. 308)

As we observed in Chapter 10, approximately 5 percent of people with chronic alcoholism develop Korsakoff's syndrome. A combination of excessive drinking and improper diet produce a deficiency of *vitamin B* (*thiamine*), which leads to damage in portions of the *diencephalon* (Harding et al., 2000). Sufferers

Alzheimer's disease may last for as many as 20 years. It usually begins with mild memory problems, lapses of attention, and difficulties in language and communication (Shenk, 2001). As symptoms worsen, the person has trouble completing complicated tasks or remembering important appointments. Eventually sufferers also have difficulty with simple tasks, distant memories are forgotten, and changes in personality often become very noticeable. For example, a man may become uncharacteristically aggressive (Revetz, 1999).

People with Alzheimer's disease may at first deny that they have a problem (Shenk, 2001), but they soon become anxious or depressed about their state of mind; many also become agitated (Janzing, 2003; Zal, 1999). A woman from Virginia describes her memory loss as the disease progresses:

> Very often I wander around looking for something which I know is very pertinent, but then after a while I forget about what it is I was looking for. . . . Once the idea is lost, everything is lost and I have nothing to do but wander around trying to figure out what it was that was so important earlier.
>
> *(Shenk, 2001, p. 43)*

of this disorder primarily lose memories of factual knowledge, but still maintain their intellectual and language skills (Verfaellie et al., 1990). This may explain why Korsakoff's patients tend to *confabulate*. Like Fred, they use their general intellect to make up elaborate stories and lies in an effort to replace the factual memories they keep losing.

Head Injuries and Brain Surgery

Both head injuries and brain surgery can cause amnestic disorders (Richardson, 2002; Zec et al., 2002, 2001). Either may destroy memory-related brain structures. Television shows and movies often portray bumps on the head as a quick and easy way to lose one's memory. In fact, *mild* head injuries, such as a concussion that does not result in coma or a period of unconsciousness, rarely cause much memory loss, and what loss there is usually disappears within days or at most months. In contrast, almost half of all *severe* head injuries do cause some permanent learning and memory problems, both anterograde and retrograde. Altogether, 2 million people in the United States suffer traumatic brain injuries each year (Waxweiler et al., 1995). More than 20 percent of them experience lifelong aftereffects (NCIPC, 1999).

The leading causes are car accidents and falls.

Brain surgery may create more specific memory problems. The most famous case of memory loss as a result of brain surgery is that of H.M., a man whose identity has been protected for decades (Kensinger et al., 2001; Corkin, 1984, 1968; Milner, 1971). H.M. suffered from severe *brain seizure disorder*, or *epilepsy*, a disorder that produced seizures in his temporal lobes. To reduce his symptoms, doctors removed parts of both his temporal lobes in 1953, along with two other brain structures—the amygdala and hippocampus. At that time, the key involvement of these brain areas in the formation of memories was not known. (Today temporal lobe surgery is usually limited to either

the right or left side of the brain.) H.M. has experienced severe anterograde amnesia ever since his surgery a half-century ago. He is unable to recognize anyone he has met since the day of his operation.

Part of the game? *Hard blows to the head are common in contact sports such as hockey, football, and boxing and often result in concussions and at least temporary losses of memory. Repeated blows may, in fact, lead to repeated concussions, further affecting memory and other cognitive functions and, in some cases, endangering the athlete's physical integrity or life.*

Table 15-1 DSM-IV Checklist

DEMENTIA OF THE ALZHEIMER'S TYPE

1. The development of multiple cognitive deficits manifested by both memory impairment and at least one of the following cognitive disturbances:
   a. Aphasia.
   b. Apraxia.
   c. Agnosia.
   d. Disturbance in executive functioning.
2. Significant impairment in social or occupational functioning, along with significant decline from a previous level of functioning.
3. Gradual onset and continuing cognitive decline.

Based on APA, 2000, 1994.

Richard Falco/Black Star

Losing one's mind *Because of their short-term memory problems, people with advanced cases of Alzheimer's disease, one source of dementia, are often unable to complete simple tasks such as painting a picture. In addition, their long-term memory deficits may prevent them from recognizing even close relatives or friends.*

As the symptoms of dementia intensify, people with Alzheimer's disease show less and less awareness of their limitations. They may withdraw from others during the late stages of the disorder, become more confused about time and place, wander, and show very poor judgment. Eventually they become fully dependent on other people. They may lose almost all knowledge of the past and fail to recognize the faces of even close relatives. They also become more and more uncomfortable at night and take frequent naps during the day. The late phase of the disorder can last from two to five years, with the individuals requiring constant care (Mace & Rabins, 1991).

Alzheimer's victims usually remain in fairly good health until the later stages of the disease. As their mental functioning declines, however, they become less active and spend much of their time just sitting or lying in bed. As a result, they are prone to develop illnesses such as pneumonia, which can result in death. Alzheimer's disease is responsible for 23,000 deaths each year in the United States, which makes it the eighth leading cause of death in elderly people (NCHS, 1999).

In most cases, Alzheimer's disease can be diagnosed with certainty only after death (APA, 2000), when structural changes in the person's brain, such as excessive *neurofibrillary tangles* and *senile plaques*, can be fully examined. **Neurofibrillary tangles**, twisted protein fibers found *within* the cells of the hippocampus and certain other brain areas, occur in all people as they age, but people with Alzheimer's disease form a very high number of them (Thompson, 2000; Selkoe, 1992). **Senile plaques** are sphere-shaped deposits of a small molecule known as the *beta-amyloid protein* that form in the spaces *between* cells in the hippocampus, cerebral cortex, and certain other brain regions, as well as in some nearby blood vessels. The formation of plaques is also a normal part of aging, but again it is exceptionally high in people with Alzheimer's disease (Selkoe, 2002, 2000, 1992). Plaques may interfere with communications between cells and so cause cell breakdown or cell death. Scientists do not fully understand why some people develop these problems and the disease. Research has suggested several possible causes, however, including genetic factors and abnormalities in brain structure and brain chemistry.

WHAT ARE THE GENETIC CAUSES OF ALZHEIMER'S DISEASE? It appears that Alzheimer's disease often has a genetic basis (Williams, 2003). Studies have found that particular genes are responsible for the production of proteins called *beta-amyloid precursor protein (beta-APP)*, *presenilin*, and *interleukin-1*. Many theorists now believe that some families transmit mutations, or abnormal forms, of these genes, increasing the likelihood of plaque and tangle formations and, in turn, of Alzheimer's disease (Farlow et al., 2001; St. George-Hyslop, 2000; Selkoe, 1999, 1998, 1996). Genetic studies have also linked certain kinds of Alzheimer's disease to defects on chromosomes 1, 14, 19, and 21 (Turkington & Harris, 2001; Higgins et al., 1997).

WHAT ARE THE STRUCTURAL AND BIOCHEMICAL CAUSES OF ALZHEIMER'S DISEASE? Whether the factors that predispose individuals to Alzheimer's disease are genetic or otherwise, we still need to know what brain abnormalities they set in motion. That is, what abnormalities in brain structure or brain chemistry lead to Alzheimer's disease and to the excessive numbers of tangles and plaques that are its hallmark? Researchers have identified a number of possibilities.

As new memories are formed, proteins are produced in key brain cells. One line of research suggests that some of these proteins may take an abnormal form and essentially run amok in people with Alzheimer's disease (Hardy & Selkoe, 2002; Turkington & Harris, 2001). Studies suggest, for example, that two key memory proteins—*beta-amyloid protein* and *tau protein*—operate abnormally in such individuals. As we observed earlier, abnormal activity by the beta-amyloid protein is involved in the formation of plaques in the hippocampus and certain other brain areas. Similarly, abnormal activity of the tau protein leads to the formation of tangles in those brain areas (see Figure 15-3).

Another line of research points to abnormal activity by the neurotransmitters and related chemicals that help produce memory proteins. Many studies have found, for example, that *acetylcholine* and *glutamate* are in low supply, or at least function differently, in the brains of Alzheimer victims (Bissette et al., 1996; Lee et al., 1996). Other studies suggest that victims may display an imbalance in *calcium*.

A third explanation for Alzheimer's disease holds that certain substances found in nature may act as toxins and damage the brain. For example, researchers have detected high levels of *zinc* in the brains of some Alzheimer's victims. This finding has gained particular attention because in some animal studies zinc was

NEUROFIBRILLARY TANGLES Twisted protein fibers that form within certain brain cells as people age. People with Alzheimer's disease have an excessive number of such tangles.

SENILE PLAQUES Sphere-shaped deposits of beta-amyloid protein that form in the spaces between certain brain cells and in certain blood vessels as people age. People with Alzheimer's disease have an excessive number of such plaques.

FIGURE 15-3 **The aging brain** *In old age, our brain undergoes changes that affect memory, learning, and reasoning to some degree. These same changes occur to an excessive degree in people with Alzheimer's disease. (Adapted from Selkoe, 1992, p. 136.)*

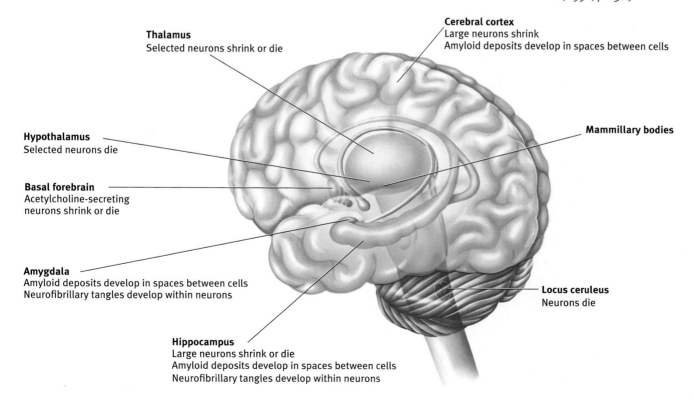

Thalamus
Selected neurons shrink or die

Cerebral cortex
Large neurons shrink
Amyloid deposits develop in spaces between cells

Hypothalamus
Selected neurons die

Mammillary bodies

Basal forebrain
Acetylcholine-secreting neurons shrink or die

Amygdala
Amyloid deposits develop in spaces between cells
Neurofibrillary tangles develop within neurons

Locus ceruleus
Neurons die

Hippocampus
Large neurons shrink or die
Amyloid deposits develop in spaces between cells
Neurofibrillary tangles develop within neurons

>>LOOKING AROUND
The Case of Ronald Reagan

Ronald Reagan's mother and older brother both suffered from dementia.<<

- -

Mildly forgetful during the late years of his presidency (1980–1988), Reagan experienced bouts of forgetfulness that began to interfere with his daily functioning by 1992.<<

- -

At the conclusion of a medical exam in 1992, Reagan looked up at his doctor of many years with an utterly blank face and said, "What am I supposed to do next?"<<

- -

In 1994 Reagan's doctors arrived at a formal diagnosis of Alzheimer's disease.<<

(Shenk, 2001)

Victim of Parkinson's disease *The world cheered when Muhammad Ali, considered the most skilled and influential athlete of his generation, lit the Olympic flame in 1996. At the same time, Ali's slow gait, halting verbal responses, and shaking hands and limbs demonstrated the impairment that Parkinson's disease can bring.*

observed to trigger a clumping of the beta-amyloid protein, similar to the plaques found in the brains of Alzheimer patients (Turkington & Harris, 2001).

Finally, two other explanations for Alzheimer's disease have been offered. One is the *autoimmune theory*. On the basis of certain irregularities found in the immune systems of people with Alzheimer's disease, several researchers have speculated that changes in aging brain cells may trigger an *autoimmune response* (that is, a mistaken attack by the immune system against itself) that leads to this disease (Hüll et al., 1996; McGeer & McGeer, 1996). The other explanation is a *viral theory*. Because Alzheimer's disease resembles *Creutzfeldt-Jacob disease*, another form of dementia that is known to be caused by a slow-acting virus, some researchers propose that a similar virus may cause Alzheimer's disease (Prusiner, 1991). However, no such virus has been detected in the brains of Alzheimer's victims.

OTHER FORMS OF DEMENTIA A number of other disorders may also lead to dementia. **Vascular dementia**, also known as **multi-infarct dementia**, may follow a cerebrovascular accident, or *stroke*, during which blood flow to specific areas of the brain was cut off, thus damaging the areas (Ghika & Bogousslavsky, 2002). In many cases, the patient may not even be aware of the stroke. Like Alzheimer's disease, vascular dementia is progressive, but its symptoms begin suddenly rather than gradually. Moreover, cognitive functioning may continue to be normal in areas of the brain that have not been affected by the stroke, in contrast to the broad cognitive deficiencies usually displayed by Alzheimer patients. Some people have both Alzheimer's disease and vascular dementia (Desmond et al., 2000).

Pick's disease, a rare disorder that affects the frontal and temporal lobes, offers a clinical picture similar to Alzheimer's disease, but the two diseases can be distinguished at autopsy (Hodges, 2001). *Creutzfeldt-Jakob disease,* another source of dementia, has symptoms that often include spasms of the body. As we observed earlier, this disease is caused by a slow-acting virus that may live in the body for years before the disease develops (APA, 2000). Once launched, however, the disease has a rapid course. *Huntington's disease* is an inherited progressive disease in which memory problems worsen over time, along with personality changes and mood difficulties (Ranen, 2002). Huntington's victims have movement problems, too, such as severe twitching and spasms. Children of people with Huntington's disease have a 50 percent chance of developing it. *Parkinson's disease,* the slowly progressive neurological disorder marked by tremors, rigidity, and unsteadiness, causes dementia in 20 to 60 percent of cases, particularly in older people or individuals whose cases are advanced (APA, 2000). And, lastly, cases of dementia may also be caused by viral and bacterial *infectious disorders* such as HIV and AIDs, meningitis, and advanced syphilis; by *brain seizure disorder;* by *drug abuse;* or by *toxins* such as *mercury, lead,* or *carbon monoxide*.

WHAT TREATMENTS ARE AVAILABLE FOR DEMENTIA? Treating dementia is a frustrating and difficult challenge. No single approach is effective in all cases, and treatment tends to offer modest help. However, the growing research on the causes of diseases that produce dementia has encouraged hope that dementia may be treated more effectively or even prevented in the years to come (Kalb, 2000).

Currently the first step in treatment is to identify as clearly as possible the precise type and nature of the individual's disease. Clinicians will typically take a complete history of the patient (knowing about a person's abuse of alcohol or a family history of Alzheimer's disease, for example, helps narrow the diagnosis), do extensive neuropsychological testing, and conduct brain scans to help pinpoint the biological causes of the patient's dysfunctioning (Zal, 1999; Gonzalez, 1996).

THE CURRENT SCENE

Mad Human Disease?

In the 1980s British farmers first became aware of *bovine spongiform encephalopathy*, or *mad cow disease*. Cows with this disease became disoriented, uncoordinated, and irritable, and eventually died. Autopsies revealed holes and tangles of protein in their brains. Researchers traced the disease to a particular feeding practice: sick cattle and parts of cattle that could not be sold for meat were ground up and fed to other cattle. British officials promptly banned the practice, but symptoms of the disease do not appear until years after the infection is contracted, so a continuing epidemic unfolded (Hileman, 2001). Some 200,000 cows have now died of the disease.

What does mad cow disease have to do with abnormal psychology in humans? Clinicians have come to appreciate that *Creutzfeldt-Jakob disease (CJD)*, a form of human dementia, is somewhat similar, clinically and biologically, to mad cow disease. CJD is a rare progressive dementia—incurable and fatal—apparently caused by an infectious protein that stays in the body for decades before producing symptoms (APA, 2000; Prusiner, 1995).

Although scientists at first believed that it was impossible for mad cow disease to "jump species," many now be-

Martyn Hayhow/AP/Wide World Photos

lieve that a new variant of CJD, called *vCJD*, may be contracted by people who eat the meat of cows infected with mad cow disease. To date, about 100 people in Europe have died of vCJD, but nobody knows how many have been infected—like mad cow disease and conventional CJD, vCJD may take years to produce symptoms. Although the absolute number of cases remains small, the rate of residents in the United Kingdom infected with vCJD has grown by 23 percent each year since 1994 (Hileman, 2001).

Once people became aware of the possible connection between mad cow disease and vCJD, panic swept across the United Kingdom and around the world. Most nations banned imports of British beef. Healthy cows could not be distinguished from infected ones, and so the United Kingdom agreed to destroy almost half of the nation's herd. By 2000, the number of slaughtered cows had reached 8 million.

The United States tried to avoid this health problem by taking measures to prevent the spread of mad cow disease and the emergence of vCJD. In 1997, for example, the Food and Drug Administration (FDA) banned the feeding of meat made from cud-chewing animals to other cud-chewing animals (cows and sheep). Also, beginning in 1989, the Department of Agriculture banned imports of live cattle and sheep from countries where mad cow disease has been identified.

However, such measures had limitations. For example, banned meals could still be fed to poultry, fish, and pigs, whose remains, in turn, could be fed to cattle (Burros, 2001). Moreover, the government's monitoring of farms and slaughterhouses for compliance with feed regulations and other safeguards was often unsystematic (Burros, 2001). Thus, it was not a total surprise when a cow in the United States was found to have mad cow disease in December, 2003. Federal authorities quickly quarantined three cattle herds and even decided to slaughter an entire herd. In addition, the government announced that meat from cattle who cannot walk unassisted would no longer be allowed to enter the food chain. Despite such measures, many countries cancelled imports of U.S. beef.

A common approach to the treatment of dementia is the use of drugs that affect the neurotransmitters known to play important roles in memory. Three such drugs, *tacrine* (trade name Cognex), *donepezil* (Aricept), and *rivastigmine* (Exelon), prevent the breakdown of acetylcholine, the neurotransmitter in low supply among people with Alzheimer's disease (Grilly, 2002). Some Alzheimer patients who take these drugs improve slightly in short-term memory and reasoning ability, as well as in their use of language and their ability to cope under pressure (Krall et al., 1999; Lyketsos et al., 1996). Although the benefits of the drugs are limited and the risk of harmful effects (particularly for tacrine) is sometimes high, the drugs have been approved by the Food and Drug Administration. Clinicians believe that they may be of most use to persons in the early stages of Alzheimer's disease or those with a mild form of dementia (Keltner & Folks, 2001; Turkington & Harris, 2001).

VASCULAR DEMENTIA Dementia caused by a cerebrovascular accident, or stroke, which restricts blood flow to certain areas of the brain. Also known as *multi-infarct dementia*.

Overcoming strokes *Cerebrovascular accidents, or strokes, may cause severe damage, psychologically as well as physically. They may produce vascular dementia, for example, or leave victims markedly depressed and anxious. Thus, groups such as the Handicapables in Sun City, Arizona, a water-therapy and support club for stroke victims, are often critical to a successful physical and psychological recovery.*

Tacrine and related drugs are prescribed *after* a person has developed Alzheimer's disease. A number of studies seem to suggest, however, that certain substances may actually help prevent or delay the onset of the disease. For example, one team of researchers concluded that women who take *estrogen*, the female sex hormone, for years after menopause cut their risk of developing Alzheimer's disease in half (Kawas et al., 1997). Similarly, long-term use of *nonsteroid anti-inflammatory drugs* such as *ibuprofen* and *naprosyn* (drugs found in Advil, Motrin, Nuprin, and other pain relievers) seems to greatly reduce the risk of Alzheimer's disease.

Behavioral interventions have been tried in cases of dementia, with modest success. They typically focus on changing everyday patient behaviors that are stressful for the family, such as wandering at night, loss of bladder control, demands for attention, and poor personal care (Fisher & Carstensen, 1990). In these techniques therapists use a combination of role-playing exercises, modeling, and practice to teach family members how and when to apply reinforcement in order to shape more positive behaviors (Pinkston & Linsk, 1984).

Caregiving can take a heavy toll on the close relatives of people with dementia (Kiecolt-Glaser et al., 2002, 1996; Schulz et al., 2002). It is hard to take care of someone who is becoming increasingly lost, helpless, and medically ill. And it is very painful to witness the decline of someone you love. One of the most frequent reasons for the institutionalization of Alzheimer's victims is that overwhelmed caregivers can no longer cope with the difficulties of keeping them at home (Kaplan, 1998). Many caregivers experience anger and depression, and their own physical and mental health often declines (Graesel, 2002; Powers et al., 2002). Clinicians now recognize that one of the most important aspects of treating Alzheimer's disease and other forms of dementia is to focus on the emotional needs of the caregivers: their need for regular time out, for education about the

Day treatment *Two women go their separate ways in a New Jersey day facility for patients with Alzheimer's disease. Such facilities, which are growing in number, provide special programs and activities for patients. The individuals return to their families each night.*

ABNORMALITY AND THE ARTS

"You Are the Music, while the Music Lasts" *Clayton S. Collins*

Oliver Sacks [a well-known neurologist and writer] danced to the Dead. For three solid hours. At 60. And with "two broken knees." . . .

The power of music—. . . to "bring back" individuals rendered motionless and mute by neurological damage and disorders—is what's driving Sacks these days. The . . . author (*Migraine, A Leg to Stand On, The Man Who Mistook His Wife for a Hat, Seeing Voices* and *Awakenings*) . . . is working on another case-study book, one that deals in part with the role of music as a stimulus to minds that have thrown up stiff sensory barriers. . . .

"One sees how robust music is neurologically," Sacks says. "You can lose all sorts of particular powers but you don't tend to lose music and identity." . . .

Much of what he has encountered, particularly in working with patients at Beth Abraham Hospital, Bronx, N.Y., . . . relates to music. . . .

"Deeply demented people respond to music, babies respond to music, fetuses probably respond to music. Various animals respond to music," Sacks says. "There is something about the animal nervous system . . . which seems to respond to music all the way down . . . ," Sacks says, citing the case of a patient with damage to the frontal lobes of his brain.

"When he sings, one almost has the strange feeling that [music] has given him his frontal lobes back, given him back, temporally, some function that has been lost on an organic basis," Sacks says, adding a quote from T. S. Eliot: "You are the music, while the music lasts."

The effects of music therapy may not always last. Sacks will take what he can

Musical awakenings *Over the years, Oliver Sacks has treated neurological disorders with techniques ranging from medication to the music of the Grateful Dead.*

get. "To organize a disorganized person for a minute is miraculous. And for half an hour, more so." . . .

The key, says Sacks, is for patients to "learn to be well" again. Music can restore to them, he says, the identity that predates the illness. . . .

"Greg" was an amnesiac with a brain tumor and no coherent memories of life since about 1969—but an encyclopedic memory of the years that came before, and a real love of Grateful Dead tunes.

Sacks took Greg to that night's [Grateful Dead] performance. "In the first half of the concert they were doing early music, and Greg was enchanted by everything," Sacks recalls. "I mean, he

was not an amnesiac. He was completely oriented and organized and with it." Between sets Sacks went backstage and introduced Greg to band member Micky Hart, who was impressed with Greg's knowledge of the group but quite surprised when Greg asked after Pigpen. When told the former band member had died 20 years before, "Greg was very upset," Sacks recalls. "And then 30 seconds later he asked 'How's Pigpen?' "

During the second half, the band played its newer songs. And Greg's world began to fall apart. "He was bewildered and enthralled and frightened. Because the music for him—and this is an extremely musical man, who understands the idiom of the Grateful Dead—was both familiar and unfamiliar. . . . He said, 'This is like the music of the future.' "

Sacks tried to keep the new memories fresh. But the next day, Greg had no memory of the concert. It seemed as if all had been lost. "But—and this is strange—when one played some of the new music, which he had heard for the first time at the concert, he could sing along with it and remember it."

It is an encouraging development. . . . Children have been found to learn quickly lessons that are embedded in song. Sacks, the one-time quiet researcher, is invigorated by the possibilities. He wonders whether music could carry such information, to give his patient back a missing part of his life. To give Greg "some sense of what's been happening in the last 20 years, where he has no autobiography of his own."

That would have Sacks dancing in the aisles.

(Excerpted by permission from Profiles, *the magazine of Continental Airlines, February 1994.)*

disease, and for psychotherapy when stress begins to build (Gaugler et al., 2003; Clyburn et al., 2000). Some clinicians also provide caregiver support groups (Pillemer & Suitor, 2002; Gallagher-Thompson et al., 2000, 1991).

In recent years, sociocultural approaches have begun to play an important role in treatment (Kalb, 2000). A number of *day care facilities* for patients with dementia have been developed, providing treatment programs and activities for outpatients during the day and returning them to their homes and families at night.

In addition, many *assisted living* facilities have been built, in which individuals suffering from dementia live in cheerful apartments, receive needed supervision, and take part in various activities that bring more joy and stimulation to their lives. These apartments are typically designed to meet the special needs of the residents—providing more light, for example, or enclosing gardens with circular paths so the individuals can go for strolls alone without getting lost (Kalb, 2000). Studies suggest that such facilities often help slow the cognitive decline of residents and enhance their enjoyment of life.

Rather than being discouraged by the present limitations in the understanding and treatment of dementia, researchers are looking forward to advances in the coming years. The brain changes responsible for dementia are tremendously complex, but given the amount of research under way and present reports of progress, most investigators believe that exciting breakthroughs are just over the horizon.

SUMMING UP

Disorders of Cognition

Older people are more likely than people of other age groups to experience delirium, a clouding of consciousness in which a person has great difficulty concentrating, focusing attention, and following an orderly sequence of thought. Dementia, a syndrome marked by severe memory loss and other cognitive disturbances, also becomes increasingly common in older age groups. It can result from dozens of brain illnesses or injuries, most commonly Alzheimer's disease. Alzheimer's disease has been linked to an unusually high number of neurofibrillary tangles and senile plaques in the brain. A number of causes have been proposed for this disease, including genetic factors, protein abnormalities, abnormal neurotransmitter activity, high levels of zinc in the brain, autoimmune responses, and viral infections. Drug, behavioral, and sociocultural interventions have been provided for people with dementia, with varying degrees of success. Addressing the needs of caregivers is now also recognized as a key part of treatment.

Stimulating effects *When long-term care institutions offer stimulating programs (such as this exercise class for people with Alzheimer's disease), allow patients to control their lives, and involve family members and friends, elderly persons are generally happier and show better cognitive functioning.*

Issues Affecting the Mental Health of the Elderly

As the study and treatment of elderly people have progressed, three issues have raised concern among clinicians: the problems faced by elderly members of racial and ethnic minority groups, the inadequacies of long-term care, and the need for a health-maintenance approach to medical care in an aging world (Gallagher-Thompson & Thompson, 1995).

Discrimination due to race and ethnicity has long been a problem in the United States (see Chapter 2), and many people suffer as a result, particularly those who are old (Utsey et al., 2002; Cavanaugh, 1990). To be both old and a member of a minority group is considered a kind of "double jeopardy" by many observers. For older women in minority groups, the difficulties are sometimes termed "triple jeopardy," as many more older women than older men live alone, are widowed, and are poor. Clinicians must take into account their older patients' race, ethnicity, and gender as they try to diagnose and treat their mental health problems (Hinton, 2002; Olson, 2002) (see Figure 15-4).

Some elderly people in minority groups face language barriers that interfere with their medical and mental health care. Others may hold cultural beliefs that prevent them from seeking services. Moreover, many members of minority groups do not trust the majority establishment or do not know about medical and mental health services that are sensitive to their culture and their particular needs (Ayalon & Huyck, 2001; Ralston, 1991; Jackson, 1988).

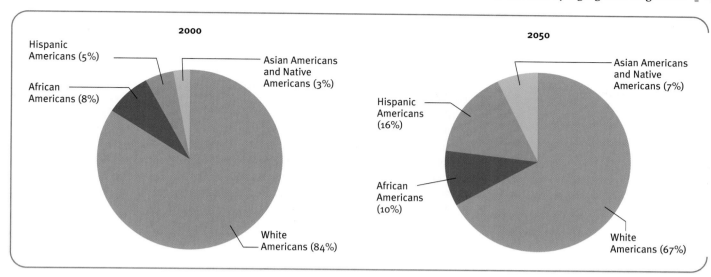

2000

Hispanic Americans (5%)

African Americans (8%)

Asian Americans and Native Americans (3%)

White Americans (84%)

2050

Asian Americans and Native Americans (7%)

Hispanic Americans (16%)

African Americans (10%)

White Americans (67%)

FIGURE 15-4 **Ethnicity and old age** *The elderly population is becoming racially and ethnically more diverse. In the United States today, 84 percent of all people over the age of 65 are white Americans. By 2050, only 67 percent of the elderly will be in this group. (Adapted from U.S. Census, 2000; Hobbs, 1997; NIA, 1996.)*

As a result, it is common for elderly members of racial and ethnic minority groups to rely largely on family members or friends for remedies and health care.

Many older people require *long-term care*, a general term that may refer variously to the services offered in a partially supervised apartment, in a senior housing complex for mildly impaired elderly persons, or in a nursing home where skilled medical and nursing care are available around the clock. The quality of care in such residences varies widely.

At any given time in the United States, only about 5 percent of the elderly population actually live in nursing homes, but as many as 30 percent eventually wind up being placed in such facilities (Fisher et al., 2001). Thus many older adults live in fear of being "put away." They fear having to move, losing independence, and living in a medical environment. Many elderly people know someone who died shortly after being admitted to a long-term care facility, and this increases their fears about life in such settings (Gallagher-Thompson & Thompson, 1995).

Many also worry about the cost of long-term care facilities. Families today are trying to keep elderly relatives at home longer, and so most older people enter nursing homes only in the last stages of a disease and in need of almost total care. Around-the-clock nursing care is expensive, and nursing home costs continue to rise. The health insurance plans available today do not even begin to cover the costs of long-term or permanent placement (Gallagher-Thompson & Thompson, 1995). Worry over these issues can greatly harm the mental health of older adults, perhaps leading to depression and anxiety as well as family conflict (Banerjee & Macdonald, 1996).

Finally, medical scientists suggest that the current generation of young adults should take a *health-maintenance*, or *wellness*, approach to their own aging process. In other words, they should do things that promote physical and mental health—avoid smoking, eat well-balanced and healthful meals, exercise regularly, and take advantage of psychoeducational, stress management, and other mental health programs. There is a growing belief that older adults will adapt more readily to changes and negative events if their physical and psychological health is good (Gallagher-Thompson & Thompson, 1995).

SUMMING UP

Key Issues Affecting the Elderly

In studying and treating the problems of old age, clinicians have become concerned about three issues: the problems of elderly members of racial and ethnic minority groups, the inadequacies of long-term care, and the need for health maintenance by young adults.

>>BY THE NUMBERS

Eye of the Beholder

67 years old	The age at which old age begins, according to surveys of people under age 30.‹‹
77 years old	The age at which old age begins, according to surveys of people over age 60.‹‹

(Roper Reports, 1998)

CROSSROADS:
Clinicians Discover the Elderly

Early in the twentieth century, mental health professionals focused little on the elderly. But like the problems of children, those of aging persons have now caught the attention of researchers and clinicians. Current work is bringing important changes in how we understand and treat the psychological problems of the elderly. No longer do clinicians simply accept depression or anxiety in elderly people as inevitable. No longer do they overlook the dangers of prescription drug misuse by the elderly. And no longer do they underestimate the dangers of delirium or the prevalence of dementia. Similarly, geropsychologists have become more aware of the importance of addressing the health care and financial needs of the elderly as keys to their psychological well-being.

As the elderly population grows ever larger, the special needs of people in this age group are becoming more apparent. Thus the study and treatment of their psychological problems, like those of children, will probably continue at a rapid pace. Clinicians and public officials are not likely to underestimate their needs and importance again.

Particularly urgent is dementia and its devastating impact on the elderly and their families. The complexity of the brain makes dementia difficult to understand, diagnose, and treat. However, researchers announce exciting new discoveries almost daily. To date, this research has been largely biological; but dementia has such a powerful impact on patients and their families that psychological and sociocultural investigations will not lag behind for long. In fact, society's special interest in and focus on Alzheimer's disease have reminded everyone about the importance of memory and related cognitive faculties. Memory is so central to our lives and to our self-concept that psychological and sociocultural research in this area is of potential value to every person's well-being. Thus, we can expect such work to grow and expand in the years to come.

"As I get older, I find I rely more and more on these sticky notes to remind me."

CRITICAL THOUGHTS

1. Need aging lead to depression and other psychological problems? What kinds of attitudes, preparations, and activities might help an individual enter old age with peace of mind and even a positive outlook? *pp. 450–456*

2. What changes in medical practice, patient education, or family interactions might address the growing problem of prescription drug misuse among the elderly? *p. 455*

3. Current research developments suggest that diagnosticians may eventually be able to identify victims of Alzheimer's disease years before a decline in their memory becomes noticeable. Would people be better off knowing or not knowing that they will eventually develop a disease that currently has no known cure? *pp. 457–466*

4. Initially, some scientists argued that mad cow disease could not be transmitted from one species to another, while others countered that it was indeed possible (Aldhous, 1996). When scientists disagree, how should the public proceed? *p. 463*

KEY TERMS

geropsychology p. 450

delusional disorder p. 455

delirium p. 456

dementia p. 457

Alzheimer's disease p. 457

neurofibrillary tangles p. 460

senile plaques p. 460

beta-amyloid protein p. 460

beta-amyloid precursor protein p. 461

presenilin p. 461

interleukin-1 p. 461

tau protein p. 461

acetylcholine p. 461

glutamate p. 461

calcium p. 461

zinc p. 461

autoimmune theory p. 462

viral theory p. 462

vascular dementia p. 462

Pick's disease p. 462

Creutzfeldt-Jakob disease p. 462

Huntington's disease p. 462

Parkinson's disease p. 462

tacrine p. 463

estrogen p. 464

nonsteroid anti-inflammatory drugs p. 464

day care facilities p. 465

assisted living facilities p. 466

discrimination p. 466

long-term care p. 467

QUICK QUIZ

1. What is geropsychology? What kinds of special pressures and up-sets are faced by elderly persons? *pp. 450–451*

2. How common is depression among the elderly? What are the possible causes of this disorder in aged persons, and how is it treated? *pp. 451–452*

3. How prevalent are anxiety disorders among the elderly? How do theorists explain the onset of these disorders in aged persons, and how do clinicians treat them? *pp. 453–454*

4. Describe and explain the kinds of substance abuse patterns that sometimes emerge among the elderly. *pp. 454–455*

5. What kinds of psychotic disorders may be experienced by elderly persons, and how are they treated? *p. 455*

6. What is delirium, and how does it differ from dementia? *pp. 456–457*

7. How common is dementia among the elderly? What are some of the diseases and problems that may produce dementia? *pp. 457–462*

8. Describe the clinical features and course of Alzheimer's disease. What are its possible causes? *pp. 457–462*

9. What kinds of interventions are applied in cases of Alzheimer's disease and other forms of dementia? *pp. 462–466*

10. What issues regarding aging have raised particular concern among clinicians? *pp. 466–467*

CYBER STUDY

SEARCH THE *FUNDAMENTALS OF ABNORMAL PSYCHOLOGY* CD-ROM FOR

▲ Chapter 15 Video Case Enrichment
  What problems are faced by sufferers of dementia and their caregivers?
  Observe a severe case of organic memory loss.

▲ Chapter 15 Practical, Research, and Decision-Making Exercises
  Experiencing the physical and psychological changes of aging

▲ Chapter 15 Practice Test and Feedback

LOG ON TO THE COMER WEB PAGE FOR

▲ Suggested Web links, exercises, FAQ page, additional Chapter 15 practice test questions
  <www.worthpublishers.com/comer>

<<<

EVELYN WILLIAMS, 1984

Law, Society, and the Mental Health Profession

Dear Jodie:

There is a definite possibility that I will be killed in my attempt to get Reagan. It is for this very reason that I am writing you this letter now. As you well know by now, I love you very much. The past seven months I have left you dozens of poems, letters and messages in the faint hope you would develop an interest in. . . . Jodie, I would abandon this idea of getting Reagan in a second if I could only win your heart and live out the rest of my life with you, whether it be in total obscurity or whatever. I will admit to you that the reason I'm going ahead with this attempt now is because I just cannot wait any longer to impress you. I've got to do something now to make you understand in no uncertain terms that I am doing all of this for your sake. By sacrificing my freedom and possibly my life I hope to change your mind about me. This letter is being written an hour before I leave for the Hilton Hotel. Jodie, I'm asking you please to look into your heart and at least give me the chance with this historical deed to gain your respect and love. I love you forever.

JOHN HINCKLEY

John W. Hinckley Jr. wrote this letter to the actress Jodie Foster in March 1981. Soon after writing it, he stood waiting, pistol ready, outside the Washington Hilton Hotel. Moments later, President Ronald Reagan came out of the hotel, and the popping of pistol fire was heard. As Secret Service men pushed Reagan into the limousine, a policeman and the president's press secretary fell to the pavement. The president had been shot, and by nightfall most of America had seen the face and heard the name of the disturbed young man from Colorado.

We have observed throughout this book that the psychological dysfunctioning of an individual does not occur in isolation. It is influenced—sometimes caused—by societal and social pressures, and it affects the lives of relatives, friends, and acquaintances. The case of John Hinckley demonstrates in powerful terms that individual dysfunction may, in some cases, also affect the well-being and rights of people the person does not know.

By the same token, clinical scientists and practitioners do not conduct their work in isolation. As they study and treat people with psychological problems, they are affecting and being affected by other institutions of society. We have seen, for example, how the government regulates the use of psychotropic medications, how clinicians have helped carry out the government's policy of deinstitutionalization, and how clinicians have called the psychological ordeal of Vietnam veterans to the attention of society.

In short, like their clients, clinical professionals operate within a complex social system, and in fact, that system assigns responsibilities to these professionals. Just as we must understand the social context in which abnormal behavior occurs in order to understand the behavior, so must we understand the context in which this behavior is studied and treated.

FORENSIC PSYCHOLOGY The branch of psychology concerned with intersections between psychological practice and research and the judicial system. Also related to the field of *forensic psychiatry*.

CRIMINAL COMMITMENT A legal process by which people accused of a crime are instead judged mentally unstable and sent to a mental health facility for treatment.

NOT GUILTY BY REASON OF INSANITY (NGRI) A verdict stating that defendants are not guilty of committing a crime because they were insane at the time of the crime.

M'NAGHTEN TEST A widely used legal test for insanity that holds people to be insane at the time they committed a crime if, because of a mental disorder, they did not know the nature of the act or did not know right from wrong.

IRRESISTIBLE IMPULSE TEST A legal test for insanity that holds people to be insane at the time they committed a crime if they were driven to do so by an uncontrollable "fit of passion."

DURHAM TEST A legal test for insanity that holds people to be insane at the time they committed a crime if their act was the result of a mental disorder or defect.

AMERICAN LAW INSTITUTE TEST A legal test for insanity that holds people to be insane at the time they committed a crime if, because of a mental disorder, they did not know right from wrong or could not resist an uncontrollable impulse to act.

Two social institutions have a particularly strong impact on the mental health profession—the legislative and judicial systems. These institutions—collectively, the *legal field*—have long been responsible for protecting both the public good and the rights of individuals. Sometimes the relationship between the legal field and the mental health field has been friendly, and they have worked together to protect the rights and meet the needs of troubled individuals and of society at large. At other times they have clashed, and one field has imposed its will on the other.

This relationship has two aspects. On the one hand, mental health professionals often play a role in the criminal justice system, as when they are called on to help the courts assess the mental stability of people accused of crimes. They responded to this call in the Hinckley case, as we shall see, and in thousands of other cases. This aspect of the relationship is sometimes termed *psychology in law;* that is, clinical practitioners and researchers operate within the legal system. On the other hand, there is another aspect to the relationship, called *law in psychology*. The legislative and judicial systems act upon the clinical field, regulating certain aspects of mental health care. The courts may, for example, force some individuals to enter treatment, even against their will. In addition, the law protects the rights of patients.

The intersections between the mental health field and the legal and judicial systems are referred to as **forensic psychology** (Otto & Heibrun, 2002). Forensic psychologists or psychiatrists (or related mental health professionals) may perform such varied activities as testifying in trials, researching the reliability of eyewitness testimony, or helping police profile the personality of a serial killer on the loose.

Psychology in Law: How Do Clinicians Influence the Criminal Justice System?

To arrive at just and appropriate punishments, the courts need to know whether defendants are *responsible* for the crimes they commit and *capable* of defending themselves in court. If not, it would be inappropriate to find individuals guilty or punish them in the usual manner. The courts have decided that in some instances people who suffer from severe *mental instability* may not be responsible for their actions or may not be able to defend themselves in court, and so should not be punished in the usual way. Although the courts make the final judgment as to mental instability, their decisions are guided to a large degree by the opinions of mental health professionals.

When people accused of crimes are judged to be mentally unstable, they are usually sent to a mental institution for treatment, a process called **criminal commitment**. Actually there are several forms of criminal commitment. In one, individuals are judged mentally unstable *at the time of their crimes* and so innocent of wrongdoing. They may plead **not guilty by reason of insanity** (**NGRI**) and bring mental health professionals into court to support their claim. When people are found not guilty on this basis, they are committed for treatment until they improve enough to be released.

In a second form of criminal commitment, individuals are judged mentally unstable *at the time of their trial* and so are considered unable to understand the trial procedures and defend themselves in court. They are committed for treatment until they are competent to stand trial. Once again, the testimony of mental health professionals helps determine the defendant's psychological functioning.

These judgments of mental instability have stirred many arguments. Some people consider the judgments to be loopholes in the legal system that allow criminals to escape proper punishment for wrongdoing. Others argue that a legal system simply cannot be just unless it allows for extenuating circumstances, such as mental instability. The practice of criminal commitment differs from country to country. In this chapter we shall observe primarily how it operates in the United States. Although the specific principles and procedures of each country may differ, most countries grapple with the same issues, concerns, and decisions that we shall be examining.

Criminal Commitment and Insanity during Commission of a Crime

Consider once again the case of John Hinckley. Was he insane at the time he shot the president? If insane, should he be held responsible for his actions? On June 21, 1982, 15 months after he shot four men in the nation's capital, a jury pronounced Hinckley not guilty by reason of insanity. Hinckley thus joined Richard Lawrence, a house painter who shot at Andrew Jackson in 1835, and John Schrank, a saloonkeeper who shot former president Teddy Roosevelt in 1912, as a would-be assassin who was found not guilty by reason of insanity.

It is important to recognize that "insanity" is a legal term. That is, the definition of "insanity" used in criminal cases was written by legislators, not by clinicians. Defendants may have mental disorders but not necessarily qualify for a legal definition of insanity. Modern Western definitions of insanity can be traced to the murder case of Daniel M'Naghten in England in 1843. M'Naghten shot and killed Edward Drummond, the secretary to British Prime Minister Robert Peel, while trying to shoot Peel. Because of M'Naghten's apparent delusions of persecution, the jury found him to be not guilty by reason of insanity. The public was outraged by this decision, and their angry outcry forced the British law lords to define the insanity defense more clearly. This legal definition, known as the **M'Naghten test**, or **M'Naghten rule**, stated that experiencing a mental disorder at the time of a crime does not by itself mean that the person was insane; the defendant also had to be *unable to know right from wrong*. The state and federal courts in the United States adopted this test as well.

In the late nineteenth century some state and federal courts in the United States, dissatisfied with the M'Naghten rule, adopted a different test—the **irresistible impulse test**. This test, which had first been used in Ohio in 1834, emphasized the inability to control one's actions. A person who committed a crime during an uncontrollable "fit of passion" was considered insane and not guilty under this test.

For years state and federal courts chose between the M'Naghten test and the irresistible impulse test to determine the sanity of criminal defendants. For a while a third test, called the **Durham test**, also became popular, but it was soon replaced in most courts. This test, based on a decision handed down by the Supreme Court in 1954 in the case of *Durham v. United States*, stated simply that people are not criminally responsible if their "unlawful act was the product of mental disease or mental defect." This test was meant to offer more flexibility in court decisions, but it proved too flexible. Insanity defenses could point to such problems as alcoholism or other forms of substance dependence and conceivably even headaches or ulcers, which were listed as psychophysiological disorders in DSM-I.

In 1955 the American Law Institute (ALI) developed a test that combined aspects of the M'Naghten, irresistible impulse, and Durham tests. The **American Law Institute test** held that people are not criminally responsible if at the time of a crime they had a mental disorder or defect that prevented them from knowing right from wrong *or* from being able to control themselves and to follow the law. For a time the new test became the most widely accepted legal test of insanity. After the Hinckley verdict, however, there was a public uproar over the "liberal" ALI guidelines, and people called for tougher standards.

Partly in response to this uproar, the American Psychiatric Association recommended in 1983 that people should be found not guilty by reason of insanity *only* if they did not know right from wrong at the time of the crime; an inability to control themselves and to follow the law should no longer be sufficient grounds

Would-be assassin *Few courtroom decisions have spurred as much debate as the jury's verdict that John Hinckley, having been captured in the act of shooting President Ronald Reagan, was not guilty by reason of insanity.*

>>**IN THEIR WORDS**

"John Hinckley suffers [from] schizophrenia."<<

Expert defense witness, June 7, 1982

"Hinckley does not suffer from schizophrenia."<<

Expert prosecution witness, June 7, 1982

"[Hinckley had] a very severe depressive disorder."<<

Expert defense witness, May 20, 1982

"There is little to suggest he was seriously depressed [the day of the shootings]."<<

Expert prosecution witness, June 4, 1982

STEPPING BACK

Famous Insanity Defense Cases

1977 In Michigan, Francine Hughes poured gasoline around the bed where her husband, Mickey, lay in a drunken stupor. Then she lit a match and set him on fire. At her trial she explained that he had beaten her repeatedly for 14 years, and he had threatened to kill her if she tried to leave him. The jury found her not guilty by reason of temporary insanity, making her into a symbol for many abused women across the nation. Some people saw the decision as confirmation of a woman's right to self-defense in her own home.

1978 David "Son of Sam" Berkowitz, a serial killer in New York City, explained that a barking dog had sent him demonic messages to kill. Although two psychiatrists assessed him as psychotic, he was found guilty of his crimes. Long after his trial, he said that he had actually made up the delusions.

1979 Kenneth Bianchi, one of the pair known as the Hillside Strangler, entered a plea of not guilty by reason of insanity but was found guilty along with his cousin of sexually assaulting and murdering women in the Los Angeles area in late 1977 and early 1978. He claimed that he had multiple personality disorder.

1980 In December, Mark David Chapman murdered John Lennon. Chapman later explained that he had killed the rock music legend because he believed Lennon to be a "sell-out." He also described hearing the voice of God, considered himself his generation's "catcher in the rye" (from the J. D. Salinger novel), and compared himself to Moses. Despite clinical testimony that supported Chapman's plea of not guilty by reason of insanity, he was ultimately convicted of murder.

1981 In an attempt to prove his love for the actress Jodie Foster, John Hinckley Jr. tried to assassinate President Ronald Reagan. Hinckley was found not guilty by reason of insanity and was committed to St. Elizabeths Hospital for the criminally insane in Washington, D.C., where he remains today.

1992 Jeffrey Dahmer, a 31-year-old mass murderer in Milwaukee, was tried for the killings of 15 young men. Dahmer apparently drugged some of his victims and performed crude lobotomies on them in an attempt to create zombielike companions for himself. He also dismembered his victims' bodies and stored their parts to be eaten. Although his defense attorney argued that Dahmer was not guilty by reason of insanity, the jury found him guilty as charged. He was beaten to death by another inmate in 1995.

1994 On June 23, 1993, 24-year-old Lorena Bobbitt cut off her husband's penis with a 12-inch kitchen knife while he slept. During her trial, defense attorneys argued that after years of abuse by John Bobbitt, his wife suffered a brief psychotic episode and was seized by an "irresistible impulse" to cut off his penis after he came home drunk and raped her. In 1994, the jury acquitted her of the charge of malicious wounding by reason of temporary insanity. She was committed to a state mental hospital for further assessment and treatment and released a few months later.

1997 John E. Du Pont, 57-year-old heir to his family's chemical fortune, shot and killed the Olympic wrestling champion Dave Schultz in January 1995. The murder took place on Du Pont's 800-acre estate, where he had built a sports center for amateur athletes. Schultz, his close friend, had coached wrestlers at the center. In 1997 Du Pont was found guilty of third-degree murder, but mentally ill. He was sentenced to prison for 13 to 30 years and assigned to receive treatment at the prison's mental health unit.

2002 On June 20, 2001, Andrea Yates, a 36-year-old woman, drowned each of her five children in the bathtub. Yates had a history of postpartum depression and postpartum psychosis: she believed that she was the devil, that she had failed to be a good mother, and that her children were not developing correctly. She had in fact been hospitalized twice

A verdict of guilty *Andrea Yates is led into a district court in Texas for arraignment on multiple counts of murder in the drowning of her five children.*

for her disorder and was in treatment just prior to the killings. Given such problems and history, she pleaded not guilty by reason of insanity. The jury agreed that she had a profound disorder, but it concluded that she did know right from wrong at the time of the murders. In 2002 she was found guilty and sentenced to life in prison in Texas.

2003 For three weeks in October 2002, John Allen Muhammad and Lee Boyd Malvo went on a sniping spree in the Washington, D.C., area, shooting 10 people dead and wounding three others. Attorneys for Malvo, a teenager, argued that he had acted under the influence of the middle-aged Muhammad and that he should be found not guilty of the crimes by reason of insanity. The jury, however, found Malvo guilty of capital murder, and sentenced him to life in prison.

for a judgment of insanity. In short, the association was calling for a return to the M'Naghten test. This test now is used in all cases tried in federal courts and in about half of the state courts (Steadman et al., 1993). The more liberal ALI standard is still used in the remaining state courts, except in Idaho, Montana, and Utah, which have done away with the insanity plea altogether. Research has not found, however, that the stricter M'Naghten definition actually reduces the likelihood of verdicts of not guilty by reason of insanity (Ogloff et al., 1992; Finkel, 1991, 1990, 1989).

People suffering from severe mental disorders in which confusion is a major feature may not be able to tell right from wrong or to control their behavior. It is therefore not surprising that approximately two-thirds of defendants who are acquitted of a crime by reason of insanity qualify for a diagnosis of schizophrenia (Steadman et al., 1993). The vast majority of these acquitted defendants have a history of past hospitalization, arrest, or both. About half who successfully plead insanity are white, and 86 percent are male. Their mean age is 32 years. The crimes for which defendants are found not guilty by reason of insanity vary greatly. However, approximately 65 percent are violent crimes of some sort (Steadman et al., 1993). Close to 15 percent of those acquitted are accused specifically of murder (see Figure 16-1).

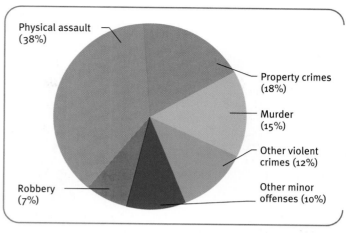

FIGURE 16-1 Crimes for which persons are found not guilty by reason of insanity (NGRI) *A review of NGRI verdicts in eight states revealed that most people who were acquitted on this basis had been charged with a crime of violence. (Based on Steadman et al., 1993; Callahan et al., 1991.)*

WHAT CONCERNS ARE RAISED BY THE INSANITY DEFENSE? Despite the changes in the insanity tests, criticism of the insanity defense continues (Slovenko, 2002, 1995). One concern is the fundamental difference between the law and the science of human behavior. The law assumes that individuals have free will and are generally responsible for their actions. Several models of human behavior, in contrast, assume that physical or psychological forces act to determine the individual's behavior. Inevitably, then, legal definitions of insanity and responsibility will differ from those suggested by clinical research.

A second criticism points to the uncertainty of scientific knowledge about abnormal behavior. During a typical insanity defense trial, the testimony of defense clinicians conflicts with that of clinicians hired by the prosecution, and so the jury must weigh the claims of "experts" who disagree in their assessments. Some people see this lack of professional agreement as evidence that clinical knowledge in some areas may be too limited to be allowed to influence important legal decisions (Slovenko, 1995). Others counter that the field has made great advances—for example, developing several psychological scales to help clinicians discriminate more consistently between the sane and insane as defined by the M'Naghten test (Rogers & Shuman, 2000).

Even with helpful scales in hand, however, clinicians making judgments of legal insanity face a problem that is hard to overcome: they must evaluate a defendant's state of mind during an event that occurred weeks, months, or years earlier. Because mental states can and do change over time and across situations, clinicians can never be entirely certain that their assessments of mental instability at the time of the crime are accurate.

Perhaps the most often heard criticism of the insanity defense is that it allows dangerous criminals to escape punishment. Granted, some people who successfully plead insanity are released from treatment facilities just months after their acquittal. Yet the number of such cases is quite small. According to surveys, the public dramatically overestimates the percentage of defendants who plead insanity, guessing it to be 30 to 40 percent, when in fact it is less than 1 percent (Steadman et al., 1993). Moreover, only a minority of these persons fake or exaggerate their psychological symptoms (Resnick & Harris, 2002), and only one-quarter of defendants who plead insanity are actually found not guilty on this basis (Callahan et al., 1991). In the end, fewer than 1 of every 400 defendants in the United States is found not guilty by reason of insanity.

>>**IN THEIR WORDS**

"I feel the insanity defense should be retained. I bear no grudge against John Hinckley, but I sure don't hope he wins the Irish Sweepstakes."<<

James Brady, presidential news secretary shot by John Hinckley

Stephen Ferry/Gamma Liaison

Legal experts *Forensic specialists perform much of their clinical work in the courts and legislatures. Forensic psychologists, psychiatrists, and social workers typically receive special training in such duties as evaluating the functioning of criminal defendants, making recommendations concerning patients' rights, and assessing the psychological trauma experienced by crime victims.*

During most of U.S. history, a successful insanity plea amounted to the equivalent of a long-term prison sentence (Miller, 2002). In fact, treatment in a mental hospital often resulted in a longer period of confinement than a verdict of guilty would have brought (Perlin, 2000). Because hospitalization resulted in little, if any, improvement, clinicians were reluctant to predict that the offenders would not repeat their crimes. Today, however, offenders are being released from mental hospitals earlier and earlier. This trend is the result of the increasing effectiveness of drug therapy and other treatments in institutions, the growing reaction against extended institutionalization, and a greater emphasis on patients' rights (Salekin & Rogers, 2001; Blackburn, 1993). In 1992, in the case of *Foucha v. Louisiana*, the U.S. Supreme Court ruled that the *only* acceptable basis for determining the release of hospitalized offenders is whether or not they are still "insane"; they cannot be kept indefinitely in mental hospitals solely because they are dangerous. Some states are able to maintain control over offenders even after their release from hospitals (Hilday, 1999). The states may insist on community treatment, observe the patients closely, and rehospitalize them if necessary.

WHAT OTHER VERDICTS ARE AVAILABLE? In recent years 13 states have added another verdict option—**guilty but mentally ill**. Defendants who receive this verdict are found to have had a mental illness at the time of their crime, but the illness was not fully related to or responsible for the crime. The guilty-but-mentally-ill option enables jurors to convict a person they view as dangerous while also suggesting that the individual receive needed treatment. Defendants found to be guilty but mentally ill are given a prison term with the added recommendation that they also undergo treatment if necessary.

In Georgia, juries given the option of finding a person guilty but mentally ill have delivered fewer insanity acquittals (Callahan et al., 1992). Studies with mock juries have found that many jurors prefer having this third option, seeing it as "moral, just and an adequate means of providing for the treatment needs of mentally ill offenders" (Boudouris, 2000; Roberts et al., 1987). However, those who criticize this option point out that appropriate mental health care is supposed to be available to all prisoners anyway, regardless of the verdict. They argue that the new option differs from a guilty verdict in name only (Melville & Naimark, 2002). Critics also believe that the option may confuse jurors.

Some states allow still another kind of defense, *guilty with diminished capacity*. Here a defendant's mental dysfunctioning is viewed as an extenuating circumstance that the court should take into consideration in determining the precise crime of which he or she is guilty (Leong, 2000). The defense lawyer argues that because of mental dysfunctioning, the defendant could not have *intended* to commit a particular crime. The person can then be found guilty of a lesser crime—of manslaughter (unlawful killing without intent), say, instead of murder in the first degree (planned murder). The case of Dan White, who shot and killed Mayor George Moscone and City Supervisor Harvey Milk of San Francisco in 1978, illustrates the use of this verdict.

GUILTY BUT MENTALLY ILL A verdict stating that defendants are guilty of committing a crime but are also suffering from a mental illness that should be treated during their imprisonment.

> . . . Defense attorney Douglas Schmidt argued that a patriotic, civic-minded man like Dan White—high school athlete, decorated war veteran, former fireman, policeman, and city supervisor—could not possibly have committed such an act unless something had snapped inside him. The brutal nature of the two final shots to each man's head only proved that White had lost his wits. White was not fully responsible for his actions because he suffered from "diminished capacity." Although White killed Mayor George Moscone and Supervisor Harvey Milk, he had not planned his actions. On the day of the shootings, White was mentally incapable of planning to kill, or even of wanting to do such a thing.

Well known in forensic psychiatry circles, Martin Blinder, professor of law and psychiatry at the University of California's Hastings Law School in San Francisco, brought a good measure of academic prestige to White's defense. White had been, Blinder explained to the jury, "gorging himself on junk food: Twinkies, Coca-Cola. . . . The more he consumed, the worse he'd feel and he'd respond to his ever-growing depression by consuming ever more junk food." Schmidt later asked Blinder if he could elaborate on this. "Perhaps if it were not for the ingestion of this junk food," Blinder responded, "I would suspect that these homicides would not have taken place." From that moment on, Blinder became known as the author of the Twinkie defense. . . .

Dan White was convicted only of voluntary manslaughter, and was sentenced to seven years, eight months. (He was released on parole January 6, 1984.) Psychiatric testimony convinced the jury that White did not wish to kill George Moscone or Harvey Milk.

(Coleman, 1984, pp. 65–70)

Because of possible miscarriages of justice, many legal experts have argued against the "diminished capacity" defense (Slovenko, 2002, 1992; Coleman, 1984), and a number of states have eliminated it. Some studies find, however, that jurors are often capable of using the option in careful and appropriate ways (Finkel & Duff, 1989).

WHAT ARE SEX-OFFENDER STATUTES? Since 1937, when Michigan passed the first "sex psychopath" law, some states have placed sex offenders in a special legal category (Reid, 2002; Bumby & Maddox, 1999). These states believe that people who are repeatedly found guilty of certain sex crimes have a mental disorder, and so the states categorize them as *mentally disordered sex offenders*.

People classified in this way have been convicted of a criminal offense and are thus judged to be responsible for their actions. Nevertheless, like people found not guilty by reason of insanity, mentally disordered sex offenders are committed to a mental health facility. In part, such laws reflect a belief held by some legislators that such sex offenders are psychologically disturbed. On a practical level, the laws help protect sex offenders from the physical abuse that they often receive in prison society.

Over the last two decades, a growing number of states have been changing or abolishing these sex-offender laws. There are several reasons for this trend. First,

>>LOOKING AROUND
The Aftermath

Dan White Convicted of involuntary manslaughter in the killings of San Francisco Mayor George Moscone and City Supervisor Harvey Milk in 1978, Dan White was released from prison in 1984 and spent a year on parole. He committed suicide in 1985.‹‹

Daniel M'Naghten After being judged not guilty by reason of insanity, Daniel M'Naghten lived in a mental hospital until his death 22 years later (Slovenko, 2002, 1995).‹‹

John Hinckley In December 2003, a U.S. District judge ruled that John Hinckley may make six day visits to see his parents in the Washington, D.C., area, without being accompanied by an escort from St. Elizabeths Hospital, the facility in which he has been confined since his attempt to assassinate President Ronald Reagan in 1981.‹‹

Justice served? *Mass protests were held in San Francisco after Dan White was convicted of voluntary manslaughter rather than premeditated murder in the killings of Mayor George Moscone and Supervisor Harvey Milk, one of the nation's leading gay activists. For many observers, the 1979 verdict highlighted the pitfalls of the "diminished capacity" defense.*

Bill Nation/Sygma

MENTAL INCOMPETENCE A state of mental instability that leaves defendants unable to understand the legal charges and proceedings they are facing and unable to prepare an adequate defense with their attorney.

CIVIL COMMITMENT A legal process by which an individual can be forced to undergo mental health treatment.

certain states have found the laws difficult to apply. Some state laws, for example, require that the offender be found "sexually dangerous beyond a reasonable doubt"—a judgment that is often beyond the reach of the clinical field's expertise (Szasz, 1991). Furthermore, there is evidence that racial bias can affect the use of the sex-offender classification (Sturgeon & Taylor, 1980). White Americans are twice as likely to be granted sex-offender status as African Americans or Hispanic Americans who have been convicted of similar crimes. Finally, the courts have become less concerned about the rights and needs of sex offenders in recent years as the public has increasingly expressed outrage over the high number of sex crimes taking place across the country, particularly those in which children are victims. In fact, in the 1997 case of *Kansas v. Hendricks* the Supreme Court ruled (5 to 4) that individuals who have been convicted of sex crimes may be removed from criminal confinement before their release and subjected to involuntary civil commitment in a mental hospital if a court judges them likely to engage in further "predatory acts of sexual violence" as a result of "mental abnormality" or "personality disorder."

Criminal Commitment and Incompetence to Stand Trial

Regardless of their state of mind at the time of a crime, defendants may be judged to be **mentally incompetent** to stand trial. The competence requirement is meant to ensure that defendants understand the charges they are facing and can work with their lawyers to prepare and run an adequate defense (Grisso, 2003). This minimum standard of competence was specified by the Supreme Court in the case of *Dusky v. United States* (1960).

The issue of competence is most often raised by the defendant's attorney, although prosecutors, arresting police officers, and even the judge may raise it as well (Meyer, 1992). They prefer to err on the side of caution, because some convictions have been reversed on appeal when a defendant's competence was not established at the beginning. When the issue of competence is raised, the judge orders a psychological evaluation, usually on an inpatient basis. Approximately 20 percent of defendants who receive such an evaluation are in fact found to be incompetent to stand trial (Hiday, 1999). If the court decides that the defendant is incompetent, the person is assigned to a mental health facility until competent to stand trial (Bennett & Kish, 1990).

Many more cases of criminal commitment result from decisions of mental incompetence than from verdicts of not guilty by reason of insanity (Roesch et al.,

Population unserved *Given the overcrowded and unsafe conditions in most prisons, the prevalence of psychological problems among prisoners is extraordinarily high. Yet only a fraction of those who need treatment are afforded mental health services.*

1999). However, the majority of criminals currently institutionalized for psychological treatment in the United States are not from either of these two groups. Rather, they are convicted inmates whose psychological problems have led prison officials to decide they need treatment—either in mental health units within the prison or in mental hospitals (Ogloff, 2002) (see Figure 16-2).

It is possible that an innocent defendant, ruled incompetent to stand trial, could spend years in a mental health facility with no chance to disprove the criminal accusations. Some defendants have, in fact, served longer "sentences" in mental health facilities awaiting a ruling of competence than they would have served in prison had they been convicted (Meyer, 1992). Such a possibility was reduced when the Supreme Court ruled, in the case of *Jackson v. Indiana* (1972), that an incompetent defendant cannot be indefinitely committed. After a reasonable amount of time, he or she should either be found competent and tried, set free, or transferred to a mental health facility under *civil* commitment procedures.

Until the early 1970s, most states required the commitment of mentally incompetent defendants to maximum-security institutions for the "criminally insane" (Winick, 1983). Under current law, the courts have greater flexibility. In some cases, particularly when the charge is a minor one, the defendant may even be treated on an outpatient basis.

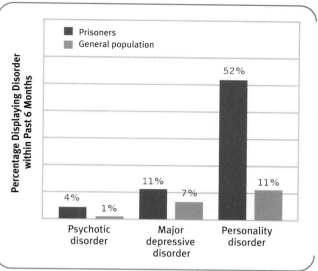

FIGURE 16-2 **Prison and mental health**
According to studies conducted in several Western countries, psychological disorders are much more common in prison populations than in the general population. For example, schizophrenia is 4 times more common and personality disorders are 5 times more common among prisoners than among nonprisoners. In fact, antisocial personality disorder is 10 times more common. (Based on Fazel & Danesh, 2002.)

SUMMING UP | **How Do Clinicians Influence the Criminal Justice System?**

One way in which the mental health profession and the legislative and judicial systems interact is in the help offered by clinicians in assessing the mental stability of people accused of crimes. Evaluations by clinicians may help judges and juries decide whether defendants are (1) responsible for crimes or (2) capable of defending themselves in court.

If defendants are judged to have been mentally unstable at the time they committed a crime, they may be found not guilty by reason of insanity and placed in a treatment facility rather than a prison (criminal commitment). In federal courts and about half the state courts, insanity is judged in accordance with the M'Naghten test. Other states use the broader American Law Institute test.

The insanity defense has been criticized on several grounds, and some states have added an additional option, guilty but mentally ill. Still another optional verdict is guilty with diminished capacity. In a related category are convicted sex offenders, who are considered in some states to have a mental disorder and are therefore assigned to treatment in a mental health facility.

Regardless of their state of mind at the time of the crime, defendants may be found mentally incompetent to stand trial, that is, incapable of fully understanding the charges or legal proceedings that confront them. If so, they are typically sent to a mental health facility until they are competent to stand trial (another form of criminal commitment).

Law in Psychology: How Do the Legislative and Judicial Systems Influence Mental Health Care?

Just as clinical science and practice have influenced the legal system, so the legal system has had a major impact on clinical practice. First, courts and legislatures have developed the process of **civil commitment**, which allows certain people to be forced into mental health treatment. Although many people who show signs

A CLOSER LOOK

The Separation of Mind and State

*D*uring the presidential campaigns of 1992 and 1996, the independent candidate Ross Perot was branded "emotionally unbalanced" by some of his detractors. Perot reacted with good humor and even adopted Willie Nelson's "Crazy" as his theme song. The strategy of questioning the psychological stability of political opponents was taken to the extreme in the former Soviet Union, particularly under the rule of Joseph Stalin, when many political opponents were placed in mental hospitals to get them out of the way.

Politically motivated labeling was at work during the mid-nineteenth-century debate over slavery in the United States, when those who favored slavery attacked Abraham Lincoln in the press as "insane" for his antislavery stance (Gamwell & Tomes, 1995). Many people, even among those who were against slavery, feared radical abolitionists and called them mentally unbalanced, blaming them for the nation's turmoil.

The trial of the abolitionist John Brown brought the issue out front for all to see. Brown, a white opponent of slavery, organized a small force of African Americans and white Americans to attack the federal armory at Harpers Ferry in Virginia. He was captured after

The Metropolitan Museum of Art, New York

"The Last Moments of John Brown" *The abolitionist John Brown's journey to execution is portrayed in Thomas Hovenden's painting* The Last Moments of John Brown, *1884.*

two days and tried for murder and treason. Many of Brown's supporters, including his own defense attorneys, urged him to plead not guilty by reason of insanity to avoid the death penalty (Gamwell & Tomes, 1995). Some fellow abolitionists, however, were offended by

the suggestion that Brown's actions represented insanity, and Brown himself proudly maintained that he was mentally stable. In the end, Brown was convicted and executed.

As the historians Lynn Gamwell and Nancy Tomes (1995) point out, it was in the interests of both sides of the case to have Brown declared legally insane. Many people who opposed slavery believed that an insanity verdict would distance Brown's radical behavior from their own abolitionist behaviors in the public's mind and would thus calm public fears of violence by abolitionists. Many of those who defended slavery believed that a judgment of insanity would hurt Brown's reputation and prevent him from becoming a martyr for the abolitionist cause—as in fact he did become. Obviously, the verdict pleased neither side.

Clinical labels have been used for political gain throughout the ages. We may not always be able to stop the practice, but we should at least be aware of it. As we read about historical events, we must be careful to separate mental health labels that are used correctly from those that seek merely to further a political cause.

of mental disturbance seek treatment voluntarily, a large number are not aware of their problems or are simply not interested in undergoing therapy. What are clinicians to do for these people? Should they force treatment upon them? Or do people have the right to feel miserable and function poorly? The law has answered this question by developing civil commitment guidelines under which certain people can be forced into treatment (Stafford, 2002; Douglas & Koch, 2001).

Second, the legal system, on behalf of the state, has taken on the responsibility for protecting patients' rights during treatment. This protection extends not only to patients who have been involuntarily committed but also to those who seek treatment voluntarily, even on an outpatient basis.

Civil Commitment

Every year in the United States large numbers of people with mental disorders are involuntarily committed to treatment. Typically they are committed to *mental institutions*, but 27 states also have *outpatient civil commitment* laws that allow patients to be forced into community treatment programs (Allbright et al., 2002).

Civil commitments have long caused controversy and debate. In some ways the law provides greater protection for suspected criminals than for people suspected of psychosis (Burton, 1990).

WHY COMMIT? Generally our legal system permits involuntary commitment of individuals when they are considered to be *in need of treatment* and *dangerous to themselves or others*. People may be dangerous to themselves if they are suicidal or if they act recklessly (for example, drinking a drain cleaner to prove that they are immune to its chemicals). They may be dangerous to others if they seek to harm them or if they unintentionally place others at risk. The state's authority to commit disturbed individuals rests on its duties to protect the interests of the individual and of society: the principles of *parens patriae* ("parent of the country") and *police power* (Taxman & Messina, 2002; Perlin, 2000).

WHAT ARE THE PROCEDURES FOR CIVIL COMMITMENT? Civil commitment laws vary from state to state (Winick, 2001). Some basic procedures, however, are common to most of these laws. Often family members begin commitment proceedings. In response to a son's psychotic behavior and repeated assaults on other people, for example, his parents may try to persuade him to seek admission to a mental institution. If the son refuses, the parents may go to court and seek an involuntary commitment order. If the son is a minor, the process is simple. The Supreme Court has ruled that a hearing is not necessary in such cases, as long as a mental health professional considers commitment necessary. If the son is an adult, however, the process is more involved. The court will usually order a mental examination and allow the person to challenge the commitment in court, often represented by a lawyer (Perlin, 2000; Holstein, 1993).

Although the Supreme Court has offered few guidelines concerning specific procedures of civil commitment, one important decision, in the case of *Addington v. Texas* (1979), outlined the *minimum standard of proof* needed for commitment. Here the Court ruled that before an individual can be committed, there must be "clear and convincing" proof that he or she is mentally ill and has met the state's criteria for involuntary commitment. The ruling does not suggest what criteria should be used. That matter is still left to each state. But, whatever the state's criteria, clinicians must offer clear and convincing proof that the individual meets those criteria. When is proof clear and convincing, according to the Court? When it provides 75 percent certainty that the criteria of commitment have been met. This is far less than the near-total certainty ("beyond a reasonable doubt") required to convict people of committing a crime.

EMERGENCY COMMITMENT Many situations require immediate action; no one can wait for commitment proceedings when a life is at stake. Consider, for example, an emergency room patient who is suicidal or hearing voices demanding hostile actions against others. He or she may need immediate treatment and round-the-clock supervision. If treatment could not be given in such situations without the patient's full consent, the consequences could be tragic.

Therefore, many states give clinicians the right to certify that certain patients need temporary commitment and medication (Winick, 2001). In past years, these states required certification by two *physicians* (not necessarily psychiatrists in some of the states). Today states may allow certification by other mental health professionals as well. The clinicians must declare that the state of mind of the patients makes them dangerous to themselves or others. By tradition, the certifications are often referred to as *two-physician certificates*, or *2 PCs*. The length of such emergency commitments varies from state to state, but three days is often the limit (Holstein, 1993). Should clinicians come to believe that a longer stay is necessary, formal commitment proceedings may be initiated during the period of emergency commitment.

WHO IS DANGEROUS? In the past, people with mental disorders were actually less likely than others to commit violent or dangerous acts. This low rate of violence

>>**LOOKING AROUND**
Arresting the Homeless

Many homeless people with severe mental disorders currently wind up in jail rather than in treatment. Most of them are charged with such infractions as disorderly conduct, trespassing, not paying for a meal, menacing, panhandling, loitering, or "lewd and lascivious behavior" (for example, urinating on a street corner) (Mulhern, 1990; Valdiserri, Carroll, & Harti, 1986).<<

>>**LOOKING AROUND**
Patient Dumping

Two-thirds of mental hospitals in the United States currently engage in "patient dumping"—denying care to patients or transferring them largely because they require costly care or are underinsured (Grinfield, 1998; Schlesinger et al., 1997).<<

Save the brain? *In order to understand criminal behavior and to predict dangerousness more accurately, clinical researchers often study individuals who have committed crimes, particularly brutal crimes. In a celebrated case, authorities temporarily had the brain of the serial murderer Jeffrey Dahmer stored in formaldehyde after he died in 1995, hoping that investigators could dissect and study it. However, in response to a petition from Dahmer's father, a judge ordered that the brain be cremated.*

was apparently tied to the fact that so many such individuals lived in institutions. As a result of deinstitutionalization, however, hundreds of thousands of people with severe disturbances now live in the community and receive little, if any, treatment. Some of these individuals are indeed dangerous to themselves or others (Nottestad & Linkaer, 2002; Torrey, 2001).

Although approximately 90 percent of people with mental disorders are in no way violent or dangerous (Swanson et al., 1990), studies now suggest at least a small relationship between severe mental disorders and violent behavior (Walsh et al., 2002; Monahan, 2001). After reviewing a number of studies, John Monahan (1993, 1992), a law and psychology professor, concluded that the rate of violent behavior among persons with severe mental disorders, particularly psychotic disorders, is at least somewhat higher than that of people without such disorders:

- Approximately 15 percent of patients in mental hospitals have assaulted another person prior to admission.
- Around 25 percent of patients in mental hospitals assault another person during hospitalization.
- Approximately 12 percent of all people with schizophrenia, major depression, or bipolar disorder have assaulted other people, compared with 2 percent of persons without a mental disorder.
- Approximately 4 percent of people who report having been violent during the past year suffer from schizophrenia, whereas 1 percent of nonviolent persons suffer from schizophrenia.

Monahan cautions that the findings do not suggest that people with mental disorders are generally dangerous. But they do indicate that a severe mental disorder may be more of a risk factor for violence than mental health experts used to believe.

A judgment of *dangerousness* is often required for involuntary civil commitment. But can mental health professionals accurately predict who will commit violent acts? Research suggests that psychiatrists and psychologists are wrong more often than right when they make *long-term* predictions of violence (West, 2001; Buchanan, 1999, 1997). Most often they overestimate the likelihood that a patient will eventually be violent. On the other hand, studies suggest that *short-term* predictions—that is, predictions of imminent violence—can be more accurate (Binder, 1999). Researchers are now working, with some success, to develop new assessment techniques that use statistical approaches and are more objective in their predictions of dangerousness than the subjective judgments of clinicians (Franklin, 2003; Harris et al., 2002).

WHAT ARE THE PROBLEMS WITH CIVIL COMMITMENT? Civil commitment has been criticized on several grounds. First is the difficulty of assessing a person's dangerousness. If judgments of dangerousness are often inaccurate, how can one justify their being used to deprive people of liberty (Ennis & Emory, 1978)? Second, the legal definitions of "mental illness" and "dangerousness" are vague. The terms may be defined so broadly that they could be applied to almost anyone an evaluator views as undesirable. Indeed, many civil libertarians worry about the use of involuntary commitment to control people, as occurred in the former Soviet Union and certain other countries where mental hospitals routinely housed people with unpopular political views (Morse, 1982; Ennis & Emory, 1978). A third problem is the sometimes questionable therapeutic value of civil commitment. Research indicates that a number of people committed involuntarily do not respond well to treatment (Winick, 2002; Wanck, 1984). On the basis of these and other arguments, some clinicians suggest that involuntary commitment should be abolished (Szasz, 1977, 1963).

TRENDS IN CIVIL COMMITMENT The flexibility of the involuntary commitment laws probably reached a peak in 1962. That year, in the case of *Robinson v. California*, the Supreme Court ruled that imprisoning people who suffered from

Failure to predict *The 1990s witnessed the growth of a new form of dangerousness— children and adolescents who shoot family members, schoolmates, and teachers. A school cafeteria surveillance camera captures Dylan Klebold and Eric Harris in the midst of their killing rampage at Columbine High School in Littleton, Colorado, on April 20, 1999. Earlier videos made by the two boys suggest that they had planned their attack for more than a year. Despite building a violent Web site, threatening other students, having problems with the law, and, in the case of one boy, receiving treatment for psychological problems, professionals were not able to predict or prevent their violent behavior.*

drug addiction might violate the Constitution's ban on cruel and unusual punishment, and it recommended involuntary civil commitment to a mental hospital as a more reasonable action. This ruling encouraged the civil commitment of many kinds of "social deviants." In the years immediately following, civil commitment procedures granted far fewer rights to "defendants" than the criminal courts did (Holstein, 1993). In addition, involuntarily committed patients found it particularly difficult to obtain release.

During the late 1960s and early 1970s, reporters, novelists, civil libertarians, and others spoke out against the ease with which so many people were being unjustifiably committed to mental hospitals. As the public became more aware of these issues, state legislatures started to pass stricter standards for involuntary commitment (Benditt, 2002; Perlin, 2000). Some states, for example, spelled out specific types of behavior that had to be observed before an assessment of dangerousness could be made. Rates of involuntary commitment then declined and release rates rose.

Fewer people are institutionalized through civil commitment procedures today than in the past. The lower commitment rate has not led to more criminal behavior or more arrests of people who would have been committed under more flexible criteria (Teplin et al., 1994; Hiday, 1992). Nevertheless, some states are concerned that commitment criteria are now too strict, and they are moving toward broadening the criteria once again (Taxman & Messina, 2002; Beck & Parry, 1992). It is not yet clear whether this broadening will lead to a return to the vague commitment procedures of the past.

Protecting Patients' Rights

Over the past two decades, court decisions and state and federal laws have greatly expanded the rights of patients with mental disorders, in particular the *right to treatment* and the *right to refuse treatment* (Saks, 2002).

HOW IS THE RIGHT TO TREATMENT PROTECTED? When people are committed to mental institutions and do not receive treatment, the institutions become, in effect, prisons for the unconvicted. To many patients in the late 1960s and the 1970s, large state mental institutions were just that. Thus some patients and their

Hospital neglect *While some countries have attended increasingly to the rights of patients in recent decades, including their rights to treatment and to humane conditions, many countries have lagged behind. This heart-wrenching scene inside a mental hospital in the southern Philippines underscores this point.*

attorneys began to demand that the state honor their **right to treatment**. In the important case of *Wyatt v. Stickney*, a suit on behalf of institutionalized patients in Alabama in 1972, a federal court ruled that the state was constitutionally obligated to provide "adequate treatment" to all people who had been committed involuntarily. Because conditions in the state's hospitals were so terrible, the judge laid out goals that state officials had to meet, including more therapists, better living conditions, more privacy, more social interactions and physical exercise, and a more proper use of physical restraint and medication. Other states have since adopted many of these standards.

Another important decision was handed down in 1975 by the Supreme Court in the case of *O'Connor v. Donaldson*. After being held in a Florida mental institution for more than 14 years, Kenneth Donaldson sued for release. Donaldson had repeatedly sought release and had been overruled by the institution's psychiatrists. He argued that he and his fellow patients were receiving poor treatment, were being largely ignored by the staff, and were allowed little personal freedom. The Supreme Court ruled in his favor, fined the hospital's superintendent, and said that such institutions must review patients' cases periodically. The justices also ruled that the state cannot continue to institutionalize against their will people who are not dangerous and who are capable of surviving on their own or with the willing help of responsible family members or friends. In a later case, *Youngberg v. Romeo* (1982), the Supreme Court further ruled that people committed involuntarily have a right to "reasonably nonrestrictive confinement conditions" as well as "reasonable care and safety."

To help protect the rights of patients, Congress passed the *Protection and Advocacy for Mentally Ill Individuals Act* in 1986 (Woodside & Legg, 1990). This law set up *protection and advocacy systems* in all states and U.S. territories and gave public advocates who worked for patients the power to investigate possible abuse and neglect and to correct those problems legally.

In recent years public advocates have argued that the right to treatment should also be extended to the tens of thousands of people with severe mental disorders who are repeatedly released from hospitals into ill-equipped communities. Many such people have no place to go and are unable to care for themselves, often winding up homeless or in prisons (Torrey, 2001). A number of advocates are now suing federal and state agencies throughout the country, demanding that they fulfill the promises of the community mental health movement (see Chapter 12).

HOW IS THE RIGHT TO REFUSE TREATMENT PROTECTED? During the past two decades the courts have also decided that patients, particularly those in institutions, have the **right to refuse treatment** (Perlin, 2000). The courts have been reluctant to make a single general ruling on this right because there are so many different kinds of treatment, and a general ruling based on one of them might have unintended effects. Therefore, rulings usually target one specific treatment at a time.

Most of the right-to-refuse-treatment rulings center on *biological treatments* (Wettstein, 1999). These treatments are easier to force on patients without their cooperation than psychotherapy, and they often seem more hazardous. For example, state rulings have consistently granted patients the right to refuse *psychosurgery*, the most irreversible form of physical treatment—and therefore the most dangerous.

Some states have also acknowledged a patient's right to refuse *electroconvulsive therapy* (*ECT*), the treatment used in many cases of severe depression (see Chapter

RIGHT TO TREATMENT The legal right of patients, particularly those who are involuntarily committed, to receive adequate treatment.

RIGHT TO REFUSE TREATMENT The legal right of patients to refuse certain forms of treatment.

7). However, the right-to-refuse issue is more complex with regard to ECT than to psychosurgery. ECT is very effective for many people with severe depression; yet it can cause great upset and can also be misused. Today many states grant patients—particularly voluntary patients—the right to refuse ECT. Usually a patient must be informed fully about the nature of the treatment and must give written consent to it. A number of states continue to permit ECT to be forced on committed patients (Baldwin & Oxlad, 2000), whereas others require the consent of a close relative or other third party in such cases.

In the past, patients did not have the right to refuse *psychotropic medications*. As we have seen, however, many psychotropic drugs are very powerful, and some can produce effects that are unwanted and dangerous. As these harmful effects have become more apparent, some states have granted patients the right to refuse medication. Typically, these states require physicians to explain the purpose of the medication to patients and obtain their written consent. If a patient's refusal is considered incompetent, dangerous, or irrational, the state may allow it to be overturned by an independent psychiatrist, medical committee, or local court (Wettstein, 1999, 1988). However, the refusing patient is supported in this process by a lawyer or other patient advocate.

WHAT OTHER RIGHTS DO PATIENTS HAVE? Court decisions have protected still other patient rights over the past several decades. Patients who perform work in mental institutions, particularly private institutions, are now guaranteed at least a minimum wage. In addition, a district court ruled in 1974 that patients released from state mental hospitals have a right to aftercare and to an appropriate community residence, such as a group home. And in the 1975 case of *Dixon v. Weinberger*, another district court ruled that people with psychological disorders should receive treatment in the least restrictive facility available. If an inpatient program at a community mental health center is available, for example, then that is the facility to which they should be assigned, not a mental hospital. In the 1999 case of *Olmstead v. L.C. et al.*, the Supreme Court again confirmed that patients have a right to community treatment.

THE "RIGHTS" DEBATE Certainly, people with psychological disorders have civil rights that must be protected at all times. However, many clinicians express concern that the patients' rights rulings and laws may unintentionally deprive these patients of opportunities for recovery. Consider the right to refuse medication. If medications can help a patient with schizophrenia to recover, doesn't the patient have the right to that recovery? If confusion causes the patient to refuse medication, can clinicians in good conscience delay medication while legal channels are pursued? The psychologist Marilyn Whiteside raised similar concerns in her description of a 25-year-old patient with mental retardation:

> He was 25 and severely retarded. And after his favorite attendant left, he became self-abusive. He beat his fists against the side of his head until a football helmet had to be ordered for his protection. Then he clawed at his face and gouged out one of his eyes.
>
> The institution psychologists began a behavior program that had mildly aversive consequences: they squirted warm water in his face each time he engaged in self-abuse. When that didn't work, they requested permission to use an electric prod. The Human Rights Committee vetoed this "excessive and inhumane form of correction" because, after all, the young man was retarded, not criminal.
>
> Since nothing effective could be done that abridged the rights and negated the dignity of the developmentally disabled patient, he was verbally reprimanded for his behavior—and allowed to push his thumb through his remaining eye. He is now blind, of course, but he has his rights and presumably his dignity.
>
> *(Whiteside, 1983, p. 13)*

Despite such legitimate concerns, we should keep in mind that the clinical field has not always done an effective job of protecting patients' rights. Over the years, many patients have been overmedicated and received improper treatments (Crane, 1973). Furthermore, one must ask whether the field's present state of knowledge justifies clinicians' overriding of patients' rights. Can clinicians confidently say that a given treatment will help a patient? Can they predict when a treatment will have harmful effects? Since clinicians themselves often disagree, it seems appropriate for patients, their advocates, and outside evaluators to play key roles in decision making.

SUMMING UP | **How Does the Legal System Influence Mental Health Care?**

Courts may be called upon to commit noncriminals to mental hospitals for treatment, a process called civil commitment. Society allows involuntary commitment of people considered to be in need of treatment and dangerous to themselves or others. Laws governing civil commitment procedures vary from state to state, but a minimum standard of proof has been defined by the Supreme Court.

The courts and legislatures also significantly affect the mental health profession by specifying legal rights to which patients are entitled. The rights that have received the most attention are the right to treatment and the right to refuse treatment.

In What Other Ways Do the Clinical and Legal Fields Interact?

Mental health and legal professionals may influence each other's work in other ways as well (Miller et al., 2003). During the past two decades, their paths have crossed in four key areas: *malpractice suits*, *professional boundaries*, *jury selection*, and *psychological research of legal topics*.

Law in Psychology: Malpractice Suits

The number of *malpractice suits* against therapists has risen sharply in recent years. Claims have been made against clinicians in response to a patient's attempted suicide, sexual activity with a patient, failure to obtain informed consent for a treatment, negligent drug therapy, omission of drug therapy that would speed improvement, improper termination of treatment, and wrongful commitment (Ash, 2002; Switzer, 2000; Slovenko, 1999). Studies suggest that a malpractice suit, or the fear of one, can have significant effects on clinical decisions and practice, for better or for worse (Switzer, 2000).

Law in Psychology: Professional Boundaries

During the past several years the legislative and judicial systems have helped to change the *boundaries* that separate one clinical profession from another. In particular, they have given more authority to psychologists and blurred the lines that once separated psychiatry from psychology. A growing number of states, for example, are ruling that psychologists can admit patients to the state's hospitals, a power previously held only by psychiatrists (Halloway, 2004).

In 1991, with the blessings of Congress, the Department of Defense (DOD) started to reconsider the biggest difference of all between the practices of psychiatrists and psychologists—the authority to prescribe drugs, a role heretofore denied to psychologists. The DOD set up a trial training program for Army psychologists. Given the apparent success of this trial program, the American Psychological Association recommended in 1996 that all psychologists be allowed to attend a special educational program in prescription services and receive certification to prescribe medications if they pass. In turn, several states introduced legislation regarding the expansion of prescription privileges, and in 2002 New Mexico became the first one to grant prescription privileges to specially trained psychologists (Hayes et al., 2002; Saeman, 2002).

Psychology in Law: Jury Selection

During the past 25 years, more and more lawyers have turned to clinicians for psychological advice in conducting trials (Kressel & Kressel, 2002; Strier, 1999). A new breed of clinical specialists, known as "jury specialists," has evolved. They advise lawyers about which jury candidates are likely to favor their side and which strategies are likely to win jurors' support during trials. The jury specialists make their suggestions on the basis of surveys, interviews, analyses of jurors' backgrounds and attitudes, and laboratory enactments of upcoming trials. However, it is not clear that a clinician's advice is more valid than a lawyer's instincts or that either's judgments are particularly accurate.

Psychology in Law: Psychological Research of Legal Topics

Psychologists have sometimes conducted studies on topics of great importance to the criminal justice system. In turn, these studies influence how the system carries out its work. Psychological investigations of two topics, *eyewitness testimony* and *patterns of criminality*, have gained particular attention.

EYEWITNESS TESTIMONY In criminal cases testimony by eyewitnesses is extremely influential. It often determines whether a defendant will be found guilty or not guilty. But how accurate is eyewitness testimony? This question has become urgent, as a troubling number of prisoners (many on death row) have recently had their convictions overturned after DNA evidence revealed that they could not have committed the crimes of which they had been convicted. To date, at least 123 such prisoners have been freed after new DNA evidence indicated their innocence.

Most eyewitnesses try to tell the truth about what or who they saw. Yet research indicates that eyewitness testimony can be highly unreliable (Loftus, 2003; Geiselman et al., 2002), partly because crimes are typically unexpected and fleeting, and so are not set up for optimal remembering. During the crime, for example, lighting may be poor or other distractions may be present. Witnesses may have other things on their minds, such as concern for their own safety or that of bystanders. Psychological studies indicate that such concerns may greatly impair later recall (Yarmey, 2004).

Moreover, in laboratory studies researchers have found it easy to fool subjects who are trying to recall the details of an observed event simply by introducing misinformation. After a suggestive description by the researcher, stop signs can be transformed into yield signs, white cars into blue ones, and Mickey Mouse into Minnie Mouse (Pickel, 2004; Loftus, 2003). In addition, laboratory studies indicate that persons who are generally suggestible have the poorest recall of observed events (Liebman et al., 2002).

As for identifying actual perpetrators, research has found that accuracy is greatly affected by the method used in identification (Wells & Olsen, 2003). The traditional police lineup, for example, is not always a highly reliable technique, and witnesses' errors committed during lineups tend to stick (Koehnken et al.,

"It was this big! Honest!"

1996). Researchers have also learned that witnesses' confidence is not necessarily related to accuracy. Witnesses who are "absolutely certain" are no more likely to be correct in their recollections than those who are only "fairly sure." Yet the degree of a witness's confidence often influences whether jurors believe the testimony (Smith et al., 1989; Brigham, 1988).

Psychological investigations into eyewitnesses' memory have not yet undone the judicial system's reliance on those witnesses' testimony (Kassin et al., 2001). Nor should it. The distance between laboratory studies and real-life events is often great, and the implications of such research must be carefully considered and applied. Still, eyewitness research has begun to make an impact. Studies of hypnosis and of its ability to create false memories, for example, have led most states to prohibit eyewitnesses from testifying about events if their recall of the events was initially helped by hypnosis.

PATTERNS OF CRIMINALITY A growing number of television shows, movies, and books suggest that clinicians often play a major role in criminal investigations by providing police with *psychological profiles* of perpetrators—"He's probably white, in his 30s, has a history of animal torture, has few friends, and is subject to emotional outbursts." The study of criminal behavior patterns and the practice of profiling has increased in recent years; however, it is not nearly as revealing or influential as the media and the arts would have us believe (Kocsis et al., 2002).

THE CURRENT SCENE

Serial Murderers: Madness or Badness?

Photo by Alex Wong/Getty Images

Murder by mail *A hazardous-material worker sprays his colleagues as they depart the Senate Office Building after searching the building for traces of anthrax, a spore-forming bacterium that causes an acute infectious disease. In late 2001, a number of anthrax-tainted letters were mailed to people throughout the eastern United States, leading to 5 deaths and to severe illness in 13 other people. As of 2004, the serial killer responsible for these acts had continued to elude criminal investigators.*

California, Berkeley, he seemed destined for fame and success. But . . . two years into his stint at Berkeley, he decided to drop out of society—opting instead for a grubby . . . existence in rural Montana.

It was here, alone in a 10-foot-by-12-foot shack, that this reclusive eccentric produced his most renowned works: sixteen bombs, three deaths, twenty-three maimings, several taunting letters to *The New York Times*, and a 35,000-word antitechnology manifesto. By the end of his eighteen-year rampage, "Unabomber"—his FBI code name—had become a household word. On April 3, 1996, federal agents raided Theodore Kaczynski's Montana cabin, and his reign of mail bomb terror, which had captured the attention of a nation, was finally put to an end. ▮

(DUFFY, 1996; THOMAS, 1996)

Theodore Kaczynski is one of a growing list of serial killers who have fascinated and horrified the public over the years: Ted Bundy, David Berkowitz ("Son of Sam"), John Wayne Gacy, Jeffrey Dahmer, John Allen Muhammad, Lee Boyd Malvo. Serial murderers often seem to kill for the

▮ A shy, brilliant boy, he skipped two grades in school and entered Harvard at age 16. He went on to receive a Ph.D. in mathematics from the University of Michigan in 1967. Securing a highly prestigious position at the University of

Failure of profiling *Massive numbers of police search for clues outside a Home Depot in Virginia in 2002, hoping to identify the serial sniper who killed 10 people and terrorized residents throughout Washington, D.C., Maryland, and Virginia. As it turned out, psychological profiling in this case offered limited help and in fact misled the police in certain respects.*

On the positive side, researchers have gathered information about the psychological features of various criminals, and they have indeed found that perpetrators of particular kinds of crimes—serial murder or serial sexual assault, for example—frequently share a number of traits and background features (Palermo, 2002; Smith, 2002). But while such traits are *often* present, they are not *always* present, and so applying profile information to a particular crime can be wrong and misleading. Increasingly police are employing psychological profilers, and this practice appears to be helpful as long as the limitations of profiling are recognized and the contributions of profilers are combined with

sheer thrill of the experience. Clinical theorists do not yet understand these individuals, but they are beginning to use the information that has been gathered about them to speculate on the psychology behind their violence.

Although each follows his own pattern (Palermo, 2002), many serial killers appear to have certain characteristics in common. Most are white males between 25 and 34 years old, of average to high intelligence, generally clean-cut, smooth-talking, attractive, and skillful manipulators. For the most part, these men have no permanent ties to any community and move from place to place in pursuit of the kill. They typically select their victims carefully. Many are fascinated by police work and the popular media and follow their crimes closely in the news (Ressler & Schactman, 1992; Holmes & DeBurger, 1985). Only 8 percent of the serial killers in the United States are women, although this represents a much higher percentage than that found in any other country (Hickey, 2002).

Many serial killers have mental disorders, but they do not typically fit the legal criteria of insanity (Kelleher & Van Nuys, 2002; Ferreira, 2000). Park Dietz,

a psychiatrist and highly regarded expert on the subject, offers this explanation:

❙ None of the serial killers I've had the occasion to study or examine has been legally insane, but none has been normal, either. They've all been people who've got mental disorders. But despite their mental disorders, which have to do with their sexual interests and their character, they've been people who knew what they were doing, knew what they were doing was wrong, but chose to do it anyway. ❙

(DOUGLAS, 1996, PP. 344–345)

As a result, the plea of not guilty by reason of insanity is generally unsuccessful for serial killers. This outcome may also be influenced by the concern of communities that a defendant found not guilty by reason of insanity may be released too quickly (Gresham, 1993).

A number of serial killers seem to display severe personality disorders (Papazian, 2001). Lack of conscience and an utter disregard for people and the rules of society—key features of antisocial personality disorder—are typical. Narcissistic thinking is quite common as well. The feeling of being special may

even give the killer an unrealistic belief that he will not get caught (Scarf, 1996). Often it is this sense of invincibility that leads to his capture.

Sexual dysfunction and fantasy also seem to play a part (Ressler & Schactman, 1992). Studies have found that vivid fantasies, often sexual and sadistic, may help drive the killer's behavior (Lachmann & Lachmann, 1995; Ressler & Schactman, 1992). Some clinicians also believe that the killers may be trying to overcome general feelings of powerlessness by controlling, hurting, or eliminating those who are momentarily weaker (Fox & Levin, 1999; Levin & Fox, 1985). Studies show that the majority of serial killers were abused as children—physically, sexually, and emotionally (Pincus, 2001; Ressler & Schactman, 1992).

Despite such profiles and suspicions, clinical theorists do not yet understand why serial killers behave as they do. Thus most agree with Dietz when he asserts, "It's hard to imagine any circumstance under which they should be released to the public again" (Douglas, 1996, p. 349).

other, often more compelling clues to help the police pursue and narrow their investigations (Palermo, 2002; Smith, 2002).

A reminder of the limitations of profiling information comes from the case of the snipers who terrorized the Washington, D.C., area for three weeks in October 2002, shooting 10 people dead and seriously wounding 3 others. Most of the profiling done by FBI psychologists had suggested that the sniper was acting alone; it turned out that the attacks were conducted by a pair: a middle-aged man, John Allen Muhammad, and a teenaged boy, Lee Boyd Malvo. Although profiles had suggested a young thrill-seeker, Muhammad was 41. Profilers had believed the attacker to be white, but neither Muhammad nor Malvo is white. The prediction of a male attacker was correct, but then again, female serial killers are rare.

SUMMING UP

Other Clinical-Legal Interactions

Mental health and legal professionals also cross paths in four other areas. First, malpractice suits against therapists have increased in recent years. Second, the legislative and judicial systems help define professional clinical boundaries. Third, lawyers may seek the advice of mental health professionals regarding the selection of jurors and case strategies. Fourth, psychologists may investigate legal phenomena such as eyewitness testimony and patterns of criminality.

The ethics of giving professional advice *Like the enormously popular psychologist Phil McGraw ("Dr. Phil"), many of today's clinicians offer advice in books, at workshops, on television and radio programs, and in tape packages. Their presentations often affect people greatly, and so they, too, are bound by the field's ethics code to act responsibly and professionally and to base their advice on appropriate psychological findings and practices.*

What Ethical Principles Guide Mental Health Professionals?

Discussions of the legal and mental health systems may sometimes give the impression that clinicians as a group are uncaring and are considerate of patients' rights and needs only when they are forced to be. This, of course, is not true. Most clinicians care greatly about their clients and try to help them while at the same time respecting their rights and dignity. In fact, clinicians do not rely exclusively on the legislative and court systems to ensure proper and effective clinical practice. They also regulate themselves by continually developing and revising ethical guidelines for members of the clinical field. Many legal decisions do nothing more than place the power of the law behind these already existing professional guidelines.

Each profession within the mental health field has its own **code of ethics** (Radden, 2002; Ford, 2001; Nagy, 2000). The code of the American Psychological Association (2002, 1992) is typical. This code, highly respected by other mental health professionals and public officials, includes specific guidelines:

1. **Psychologists are permitted to offer advice** in self-help books, on television and radio programs, in newspaper and magazine articles, through mailed material, and in other places, provided they do so responsibly and professionally and base their advice on appropriate psychological literature and practices.

2. **Psychologists may not conduct fraudulent research, plagiarize the work of others, or publish false data**. During the past 25 years cases of scientific fraud or misconduct have been discovered in all of the sciences, including psychology. These acts have led to misunderstandings of important issues, taken scientific research in the wrong direction, and damaged public trust. Unfortunately, the impressions created by false findings may continue to influence the thinking of both the public and other scientists for years (Pfeifer & Snodgrass, 1990).

3. **Psychologists must acknowledge their limitations** with regard to patients who are disabled or whose gender, ethnicity, language, socioeconomic status, or sexual orientation differs from that of the therapist. This guideline often requires psychotherapists to obtain additional training or supervision, consult with more knowledgeable colleagues, or refer clients to more appropriate professionals.

4. **Psychologists who make evaluations and testify in legal cases must base their assessments on sufficient information and substantiate their findings appropriately**. If an adequate examination of the individual in question is not possible, psychologists must make clear the limited nature of their testimony.

5. **Psychologists may not take advantage of clients and students, sexually or otherwise**. This guideline relates to the widespread social problem of sexual harassment, as well as the problem of therapists who take sexual advantage of clients in therapy. The code specifically forbids a sexual relationship with a present or former therapy client for at least two years after the end of treatment; and even then such a relationship is permitted only in "the most unusual circumstances." Furthermore, psychologists may not accept as clients people with whom they have previously had a sexual relationship.

    Clients may suffer great emotional damage from sexual involvement with their therapists (Malley & Reilly, 1999; Lazarus, 1995). A number of therapists are now treating clients whose primary problem is that they previously experienced some form of sexual misconduct by a therapist (Bloom et al., 1999; Wincze et al., 1996). Many such clients experience the symptoms of posttraumatic stress disorder or major depressive disorder (Luepker, 1999; Hankins et al., 1994).

    How many therapists actually have a sexual relationship with a client? On the basis of various surveys, reviewers have estimated that some form of sexual misconduct with patients may be engaged in by around 8 percent of today's male therapists and 2 percent of female therapists (Malley & Reilly, 1999; Illingworth, 1995; Hankins et al., 1994). Although the vast majority of therapists keep their sexual behavior within appropriate professional bounds, their ability to control private feelings is apparently another matter. In surveys, close to 90 percent of therapists reported having been sexually attracted to a client, at least on occasion (Pope, 2000; Pope & Tabachnick, 1993). Although few of these therapists acted on their feelings, most of them felt guilty, anxious, or concerned about the attraction (Pope et al., 1986). Given such sexual issues, it is not surprising that in recent years sexual ethics training has been given high priority in many clinical training programs (Housman & Stake, 1999).

6. **Psychologists must adhere to the principle of confidentiality**. All of the state courts uphold laws protecting therapist **confidentiality**, and in the 1996 case of *Jaffee v. Redmond*, the Supreme Court applied this principle to federal courts as well. For peace of mind and to ensure effective therapy, clients must be able to trust that their private exchanges with a therapist will not be repeated to others (Lowenthal, 2002; Welfel, 2001). There are times, however, when the principle of confidentiality must be compromised (Gross, 2002). A therapist in training, for example, must discuss cases on a regular basis with a supervisor (Bernard & Goodyear, 2004). Clients, in turn, must be informed when such discussions are occurring.

    A second exception arises in cases of outpatients who are clearly dangerous. The 1976 case of *Tarasoff v. Regents of the University of California*, one of the most important cases to affect client–therapist relationships, concerned an outpatient at a University of California hospital. He had confided to his therapist that he wanted to harm his former girlfriend, Tanya Tarasoff. Several days after ending therapy, the former patient fulfilled his promise. He stabbed Tanya Tarasoff to death.

>>IN THEIR WORDS
"Our [legal] confusion is eliminated, we believe, if we resort to that quintessential twentieth-century solution to hard problems: We refer the problem to an expert."<<
Winslade & Ross, 1983

CODE OF ETHICS A body of principles and rules for ethical behavior, designed to guide decisions and actions by members of a profession.

CONFIDENTIALITY The principle that certain professionals will not divulge the information they obtain from a client.

DUTY TO PROTECT The principle that therapists must break confidentiality in order to protect a person who may be the intended victim of a client.

EMPLOYEE ASSISTANCE PROGRAM A mental health program offered by a business to its employees.

STRESS-REDUCTION AND PROBLEM-SOLVING SEMINAR A workshop or series of group sessions offered by a business in which mental health professionals teach employees how to cope with and solve problems and reduce stress.

MANAGED CARE PROGRAM An insurance program in which the insurance company decides the cost, method, provider, and length of treatment.

PEER REVIEW SYSTEM A system by which clinicians paid by an insurance company may periodically review a patient's progress and recommend the continuation or termination of insurance benefits.

Should confidentiality have been broken in this case? The therapist, in fact, felt that it should. Campus police were notified, but the patient was released after some questioning. In their suit against the hospital and therapist, the victim's parents argued that the therapist should have also warned them and their daughter that the patient intended to harm Ms. Tarasoff. The California Supreme Court agreed: "The protective privilege ends where the public peril begins."

The current code of ethics for psychologists thus declares that therapists have a **duty to protect**—a responsibility to break confidentiality, even without the client's consent, when it is necessary "to protect the client or others from harm." Since the *Tarasoff* ruling, California's courts have further held that therapists must also protect people who are close to a client's intended victim and thus in danger. A child, for example, is likely to be at risk when a client plans to assault the child's mother. The California courts have also clarified that the duty to protect applies only when the intended victim is readily identifiable, as opposed to the public at large, and only when the intended object of violence is a person, as opposed to property. Many, but not all, states have adopted the California court rulings or similar ones (Bloom, 1990; Pietrofesa et al., 1990), and a number have passed "duty to protect" bills that clarify the rules of confidentiality for therapists and protect them from certain kinds of civil suits (Simon, 2001; Bersoff, 1999).

Mental Health, Business, and Economics

The legislative and judicial systems are not the only social institutions with which mental health professionals interact. The *business* and *economic* fields are two other sectors that influence and are influenced by clinical practice and study.

Bringing Mental Health Services to the Workplace

Collectively, psychological disorders are among 10 leading categories of work-related disorders and injuries in the United States. In fact, almost 12 percent of all employees are said to experience psychological problems that are serious enough to affect their work. Psychological problems contribute to 60 percent of all absenteeism from work, up to 90 percent of industrial accidents, and 65 percent of work terminations (Kemp, 1994). Alcohol abuse and other substance-related disorders are particularly damaging, increasing absences by as much as six times, accidents by four times, and workers' compensation claims by five times (Martin et al., 1994; Wright, 1984). The business world has often turned to clinical professionals to help prevent and correct such problems (Schott, 1999; Millar, 1990, 1984). Two common means of providing mental health care in the workplace are *employee assistance programs* and *problem-solving seminars*.

Employee assistance programs, mental health services made available by a place of business, are run either by mental health professionals who work directly for a company or by outside mental health agencies (Cagney, 2003; Cooper et al., 2003). Companies publicize such programs at the work site, educate workers about psychological dysfunctioning, and teach supervisors how to identify workers who are having psychological problems. Businesses believe that employee assistance programs save them money in the long run by preventing psychological problems from interfering with work performance and by reducing employee insurance claims, although these beliefs have not undergone extensive testing (Longwell-Grice & Sandhu, 2002; Kemp, 1994).

Stress-reduction and problem-solving seminars are workshops or group sessions in which mental health professionals teach employees techniques for coping, solving problems, and handling and reducing stress (Daw, 2001; Kagan et al., 1995). Programs of this kind are just as likely to be aimed at high-level

>>LOOKING AROUND

A Public View

In a survey of 1,000 people across the United States, 67 percent of respondents said the government should spend more money to treat people with mental disorders who cannot afford to pay (Time/CNN, 1999).<<

executives as at assembly-line workers. Often employees are required to attend such workshops, which may run for several days, and are given time off from their jobs to do so. Again, the businesses expect these programs to save money by helping workers to achieve a healthier state of mind, suffer less dysfunction on the job, and improve their performance.

The Economics of Mental Health

We have already seen how economic decisions by the government may influence the clinical field's treatment of people with severe mental disorders. For example, the desire of the state and federal governments to reduce costs was an important consideration in the country's deinstitutionalization movement, which contributed to the premature release of hospital patients into the community. Economic decisions by government agencies may affect other kinds of clients and treatment programs as well.

On the one hand, government funding for people with psychological disorders has risen sharply over the past three and a half decades, from $3 billion in 1969 to $61 billion today (Torrey, 2001, 1997; Redick et al., 1992). On the other hand, much of that money is spent on income support, housing subsidies, and other such expenses, rather than directly on mental health services. Government funding for services actually appears to be decreasing. It currently covers less than half the cost of all mental health services, leaving most of the expense to individual patients and their private insurance companies (Taube, 1990).

The growing economic role of private insurance companies has had a significant effect on the way clinicians go about their work. As we observed in Chapter 1, to reduce their expenses and keep track of their payments, most of these companies have developed **managed care programs**, in which the insurance company decides such questions as which therapists clients may choose, the cost of sessions, and the number of sessions for which a client may be reimbursed (Feldman, 2003). These and other insurance plans may also control expenses through the use of **peer review systems**, in which clinicians who work for the insurance company periodically review a client's treatment program and recommend that insurance benefits be either continued or stopped. Typically, insurers require detailed reports or session notes from the therapist, often including intimate personal information about the patient.

As we also saw in Chapter 1, many therapists and clients dislike managed care programs and peer reviews (Lazarus & Sharfstein, 2002). They believe that the reports required of therapists breach confidentiality, even when efforts are made

>>LOOKING AROUND

Declining Costs Mental health expenditures by insurance companies fell 54 percent during the 1990s. Total health care spending fell just 7 percent during the same decade (*Wall Street Journal*, 1998).

Mandatory Coverage Thirty-three states in the United States mandate that every private health insurance policy must include coverage for mental health services.

Without Coverage The number of people in the United States who do not have health insurance is 44 million.

Insurance Bias Even after controlling for age, income, and employment status, studies reveal that United States citizens who were born in a foreign country are twice as likely to be uninsured as those who are native born.**<<**

"You can rest assured, Mrs. Wilson, that your husband will receive the best care known to medical coverage."

to protect anonymity, and that the value of therapy in a given case is sometimes difficult to present in a brief report. They also argue that the priorities of managed care programs inevitably shorten therapy, even if longer-term treatment would be advisable in particular cases. The priorities may also favor treatments that offer short-term results (for example, drug therapy) over more costly approaches that might achieve a more promising long-term improvement. As in the medical field, disturbing stories are often heard about patients who are prematurely cut off from mental health services by their managed care programs. In short, many clinicians fear that the current system amounts to regulation of therapy by insurance companies rather than by therapists.

SUMMING UP
Ethical, Economic, and Personal Factors

Each clinical profession has a code of ethics. The psychologists' code includes prohibitions against engaging in fraudulent research and against taking advantage of clients or students, sexually or otherwise. It also establishes guidelines for respecting patient confidentiality. The case of *Tarasoff v. Regents of the University of California* helped to determine the circumstances in which therapists have a duty to protect the public from harm and must break confidentiality.

Clinical practice and study also intersect with the business and economic worlds. Clinicians often help to address psychological problems in the workplace. In addition, private insurance companies are setting up managed care programs whose procedures influence and often reduce the length, nature, and quality of therapy.

Finally, mental health activities are affected by the personal needs, values, and goals of the human beings who provide the clinical services. These factors inevitably affect their practices and decisions and even the quality of their work.

The Person within the Profession

The actions of clinical researchers and practitioners not only influence and are influenced by other institutions but are closely tied to their personal needs and goals. We have seen that the human strengths, imperfections, wisdom, and clumsiness of clinical professionals may affect their theoretical orientations, their interactions with clients, and the kinds of clients with whom they choose to work. We have also looked at how personal leanings may sometimes override professional standards and scruples and, in extreme cases, lead clinical scientists to commit research fraud and clinical practitioners to engage in sexual misconduct with clients.

A national survey of the mental health of therapists found that 84 percent reported being in therapy at least once (Pope & Brown, 1996; Pope & Tabachnick, 1994). Their reasons were largely the same as those of other clients, with emotional problems, depression, and anxiety topping the list. It is not clear why so many therapists report having psychological problems. Perhaps their jobs are highly stressful; perhaps therapists are simply more aware of their own negative feelings or are more likely to pursue treatment for their problems; or perhaps individuals with personal concerns are more inclined to choose clinical work as a profession. Whatever the reason, clinicians bring to their work a set of psychological concerns and emotions that may, along with other important factors, affect how they listen and respond to clients.

The science and profession of abnormal psychology seeks to understand, predict, and change abnormal functioning. But we must not lose sight of the broader environment in which its activities are conducted. Mental health researchers and clinicians are human beings, living within a society of human beings, working to

A CLOSER LOOK

Therapists under Attack

According to surveys, more than 80 percent of therapists have on at least one occasion feared that a client might physically attack them (Pope & Tabachnick, 1993). Are such concerns exaggerated? Not always. In fact, a number of therapists have found out that their rights—including the right to a safe practice—may be violated (Fry et al., 2002; Flannery et al., 2000; Brasic & Fogelman, 1999). More than 10 percent of therapists have been attacked by a patient at least once in private therapy, and an even larger percentage have been assaulted in mental hospitals (Tryon, 1987; Bernstein, 1981). Similarly, a number of therapists have

been stalked or harassed by patients (Dinkelmeyer & Johnson, 2002).

© 2003 The New Yorker Collection, from cartoonbank.com

Patients have used a variety of weapons in their attacks, including such common objects as shoes, lamps, fire extinguishers, and canes. Some have used guns or knives and have severely wounded or even killed a therapist.

Many therapists who have been attacked continue to feel anxious and insecure in their work for a long time afterward. Some try to be more selective in accepting patients and look for cues that signal impending violence. It is possible that such concerns represent a significant distraction from the task at hand when they are in session with certain clients.

serve human beings. The mixture of discovery, misdirection, promise, and frustration that we have encountered throughout this book is thus to be expected. When one thinks about it, could the study and treatment of human behavior really proceed in any other way?

CROSSROADS:
Operating within a Larger System

At one time clinical researchers and professionals conducted their work largely in isolation. Today, however, their activities have many ties to the legislative, judicial, economic, and other established systems. One reason for this growing interconnectedness is that the clinical field has achieved a high level of respect and acceptance in our society. Clinicians now serve millions of people in many ways. They have much to say about almost every aspect of society, from education to ecology, and are widely looked to as sources of expertise. When a field achieves such prominence, it inevitably affects how other institutions are run. It also attracts public attention, and various institutions begin to keep an eye on its activities.

Today, when people with psychological problems seek help from a therapist, they are entering a complex system consisting of many interconnected parts. Just as their personal problems have grown within a social structure, so will their treatment be affected by the various parts of a larger system—the therapist's values and needs, legal and economic forces, societal attitudes, and yet other forces. These various forces influence clinical research as well.

The effects of this larger system on an individual's psychological needs can be positive or negative, like a family's impact on each of its members. When the system protects a client's rights and confidentiality, for example, it is serving the

>>IN THEIR WORDS

"I spent . . . two hours chatting with Einstein. . . . He is cheerful, assured and likable, and understands as much about psychology as I do about physics, so we got on together very well."

Sigmund Freud, 1927

client well. When economic, legal, or other societal forces limit treatment options, cut off treatment prematurely, or stigmatize a person, the system is adding to the person's problems.

Because of the enormous growth and impact of the mental health profession in our society, it is important that we understand its strengths and weaknesses. As we have seen throughout this book, the field has gathered much knowledge, especially during the past several decades. What mental health professionals do not know and cannot do, however, still outweighs what they do know and can do. Everyone who turns to the clinical field—directly or indirectly—must recognize that it is young and imperfect. Society is vastly curious about behavior and often in need of information and help. What we as a society must remember, however, is that the field is truly at a *crossroads*.

CRITICAL THOUGHTS

1. In some states, a defendant who pleads not guilty by reason of insanity must prove that he or she was not sane at the time the crime was committed, while in other states the prosecution must prove that a defendant making this plea was not insane. Which burden of proof is more appropriate? *pp. 472–475*

2. After a patient has been criminally committed to an institution, why might a clinician be reluctant to declare that the person is mentally stable and unlikely to commit the same crime again, even if the patient shows significant improvement? *pp. 475–476*

3. How are people who have been institutionalized viewed and treated by other members of society today? Is the stigma of hospitalization a legitimate argument against civil commitment? *pp. 481–483*

4. Most psychiatrists do not want psychologists to be granted the authority to prescribe psychotropic medications. Surprisingly, many psychologists oppose the idea as well (Heiby, 2002). Why might they take this position? *pp. 486–487*

5. How might lingering anxiety affect the behavior and effectiveness of clinicians who have been attacked by a patient? What do patients' attacks on therapists suggest about therapists' ability to predict dangerousness? *p. 495*

KEY TERMS

criminal commitment p. 472
not guilty by reason of insanity (NGRI) p. 472
M'Naghten test p. 473
irresistible impulse test p. 473
Durham test p. 473
American Law Institute (ALI) test p. 473
guilty but mentally ill p. 476
guilty with diminished capacity p. 476
mentally disordered sex offenders p. 477

mental incompetence p. 478
civil commitment p. 479
two-physician certificate (2 PC) p. 481
dangerousness p. 482
right to treatment p. 484
right to refuse treatment p. 484
malpractice lawsuit p. 486
professional boundaries p. 486
jury selection p. 487

eyewitness testimony p. 487
psychological profiles p. 488
code of ethics p. 490
confidentiality p. 491
duty to protect p. 492
employee assistance programs p. 492
stress-reduction seminars p. 492
managed care program p. 493
peer review system p. 493

QUICK QUIZ

1. Briefly explain the M'Naghten, irresistible impulse, Durham, and ALI tests of insanity. Which tests are used today to determine whether defendants are not guilty by reason of insanity? *pp. 473–475*

2. Explain the guilty-but-mentally-ill, diminished-capacity, and mentally-disordered-sex-offender verdicts. *pp. 476–478*

3. What are the reasons behind and the procedures for determining whether defendants are mentally incompetent to stand trial? *pp. 478–479*

4. What are the reasons for civil commitment, and how is it carried out? What criticisms have been made of civil commitment? *pp. 479–483*

5. What rights have court rulings and legislation guaranteed to patients with psychological disorders? *pp. 483–486*

6. How do the legislative and judicial systems affect the professional boundaries of clinical practice? *pp. 486–487*

7. What have clinical researchers learned about eyewitnesses' memories and about patterns of criminality? How accurate and influential is the practice of psychological profiling in criminal cases? *pp. 487–490*

8. What key issues are covered by the psychologist's code of ethics? Under what conditions must therapists break the principle of confidentiality? *pp. 490–492*

9. What kinds of programs for the prevention and treatment of psychological problems have been established in business settings? *pp. 492–493*

10. What trends have emerged in recent years in the funding and insurance of mental health care? *pp. 493–494*

CYBER STUDY

SEARCH THE *FUNDAMENTALS OF ABNORMAL PSYCHOLOGY* CD-ROM FOR

▲ **Chapter 16 Video Case Enrichment**
   Can clinicians predict antisocial, dangerous, or violent behavior?
   Where do the clinical and judicial fields intersect?
   Did hospital treatments of past times violate patients' rights?

▲ **Chapter 16 Practical, Research, and Decision-Making Exercises**
   Resolving ethical dilemmas in clinical practice
   Predicting dangerousness

▲ **Chapter 16 Practice Test and Feedback**

LOG ON TO THE COMER WEB PAGE FOR

▲ Suggested Web links, exercises, FAQ page, additional Chapter 16 practice test questions
   <www.worthpublishers.com/comer>

〈〈〈

Abnormal psychology The scientific study of abnormal behavior in order to describe, predict, explain, and change abnormal patterns of functioning.

Acute stress disorder An anxiety disorder in which fear and related symptoms are experienced soon after a traumatic event and last less than a month.

Affect An experience of emotion or mood.

Aftercare A program of posthospitalization care and treatment in the community.

Agoraphobia An anxiety disorder in which a person is afraid to be in places or situations from which escape might be difficult (or embarrassing) or help unavailable if paniclike symptoms were to occur.

Alcohol Any beverage containing ethyl alcohol, including beer, wine, and liquor.

Alcoholics Anonymous (AA) A self-help organization that provides support and guidance for persons with patterns of alcohol abuse or dependence.

Alcoholism A pattern of behavior in which a person repeatedly abuses or develops a dependence on alcohol.

Alogia A symptom of schizophrenia in which the individual shows a decrease in speech or speech content. Also known as *poverty of speech*.

Alprazolam A benzodiazepine drug shown to be effective in the treatment of anxiety disorders. Marketed as Xanax.

Altruistic suicide Suicide committed by people who intentionally sacrifice their lives for the well-being of society.

Alzheimer's disease The most common form of dementia, usually occurring after the age of 65.

Amenorrhea The absence of menstrual cycles.

American Law Institute (ALI) test A legal test for insanity that holds people to be insane at the time of committing a crime if, because of a mental disorder, they did not know right from wrong or they could not resist an uncontrollable impulse to act.

Amnesia Loss of memory.

Amnestic disorders Organic disorders in which the primary symptom is memory loss.

Amphetamine A stimulant drug that is manufactured in the laboratory.

Analog observation A method for observing behavior in which people are observed in artificial settings such as clinicians' offices or laboratories.

Analogue experiment A research method in which the experimenter produces abnormal-like behavior in laboratory subjects and then conducts experiments on the subjects.

Anomic suicide Suicide committed by individuals whose social environment fails to provide stability, thus leaving them without a sense of belonging.

Anorexia nervosa A disorder marked by the pursuit of extreme thinness and by an extreme loss of weight.

Antagonist drugs Drugs that block or change the effects of an addictive drug.

Anterograde amnesia The inability to remember new information acquired after the event that triggered amnesia.

Antianxiety drugs Psychotropic drugs that help reduce tension and anxiety. Also called *minor tranquilizers* or *anxiolytics*.

Antibipolar drugs Psychotropic drugs that help stabilize the moods of people suffering from a bipolar mood disorder.

Antibodies Bodily chemicals that seek out and destroy foreign invaders such as bacteria or viruses.

Antidepressant drugs Psychotropic drugs that improve the mood of people with depression.

Antigen A foreign invader of the body, such as a bacterium or virus.

Antipsychotic drugs Drugs that help correct grossly confused or distorted thinking, such as that found in psychotic disorders.

Antisocial personality disorder A personality disorder marked by a general pattern of disregard for and violation of other people's rights.

Anxiety The central nervous system's physiological and emotional response to a vague sense of threat or danger.

Anxiety sensitivity A tendency of certain persons to focus on their bodily sensations, assess them illogically, and interpret them as harmful.

Anxiolytics Drugs that reduce anxiety.

Assessment The process of collecting and interpreting relevant information about a client or subject.

Asthma A medical problem marked by narrowing of the trachea and bronchi, which results in shortness of breath, wheezing, coughing, and a choking sensation.

Asylum A type of institution first established in the sixteenth century to provide care for persons with mental disorders. Most became virtual prisons.

Attention-deficit/hyperactivity disorder (ADHD) A disorder in which persons behave overactively and impulsively or are unable to focus their attention, or both.

Attribution An explanation of things we see going on around us which points to particular causes.

Atypical antipsychotic drugs A new group of antipsychotic drugs that operate in a biological manner that is different from the way traditional antipsychotic drugs operate.

Auditory hallucination A hallucination in which a person hears sounds or voices that are not actually present.

Augmentative communication system A method for teaching communication skills to individuals with autism, mental retardation, or cerebral palsy by pointing to pictures, symbols, letters, or words on a communication board or computer.

Autistic disorder A long-term disorder marked by extreme unresponsiveness to others, poor communication skills, and highly repetitive and rigid behavior. Also known as *autism*.

Automatic thoughts Numerous unpleasant thoughts that come into the mind, helping to cause or maintain depression, anxiety, or other forms of psychological dysfunction.

Autonomic nervous system (ANS) The network of nerve fibers that connect the central nervous system to all the other organs of the body.

Aversion therapy A treatment based on the principles of classical conditioning in which people are repeatedly presented with shocks or another unpleasant stimulus while they are performing undesirable behaviors such as taking a drug.

Avoidant personality disorder A personality disorder in which an individual is consistently uncomfortable and restrained in social situations, overwhelmed by feelings of inadequacy, and extremely sensitive to negative evaluation.

Avolition A symptom of schizophrenia marked by apathy and an inability to start or complete a course of action.

Axon A long fiber extending from the body of a neuron.

Barbiturates A group of addictive sedative-hypnotic drugs used to reduce anxiety or to help persons fall asleep.

Basic irrational According to Albert Ellis, the inaccurate and inappropriate beliefs held by people with various psychological problems.

Battery A series of tests, each of which measures a specific skill area.

B-cell A lymphocyte that produces antibodies.

Behavioral medicine A field of treatment that combines psychological and physical interventions to treat or prevent medical problems.

Behavioral self-control training (BSCT) A cognitive-behavioral approach to treating alcohol abuse and dependence in which people are taught to keep track of their drinking behavior and to apply coping strategies in situations that typically trigger excessive drinking.

Behavioral therapy A therapeutic approach that seeks to identify problem-causing behaviors and change them. Also known as *behavior modification*.

Benzodiazepines The most common group of antianxiety drugs, including Valium and Xanax.

Bereavement The process of working through the grief that one feels when a loved one dies.

Beta-amyloid protein A small molecule that forms sphere-shaped deposits called senile plaques, linked to aging and to Alzheimer's disease.

Binge An episode of uncontrollable eating during which a person eats a very large quantity of food.

Binge-eating disorder A type of eating disorder in which a person displays a pattern of binge eating without accompanying compensatory behaviors.

Biofeedback training A treatment technique in which a person is given information about physiological reactions as they occur and learns to control the responses voluntarily.

Biological challenge test A procedure used to produce panic in subjects or clients by having them exercise vigorously or perform other tasks in the presence of a researcher or therapist.

Bipolar disorder A disorder marked by alternating or intermixed periods of mania and depression.

Bipolar I disorder A type of bipolar disorder in which a person experiences full manic and major depressive episodes.

Bipolar II disorder A type of bipolar disorder in which a person experiences mildly manic (hypomanic) episodes and major depressive episodes.

Blind design An experiment in which subjects do not know whether they are in the experimental or the control condition.

Body dysmorphic disorder A somatoform disorder marked by excessive worry that some aspect of one's physical appearance is defective. Also known as *dysmorphophobia*.

Borderline personality disorder A personality disorder in which an individual displays repeated instability in interpersonal relationships, self-image, and mood, as well as extremely impulsive behavior.

Bulimia nervosa A disorder marked by frequent eating binges that are followed by forced vomiting or other extreme compensatory behaviors. Also known as *binge-purge syndrome*.

Caffeine A stimulant drug that is commonly consumed in the form of coffee, tea, cola, and chocolate.

Cannabis drugs Drugs produced from the different varieties of the hemp plant, *Cannabis sativa*. They cause a mixture of hallucinogenic, depressant, and stimulant effects.

Case manager A community therapist who offers a full range of services for persons with schizophrenia or other severe disorders, including therapy, advice, medica-

tion, guidance, and protection of patients' rights.

Case study A detailed account of a person's life and psychological problems.

Catatonia A pattern of extreme psychomotor symptoms, found in some forms of schizophrenia, that may include catatonic stupor, rigidity, or posturing.

Catatonic type of schizophrenia A type of schizophrenia dominated by severe psychomotor disturbances.

Catharsis The reliving of past repressed feelings in order to settle internal conflicts and overcome problems.

Caudate nuclei Structures in the brain, within the region known as the basal ganglia, that help convert sensory information into thoughts and actions.

Central nervous system The brain and spinal cord.

Cerebellum An area of the brain that coordinates movement in the body and perhaps helps control a person's rapid attention to things.

Chromosomes The structures, located within a cell, that contain genes.

Civil commitment A legal process by which certain individuals can be forced to undergo mental health treatment.

Classical conditioning A process of learning by temporal association in which two events that repeatedly occur close together in time become fused in a person's mind and so produce the same response.

Classification system A list of disorders, along with descriptions of symptoms and guidelines for making appropriate diagnoses.

Cleaning compulsion A common compulsion in which people feel compelled to keep cleaning themselves, their clothing, and their homes.

Client-centered therapy The humanistic therapy developed by Carl Rogers in which clinicians try to help clients by being accepting, empathizing accurately, and conveying genuineness.

Clinical interview A face-to-face encounter in which clinicians ask questions of clients, weigh their responses and reactions, and learn about them and their psychological problems.

Clinical psychologist A mental health professional who has earned a doctorate in clinical psychology.

Cocaine An addictive stimulant taken from the coca plant; the most powerful natural stimulant known.

Code of ethics A body of principles and rules for ethical behavior, designed to guide decisions and actions by members of a profession.

Cognitive behavior Thoughts and beliefs, many of which remain private.

Cognitive therapy A therapy developed by Aaron Beck that helps people identify and

change the maladaptive assumptions and ways of thinking that help cause their psychological disorders.

Cognitive triad The three forms of negative thinking that theorist Aaron Beck says lead people to feel depressed. The triad consists of a negative view of one's experiences, oneself, and the future.

Community mental health treatment A treatment approach that emphasizes community care.

Community mental health center A community treatment facility that provides medication, psychotherapy, and, ideally, emergency care to patients and coordinates their treatment in the community.

Comorbidity The occurrence of two or more disorders in the same person.

Compulsion A repetitive and rigid behavior or mental act that persons feel they must perform in order to prevent or reduce anxiety.

Computerized axial tomography (CAT scan) A composite image of the brain created by compiling X-ray images taken from many angles.

Conditioning A simple form of learning in which a given stimulus comes to produce a given response.

Conduct disorder A childhood disorder in which the child repeatedly violates the basic rights of others, displaying aggression and sometimes destroying others' property, lying, or running away from home.

Confidentiality The principle that certain professionals will not divulge the information they obtain from a client.

Confound In an experiment, a variable other than the independent variable that may also be acting on the dependent variable.

Control group In an experiment, a group of subjects who are not exposed to the independent variable.

Conversion disorder A somatoform disorder in which a psychosocial need or conflict is converted into dramatic physical symptoms that affect voluntary motor or sensory function.

Convulsion A brain seizure.

Coronary heart disease Illness of the heart caused by a blocking of the coronary arteries.

Correlation The degree to which events or characteristics vary along with each other.

Correlational method A research procedure used to determine how much events or characteristics vary along with each other.

Corticosteroids A group of hormones released by the adrenal glands at times of stress.

Couple therapy A therapy format in which the therapist works with two people who share a long-term relationship. Also called *marital therapy*.

Crack A powerful, ready-to-smoke freebase cocaine.

Creutzfeldt-Jakob disease A form of dementia caused by a slow-acting virus that may live in the body for years before the disease unfolds.

Criminal commitment A legal process by which persons accused of a crime are instead judged mentally unstable and sent to a mental health facility for treatment.

Crisis intervention A treatment approach that tries to help people in a psychological crisis view their situation more accurately, make better decisions, act more constructively, and overcome the crisis.

Critical incident stress debriefing Training in how to help victims of disasters or other horrifying events talk about their feelings and reactions to the traumatic incidents.

Culture A people's common history, values, institutions, habits, skills, technology, and arts.

Culture-sensitive therapies Treatment approaches that seek to address the unique issues faced by members of various cultural and ethnic groups.

Cyclothymic disorder A disorder marked by numerous periods of hypomanic symptoms and mild depressive symptoms.

D-2 receptors The subgroup of dopamine receptors that have been linked to schizophrenia.

Day center A program that offers hospital-like treatment during the day only. Also called *day hospital*.

Death darer A person who is ambivalent about the wish to die even as he or she attempts suicide.

Death ignorer A person who attempts suicide without recognizing the finality of death.

Death initiator A person who attempts suicide believing that the process of death is already under way and that he or she is simply quickening the process.

Death seeker A person who clearly intends to end his or her life at the time of a suicide attempt.

Deinstitutionalization The discharge of large numbers of patients from long-term institutional care so that they might be treated in community programs.

Delirium A rapidly developing clouded state of consciousness in which a person has great difficulty concentrating, focusing attention, and keeping a straightforward stream of thought.

Delirium tremens (DTs) A dramatic withdrawal reaction experienced by some people who are alcohol-dependent; consists of mental confusion, clouded consciousness, and terrifying visual hallucinations. Also called *alcohol withdrawal delirium*.

Delusion A strange false belief firmly held despite evidence to the contrary.

Delusional disorder A disorder consisting of persistent, nonbizarre delusions that are not part of a schizophrenic disorder.

Dementia A syndrome marked by severe problems in memory and at least one other cognitive function.

Demonology The belief that abnormal behavior results from supernatural causes such as evil spirits.

Dendrite An extension located at one end of a neuron that receives impulses from other neurons.

Dependent personality disorder A personality disorder characterized by a pattern of clinging and obedience, fear of separation, and a persistent, excessive need to be taken care of.

Dependent variable The variable in an experiment that is expected to change as the independent variable is manipulated.

Depression A low state marked by significant levels of sadness, lack of energy, low self-worth, guilt, or related symptoms.

Desensitization See *systematic desensitization*.

Desire phase The phase of the sexual response cycle consisting of an urge to have sex, sexual fantasies, and sexual attraction to others.

Detoxification Systematic and medically supervised withdrawal from a drug.

Diagnosis A determination that a person's problems reflect a particular disorder.

***Diagnostic and Statistical Manual of Mental Disorders* (DSM)** The classification system for mental disorders developed by the American Psychiatric Association.

Diathesis-stress view The view that a person must first have a predisposition to a disorder and then be subjected to immediate psychosocial stress in order to develop the disorder.

Dichotomous thinking Viewing problems and solutions in rigid "either/or" terms.

Diencephalon A brain area (consisting of the mammillary bodies, thalamus, and hypothalamus) that plays a key role in transforming short-term to long-term memory, among other functions.

Directed masturbation training A sex therapy approach that teaches women with female arousal or orgasmic disorders how to masturbate effectively and eventually to reach orgasm during sexual interactions.

Disaster Response Network (DRN) A network of thousands of volunteer mental health professionals who mobilize to provide free emergency psychological services at disaster sites throughout North America.

Disorganized type of schizophrenia A type of schizophrenia marked primarily by confusion, incoherence, and flat or inappropriate affect.

Dissociative amnesia A dissociative disorder marked by an inability to recall important personal events and information.

Dissociative disorders Disorders marked by major changes in memory that are not due to clear physical causes.

Dissociative fugue A dissociative disorder in which a person travels to a new location and may assume a new identity, simultaneously forgetting his or her past.

Dissociative identity disorder A disorder in which a person develops two or more distinct personalities. Also called *multiple personality disorder*.

Disulfiram (Antabuse) An antagonist drug used in treating alcohol abuse or dependence.

Dopamine The neurotransmitter whose high activity has been shown to be related to schizophrenia.

Dopamine hypothesis The theory that schizophrenia results from excessive activity of the neurotransmitter dopamine.

Down syndrome A form of mental retardation related to an abnormality in the twenty-first chromosome.

Dream A series of ideas and images that form during sleep and are interpreted by psychodynamic theorists as clues to the unconscious.

Drug Any substance other than food that affects the body or mind.

DSM-IV The fourth, and current, edition of the *Diagnostic and Statistical Manual of Mental Disorders*.

Durham test A legal test for insanity that holds people to be insane at the time of committing a crime if the act was the result of a mental disorder or defect.

Duty to protect The principle that therapists must break confidentiality in order to protect a person who may be the intended victim of a client.

Dyslexia A disorder in which persons show a marked impairment in the ability to recognize words and to comprehend what they read. Also known as *reading disorder*.

Dyspareunia A disorder in which a person experiences severe pain in the genitals during sexual activity.

Dysthymic disorder A mood disorder that is similar to but longer-lasting and less disabling than a major depressive disorder.

Ego According to Freud, the psychological force that employs reason and operates in accordance with the reality principle.

Ego defense mechanisms According to psychoanalytic theory, strategies developed by the ego to control unacceptable id impulses and to avoid or reduce the anxiety they arouse.

Ego theory The psychodynamic theory that emphasizes the ego and considers it an independent force.

Egoistic suicide Suicide committed by people over whom society has little or no control, people who are not concerned with the norms or rules of society.

Electroconvulsive therapy (ECT) A form of treatment, used primarily in cases of unipolar depression, in which electrodes attached to a person's head send an electric current through the brain, causing a brain seizure.

Electroencephalograph (EEG) A device that records electrical impulses in the brain.

Electromyograph (EMG) A device that provides feedback about the level of muscular tension in the body.

Employee assistance program A mental health program that some businesses offer to their employees.

Encopresis A childhood disorder characterized by repeated defecation into inappropriate places, such as one's clothing.

Endocrine system The system of glands located throughout the body that helps control important activities such as growth and sexual activity.

Endorphins Neurotransmitters that help relieve pain and reduce emotional tension; sometimes referred to as the body's own opioids.

Enmeshed family pattern A family system in which members are overinvolved with each other's affairs and overconcerned about each other's welfare.

Enuresis A childhood disorder marked by repeated bed-wetting or wetting of one's clothes.

Epidemiological study A study that measures the incidence and prevalence of a disorder in a given population.

Estrogen The primary female sex hormone.

Excitement phase The phase of the sexual response cycle marked by changes in the pelvic region, general physical arousal, and increases in heart rate, muscle tension, blood pressure, and rate of breathing.

Exhibitionism A paraphilia in which persons have repeated sexually arousing urges or fantasies about exposing their genitals to another person and may act upon those urges.

Existential anxiety According to existential theorists, a universal fear of the limits and responsibilities of one's existence.

Existential therapy A therapy that encourages people to accept responsibility for their lives and to live with greater meaning and values.

Exorcism The practice in early societies of treating abnormality by coaxing evil spirits to leave the person's body.

Experiment A research procedure in which a variable is manipulated and the effect of the manipulation is observed.

Experimental group In an experiment, the subjects who are exposed to the independent variable under investigation.

Exposure and response prevention A behavioral treatment for obsessive-compulsive disorder in which individuals are exposed to anxiety-arousing thoughts or situations and then prevented from performing their compulsive acts.

Exposure treatments Behavioral treatments in which persons with fears are exposed to their dreaded objects or situations.

Expressed emotion The general level of criticism, disapproval, hostility, and intrusiveness expressed in a family.

Extrapyramidal effects Unwanted movements, such as severe shaking, bizarre-looking twisting of the face and body, and extreme restlessness, sometimes produced by traditional antipsychotic drugs.

Eye movement desensitization and reprocessing A behavioral exposure treatment in which clients move their eyes in a saccadic (rhythmic) manner from side to side while flooding their minds with images of objects and situations they ordinarily avoid.

Factitious disorder An illness with no identifiable physical cause, in which the patient is believed to be intentionally producing or faking symptoms in order to assume a sick role.

Family pedigree study A research design in which investigators determine how many and which relatives of a person with a disorder have the same disorder.

Family systems theory A theory that views the family as a system of interacting parts and proposes that members interact in consistent ways and operate by unstated rules.

Family therapy A therapy format in which the therapist meets with all members of a family and helps them change in therapeutic ways.

Fear The central nervous system's physiological and emotional response to a serious threat to one's well-being.

Fear hierarchy A list of objects or situations that frighten a person, starting with those that are slightly feared and ending with those that are greatly feared; used in systematic desensitization.

Female orgasmic disorder A dysfunction in which a woman rarely has an orgasm or repeatedly experiences a very delayed one following a normal sexual excitement phase.

Female sexual arousal disorder A female dysfunction marked by a persistent inability to attain or maintain adequate lubrica-tion or genital swelling during sexual activity.

Fetal alcohol syndrome A group of problems in a child, including lower intellectual functioning, low birth weight, and irregularities in the hands and face, that result from excessive alcohol intake by the mother during pregnancy.

Fetishism A paraphilia consisting of recurrent and intense sexual urges, fantasies, or behaviors that involve the use of a nonliving object, often to the exclusion of all other stimuli.

Fixation According to Freud, a condition in which the id, ego, and superego do not mature properly, causing the person to become entrapped at an early stage of development.

Flashback The recurrence of LSD-induced sensory and emotional changes long after the drug has left the body. Or, in post-traumatic stress disorder, the reexperiencing of past traumatic events.

Flat affect A symptom of schizophrenia in which the person shows almost no emotion at all.

Flooding A treatment for phobias in which a person is exposed repeatedly and intensively to a feared object and made to see that it is actually harmless.

Forensic psychology The branch of psychology concerned with intersections between psychological practice and research and the judicial system. Also related to the field of *forensic psychiatry*.

Formal thought disorder A disturbance in the production and organization of thought.

Free association A psychodynamic technique in which a person describes any thought, feeling, or image that comes to mind, even if it seems unimportant.

Free-base A technique for ingesting cocaine in which the pure-cocaine basic alkaloid is chemically separated from processed cocaine, vaporized by heat from a flame, and inhaled through a pipe.

Frotteurism A paraphilia consisting of repeated and intense sexual urges, fantasies, or behaviors that involve touching and rubbing against a nonconsenting person.

Fusion The final merging of two or more subpersonalities in multiple personality disorder.

Galvanic skin response (GSR) Changes in the electrical resistance of the skin.

Gamma aminobutyric acid (GABA) A neurotransmitter whose low activity has been linked to generalized anxiety disorder.

Gender identity disorder A disorder in which a person persistently feels extremely uncomfortable about his or her assigned sex and strongly wishes to be a member of the opposite sex. Also called *transsexualism*.

Gender-sensitive therapies Treatment approaches geared to the special pressures of being a woman in Western society. Also called *feminist therapies*.

Generalized anxiety disorder A disorder marked by persistent and excessive feelings of anxiety and worry about numerous events and activities.

Genes Chromosome segments that control the characteristics and traits we inherit.

Genetic linkage study A research approach in which extended families with high rates of a disorder over several generations are observed in order to determine whether the disorder closely follows the distribution pattern of other family traits.

Geropsychology The field of psychology concerned with the mental health of elderly people.

Gestalt therapy The humanistic therapy developed by Fritz Perls in which clinicians actively move individuals toward self-recognition and self-acceptance by using techniques such as role playing and skillful frustration.

Grief The reaction one experiences when a loved one is lost.

Group home Special homes where people with disorders or disabilities live and are taught self-help, living, and working skills.

Group therapy A therapy format in which a group of people with similar problems meet together with a therapist to work on their problems.

Guilty but mentally ill A verdict stating that defendants are guilty of committing a crime but are also suffering from a mental illness that should be treated during their imprisonment.

Habituation training A therapeutic technique in which a therapist tries to call forth a client's obsessive thoughts again and again, with the expectation that the thoughts will eventually lose their threatening meaning and cause less anxiety.

Halfway house A residence for people with severe psychological problems who cannot yet live alone or with their families; often staffed by paraprofessionals. Also known as *group home*.

Hallucination The experiencing of imagined sights, sounds, or other sensory experiences as if they were real.

Hallucinogens Substances that primarily cause powerful changes in sensory perception, including strengthening a person's perceptions and producing illusions and hallucinations. Also called *psychedelic drugs*.

Helper T-cell A lymphocyte that identifies foreign invaders and then both multiplies and triggers the production of other kinds of immune cells.

Heroin A highly addictive substance derived from morphine; illegal in the United States under all circumstances.

Histrionic personality disorder A personality disorder in which an individual displays a pattern of excessive emotionality and attention seeking. Once called *hysterical personality disorder*.

Hopelessness A pessimistic belief that one's present circumstances, problems, or mood will not change.

Hormones The chemicals released by glands into the bloodstream.

Humors According to ancient Greek and Roman physicians, bodily chemicals that influence mental and physical functioning.

Huntington's disease An inherited disease, characterized by progressive problems in cognition, emotion, and movement, which results in dementia.

Hypertension Chronic high blood pressure.

Hypnosis A sleeplike suggestible state during which a person can be directed to act in unusual ways, to experience unusual sensations, to remember seemingly forgotten events, or to forget remembered events.

Hypnotic amnesia Loss of memory produced by hypnotic suggestion.

Hypnotic therapy A treatment in which a person undergoes hypnosis and is then guided to recall forgotten events or perform other therapeutic activities. Also called *hypnotherapy*.

Hypoactive sexual desire disorder A disorder marked by a lack of interest in sex.

Hypochondriasis A somatoform disorder in which people mistakenly fear that minor changes in their physical functioning indicate a serious disease.

Hypomanic pattern A pattern in which a person displays symptoms of mania, but the symptoms are less severe and cause less impairment than a manic episode.

Hypothalamic-pituitary-adrenal (HPA) pathway One route by which the brain and body produce arousal and fear. At times of stress, the hypothalamus signals the pituitary gland, which in turn signals the adrenal glands. Stress hormones are then released to various body organs.

Hypothalamus A part of the brain that helps maintain various bodily functions, including eating and hunger.

Hypothesis A hunch or prediction that certain variables are related in certain ways.

Hysterical somatoform disorders Somatoform disorders in which people experience actual changes in their physical functioning.

Iatrogenic disorder A disorder that is unintentionally produced by a practitioner.

Id According to Freud, the psychological force that produces instinctual needs, drives, and impulses.

Idiographic understanding An understanding of the behavior of a particular individual.

Immune system The body's network of activities and cells that identify and destroy antigens and cancer cells.

Impulse-control disorders Disorders in which people repeatedly fail to resist an impulse, drive, or temptation to perform an act that is harmful to themselves or to others.

Inappropriate affect A symptom of schizophrenia in which a person displays emotions that are unsuited to the situation.

Incidence The number of new cases of a disorder occurring in a population over a specific period of time.

Independent variable The variable in an experiment that is manipulated to determine whether it has an effect on another variable.

Insanity defense A legal defense in which persons charged with a criminal offense claim to be not guilty by reason of insanity at the time of the crime.

Insomnia The most common dyssomnia, characterized by difficulties initiating and maintaining sleep.

Intelligence quotient (IQ) A general score derived from an intelligence test that theoretically represents a person's overall intellectual capacity.

Intelligence test A test designed to measure a person's intellectual ability.

International Classification of Diseases (ICD) The classification system for medical and mental disorders that is used by the World Health Organization.

Interpersonal psychotherapy (IPT) A treatment for unipolar depression that is based on the belief that clarifying and changing one's interpersonal problems will help lead to recovery.

Intoxication A temporary drug-induced state in which people display symptoms such as impaired judgment, mood changes, irritability, slurred speech, and loss of coordination.

Irresistible impulse test A legal test for insanity that holds people to be insane at the time of committing a crime if they were driven to do so by an uncontrollable "fit of passion."

Isolation An ego defense mechanism in which people unconsciously isolate and disown undesirable and unwanted thoughts, experiencing them as foreign intrusions.

Killer T-cell A lymphocyte that seeks out and destroys body cells that have been infected by viruses.

Korsakoff's syndrome An amnestic disorder marked by extreme confusion, memory impairment, and other neurological symptoms; caused by long-term alcoholism, an accompanying poor diet, and, in turn, a deficiency of vitamin B (thiamine).

L-dopa A drug used in the treatment of Parkinson's disease, a disease in which dopamine is low.

Lateral hypothalamus (LH) The region of the hypothalamus that, when activated, produces hunger.

Learned helplessness The perception, based on past experiences, that one has no control over one's reinforcements.

Learning disorder A developmental disorder marked by impairments in cognitive skills such as reading, mathematics, or language.

Light therapy A treatment for seasonal affective disorder in which patients are exposed to extra light for several hours. Also called *phototherapy*.

Lithium A metallic element that occurs in nature as a mineral salt and is a highly effective treatment for bipolar disorders.

Lobotomy Psychosurgery in which a surgeon cuts the connections between the brain's frontal lobes and the lower centers of the brain.

Locus ceruleus A small area of the brain that seems to be active in the regulation of emotions. Many of its neurons use norepinephrine.

Longitudinal study A study that observes the same subjects on many occasions over a long period of time.

Long-term memory The memory system that contains all the information that a person has stored over the years.

Loose associations A common thinking disturbance in schizophrenia, involving rapid shifts from one topic of conversation to another. Also known as *derailment*.

Lymphocytes White blood cells that circulate through the lymph system and bloodstream, helping the body identify and destroy antigens and cancer cells.

Lysergic acid diethylamide (LSD) A hallucinogenic drug derived from ergot alkaloids.

Magnetic resonance imaging (MRI) The use of the magnetic property of certain atoms in the brain to create a detailed picture of the brain's structure.

Mainstreaming An approach to educating children with mental retardation in which they are placed in regular classes with children who are not mentally retarded.

Major depressive disorder A severe pattern of depression that is disabling and is not caused by such factors as drugs or a general medical condition.

Male erectile disorder A dysfunction in which a man persistently fails to attain or maintain an erection during sexual activity.

Male orgasmic disorder A male dysfunction characterized by a repeated inability to reach orgasm or by long delays in reaching orgasm after normal sexual excitement.

Managed care program A system of health-care coverage in which the insurance company largely controls the cost, method, provider, and length of treatment.

Mania A state or episode of euphoria or frenzied activity in which people may have an exaggerated belief that the world is theirs for the taking.

MAO inhibitor An antidepressant drug that prevents the action of the enzyme monoamine oxidase.

Marijuana One of the cannabis drugs, derived from the leaves and flowering tops of the hemp plant, *Cannabis sativa*.

Marital therapy A therapy approach in which the therapist works with two people who share a long-term relationship. Also known as *couple therapy*.

Masturbation Self-stimulation of the genitals to achieve sexual arousal.

Masturbatory satiation A behavioral treatment in which a client masturbates for a very long period of time while fantasizing in detail about a paraphilic object. The procedure is expected to produce a feeling of boredom that in turn becomes linked to the object.

Meditation A technique of turning one's concentration inward and achieving a slightly changed state of consciousness.

Melatonin A hormone released by the pineal gland when a person's surroundings are dark.

Memory The faculty for recalling past events and past learning.

Mental incompetence A state of mental instability that leaves defendants unable to understand the legal charges and proceedings they are facing and unable to adequately prepare a defense with their attorneys.

Mentally ill chemical abusers (MICAs) Persons suffering from both schizophrenia (or another severe psychological disorder) and a substance-related disorder.

Mental retardation A disorder in which people display general intellectual functioning and adaptive behavior that are well below average.

Mental status exam A set of interview questions and observations designed to reveal the degree and nature of a person's abnormal functioning.

Methadone A laboratory-made opioidlike drug.

Methadone maintenance program An approach to treating heroin dependence in which people are given legally and medically supervised doses of methadone, a laboratory-produced opioid, as a substitute for heroin.

Methylphenidate A stimulant drug, known better by the trade name Ritalin, commonly used to treat ADHD.

Migraine headache An extremely severe headache that occurs on one side of the head, often preceded by a warning sensation and sometimes accompanied by dizziness, nausea, or vomiting.

Mild retardation A level of mental retardation (IQ between 50 and 70) in which persons can benefit from education and support themselves as adults.

Milieu therapy A humanistic approach to institutional treatment based on the belief that institutions can help patients recover by creating a climate that builds self-respect, individual responsibility, and meaningful activity.

Minnesota Multiphasic Personality Inventory (MMPI) A widely used personality inventory consisting of a large number of statements that subjects mark as being true or false for them.

M'Naghten test A widely used legal test for insanity that holds people to be insane at the time of committing a crime if, because of a mental disorder, they did not know the nature of the act or did not know right from wrong.

Model A set of assumptions and concepts that helps scientists explain and interpret observations. Also called *paradigm*.

Modeling A process of learning in which an individual acquires responses by observing and imitating others. Also, a therapy approach based on the same principle.

Moderate retardation A level of mental retardation (IQ between 35 and 49) in which persons can learn to care for themselves and benefit from vocational training.

Moral treatment A nineteenth-century approach to treating people with mental dysfunction which emphasized moral guidance and humane and respectful treatment.

Morphine A highly addictive substance derived from opium that is particularly effective in relieving pain.

Multidimensional risk perspective A theory that identifies several different kinds of risk factors that may combine to help cause a disorder. The more such factors present, the greater the risk of developing the disorder.

Multiple personality disorder A dissociative disorder in which a person develops two or more distinct personalities. Also called *dissociative identity disorder*.

Munchausen syndrome An extreme and long-term form of factitious disorder in which a person produces symptoms, gains admission to a hospital, and receives treatment.

Munchausen syndrome by proxy A factitious disorder in which parents make up or produce physical illnesses in their children.

Muscle contraction headache A headache caused by the narrowing of muscles surrounding the skull. Also called *tension headache*.

Narcissistic personality disorder A personality disorder marked by a broad pattern of grandiosity, need for admiration, and lack of empathy.

Narcotic Any natural or synthetic opioid-like drug.

Narcotic antagonist A substance that attaches to opioid receptors in the brain and, in turn, blocks the effects of opioids.

Natural experiment An experiment in which nature, rather than an experimenter, manipulates an independent variable.

Naturalistic observation A method of observing behavior in which clinicians or researchers observe people in their everyday environments.

Negative symptoms Symptoms of schizophrenia that seem to be deficits of normal thought, emotion, or behavior.

Nerve ending The region at the end of a neuron from which an impulse is sent to a neighboring neuron.

Neurofibrillary tangles Twisted protein fibers that form within certain brain cells as people age.

Neuroimaging techniques Neurological tests that provide images of brain structure or brain activity, including CT scans, PET scans, and MRIs.

Neurological Relating to the structure or activity of the brain.

Neurological test A test that directly measures brain structure or activity.

Neuron A nerve cell. The brain contains billions of neurons.

Neuropsychological test A test that detects brain impairment by measuring a person's cognitive, perceptual, and motor performances.

Neurotransmitter A chemical that, released by one neuron, crosses the synaptic space to be received at receptors on the dendrites of neighboring neurons.

Neutralizing A person's attempt to eliminate unwanted thoughts by thinking or behaving in ways that put matters right internally, that make up for the unacceptable thoughts.

Nocturnal penile tumescence (NPT) The occurrence of erections during sleep.

Nomothetic understanding A general understanding of the nature, causes, and treatments of abnormal psychological functioning in the form of laws or principles.

Norepinephrine A neurotransmitter whose abnormal activity is linked to depression and panic disorder.

Normalization The principle that institutions and community residences should expose persons with mental retardation to living conditions and opportunities similar to those found in the rest of society.

Norms A society's stated and unstated rules for proper conduct.

Not guilty by reason of insanity (NGRI) A verdict stating that defendants are not guilty of committing a crime because they were insane at the time of the crime.

Object relations theory The psychodynamic theory that views the desire for relationships as the key motivating force in human behavior.

Obsession A persistent thought, idea, impulse, or image that is experienced repeatedly, feels intrusive, and causes anxiety.

Obsessive-compulsive disorder A disorder in which a person has recurrent and unwanted thoughts and/or a need to perform repetitive and rigid actions or mental acts.

Obsessive-compulsive personality disorder A personality disorder in which an individual is so focused on orderliness, perfectionism, and control that he or she loses flexibility, openness, and efficiency.

Operant conditioning A process of learning in which behavior that leads to satisfying consequences, or rewards, is likely to be repeated.

Opioid Opium or any of the drugs derived from opium, including morphine, heroin, and codeine.

Opium A highly addictive substance made from the sap of the opium poppy seed.

Oppositional defiant disorder A childhood disorder in which children argue repeatedly with adults, lose their temper, and feel great anger and resentment.

Orbital frontal cortex The brain region in which impulses involving excretion, sexuality, violence, and other primitive activities normally arise.

Orgasm A peaking of sexual pleasure, consisting of rhythmic muscular contractions in the pelvic region, during which a man's semen is ejaculated and the outer third of a woman's vaginal wall contracts.

Orgasm phase The phase of the sexual response cycle during which an individual's sexual pleasure peaks and sexual tension is released as muscles in the pelvic region contract rhythmically.

Orgasmic reorientation A procedure for treating certain paraphilias by teaching clients to respond to new, more appropriate sources of sexual stimulation.

Pain disorder associated with psychological factors A somatoform disorder marked by pain, with psychosocial factors playing a central role in the onset, severity, or continuation of the pain.

Panic attack A short bout of panic that occurs suddenly, reaches a peak within minutes, and gradually passes.

Panic disorder An anxiety disorder marked by recurrent and unpredictable panic attacks.

Panic disorder with agoraphobia A panic disorder in which panic attacks lead to agoraphobic patterns of behavior.

Paranoid personality disorder A personality disorder marked by a pattern of extreme distrust and suspiciousness of others.

Paranoid type of schizophrenia A type of schizophrenia in which the person has an organized system of delusions and hallucinations.

Paraphilias Disorders characterized by recurrent and intense sexual urges, fantasies, or behaviors involving nonhuman objects, children, nonconsenting adults, or experiences of suffering or humiliation.

Paraprofessional A person without previous professional training who provides services under the supervision of a mental health professional.

Parasuicide A suicide attempt that does not result in death.

Parasympathetic nervous system The group of nerve fibers of the autonomic nervous system that help maintain normal organ functioning. They slow organ functioning after stimulation and help return other bodily processes to normal.

Parkinson's disease A slowly progressive neurological disease, marked by tremors and rigidity, that may also cause dementia.

Participant modeling A behavioral treatment in which people with fears observe a therapist (model) interacting with a feared object and then interact with the object themselves.

Passive-aggressive personality disorder A category of personality disorder, listed in past versions of DSM, marked by a pattern of negative attitudes and resistance to the demands of others.

Pedophilia A paraphilia in which a person has repeated and intense sexual urges or fantasies about watching, touching, or engaging in sexual acts with prepubescent children, and may carry out these urges or fantasies.

Peer review system A system by which clinicians paid by an insurance company may periodically review a patient's progress and recommend the continuation or termination of insurance benefits.

Performance anxiety The fear of performing inadequately and a related tension experienced during sex.

Perseveration The persistent repetition of words and statements.

Personality A unique and long-term pattern of inner experience and outward behavior, which leads to consistent reactions across various situations.

Personality disorder A very rigid pattern of inner experience and outward behavior that differs from the expectations of one's culture and leads to dysfunctioning.

Personality inventory A test designed to measure broad personality characteristics that consists of statements about behaviors, beliefs, and feelings. People evaluate the statements as either characteristic or uncharacteristic of themselves.

Pervasive developmental disorders A broad category of disorders beginning in early childhood, characterized by severe and pervasive impairments in social interaction and communication, or the presence of rigid and repetitive behaviors, interests, and activities.

Phenothiazines A group of antihistamine drugs that became the first group of effective antipsychotic medications.

Phobia A persistent and unreasonable fear of a particular object, activity, or situation.

Pick's disease A neurological disease that affects the frontal and temporal lobes, causing dementia.

Placebo A sham treatment that a subject believes to be genuine.

Play therapy An approach to treating childhood disorders that helps children express their conflicts and feelings indirectly by drawing, playing with toys, and making up stories.

Polygraph A test that seeks to determine whether or not the test taker is telling the truth by measuring physiological responses such as respiration level, perspiration level, and heart rate. Also known as a *lie-detector test*.

Polysubstance use The use of two or more substances at the same time.

Polysubstance-related disorder A long-term pattern of maladaptive behavior centered around the abuse of or dependence on a combination of drugs.

Positive psychology The study and enhancement of positive feelings, traits, and abilities.

Positive symptoms Symptoms of schizophrenia that seem to be excesses, that is, bizarre additions to normal thoughts, emotions, or behaviors.

Positron emission tomography (PET scan) A computer-produced motion picture showing rates of metabolism throughout the brain.

Postpartum depression An episode of depression that may begin for some new mothers within four weeks after childbirth.

Postpartum psychosis An episode of psychosis that may begin for a small percentage of new mothers within days or weeks after childbirth.

Posttraumatic stress disorder An anxiety disorder in which fear and related symptoms continue to be experienced long after a traumatic event.

Predisposition An inborn or acquired vulnerability for developing certain symptoms or disorders.

Prefrontal lobes Regions of the brain that play a key role in short-term memory, among other functions.

Premature ejaculation A dysfunction in which a man reaches orgasm and ejaculates before, on, or shortly after penetration and before he wishes it.

Premorbid The period prior to the onset of a disorder.

Preoccupation somatoform disorders Somatoform disorders in which people misinterpret and overreact to minor, even normal, bodily symptoms or features.

Preparedness A predisposition to develop certain fears.

Prevalence The total number of cases of a disorder occurring in a population over a specific period of time.

Prevention A key feature of community mental health programs, which seek to prevent or minimize psychological disorders.

Primary gain In psychodynamic theory, the gain achieved when hysterical symptoms keep internal conflicts out of awareness.

Private psychotherapy An arrangement in which a person directly pays a therapist for counseling services.

Profound retardation A level of mental retardation (IQ below 20) in which individuals need a very structured environment with constant aid and supervision.

Projective test A test that consists of vague material that people interpret or respond to.

Protection and advocacy system The system by which lawyers and advocates who work for patients may investigate and protect the patients' rights during treatment.

Prozac Trade name for fluoxetine; a second-generation antidepressant.

Psychedelic drugs Substances, such as LSD, that cause profound perceptual changes. Also called *hallucinogenic drugs*.

Psychiatric social worker A mental health specialist who is qualified to conduct psychotherapy upon earning a master's degree or doctorate in social work.

Psychiatrist A physician who in addition to medical school has completed three to four years of residency training in the treatment of abnormal mental functioning.

Psychoanalysis Either the theory or the treatment of abnormal psychological functioning that emphasizes unconscious psychological forces as the cause of psychopathology.

Psychodynamic therapy A system of therapy whose goals are to help clients uncover past traumatic events and the inner conflicts that have resulted from them, settle those conflicts, and resume personal development.

Psychogenic perspective The view that the chief causes of abnormal functioning are psychological.

Psychoneuroimmunology The study of the connections among stress, the body's immune system, and illness.

Psychopathy See *antisocial personality disorder*.

Psychopharmacologist A psychiatrist who primarily prescribes medications.

Psychophysiological disorders Illnesses that result from an interaction of both psychosocial and physical factors. DSM-IV labels these illnesses *psychological factors affecting medical condition*. Also called *psychosomatic disorders*.

Psychophysiological test A test that measures physical responses (such as heart rate and muscle tension) as possible indicators of psychological problems.

Psychosis A state in which a person loses contact with reality in key ways.

Psychosomatic illnesses See *psychophysiological illnesses*.

Psychosurgery Brain surgery for mental disorders.

Psychotherapy A treatment system in which words and acts are used by a client (patient) and therapist in order to help the client overcome psychological difficulties.

Psychotropic medications Drugs that primarily affect the brain and reduce various symptoms of mental dysfunctioning.

Quasi-experiment An experiment in which investigators do not randomly assign the subjects to control and experimental groups but instead make use of groups that already exist in the world at large. Also called a *mixed design*.

Random assignment A selection procedure that ensures that subjects are randomly placed either in the control group or in the experimental group.

Rap group A group that meets to help members talk about and explore problems in an atmosphere of mutual support.

Rape Forced sexual intercourse or another sexual act upon a nonconsenting person or intercourse with an underage person.

Rapid eye movement (REM) sleep The period of the sleep cycle during which the eyes move quickly back and forth, indicating that the person is dreaming.

Rapprochement movement An effort to identify a set of common strategies that characterize the work of all effective therapists.

Rational-emotive therapy A cognitive therapy developed by Albert Ellis that helps people identify and change the irrational assumptions and thinking that help cause their psychological disorders.

Reaction formation An ego defense mechanism in which an unacceptable desire is countered by taking on a lifestyle that directly opposes the unwanted impulse.

Receptor A site on a neuron that receives a neurotransmitter.

Regression An ego defense mechanism in which a person returns to a more primitive mode of interacting with the world.

Reinforcement The desirable or undesirable stimuli that follow as a result of an organism's behavior.

Relapse-prevention training An approach to treating alcohol abuse that is similar to BSCT but also has people plan ahead for risky situations and reactions.

Relaxation training A treatment procedure that teaches people to relax at will.

Reliability A measure of the consistency of test or research results.

Repression A defense mechanism in which the ego prevents unacceptable impulses from reaching consciousness.

Residential treatment center A place where people formerly dependent on drugs live, work, and socialize in a drug-free environment. Also called a *therapeutic community*.

Residual type of schizophrenia A type of schizophrenia in which the acute symptoms of the disorder have lessened in strength and number yet remain in residual form.

Resistance A defense mechanism that blocks a person's free associations or causes the person to change the subject to avoid a painful discussion.

Response inventories Tests designed to measure a person's responses in one specific area of functioning, such as affect, social skills, or cognitive processes.

Retrograde amnesia A lack of memory about events that occurred before the event that triggered amnesia.

Retrospective analysis A psychological autopsy in which clinicians and researchers piece together information about a person's suicide from the person's past.

Reward A pleasurable stimulus given to an organism which encourages a specific behavior.

Reward center A dopamine-rich pathway in the brain which produces feelings of pleasure when activated.

Reward-deficiency syndrome A condition, suspected to be present in some individuals, in which the brain's reward center is not readily activated by the usual events in their lives.

Right to refuse treatment The legal right of patients to refuse certain forms of treatment.

Right to treatment The legal right of patients, particularly those who are involuntarily committed, to receive adequate treatment.

Ritalin Trade name of methylphenidate, a stimulant drug that is helpful in many cases of attention-deficit/hyperactivity disorder (ADHD).

Role play A therapy technique in which clients are instructed to act out roles assigned to them by the therapist.

Rorschach test A projective test in which a person reacts to inkblots, designed to help reveal psychological features of the person.

Rosenthal effect The general finding that the results of any experiment often conform to the expectations of the experimenter.

Sample A group of subjects that is representative of the larger population about which a researcher wishes to make a statement.

Savant A person with a mental disorder or significant intellectual deficits who has some extraordinary ability despite the disorder or deficits.

Schizoid personality disorder A personality disorder in which a person persistently avoids social relationships and shows little emotional expression.

Schizophrenia A psychotic disorder in which personal, social, and occupational functioning deteriorate as a result of strange perceptions, disturbed thought processes, unusual emotions, and motor abnormalities.

Schizophrenogenic mother A type of mother—supposedly cold, domineering, and uninterested in the needs of others—who was once thought to cause schizophrenia in the child.

Schizotypal personality disorder A personality disorder in which a person displays a pattern of interpersonal problems marked by extreme discomfort in close relationships, odd forms of thinking and perceiving, and behavioral eccentricities.

School phobia A childhood pattern in which children fear going to school and often stay home for a long period of time. Also called *school refusal*.

Scientific method The process of systematically gathering and evaluating information through careful observations to gain an understanding of a phenomenon.

Seasonal affective disorder (SAD) A mood disorder in which mood episodes are related to changes in season.

Second-generation antidepressants New antidepressant drugs that differ structurally from tricyclics and MAO inhibitors.

Second messengers Chemical changes within a neuron just after the neuron receives a neurotransmitter message and just before it responds.

Secondary gain In psychodynamic theory, the gain achieved when hysterical symptoms elicit kindness from others or provide an excuse for avoiding unpleasant activities.

Sedative-hypnotic drug A drug used in low doses to reduce anxiety and in higher doses to help people sleep. Also called *anxiolytic drug*.

Selective serotonin reuptake inhibitors (SSRIs) A group of second-generation antidepressant drugs that increase serotonin activity specifically, without affecting other neurotransmitters.

Self-actualization The humanistic process by which people fulfill their potential for goodness and growth.

Self-efficacy The judgment that one can master and perform needed behaviors whenever necessary.

Self-help group A group made up of people with similar problems who help and support one another without the direct leadership of a clinician. Also called *mutual help group*.

Self-hypnosis The process of hypnotizing oneself—for example, to forget unpleasant events.

Self-instruction training A cognitive treatment developed by Donald Meichenbaum that teaches people to use coping self-statements at times of stress or discomfort. Also called *stress inoculation training*.

Self-monitoring A technique for observing behavior in which clients observe themselves.

Self theory The psychodynamic theory that emphasizes the role of the self—a person's unified personality.

Senile Typical of or occurring in people over the age of 65.

Senile plaques Sphere-shaped deposits of beta-amyloid protein that form in the spaces between certain brain cells and in certain blood vessels as people age.

Sensate focus A treatment for sexual disorders that instructs couples to take the focus away from orgasm or intercourse and instead spend time concentrating on the pleasure achieved by such acts as kissing, hugging, and mutual massage. Also known as *nondemand pleasuring.*

Separation anxiety disorder A childhood disorder marked by excessive anxiety, even panic, whenever the child is separated from home or a parent.

Serotonin A neurotransmitter whose abnormal activity is linked to depression, obsessive-compulsive disorder, and eating disorders.

Severe retardation A level of mental retardation (IQ between 20 and 34) in which individuals require careful supervision and can learn to perform basic work in structured and sheltered settings.

Sex-change surgery A surgical procedure that changes a person's sex organs and features, and, in turn, sexual identity.

Sexual aversion disorder A disorder characterized by an aversion to and avoidance of genital sexual interplay.

Sexual dysfunction A disorder marked by a persistent inability to function normally in some area of the human sexual response cycle.

Sexual masochism A paraphilia characterized by repeated and intense sexual urges, fantasies, or behaviors that involve being humiliated, beaten, bound, or otherwise made to suffer.

Sexual response cycle The general sequence of behavior and feelings that occurs during sexual activity, consisting of desire, excitement, orgasm, and resolution.

Sexual sadism A paraphilia characterized by repeated and intense sexual urges, fantasies, or behaviors that involve inflicting suffering on others.

Shaping A learning procedure in which successive approximations of the desired behavior are rewarded until, finally, the exact and complete behavior is learned.

Sheltered workshop A protected and supervised workplace that offers job opportunities and training at a pace and level tailored to people with various disabilities.

Short-term memory The memory system that collects new information. Also known as *working memory.*

Sildenafil A drug, used to treat erectile disorder, which helps increase blood flow to the penis during sexual activity. Marketed as Viagra.

Single-subject experiment A research method in which a single subject is observed and measured both before and after the manipulation of an independent variable.

Situation anxiety The various levels of anxiety produced in a person by different situations. Also called *state anxiety.*

Social phobia A severe and persistent fear of social or performance situations in which embarrassment may occur.

Social skills training A therapy approach that helps people learn or improve social skills and assertiveness through the use of role playing and rehearsing of desirable behaviors.

Social therapy An approach to therapy in which the therapist makes practical advice and life adjustment a central focus of treatment for schizophrenia. Therapy also focuses on problem solving, decision making, development of social skills, and management of medications. Also known as *personal therapy.*

Sociopathy See *antisocial personality disorder.*

Somatization disorder A somatoform disorder marked by numerous recurring physical ailments without an organic basis. Also called *Briquet's syndrome.*

Somatoform disorder A physical illness or ailment that is largely explained by psychosocial causes, in which the patient experiences no sense of wanting or guiding his or her symptoms.

Somatogenic perspective The view that abnormal psychological functioning has physical causes.

Special education An approach to educating children with mental retardation in which they are grouped together and given a separate, specially designed education.

Specific phobia A severe and persistent fear of a specific object or situation (other than agoraphobia and social phobia).

Spectator role A state of mind that some people experience during sex in which they focus on their sexual performance to such an extent that their performance and their enjoyment are reduced.

Standardization The process in which a test is administered to a large group of persons whose performance then serves as a common standard or norm against which any individual's score can be measured.

State-dependent learning Learning that becomes associated with the conditions under which it occurred, and so is best remembered under the same conditions.

State hospitals State-run public mental institutions in the United States.

State school A state-supported institution for individuals with mental retardation.

Statistical analysis The application of principles of probability to the findings of a study in order to learn how likely it is that the findings have occurred by chance.

Statistical significance A measure of the probability that a study's findings occurred by chance rather than because of the experimental manipulation.

Stimulus generalization A phenomenon in which responses to one stimulus are also produced by similar stimuli.

Stress management program An approach to treating generalized and other anxiety disorders that teaches people techniques for reducing and controlling stress.

Stress response A person's particular reactions to stress.

Stressor An event that creates a sense of threat by confronting a person with a demand or opportunity for change of some kind.

Stress-reduction seminar A workshop or series of group sessions offered by a business in which mental health professionals teach employees how to cope with and solve problems and reduce stress. Also known as *problem-solving seminar.*

Structured interview An interview format in which the clinician asks prepared questions.

Stutter A disturbance in the normal fluency and timing of speech.

Subintentional death A death in which the victim plays an indirect, hidden, partial, or unconscious role.

Subject An individual chosen to participate in a study. Also called a *participant.*

Subpersonalities The distinct personalities found in individuals suffering from multiple personality disorder. Also known as *alternate personalities.*

Substance abuse A pattern of behavior in which people rely on a drug excessively and repeatedly, thus disrupting their lives.

Substance dependence A pattern of behavior in which people rely on a drug excessively, center their lives around it, and perhaps build a tolerance to it or experience withdrawal symptoms when they stop taking it, or both. Also known as *addiction.*

Suicide A self-inflicted death in which the person acts intentionally, directly, and consciously.

Suicide prevention program A program that tries to identify people who are at risk of killing themselves and to offer them crisis intervention.

Superego According to Freud, the psychological force that emphasizes one's conscience, values, and ideals.

Symbolic loss According to Freudian theory, the loss of a valued object (for example, a loss of employment) which is unconsciously interpreted as the loss of a loved one. Also called *imagined loss.*

Sympathetic nervous system The nerve fibers of the autonomic nervous system that quicken the heartbeat and produce other changes experienced as fear or anxiety.

Symptom A physical or psychological sign of a disorder.

Synapse The tiny space between the nerve ending of one neuron and the dendrite of another.

Syndrome A cluster of symptoms that usually occur together.

Synergistic effect In pharmacology, an increase of effects that occurs when more than one drug is acting on the body at the same time.

Systematic desensitization A behavioral treatment that uses relaxation training and a fear hierarchy to help people with phobias react calmly to the objects or situations they dread.

Tardive dyskinesia A condition characterized by extrapyramidal effects that appear in some patients after they have taken traditional antipsychotic drugs for an extended time.

Temporal lobes Regions of the brain that play a key role in transforming short-term memory to long-term memory, among other functions.

Tension headache See *muscle contraction headache*.

Test A device for gathering information about a few aspects of a person's psychological functioning from which broader information about the person can be inferred.

Testosterone The principal male sex hormone.

Tetrahydrocannabinol (THC) The main active ingredient of cannabis substances.

Thematic Apperception Test (TAT) A projective test using pictures that show people in somewhat unclear situations.

Theory of mind Awareness that other people base their behaviors on their own beliefs, intentions, and mental states, not on information they have no way of knowing.

Therapist A professional clinician who applies a system of therapy to help a person overcome psychological difficulties.

Therapy A systematic process for helping persons overcome their psychological problems. It consists of a patient, a trained therapist, and a series of contacts between them.

Token economy program A behavioral program in which a person's desirable behaviors are reinforced systematically throughout the day by the awarding of tokens that can be exchanged for goods or privileges.

Tolerance Upon regular use of a drug, the need of the brain and the body for ever-larger doses in order to achieve the drug's earlier effects.

Trait anxiety The general level of anxiety that a person brings to the various events in his or her life.

Tranquilizer A drug that reduces anxiety.

Transference According to psychodynamic theorists, a process in which persons, during psychotherapy, act toward the therapist as they did or do toward important figures in their lives.

Transvestic fetishism A paraphilia consisting of repeated and intense sexual urges, fantasies, or behaviors that involve dressing in clothes of the opposite sex. Also known as *transvestism* or *cross-dressing*.

Treatment A procedure designed to help change abnormal behavior into more normal behavior. Also called *therapy*.

Trephination An ancient operation in which a stone instrument was used to cut away a circular section of the skull, perhaps to treat abnormal behavior.

Trichotillomania An impulse-control disorder (or compulsion) in which people repeatedly pull at and even yank out their hair, eyelashes, and eyebrows.

Tricyclic An antidepressant drug, such as imipramine, that has three rings in its molecular structure.

Type A personality style A personality pattern characterized by hostility, cynicism, drivenness, impatience, competitiveness, and ambition.

Type B personality style A personality pattern in which persons are more relaxed, less aggressive, and less concerned about time.

Type I schizophrenia A type of schizophrenia characterized mainly by positive symptoms, such as delusions, hallucinations, and certain formal thought disorders.

Type II schizophrenia A type of schizophrenia in which persons experience mostly negative symptoms, such as flat affect, poverty of speech, and loss of volition.

Ulcer A lesion that forms in the wall of the stomach or of the duodenum.

Unconditional positive regard Full, warm acceptance of a person regardless of what he or she says, thinks, or feels; a critical component of client-centered therapy.

Unconscious The deeply hidden mass of memories, experiences, and impulses that is viewed in Freudian theory as the source of much behavior.

Undifferentiated type of schizophrenia A type of schizophrenia in which no single set of psychotic symptoms (incoherence, psychomotor disturbances, delusions, or hallucinations) dominates.

Undoing An ego defense mechanism in which a person unconsciously cancels out an unacceptable desire or act by performing another act.

Unipolar depression Depression without a history of mania.

Unstructured interview An interview format in which the clinician asks spontaneous questions that are based on issues that arise during the interview.

Vaginismus A condition marked by involuntary contractions of the muscles around the outer third of the vagina during sexual activity, preventing entry of the penis.

Validity The accuracy of a test's or study's results; that is, the extent to which the test or study actually measures or shows what it claims to.

Variable Any characteristic or event that can vary across time, locations, or persons.

Vascular dementia Dementia caused by a cerebrovascular accident, or stroke, that restricts blood flow to certain areas of the brain. Also called *multi-infarct dementia*.

Ventromedial hypothalamus (VMH) The region of the hypothalamus that, when activated, depresses hunger.

Voyeurism A paraphilia in which a person has repeated and intense sexual desires or urges to secretly observe unsuspecting people as they undress or have intercourse. The person may also act on these desires.

Weight set point The weight level that a person is predisposed to maintain, controlled, in part, by the hypothalamus.

Withdrawal Unpleasant, sometimes dangerous reactions that may occur when people who use a drug regularly stop taking or reduce their dosage of the drug.

Working through The psychodynamic treatment process of repeatedly facing conflicts, reinterpreting feelings, and overcoming one's problems.

references

Journal Abbreviations

Academ. Med. *Academic Medicine*
Acta Genet. Med. Gemellol. *Acta Geneticae Medicae et Gemoliologiae*
Acta Paediatr. *Acta Paediatrica*
Acta Psychiatr. Belg. *Acta Psychiatrica Belgica*
Acta Psychiatr. Scandin. *Acta Psychiatrica Scandinavica*
Adap. Phys. Activ. Q. *Adapted Physical Activity Quarterly*
Addic. Behav. *Addictive Behaviors*
Admin. Pol. Ment. Hlth. *Administration and Policy in Mental Health*
Adol. Psychiat. *Adolescent Psychiatry*
Adv. Behav. Res. Ther. *Advances in Behavior Research and Therapy*
Adv. In Biochem. & Psychopharm. *Advances in Biochemical Psychopharmacology*
Adv. Drug React. Toxicol. Rev. *Advanced Drug Reaction and Toxicology Review*
Adv. Mind-Body Med. *Advances in Mind-Body Medicine*
Aggress. Viol. Behav. *Aggression and Violent Behavior*
Alcohol Alcoholism *Alcohol and Alcoholism*
Alcohol.: Clin. Exp. Res. *Alocholism: Clinical and Experimental Research*
Alochol. Treat Q. *Alcoholism: Treatment Quarterly*
Alc. Res. Hlth. *Alcohol Research and Health*
Alz. Disease Assoc. Disord. *Alzheimer's Disease and Associated Disorders*
Am. Demogr. *American Demographics*
Am. Heart J. *American Heart Journal*
Amer. Fam Physician. *American Family Physician*
Amer. Hlth. *American Health*
Amer. J. Addict. *American Journal on Addictions*
Amer. J. Cardiol. *American Journal of Cardiology*
Amer. J. Clin. Hyp. *American Journal of Clinical Hypnosis*
Amer. J. Clin. Hypnother. *American Journal of Clinical Hypnotherapy*
Amer. J. Clin. Nutr. *American Journal of Clinical Nutrition*
Amer. J. Comm. Psych. *American Journal of Community Psychology*
Amer. J. Criminal Justice *American Journal of Criminal Justice*
Amer. J. Digestional Dis. *American Journal of Digestive Diseases*
Amer. J. Drug Alch. Ab. *American Journal of Drug and Alcohol Abuse*
Amer. Educ. Res. J *American Educational Research Journal*
Amer. Fam. Physician *American Family Physician*
Amer. J. Epidemiol. *American Journal of Epidemiology*
Amer. J. Forens. Psychol. *American Journal of Forensic Psychology*
Amer. J. Ger. Psychiat. *American Journal of Geriatric Psychiatry*
Amer. J. Hlth. Sys. Pharmacol. *American Journal of Health Systems and Pharmacology*
Amer. J. Hospice Pall. Care *American Journal of Hospice and Palliative Care*
Amer. J. Med. Genet. *American Journal of Medical Genetics*
Amer. J. Ment. Def. *American Journal of Mental Deficiency*
Amer. J. Ment. Retard. *American Journal on Mental Retardation*
Amer. J. Obstet. Gynecol. *American Journal of Obstetrics and Gynecology*
Amer. J. Orthopsychiat. *American Journal of Orthopsychiatry*
Amer. J. Psychiat. *American Journal of Psychiatry*
Amer. J. Psychother. *American Journal of Psychotherapy*
Amer. J. Pub. Hlth. *American Journal of Public Health*
Amer. Psychiat. Assoc. Res. Rep.
Amer. Psychologist *American Psychologist*
Amer. Sci. *American Scientist*

Amer. Sociol. Rev. *American Sociological Review*
Anális. Modif. Cond. *Análisis y Modificación de Conducta*
Ann. Amer. Psychother. Assn. *Annals of the American Psychotherapy Association*
Ann. Behav. Med. *Annals of Behavioral Medicine*
Ann. Clin. Psychiat. *Annals of Clinical Psychiatry*
Ann. Internal Med. *Annals of Internal Medicine*
Ann. Med. *Annals of Medicine*
Ann. Neurol. *Annals of Neurology*
Ann. N.Y. Acad. Sci. *Annals of the New York Academy of Sciences*
Ann. Pharmacother. *Annals of Pharmacotherapy*
Annu. Rev. Med. *Annual Review of Medicine*
Annu. Rev. Neurosci. *Annual Review of Neuroscience*
Annu. Rev. Psychol. *Annual Review of Psychology*
Anx., Stress, Coping Inter. J. *Anxiety, Stress, and Coping: An International Journal*
Appl. Cog. Psychol. *Applied Cognitive Psychology*
Appl. Dev. Sci. *Applied Developmental Science*
Appl. Neuropsychol. *Applied Neuropsychology*
Appl. Prev. Psychol. *Applied and Preventive Psychology*
Appl. Psychophysiol. Biofeedback *Applied Psychophysiology and Biofeedback*
Arch. Fam. Med. *Archives of Family Medicine*
Arch. Gen. Psychiat. *Archives of General Psychiatry*
Arch. Internal Med. *Archives of Internal Medicine*
Arch. Neurol. *Archives of Neurology*
Arch. Neurol. Psychiat. *Archives of Neurology and Psychiatry Chicago*
Arch. Pediatr. Adoles. *Archives of Pediatric Adolescent Medicine*
Arch. Psychiatr. Nursing *Archives of Psychiatric Nursing*
Arch. Sex. Behav. *Archives of Sexual Behavior*
Arch. Suic. Res. *Archives of Suicide Research*
Assoc. Res. Nerv. Ment. Dis.
Austral. Fam. Physician. *Australian Family Physician*
Austral. J. Clin. Exp. Hyp. *Australian Journal of Clinical and Experimental Hypnosis*
Austral. New Zeal. J. Ment. Hlth. Nurs. *Australian and New Zealand Journal of Mental Health Nursing*
Austral. New Zeal. J. Psychiat. *Australian and New Zealand Journal of Psychiatry*
Austral. Psychologist *Australian Psychologist*
Aviat. Space, Envir. Med. *Aviation, Space, and Environmental Medicine*

Basic Appl. Soc. Psychol. *Basic and Applied Social Psychology*
Behav. Brain Res. *Behavioral Brain Research*
Behav. Change *Behaviour-Change*
Behav. Cog. Psychother. *Behavioral and Cognitive Psychotherapy*
Behav. Genet. *Behavioral Genetics*
Behav. Hlth. Manage.
Behav. Intervent. *Behavioral Interventions*
Behav. Med. *Behavioral Medicine*
Behav. Mod. *Behavior Modification*
Behav. Neurosci. *Behavioral Neuroscience*
Behav. Pharmacol. *Behavioural Pharmacology*
Behav. Psychother. *Behavioural Psychotherapy*
Behav. Res. Meth. Instru. Computers *Behavioral Research Methods, Instruments, and Computers*
Behav. Res. Ther. *Behavior Research and Therapy*
Behav. Sci. *Behavioral Science*
Behav. Sci. Law *Behavioral Sciences and the Law*
Behav. Ther. *Behavior Therapy*
Behav. Therapist *Behavior Therapist*
Biofeed. Self-Reg. *Biofeedback and Self-Regulation*
Biol. Psychiat. *Biological Psychiatry*
Biol. Psychol. *Biological Psychology*
Biol. Signals Recept. *Biological Signals and Receptors*
Bipolar Disord. *Bipolar Disorders*
Bull. Suicidol. *Bulletin of Suicidology*
Br. J. Clin. Psychol. *British Journal of Clinical Psychology*

Brain Behav. Immun. *Brain, Behavior, and Immunity*
Brain Cognit. *Brain and Cognition*
Brain Inj. *Brain Injury*
Brain Res. *Brain Research Reviews*
Brit. J. Addic. *British Journal of Addiction*
Brit. J. Cog. Psychother. *British Journal of Cognitive Psychotherapy*
Brit. J. Dev. Psychol. *British Journal of Developmental Psychology*
Brit. J. Forensic Prac. *British Journal of Forensic Practice*
Brit. J. Guid. Couns. *British Journal of Guidance and Counselling*
Brit. J. Med. Psychol. *British Journal of Medicinal Psychology*
Brit. J Prev. Soc. Med. *British Journal of Preventive and Social Medicine*
Brit. J. Psychiat. *British Journal of Psychiatry*
Brit. J. Psychother. *British Journal of Psychotherapy*
Brit. J. Urol. *British Journal of Urology*
Brit. Med. J. *British Medical Journal*
Bull. Assoc. Amer. Med. Colleges *Bulletin of the Association of American Medical Colleges*
Bull. Amer. Acad. Psychiat. Law *Bulletin of the American Academy of Psychiatry Law*
Bull. Menninger Clin. *Bulletin of the Menninger Clinic*
Bull. Psychol. *Bulletin de Psychologie*
Bull. Psychon. Soc. *Bulletin of the Psychonomic Society*
Bull. Psychosom. Soc. *Bulletin of the Psychosomatic Society*

Calif. Law Rev. *California Law Review*
Can. J. Behav. Sci. *Canadian Journal of Behavioural Science*
Canad. J. Couns. *Canadian Journal of Counselling*
Canad. J. Neurol. Sci. *Canadian Journal of Neurological Science*
Canad. J. Psychiat. *Canadian J. Psychiatry*
Canad. Psychol. *Canadian Psychology*
Cesko. Psychol. *Ceskoslovenska Psychologie*
Chem. Eng. News *Chemical and Engineering News*
Chin. Ment. Hlth. J. *Chinese Mental Health Journal*
Child Abuse Negl. *Child Abuse and Neglect*
Child Adol. Ment. Hlth. *Child and Adolescent Mental Health*
Child Adol. Psychiat. Clin. N. Amer. *Child and Adolescent Psychiatric Clinics of North America*
Child Dev. *Child Development*
Child. Maltreat: J. Amer. Profess. Soc. Abuse Child. *Child Maltreatment: Journal of the American Professional Society on the Abuse of Children*
Child Psychol. Psychiat. Rev. *Child Psychology and Psychiatry Review*
Child Psychiat. Human Dev. *Child Psychiatry and Human Development*
Chin. J. Clin. Psychol. *Chinese Journal of Clinical Psychology*
Chron. Higher Educ. *Chronicle of Higher Education*
Clin. Child Psychol. Psychiat. *Clinical Child Psychology and Psychiatry*
Clin. Electroencephalogr. *Clinical Electroencephalography*
Clin. Geront. *Clinical Gerontologist*
Clin. Neuropharmacol. *Clinical Neuropharmacology*
Clin. Pediatr. *Clinical Pediatrics*
Clin. Pharmacol. Ther. *Clinical and Pharmacological Therapy*
Clin. Psychol. Rev. *Clinical Psychology Review*
Clin. Psychol.: Sci. Prac. *Clinical Psychology: Science and Practice*
Clin. Psychologist *Clinical Psychologist*
Clin. Rehab. *Clinical Rehabilitation*
Clin. Soc. Work J. *Clinical Social Work Journal*
Clin. Ther.: Inter. J. Drug Ther. *Clinical Therapeutics: The International Journal of Drug Therapy*
Cog. Emot. *Cognition & Emotion*
Cog. Neuropsychiat. *Cognitive Neuropsychiatry*

Cog. Ther. Res. *Cognitive Therapy and Research*
Community Dent. Oral Epidemiol. *Community Dentistry and Oral Epidemiology*
Comm. Ment. Hlth. J. *Community Mental Health Journal*
Communic. Res. *Communication Research*
Comprehen. Psychiat. *Comprehensive Psychiatry*
Comprehen. Ther. *Comprehensive Therapy*
Comp. Hum. Behav. *Computers in Human Behavior*
Consciousness Cog. *Consciousness and Cognition: An International Journal*
Contemp. Fam. Therap: Internat. J. *Contemporary Family Therapy: An International Journal*
Contemp. Hyp. *Contemporary Hypnosis*
Contemp. Psychol. *Contemporary Psychology*
Couns. Psychology. *Counselling Psychology Quarterly*
Criminal Justice Behav. *Criminal Justice and Behavior*
Cult. Div. Ethnic Minority Psychol. *Cultural Diversity and Ethnic Minority Psychology*
Cult. Med. Psychiat. *Culture, Medicine, and Psychiatry*
Curr. Direct. Psychol. Sci. *Current Directions in Psychological Science*
Curr. Opin. Neurobiol. *Current Opinion in Neurobiology*
Curr. Opin. Psychiat. *Current Opinion in Psychiatry*
Curr. Probl. Pediatr., *Current Problems in Pediatrics*
CyberPsych. Behav. *CyberPsychology and Behavior*

Death Stud. *Death Studies*
Dement. Ger. Cogn. Disord. *Dementia and Geriatric Cognitive Disorders*
Depress. Anx. *Depression and Anxiety*
Dev. Disabil. Bull. *Developmental Disabilities Bulletin*
Dev. Med. Child Neurol. *Developmental Medicine and Child Neurology*
Dev. Neuropsychol. *Developmental Neuropsychology*
Dev. Psychol. *Developmental Psychology*
Dev. Psychopathol. *Developmental Psychopathology*
Dis. Nerv. Syst. *Diseases of the Nervous System*
Diss. Abstr. Inter. *Dissertation Abstracts International*
Diss. Abstr. Inter.: Sect. A: Human Soc. Sci. *Dissertation Abstracts International: Section A: Humanities and Social Sciences*
Diss. Abstr. Inter.: Sect. B: Sci. Eng. *Dissertation Abstracts International: Section B: The Sciences and Engineering*
Dissociat. Prog. Dissociat. Disorders *Dissociation Progress in the Dissociative Disorders*
Drug. Alc. Dep. *Drug and Alcohol Dependence*
Drug. Alc. Rev. *Drug and Alcohol Review*
Drug Benef. Trends *Drug Benefit Trends*

Early Ed. Dev. *Early Education and Development*
Eat. Behav. *Eating Behaviors*
Eat. Disord.: J. Treat. Prev. *Eating Disorders: The Journal of Treatment and Prevention*
Eat. Weight Disord. *Eating and Weight Disorders*
Educ. Psychol. Meas. *Educational and Psychological Measurement*
eMed. J. *eMedicine Journal*
Empir. Stud. Arts *Empirical Studies of the Arts*
Endocrine Res. *Endocrine Research*
Ethics Behav. *Ethics & Behavior*
Eur. Arch. Psychiat. Clin. Neurosci. *European Archives of Psychiatry and Clinical Neuroscience*
Eur. Arch. Psychiat. Neurol. Sci. *European Archives of Psychiatry and Neurological Science*
Eur. Child Adolesc. Psychiatry *European Child and Adolescent Psychiatry*
Eur. Eat. Disord. Rev. *European Eating Disorders Review*
Eur. J. Cog. Psychol. *European Journal of Cognitive Psychology*
Eur. J. Med. Res. *European Journal of Medical Research*
Eur. J. Pers. *European Journal of Personality*
Eur. J. Psychiat. *European Journal of Psychiatry*

Eur. J. Psychol. Assess. *European Journal of Psychological Assessment*
Eur. Neurol. *European Neurology*
Eur. Neuropsychopharmacology *European Neuropsychopharmacology*
Eur. Psychiat. *European Psychiatry*
Eur. Psycholog. *European Psychologist*
Eur. Urol. *European Urology*
Evolution Psychiatr. *Evolution Psychiatrique*
Exp. Clin. Psychopharmacol. *Experimental and Clinical Psychopharmacology*

Fam. Hlth. *Family Health*
Fam. J. Counsel. Ther. Couples Fam. *Family Journal Counseling and Therapy for Couples and Families*
Fam. Pract. Res. J. *Family Practice Research Journal*
Fam. Process *Family Process*
Fed. Probation *Federal Probation*
Focus Autism Other Dev. Disabil *Focus on Autism and Other Developmental Disabilities*
Focus Autistic Behav. *Focus on Autistic Behavior*

G. Ital. Suic. *Giornale Italiano di Suicidologia*
Gedragstherapie *Gedragstherapie*
Gerontol. Geriat. Educ. *Gerontology and Geriatrics Education*
Gen. Hosp. Psychiat. *General Hospital Psychiatry*
Gender Soc. *Gender and Society*

Harvard Educ. Rev. *Harvard Educational Review*
Harv. Rev. Psychiat. *Harvard Review of Psychiatry*
Hist. Psychiat. *History of Psychiatry*
Hlth. Affairs *Health Affairs*
Hlth. Care Women Inter. *Health Care for Women International*
Hlth. Psychol. *Health Psychology*
Hlth. Soc. Work *Health and Social Work*
Homeostasis Hlth. Dis. *Homeostasis Health and Disease*
Hosp. Comm. Psychiat. *Hospital and Community Psychiatry*
Hosp. Practitioner *Hospital Practitioner*
Human Mutat. *Human Mutation*
Human Psychopharmacol. Clin. Exp. *Human Psychopharmacology Clinical and Experimental*
Humanist. Psycholog. *Humanistic Psychologist*

Imag. Cog. Pers. *Imagination, Cognition and Personality*
Indian Med. *Indian Medical Journal*
Indian J. Clin. Psychol. *Indian Journal of Clinical Psychology*
Indiv. Psychol. J. Adlerian Theory Res. Prac. *Individual Psychology: A Journal of Adlerian Theory, Research, and Practice*
Injury Prev. *Injury Prevention*
Int. For. Logotherapy *International Forum for Logotherapy*
Integ. Physiol. Behav. Sci. *Integrative Physiological and Behavioral Science*
Integ. Psychiat. *Integrated Psychiatry*
Inter. Clin. Psychopharmacology *International Clinical Psychopharmacology*
Inter. Forum Psychoanal. *International Forum of Psychoanalysis*
Inter. J. Addic. *International Journal of Addiction*
Inter. J. Aging Human Dev. *International Journal of Aging and Human Development*
Inter. J. Behav. Dev. *International Journal of Behavioral Development*
Inter. J. Behav. Med. *International Journal of Behavioral Medicine*
Inter. J. Clin. Exp. Hyp. *International Journal of Clinical and Experimental Hypnosis*

Inter. J. Eat. Disorders *International Journal of Eating Disorders*
Inter. J. Epidemiol. *International Journal of Epidemiology*
Inter. J. Ger. Psychiat. *International Journal of Geriatric Psychiatry*
Inter. J. Group Psychother. *International Journal of Group Psychotherapy*
Inter. J. Law Psychiat. *International Journal of Law and Psychiatry*
Inter. J. Ment. Hlth. *International Journal of Mental Health*
Inter. J. Ment. Hlth. Nurs. *International Journal of Mental Health Nursing*
Inter. J. Methods Psychiatr. Res. *International Journal of Methods in Psychiatric Research*
Inter. J. Neurosci. *International Journal of Neuroscience*
Inter. J. Nurs. Stud. *International Journal of Nursing Studies*
Inter. J. Obesity *International Journal of Obesity*
Inter. J. Offend. Ther. Compar. Crimin. *International Journal of Offender Therapy and Comparative Criminology*
Inter. J. Psychiat. Clin. Prac. *International Journal of Psychiatry in Clinical Practice*
Inter. J. Psychiat. Med. *International Journal of Psychiatry in Medicine*
Inter. J. Psychoanal. *International Journal of Psychoanalysis*
Inter. J. Psychoanal.-Psychother. *International Journal of Psychoanalytic-Psychotherapy*
Inter. J. Psychol. Religion *International Journal for the Psychology of Religion*
Inter. J. Psychophysiol. *International Journal of Psychophysiology*
Inter. J. Psychosoc. Rehab. *International Journal of Psychosocial Rehabilitation*
Inter. J. Psychosom. *International Journal of Psychosomatics*
Inter. J. Soc. Psychiat. *International Journal of Social Psychiatry*
Inter. J. Sport Psychol. *International Journal of Sport Psychology*
Inter. J. STD AIDS *International Journal of STD and AIDS*
Inter. J. Stress Manag. *International Journal of Stress Management*
Inter. Med. J. *International Medical Journal*
Inter. Psychoger. *International Psychogeriatrics*
Intern. Rev. Psychiat. *International Review of Psychiatry*
Inter. Rev. Psychoanal. *International Review of Psychoanalysis*
Irish J. Psychol. Med. *Irish Journal of Psychological Medicine*
Israel J. Psychiat. Rel. Sci. *Israel Journal of Psychiatry and Related Sciences*
Issues Ment. Hlth. Nurs. *Issues in Mental Health Nursing*
Ital. J. Neurol. Sci. *Italian Journal of Neurological Sciences*

J. Abnorm. Behav. *Journal of Abnormal Behavior*
J. Abnorm. Child Psychol. *Journal of Abnormal Child Psychology*
J. Abnorm. Psychol. *Journal of Abnormal Psychology*
J. Abnorm. Soc. Psychol. *Journal of Abnormal and Social Psychology*
J. Adol. Hlth. *Journal of Adolescent Health*
J. Adolescence *Journal of Adolescence*
J. Adv. Nurs. *Journal of Advanced Nursing*
J. Affect. Disorders *Journal of Affective Disorders*
J. Aggress. Maltreat. Trauma *Journal of Aggression, Maltreatment, and Trauma*
J. Alcohol Drug Educ. *Journal of Alcohol and Drug Education*

J. Amer. Acad. Child Adol. Psychiat. *Journal of the American Academy of Child and Adolescent Psychiatry*

J. Amer. Acad. Child Psychiat. *Journal of the American Academy of Child Psychiatry*

J. Amer. Acad. Psychiat. Law *Journal of the American Academy of Psychiatry and the Law*

J. Amer. Acad. Psychoanal. *Journal of the American Academy of Psychoanalysis*

J. Amer. Board Fam. Pract. *Journal of American Board of Family Practitioners*

J. Amer. Coll. Hlth. *Journal of American College Health*

J. Amer. Coll. Nutr. *Journal of the American College of Nutrition*

J. Amer. Ger. Soc. *Journal of the American Geriatric Society*

J. Amer. Med. Women's Assoc. *Journal of American Medical Women's Association*

J. Amer. Osteopath Assoc. *Journal of American Osteopath Associates*

J. Amer. Psychiat. Nurs. Assoc. *Journal of the American Psychiatric Nurses Association*

J. Amer. Psychoanal. Assoc. *Journal of the American Psychoanalytical Association*

J. Anx. Dis. *Journal of Anxiety Disorders*

J. App. Psychol. *Journal of Applied Psychology*

J. App. Cog. Psychol. *Journal of Applied Cognitive Pscyhology*

J. Appl. Behav. Anal. *Journal of Applied Behavior Analysis*

J. Appl. Behav. Sci. *Journal of Applied Behavioral Sciences*

J. Appl. Physiol. *Journal of Applied Physiology*

J. Appl. Psychol. *Journal of Applied Psychology*

J. Appl. Rehabil. Counsel. *Journal of Applied Rehavilitation Counseling*

J. Appl. Soc. Psychol. *Journal of Applied Social Psychology*

J. Appl. Soc. Sci. *Journal of Applied Social Sciences*

J. Asthma *Journal of Asthma*

J. Autism Child. Schizo. *Journal of Autism and Childhood Schizopherenia*

J. Autism Dev. Disorders *Journal of Autism and Developmental Disorders*

J. Behav. Decis. Making *Journal of Behavioral Decision Making*

J. Behav. Hlth. Serv. Res. *Journal of Behavioral Health Services and Research*

J. Behav. Ther. Exp. Psychiat. *Journal of Behavior Therapy and Experimental Psychiatry*

J. Black Psychol. *Journal of Black Psychology*

J. Cardiovasc. Pharmacol. Ther. *Journal of Cardiovascular Pharmacology and Therapy*

J. Child Adolecs. Group Ther. *Journal of Child and Adolescence Group Therapy*

J. Child Adol. Psychopharmacol. *Journal of Child and Adolescent Psychopharmacology*

J. Child Psychol. Psychiat. Allied Disc. *Journal of Child Psychology, Psychiatry, and Allied Disciplines*

J. Child Psychol. Psychiat. *Journal of Child Psychology and Psychiatry*

J. Child Sex. Abuse *Journal of Child Sexual Abuse*

J. Clin. Child Adol. Psychol. *Journal of Clinical Child and Adolescent Psychology*

J. Clin. Child Psychol. *Journal of Clinical Child Psychology*

J. Clin. Exp. Neuropsychol. *Journal of Clinical and Experimental Neuropsychology*

J. Clin. Geropsychol. *Journal of Clinical Geropsychology*

J. Clin. Psychiat. *Journal of Clinical Psychiatry*

J. Clin. Psychol. *Journal of Clinical Psychology*

J. Clin. Psychol. Med. Settings *Journal of Clinical Psychology in Medical Settings*

J. Clin. Psychopharmacol. *Journal of Clinical Psychopharmacology*

J. Clin. Exp. Psychopathol. *Journal of Clinical and Experimental Psychopathology*

J. Cog. Psychother. *Journal of Cognitive Psychotherapy*

J. Coll. Student Dev. *Journal of College Student Development*

J. Comm. Psychol. *Journal of Community Psychology*

J. Compar. Physiol. Psychol. *Journal of Comparative and Physiological Psychology*

J. Cons. Clin. Psychol. *Journal of Consulting and Clinical Psychology*

J. Cons. Stud. *Journal of Consciousness Studies*

J. Contemporary Health Law and Policy *The Journal of Contemporary Health Law and Policy*

J. Couns. Dev. *Journal of Counseling & Development*

J. Couns. Psychol. *Journal of Counseling Psychology*

J. Cross-Cult. Psychol. *Journal of Cross-Cultural Psychology*

J. Dev. Behav. Pediatr. *Journal of Development and Behavioral Pediatrics*

J. Dev. Phys. Disabil. *Journal of Developmental and Physical Disabilities*

J. Drug Edu. *Journal of Drug Education*

J. Drug Issues *Journal of Drug Issues*

J. Early Adolescence *Journal of Early Adolescence*

J. Epidemiol. Comm. Hlth. *Journal of Epidemiology and Community Health*

J. Exp. Anal. Behav. *Journal of Experimental Analysis of Behavior*

J. Exp. Child Psychol. *Journal of Experimental Child Psychology*

J. Exp. Psychol. Gen. *Journal of Experimental Psychology General*

J. Exp. Psychol. *Journal of Experimental Psychology*

J. Exp. Soc. Psychol. *Journal of Experimental Social Psychology*

J. Fam. Issues *Journal of Family Issues*

J. Fam. Prac. *Journal of Family Practice*

J. Fam. Psychother. *Journal of Family Psychotherapy*

J. Forensic Sci. *Journal of Forensic Sciences*

J. Gamb. Stud. *Journal of Gambling Studies*

J. Gend. Specif. Med. *Journal of Gender Specific Medicine*

J. Gen. Internal Med. *Journal of General Internal Medicine*

J. Gen. Psychol. *Journal of Genetic Psychology*

J. Ger. *Journal of Gerontology*

J. Ger. A Biol. Sci. Med. Sci. *Journal of Gerontology, A: Biological Science and Medical Science*

J. Ger. B Psychol. Sci. Soc. Sci. *Journal of Gerontology, B. Psychological Science and Social Science*

J. Ger. Psychiat. *Journal of Geriatric Pschiatry*

J. Geriat. Psychiat. Neurol. *Journal of Geriatric Psychiatry and Neurology*

J. History Behav. Sci. *Journal of the History of the Behavioral Sciences*

J. Hist. Neurosci. *Journal of the History of the Neurosciences*

J. Hellenic Psychol. Soc. *Journal of the Hellenic Psychological Society*

J. Hlth. Care Poor Underserved. *Journal of Health Care for the Poor and Underserved*

J. Hlth. Soc. Behav. *Journal of Health and Social Behavior*

J. Homosex. *Journal of Homosexuality*

J. Human. Psychol. *Journal of Humanistic Psychology*

J. Individ. Psychol. *Journal of Individual Psychology*

J. Intell. Disab. Res. *Journal of Intellectual Disability Research*

J. Inter. Neuropsychol. *Journal of the International Neuropsychological Society*

J. Inter. Soc. Life Info. Sci. *Journal of International Society of Life Information Science*

J. Interpers. Violence *Journal of Interpersonal Violence*

J. Law Health *Journal of Law and Health*

J. Learn. Dis. *Journal of Learning Disorders*

J. Marital Fam. Ther. *Journal of Marital and Family Therapy*

J. Marr. Fam. *Journal of Marriage and Family*

J. Med. Genet. *Journal of Medical Genetics*

J. Ment. Hlth. Admin. *Journal of Mental Health Administration*

J. Ment. Hlth. Couns. *Journal of Mental Health Counseling*

J. Ment. Hlth. UK *Journal of Mental Health UK*

J. Ment. Imagery *Journal of Mental Imagery*

J. Mind Behav. *Journal of Mind and Behavior*

J. Nerv. Ment. Dis. *Journal of Nervous and Mental Diseases*

J. Neurochem. *Journal of Neurochemistry*

J. Neurol. Neurosurg. Psychiat. *Journal of Neurology and Neurosurgical Psychiatry*

J. Neuropsych. Clin. Neurosci. *Journal of Neuropsychiatry and Clinical Neurosciences*

J. Neurosci. *Journal of Neuroscience*

J. Neurotrauma *Journal of Neurotrauma*

J. Occup. Med. *Journal of Occupational Medicine*

J. Occup. Hlth. Psychol. *Journal of Occupational Health Psychology*

J. Pediatr. Psychol. *Journal of Pediatric Psychology*

J. Perinat. Med. *Journal of Perinatal Medicine*

J. Pers. Assess. *Journal of Personality Assessment*

J. Pers. Disorders *Journal of Personality Disorders*

J. Pers. Soc. Psychol. *Journal of Personality and Social Psychology*

J. Pharmacol. Exp. Ther. *Journal of Pharmacology and Experimental Therapeutics*

J. Pineal Res. *Journal of Pineal Research*

J. Positive Behav. Interventions *Journal of Positive Behavior Interventions*

J. Prev. Psychiat. *Journal of Preventive Psychiatry*

J. Primary Prev. *Journal of Primary Prevention*

J. Psychoactive Drug. *Journal of Psychoactive Drugs*

J. Psychiat. Law *Journal of Psychiatry and Law*

J. Psychiat. Neurosci. *Journal of Psychiatry & Neuroscience*

J. Psychiatr. Ment. Hlth. Nurs. *Journal of Psychiatric and Mental Health Nursing*

J. Psychiatr. Prac. *Journal of Psychiatric Practice*

J. Psychiatr. Res. *Journal of Psychiatric Research*

J. Psychoact. Drugs. *Journal of Psychoactive Drugs*

J. Psychol. Human Sex. *Journal of Psychology and Human Sexuality*

J. Psychol. *Journal of Psychology*

J. Psychol. Pract. *Journal of Psychological Practice*

J. Psychol. Theol. *Journal of Psychology and Theology*

J. Psychopharmacol. *Journal of Psychopharmacology*

J. Psychopath. Behav. Ass. *Journal of Psychopathology and Behavioral Assessment*

J. Psychosom. Med. *Journal of Psychosomatic Medicine*

J. Psychosom. Res. *Journal of Psychosomatic Research*

J. Psychother. Prac. Res. *Journal of Psychotherapy Practice and Research*

J. Rat.-Emot. & Cog.-Behav. Ther. *Journal of Rational-Emotive & Cognitive-Behavior Therapy*

J. Rehab. *Journal of Rehabilitation*

J. Res. Adol. *Journal of Research on Adolescence*

J. Res. Pers. *Journal of Research in Personality*

J. Rural Commun. Psychol. *Journal of Rural Community Psychology*

J. Sci. Study Religion *Journal for the Scientific Study of Religion*

J. Sex Educ. Ther. *Journal of Sex Education and Therapy*

J. Sex Marital Ther. *Journal of Sex and Marital Therapy*

J. Sex Res. *Journal of Sex Research*

J. Soc. Behav. Pers. *Journal of Social Behavior and Personality*

J. Soc. Clin. Psychol. *Journal of Social and Clinical Psychology*

J. Soc. Issues *Journal of Social Issues*

J. Soc. Pers. Relationships *Journal of Social and Personal Relationships*

J. Soc. Psychol. *Journal of Social Psychology*

J. Sociol. *Journal of Sociology*

J. Sociol. Soc. Welfare *Journal of Sociology and Social Welfare*

J. Spec. Group Work *Journal of Specialists in Group Work*

J. Sport Behav. *Journal of Sport Behavior*
J. Sport Exercise Psychol. *Journal of Sport and Exercise Psychology*
J. Sport. Psychol. *Journal of Sport Psychology*
J. Stud. Alc. *Journal of Studies on Alcohol*
J. Substance Abuse. *Journal of Substance Abuse*
J. Subst. Abuse Treatm. *Journal of Substance Abuse Treatments*
J. Toxicol. Clin. Toxicol. *Journal of Toxicology Clinical Toxicology*
J. Traum. Dissoc. *Journal of Trauma and Dissociation*
J. Traum. Stress. *Journal of Traumatic Stress*
J. Urology *Journal of Urology*
J. Youth Adolescence *Journal of Youth and Adolescence*
JAMA *Journal of the American Medical Association*
Jap. J. Hyp. *Japanese Journal of Hypnosis*
Jpn. J. Psychiatry. *Japanese Journal of Psychiatry*

Law Human Behav. *Law and Human Behavior*
Law Med. Health Care *Law Medicine and Health Care*
Law Psychol. Rev. *Law and Psychology Review*

Marriage Fam. Rev. *Marriage and Family Review*
Med. Anthropol. *Medical Anthropology*
Med. Aspects Human Sex. *Medical Aspects of Human Sexuality*
Med. Sci. Law *Medicine, Science and the Law*
Mem. Cog. *Memory and Cognition*
Ment. Hlth. Religion Cult. *Mental Health, Religion and Culture*
Ment. Physi. Disabil. Law. *Mental and Physical Disability Law*
Ment. Retard. *Mental Retardation*
Ment. Retard. Disabil. Res. Rev. *Mental Retardation and Developmental Disabilities Research Reviews*
Med. J. Austral. *Medical Journal of Australia*
Merrill Palmer Quart. *Merrill Palmer Quarterly*
Military Med. *Military Medicine*
MMW Fortschr. Med. *MMW Fortschritte der Medizin*
Mol. Psychiat. *Molecular Psychiatry.*
Monit. Psychol. *Monitor on Psychology*

Nat. Genet. *Nature Genetics*
Natl. Geogr. *National Geographic Magazine*
Natl. Psychol. *National Psychology*
N. Engl. J. Med. *New England Journal of Medicine*
Ned. Tidjschr. Geneeskd. *Nederlands Tijdschrift voor Geneeskunde*
Nerv. Child. *Nervous Child*
Neurol. Clin. *Neurologic Clinics*
Neurosci. Biobehav. Rev. *Neuroscience and Biobehavioral Reviews*
Neuropsychiat., Neuropsychol., Behav. Neurol. *Neuropsychiatry, Neuropsychology, and Behavioral Neurology*
New Zeal. Med. J. *New Zealand Medical Journal*
NORC *National Opinion Research Center*
Nord. Sex. *Nordisk Sexologi*
NY St. J. Med. *New York State Journal of Medicine*

Obesity Hlth. *Obesity and Health*
Obstet. Gynecol. Clin. North Am. *Obstetrics and Gynecology Clinics of North America*
Omega: J. Death Dying *Omega: Journal of Death and Dying*

Pain Med. *Pain Medicine*
Patient Educ. *Counsel Patient Education and Counseling*
Pediatr. Clin. N. Amer. *Pediatric Clinics of North America*
Percept. Motor Skills *Perceptual and Motor Skills*
Pers. Individ. Diff. *Personality and Individual Differences*

Pers. Soc. Psychol. Bull. *Personality and Social Psychology Bulletin*
Pharmacol. Biochem. Behav. *Pharmacological Biochemical Behavior*
Pharmacol. Rev. *Pharmacological Reviews*
Philos. Psychiat. Psychol. *Philosophy, Psychiatry, and Psychology*
Physician Sports Med. *The Physician and Sports Medicine*
Physiol. Behav. *Physiology and Behavior*
Police J. *Police Journal*
Postgrad. Med. J. *Postgraduate Medical Journal*
Prevent. Sci. *Prevention Science*
Proc. Natl. Acad. Sci. USA *Proceedings of the National Academy of Science USA*
Proc. R. Soc. Med. *Proceedings of the Royal Society of Medicine*
Prim. Care Psychiat. *Primary Care Psychiatry*
Profess. Psychol.: Res. Pract. *Professional Psychology: Research and Practice*
Profess. Psychologist. *Professional Psychologist*
Profess. School Couns. *Professional School Counseling*
Prog. Neuropsychopharmacol. Biol. Psychiat. *Progressive Neuropsychopharmacological Biological Psychiatry*
Prog. Neuropsychopharmacol. *Progressive Neuropsychopharmacology*
Psychiat. Clin. Neurosci. *Psychiatry and Clinical Neurosciences*
Psychiat. Genet. *Psychiatric Genetics*
Psychiat. & Psychoanal. *Psychiatry and Psychoanalysis*
Psychiat. Res. *Psychiatry Research*
Psychiat. Res.: Neuroimaging *Psychiatric Research and Neuroimaging*
Psychiatr. Ann. *Psychiatric Annals*
Psychiatr. Bull. *Psychiatric Bulletin*
Psychiatr. Clin. N. Amer. *Psychiatric Clinics of North America*
Psychiatr. Hosp. *Psychiatric Hospital*
Psychiatr. J. Univ. Ottawa *Psychiatric Journal of the University of Ottawa*
Psychiatr. News. *Psychiatric News*
Psychiatr. Quart. *Psychiatric Quarterly*
Psychiatr. Rehab. J. *Psychiatric Rehabilitation Journal*
Psychiatr. Serv. *Psychiatric Services*
Psychiatr. Times *Psychiatric Times*
Psychiatry, Psychol. Law. *Psychiatry Psychology and Law*
Psychoanal. Inq. *Psychoanalytic Inquiry*
Psychoanal. Psychol. *Psychoanalytic Psychology*
Psychoanalytic Psychother. *Psychoanalytic Psychotherapy*
Psychoanal. Q. *Psychoanalytic Quarterly*
Psychoanal. Rev. *Psychoanalytic Review*
Psychohist. Rev. *Psychohistory Review*
Psychol. Addict. Behav. *Psychology of Addictive Behavior*
Psychol. Aging *Psychology and Aging*
Psychol. Assess. *Psychological Assessment*
Psychol. Bull. *Psychological Bulletin*
Psychol. Crime Law *Psychology, Crime, and Law*
Psychol. Health Med. *Psychology Health and Medicine*
Psychology: J. of Human Behav. *Psychology: A Journal of Human Behavior*
Psychol. Med. *Psychological Medicine*
Psychol. Psychother.: Theory, Res. Prac. *Psychology and Psychotherapy Theory Research and Practice*
Psychol. Pub. Pol. Law *Psychology Public Policy and Law*
Psychol. Rec. *Psychological Record*
Psychol. Rep. *Psychological Reports*
Psychol. Rev. *Psychological Review*
Psychol. Schools *Psychology in the Schools*
Psychol. Sci. *Psychological Science*
Psychol. Sci. Pub. Interest *Psychological Science in the Public Interest*

Psychol. Today *Psychology Today*
Psychol. Women Quart. *Psychology of Women Quarterly*
Psychopharmacol. Bull. *Psychopharmacology Bulletin*
Psychopharmacology (Berl.) *Psychopharmacology (Berlin)*
Psychosom. J. Cons. Liaison Psychiat. *Psychosomatics: Journal of Consultation Liaison Psychiatry*
Psychosom. Med. *Psychosomatic Medicine*
Psychother. Priv. Prac. *Psychotherapy in Private Practice*
Psychother. Psychosom. *Psychotherapy and Psychosomatics*
Psychother. Res. *Psychotherapy Research*
Psychother. Theory Res. Prac. *Psychotherapy: Theory, Research, and Practice*
Pub. Hlth. Rep. *Public Health Reports*
Public Pers. Manag. *Public Personnel Management*

Quart. J. Stud. Alcohol. *Quarterly Journal on the Studies of Alcoholism*

Rehab. Couns. Bull. *Rehabilitation Counseling Bulletin*
Rehab. Nursing *Rehabilitation Nursing*
Rehab. Psychol. *Rehabilitation Psychology*
Remed. Spec. Educ. *Remedial and Special Education*
Reprod. Nutr. Dev. *Reproductive and Nutritional Development*
Res. Aging *Research on Aging*
Res.Dev. Disabil. *Research in Developmental Disabilities*
Res. Nursing Hlth. *Research in Nursing and Health*
Res. Soc. Work Prac. *Research on Social Work Practice*
Rev. Bras. Psicanal *Revista Brasileira De Psicanalise*
Roper Rev. *Roper Review*

S. Afr. J. Psychol. *South African Journal of Psychology*
Scand. J. Psychol. *Scandinavian Journal of Psychology*
Scand. J. Work Envir. Hlth. *Scandinavian Journal of Work and Environment Health*
Schizo. Bull. *Schizophrenic Bulletin*
Schizo. Res. *Schizophrenia Research*
Sci. News *Science News*
Scientif. Amer. *Scientific American*
Sem. in Neuro. *Seminars in Neurology*
Sex. Abuse J. Res. Treat. *Sexual Abuse Journal of Research and Treatment*
Sex. Disability *Sexual Disability*
Sex. Marital Ther. *Sexual and Marital Therapy*
Sex. Relat. Ther. *Sexual and Relationship Therapy*
Sleep Hyp. *Sleep and Hypnosis*
Soc. Behav. Pers. *Social Behavior and Personality*
Soc. Forces *Social Forces*
Soc. Indicators Res. *Social Indicators Research*
Soc. Psychiat. *Social Psychiatry*
Soc. Psychiat. Psychiatr. Epidemiol. *Social Psychiatry and Psychiatric Epidemiology*
Soc. Sci. Med. *Social Science and Medicine*
Soc. Sci. Res. *Social Science Research*
Soc. Work *Social Work*
Soc. Work Hlth. Care *Social Work Health Care*
Sport Psychol. *Sport Psychologist*
Subs. Abuse *Substance Abuse*
Substance Use Misuse *Substance Use and Misuse*
Suic. Life-Threat. Behav. *Suicide and Life-Threatening Behavior*

Tex. Mon. Mag. *Texas Monthly Magazine*
Topics Early Childhood Spec. Ed. *Topics in Early Childhood Special Education*
Transcult. Psychiatr. Res. Rev. *Transcultural Psychiatric Research Review*
Transplant Proc. *Transplant Proceedings*

Trends Cell Biol. *Trends in Cell Biology*
Trend Cog. Sci. *Trends in Cognitive Sciences*
Trends Neurosci. *Trends in Neuroscience*
Trends Pharmacol. Sci. *Trends in Pharmacological Sciences*

Vet. Hum. Toxicol. *Veterinary and Human Toxicology*

Women Hlth. *Women & Health*

Zeitschr. Klin. Psychol. Psychother.: Forsch. Prax. *Zeitschrift Fuer Klinische Psychologie und Psychotherapie Forschung und Praxis*

References

AA (Alcoholics Anonymous) World Services (2003). *About A.A.*

AAMR (American Association on Mental Retardation). (1992). *Mental retardation: Definition, classification, and systems of supports* (9th ed.). Washington, DC: Author.

Aasland, O. G., Ekeberg, O., & Schweder, T. (2001). Suicide rates from 1960 to 1989 in Norwegian physicians compared with other educational groups. *Soc. Sci. Med., 52(2),* 259–265.

Abdulhamid, I. (2002). Munchausen by proxy. *eMed. J., 3(1).*

Abel, G. G., Becker, J. V., & Cunningham-Rathner, J. (1984). Complications, consent, and cognitions in sex between children and adults. *Inter. J. Law Psychiat., 7,* 89–103.

Abel, G. G., Jordan, A., Hand, C. G., Holland, L. A., & Phipps, A. (2001). Classification models of child molesters utilizing the Abel Assessment for child sexual abuse interest. *Child Abuse Negl., 25(5),* 703–718.

Abel, G. G., & Osborn, C. (1992). The paraphilias: The extent and nature of sexually deviant and criminal behavior. *Psychiatr. Clin. N. Amer., 15(3),* 675–687.

Abraham, K. (1911). Notes on the psychoanalytic investigation and treatment of manic-depressive insanity and allied conditions. In *Selected papers on psychoanalysis* (pp. 137–156). New York: Basic Books, 1960.

Abraham, K. (1916). The first pregenital stage of the libido. In *Selected papers on psychoanalysis* (pp. 248–279). New York: Basic Books, 1960.

Abraham, S., & Llewellyn-Jones, D. (1984). *Eating disorders: The facts.* New York: Oxford University Press.

Abram, K. M., & Teplin, L. A. (1990). Drug disorder, mental illness, and violence. *Nat. Inst. Drug Abuse Res. Monogr. Ser., 103,* 222–238.

Abrams, K. M., & Robinson, G. E. (1998). Stalking: Part I. An overview of the problem. *Canad. J. Psychiat., 43(5),* 473–476.

Abramson, L. Y., Alloy, L. B., Hankin, B. L., Haeffel, G. J., MacCoon, D. G., & Gibb, B. E. (2002). Cognitive vulnerability—Stress models of depression in a self-regulatory and psychobiological context. In I. H. Gotlib & C. L. Hammen (Eds.), *Handbook of depression* (pp. 268–294). New York: Guilford Press.

Abramson, L. Y., Metalsky, G. I., & Alloy, L. B. (1989). Hopelessness depression: A theory-based subtype of depression. *Psychol. Rev., 96(2),* 358–372.

Abramson, L. Y., Seligman, M. E., & Teasdale, J. D. (1978). Learned helplessness in humans: Critique and reformulation. *J. Abnorm. Psychol., 87(1),* 49–74.

Acocella, J. (1999). *Creating hysteria: Women and multiple personality disorder.* San Francisco: Jossey-Bass.

Adam, K. S., Bouckoms, A., & Streiner, D. (1982). Parental loss and family stability in attempted suicide. *Arch. Gen. Psychiat., 39 (9),* 1081–1085.

Adams, W. L., & Cox, N. S. (1997). Epidemiology of problem drinking among elderly people. In A. Gurnack (Ed.), *Older adults' misuse of alcohol, medicines, and other drugs.* New York: Springer.

Ader, R., Felten, D. L., & Cohen, N. (Eds.). (2001). *Psychoneuroimmunology* (3rd ed., Vols. 1 & 2). San Diego, CA: Academic Press.

Adler, G. (2000). The alliance and the more disturbed patient. In S. T. Levy et al. (Eds.), *The therapeutic alliance. Workshop series of the American Psychoanalytic Association, Monograph 9.* Madison, CT: International Universities Press.

Adler, J. (1998, May 4). Take a pill and call me tonight. *Newsweek,* p. 48.

Adler, T. (1992). Prenatal cocaine exposure has subtle, serious effects. *APA Monitor, 23 (11),* 17.

Advertising Council and Caravan Opinion Research, (1995).

Agras, W. S. (1995). Treatment of eating disorders. In A. F. Schatzberg & C. B. Nemeroff (Eds.), *The American Psychiatric Press textbook of psychopharmacology.* Washington, DC: American Psychiatric Press.

Agras, W. S., Sylvester, D., & Oliveau, D. (1969). The epidemiology of common fears and phobias. *Comprehen. Psychiat., 10(2),* 151–156.

Aiken, L. R. (1985). *Psychological testing and assessment* (5th ed.). Boston: Allyn & Bacon.

Aikins, D. E., & Craske, M. G. F. (2001). Cognitive theories of generalized anxiety disorder. *Psychiatr. Clin. North Am., 24(1),* 57–74.

Akechi, T., Okamura, H., Yamawaki, S., & Uchitomi, Y. (2001). Why do some cancer patients with depression desire an early death and others do not? *Psychosomatics, 42(2),* 141–145.

Akhtar, S., Wig, N. H., Verma, V. K., Pershod, D., & Verma, S. K. (1975). A phenomenological analysis of symptoms in obsessive-compulsive neuroses. *Brit. J. Psychiat., 127,* 342–348.

Albano, A. M., Chorpita, B. F., & Barlow, D. H. (2003). Childhood anxiety disorders. In E. J. Mash & R. A. Barkley (Eds.), *Child psychopathology* (2nd ed.) New York: Guilford Press.

Albano, A. M., & Kendall, P. C. (2002). Cognitive behavioural therapy for children and adolescents with anxiety disorders: Clinical research advances. *Intern. Rev. Psychiat., 14(2),* 129–134.

Albertini, R. S., & Phillips, K. A. (1999). Thirty-three cases of body dysmorphic disorder in children and adolescents. *J. Amer. Acad. Child Adol. Psychiat., 38(4),* 453–459.

Aldridge, D. (1998). *Suicide: The tragedy of hopelessness.* London: Jessica Kingsley Pub.

Alegria, M., Kessler, R. C., Bijl, R., Lin, E., Heeringa, S. G., Takeuchi, D. T., & Kolody, B. (2000). Comparing data on mental health service use between countries. In G. Andrews & S. Henderson (Eds.), *Unmet need in psychiatry: Problems, resources, responses* (pp. 97–118). New York: Cambridge University Press.

Alexander, J. F., Sexton, T. L., & Robbins, M. S. (2002). The developmental status of family therapy in family psychology intervention science. In H. A.Liddle, D. A. Santiseban, R. F. Levant, & J. H. Bray (Eds.), *Family psychology: Science-based interventions.* (pp. 17–40) Washington, DC: APA.

Allison, R. B. (1978). A rational psychotherapy plan for multiplicity. *Svensk Tidskrift Hyp., 3,* 9–16.

Allan, C. A., Smith, I., & Mellin, M. (2000). Detoxification from alcohol: A comparison of home detoxification and hospital-based day patient care. *Alcohol Alcoholism, 35(1),* 66–69.

Allan, C. A., Smith, I., & Mellin, M. (2002). Changes in psychological symptoms during ambulant detoxification. *Alcohol Alcoholism, 37(3),* 241–244.

Allard, R., Marshall, M., & Plante, M. C. (1992). Intensive follow-up does not decrease the risk of repeat suicide attempts. *Suic. Life-Threat. Behav., 22,* 303–314.

Allbright, A., Levy, F., & Wagle, N. C. (2002). Outpatient civil commitment laws: An overview. *Ment. Physi. Disabil. Law. 26(2),* 179–182.

Allen, J. J. B. (2002). The role of psychophysiology in clinical assessment: ERPs in the evaluation of memory. *Psychophysiology, 39(3),* 261–280.

Allen, L. A., Woolfolk, R. L., Lehrer, P. M., Gara, M. A., & Escobar, J. I. (2001). Cognitive behavior therapy for somatization disorder: A preliminary investigation. *J. Behav. Ther. Exp. Psychiat., 32(2),* 53–62.

Allsop, S., Saunders, B., & Phillips, M. (2000). The process of relapse in severely dependent male problem drinkers. *Addiction, 95(1),* 95–106.

Althof, S. E. (1995). Pharmacologic treatment of rapid ejaculation. Special issue: Clinical sexuality. *Psychiatr. Clin. N. Amer., 18(1),* 85–94.

Althof, S. E., Levine, S. B., Corty, E., Risen, C., & Stern, E. (1994, March). *The role of clomipramine in the treatment of premature ejaculation.* Paper presented at the 16th annual meeting of the Society for Sex Therapy and Research.

Althof, S. E., & Seftel, A. D. (1995). The evaluation and management of erectile dysfunction. *Psychiatr. Clin. N. Amer., 18(1),* 171–191.

Altman, C. A. (2001). Effects of selective-serotonin reuptake inhibitors on sexual function. *J. Clin. Psychopharmacol., 21(2),* 241–242.

Alvarez, E., Bobes, J., Gomez, J. C., Sacristan, J. A., Canas, F., Carrasco, J. L., Lascon, J., Gibert, J., & Gutierrez, M. (2003). Safety of olanzapine versus conventional antipsychotics in the treatment of patients with acute schizophrenia: A naturalistic study. *Eur. Neuropsychopharmacology, 13(1),* 38–48.

Alzheimer's Association. (1997, February 17). Survey: Stress on Alzheimer caregivers. Cited in *USA Today,* p. 1D.

Amass, L., Kamien, J. B., & Mikulich, S. K. (2000). Efficacy of daily and alternate-day dosing regimens with the combination buprenorphine-naloxone tablet. *Drug Alc. Dep., 58(1–2),* 143–152.

Americans' Use of Time Project. (1995). Survey. As cited in J. P. Robinson & G. Godbey, The great American slowdown. *American Demographics, 13(6),* 34–41.

Amminger, G. P., Pape, S., Rock, D., Roberts, S. A., Ott, S. L., Squires-Wheeler, E., Kestenbaum, C., & Erlenmeyer, K. L. (1999). Relationship between childhood behavioral disturbance and later schizophrenia in the New York High-Risk Project. *Amer. J. Psychiat., 156(4),* 525–530.

Andersen, A. E. (1985). *Practical comprehensive treatment of anorexia nervosa and bulimia.* Baltimore: Johns Hopkins University Press.

Anderson, D. (1994). *Breaking the tradition on college campuses: Reducing drug and alcohol misuse.* Fairfax, VA: George Mason University Press.

Anderson, K. G., Sankis, L. M., & Widiger, T. A. (2001). Pathology versus statistical infrequency: Potential sources of gender bias in personality disorder criteria. *J. Nerv. Ment. Dis., 189(10),* 661–668.

Anderson, S. C. (1993). Anti-stalking laws: Will they ccccurb the erotomanic's obsessive pursuit? *Law Psychol. Rev., 17,* 171–191.

Andrade, V. M. (1996). Superego, narcissism and culture. *Revista Brasileira de Psicanalise, 30*(2), 385–405.

Andrasik, F. (2000). Biofeedback. In D. I. Mostofsky & D. H. Barlow (Eds.), *The management of stress and anxiety in medical disorders.* Needham Heights, MA: Allyn & Bacon.

Andreasen, N. C. (2001). *Brave new brain: Conquering mental illness in the era of the genome.* New York: Oxford University Press.

Andresen, J. (2000). Meditation meets behavioral medicine: The story of experimental research on meditation. *J. Consciousness. Stud., 7*(11–12), 17–73.

Angier, N. (2001, May 20). Bully for you: Why push comes to shove. *New York Times,* Sect. 4, p. 1.

Anonymous. (1996). First person account: Social, economic, and medical effects of schizophrenia. *Schizo. Bull., 22*(1), 183.

Anooshian, J., Streltzer, J., & Goebert, D. (1999). Effectiveness of a psychiatric pain clinic. *Psychosomatics, 40*(3), 226–232.

Anthony, J. C., Arria, A. M., & Johnson, E. O. (1995). Epidemiological and public health issues for tobacco, alcohol, and other drugs. In J. M. Oldham & M. B. Riba (Eds.), *American Psychiatric Press review of psychiatry* (Vol. 14). Washington, DC: American Psychiatric Press.

Antony, M. M., & Barlow, D. H. (2002). Specific phobias. In D. H. Barlow (Ed.), *Anxiety and its disorders: The nature and treatment of anxiety and panic* (2nd ed., pp. 380–417). New York: Guilford Press.

Antony, M. M., & Swinson, R. P. (2000). *Phobic disorders and panic in adults: A guide to assessment and treatment.* Washington, DC: American Psychological Association.

APA (American Psychiatric Association). (1994). *Diagnostic and statistical manual of mental disorders* (4th ed.). Washington, DC: Author.

APA (American Psychiatric Association). (1995). Survey: Healthy mind over matter. In *USA Today,* May 23, 1995, p. 1D.

APA (American Psychological Association). (1992). Ethical principles of psychologists and code of conduct. *APA.* Retrieved December 24, 2002, from www.apa.org/ethics/code1992.html

APA (American Psychological Association). (1993). *Practice guideline for major depressive disorder in adults.* Washington, DC: Author.

APA (American Psychological Association). (1996). Interim report of the working group on investigation of memories of childhood abuse. In K. Pezdek & W. P. Banks (Eds.), *The recovered memory/false memory debate.* San Diego: Academic Press.

APA (American Psychological Association). (2000). *DSM-IV text revision.* Washington, DC: Author.

APA (American Psychological Association). (2002). Ethical principles of psychologists and code of conduct. *APA.* Retrieved December 24, 2002, from www.apa.org/ethics/code2002.html

Archer, D., & McDaniel, P. (1995). Violence and gender: Differences and similarities across societies. In R. B. Ruback & N. A. Weiner (Eds.), *Interpersonal violent behaviors: Social and cultural aspects.* New York: Springer.

Arieti, S. (1974). *Interpretation of schizophrenia.* New York: Basic Books.

Arieti, S., & Bemporad, J. (1978). *Severe and mild depression: The psychotherapeutic approach.* New York: Basic Books.

Aring, C. D. (1974). The Gheel experience: Eternal spirit of the chainless mind! *JAMA, 230*(7), 998–1001.

Aring, C. D. (1975). Gheel: The town that cares. *Fam. Hlth., 7*(4), 54–55, 58, 60.

Asaad, G. (2000). Somatization disorder. In M. Hersen & M. Biaggio (Eds.), *Effective brief therapies: A clinician's guide* (pp. 179–190). San Diego, CA: Academic Press.

Asarnow, J. R., Asarnow, R. F., Hornstein, N., & Russell, A. (1991). Childhood-onset schizophrenia: Developmental perspectives on schizophrenic disorders. In E. F. Walker (Ed.), *Schizophrenia: A life-course developmental perspective.* San Diego: Academic Press.

Asberg, M., Traskman, L., & Thoren, P. (1976). 5 HIAA in the cerebrospinal fluid: A biochemical suicide predictor? *Arch. Gen. Psychiat., 33*(10), 1193–1197.

Aserinsky, E., & Kleitman, N. (1953). Eye movements during sleep. *Fed. Process, 13,* 6–7.

Ash, R. (1998). *The top 10 of everything 1999.* New York: DK Publishing.

Ash, R. (1999). *Fantastic book of 1001 facts.* New York: DK Publishing.

Ash, R. (2001). *The top 10 of everything 2002* (American ed.). New York: DK Publishing.

Ashton, C. H. (2001). Pharmacology and effects of cannabis: A brief review. *Brit. J. Psychiat., 178,* 101–106.

Ashton, J. R., & Donnan, S. (1981). Suicide by burning as an epidemic phenomenon: An analysis of 82 deaths and inquests in England and Wales in 1978–9. *Psychol. Med., 11*(4), 735–739.

Asimov, I. (1997). *Isaac Asimov's book of facts.* New York: Random House (Wings Books).

Auchincloss, E. L., & Weiss, R. W. (1992). Paranoid character and the intolerance of indifference. *J. Amer. Psychoanal. Assoc., 40*(4), 1013–1037.

Ayalon, L., & Huyck, M. H. (2001). Latino caregivers of relatives with Alzheimer's disease. *Clin. Geront., 24*(3–4), 93–106.

Ayalon, L., & Young, M. A. (2003). A comparison of depressive symptoms in African Americans and Caucasian Americans. *J. Cross-Cult. Psychol. 34*(1), 111–124.

Ayd, F. J., Jr. (1956). A clinical evaluation of Frenquel. *J. Nerv. Ment. Dis., 124,* 507–509.

Ayllon, T. (1963). Intensive treatment of psychotic behavior by stimulus satiation and food reinforcement. *Behav. Res. Ther., 1,* 53–62.

Ayllon, T., & Michael, J. (1959). The psychiatric nurse as a behavioural engineer. *J. Exp. Anal. Behav., 2,* 323–334.

Ayoub, C. C., Deutsch, R. M., & Kinscherff, R. (2000). Munchausen by proxy: Definitions, identification, and evaluation. In R. M. Reece (Ed.), *Treatment of child abuse: Common ground for mental health, medical, and legal practitioners* (pp. 213– 226). Baltimore: Johns Hopkins University Press.

Ayoub, C. C., Deutsch, R. M., & Kinscherff, R. (2000). Psychosocial management issues in Munchausen by proxy. In R. M. Reese (Ed.), *Treatment of child abuse: Common ground for mental health, medical, and legal practitioners* (pp. 226–235). Baltimore: Johns Hopkins University Press.

Azar, B. (1995). Mental disabilities and the brain-gene link. *APA Monitor, 26*(12), 18.

Azar, S.T., Ferraro, M.H., & Breton, S.J. (1998). Intrafamilial child maltreatment. In T.H. Ollendick & M. Hersen (Eds.), *Handbook of child psychopathology* (3rd ed.). New York: Plenum.

Azar, S. T., & Siegal, B. R. (1990). Behavioral treatment of child abuse: A developmental perspective. *Behav. Mod., 14* (3), 279–300.

Azima, F. J. C. (1993). Group psychotherapy with personality disorders. In H. I. Kaplan & B. J. Sadock (Eds.), *Comprehensive group psychotherapy* (3rd ed.). Baltimore: Williams & Wilkins.

Bach, A.K., Wincze, J.P., & Barlow, D.H. (2001). Sexual dysfunction. In D.H. Barlow (Ed.), *Clinical handbook of psychological disorders: A step-by-step treatment manual* (3rd ed., pp. 562–608). New York: Guilford Press.

Backmund, M., Meyer, K., Eichenlaub, D., & Schuetz, C.G. (2001). Predictors for completing an inpatient detoxification program among intravenous heroin users, methadone substituted and codeine substituted patients. *Drug and Alcohol Dependence, 64*(2), 173–180.

Badner, J. A., & Gershon, E. S. (2002). Meta-analysis of whole-genome linkage scans of bipolar disorder and schizophrenia. *Mol. Psychiat.,7*(4), 405–411.

Baer, L. (2001). *The imp of the mind: Exploring the silent epidemic of obsessive bad thoughts.* New York: Dutton/Penguin Books.

Bagby, E. (1922). The etiology of phobias. *J. Abnorm. Psychol., 17,* 16–18.

Baggot, M., & Mendelson, J. (2001). Does MDMA cause brain damage? In J. Holland (Ed.), *Ecstasy: The complete guide: A comprehensive look at the risks and benefits of MDMA* (pp. 110–145). Rochester, VT: Park Street Press.

Bagley, C. (1991). Poverty and suicide among Native Canadians: A replication. *Psychol. Rep., 69* (1), 149–150.

Bahrick, H. (1996, January). Cited in G. Neimeyer, Anecdotes for education. *Newsletter for Abnormal Psychology.*

Bailey, J. M., & Pillard, R. C. (1991). A genetic study of male sexual orientation. *Arch Gen Psychiatry, 48*(12), 1089–1096.

Bailey, J. M., Pillard, R. C., Neale, M. C., et al. (1993). Heritable factors influence sexual orientation in women. *Arch. Gen. Psychiat., 50*(3), 217–223.

Bakken, J., Miltenberger, R. G., & Schauss, S. (1993). Teaching parents with mental retardation: Knowledge versus skills. *Amer. J. Ment. Retard., 97*(4), 405–417.

Bal, S., De Bourdeaudhuij, I., Crombez, G., & Van Oost, P. (2004). Differences in trauma symptoms and family functioning in intra- and extra-familial sexually abused adolescents. *J. Interpers. Violence, 19*(1), 108–123.

Baldessarini, R. J., Tondo, L., & Hennen, J. (1999). Effects of lithium treatment and its discontinuation on suicidal behavior in bipolar manic-depressive disorders. *J. Clin. Psychiat., 60*(Suppl. 2), 77–84.

Baldwin, S., & Oxlad, M. (2000). *Electroshock and minors: A fifty-year review.* Westport, CT: Greenwood.

Ball, S. G., Baer, L., & Otto, M. W. (1996). Symptom subtypes of obsessive-compulsive disorder in behavioral treatment studies: A quantitative review. *Behav. Res. Ther., 34*(1), 47–51.

Ballenger, J. C. (1998). Treatment of panic disorder in the general medical setting. *J. Psychosom. Res., 44*(1), 5–15.

Bancroft, J. (1989). *Human sexuality and its problems.* New York: Churchill-Livingstone.

Bandura, A. (1971). Psychotherapy based upon modeling principles. In A. E. Bergin & S. L. Garfield (Eds.), *Handbook of psychotherapy and behavior change.* New York: Wiley.

Bandura, A. (1971). Vicarious and self-reinforcement processes. In R. Glaser (Ed.), *The nature of reinforcement.* New York: Academic Press.

Bandura, A. (1977). Self-efficacy: Toward a unifying theory of behavioral change. *Psychol. Rev., 84*(2), 191–215.

Bandura, A., Adams, N. E., & Beyer, J. (1977). Cognitive processes mediating behavioral change. *J. Pers. Soc. Psychol., 35* (3), 125–139.

Bandura, A., & Rosenthal, T. (1966). Vicarious classical conditioning as a function of arousal level. *J. Pers. Soc. Psychol., 3,* 54–62.

Bandura, A., Roth, D., & Ross, S. (1963). Imitation of film-mediated aggressive models. *J. Abnorm. Soc. Psychol., 66,* 3–11.

Banerjee, S., & Macdonald, A. (1996). Mental disorder in an elderly home care population: Associations with health and social service use. *Brit. J. Psychiat., 168,* 750–756.

Banister, P., Burman, E., Parker, I., Taylor, M., & Tindall, C. (1994). *Qualitative methods in psychology: A research guide.* Buckingham, UK: Open University Press.

Barber, A. (1999, March). HerZines. Some yet-to-be exploited niches in the women's magazine market. *American Demographics.*

Barber, T. X. (1984). Hypnosis, deep relaxation, and active relaxation: Data, theory and clinical applications. In F. L. Woolfolk & P. M. Lehrer (Eds.), *Principles and practice of stress management.* New York: Guilford Press.

Barber, T. X. (1993). Hypnosuggestive approaches to stress reduction: Data, theory, and clinical applications. In P. M. Lehrer & R. L. Woolfolk (Eds.), *Principles and practice of stress management* (2nd ed.). New York: Guilford Press.

Barker, C., Pistrang, N., & Elliott, R. (1994). *Research methods in clinical and counseling psychology.* Chichester, England: Wiley.

Barkley, R. A. (1998). *Attention-deficit hyperactivity disorder: A handbook for diagnosis and treatment* (2nd ed.). New York: Guilford Press.

Barkley, R. A. (1998). Attention-deficit hyperactivity disorder. In E. J. Mash & R. A. Barkley (Eds.), *Treatment of childhood disorders* (2nd ed.). New York: Guilford Press.

Barkley, R. A. (Ed.) (2002). Taking charge of ADHD: The complete authoritative guide for parents, revised edition. *J. Amer. Acad. Child Adol. Psychiat., 41*(1), 101–102.

Barlow, D. H. (Ed.). (2001). *Clinical handbook of psychological disorders: A step-by step treatment manual* (3rd ed.). New York: Guilford Press.

Barlow, D. H. (Ed.) (2002). *Anxiety and its disorders: The nature and treatment of anxiety and panic* (2nd ed.). New York: Guilford Press.

Barlow, D. H., Gorman, J. M., Shear, M. K., & Woods, S. W. (2000). Cognitive-behavioral therapy, imipramine, or their combination for panic disorder: A randomized controlled trial. *JAMA, 283*(19), 2529–2536.

Barlow, D. H., Raffa, S. D., & Cohen, E. M. (2002). Psychosocial treatments for panic disorders, phobias, and generalized anxiety disorder. In P. E. Nathan & J. M. Gorman (Eds.), *A guide to treatments that work* (2nd ed., pp. 301–335). London: Oxford University Press.

Barnes, G. E., & Prosen, H. (1985). Parental death and depression. *J. Abnorm. Psychol., 94*(1), 64–69.

Barnier, A. (2002). Remembering and forgetting autobiographical events: Instrumental uses of hypnosis. *Contemp. Hyp., 19*(2), 51–61.

Baroff, G. S., & Olley, J. G. (1999). *Mental retardation: Nature, cause, and management* (3rd ed.). Philadelphia: Brunner/Mazel.

Baron, M. (2002). Manic-depression genes and the new millennium: Poised for discovery. *Mol. Psychiat., 7*(4), 342–358.

Barrett, P. M., Dadds, M. R., & Rapee, R. M. (1996). Family treatment of childhood anxiety: A controlled trial. *J. Cons. Clin. Psychol., 64*(2), 333–342.

Barrett, P. M., Rapee, R. M., Dadds, M. M., & Ryan, S. M. (1996). Family enhancement of cognitive style in anxious and aggressive children. *J. Abnorm. Child Psychol., 24*(2), 187–203.

Barrett, P. M., & Shortt, A. L. (2003). Parental involvement in the treatment of anxious children. In A. E. Kazdin & J. R. Weisz (Eds.), *Evidence-based psychotherapies for children and adolescents.* New York: Guilford Press.

Barrington, M. R. (1980). Apologia for suicide. In M. P. Battin & D. J. Mayo (Eds.), *Suicide: The philosophical issues.* New York: St. Martin's Press.

Bartholomew, K. (2000). Clinical protocol. *Psychoanal. Inq., 20*(2), 227–248.

Bartholomew, K., Kwong, M. J., & Hart, S. D. (2001). Attachment. In W. J. Livesley (Ed.), *Handbook of personality disorders: Theory, research, and treatment* (pp. 196–230). New York: Guilford Press.

Bartrop, R. W., Lockhurst, E., Lazarus, L., Kiloh, L. G., & Penny, R. (1977). Depressed lymphocyte function after bereavement. *Lancet, 1,* 834–836.

Baruss, I. (2003). Dreams. In I. Baruss, *Alterations of consciousness: An empirical analysis for social scientists.* Washington, DC: American Psychological Association.

Basson, R., Berman, J., Burnett, A., Derogatis, L., Ferguson, J., Fourcroy, J., Goldstein, I., Graziottin, A., Heiman, J., Laan, E., Leiblum, S., Padma-Nathan, H., Rosen, R., Segraves K., Segraves, R. T., Shabsigh, R., Sipski, M., Wagner, G., & Whipple, B. (2001). Report of the International Consensus Development Conference on Female Dysfunction: Definitions and classifications. *J. Sex Marital Ther., 27*(2), 83–94.

Bastiani, A. M., Altemus, M., Pigott, T. A., Rubenstein, C., et al. (1996). Comparison of obsessions and compulsions in patients with anorexia nervosa and obsessive-compulsive disorder. *Biol. Psychiat., 39,* 966–969.

Bates, G. W., Thompson, J. C., & Flanagan, C. (1999). The effectiveness of individual versus group induction of depressed mood. *J. Psychol., 133*(3), 245–252.

Baucom, D. H., Epstein, N., & Gordon, K. C. (2000). Marital therapy: Theory, practice, and empirical status. In C. R. Snyder & R. E. Ingram (Eds.), *Handbook of psychological change: Psychotherapy processes & practices for the 21st century* (pp. 280–308). New York: Wiley.

Baucom, D. H., Shoham, V., Mueser, K. T., Daiuto, A. D., & Stickle, T. R. (1998). Empirically supported couple and family interventions for marital distress and adult mental health problems. *J. Cons. Clin. Psychol., 66*(1), 53–88.

Baum, A. (1990). Stress, intrusive imagery, and chronic stress. *Hlth. Psychol., 9,* 653–675.

Baum, A., Gatchel, R. J., & Schaeffer, M. (1983). Emotional, behavioural and physiological effects of chronic stress at Three Mile Island. *J. Cons. Clin. Psychol., 51,* 565–572.

Baum, A., Revenson, T. A., & Singer, J. E. (2001). *Handbook of health psychology.* Mahwah, NJ: Erlbaum.

Baxter, L. R., Jr., Clark, E. C., Iqbal, M., & Ackermann, R. F. (2001). Cortical-subcortical systems in the mediation of obsessive-compulsive disorder: Modeling the brain's mediation of a classic "neurosis." In D. G. Lichter & J. L. Cummings (Eds.), *Frontal-subcortical circuits in psychiatric and neurological disorders* (pp. 207–230). New York: Guilford Press.

Baxter, L. R., Schwartz, J. M., Bergman, K. S., Szuba, M. P., Guze, B. H., Mazziotta, J. C.,

Alazraki, A., Selin, C. E., Ferng, H. K., Munford, P., & Phelps, M. E. (1992). Caudate glucose metabolic rate changes with both drug and behavior therapy for obsessive-compulsive disorder. *Arch. Gen. Psychiat., 49,* 681–689.

Baxter, L. R., Schwartz, J. M., Guze, B. H., Bergman, K., et al. (1990). PET imaging in obsessive compulsive disorder with and without depression. Symposium: Serotonin and its effects on human behavior (1989, Atlanta, GA). *J. Clin. Psychiat., 51*(Suppl.), 61–69.

Beach, S. R. H., & Jones, D. J. (2002). Marital and family therapy for depression in adults. In I. H. Gotlib & C. L. Hammen (Eds.), *Handbook of depression* (pp. 422–440). New York: Guilford Press.

Beadry, M. (2002). Profiles: Guerlain Chicherit. Retrieved October 17, 2002, http://www.freezeonline.com.

Beaty, L. A. (1999). *Identity development of homosexual youth and parental and familial influences on the coming out process.* Chicago: Northeastern Illinois University Press.

Beautrais, A., Joyce, P., & Mulder, R. (2000). Unmet need following serious suicide attempt: Follow-up of 302 individuals for 30 months. In G. Andrews, S. Henderson, et al. (Eds.), *Unmet need in psychiatry: Problems, resources, responses.* New York: Cambridge University Press.

Bebbington, P., Johnson, S., & Thornicroft, G. (2002). Community mental health care: Promises and pitfalls. In N. Sartorius & W. Gaebel, et al. (Eds.), *Psychiatry in society* (pp. 131–170). New York: Wiley.

Beck, A. T. (1967). *Depression: Clinical, experimental and theoretical aspects.* New York: Harper & Row.

Beck, A. T. (1976). *Cognitive therapy and the emotional disorders.* New York: International University Press.

Beck, A. T. (1985). Theoretical perspectives on clinical anxiety. In A. H. Tuma & J. D. Maser (Eds.), *Anxiety and the anxiety disorders.* Hillsdale, NJ: Erlbaum.

Beck, A. T. (1991). Cognitive therapy: A 30-year retrospective. *Amer. Psychologist, 46*(4), 368–375.

Beck, A. T. (1997). Cognitive therapy: Reflections. In J. K. Zeig (Ed.), *The evolution of psychotherapy: The third conference.* New York: Brunner/Mazel.

Beck, A. T. (2002). Cognitive models of depression. In R. L. Leahy & E. T. Dowd (Eds.), *Clinical advances in cognitive psychotherapy: Theory and application* (pp. 29–61). New York: Springer.

Beck, A. T., Butler, A. C., Brown, G. K., Dahlsgaard, K. K., Newman, C. F., & Beck, J. S. (2001). Dysfunctional beliefs discriminate personality disorders. *Behav. Res. Ther., 39*(10), 1213–1225.

Beck, A. T., & Emery, G., with Greenberg, R. L. (1985). Differentiating anxiety and depression: A test of the cognitive content-specificity hypothesis. *J. Abnorm. Psychol., 96,* 179–183.

Beck, A. T., & Freeman, A. (1990). *Cognitive therapy of personality disorders.* New York: Guilford Press.

Beck, A. T., Freeman, A., Davis, D. D., et al. (2004). *Cognitive therapy of personality disorders* (2nd ed.). New York: Guilford Press.

Beck, A. T., Resnik, H., & Lettieri, D. (Eds.). (1974). *The prediction of suicide.* Philadelphia: Charles Press.

Beck, A. T., Rush, A. J., Shaw, B. F., & Emery, G. (1979). *Cognitive therapy of depression.* New York: Guilford Press.

Beck, J. C., & Parry, J. W. (1992). Incompetence, treatment refusal, and hospitalization. *Bull. Amer. Acad. Psychiat. Law, 20*(3), 261–267.

Beck, J. G. (1993). Vaginismus. In W. O'Donohue & J. H. Geer (Eds.), *Handbook of sexual dysfunctions:*

Assessment and treatment (pp. 381–397). Needham Heights, MA: Allyn & Bacon.

Beck, J. G., & Bozman, A. (1996). Gender differences in sexual desire: The effects of anger and anxiety. *Arch. Sex. Behav., 24*(6), 595–612.

Beebe, D. K. (1991). Emergency management of the adult female rape victim. *Amer. Fam. Physician, 43*, 2041–2046.

Begley, S. (2000, May 8). A world of their own. *Newsweek*, pp. 52–63.

Beidel, D. C., Turner, S. M., & Morris, T. L. (1995). A new inventory to assess childhood social anxiety and phobia: The social phobia and anxiety inventory for children. *Psychol. Assess., 7*(1), 73–79.

Beidel, D. C., Turner, S. M., & Morris, T. L. (2000). Behavioral treatment of childhood social phobia. *J. Cons. Clin. Psychol., 68*(6), 1072–1080.

Bejerot, S. (2003). Psychosurgery for obsessive-compulsive disorder: Concerns remain. *Acta Psychiatr. Scandin., 107*(4), 241–243.

Belkin, L. (1990, June 6). Doctor tells of first death using his suicide device. *New York Times*, A1, p. 3.

Bell, M. D., Lysaker, P. H., & Milstein, R. M. (1996). Clinical benefits of paid work activity in schizophrenia. *Schizo. Bull., 22*(1), 51–67.

Belle, D. (1990). Poverty and women's mental health. *Amer. Psychologist., 45*(3), 385–389.

Bellinger, D. L., Madden, K. S., Felten, S. Y., & Felten, D. L. (1994). Neural and endocrine links between the brain and the immune system. In C. S. Lewis, C. O'Sullivan, & J. Barraclough (Eds.), *The psychoimmunology of cancer: Mind and body in the fight for survival.* Oxford, England: Oxford University Press.

Belluck, P. (1996, December 1). The symptoms of Internet addiction. *New York Times*, p. 5.

Bemporad, J. R. (1992). Psychoanalytically orientated psychotherapy. In E. S. Paykel (Ed.), *Handbook of affective disorders.* New York: Guilford Press.

Bender, D. S., Farber, B. A., & Geller, J. D. (2001). Cluster B personality traits and attachment. *J. Amer. Acad. Psychoanal., 29*(4), 551–563.

Bender, L. (1938). *A visual motor gestalt test and its clinical use.* New York: American Orthopsychiatric Assoc.

Benditt, T. (2002). Mental illness and commitment. In J. M. Humber & R. F. Almeder (Eds.), *Mental illness and public health care: Biomedical ethics reviews. Contemporary issues in biomedicine, ethics, and society* (pp. 1–24). Totowa, NJ: Humana.

Benezech, M., DeWitte, J. J. E., & Bourgeois, M. (1989). A lycanthropic murderer [Letter to the editor]. *Amer. J. Psychiat., 146*(7), 942.

Bennett, F. C., Brown, R. T., Craver, J., & Anderson, D. (1999). Stimulant medication for the child with attention-deficit/hyperactivity disorder. *Pediatr. Clin. N. Amer., 46*(5), 929–944, vii.

Bennett, G. T., & Kish, G. R. (1990). Incompetency to stand trial: Treatment unaffected by demographic variables. *J. Forensic Sci., 35*(2), 403–412.

Bennett, J. B., & Lehman, W. E. K. (Eds.). (2003). *Preventing workplace substance abuse: Beyond drug testing to wellness.* Washington, D. C.: American Psychological Association.

Benson, J. (1996, January 15). Crime: Law and order. *Newsweek*, pp. 48–54.

Bentovim, A. (2001). A 20-year overview. In G. Adshead & D. Brooke (Eds.), *Munchausen's syndrome by proxy: Current issues in assessment, treatment and research* (pp. 1–12). London: Imperial College Press.

Bergin, A. E., & Richards, P. S. (2001). Religious values and mental health. In A. E. Kazdin (Ed.), *Encyclopedia of psychology.* New York: APA & Oxford University Press.

Bergler, E. (1951). *Neurotic counterfeit sex.* New York: Grune & Stratton.

Berk, S. N., & Efran, J. S. (1983). Some recent developments in the treatment of neurosis. In C. E. Walker et al. (Eds.), *The handbook of clinical psychology: Theory, research, and practice*(Vol. 2). Homewood, IL: Dow Jones-Irwin.

Berlin, F. S. (2000). The etiology and treatment of sexual offending. In D. H. Fishbein (Ed.), *The science, treatment, and prevention of antisocial behaviors: Application to the criminal justice system*(pp. 21-1–21-15). Kingston, NJ: Civic Research Institute.

Berman, A. L. (1986). Helping suicidal adolescents: Needs and responses. In C. A. Corr & J. N. McNeil (Eds.), *Adolescence and death.* New York: Springer.

Berman, A. L., & Jobes, D. A. (1991). *Adolescent suicide: Assessment and intervention.* Washington, DC: APA.

Berman, A. L., & Jobes, D. A. (1995). Suicide prevention in adolescents (age 12–18). [Special issue: Suicide prevention: Toward the year 2000.] *Suic. Life-Threat. Behav., 25*(1), 143–154.

Bernard, J. M., & Goodyear, R. K. (2004). *Fundamentals of clinical supervision* (3rd ed.). Needham Heights, MA: Allyn and Bacon.

Berney, B. (1993). Round and round it goes: The epidemiology of childhood lead poisoning, 1950–1990. *Milbank Quarterly, 71*(1), 3–39.

Bernstein, H. A. (1981). Survey of threats and assaults directed toward psychotherapists. *Amer. J. Psychother., 35*, 542–549.

Berrettini, W. H. (2000). Susceptibility loci for bipolar disorder: Overlap with inherited vulnerability to schizophrenia. *Biol. Psychiat., 47*(3), 245–251.

Bersoff, D. M. (Ed.). (1999). *Ethical conflicts in psychology* (2nd ed.). Washington, DC: American Psychological Association.

Berthier, M. L., Kulisevsky, J., Gironell, A., & Lopez, O. L. (2001). Obsessive-compulsive disorder and traumatic brain injury: Behavioral, cognitive, and neuroimaging findings. *Neuropsychiat., Neuropsychol., Behav. Neurol., 14*(1), 23–31.

Beutler, L. E. (1991). Have all won and must all have prizes? Revisiting Luborsky et al.'s verdict. *J. Cons. Clin. Psychol., 59*, 226–232.

Beutler, L. E. (2000). David and Goliath: When empirical and clinical standards of practice meet. *Amer. Psychologist, 55*(9), 997–1007.

Beutler, L. E. (2002). The dodo bird is extinct. *Clin. Psychol.: Sci. Prac., 9*(1), 30–34.

Beutler, L. E., & Malik, M. L. (Eds.) (2002). *Rethinking the DSM: A psychological perspective. Decade of behavior.* Washington,DC: APA.

Beutler, L. E., Williams, R. E., Wakefield, P. J., & Entwistle, S. R. (1995). Bridging scientist and practitioner perspectives in clinical psychology. *Amer. Psychologist., 50*(12), 984–994.

Beyer, H. A. (1991). Litigation involving people with mental retardation. In J. L. Matson & J. A. Mulick (Eds.), *Handbook of mental retardation* (2nd ed.). New York: Pergamon Press.

Bichsel, S. (2001). Schizophrenia and severe mental illness: Guidelines for assessment, treatment, and referral. In E. R. Welfel & R. E. Ingersoll (Eds.), *The mental health desk reference* (pp. 142–154). New York: Wiley.

Bickman, L., & Dokecki, P. (1989). Public and private responsibility for mental health services. *Amer. Psychologist., 44*(8), 1133–1137.

Biederman, J., Mick, E., Faraone, S. V., & Burback, M. (2001). Patterns of remission and symptom decline in conduct disorder: A four-year prospective study of an ADHD sample. *J. Amer. Acad. Child Adol. Psychiat., 40*(3), 290–298.

Biegon, A., & Kerman, I. (1995). Quantitative autoradiography of cannabinoid receptors in the human brain post-mortem. In A. Biegon & N. D. Volkow (Eds.), *Sites of drug action in the human brain.* Boca Raton, FL: CRC Press.

Binder, R. L. (1999). Are the mentally ill dangerous? *J. Amer. Acad. Psychiat. Law, 27*(2), 189–201.

Binet, A., & Simon, T. (1916). *The development of intelligence in children (The Binet-Simon Scale).* Baltimore: Williams & Wilkins.

Binik, Y. M., Bergeron, S., & Khalife, S. (2000). Dyspareunia. In S. R. Leiblum & R. C. Rosen (Eds.), *Principles and practice of sex therapy* (3rd ed., pp. 154–180). New York: Guilford Press.

Binik, Y. M., Reissing, E., Pukall, C., Flory, N., Payne, K. A., & Khalife, S. (2002). The female sexual pain disorders: Genital pain or sexual dysfunction? *Arch. Sex. Behav., 31*(5), 425–429.

Birch, H. G., Richardson, S. A., Baird, D., et al. (1970). *Mental subnormality in the community—A clinical and epidemiological study.* Baltimore: Williams & Wilkins.

Birket-Smith, M., & Mortensen, E. L. (2002). Pain in somatoform disorders: Is somatoform pain disorder a valid diagnosis? *Acta Psychiatr. Scandin., 106*(2), 103–108.

Birren, J. E., & Schroots, J. F. (Eds.). (2000). *A history of geropsychology in autobiography.* Washington, DC: APA.

Birren, J. E., & Schroots, J. J. F. (2001). History of geropsychology. In J.E. Birren, et al. (Eds.), *Handbook of the psychology of aging* (5th ed., pp. 3–28). San Diego, CA: Academic.

Birtchnell, J. (1996). Detachment. In C. G. Costello (Ed.), *Personality characteristics of the personality disordered.* New York: Wiley.

Bissette, G., Seidler, F. J., Nemeroff, C. B., & Slotkin, T. A. (1996). High affinity choline transporter status in Alzheimer's disease tissue from rapid autopsy. In R. J. Wurtman, S. Corkin, J. H. Growdon, & R. M. Nitsch (Eds.), *The neurobiology of Alzheimer's disease.* New York: New York Academy of Sciences.

Bisson, J. I., & Deahl, M. P. (1994). Psychological debriefing and prevention of post-traumatic stress: More research is needed. *Brit. J. Psychiat., 165*(6), 717–720.

Blacher, J., & Baker, B. L. (1992). Toward meaningful involvement in out-of-home placement settings. *Ment. Retard., 30*(1), 35–43.

Blacher, J., & Baker, B. L. (1994). Family involvement in residential treatment of children with retardation: Is there evidence of detachment? *J. Child Psychol. Psychiat. Allied Disc., 35*(3), 505–520.

Black, D. W., & Andreasen, N. C. (1994). Schizophrenia, schizophreniform disorder, and delusional (paranoid) disorder. In R. E. Hales, S. C. Yudofsky, & J. A. Talbott (Eds.), *The American Psychiatric Press textbook of psychiatry* (2nd ed.). Washington, DC: American Psychiatric Press.

Black, D. W., Belsare, G., & Schlosser, S. (1999). Clinical features, psychiatric comorbidity, and health-related quality of life in persons reporting compulsive computer use behavior. *J. Clin. Psychiat., 60*(12), 839–844.

Black, S. T. (1993). Comparing genuine and simulated suicide notes: A new perspective. *J. Cons. Clin. Psychol., 61*(4), 699–702.

Black, S. T. (1995). Comparing genuine and simulated suicide notes: Response to Diamond et al. (1995). *J. Cons. Clin. Psychol., 63*(1), 49–51.

Blackburn, R. (1993). *The psychology of criminal conduct: Theory, research, and practice.* New York: Wiley.

Blanchard, J. J., Brown, S. A., Horan, W. P., & Sherwood, A. R. (2000). Substance use disorders in schizophrenia: Review, integration, and a proposed model. *Clin. Psychol. Rev., 20*(2), 207–234.

Blanchard, E. B., & Hickling, E. J. (2004). *After the crash: Psychological assessment and treatment of survivors of motor vehicle accidents* (2nd ed.). Washington, DC: American Psychological Association.

Blanchard, R., & Hucker, S. J. (1991). Age, transvestism, bondage, and concurrent paraphilic activities in 117 fatal cases of autoerotic asphyxia. *Brit. J. Psychiat., 159*, 371–377.

Blanco, C., Ibanez, A., Saiz-Ruiz, J., Blanco-Jerez, C., & Nunes E. V. (2000). Epidemiology, pathophysiology and treatment of pathological gambling. *CNS Drugs, 13*(6), 397–407.

Blatt, S. J. (1995). The destructiveness of perfectionism. Implications for the treatment of depression. *Amer. Psychologist., 50*(12), 1003–1020.

Blatt, S. J. (1999). Personality factors in brief treatment of depression: Further analyses of the NIMH-sponsored Treatment for Depression Collaborative Research Program. In D. S. Janowsky et al. (Eds.), *Psychotherapy indications and outcomes.* Washington, DC: American Psychiatric Press.

Blazer, D. (2002). *Depression in late life* (3rd ed.). New York: Springer.

Blazer, D. G., George, L. K., & Hughes, D. (1991). The epidemiology of anxiety disorders: An age comparison. In C. Salzman & B. D. Lebowitz (Eds.), *Anxiety in the elderly.* New York: Springer.

Blazer, D. G., Hughes, D., George, L. K., Swartz, M., & Boyer, R. (1991). Generalized anxiety disorder. In L. N. Robins & D. A. Regier (Eds.), *Psychiatric disorders in America: The epidemiologic catchment area study.* New York: Maxwell Macmillan International.

Bliss, E. L. (1980). Multiple personalities: A report of 14 cases with implications for schizophrenia and hysteria. *Arch. Gen. Psychiat., 37*(12), 1388–1397.

Bliss, E. L. (1980). *Multiple personality, allied disorders and hypnosis.* New York: Oxford University Press.

Bliss, E. L. (1985). "How prevalent is multiple personality?": Dr. Bliss replies. *Amer. J. Psychiat., 142*(12), 1527.

Bloom, B. L. (1984). *Community mental health: A general introduction* (2nd ed.). Monterey, CA: Brooks/Cole.

Bloom, F., Lazerson, A., & Hofstadter, L. (1985). *Brain, mind, and behavior.* New York: W. H. Freeman.

Bloom, J. D. (1990). The *Tarasoff* decision & gun control legislation. *Inter. J. Offend. Ther. Compar. Criminol., 34*(1), v–viii.

Bloom, J. D., Nadelson, C. C., & Notman, M. T. (Eds.). (1999). *Physician sexual misconduct.* Washington, DC: American Psychiatric Press.

Bluglass, K. (2001). Treatment of perpetrators. In G. Adshead & D. Brooke (Eds.), *Munchausen's syndrome by proxy: Current issues in assessment, treatment and research* (pp. 175–184). London: Imperial College Press.

Blum, K., Braverman, E. R., Holder, J. M., Lubar, J. F., Monastra, V. J., Miller, D., Lubar, J. O., Chen, T. J. H., & Comings, D. E. Reward deficiency syndrome: A biogenetic model for the diagnosis and treatment of impulsive, addictive, and compulsive behaviors. *J. Psychoact. Drugs, 32* (Suppl.), 1–68.

Blum, K., & Noble, E. (1993). Drug dependence and the A1 allele gene. *Drug Alc. Dep., 33*(5).

Blumer, D. (2002). The illness of Vincent van Gogh. *Amer. J. Psychiat., 159*(4), 519–526.

Blyler, C. R. (2003). Understanding the employment rate of people with schizophrenia: Different approaches lead to different implications for policy. In M. F. Lenzenweger & J. M. Hooley (Eds.), *Principles of experimental psychopathology: Essays in honor of Brendan A. Maher* (pp. 107–115). Washington, DC: APA.

Bockoven, J. S. (1963). *Moral treatment in American psychiatry.* New York: Springer.

Boegels, S. M., & Zigterman, D. (2000). Dysfunctional cognitions in children with social phobia, separation anxiety disorder, and generalized anxiety disorder. *J. Abnorm. Child Psychol., 28*(2), 205–211.

Boergers, J., Spirito, A., & Donaldson, D. (1998). Reasons for adolescent suicide attempts: Associations with psychological functioning. *J. Amer. Acad. Child Adol. Psychiat., 37*(12), 1287–1293.

Bogdan, R., & Taylor, S. (1976, January). The judged, not the judges: An insider's view of mental retardation. *Amer. Psychologist., 31*(1), 47–52.

Bohart, A. C. (2003). Person-centered psychotherapy and related experiential approaches. In A. S. Gurman & S. B. Messer (Eds.), *Essential psychotherapies: Theory and practice* (2nd ed.). New York: Guilford Press.

Bohne, A., Keuthen, N., Wilheim, S., Deckersback, T., & Jenike, M. (2002). Prevalence of symptoms of body dysmorphic disorder and its correlates: A cross-cultural comparison. *Psychosom. J. Cons. Liaison Psychiat., 43*(6), 486–490.

Boland, R. J., & Keller, M. B. (2002). Course and outcome of depression. In I. H. Gotlib & C. L. Hammen (Eds.), *Handbook of depression* (pp. 43–60). New York: Guilford Press.

Bolgar, H. (1965). The case study method. In B. B. Wolman (Ed.), *Handbook of clinical psychology.* New York: McGraw-Hill.

Bongar, B., Lomax, J. W., & Marmatz, M. (1992). Training and supervisory issues in the assessment and management of the suicidal patient. In B. Bongar (Ed.), *Suicide: Guidelines for assessment, management and treatment* (pp. 253–267). New York: Oxford University Press.

Bonner, R. L. (1992). Isolation, seclusion, and psychosocial vulnerability as risk factors for suicide behind bars. In R. W. Maris, A. L. Berman, J. T. Maltsberger, & R. I. Yufit (Eds.), *Assessment and prediction of suicide.* New York: Guilford Press.

Bornstein, R. A., Schwarzkopf, S. B., Olson, S. C., & Nasrallah, H. A. (1992). Third-ventricle enlargement and neuropsychological deficit in schizophrenia. *Biol. Psychiat., 31*(9), 954–961.

Bornstein, R. F. (1998). Dependency in the personality disorders: Intensity, sight, expression, and defense. *J. Clin. Psychol., 54*(2), 175–189.

Boros, S., Ophoven, J., Anderson, R., & Brubaker, L. (1995). Munchausen syndrome by proxy: A profile for medical child abuse. *Austral. Fam. Physician, 24*(5), 768–773.

Borthwick, A., Holman, C., Kennard, D., McFetridge, M., Messruther, K., & Wilkes, J. (2001). The relevance of moral treatment to contemporary mental health care. *J. Ment. Hlth. UK., 10*(4), 427–439.

Bossolo, L., & Lichtenstein, B. (2002). Many Americans still feeling effects of September 11th; Are reexamining their priorities in life. *APA Online.*

Bott, E. (1928). Teaching of psychology in the medical course. *Bull. Assoc. Amer. Med. Colleges, 3,* 289–304.

Bouchard, C., Rheaume, J., & Ladouceur, R. (1999). Responsibility and perfectionism in OCD: An experimental study. *Behav. Res. Ther., 37*(3), 239–248.

Boudouris, J. (2000). The insanity defense in Polk County, Iowa. *Amer. J. Forens. Psychol., 18*(1), 41–79.

Bourgeois, M. (1991). Serotonin, impulsivity and suicide. *Human Psychopharmacol. Clin. Exp., 6*(Suppl.), 31–36.

Bourin, M., Malinge, M., & Guitton, B. (1995). [Provocative agents in panic disorder.] *Therapie 50*(4), 301–306. [French]

Bowden, C. L. (2001). Strategies to reduce misdiagnosis of bipolar depression. *Psychiatr. Serv., 52*(1), 51–55.

Bowen, K. (2000). Child abuse and domestic violence in families of children seen for suspected sexual abuse. *Clin. Pediatr., 39*(1), 33–40.

Bower, B. (1995). Deceptive appearances: Imagined physical defects take an ugly personal toll. *Sci. News, 148*, 40–41.

Bower, G. H. (1981). Mood and memory. *Amer. Psychologist, 36*(2), 129–148.

Bowman, D. H. (2002). Lethal school shootings resemble workplace rampages, report says. *Education Week, 21*(38), 10.

Boyce, W. T., Chesney, M., Alkon, A., Tschann, J. M., et al. (1995). Psychobiologic reactivity to stress and childhood respiratory illnesses: Results of two prospective studies. *Psychosom. Med., 57*, 411–422.

Boyd, C. J., McCabe, S. E., & d'Arcy, H. (2003). Ecstasy use among college undergraduates: Gender, race and sexual identity. *J. Subst. Abuse Treatm., 24*(3), 209–215.

Boye, B., Bentsen, H., & Malt, U. F. (2002). Does guilt proneness predict acute and long-term distress in relatives of patients with schizophrenia? *Acta Pyschiatr. Scandin., 106*(5), 351–357.

Boyles, S. (2002, Jan. 8). More people seeking treatment for depression. *WebMDHealth.* Retrieved Jan. 9, 2002, from www.webcenter.health.web.

Bozarth, J. D. Zimring, F. M., & Tausch, R. (2002). Client-centered therapy: The evolution of a revolution. In D. J. Cain & J. Seeman (Eds.), *Humanistic psychotherapies: Handbook of research and practice* (pp. 147–188). Washington, DC: APA.

Braback, L., & Humble, M. (2001). Young woman dies of water intoxication after taking one tablet of ecstasy. Today's drug panorama calls for increased vigilance in health care. *Lakartidningen, 98*(9), 817–819.

Bradford, J. M. W. (1995). Pharmacological treatment of the paraphilias. In J. M. Oldham & M. B. Riba (Eds.), *American Psychiatric Press review of psychiatry* (Vol. 14). Washington, DC: American Psychiatric Press.

Bradford, J. M. W. (1999). The paraphilias, obsessive compulsive spectrum disorder, and the treatment of sexually deviant behaviour. *Psychiatr. Quart., 70*(3), 209–219.

Bradley, B. P., Mogg, K., Falla, S. J., & Hamilton, L. R. (1998). Attentional bias for threatening facial expressions in anxiety: Manipulation of stimulus duration. *Cog. Emot., 12*(6), 737–753.

Bradley, S. J. (1995). Psychosexual disorders in adolescence. In J. M. Oldham & M. B. Riba (Eds.), *American Psychiatric Press review of psychiatry,* (Vol. 14). Washington, DC: American Psychiatric Press.

Brasic, J. R., & Fogelman, D. (1999). Clinician safety. *Psychiatr. Clin. N. Amer., 22*(4), 923–940.

Brauer, A. (1999). Biofeedback and anxiety. *Psychiatr. Times, XVI*(2).

Braun, D. L. (1996, July 28). Interview. In S. Gilbert, More men may seek eating-disorder help. *New York Times.*

Brawman-Mintzer, O. (2001). Pharmacologic treatment of generalized anxiety disorder. *Psychiatr. Clin. N. Amer., 24*(1), 119–137.

Breier, A. (2001). A new era in the pharmacotherapy of psychotic disorders. *J. Clin. Psychiat., 62*(Suppl. 2), 3–5.

Bremner, J. D. (2002). *Does stress damage the brain? Understanding trauma-related disorders from a mind-body perspective.* New York: Norton.

Bremner, J. D., Southwick, S. M., & Charney, D. S. (1999). The neurobiology of posttraumatic stress disorder: An integration of animal and human research. In P. A. Saigh, J. D. Bremner, et al. (Eds.), *Posttraumatic stress disorder: A comprehensive text.* Boston: Allyn & Bacon.

Bremner, J. D., Southwick, S. M., Johnson, D. R., Yehuda, R., & Charney, D. S. (1993). Childhood physical abuse and combat-related posttraumatic stress disorder in Vietnam veterans. *Amer. J. Psychiat., 150*(2), 235–239.

Brems, C. (1995). Women and depression: A comprehensive analysis. In W. Beckham & W. Leber (Eds.), *Handbook of depression* (2nd ed.). New York: Guilford Press.

Brende, J. O., & Parson, E. R. (1985). *Vietnam veterans.* New York: Plenum.

Brenner, I. (1999). Deconstructing DID. *Amer. J. Psychother., 53*(3), 344–360.

Brent, D. A. (2001). Assessment and treatment of the youthful suicidal patient. In H. Hendin & J. J. Mann (Eds.), *The clinical science of suicide prevention.* (Vol. 932, pp. 106–131). New York: Annals of the New York Academy of Sciences.

Brent, D. A., Bridge, J., Johnson, B. A., & Connolly, J. (1996). Suicidal behavior runs in families. A controlled family study of adolescent suicide victims. *Arch. Gen. Psychiat., 53,* 1145–1152.

Brent, D. A., Bridge, J., Johnson, B. A., & Connolly, J. (1998). Suicidal behavior runs in families: A controlled family study of adolescent suicide victims. In R. J. Kosky, H. S. Eshkevari, & R. Hassan (Eds.), *Suicide prevention: The global context.* New York: Plenum Press.

Brent, D. A., Kupfer, D. J., Bromet, E. J., & Dew, M. A. (1988). The assessment and treatment of patients at risk for suicide. In A. J. Frances & R. E. Hales (Eds.), *American Psychiatric Press review of psychiatry* (Vol. 7). Washington, DC: American Psychiatric Press.

Brent, D. A., Moritz, G., Liotus, L., Schweers, J., Balach, L., Roth, C., & Perper, J. A. (1998). Familial risk factors for adolescent suicide: A case-control study. In R. J. Kosky, H. S. Eshkevari, & R. Hassan, *Suicide prevention: The global context.* New York: Plenum Press.

Bresnahan, M. J., & Murray-Johnson, L. (2002). The healing web. *Hlth. Care Women Inter. 23*(4), 398–407.

Brewerton, T. D., Lydiard, R. B., Herzog, D. B., Brotman, A. W., et al. (1995). Comorbidity of Axis I psychiatric disorders in bulimia nervosa. *J. Clin. Psychiat., 56*(2), 77–80.

Brigham, J. C. (1988). Is witness confidence helpful in judging eyewitness accuracy? In M. M. Gruneberg & P. J. Morris (Eds.), *Practical aspects of memory: Current research and issues, Vol. 1: Memory in everyday life* (pp. 77–82). Chichester: Wiley.

Britton, W. H., & Eaves, R. C. (1986). Relationship between the Vineland Adaptive Behavior Scales-Classroom Edition of the Vineland Social Maturity Scales. *Amer. J. Ment. Def., 91*(1), 105–107.

Brock, D. W. (2001). Physician-assisted suicide—The worry about abuse. In L. M. Kopelman & K. A. De Ville (Eds.), *Physician-assisted suicide: What are the issues?*(pp. 59–74). Dordrecht, Netherlands: Kluwer Academic.

Brody, H. (2000). Better health from your inner pharmacy. *Psychology Today, 32*(4), 60–67.

Bromet, E. J., Hough, L., & Connell, M. (1984). Mental health of children near the Three Mile Island reactor. *J. Prev. Psychiat., 2,* 275–301.

Bromet, E. J., Schulberg, H. C., & Dunn, L. (1982). Reactions of psychiatric patients to the Three Mile Island nuclear accident. *Arch. Gen. Psychiat., 39*(6), 725–730.

Brooks, G. R., & Richardson, F. C. (1980). Emotional skills training: A treatment program for duodenal ulcer. *Behav. Ther., 11*(2), 198–207.

Brooner, R. K., King, V. L., Kidorf, M., Schmidt, C. W., & Bigelow, G. E. (1997). Psychiatric and substance use comorbidity among treatment-seeking opioid abusers. *Arch. Gen. Psychiat., 54,* 71–80.

Brown, G. P., & Beck, A. T. (2002). Dysfunctional attitudes, perfectionism, and models of vulnerability to depression. In G. L. Flett & P. L. Hewitt (Eds.), *Perfectionism: Theory, research, and treatment* (pp. 231–251). Washington, DC: APA.

Brown, G. R., & Ceniceros, S. (2001). Human sexuality in health and disease. In D. Wedding (Ed.), *Behavior and medicine* (3rd ed. pp. 171–184). Seattle: Hogrefe & Huber.

Brown, G. R., Wise, T. N., Costa, P. T., Herbst, J. H., & Fagan, P. J. (1996). Personality characteristics and sexual functioning of 188 cross-dressing men. *J. Nerv. Ment. Dis., 184*(5), 265–273.

Brown, G. W., & Harris, T. O. (1978). *Social origins of depression: A study of psychiatric disorder in women.* London: Tavistock.

Brown, G. W., Harris, T. O., & Hepworth, C. (1995). Loss, humiliation and entrapment among women developing depression: A patient and non-patient comparison. *Psychol. Med., 25,* 7–21.

Brown, G. W., Monck, E. M., Carstairs, G. M., & Wing, J. K. (1962). Influence on family life on the course of schizophrenic illness. *Brit. J. Prev. Soc. Med., 16,* 55–68.

Brown, J. H., Henteleff, P., Barakat, S., & Rowe, C. J. (1986). Is it normal for terminally ill patients to desire death? *Amer. J. Psychiat., 143*(2), 208–211.

Brown, L. (1993). Enrollment of drug abusers in HIV clinical trials: A public health imperative for communities of color. *J. Psychoactive Drugs, 25*(1), 45–48.

Brown, M. L., & Rounsley, C. A. (1996). *True selves: Understanding transsexualism—for families, friends, coworkers, and helping professionals.* San Francisco: Jossey-Bass/Pfeiffer.

Brown, P. J., Read, J. P., & Kahler, C. W. (2003). Comorbid posttraumatic stress disorder and substance use disorders: Treatment outcomes and the role of coping. In P. Ouimette & P. J. Brown (Eds.), *Trauma and substance abuse: Causes, consequences, and treatment of comorbid disorders.* Washington, DC: APA.

Brown, R. J. (2002). The cognitive psychology of dissociative states. *Cog. Neuropsychiat., 7*(3), 221–235.

Brown, R. T., & LaRosa, A. (2002). Recent developments in the pharmacotherapy of attention-deficit/hyperactivity disorder (ADHD). *Profess. Psychol.: Res. Pract., 33*(6), 591–595.

Brown, T. A., Hertz, R. M., & Barlow, D. H. (1992). New developments in cognitive-behavioral treatment of anxiety disorders. In A. Tasman & M. B. Riba (Eds.), *Review of psychiatry* (Vol. 11). Washington, DC: American Psychiatric Press.

Brown, T. A., O'Leary, T. A., & Barlow, D. A. (2001). Generalized anxiety disorder. In D. H. Barlow (Ed.), *Clinical handbook of psychological disorders: A step-by-step treatment manual*(3rd ed. pp. 154–208). New York: Guilford Press.

Brown, W. S. (2002). Psychoneuroimmunology and Western religious traditions. In H. G. Koenig & H. J. Cohen (Eds.), *The link between religion and health: Psychoneuroimmunology and the faith factor*(pp. 262–274). New York: Oxford University Press.

Browne, A., & Finklehor, D. (1986). Impact of child sexual abuse: A review of the research. *Psychol. Bull., 99*(1), 66–77.

Brownell, K. D., & Napolitano, M. A. (1995). Distorting reality for children: Body size proportions of Barbie and Ken dolls. *Inter. J. Eat. Disorders, 18*(3), 295–298.

Brownell, K. D., & O'Neil, P. M. (1993). Obesity. In D. H. Barlow (Ed.), *Clinical handbook of psychological disorders: A step-by-step treatment manual*(2nd ed.). New York: Guilford Press.

Brownell, K. D., & Wadden, T. A. (1992). Etiology and treatment of obesity: Understanding a serious, prevalent, and refractory disorder. *J. Cons. Clin. Psychol., 60*(4), 505–517.

Bruce, E. J., Schultz, C. L., & Smyrnios, K. X. (1996). A longitudinal study of the grief of mothers and fathers of children with intellectual disability. *Brit. J. Med. Psychol., 69,* 33–45.

Bruce, M. L., & Kim, K. M. (1992). Differences in the effects of divorce on major depression in men and women. *Amer. J. Psychiat., 149*(7), 914–917.

Bruch, H. (1962). Perceptual and conceptual disturbances in anorexia nervosa. *Psychosom. Med., 24,* 187–194.

Bruch, H. (1973). *Eating disorders: Obesity, anorexia nervosa and the person within.* New York: Basic Books.

Bruch, H. (1973). Psychiatric aspects of obesity. *Psychiatr. Ann., 3*(7), 6–10.

Bruch, H. (1978). *The golden cage: The enigma of anorexia nervosa.* Cambridge, MA: Harvard University Press.

Bruch, H. (1982). Anorexia nervosa: Therapy and theory. *Amer. J. Psychiat., 139,* 1531–1538.

Bruch, H. (1991). The sleeping beauty: Escape from change. In S. I. Greenspan & G. H. Pollock (Eds.), *The course of life: Vol. 4. Adolescence.*Madison, CT: International Universities Press.

Brumberg, J. J. (1988). *Fasting girls: The history of anorexia nervosa.* New York: Penguin Books.

Bruni, F. (1998, November 22). Behind the jokes, a life of pain and delusion; For Letterman stalker, mental illness was family curse and scarring legacy. *New York Times,* Sect. 1, p. 45.

Brust, J. C. M., & Caplan, L. R. (2001). Agitation and delirium. In J. Bogousslavsky & L. R. Caplan (Eds.), *Stroke syndromes* (2nd ed., pp. 222–231). New York: Cambridge University Press.

Bryant, R. A., Guthrie, R. M., & Moulds, M. L. (2001). Hypnotizability in acute stress disorder. *Amer. J. Psychiat., 158*(4), 600–604.

Bryant, R. A., & Harvey, A. G. (1995). Posttraumatic stress in volunteer firefighters: Predictors of stress. *J. Nerv. Ment. Dis., 183*(4), 267–271.

Buchanan, A. (1997). The investigation of acting on delusions as a tool for risk assessment in the mentally disordered. *Brit. J. Psychiat., 170*(Suppl. 32), 12–14.

Buchanan, A. (1999). Risk and dangerousness. *Psychol. Med., 29*(2), 465–473.

Buhlmann, U., McNally, R. J., Wilhelm, S., & Florin, I. (2002). Selective processing of emotional information in body dysmorphic disorder. *J. Anx. Dis., 16*(3), 289–298.

Bujold, A., Ladouceur, R., Sylvain, C., & Boisvert J. M. (1994). Treatment of pathological gamblers: An experimental study. *J. Behav. Ther. Exp. Psychiat., 25*(4), 275–282.

Bulik, C. M., Sullivan, P. F., Carter, F. A., McIntosh, V. V., & Joyce, P. R. (1998). The role of exposure with response prevention in the cognitive-behavioural therapy for bulimia nervosa. *Psychol. Med., 28*(3), 611–623.

Bumby, K. M., & Maddox, M. C. (1999). Judges' knowledge about sexual offenders, difficulties presiding over sexual offense cases, and opinions on sentencing, treatment, and legislation. *Sex. Abuse J. Res. Treat.*, 11(4), 305–315.

Bureau of Justice Statistics. (1999). *Report on U.S. prison population.* Washington, DC.

Burnette, E., & Murray, B. (1996). Conduct disorders need early treatment. *APA Monitor*, 27(10), 40.

Burns, L. H. (1995). An overview of sexual dysfunction in the infertile couple. *J. Fam. Psychother.*, 6(1), 25–46.

Burr, J. A., Hartman, J. T., & Matteson, D. W. (1999). Black suicide in U.S. metropolitan areas: An examination of the racial inequality and social integration-regulation hypotheses. *Soc. Forces*, 77(3), 1049–1080.

Burros, M. (2001, May 8). Experts see flaws in U.S. mad cow safeguards. *New York Times.*

Burt, D. R., Creese, I., & Snyder, S. H. (1977). Anti-schizophrenic drugs: Chronic treatment elevates dopamine receptor binding in brain. *Science*, 196(4287), 326–328.

Burton, D. (1988). Do anxious swimmers swim slower? Reexamining the elusive anxiety-performance relationship. *J. Sport Psychol.*, 10, 45–61.

Burton, V. S. (1990). The consequences of official labels: A research note on rights lost by the mentally ill, mentally incompetent, and convicted felons. *Comm. Ment. Hlth. J.*, 26(3), 267–276.

Burvill, P. W. (1998). Migrant suicide rates in Australia and in country of birth. *Psychol. Med.*, 28(1), 201–208.

Busch, B., Biederman, J., Cohen, L. G., Sayer, J. M., Monuteaux, M. C., Mick, E., Zallen, B., & Faraone, S. V. (2002). Correlates of ADHD among children in pediatric and psychiatric clinics. *Psychiatr. Serv.*, 53(9), 1103–1111.

Bushman, B. J., & Anderson, C. A. (2001). Media violence and the American public: Scientific facts versus media misinformation. *Amer. Psychologist*, 56(6/7), 477–489.

Bushman, B. J., Baumeister, R. F., & Stack, A. D. (1999). Catharsis, aggression, and persuasive influence: Self-fulfilling or self-defeating prophecies? *J. Pers. Soc. Psychol.*, 76(3), 367–376.

Buss, D. M. (2000). *The dangerous passion: Why jealousy is as necessary as love and sex.* New York: Free Press.

Bustillo, J. R., Lauriello, J., Horan, W. P., & Keith, S. J. (2001). The psychosocial treatment of schizophrenia: An update. *Amer. J. Psychiat.*, 158(2), 163–175.

Butcher, J. N. (Ed.). (2000). *Basic sources on the MMPI-2.* Minneapolis, MN: University of Minnesota Press.

Butler, G., Fennel, M., Robson, P., & Gelder, M. (1991). A comparison of behavior therapy and cognitive behavior therapy in the treatment of generalized anxiety disorder. *J. Cons. Clin. Psychol.*, 59(1), 167–175.

Butler, P. D., DeSanti, L. A., Maddox, J., Harkavy-Friedman, J. M., Amador, X. F., Goetz, R. R., Javitt, D. C., & Gorman, J. M. (2003). Visual backward-masking deficits in schizophrenia: Relationship to visual pathway function and symptomatology. *Schizo. Res.*, 59(2–3), 199–209.

Butler, R. N. (1975). Psychiatry and the elderly: An overview. *Amer. J. Psychiat.*, 132, 893–900.

Button, E. (1993). *Eating disorders: Personal construct therapy and change.* Chichester, England: Wiley.

Button, E. J., & Warren, R. L. (2001). Living with anorexia nervosa: The experience of a cohort of sufferers from anorexia nervosa 7.5 years after initial presentation to a specialized eating disorders service. *Eur. Eating Disord. Rev.*, 9(2), 74–96.

Buttross, S. (2000). Attention deficit-hyperactivity disorder and its deceivers. *Curr. Probl. Pediatr.*, 30(2), 37–50.

Cadoret, R. J., Yates, W. R., Troughton, E., Woodworth, G., & Stewart, M. A. (1995). Adoption study demonstrating two genetic pathways to drug abuse. *Arch. Gen. Psychiat.*, 52, 42–52.

Cagney, T. (2003). Employee assistance programs. In S. Feldman (Ed.), *Managed behavioral health services: Perspectives and practice.* Springfield, IL: Charles C. Thomas Publisher, Ltd.

Cahn, W., Pol, H. E. H., Bongers, M., Schnack, H. G., Mandi, R. C. W., Van Haren, N. E. M., Durston, S., Koning, H., Van Der Linden, J. A., & Kahn, R. S. (2002). Brain morphology in antipsychotic-naïve schizophrenia: A study of multiple brain structures. *Brit. J. Psychiat.*, 181(Suppl 43), s66-s72.

Calamari, J. E., & Cassiday, K. L. (1999). Treating obsessive-compulsive disorder in older adults: A review of strategies. In M. Duffy (Ed.), *Handbook of counseling and psychotherapy with older adults.* New York: Wiley.

Calev, A., Gaudino, E. A., Squires, N. K., Zervas, I. M., & Fink, M. (1995). ECT and non-memory cognition: A review. *Br. J. Clin. Psychol.*, 34, 505–515.

Calev, A., Nigal, D., Shapira, B., Tubi, N., et al. (1991). Early and long-term effects of electroconvulsive therapy and depression on memory and other cognitive functions. *J. Nerv. Ment. Dis.*, 179(9), 526–533.

Callahan, L. A., Steadman, H. J., McGreevy, M. A., & Robbins, P. C. (1991). The volume and characteristics of insanity defense pleas: An eight-state study. *Bull. Amer. Acad. Psychiat. Law*, 19(4), 331–338.

Cameron, D. J., Thomas, R. I., Mulvhill, M., & Bronheim, H. (1987). Delirium: A test of the Diagnostic and Statistical Manual III criteria on medical inpatients. *J. Amer. Ger. Soc.*, 35, 1007–1010.

Campbell, F. A., Ramey, C. T., Pungelli, E., Sparling, J., & Miller-Johnson, S. (2002). Early childhood education: Young adult outcomes from the Abecedarian Project. *Appl. Dev. Sci.*, 6(1), 42–57.

Canals, J., Blade, J., Carbvajo, G., & Domenech-Llaberia, E. (2001). The Beck Depression Inventory: Psychometric characteristics and usefulness in nonclinical adolescents. *Eur. J. Psychol. Assess.*, 17(1), 63–68.

Canetto, S. S. (1995). Elderly women and suicidal behavior. In S. S. Canetto & D. Lester (Eds.), *Women and suicidal behavior.* New York: Springer.

Canetto, S. S. (1995). Suicidal women: Prevention and intervention strategies. In S. S. Canetto & D. Lester (Eds.), *Women and suicidal behavior.* New York: Springer.

Canetto, S. S., & Lester, D. (1995). Gender and the primary prevention of suicide mortality. [Special issue]. *Suic. Life-Threat. Behav.*, 25(1), 58–69.

Capaldi, D. M., & Patterson, G. R. (1994). Interrelated influences of contextual factors on antisocial behavior in childhood and adolescence for males. In D. C. Fowles, P. Sutker, & S. H. Goodman (Eds.), *Progress in experimental personality and psychopathology research.* New York: Springer.

Caplan, R., Perdue, S., Tanguay, P. E., & Fish, B. (1990). Formal thought disorder in childhood onset schizophrenia and schizotypal personality disorder. *J. Child Psychol. Psychiat. Allied Disc.*, 31(7), 1103–1114.

Caporael, L. R. (2001). Evolutionary psychology: Toward a unifying theory and a hybrid science. *Annu. Rev. Psychol.*, 53, 607–628.

Carducci, B. (2000). Shyness: The new solution. *Psychology Today*, 33(1), 38–45.

Carek, P. J., & Dickerson, L. M. (1999). Current concepts in the pharmacological management of obesity. *Drugs*, 57(6), 883–904.

Carey, R. J., Pinheiro-Carrera, M., Dai, H., Tomaz, C., et al. (1995). L-DOPA and psychosis: Evidence for L-DOPA-induced increases in prefrontal cortex dopamine and in serium corticosterone. *Biol. Psychiat.*, 38(10), 669–676.

Carlbring, P., Gustafsson, H., Ekselius, L., & Andersson, G. (2002). 12-month prevalence of panic disorder with or without agoraphobia in the Swedish general population. *Soc. Psychiat. Psychiatr. Epidemiol.*, 37(5), 207–211.

Carlson, G. A., Asarnow, J. R., & Orbach, I. (1994). Developmental aspects of suicidal behavior in children and developmentally delayed adolescents. In G. Noam & S. Borst (Eds.), *Children, youth, and suicide: Developmental perspectives. New directions for child development* (pp. 93–107). San Francisco:Jossey-Bass/Pfieffer.

Carlson, G. A., Rich, C. L., Grayson, P., & Fowler, R. C. (1991). Secular trends in psychiatric diagnosis of suicide victims. *J. Affect. Disorders*, 21(2), 127–132.

Carlson, M. (1998, June 22). The best things in life aren't free. *Time*, 151, 21.

Carpenter, S. (2001). Research on Teen Smoking Cessation gains momentum. *APA Monitor*, 32(6), 54–55.

Carper, R. A., & Courchesne, E. (2000). Inverse correlation between frontal lobe and cerebellum sizes in children with autism. *Brain*, 123(Pt. 4), 836–844.

Carr, J. E. (1994). Annotation: Long term outcome for people with Down syndrome. *J. Child Psychol. Psychiat. Allied Disc*, 35(3), 425–439.

Carr, J. E. (2001). Stress and illness. In D. Wedding (Ed.), *Behavior and medicine* (3rd ed., pp. 231–246). Seattle: Hogrefe & Huber.

Carrasco, J. L., Diaz-Marsa, M., Hollander, E., Cesar, J., & Saiz-Ruiz, J. (2000). Decreased platelet monoamine oxidase activity in female bulimia nervosa. *Eur. Neuropsychopharmacology*, 10(2), 113–117.

Carrington, P. (1978). *Clinically standardized meditation (CSM) instructors kit.* Kendall Park, NJ: Pace Educational Systems.

Carrington, P. (1993). Modern forms of meditation. In P. M. Lehrer & R. L. Woolfolk (Eds.), *Principles and practice of stress management* (2nd ed.). New York: Guilford Press.

Carroll, K. M., & Rounsaville, B. J. (1995). Psychosocial treatments. In J. M. Oldham & M. B. Riba (Eds.), *American Psychiatric Press review of psychiatry*, (Vol. 14). Washington, DC: American Psychiatric Press.

Carstairs K. (1992). Paranoid-schizoid or symbiotic? *Inter. J. Psychoanal.*, 73(1), 71–85.

Cartwright, R. D. (2001). Sleep and sleep disturbances. In D. Wedding (Ed.), *Behavior and medicine* (3rd ed., pp. 219–230). Seattle: Hogrefe & Huber.

Cartwright, R. D., & Lamberg, L. (1992). *Crisis dreaming: Using your dreams to solve your problems.* New York: HarperCollins.

Casey, P. (2001). Multiple personality disorder. *Prim. Care Psychiat.*, 7(1), 7–11.

Cash, T. F., & Henry, P. E. (1995). Women's body images: The results of a national survey in the U. S. A. *Sex Roles*, 33(1/2), 19–28.

Casper, R. C. (1995). Biology of eating disorders. In A. F. Schatzberg & C. B. Nemeroff (Eds.), *The American Psychiatric Press textbook of psychopharma-*

cology. Washington, DC: American Psychiatric Press.

Castellani, B. (2000). *Pathological gambling: The making of a medical problem*. Albany: State University of New York Press.

Castelnuovo, G., Gaggioli, A., & Riva, G. (2001). Cyberpsychology meets clinical psychology: The emergence of e-therapy in mental health care. In G. Riva & C. Galimberti (Eds.), *Towards cyberpsychology: Mind, cognition, and society in the Internet age* (pp. 229–252). Amsterdam: IOS Press.

Castrogiovanni, P., Pieraccini, F., & Di Muro, A. (1998). Suicidality and aggressive behavior. *Acta Psychiatr. Scandin.*, 97(2), 144–148.

Cathebras, P. (2002). Cure. *Lancet*, 359(9325), 2273.

Catherall, D. R. (1999). Family as a group treatment for PTSD. In B. H. Young & D. D. Blake (Eds.), *Group treatments for post-traumatic stress disorder*. Philadelphia: Brunner/Mazel.

Cauchon, D. (1999, February). Patients often aren't informed of danger. *USA Today*.

Cautela, J. R. (2000). Rationale and procedures for covert conditioning. *Psicoterapia Cognitiva e Comportamentale*, 6(2), 194–205.

Cauwels, J. M. (1983). *Bulimia: The binge-purge compulsion*. New York: Doubleday.

Cavanaugh, J. C. (1990). *Adult development and aging*. Belmont, CA: Wadsworth.

CDC (Centers for Disease Control and Prevention). (1997). Cited in NCIPC (National Center for Injury Prevention and Control), *Impaired driving fact sheet*. Atlanta, GA: Author.

CDC (Centers for Disease Control and Prevention). (2002). Alcohol use. NCHS fast stats. Retrieved November 24, 2002, from www.cdc.gov/nchs/fastats/alcohol.

Cerletti, U., & Bini, L. (1938). L'elettroshock. *Arch. Gen. Neurol. Psychiat. & Psychoanal.*, 19, 266–268.

Chait, L. D., Fishman, M. W., & Schuster, C. R. (1985). "Hangover" effects the morning after marijuana smoking. *Drug Alc. Dep.*, 15(3), 229–238.

Chakos, M. H., Lieberman, J. A., Hoffman, E., Bradford, D., & Sheitman, B. (2001). Effectiveness of second-generation antipsychotics in patients with treatment-resistant schizophrenia: A review and meta-analysis of randomized trials. *Amer. J. Psychiat.*, 158(4), 518–526.

Chamberlain, P., & Smith, D. K. (2003). Antisocial behavior in children and adolescents: The Oregon multidimensional treatment foster care model. In A. E. Kazdin & J. R. Weisz (Eds.), *Evidence-based psychotherapies for children and adolescents*. New York: Guilford Press.

Chambless, D. L. (2002). Identification of empirically supported counseling psychology interventions: Commentary. *Counseling Psychologist*, 30(2), 302–308.

Chambless, D. L., & Ollendick, T. H. (2001). Empirically supported psychological interventions: Controversies and evidence. *Annu. Rev. Psychol.*, 52, 685–716.

Chamorro, R., & Flores-Ortiz, Y. (2000). Acculturation and disordered eating patterns among Mexican American women. *Inter. J. Eat. Disorders*, 28, 125–129.

Char, W. F. (1985). The hysterical spouse. *Med. Aspects Human Sex.*, 19(9), 123–133.

Charman, D. P. (Ed.). (2004). *Core processes in brief psychodynamic psychotherapy: Advancing effective practice*. Mahwah, NJ: Lawrence Erlbaum Associates.

Charney, D. S., Woods, S. W., Goodman, W. K., & Heninger, G. R. (1987). Neurobiological mechanisms of panic anxiety: Biochemical and behavioral correlates of yohimbine-induced anxiety. *Amer. J. Psychiat.*, 144(8), 1030–1036.

Charney, D. S., Woods, S. W., Price, L. H., Goodman, W. K., Glazer, W. M., & Heninger, G. R. (1990). Noradrenergic dyssregulation in panic disorder. In J. C. Ballenger (Ed.), *Neurobiology of panic disorder*. New York: Wiley-Liss.

Chase, M. (1993, May 28). Psychiatrists declare severe PMS a depressive disorder. *Wall Street Journal*, pp. B1, B6.

Chassin, L., Collins, R. L., Ritter, J., & Shirley, M. C. (2001). Vulnerability to substance use disorders across the life span. In R. E. Ingram & J. M. Price (Eds.), *Vulnerability to psychopathology: Risk across the lifespan*, (pp. 165–172). New York: Guilford Press.

Chen, Y. R., Swann, A. C., & Burt, D. B. (1996). Stability of diagnosis in schizophrenia. *Amer. J. Psychiat.*, 153(5), 682–686.

Cherland, E., & Fitzpatrick, R. (1999). Psychotic side effects of psychostimulants: A 5-year review. *Canad. J. Psychiat.*, 44(8), 811–813.

Chiu, L. H. (1971). Manifested anxiety in Chinese and American children. *J. Psychol.*, 79, 273–284.

Chochinov, H. M., & Schwartz, L. (2002). Depression and the will to live in the psychological landscape of terminally ill patients. In K. Foley & H. Hendin (Eds.), *The case against assisted suicide: For the right to end-of-life care* (pp. 261–278). Baltimore, MD: The John Hopkins University Press.

Chodoff, P. (1989). Histrionic personality disorder. In American Psychiatric Association (Ed.), *Treatments of psychiatric disorders: A task force report of the American Psychiatric Association.* Washington, DC: American Psychiatric Press.

Chou, K. R., Liu, S. Y., & Chu, H. (2002). The effects of support groups on caregivers of patients with schizophrenia. *Inter. J. Nurs. Stud.*, 39(7), 713–722.

Chou, T. (1992). Wake up and smell the coffee: Caffeine, coffee and the medical consequences. *Western Journal of Medicine*, 157, 544–553.

Christie, D. (2000). Cognitive-behavioral therapeutic techniques for children with eating disorders. In B. Lask & R. Bryant-Waugh (Eds.), *Anorexia nervosa and related eating disorders in childhood and adolescence* (2nd ed., pp. 205–226). Hove, England: Psychology Press/Taylor & Francis.

Christison, G. W., Haviland, M. G., & Riggs, M. L. (2002). The medical condition regard scale: Measuring reactions to diagnoses. *Academ. Med.*, 77(3), 257–262.

Chu, J. A. (2000). "Memories of childhood abuse: Dissociation, amnesia, and corroboration": Reply. *Amer. J. Psychiat.*, 157(8), 1348–1349.

Citrome, L., Bilder, R. M., & Volavka, J. (2002). Managing treatment-resistant schizophrenia: Evidence from randomized clinical trials. *J. Psychiatr. Prac.*, 8(4), 205–215.

Claes, L., Vandereycken, W., & Vertommen, H. (2002). Impulsive and compulsive traits in eating disordered patients compared with controls. *Pers. Individ. Diff.*, 32(4), 707–714.

Clark, D. C. (1999). The puzzle of suicide in later life. In M. T. Stimming, M. Stimming, et al. (Eds.), *Before their time: Adult children's experiences of parental suicide*. Philadephia: Temple University Press.

Clark, H. W. (2001). Residential substance abuse treatment for pregnant and postpartum women and their children: Treatment and policy implications. *Child Welfare*, 80(2), 179–198.

Clark, L. A. (2002). Evaluation and devaluation in personality assessment. In J. Z. Sadler (Ed.), *Descriptions and prescriptions: Values, mental disorders, and the DSMs* (pp. 131–147). Baltimore, MD: Johns Hopkins University Press.

Clark, L. A., & Harrison, J. A. (2001). Assessment instruments. In W. J. Livesley (Ed.), *Handbook of personality disorders: Theory, research, and treatment* (pp. 277–306). New York: Guilford Press.

Clark, R., Anderson, N. B., Clark, V. R., & Williams, D. R. (1999). Racism as a stressor for African Americans: A biopsychosocial model. *Amer. Psychologist.*, 54(10), 805–816.

Clark, S. E., & Goldney, R. D. (2000). The impact of suicide on relatives and friends. In K. Hawton & K. van Heeringen (Eds.), *The international handbook of suicide and attempted suicide*. Chichester: Wiley.

Clarke, J. C., & Saunders, J. B. (1988). *Alcoholism and problem drinking: Theories and treatment*. Sydney: Pergamon Press.

Clarke, J., Stein, M. D., Sobota, M., Marisi, M., & Hanna, L. (1999). Victims as victimizers: Physical aggression by persons with a history of childhood abuse. *Arch. Internal Med.*, 159(16), 1920–1924.

Clary, G. L., & Krishnan, K. R. (2001). Delirium: Diagnosis, neuropathogenesis and treatment. *J. Psychiatr. Prac.*, 7(5), 310–323.

Clay, R. A. (1996). Psychologists' faith in religion begins to grow. *APA Monitor*, 27(8), 1, 48.

Clayton, A. H., Pradko, J. F., Croft, H. A., Montano, C. B., Leadbetter, R. A., Bolden-Watson, C., Bass, K. I., Donahue, R. M. J., Jamerson, B. D., & Metz, A. (2002). Prevalence of sexual dysfunction among newer antidepressants. *J. Clin. Psychiat.*, 63(4), 357–366.

Clum, G. A., & Febbraro, G. A. R. (2001). Phobias. In H. S. Friedman (Ed.), *Specialty articles from the encyclopedia of mental health*. San Diego: Academic Press.

Clyburn, L. D., Stones, M. J., Hadjistavropoulos, T., & Tuokko, H. (2000). Predicting caregiver burden and depression in Alzheimer's disease. *J. Ger. B Psychol. Sci. Soc. Sci.*, 55(1), S2–13.

Coambs, R. B., & McAndrews, M. P. (1994). The effects of psychoactive substances on workplace performance. In S. Macdonald & P. Roman (Eds.), *Research advances in alcohol and drug problems: Vol. 11. Drug testing in the workplace*. New York: Plenum Press.

Cobb, J. M. T., & Steptoe, A. (1998). Psychosocial influences on upper respiratory infectious illness in children. *J. Psychosom. Res.*, 45(4), 319–330.

Coccaro, E. F. (2001). Biological and treatment correlates. In W. J. Livesley (Ed.), *Handbook of personality disorders: Theory, research, and treatment* (pp. 124–135). New York: Guilford Press.

Coffey, C., Carlin, J. B., Lynskey, M., Li, N., & Patton, G. C. (2003). Adolescent precursors of cannabis dependence: Findings from the Victorian Adolescent Health Cohort Study. *Brit. J. Psychiat.*, 182(4), 330–336.

Coffey, S. F., Gudleski, G. D., Saladin, M. E., & Brady, K. T. (2003). Impulsivity and rapid discounting of delayed hypothetical rewards in cocaine-dependent individuals. *Exp. Clin. Psychopharmacol.*, 11(1), 18–25.

Cohen, C., & Regan, T. (2001). *Animal rights debate*. Lanham, MD: Rowan and Littlefield.

Cohen, L., Ardjoen, R. C., & Sewpersad, K. S. M. (1997). Type A behaviour pattern as a risk factor after myocardial infarction: A review. *Psychology and Health*, 12, 619–632.

Cohen, L. J., & Galynker, I. I. (2002). Clinical features of pedophilia and implications for treatment. *J. Psychiatr. Prac.*, 8(5), 276–289.

Cohen, R. M., Semple, W. E., Gross, M., & Nordahl, T. E. (1988). From syndrome to illness: Delineating the pathophysiology of schizophrenia with PET. *Schizo. Bull.*, 14(2), 169–176.

Cohen, S. (2002). Psychosocial stress, social networks, and susceptibility to infection. In H. G.

Koenig & H. J. Cohen (Eds.), *The link between religion and health: Psychoneuroimmunology and the faith factor.* New York: Oxford University Press (pp. 101–123).

Cohen, S., & Herbert, T. B. (1996). Health psychology: Psychological factors and physical disease from the perspective of human psychoneuroimmunology. In J. T. Spence, J. M. Darley, & D. J. Foss (Eds.), *Annual review of psychology* (Vol. 47). Palo Alto, CA: Annual Reviews.

Cohen-Kettenis, P. T. (2001). Gender identity disorder in DSM? *J. Amer. Acad. Child Adol. Psychiat., 40*(4), 391.

Cohen-Kettenis, P. T., & Gooren, L. J. (1999). Transsexualism: A review of etiology, diagnosis and treatment. *J. Psychosom. Res., 46*(4), 315–333.

Cohen-Kettenis, P. T., & van Goozen, S. H. M. (1997). Sex reassignment of adolescent transsexuals: A follow-up study. *J. Amer. Acad. Child Adol. Psychiat., 36*(2), 263–271.

Colbach, E. M. (1987). Hysteria again and again and again. *Inter. J. Offend. Ther. Compar. Crimin., 31*(1), 41–48.

Colburn, D. (1996, November 19). Singer's suicide doesn't lead to "copycat" deaths. *Washington Post Health,* p. 5.

Cole, D. A., & Turner, J. E., Jr. (1993). Models of cognitive mediation and moderation in child depression. *J. Abnorm. Psychol., 102*(2), 271–281.

Cole, J. O., & Yonkers, K. A. (1995). Nonbenzodiazepine anxiolytics. In A. F. Schatzberg & C. B. Nemeroff (Eds.), *The American Psychiatric Press textbook of psychopharmacology.* Washington, DC: American Psychiatric Press.

Coleman, L. (1984). *The reign of error: Psychiatry, authority, and law.* Boston: Beacon.

Colom, F., Vieta, E., Martinez, A. A., Reinares, M., Goikolea, J. M., Benabarre, A., Torrent, C., Comes, M., Corbella, B., Parramon, G., & Corominas, J. (2003). A randomized trial on the efficacy of group psychoeducation in the prophylaxis of recurrences in bipolar patients whose disease is in remission. *Arch. Gen. Psychiat., 60*(4), 402–407.

Colom, F., Vieta, E., Reinares, M., Martinez, A. A., Torrent, C., Goikolea, J. M., & Gasto, C. (2003). Psychoeducation efficacy in bipolar disorders: Beyond compliance enhancement. *J. Clin. Psychiat., 64*(9), 1101–1105.

Comer, R. (1973). *Therapy interviews with a schizophrenic patient.* Unpublished manuscript.

Compas, B. E., & Gotlib, I. H. (2002). *Introduction to clinical psychology: Science and practice.* Boston: McGraw-Hill.

Compas, B. E., Haaga, D. A. F., Keefe, F. J., Leitenberg, H., & Williams, D. A. (1998). Sampling of empirically supported psychological treatments from health psychology: Smoking, chronic pain, cancer, and bulimia nervosa. *J. Cons. Clin. Psychol., 66*(1), 89–112.

Connelly, M., & Dutton, S. (2002). Bearing the brunt: New Yorkers react to 9/11. The Roper Center for Public Opinion Research, *13*(5), 25.

Connor, J. P., Young, R. McD., Lawford, B. R., Ritchie, T. L., & Noble, E. P. (2002). D₂ dopamine receptor (DRD2) polymorphism is associated with severity of alcohol dependence. *Eur. Psychiat., 17*(1), 17–23.

Conrad, N. (1992). Stress and knowledge of suicidal others as factors in suicidal behavior of high school adolescents. *Issues Ment. Hlth. Nurs., 13*(2), 95–104.

Conwell, Y., Caine, E. D., & Olsen, K. (1990). Suicide and cancer in late life. *Hosp. Comm. Psychiat., 43,* 1334–1338.

Conwell, Y., & Duberstein, P. (2001). Suicide in elders. In H. Hendin & J. J. Mann (Eds.), *The clini-*

cal science of suicide prevention (Vol. 932, pp. 132–148). *New York: Annals of the New York Academy of Sciences, 932,* 132.

Cook, C. C. H., & Gurling, H. H. D. (2001). Genetic predisposition to alcohol dependence and problems. In N. Heather, T. J. Peters, et al. (Eds.), *International handbook of alcohol dependence and problems* (pp. 257–279). New York: Wiley.

Cook, C. E., Jeffcoat, A. R., & Perez-Reyes, M. (1985). Pharmacokinetic studies of cocaine and phencyclidine in man. In G. Barnett & C. N. Chiang (Eds.), *Pharmacokinetics and pharmacodynamics of psychoactive drugs.* Foster City, CA: Biomedical Publications.

Coon, D. W., & Thompson, L. W. (2003). The relationship between homework compliance and treatment outcomes among older adult outpatients with mild to moderate depression. *Amer. J. Ger. Psychiat., 11*(1), 53–61.

Coons, P. M. (1980). Multiple personality: Diagnostic considerations. *J. Clin. Psychiat., 41*(10), 330–336.

Coons, P. M. (1998). The dissociative disorders. Rarely considered and underdiagnosed. *Psychiatr. Clin. N. Amer., 21*(3), 637–648.

Coons, P. M., Bowman, E. S., & Milstein, V. (1988). Multiple personality disorder: A clinical investigation of 50 cases. *J. Nerv. Ment. Dis., 176*(9), 519–527.

Cooper, A. M., & Ronningstam, E. (1992). Narcissistic personality disorder. In A. Tasman & M. B. Riba (Eds.), *American Psychiatric Press review of psychiatry* (Vol. 11). Washington, DC: American Psychiatric Press.

Cooper, C. L., Dewe, P., & O'Driscoll, M. (2003). Employee assistance programs. In J. C. Quick, & L. E. Tetrick (Eds.), *Handbook of occupational health psychology* (pp. 289–304). Washington DC: APA.

Cooper, M. L. (1994). Motivations for alcohol use among adolescents: Development and validation of a four-factor model. *Psychol. Assess., 6*(2), 117–128.

Corey, G. (2001). *Theory and practice of counseling and psychotherapy* (6th ed.). Belmont, CA: Brooks/Cole.

Corey, M. S., & Corey, G. (2002). *Groups: Process and practice* (6th ed.). Pacific Grove, CA: Brooks/Cole.

Corkin, S. (1968). Acquisition of motor skill after bilateral medial temporal-lobe excision. *Neuropsychologia, 6,* 255–264.

Corkin, S. (1984). Lasting consequences of bilateral medial temporal lobectomy: Clinical course and experimental findings in H.M. *Sem. in Neuro., 4,* 249–259.

Cornblatt, B. A., & Keilp, J. G. (1994). Impaired attention, genetics, and the pathophysiology of schizophrenia. *Schizo. Bull., 20*(1), 31–46.

Cornelius, J. R., Salloum, I. M., Mezzich, J., Cornelius, M. D., Fabrega, H., Ehler, J. G., Ulrich, R. F., Thase, M. E., & Mann, J. J. (1995). Disproportionate suicidality in patients with comorbid major depression and alcoholism. *Amer. J. Psychiat., 152*(3), 358–364.

Cornish, J. W., McNicholas, L. F., & O'Brien, C. P. (1995). Treatment of substance-related disorders. In A. F. Schatzberg & C. B. Nemeroff (Eds.), *The American Psychiatric Press textbook of psychopharmacology.* Washington, DC: American Psychiatric Press.

Corrigan, P. W., & Penn, D. L. (Eds.). (2001). *Social cognition and schizophrenia.* Washington, DC: APA.

Coryell, W., Miller, D. D., & Perry, P. J. (1998). Haloperidol plasma levels and dose optimization. *Amer. J. Psychiat., 155,* 48–53.

Cosimides, L., & Tooby, J. (2000). Psychology and the emotions. In M. Lewis & J. M. Haviland (Eds.), *Handbook of emotions* (2nd ed.). New York: Guilford Press.

Costa, E. (1983). Are benzodiazepine recognition sites functional entities for the action of endogenous effectors or merely drug receptors? *Adv. in Biochem. & Psychopharm., 38,* 249–259.

Costa, E. (1985). Benzodiazepine-GABA interactions: A model to investigate the neurobiology of anxiety. In A. H. Tuma & J. Maser (Eds.), *Anxiety and the anxiety disorders.* Hillsdale, NJ: Erlbaum.

Costa, E., & Guidotti, A. (1996). Benzodiazepines on trial: A research strategy for their rehabilitation. *Trends Pharmacol. Sci., 17,* 192–200.

Costa, J. L., Brennen, M. B., & Hochgeschwender, U. (2002). The human genetics of eating disorders: Lessons from the leptin/melanocortin system. *Child Adol. Psychiat. Clin. N. Amer., 11*(2), 387–397.

Costa, P. T., Jr., & Widiger, T. A. (Eds.). (2002). *Personality disorders and the five-factor model of personality* (2nd ed.). Washington, DC: APA.

Costantino, G., Flanagan, R., & Malgady, R. G. (2001). Narrative assessments: TAT, CAT, and TEMAS. In L. A. Suzuki, J. G. Ponterotto, et al. (Eds.), *Handbook of multicultural assessment: Clinical, psychological, and educational applications* (2nd ed., pp. 217–236). San Francisco: Jossey-Bass.

Costello, C. G. (1996). The advantages of focusing on the personality characteristics of the personality disordered. In C. G. Costello (Ed.), *Personality characteristics of the personality disordered.* New York: Wiley.

Cottrell, D., & Boston, P. (2002). Practitioner review: The effectiveness of systemic family therapy for children and adolescents. *J. Child Psychol. Psychiat. Allied Disc., 43* (5), 573–586.

Coulson, B. S., & Almeida, O. P. (2002). Delirium: Moving behind the clinical diagnosis. *Revista Brasileora de Psiquiatria, 24*(Suppl. 1), 28–33.

Courtois, C. A. (2001). Implications of the memory controversy for clinical practice: An overview of treatment recommendations and guidelines. *J. Child Sex. Abuse, 9*(3–4), 183–210.

Cowan, D., & Brunero, S. (1997). Group therapy for anxiety disorders using rationale emotive behaviour therapy. *Austral. New Zeal. J. Ment. Hlth. Nurs., 6*(4), 164–168.

Cowan, S. (2002). Public arguments for and against the establishment of community mental health facilities: Implications for mental health practice. *J. Ment. Hlth. UK, 11*(1), 5–15.

Cowley, G. (2000, January 31). Alzheimer's: Unlocking the mystery. *Newsweek,* pp. 46–51.

Cox, A., Rutter, M., Newman, S., & Bartak, L. (1975). A comparative study of infantile autism and specific developmental receptive language disorder: II. Parental characteristics. *Brit. J. Psychiat., 126,* 146–159.

Cox, B. J., Enns, M. W., Borger, S. C., & Parker, J. D. A. (1999). The nature of the depressive experience in analogue and clinically depressed samples. *Behav. Res. Ther., 37*(1), 15–24.

Cox, D. J., Morris, J. B. Jr., Borowitz, S. M., & Sutphen, J. L. (2002). Psychological differences between children with and without chronic encopresis. *J. Pediatr. Psychol., 27*(7), 585–591.

Cox, W. M., Yeates, G. N., Gilligan, P. A. T., & Hosier, S. G. (2001). Individual differences. In N. Heather, T. Peters et al. (Eds.), *International handbook of alcohol dependence and problems.* New York: Wiley.

Coy, T. V. (1998). The effect of repressive coping style on cardiovascular reactivity and speech disturbances during stress. *Diss. Abstr. Inter.: Sect. B: Sci. Eng., 58*(8–B), 4512.

Coyne, J. C. (2001). Depression and the response of others. In W. G. Parrott (Ed.), *Emotions in social psychology: Essential readings* (pp. 231–238). Philadelphia: Psychology Press/Taylor & Francis.

Coyne, J. C., Schwenk, T. L., & Fechner-Bates, S. (1995). Nondetection of depression by primary care physicians reconsidered. *Gen. Hosp. Psychiat.,* 17(1), 3–12.

Crabbé, J. C. (2001). Use of genetic analyses to refine phenotypes related to alcohol tolerance and dependence. *Alcohol.: Clin. Exp. Res.,* 252, 288–292.

Crabbé, J. C. (2002). Genetic contributions to addiction. *Annu. Rev. Psychol.,* 53, 435–462.

Craddock, N., & Jones, I. (1999). Genetics of bipolar disorder. *J. Med. Genet.,* 36(8), 585–594.

Crandall, C. S., Preisler, J. J., & Aussprung, J. (1992). Measuring life events stress in the lives of college students: The Undergraduate Stress Questionnaire (USQ). *Journal of Behavioral Medicine,* 15(6), 627–662.

Crane, G. E. (1973). Persistent dyskinesia. *Brit. J. Psychiat.,* 22, 395–405.

Craske, M. G., & Barlow, D. H. (2001). Panic disorder and agoraphobia. In D. H. Barlow (Ed.), *Clinical handbook of psychological disorders: A step-by-step treatment manual* (3rd ed., pp. 1–59). New York: Guilford Press.

Creer, C., & Wing, J. K. (1974). *Schizophrenia at home.* London: National Schizophrenia Fellowship.

Creese, I., Burt, D. R., & Snyder, S. H. (1977). Dopamine receptor binding enhancement accompanies lesion-induced behavioral supersensitivity. *Science,* 197, 596–598.

Crijnen, A. A., Achenbach, T. M., & Verhulst, F. C. (1999). Problems reported by parents of children in multiple cultures: The Child Behavior Checklist syndrome constructs. *Amer. J. Psychiat.,* 156(4), 569–574.

Crisp, A. H. (1981). Anorexia nervosa at a normal weight?: The abnormal-normal weight control syndrome. *Inter. J. Psychiat. Med.,* 11, 203–233.

Crisp, M. (2001, April 8). Sticks & stones: 'New Kid' puts comic spin on a serious situation. *Sunday News* (Lancaster, PA), p. H-1.

Crits-Christoph, P. (2002). Psychodynamic-interpersonal treatment of generalized anxiety disorder. *Clin. Psychol.: Sci. Prac.,* 9(1), 81–84.

Crits-Christoph, P., & Barber, J. P. (2002). Psychological treatments for personality disorders. In P. E. Nathan & J. M. Gorman (Eds.), *A guide to treatments that work* (2nd ed., pp. 611–623). London: Oxford University Press.

Crow, S. J., Thuras, P., Keel, P. K., & Mitchell, J. E. (2002). Long-term menstrual and reproductive function in patients with bulimia nervosa. *Amer. J. Psychiat.,* 159(6), 1048–1050.

Crow, T. J. (1980). Positive and negative schizophrenic symptoms and the role of dopamine: II. *Brit. J. Psychiat.,* 137, 383–386.

Crow, T. J. (1982). Positive and negative symptoms and the role of dopamine in schizophrenia. In G. Hemmings (Ed.), *Biological aspects of schizophrenia and addiction.* New York: Wiley.

Crow, T. J. (1985). The two-syndrome concept: Origins and current status. *Schizo. Bull.,* 11(3), 471–486.

Crow, T. J. (1995). Brain changes and negative symptoms in schizophrenia. *Psychopathology,* 28(1), 18–21.

Crowley, T. J., Macdonald, M. J., Whitmore, E. A., & Mikulich, S. K. (1998). Cannabis dependence, withdrawal, and reinforcing effects among adolescents with conduct symptoms and substance use disorder. *Drug Alc. Dep.,* 50(1), 27–37.

Crowther, J. H., Snaftner, J., Bonifazi, D. Z., & Shepherd, K. L. (2001). The role of daily hassles in binge eating. *Inter. J. Eat. Disorders,* 29 (4), 449–454.

Csernansky, J. G., & Schuchart, E. K. (2002). Relapse and rehospitalisation rates in patients with schizophrenia: Effects of second generation antipsychotics. *CNS Drugs,* 16(7), 473–484.

Cukan, A. (2001, March 8). Confronting a culture of cruelty. General feature release. *United Press International.*

Culp, A. M., Clyman, M. M., & Culp, R. E. (1995). Adolescent depressed mood, reports of suicide attempts, and asking for help. *Adolescence,* 30(120), 827–837.

Cumming, J., & Cumming, E. (1962). *Ego and milieu: Theory and practice of environmental therapy.* New York: Atherton.

Cuneo, M. W. (2000, November 28). Interviewed for article by J. W. Fountain. Exorcists and exorcisms proliferate across U.S. *New York Times,* A:16.

Cunningham-Owens, D. G. (2000). The challenges of diagnosis and continuing patient assessment. *Inter. J. Psychiat Clin. Pract.,* 4(Suppl. 1), S13–S18.

Curtis, G. C., Magee, W. J., Eaton, W. W., Wittchen, H.-U., & Kessler, R. C. (1998). Specific fears and phobias: Epidemiology and classification. *Brit. J. Psychiat.,* 173, 212–217.

Curtis, J. M., & Cowell, D. R. (1993). Relation of birth order and scores on measures of pathological narcissism. *Psychol. Rep.,* 72(1), 311–315.

Curtiss, L. M. (April, 2002). *The marketing of psychotropic drugs: Mind games with mind drugs or meeting the demand for information?* Unpublished thesis, Princeton University.

Cusack, J. R. (2002). Challenges in the diagnosis and treatment of bipolar disorder. *Drug Benef. Trends,* 14(10), 34–38.

Cuticchia, A. J. (2000). Future vision of the GDB human genome database. *Human Mutat.,* 15(1), 62–67.

Cutler, D. M., Glaeser, E. L., & Norberg, K. E. (2001). Explaining the rise in youth suicide. In J. Gruber (Ed.), *Risky behavior among youths: An economic analysis* (pp. 219–269). Chicago: University of Chicago Press.

Cutright, P., & Fernquist, R. M. (2001). The relative gender gap in suicide: Societal integration, the culture of suicide and period effects in 20 developed countries, 1955–1994. *Soc. Sci. Res.,* 30(1), 76–99.

Cuvelier, M. (2002). Victim, not villain. The mentally ill are six to seven times more likely to be murdered. *Psychology Today,* 35(3), 23.

Cytryn, L., & McKnew, D. H., Jr. (1996). *Growing up sad: Childhood depression and its treatment.* New York: Norton.

D'Onofrio, G., Rathlev, N. K., Ulrich, A. S., Fish, S. S., & Freedland, E. S. (1999). Lorazepam for the prevention of recurrent seizures related to alcohol. *N. Engl. J. Med.,* 340(12), 915–919.

Dada, F., Sethi, S., & Grossberg, S. T. (2001). Generalized anxiety disorder in the elderly. *Psychiatr. Clin. N. Amer.* 24(1), 155–164.

Dahlgren, S., Sandberg, A. D., & Hjelmquist, E. (2003). The non-specificity of theory of mind deficits: Evidence from children with communicative disabilities. *Eur. J. Cog. Psychol.,* 15(1), 129–155.

Dalgleish, T., Taghavi, R. Neshat-Doost, H., Moradi, A., Canterbury, R., & Yule, W. (2003). Patterns of processing bias for emotional information across clinical disorders: A comparison of attention, memory, and prospective cognition in children and adolescents with depression, generalized anxiety, and posttraumatic stress disorder. *J. Clin. Child Adol. Psychol.,* 32(1), 10–21.

Damasio, A. R. (1994). *Descartes' error: Emotion, reason, and the human brain.* New York: Avon Books.

Dancyger, I., Fornari, V., Schneider, M., Fisher, M., Frank, S., Goodman, B., Sison, C., & Wisotsky, W. (2003). Adolescents and eating disorders: An examination of a day treatment program. *Eat. Weight Disord.,* 8(3), 242–248.

Daniels, C. W. (2002). Legal aspects of polygraph admissibility in the United States. In M. Klener (Ed.), *The handbook of polygraph testing.* San Diego, CA: Academic.

Dare, C., & Crowther, C. (1995). Living dangerously: Psychoanalytic psychotherapy of anorexia nervosa. In G. Szmukler, C. Dare, & J. Treasure (Eds.), *Handbook of eating disorders: Theory, treatment and research.* Chichester, England: Wiley.

Dare, C., & Crowther, C. (1995). Psychodynamic models of eating disorders. In G. Szmukler, C. Dare, & J. Treasure (Eds.), *Handbook of eating disorders: Theory, treatment and research.* Chichester, England: Wiley.

Darvres-Bornoz, J., Lemperiere, T., Degiovanni, A., & Gaillard, P. (1995). Sexual victimization in women with schizophrenia and bipolar disorder. *Soc. Psychiat. Psychiatr. Epidemiol.,* 30(2), 78–84.

Dass, R., & Levine, S. (2002). Guided meditation. In A. A. Sheikh (Ed.), *Handbook of therapeutic imagery techniques. Imagery and human development series* (pp. 351–353). Amityville, NY: Baywood Publishing Co., IncDass & Levine, 2002.

Davidson, J. R. T., Weisler, R. H., Butterfield, M. I., Casat, C. D., Connor, K. M., Barnett, S., & van Meter, S. (2003). Mirtazapine vs. placebo in posttraumatic stress disorder: A pilot trial. *Biol. Psychiat.,* 53(2), 188–191.

Davidson, J. R., Hughes, D., Blazer, D. G., & George, L. K. (1991). Posttraumatic stress disorder in the community: An epidemiological study. *Psychol. Med.,* 21(3), 713–721.

Davidson, M. (2002). "Risk of cardiovascular disease and sudden death in schizophrenia": Erratum. *J. Clin. Psychiat.,* 63(8), 744.

Davidson, P. R., & Parker, K. C. (2001). Eye movement desensitization and reprocessing (EMDR): A meta-analysis. *J. Cons. Clin. Psychol.,* 69, 305–316.

Davis, M. (1992). Analysis of aversive memories using the fear potentiated startle paradigm. In N. Butters & L. R. Squire (Eds.), *The neuropsychology of memory* (2nd ed.). New York: Guilford Press.

Davis, R., Olmsted, M., Rockert, W., Marques, T., & Dolhanty, J. (1997). Group psychoeducation for bulimia nervosa with and without additional psychotherapy process sessions. *Inter. J. Eat. Disorders,* 22, 25–34.

Davis, R. A. (2001). A cognitive-behavioral model of pathological Internet use. *Computers Hum. Behav.,* 17(2), 187–195.

Davis, R. C., Brickman, E., & Baker, T. (1991). Supportive and unsupportive responses of others to rape victims: Effects on concurrent victim adjustment. *Amer. J. Comm. Psychol.,* 19, 443–451.

Davis, S. (2000). Testosterone and sexual desire in women. *J. Sex Educ. Ther.,* 25(1), 25–32.

Davis, S. R. (1998). The clinical use of androgens in female sexual disorders. *J. Sex Marital Ther.,* 24(3), 153–163.

Davis, T., Gunderson, J. G., & Myers, M. (1999). Borderline personality disorder. In D. G. Jacobs (Ed.), *The Harvard Medical School guide to suicide assessment and intervention.* San Francisco: Jossey-Bass.

Davison, K. P., Pennebaker, J. W., & Dickerson, S. S. (2000). Who talks? The social psychology of illness support groups. *Amer. Psychologist,* 55(2), 205–217.

Daw, J. (2001). APA's disaster response network: Help on the scene. *Monit. Psychol., 32*(10), 14–15.

Daw, J. (2002). What have we learned since 9/11? *Monit. Psychol., 33*(8), 32–34.

DAWN (Drug Abuse Warning Network). (1998). Highlights from 1998 Report. *Drug Abuse Warning Network.*

DAWN (Drug Abuse Warning Network). (2002). Publications and tables from DAWN Emergency Department Data. Retrieved November 24, 2002, from www.dawninfo.net.

Dawood, K., Pillard, R. C., Horvath, C., Revelle, W., & Bailey, J. M. (2000). Familial aspects of male homosexuality. *Arch. Sex. Behav., 29*(2), 155–163.

Dawson, G., & Castelloe, P. (1992). Autism. In C. E. Walker (Ed.), *Clinical psychology: Historical and research foundations.* New York: Plenum Press.

DeAngelis, T. (1993, September). Controversial diagnosis is voted into latest DSM. *APA Monitor, 24*(9), 32–33.

DeAngelis, T. (2001). Surviving a patient's suicide. *Monit. Psychol., 32*(1), 70–73.

DeAngelis, T. (2002). Binge-eating disorder: What's the best treatment? *Monit. Psychol., 33*(3), 30–32.

DeAngelis, T. (2002). A bright future for PNI. *Monit. Psychol., 33*(6), 46–50.

DeCarlis, L., De Gasperi, A., Slim, A. O., Giacomoni, A., Corti, A., Mazza, E., Di Beneditto, F., Lauterio, A., Arcieri, K., Maione, G., Rondinara, G. F., & Forti, D. (2001). Liver transplantation for ecstasy-induced fulminant hepatic failure. *Transplant Proc., 33*(5), 2743–2744.

DeCubas, M., & Field, T. (1993). Children of methadone-dependent women: Developmental outcomes. *Amer. J. Orthopsychiat., 63*(2), 266–269.

Dedman, B. (2000). Deadly lessons: School shooters tell why. *Chicago Sun-Times,* Digital Chicago, Inc., October 15, 2000.

Degun-Mather, M. (2002). Hypnosis in the treatment of a case of dissociative amnesia for a 12-year period. *Contemp. Hyp., 19*(1), 34–31.

Deitz, S. M. (1977). An analysis of programming DRL schedules in educational settings. *Behav. Res. Ther., 15*(1), 103–111.

Delahanty, J., Ram, R., Postrado, L., Balis, T., Green-Paden, L., & Dixon, L. (2001). Differences in rates of depression in schizophrenia by race. *Schizo. Bull., 27*(1), 29–38.

De Leo, D., Padoani, W., Scocco, P., Lie, D., Bille-Brahe, U., Årensman, E., Hjelmeland, H., Crepet, P., Haring, C., Hawton, K., Lonnqvist, J., Michel, K., Pommereau, X., Querejeta, I., Phillipe, J., Salander-Renberg, E., Schmidtke, A., Fricke, S., Weinacker, B., Tamesvary, B., Wasserman, D., & Faria, S. (2001). Attempted and completed suicide in older subjects: Results from the WHO/EURO Multicentre Study of Suicidal Behavior. *Inter. J. Ger. Psychiat., 16*(3), 300–310.

DeLeon, M. J., Convit, A., George, A. E., Golomb., J., De Santi, S., Tarshish, C., Rusinek, H., Bobinski, M., Ince, C., Miller, D., & Wisniewski, H. (1996). In vivo structural studies of the hippocampus in normal aging and in incipient Alzheimer's disease. In R. J. Wurtman, S. Corkin, J. H. Growdon, & R. M. Nitsch (Eds.), *The neurobiology of Alzheimer's disease.* New York: New York Academy of Sciences.

Delgado, P. L., & Moreno, F. A. (2000). Role of norepinephrine in depression. *J. Clin. Psychiat., 61*(Suppl.), 5–12.

Delisle, J. R. (1986). Death with honors: Suicide among gifted adolescents [Special issue]. *J. Couns. Dev., 64*(9), 558–560.

Dell, P. F. (2002). Dissociative phenomenology of dissociative identity disorder. *J. Nerv. Ment. Dis., 190*(1), 10–15.

de Messias, E. L. M., Cordeiro, N.-F., Sampaio, J. J. C., Bartko, J. J., & Kirkpatrick, B. (2001). Schizophrenia and season of birth in a tropical region: Relationship to rainfall. *Schizo. Res., 48*(2–3), 227–234.

Dencker, S. J., & Dencker, K. (1995). The need for quality assurance for a better compliance and increased quality of life in chronic schizophrenic patients. XIIth AEP Congress: Improvement of compliance: Quality assurance: Increased quality of life in community care in schizophrenia. *Inter. Clin. Psychopharmacology, 9*(Suppl 5), 35–40.

Denton, W. H. (2003). Depression, marital discord and couple therapy. *Curr Opin. Psychiat., 16*(1), 29–34.

DeRubeis, R. J., Tang, T. Z., & Beck, A. T. (2001). Cognitive therapy. In K. S. Dobson (Ed.). *Handbook of cognitive-behavioral therapies* (2nd ed., pp. 349–392). New York: Guilford Press.

Desmond, D. W., Morony, J. T., Paik, M. C., Sano, M., Mohr, J. P., Aboumatar, S., Tseng, C. L., Chan, S., Williams, J. B., Remien, R. H., Hauser, W. A., & Stern, Y. (2000). Frequency and clinical determinants of dementia after ischemic stroke. *Neurology, 54*(5), 1124–1131.

Devanand, D. P. (2002). Comorbid psychiatric disorders in late life depression. *Biol. Psychiat., 52*(3), 236–242.

DeVeaugh-Geiss, J., Moroz, G., Biederman, J., Cantwell, D. P. et al. (1992). Clomipramine hydrochloride in childhood and adolescent obsessive compulsive disorder. A multicenter trial. *J. Amer. Acad. Child Adol. Psychiat., 31*(1), 45–49.

Dew, M. A., Bromet, E. J., Brent, D., & Greenhouse, J. B. (1987). A quantitative literature review of the effectiveness of suicide prevention centers. *J. Cons. Clin. Psychol., 55*, 239–244.

DHHS (Department of Health and Human Services). (1999). Mental health: A report of the surgeon general, executive summary. Rockville, MD: U. S. Department of Health and Human Services.

Dhossche, D., van-der-Steen, F., Ferdinand, R. (2002). Somatoform disorders in children and adolescents: A comparison with other internalizing disorders. *Ann. Clin. Psychiat., 14*(1), 23–31.

Diamond, G. S., & Diamond, G. M. (2002). Studying a matrix of change mechanisms: An agenda for family-based process research. In H. A. Liddle, D. A. Santisteban, R. F. Levant, & J. H. Bray (Eds.), *Family psychology: Science-based interventions* (pp. 41–66). Washington, DC: APA.

Dickey, R., Nussbaum, D., Chevolleau, K., & Davidson, H. (2002). Age as a differential characteristic of rapists, pedophiles, and sexual sadists. *J. Sex Marital Ther., 28*(3), 211–218.

Diekstra, R. F. W. (1989). Suicidal behavior in adolescents and young adults: The international picture. *Crisis, 10*, 16–35.

Diekstra, R. F. W. (1989). Suicide and attempted suicide: An international perspective. *Acta Psychiatr. Scandin., 80*(Suppl. 354), 1–24.

Diekstra, R. F. W., Kienhorst, C. W. M., & de Wilde, E. J. (1995). Suicide and suicidal behaviour among adolescents. In M. Rutter & D. J. Smith, *Psychosocial disorders in young people.* Chichester, England: Wiley.

Diener, E. (2000, January). Subjective well-being: The science of happiness and a proposal for a national index. *Amer. Psychologist, 55*(1), 34–43.

Diener, E., & Diener, C. (1996). Most people are happy. *Psychol. Sci., 7*(3), 181–185.

Diener, E., Sandvik, E., Pavot, W., & Fujita, F. (1992). Extraversion and subjective well-being in a U. S. national probability sample. *J. Res. Pers., 26*(3), 205–215.

Diener, E., Sandvik, E., Seidlitz, L., & Diener, M. (1993). The relationship between income and subjective well-being: Relative or absolute? *Soc. Indicators Res., 28*(3), 195–223.

Dies, R. R. (2003). Group psychotherapies. In A. S. Gurman & S. B. Messer (Eds.), *Essential Psychotherapies: Theory and Practice* (2nd ed.). New York: Guilford Press.

Dietch, J. T. (2001). Old age. In D. Wedding (Ed.), *Behavior and medicine* (3rd ed., pp. 185–194). Seattle: Hogrefe & Huber.

Diller, L. H. (1999). Attention-deficit/hyperactivity disorder. *N. Engl. J. Med, 340*, 1766.

Dinkelmeyer, A., & Johnson, M. B. (2002). Stalking and harassment of psychotherapists. *Amer. J. Forens. Psychol., 20*(4), 5–20.

Dinn, W. M., & Harris, C. L. (2000). Neurocognitive function in antisocial personality disorder. *Psychiat. Res., 97*(2–3), 173–190.

Dinwiddie, S. H., Heath, A. C., Dunne, M. P., Bucholz, K. K., Madden, P. A. F., Slutske, W. F., Bierut, L. J., Statham, D. B., & Martin, N. G. (2000). Early sexual abuse and lifetime psychopathology: A co-twin-control study. *Psychol. Med., 30*(1), 41–52.

di Tomaso, E., Beltramo, M., & Piomelli, D. (1996, August 22). Brain cannabinoids in chocolate. *Nature* (London), *382*, 677–678.

Dittman, M. (2004). Expanding geropsychology training. *Monit. Psychol., 35*(1), 40–41.

Dittrich, E. A. (1997). Sociocultural factors that influence body image satisfaction in women. *Diss. Abstr. Inter.*

Dobkin, P. L., & Da Costa, D. (2000). Group psychotherapy for medical patients. *Psychol., Health Med., 5*(1), 87–96.

Dobson, D. J. G., McDougall, G., Busheikin, J., & Aldous, J. (1995). Effects of social skills training and social milieu treatment on symptoms of schizophrenia. *Psychiatr. Serv., 46*(4), 376–380.

Dobson, V., & Sales, B. (2000). The science of infanticide and mental illness. *Psychol. Pub. Pol. Law, 6*(4), 19–25.

Doctor, R. M., & Neff, B. (2001). Sexual disorders. In H. S. Friedman (Ed.), *Specialty articles from the encyclopedia of mental health.* San Diego: Academic Press.

Dohrmann, R. J., & Laskin, D. M. (1978). An evaluation of electromyographic feedback in the treatment of myofascial pain-dysfunction syndrome. *JAMA, 96*, 656–662.

Dohrenwend, B. P. (2000). The role of adversity and stress in psychopathology: Some evidence and its implications for theory and research. *J. Hlth. Soc. Behav., 41*(1), 1–19.

Dolan, B., Evans, C., & Norton, K. (1995). Multiple Axis-II diagnoses of personality disorder. *Brit. J. Psychiat., 166*, 107–112.

Dolan, M., Deakin, W. J. F., Roberts, N., & Anderson, I. (2002). Serotonergic and cognitive impairment in impulsive aggressive personality disordered offenders: Are there implications for treatment? *Psychol. Med., 32*(1), 105–117.

Dole, V. P., & Nyswander, M. (1965). A medical treatment for heroin addiction. *JAMA, 193*, 646–650.

Dole, V. P., & Nyswander, M. (1967). Heroin addiction, a metabolic disease. *Arch. Internal Med., 120*, 19–24.

Dorfman, W. I., & Leonard, S. (2001). The Minnesota Multiphasic Personality Inventory-2 (MMPI-2). In W. I. Dorfman & M. Hersen (Eds.), *Understanding psychological assessment. Perspectives on individual differences* (pp. 145–171). New York: Kluwer Academic/Plenum Press.

Dorwart, R. A., & Ostacher, M. J. (1999). A community psychiatry approach to preventing suicide. In D. G. Jacobs (Ed.), *The Harvard Medical School guide to suicide assessment and intervention.* San Francisco: Jossey-Bass.

Dougall, A. L., & Baum, A. (2001). Stress, health, and illness. In A. Baum, T. A. Revenson, & J. E. Singer (Eds.), *Handbook of health psychology.* Mahwah, NJ: Erlbaum.

Douglas, J. (1996). *Mind hunter: Inside the FBI's elite serial crime unit.* New York: Pocket Star.

Douglas, K. S., & Koch, W. J. (2001). Civil commitment and civil competence: Psychological issues. In R. A. Schuller & J. R. P. Ogloff (Eds.), *Introduction to psychology and law: Canadian perspectives* (pp. 353–374). Toronto, Ont., Can.: University of Toronto Press.

Dowdney, L., & Skuse, D. (1993). Parenting provided by adults with mental retardation. *J. Child Psychol. Psychiat. Allied Disc., 34*(1), 25–47.

Doweiko, H. E. (1999). *Concepts of chemical dependency* (4th ed.). Pacific Grove, CA: Brooks/Cole.

Doweiko, H.E. (2002). *Concepts of chemical dependency.* Australia: Brooks/Cole.

Downey, A. M. (1991). The impact of drug abuse upon adolescent suicide. *Omega: J. Death Dying, 22*(4), 261–275.

Downey, R. G., Sinnett, E. R., & Seeberger, W. (1998). The changing face of MMPI practice. *Psychol. Rep., 83*(3, Pt. 2), 1267–1272.

Downhill, J. E., Jr., Buchsbaum, M. S., Hazlett, E. A., Barth, S., Roitman, S. L., Nunn, M., Lekarev, O., Wei, T., Shihabuddin, L., Mitropoulou, V., Silverman, J., & Siever, L. J. (2001). Temporal lobe volume determined by magnetic resonance imaging in schizotypal personality disorder and schizophrenia. *Schizo. Res., 48*(2–3), 187–199.

Doyle, K. O., & Youn, S. (2000). Exploring the traits of happy people. *Soc. Indicators Res., 52*(2), 195–209.

Dozier, M. (1996). Personal correspondence. University of Delaware, Newark.

Draine, J., Salzer, M. S., Culahne, D. P., & Hadley, T. R. (2002). Role of social disadvantage in crime, joblessness, and homelessness among persons with serious mental illness. *Psychiatr. Serv., 53*(5), 565–573.

Drake, R. E., McHugo, G. J., Becker, D. R., Anthony, W. A., & Clark, R. E. (1996). The New Hampshire study of supported employment for people with severe mental illness. *J. Cons. Clin. Psychol., 64*(2), 391–399.

Drake, R. E., & Wallach, M. A. (1992). Mental patients' attraction to the hospital: Correlates of living preference. *Comm. Ment. Hlth. J., 28*(1), 5–12.

Dratcu, L. (2000). Panic, hyperventilation and perpetuation of anxiety. *Prog. Neuropsychopharmacol. Biol. Psychiat., 24*(7), 1069–1089.

Drobes, D. J., Saladin, M. E., & Tiffany, S. T. (2001). Classical conditioning mechanisms in alcohol dependence. In N. Heather, T. J. Peters, et al. (Eds.), *International handbook of alcohol dependence and problems* (pp. 281–297). New York: Wiley.

Drug Enforcement Administration (DEA). (1996). *Consumption of ritalin.* Washington, DC: Author.

Drug Enforcement Administration (DEA). (2000, May 16). DEA congressional testimony before the committee on education and the workforce: Subcommittee on early childhood and families.

Druss, B. G., & Rosenheck, R. A. (1998). Mental disorders and access to medical care in the United States. *Amer. J. Psychiat., 155*(12), 1775–1777.

Dryden, W., & Ellis, A. (2001). Rational emotive behavior therapy. In K. S. Dobson (Ed.), *Handbook of cognitive-behavioral therapies* (2nd ed., pp 295–348). New York: Guilford Press.

Dubbert, P. M. (1995). Behavioral (life-style) modification in the prevention and treatment of hypertension. *Clin. Psychol. Rev., 15*(3), 187–216.

Duberstein, P. R., Conwell, Y., & Cox, C. (1998). Suicide in widowed persons: A psychological autopsy comparison of recently and remotely bereaved older subjects. *Amer. J. Ger. Psychiat., 6*(4), 328–334.

Duberstein, P. R., Conwell, Y., Cox, C., Podgorski, C., Glazer, R., & Caine, E. (1995). Attitudes toward self-determined death: A survey of primary care physicians. *J. Amer. Ger. Soc., 43,* 395–400.

Duffy, B. (1996, April 15). The mad bomber? *U. S. News & World Report,* pp. 29–36.

Dugas, M. J., Buhr, K., & Ladouceur, R. (2002). The role of intolerance of uncertainty in the etiology and maintenance of generalized anxiety disorder. In R. G. Heimberg, C. L. Turk, & D. S. Mennin (Eds.), *Generalized anxiety disorder: Advances in research and practice.* New York: Guilford Press.

Duggan, J. P., & Booth, D. A. (1986). Obesity, overeating, and rapid gastric emptying in rats with ventromedial hypothalamic lesions. *Science, 231*(4738), 609–611.

Dunbar, F. (1948). *Synopsis of psychosomatic diagnosis and treatment.* St. Louis: Mosby.

Duncan, B. L. (2002). Does drug company marketing now include product placement in the movies? *Ethical Human Sciences and Services, 4*(2), 147–150.

Dunn, E. F., & Steiner, M. (2000). The functional neurochemistry of mood disorders in women. In M. Steiner, K.A. Yonkers, & E. Erikson (Eds.), *Mood disorders in women* (pp. 71–82). London: Martin Dunitz.

Dunn, K. M., Croft, P. R., & Hackett, G. I. (1999). Association of sexual problems with social, psychological, and physical problems in men and women: A cross sectional population survey. *J. Epidemiol. Comm. Hlth., 53*(3), 144–148.

Dupont, S. (1995). Multiple sclerosis and sexual functioning: A review. *Clin. Rehab. 9*(2), 135–141.

Dupree, L. W., & Schonfeld, L. (1999) Management of alcohol abuse in older adults. In M. Duffy (Ed.), *Handbook of counseling and psychotherapy with older adults.* New York: Wiley.

Durkheim, E. (1951). *Suicide.* New York: Free Press. (Original work published 1897.)

Dykens, E. M., & Hodapp, R. M. (2001). Research in mental retardation: Toward an etiologic approach. *J. Child Psychol. Psychiat. Allied Discl., 42*(1), 49–71.

Eakes, G. G. (1995). Chronic sorrow: The lived experience of parents of chronically mentally ill individuals. *Arch. Psychiatr. Nursing, 9*(2), 77–84.

Eaton, W. W., Dryman, A., & Weissman, M. M. (1991). Panic and phobia. In L. N. Robins & D. A. Regier (Eds.), *Psychiatric disorders in America: The Epidemiologic Catchment Area Study.* New York: Maxwell Macmillan International.

Ebstein, R. P., & Kotler, M. (2002). Personality, substance abuse, and genes. In J. Benjamin, R. P. Ebstein, et al. (Eds.), *Molecular genetics and the human personality* (pp. 151–163). Washington, DC: APA.

Echeburúa, E., Báez, C., & Fernández-Montalvo, J. (1996). Comparative effectiveness of three therapeutic modalities in the psychological treatment of pathological gambling: Long-term outcome. *Behav. Cog. Psychother., 24,* 51–72.

Edelman, R. E., & Chambless, D. L. (1995). Adherence during sessions and homework in cognitive-behavioral group treatment of social phobia. *Behav. Res. Ther., 33*(5), 573–577.

Edlund, M. J., Wamg, P. S., Berglund, P. A., Katz, S. J., Lin, E., & Kessler, R. C. (2002). Dropping out of mental health treatment: Patterns and predictors among epidemiological survey respondents in the United States and Ontario. *Amer. J. Psychiat., 159*(5), 845–851.

Efron, S. (1997, October 21). Eating disorders in Asia. *Los Angeles Times.*

Ehrman, M. (1995, June 25). Reaching out for virtual therapy. *Los Angeles Times,* pp. E1, E4.

Eisenberg, L. (1958). School phobia: A study in the communication of anxiety. *Amer. J. Psychiat., 114,* 712–718.

Eisenthal, S., Koopman, C., & Lazare, A. (1983). Process analysis of two dimensions of the negotiated approach in relation to satisfaction in the initial interview. *J. Nerv. Ment. Dis., 171,* 49–54.

Eisler, I. (1995). Family models of eating disorders. In G. Szmukler, C. Dare, & J. Treasure (Eds.), *Handbook of eating disorders: Theory, treatment and research.* Chichester, UK: Wiley.

Eisler, I., et al. (2000). Family therapy for adolescent anorexia nervosa: The results of a controlled comparison of two family interventions. *J. Child Psychol. Psychiat., 41*(6), 727–736.

Elias, M. (1995, April 18). Therapist's program to go on-line. *USA Today,* p. 1D.

Elias, M. (1999, August 26). Teen mags hurt fat-fearful girls. *USA Today,* 5D.

Elias, M. (2000, March 7). Online mental-health therapy in its formative years. *USA Today,* p. 3D.

Eliez, S., & Feinstein, C. (2001). The fragile X syndrome: Bridging the gap from gene to behavior. *Curr. Opin. Psychiat., 14*(5), 443–449.

Elkins, I. J., & Cromwell, R. L. (1994). Priming effects in schizophrenia: Associative interference and facilitation as a function of visual context. *J. Abnorm. Psychol., 103*(4), 791–800.

Ellenberger, H. F. (1970). *The discovery of the unconscious.* New York: Basic Books.

Ellenberger, H. F. (1972). The story of "Anna O.": A critical review with new data. *J. History Behav. Sci., 8,* 267–279.

Elliott, R. (2002). The effectiveness of humanistic therapies. In D.J. Cain & J. Seeman (Eds.), *Humanistic psychotherapies: Handbook of research and practice* (pp. 57–82). Washington, DC: APA.

Elliott, D. S., Hamburg, B., & Williams, K. R. (2002). Violence in American schools: An overview. In CSPV (Center for the Study and Prevention of Violence, University of Colorado) *Violence in American Schools.* Cambridge, UK: Cambridge University Press.

Ellis, A. (1962). *Reason and emotion in psychotherapy.* Secaucus, NJ: Lyle Stuart.

Ellis, A. (1977). The basic clinical theory of rational-emotive therapy. In A. Ellis & R. Grieger (Eds.), *Handbook of rational-emotive therapy.* New York: Springer.

Ellis, A. (2001). *Overcoming destructive beliefs, feelings, and behaviors: New directions for rational emotive behavior therapy.* Amherst, NY: Prometheus.

Ellis, A. (2002). The role of irrational beliefs in perfectionism. In G. L. Flett & P. L. Hewitt (Eds.) *Perfectionism: Theory, research, and treatment* (pp. 217–229). Washington, DC: APA.

El-Mallakh, R. S., & Huff, M. O. (2001). Mood stabilizers and ion regulation. *Harv. Rev. Psychiatry, 9*(1), 23–32.

Emmelkamp, P. M. (1982). Exposure in vivo treatments. In A. Goldstein & D. Chambless (Eds.), *Agoraphobia: Multiple perspectives on theory and treatment.* New York: Wiley.

Emmelkamp, P. M. (1994). Behavior therapy with adults. In A. E. Bergin & S. L. Garfiel (Eds.),

Handbook of psychotherapy and behavior change(4th ed.). New York: Wiley.

Ennis, B. J., & Emery, R. D. (1978). *The rights of patients* (ACLU Handbook Series). New York: Avon.

Enoch, M. A., Kaye, W. H., Rotondo, A., et al. (1998). 5-HT2A promoter polymorphism-1438G/A, anorexia nervosa, and obsessive-compulsive disorder [Letter]. *Lancet, 351,* 1785–1786.

Epstein, S. (1983). Hypnotherapeutic control of exhibitionism: A brief communication. *Inter. J. Clin. Exp. Hyp., 31*(2), 63–66.

Erba, H. W. (2000). Early intervention programs for children with autism: Conceptual frameworks for implementation. *Amer. J. Orthopsychiat., 70*(1), 82–94.

Erickson, M. T. (1992). *Behavior disorders of children and adolescents.* Englewood Cliffs, NJ: Prentice Hall.

Erikson, E. (1963). *Childhood and society.* New York: Norton.

Ernst, N. D., & Harlan, W. R. (1991). Obesity and cardiovascular disease in minority populations: Executive summary. Conference highlights, conclusions, and recommendations. *Amer. J. Clin. Nutr., 53*(Suppl.), 1507–1511.

Erwin, E. (2000). Is a science of psychotherapy possibile: Subjectivity problems. *Amer. Psychologist, 55*(10), 1133–1138.

Eser, A. (1981). "Sanctity" and "quality" of life in a historical comparative view. In S. E. Wallace & A. Eser (Eds.), *Suicide and euthanasia: The rights of personhood.* Knoxville: University of Tennessee Press.

Espie, C. A. (2002). Insomnia: Conceptual issues in the development, persistence, and treatment of sleep disorder in adults. *Annu. Rev. Psychol., 53,* 215–243.

Espina, A., Ortego, A., Ochoa-de-Alda, I., & Aleman, A. (2002). Alexitimia en low trastornos alimentarios./Alexithyma in eating disorders. *Analis. Modif. Cond., 28*(117), 25–42.

Everly, G. S., Jr., & Lating, J. M. (2004). *Personality-guided therapy for posttraumatic stress disorder.* Washington, DC: American Psychological Association.

Everson, S. A., Goldberg, D. E., Kaplan, G. A., Cohen, R. D., et al. (1996). Hopelessness and risk of mortality and incidence of myocardial infarction and cancer. *Psychosom. Med., 58,* 113–121.

Express Scripts, Inc. (1999, June 29). *1998 Express Scripts Trend Report.* St. Louis: Author.

Fábrega, H., Jr. (2002). *Origins of psychopathology: The phylogenetic and cultural basis of mental illness.* New Brunswick, NJ: Rutgers University Press.

Fábrega, H., Ulrich, R., Pilkonis, P., & Mezzich, J. (1991). On the homogeneity of personality disorder clusters. *Comprehen. Psychiat., 32*(5), 373–386.

Fahrenberg, J., Foerster, F., & Wilmers, F. (1995). Is elevated blood pressure level associated with higher cardiovascular responsiveness in laboratory tasks and with response specificity? *Psychophysiology, 32*(1), 81–91.

Fairbank, J. A., & Keane, T. M. (1982). Flooding for combat-related stress disorders: Assessment of anxiety reduction across traumatic memories. *Behav. Ther., 13,* 499–510.

Fairburn, C. G. (1985). Cognitive-behavioural treatment for bulimia. In D. M. Garner & P. E. Garfinkel (Eds.), *Handbook of psychotherapy for anorexia nervosa and bulimia.* New York: Guilford Press.

Fairburn, C. G., Cooper, Z., & Shafran, R. (2003). Cognitive behaviour therapy for eating disorders: A "transdiagnostic" theory and treatment. *Behav. Res. Ther., 41*(5), 509–528.

Falloon, I. R. H. (2002). Cognitive-behavioral family and educational interventions for schizophrenic disorders. In S. G. Hofmann & M. C. Tompson (Eds.), *Treating chronic and severe mental disorders: A handbook of empirically supported interventions.* New York: Guilford Press.

Faraone, S. V. (2000). Attention deficit hyperactivity disorder in adults: Implications for theories of diagnosis. *Curr. Direct. Psychol. Sci., 9,* 33–36.

Farberow, N. L., & Litman, R. E. (1970). *A comprehensive suicide prevention program.* Unpublished final report, Suicide Prevention Center of Los Angeles, Los Angeles.

Farlow, M. R., Murrell, J. R., Unverzagt F. W., Phillips, M., Takao, M., Hulette, C., & Ghetti, B. (2001). Familial Alzheimer's disease with spastic paraparesis associated with a mutation at codon 261 of the presenilin 1 gene. In I. Khalid, S. S. Sisodia, & B. Winblad (Eds.), *Alzheimer's disease: Advances in etiology, pathogenesis and therapeutics.* Chichester: Wiley.

Farrington, D. P. (1991). Psychological contributions to the explanations of offending. *Issues Criminol. & Legal Psychol., 1*(17), 7–19.

Fasko, S. N., & Fasko, D. (1991). Suicidal behavior in children. *Psychology: J. of Human Behav., 27* (4)-*28*(1), 10–16.

Fava, M., Farabaugh, A. H., Sickinger, A. H., Wright, E., Alpert, J. E., Sonawalla, S., Nierenberg, A. A., & Worthington, J. J. (2002). Personality disorders and depression. *Psychol. Med., 32*(4), 1049–1057.

Favaro, A., & Santonastaso, P. (2002). The spectrum of self-injurious behavior in eating disorders. *Eat. Disord.: J. Treat. Prev., 10*(3), 215–225.

Favaro, A., Maiorani, M., Colombo, G., & Santonastaso, P. (1999). Traumatic experiences, posttraumatic stress disorder, and dissociative symptoms in a group of refugees from former Yugoslavia. *J. Nerv. Ment. Dis., 187*(5), 306–308.

Fay, B. P. (1995). The individual versus society: The cultural dynamics of criminalizing suicide. *Hastings International and Comparative Law Review, 18,* 591–615.

Fazel, S., & Danesh, J. (2002). Serious mental disorder in 23,000 prisoners: A systematic review of 62 surveys. *Lancet, 359*(9306), 545–550.

FBI Uniform Crime Reports. (1996). *Crime in the United States: 1996 Uniform Crime Reports.* Washington, DC: FBI.

Feldman, H. A., Goldstein, I., Hatzichristou, D. G., Krane, R. J., & McKinlay, J. B. (1994). Impotence and its medical and psychosocial correlates: Results of the Massachusetts Male Aging Study. *J. Urology, 151,* 54–61.

Feldman, M. D., Ford, C. V., & Reinhold, T. (1994). *Patient or pretender: Inside the strange world of factitious disorders.* New York: Wiley.

Feldman, S. (Ed.). (2003). *Managed behavioral health services: Perspectives and practice.* Springfield, IL: Charles C. Thomas Publisher, Ltd.

Feldman, S., Bachman, J., & Bayer, J. (2002). Mental health parity: A review of research and a bibliography. *Admin. Pol. Ment. Hlth., 29*(3), 215–228.

Felner, R. D., Felner, T. Y., & Silverman, M. M. (2000). Prevention in mental health and social intervention: Conceptual and methodological issues in the evolution of the science and practice of prevention. In J. Rappaport & E. Seidman (Eds.), *Handbook of community psychology* (pp. 9–42). New York: Kluwer Academic/Plenum Publishers.

Fenichel, O. (1945). *The psychoanalytic theory of neurosis.* New York: Norton.

Fenigstein, A. (1996). Paranoia. In C. G. Costello (Ed.), *Personality characteristics of the personality disordered.* New York: Wiley.

Fennig, S., Fennig, S., & Roe, D. (2002). Cognitive-behavioral therapy for bulimia nervosa: Time course and mechanisms of change. *Gen. Hosp. Psychiat., 24*(2), 87–92.

Fennig, S., Schwartz, J. E., & Bromet, E. J. (1994). Are diagnostic criteria, time of episode and occupational impairment important determinants of the female:male ratio for major depression? *J. Affect. Disorders, 30,* 147–154.

Fenton, W. S., Hoch, J. S., Herrell, J. M., Mosher, L., & Dixon, L. (2002). Cost and cost-effectiveness of hospital vs. residential crisis care for patients who have serious mental illness. *Arch. Gen. Psychiat., 59*(4), 357–364.

Fergusson, D. M., Woodward, L. J., & Horwood, L. J. (2000). Risk factors and life processes associated with the onset of suicidal behavior during adolescence and early adulthood. *Psychol. Med., 30*(1), 23–39.

Ferrada, N. M., Asberg, M., Ormstad, K., & Nordstrom, P. (1995). Definite and undetermined forensic diagnoses of suicide among immigrants in Sweden. *Acta Psychiatr. Scandin., 91*(2), 130–135.

Ferrando, S. J. (2001). Substance abuse and HIV infection. *Psychiatr. Ann., 31*(1), 57–62.

Ferreira, C. (2000). Serial killers—Victims of compulsion or masters of control? In D. H. Fishbein (Ed.), *The science, treatment, and prevention of antisocial behaviors: Application to the criminal justice system*(pp. 15-1–15-8). Kingston, NJ: Civic Research Institute.

Fetto, J. (2001, Oct. 1). Pencil me in. *Amer. Demog.* Retrieved on Sept. 15, 2002, from www.industryclick.com.

Fetto, J. (2002, May 1). Drugged out. *Amer. Demog.* Retrieved September 15, 2002, from www.americandemographics.com.

Fetto, J. (2002, Apr. 1). What seems to be the problem? *Amer. Demog.* Retrieved Sept. 15, 2002, from www.industryclick.com.

Fetto, J. (2002, May 1). You never call. *Amer. Demog. 4, (1),* 8–9. Retrieved September 15, 2002, from www.americandemographics.com.

Fichter, M. M., & Pirke, K. M. (1995). Starvation models and eating disorders. In G. Szmukler, C. Dare, & J. Treasure (Eds.), *Handbook of eating disorders: Theory, treatment and research.* Chichester, England: Wiley.

Fichtner, C. G., Kuhlman, D. T., Gruenfeld, M. J., & Hughes, J. R. (1990). Decreased episodic violence and increased control of dissociation in a carbamazepine-treated case of multiple personality. *Biol. Psychiat., 27*(9), 1045–1052.

Field, A. P., & Davey, G. C. L. (2001). Conditioning models of childhood anxiety. In W. K. Silverman & P. S. A. Treffers (Eds.), *Anxiety disorders in children and adolescents: Research, assessment and intervention* (pp. 187–211). New York: Cambridge University Press.

Fieve, R. R. (1975). *Moodswing.* New York: Morrow.

Figley, C. R. (1978). Symptoms of delayed +combat stress among a college sample of Vietnam veterans. *Military Med., 143*(2), 107–110.

Figley, C. R., & Leventman, S. (1990). Introduction: Estrangement and victimization. In C. R. Figley & S. Leventman (Eds.), *Strangers at home: Vietnam veterans since the war.* New York: Praeger.

Finckh, U. (2001). The dopamine D2 receptor gene and alcoholism: Association studies. In D. P. Agarwal & H. K. Seitz (Eds.), *Alcohol in health and disease* (pp. 151–176). New York: Marcel Dekker.

Fine, C. G., & Madden, N. E. (2000). Group psychotherapy in the treatment of dissociative identity disorder and allied dissociative disorders. In R. H. Klein & V. L. Schermer (Eds.), *Group psychotherapy for psychological trauma* (pp. 298–325). New York: Guilford Press.

Finfgeld, D. L. (2002). Anorexia nervosa: Analysis of long-term outcomes and clinical implications. *Arch. Psychiatr. Nursing, 16*(4), 176–186.

Fink, M. (1992). Electroconvulsive therapy. In E. S. Paykel (Ed.), *Handbook of affective disorders.* New York: Guilford Press.

Fink, M. (2001). Convulsive therapy: A review of the first 55 years. *J. Affect. Disorders, 63*(1–3), 1–15.

Finkel, N. J. (1989). The Insanity Defense Reform Act of 1984: Much ado about nothing. *Behav. Sci. Law, 7*(3), 403–419.

Finkel, N. J. (1990). De facto departures from insanity instructions. *Law Human Behav., 14*(2), 105–122.

Finkel, N. J. (1991). The insanity defense. *Law Human Behav., 15*(5), 533–555.

Finkel, N. J., & Duff, K. (1989). The insanity defense: Giving jurors a third option. *Forensic Reports, 1*, 65–70.

Finkelhor, D., Asdigian, N., & Dziuba-Leatherman, J. (1995). Victimization prevention programs for children: A follow-up. *Amer. J. Pub. Hlth., 85*(12), 1684–1689.

Finn, P. R., Sharkansky, E. J., Brandt, K. M., & Turcotte, N. (2000). The effects of familial risk, personality, and expectancies on alcohol use and abuse. *J. Abnorm. Psychol., 109*(1), 122–133.

Fischer, C. T. (Ed.). (2002). Introduction: Special issue on humanistic approaches to psychological assessment. *Humanist. Psycholog., 30*(1–2), 3–9.

Fishbain, D. A. (2000). Re: The meeting of pain and depression. Comorbidity in women. *Canad. J. Psychiat., 45*(1), 88.

Fisher, D., Beech, A., & Browne, K. (2000). The effectiveness of relapse prevention training in a group of incarcerated child molesters. *Psychol. Crime Law, 6*(3), 181–195.

Fisher, J. E., & Carstensen, L. L. (1990). Behavior management of the dementias. *Clin. Psychol. Rev., 10*, 611–629.

Fisher, J. E., Zeiss, A. M., & Carstensen, L. L. (2001). Psychopathology in the aged. In P. B. Sutker & H. E. Adams (Eds.), *Comprehensive handbook of psychopathology* (3rd ed., pp. 921–952). New York: Kluwer Academic/Plenum.

Fisher, J. O., & Birch, L. L. (1999). Restricting access to palatable foods affects children's behavioral response, food selection, and intake. *Amer. J. Clin. Nutr., 69*(6), 1264–1272.

Fitz, A. (1990). Religious and familial factors in the etiology of obsessive-compulsive disorder: A review. *J. Psychol. Theol., 18*(2), 141–147.

Fitzgibbon, M. L., Spring, B., Avellone, M. E., Blackman, L. R., Pingitore, R., & Stolley, M. R. (1998). Correlates of binge eating among Hispanic, Black and White women. *Inter. J. Eat. Disorders, 24*, 43–52.

Fivush, R., Sales, J. M., Goldberg, A., Bahrick, L., & Parker, J. (2004). Weathering the storm: Children's long-term recall of Hurricane Andrew. *Memory, 12*(1), 104–118.

Flament, M. F., Godart, N. T., Fermanian, J., & Jeammet, P. (2001). Predictive factors of social disability in patients with eating disorders. *Eat. Weight Disord., 6*(2), 99–106.

Flannery, R. B., Jr., Fisher, W., Walker, A., Kolodziej, K., & Spillane, M. J. (2000). Assaults on staff by psychiatric patients in community residences. *Psychiatr. Serv., 51*(1), 111–113.

Fletcher, K. E. (2003). Childhood posttraumatic stress disorder. In E. J. Mash & R. A. Barkley (Eds.), *Child psychopathology* (2nd ed.)(pp. 330–371). New York: Guilford Press.

Fletcher, T. B. (2000). Primary nocturnal enuresis: A structural and strategic family systems approach. *J. Ment. Hlth Couns., 22*(1), 32–44.

Flick, S. N., Roy-Byrne, P. P., Cowley, D. S., Shores, M. M., & Dunner, D. L. (1993). DSM-III-R personality disorders in a mood and anxiety disorders clinic: Prevalence, comorbidity, and clinical correlates. *J. Affect. Disorders, 27*, 71–79.

Flint, A. J. (1994). Epidemiology and comorbidity of anxiety disorders in the elderly. *Amer. J. Psychiat., 151*(5), 640–649.

Foa, E. B., & Franklin, M. E. (2001). Obsessive-compulsive disorder. In D.H. Barlow (Ed.), *Clinical handbook of psychological disorders: A step-by-step treatment manual*(3rd ed.). New York: Guilford Press.

Foa, E. B., Hearst-Ikeda, D., & Perry, K. L. (1995). Evaluation of a brief cognitive-behavioral program for the prevention of chronic PTSD in recent assault victims. *J. Cons. Clin. Psychol., 63*, 948–955.

Foderaro, L. (1995, June 16). The mentally ill debate what to call themselves. *New York Times*, p. B1.

Fog, R. (1995). New diagnostic vistas. XIIth AEP Congress: Improvement of compliance: Quality assurance: Increased quality of life in community care in schizophrenia. *Inter. Clin. Psychopharmacology, 9*(Suppl. 5), 71–73.

Foley, K., & Hendin, H. (Eds.). (2002). *The case against assisted suicide: For the right to end-of-life care.* Baltimore, MD: The John Hopkins University Press.

Foley, K., & Hendin, H. (2002). Introduction: A medical, ethical, legal, and psychosocial perspective. In K. Foley & H. Hendin (Eds.), *The case against assisted suicide: For the right to end-of-life care* (pp. 1–16). Baltimore, MD: The John Hopkins University Press.

Foley, K., & Hendin, H. (Eds.). (2003). The case against assisted suicide: For the right to-end-life care. *J. Nerv. Ment. Dis., 191*(1), 62–64.

Fombonne, E. (1995). Eating disorders: Time trends and possible explanatory mehanisms. In M. Rutter & D.J Smith, *Psychosocial disorders in young people.* Chichester, England: Wiley.

Ford, G. G. (2001). *Ethical reasoning in the mental health professions.* Boca Raton, FL: CRC Press.

Ford, J. D., & Stewart, J. (1999). Group psychotherapy for war-related PTSD with military veterans. In B. H. Young & D. D. Blake (Eds.), *Group treatments for post-traumatic stress disorder.* Philadelphia: Brunner/Mazel.

Ford, M. R., & Widiger, T. A. (1989). Sex bias in the diagnosis of histrionic and antisocial personality disorders. *J. Cons. Clin. Psychol., 57* (2), 301–305.

Foreyt, J. P., Poston, W. S. C., & Goodrick, G. K. (1996). Future directions in obesity and eating disorders. *Addic. Behav., 21*(6), 767–778.

Foster, P. S., & Eisler, R. M. (2001). An integrative approach to the treatment of obsessive-compulsive disorder. *Comprehen. Psychiat., 42*(1), 24–31.

Fountain, J. W. (2000, November 28). Exorcists and exorcisms proliferate across U.S. *New York Times*, A-16.

Fowler, J. S., Volkow, N. D., & Wolf, A. P. (1995). PET studies of cocaine in human brain. In A. Biegon & N. D. Volkow (Eds.), *Sites of drug action in the human brain.* Boca Raton, FL: CRC Press.

Fowler, R. (1999, June 10). Cited in Associated Press release (Philadelphia), Outrage over sex abuse study.

Fox, V. (2000). Empathy: The wonder quality of mental health treatment. *Psychiatr. Rehab. J., 23*(3), 292–293.

Foxhall, K. (2001). Preventing relapse: Looking at data differently led to today's influential relapse prevention therapy. *APA Monitor, 32*(6), 46–47.

Frances, R. J., & Franklin, J. E. (1988). Alcohol and other psychoactive substance use disorders. In J. A. Talbott, R. E. Hales, & S. C. Yudofsky (Eds.), *Textbook of psychiatry.* Washington, DC: American Psychiatric Press.

Frank, J. D. (1973). *Persuasion and healing* (Rev. ed.). Baltimore: Johns Hopkins University Press.

Frankel, F. H. (1993). Adult reconstruction of childhood events in the multiple personality literature. *Amer. J. Psychiat., 150*(6), 954–958.

Frankish, C. J. (1994). Crisis centers and their role in treatment: Suicide prevention versus health promotion. In A. A. Leenaars, J. T. Maltsberger, & R. A. Neimeyer (Eds.), *Treatment of suicidal people.* Washington, DC: Taylor & Francis.

Franklin R. D. (Ed.) (2003). *Prediction in forensic and neuropsychology: Sound statistical practices.* Mahwah, NJ: Erlbaum.

Frayn, D. H. (1991). The incidence and significance of perceptual qualities in the reported dreams of patients with anorexia nervosa. *Canad. J. Psychiat., 36*(7), 517–520.

Frederick, C. J. (1969). Suicide notes: A survey and evaluation. *Bull. Suicidol., 8*, 17–26.

Fredericks, L. E. (2001). *The use of hypnosis in surgery and anesthesiology: Psychological preparation of the surgical patient.* Springfield, IL: Thomas.

Freeman, A. (2002). Cognitive-behavioral therapy for severe personality disorders. In S. G. Hofmann & M. C. Tompson (Eds.), *Treating chronic and severe mental disorders: A handbook of empirically supported interventions* (pp. 382–402). New York: Guilford Press.

Freeman, C. (1995). Cognitive therapy. In G. Szmukler, C. Dare, & J. Treasure (Eds.), *Handbook of eating disorders: Theory, treatment and research.* Chichester, England: Wiley.

Freeman, E. W. (2003). Premenstrual syndrome and premenstrual dysphoric disorder: Definitions and diagnosis. *Psychoneuroendocrinology, 28*(Supp 3), 25–37.

Freeman, S. F. N., & Alkin, M. C. (2000). Academic and social attainments of children with mental retardation in general education and special education settings. *Remed. Spec. Educ., 21*(1), 3–18.

Freeston, M. H., Ladouceur, R., Gagnon, F., & Thibodeau, N. (1992). *Beliefs about obsessional thoughts.* Unpublished manuscript, Laval University, Quebec City, Quebec.

Freeston, M. H., Rhéaume, J., & Ladouceur, R. (1996). Correcting faulty appraisals of obsessional thoughts. *Behav. Res. Ther., 34*(5/6), 433–446.

Freud, S. (1885). On the general effects of cocaine. *Med. Chir. Centralb., 20*, 373–375.

Freud, S. (1894). The neuropsychoses of defense. In J. Strachey (Ed.), *The standard edition of the complete psychological works of Sigmund Freud*(Vol. 3). London: Hogarth Press, 1962.

Freud, S. (1900). *The interpretation of dreams* (J. Strachey, Ed. & Trans.). New York: Wiley.

Freud, S. (1915). A case of paranoia counter to psychoanalytic theory. In *Complete psychological works* (Vol. 14). London: Hogarth, 1957.

Freud, S. (1917). *A general introduction to psychoanalysis*(J. Riviere, Trans.). New York: Liveright, 1963.

Freud, S. (1924). The loss of reality in neurosis and psychosis. In *Sigmund Freud's collected papers*, (Vol. 2), pp. 272–282. London: Hogarth Press.

Freud, S. (1933). *New introductory lectures on psychoanalysis.* New York: Norton.

Freud, S. (1961). *The future of an illusion.* New York: W.W. Norton.

Frey, K. A., Koeppe, R. A., & Holthoff, V. A. (1995). *In vivo imaging of benzodiazepine receptors with positron emission tomography.* In A. Biegon & N. D. Volkow (Eds.), *Sites of drug action in the human brain.* Boca Raton, FL: CRC Press.

Frick, P. J., & McCoy, M. G. (2001). Conduct disorder. In H. Orvaschel, J. Faust, et al. (Eds.), *Handbook of conceptualization and treatment of child psychopathology* (pp. 57–76). Amsterdam: Pergamon/Elsevier Science.

Friedman, M., & Rosenman, R. (1959). Association of specific overt behavior pattern with blood and cardiovascular findings. *JAMA, 169,* 1286.

Friedman, M., & Rosenman, R. (1974). *Type A behavior and your heart.* New York: Knopf.

Friman, P. C., Allen, K. D., Kerwin, M. L. E., & Larzelere, R. (1993). Changes in modern psychology: A citation analysis of the Kuhnian displacement thesis. *Amer. Psychologist, 48*(6), 658–664.

Frith, U. (2000). Cognitive explanations of autism. In K. Lee et al. (Eds.), *Childhood cognitive development: The essential readings. Essential readings in development psychology.* Malden, MA: Blackwell.

Froelich, J., von Gontard, A., Lehmkuhl, G., Pfeiffer, E., & Lehmkuhl, U. (2001). Pericardial effusions in anorexia nervosa. *Eur. Child Adolesc. Psychiatry, 10*(1), 54–57.

Frohman, E. M. (2002). Sexual dysfunction in neurological disease. *Clin. Neuropharmacol., 25*(3), 126–132.

Fromm-Reichmann, F. (1948). Notes on the development of treatment of schizophrenia by psychoanalytic psychotherapy. *Psychiatry, 11,* 263–273.

Frosch, W. A., Robbins, E. S., & Stern, M. (1965). Untoward reactions to lysergic acid diethylamide (LSD) resulting in hospitalization. *N. Engl. J. Med., 273,* 1235–1239.

Frost, R. O., & Steketee, G. (2001). Obsessive-compulsive disorder. In H. S. Friedman (Ed.), *Specialty articles from the encyclopedia of mental health.* San Diego: Academic Press.

Fry, A. J., O'Riordan, D., Turner, M., & Mills, K. L. (2002). Survey of aggressive incidents experienced by community mental health staff. *Inter. J. Ment. Hlth. Nurs., 11*(2), 112–120.

Fry, R. (1993). Adult physical illness and childhood sexual abuse. *J. Psychosom. Res., 37*(2), 89–103.

Fuentes, K., & Cox, B. (2000). Assessment of anxiety in older adults: A community-based survey and comparison with younger adults. *Behav. Res. Ther., 38*(3), 297–309.

Fukunishi, I. (1998). Eating attitudes in female college students with self-reported alexithymic characteristics. *Psychol. Rep., 82,* 35–41.

Fulwiler, C., & Pope, H. G., Jr. (1987). Depression in personality disorder. In O. G. Cameron (Ed.), *Presentations of depression: Depressive symptoms in medical and other psychiatric disorders.* New York: Wiley.

Furukawa, T. A. (2003). Effectiveness: The treatment of panic disorder in the real world. *Curr. Opin. Psychiat., 16*(1), 45–48.

Gaal, E., VanWeeghel, J., VanCampen, M., & Linszen, D. (2002). The trainee project: Family-aided vocational rehabilitation of young people with schizophrenia. *Psychiatr. Rehab. J., 26*(1), 101–105.

Gabbard, G. O. (1990). *Psychodynamic psychiatry in clinical practice.* Washington, DC: American Psychiatric Press.

Gabbard, G. O. (2001). Psychoanalysis and psychoanalytic psychotherapy. In W. J. Livesley (Ed.), *Handbook of personality disorders: Theory, research, and treatment* (pp. 359–376). New York: Guilford Press.

Gabbard, G. O., & Coyne, L. (1987). Predictors of response of antisocial patients to hospital treatment. *Hosp. Comm. Psychiat., 38*(11), 1181–1185.

Gaffney, M. (2003). Factor analysis of treatment response in posttraumatic stress disorder. *J. Traum. Stress., 16*(1), 77–80.

Galambos, N. L., Leadbeater, B. J., & Barker, E. T. (2004). Gender differences in and risk factors for depression in adolescence: A 4-year longitudinal study. *Inter. J. Behav. Dev., 28*(1), 16–25.

Galanter, M., & Brooks, D. (2001). Network therapy for addiction: Bringing family and peer support into office practice. *Inter. J. Group Psychother., 51*(1), 101–122.

Galanter, M., Talbott, D., Gallegos, K., & Rubenstone, E. (1990). Combined Alcoholics Anonymous and professional care for addicted physicians. *Amer. J. Psychiat., 147*(1), 64–68.

Gallagher, R. (1998, December 17). Interviewed in R. Vigoda, More college students showing signs of stress. *The Seattle Times.*

Gallagher-Thompson, D., & Thompson, L. W. (1995). Problems of aging. In R. J. Comer (Ed.), *Abnormal psychology.* New York: W. H. Freeman.

Gallup Organization. (1995). *Child abuse survey.* Princeton, NJ: Author.

Gamwell, L., & Tomes, N. (1995). *Madness in America: Cultural and medical perceptions of mental illness before 1914.* Ithaca, NY: Cornell University Press.

Ganaway, G. K. (1989). Historical versus narrative truth: Clarifying the role of exogenous trauma in the etiology of MPD and its variants. *Dissociation, 2,* 205–222.

Ganzini, L., Leong, G. B., Fenn, D. S., Silva, J. A., & Weinstock, R. (2000). Evaluation of competence to consent to assisted suicide: Views of forensic psychiatrists. *Amer. J. Psychiat., 157*(4), 595–600.

Garber, J., & Horowitz, J. L. (2002). Depression in children. In I. H. Gotlib & C. L. Hammen (Eds.), *Handbook of depression* (pp. 510–540). New York: Guilford Press.

Garbino, J., Henry, J. A., Mentah, G., & Romand, J. A. (2001). Ecstasy ingestion and fulminant hepatic failure: Liver transplantation to be considered as a last therapeutic option. *Vet. Hum. Toxicol., 43*(2), 99–102.

Gardyn, R. (2002). Family matters. *Amer. Demog., 24*(8), 34. Retrieved Sept. 22, 2002, from www.proquest.umi.com.

Gardyn, R. (2002, March 1). What's cooking. *Amer. Demog.* Retreived, Sept. 15, 2002 from www.industryclick.com.

Garety, P. (1991). Reasoning and delusions. *Brit. J. Psychiat., 159*(Suppl. 14), 14–18.

Garfield, D. A., & Havens, L. (1991). Paranoid phenomena and pathological narcissism. *Amer. J. Psychother., 45*(2), 160–172.

Garner, D. M., & Bemis, K. M. (1982). A cognitive-behavioral approach to anorexia nervosa. *Cog. Ther. Res., 6*(2), 123–150.

Garner, D. M., & Bemis, K. M. (1985). Cognitive therapy for anorexia nervosa. In D. M. Garner & P. E. Garfinkel (Eds.), *Handbook of psychotherapy for anorexia nervosa and bulimia.* New York: Guilford Press.

Garner, D. M., Cooke, A. K., & Marano, H. E. (1997). The 1997 body image survey results. *Psychol. Today,* pp. 30–44.

Garner, D. M., & Fairburn, C. G. (1988). Relationship between anorexia nervosa and bulimia nervosa: Diagnostic implications. In D. M. Garner & P. E. Garfinkel (Eds.), *Diagnostic issues in anorexia nervosa and bulimia nervosa.* Brunner/Mazel eating disorders monograph series, No. 2. New York: Brunner/Mazel.

Garner, D. M., Garfinkel, P. E., & O'Shaughnessy, M. (1985). The validity of the distinction between bulimia with and without anorexia nervosa. *Amer. J. Psychiat., 142,* 581–587.

Garner, D. M., Garfinkel, P. E., Schwartz, D., & Thompson, M. (1980). Cultural expectations of thinness in women. *Psychol. Rep., 47,* 483–491.

Garner, D. M., & Kearney-Cooke, A. (1997). The 1997 body image survey results. *Psychol. Today,* 30–44, 75–76, 78, 80, 84.

Garner, D. M., & Magana, C. G. (2002). Anorexia nervosa. In M. Hersen (Ed.), *Clinical behavior therapy: Adults and children* (pp. 345–360). New York: Wiley.

Garner, D. M., Olmsted, M. P., & Polivy, J. (1984). *The EDI.* Odessa, FL: Psychological Assessment Resources.

Gamwell, L., & Tomes, N. (1995). *Madness in America: Cultural and medical perceptions of mental illness before 1914.* Ithaca, NY: Cornell University Press.

Garralda, M. E. (1996). Somatisation in children. *J. Child Psychol. Psychiat., 37*(1), 13–33.

Garssen, B., & Goodkin, K. (1999). On the role of immunological factors as mediators between psychosocial factors and cancer progression. *Psychiat. Res., 85*(1), 51–61.

Garvin, V., Striegel-Moore, R. H., Kaplan, A., Wonderlich, S. A. (2001). The potential of professionally developed self-help interventions for the treatment of eating disorders. In R. H. Striegel-Moore & L. Smolak (Eds.), *Eating disorders: Innovative directions in research and practice* (pp. 153–172). Washington, DC: APA.

Gatchel, R. J. (2001). Biofeedback and self-regulation of physiological activity: A major adjunctive treatment modality in health psychology. In A. Baum, T. A. Revenson, & J. E. Singer (Eds.), *Handbook of health psychology* (pp. 95–104). Mahwah, NJ: Erlbaum.

Gaugler, J. E., Jarrott, S. E., Zarit, S. H., Stephens, M. A. P., Townsend, A., & Greene, R. (2003). Adult day service use and reductions in caregiving hours: Effects on stress and psychological well-being for dementia caregivers. *Inter. J. Ger. Psychiat., 18*(1), 55–62.

Gaw, A. C. (2001). *Concise guide to cross-cultural psychiatry.* Washington, DC: American Psychiatric Publishing.

Gay, P. (1999, March 29). Psychoanalyst Sigmund Freud. *Time,* pp. 66–69.

Gebhard, P. H. (1965). Situational factors affecting human sexual behavior. In F. Beach (Ed.), *Sex and behavior.* New York: Wiley.

Geiselman, R. E., Putman, C., Korte, R., Shahriary, M., Jachimowicz, G., & Irzhevsky, V. (2002). Eyewitness expert testimony and juror decisions. *Amer. J. Forens. Psychol., 20*(3), 21–36.

Geisthardt, C., & Munsch, J. (1996). Coping with school stress: A comparison of adolescents with and without learning disabilities. *J. Learn. Dis., 29*(3), 287–296.

Gelfand, D. M., Jenson, W. R., & Drew, C. J. (1982). *Understanding child behavior disorders.* New York: Holt, Rinehart & Winston.

General Social Survey, University of Chicago (GSS). (1998, February). Cited in *J. Student,* American Demographics.

George, E. L., Friedman, J. C., & Miklowitz, D. J. (2000). Integrated family and individual therapy for bipolar disorder. In S. L. Johnson, A. M. Hayes, et al. (Eds.), *Stress, coping, and depression.* Mahwah, NJ: Erlbaum.

Gerardin, P., Cohen, D., Mazet, P., & Flament, M. F. (2002). Drug treatment of conduct disorder in young people. *Eur. Neuropsychopharmacology, 12*(5), 361–370.

Gershon, E. S. (2000). Bipolar illness and schizophrenia as oligogenic diseases: Implications for the future. *Biol. Psychiat., 47*(3), 240–244.

Gershon, E. S., & Nurnberger, J. I. (1995). Bipolar illness. In J. M. Oldham & M. B. Riba (Eds.), *American Psychiatric Press review of psychiatry* (Vol. 14). Washington, DC: American Psychiatric Press.

Ghaemi, S. N., Boiman, E. E., & Goodwin, F. K. (1999). Kindling and second messengers: An approach to the neurobiology of recurrence in bipolar disorder. *Biol. Psychiat., 45*(2), 137–144.

Gheorghiu, V. A., & Orleanu, P. (1982). Dental implant under hypnosis. *Amer. J. Clin. Hyp., 25*(1), 68–70.

Gherardelli, S., Pucci, D., & Bersani, G. (2002). The birth season and schizophrenia. *Psichiatria E Psicoterapia Analitica, 21*(2), 150–159.

Ghika, J., & Bogousslavsky, J. (2002). Vascular dementia after stroke. In J. Bogousslavsky (Ed.), *Long-term effects of stroke* (pp. 235–262). New York: Marcel Dekker.

Gianoulakis, C. (2001). Influence of the endogenous opioid system on high alcohol consumption and genetic predisposition to alcoholism. *J. Psychiat. Neurosci., 26*(4), 304–318.

Gidron, Y., Davidson, K., & Bata, I. (1999). The short-term effects of a hostility-reduction intervention on male coronary heart disease patients. *Hlth. Psychol., 18*(4), 416–420.

Gilbert, P. L., Harris, M. J., McAdams, L. A., & Jeste, D. V. (1995). Neuroleptic withdrawal in schizophrenic patients: Review of the literature. *Arch. Gen. Psychiat., 52*(3), 173–188.

Gill, A. D. (1982). Vulnerability to suicide. In E. L. Bassuk, S. C. Schoonover, & A. D. Gill (Eds.), *Lifelines: Clinical perspectives on suicide.* New York: Plenum Press.

Gillham, J. E., Reivich, K. J., Jaycox, L. H., & Seligman, M. E. (1995). Prevention of depressive symptoms in schoolchildren: Two-year follow-up. *Psychol. Sci., 6*(6), 343–351.

Gillham, J. E., Shatte, A. J., & Freres, D. R. (2000). Preventing depression: A review of cognitive-behavioral and family interventions. *Appl. Prev. Psychol., 9,* 63–88.

Gilligan, J. (2001). The last mental hospital. *Psychiatr. Quart., 72*(1), 45–61.

Gist, R., & Woodall, S. J. (1999). There are no simple solutions to complex problems: The rise and fall of critical incident stress debriefing as a response to occupational stress in the fire service. In R. Gist & B. Lubin (Eds.), *Response to disaster.* Philadelphia: Brunner/Mazel.

Gitlin, M. J. (2002). Pharmacological treatment of depression. In I. H. Gotlib & C. L. Hammen (Eds.), *Handbook of depression* (pp. 360–382). New York: Guilford Press.

Glass, C. R., & Merluzzi, T. V. (2000). Cognitive and behavioral assessment. In C. E. Watkins, Jr., V. L. Campbell, et al. (Eds.), *Testing and assessment in counseling practice* (2nd ed). Mahwah, NJ: Erlbaum.

Globisch, J., Hamm, A. O., Esteves, F., & Oehman, A. (1999). Fear appears fast: Temporal course of startle reflex potentiation in animal fearful subjects. *Psychophysiology, 36*(1), 66–75.

Glogower, F. D., Fremouw, W. J., & McCroskey, J. C. (1978). A component analysis of cognitive restructuring. *Cog. Ther. Res., 2*(3), 209–223.

Glynn, S. M., Eth, S., Randolph, E. T., Foy, D. W. et al. (1995). Behavioral family therapy for

Vietnam combat veterans with posttraumatic stress disorder. *J. Psychother. Prac. Res., 4*(3), 214–223.

Godenzi, A., & De Puy, J. (2001). Overcoming boundaries: A cross-cultural inventory of primary prevention programs against wife abuse and child abuse. *J. Primary Prev., 21*(4), 455–475.

Godt, K. (2002). Personality disorders and eating disorders: The prevalence of personality disorders in 176 female outpatients with eating disorders. *Eur. Eat. Disord. Rev., 10*(2), 102–109.

Goin, M. K. (2001). Borderline personality disorder: The importance of establishing a treatment framework. *Psychiatr. Serv., 52*(2), 167–168.

Goisman, R. M., Warshaw, M. G., & Keller, M. B. (1999). Psychosocial treatment prescriptions for generalized anxiety disorder, panic disorder, and social phobia, 1991–1996. *Amer. J. Psychiat., 156*(11), 1819–1821.

Gold, E. R., (1986). Long-term effects of sexual victimization in childhood: An attributional approach. *J. Cons. Clin. Psychol., 54,* 471–475.

Gold, J. H. (1998). Gender differences in psychiatric illness and treatments: A critical review. *J. Nerv. Ment. Dis., 186*(12), 769–775.

Gold, J., deGirolamo, J., Brambilla, L., Cappa, S., Mazzi, F., O'Donnell, K., Scala, V., & Pioli, R. (2002). Schizophrenia and cognitive functioning: Meaning, implications and treatment of cognitive deficits. *Rivista di Psichiatria, 37*(2), 53–60.

Gold, J. M., & Thaker, G. K. (2002). Current progress in schizophrenia research. Cognitive phenotypes of schizophrenia: Attention. *J. Nerv. Ment. Dis., 190*(9), 638–639.

Golden, N. H. (2002). A review of the femal athlete triad (amenorrhea, osteoporosis and disordered eating). *International Journal of Adolescent Medicine and Health, 14* (1), 9–17.

Goldfried, M. R., & Wolfe, B. E. (1996). Psychotherapy practice and research. Repairing a strained alliance. *Amer. Psychologist, 51*(10), 1007–1016.

Goldiamond, I. (1965). Self-control procedures in personal behavior problems. *Psychol. Rep., 17,* 851–868.

Goldman, J. G. (1995). A mutual story-telling technique as an aid to integration after abreaction in the treatment of MPD. *Dissociat. Prog. Dissociat. Disorders 8*(1), 53–60.

Goldman, S., & Beardslee, W. R. (1999). Suicide in children and adolescents. In D. G. Jacobs (Ed.), *The Harvard Medical School guide to suicide assessment and intervention.* San Francisco: Jossey-Bass.

Goldney, R. D. (1998). Suicide prevention is possible: A review of recent studies. *Arch. Suic. Res., 4*(4): 329–339.

Goldstein, A. (1994). *Addiction: From biology to drug policy.* New York: W. H. Freeman.

Goldstein, S., & Ellison, A. T. (Eds.), (2002). *Clinicians' guide to adult ADHD: Assessment and intervention.* San Diego: Academic Press.

Goleman, D., & Gurin, J. (1993). Mind/body medicine—At last. *Psychol. Today, 26*(2), 16, 80.

Gollan J. K., & Jacobson N. S. (2002). Developments in couple therapy research. In H. A. Liddle, D. A. Santiseban, R. F. Levant, & J. H. Bray & (Eds.), *Family psychology: Science-based interventions.* Washington, DC: APA.

Gonzalez, R. G. (1996). Molecular and functional magnetic resonance neuroimaging for the study of dementia. In R. J. Wurtman, S. Corkin, J. H. Growdon, & R. M. Nitsch (Eds.), *The neurobiology of Alzheimer's disease.* New York: New York Academy of Sciences.

Goodman, N. (2002). The serotonergic system and mysticism: Could LSD and the nondrug-induced mystical experience share common neural mechanisms? *J. Psychoactive Drugs, 34*(3), 263–272.

Goodman, S. H. (2002). Depression and early adverse experiences. In I. H. Gotlib & C. L. Hammen (Eds.), *Handbook of depression* (pp. 245–267). New York: Guilford Press.

Goodman-Brown, T. B., Edelstein, R. S., Goodman, G. S., Jones, D. P. H., & Gordon, D. S. (2003). Why children tell: A model of children's disclosure of sexual abuse. *Child Abuse Negl., 27*(5), 525–540.

Goodwin, C. J. (2002). *Research in psychology: Methods and design* (3rd ed.). New York: Wiley.

Gopaul-McNicol, S., & Armour-Thomas, E. (2002). *Assessment and culture: Psychological tests with minority populations.* San Diego, CA: Academic.

Gorman, C. (1998, August 17). E-mail your doctor. *Time.*

Gorman, J. M. (2002). Treatment of generalized anxiety disorder. *J. Clin. Psychiat., 63*(Suppl 8), 17–23.

Gorman, J. M., Kent, J. M., Sullivan, G. M., & Coplan, J. D. (2000). Neuroanatomical hypothesis of panic disorder, revised. *Amer. J. Psychiat., 157*(4), 493–505.

Gorman, J. M., Papp, L. A., & Coplan, J. D. (1995). Neuroanatomy and neurotransmitter function in panic disorder. In S. P. Roose & R. A. Glick (Eds.), *Anxiety as symptom and signal.* Hillsdale, NJ: Analytic Press.

Gorwood, P., Bouvard, M., Mouren-Simeoni, et al. (1998). Genetics and anorexia nervosa: A review of candidate genes. *Psychiat. Genet., 8,* 1–12.

Goshen, C. E. (1967). *Documentary history of psychiatry: A source book on historical principles.* New York: Philosophy Library.

Gossop, M., Marsden, J., Stewart, D., & Treacy, S. (2001). Outcomes after methadone maintenance and methadone reduction treatments: Two-year follow-up results from the National Treatment Outcome Research Study. *Drug Alc. Dep., 62*(3), 255–264.

Gottesman, I. I. (1991). *Schizophrenia genesis.* New York: Freeman.

Gottesman, I. I., & Reilly, J. L. (2003). Strengthening the evidence for genetic factors in schizophrenia (without abetting genetic discrimination). In M. F. Lenzenweger & J. M. Hooley (Eds.), *Principles of experimental psychopathology: Essays in honor of Brendan A. Maher* (pp. 31–44). Washington, DC: APA.

Gottesman, I. I., & Shields, J. (1984). Genetic theorizing and schizophrenia. In T. Millon (Ed.), *Theories of personality and psychopathology* (3rd ed.). New York: Holt, Rinehart and Winston.

Gottfredson, D. C., & Wilson, D. B. (2003). Characteristics of effective school-based substance abuse prevention. *Prevent. Sci., 4*(1), 27–38.

Gottlieb, J. (1981). Mainstreaming: Fulfilling the promise? *Amer. J. Ment. Def., 86*(2), 115–126.

Gottlieb, J., Alter, M., & Gottlieb, B. W. (1991). Litigation involving people with mental retardation. In J. L. Matson & J. A. Mulick (Eds.), *Handbook of mental retardation.* New York: Pergamon Press.

Gottman, J. M., Ryan, K. D., Carrère, S., & Erley, A. M. (2001). Chapter 8: Toward a scientifically based marital therapy. In H. A.Liddle, D. A. Santiseban, R. F. Levant, & J. H. Bray (Eds.), *Family psychology: Science-based interventions.* Washington, DC: APA.

Gould, D., Petchlikoff, L., & Weinberg, R. S. (1984). Antecedents of, temporal changes in, and relationship between the CSAI-2 sub components. *J. Sport Psychol., 6,* 289–304.

Gould, J. E. (2002). *Concise handbook of experimental methods for the behavioral and biological sciences.* Boca Raton, FL: CRC Press.

Gould, M. S. (2001). Suicide and the media. In H. Hendin & J. J. Mann (Eds.), *The clinical science of suicide prevention* (Vol. 932, pp. 200–224). New York: Annals of the New York Academy of Sciences.

Gowers, S. G., North, C. D., & Byram, V. (1996). Life event precipitants of adolescent anorexia nervosa. *J. Child Psychol. Psychiat.*, *37*(4), 469–477.

Graesel, E. (2002). When home care ends—Changes in the physical health of informal caregivers caring for dementia patients: A longitudinal study. *J. Amer. Ger. Soc. 50*(5), 843–849.

Graham, J. R. (2000). *MMPI-2: Assesssing personality and psychopathology* (3rd ed.). New York: Oxford University Press.

Graham, J. R., Barthlow, D. L., Stein, L. A. R., Ben-Porath, Y. S., & McNulty, J. L. (2002). Assessing general maladjustment with the MMPI-2. *J. Pers. Assess.*, *78*(2), 334–347.

Graham, K., Clarke, D., Bois, C., Carver, V. et al. (1996). Addictive behavior of older adults. *Addic. Behav.*, *21*(3), 331–346.

Grant, B. F., & Dawson, D. A. (1997). Age at onset of alcohol use and its association with DSM-IV alcohol abuse and dependence: Results from the National Longitudinal Alcohol Epidemiologic Survey. *J. Substance Abuse*, *9*, 103–110.

Grawe, K., Donate, R., & Bernauer, F. (1998). *Psychotherapy in transition.* Seattle: Hogrefe & Huber.

Gray, H. (1959). *Anatomy of the human body* (27th ed.). Philadelphia: Lea & Febiger.

Gray, J., Nielsen, D. R., Wood, L. E., Andresen, M., & Dolce, K. (2000). Academic progress of children who attended a preschool for abused children: A follow-up of the Keepsafe Project. *Child Abuse Negl.* 24(1), 25–32.

Greeley, A. M. (1991). *Faithful attraction.* New York: Tor Books.

Green, R. (2000). Family cooccurrence of "gender dysphoria": Ten siblings or parent-child pairs. *Arch. Sex. Behav.*, *29*(5), 499–507.

Green, S. A. (1985). *Mind and body: The psychology of physical illness.* Washington, DC: American Psychiatric Press.

Greenberg, I., Chan, S., & Blackburn, G. L. (1999). Nonpharmacologic and pharmacologic management of weight gain. *J. Clin. Psychiat.*, *60*(Suppl. 21), 31–36.

Greenberg, L. S., Elliott, R., & Lietaer, G. (1994). Research on experiential psychotherapies. In A. E. Bergin & S. L. Garfield (Eds.), *Handbook of psychotherapy and behavior change.* New York: Wiley.

Greenberg, L. S., Watson, J. C., & Lietaer, G. (Eds.) (1998). *Handbook of experiential psychotherapy.* New York: Guilford Press.

Greenberg, P. E., Sisitsky, T., Kessler, R. C., Finkelstein, S. N., Berndt, E. R., Davidson, J. R., Ballenger, J. C., & Fyer, A. J. (1999). The economic burden of anxiety disorders in the 1990s. *J. Clin. Psychiat.*, *60*(7), 427–435.

Greenberg, R. P., & Bornstein, R. F. (1988). The dependent personality: II. Risk for psychological disorders. *J. Pers. Disord.*, *2*(2), 136–143.

Greenfield, D. N. (1999). Psychological characteristics of compulsive internet use: A preliminary analysis. *CyberPsych. Behav.*, *2*(5), 403–412.

Greenfield, D. N. (1999). *Virtual addiction: Help for netheads, cyberfreaks, and those who love them.* Oakland, CA: New Harbinger Publications, Inc.

Gregory, R. J. (2004). *Psychological testing: History, principles, and applications.* Needham Heights, MA: Allyn and Bacon.

Gresham, A. C. (1993). The insanity plea: A futile defense for serial killers. *Law Psychol. Rev.*, *17*, 193–208.

Grice, D. E., Halmi, K. A., Fichter, M. M., Strober, M., Woodside, D. B., Treasure, J. T.,

Kaplan, A. S., Magistretti, P. J., Goldman, D., Bulik, C. M., Kaye, W. H., & Berrettini, W. H. (2002). Evidence for a susceptibility gene for anorexia nervosa on chromosome 1. *American Journal of Human Genetics, 70*(3), 787–792.

Griffiths, M. (2002). Invisibility: The major obstacle in understanding and diagnosing transsexualism. *Clin. Child Psychol. Psychiat.*, *7*(3), 493–496.

Griffiths, R., Gross, G., Russell, J., Thornton, C., Beumont, P. J. V., Schotte, D., & Touyz, S. W. (1998). Perceptions of bed rest of anorexic patients. *Inter. J. Eat. Disorders*, *23*, 443–447.

Grigg, J. R. (1988). Imitative suicides in an active duty military population. *Military Med.*, *153*(2), 79–81.

Grigorenko, E. L. (2001). Developmental dyslexia: An update on genes, brains, and environments. *J. Child Psychol. Psychiat. Allied Disc.*, *42*(1), 91–125.

Grilo, C. M., & Masheb, R. M. (2002). Childhood maltreatment and personality disorders in adult patients with binge eating disorder. *Acta Psychiatr. Scandin.*, *106*(3), 183–188.

Grilo, C. M., Sanislow, C. A., & McGlashan, T. H. (2002). Co-occurrence of DSM-IV personality disorders with borderline personality disorder. *J. Nerv. Ment. Dis.*, *190*(8), 552–553.

Grilly, D. M. (2002). *Drugs and human behavior* (4th ed.). Boston: Allyn and Bacon.

Grinfield, M. J. (1993, July). Report focuses on jailed mentally ill. *Psychiatr. Times*, pp. 1–3.

Grinfield, M. J. (1998, February). "Patient dumping"—Mentally ill get shortchanged. *Psychiatr. Times*, *XV* (2).

Grinspoon, L., et al. (Eds.). (1986). Paraphilias. *Harv. Med. Sch. Ment. Health Newsl.*, *3*(6), 1–5.

Grisso, T. (2003) *Evaluating competencies: Forensic assessments and instruments* (2nd ed.). New York: Kluwer Academic/Plenum Pub.

Grob, G. N. (1966). *State and the mentally ill: A history of Worcester State Hospital in Massachusetts, 1830-1920.* Chapel Hill: University of North Carolina Press.

Gross, B. (2002). The constraints of confidentiality. *Ann. Amer. Psychother. Assn.*, *5*(2), 31.

Grossman, J. A., & Kruesi, M. J. P. (2000). Innovative approaches to youth suicide prevention: An update of issues and research findings. In R. W. Maris, S. S. Canetto et al. (Eds.), *Review of suicidology, 2000* (pp. 170–201). New York: Guilford Press.

Gunderson, J. G., & Ronningstam, E. (2001). Differentiating narcissistic and antisocial personality disorders. *J. Pers. Disorders*, *15*(2), 103–109.

Gurman, A. S. (2003). Marital therapies. In A. S. Gurman & S. B. Messer (Eds.), *Essential psychotherapies: Theory and practice* (2nd ed.). New York: Guilford Press.

Gurman, A. S., & Messer, S. B. (Eds.). (2003). *Essential psychotherapies: Theory and practice* (2nd ed.). New York: Guilford Press.

Gurman, A. S., & Messer, S. B. (2003). Contemporary issues in the theory and practice of psychotherapy: A framework for comparative study. In A. S. Gurman & S. B. Messer (Eds.), *Essential psychotherapies: Theory and practice* (2nd ed.). New York: Guilford Press.

Gurnack, A. M., Atkinson, R., & Osgood, N. J. (Eds.) (2002). *Treating alcohol and drug abuse in the elderly.* New York: Springer.

Guttman, H. A. (2002). The epigenesis of the family system as a context for individual development. *Fam. Process*, *41*(3), 533–545.

Hadley, S. W., & Strupp, H. H. (1976). Contemporary views of negative effects in psychotherapy: An integrated account. *Arch. Gen. Psychiat.*, *33*(1), 1291–1302.

Hafner, H., & an der Heiden, W. (1988). The mental health care system in transition: A study in organization, effectiveness, and costs of complementary care for schizophrenic patients. In C. N. Stefanis & A. D. Rabavilis (Eds.), *Schizophrenia: Recent biosocial developments.* New York: Human Sciences Press.

Hagan, P. (2002, Sept. 20). Fearless kids said to make the best athletes. *Reuters Health.*

Halaas, J. L., Gajiwala, K. F., Maffei, M., Cohen, S. L., et al. (1995). Weight-reducing effects of the plasma protein encoded by the obese gene. *Science, 269*, 543–546.

Hale, E. (1983, April 17). Inside the divided mind. *New York Times Magazine*, pp. 100–106.

Hall, C. (1997, March 17). It's not only the string section that's highly strung. *Electronic Telegraph.*

Hall, C. W., & Webster, R. E. (2002). Traumatic symptomatology characteristics of adult children of alcoholics. *J. Drug Edu.*, *32*(3), 195–211.

Hall, L., with Cohn, L. (1980). *Eat without fear.* Santa Barbara, CA: Gurze.

Hall, N. W., & Zigler, E. (1997). Drug-abuse prevention efforts for young children: A review and critique of existing programs. *Amer. J. Orthopsychiat.*, *67*(1), 134–143.

Hall, T. M., Kaduson, H. G., & Schaefer, C. E. (2002). Fifteen effective play therapy techniques. *Profess. Psychol.: Res. Pract.*, *33*(6), 515–522.

Halloway, J. D. (2004). California psychologists prepare for hospital privileges battle. *APA Monitor on Psychology, 35*(1), 28–29.

Halmi, K. A. (1995). Current concepts and definitions. In G. Szmukler, C. Dare, & J. Treasure (Eds.), *Handbook of eating disorders: Theory, treatment and research.* Chichester, England: Wiley.

Halmi, K. A., Agras, W. S., Kaye, W. H., & Walsh, B. T. (1994). Evaluation of pharmacologic treatments in eating disorders. In R. F. Prien & D. S. Robinson (Eds.), *Clinical evaluation of psychotropic drugs: Principles and guidelines.* New York: Raven Press, Ltd.

Ham, L. S., Hope, D. A., White, C. S., & Rivers, P. C. (2002). Alcohol expectancies and drinking behavior in adults with social anxiety disorder and dysthymia. *Cog. Ther. Res.*, *26*(2), 275–288.

Hamer, D. H., Hu, S., Magnuson, V. L., Hu, N., et al. (1993). A linkage between DNA markers on the X chromosome and male sexual orienation. *Science, 261*, 321–327.

Hamilton, N. (1991). Intake and diagnosis of drug-dependent women. In *National Conference on Drug Abuse Research and Practice Conference highlights.* Rockville, MD: National Institute on Drug Abuse.

Hamilton, S., Rothbart, M., & Dawes, R. N. (1986). *Sex Roles*, *15*(5–6), 269–274.

Hammen, C. L., Gitlin, M., & Altshuler, L. (2000). Predictors of work adjustment in bipolar I patients: A naturalistic longitudinal follow-up. *J. Cons. Clin. Psychol.*, *68*(2), 220–225.

Hammen, C. L., & Glass, D. R. (1975). Expression, activity, and evaluation of reinforcement. *J. Abnorm. Psychol.*, *84*(6), 718–721.

Hammen, C. L., & Krantz, S. (1976). Effect of success and failure on depressive cognitions. *J. Abnorm. Psychol.*, *85*(8), 577–588.

Handy, B. (1998, May 4). The Viagra craze. *Newsweek*, pp. 56–61.

Hankin, B. L., & Abramson, L. Y. (1999). Development of gender differences in depression: Description and possible explanations. *Ann. Med.*, *31*(6), 372–379.

Hankin, B. L., & Abramson, L. Y. (2001). Development of gender differences in depression: An elaborated cognitive vulnerability-transactional stress theory. *Psychol. Bull.*, *127*, 773–796.

Hankin, J. R. (2002). Fetal alcohol syndrome prevention research. *Alc. Res. Hlth.*, 26(1), 58–65.

Hankins, G. C., Vera, M. I., Barnard, G. W., & Herkov, M. J. (1994). Patient-therapist sexual involvement: A review of clinical and research data. *Bull. Amer. Acad. Psychiat. Law.*, 22(1), 109–126.

Hanson, M., Tiberius, R., Hodges, B., MacKay, S., McNaughton, N., Dickens, S., & Regehr, G. (2002). Implications of suicide contagion for the selection of adolescent standardized patients. *Academ. Med.*, 77(Suppl. 10), S100–S102.

Hanton, S., Jones, G., & Mullen, R. (2000). Intensity and direction of competitive state anxiety as interpreted by rugby players and rifle shooters. *Percept. Motor Skills*, 90(2), 513–521.

Hanton, S., Mallalieu, S. D., & Hall, R. (2002). Re-examining the competitive anxiety trait-state relationship. *Pers. Individ. Diff.*, 33(7), 1126–1136.

Hanton, S., O'Brien, M., & Mellalieu, S. D. (2003). Individual differences, perceived control and competitive trait anxiety. *J. Sport Behav.*, 26(1), 39–55.

Happé, F. G. E. (1995). The role of age and verbal ability in the theory of mind task performance of subjects with autism. *Child Dev.*, 66, 843–855.

Happé, F. G. E. (1997). Central coherence and theory of mind in autism: Reading homographs in context. *Brit. J. Dev. Psychol.*, 15, 1–12.

Harding, A., Halliday, G., Caine, D., & Kril, J. (2000). Degeneration of anterior thalamic nuclei differentiates alcoholics with amnesia. *Brain*, 123(1), 141–154.

Hardy, J., & Selkoe, D. J. (2002). The amyloid hypothesis of Alzheimer's disease: Progress and problems on the road to therapeutics. *Science*, 297(5580), 353–356.

Hardy, L., Jones, G., & Gould, D. (1996). *Understanding psychological preparation for sport: Theory and practice of elite performers.* Chichester: Wiley.

Hare, R. D. (1993). *Without conscience: The disturbing world of the psychopaths among us.* New York: Pocket Books.

Hargreaves, R. J., & Shepheard, S. L. (1999). Pathophysiology of migraine—New insights. *Canad. J. Neurol. Sci.*, 26(Suppl. 3), S12–S19.

Harkavy, J. M., & Asnis, G. (1985). Suicide attempts in adolescence: Prevalence and implications. *N. Engl. J. Med.*, 313, 1290–1291.

Harrington, R. C., Fudge, H., Rutter, M. L., Bredenkamp, D., Groothues, C., & Pridham, J. (1993). Child and adult depression: A test of continuities with data from a family study. *Brit. J. Psychiat.*, 162, 627–633.

Harris, E. C., & Barraclough, B. (1998). Excess mortality of mental disorder. *Brit. J. Psychiat.*, 173, 11–53.

Harris, G. T., Rice, M. E., & Cormier, C. A. (2002). Prospective replication of the Violence Risk Appraisal Guide in predicting violent recidivism among forensic patients. *Law Human Behav.*, 26 (4), 377–394.

Harris, S. L. (1995). Autism. In M. Hersen & R. T. Ammerman (Eds.), *Advanced abnormal psychology.* Hillsdale, NJ: Erlbaum.

Harris, S. L. (2000). Pervasive developmental disorders: The spectrum of autism. In M. Hersen, R. T. Ammerman, et al. (Eds.), *Advanced abnormal child psychology* (2nd ed.). Mahwah, NJ: Erlbaum.

Hart, K., & Kenny, M. E. (1995, August). *Adherence to the superwoman ideal and eating disorder symptoms among college women.* Paper presented at the American Psychological Association, New York.

Hartman, M., Steketee, M. C., Silva, S., Lanning, K., & McCann, H. (2003). Working memory and schizophrenia: Evidence for slowed encoding. *Schizo. Res.*, 59(2–3), 99–113.

Harvard School of Public Health. (1995). *Binge drinking on American college campuses: A new look at an old problem.* Boston: Author.

Harvey, J. (2003). Novel actions of leptin in the hippocampus. *Annals of Medicine*, 35(3), 197–206.

Harvey, S. C., Foster, K. L., McKay, P. F., Carroll, M. R., Seyoum, R., Woods, J. E., Grey, C., Jones C. M., McCane, S., Cummings, R., Mason, D., Ma, C., Cook, J. M., & June, H. L. (2002). The GABA-sub(A) receptor alpha-sub-1 subtype in the ventral pallidum regulates alcohol-seeking behaviors. *J. Neurosci.*, 22(9), 3765–3775.

Harwood, D., Hawton, K., Hope, T., & Jacoby, R. (2001). Psychiatric disorder and personality factors associated with suicide in older people: A descriptive and case-control study. *Inter. J. Ger. Psychiat.*, 16(2), 155–165.

Hasin, D., Endicott, J., & Lewis, C. (1985). Alcohol and drug abuse in patients with affective syndromes. *Comprehen. Psychiat.*, 26, 283–295.

Haslam, N., Reichert, T., & Fiske, A. P. (2002). Aberrant social relations in the personality disorders. *Psychol. Psychother.: Theory, Res. Prac.*, 75 (1), 19–31.

Hassan, R. (1998). One hundred years of Emile Durkheim's *Suicide: A Study in Sociology. Austral. New Zeal. J. Psychiat.*, 32(2), 168–171.

Hauri, P. J. (2000). The many faces of insomnia. In D. Mostofsky & D. H. Barlow (Eds.), The management of stress and anxiety in medical disorders (pp. 143–159). Needham Heights, MA: Allyn & Bacon.

Haworth-Hoeppner, S. (2000). The critical shapes of body image: The role of culture and family in the production of eating disorders. *J. Marr. Fam.*, 62(1), 212–227.

Hawton, K. (2001). The treatment of suicidal behavior in the context of the suicidal process. In K. van Heeringen (Ed.), *Understanding suicidal behavior: The suicidal process approach to research, treatment and prevention* (pp. 212–229). Chichester, UK: Wiley.

Hawton, K., Fagg, J., Simkin, S., Bale, E., & Bond, A. (2000). Deliberate self-harm in adolescents in Oxford, 1985–1995. *J. Adolescence*, 23(1), 47–55.

Hayaki, J., Friedman, M. A., & Brownell, K. D. (2002). Shame and severity of bulimic symptoms. *Eat. Behav.*, 3(1), 73–83.

Hayday, G. (2002, August 26). Internet addicts surf on work time. *ZDNet.*

Hayden, L. A. (1998). Gender discrimination within the reproductive health care system: Viagra v. birth control. *J. Law Health*, 13, 171–198.

Hayes, L. M., & Rowan, J. R. (1988). *National study of jail suicides: Seven years later.* Alexandria, VA: National Center for Institutions and Alternatives.

Hayes, S. C., Walser, R. D., & Bach, P. (2002). Prescription privileges for psychologists: Constituencies and conflicts. *J. Clin. Psychol.*, 58(6), 697–708.

Haynes, S. G., Feinleib, M., & Kannel, W. B. (1980). The relationship of psychosocial factors to coronary heart disease in the Framingham study: III. Eight-year incidence of coronary heart disease. *Amer. J. Epidemiol.*, 111, 37–58.

Haynes, S. N. (2001). Clinical applications of analog behavioral observations: Dimensions of psychometric evaluations. *Psychol. Assess.*, 13(1), 73–85.

Haynes, S. N. (2001). Introduction to the special section on clinical applications of analogue behavioral observation. *Psychol. Assess.*, 13(1), 3–4.

Haynes, S. N., & O'Brien, W. H. (2000). *Principles and practice of behavioral assessment.* New York: Kluwer Academic/Plenum Press.

Haynie, D. L., Nansel, T., Eitel, P., Crump, A. D., Saylor, K., Yu, K., & Simons, M. B. (2001). Bullies, victims, and bully/victims: Distinct groups of at-risk youth. *J. Early Adolescence*, 21(1), 29–49.

Hazell, P., & Lewin, T. (1993). Friends of adolescent suicide attempters and completers. *J. Amer. Acad. Child Adol. Psychiat.*, 32(1), 76–81.

Heap, L. C., Pratt, O. E., Ward, R. J. Waller, S., Thomson, A. D., & Shaw, G. K. (2002). Individual susceptibility to Wernicke-Korsakoff syndrome and alcoholism-induced cognitive deficit impaired thiamine utilization found in alcoholics and alcohol abusers. *Psychiat. Genet.*, 12(4), 217–224.

Heavey, L. (2003). Arithmetical savants. In A. J. Baroody & A. Dowker (Eds.). *The development of arithmetic concepts and skills: Constructing adaptive expertise.* Mahwah, NJ: Lawrence Erlbaum Associates.

Heavey, L., Pring, L., & Hermelin, B. (1999). A date to remember: The nature of memory in savant calendrical calculators. *Psychol. Med.*, 29(1), 145–160.

Heffernan, T. M., Jarvis, H., Rodgers, J., Scholey, A. B., & Ling, J. (2001). Prospective memory, everyday cognitive failure and central executive function in recreational users of Ecstasy. *Human Psychopharmacol. Clin. Exp.*, 16(8), 607–612.

Heiman, J. R. (2000). Organic disorders in women. In S. R. Leiblum & R. C. Rosen (Eds.), *Principles and practice of sex therapy* (3rd ed., pp. 118–153). New York: Guilford Press.

Heiman, J. R. (2002). Sexual dysfunction: Overview of prevalence, etiological factors, and treatments. *J. Sex Res.*, 39(1), 73–78.

Heiman, J. R., Gladue, B. A., Roberts, C. W., & LoPiccolo, J. (1986). Historical and current factors discriminating sexually functional from sexually dysfunctional married couples. *J. Marital Fam. Ther.*, 12(2), 163–174.

Heiman, J. R., & LoPiccolo, J. (1988). *Becoming orgasmic: A personal and sexual growth program for women.* New York: Prentice Hall.

Heimberg, R. G. (2001). Current status of psychotherapeutic interventions for social phobia. *J. Clin. Psychiat.*, 62(Suppl. 1), 36–42.

Heinlen, K. T., Welfel, E. R., Richmond, E. N., & O'Donnell, M. S. (2003). The nature, scope, and ethics of psychologists' e-therapy Web sites: What consumers find when surfing the Web. *Psychotherapy, Theory, Research, Practice, Training*, 40(1–2), 112–124.

Heinz, A., Mann, K., Weinberger, D. E., & Goldman, D. (2001). Serotonergic dysfunction, negative mood states, and response to alcohol. *Alcohol.: Clin. Exp. Res.*, 25(4), 487–495.

Helgeson, V. S. (2002). *The psychology of gender.* Upper Saddle River, NJ: Prentice Hall.

Helzer, J. E., Burnam, A., & McEvoy, L. T. (1991). Alcohol abuse and dependence. In L. N. Robins & D. S. Regier (Eds.), *Psychiatric disorders in America: The Epidemiological Catchment Area Study.* New York: Free Press.

Hendin, H. (1999). Suicide, assisted suicide, and medical illness. *J. Clin. Psychiat.*, 60(Suppl. 2), 46–50.

Hendin, H. (2002). The Dutch experience. In K. Foley & H. Hendin (Eds.), *The case against assisted suicide: For the right to end-of-life care* (pp. 97–121). Baltimore, MD: The John Hopkins University Press.

Hendin, H., Maltsberger, J. T., Lipschitz, A., Haas, A. P., & Kyle, J. (2001). Recognizing and responding to a suicide crisis. In H. Hendin & J. J. Mann (Eds.), *The clinical science of suicide prevention* (Vol. 932, pp. 169–187). New York: Annals of the New York Academy of Sciences.

Henggeler, S. W., & Lee, T. (2003). Multisystemic treatment of serious clinical problems. In A. E. Kazdin & J. R. Weisz (Eds.), *Evidence-based psychotherapies for children and adolescents.* New York: Guilford Press.

Henley, D. R. (2003). Bright splinters of the mind: A personal story of research with autistic savants. *Art Therapy, 20*(3), 178–180.

Henning, C. W., Crabtree, C. R., & Baum, D. (1998). Mental health CPR: Peer contracting as a response to potential suicide in adolescents. *Arch. Suic. Res., 4*(2), 169–187.

Hepp, U., Klaghofer, R., Burkhard, K., & Buddeberg, C. (2002). Treatment history of transsexual patients: A retrospective follow-up study., *Nervenarzt, 73*(3), 283–288.

Herek, G. M., & Capitanio, J. P. (1993). Public reaction to AIDS in the U.S.: A 2nd generation of stigma. *Amer. J. Pub. Hlth., 83*(4), 574–577.

Hersen, M., Bellack, A. S., Himmelhoch, J. M., & Thase, M. E. (1984). Effects of social skill training, amitriptyline, and psychotherapy in unipolar depressed women. *Behav. Ther., 15*, 21–40.

Hertel, P. (1998). Relation between rumination and impaired memory in dysphoric moods. *J. Abnorm. Psychol., 107*(1), 166–172.

Herz, M. I., & Marder, S. R. (2002). *Schizophrenia: Comprehensive treatment and management.* Philadelphia: Lippincott, Williams & Wilkins.

Herzog, D. B., Dorer, D. J., Keel, P. K., Selwin, S. E., Ekeblad, E. R., Flores, A. T., Greenwood, D. N., Burwell, R. A., & Keller, M. B. (1999). Recovery and relapse in anorexia and bulimia nervosa: A 7.5-year follow-up study. *J. Amer. Acad. Child Adol. Psychiat., 38*(7), 829–837.

Hess, N. (1995). Cancer as a defence against depressive pain. University College Hospital/Middlesex Hospital Psychotherapy Department. *Psychoanalytic Psychother., 9*(2), 175–184.

Hester, R. K. (1995). Behavioral self-control training. In R. K. Hester & W. R. Miller (Eds.), *Handbook of alcoholism treatment approaches: Effective alternatives* (2nd ed.). Boston: Allyn & Bacon.

Heston, L. L. (1992). *Mending minds: A guide to the new psychiatry of depression, anxiety, and other serious mental disorders.* New York: W. H. Freeman.

Hettema, J. M., Neale, M. C., & Kendler, K. S. (2001). A review and meta-analysis of genetic epidemiology off anxiety disorders. *Amer. J. Psychiat. 158*(10), 1568–1578.

Hettema, J. M., Prescott, C. A., & Kendler, K. S. (2001). A population-based twin study of generalized anxiety disorder in men and women. *J. Nerv. Ment. Dis., 189*(7), 413–420.

HEW (Health, Education and Welfare). (1976). *Even my kids didn't know I was an alcoholic: An interview with Dick Van Dyke* (ADM 76–348). Washington, DC: U.S. Government Printing Office.

Hewitt, P. L., Newton, J., Flett, G. L., & Callander, L. (1997). Perfectionism and suicide ideation in adolescent psychiatric patients. *J. Abnorm. Child Psychol., 25*(2), 95–101.

Heyman, R. E., & Slep, A. M. S. (2002). Do child abuse and interparental violence lead to adulthood family violence? *J. Marr. Fam., 64*(4), 864–870.

Heyne, D., King, N. J., Tonge, B. J., Rollings, S., Young, D., Pritchard, M., & Ollendick, T. H. (2002). Evaluation of child therapy and caregiver training in the treatment of school refusal. *J. Amer. Acad. Child Adol. Psychiat., 41*(6), 687–695.

Hickey, E. (2002). *Serial murderers and their victims*(3rd ed.). Belmont: Wadsworth.

Hickie, I., Pols, R. G., Koschera, A., & Davenport, T. (2000). Why are somatoform disorders so poorly recognized and treated? In G. Andrews, S. Henderson, et al. (Eds.), *Unmet need in psychiatry: Problems, resources, responses.* New York: Cambridge University Press.

Hiday, V. A. (1999). Mental illness and the criminal justice system. In A. V. Horwitz & T. L. Scheid

(Eds.), *A handbook for the study of mental health: Social contexts, theories, and systems.* Cambridge, England: Cambridge University Press.

Higgins, G. A., Large, C. H., Rupniak, H. T., & Barnes, J. C. (1997). Apolipoprotein E and Alzheimer's disease: A review of recent studies. *Pharmacol. Biochem. Behav., 56*(4), 675–685.

Higgins, S. T., Budney, A. J., Bickel, W. K., Hughes, J., Foerg, F., & Badger, G. (1993). Achieving cocaine abstinence with a behavioral approach. *Amer. J. Psychiat., 150*(5), 763–769.

Hileman, B. (2001, April 9). The "mad" disease has many forms: Has the U.S. government taken sufficient measures to keep it from infecting humans? *Chem. Eng. News.*

Hilgard, E. R. (1977). Controversies over consciousness and the rise of cognitive psychology. *Austral. Psychologist, 12*(1), 7–26.

Hill, A. J., & Robinson, A. (1991). Dieting concerns have a functional effect on the behaviour of nine-year-old girls. *Brit. J. Clin. Psychol., 30*(3), 265–267.

Hill, J. (2003). Childhood trauma and depression. *Curr. Opin. Psychiat., 16*(1), 3–6.

Hilliard, R. B., & Spitzer, R. L. (2002). Change in criterion for paraphilias in DSM-IV-TR. *Amer. J. Psychiat., 159*(7), 1249.

Hindmarch, T. (2000). *Eating disorders: A multiprofessional approach.* London: Whurr.

Hingson, R., Heeren, T., Zakocs, R., Kopstein, A., & Wechsler, H. (2002). Magnitude of alcohol-related morbidity, mortality, and alcohol dependence among U.S. college students age 18–24. *J. Stud. Alc., 63*(2), 136–144.

Hinrichsen, G. A. (1999). Interpersonal psychotherapy for late-life depression In M. Duffy (Ed.), *Handbook of counseling and psychotherapy with older adults.* New York: Wiley.

Hinton, L. (2002). Improving care for ethnic minority elderly and their family caregivers across the spectrum of dementia severity. *Alz. Disease Assoc. Disord., 16*(Suppl. 2), S50–S55.

Hiroeh, U., Appleby, L., Mortensen, P.-B., & Dunn, G. (2001). Death by homicide, suicide, and other unnatural causes in people with mental illness: A population-based study. *Lancet, 358*(9299), 2110–2112.

Hirsch, S., Adams, J. K., Frank, L. R., Hudson, W., Keene, R., Krawitz-Keene, G., Richman, D., & Roth, R. (Eds.). (1974). *Madness: Network news reader.* San Francisco: Glide Publications.

Hirschfeld, R. M. (1992). The clinical course of panic disorder and agoraphobia. In G. D. Burrows, S. M. Roth, & R. Noyes, Jr. (Eds.), *Handbook of anxiety* (Vol. 5). Oxford: Elsevier.

Hirschfeld, R. M. (1999). Efficacy of SSRIs and newer antidepressants in severe depression: Comparison with TCAs. *J. Clin. Psychiat., 60*(5), 326–335.

Hirschfeld, R. M., & Russell, J. M. (1997). Assessment and treatment of suicidal patients. *N. Engl. J. Med., 337*, 910–915.

Hjerl, K., Andersen, E. W., Keiding, N., Mouridsen, H. T., Mortensen, P. B., & Jorgensen, T. (2003). Depression as a prognostic for breast cancer mortality. *Psychosom. J. Cons. Liaison Psychiat., 44*(1), 24–30.

Hlastala, S. A., Frank, E., Mallinger, A. G., Thase, M. E., Ritenour, A. M., & Kupfer, D. J. (1997). Bipolar depression: An underestimated treatment challenge. *Depress. Anx., 5*, 73–83.

Ho, T. P., Hung, S. F., Lee, C. C., Chung, K. F., et al. (1995). Characteristics of youth suicide in Hong Kong. *Soc. Psychiat. Psychiatr. Epidemiol., 30*(3), 107–112.

Hoagwood, K., Kelleher, K. J., Feil, M., & Comer, D. M. (2000). Treatment services for children

with ADHD: A national perspective. *J. Amer. Acad. Child Adol. Psychiat., 39*(2), 198–206.

Hobbs, F. B. (1997). The elderly population. *U.S. Census Bureau: The official statistics.* Washington, DC: U.S. Census Bureau.

Hobson, C. J., Kamen, J., Szostek, J., Nethercut, C. M., Tiedmann, J. W., & Wojnarowicz, S. (1998). Stressful life events: A revision and update of the Social Readjustment Rating Scale. *Inter. J. Stress Manag., 5*(1), 1–23.

Hochman, G. (2000, Oct. 22). Portrait of madness. *The Philadelphia Inquirer* (*Inquirer Magazine*).

Hodapp, R. M., & Dykens, E. M. (2003). Mental retardation (intellectual disabilities). In E. J. Mash & R. A. Barkley (Eds.), *Child psychopathology*(2nd ed.). New York: Guilford Press.

Hodges, J. R. (2001). Frontotemporal dementia (Pick's disease): Clinical features and assessment. *Neurol., 56*(Suppl. 4), S6–S10.

Hodgson, R. J., & Rachman, S. (1972). The effects of contamination and washing in obsessional patients. *Behav. Res. Ther., 10*, 111–117.

Hoffman, J. H., Barnes, G. M., Welte, J. W., & Dintcheff, B. A. (2000). Trends in combinational use of alcohol and illicit drugs among minority adolescents, 1983–1994. *Amer. J. Drug Alc. Abuse, 26*(2), 311–324.

Hofmann, S. G., & Barlow, D. H. (2002). Social phobia (social anxiety disorder). In D. H. Barlow (Ed.), *Anxiety and its disorders: The nature and treatment of anxiety and panic* (2nd ed., pp. 454–476). New York: Guilford Press.

Hogan, R. A. (1968). The implosive technique. *Behav. Res. Ther., 6*, 423–431.

Hogarty, G. E., et al. (1974). Drug and sociotherapy in the aftercare of schizophrenic patients: III. Two-year relapse rates. *Arch. Gen. Psychiat., 31*(5), 609–618.

Hogarty, G. E., et al. (1986). Family psychoeducation, social skills training, and maintenance chemotherapy in the aftercare treatment of schizophrenia: I. One-year effects of a controlled study on relapse and expressed emotion. *Arch. Gen. Psychiat., 43*(7), 633–642.

Hohagen, F., Winkelmann, G., Rasche-Raeuchle, H., Hand, I., Koenig, A., Muenchau, N., Hiss, H., Geiger-Kabisch, C., Kaeppler, C., Schramm, P., Rey, E., Aldenhoff, J., & Berger, M. (1998). Combination of behaviour therapy with fluvoxamine in comparison with behaviour therapy and placebo: Results of a multicentre study. *Brit. J. Psychiat., 173*(Suppl. 35), 71–78.

Holder, H., Longabaugh, R., Miller, W. et al. (1991). The cost effectiveness of treatment for alcoholism: A first approximation. *J. Stud. Alc., 52*, 517–540.

Holder-Perkins, V., & Wise, T. N. (2001). Somatization disorder. In K. A. Phillips (Ed.), *Somatoform and factitious disorders. Review of psychiatry* (Vol. 20, pp. 1–26). Washington, DC: American Psychiatric Association.

Holinger, P. C., & Offer, D. (1982). Prediction of adolescent suicide: A population model. *Amer. J. Psychiat., 139*, 302–307.

Holinger, P. C., & Offer, D. (1991). Sociodemographic, epidemiologic, and individual attributes. In L. Davidson & M. Linnoila (Eds.), *Risk factors for youth suicide.* New York: Hemisphere.

Holinger, P. C., & Offer, D. (1993). *Adolescent suicide.* New York: Guilford Press.

Holland, J. (Ed.). (2001). *Ecstasy: The complete guide: A comprehensive look at the risks and benefits of MDMA.* Rochester, VT: Park Street Press.

Holland, J. (2001). The history of MDMA. In J. Holland (Ed.), *Ecstasy: The complete guide: A com-*

prehensive look at the risks and benefits of MDMA (pp. 11–20). Rochester, VT: Park Street Press.

Holland, J. C. (1996, September). Cancer's psychological challenges. *Scientif. Amer.*, pp. 158–160.

Hollander, M. H. (1988). Hysteria and memory. In H. M. Pettinati (Ed.), *Hypnosis and memory.* New York: Guilford Press.

Hollon, S. D., Haman, K. L., & Brown, L. L. (2002). Cognitive behavioral treatment of depression. In I. H. Gotlib & C. L. Hammen (Eds.), *Handbook of depression* (pp. 383–403). New York: Guilford Press.

Holmes, J. (2002). All you need is cognitive behavior therapy? *Brit. Med. J.*, 324(7332), 288–290.

Holmes, R. M., & DeBurger, J. E. (1985). Profiles in terror: The serial murderer. *Fed. Probation*, 49, 29–34.

Holmes, S. B., Banerjee, A. K., & Alexander, W. D. (1999). Hyponatreaemia and seizures after ecstasy use. *Postgrad. Med. J.*, 75(879), 32–33.

Holmes, T. H., & Rahe, R. H. (1967). The Social Readjustment Rating Scale. *J. Psychosom. Res.*, 11, 213–218.

Holmes, T. H., & Rahe, R. H. (1989). The Social Readjustment Rating Scale. In T. H. Holmes & E. M. David (Eds.), *Life change, life events, and illness: Selected papers.* New York: Praeger.

Holsboer, F. (2001). Stress, hypercortisolism and corticosteroid receptors in depression: Implications for therapy. *J. Affect. Disorders*, 62(1–2), 77–91.

Holstein, J. A. (1993). *Court-ordered insanity: Interpretive practice and involuntary commitment.* New York: Aldine de Gruyter.

Honikman, J. I. (1999). Role of self-help techniques for postpartum mood disorders. In L. J. Miller et al. (Eds.), *Postpartum mood disorders.* Washington, DC: American Psychiatric Press.

Honkonen, T., Karlsson, H., Koivisto, A. M., Stengard, E., Salokangas, R. K. R. (2003). Schizophrenic patients in different treatment settings during the era of deinstitutionalization: Three-year follow-up of three discharge cohorts in Finland. *Austral. New Zeal. J. Psychiat.*, 37(2), 160–168.

Hooley, J. M., & Hiller, J. B. (2000). Personality and expressed emotion. *J. Abnorm. Psychol.*, 109(1), 40–44.

Hopkins, J., Marcus, M., & Campbell, S. (1984). Postpartum depression: A critical review. *Psychol. Bull.*, 95(3), 498–515.

Hopper, E. (1995). A psychoanalytical theory of "drug addiction": Unconscious fantasies of homosexuality, compulsions and masturbation within the context of traumatogenic processes. *Inter. J. Psychoanal.*, 76(6), 1121–1142.

Horley, J. (2001). Frotteurism: A term in search of an underlying disorder? *J. Sex. Aggress.*, 7(1), 51–55.

Horner, A. J. (1975). Stages and processes in the development of early object relations and their associated pathologies. *Inter. Rev. Psychoanal.*, 2, 95–105.

Horner, A. J. (1991). *Psychoanalytic object relations therapy.* Northvale, NJ: Jason Aronson.

Horney, K. (1937). *The neurotic personality of our time.* New York: Norton.

Hornyak, L. M., Green, J. P. et al. (Eds.). (2000). *Healing from within: The use of hypnosis in women's health care. Dissociation, trauma, memory, and hypnosis book series.* Washington, DC: American Psychological Association.

Horowitz, J., Damato, E., Solon, L., Metzsch, G., & Gill, V. (1995). Postpartum depression: Issues in clinical assessment. *J. Perinat. Med.*, 15(4), 268–278.

Hou, C., Miller, B. L., Cummings, J. L., Goldberg, M., Mychack, P., Bottino, V., &

Benson, D. F. (2000). Artistic savants. *Neuropsychiat., Neuropsychol., Behav. Neurol.*, 13(1), 29–38.

Housman, L. M., & Stake, J. E. (1999). The current state of sexual ethics training in clinical psychology: Issues of quantity, quality and effectiveness. *Profess. Psychol.: Res. Pract.*, 30(3), 302–311.

Houston, K., Hawton, K., & Sheppard, R. (2001). Suicide in young people aged 15–24: A psychological autopsy study. *J. Affect. Disorders*, 63 (1–3), 159–170.

Houts, A. C. (2003). Behavioral treatment for enuresis. In A. E. Kazdin & J. R. Weisz (Eds.), *Evidence-based psychotherapies for children and adolescents.* New York: Guilford Press.

Howe, R., & Nugent, T. (1996, April 22). The gory details. *People*, pp. 91–92.

Howitt, D. (1995). *Paedophiles and sexual offences against children.* Chichester, England: Wiley.

Hoyert, D. L., Arias, E., Smith, B. L., Murphy, S. L., & Kochanek, K. D. (2001). Deaths: Final data for 1999. In National Vital Statistics Report, 49(8). Hyattsville, MD: National Center for Health Statistics.

Hoyt, M. F. (2003). Brief psychotherapies. In A. S. Gurman & S. B. Messer (Eds.), *Essential psychotherapies: Theory and practice* (2nd ed.). New York: Guilford Press.

Hrobjartsson, A., & Gotzsche, P. C. (2001). Is the placebo powerless? An analysis of clinical trials comparing placebo with no treatment. *N. Engl. J. Med.*, 344(21), 1594–1602.

Hsu, L. K. G., Crisp, A. H., & Callender, J. S. (1992). Psychiatric diagnoses in recovered and unrecovered anorectics 22 years after onset of illness: A pilot study. *Comprehen. Psychiat.*, 33(2), 123–127.

Hsu, L. K. G., & Holder, D. (1986). Bulimia nervosa: Treatment and short-term outcome. *Psychol. Med.*, 16, 65.

Hu, S., Pattatucci, A. M. L., Patterson, C., Li, L. et al. (1995, November). Linkage between sexual orientation and chromosome Xq28 in males but not in females. *Nat. Genet.*, 11, 248–256.

Hugdahl, K. (1995). *Psychophysiology: The mind-body perspective.* Cambridge, MA: Harvard University Press.

Hüll, M., Berger, M., Volk, B., & Bauer, J. (1996). Occurrence of interleukin-6 in cortical plaques of Alzheimer's disease patients may precede transformation of diffuse into neuritic plaques. In R. J. Wurtman, S. Corkin, J. H. Growdon, & R. M. Nitsch (Eds.), *The neurobiology of Alzheimer's disease.* New York: New York Academy of Sciences.

Humphreys, K. (1996). Clinical psychologists as psychotherapists. History, future, and alternatives. *Amer. Psychologist*, 51(3), 190–197.

Humphreys, K., & Rappaport, J. (1993). From the community mental health movement to the war on drugs: A study in the definition of social problems. *Amer. Psychologist*, 48(8), 892–901.

Humphry, D., & Wickett, A. (1986). *The right to die: Understanding euthanasia.* New York: Harper & Row.

Hunnicutt, C. P., & Newman, I. A. (1993). Adolescent dieting practices and nutrition knowledge. Health values. *Journal of Health Behavior, Education and Promotion*, 17(4), 35–40.

Hunt, C., & Andrews, G. (1995). Comorbidity in the anxiety disorders: The use of a life-chart approach. *J. Psychiatr. Res.*, 29(6), 467–480.

Huntington, D. D., & Bender, W. N. (1993). Adolescents with learning disabilities at risk: Emotional well-being, depression, suicide. *J. Learn. Dis.*, 26(3), 159–166.

Hurlbert, D. F. (1991). The role of assertiveness in female sexuality: A comparative study between sexually assertive and sexually nonassertive women. *J. Sex Marital Ther.*, 17(3), 183–190.

Hurlbert, D. F. (1993). A comparative study using orgasm consistency training in the treatment of women reporting hypoactive sexual desire. *J. Sex Marital Ther.*, 19, 41–55.

Hurt, S., & Oltmanns, T. F. (2002). Personality traits and pathology in older and younger incarcerated women. *J. Clin. Psychol.*, 58(4), 457–464.

Hyde, J. S. (1990). *Understanding human sexuality* (4th ed.). New York: McGraw-Hill.

Hyman, Jr, I. E., & Loftus, E. F. (2002). False childhood memories and eyewitness memory errors. In M. L. Eisen (Ed.), *Memory and suggestibility in the forensic interview. Personality and clinical psychology series* (pp. 63–84). Mahwah, NJ: Lawrence Erlbaum Associates.

Iketani, T., Kiriike, N., Nakanishi, S., & Nakasuji, T. (1995). Effects of weight gain and resumption of menses on reduced bone density in patients with anorexia nervosa. *Biol. Psychiat.*, 37(80), 521–527.

Illingworth, P. M. L. (1995). Patient-therapist sex: Criminalization and its discontents. *J. Contemporary Health Law and Policy*, 11, 389–416.

Infoplease (2003). *A time line of recent worldwide school shootings.* Pearson Education. December 5, 2003.

Ingersoll, R. E., & Burns, L. (2001). Prevalence of adult disorders. In E. R. Welfel & R. E. Ingersoll (Eds.), *The mental health desk reference* (pp. 3–9). New York: Wiley.

Innes, M. (2002). Satir's therapeutically oriented educational process: A critical appreciation. *Contemp. Fam. Therap: Internat. J.*, 24(1), 35–56.

Inouye, S. K. (1998). Delirium in hospitalized older patients: Recognition and risk factors. *J. Geriat. Psychiat. Neurol.*, 11(3), 118–125.

Inouye, S. K. (1999). Predisposing and precipitating factors for delirium in hospitalized older patients. *Dement. Ger. Cogn. Disord.*, 10(5), 393–400.

Isometsae, E. T., & Loennqvist, J. K. (1998). Suicide attempts preceding completed suicide. *Brit. J. Psychiat.*, 173, 531–535.

Jablensky, A. (2002). The classification of personality disorders: Critical review and need for rethinking. *Psychopathology*, 35(2–3), 112–116.

Jackson, J. L., Calhoun, K. S., Amick, A. A., Madever, H. M., & Habif, V. L. (1990). Young adult women who report childhood intrafamilial sexual abuse: Subsequent adjustment. *Arch. Sex. Behav.*, 19(3), 211–221.

Jackson, J. S. (Ed.). (1988). *The black American elderly: Research on physical and psychosocial health.* New York: Springer.

Jacobs, B. L. (Ed.). (1984). *Hallucinogens: Neurochemical, behavioral, and clinical perspectives.* New York: Raven Press.

Jacobs, B. L. (1994). Serotonin, motor activity and depression-related disorders. *Amer. Sci.*, 82, 456–463.

Jacobs, D. G. (Ed.). (1999). *The Harvard Medical School guide to suicide assessment and intervention.* San Francisco: Jossey-Bass.

Jacobs, D. G., Brewer, M., & Klein-Benheim, M. (1999). Suicide assessment: An overview and recommended protocol. In D. G. Jacobs (Ed.), *The*

Harvard Medical School guide to suicide assessment and intervention. San Francisco: Jossey-Bass.

Jacobs, M. K., Christensen, A., Snibbe, J. R., Dolezal-Wood, S., Huber, A., & Polterok, A. (2001). A comparison of computer-based versus traditional individual psychotherapy. *Profess. Psychol.: Res. Pract.*, 32(1), 92–96.

Jacobsen, L. K., Rabinowitz, I., Popper, M. S., Solomon, R. J., Sokol, M. S., & Pfeffer, C. R. (1994). Interviewing prepubertal children about suicidal ideation and behavior. *J. Amer. Acad. Child Adol. Psychiat.*, 33(4), 439–452.

Jacobson, G. (1999). The inpatient management of suicidality. In D. G. Jacobs (Ed.), *The Harvard Medical School guide to suicide assessment and intervention.* San Francisco: Jossey-Bass.

Jacobson, N. S., Dobson, K. S., Truax, P. A., Addis, M. E. et al. (1996). A component analysis of cognitive-behavioral treatment for depression. *J. Cons. Clin. Psychol.*, 64(2), 295–304.

Jaffe, J. H. (1985). Drug addiction and drug abuse. In Goodman & Gilman (Eds.), *The pharmacological basis of therapeutic behavior.* New York: Macmillan.

Jahangir, F., ur-Rehman, H., & Jan, T. (1998). Degree of religiosity and vulnerability to suicidal attempt/plans in depressive patients among Afghan refugees. *Inter. J. Psychol. Religion*, 8(4), 265–269.

Jambor, E. (2001). Media involvement and the idea of beauty. In R. McComb & J. Jacalyn (Eds.), *Eating disorders in women and children: Prevention, stress management, and treatment*(pp. 179–183). Boca Raton, FL: CRC Press.

James, W. (1890). *Principles of psychology* (Vol. 1). New York: Holt, Rinehart & Winston.

Jamison, K. R. (1995, February). Manic-depressive illness and creativity. *Scientif. Amer.*, pp. 63–67.

Jamison, K. R. (1995). *An unquiet mind.* New York: Vintage Books.

Jang, K. L., & Vernon, P. A. (2001). Genetics. In W. J. Livesley (Ed.), *Handbook of personality disorders: Theory, research, and treatment* (pp. 177–195). New York: Guilford Press.

Janicak, P. G., Davis, J. M., Preskorn, S. H., & Ayd, F. J. (2001). *Principles and practice of psychopharmacotherapy* (3rd ed.). Philadelphia: Lippincott Williams & Wilkin.

Janowsky, D. S., El-Yousef, M. K., Davis, J. M., & Sekerke, H. J. (1973). Provocation of schizophrenic symptoms by intravenous administration of methylphenidate. *Arch. Gen. Psychiat.*, 28, 185–191.

Jansen, K. L. R. (2001). Mental health problems associated with MDMA use. In J. Holland (Ed.), *Ecstasy: The complete guide: A comprehensive look at the risks and benefits of MDMA* (pp. 87–109). Rochester, VT: Park Street Press.

Janus, S. S., & Janus, C. L. (1993). *The Janus report on sexual behavior.* New York: Wiley.

Janzing, J. G. E. (2003). Depression and dementia: Missing the link. *Curr. Opin. Psychiat.*, 16(1), 13–16.

Javitt, D. C., & Coyle, J. T. (2004). Decoding schizophrenia. *Scientific American*, 290(1), 48–55.

Jaycox, L. H., & Foa, E. B. (2001). Posttraumatic stress. In H.S. Friedman (Ed.), *Specialty articles from the encyclopedia of mental health.* San Diego: Academic Press.

Jefferson, J. W., & Greist, J. H. (1994). Mood disorders. In R. E. Hales, S. C. Yudofsky, & J. A. Talbott (Eds.), *The American Psychiatric Press textbook of psychiatry*(2nd ed.). Washington, DC: American Psychiatric Press.

Jefferson, L. (1948). *These are my sisters.* Tulsa, OK: Vickers.

Jenike, M. A. (1992). New developments in treatment of obsessive-compulsive disorder. In A.

Tasman & M. B. Riba (Eds.), *Review of psychiatry*(Vol. 11). Washington, DC: American Psychiatric Press.

Jenkins, R. L. (1968). The varieties of children's behavioral problems and family dynamics. *Amer. J. Psychiat.*, 124(10), 1440–1445.

Jensen, G. M. (1998). The experience of injustice: Health consequences of the Japanese American internment. *Diss. Abstr. Inter.: Sect. A: Human Soc. Sci.*, 58(7–A), 2718.

Jessen, G., Jensen, B. F., Arensman, E., Bille-Brahe, U., Crepet, P., De Leo, D., Hawton, K., Haring, C., Hjelmeland, H., Michel, K., Ostamo, A., Salander-Renberg, E., Schmidtke, A., Temesvary, B., & Wasserman, D. (1999). Attempted suicide and major public holidays in Europe: Findings from the WHO/EURO multicentre study on parasuicide. *Acta Psychiatr. Scandin.*, 99(6), 412–418.

Joffe, H., Brodaty, H., Luscombe, G., & Ehrlich, F. (2003). The Sydney Holocaust study: Posttraumatic stress disorder and other psychosocial morbidity in an aged community sample. *J. Traum. Stress.*, 16(1), 39–47.

Johns, A. (2001). Psychiatric effects of cannabis. *Brit. J. Psychiat.*, 178, 116–122.

Johns, L. C., Sellwood, W., McGovern, J., & Haddock, G. (2002). Battling boredom: Group cognitive behaviour therapy for negative symptoms of schizophrenia. *Behav. Cog. Psychother.*, 30(3), 341–346.

Johnsen, F. (1994). *The encyclopedia of popular misconceptions.* New York: Citadel Press.

Johnson, B. R., & Becker, J. V. (1997). Natural born killers?: The development of the sexually sadistic serial killer. *J. Amer. Acad. Psychiat. Law.*, 25(3), 335–348.

Johnson, C. (1995, February 8). National Collegiate Athletic Association study. In *The Hartford Courant.*

Johnson, D. L. (2002). A brief history of the international movement of family organization for persons with mental illness. In H. P. Lefley & D. L. Johnson (Eds.), *Family intervention in mental illness: International perspectives.* Westport, CT: Praeger.

Johnson, D. R., Feldman, S., & Lubin, H. (1995). Critical interaction therapy: Couples therapy in combat-related posttraumatic stress disorder. *Fam. Process*, 34, 401–412.

Johnson, E. H., Gentry, W. D., & Julius, S. (Eds.). (1992). *Personality, elevated blood pressure, and essential hypertension.* Washington, DC: Hemisphere.

Johnson, J. G., Cohen, P., Smailes, E. M., Skodol, A. E., Brown, J., & Oldham, J. M. (2001). Childhood verbal abuse and risk for personality disorders during adolescence and early adulthood. *Comprehen. Psychiat.*, 42(1), 16–23.

Johnson, M. E., Jones, G., & Brems, C. (1996). Concurrent validity of the MMPI-2 feminine gender role (GF) and masculine gender role (GM) scales. *J. Pers. Assess.*, 66(1), 153–168.

Johnson, W. D. (1991). Predisposition to emotional distress and psychiatric illness amongst doctors: The role of unconscious and experiential factors. *Brit. J. Med. Psychol.*, 64(4), 317–329.

Johnston, L. D., O'Malley, P. M., & Bachman, J. G. (1993). *National survey results on drug use from the Monitoring the Future Study, 1975–1992.* Rockville, MD: National Institute on Drug Abuse.

Johnston, L. D., O'Malley, P. M., & Bachman, J. G. (2002). *Monitoring the future: National results on adolescent drug use. Overview of key findings, 2001.*Bethesda, MD: National Institute on Drug Abuse.

Johnstone, L. (2000). *Users and abusers of psychiatry: A critical look a psychiatric practice* (2nd ed.). London: Routledge.

Joiner, T. E. (1995). The price of soliciting and receiving negative feedback: Self-verification theory as a vulnerability to depression theory. *J. Abnorm. Psychol.*, 104(2), 364–372.

Joiner, T. E., Jr., (2002). Depression in its interpersonal context. In I. H. Gotlib & C. L. Hammen (Eds.), *Handbook of depression* (pp. 295–313). New York: Guilford Press.

Jones, G., Swain, A. B. J., & Cole, A. (1990). Antecedents of multidimensional competitive state anxiety and self confidence in elite intercollegiate middle distance runners. *Sport Psychol.*, 4, 107–118.

Jones, M. C. (1968). Personality correlates and antecedants of drinking patterns in males. *J. Cons. Clin. Psychol.*, 32, 2–12.

Jones, M. C. (1971). Personality antecedents and correlates of drinking patterns in women. *J. Cons. Clin. Psychol.*, 36, 61–69.

Joober, R., Boksa, P, Benkelfat, C., & Rouleau, G. (2002). Genetics of schizophrenia: From animal models to clinical studies. *J. Psychiat. Neurosci.*, 27(5), 336–347.

Jordan, D. (1997). *1001 more facts somebody screwed up.* Atlanta, GA: Longtreet Press.

Jorenby, D. E., Leischow, S. J., Nides, M. A., Rennard, S. I., Johnston, J. A., Hughes, A. R., Smith, S. S., Muramoto, M. L., Daughton, D. M., Doan, K., Fiore, M. C., & Baker, T. B. (1999). A controlled trial of sustained-release bupropion, a nicotine patch, or both for smoking cessation. *N. Engl. J. Med.*, 340(9), 685–691.

Juel-Nielsen, N., & Videbech, T. (1970). A twin study of suicide. *Acta Genet. Med. Gemellol.*, 19, 307–310.

Julius, S. (1992). Relationship between the sympathetic tone and cardiovascular responsiveness in the course of hypertension. In E. H. Johnson, E. D. Gentry, & S. Julius (Eds.), *Personality, elevated blood pressure, and essential hypertension.* Washington, DC: Hemisphere.

Juster, H. R., Heimberg, R. G., & Holt, C. S. (1996). Social phobia: Diagnostic issues and review of cognitive behavioral treatment strategies. In M. Hersen, R. M. Eisler, & P. M. Miller (Eds.), *Progress in behavior modification* (Vol. 30). Pacific Grove, CA: Brooks/Cole.

Kabat-Zinn, J., Massion, A. O., Kristeller, J., Peterson, L. G. et al. (1992). Effectiveness of a meditation-based stress reduction program in the treatment of anxiety disorders. *Amer. J. Psychiat.*, 149(7), 936–943.

Kabot, S., Masi, W., & Segal, M. (2003). Advances in the diagnosis and treatment of autism spectrum disorders. *Profess. Psychol.: Res. Pract.*, 34(1), 26–33.

Kafka, M. P. (2000). The paraphilia-related disorders: Nonparaphilic hypersexuality and sexual compulsivity/addiction. In S. R. Leiblum & R. C. Raymond (Eds.), *Principles and practice of sex therapy* (3rd ed., pp. 471–503). New York: Guilford Press.

Kagan, J., & Snidman, N. (1991). Infant predictors of inhibited and uninhibited profiles. *Psychol. Sci.*, 2, 40–44.

Kagan, J., & Snidman, N. (1999). Early childhood predictors of adult anxiety disorders. *Biol. Psychiat.*, 46(11), 1536–1541.

Kagan, N. I., Kagan, H., & Watson, M. G. (1995). Stress reduction in the workplace: The effectiveness of psychoeducational progams. *J. Couns. Psychol.*, 42(1), 71–78.

Kahn, A. P., & Fawcett, J. (1993). *The encyclopedia of mental health.* New York: Facts on File.

Kaij, L. (1960). *Alcoholism in twins: Studies on the etiology and sequels of abuse of alcohol.* Stockholm: Almquist & Wiksell.

Kail, R. (1992). General slowing of information-processing by persons with mental retardation. *Amer. J. Ment. Retard., 97*(3), 333–341.

Kaiser Family Foundation (2001, November). *Understanding the effects of direct-to-consumer prescription drug advertising.* The Health Care Marketplace Project Publications: Menlo Park, CA.

Kaiser Family Foundation (2002, May 1). Direct-to-consumer promotional spending by pharmaceutical manufacturers. *Amer. Demog.* Retrieved September 15, 2002, from www.industryclick.com

Kalafat, J., & Ryerson, D. M. (1999). The implementation and institutionalization of a school-based youth suicide prevention program. *J. Primary Prev., 19*(3), 157–175.

Kalayjian, L. A., & Morrell, M. J. (2000). Female sexuality and neurological disease. *J. Sex Educ. Ther., 25*(1), 89–95.

Kalb, C. (2000, January 31). Coping with the darkness: Revolutionary new approaches in providing care for helping people with Alzheimer's stay active and feel productive. *Newsweek,* pp. 52–54.

Kalb, C. (2003, November 10). Faith and healing. *Newsweek,* 44–56.

Kalin, N. H. (1993, May). The neurobiology of fear. *Scientif. Amer.,* pp. 94–101.

Kalska, H., Punamaeki, R. L., Maekinen-Pelli, T., & Saarinen, M. (1999). Memory and metamemory functioning among depressed patients. *Appl. Neuropsychol., 6*(2), 96–107.

Kaminer, Y., Burleson, J. A., & Jadamec, A. (2002). Gambling behavior in adolescent substance abuse. *Substance Abuse, 23*(3), 191–198.

Kamphaus, R. W., & Frick, P. J. (2002). *Clinical assessment of child and adolescent personality and behavior* (2nd ed.). Boston: Allyn and Bacon.

Kamphuis, J. H., & Emmelkamp, P. M. G. (2001). Traumatic distress among support-seeking female victims of stalking. *Amer. J. Psychiat., 158*(5), 795–798.

Kane, J. M. (1992). Clinical efficacy of clozapine in treatment-refractory schizophrenia: An overview. *Brit. J. Psychiat., 160*(Suppl. 17), 41–45.

Kane, J. M. (2001). Progress defined—short-term efficacy, long-term effectiveness. *Inter. Clin. Psychopharmacol., 16*(Suppl. 1), S1–S8.

Kane, J. M. (2001). Schizophrenia: Editorial review. *Curr. Opin. Psychiat., 14*(1), 1.

Kanner, B. (1995). *Are you normal?: Do you behave like everyone else?* New York: St. Martin's Press.

Kanner, B. (1998, February). Are you normal? Turning the other cheek. *American Demog.*

Kanner, B. (1998, May). Are you normal? Creatures of habit. *Am. Demogr.*

Kanner, B. (1998, August). Are you normal? Summertime. *Am. Demogr.*

Kanner, B. (1999, January). Hungry, or just bored? *Am. Demogr.*

Kanner, L. (1943). Autistic disturbances of affective contact. *Nerv. Child. 2,* 217.

Kanner, L. (1954). To what extent is early infantile autism determined by constitutional inadequacies? *Proceedings of the Assoc. Res. Nerv. Ment. Dis., 33,* 378–385.

Kaplan, A. (1998, September). Caring for the caregivers: Family interventions and Alzheimer's disease. *Psychiatr. Times, XV*(9).

Kaplan, A. (1999). China's suicide patterns challenge depression theory. *Psychiatr. Times., XVI*(1).

Kaplan, A. S., & Garfinkel, P. E. (1999). Difficulties in treating patients with eating disorders: A review of patient and clinician variables. *Canad. J. Psychiat., 44*(7), 665–670.

Kaplan, H. S. (1974). *The new sex therapy: Active treatment of sexual dysfunction.* New York: Brunner/Mazel.

Kaplan, R. M. (2000). Two pathways to prevention. *Amer. Psychologist, 55*(4), 382–396.

Kapp, M. B. (2002). Regulating research for the decisionally impaired: Implications for mental health professionals. *J. Clin. Geropsychol., 8*(1), 35–51.

Kardiner, A. (1977). *My analysis with Freud: Reminiscences.* New York: Norton.

Karel, R. (1992, May 1). Hopes of many long-term sufferers dashed as FDA ends medical marijuana program. *Psychiatr. News.*

Karon, B. P., & Vandenbos, G. R. (1996). *Psychotherapy of schizophrenia: The treatment of choice.* Northvale, NJ: Jason Aronson.

Kasai, K., Shenton, M. E., Salisbury, D. F., Hirayasu, Y., Lee, C. U., Ciszewski, A. A., Yurgelun-Todd, D., Kinikis, R., Jolesz, F. A., & McCarley, R. W. (2003). Progressive decrease of left superior temporal gyrus gray matter volume in patients with first-episode schizophrenia. *Amer. J. Psychiat., 160*(1), 156–164.

Kaslow, N. J., Dausch, B. M., & Celano, M. (2003). In A. S. Gurman & S. B. Messer (Eds.), *Essential psychotherapies: Theory and practice* (2nd ed.). New York: Guilford Press.

Kaslow, N. J., Reviere, S. L., Chance, S. E., Rogers, J. H., Hatcher, C. A., Wasserman, F., Smith, L., Jessee, S., James, M. E., & Seelig, B. (1998). An empirical study of the psychodynamics of suicide. *J. Amer. Psychoanal. Assoc., 46*(3), 777–796.

Kassel, J. D., Wagner, E. F., & Unrod, M. (1999). Alcoholism-behavior therapy. In M. Hersen & A. S. Bellack (Eds.), *Handbook of comparative interventions for adult disorders* (2nd ed.). New York: Wiley.

Kassin S. M., Tubb, V. A., Hosch, H. M., & Memon, A. (2001). On the "general acceptance" of eyewitness testimony research: A new survey of the experts. *Amer. Psychologist, 56*(5), 405–416.

Kate, N. T. (1998, May). Freshmen get wholesome. *Am. Demogr.*

Katel, P., & Beck, M. (1996, March 29). Sick kid or sick Mom? *Newsweek,* p. 73.

Katz, E. C., Gruber, K., Chutuape, M. A., & Stitzer, M. L. (2001). Reinforcement-based outpatient treatment for opiate and cocaine abusers. *J. Subst. Abuse Treatm., 20*(1), 93–98.

Katzman, R. (2001). Epidemiology of Alzheimer's disease and dementia: Advances and challenges. In K. Iqbal, S. S. Sisodia, & B. Winblad (Eds.), *Alzheimer's disease: Advances in etiology, pathogenesis and therapeutics* (pp. 11–22). New York: Wiley.

Kaufman, M. (1999, June 8). White House decries stigma: "A health issue—no more and no less." *Washington Post,* p. Z07.

Kawas, C., Resnick, S., Morrison, A., Brookmeyer, R., Corrada, M., Zonderman, A., Bacal, C., Lingle, D. D., & Metter, E. J. (1997). A prospective study of estrogen replacement therapy and the risk of developing Alzheimer's disease: The Baltimore Longtitudinal Study of Aging. *Neurology, 48*(6), 1517–1521.

Kaye, W. H., Gendall, K. A., Fernstrom, M. H., Fernstrom, J. D., McConaha, C. W., & Weltzin, T. E. (2000). Effects of acute tryptophan depletion on mood in bulimia nervosa. *Biol. Psychiat., 47*(2), 151–157.

Kaye, W. H., Strober, M., & Rhodes, L. (2002). Body image disturbance and other core symptoms in anorexia and bulimia nervosa. In D. J. Castle & K. A. Phillips (Eds.), *Disorders of body image* (pp. 67–82). Petersfield, UK: Wrightson Biomedical.

Kazdin, A. E. (1994). Methodology, design, and evaluation in psychotherapy research. In A. E. Bergin & S. L. Garfiel (Eds.), *Handbook of psychotherapy and behavior change*(4th ed.). New York: Wiley.

Kazdin, A. E. (2000). Adolescent development, mental disorders, and decision making of delinquent youths. In T. Grisso & R. G. Schwartz (Eds.), *Youth on trial: A developmental perspective on juvenile justice* (pp. 33–65). Chicago: University of Chicago Press.

Kazdin, A. E. (2000). *Psychotherapy for children and adolescents: Directions for research and practice.* New York: Oxford University Press.

Kazdin, A. E. (2002). Psychosocial treatments for conduct disorder in children and adolescents. In P. E. Nathan & J. M. Gorman (Eds.), *A guide to treatments that work*(2nd ed., pp. 57–85). London: Oxford University Press.

Kazdin, A. E. (2003). Problem-solving skills training and parent management training for conduct disorder. In A. E. Kazdin & J. R. Weisz (Eds.), *Evidence-based psychotherapies for children and adolescents.* New York: Guilford Press.

Kazdin, A. E. (Ed.) (2003). *Methodological issues & strategies in clinical research* (3rd ed.). Washington, DC: American Psychological Association.

Kazdin, A. E., & Weisz, J. R. (1998). Identifying and developing empirically supported child and adolescent treatments. *J. Cons. Clin. Psychol., 66*(1), 19–36.

Kazdin, A. E., & Weisz, J. R. (2003). Introduction: Context and background of evidence-based psychotherapies for children and adolescents. In A. E. Kazdin & J. R. Weisz (Eds.), *Evidence-based psychotherapies for children and adolescents.* New York: Guilford Press.

Kazdin, A. E., & Weisz, J. R. (Eds.). (2003). *Evidence-based psychotherapies for children and adolescents.* New York: Guilford Press.

Keane, T. M., & Barlow, D. H. (2002). Posttraumatic stress disorder. In D. H. Barlow (Ed.), *Anxiety and its disorders: The nature and treatment of anxiety and panic*(2nd ed., pp. 418–453). New York: Guilford Press.

Kearney-Cooke, A., & Steichen-Asch, P. (1990). Men, body image, and eating disorders. In A. E. Andersen (Ed.), *Males with eating disorders.* New York: Brunner/Mazel.

Keefe, R. S. E., Arnold, M. C., Bayen, U. J., McEvoy, J. P., & Wilson, W. H. (2002). Source-monitoring deficits for self-generated stimuli in schizophrenia: Multinomial modeling of data from three sources. *Schizo. Res., 57*(1), 51–68.

Keel, P. K., & Mitchell, J. E. (1997). Outcome in bulimia nervosa. *Amer. J. Psychiat., 154,* 313–321.

Keel, P. K., Mitchell, J. E., Miller, K. B., Davis, T. L., & Crow, S. J. (1999). Long-term outcome of bulimia nervosa. *Arch. Gen. Psychiat., 56*(1), 63–69.

Keel, P. K., Mitchell, J. E., Miller, K. B., Davis, T. L., & Crow, S. J. (2000). Social adjustment over 10 years following diagnosis with bulimia nervosa. *Inter. J. Eat. Disorders, 27*(1), 21–28.

Keen, E. (1970). *Three faces of being: Toward an existential clinical psychology.* By the Meredith Corp. Reprinted by permission of Irvington Publishers.

Keesey, R. E., & Corbett, S. W. (1983). Metabolic defense of the body weight set-point. In A. J. Stunkard & E. Stellar (Eds.), *Eating and its disorders.* New York: Raven Press.

Keith, S. J., Regier, D. A., & Rae, D. S. (1991). Schizophrenic disorders. In L. N. Robins & D. S. Regier (Eds.), *Psychiatric disorders in America: The Epidemiological Catchment Area Study.* New York: Free Press.

Kelleher, M. D., & Van Nuys, D. (2002). *This is the Zodiac speaking: Into the mind of a serial killer.* Westport, CT: Praeger/Greenwood.

Keller, M. B. (2002). The long-term clinical course of generalized anxiety disorder. *J. Clin. Psychiat.*, 63(Suppl 8), 11–16.

Keller, R., & Shaywitz, B. A. (1986). Amnesia or fugue state: A diagnostic dilemma. *J. Dev. Behav. Pediatr.*, 7(8), 131–132.

Kelley, A. E., & Berridge, K. C. (2002). The neuroscience of natural rewards: Relevance to addictive drugs. *J. Neurosci.*, 22(9), 3306–3311.

Kellner, M., & Yehuda, R. (1999). Do panic disorder and posttraumatic stress disorder share a common psychoneuroendocrinology? *Psychoneuroendocrinology*, 24(5), 485–504.

Kelly, K. A. (1993). Multiple personality disorders: Treatment coordination in a partial hospital setting. *Bull. Menninger Clin.*, 57(3), 390–398.

Kelly, K. G., Zisselman, M., Cutillo-Schmitter, T., Reichard, R., Payne, D., & Denman, S. J. (2001). Severity and course of delirium in medically hospitalized nursing facility residents. *Amer. J. Ger. Psychiat.*, 9(1), 72–77.

Kelly, M. P., Strassberg, D. S., & Kircher, J. R. (1990). Attitudinal and experiental correlates of anorgasmia. *Arch. Sex. Behav.*, 19, 165–172.

Keltner, N. L., & Folks, D. G. (2001). *Psychotropic drugs* (3rd ed.). St. Louis, MO: Mosby.

Kemp, A., Green, B. L., Hovanitz, C., & Rawlings, E. I. (1995). Incidence and correlates of posttraumatic stress disorder in battered women: Shelter and community samples. *J. Interpers. Violence*, 10(1), 43–55.

Kemp, D. R. (1994). *Mental health in the workplace: An employer's and manager's guide.* Westport, CT: Quorum Books.

Kendall, P. C. (2000). *Childhood disorders.* Hove, England: Psychology Press/Taylor & Francis.

Kendell, R. E. (2002). Personality disorder: Author's reply. *Brit. J. Psychiat.*, 181(1), 77–78.

Kendler, K. S., Heath, A., & Martin, N. G. (1987). A genetic epidemiologic study of self-report suspiciousness. *Comprehen. Psychiat.*, 28(3), 187–196.

Kendler, K. S., Heath, A., Neale, M., Kessler, R., & Eaves, L. (1992). A population-based twin study of alcoholism in women. *JAMA*, 268(14), 1877–1882.

Kendler, K. S., Karkowski, L. M., & Prescott, C. A. (1998). Stressful life events and major depression: Risk period, long-term contextual threat and diagnostic specificity. *J. Nerv. Ment. Dis.*, 186(11), 661–669.

Kendler, K. S., Myers, J. M., O'Neill, F. A., Martin, R., Murphy, B., MacLean, C. J., Walsh, D., & Straub, R. E. (2000). Clinical features of schizophrenia and linkage to chromosomes 5q, 6p, 8p, and 10p in the Irish study of high-density schizophrenia families. *Amer. J. Psychiat.*, 157(3), 402–408.

Kendler, K. S., Neale, M. C., Heath, A. C., Kessler, R. C., & Eaves, L. J. (1994). A twin-family study of alcoholism in women. *Amer. J. Psychiat.*, 151(5), 707–715.

Kendler, K. S., Neale, M. C., Kessler, R. C., Heath, A. C., & Eaves, L. J. (1993). Panic disorder in women: A population-based twin study. *Psychol. Med.*, 23, 397–406.

Kendler, K. S., Ochs, A. L., Gorman, A. M., Hewitt, J. K., Ross, D. E., & Mirsky, A. F. (1991). The structure of schizotypy: A pilot multi-trait twin study. *Psychiat. Res.*, 36(1), 19–36.

Kendler, K. S., Walters, E. E., & Kessler, R. C. (1997). The prediction of length of major depressive episodes: Results from an epidemiological sample of female twins. *Psychol. Med.* 27(1), 107–117.

Kendler, K. S., Walters, E. E., Neale, M. C., Kessler, R. C., et al. (1995). The structure of the genetic and environmental risk factors for six major psychiatric disorders in women: Phobia, generalized anxiety disorder, panic disorder, bulimia, major depression, and alcoholism. *Arch. Gen. Psychiat.*, 52(5), 374–383.

Kensinger, E. A., Ullman, M. T., & Corkin, S. (2001). Bilateral medial temporal lobe damage does not affect lexical or grammatical processing: Evidence from amnesic patient H. M. *Hippocampus*, 11(4), 347–360.

Keown, P., Holloway, F., & Kuipers, E. (2002). The prevalence of personality disorders, psychotic disorders and affective disorders amongst the patients seen by a community mental health team in London. *Soc. Psychiat. Psychiatr. Epidemiol.*, 37(5), 225–229.

Kernberg, O. F. (1976). *Object-relations theory and clinical psychoanalysis.* New York: Jason Aronson.

Kernberg, O. F. (1989). Narcissistic personality disorder in childhood. *Psychiatr. Clin. N. Amer.*, 12(3), 671–694.

Kernberg, O. F. (1997). Convergences and divergences in contemporary psychoanalytic technique and psychoanalytic psychotherapy. In J. K. Zeig (Ed.), *The evolution of psychotherapy: The third conference.* New York: Brunner/Mazel.

Kernberg, O. F. (2001). The concept of libido in the light of contemporary psychoanalytic theorizing. In P. Hartocollis (Ed.), *Mankind's oedipal destiny: Libidinal and aggressive aspects of sexuality* (pp. 95–111). Madison, CT: International Universities Press.

Kernberg, O. F. (2002). Psychoanalytic contributions to psychiatry. *Arch. Gen. Psychiat.*, 59(6), 497–498.

Kessler, D. A., & Pines, W. L. (1990). The federal regulation of prescription drug advertising and promotion. *JAMA*, 264(18), 2409–2415.

Kessler, R. C. (2002). Epidemiology of depression. In I. H. Gotlib & C. L. Hammen (Eds.), *Handbook of depression* (pp. 23–42). New York: Guilford Press.

Kessler, R. C., DuPont, R. L., Berglund, P., & Wittchen, H. U. (1999). Impairment in pure and comorbid generalized anxiety disorder and major depression at 12 months in two national surveys. *Amer. J. Psychiat.*, 156(12), 1915–1923.

Kessler, R. C., Keller, M. B., & Wittchen, H. U. (2001). The epidemiology of generalized anxiety disorder. *Psychiatr. Clin. N. Amer.*, 24(1), 19–39.

Kessler, R. C., McGonagle, K. A., Zhao, S., Nelson, C. B., Hughes, M., Eshleman, S., Wittchen, H. U., & Kendler, K. S. (1994). Lifetime and 12-month prevalence of DSM-III-R psychiatric disorders among persons aged 15–54 in the United States: Results from the National Comorbidity Survey. *Arch. Gen. Psychiat.*, 51(1), 8–19.

Kessler, R. C., Olfson, M., & Berglund, P. A. (1998). Patterns and predictors of treatment contact after first onset of psychiatric disorders. *Amer. J. Psychiat.*, 155(1), 62–69.

Kessler, R. C., Sonnega, A., Bromet, E., Hughes, M., & Nelson, C. B. (1995). Posttraumatic stress disorder in the National Comorbidity Survey. *Arch. Gen. Psychiat.*, 52, 1048–1060.

Kessler, R. C., & Walters, E. (2002). The national comorbidity survey. In M. T. Tsuang & M. Tohen (Eds.), *Textbook in psychiatric epidemiology* (2nd ed.). New York: Wiley-Liss.

Kessler, R. C., & Zhao, S. (1999). The prevalence of mental illness. In A. V. Horwitz & T. L. Scheid (Eds.), *A handbook for the study of mental health: Social contexts, theories, and systems.* Cambridge, England: Cambridge University Press.

Kettl, P. (1998). Alaska native suicide: Lessons for elder suicide. *Inter. Psychoger.*, 110(2), 205–211.

Kety, S. S., Rosenthal, D., Wender, P. H., et al. (1968). The types and prevalence of mental illness in the biological and adoptive families of schizophrenics. *J. Psychiatr. Res.*, 6, 345–362.

Keys, A., Brozek, J., Henschel, A., Mickelson, O., & Taylor, H. L. (1950). *The biology of human starvation.* Minneapolis: University of Minnesota Press.

Khan, S., Murray, R. P., & Barnes, G. E. (2002). A structural equation model of the effect of poverty and unemployment on alcohol abuse. *Addic. Behav.*, 27(3), 405–423.

Kiecolt-Glaser, J. K., Dura, J. R., Speicher, C. E., Trask, O. J., & Glaser, R. (1991). Spousal caregivers of dementia victims: Longitudinal changes in immunity and health. *Psychosom. Med.*, 53, 345–362.

Kiecolt-Glaser, J. K., & Glaser, R. (1988). Methodological issues in behavioral immunology research with humans. *Brain Behav. Immun.*, 2, 67–68.

Kiecolt-Glaser, J. K., & Glaser, R. (1999). Psychoneuroimmunology and immunotoxicology: Implications for carcinogenesis. *Psychosom. Med.*, 61(3), 271–272.

Kiecolt-Glaser, J. K., & Glaser, R. (2001). Stress and immunity: Age enhances the risks. *Curr. Direct. Psychol. Sci.*, 10(1), 18–21.

Kiecolt-Glaser, J. K., Glaser, R., Gravenstein, S., Malarkey, W. B., & Sheridan, J. (1996). Chronic stress alters the immune response to influenza virus vaccine in older adults. *Proc. Natl. Acad. Sci. USA*, 93, 3043–3047.

Kiecolt-Glaser, J. K., Glaser, R., Shuttleworth, E. C., Dyer, C. S., Ogrocki, P., & Speicher, C. E. (1987). Chronic stress and immunity in family caregivers of Alzheimer's disease victims. *Psychosom. Med.*, 49, 523–535.

Kiecolt-Glaser, J. K., Kennedy, S., Malkoff, S., Fisher, L., Speicher, C. E., & Glaser, R. (1988). Marital discord and immunity in males. *Psychosom. Med.*, 50, 213–229.

Kiecolt-Glaser, J. K., McGuire, L., Robles, T. F., & Glaser, R. (2002). Psychoneuroimmunology: Psychological influences on immune function and health. *J. Cons. Clin. Psychol.*, 70(3), 537–547.

Kiecolt-Glaser, J. K., Page, G. G., Marucha, P. T., MacCallum, R. C., & Glaser, R. (1998). Psychological influences on surgical recovery. Perspectives from psychoneuroimmunology. *Amer. Psychologist*, 53(11), 1209–1218.

Kiefer, F., Jahn, H., Tamaske, T., Helwig, H., Briken, P., Holzbach, R., Kaempf, P., Stracke, R., Baehr, M., Naber, D., & Wiedermann, K. (2003). Comparing and combining naltrexone and acamprosate in relapse prevention of alcoholism: A double-blind, placebo-controlled study. *Arch. Gen. Psychiat.*, 60(1), 92–99.

Kienhorst, C. W. M., de Wilde, E. J., & Diekstra, R. F. W. (1995). Suicidal behaviour in adolescents. *Arch. Suic. Res.*, 1(3), 185–209.

Kienhorst, C. W. M., de Wilde, E. J., Diekstra, R. F. W., & Wolters, W. H. G. (1995). Adolescents' image of their suicide attempt. *J. Amer. Acad. Child Adol. Psychiat.*, 34(5), 623–628.

Kiernan, W. (2000). Where we are now: Perspectives on employment of persons with mental retardation. *Focus Autism Other Dev. Disabil.*, 15(2), 90–96.

Kiesler, C. A. (2000). The next wave of change for psychology and mental health services in the health care revolution. *Amer. Psychologist*, 55(5), 481–487.

Kiesler, D. J. (1966). Some myths of psychotherapy research and the search for a paradigm. *Psychol. Bull.*, 65, 110–136.

Kiesler, D. J. (1995). Research classic: "Some myths of psychotherapy research and the search for a paradigm": Revisited. *Psychother. Res.*, 5(2), 91–101.

Kiev, A. (1989). Suicide in adults. In J. G. Howells (Ed.), *Modern perspectives in the psychiatry of the affective disorders.* New York: Brunner/Mazel.

Kihlstrom, J.F. (1994) *The social construction of memory.* Paper presented at the American Psychological Society convention.

Kihlström, J. F. (2001). *Dissociative disorders.* New York: Kluwer Academic/Plenum.

Kihlström, J. F. (2002). To honor Kraepelin. . . : From symptoms to pathology in the diagnosis of mental illness. In L. E. Beutler & M. L. Malik (Eds.), *Rethinking the DSM: A psychological perspective. Decade of behavior.* Washington, DC: APA.

Kihlström, J. F., Tataryn, D. J., & Hoyt, I. P. (1993). Dissociative disorders. In P. B. Sucker & H. E. Adams (Eds.), *Comprehensive handbook of psychopathology*(2nd ed.). New York: Plenum Press.

Kim, C. H., Chang, J. W., Koo, M. S., Kim, J. W., Suh, H. S., Park, I. H., & Lee, H.S. (2003). Anterior cingulotomy for refractory obsessive-compulsive disorder. *Acta Psychiatr. Scandin., 107*(4), 283–290.

Kim, C. H., Jayathilake, K., & Meltzer, H. Y. (2003). Hopelessness, neurocognitive function, and insight in schizophrenia: Relationship to suicidal behavior. *Schizo. Res., 60*(1), 71–80.

Kimball, A. (1993). Nipping and tucking. In Skin deep: Our national obsession with looks. *Psychol. Today, 26*(3), 96.

Kinard, E. M. (1982). Child abuse and depression: Cause or consequence? *Child Welfare, 61,* 403–413.

Kinderman, P., & Bentall, R. P. (1997). Causal attributions in paranoia and depression: Internal, personal, and situational attributions for negative events. *J. Abnorm. Psychol., 106*(3), 341–345.

King, D. W., King, L. A., Foy, D. W., & Gudanowski, D. M. (1996). Prewar factors in combat related posttraumatic stress disorder: Structural equation modeling with a national sample of female and male Vietnam veterans. *J. Cons. Clin. Psychol., 64,* 520–531.

King, G. A., Polivy, J., & Herman, C. P. (1991). Cognitive aspects of dietary restraint: Effects on person memory. *Inter. J. Eat. Disorders, 10*(3), 313–321.

King, L. (2002, March 19). Interview with Russell Yates. *Larry King Live, CNN.*

King, M., & Bartlett, A. (1999). British psychiatry and homosexuality. *Brit. J. Psychiat., 175,* 106–113.

King, M. B., & Mezey, G. (1987). Eating behaviour of male racing jockeys. *Psychol. Med., 17,* 249–253.

King, M. P., & Tucker, J. A. (2000). Behavior change patterns and strategies distinguishing moderation drinking and abstinence during the natural resolution of alcohol problems without treatment. *Psychol. Addict. Behav., 14*(1), 48–55.

King, N. (2001). Young adult women: Reflections on recurring themes and a discussion of the treatment process and setting. In B. Kinoy (Ed.), *Eating disorders: New directions in treatment and recovery* (2nd ed., pp. 148–158). New York: Columbia University Press.

Kinzie, J., Leung, P., Boehnlein, J., & Matsunaga, D. (1992). Psychiatric epidemiology of an Indian village: A 19-year replication study. *J. Nerv. Ment. Dis., 180*(1), 33–39.

Kirby, M. (2000). Psychiatry, psychology, law and homosexuality—Uncomfortable bedfellows. *Psychiatry, Psychol. Law, 7*(2), 139–149.

Kirchmayer, U., Davoli, M., Verster, A. D., Amato, L., Ferri, M., & Perucci, C. A. (2002). A systematic review on the efficacy of naltrexone maintenance treatment in opioid dependence. *Addiction, 97*(10), 1241–1249.

Kirk, S. A., & Kutchins, H. (1992). *The selling of DSM: The rhetoric of science in psychiatry.* New York: Aldine de Gruyter.

Kirkby, K. (2003). Obsessive-compulsive disorder: Towards better understanding and outcomes. *Curr. Opin Psychiat., 16*(1), 49–55.

Kirley, A., Hawi, Z., Daly, G., McCarron, M., Mullins, C., Millar, N., Waldman, I., Fitzgerald, M., & Gill, M. (2002). Dopaminergic system genes in ADHD: Toward a biological hypothesis. *Neuropsychopharm., 27*(4), 607–619.

Kirmayer, L. J., Robbins, J. M., & Paris, J. (1994). Somatoform disorders: Personality and the social matrix of somatic distress. *J. Abnorm. Psychol., 103*(1), 125–136.

Kirsch, I., & Scoboria, A. (2001). Apples, oranges, and placebos: Heterogeneity in a meta-analysis of placebo effects. *Adv. Mind-Body Med., 17*(4), 307–309.

Kisker, G. W. (1977). *The disorganized personality.* New York: McGraw-Hill.

Klassen, A., Miller, A., Raina, P., Lee, S. K., & Olsen, L. (1999). Attention-deficit hyperactivity disorder in children and youth: A quantitative systematic review of the efficacy of different management strategies. *Canad. J. Psychiat., 44*(10), 1007–1016.

Kleber, H. D. (1981). Detoxification from narcotics. In J. H. Lowinson & P. Ruiz (Eds.), *Substance abuse: Clinical problems and perspectives.* Baltimore: William & Wilkins.

Klein, D. F. (1964). Delineation of two drug-responsive anxiety syndromes. *Psychopharmacologia, 5,* 397–408.

Klein, D. F., & Fink, M. (1962). Psychiatric reaction patterns to imipramine. *Amer. J. Psychiat., 119,* 432–438.

Klein, M. (1998, March). Looking out for Fido. *Am. Demogr.*

Klein, M. (1998, March). Stalking situations. *Am. Demogr.*

Klein, W. C., & Jess, C. (2002). One last pleasure? Alcohol use among elderly people in nursing homes. *Hlth. Soc. Work., 27*(3), 193–203.

Kleiner, M. (Ed.). (2002). *Handbook of polygraph testing.* San Diego, CA: Academic.

Klerman, G. L., & Weissman, M. M. (1992). Interpersonal psychotherapy. In E. S. Paykel (Ed.), *Handbook of affective disorders.* New York: Guilford Press.

Klerman, G. L., Weissman, M. M., Markowitz, J., Glick, I., Wilner, P. J., Mason, B., & Shear, M. K. (1994). Medication and psychotherapy. In A. E. Bergin & S. L. Garfield (Eds.), *Handbook of psychotherapy and behavior change* (4th ed.). New York: Wiley.

Kline, N. S. (1958). Clinical experience with iproniazid (Marsilid). *J. Clin. Exp. Psychopathol., 19*(1, Suppl.), 72–78.

Kling, K. C., Hyde, J. S., Showers, C. J., & Buswell, B. N. (1999). Gender differences in self-esteem: A meta-analysis. *Psychol. Bull., 125*(4), 470-500.

Klocek, J. W., Oliver, J. M., & Ross, M. J. (1997). The role of dysfunctional attitudes, negative life events, and social support in the prediction of depressive dysphoria: A prospective longitudinal study. *Soc. Behav. Pers., 25*(2), 123–136.

Kluft, R. P. (1984). Treatment of multiple personality disorder: A study of 33 cases. *Psychiatr. Clin. N. Amer., 7*(1), 9–29.

Kluft, R. P. (1985). Hypnotherapy of childhood multiple personality disorder. *Amer. J. Clin. Hyp., 27*(4), 201–210.

Kluft, R. P. (1987). The simulation and dissimulation of multiple personality disorder. *Amer. J. Clin. Hyp., 30*(2), 104–118.

Kluft, R. P. (1988). The dissociative disorders. In J. Talbott, R. Hales, & S. Yudofsky (Eds.), *Textbook of psychiatry.* Washington, DC: American Psychiatric Press.

Kluft, R. P. (1991). Multiple personality disorder. In A. Tasman & S. M. Goldfinger (Eds.), *American Psychiatric Press review of psychiatry* (Vol. 10). Washington, DC: American Psychiatric Press.

Kluft, R. P. (1992). Discussion: A specialist's perspective on multiple personality disorder. *Psychoanal. Inq., 12*(1), 139–171.

Kluft, R. P. (1993). Basic principles in conducting the psychotherapy of multiple personality disorder. In R. P. Kluft & C. G. Fine (Eds.), *Clinical perspectives on multiple personality disorder.* Washington, DC: American Psychiatric Press.

Kluft, R. P. (1999). An overview of the psychotherapy of dissociative identity disorder. *Amer. J. Psychother., 53*(3), 289–319.

Kluft, R. P. (2000). The psychoanalytic psychotherapy of dissociative identity disorder in the context of trauma therapy. *Psychoanal. Inq., 20*(2), 259–286.

Kluft, R. P. (2001). Dissociative disorders. In H.S. Friedman (Ed.), *Specialty articles from the encyclopedia of mental health.* San Diego: Academic Press.

Knapp, S., & VandeCreek, L. (2000). Recovered memories of childhood abuse: Is there an underlying professional consensus? *Profess. Psychol. Res. Pract., 31*(4), 365–371.

Knowlton, L. (1995, August 29). Licensed to heal. *Los Angeles Times,* p. E3.

Knowlton, L. (1997, May). Outreach Program aids homeless mentally ill. *Psychiatr. Times, XIV*(5).

Knowlton, L. (1998). "Women Healing" conference examines women in recovery. *Psychiatr. Times, XV*(7).

Kocsis, R. N., Hayes, A. F., & Irwin, H. J. (2002). Investigative experience and accuracy in psychological profiling of a violent crime. *J. Interpers. Violence, 17*(8), 811–823.

Koegel, L. K., Koegel, R. L., Hurley, C., & Frea, W. D. (1992). Improving social skills and disruptive behavior in children with autism through self-management. *J. Appl. Behav. Anal., 25*(2), 341–353.

Koehnken, G., Malpass, R. S., & Wogalter, M. S. (1996). Forensic applications of line-up research. In S. L. Sporer, R. S. Malpass, & G. Koehnken (Eds.), *Psychological issues in eyewitness identification* (pp. 205–231). Hillsdale, NJ: Erlbaum.

Koenen, K. C., Goodwin, R., Struening, E., Hellman, F., & Guardino, M. (2003). Posttraumatic stress disorder and treatment seeking in a national screening sample. *J. Traum. Stress., 16*(1), 5–16.

Koenig, H. G. (2002). The connection between psychoneuroimmunology and religion. In H. G. Koenig & H. J. Cohen (Eds.), *The link between religion and health: Psychoneuroimmunology and the faith factor.* New York: Oxford University Press.

Koenig, H. G., & Cohen, H.J. (Eds.). (2002). *The link between religion and health: Psychoneuroimmunology and the faith factor.* Oxford: Oxford University Press.

Koenig, H. G., Hays, J. C., Larson, D. B., George, L. K., Cohen, H. J., McCullough, M. E., Meador, K. G., & Blazer, D. G. (1999). Does religious attendance prolong survival? A six-year follow-up study of 3,968 older adults. *J. Ger. A Biol. Sci. Med. Sci., 54*(7), M370–M376.

Koenigsberg, H. W., Anwunah, I., New, A. S., Mitropoulou, V., Schopick, F., & Siever, L. J. (1999). Relationship between depression and borderline personality disorder. *Depress. Anx., 10*(4), 158–167.

Koenigsberg, H. W., Harvey, P. D., Mitropoulou, V., Schmeidler, J., New, A. S., Goodman, M., Silverman, J. M., Serby, M., Schopick, F., &

Siever, L. J. (2002). Characterizing affective instability in borderline personality disorder. *Amer. J. Psychiat.*, 159(5), 784–788.

Koenigsberg, H. W., Woo-Ming, A. M., & Siever, L. J. (2002). Pharmacological treatments for personality disorders. In P. E. Nathan & J. M. Gorman (Eds.), *A guide to treatments that work* (2nd ed., pp. 625–641). London: Oxford University Press.

Koh, M., Nishimatsu, Y., & Endo, S. (2000). Dissociative disorder. *J. Inter. Soc. Life Info. Sci.*, 18(2), 495–498.

Kohut, H. (1977). *The restoration of the self.* New York: International Universities Press.

Kohut, H. (1984). *How does analysis cure?* Chicago: University of Chicago Press.

Kolff, C. A., & Doan, R. N. (1985). Victims of torture: Two testimonies. In E. Stover & E. O. Nightingale (Eds.), *The breaking of bodies and minds: Torture, psychiatric abuse, and the health professions.* New York: W. H. Freeman.

Kolodny, R., Masters, W. H., & Johnson, J. (1979). *Textbook of sexual medicine.* Boston: Little, Brown.

Komaroff, A. L., Masuda, M., & Holmes, T. H. (1986). The Social Readjustment Rating Scale: A comparative study of Negro, white, and Mexican Americans. *J. Psychosom. Res.*, 12, 121–128.

Komaroff, A. L., Masuda, M., & Holmes, T. H. (1989). The Social Readjustment Rating Scale: A comparative study of Black, white, and Mexican Americans. In T. H. Holmes and E. M. David (Eds.), *Life change, life events, and illness.* New York: Praeger.

Kong, D. (1998, November 18). Still no solution in the struggle on safeguards—Doing harm: Research on the mentally ill. *Boston Globe*, p. A1.

Kopelowicz, A., Liberman, R. P., & Zarate, R. (2002). Psychosocial treatments for schizophrenia. In P. E. Nathan & J. M. Gorman (Eds.), *A guide to treatments that work* (2nd ed., pp. 201–228). London: Oxford University Press.

Korchin, S. J., & Sands, S. H. (1983). Principles common to all psychotherapies. In C. E. Walker et al. (Eds.), *The handbook of clinical psychology.* Homewood, IL: Dow Jones-Irwin.

Koss, M. P. (1992). The underdetection of rape: Methodological choices influence incidence estimates. *J. Soc. Issues*, 48(1), 61–75.

Koss, M. P. (1993). Rape: Scope, impact, interventions, and public policy responses. *Amer. Psychologist*, 48(10), 1062–1069.

Koss, M. P., & Heslet, L. (1992). Somatic consequences of violence against women. *Arch. Fam. Med.*, 1(1), 53–59.

Koss, M. P., & Kilpatrick, D. G. (2001). Rape and sexual assault. In E. Gerrity, T. M. Keane, et al. (Eds.), *The mental health consequences of torture* (pp. 177–193). New York: Kluwer Academic/Plenum.

Koss, M. P., Woodruff, W. J., & Koss, P. (1991). Criminal victimization among primary care medical patients: Prevalence, incidence, and physician usage. *Behav. Sci. Law*, 9, 85–96.

Kosslyn, S. M., Cacioppo, J. T., Davidson, R. J., Hugdahl, K., Lovallo, W. R., Speigel, D., & Rose, R. (2002). Bridging psychology and biology: The analysis of individuals in groups. *Amer. Psychologist*, 57(5), 341–351.

Kotler, M., Iancu, J., Efroni, R., & Amir, M. (2001). Anger, impulsivity, social support, and suicide risk in patients with posttraumatic stress disorder. *J. Nerv. Ment. Dis.*, 189(3), 162–167.

Kouri, E. M., & Pope, H. G., Jr. (2000). Abstinence symptoms during withdrawal from chronic marijuana use. *Exp. Clin. Psychopharmacol.*, 8(4), 483–492.

Kovacs, M., Goldston, D., & Gatsonis, C. (1993). Suicidal behaviors and childhood-onset depressive disorders: A longitudinal investigation. *J. Amer. Acad. Child Adol. Psychiat.*, 32, 8–20.

Kraines, S. H., & Thetford, E. S. (1972). *Help for the depressed.* Springfield, IL: Thomas.

Krakauer, S. Y. (2001). *Treating dissociative identity disorder: The power of the collective heart.* Philadelphia: Brunner-Routledge.

Krall, W. J., Sramek, J. J., & Cutler, N. R. (1999). Cholinesterase inhibitors: A therapeutic strategy for Alzheimer's disease. *Ann. Pharmacother.*, 33(4), 441–450.

Kramer, M. (1989, August 14). Cited in S. Begley, "The stuff that dreams are made of." *Newsweek*, p. 40.

Kramer, M. (2000). Dreamspeak. *Psychol. Today*, 33(5), 56.

Krane, V., Joyce, D., & Rafeld, J. (1994). Competitive anxiety, situation criticality, and softball performance. *Sport Psychol.*, 8, 58–72.

Krantz, L. (1992). *What the odds are.* New York: Harper Perennial.

Krapohl, D. J. (2002). The polygraph in personnel screening. In M. Kleiner (Ed.), *The handbook of polygraph testing.* San Diego, CA: Academic.

Kratochwill, T. R. (1992). Single-case research design and analysis: An overview. In T. R. Kratochwill & J. R. Levin (Eds.), *Single-case research design and analysis: New directions for psychology and education.* Hillsdale, NJ: Erlbaum.

Krauss, M. W., Seltzer, M. M., & Goodman, S. J. (1992). Social support networks of adults with mental retardation who live at home. *Amer. J. Ment. Retard.*, 96(4), 432–441.

Kresin, D. (1993). Medical aspects of inhibited sexual desire disorder. In W. O'Donohue & J. Geer (Eds.), *Handbook of sexual dysfunctions.* Boston: Allyn & Bacon.

Kressel, N. J., & Kressel, D. F. (2002). *Stack and sway: The new science of jury consulting.* Boulder, CO: Westview.

Kring, A. M., & Neale, J. M. (1996). Do schizophrenic patients show a disjunctive relationship among expressive, experiential, and psychophysiological components of emotion? *J. Abnorm. Psychol.*, 105(2), 249–257.

Krippner, S., & Weinhold, J. (2002). Gender differences in a content analysis study of 608 dream reports from research participants in the United States. *Soc. Behav. Pers.*, 30(4), 399–410.

Kropp, P. R., Hart, S. D., & Lyon, D. R. (2002). Risk assessment of stalkers: Some problems and possible solutions. *Criminal Justice Behav.*, 29(5), 590–616.

Krueger, R. G., & Kaplan, M. S. (2000). Evaluation and treatment of sexual disorders: Frottage. In L. Vandecreed & T. L. Jackson (Eds.), *Innovations in clinical practice: A source book* (Vol. 18, pp. 185–197). Sarasota, FL: Professional Resource Press.

Krueger, R. G., & Kaplan, M. S. (2002). Behavioral and psychopharmacological treatment of the paraphilic and hypersexual disorders. *J. Psychiatr. Prac.*, 8(1), 21–32.

Kuechenhoff, J. (2002). Hysterie heute—eine Revision. [Hysteria today—A revision]. *For. Psychoanal.: Zeitshr. Klin. Theor. Prax.*, 18(3), 224–244.

Kuhn, R. (1958). The treatment of depressive states with G-22355 (imipramine hydrochloride). *Amer. J. Psychiat.*, 115, 459–464.

Kuhn, T. S. (1962). *The structure of scientific revolutions.* Chicago: University of Chicago Press.

Kulhara, P., Basu, D., Mattoo, S. K., Sharan, P., & Chopra, R. (1999). Lithium prophylaxis of recurrent bipolar affective disorder: Long-term outcome and its psychosocial correlates. *J. Affect. Disorders*, 54(1–2), 87–96.

Kupfer, D. J., & Frank, E. (2001). The interaction of drug- and psychotherapy in the long-term treatment of depression. *J. Affect. Disorders*, 62(1–2), 131–137.

Kuriansky, J. B. (1988). Personality style and sexuality. In R. A. Brown & J. R. Field (Eds.), *Treatment of sexual problems in individual and couples therapy.* Costa Mesa, CA: PMA Publishing.

Kurtz, D. L., Stewart, R. B., Zweifel, M., Li, T.-K., & Froehlich, J. C. (1996). Genetic differences in tolerance and sensitization to the sedative/hypnotic effects of alcohol. *Pharmacol. Biochem. Behav.*, 53(3), 585–591.

Lachmann, A., & Lachmann, F. M. (1995). The personification of evil: Motivations and fantasies of the serial killer. *Inter. Forum Psychoanal.*, 4(1), 17–23.

Lacks, P. (1984). *Bender Gestalt screening for brain dysfunction.* New York: Wiley.

Ladouceur, R., Freeston, M. H., Gagnon, F., Thibodeau, N., et al. (1995). Cognitive-behavioral treatment of obsessions. *Behav. Mod.*, 19(2), 247–257.

Ladwig, K. H., Marten, M. B., Erazo, M., & Guendel, H. (2001). Identifying somatization disorder in a population-based health examination survey: Psychosocial burden and gender differences. *Psychosomatics*, 42(6), 511–518.

Lakin, K. C., Anderson, L., Prouty, R., & Polister, B. (1999). State institution populations less than one third of 197, residents older with more impairments. *Mental Retardation*, 37, 85–86.

Lakin, K. C., Prouty, B., Smith, G., & Braddock, D. (1996). Nixon goal surpassed: Two-fold. *Mental Retardation*, 34, 67.

Lambert, M. J., & Bergin, A. E. (1994). The effectiveness of psychotherapy. In A. E. Bergin & S. L. Garfield (Eds.), *Handbook of psychotherapy and behavioral change* (4th ed.). New York: Wiley.

Lambert, M. J., Shapiro, D. A., & Bergin, A. E. (1986). The effectiveness of psychotherapy. In S. L. Garfield & A. E. Bergin (Eds.), *Handbook of psychotherapy and behavioral change* (3rd ed.). New York: Wiley.

Lambert, M. T. (2003). Suicide risk assessment and management: Focus on personality disorders. *Curr. Opin. Psychiat.*, 16(1), 71–76.

Landau, B. M. (2001). Psychotherapy online in 2001: For psychotherapists new to the Internet. *J. Ment. Imagery*, 25(1–2), 65–82.

Landry, M. J. (1994). *Understanding drugs of abuse: The processes of addiction, treatment, and recovery.* Washington, DC: American Psychiatric Press.

Landsbergis, P. A., Schnall, P. L., Warren, K., Pickering, T. G., & Schwartz, J. E. (1994). Association between ambulatory blood pressure and alternative formulations of job strain. *Scand. J. Work Envir. Hlth.*, 20, 349–363.

Lang, J. (1999, April 16). Local jails dumping grounds for mentally ill. *Detroit News.*

Langevin, R., Bain, J., Wortzman, G., Hucker, S., et al. (1988). Sexual sadism: Brain, blood, and behavior. *Ann. N.Y. Acad. Sci.*, 528, 163–171.

Lara, M. E., & Klein, D. N. (1999). Psychosocial processes underlying the maintenance and persistence of depression: Implications for understanding chronic depression. *Clin. Psychol. Rev.*, 19(5), 553–570.

Larsson, B., & Ivarsson, T. (1998). Clinical characteristics of adolescent psychiatric inpatients who have attempted suicide. *Eur. Child Adol. Psychiat.*, 7(4), 201–208.

Lask, B. (2000). Aetiology. In B. Lask, R. Bryant-Waugh, et al. (Eds.), *Anorexia nervosa and related eating disorders in childhood and adolescence* (2nd ed.). Hove, England: Psychology Press/Taylor & Francis.

Lask, B., & Bryant-Waugh, R. (Eds.). (2000). *Anorexia nervosa and related eating disorders in childhood and adolescence* (2nd ed.). Hove, England: Psychology Press/Taylor & Francis.

Latner, J. D., & Wilson, G. T. (2002). Self-monitoring and the assessment of binge eating. *Behav. Ther., 33*(3), 465–477.

Laumann, E. O., Gagnon, J. H., Michael, R. T., & Michaels, S. (1994). *The social organization of sexuality.* Chicago: University of Chicago Press.

Laumann, E. O., Paik, A., & Rosen, R. C. (1999). Sexual dysfunction in the United States: Prevalence and predictors. *JAMA, 281*(13), 1174.

Lautenbacher, S., & Rollman, G. B. (1999). Somatization, hypochondriasis, and related conditions. In A. R. Block, E. F. Kremer, et al. (Eds.), *Handbook of pain syndromes: Biopsychosocial perspectives.* Mahwah, NJ: Erlbaum.

Lavan, H., & Johnson, J. G. (2002). The association between Axis I and II psychiatric symptoms and high-risk sexual behavior during adolescence. *J. Pers. Disorders, 16*(1), 73–94.

Lawford, B. R., Young, R. McD., Rowell, J. A., Gibson, J. N., et al. (1997). Association of the D2 dopamine receptor A1 allele with alcoholism: Medical severity of alcoholism and type of controls. *Biol. Psychiat., 41,* 386–393.

Lawlor, B. A., McCarron, M., Wilson, G., & McLoughlin, M. (2001). Temporal lobe-oriented CT scanning and dementia in Down's syndrome. *Inter. J. Ger. Psychiat., 16* (4), 427–429.

Lawrence, C. (1987). An integrated spiritual and psychological growth model in the treatment of narcissism. *J. Psychol. Theol., 15*(3), 205–213.

Lay, B., Jennen-Steinmetz, C., Reinhard I., & Schmidt, M. H. (2002). Characteristics of inpatient weight gain in adolescent anorexia nervosa: Relation to speed of relapse and re-admission. *Eur. Eat. Disord. Rev., 10*(1), 22–40.

Lazarus, A. A. (1965). The treatment of a sexually inadequate man. In L. P. Ullman & L. Krasner (Eds.), *Case studies in behavior modification.* New York: Holt, Rinehart & Winston.

Lazarus, J. A. (1995). Ethical issues in doctor-patient sexual relationships. [Special issue: Clinical sexuality]. *Psychiatr. Clin. N. Amer., 18*(1), 55–70.

Lazarus, J. A., & Sharfstein, S. S. (2002). Ethics in managed care. *Psychiatr. Clin. N. Amer., 25*(3), 561–574.

Lazarus, R. S. (2003). Does the positive psychology movement have legs? *Psychological Inquiry, 14*(2), 93–109.

Lazarus, R. S., & Folkman, S. (1984). *Stress, appraisal, and coping.* New York: Springer.

Lean, M. E., Han, T. S., & Seidell, J. C. (1999). Impairment of health and quality of life using new U.S. federal guidelines for the identification of obesity. *Arch. Internal Med., 159*(8), 837–843.

Leavitt, F. (2001). Iatrogenic recovered memories: Examining the empirical evidence. *Amer. J. Forens. Psychol., 19*(2), 21–32.

Leavitt, F. (2002). "The reality of repressed memories" revisited and principles of science. *J. Trauma. Dissoc., 3*(1), 19–35.

Lebegue, B. (1991). Paraphilias in U.S. pornography titles: "Pornography made me do it" (Ted Bundy). *Bull. Amer. Acad. Psychiat. Law, 19*(1), 43–48.

Ledoux, S., Miller, P., Choquet, M., & Plant, M. (2002). Family structure, parent-child relationships, and alcohol and other drug use among teenagers in France and the United Kingdom. *Alcohol Alcoholism, 37*(1), 52–60.

Lee, D. E. (1985). Alternative self-destruction. *Percept. Motor Skills, 61*(3, Part 2), 1065–1066.

Lee, J., & Sue, S. (2001). Clinical psychology and culture. In D. Matsumoto (Ed.), *The handbook of culture and psychology.* New York: Oxford University Press.

Lee, P. W. H., Lieh-Mak, F., Yu, K. K., & Spinks, J. A. (1993). Coping strategies of schizophrenic patients and their relationship to outcome. *Brit. J. Psychiat., 163,* 177–182.

Lee, R. K. K., Jimenez, J., Cox, A. J., & Wurtman, R. J. (1996). Metabotropic glutamate receptors regulate APP processing in hippocampal neurons and cortical astrocytes derived from fetal rats. In R. J. Wurtman, S. Corkin, J. H. Growdon, & R. M. Nitsch (Eds.), *The neurobiology of Alzheimer's disease.* New York: New York Academy of Sciences.

Leenaars, A. A. (1989). *Suicide notes: Predictive clues and patterns.* New York: Human Sciences Press.

Leenaars, A. A. (1991). Suicide in the young adult. In A. A. Leenaars (Ed.), *Life span perspectives of suicide: Time-lines in the suicide process.* New York: Plenum Press.

Leenaars, A. A., Connolly, J., Cantor, C., EchoHawk, M., He, Z.-X., Kokorina, N., Lester, D., Lopatin, A. A., Rodriguez, M., Schlebusch, L., Takahashi, Y., & Vijayakuman, L. (2001). Suicide, assisted suicide and euthanasia: International perspectives. *Irish J. Psychol. Med., 18*(1), 33–37.

Leenstra, A. S., Ormel, J., & Giel, R. (1995). Positive life change and recovery from depression and anxiety: A three-stage longitudinal study of primary care attenders. *Brit. J. Psychiat., 166*(3), 333–343.

LeGrange, D., & Lock, J. (2002). Bulimia nervosa in adolescents: Treatment, eating pathology and comorbidity. *S. Afr. Psychiat. Rev., 5*(3), 19–22, 24–25.

Lehmann, H. E. (1985). Current perspectives on the biology of schizophrenia. In M. N. Menuck & M. V. Seeman. *New perspectives in schizophrenia.* New York: Macmillan.

Lehoux, P. M., Steiger, H., & Jabalpurlawa, S. (2000). State/trait distinctions in bulimic syndromes. *Inter. J. Eat. Disorders, 27*(1), 36–42.

Leiblum, S. R. (1996). Sexual pain disorders. In *Treatment of psychiatric disorders: The DSM-IV edition.* Washington, DC: American Psychiatric Press.

Leiblum, S. R. (2001). Critical overview of the new consensus-based definitions and classification of female sexual dysfunction. *J. Sex. Marital Ther., 27*(2), 159–168.

Leiblum, S. R. (2002). After sildenafil: Bridging the gap between pharmacologic treatment and satisfying sexual relationships. *J. Clin. Psychiat., 63*(Suppl. 5), 17–33.

Leiblum, S. R., & Rosen, R. C. (Eds.). (2000). *Principles and practice of sex therapy* (3rd ed.). New York: Guilford Press.

Leiblum, S. R., & Segraves, R. T. (1995). Sex and aging. In J. M. Oldham & M. B. Riba (Eds.), *American Psychiatric Press review of psychiatry* (Vol. 14). Washington, DC: American Psychiatric Press.

Leibowitz, S. F., & Hoebel, B. G. (1998). Behavioral neuroscience of obesity. In G. A. Bray, C. Bouchard, & P. T. James (Eds.), *The handbook of obesity.* New York: Dekker.

Leichsenring, F. (2001). Comparative effects of short-term psychodynamic psychotherapy and cognitive-behavioral therapy in depression. A meta-analytic approach. *Clin. Psychol. Rev., 21*(3), 401–419.

Lekander, M. (2002). Ecological immunology: The role of the immune system in psychology and neuroscience. *Eur. Psychiat., 7*(2), 98–115.

Leland, H. (1991). Adaptive behavior scales. In J. L. Matson & J. A. Mulick (Eds.), *Handbook of mental retardation.* New York: Pergamon Press.

LeMarquand, D., Tremblay, R. E., & Vitaro, F. (2001). The prevention of conduct disorder: A review of successful and unsuccessful experiments. In J. Hill & B. Maughan (Eds.), *Conduct disorders in childhood and adolescence* (pp. 449–477). New York: Cambridge University Press.

Lemonick, M. D., & Goldstein, A. (2002, April 14). At your own risk. *Time,* 46–57.

Lennkh, C., & Simhandl, C. (2000). Current aspects of valproate in bipolar disorder. *Inter. Clin. Psychopharmacology, 15*(1), 1–11.

Lenzenweger, M. F., Cornblatt, B. A., & Putnick, M. (1991). Schizotypy and sustained attention. *J. Abnorm. Psychol., 100*(1), 84–89.

Leon, G. R. (1984). *Case histories of deviant behavior* (3rd ed.). Boston: Allyn & Bacon.

Leong, G. B. (2000). Diminished capacity and insanity in Washington State: The battle shifts to admissibility. *J. Amer. Acad. Psychiat. Law, 28*(1), 77–81.

Leri, F., Bruneau, J., & Stewart, J. (2003). Understanding polydrug use: Review of herion and cocaine co-use. *Addiction, 98*(1), 7–22.

Lerner, A. G., Gelkopf, M., Skladman, I., Oyffe, I., Finkel, B., Sigal, M., & Weizman, A. (2002). Flashback and hallucinogen persisting perception disorder: Clinical aspects and pharmacological treatment approach. *Israel J. Psychiat. Rel. Sci., 39*(2), 92–99.

Lerner, R. M. (2002). *Adolescence: Development, diversity, context, and application.* Upper Saddle River, NJ: Pearson Education.

Lerner, V., Fotyanov, M., Liberman, M., Shlafman, M., & Bar-El, Y. (1995). Maintenance medication for schizophrenia and schizoaffective patients. *Schizo. Bull., 21*(4), 693–701.

Leroux, J. A. (1986). Suicidal behavior and gifted adolescents. *Roeper Rev., 9*(2), 77–79.

Leserman, J., Drossman, D. A., Li, Z., Toomey, T. C., et al. (1996). Sexual and physical abuse history in gastroenterology practice: How types of abuse impact health status. *Psychosom. Med., 58*(1), 4–15.

Leshner, A. I., et al. (1992). *Outcasts on the main street: Report of the Federal Task Force on Homelessness and Severe Mental Illness.* Washington, DC: Interagency Council on the Homeless.

Leslie, A. (1997, May 23). *Theory of mind impairment in autism: Its nature and significance.* Keynote address at The Eden Institute Foundation Princeton Lecture Series on Autism.

Lester, D. (1972). Myth of suicide prevention. *Comprehen. Psychiat., 13*(6), 555–560.

Lester, D. (1974). The effects of suicide prevention centers on suicide rates in the United States. *Pub. Hlth. Rep., 89,* 37–39.

Lester, D. (1985). The quality of life in modern America and suicide and homicide rates. *J. Soc. Psychol., 125*(6), 779–780.

Lester, D. (1991). The etiology of suicide and homicide in urban and rural America. *J. Rural Commun. Psychol., 12*(1), 15–27.

Lester, D. (1997). Effect of suicide prevention centers in Ireland and Great Britain. *Psychol. Rep., 81,* 1186.

Lester, D. (1998). Suicide and homicide after the fall of communist regimes. *Eur. Psychiat., 13*(2), 98–100.

Lester, D. (2000). *Why people kill themselves: A 2000 summary of research on suicide.* Springfield, IL: Charles C. Thomas

Lester, D., & Linn, M. (1998). The content of suicide notes written by those using different methods for suicide. *Percept. Motor Skills, 87*(2), 722.

Letourneau, E., & O'Donohue, W. (1993). Sexual desire disorders. In W. O'Donohue & J. Geer (Eds.), *Handbook of sexual dysfunctions.* Boston: Allyn & Bacon.

Le Unes, A. D., Nation, J. R., & Turley, N. M. (1980). Male-female performance in learned helplessness. *J. Psychol., 104,* 255–258.

Leutwyler, K. (1996). Paying attention: The controversy over ADHD and the drug Ritalin is obscuring a real look at the disorder and its underpinnings. *Scientif. Amer., 272*(2), 12–13.

LeVay, S., & Hamer, D. H. (1994). Evidence for a biological influence in male homosexuality. [Review]. *Scientif. Amer., 270*(5), 44–49.

Levesque, R. J. R. (1996). Regulating the private relations of adults with mental disabilities: Old laws, new policies, hollow hopes. *Behav. Sci. Law, 14,* 83–106.

Levesque, R. J. R. (2002). *Dangerous adolescents, model adolescents: Shaping the role and promise of education.* New York: Kluwer Academic/Plenum Publishers.

Levin, E. (1983, February 21). A sweet surface hit a troubled soul in the late Karen Carpenter, a victim of anorexia nervosa. *People Weekly* (quoting Cherry Boone O'Neill).

Levin, J., & Fox, J. A. (1985). *Mass murder.* New York: Plenum Press.

Levine, M. D. (1975). Children with encopresis: A descriptive analysis. *Pediatrics, 56,* 412–416.

Levine, M. D. (1987). *How schools can help combat student eating disorders: Anorexia nervosa and bulimia.* Washington, DC: National Education Assoc.

Levitan, H. L. (1981). Implications of certain dreams reported by patients in a bulimic phase of anorexia nervosa. *Canad. J. Psychiat., 26*(4), 228–231.

Lewins, F. (2002). Explaining stable partnerships among FTMs and MTFs: A significant difference? *J. Sociol., 38*(1), 76–88.

Lewinsohn, P. M., Antonuccio, D. O., Steinmetz, J. L., & Teri, L. (1984). *The coping with depression course.* Eugene, OR: Castalia.

Lewinsohn, P. M., Clarke, G. N., Hops, H., & Andrews, J. (1990). Cognitive-behavioral treatment for depressed adolescents. *Behav. Ther., 21,* 385–401.

Lewinsohn, P. M., & Essau, C. A. (2002). Depression in adolescents. In I. H. Gotlib & C. L. Hammen (Eds.), *Handbook of depression* (pp. 541–559). New York: Guilford Press.

Lewinsohn, P. M., Rohde, P., Teri, L., & Tilson, M. (1990, April). Presentation. Western Psychological Association.

Lewinsohn, P. M., Sullivan, J. M., & Grosscup, S. J. (1982). Behavioral therapy: Clinical applications. In A. T. Rush (Ed.), *Short-term psychotherapies for the depressed patient.* New York: Guilford Press.

Lewinsohn, P. M., Youngren, M. A., & Grosscup, S. J. (1979). Reinforcement and depression. In R. A. Depue (Ed.), *The psychobiology of the depressive disorders.* New York: Academic Press.

Lewis, O., & Chatoor, I. (1994). Eating disorders. In J. M. Oldham & M. B. Riba (Eds.), *Review of psychiatry* (Vol. 13). Washington, DC: American Psychiatric Press.

Lewis-Harter, S. (2000). Psychosocial adjustment of adult children of alcoholics: A review of the recent empirical literature. *Clin. Psychol. Rev., 20*(3), 311–337.

Li, T. K. (2000). Pharmacogenetics of responses to alcohol and genes that influence alcohol drinking. *J. Stud. Alc., 61*(1), 5–12.

Libow, J. A. (1995). Munchausen by proxy victims in adulthood: A first look. *Child Abuse Negl., 19*(9), 1131–1142.

Libow, J. A., & Schreirer, H. A. (1998) Factitious disorder by proxy. In R. T. Ammerman & J. V. Campo (Eds.), *Handbook of pediatric psychology and psychiatry: Vol. 1. Psychological and psychiatric issues in the pediatric setting.* Boston: Allyn & Bacon.

Lickey, M. E., & Gordon, B. (1991). *Medicine and mental illness: The use of drugs in psychiatry.* New York: W. H. Freeman.

Lieb, R., Merikangas, K. R., Hoefler, M., Pfister, H., Isensee, B., & Wittchen, H. U. (2002). Parental alcohol use disorders and alcohol use and disorders in offspring: A community study. *Psychol. Med., 32*(1), 63–78.

Lieb, R., Pfister, H., Mastaler, M., & Wittchen, H. U. (2000). Somatoform syndromes and disorders in a representative population sample of adolescents and young adults: Prevalence, comorbidity and impairments. *Acta Psychiatr. Scandin., 101*(3), 194–208.

Lieberman, J. A., Alvir, J. Ma., Koreen, A., Geisler, S., Chakos, M., Scheitman, B., & Woerner, M. (1996). Psychobiologic correlates of treatment response in schizophrenia. *Neuropsychopharmacology, 14,* 13S–21S.

Lieberman, J. A., Chakos, M., Wu, H., Alvir, J., Hoffman, E., Robinson, D., & Bilder, R. (2001). Longitudinal study of brain morphology in first episode schizophrenia. *Biol. Psychiat., 49*(6), 487–499.

Liebman, J. I., McKinley-Pace, M. J., Leonard, A. M., Sheesley, L. A., Gallant, C. L., Renkey, M. E., & Lehman, E. B. (2002). Cognitive and psychosocial correlates of adults' eyewitness accuracy and suggestibility. *Pers. Individ. Diff., 33*(1), 49–66.

Liebowitz, M. R., Stone, M., & Turkat, I. D. (1986). Treatment of personality disorders. In A. Frances & R. Hales (Eds.), *American Psychiatric Association annual review* (Vol. 5). Washington, DC: American Psychiatric Press.

Liedl, B. (1999). Sex-adjusting surgery in transsexualism (in German). *MMW Fortschr. Med., 141*(23), 41–45.

Lilienfield, S. O., & Lynn, S. J. (2003). Dissociative identity disorder: Multiple personalities, multiple controversies. In S. O. Lilienfeld, S. J. Lynn, et al. (Eds.), *Science and pseudoscience in clinical psychology.* New York: Guilford Press.

Lilienfeld, S. O., Lynn, S. J., Kirsch, I., Chaves, J. F., Sarbin, T. R., Ganaway, G. K., & Powell, R. A. (1999). Dissociative identity disorder and the sociocognitive model: Recalling the lessons of the past. *Psychol. Bull., 125*(5), 507–523.

Lindner, M. (1968). *Hereditary and environmental influences upon resistance to stress.* Unpublished doctoral dissertation, University of Pennsylvania, Philadelphia.

Lindsay, D. S. (1994). Contextualizing and clarifying criticisms of memory work in psychotherapy. *Consciousness Cog., 3,* 426–437.

Lindsay, D. S. (1996). Contextualizing and clarifying criticisms of memory work in psychotherapy. In K. Pezdek & W. P. Banks (Eds.), *The recovered memory/false memory debate.* San Diego: Academic Press.

Lindsay, D. S., Wade, K. A., Hunter, M. A., & Read, J. D. (2004). Adults' memories of childhood: Affect, knowing, and remembering. *Memory, 12*(1), 27–43.

Linehan, M. M. (1992). Behavior therapy, dialectics, and the treatment of borderline personality disorder. In D. Silver & M. Rosenbluth (Eds.), *Handbook of borderline disorders.* Madison, CT: International Universities Press.

Linehan, M. M. (1993). *Cognitive-behavioral therapy of borderline personality disorder.* New York: Guilford Press.

Linehan, M. M., Cochran, B. N., & Kehrer, C. A. (2001). Dialectical behavior therapy for borderline personality disorder. In D. H. Barlow (Ed.), *Clinical handbook of psychological disorders: A step-by-step treatment manual* (3rd ed.). New York: Guilford Press.

Ling, W., Huber, A., & Rawson, R. A. (2001). New trends in opiate pharmacotherapy. *Drug Alc. Rev., 20*(1), 79–94.

Link, B. G., Struening, E. L., Neese-Todd, S., Asmussen, S., & Phelan, J. C. (2001). Stigma as a barrier to recovery: The consequences of stigma for the self-esteem of people with mental illness. *Psychiatr. Serv., 52*(12), 1621–1626.

Linszen, D. H., Dingemans, P. M., Nugter, M. A., Willem, A. J., et al. (1997). Patient attributes and expressed emotion as risk factors for psychotic relapse. *Schizo. Bull., 23*(1), 119–130.

Linz, D., & Imrich, D. (2001). Child pornography. In S. O. White (Ed.), *Handbook of youth and justice* (pp. 79–111). New York: Kluwer Academic/Plenum Press.

Lisansky-Gomberg, E. (1993). Women and alcohol: Use and abuse. *J. Nerv. Ment. Dis., 181*(4), 211–216.

Litman, R. E. (1995). Suicide prevention in a treatment setting [Special issue: Suicide prevention: Toward the year 2000]. *Suic. Life-Threat. Behav., 25*(1), 134–142.

Liu, T., Hau, W., Wang, X., He, J., Li, H., Xiong, P., Fan, C., Tang, W., & Chen, S. (2002). Negative consequences of recreational use of amphetamine-type stimulants. *Chin. Ment. Hlth. J., 16*(5), 293–295.

Livesley, W. J. (2000). A practical approach to the treatment of patients with borderline personality disorder. *Psychiatr. Clin. N. Amer., 23*(1), 211–232.

Livesley, W. J., Schroeder, M. L., Jackson, D. N., & Jang, K. L. (1994). Categorical distinctions in the study of personality disorder: Implications for classification. *J. Abnorm. Psychol., 103*(1), 6–17.

Lloyd, G. K., Fletcher, A., & Minchin, M. C. W. (1992). GABA agonists as potential anxiolytics. In G. D. Burrows, S. M. Roth, & R. Noyes, Jr., (Eds.), *Handbook of anxiety* (Vol. 5). Oxford, England: Elsevier.

Lock, J. (2002). Treating adolescents with eating disorders in the family context: Empirical and theoretical considerations. *Child Adol. Psychiat. Clin. N. Amer., 11*(2), 331–342.

Loebel, J. P., Loebel, J. S., Dager, S. R., Centerwall, B. S., et al. (1991). Anticipation of nursing home placement may be a precipitant of suicide among the elderly. *J. Amer. Ger. Soc., 39*(4), 407–408.

Loerch, B., Graf-Morgenstern, M., Hautzinger, M., & Schlegel, S. (1999). Randomised placebo-controlled trial of moclobemide, cognitive-behavioural therapy and their combination in panic disorder with agoraphobia. *Brit. J. Psychiat., 174,* 205–212.

Loewenstein, R. J. (1991). Psychogenic amnesia and psychogenic fugue: A comprehensive review. In A. Tasman & S. M. Goldfinger (Eds.), *American Psychiatric Press review of psychiatry* (Vol. 10). Washington, DC: American Psychiatric Press.

Loftus, E. F. (1993). The reality of repressed memories. *Amer. Psychologist, 48,* 518–537.

Loftus, E. F. (1997). Repressed memory accusations: Devastated families and devastated patients. *Appl. Cog. Psychol., 11,* 25–30.

Loftus, E. F. (2000). Remembering what never happened. In E. Tulving, et al. (Eds.), *Memory,* *consciousness, and the brain: The Tallinn Conference.* Philadelphia: Psychology Press/Taylor & Francis.

Loftus, E. F. (2001). Imagining the past. *Psychologist,* 14(11), 584–587.

Loftus, E. F. (2003). Make-believe memories. *American Psychologist,* 58(11), 867–873.

Loftus, E. F. (2003). Our changeable memories: Legal and practical implications. *Nature Reviews: Neuroscience, 4,* 231–234.

Logue, A. W. (1991). *The psychology of eating and drinking.* New York: W. H. Freeman.

Longwell-Grice, R. M., & Sandhu, D. S. (2002). Evaluating employee assistance programs. In D. S. Sandhu (Ed.), *Counseling employees: A multifaceted approach* (pp. 351–363). Alexandria, VA: American Counseling Association.

Lonigan, C. J., Shannon, M. P., Taylor, C. M., et al. (1994). Children exposed to disaster: II. Risk factors for the development of post-traumatic symptomatology. *J. Amer. Acad. Child Adol. Psychiat., 33,* 94–105.

Looper, K. J., & Kirmayer, L. J. (2002). Behavioral medicine approaches to somatoform disorders. *J. Cons. Clin. Psychol.,* 70(3), 810–827.

Looper, K. J., & Paris, J. (2000). What dimensions underlie Cluster B personality disorders? *Comprehen. Psychiat.,* 41(6), 432–437.

LoPiccolo, J. (1985). Advances in diagnosis and treatment of male sexual dysfunction. *J. Sex Marital Ther.,* 11(4), 215–232.

LoPiccolo, J. (1991). Post-modern sex therapy for erectile failure. In R. C. Rosen & S. R. Leiblum (Eds.), *Erectile failure: Diagnosis and treatment.* New York: Guilford Press.

LoPiccolo, J. (1992). Paraphilias. *Nord. Sex., 10*(1), 1–14.

LoPiccolo, J. (1995). Sexual disorders and gender identity disorders. In R. J. Comer, *Abnormal psychology* (2nd ed.). New York: W. H. Freeman.

LoPiccolo, J. (1997). Sex therapy: A post-modern model. In S. J. Lynn & J. P. Garske (Eds.), *Contemporary psychotherapies: Models and methods* (2nd ed.). Columbus, OH: Merrill.

LoPiccolo, J., & Stock, W. E. (1987). Sexual function, dysfunction, and counseling in gynecological practice. In Z. Rosenwaks, F. Benjamin, & M. L. Stone (Eds.), *Gynecology.* New York: Macmillan.

Lorand, S. (1968). Dynamics and therapy of depressive states. In W. Gaylin (Ed.), *The meaning of despair.* New York: Jason Aronson.

Lord, M. (2002). One year after 9/11–A nation changed. *U. S. News World Rep., 133*(7), 33.

Lovaas, O. I. (1987). Behavioral treatment and normal educational/intellectual functioning in young autistic children. *J. Cons. Clin. Psychol., 55,* 3–9.

Lovaas, O. I. (2003). *Teaching individuals with developmental delays: Basic intervention techniques.* Austin, TX: PRO-ED.

Love, S. R., Matson, J. L., & West, D. (1990). Mothers as effective therapists for autistic children's phobias. *J. Appl. Behav. Anal., 23*(3), 379–385.

Lovejoy, M. (1982). Expectations and the recovery process. *Schizo. Bull., 8*(4), 605–609.

Lovejoy, M. (2001). Disturbances in the social body: Differences in body image and eating problems among African-American and white women. *Gender Soc., 15*(2), 239–261.

Lovett, M. W. (2000). Developmental reading disorders. In M. J. Farah & T. E. Feinberg (Eds.), *Patient-based approaches to cognitive neuroscience: Issues in clinical and cognitive neuropsychology* (pp. 247–261). Cambridge, MA: MIT Press.

Lowenthal, D. (2002). Case studies in confidentiality. *J. Psychiatr. Prac., 8*(3), 151–159.

Lu, L. (1999). Personal or environmental causes of happiness: A longitudinal analysis. *J. Soc. Psychol., 139*(1), 79–90.

Lublin, H. (2001). Cognitive dysfunction in schizophrenia. *Acta Psychiatr. Scandin., 104*(Suppl. 508), 5–9.

Luborsky, L. (1973). Forgetting and remembering (momentary forgetting) during psychotherapy. In M. Mayman (Ed.), *Psychoanalytic research and psychological issues*(Monograph 30). New York: International Universities Press.

Luborsky, L., Diguer, L., Luborsky, E., & Schmidt, K. A. (1999). The efficacy of dynamic versus other psychotherapies: Is it true that "everyone has won and all must have prizes"?—An Update. In D. S. Janowsky, et al. (Eds.), *Psychotherapy indications and outcomes.* Washington, DC: American Psychiatric Press.

Luborsky, L., Rosenthal, R., Diguer, L., Andrusyna, T. P., Berman, J. S., Levitt, J. T., Seligman, D. A., & Krause, E. D. (2002). The dodo bird verdict is alive and well—mostly. *Clin. Psychol.: Sci. Prac., 9*(1), 2–12.

Luborsky, L., Singer, B., & Luborsky, L. (1975). Comparative studies of psychotherapies. *Arch. Gen. Psychiat., 32,* 995–1008.

Lucas, R. E., Clark, A. E., Georgellis, Y., & Diener, E. (2003). Reexamining adaptation and the set point model of happiness: Reactions to changes in marital status. *J. Pers. Soc. Psychol., 84*(3), 527–539.

Ludwig, A. M. (1994). Creative activity and mental illness in female writers. *Amer. J. Psychiat., 151,* 1650–1656.

Ludwig, A. M. (1995). *The price of greatness: Resolving the creativity and madness controversy.* New York: Guilford Press.

Luepker, E. T. (1999). Effects of practitioners' sexual misconduct: A follow-up study. *J. Amer. Acad. Psychiat. Law, 27*(1), 51–63.

Lumley, V. A., & Scotti, J. R. (2001). Supporting the sexuality of adults with mental retardation: Current status and future directions. *J. Positive Behav. Interventions, 3*(2), 109–119.

Lyketsos, C. G., Hoover, D. R., Guccione, M., Dew, M. A., et al. (1996). Changes in depressive symptoms as AIDS develops. *Amer. J. Psychiat., 153*(11), 1430–1437.

Lykken, D. T. (1957). A study of anxiety in the sociopathic personality. *J. Abnorm. Soc. Psychol., 55,* 6–10.

Lykken, D. T. (1995). *The antisocial personalities.* Hillsdale, NJ: Erlbaum.

Lykken, D. T., & Tellegen, A. (1996). Happiness is a stochastic phenomenon. *Psychol. Sci., 7*(3), 186–189.

Lyman, B. (1982). The nutritional values and food group characteristics of foods preferred during various emotions. *J. Psychol., 112,* 121–127.

Lyon, K. A. (1992). Shattered mirror: A fragment of the treatment of a patient with multiple personality disorder. *Psychoanal. Quarter., 12*(1), 71–94.

Lyon, M., Chatoor, I., Atkins, D., Silber, T., et al. (1997, Spring). Testing the hypothesis of the multidimensional model of anorexia nervosa in adolescents. *Adolescence, 32*(125), 101–111.

Lysaker, P., & Bell, M. (1995). Work and meaning: Disturbance of volition and vocational dysfunction in schizophrenia. *Psychiatry, 58*(4), 392–400.

MacDonald, W. L. (1998). The difference between blacks' and whites' attitudes toward voluntary euthanasia. *J. Sci. Study Religion, 37*(3), 411–426.

Mace, N., & Rabins, P. (1991). *The 36-hour day* (2nd ed.). Baltimore: Johns Hopkins University Press.

Macera, C. A., Armstead, C. A., & Anderson, N. B. (2001). Sociocultural influences on health. In A. Baum, T. A. Revenson, & J. E. Singer (Eds.), *Handbook of health psychology.* Mahwah, NJ: Erlbaum.

Maciejewski, P. K., Prigerson, H. G., & Mazure, C. M. (2001). Sex differences in event-related risk for major depression. *Psychol. Med., 31,* 593–604.

MacIntyre, D., & Carr, A. (1999). Helping children to the other side of silence: A study of the impact of the stay safe program on Irish children's disclosures of sexual victimization. *Child Abuse Negl., 23*(12), 1327–1340.

Mack, A., & Joy, J. (2001). *Marijuana as medicine? The science beyond the controversy.* Washington, DC: National Academy Press.

MacKenzie, K. R. (2001). Group psychotherapy. In W. J. Livesley (Ed.), *Handbook of personality disorders: Theory, research, and treatment* (pp. 497–526). New York: Guilford Press.

MacLaren, V. V. (2001). A qualitative review of the Guilty Knowledge Test. *J. Appl. Psychol., 86*(4), 674–683.

MacQueen, G. M., & Young, L. T. (2001). Bipolar II disorder: Symptoms, course, and response to treatment. *Psychiatr. Serv., 52*(3), 358–361.

Madge, N., & Harvey, J. G. (1999). Suicide among the young: The size of the problem. *J. Adolescence, 22*(1), 145–155.

Maes, M., DeVos, N., VanHunsel, F., VanWest, D., Westenberg, H., Cosyns, P., & Neels, H. (2001). Pedophilia is accompanied by increased plasma concentrations of catecholamines, in particular, epinephrine. *Psychiat. Res., 103*(1), 43–49.

Magarinos, M., Zafar, U., Nissenson, K., & Blanco, C. (2002). Epidemiology and treatment of hypochondriasis. *CNS Drugs, 16*(1), 9–22.

Magee, W. J., Eaton, W. W., Wittchen, H.-U., McGonagle, K. A., & Kessler, R. C. (1996). Agoraphobia, simple phobia, and social phobia in the National Comorbidity Survey. *Arch. Gen. Psychiat., 53,* 159–168.

Maher, B. A. (1974). Delusional thinking and perceptual disorder. *J. Individ. Psychol., 30*(1), 98–113.

Mahrer, A. R. (2000). Philosophy of science and the foundations of psychotherapy. *APA, 55*(10), 1117–1125.

Maier, W., Gansicke, M., Freyberger, H. J., Linz, M., Heun, R., & Lecrubier, Y. (2000). Generalized anxiety disorder (ICD-10) in primary care from a cross-cultural perspective: A valid diagnostic entity? *Acta Psychiatr. Scandin., 101*(1), 29–36.

Maina, G., Albert, U., & Bogetto, F. (2001). Relapses after discontinuation of drugs associated with increased resistance to treatment in obsessive-compulsive disorder. *Inter. Clin. Psychopharmacology, 16*(1), 33–38.

Malberg, J. E., & Bonson, K. R. (2001). How MDMA works in the brain. In J. Holland (Ed.), *Ecstasy: The complete guide: A comprehension look at the risks and benefits of MDMA* (pp. 29–38). Rochester, VT: Park Street Press.

Malcolm, A. H. (1990, June 9). Giving death a hand. *New York Times,* p. A6.

Malcolm, R., Myrick, H., Roberts, J., Wang, W., & Anton, R. F. (2002). The differential effects of medication on mood, sleep disturbance, and work ability in outpatient alcohol detoxification. *Amer. J. Addict., 11*(2), 141–150.

Maldonado, J. R., Butler, L. D., & Spiegel, D. (2002). Treatments for dissociative disorders. In P. E. Nathan & J. M. Gorman (Eds.), *A guide to treatments that work* (2nd ed., pp. 463–496). London: Oxford University Press.

Maletzky, B. M. (2000). Exhibitionism. In M. Hersen & M. Biaggio (Eds.), *Effective brief therapies: A clinician's guide.* San Diego, CA: Academic.

Maletzky, B. M. (2002). The paraphilias: Research and treatment. In P. E. Nathan & J. M. Gorman (Eds.), *A guide to treatments that work* (2nd ed., pp. 525–557). London: Oxford University Press.

Malik, M. L., & Beutler, L. E. (2002). The emergence of dissatisfaction with the DSM. In L. E. Beutler & M. L. Malik (Eds.), *Rethinking the DSM: A psychological perspective. Decade of behavior.* Washington, DC: APA.

Maller, R. G., & Reiss, S. (1992). Anxiety sensitivity in 1984 and panic attacks in 1987. *J. Anx. Dis., 6*(3), 241–247.

Malley, P. B., & Reilly, E. P. (1999). *Legal and ethical dimensions for mental health professionals.* Philadelphia: Taylor & Francis.

Maltsberger, J. T. (1999). The psychodynamic understanding of suicide. In D. G. Jacobs et al. (Eds.), *The Harvard Medical School guide to suicide assessment and intervention.* San Francisco: Jossey-Bass.

Mamounas, J., Lykouras, E., Oulis, P., & Christodoulou, G. N. (2001). Premorbid adjustment in schizophrenia: Associations with clinical variables. *Psychiatriki, 12*(2), 134–141.

Manji, H. K., Bebchuk, J. M., Moore, G. J., Glitz, D., Hasanat, K. A., & Chen, G. (1999). Modulation of CNS signal transduction pathways and gene expression by mood-stabilizing agents: Therapeutic implications. *J. Clin. Psychiat., 60*(Suppl. 2), 27–39.

Manley, R. S., & Needham, L. (1995). An antibulimia group for adolescent girls. *J. Child Adolesc. Group Ther., 5*(1), 19–33.

Mann, B. J. (1995). The North Carolina Dissociation Index: A measure of dissociation using items from the MMPI-2. *J. Pers. Assess., 64*(2), 349–359.

Mann, J. J., & Arango, V. (1999). The neurobiology of suicidal behavior. In D. G. Jacobs (Ed.), *The Harvard Medical School guide to suicide assessment and intervention.* San Francisco: Jossey-Bass.

Mann, J. J., Brent, D. A., & Arango, V. (2001). The neurobiology and genetics of suicide and attempted suicide: A focus on the serotonergic system. *Neurosychopharmacology, 24*(5), 467–477.

Mannuzza, S., & Klein, R. G. (1991). "Criminality and childhood hyperactivity": Reply. *Arch. Gen. Psychiat., 48*(7), 667–668.

Manschreck, T. C. (2003). The role of motor behavior in the pathogenesis of schizophrenia. In M. F. Lenzenweger & J. M. Hooley (Eds.), *Principles of experimental psychopathology: Essays in honor of Brendan A. Maher* (pp. 45–66). Washington, DC: APA.

Manson, J. E., Willett, W. C., Stampfer, M. J., Colditz, G. A., et al. (1995). Body weight and mortality among women. *N. Engl. J. Med., 333*(11), 677–685.

Manson, S. M., & Good, B. J. (1993). *Cultural considerations in the diagnosis of DSM-IV mood disorders. Cultural proposals and supporting papers for DSM-IV.* Submitted to the DSM-IV Task Force by the Steering Committee, NIMH-Sponsored Group on Culture and Diagnosis.

Manuck, S. B., Cohen, S., Rabin, B. S., Muldoon, M. F., & Bachen, E. A. (1991). Individual differences in cellular immune responses to stress. *Psychol. Sci., 2,* 1–5.

Marazitti, D., Akiskal, H. S., Rossi, A., & Cassano, G. B. (1999). Alteration of the platelet serotonin transporter in romantic love. *Psychol. Med., 29*(3), 741–745.

Marder, S. R. (1996). Management of schizophrenia. *J. Clin. Psychiat., 57*(Suppl. 3), 9–13.

Margo, J. L. (1985). Anorexia nervosa in adolescents. *Brit. J. Med. Psychol., 58*(2), 193–195.

Margraf, J., Ehlers, A., Roth, W. T., Clark, D. B., et al. (1991). How "blind" are double-blind studies? *J. Cons. Clin. Psychol., 59*(1), 184–187.

Maris, R. W. (2001). Suicide. In H. S. Friedman (Ed.), *Specialty articles from the encyclopedia of mental health.* San Diego: Academic Press.

Mark, T. L., Dirani, R., Slade, E., & Russo, P. A. (2002). Access to new medications to treat schizophrenia. *J. Behav. Hlth. Serv. Res., 29*(1), 15–29.

Markovitz, P. (2001). Pharmacotherapy. In W. J. Livesley (Ed.), *Handbook of personality disorders: Theory, research, and treatment* (pp. 475–494). New York: Guilford Press.

Marks, I. M. (1977). Phobias and obsessions: Clinical phenomena in search of a laboratory model. In J. Maser and M. Seligman (Eds.), *Psychopathology: Experimental models.* San Francisco: Freeman.

Marks, I. M. (1987). *Fears, phobias and rituals: Panic, anxiety and their disorders.* New York: Oxford University Press.

Marks, I. M., & Gelder, M. G. (1967). Transvestism and fetishism: Clinical and psychological changes during faradic aversion. *Brit. J. Psychiat., 113,* 711–730.

Marks, I. M., Green, R., & Mataix-Cols, D. (2000). Adult gender identity disorder can remit. *Comprehen. Psychiat., 41*(4), 273–275.

Marks, I. M., & Swinson, R. (1992). Behavioral and/or drug therapy. In G. D. Burrows, S. M. Roth, & R. Noyes, Jr. (Eds.), *Handbook of anxiety* (Vol. 5). Oxford, England: Elsevier.

Marks, J. (1998, October 12). Mayor vs. drug czar. *U.S. News & World Report.*

Marlatt, G. A. (1985). Controlled drinking: The controversy rages on. *Amer. Psychologist, 40*(3), 374–375.

Marlatt, G. A., Blume, A. W., & Parks, G. A. (2001). Integrating harm reduction therapy and traditional substance abuse treatment. *J. Psychoact. Drugs, 33*(1), 13–21.

Marlatt, G. A., Kosturn, C. F., & Lang, A. R. (1975). Provocation to anger and opportunity for retaliation as determinants of alcohol consumption in social drinkers. *J. Abnorm. Psychol., 84*(6), 652–659.

Marmar, C. R., Foy, D., Kagan, B., & Pynoos, R. S. (1993). An integrated approach for treating posttraumatic stress. In J. M. Oldham, M. B. Riba, & A. Tasman (Eds.), *Review of psychiatry* (Vol. 12). Washington, DC: American Psychiatric Press.

Marquis, J. N., & Morgan, W. G. (1969). *A guidebook for systematic desensitization.* Palo Alto, CA: Veterans Administration Hospital.

Marshall, J. (1997). Personal communication.

Marshall, W. L., & Kennedy, P. (2003). Sexual sadism in sexual offenders. An elusive diagnosis. *Aggress. Viol. Behav., 8* (1), 1–22.

Marston, W. M. (1917). Systolic blood pressure changes in deception. *J. Exp. Physiol., 2,* 117–163.

Martin, J. K., Kraft, J. M., & Roman, P. M. (1994). Extent and impact of alcohol and drug use problems in the workplace: A review of the empirical evidence. In S. Macdonald & P. Roman (Eds.), *Research advances in alcohol and drug problems: Vol. 11. Drug testing in the workplace.* New York: Plenum Press.

Martin, P. L. (2000). Potency and pregnancy in Japan: Did Viagra push the pill? *Tulsa Law. J., 35,* 651–677.

Martin, S. (2002). Easing migraine pain. *Monit. Psychol., 33*(4), 71.

Marzuk, P. M., Tardiff, K., Leon, A. C., Stajic, M., Morgan, E. B., & Mann, J. J. (1992). Prevalence of cocaine use among residents of New York City who committed suicide during a one-year period. *Amer. J. Psychiat., 149*(3), 371–375.

Masi, G., Mucci, M., & Millepiedi, S. (2001). Separation anxiety disorder in children and adolescents: Epidemiology, diagnosis and management. *CNS Drugs, 15*(2), 93–104.

Maslow, A. H. (1970). *Motivation and personality* (2nd ed.). New York: Harper & Row.

Masters, W. H., & Johnson, V. E. (1966). *Human sexual response.* Boston: Little, Brown.

Masters, W. H., & Johnson, V. E. (1970). *Human sexual inadequacy.* Boston: Little, Brown.

Mathew, R. J., & Wilson, W. H. (1993). Acute changes in cerebral blood flow after smoking marijuana. *Life Sciences, 52*(8), 757–767.

Mathew, R. J., Wilson, W. H., Humphreys, D., Lowe, J. V., et al. (1993). Depersonalization after marijuana smoking. *Biol. Psychiat., 33*(6), 431–441.

Matson, J. L., Bamburg, J. W., Mayville, E. A., Pinkston, J., Bielecki, J., Kuhn, D., Smalls, Y., & Logan, J. R. (2000). Psychopharmacology and mental retardation: A 10-year review (1990–1999). *Res. Dev. Disabil., 21*(4), 263–296.

Matsumoto, D. (1994). *Cultural influence on research methods and statistics.* Pacific Grove, CA: Brooks/Cole.

Matsunaga, H., Kaye, W. H., McConaha, C., Plotnicov, K., Pollice, C., & Rao, R. (2000). Personality disorders among subjects recovering from eating disorders. *Inter. J. Eat. Disorders, 27*(3), 353–357.

Mattia, J. I., & Zimmerman, M. (2001). Epidemiology. In W. J. Livesley (Ed.), *Handbook of personality disorders: Theory, research, and treatment* (pp. 107–123). New York: Guilford Press.

Maugh, T. H., II. (1995, May 31). Researchers hone in on gene that may cause "werewolf" disorder. *Los Angeles Times,* p. A3.

Mauk, G. W., & Sharpnack, J. D. (1998). A light unto the darkness: The psychoeducational imperative of school-based suicide postvention. In A. H. Esman, L. T. Flaherty, et al. (Eds.), *Adolescent psychiatry: Developmental and clinical studies* (Vol. 23). Annals of the American Society for Adolescent Psychiatry. Hillsdale, NJ: Analytic Press.

Maurice, T., Martin-Fardon, R., Romieu, P., & Matsumoto, R. R. (2002). Sigma-sub-1 receptor antagonists represent a new strategy against cocaine addiction and toxicity. *Neurosci. Biobehav. Rev., 26*(4), 499–527.

Mavissakalian, M. R., Hamann, M. S., & Jones, B. (1990). Correlates of DSM III personality disorder in obsessive-compulsive disorder. *Comprehen. Psychiat., 31*(6), 481–489.

May, P. R. A., & Tuma, A. H. (1964). Choice of criteria for the assessment of treatment outcome. *J. Psychiatr. Res., 2*(3), 16–527.

May, P. R. A., Tuma, A. H., & Dixon, W. J. (1981). Schizophrenia: A follow-up study of the results of five forms of treatment. *Arch. Gen. Psychiat., 38,* 776–784.

May, P. A., & Gossage, J. P. (2001). Estimating the prevalence of fetal alcohol syndrome: A summary. *Alc. Res. Hlth., 25*(3), 159–167.

May, R., Angel, E., & Ellenberger, H. F. (1958). *Existence: A new dimension in psychiatry and psychology.* New York: Basic Books.

May, R., & Yalom, I. (1989). Existential psychotherapy. In R. J. Corsini & D. Wedding (Eds.), *Current psychotherapies.* Itasca, IL: Peacock.

May, R., & Yalom, I. (1995). Existential psychotherapy. In R. J. Corsini & D. Wedding (Eds.), *Current psychotherapies* (5th ed.). Itasca, IL: Peacock.

Mayahara, K., & Ito, H. (2002). Readmission of discharged schizophrenic patients with and without day care in Japan. *Inter. Med. J., 9*(2), 121–123.

Mazarakis, N. K., & Nestoros, I. N. (2001). The neurophysiological substrate of anxiety: The role of the GABAergic system. *Psychol.: J. Hellenic Psychol. Soc., 8*(1), 40–59.

McAnulty, R. D., Adams, H. E., & Dillon, J. (2001). Sexual disorders: The paraphilias. In P. B. Sutker & H. E. Adams (Eds.), *Comprehensive handbook of psychopathology*(3rd ed.). New York: Kluwer Academic/Plenum.

McBrien, J. A. (2003). Assessment and diagnosis of depression in people with intellectual disability. *J. Intell. Disab. Res., 47*(1), 1–13.

McCabe, R., Roder-Wanner, U. U., Hoffmann, K., & Priebe, S. (1999). Therapeutic relationships and quality of life: Association of two subjective constructs in schizophrenia patients. *Inter. J. Soc. Psychiat., 45*(4), 276–283.

McCarroll, J. E., Fullerton, C. S., Ursano, R. J., & Hermsen, J. M. (1996). Posttraumatic stress symptoms following forensic dental identification: Mt. Carmel, Waco, Texas. *Amer. J. Psychiat., 153,* 778–782.

McClelland, G. M., & Teplin, L. A. (2001). Alcohol intoxication and violent crime: Implications for public health policy. *Amer. J. Addict., 10*(Suppl.), 70–85.

McClelland, S. (1998, September 21). Grief crisis counsellors under fire: Trauma teams were quick to descend on Peggy's Cove. Susan McClelland asks whether they do more harm than good. *Ottawa Citizen,* p. A4.

McCormick, L. H. (2000). Improving social adjustment in children with attention-deficit/hyperactivity disorder. *Arch. Fam. Med., 9*(2), 191–194.

McCoy, S. A. (1976). Clinical judgments of normal childhood behavior. *J. Cons. Clin. Psychol., 44*(5), 710–714.

McDermut, W., Miller, I. W., & Brown, R. A. (2001). The efficacy of group psychotherapy for depression: A meta-analysis and review of the empirical research. *Clin. Psychol.: Sci. Prac., 8*(1), 98–116.

McDowell, D. M., & Clodfelter, R. C., Jr. (2001). Depression and substance abuse: Considerations of etiology, comorbidity, evaluation, and treatment. *Psychiatr. Ann., 31*(4), 244–251.

McEachin, J. J., Smith, T., & Lovaas, O. I. (1993). Long-term outcome for children with autism who received early intensive behavioral treatment. *Amer. J. Ment. Retard., 97*(4), 359–372.

McElroy, S. L., Hudson, J. L., Pope, H. G., & Keck, P. E. (1991). Kleptomania: Clinical characteristics and associated psychopathology. *Psychol. Med., 21*(1), 93–108.

McGaugh, J. (1999, March 30). Interviewed in L. Muhammad. Experts brainstorming over memory loss. *USA Today,* p. 6D.

McGeer, P. L., & McGeer, E. G. (1996). Anti-inflammatory drugs in the fight against Alzheimer's disease. In R. J. Wurtman, S. Corkin, J. H. Growdon & R. M. Nitsch (Eds.), *The neurobiology of Alzheimer's disease.* New York: New York Academy of Sciences.

McGehee, D. S., Heath, M. J. S., Gelber, S., Devay, P., & Role, L. W. (1995). Nicotine enhancement of fast excitatory synaptic transmission in CNS by presynaptic receptors. *Science, 269,* 1692–1696.

McGhie, A., & Chapman, J. S. (1961). Disorders of attention and perception in early schizophrenia. *Brit. J. Med. Psychol., 34,* 103–116.

McGowen, K. R. (2001). Clinical assessment of children and adolescents: A place to begin. *In H. B. Vance & A. Pumariega (Eds.), Clinical assessment of child and adolescent behavior* (pp. 19–31). Hoboken, NJ: Wiley.

McGrady, A., Lynch, D., Nagel, R., & Zsembik, C. (1999). Application of the High Risk Model of Threat Perception to a primary care patient population. *J. Nerv. Ment. Dis., 187*(6), 369–375.

McGrath, M. L., Mellon, M. W., & Murphy, L. (2000). Empirically supported treatments in pediatric psychology: Constipation and encopresis. *J. Pediatr. Psychol., 25*(4), 225–254.

McGrath, P. A., & Hillier, L. M. (2001). Recurrent headache: Triggers, causes, and contributing factors. In P. A. McGrath & L. M. Hiller (Eds.), *The child with headache: Diagnosis and treatment* (pp. 77–107). Seattle, WA: IASP Press.

McGuffin, P., Katz, R., Watkins, S., & Rutherford, J. (1996). A hospital-based twin register of the heritability of DSM-IV unipolar depression. *Arch. Gen. Psychiat., 53,* 129–136.

McGuire, D. (1982). The problem of children's suicide: Ages 5–14. *Inter. J. Offend. Ther. Compar. Crimin., 26*(1), 10–17.

McGuire, P. A. (2000, February). New hope for people with schizophrenia. *Monitor on Psychology, 31*(2), 24–28.

McGuire, P. K., Shah, G. M. S., & Murray, R. M. (1993). Increased blood flow in Broca's area during auditory hallucinations in schizophrenia. *Lancet, 342,* 703–706.

McGuire, P. K., Silbersweig, D. A., Wright, I., Murray, R. M., et al. (1995). Abnormal monitoring of inner speech: A physiological basis for auditory hallucinations. *Lancet, 346,* 596–600.

McGuire, P. K., Silbersweig, D. A., Wright, I., Murray, R. M., Frackowiak, R. S., & Frith, C. D. (1996). The neural correlates of inner speech and auditory verbal imagery in schizophrenia: Relationship to auditory verbal hallucinations. *Brit. J. Psychiat., 169*(2), 148–159.

McIntosh, J. L. (1991). Epidemiology of suicide in the U.S. In A. A. Leenaars (Ed.), *Life span perspectives of suicide.* New York: Plenum Press.

McIntosh, J. L. (1992). Epidemiology of suicide in the elderly. *Suic. Life-Threat. Behav., 22*(1), 15–35.

McIntosh, J. L. (1992). Methods of suicide. In R. W. Maris, A. L. Berman, J. T. Maltsberger, & R. I. Yufit (Eds.), *Assessment and prediction of suicide.* New York: Guilford Press.

McIntosh, J. L. (1995). Suicide prevention in the elderly (age 65–99) [Special issue: Suicide prevention: Toward the year 2000]. *Suic. Life-Threat. Behav., 25*(1), 180–192.

McIntosh, J. L. (1996). *U.S. suicide rates 1932–1992.* Washington, DC: National Center for Health Statistics.

McIntosh, J. L., & Santos, J. F. (1982). Changing patterns in methods of suicide by race and sex. *Suic. Life-Threat. Behav., 12,* 221–233

McKisack, C., & Waller, G. (1997). Factors influencing the outcome of group psychotherapy for bulimia nervosa. *Inter. J. Eat. Disorders, 22,* 1–13.

McLean, P. D., & Woody, S. R. (2001). *Anxiety disorders in adults: An evidence-based approach to psychological treatment.* New York: Oxford University Press.

McNally, R. J. (1999). Anxiety sensitivity and information-processing biases for threat. In S. Taylor et al. (Eds.), *Anxiety sensitivity: Theory, research, and treatment of the fear of anxiety. The LEA series in personality and clinical psychology.* Mahwah, NJ: Erlbaum.

McNally, R. J. (2001a). The cognitive psychology of repressed and recovered memories of childhood sexual abuse: Clinical implications. *Psychiatr. Ann., 31*(8), 509–514.

McNally, R. J. (2001b). Vulnerability to anxiety disorders in adulthood. In R. E. Ingram & J. M. Price (Eds.), *Vulnerability to psychopathology: Risk across the lifespan* (pp. 304–321). New York: Guilford Press.

McNally, R. J. (2003). Experimental approaches to the recovered memory controversy. In M. F. Lenzenweger & J. M. Hooley (Eds.), *Principles of experimental psychopathology: Essays in honor of Brendan A. Maher* (pp. xviii, 305), Washington, DC: American Psychological Association.

McNally, R. J. (2003). Progress and controversy in the study of posttraumatic stress disorder. *Annu. Rev. Psychol., 54,* 229–252.

McNally, R. J. (2003). Psychological mechanisms in acute response to trauma. *Biol. Psychiat., 53*(9), 779–786.

McNally, R. J. (2003). Recovering memories of trauma: A view from the laboratory. *Curr. Direct. Psychol. Sci., 12*(1), 32–35.

McNally, R. J. (2003). *Remembering trauma.* Cambridge: Belknap Press/Harvard University Press.

McNally, R. J., Hornig, C. D., & Donnell, C. D. (1995). Clinical versus nonclinical panic: A test of suffocation false alarm theory. *Behav. Res. Ther., 33*(2), 127–131.

McNamara, S. (2000). *Stress in young people: What's new and what can we do?* London: Continuum International Publishing Group.

McNeil, E. B. (1967). *The quiet furies.* Englewood Cliffs, NJ: Prentice Hall.

McNeil, T. F., & Cantor-Graae, E. (2001). Obstetric complications as risk factors for schizophrenia. *Inter. J. Ment. Hlth, 29*(4), 73–83.

McParland, E., Neugroschl, J., & Marin, D. (2002). Women as caregivers for patients with Alzheimer's disease. In F. Lewis-Hall, T. S. Williams, et al. (Eds.), *Psychiatric illness in women: Emerging treatments and research* (pp. 427–444). Washington, DC: American Psychiatric.

Mednick, S. A. (1971). Birth defects and schizophrenia. *Psychol. Today, 4,* 48–50.

Meehl, P. E. (1960). The cognitive activity of the clinician. *Amer. Psychologist, 15,* 19–27.

Meehl, P. E. (1996). *Clinical versus statistical prediction: A theoretical analysis and a review of the evidence.* Northvale, NJ: Jason Aronson.

Meichenbaum, D. H. (1972). Cognitive modification of test-anxious college students. *J. Cons. Clin. Psychol., 39,* 370–380.

Meichenbaum, D. H. (1972). Examination of model characteristics in reducing avoidance behavior. *J. Behav. Ther. Exp. Psychiat., 3,* 225–227.

Meichenbaum, D. H. (1975). A self-instructional approach to stress management: A proposal for stress inoculation training. In I. Sarason & C. D. Spielberger (Eds.), *Stress and anxiety* (Vol. 2). New York: Wiley.

Meichenbaum, D. H. (1975). Enhancing creativity by modifying what subjects say to themselves. *Amer. Educ. Res. J., 12*(2), 129–145.

Meichenbaum, D. H. (1975). Theoretical and treatment implications of development research on verbal control of behavior. *Canad. Psychol. Rev., 16*(1), 22–27.

Meichenbaum, D. H. (1975). Toward a cognitive theory of self-control. In G. Schwartz & D. Shapiro (Eds.), *Consciousness and self-regulation: Advances in research.* New York: Plenum Press.

Meichenbaum, D. H. (1977). *Cognitive-behavior modification: An integrative approach.* New York: Plenum Press.

Meichenbaum, D. H. (1993). Stress inoculation training: A 20-year update. In P. M. Lehrer & R. L. Woolfolk (Eds.), *Principles and practice of stress management* (2nd ed.). New York: Guilford Press.

Meichenbaum, D. H. (1997). The evolution of a cognitive-behavior therapist. In J. K. Zeig (Ed.), *The* evolution of psychotherapy: The third conference. New York: Brunner/Mazel.

Meichenbaum, D. (2003). Cognitive behavior therapy: Folktales and the unexpurgated history. *Cog. Ther. Res.*, 27(1), 125–129.

Melamed, B. G., Kaplan, B., & Fogel, J. (2001). Childhood health issues across the life span. In A. Baum, T. A. Revenson, & J. E. Singer (Eds.), *Handbook of health psychology* (pp. 449–458). Mahwah, NJ.

Melfi, C. A., Croghan, T. W., & Hanna, M. P. (1999). Access to treatment for depression in a Medicaid population. *J. Hlth. Care Poor Underserved*, 10(2), 201–215.

Melle, I., Friis, S., Hauff, E., & Vaglum, P. (2000). Social functioning of patients with schizophrenia in high-income welfare societies. *Psychiatr. Serv.*, 51(2), 223–228.

Mellinger, G. D., Balter, M. B., & Uhlenhuth, E. H. (1985). Insomnia and its treatment. *Arch. Gen. Psychiat.*, 42, 225–232.

Melo, J. A., Shendure, J., Pociask, K., & Silver, L. M. (1996, June). Identification of sex-specific quantiative trait loci controlling alcohol preference in C57BL/6 mice. *Nature Genetics*, 13, 147–153.

Meltzer, H. Y. (1991). The mechanism of action of novel antipsychotic drugs. *Schizo. Bull.*, 17(2), 263–287.

Meltzer, H. Y. (2000). Genetics and etiology of schizophrenia and bipolar disorder. *Biol. Psychiat.*, 47(3), 171–173.

Meltzer, H. Y. (2002). Commentary on "Clinical studies on the mechanism of action of clozapine: The dopamine-serotonin hypothesis of schizophrenia. *Psychopharmacology (Berl)*, 163(1), 1–3.

Melville, J. (1978). *Phobias and obsessions*. New York: Penguin.

Melville, J. D., & Naimark, D. (2002). Punishing the insane: The verdict of guilty but mentally ill. *J. Amer. Acad. Psychiat. Law*, 30(4), 553–555.

Menzies, R. P. D., Federoff, J. P., Green, C. M., & Isaacson, K. (1995). Prediction of dangerous behaviour in male erotomania. *Brit. J. Psychiat.*, 116(4), 529–536.

Merskey, H. (1986). Classification of chronic pain: Descriptions of chronic pain syndromes and definitions of pain terms. *Pain*, 3, 226.

Merskey, H. (1992). The manufacture of personalities: The production of multiple personality disorder. *Brit. J. Psychiat.*, 160, 327–340.

Merskey, H. (1995). Multiple personality disorder and false memory syndrome. *Brit. J. Psychiat.*, 166(3), 281–283.

Merzenich, M. M., Jenkins, W. M., Johnston, P., Schreiner, C., et al. (1996). Temporal processing deficits of language-learning impaired children ameliorated by training. *Science*, 271, 77–84.

Messer, S. B. (2001). What makes brief psychodynamic therapy time efficient. *Clin. Psychol.: Sci. Prac.*, 8(1), 5–22.

Messer, S. B., & Wampold, B. E. (2002). Let's face facts: Common factors are more potent than specific therapy ingredients. *Clin. Psychol.: Sci. Prac.*, 9(1), 21–25.

Metz, M. E., & Epstein, N. (2002). Assessing the role of relationship conflict in sexual dysfunction. *J. Sex Marital Ther.*, 28(2), 139–164.

Metz, M. E., & Pryor, J. L. (2000). Premature ejaculation: A psychophysiological approach for assessment and management. *J. Sex Marital Ther.*, 26(4), 293–320.

Meyer, B., & Carver, C. S. (2000). Negative childhood accounts, sensitivity and pessimism: A study of avoidant personality disorder features in college students. *J. Pers. Disorders*, 14(3), 233–248.

Meyer, G. J. (2001). Introduction to the final special section in the special series on the utility of the Rorschach for clinical assessment. *Psychol. Assess.* 13(4), 419–422.

Meyer, G. J., Finn, S. E., Eyde, L. D., Kay, G. G., Moreland, K. L., Dies, R. R., Eisman, E. J., Kubiszyn, T. W., & Reed, G. M. (2001). Psychological testing and psychological assessment: A review of evidence and issues. *Amer. Psychologist*, 56(2), 128–165.

Meyer, G. J., Finn, S. E., Eyde, L. D., Kay, G. G., Moreland, K. L., Dies, R. R., Eisman, E. J., Kubiszyn, T. W., & Reed, G. M. (2003). Psychological testing and psychological assessment: A review of evidence and issues. In A. E. Kazdin (Ed.), *Methodological issues and strategies in clinical research*(3rd ed., pp. 265–345). Washington, DC: American Psychological Association.

Meyer, R. E., Murray, R. F., Jr., Thomas, F. B., et al. (1989). *Prevention and treatment of alcohol problems: Research opportunities*. Washington, DC: National Academy Press.

Meyer, R. G. (1992). *Abnormal behavior and the criminal justice system*. New York: Lexington Books.

Meyer, V. (1966). Modification of expectations in cases with obsessional rituals. *Behav. Res. Ther.*, 4, 273–280.

Michael, R. T., Gagnon, J. H., Laumann, E. O., & Kolata, G. (1994). *Sex in America: A definitive survey*. Boston: Little, Brown.

Michaelson, R. (1993). Flood volunteers build emotional levees. *APA Monitor*, 24(10), 30.

Michel, A., Ansseau, M., Legros, J.-J., Pitchot, W., & Mormont, C. (2002). The transsexual: What about the future. *Eur. Psychiat.*, 17(6), 353–362.

Mickalide, A. D. (1990). Sociocultural factors influencing weight among males. In A. E. Andersen (Ed.), *Males with eating disorders*. New York: Brunner/Mazel.

Mickley, D. W. (2001). Medical aspects of anorexia and bulimia. In B. Kinoy (Ed.), *Eating disorders: New directions in treatment and recovery*(2nd ed., pp. 7–16). New York: Columbia University Press.

Mikkelsen, E. J. (2001). Enuresis and encopresis: Ten years of progress. *J. Amer. Acad. Child Adol. Psychiat.*, 40(10), 1146–1158.

Millar, J. D. (1984). The NIOSH-suggested list of the ten leading work-related diseases and injuries. *J. Occup. Med.*, 26, 340–341.

Millar, J. D. (1990). Mental health and the workplace: An interchangeable partnership. *Amer. Psychologist*, 45(10), 1165–1166.

Miller, A. (1999). Appropriateness of psychostimulant prescription to children: Theoretical and empirical perspectives. *Canad. J. Psychiat.*, 44(10), 1017–1024.

Miller, M., & Kantrowitz, B. (1999, January 25). Unmasking Sybil: A re-examination of the most famous psychiatric patient in history. *Newsweek*, pp. 66–68.

Miller, M. A., & Rahe, R. H. (1997). Life changes scaling for the 1990s. *J. Psychosom. Res.*, 43(3), 279–292.

Miller, M. C., Jacobs, D. G., & Gutheil, T. G. (1998). Talisman or taboo: The controversy of the suicide-prevention contract. *Harvard Review of Psychiatry*, 6(2), 78–87.

Miller, M. O., Sales, B. D., & Delgado, J. B. (2003). *Law & mental health professionals: Arizona* (2nd ed.). Washington, DC: American Psychological Association.

Miller, N. E. (1948). Studies of fear as an acquirable drive: I. Fear as motivation and fear-reduction as reinforcement in the learning of new responses. *J. Exp. Psychol.*, 38, 89–101.

Miller, N. S., & Gold, M. S. (1990). Benzodiazepines: Tolerance, dependence, abuse, and addiction. *J. Psychoactive Drugs*, 22(1), 23–33.

Miller, P. M., Ingham, J. G., & Davidson, S. (1976). Life events, symptoms, and social support. *J. Psychiatr. Res.*, 20(6), 514–522.

Miller, R. D. (2002). Automatic commitment of insanity acquittees: Keeping up with the Joneses? *J. Psychiat. Law.*, 30(1), 59–96.

Miller, W. R. (1983). Controlled drinking, *Quart. J. Stud. Alcohol.*, 44, 68–83.

Miller, W. R., Leckman, A. L., Delaney, H. D., & Tinchom, M. (1992). Long-term follow-up of behavioral self-control training. *J. Stud. Alc.*, 51, 108–115.

Miller, W. R., & Seligman, M. E. (1975). Depression and learned helplessness in man. *J. Abnorm. Psychol.*, 84(3), 228–238.

Miller, W. R., Walters, S. T., & Bennett, M. E. (2001). How effective is alcoholism treatment in the United States? *J. Stud. Alc*, 62 (2), 211–220.

Millon, T. (1969). *Modern psychopathology: A biosocial approach to maladaptive learning and functioning*. Philadelphia: Saunders.

Millon, T. (1987). *Millon Clinical Multiaxial Inventory-II: Manual for the MCMI-II* (2nd ed.). Minneapolis, MN: National Computer Systems.

Millon, T. (1990). The disorders of personality. In L. A. Pervin (Ed.), *Handbook of personality theory and practice*. New York: Guilford Press.

Millon, T. (1990). *Toward a new personology*. New York: Wiley.

Millon, T. (1999). *Personality-guided therapy*. New York: Wiley.

Millon, T. (2002). Assessment is not enough: The SPA should participate in constructing a comprehensive clinical science of personality. *J. Pers. Assess.*, 78(2), 209–218.

Millon, T., Davis, R., Millon, C., Escovar, L., & Meagher, S. (2000). *Personality disorders in modern life*. New York: Wiley.

Milos, G., Sprindler, A., Ruggiero, G., Klaghofer, R., & Schnyder, U. (2002). Comorbidity of obsessive-compulsive disorders and duration of eating disorders. *Inter. J. Eat. Disorders*, 31(3), 284–289.

Milosevic, A., Agrawal, N., Redfearn, P., & Mair, L. (1999). The occurrence of toothwear in users of Ecstasy (3,4-methylenedioxymethamphetamine). *Community Dent. Oral Epidemiol.* 27(4), 283–287.

Milrod, B. (2002). A 9-year-old with conversion disorder, successfully treated with psychoanalysis. *Inter. J. Psychoanal.*, 83(3), 623–631.

Mineka, S., & Ohman, A. (2002). Phobias and preparedness: The selective, automatic, and encapsulated nature of fear. *Biol. Psychiat.*, 51(9), 927–937.

Minton, H. L. (2002). *Departing from deviance: A history of homosexual rights and emancipatory science in America*. Chicago: University of Chicago Press.

Minuchin, S. (1974). *Families and family therapy*. Cambridge, MA: Harvard University Press.

Minuchin, S. (1987). My many voices. In J. K. Zeig (Ed.), *The evolution of psychotherapy*. New York: Brunner/Mazel.

Minuchin, S. (1997). The leap to complexity: Supervision in family therapy. In J. K. Zeig (Ed.), *The evolution of psychotherapy: The third conference*. New York: Brunner/Mazel.

Minuchin, S., Rosman, B. L., & Baker, L. (1978). *Psychosomatic families: Anorexia nervosa in context*. Cambridge, MA: Harvard University Press.

Mirin, S. M., & Weiss, R. D. (1991). Substance abuse and mental illness. In R. J. Frances & S. I. Miller (Eds.), *Clinical textbook of addictive disorders*. New York: Guilford Press.

Mirsky, I. A. (1958). Physiologic, psychologic, and social determinants of the etiology of duodenal ulcer. *Amer. J. Digestional Dis.*, 3, 285–314.

Mishara, B. L. (1999). Conceptions of death and suicide in children ages 6–12 and their implications for suicide prevention. *Suic. Life-Threat. Behav.*, *29*(2), 105–118.

Mishna, F. (1996). Clinical report. In their own words: Therapeutic factors for adolescents who have learning disabilities. *Inter. J. Group Psychother.*, *46*(2), 265–273.

Mitchell, I. (2001). Treatment and outcome for victims. In G. Adshead & D. Brooke (Eds.), *Munchausen's syndrome by proxy: Current issues in assessment, treatment and research* (pp. 185–196). London: Imperial College Press.

Mitchell, J. E. (2001). Psychopharmacology of eating disorders: Current knowledge and future directions. In R. H. Striegel-Moore & L. Smolak (Eds.), *Eating disorders: Innovative directions in research and practice* (pp. 197–212). Washington, DC: APA.

Mitchell, J. E., Halmi, K., Wilson, G. T., Agras, W. S., Kraemer, H., & Crow, S. (2002). A randomized secondary treatment study of women with bulimia nervosa who fail to respond to CBT. *Inter. J. Eat. Disorders*, *32*(3), 271–281.

Mitchell, J. E., & Peterson, C. B. (1997). Cognitive-behavioral treatment of eating disorder. In L. J. Dickstein, M. B. Riba, & J. M. Oldham (Eds.), *Review of psychiatry* (Vol. 16). Washington, D.C.: American Psychiatric Press.

Mitchell, J. E., Pyle, R. L., & Miner, R. A. (1982). Gastric dilation as a complication of bulimia. *Psychosomatics*, *23*, 96–97.

Mittleman, M. A., Mintzer, D., Maclure, M., Tofler, G. H., Sherwood, J. B., & Muller, J. E. (1999). Triggering of myocardial infarction by cocaine. *Circulation*, *99*(21), 2737–2741.

Mizes, J. S. (1993). Bulimia nervosa. In A. S. Bellack & M. Hersen (Eds.), *Handbook of behavior therapy in the psychiatric setting. Critical issues in psychiatry* (pp. 311–327). New York: Plenum Press.

Mizes, J. S. (1995). Eating disorders. In M. Hersen & R. T. Ammerman (Eds.), *Advanced abnormal child psychology*. Hillsdale, NJ: Erlbaum.

Mizes, J. S., & Bonifazi, D. Z. (2002). Bulimia nervosa. In M. Hersen (Ed.), *Clinical behavior therapy: Adults and children* (pp. 144–159). New York: Wiley.

Modestin, J., & Villiger, C. (1989). Follow-up study on borderline versus nonborderline personality disorders. *Comprehen. Psychiat.*, *30*(3), 236–244.

Modlin, T. (2002). Sleep disorders and hypnosis: To cope or cure? *Sleep Hyp.*, *4*(1), 39–46.

Modrow, J. (1992). *How to become a schizophrenic: The case against biological psychiatry.* Everett, WA: Apollyon Press.

Moene, F. C., Spinhoven, P., Hoogduin, K. A. L., & van Dyck, R. (2002). A randomised controlled clinical trial on the additional effect of hypnosis in a comprehensive treatment programme for in-patients with conversion disorder of the motor type. *Psychother. Psychosom.*, *71*(2), 66–76.

Mohler, H., & Okada, T. (1977). Benzodiazepine receptor: Demonstration in the central nervous system. *Science*, *198*(4319), 849–851.

Mohler, H., Richards, J. G., & Wu, J.-Y. (1981). Autoradiographic localization of benzodiazepine receptors in immunocytochemically identified Y-aminobutyric synapses. *Proc. Natl. Acad. Sci., USA*, *78*, 1935–1938.

Mohlman, J., Gorenstein, E. E., Kleber, M., de Jesus, M., Gorman, J. M., & Papp, L. A. (2003). Standard and enhanced cognitive-behavior therapy for late-life generalized anxiety disorder: Two pilot investigations. *Amer. J. Ger. Psychiat.*, *11*(1), 24–32.

Mohr, D. C., & Beutler, L. E. (1990). Erectile dysfunction: A review of diagnostic and treatment procedures. *Clin. Psychol. Rev.*, *10*(1), 123–150.

Mollinger, R. N. (1980). Antithesis and the obsessive-compulsive. *Psychoanal. Rev.*, *67*(4), 465–477.

Molnar, B. E., Buka, S. L., & Kessler, R. C. (2001). Child sexual abuse and subsequent psychopathology: Results from the National Comorbidity Survey. *Amer. J. Pub. Hlth.*, *91*(5), 753–760.

Monahan, J. (1992). Mental disorder and violent behavior: Perceptions and evidence. *Amer. Psychologist*, *47*(4), 511–521.

Monahan, J. (1993). Limiting therapist exposure to Tarasoff liability: Guidelines for risk containment. *Amer. Psychologist*, *48*(3), 242–250.

Monahan, J. (1993). Mental disorder and violence: Another look. In S. Hodgins (Ed.), *Mental disorder and crime*. Newbury Park, CA: Sage.

Monahan, J. (2001). Major mental disorder and violence: Epidemiology and risk assessment. In G. F. Pinard & L. Pagani (Eds.), *Clinical assessment of dangerousness: Empirical contributions* (pp. 89–102). New York: Cambridge University Press.

Moncrieff, J. (1997). Lithium: Evidence reconsidered. *Brit. J. Psychiat.*, *171*, 113–119.

Monette, J., du Fort, G. G., Fung, S. H., Massoud, F., Moride, Y., Arsenault, L., & Afilalo, M. (2001). Evaluation of the Confusion Assessment Method (CAM) as a screening tool for delirium in the emergency room. *Gen. Hosp. Psychiat.*, *23*(1), 20–25.

Monroe, S. M., & Hadjiyannakis, K. (2002). The social environment and depression: Focusing on severe life stress. In I. H. Gotlib & C. L. Hammen (Eds.), *Handbook of depression: Research and treatment* (pp. 314–340). New York: Guilford Press.

Montgomery, S. A., Bebbington, P., Cowen, P., Deakin, W., et al. (1993). Guidelines for treating depressive illness with antidepressants. *J. Psychopharmacol.*, *7*(1), 19–23.

Moore, M. T. (1997, October 30). Maine initiative would give the vote to all mentally ill. *USA Today*, p. 12A.

Moorhead, D. J., Stashwick, C. K., Reinherz, H. Z., Giaconia, R. M., Streigel-Moore, R. M., & Paradis, A. D. (2003). Child and adolescent predictors for eating disorders in a community population of young adult women. *Inter. J. Eat. Disorders*, *33*(1), 1–9.

Moos, R. H., & Cronkite, R. C. (1999). Symptom-based predictors of a 10-year chronic course of treated depression. *J. Nerv. Ment. Dis.*, *187*(6), 360–368.

Morgan, C. D., & Murray, H. A. (1935). A method of investigating fantasies: The Thematic Apperception Test. *Arch. Neurol. Psychiat.*, *34*, 289–306.

Moriarty, P. J., Lieber, D., Bennett, A., White, L., Parrella, M., Harvey, P. D., & Davis, K. L. (2001). Gender differences in poor outcome patients with lifelong schizophrenia. *Schizo. Bull.*, *27*(1), 103–113.

Morokoff, P. J., & Gillilland, R. (1993). Stress, sexual functioning, and marital satisfaction. *J. Sex Res.*, *30*(1), 43–53.

Morral, A. R., McCaffrey, D., & Iguchi, M. Y. (2000). Hardcore drug users claim to be occasional users: Drug use frequency underreporting. *Drug Alc. Dep.*, *57*(3), 193–202.

Morris, P., Hopwood, M., Maguire, K., Norman, T., & Schweitzer, I. (2004). Blunted growth hormone response to clonidine in post-traumatic stress disorder. *Psychoneuroendocrinology*, *29*(2), 269–278.

Morse, S. J. (1982). A preference for liberty: The case against involuntary commitment of the mentally disordered. *Calif. Law Rev.*, *70*, 55–106.

Morton, W. J. (2002). Historical note: The ability of mentally ill persons to live in the community, 1880. *J. Nerv. Ment. Dis.*, *190*(6), 398.

Moscicki, E. K. (1999). Epidemiology of suicide. In D. G. Jacobs (Ed.), *The Harvard Medical School guide to suicide assessment and intervention*. San Francisco: Jossey-Bass.

Moskowitz, E. S. (2001). *In therapy we trust: America's obsession with self-fulfillment.* Baltimore: Johns Hopkins University Press.

Moss, D. (2002). Biofeedback. In S. Shannon (Ed.), *Handbook of complementary and alternative therapies in mental health* (pp. 135–158). San Diego, Ca: Academic Press.

Moss, H. B. (1999). Pharmacotherapy. In M. Hersen & A. S. Bellack (Eds.), *Handbook of comparative interventions for adult disorders* (2nd ed.). New York: Wiley.

Mowbray, C. T., Grazier, K. L., & Holter, M. (2002). Managed behavioral health care in the public sector: Will it become the third shame of the States? *Psychiatr. Serv.*, *53*(2), 157–170.

Mowrer, O. H. (1939). *An experimentally produced "social problem" in rats* [Film]. Bethlehem, PA: Lehigh University, Psychological Cinema Register.

Mowrer, O. H. (1939). A stimulus-response analysis of anxiety and its role as a reinforcing agent. *Psychol. Rev.*, *46*, 553–566.

Mowrer, O. H. (1947). On the dual nature of learning: A reinterpretation of "conditioning" and "problem-solving." *Harvard Educ. Rev.*, *17*, 102–148.

Mowrer, O. H., & Mowrer, W. M. (1938). Enuresis: A method for its study and treatment. *Amer. J. Orthopsychiat.*, *8*, 436–459.

MRI (Matrix Research Institute). (1998). *The facts about mental illness and work.* Philadelphia, PA: Author.

Mueller, R. A., & Courchesne, E. (2000). Autism's home in the brain: Reply. *Neurology*, *54*(1), 270.

Mufson, L., Nomura, Y., & Warner, V. (2002). The relationship between parental diagnosis, offspring temperament and offspring psychopathology: A longitudinal analysis. *J. Affect. Disorders*, *71*(1–3), 61–69.

Muhammad, L. (1999, March 30). Experts brainstorming over memory loss. *USA Today*, p. 6D.

Muir, J. L. (1997). Acetylcholine, aging, and Alzheimer's disease. *Pharmacol. Biochem. Behav.*, *56*(4), 687–696.

Mulder, R. T. (2002). Personality pathology and treatment outcome in major depression: A review. *Amer. J. Psychiat.*, *159*(3), 359–371.

Mulhern, B. (1990, December 15–18). Everyone's problem, no one's priority. *Capital Times.*

Mulholland, A. M., & Mintz, L. B. (2001). Prevalence of eating disorders among African American women. *J. Couns. Psychol.*, *48*(1), 111–116.

Munk, J. P., & Mortensen, P. B. (1992). Social outcome in schizophrenia: A 13-year follow-up. *Soc. Psychiat. Psychiatr. Epidemiol.*, *27*(3), 129–134.

Muñoz, R. F., Le, H.-N., Clarke, G., & Jaycox, L. (2002). Preventing the onset of major depression. In I. H. Gotlib & C. L. Hammen (Eds.), *Handbook of depression* (pp. 343–359). New York: Guilford Press.

Muris, P., Schmidt, H., Merckelbach, H., & Schouten, E. (2001). Anxiety sensitivity in adolescents: Factors structure and relationships to trait and symptoms of anxiety disorders and depression. *Behav. Res. Ther.*, *39*(1), 89–100.

Murphy, E., & Carr, A. (2000). Enuresis and encopresis. In A. Carr (Ed.), *What works with children and adolescents?: A critical review of psychological interventions with children, adolescents and their fami-*

lies (pp. 49–64). Florence, KY: Taylor & Francis/Routledge.

Murphy, J. B., & Lipshultz, L. I. (1988). Infertility in the paraplegic male. In E. A. Tanagho, T. F. Lue, & R. D. McClure (Eds.), *Contemporary management of impotence and infertility.* Baltimore: Williams & Wilkins.

Murphy, S. M. (1990). Rape, sexually transmitted diseases and human immunodeficiency virus infection. *Inter. J. STD AIDS, 1,* 79–82.

Murphy, S. M., & Woolfolk, R. L. (1987). The effects of cognitive interventions on competitive anxiety and performance on a fine motor skill accuracy task. *Inter. J. Sport Psychol., 18*(2), 152–166.

Murray, B. (1996). Computer addictions entangle students. *APA Monitor, 27*(6), 38–39.

Murray, J. B. (2001). Ecstasy is a dangerous drug. *Psychol. Rep., 88*(3, Pt. 1), 895–902.

Murray, K. (1993, May 9). When the therapist is a computer. *New York Times,* Section 3, p. 25.

Mustaine, E. E., & Tewksbury, R. (1998). Specifying the role of alcohol in predatory victimization. *Deviant Behavior: An Interdisciplinary Journal, 19,* 173–199.

Muuss, R. E. (1986). Adolescent eating disorder: Bulimia. *Adolescence, 21*(82), 257–267.

Mydans, S. (1996, October 19). New Thai tourist sight: Burmese "giraffe women." *New York Times,* p. C1.

Myers, D. G. (2000). The funds, friends, and faith of happy people. *Amer. Psychologist, 55*(1), 56–67.

Myers, D. G., & Diener, E. (1996, May). The pursuit of happiness. *Scientif. Amer.,* pp. 70–72.

Myers, M. G., Stewart, D. G., & Brown, S. A. (1998). Progression from conduct disorder to antisocial personality disorder following treatment for adolescent substance abuse. *Amer. J. Psychiat., 155*(4), 479–485.

Mylant, M. L., Ide, B., Guevas, E., & Meehan, M. (2002). Adolescent children of alcoholics: Vulnerable or resilient? *J. Amer. Psychiat. Nurs. Assoc., 8*(2), 57–64.

Nagy, T. F. (2000). *Ethics in plain English: An illustrative casebook for psychologists.* Washington, DC: American Psychological Association.

Nahas, G. G., Sutin, K. M., Harvey, D., Agurell, S., Pace, N., & Cancro, R. (Eds.). (1999). *Marihuana and medicine.* Clifton, NJ: Humana Press.

Najman, J. M., Andersen, M. J., Bor, W., O'Callaghan, M. J., & Williams, G. M. (2000). Postnatal depression—Myth and reality: Maternal depression before and after the birth of a child. *Soc. Psychiat. Psychiatr. Epidemiol., 35*(1), 19–27.

NAMI (National Alliance for the Mentally Ill). (1996, February 7). Survey on mental health insurance. Cited in *USA Today,* p. 4D.

NAPHS (National Association of Psychiatric Health Systems). (1999). *The NAPHS 1998 annual survey report—trends in psychiatric health systems: A benchmarking report.* Washington, DC: Author.

Narash-Eisikovits, O., Dierberger, A., & Westen, D. (2002). A multidimensional meta-analysis of pharmacotherapy for bulimia nervosa: Summarizing the range of outcomes in controlled clinical trials. *Harv. Rev. Psychiat., 10*(4), 193–211.

Narrow, W. E., Rae, D. S., Robins, L. N., & Regier, D. A. (2002). Revised prevalence based estimates of mental disorders in the United States: Using a clinical significance criterion to reconcile 2 surveys' estimates. *Arch. Gen. Psychiat., 59*(2), 115–123.

Narrow, W. E., Regier, D. A., Rae, D. S., Manderscheid, R. W., & Locke, B. Z. (1993). Use of services by persons with mental and addictive disorders: Findings from the National Institute of Mental Health Epidemiologic Catchment Area Program. *Arch. Gen. Psychiat., 50,* 95–107.

Nasar, S. (2002, March 11). The man behind "A Beautiful Mind." *Newsweek,* p. 52.

Nasar, S. (2002, March 18). A majestic person, despite flaws: Some recent reports about mathematician John Nash distort the truth. *Los Angeles Times,* p. B3.

Nash, J. M. (1997). Special report: Fertile minds. *Newsweek, 149*(5), 48–56.

Nash, J. M. (1997, May 5). Addicted. *Time,* pp. 68–76.

Nash, M. R. (2001, July). The truth and the hype of hypnosis. *Scientif. Amer.,* pp. 47–55.

Nasser, M., Katzman, M. A., & Gordon, R. A. (Eds.). (2001). *Eating disorders and cultures in transition.* New York: Brunner-Routledge.

Nathan, P. E., & Lagenbucher, J. W. (1999). Psychopathology: Description and classification. *Annu. Rev. Psychol., 50,* 79–107.

NCHS (National Center for Health Statistics). (1999). *Fastats A to Z. Divorce.* Washington, DC: Center for Disease Control.

NCHS (National Center for Health Statistics). (2000). *Births, marriages, divorces, and deaths: Provisional data for January 1999.* Centers for Disease Control and Prevention (National Vital Statistics Reports, vol. 48, no. 1).

NCHS (National Center for Health Statistics). (2002). *Health, United States, 2002. With chartbook on trends in the health of Americans.* Hyattsville, MD: Author.

NCHS (National Center for Health Statistics). (2002). *Illegal drug use.* Retrieved November 24, 2002, from www.cdc.gov.

NCHS (National Center for Health Statistics). (2002). *With chartbook on trends of the health of Americans.* Hyattsville, MD: Author.

NCIPC (National Center for Injury Prevention and Control). (1999, October 25). *Epidemiology of traumatic brain injury in the United States.* Centers for Disease Control and Prevention.

NCVS (National Crime Victimization Survey). (1993). Highlights from 20 years of surveying crime victims: The National Crime Victimization Survey, 1973–1992. Washington, DC: Bureau of Justice Statistics.

NCVS (National Crime Victimization Survey). (1996). Washington, DC: Bureau of Justice Statistics.

NCVS (National Crime Victimization Survey) (1998). Washington, DC: Bureau of Justice Statistics.

Neeleman, J., Wessely, S., & Lewis, G. (1998). Suicide acceptability in African- and white Americans: The role of religion. *J. Nerv. Ment. Dis., 186*(1), 12–16.

Neimeyer, R. A., & Bonnelle, K. (1997). The suicide intervention response inventory: A revision and validation. *Death Stud., 21,* 59–81.

Neisser, U., Boodoo, G., Bouchard, T. J., Jr., Boykin, A. W., et al. (1996). Intelligence: Knowns and unknowns. *Amer. Psychologist, 51*(2), 77–101.

Nemecek, S. (1996, September). Mysterious maladies. *Sci. Amer.,* Retrieved Jan. 25, 2002, from www.sciam.com.

Nemeroff, C. B., Compton, M. T., & Berger, J. (2001). The depressed suicidal patient: Assessment and treatment. In H. Hendin & J. J. Mann (Eds.), *The clinical science of suicide prevention* (Vol. 932, pp. 1–23). New York: Annals of the New York Academy of Sciences.

Ness, R. B., Grisso, J. A., Herschinger, N., Markovic, N., Shaw, L. M., Day, N. L., & Kline, J. (1999). Cocaine and tobacco use and the risk of spontaneous abortion. *N. Engl. J. Med., 340*(5), 333–339.

Nestadt, G., Romanoski, A. J., Chahal, R., Merchant, A., Folstein, M. F., Gruenberg, E. M., & McHugh, P. R. (1990). An epidemiological study of histrionic personality disorder. *Psychol. Med., 29,* 413–422.

Netting, N. S. (1992). Sexuality in youth culture: Identity and change. *Adolescence, 27*(108), 961–976.

Neumarker, K. J. (1997). Mortality and sudden death in anorexia nervosa. *Inter. J. Eat. Disorders, 21*(3), 205–212.

Newman, J. P., Kosson, D. S., & Patterson, C. M. (1987). Response perseveration in psychopaths. *J. Abnorm. Psychol., 96,* 145–149.

Newman, J. P., Kosson, D. S., & Patterson, C. M. (1992). Delay of gratification in psychopathic and nonpsychopathic offenders. *J. Abnorm. Psychol., 101*(4), 630–636.

Newman, R., et al. (1996). State leadership conference mobilizes practitioners for community outreach. *Practitioner Update, 4*(1), 1.

Neziroglu, F., McKay, D., Todaro, J., & Yaryura-Tobias, J. A. (1996). Effect of cognitive behavior therapy on persons with body dysmorphic disorder and comorbid Axis II diagnoses. *Behav. Ther., 27,* 67–77.

Nezlek, J. B., Hampton, C. P., & Shean, G. D. (2000). Clinical depression and day-to-day social interaction in a community sample. *J. Abnorm. Psychol., 109*(1), 11–19.

NHSDA (National Household Survey on Drug Abuse). (1998). *1998 national estimates of rates of use and other measures related to drugs, alcohol, cigarettes, and other forms of tobacco.* Washington, DC: U.S. Department of Health and Human Services.

NHSDA (National Household Survey on Drug Abuse). (2002). *The NHSDA Report: Substance abuse or dependence.* Retrieved February 15, 2003, from www.samhsa.gov.

NIA (National Institute on Aging). (1996). *Aging America poses unprecendented challenge. 65+.* Washington, DC: Office of the Demography of Aging.

NIAAA (National Institute on Alcohol Abuse and Alcoholism). (1992). *Alcohol alert #15. Alcohol and AIDS.* Rockville, MD: Author.

Nichols, D. S. (2001). *Essentials of MMPI-2 assessment.* New York: Wiley.

Nichter, M., & Nichter, M. (1991). Hype and weight. *Med. Anthropol., 13*(3), 249–284.

Nicolson, P. (1999). Loss, happiness and postpartum depression: The ultimate paradox. *Canad. Psychol., 40*(2), 162–178.

NIDA (National Institute on Drug Abuse). (1995). *Facts about teenagers and drug abuse. NIDA Capsule.* Rockville, MD: Author.

NIDA (National Institute on Drug Abuse). (1998). *Economic costs of alcohol and drug abuse.* Washington, DC: Author.

NIDA (National Institute on Drug Abuse). (2002). *Marijuana abuse.* Retrieved November 24, 2002, from www.drugabuse.gov.

NIDA (National Institute on Drug Abuse). (2002). MDMA (Ecstasy). *NIDA Info Facts.* Retrieved November 24, 2002, from www.nida.nih.gov.

Nielsen, S., Møller-Madsen, S., Isager, T., Jørgensen, J., Pagsberg, K., & Theander, S. (1998). Standardized mortality in eating disorders—A quantitative summary of previously published and new evidence. *J. Psychosom. Res., 14*(3/4), 413–434.

Nietzel, M. T., Bernstein, D. A., & Milich, R. (1994). *Introduction to clinical psychology* (4th ed.). Englewood Cliffs, NJ: Prentice Hall.

NIH (National Institutes of Health). (1999, February 19). *American Indian: Facts-at-a-glance for women's health.* Washington, DC: Author.

Nishino, S., Mignot, E., & Dement, W. C. (1995). Sedative hypnotics. In A. F. Schatzberg & C. B. Nemeroff (Eds.), *The American Psychiatric Press Textbook of Psychopharmacology.* Washington, DC: American Psychiatric Press.

NMHA (National Mental Health Association). (1999, June 5). Poll. *U.S. Newswire.*

Nock, M. K., & Marzuk, P. M. (1999) Murder-suicide: Phenomenology and clinical implications. In D. G. Jacobs (Ed.), *The Harvard Medical School guide to suicide assessment and intervention.* San Francisco: Jossey-Bass.

Nolen-Hoeksema, S. (1987). Sex differences in unipolar depression: Evidence and theory. *Psychol. Bull., 101*(2), 259-282.

Nolen-Hoeksema, S. (1990). *Sex differences in depression.* Stanford, CA: Stanford University Press.

Nolen-Hoeksema, S. (1995). Gender differences in coping with depression across the lifespan. *Depression, 3,* 81-90.

Nolen-Hoeksema, S. (1998). The other end of the continuum: The costs of rumination: *Psychological Inquiry, 9*(3), 216-219.

Nolen-Hoeksema, S. (2000). The role of rumination in depressive disorders and mixed anxiety/depressive symptoms. *J. Abnorm. Psychol., 109,* 504-511.

Nolen-Hoeksema, S. (2002). Gender differences in depression. In I. H. Gotlib & C. L. Hammen (Eds.), *Handbook of depression* (pp. 492-509). New York: Guilford Press.

Nolen-Hoeksema, S. (2002). The role of rumination in depressive disorders and mixed anxiety/depressive symptoms. *J. Abnorm. Psychol., 109,* 504-511.

Nolen-Hoeksema, S., & Girgus, J. (1995). Explanatory style and achievement, depression, and gender differences in childhood and early adolescence. In G. Buchanan & M. Seligman (Eds.), *Explanatory style.* Hillsdale, NJ: Erlbaum.

Nolen-Hoeksema, S., Larson, J., & Grayson, C. (1999). Explaining the gender difference in depressive symptoms. *J. Pers. Soc. Psychol., 77*(5), 1061-1072.

Noll, R., & Turkington, C. (1994). *The encyclopedia of memory and memory disorders.* New York: Facts on File.

Nonacs, R. (2002, March 12). Postpartum psychiatric illness. *eMed. J., 3*(3).

Nonacs, R., & Cohen, L. S. (1998). Postpartum mood disorders: Diagnosis and treatment guidelines. *J. Clin. Psychiat., 59*(Suppl. 2), 34-40.

Norcross, J. C., Karg, R. S., & Prochaska, J. O. (1997). Clinical psychologists in the 1990s. *Clin. Psychol., 50*(2), 4-9.

Norcross, J. C., Prochaska, J. O., & Farber, J. A. (1993). Psychologists conducting psychotherapy: New findings and historical comparisons on the psychotherapy division membership. *Psychotherapy, 30*(4), 692-697.

Nordstrom, P., Samuelsson, M., & Asberg, M. (1995). Survival analysis of suicide risk after attempted suicide. *Acta Psychiatr. Scandin., 91*(5), 336-340.

Norra, C., Mrazek, M., Tuchtenhagen, F., Gobbele, R., Buchner, H., Sass, H., & Herpertz, S. C. (2003). Enhanced intensity dependence as a marker of low serotonergic neurotransmission in borderline personality disorder. *J. Psychiatr. Res., 37*(1), 23-33.

North, C. S., Nixon, S. J., Shariat, S., Mallonee, S., McMillen, J. C., Spitznagel, E. L., & Smith, E. M. (1999). Psychiatric disorders among survivors of the Oklahoma City bombing. *JAMA, 282*(8), 755-762.

Nott, K. H., & Vedhara, K. (1999). Nature and consequences of stressful life events in homosexual HIV-positive men: A review. *AIDS Care, 11*(2), 235-243.

Nottestad, J. A., & Linkaer, O. M. (2002). Predictors for attacks on people after deinstitutionalization. *J. Intell. Disab. Res., 46*(6), 493-502.

Noyes, R., Jr. (2001). Comorbidity in generalized anxiety disorder. *Psychiatr. Clin. N. Amer., 24*(1), 41-55.

Nutt, D. J., & Maizia, A. L. (2001). New insights into the role of the GABA-sub(A) benzodiazepine receptor in psychiatric disorder. *Brit. J. Psychiat., 179,* 390-396.

O'Brien, C. P., & McKay, J. (2002). Pharmacological treatments for substance use disorders. In P. E. Nathan & J. M. Gorman (Eds.), *A guide to treatments that work* (2nd ed). London: Oxford University Press.

O'Brien, C. P., O'Brien, T. J., Mintz, J., & Brady, J. P. (1975). Conditioning of narcotic abstinence symptoms in human subjects. *Drug. Alc. Dep., 1,* 115-123.

O'Brien, K. M., & Vincent, N. K. (2003). Psychiatric comorbidity in anorexia and bulimia nervosa: Nature, prevalence and causal relationships. *Clin. Psychol. Rev., 23*(1), 57-74.

O'Connor, S., Deeks, J. J., Hawton, K., Simkin, S., Keen, A., Altman, D. G., Philo, G., & Bulstrode, C. (1999). Effects of a drug overdose in a television drama on knowledge of specific dangers of self poisoning: Population based surveys. *Brit. Med. J., 318*(7189), 955-956.

Oei, T. P., Lim, B., & Hennessy, B. (1990). Psychological dysfunction in battle: Combat stress reactions and posttraumatic stress disorder. *Clin. Psychol. Rev., 10*(3), 355-388.

Oest, L. G., & Treffers, P. D. A. (2001). Onset, course, and outcome for anxiety disorders in children. In W. K. Silverman & P. D. A. Treffers (Eds.), *Anxiety disorders in children and adolescents: Research, assessment and intervention* (pp. 293-312). New York: Cambridge University Press.

Ouellette, S. C. (1993). Inquiries into hardiness. In L. Goldberger & S. Beznitz (Eds.), *Handbook of stress: Theoretical and clinical aspects* (2nd ed.). New York: Free Press.

Ouellette, S. C., & DiPlacido, J. (2001). Personality's role in the protection and enhancement of health: Where the research has been, where it is stuck, how it might move. In A. Baum, T. A. Revenson, & J. E. Singer (Eds.), *Handbook of health psychology.* Mahwah, NJ: Erlbaum.

Ogden, J., & Ward, E. (1995). Help-seeking behavior in sufferers of vaginismus. *Sex. Marit. Ther., 10*(1), 23-30.

Ogloff, J. R. P. (2002). Identifying and accommodating the needs of mentally ill people in gaols and prisons. *Psychiatr. Psychol. Law., 9*(1), 1-33.

Ogloff, J. R. P., Schweighofer, A., Turnbull, S. D., & Whittemore, K. (1992). Empirical research regarding the insanity defense: How much do we really know? In J. R. P. Ogloff (Ed.), *Law and psychology: The broadening of the discipline* (pp. 171-210). Durham, NC: Carolina Academic Press.

O'Hara, M. W. (2003). Postpartum depression. *Clinicians Research Digest, Supplemental Bulletin 29.*

Ohayon, M. M., & Roth, T. (2003). Place of chronic insomnia in the course of depressive and anxiety disorders. *J. Psychiatr. Res., 37*(1), 9-15.

Ohman, A., Erixon, G., & Lofberg, I. (1975). Phobias and preparedness: Phobic versus neutral pictures as continued stimuli for human autonomic responses. *J. Abnorm. Psychol., 84,* 41-45.

Ohman, A., & Soares, J. J. F. (1993). On the automatic nature of phobic fear: Conditioned electrodermal responses to masked fear-relevant stimuli. *J. Abnorm. Psychol., 102*(1), 121-132.

Olfson, M., Mechanic, D., Hansell, S., Boyer, C.A., Walkup, J., & Weiden, P. J. (2000). Predicting medication noncompliance after hospital discharge among patients with schizophrenia. *Psychiatr. Serv., 51*(2), 216-222.

Olivardia, R., Pope, H. G., Jr., & Phillips, K. A. (2000). *The Adonis complex: The secret crisis of male body.* New York: Free Press.

Ollendick, T. H., King, N. J., & Muris, P. (2002). Fears and phobias in children: Phenomenology, epidemiology, and aetiology. *Child Adol. Ment. Hlth., 7*(3), 98-106.

Olmos de Paz, T. (1990). Working-through and insight in child psychoanalysis. *Melanie Klein & Object Relations, 8*(1), 99-112.

Olmsted, M. P., Kaplan, A. S., & Rockert, W. (1994). Rate and prediction of relapse in bulimia nervosa. *Amer. J. Psychiat., 151*(5), 738-743.

Olson, L. K. (Ed.). (2002). Age through ethnic lenses: Caring for the elderly in a multicultural society. *Amer. J. Ger. Psychiat., 10*(3), 351.

O'Malley, S. S., Jaffe, A. J., Chang, G., Schottenfeld, R., Meyer, R., & Rounsaville, B. (1992). Naltrexone and coping skills therapy for alcohol dependence. *Arch. Gen. Psychiat., 49,* 881-888.

O'Malley, S. S., Jaffe, A. J., Rode, S., & Rounsaville, B. J. (1996). Experience of a "slip" among alcoholics treated with naltrexone or placebo. *Amer. J. Psychiat., 153,* 281-283.

O'Malley, S. S., Krishnan-Sarin, S., Farren, C., & O'Connor, P. G. (2000). Naltrexone-induced nausea in patients treated for alcohol dependence: Clinical predictors and evidence for opioid-mediated effects. *J. Clin. Psychopharmacol., 20*(1), 69-76.

ONDCP (Office of National Drug Control Policy) (2000). Methadone. *ONDCP Drug Policy Information Clearinghouse Fact Sheet.*

ONDCP (Office of National Drug Control Policy) (2002). Methadone. *ONDCP Drug Policy Information Clearinghouse Fact Sheet.*

Oquendo, M. A., Placidi, G. P. A., Malone, K. M., Campbell, C., Keilp, J., Brodsky, B., Kegeles, L. S., Cooper, T. B., Parsey, R. V., Van Heertum, R. L., & Mann. J. J. (2003). Positron emission tomography of regional brain metabolic responses to a serotonergic challenge and lethality of suicide attempts in major depression. *Arch. Gen. Psychiat., 60*(1), 14-22.

Orsillo, S. M., Weathers, F. W., Litz, B. T., Steinberg, H. R., et al. (1996). Current and lifetime psychiatric disorders among veterans with war zone-related posttraumatic stress disorder. *J. Nerv. Ment. Dis., 184,* 307-313.

Orzack, M. H. (1996, December 1). Interview in P. Belluck, The symptoms of Internet addiction. *New York Times,* p. 5.

Orzack, M. H. (1998). Computer addiction: What is it? *Psychiatr. Times, XV*(8).

Oslin, D. W., & Holden, R. (2002). Recognition and assessment of alcohol and drug dependence in the elderly. In A. M. Gurnack, R. Atkinson, et al. (Eds.), *Treating alcohol and drug abuse in the elderly.* New York: Springer.

Ostrove, N. M. (2001, July 24). Statement before the subcommittee on consumer affairs, foreign commerce, and tourism, Senate committee on commerce, science, and transportation. Retrieved from www.fda.gov.

Oswalt, R., & Finkelberg, S. (1995). College depression: Causes, duration, and coping. *Psychol. Rep., 77*, 858.

Otto, R. K., & Heilbrun, K. (2002). The practice of forensic psychology: A look toward the future in light of the past. *Amer. Psychologist, 57*(1), 5–18.

Overholser, J. C. (1996). The dependent personality and interpersonal problems. *J. Nerv. Ment. Dis., 184*(1), 8–16.

Overholser, J. C., & Nasser, E. H. (2000). Cognitive-behavioral treatment for generalized anxiety disorder. *Journal of Contemporary Psychotherapy, 30*(2), 149–161.

Overton, D. (1966). State-dependent learning produced by depressant and atropine-like drugs. *Psychopharmacologia, 10*, 6–31.

Owen, M. J., & O'Donovan, M. C. (2003). Schizophrenia and genetics. In R. Plomin, J. C. DeFries, et al. (Eds.), *Behavioral genetics in the postgenomic era* (pp. 463–480). Washington, DC: American Psychological Association.

Owen, M. K., Lancee, W. J., & Freeman, S. J. (1986). Psychological factors and depressive symptoms. *J. Nerv. Ment. Dis., 174*(1), 15–23.

Owen-Howard, M. (2001). Pharmacological aversion treatment of alcohol dependence. I. Production and prediction of conditioned alcohol aversion. *Amer. J. Drug Alch. Ab., 27*(3), 561–585.

Oxley, D. (2000). The school reform movement: Opportunities for community psychology. In J. Rappaport & E. Seidman (Eds.), *Handbook of community psychology.* New York: Kluwer Academic/ Plenum Publishers.

Ozer, E. J., Best, S. R., Lipsey, T. L., & Weiss, D. S. (2003). Predictors of posttraumatic stress disorder and symptoms in adults: A meta-analysis. *Psychol. Bull., 129*(1), 52–73.

Padwa, L. (1996). *Everything you pretend to know and are afraid someone will ask.* New York: Penguin.

Painot, D., Jotterand, S., Kammer, A., Fossati, M., & Golay, A. (2001). Simultaneous nutritional cognitive-behavioral therapy in obese patients. *Patient Educ. Counsel., 42*(1), 47–52.

Pajer, K. (1995). New strategies in the treatment of depression in women. *J. Clin. Psychiat., 56*(Suppl. 2), 30–37.

Palermo, G. B. (2002). Criminal profiling: The uniqueness of the killer. *Inter. J. Offend. Ther. Compar. Crimin., 46*(4), 383–385.

Palmer, C. J., Jr. (2001). African Americans, depression, and suicide risk. *J. Black Psychol., 27*(1), 100–111.

Palmer, R. L., Birchall, H., McGrain, L., & Sullivan, V. (2002). Self-help for bulimic disorders: A randomised controlled trial comparing minimal guidance with face-to-face or telephone guidance. *Brit. J. Psychiat., 181*(3), 230–235.

Palmer, S., (2002). Suicide reduction and prevention: Strategies and interventions. *Brit. J. Guid. Couns., 30*(4), 341–352.

Panati, C. (1987). *Panati's extraordinary origin of everyday things.* New York: Harper & Row.

Papazian, L. M. (2001). Literature review on the personalities and patterns of serial killers. *Diss. Abstr. Inter.: Sect. B: Sci. Eng., 61*(11-B), 6144.

Paris, J. (1991). Personality disorders, parasuicide, and culture. *Transcult. Psychiatr. Res. Rev., 28*(1), 25–39.

Paris, J. (2001). Cultural risk factors in personality disorders. In J. F. Schumaker & T. Ward (Eds.), *Cultural cognition and psychopathology.* Westport, CT: Praeger.

Paris, J. (2001). Psychosocial adversity. In W. J. Livesley (Ed.), *Handbook of personality disorders: Theory, research, and treatment* (pp. 231–241). New York: Guilford Press.

Parker, A., & Bhugra, D. (2000). Attitudes of British medical students towards male homosexuality. *Sex. Relat. Ther., 15*(2), 141–149.

Parker, G. (1983). Parental "affectionless control" as an antecedent to adult depression. *Arch. Gen. Psychiat., 48*, 956–960.

Parker, G. (1992). Early environment. In E. S. Paykel (Ed.), *Handbook of affective disorders.* New York: Guilford Press.

Parker, G., Hadzi-Pavlovic, D., Greenwald, S., & Weissman, M. (1995). Low parental care as a risk factor to lifetime depression in a community sample. *J. Affect. Disorders, 33*(3), 173–180.

Parker, S., Nichter, M., Vuckovic, N., Sims, C., & Ritenbaugh, C. (1995). Body image and weight concerns among African American and white adolescent females: Differences that make a difference. *Human Organization, 54*(2), 103–114.

Parks, G. A., & Marlatt, G. A. (1999). Relapse prevention therapy for substance-abusing offenders: A cognitive-behavioral approach. In E. L. Lanham (Ed.), *What works: Strategic solutions* (pp. 161–233). New York: American Correctional Association.

Parks, G. A., & Marlatt, G. A. (2000). Relapse prevention therapy: A cognitive-behavioral approach. *Natl. Psychol., 9*(5).

Parmelee, P. A., Katz, I. R., & Lawton, M. P. (1991). The relations of pain to depression among institutionalized aged. *J. Ger., 46*, P15–P21.

Parrott, A. C. (1999). Does cigarette smoking cause stress? *Amer. Psychologist, 54*(10), 817–820.

Parrott, A. C. (2000). Cigarette smoking does cause distress. *Amer. Psychologist, 55*(10), 1159–1160.

Parry, B. L. (1999). Postpartum depression in relation to other reproductive cycle mood changes. In L. J. Miller et al. (Eds.), *Postpartum mood disorders.* Washington, DC: American Psychiatric Press.

Pathe, M. (2002). *Surviving stalking.* New York: Cambridge University Press.

Paton, C., & Beer, D. (2001). Caffeine: The forgotten variable. *Inter. J. Psychiat. Clin. Prac., 5*(4), 231–236.

Patrick, C. J., Bradley, M. M., & Lang, P. J. (1993). Emotion in the criminal psychopath: Startle reflex modulation. *J. Abnorm. Psychol., 102*(1), 82–92.

Patrick, C. J., Cuthbert, B. N., & Lang, P. J. (1990). Emotion in the criminal psychopath: Fear imagery. *Psychophysiology, 27*(Suppl.), 55.

Patterson, C. H. (2000). *Person-centered approach and client-centered therapy: Essential readers.* Ross-on-Wye, England: PCCS Books.

Patterson, G. R. (1982). *Coercive family process.* Eugene, OR: Castalia.

Patterson, G. R. (1986). Performance models for antisocial boys. *Amer. Psychologist, 41*, 432–444.

Patterson, G. R. (1996). Some characteristics of a developmental theory for early-onset delinquency. In M. F. Lenzenweger & J. J. Haugaard (Eds.), *Frontiers of developmental psychopathology.* New York: Oxford University Press.

Patterson, T. L., Lacro, J. P., & Jeste, D. V. (1999). Abuse and misuse of medications in the elderly. *Psychiatr. Times, XVI*(4).

Patton, G. C., Selzer, R., Coffee, C., Carlin, J. B., & Wolfe, R. (1999). Onset of adolescent eating disorders: Population based cohort study over 3 years. *Brit. Med. J., 318*(7186), 765–768.

Patton, J. R., Polloway, E. A., & Smith, T. E. C. (2000). Educating students with mild mental retardation. *Focus Autism Other Dev. Disabil., 15*(2), 80–89.

Paul, G. L. (1967). The strategy of outcome research in psychotherapy. *J. Couns. Psychol., 31*, 109–118.

Paul, G. L., & Lentz, R. (1977). *Psychosocial treatment of the chronic mental patient.* Cambridge, MA: Harvard University Press.

Paul, P. (2002, March 1). Global generation gap. *Amer. Demog.* Retrieved September 15, 2002, from www.industryclick.com.

Paurohit, N., Dowd, E. T., & Cottingham, H. F. (1982). The role of verbal and nonverbal cues in the formation of first impressions of black and white counselors. *J. Couns. Psychol., 4*, 371–378.

Paxton, S. J., & Diggens, J. (1997). Avoidance coping, binge eating, and depression: An examination of the escape theory of binge eating. *Inter. J. Eat. Disorders, 22*, 83–87.

Paykel, E. S. (Ed.). (1982). *Handbook of affective disorders.* New York: Guilford Press.

Paykel, E. S., & Cooper, Z. (1992). Life events and social stress. In E. S. Paykel (Ed.), *Handbook of affective disorders.* New York: Guilford Press.

Paykel, E. S., Rao, B. M., & Taylor, C. N. (1984). Life stress and symptom pattern in outpatient depression. *Psychol. Med., 14*(3), 559–568.

Payne, A. F. (1928). *Sentence completion.* New York: New York Guidance Clinics.

Payte, T. J. (1989). Combined treatment modalities: The need for innovative approaches. Third National Forum on AIDS and Chemical Dependency of the American Society of Addiction Medicine. *J. Psychoactive Drugs, 21*(4), 431–434.

Pearson, J. L. (2000). Suicidal behavior in later life: Research update. In R. W. Maris, S. S. Canetto, et al. (Eds.), *Review of suicidology, 2000.* New York: Guilford Press.

Pedersen, N. P., & Blessing, W. W. (2001). Cutaneous vasoconstriction contributes to hyperthermia induced by 3,4-methylenedioxymethamphetamine (ecstasy) in conscious rabbits. *J. Neurosci., 21*(21), 8648–8654.

Peele, S. (1989). *Diseasing of America: Addiction treatment out of control.* Lexington, MA: Lexington Books/D.C. Heath.

Peele, S. (1992). Alcoholism, politics, and bureaucracy: The consensus against controlled-drinking therapy in America. *Addic. Behav., 17*, 49–62.

Pelham, W. E., Gnagy, E. M., Greiner, A. R., Hoza, B., Hinshaw, S. P., Swanson, J. M., Simpson, S., Shapiro, C., Bukstein, O., Baron-Myak, C., & McBurnett, K. (2000). Behavioral versus behavioral and pharmacological treatment in ADHD children attending a summer treatment program. *J. Abnorm. Child Psychol., 28*, 507–525.

Pelham, W. E., Wheeler, T., & Chronis, A. (1998). Empirically supported psychosocial treatments for attention deficit hyperactivity disorder. *J. Clin. Child Psychol., 27*, 190–205.

Pelissier, M. C., & O'Connor, K. (2004). Cognitive-behavioral treatment of trichotillomania, targeting perfectionism. *Clinical Case Studies, 3*(1), 57–69.

Pendery, M. L., Maltzman, I. M., & West, L. J. (1982). Controlled drinking by alcoholics? New findings and a reevaluation of a major affirmative study. *Science, 217*(4555), 169–175.

Penn, D. L., & Nowlin-Drummond, A. (2001). Politically correct labels and schizophrenia: A rose by any other name? *Schizo. Bull., 27*(2), 197–203.

Pennington, B. F. (2002). *The development of psychopathology: Nature and nurture.* New York: Guilford Press.

Pepe, M. (2002). Cited in Getting past the trauma. *Psychology Today, 35*(1), 54.

Perelman, M. A. (2002). FSD partner issues: Expanding sex therapy with sildenafil. *J. Sex Marital Ther., 28*(Suppl. 1), 195–204.

Perez, A., Leifman, S., & Estrada, A. (2003). Reversing the criminalization of mental illness. *Crime and Delinquency, 49*(1), 62–78.

Perkins, K., Grobe, J., DiAmico, D., Fonte, C., Wilson, A., & Stiller, R. (1996). Low-dose nicotine nasal spray use and effects during initial smoking cessation. *Exp. Clin. Psychopharmacol., 4*(2), 191–197.

Perlick, D. A., Rosenheck, R. A., Clarkin, J. F., Sirey, J., Salahi, J., Struening, E. L., & Link, B. G. (2001). Stigma as a barrier to recovery: Adverse effects of perceived stigma on social adaptation of persons diagnosed with bipolar affective disorder. *Psychiatr. Serv., 52*(12), 1627–1632.

Perlin, M. L. (2000). *The hidden prejudice: Mental disability on trial.* Washington, DC: American Psychological Association.

Perris, C. (1988). Decentralization, sectorization, and the development of alternatives to institutional care in a northern county in Sweden. In C. N. Stefanis & A. D. Rabavilis (Eds.), *Schizophrenia: Recent biosocial developments.* New York: Human Sciences Press.

Perry, J. C. (1989). Dependent personality disorder. In American Psychiatric Association (Eds.), *Treatments of psychiatric disorders: A task force report of the American Psychiatric Association.* Washington, DC: American Psychiatric Press.

Perry, J. C., & Jacobs, D. (1982). Overview: Clinical applications of the amytal interview in psychiatric emergency settings. *Amer. J. Psychiat., 139*(5), 552–559.

Perske, R. (1972). The dignity of risk and the mentally retarded. *Ment. Retard., 10,* 24–27.

Pesce, V., Seidman, S. N., & Roose, S. P. (2002). Depression, antidepressants and sexual functioning in men. *Sex. Relation. Ther., 17*(3), 281–287.

Peterson, B. D., West, J., Pincus, H. A., Kohout, J., et al. (1996). An update on human resources in mental health. In R. W. Manderscheid & M. A. Sonnenschein (Eds.), *Mental health, United States, 1996* (DHHS Publ. No. SMA 96–3098). Washington, DC: U.S. Department of Health and Human Services.

Peterson, B. S., Leckman, J. F., Arnsten, A., Anderson, G. M., Staib, L. H., Gore, J. C., Bronen, R. A., Malison, R., Scahill, L., & Cohen, D. J. (1999). Neuroanatomical circuitry. In J. F. Leckman & D. J. Cohen (Eds.), *Tourette's syndrome—Tics, obsessions compulsions: Developmental psychopathology and clinical care* (pp. 230–260). New York: John Wiley & Sons.

Peterson, C. (1993). Helpless behavior. *Behav. Res. Ther., 31*(3), 289–295.

Peterson, L., & Roberts, M. C. (1991). Treatment of children's problems. In C. E. Walker (Ed.), *Clinical psychology: Historical and research foundations.* New York: Plenum Press.

Pet Food Institute. http://www.petfoodinstitute.org.

Petrocelli, J. V. (2002). Effectiveness of group cognitive-behavioral therapy for general symptomatology: A meta-analysis. *J. Spec. Group Work, 27*(1), 92–115.

Petry, N. M. (2000). A comprehensive guide to the application of contingency management procedures in clinical settings. *Drug Alc. Dep., 58*(1–2), 9–25.

Petry, N. M. (2001). Substance abuse, pathological gambling, and impulsiveness. *Drug Alc. Dep., 63*(1), 29–38.

Pew Research Center for the People and the Press. (1997). *Trust and citizen engagement in metropolitan Philadelphia: A case study.* Washington, DC: Author.

Pfeffer, C. R. (1986). *The suicidal child.* New York: Guilford Press.

Pfeffer, C. R. (1993). Suicidal children. In A. A. Leenaars (Ed.), *Suicidology.* Northvale, NJ: Jason Aronson.

Pfeffer, C. R. (2000). Suicidal behavior in prepubertal children: From the 1980s to the new millennium. In R. W. Maris, S. S. Canetto, et al. (Eds.), *Review of suicidology, 2000.* New York: Guilford Press.

Pfeffer, C. R., Zuckerman, S., Plutchik, R., & Mizruchi, M. S. (1984). Suicidal behavior in normal school children: A comparison with child psychiatric inpatients. *J. Amer. Acad. Child Adol. Psychiat., 23,* 416–423.

Pfeifer, M. P., & Snodgrass, G. L. (1990). The continued use of retractable invalid scientific literature. *JAMA, 263*(10), 1420–1427.

Pfeiffer, S. I., & Nelson, D. D. (1992). The cutting edge in services for people with autism. *J. Autism Dev. Disorders, 22*(1), 95–105.

Phares, V. (2003). *Understanding abnormal child psychology.* Hoboken, NJ: Wiley.

Phillips, D. P. (1974). The influence of suggestion on suicide: Substantive and theoretical implications of the Werther effect. *Amer. Sociol. Rev., 39,* 340–354.

Phillips, D. P., & Ruth, T. E. (1993). Adequacy of official suicide statistics for scientific research and public policy. *Suic. Life-Threat. Behav., 23*(4), 307–319.

Phillips, K. A. (Ed.). (2001). *Somatoform and factitious disorders: Review of psychiatry,* Vol. 20. Washington, DC: American Psychiatric Association.

Phillips, K. A., & Castle, D. J. (2002). Body dysmorphic disorder. In D. J. Castle & K. A. Phillips (Eds.), *Disorders of body image.* Petersfield, England: Wrightson Biomedical Publishing, Ltd.

Phillips, K. A., & Gunderson, J. G. (1994). Personality disorders. In R. E. Hales, S. C. Yudofsky, & J. A. Talbott (Eds.), *The American Psychiatric Press textbook of psychiatry* (2nd ed.). Washington, DC: American Psychiatric Press.

Phillips, K. A., McElroy, S. L., Keck, P. E., Pope, H. G., et al. (1993). Body dysmorphic disorder: 30 cases of imagined ugliness. *Amer. J. Psychiat., 150*(2), 302–308.

Phillips, M. R., Liu, H., & Zhang, Y. (1999). Suicide and social change in China. *Cult. Med. Psychiat., 23*(1), 25–50.

Phillips, P. L., Greenson, J. N., Collett, B. R., & Gimpel, G. A. (2002). Assessing ADHD symptoms in preschool children: Use of the ADHD symptoms rating scale. *Early Ed. Dev., 13*(3), 283–299.

Piacentini, J., Rotheram-Bors, M. J., Gillis, J. R., Graae, F., et al. (1995). Demographic predictors of treatment attendance among adolescent suicide attempters. *J. Cons.. Clin. Psychiat., 63*(3), 469–473.

Pickel, K. L. (2004). When a lie becomes the truth: The effects of self-generated misinformation on eyewitness memory. *Memory, 12*(1), 14–26.

Pickover, C. A. (1999). *Strange brains and genius: The secret lives of eccentric scientists and madmen.* New York: HarperCollins/Quill.

Pierce, K., & Courchesne, E. (2001). Evidence for a cerebellar role in reduced exploration and stereotyped behavior in autism. *Biol. Psychiat., 49*(8), 655–664.

Pierce, K., & Courchesne, E. (2002). "A further support to the hypothesis of a link between serotonin, autism and the cerebellum": Reply. *Biol. Psychiat., 52*(2), 143.

Pietrofesa, J. J., et al. (1990). The mental health counselor and "duty to warn." *J. Ment. Hlth Couns., 12*(2), 129–137.

Pike, K. M., & Rodin, J. (1991). Mothers, daughters, and disordered eating. *J. Abnorm. Psychol., 100*(2), 198–204.

Pillard, R. C., & Bailey, J. M. (1995). A biologic perspective on sexual orientation. Special issue: Clinical sexuality. *Psychiatr. Clin. N. Amer., 18*(1), 71–84.

Pillemer, K., & Suitor, J. J. (2002). Peer support for Alzheimer's caregivers: Is it enough to make a difference? *Res. Aging, 24*(2), 171–192.

Pilling, S., Bebbington, P., Kuipers, E., Garety, P., Geddes, J., Orbach, G., & Morgan, C. (2002). Psychological treatments in schizophrenia: I. Meta-analysis of family intervention and cognitive behaviour therapy. *Psychol. Med., 32*(5), 763–782.

Pincus, J. H. (2001). *Base instincts: What makes killers kill?* New York: Norton.

Pinel, J. P. J., Assanand, S., & Lehman, D. R. (2000). Hunger, eating, and ill health. *Amer. Psychologist, 55*(10), 1105–1116.

Pines, W. L. (1999). A history and perspective on direct-to-consumer promotion. *Food Drug Law J., 54,* 489–518.

Pinhas, L., Toner, B. B., Ali, A., Garfinkel, P. E., & Stuckless, N. (1999). The effects of the ideal of female beauty on mood and body satisfaction. *Inter. J. Eat. Disorders, 25*(2), 223–226.

Pinkston, E. M., & Linsk, N. L. (1984). Behavioral family intervention with the impaired elderly. *Gerontologist, 24,* 576–583.

Piper, W. E., & Joyce, A. S. (2001). Psychosocial treatment outcome. In W. J. Livesley (Ed.), *Handbook of personality disorders: Theory, research, and treatment* (pp. 323–343). New York: Guilford Press.

Piper, W. E., Joyce, A. S., McCallum, M., Axim, H. F., & Ogrodniczuk, J. S. (2002). *Interpretive and supportive psychotherapies: Matching therapy and patient personality.* Washington, DC: American Psychological Association.

Pirke, K. M., Kellner, M., Philipp, E., Laessle, R., Krieg, J. C., & Fichter, M. M. (1992). Plasma norepinephrine after a standardized test meal in acute and remitted patients with anorexia nervosa and in healthy controls. *Biol. Psychiat., 31,* 1074–1077.

Pirkis, J., & Burgess, P. (1998). Suicide and recency of health care contacts: A systematic review. *Brit. J. Psychiat., 173,* 462–474.

Pitschel-Waltz, G., Leucht, S., Baeuml, J., Kissling, W., & Engel, R. R. (2001). The effect of family interventions on relapse and rehospitalization in schizophrenia—A meta-analysis. *Schizo. Bull., 27*(1), 73–92.

Pithers, W. D., & Cumming, G. F. (1989). Can relapses be prevented? Initial outcome data for the Vermont Treatment Program for Sexual Aggressors. In D. R. Laws (Ed.), *Relapse prevention with sex offenders.* New York: Guilford Press.

Piven, J., Palmer, P., Jacobi, D., Childress, D., & Arndt, S. (1997). Broader autism phenotype: Evidence from a family history study of multiple-incidence autism families. *Amer. J. Psychiat., 154*(2), 185–190.

Plante, T. G. (1999). *Contemporary clinical psychology.* New York: Wiley.

Pless, M., & Carlsson, M. (2000). Effects of motor skill intervention on developmental coordination disorder: A meta-analysis. *Adap. Phys. Activ. Q., 17*(4), 381–401.

Plomin, R., DeFries, J. C., McClearn, G. E., & Rutter, M. (1997). *Behavioral genetics: A primer* (3rd ed.). New York: W. H. Freeman.

Plunkett, M. C. B., & Southall, D. P. (2001). The presentation and natural history of Munchausen syndrome by proxy. In G. Adshead & D. Brooke (Eds.), *Munchausen's syndrome by proxy: Current is-*

sues in assessment, treatment and research (pp. 77–88). London: Imperial College Press.

Polk, W. M. (1983). Treatment of exhibitionism in a 38-year-old male by hypnotically assisted covert sensitization. *Inter. J. Clin. Exp. Hyp., 31,* 132–138.

Pope, B. (1983). The initial interview. In C. E. Walker (Ed.), *The handbook of clinical psychology: Theory, research, and practice.* Homewood, IL: Dow Jones-Irwin.

Pope, H. G., Jr., Oliva, P. S., Hudson, J. I., Bodkin, J. A., & Amanda, A. J. (2000). "Attitudes toward DSM-IV dissociative disorders diagnoses among board-certified American psychiatrists": Reply. *Amer. J. Psychiat., 157*(7), 1181–1182.

Pope, H. G., Jr., Oliva, P. S., Hudson, J. I., Bodkin, J. A., & Gruber, A. J. (1999). Attitudes toward DSM-IV dissociative disorders diagnoses among board-certified American psychiatrists. *Amer. J. Psychiat., 156*(2), 321–323.

Pope, H. G. Jr., Olivardia, R., Gruber A., & Borowiecki, J. (1999). Evolving ideals of male body image as seen through action toys. *Inter. J. Eat. Disorders, 26*(1), 65–72.

Pope, K. S. (2000). Therapists' sexual feelings and behaviors: Research, trends, and quandaries. In L. T. Szuchman & F. Muscarella (Eds.), *Psychological perspectives on human sexuality* (pp. 603–658). New York: Wiley.

Pope, K. S., & Brown, L. S. (1996). *Recovered memories of abuse: Assessment, therapy, forensics.* Washington, DC: American Psychological Association.

Pope, K. S., & Tabachnick, B. G. (1993). Therapists' anger, hate, fear, and sexual feelings: National survey of therapist responses, client characteristics, critical events, formal complaints, and training. *Profess. Psychol.: Res. Pract., 24*(2), 142–152.

Pope, K. S., & Tabachnick, B. G. (1994). Therapists as patients: A national survey of pscyhologists' experiences, problems, and beliefs. *Profess. Psychol.: Res. Pract., 25*(3), 247–258.

Pope, K. S., Tabachnick, B. G., & Keith-Spiegel, P. (1986). Sexual attraction to clients: The human therapist and the (sometimes) inhuman training system. *Amer. Psychologist, 41*(2), 147–158.

Popenhagen, M. P., & Qualley, R. M. (1998). Adolescent suicide: Detection, intervention, and prevention. *Profess. School Couns., 1*(4), 30–36.

Popper, C. W. (1988). Disorders usually first evident in infancy, childhood, or adolescence. In J. Talbott, R. S. Hales, & S. C. Yudofsky (Eds.), *Textbook of psychiatry.* Washington, DC: American Psychiatric Press.

Poretz, M., & Sinrod, B. (1991). *Do you do it with the lights on?* New York: Ballantine Books.

PORT (Patient Outcomes Research Team) (1998). Cited in S. Barlas, Patient outcome research team study on schizophrenia offers grim indictment. *Psychiatr. Times, XV*(6).

Porter, S., Kelly, K. A., & Grame, C. J. (1993). Family treatment of spouses and children of patients with multiple personality disorder. *Bull. Menninger Clin., 57*(3), 371–379.

Post, R. M., et al. (1978). Cerebrospinal fluid norepinephrine in affective illness. *Amer. J. Psychiat., 135*(8), 907–912.

Post, R. M., Ballenger, J. C., & Goodwin, F. K. (1980). Cerebrospinal fluid studies of neurotransmitter function in manic and depressive illness. In J. H. Wood (Ed.), *The neurobiology of cerebrospinal fluid* (Vol. 1). New York: Plenum Press.

Potier, B. (2002). Researchers aim to understand school shootings. *Harvard University Gazette,* May 30, 2002.

Poulos, C. X., Le, A. D., & Parker, J. L. (1995). Impulsivity predicts individual susceptibility to high levels of alcohol self-administration. *Behav. Pharmacol., 6*(8), 810–814.

Poulton, R., & Milne, B. J. (2002). Dunedin Multidisciplinary Health and Development Study. *Behav. Res. Ther., 40,* 1191–1197.

Powell, L. H., Shahabi, L., & Thoresen, C. E. (2003). Religion and spirituality: Linkages to physical health. *Amer. Psychologist, 58*(1), 36–52.

Powers, D. V., Gallagher-Thompson, D., & Kraemer, H. C. (2002). Coping and depression in Alzheimer's caregivers: Longitudinal evidence of stability. *J. Ger. B Psychol. Sci. Soc. Sci., 57* B(3), 205–211.

Powers, S. W., Mitchell, M. J., Byars, K. C., Bentti, A. L., LeCates, S. L., & Hershey, A. D. (2001). A pilot study of one-session biofeedback training in pediatric headache. *Neurology, 56*(1), 133.

Pratt, S., & Mueser, K.T. (2002). Social skills training for schizophrenia. In S. G. Hofmann & M. C. Tompson (Eds.), *Treating chronic and severe mental disorders: A handbook of empirically supported interventions.* New York: Guilford Press.

Prendergast, P. J. (1995). Integration of psychiatric rehabilitation in the long-term management of schizophrenia. *Canad. J. Psychiat., 40*(3, Suppl. 1), S18–S21.

Pretzer, J. L., Beck, A. T., & Newman, C. F. (2002). Stress and stress management: A cognitive view. In R. L. Leahy, & E. T. Dowd (Eds.), *Clinical advances in cognitive psychotherapy: Theory and application* (pp. 29–61). New York: Springer.

Preuss, U. W., Schuckit, M. A., Smith, T. L., Danko, G. P., Bucholz, K. K., Hesselbrock, M. N., et al. (2003). Predictors and correlates of suicide attempts over 5 years in 1,237 alcohol-dependent men and women. *Amer. J. Psychiat., 160*(1), 56–63.

Prien, R. F., Caffey, E. M., Jr., & Klett, C. J. (1974). Factors associated with treatment success in lithium carbonate prophylaxis. *Arch. Gen. Psychiat., 31,* 189–192.

Primac, D. W. (1993). Measuring change in a brief therapy of a compulsive personality. *Psychol. Rep., 72*(1), 309–310.

Princeton Survey Research Associates. (1996). *Healthy steps for young children: Survey of parents.* Princeton: Author.

Prochaska, J. O. (1984). *Systems of psychotherapy.* Chicago: Dorsey.

Prochaska, J. O., & Norcross, J. C. (1994). *Systems of psychotherapy: A transtheoretical analysis* (3rd ed.). Pacific Grove, CA: Brooks/Cole.

Prochaska, J. O., & Norcross, J. C. (1999). *Systems of psychotherapy: A transtheoretical analysis* (4th ed.). Pacific Grove, CA: Brooks/Cole.

Prochaska, J. O., & Norcross, J. C. (2003). *Systems of psychotherapy: A transtheoretical analysis* (5th ed.). Pacific Grove, CA: Brooks/Cole.

Provini, C., Everett, J. R., & Pfeffer, C. R. (2000). Adults mourning suicide: Self-reported concerns about bereavement, needs for assistance, and help-seeking behavior. *Death Stud., 24*(1), 1–19.

Prowthrow-Stith, D., & Spivak, H. (1999) America's tragedy. *Psychiatr. Times, 16*(6).

Prusiner, S. B. (1991). Molecular biology of prion diseases. *Science, 252,* 1515–1522.

Prusiner, S. B. (1995, January). The prion diseases. *Scientif. Amer.,* pp. 48–57.

Pueschel, S. M., & Thuline, H. C. (1991). Chromosome disorders. In J. L. Matson & J. A. Mulick (Eds.), *Handbook of mental retardation.* New York: Pergamon.

Pugh, L. A. (2003). *The psychological effects of the September 11th terrorist attacks on individuals with prior exposure to traumatic events.* In press.

Pukall, C. F., Reissing, E. D., Binik, Y. M., Khalife, S., & Abbott, F. V. (2000). New clinical and research perspectives on the sexual pain disorders. *J. Sex Educ. Ther., 25*(1), 36–44.

Pulver, A. E. (2000). Search for schizophrenia susceptibility genes. *Biol. Psychiat., 47*(3), 221–230.

Pumariega, A., Gustavson, C. R., Gustavson, J. C., Stone Mkotes, P., & Ayers, S. (1994). Eating attitudes in African-American women: The essence eating disorders survey. *Eat. Disord.: J. Treat. Prev., 2*(1), 5–16.

Putnam, F. W. (1984). The psychophysiologic investigation of multiple personality disorder. *Psychiatr. Clin. N. Amer., 7,* 31–40.

Putnam, F. W. (1985). Multiple personality disorder. *Med. Aspects Human Sex., 19*(6), 59–74.

Putnam, F. W. (1988). The switch process in multiple personality disorder and other state-change disorders.

Putnam, F. W. (1992). Are alter personalities fragments of figments? *Psychoanal. Inq., 12*(1), 95–111.

Putnam, F. W. (2000). Dissocative disorders. In A. J. Sameroff, M. Lewis et al. (Eds.), *Handbook of developmental psychopathology* (2nd ed., pp. 739–754). New York: Kluwer Academic/Plenum Press.

Putnam, F. W., Zahn, T. P., & Post, R. M. (1990). Differential autonomic nervous system activity in multiple personality disorder. *J. Psychiatr. Res., 31*(3), 251–260.

Pyle, R. L. (1999). Dynamic psychotherapy. In M. Hersen & A. S. Bellack (Eds.), *Handbook of comparative interventions for adult disorders* (2nd ed.). New York: Wiley.

Quiñones-Jenab, V. (Ed.) (2001). *The biological basis of cocaine addiction.* New York: New York Academy of Sciences, Vol. 937.

Quinsey, V. L., & Earls, G. M. (1990). The modificator of sexual preferences. In W. L. Marshall, D. R. Laws, & H. E. Barbaree (Eds.), *Handbook of sexual assault.* New York: Plenum.

Quiroga, M. (2000). Cannabis: Efectos nocivos sobre la salud fisica [Cannabis: Harmful effects on health]. *Adicciones, 12*(Suppl. 2), 177–183.

Raboch, J., & Raboch, J. (1992). Infrequent orgasm in women. *J. Sex Marital Ther., 18*(2), 114–120.

Rachman, S. (1966). Sexual fetishism: An experimental analog. *Psychol. Rec., 18,* 25–27.

Radden, J. (2002). Psychiatric ethics. *Bioethics, 16*(5), 397–411.

Rahey, L., & Craig, W. M. (2002). Evaluation of an ecological program to reduce bullying in schools. *Canad. J. Couns., 36*(4), 281–296.

Raine, A., Benishay, D., Lencz, T., & Scarpa, A. (1997). Abnormal orienting in schizotypal personality disorder. *Schizo. Bull., 23*(1), 75–82.

Raine, A., Lencz, T., Bihrle, S., LaCasse, L., & Colletti, P. (2000). Reduced prefrontal gray matter volume and reduced autonomic activity in antisocial personality disorder. *Arch. Gen. Psychiat., 57*(2), 119–127.

Ralston, P. A. (1991). Senior centers and minority elders: A critical review. *Gerontologist, 31,* 325–331.

Ramey, C. T., Ramey, S. L., Lanzi, R. G., & Cotton, J. N. (2002). Early educational interventions for high-risk children: How center-based treatment can augment and improve parenting effectiveness. In J. G. Borkowski, S. L. Ramey, et al., *Parenting and the child's world: Influences on academic, intellectual, and social-emotional development. Monographs in parenting* (pp. 125–140) Mahwah, NJ: Erlbaum.

Rand, C. S., & Kuldau, J. M. (1991). Restrained eating (weight concerns) in the general population and among students. *Inter. J. Eat. Disorders, 10*(6), 699–708.

Ranen, N. G. (2002). Psychiatric management of Huntington's disease. *Psychiatr. Ann., 32*(2), 105–110.

Rapee, R. M. (2003). The influence of comorbidity on treatment outcome for children and adolescents with anxiety disorders. *Behav. Res. Ther., 41*(1), 105–112.

Rapkin, A. (2003). A review of treatment of premenstrual syndrome & premenstrual dysphoric disorder. *Psychoneuroendocrinology, 28*(Suppl 3), 39–53.

Rapoport, J. L. (1989, March). The biology of obsessions and compulsions. *Scientif. Amer.*, pp. 82–89.

Rapoport, J. L. (1991). Recent advances in obsessive-compulsive disorder. *Neuropsychopharmacology, 5*(1), 1–10.

Raskin, D. C., & Honts, C. R. (2002). The comparison question test. In M. Kleiner (Ed.), *The handbook of polygraph testing*. San Diego, CA: Academic.

Raskin, M., Peeke, H. V. S., Dickman, W., & Pinkster, H. (1982). Panic and generalized anxiety disorders: Developmental antecedents and precipitants. *Arch. Gen. Psychiat., 39*, 687–689.

Rathbone, J. (2001). *Anatomy of masochism*. New York: Kluwer Academic/Plenum.

Ray, O., & Ksir, C. (1993). *Drugs, society, and human behavior*. St. Louis: Mosby.

Raymond, N. C., Coleman, E., Ohlerking, F., Christenson, G. A., & Miner, M. (1999). Psychiatric comorbidity in pedophilic sex offenders. *Amer. J. Psychiat., 156*(5), 786–788.

Raymond, N., Robinson, B., Kraft, C., Rittberg, B., & Coleman, E. (2001). Treatment of pedophilia with leuprolide acetate: A case study. *J. Psychol. Human Sex., 13* (3–4), 79–88.

Raymont, V. (2001). Suicide in schizophrenia—how can research influence training and clinical practice? *Psychiatr. Bull., 25*(2), 46–50.

Read, J., et al. (2001). Assessing suicidality in adults: Integrating childhood trauma as a major risk factor. *Profess. Psychol.: Res. Pract., 32*, 367–372.

Rebert, W. M., Stanton, A. L., & Schwartz, R. M. (1991). Influence of personality attributes and daily moods on bulimic eating patterns. *Addic. Behav., 16*(6), 497–505.

Redfearn, P. J., Agrawakm N., & Mair, L. H. (1998). An association between the regular use of 3,4-methylenedioxy-methamphetamine (ecstasy) and excessive wear of the teeth. *Addiction, 93*(5), 745–748.

Redick, R. W., Witkin, M. J., Atay, J. E., & Manderscheid, R. W. (1992). Specialty mental health system characteristics. In R. W. Manderscheid & M. A. Sonnenschein (Eds.), *Mental health, United States, 1992*. Washington, DC: U. S. Department of Health and Human Services.

Redmond, D. E. (1977). Alterations in the function of the nucleus locus coeruleus: A possible model for studies of anxiety. In I. Hanin & E. Usdin (Eds.), *Animal models in psychiatry and neurology*. New York: Pergamon Press.

Redmond, D. E. (1979). New and old evidence for the involvement of a brain norepinephrine system in anxiety. In W. E. Fann, I. Karacan, A. D. Pokorny, & R. L. Williams (Eds.), *Phenomenology and treatment of anxiety*. New York: Spectrum.

Redmond, D. E. (1981). Clonidine and the primate locus coeruleus: Evidence suggesting anxiolytic and anti-withdrawal effects. In H. Lal & S. Fielding (Eds.), *Psychopharmacology of clonidine*. New York: Alan R. Liss.

Reeb, R. N. (2000). Classification and diagnosis of psychopathology: Conceptual foundations. *J. Psychol. Pract., 6*(1), 3–18.

Rees, W. D., & Lutkin, S. G. (1967). Mortality of bereavement. *Brit. Med. J., 4*, 13–16.

Reese, S. (1998, January). Get it together, do-gooders. *Am. Demogr.*

Regehr, C., Cadell, S., & Jansen, K. (1999). Perceptions of control and long-term recovery from rape. *Amer. J. Orthopsychiat., 69*(1), 110–115.

Regier, D. A., Narrow, W. E., Rae, D. S., Manderscheid, R. W., Locke, B. Z., & Goodwin, F. K. (1993). The de facto US Mental and Addictive Disorders Service System: Epidemiologic Catchment Area prospective 1–year prevalence rates of disorders in services. *Arch. Gen. Psychiat., 50*, 85–94.

Reich, J. H. (1990). Comparisons of males and females with DSM-III dependent personality disorder. *Psychiat. Res., 33*(2), 207–214.

Reich, J. H. (2000). The relationship of social phobia to avoidant personality disorder: A proposal to reclassify avoidant personality disorder based on clinical empirical findings. *Eur. Psychiat., 15*(3), 151–159.

Reid, R., & Lininger, T. (1993). Sexual pain disorders in the female. In W. O'Donohue & J. Geer (Eds.), *Handbook of sexual dysfunctions*. Boston: Allyn & Bacon.

Reid, S. (1998). Suicide in schizophrenia: A review of the literature. *J. Ment. Hlth. UK, 7*(4), 345–353.

Reid, W. H. (2002). Sexual predator evaluations and commitments. *J. Psychiatr. Prac., 8*(5), 320–324.

Reid, W. H., & Burke, W. J. (1989). Antisocial personality disorder. In American Psychiatric Association (Eds.), *Treatments of psychiatric disorders: A task force report of the American Psychiatric Association.* Washington, DC: American Psychiatric Press.

Reisch, T., Schlatter, P., & Tschacher, W. (1999). Efficacy of crisis intervention. *Crisis, 20*(2), 78–85.

Reissing, E. D., Binik, Y. M., Khalife, S., Cohen, D., & Amsel, R. (2003). Etiological correlates of vaginismus: Sexual and physical abuse, sexual knowledge, sexual self-schema and relationship adjustment. *J. Sex Marital Ther., 29*(1), 47–59.

Reitan, R. M., & Wolfson, D. (1996). Theoretical, methodological, and validational bases of the Halstead-Reitan neuropsychological test battery. In I. Grant & K. M. Adams (Eds.), *Neuropsychological assessment of neuropsychiatric disorders* (2nd ed., pp. 3–42). New York: Oxford University Press.

Reitan, R. M., & Wolfson, D. (2001). The Halstad-Reitan Neuropsychological Test Battery: Research findings and clinical application. In A. S. Kaufman & N. L. Kaufman (Eds.), *Specific learning disabilities and difficulties in children and adolescents: Psychological assessment and evaluation* (pp. 309–346). New York: Cambridge University Press.

Reneman, L., Booij, J., Schmand, B., van den Brink, W., & Gunning, B. (2000). Memory disturbances in "ecstasy" users are correlated with an altered brain serotonin neurotransmission. *Psychopharmacology, 148*(3), 322–324.

Resick, P. A. (2001). *Stress and trauma*. Philadelphia: Taylor & Francis.

Resick, P. A., & Calhoun, K. S. (2001). Posttraumatic stress disorder. In D. H. Barlow (Ed.), *Clinical handbook of psychological disorders: A step-by-step treatment manual* (3rd ed.). New York: Guilford Press.

Resnick, P. J., & Harris, M. R. (2002). Retrospective assessment of malingering in insanity defense cases. In R. I. Simon & D.W. Schuman (Eds.), *Retrospective assessment of mental states in litigation: Predicting the past* (pp. 101–134). Washington, DC: American Psychiatric Publishing.

Ressler, R. K., & Schactman, T. (1992). *Whoever fights monsters.* New York: St. Martin's Press.

Reuters (2003). Man dies after winning vodka-drinking contest. November 19, 2003.

Reynolds, A. J. (1998, January). Resilience among black urban youth: Prevalence, intervention effects, and mechanisms of influence. *Amer. J. Orthopsychiat., 68*(1), 84–100.

Rice, D. P., & Miller, L. S. (1998). Health economics and cost implications of anxiety and other mental disorders in the United States. *Brit. J. Psychiat., 173*(Suppl. 34), 4–9.

Rice, G., Anderson, C., Risch, N., & Ebers, G. (1999). Male homosexuality: Absence of linkage to microsatellite markers at Xq28. *Science, 284* (5414), 665–667.

Rich, C. L., Dhossche, D. M., Ghani, S., & Isacsson, G. (1998). Suicide methods and presence of intoxicating abusable substances: Some clinical and public health implications. *Ann. Clin. Psychiat., 10*(4), 169–175.

Richards, P. S., & Bergin, A. E. (Eds). (2000). Toward religious and spiritual competency for mental health professionals. In P. S. Richards & A. E. Bergin, *Handbook of psychotherapy and religious diversity*. Washington, DC: APA.

Richards, P. S., & Bergin, A. E. (Eds.). (2004). *Casebook for a spiritual strategy in counseling and psychotherapy*. Washington, DC: American Psychological Association.

Richardson, J. T. E. (2002). The aetiology, assessment, and rehabilitation of memory impairment following mild head injury. *Tidsskrift for Norsk Psykologforening, 39*(8), 700–706.

Richman, N. E., & Sokolove, R. L. (1992). The experience of aloneness, object representation, and evocative memory in borderline and neurotic patients. *Psychoanal. Psychiat., 9*(1), 77–91.

Rickels, K., & Rynn, M. (2002). Pharmacotherapy of generalized anxiety disorder. *J. Clin. Psychiat., 63*(Suppl 14), 9–16.

Ridout, N., Astell, A. J., Reid, I. C., Glen, T., & O'Carroll, R. E. (2003). Memory bias for emotional facial expressions in major depression. *Cog. Emot., 17*(1), 101–122.

Rieber, R. W. (2002). The duality of the brain and the multiplicity of minds: Can you have it both ways? *Hist. Psychiat. 13*(49, pt1), 3–18.

Riess, H. (2002). Integrative time-limited group therapy for bulimia nervosa. *Inter. J. Group Psychother., 52*(1), 1–26.

Rigby, K. (2002). Bullying in childhood. In P. K. Smith & C. H. Hart (Eds.), *Blackwell handbook of childhood social development* (pp. 549–568). Malden, MA: Blackwell.

Rihmer, Z., Rutz, W., & Pihlgren, H. (1995). Depression and suicide on Gotland. An intensive study of all suicides before and after a depression-training programme for general practitioners. *J. Affect. Disorders, 35*, 147–152.

Ritchie, K., Kildea, D., & Robine, J. M. (1992). The relationship between age and the prevalence of senile dementia: A meta-analysis of recent data. *Inter. J. Epidemiol., 21*, 763–769.

Ritter, A. (2001). Buprenorphine for the treatment of heroin dependence. *Drug Alc. Rev., 20*(1), 5–7.

Rivas-Vazquez, R. A. (2001). Antidepressants as first-line agents in the current pharmacotherapy of anxiety disorders. *Profess. Psychol.: Res. Pract., 32*(1), 101–104.

Rivas-Vazquez, R. A. (2001). Reboxetine: Refocusing on the role of norepinephrine in the treatment of depression. *Profess. Psychol.: Res. Pract., 32*(2), 211–215.

Roach, C. N., & Gross, A. M. (2002). Conduct disorder. In J. Hersen (Ed.), *Clinical behavior therapy: Adults and children* (pp. 383–399). New York: Wiley.

Roan, S. (1995, September 19) A poor state of mind. *Los Angeles Times*, pp. E1, E7.

Roazen, P. (1992). The rise and fall of Bruno Bettelheim. *Psychohist. Rev., 20*(3), 221–250.

Robb, A. S., & Dadson, M. J. (2002). Eating disorders in males. *Child Adol. Psychiat. Clin. N. Amer., 11*(2), 399–418.

Robb, A. S., Silber, T. J., Orrell-Valente, J. K., Valadez-Meltzer, A., Ellis, N., Dadson, M., & Chatoor, I. (2002). Supplemental nocturnal nasogastic refeeding for better short-term outcome in hospitalized adolescent girls with anorexia nervosa. *Amer. J. Psychiat., 159*(8), 1347–1353.

Roberts, C. F., Golding, S. L., & Fincham, F. D. (1987). Implicit theories of criminal responsibility. *Law Human Behav., 11*(3), 297–232.

Robin, A. L. (2003). Behavioral family systems: Therapy for adolescents with anorexia nervosa. In A. E. Kazdin & J. R. Weisz (Eds.), *Evidence-based psychotherapies for children and adolescents*. New York: Guilford Press.

Robin, A. L., Siegel, P. T., & Moye, A. (1995). Family versus individual therapy for anorexia: Impact on family conflict. Topical Section: Treatment and therapeutic processes. *Inter. J. Eat. Disorders, 17*(4), 313–322.

Robins, L. N., Locke, B. Z., & Regier, D. A. (1991). An overview of psychiatric disorders in America. In L. N. Robins & D. A. Regier (Eds.), *Psychiatric disorders in America: The Epidemiological Catchment Area Study*. New York: Free Press.

Robinson, D. J. (2000). *The mental status exam—explained*. Port Huron, MI: Rapid Psychler Press.

Robinson, M. S., & Alloy, L. B. (2003). Negative cognitive styles and stress-reactive rumination interact to predict depression: A prospective study. *Cog. Ther. Res., 27*(3), 275–292.

Robison, L. M., Sclar, D. A., Skaer, T. L., & Galin, R. S. (1999). National trends in the prevalence of attention-deficit/hyperactivity disorder and the prescribing of methylphenidate among school children: 1990–1995. *Clin. Pediatr., 38*(4), 209–217.

Roche, T. (2002, January 20). The Yates odyssey. *TIME.com: Nation.* Retrieved February 24, 2002, from www.time.com/time/nation

Rodgers, J. (2000). Cognitive performance amongst recreational users of "ecstasy". *Psychopharmacology (Berl), 15*(1), 19–24.

Rodier, P. M. (2000, February). The early origins of autism. *Scientif. Amer.*, pp. 56–63.

Rodin, J. (1992). Sick of worrying about the way you look? Read this. *Psychol. Today, 25*(1), 56–60.

Roelofs, K., Hoogduin, K. A. L., Keijsers, G. P. J., Naering, G. W. B., Moene, F. C., & Sandijck, P. (2002). Hypnotic susceptibility in patients with conversion disorder. *J. Abnorm. Psychol., 111*(2), 390–395.

Roemer, L., Orsillo, S. M., & Barlow, D. H. (2002). Generalized anxiety disorder. In D. H. Barlow (Ed.), *Anxiety and its disorders: The nature and treatment of anxiety and panic* (2nd ed., pp. 477–515). New York: Guilford Press.

Roehrich, L., & Kinder, B. N. (1991). Alcohol expectancies and male sexuality: Review and implications for sex therapy. *J. Sex Marital Ther., 17*(1), 45–54.

Roesch, R. (1991). *The encyclopedia of depression*. New York: Facts on File.

Roesch, R., Zapf, P. A., Golding, S. L., & Skeem, J. L. (1999). Defining and assessing competence to stand trial. In A. K. Hess, I. B. Weiner, et al. (Eds.), *The handbook of forensic psychology* (2nd ed.). New York: Wiley.

Roesler, T. A., & McKenzie, N. (1994). Effects of childhood trauma on psychological functioning of adults sexually abused as children. *J. Nerv. Ment. Dis., 182*(3), 145–150.

Rogers, C. R. (1951). *Client-centered therapy*. Boston: Houghton Mifflin.

Rogers, C. R. (1957). The necessary and sufficient conditions of therapeutic personality change. *J. Cons. Clin. Psychol., 121*, 95–203.

Rogers, C. R. (1987). Rogers, Kohut, and Erickson: A personal perspective on some similarities and differences. In J. K. Zeig (Ed.), *The evolution of psychotherapy*. New York: Brunner/Mazel.

Rogers, C. R. (1992). The necessary and sufficient conditions of therapeutic personality change. *J. Cons. Clin. Psychol., 60*(6), 827–832.

Rogers, C. R. (2000). Interview with Carl Rogers on the use of the self in therapy. In M. Baldwin (Ed.), *The use of self in therapy* (2nd ed., pp. 29–38). Binghamton, NY: Haworth.

Rogers, R., & Shuman, D. W. (2000). *Conducting insanity evaluations* (2nd ed.) New York: Guilford Press.

Roitman, S. E. L., Cornblatt, B. A., Bergman, A., Obuchowski, M., et al. (1997). Attention functioning in schizotypal personality disorder. *Amer. J. Psychiat., 154*(5), 655–660.

Roitman, S. E. L., Mitropoulou, V., Keefe, R. S. E., Silverman, J. M., Serby, M., Harvey, P. D., Reynolds, D. A., Mohs, R. C., & Siever, L. J. (2000). Visuospatial working memory in schizotypal personality disorder patients. *Schizo. Res., 41*(3), 447–455.

Rokke, P. D., & Rehm, L. P. (2001). Self-management therapies. In K. S. Dobson (Ed.), *Handbook of cognitive-behavioral therapies* (2nd ed., pp. 173–210). New York: Guilford Press.

Rollin, H. R. (1980). *Coping with schizophrenia*. London: Burnett.

Roloff, P. (2001). The nurse's role in a pilot program using a modified cognitive-behavioral approach. In B. Kinoy (Ed.), *Eating disorders: New directions in treatment and recovery* (2nd ed., pp. 127–132). New York: Columbia University Press.

Romano, E., & De Luca, R. V. (2001). Male sexual abuse: A review of effects, abuse characteristics, and links with later psychological functioning. *Aggress. Viol. Behav., 6*(1), 55–78.

Ron, M. (2001). Explaining the unexplained: Understanding hysteria. *Brain, 124*(6), 1065–1066.

Roozen, H. D., deKan, R., van den Brink, W., Kerkhof, A. J. F. M., & Geerlings, P. J. (2002). Dangers involved in rapid opioid detoxification while using opioid antagonists: Dehydration and renal failure. *Addiction, 97*(8), 1071–1073.

Roper Reports. (1998, February). Marriage: The art of compromise. *Am. Demogr.*

Rosen, E. F., Anthony, D. L., Booker, K. M., Brown, T. L., et al. (1991). A comparison of eating disorder scores among African American and white college females. *Bull. Psychon. Soc., 29*(1), 65–66.

Rosen, J. C., & Leitenberg, H. (1982). Bulimia nervosa: Treatment with exposure and response prevention. *Behav. Ther., 13*(1), 117–124.

Rosen, J. C., & Leitenberg, H. (1985). Exposure plus response prevention treatment of bulimia. In D. M. Garner & P. E. Garfinkel (Eds.), *Handbook of psychotherapy for anorexia nervosa and bulimia*. New York: Guilford Press.

Rosen, J. C., Orosan, P., & Reiter, J. (1995). Cognitive behavior therapy for negative body image in obese women. *Behav. Ther., 26*, 25–42.

Rosen, L. W., & Hough, D. O. (1988). Pathogenic weight-control behaviors of female college gymnasts. *Physician Sports Med., 16*(9), 141–144.

Rosen, L. W., McKeag, D. B., Hough, D. O., & Curley, V. (1986). Pathogenic weight-control behavior in female athletes. *The Physician and Sports Medicine, 14*(1), 79–86.

Rosen, R. C. (2000). Medical and psychological interventions for erectile dysfunction: Toward a combined treatment approach. In S. R. Leiblum & R. C. Rosen (Eds.), *Principles and practice of sex therapy* (3rd ed., pp. 276–304). New York: Guilford Press.

Rosen, R. C., & Leiblum, S. R. (1995). Hypoactive sexual desire (Special issue: Clinical sexuality). *Psychiatr. Clin. N. Amer., 18*(1), 107–121.

Rosen, R. C., Leiblum, S. R., & Spector, I. (1994). Psychologically based treatment for male erectile disorder: A cognitive-interpersonal model. *J. Sex Marital Ther., 20*, 78–85.

Rosen, R. C., & Rosen, L. R. (1981). *Human sexuality*. New York: Knopf.

Rosen, R. C., Taylor, J. F., Leiblum, S. R., & Bachmann, G. A. (1993). Prevalence of sexual dysfunction in women: Results of a survey study of 329 women in an outpatient gynecological clinic. *J. Sex Marital Ther., 19*, 171–188.

Rosenbaum, M. (1980). The role of the term schizophrenia in the decline of diagnoses of multiple personality. *Arch. Gen. Psychiat., 37*(12), 1383–1385.

Rosenberg, H. (1993). Prediction of controlled drinking by alcoholics and problem drinkers. *Psychol. Bull., 113*(1), 129–139.

Rosenfeld, M. (1998, November 22). Van Gogh's madness: Long after the painter's death, the diagnosis debate lives on. *Washington Post*, p. G1.

Rosenhan, D. L. (1973). On being sane in insane places. *Science, 179*(4070), 250–258.

Rosenthal, N. E., & Blehar, M. C. (Eds.). (1989). *Seasonal affective disorders and phototherapy*. New York: Guilford Press.

Rosenthal, R. (1966). *Experimenter effects in behavioral research*. New York: Appleton-Century-Crofts.

Rosik, C. H. (2003). Critical issues in the dissociative disorders field: Six perspectives from religiously sensitive practitioners. *J. Psychol. Theol., 31*(2), 113–128.

Ross, A. O. (1981). *Child behavior therapy: Principles, procedures and empirical basis*. New York: Wiley.

Ross, C. A., & Gahan, P. (1988). Techniques in the treatment of multiple personality disorder. *Amer. J. Psychother., 42*(1), 40–52.

Ross, C. A., Miller, S. D., Bjornson, L., Reagor, P., Fraser, G. A., & Anderson, G. (1991). Abuse histories in 102 cases of multiple personality disorder. *Canad. J. Psychiat., 36*, 97–101.

Ross, C. A., Miller, S. D., Reagor, P., & Bjornson, L., et al. (1990). Structured interview data on 102 cases of multiple personality disorder from four centers. *Amer. J. Psychiat., 147*(5), 596–601.

Ross, C. A., Norton, G. R., & Wozney, K. (1989). Multiple personality disorder: An analysis of 236 cases. *Canad. J. Psychiat., 34*(5), 413–418.

Rosselli, M., & Ardila, A. (1996). Cognitive effects of cocaine and polydrug abuse. *J. Clin. Exp. Neuropsychol., 18*(1), 122–135.

Rosser, S., Issakidis, C., & Peters, L. (2003). Perfectionism and social phobia: Relationship between the constructs and impact on cognitive behavior therapy. *Cog. Ther. Res., 27*(2), 143–151.

Rossow, I., & Amundsen, A. (1995). Alcohol abuse and suicide: A 40-year prospective study of Norwegian conscripts. *Addiction, 90*(5), 685–691.

Rossow, I., & Lauritzen, G. (2001). Shattered childhood: A key issue in suicidal behavior among drug addicts? *Addiction, 96*(2), 227–240.

Rothbaum, B. O., Foa, E. B., Riggs, D. S., Murdock, T., & Walsh, W. (1992). A prospective examination of posttraumatic stress disorder in rape victims. *J. Traum. Stress, 5*(3), 455–475.

Rothblum, E. D. (1992). The stigma of women's weight: Social and economic realities. *Feminism Psychol., 2*(1), 61–73.

Rotter, M., Way, B., Steinbacher, M., Sawyer, D., & Smith, H. (2002). Personality disorders in prison: Aren't they all antisocial? *Psychiatr. Quart., 73*(4), 337–349.

Rowa, K., Kerig, P. K., & Geller, J. (2001). The family and anorexia nervosa: Examining parent-child boundary problems. *Eur. Eat. Disord. Rev., 9*(2), 97–114.

Rowland, A. S., Lesesne, C. A., & Abramowitz, A. J. (2002). The epidemiology of attention-deficit/hyperactivity disorder (ADHD): A public health view. *Ment. Retard. Dev. Disabil. Res. Rev. 8*(3), 162–170.

Rowland, D. L., & Burnett, A. L. (2000). Pharmacology in the treatment of male sexual dysfunction. *J. Sex Res., 37*, 226–245.

Rowlands, P. (1995). Schizophrenia and sexuality. *J. Sex Marital Ther., 10*(1), 47–61.

Roy, A. (1992). Genetics, biology, and suicide in the family. In R. W. Maris, A. L. Berman, et al. (Eds.), *Assessment and prediction of suicide* (pp. xxii, 697). New York: Guilford Press.

Rozin, P., & Stoess, C. (1993). Is there a general tendency to become addicted? *Addic. Behav., 18*, 81–87.

Rubinstein, S., & Caballero, B. (2000). Is Miss America an undernourished role model? *JAMA, 283*(12), 1569.

Rudd, M. D. (2000). Integrating science into the practice of clinical suicidology: A review of the psychotherapy literature and a research agenda for the future. In R. W. Maris, S. S. Canetto, et al. (Eds.), *Review of suicidology, 2000*. New York: Guilford Press.

Rudd, M. D., Joiner, T., & Rajah, M. H. (2001). *Treating suicidal behavior: An effective time-limited approach.* New York: Guilford Press.

Ruedrich, S. L., Chu, C., & Wadle, C. V. (1985). The amytal interview in the treatment of psychogenic amnesia (Special issue). *Hosp. Comm. Psychiat., 36*(10), 1045–1046.

Rush, A. J., & Frances, A. (2000). Expert consensus guideline series: Treatment of psychiatric and behavioral problems in mental retardation. *Amer. J. Ment. Retard., 105*(3), 159–228.

Rushford, N., & Ostermeyer, A. (1997). Body image disturbances and their change with videofeedback in anorexia nervosa. *Behav. Res. Ther., 35*(5), 389–398.

Russ, S. W. (2004). *Play in child development and psychotherapy: Toward empirically supported practice.* Mahwah, NJ: Lawrence Erlbaum Associates.

Russell, G. (1979). Bulimia nervosa: An ominous variant of anorexia nervosa. *Psychol. Med., 9*(3), 429–448.

Russell, G. F. M. (1995). Anorexia nervosa through time. In G. Szmukler, C. Dare, & J. Treasure (Eds.), *Handbook of eating disorders: Theory, treatment and research.* Chichester, England: Wiley.

Ruta, N., & Cohen, L. S. (1998). Postpartum mood disorders: Diagnosis and treatment guidelines. *J. Clin. Psychiat., 59*(Suppl 2), 34–40.

Rutledge, P. C., & Sher, K. J. (2001). Heavy drinking from the freshman year into early young adulthood: The roles of stress, tension-reduction drinking motives, gender and personality. *J. Stud. Alc., 62*(4), 457–466.

Rutter, M., & O'Connor, T. G. (2004). Are there biological programming effects for psychological development? Findings from a study of Romanian adoptees. *Dev. Psychol., 40*(1), 81–94.

RWJF (The Robert Wood Johnson Foundation). (2001). Substance abuse fact sheet: The human cost of substance abuse. Retrieved November 24, 2002, from www.SALeaders.org

Rychtarik, R. G., Connors, G. J., Whitney, R. B., McGillicuddy, N. B., Fitterling, J. M., & Wirtz, P. W. (2000). Treatment settings for persons with alcoholism: Evidence for matching clients to inpatient versus outpatient care. *J. Cons. Clin. Psychol., 68*(2), 277–289.

Rzewuska, M. (2002). Drug maintenance treatment compliance and its correlation with the clinical picture and course of schizophrenia. *Prog. Neuropsychopharmacol. Biol. Psychiat., 26*(4), 811–814.

Sacks, O. (2000, May). *An anthropologist on Mars: Some personal perspectives on autism.* Keynote address. Eden Institute Foundation's Sixth Annual Princeton Lecture Series on Autism. Princeton, NJ.

Sadock, B. J., & Sadock, V. A. (2003). *Kaplan & Sadock's synopsis of psychiatry: Behavioral ciences/Clinical psychiatry* (9th ed.). Philadelphia: Lippincott Williams & Wilkins.

Saeman, H. (2002). Psychology, medicine to enforce New Mexico prescription law. *The National Psychologist, 11*(3), 1.

Safer, D. (1994). The impact of recent lawsuits on methylphenidates sales. *Clin. Pediatr., 33*(3), 166–168.

Safer, D., & Krager, J. (1992). Effect of a media blitz and a threatened lawsuit on stimulant treatment. *JAMA, 268*(8), 1004–1007.

Safren, S. A., Gershuny, B. S., Marzol, P., Otto, M. W., & Pollack, M. H. (2002). History of childhood abuse in panic disorder, social phobia, and generalized anxiety disorder. *J. Nerv. Ment. Dis., 190*(7), 453–456.

Sakheim, D. K., Hess, E. P., & Chivas, A. (1988). General principles for short-term inpatient work with multiple personality-disorder patients. *Psychotherapy, 24*, 117–124.

Saks, E. R. (2002). *Refusing care: Forced treatment and the rights of the mentally ill.* Chicago: University of Chicago Press.

Saks, E. R., Jeste, D. V., Granholm, E., Palmer, B. W., & Schneiderman, L. (2002). Ethical issues in psychosocial interventions research involving controls. *Ethics Behav., 12*(1), 87–101.

Salekin, R. T., & Rogers, R. (2001). Treating patients found not guilty by reason of insanity. In J. B. Ashford & B. D. Sales, et al. (Eds.) *Treating adult and juvenile offenders with special needs* (pp. 171–195). Washington, DC: APA.

Sales, E., Baum, M., & Shore, B. (1984). Victim readjustment following assault. *J. Soc. Issues, 40*(1), 117–136.

Salkovskis, P. M. (1985). Obsessional-compulsive problems: A cognitive-behavioural analysis. *Behav. Res. Ther., 23*, 571–584.

Salkovskis, P. M. (1989). Cognitive-behavioural factors and the persistence of intrusive thoughts in obsessional problems. *Behav. Res. Ther., 27*, 677–682.

Salkovskis, P. M. (1999). Understanding and treating obsessive-compulsive disorder. *Behav. Res. Ther., 37*(Suppl. 1), S29–S52.

Salkovskis, P. M., & Westbrook, D. (1989). Behaviour therapy and obsessional ruminations: Can failure be turned into success? *Behav. Res. Ther., 27*, 149–160.

Salzman, C., Vaccaro, B., Lieff, J., & Weiner, A. (1995). Clozapine in older patients with psychosis and behavioral disruption. *Amer. J. Ger. Psychiat., 3*(1), 26–33.

Salzman, L. (1980). *Psychotherapy of the obsessive personality.* New York: Jason Aronson.

Salzman, L. (1985). Psychotherapeutic management of obsessive-compulsive patients. *Amer. J. Psychother., 39*(3), 323–330.

Salzman, L. (1989). *Compulsive personality disorder.* In *Treatments of psychiatric disorders.* Washington, DC: American Psychiatric Press.

Samuels, J., Eaton, W. W., Bienvenu, O. J., Brown, C., Costa, P. T., Jr., & Nestadt, G. (2002). Prevalence and correlates of personality disorders in a community sample. *Brit. J. Psychiat., 180*(6), 536–542.

Sanders, M. J., & Bursch, B. (2002). Forensic assessment of illness falsification, Munchausen by proxy, and factitious disorder, NOS. *Child. Maltreat: J. Amer. Profess. Soc. Abuse Child., 7*(2), 112–124.

Sanders, S. K., & Shekhar, A. (1995). Regulation of anxiety by GABA receptors in the rat amygdala. *Pharmacol. Biochem. Behav., 52*(4), 701–706.

Sanderson, R. E., Campbell, D., & Laverty, S. G. (1963). An investigation of a new aversive conditioning treatment for alcoholism. *Quart. J. Stud. Alcohol., 24*, 261–275.

Sanderson, W. C., Beck, A. T., & McGinn, L. K. (2002). Cognitive therapy for generalized anxiety disorder: Significance of comorbid personality disorders. In R. L. Leahy & E. T. Dowd (Eds.), *Clinical advances in cognitive psychotherapy: Theory and application* (pp. 287–293). New York: Springer.

Sandler, M. (1990). Monoamine oxidase inhibitors in depression: History and mythology. *J. Psychopharmacol., 4*(3), 136–139.

Sansone, R. A., & Levitt, J. L. (2002). Self-harm behaviors among those with eating disorders: An overview. *Eat. Disord.: J. Treat. Prev., 10*(3), 205–213.

Santiseban, D. A., Muir-Malcolm, J. A., Mitrani, V. B., & Szapocznik, J. (2001). Chapter 16: Integrating the study of ethnic culture and family psychology intervention science. In H. A. Liddle, D. A. Santiseban, R. F. Levant, & J. H. Bray (Eds.), *Family psychology: Science-based interventions* (pp. 331–352). Washington, DC: APA.

Santtila, P., Sandnabba, N. K., Alison, L., & Nordling, N. (2002). Investigating the underlying structure in sadomasochistically oriented behavior. *Arch. Sex. Behav., 31*(2), 185–196.

Sarhill, N., Walsh, D., Nelson, K. A., LeGrand, S., & Davis, M. P. (2001). Assessment of delirium in advanced cancer: The use of the bedside confusion scale. *Amer. J. Hospice Pall. Care, 18*(5), 335–341.

Sarid, O., Anson, O., Yaari, A., & Margalith, M. (2004). Coping styles and changes in humoural reaction during academic stress. *Psychol. Health Med. 9*(1), 85–98.

Satir, V. (1964). *Conjoint family therapy: A guide to therapy and technique.* Palo Alto, CA: Science & Behavior Books.

Satir, V. (1967). *Conjoint family therapy* (Rev. ed.). Palo Alto, CA: Science & Behavior Books.

Satir, V. (1987). Going behind the obvious: The psychotherapeutic journey. In J. K. Zeig (Ed.), *The evolution of psychotherapy.* New York: Brunner/Mazel.

Sawle, G. A., & Kear, C. J. (2001). Adult attachment style and pedophilia: A developmental perspective. *Inter. J. Offend. Ther. Compar. Crimin., 45*(1), 32–50.

Scarf, M. (1996, June 10). The mind of the Unabomber. *New Republic,* pp. 20–23.

Scheuffgen, K., Happe, F., Anderson, M., & Frith, U. (2000). High "intelligence," low "IQ"? Speed of processing and measured IQ in children with autism. *Dev. Psychopathol., 12*(1), 83–90.

Schiffman, J., Abrahamson, A., Cannon, T., LaBrie, J., Parnas, J. Schulsinger, F., &

Mednick, S. (2001). Early rearing factors in schizophrenia. *Inter. J. Ment. Hlth.*, 30(1), 3–16.

Schiffman, J., LaBrie, J., Carter, J., Cannon, T., Schulsinger, F., Parnas, J., & Mednick, S. (2002). Perception of parent-child relationships in high-risk families, and adult schizophrenia outcome of offspring. *J. Psychiatr. Res.*, 36(1), 41–47.

Schildkraut, J. J. (1965). The catecholamine hypothesis of affective disorders: A review of supporting evidence. *Amer. J. Psychiat.*, 122(5), 509–522.

Schimmack, U., & Diener, E. (2003). Experience sampling methodology in happiness research. *Journal of Happiness Studies*, 4(1), 1–4.

Schlenger, W. E., Caddell, J. M., Ebert, L., Jordan, B. K., Rourke, K. M., Wilson, D., Thalji, L., Dennis, J. M., Fairbank, J. A., & Kulka, R. A. (2002). Psychological reactions to terrorist attacks. *JAMA*, 288(5), 581–588.

Schlesinger, M., Dorwart, R., Hoover, C., & Epstein, S. (1997). Competition, ownership, and access to hospital services: Evidence from psychiatric hospitals. *Medical Care*, 35(9), 974–992.

Schmidt, L. G., Dufeu, P., Kuhn, S., Smolka, M., & Rommelspacher, H. (2000). Transition to alcohol dependence: Clinical and neurobiological considerations. *Comprehen. Psychiat.*, 41(2, Suppl 1), 90–94.

Schmidtke, A., Weinacker, B., Apter, A., Batt, A., Berman, A., Bille-Brahe, U., Botsis, A., DeLeo, D., Doneux, A., Goldney, R., Grad, O., Haring, C., Hawton, K., Hjelmeland, H., Kelleher, M., Kerkhof, A., Leenaars, A., Lonnqvist, J., Michel, K., Ostamo, A., Salander-Renberg, E., Sayil, I., Takahashi, Y., Van Heeringen, C., Varnik, A., & Wasserman, D. (1999). Suicide rates in the world: Update. *Arch. Suic. Res.*, 5, 81–89.

Schmidtke, A., Weinacker, B., Stack, S., & Lester, D. (1999). The impact of the reunification of Germany on the suicide rate. *Arch. Suic. Res.*, 5(3), 233–239.

Schmidt, N. B., & Bates, M. J. (2003). Evaluation of a pathoplastic relationship between anxiety sensitivity and panic disorder. *Anx., Stress, Coping Inter. J.*, 16(1), 17–30.

Schneider, F., Boehner, H., Habel, U., Salloum, J. B., Stierstorfer, A., Hummel, T. C., Miller, C., Friedrichs, R., Mueller, E. E., & Sandmann, W. (2002). Risk factors for postoperative delirium in vascular surgery. *Gen. Hosp. Psychiat.*, 24(1), 28–34.

Schneider, K. J. (2003). Existential-humanistic psychotherapies. In A. S. Gurman & S. B. Messer (Eds.), *Essential psychotherapies: Theory and practice* (2nd ed.). New York: Guilford Press.

Schneiderman, L., & Baum, A. (1992). Acute and chronic stress and the immune system. In N. Schneiderman, P. McCabe, & A. Baum (Eds.), *Perspectives in behavioral medicine: Stress and disease processes*. Hillsdale, NJ: Erlbaum.

Schneiderman, N. (1999). Behavioral medicine and the management of HIV/AIDS. *Inter. J. Behav. Med.*, 6(1), 3–12.

Schneier, F. R. (2001). Treatment of social phobia with antidepressants. *J. Clin. Psychiat.*, 62(Suppl. 1), 43–49.

Schore, A. N. (2002). Advances in neuropsychoanalysis, attachment theory, and trauma research: Implications for self psychology. *Psychoanal. Inq.*, 22(3), 433–484.

Schott, R. L. (1999). Managers and mental health: Mental illness and the workplace. *Public Pers. Manag.*, 28(2), 161–183.

Schou, M. (1997). Forty years of lithium treatment. *Arch. Gen. Psychiat.*, 54, 9–13.

Schover, L. R. (2000). Sexual problems in chronic illness. In S. R. Leiblum & R. C. Rosen (Eds.), *Principles and practice of sex therapy* (3rd ed., pp. 398–422). New York: Guilford Press.

Schreiber, F. R. (1973). *Sybil*. Chicago: Regnery.

Schreiber, G. B., Robins, M., Striegel-Moore, R., Obarzanek, E., Morrison, J. A., & Wright, D. J. (1996). Weight medication efforts reported by Black and White preadolescent girls: National heart, lung, and blood institute growth and health study, *Pediatrics*, 98, 63–70.

Schuckit, M. (1999). Cited in C. Ginther, Schuckit addresses state-of-the-art addiction treatments. *Psychiatr. Times*, XVI(4).

Schuckit, M. A., Danko, G. P., Raimo, E. B., Smith, T. L., Eng, M. Y., Carpenter, K. K. T., & Hesselbrock, V. M. (2001). A preliminary evaluation of the potential usefulness of the diagnoses of polysubstance dependence. *J. Stud. Alc.*, 62(1), 54–61.

Schulenberg, J., Maggs, J. L., Long, S. W., Sher, K. J., Gotham, H. J., Baer, J. S., Kivlahan, D. R., Marlatt, G. A., & Zucker, R. A. (2001). The problem of college drinking: Insights from a developmental perspective. *Alcohol: Clin. Exp. Res.*, 25(3), 473–477.

Schultz, R., & Heckhausen, J. (1996). A life span model of successful aging. *Amer. Psychologist*, 51(7), 702–714.

Schulz, R., O'Brien, A., Czaqja, S., Ory, M., Norris, R., Martire, L. M., Belle, S. H., Burgio, L., Gitlin, L., Coon, D., Burns, R., Gallagher-Thompson, D., & Stevens, A. (2002). Dementia caregiver intervention research: In search of clinical significance. *Gerontologist*, 42(5), 589–602.

Schumaker, J. F. (2001). *The age of insanity: Modernity and mental health*. Westport, CT: Praeger.

Schuster, M. A., Stein, B. D., Jaycox, L. H., Collins, R. L., Marshall, G. N., Elliot, M. N., Zhou, A. J., Kanouse, D. E., Morrison, J. L., & Berry, S. H. (2001). A national survey of stress reactions after the September 11, 2001, terrorist attacks. *N. Engl. J. Med.*, 20, 1507–1512.

Schwalb, M. (1999). Interviewed in M. S. Baum, Autism: Locked in a solitary world. *HealthState*, 17(2), 18–22.

Schwartz, G. E. (1977). Psychosomatic disorders and biofeedback: A psychobiological model of disregulation. In J. D. Maser & M. E. P. Seligman (Eds.), *Psychopathology: Experimental models*. San Francisco: W. H. Freeman.

Schwartz, J. M., Stoessel, P. W., Baxter, L. R., Jr., Martin, K. M., & Phelps, M. E. (1996). Systematic changes in cerebral glucose metabolic rate after successful behavior modification treatment of obsessive-compulsive disorder. *Arch. Gen. Psychiat.*, 53, 109–113.

Schwartz, S. (1993). *Classic studies in abnormal psychology*. Mountain View, CA: Mayfield Publishing.

Schwartz, S., & Johnson, J. J. (1985). *Psychopathology of childhood*. New York: Pergamon Press.

Scott, A. (1995). "Reclaimed once more by the realities of life": Hysteria and the location of memory. *Brit. J. Psychother.*, 11(3), 398–405.

Scott, J. (1990, Jul. 25). Vertigo, not madness, may have tormented Van Gogh. *Los Angeles Times*, p. A14.

Scott, J. E., & Dixon, L. B. (1995). Assertive community treatment and case management for schizophrenia. *Schizo. Bull.*, 21(4), 657–668.

Scott, W. D., Winters, R. W., & Beevers, C. G. (2000). Affective distress as a central and organizing sympton in depression: Psychological mechanisms. In S. L. Johnson & A. M. Hayes (Eds.), *Stress, coping, and depression* (pp. 145–175). Mahwah, NJ: Erlbaum.

Scotti, J. R., & Morris, T. L. (2000). Diagnosis and classification. In M. Hersen & R. T. Ammerman (Eds.), *Advanced abnormal child psychology* (2nd ed., pp. 15–32). Mahwah, NJ: Erlbaum.

Seeman, J. (2002). Looking back, looking ahead: A synthesis. In D. J. Cain & J. Seeman (Eds.), *Humanistic psychotherapies: Handbook of research and practice*. Washington, DC: APA.

Segraves, R. T. (1993). Treatment-emergent sexual dysfunction in affective disorder: A review and management strategies. *J. Clin. Psychiat., Monogr. Ser.*, 11, 7–63.

Segraves, R. T. (1995). Psychopharmacological influences on human sexual behavior. In J. M. Oldham & M. B. Riba (Eds.), *American Psychiatric Press review of psychiatry* (Vol. 14). Washington, DC: American Psychiatric Press.

Segraves, R. T. (1998). Antidepressant-induced sexual dysfunction. *J. Clin. Psychiat.*, 59(Suppl. 4), 48–54.

Segraves, T., & Althof, S. (2002). Psychotherapy and pharmacotherapy for sexual dysfunctions. In P. E. Nathan & J. M. Gorman (Eds.), *A guide to treatments that work* (2nd ed., pp. 497–524). London: Oxford University Press.

Segrin, C. (2000). Social skills deficits associated with depression. *Clin. Psychol. Rev.*, 20(3), 379–403.

Segrin, C. (2001). *Interpersonal processes in psychological problems*. New York: Guilford Press.

Seiden, R. H. (1981). Mellowing with age: Factors influencing the nonwhite suicide rate. *Inter. J. Aging Human Dev.*, 13, 265–284.

Seidman, L. J., Faraone, S. V., Goldstein, J. M., Kremen, W. S., Horton, N. J., Makris, N., Tooney, R., Kennedy, D., Caviness, V. S., & Tsuang, M. T. (2002). Left hippocampal volume as a vulnerability indicator for schizophrenia: A magnetic resonance imaging morphometric study of nonpsychotic first-degree relatives. *Arch. Gen. Psychiat.*, 59(9), 839–849.

Seidman, S. N. (2002). Exploring the relationship between depression and erectile dysfunction in aging men. *J. Clin. Psychiat.*, 63 (Suppl. 5), 5–12.

Seidman, S. N., & Rieder, R. O. (1995). Sexual behavior through the life cycle: An empirical approach. In J. M. Oldham & M. B. Riba (Eds.), *American Psychiatric Press review of psychiatry* (Vol. 14). Washington, DC: American Psychiatric Press.

Seligman, M. E. P. (1971). Phobias and preparedness. *Behav. Ther.*, 2, 307–320.

Seligman, M. E. P., Castellon, C., Cacciola, J., Schulman, P., et al. (1988). Explanatory style change during cognitive therapy for unipolar depression. *J. Abnorm. Psychol.*, 97(1), 13–18.

Seligman, M. E. P., & Csikszentmihalyi, M. (2000). Positive psychology: An introduction. *Amer. Psychologist*, 55, 5–14.

Selkoe, D. J. (1992). Alzheimer's disease: New insights into an emerging epidemic. *J. Geriat. Psychiat.*, 25(2), 211–227.

Selkoe, D. J. (1998). The cell biology of beta-amyloid precursor protein and presenilin in Alzheimer's disease. *Trends Cell Biol.*, 8(11), 447–453.

Selkoe, D. J. (1999). Translating cell biology into therapeutic advances in Alzheimer's disease. *Nature*, 399(Suppl. 6738), A23–31.

Selkoe, D. J. (2000). The origins of Alzheimer's disease: A is for amyloid. *JAMA*, 283(12), 1615–1617.

Selkoe, D. J. (2002). Alzheimer's disease is a synaptic failure. *Science*, 298(5594), 789–791.

Selkoe, D. J., Yamazaki, T., Citron, M., Podlisny, M. B., Koo, E. H., Teplow, D. B., & Haass, C. (1996). The role of APP processing and trafficking pathways in the formation of amyloid B-protein. In R. J. Wurtman, S. Corkin, J. H. Growdon, & R. M. Nitsch (Eds.), *The neurobiology of Alzheimer's disease*. New York: New York Academy of Sciences.

Selling, L. S. (1940). *Men against madness.* New York: Greenberg.

Serpell, L., & Treasure, J. (2002). Bulimia nervosa: Friend or foe? The pros and cons of bulimia nervosa. *Inter. J. Eat. Disorders,* 32(2), 164–170.

Seto, M. C., Khattar, N. A., Lalumiere, M. L., & Quinsey, V. L. (1997). Deception and sexual strategy in psychopathy. *Pers. Individ. Diff.,* 22(3), 301–307.

Seto, M. C., Maric, A., & Barbaree, H. E. (2001). The role of pornography in the etiology of sexual aggression. *Aggress. Viol. Behav.,* 6(1), 35–53.

Sexton, T. L., & Alexander, J. F. (2002). Family-based empirically supported interventions. *J. Couns. Psychol.,* 30(2), 238–261.

Shafran, R. (2002). Eating disorders and obsessive compulsive disorder. In R. O. Frost & G. Steketee (Eds.), *Cognitive approaches to obsessions and compulsions: Theory, assessment, and treatment* (pp. 215–231). Amsterdam: Pergamon/Elsevier Science.

Shafran, R., Cooper, Z., & Fairburn, C. G. (2002). Clinical perfectionism: A cognitive-behavioural analysis. *Behav. Res. Ther.,* 40(7), 773–791.

Shah, R., & Waller, G. (2000). Parental style and vulnerability to depression: The role of core beliefs. *J. Nerv. Ment. Dis.,* 188(1), 19–25.

Sharf, R. S. (2000). *Theories of psychotherapy & counseling: Concepts and cases (2nd ed.).* Pacific Grove, CA: Brooks/Cole.

Sharf, R. S. (2004). *Theories of psychotherapy & counseling: Concepts and cases (3rd ed.).* Australia: Thomson-Brooks/Cole.

Shamoo, A. E. (2002). Moral and compliance issues in clinical research, Part 1: Where we are today, RAPS RA interactive (pp. 1–2). Retrieved from http:///www.raps.org/rainteractive/articleCT.cfm?article_ID=63.

Shay, J., & Munroe, J. (1999). Group and milieu therapy for veterans with complex posttraumatic stress disorder. In P. A. Saigh, J. D. Bremner, et al. (Eds.), *Posttraumatic stress disorder: A comprehensive text.* Boston: Allyn & Bacon.

Shea, M. T., Zlotnick, C., Dolan, R., Warshaw, M. G., Phillips, K. A., Brown, P., & Keller, M. B. (2000). Personality disorders, history of trauma, and posttraumatic stress disorder in subjects with anxiety disorders. *Comprehen. Psychiat.,* 41(5), 315–325.

Shear, M. K., Vander-Bilt, J., Rucci, P., Endicott, J., Lydiard, B., Otto, M. W., Pollack, M. H., Chandler, L., Williams, J., Ali, A., & Frank, D. M. (2001). Reliability and validity of a structured interview guide for the Hamilton Anxiety Rating Scale (SIGH-A). *Depress. Anx.,* 13(4), 166–178.

Shedler, J., & Block, J. (1990). Adolescent drug use and psychological health: A longitudinal inquiry. *Amer. Psychologist,* 45(5), 612–630.

Shellenbarger, S. (1998, September 28). Workers are taking more "mental health" days off. *Star Tribune,* p. 10D.

Shenefelt, P. D. (2003). Hypnosis-facilitated relaxation using self-guided imagery during dermatologic procedures. *Amer. J. Clin. Hyp.,* 45(3), 225–232.

Shenk, D. (2001). *The forgetting: Alzheimer's: Portrait of an epidemic.* New York: Doubleday.

Sheras, P. L. (2001). Problems of adolescence. In C. E. Walker & M. C. Roberts (Eds.), *Handbook of clinical child psychology* (3rd ed., pp. 619–803). New York: Wiley.

Sheras, P., & Worchel, S. (1979). *Clinical psychology: A social psychological approach.* New York: Van Nostrand.

Sherlock, R. (1983). Suicide and public policy: A critique of the "new consensus." *Bioethics,* 4, 58–70.

Sherman, R., & Thompson, R. (1990). *Bulimia: A guide for family and friends.* Lexington, MA: Lexington Books.

Shiffman, S., Gorsline, J., & Gorodetzky, C. W. (2002). Efficacy of over-the-counter nicotine patch. *Nicotine and Tobacco Research,* 4(4), 477–483.

Shiffman, S., Rolf, C. N., Hellebusch, S. J., Gorsline, J., Gorodetzky, C. W., Chiang, Y. K., Schleusener, D. S., & Di Marino, M. E. (2002). Real-world efficacy of prescription and over-the-counter nicotine replacement therapy. *Addiction,* 97(5), 505–516.

Shifren, J. L., Braunstein, G. D., Simon, J. A., Casson, P. R., Buster, J. E., Redmond, G. P., Bkurki, R. E., Ginsburg, E. S., Rosen, R. C., Leiblum, S. R., Caramelli, K. E., & Mazer, N. A. (2000). Transdermal testosterone treatment in woman with impaired sexual function after oophorectomy. *N. Engl. J. Med.,* 343, 682–731.

Shipherd, J. C., & Beck, J. G. (1999). The effects of suppressing trauma-related thoughts on women with rape-related posttraumatic stress disorder. *Behav. Res. Ther.,* 37(2), 99–112.

Shisslak, C. M., Crago, M., McKnight, K. M., Estes, L. S., Gray, G., & Parnaby, O. G. (1998). Potential risk factors associated with weight control behaviors in elementary and middle school girls. *J. Psychosom. Res.,* 44(3/4), 301–313.

Shnayerson, M. (1996, July). Natural opponents. *Vanity Fair,* pp. 98–105.

Shneidman, E. S. (1963). Orientations toward death: Subintentioned death and indirect suicide. In R. W. White (Ed.), *The study of lives.* New York: Atherton.

Shneidman, E. S. (1973). Suicide notes reconsidered. *Psychiatry,* 36, 379–394.

Shneidman, E. S. (1981). Suicide. *Suic. Life-Threat. Behav.,* 11(4), 198–220.

Shneidman, E. S. (1985). *Definition of suicide.* New York: Wiley.

Shneidman, E. S. (1987, March). At the point of no return. *Psychology Today.*

Shneidman, E. S. (1993). *Suicide as psychache: A clinical approach to self-destructive behavior.* Northvale, NJ: Jason Aronson.

Shneidman, E. S. (1999). Perturbation and lethality: A psychological approach to assessment and intervention. In D. G. Jacobs et al. (Eds.). *The Harvard Medical School guide to suicide assessment and intervention.* San Francisco: Jossey-Bass.

Shneidman, E. S. (2001). *Comprehending suicide: Landmarks in 20th-century suicidology.* Washington, DC: American Psychological Association.

Shneidman, E. S., & Farberow, N. (1968). The Suicide Prevention Center of Los Angeles. In H. L. P. Resnick (Ed.), *Suicidal behaviors: Diagnosis and management.* Boston: Little, Brown.

Showalter, E. (1985). *The female malady: Women, madness and English culture.* New York: Pantheon.

Shrout, P. E. (2002). Reliability. In J. T. Tsuang & M. Tohan (Eds.), *Textbook in psychiatric epidemiology* (2nd ed., pp. 131–147). New York: Wiley-Liss.

Siegel, R. K. (1990). In J. Sherlock, Getting high—Animals do it, too. *USA Today,* p. 1A.

Sigerist, H. E. (1943). *Civilization and disease.* Ithaca, NY: Cornell University Press.

Silberg, J., Rutter, M., D'Onofrio, B., Eaves, L. (2003). Genetic and environmental risk factors in adolescent substance use. *J. Child Psychol. Psychiat. Allied Disc.,* 44(5), 664–676.

Silbersweig, D. A., Stern, E., Frith, C., Cahill, C. et al. (1995). A functional neuroanatomy of hallucinations in schizophrenia. *Nature,* 378, 176–179.

Silva, J. A., Derecho, D. V., Leong, G. B., & Ferrari, M. M. (2000). Stalking behavior in delusional jealousy. *J. Forensic Sci.,* 45(1), 77–82.

Silver, L. B. (2004). *Attention-deficit/hyperactivity disorder: A clinical guide to diagnosis and treatment for health and mental health professionals* (3rd ed.).Washington, DC: American Psychiatric Publishing, Inc.

Silverman, K., Evans, S. M., Strain, E. C., & Griffiths, R. R. (1992). Withdrawal syndrome after the double-blind cessation of caffeine consumption. *N. Engl. J. Med.,* 327(16), 1109–1114.

Silverman, W. K., La Greca, A. M., & Wasserstein, S. (1995). What do children worry about? Worries and their relation to anxiety. *Child Dev.,* 66, 671–686.

Silverstone, T., & Hunt, N. (1992). Symptoms and assessment of mania. In E. S. Paykel (Ed.), *Handbook of affective disorders.* New York: Guilford Press.

Simmon, J. (1990). Media and market study. In skin deep: Our national obsession with looks. *Psychol. Today,* 26(3), 96.

Simon, G. E., & Gureje, O. (1999). Stability of somatization disorder and somatization symptoms among primary care patients. *Arch. Gen. Psychiat.,* 56(1), 90–95.

Simon, G. E., & Katzelnick, D. J. (1997). Depression, use of medical services and cost-offset effects. *J. Psychosom. Res.,* 42(4), 333–344.

Simon, J. A., & Martens, R. (1977). S.C.A.T. as a predictor of A-sttes in varying competitive situations. In D. M. Landers & R. W. Christina (Eds.), *Psychology of motor behavior and sport* (Vol. 2, pp. 146–156). Champaign, IL: Human Kinetics.

Simon, N. (2000). Autism's home in the brain. *Neurology,* 54(1), 269.

Simon, R. I. (2001). Duty to foresee, forewarn, and protect against violent behavior: A psychiatric perspective. In M. Shafi & S. L. Shafi (Eds.), *School violence: Assessment, management, prevention* (pp. 201–215). Washington, DC: American Psychiatric Press.

Simonds, S. L. (2001). *Depression and women: An integrative treatment approach.* New York: Springer.

Simons, R. L., Murray, V., McLoyd, V., Lin, K. H., Cutrona, C., & Rand, D. (2002). Discrimination, crime, ethnic identity, and parenting as correlates of depressive symptoms among African American children: A multilevel analysis. *Dev. Psychopathol.,* 14(2), 371–393.

Simpson, K. J. (2002). Anorexia nervosa and culture. *J. Psychiatr. Ment. Hlth. Nurs.,* 9(1), 65–71.

Sizemore, C. C., & Huber, R. J. (1988). The twenty-two faces of Eve. *Indiv.. Psychol. J. Adlerian Theory Res. Prac.,* 44(1), 53–62.

Sizemore, C., & Pittillo, E. S. (1977). *I'm Eve.* Garden City, NY: Doubleday.

Skau, K., & Mouridsen, S. (1995). Munchausen syndrome by proxy: A review. *Acta Paediatr.,* 84, 977–982.

Skodol, A. E., Gunderson, J. G., McGlashan, T. H., Dyck, I. R., Stout, R. L., Bender, D. S., Grilo, C. M., Shea, M. T., Zanarini, M. C., Morey, L. C., Sanislow, C. A., & Oldham, J. M. (2002). Functional impairment in patients with schizotypal, borderline, avoidant, or obsessive-compulsive personality disorder. *Amer. J. Psychiat.,* 159(2), 276–283.

Skodol, A. E., Stout, R. L., McGlashan, T. H., Grilo, C. M., Gunderson, J. G., Shea, M. T., Morey, L. C., Zanarini, M. C., Dyck, I. R., & Oldham, J. M. (1999). Co-occurrence of mood and personality disorders: A report from the Collaborative Longitudinal Personality Disorders Study (CLPS). *Depress. Anx.,* 10(4), 175–182.

Slade, P. (1995). Prospects for prevention. In G. Szmukler, C. Dare, & J. Treasure (Eds.), *Handbook of eating disorders: Theory, treatment and research*.Chichester, England: Wiley.

Sleek, S. (1997). Disaster victims need most long-term care, report says. *APA Monitor, 28*(10), 18.

Slovenko, R. (1992). Is diminished capacity really dead? *Psychiatr. Ann., 22*(11), 566–570.

Slovenko, R. (1995). *Psychiatry and criminal culpability.* New York: Wiley-Interscience.

Slovenko, R. (1999). Malpractice in psychotherapy: An overview. *Psychiatr. Clin. N. Amer., 22*(1), 1–15.

Slovenko, R. (2002). *Psychiatry in law/Law in psychiatry.* New York: Brunner-Routledge.

Slovenko, R. (2002). The role of psychiatric diagnosis in the law. *J. Psychiat. Law, 30*(3), 421–444.

Smith, A. L., & Weissman, M. M. (1992). Epidemiology. In E. S. Paykel (Ed.), *Handbook of affective disorders.* New York: Guilford Press.

Smith, D. (2001). Prevention: Still a young field. *APA Monitor, 32*(6), 70–72.

Smith, D. (2002). Solving crimes. *Monitor on Psychology, 33*(6), 61.

Smith, D. F. (2001). Negative emotions and coronary heart disease: Causally related or merely coexistent? *Scand. J. Psychol., 42*(1), 57–69.

Smith, G. R., Rost, K., & Kashner, T. M. (1995). A trial of the effect of a standardized psychiatric consultation on health outcomes and costs in somatizing patients. *Arch. Gen. Psychiat., 52*(3), 238–243.

Smith, M. L., & Glass, G. V. (1977). Meta-analysis of psychotherapy outcome studies. *Amer. Psychologist, 32*(9), 752–760.

Smith, M. L., Glass, G. V., & Miller, T. I. (1980). *The benefits of psychotherapy.* Baltimore: Johns Hopkins University Press.

Smith, T., Lovaas, N. W., & Lovaas, O. I. (2002). Behaviors of children with high-functioning autism when paired with typically developing versus delayed peers: A preliminary study. *Behav. Intervent., 17*(3), 129–143.

Smith, T. W., & Rasinski, K. A. (2002). Assassination and terror; Two American tragedies compared. *NORC., 13*(5), 34.

Smith, V. L., Kassin, S. M., Ellsworth, P. C., Whitley, B. E., Greenberg, M. S., Wells, G. L., Lindsay, R. C., & Ferguson, T. J. (1989). Eyewitness accuracy and confidence: Within- versus between-subjects correlations. The role of eyewitness confidence in juror perceptions of credibility: Accuracy, confidence, and juror perceptions in eyewitness identification. *J. Appl. Psychol., 74*(2), 356–359.

Smyer, M. A. (1989). Nursing homes as a setting for psychological practice: Public policy perspectives. *Amer. Psychologist, 44*(10), 1307–1314.

Smyth, J. M., & Pennebaker, J. W. (2001). What are the health effects of disclosure? In A. Baum, T. A. Revenson, & J. E. Singer (Eds.), *Handbook of health psychology* (pp. 339–348). Mahwah, NJ: Erlbaum.

Smolak, L., & Murnen, S. K. (2001). Gender and eating problems. In R. H. Striegel-Moore & L. Smolak (Eds.), *Eating disorders: Innovative directions in research and practice* (pp. 91–110). Washington, DC: American Psychological Association.

Snow, E. (1976, December). In the snow. *Tex. Mon. Mag.*

Snyder, S. (1986). *Drugs and the brain.* New York: Scientific American Library.

Snyder, S. (1991). Drugs, neurotransmitters, and the brain. In P. Corsi (Ed.), *The enchanted loom: Chapters in the history of neuroscience.* New York: Oxford University Press.

Snyder, W. V. (1947). *Casebook of non-directive counseling.* Boston: Houghton Mifflin.

Sobczak, S., Honig, A., van Duinen, M. A., & Riedel, W. J. (2002). Serotonergic dysregulation in bipolar disorders: A literature review of serotonergic challenge studies. *Bipolar Disord., 4*(6), 347–356.

Sobell, M. B., & Sobell, L. C. (1973). Individualized behavior therapy for alcoholics. *Behav. Ther., 4*(1), 49–72.

Sobell, M. B., & Sobell, L. C. (1984). The aftermath of heresy: A response to Pendery et al.'s (1982) critique of "Individualized Behavior Therapy for Alcoholics." *Behav. Res. Ther., 22*(4), 413–440.

Sobell, M. B., & Sobell, L. C. (1984). Under the microscope yet again: A commentary on Walker and Roach's critique of the Dickens Committee's enquiry into our research. *Brit. J. Addic., 79*(2), 157–168.

Sobin, C., & Sackeim, H. A. (1997). Psychomotor symptoms of depression. *Amer. J. Psychiat., 154,* 4–17.

Solms, M. (2002). Dreaming: Cholinergic and dopaminergic hypotheses. In E. Perry, H. Ashton, et al., (Eds.), *Neurochemistry of consciousness: Neurotransmitters in mind. Advances in consciousness research.* Amsterdam: John Benjamins.

Solomon, D. A., Keitner, G. I., Miller, I. W., Shea, M. T., & Keller, M. B. (1995). Course of illness and maintenance treatments for patients with bipolar disorder. *J. Clin. Psychiat., 56*(1), 5–13.

Somasundaram, D. J., & Rajadurai, S. (1995). War and suicide in northern Sri Lanka. *Acta Psychiatr. Scandin., 91*(1), 1–4.

Sommers-Flanagan, J., & Sommers-Flanagan, R. (2003). *Clinical interviewing* (3rd ed.). New York: Wiley.

Sorensen, J. L., & Copeland, A. L. (2000). Drug abuse treatment as an HIV prevention strategy: A review. *Drug Alc. Rev., 59*(1) 17–31.

Sourander, A., Helstelae, L., Haavisto, A., & Bergroth, L. (2001). Suicidal thoughts and attempts among adolescents: A longitudinal 8-year follow-up study. *J. Affect. Disorders, 63*(1–3), 59–66.

Spalter, A. R., Gwirtsman, H. E., Demitrack, M. A., & Gold, P. W. (1993). Thyroid function in bulimia nervosa. *Biol. Psychiat., 33,* 408–414.

Spaniel, F., Hajek, T., Tintera, J., Harantova, P., Dezortova, M., & Hajek, M. (2003). Differences in fMRI and MRS in a monozygotic twin pair discordant for schizophrenia (case report). *Acta Psychiatr. Scandin. 107*(2), 155–157.

Spanier, C., Shiffman, S., Maurer, A., Reynolds, W., & Quick, D. (1996). Rebound following failure to quit smoking: The effects of attributions and self-efficacy. *Exp. Clin. Psychopharmacol., 4*(2), 191–197.

Speakman, M. T., & Kloner, R. A. (1999). Viagra and cardiovascular disease. *J. Cardiovasc. Pharmacol. Ther., 4*(4), 259–267.

Sperry, L. (2003). *Handbook of diagnosis and treatment of DSM-IV-TR personality disorders* (2nd ed.), New York: Brunner-Routledge.

Spiegel, D. (1994). Dissociative disorders. In R. E. Hales, S. C. Yudofsky, & J. A. Talbott (Eds.), *The American Psychiatric Press textbook of psychiatry*(2nd ed.). Washington, DC: American Psychiatric Press.

Spiegel, D. (2002). Mesmer minus magic: Hypnosis and modern medicine. *Inter. J. Clin. Exp. Hyp., 50*(4), 397–406.

Spiegel, D., & Fawzy, F. I. (2002). Psychosocial interventions and prognosis in cancer. In H. G. Koenig & H. J. Cohen (Eds.), *The link between religion and health: Psychoneuroimmunology and the faith factor*(pp. 84–100). New York: Oxford University Press.

Spiegler, M. D., & Guevremont, D. C. (2003). *Contemporary behavior therapy.* Belmont, CA: Thomson/Wadsworth.

Spielberger, C. D. (1966). Theory and research on anxiety. In C. D. Spielberger (Ed.), *Anxiety and behavior.* New York: Academic Press.

Spielberger, C. D. (1972). Anxiety as an emotional state. In C. D. Spielberger (Ed.), *Anxiety: Current trends in theory and research* (Vol. 1). New York: Academic Press.

Spielberger, C. D. (1985). Anxiety, cognition, and affect: A state-trait perspective. In A. H. Tuma & J. Maser (Eds.), *Anxiety and the anxiety disorders.* Hillsdale, NJ: Erlbaum.

Spielrein, S. (1995). On the psychological content of a case of schizophrenia (dementia praecox). *Evolution Psychiatr., 60*(1), 69–95. [French.]

Spitzer, R. L., Gibbon, M., Skodol, A. E., Williams, J. B. W., & First, M. B. (Eds.) (1994). *DSM-IV casebook: A learning companion to the diagnostic and statistical manual of mental disorders* (4th ed.). Washington, DC: American Psychiatric Press.

Spitzer, R. L., Skodol, A., Gibbon, M., & Williams, J. B. W. (1981). *DSM-III case book* (1st ed.). Washington, DC: American Psychiatric Press.

Spitzer, R. L., Skodol, A., Gibbon, M., & Williams, J. B. W. (1983). *Psychopathology: A case book.* New York: McGraw-Hill.

Sporer, K. A. (1999). Acute heroin overdose. *Ann. Internal Med., 130*(7), 584–590.

Sprecher, S., & Hatfield, E. (1996). Premarital sexual standards among U. S. college students: Comparison with Russian and Japanese students. *Arch. Sex. Behav., 25*(3), 261–288.

Sprock, J. (2000). Gender-typed behavioral examples of histrionic personality disorder. *J. Psychopath. Behav. Ass., 22*(2), 107–122.

Squire, L. R. (1977). ECT and memory loss. *Amer. J. Psychiat., 134,* 997–1001.

Squire, L. R., & Slater, P. C. (1983). Electroconvulsive therapy and complaints of memory dysfunction: A prospective three-year follow-up study. *Brit. J. Psychiat., 142,* 1–8.

St. George-Hyslop, P. H. (2000). Molecular genetics of Alzheimer's disease. *Biol. Psychiat., 47*(3), 183–199.

St. George-Hyslop, P. H. (2000). Piecing together Alzheimer's. *Scientif. Amer., 76–83.*

St. Pierre, T. L. (2001). Strategies for community/school collaborations to prevent youth substance abuse. *J. Primary Prev., 21*(3), 381–398.

Stack, S. (1987). Celebrities and suicide: A taxonomy and analysis, 1948–1983. *Amer. Sociol. Rev., 52,* 401–412.

Stack, S. (1998). The relationship of female labor force participation to suicide: A comparative analysis. *Arch. Suic. Res., 4*(3), 249–261.

Stafford, K. P. (2002). Civil commitment. In B. Van Dorsten (Ed.), *Forensic psychology: From classroom to courtroom* (pp. 143–170). New York: Kluwer Academic/Plenum Pub.

Stahl, S. M. (2001). The psychopharmacology of sex. Part 2: Effects of drugs and disease on the 3 phases of human sexual response. *J. Clin. Psychiat., 62*(3), 147–148.

Stanley, B., Molcho, A., Stanley, M., Winchel, R., Gameroff, M. J., Parsons, B., & Mann, J. J. (2000). Association of aggressive behavior with altered serotonergic function in patients who are not suicidal. *Amer. J. Psychiat., 157*(4), 609–614.

Stanley, M. A., Hopko, D. R., Diefenbach, G. J., Bourland, S. L., Rodriguez, H., & Wagener, P. (2003). Cognitive-behavior therapy for late-life generalized anxiety disorder in primary care: Preliminary findings. *Amer. J. Ger. Psychiat., 11*(1), 92–96.

Stanley, M., Stanley, B., Traskman-Bendz, L., Mann, J. J., & Meyendorff, E. (1986). Neurochemical findings in suicide completers and suicide attempters. In R. W. Maris (Ed.), *Biology of suicide*. New York: Guilford Press.

Stanley, M., Virgilio, J., & Gershon, S. (1982). Tritiated imipramine binding sites are decreased in the frontal cortex of suicides. *Science, 216,* 1337–1339.

Steadman, H. J., Monahan, J., Robbins, P. C., Appelbaum, P., Grisso, T., Klassen, D., Mulvey, E. P., & Roth, L. (1993). From dangerousness to risk assessment: Implications for appropriate research strategies. In S. Hodgins (Ed.), *Mental disorder and crime*. New York: Sage.

Steege, J. F., & Ling, F. W. (1993). Dyspareunia: A special type of chronic pelvic pain. *Obstet. Gynecol. Clin. North Am., 20,* 779–793.

Steen, S. N., Oppliger, R. A., & Brownell, K. D. (1988). Metabolic effects of repeated weight loss and regain in adolescent wrestlers. *JAMA, 260,* 47–50.

Stein, D., Kaye, W. H., Matsunaga, H., Orbach, I., Har-Evan, D., Frank, G., McConaha, C. W., & Rao, R. (2002). Eating-related concerns, mood, and personality traits in recovered bulimia nervosa subjects: A replication study. *Inter. J. Eat. Disorders, 32*(2), 225–229.

Stein, L. I. (1993). A system approach to reducing relapse in schizophrenia. *J. Clin. Psychiat., 54*(3 Suppl.), 7–12.

Stein, M. B., Jang, K. L., & Livesley, W. J. (1999). Heritability of anxiety sensitivity: A twin study. *Amer. J. Psychiat., 156*(2), 246–251.

Stein, M. B., & Uhde, T. W. (1995). The biology of anxiety disorders. In A. F. Schatzberg & C. B. Nemeroff (Eds.), *The American Psychiatric Press textbook of psychopharmacology*. Washington, DC: American Psychiatric Press.

Stein, Z., Susser, M., Saenger, G., & Marolla, F. (1972). Nutrition and mental performance. *Science, 178,* 708–713.

Steinbrook, R. (1992). The polygraph test: A flawed diagnostic method. *N. Engl. J. Med., 327*(2), 122–123.

Steiner, H., Smith, C., Rosenkranz, R. T., & Litt, I. (1991). The early care and feeding of anorexics. *Child Psychiat. Human Dev., 21*(3), 163–167.

Steiner, M., & Tam, W. Y. K. (1999). Postpartum depression in relation to other psychiatric disorders. In L. J. Miller, et al. (Eds.), *Postpartum mood disorders*. Washington, DC: American Psychiatric Press.

Steinhausen, H. C. (2002). The outcome of anorexia nervosa in the 20th century. *Amer. J. Psychiat., 159*(8), 1284–1293.

Steinhausen, H. C., Boyadjieva, S., Grigoroiu-Serbanescu, M., Seidel, R., & Winkler-Metzke, C. (2000). A transcultural outcome study of adolescent eating disorders. *Acta Psychiatr. Scandin., 101*(1), 60–66.

Steketee, G. (1990). Personality traits and disorders in obsessive-compulsives. *J. Anx. Dis., 4*(4), 351–364.

Steketee, G., & Barlow, D. H. (2002). Obsessive-compulsive disorder. In D. H. Barlow (Ed.), *Anxiety and its disorders: The nature and treatment of anxiety and panic* (2nd ed., pp. 516–550). New York: Guilford Press.

Steptoe, A. (2001). Negative emotions in music making: The problem of performance anxiety. In P. N. Juslin & J. A. Sloboda (Eds.), *Music and emotion: Theory and research. Series in affective science* (pp. 291–307). London: Oxford University Press.

Sternberg, R. J., Grigorenko, E. L., & Bundy, D. A. (2001). The predictive value of IQ. *Merrill-Palmer Q., 47*(1), 1–41.

Stetter, F. (2000). Psychotherapy. In G. Zernig, A. Saria, et al. (Eds.), *Handbook of alcoholism. Pharmacology and toxicology*. Boca Raton, FL: CRC Press.

Stetter, F., & Kupper, S. (2002). Autogenic training: A meta-analysis of clinical outcome studies. *Appl. Psychophysiol. Biofeedback, 27*(1), 45–98.

Stevens, L. M., Lynm, C., & Glass, R. M. (2002). Postpartum depression. *JAMA, 287*(6), 802.

Stewart, D., & Oslin, D. W. (2001). Recognition and treatment of late-life addictions in medical settings. *J. Clin. Geropsychol., 7*(2), 145–158.

Stewart, S. H., Taylor, S., Jang, K. L., Cox, B. J., Watt, M. C., Fedoroff, I. C., & Borger, S. C. (2001). Causal modeling of relations among learning history, anxiety sensitivity, and panic attacks. *Behav. Res. Ther., 39*(4), 443–456.

Stice, E. (2002). The neglect of obesity. *Monitor on Psychology, 33*(3), 33.

Stice, E., & Bearman, S. K. (2001). Body-image and eating disturbances prospectively predict increases in depressive symptoms in adolescent girls: A growth curve analysis. *Dev. Psychol., 37,* 597–607.

Stillion, J. M. (1995). Through a glass darkly: Women and attitudes toward suicidal behavior. In S. S. Canetto & D. Lester (Eds.), *Women and suicidal behavior*. New York: Springer.

Stillion, J. M., & McDowell, E. E. (1996). *Suicide across the life span: Premature exits* (2nd ed.) Washington, DC: Taylor & Francis.

Stirman, S. W., & Pennebaker, J. W. (2001). Word use in the poetry of suicidal and non-suicidal poets. *Psychosom. Med., 63,* 517–522.

Stock, W. (1993). Inhibited female orgasm. In W. O'Donohue & J. Geer (Eds.), *Handbook of sexual dysfunctions*. Boston: Allyn & Bacon.

Stoil, M. (2001). Behavioral health's "finest hour." *Behav. Hlth. Manage., 21*(5), 8–10.

Stolberg, R. A., Clark, D. C., & Bongar, B. (2002). Epidemiology, assessment, and management of suicide in depressed patients. In I. H. Gotlib & C. L. Hammen (Eds.), *Handbook of depression* (pp. 581–601). New York: Guilford Press.

Stone, M. H. (1989). Schizoid personality disorder. In American Psychiatric Association (Eds.), *Treatments of psychiatric disorders: A task force report of the American Psychiatric Association.* Washington, DC: American Psychiatric Press.

Stone, M. H. (2000). Clinical guidelines for psychotherapy for patients with borderline personality disorder. *Psychiatr. Clin. N. Amer., 23*(1), 193–210.

Stone, T. H., Winslade, W. J., & Klugman, C. M. (2000). Sex offenders, sentencing laws and pharmaceutical treatment: A prescription for failure. *Behav. Sci. Law, 18*(1), 83–110.

Stoppard, J. M. (2000). *Understanding depression: Feminist social constructionist approaches*. New York: Routledge.

Stowe, Z., Casarella, J., Landry, J., & Nemeroff, C. (1995). Sertraline in the treatment of women with postpartum major depression. *Depression, 3,* 49–55.

Stratton, V. N., & Zalanowski, A. H. (1994). Affective impact of music vs. lyrics. *Empir. Stud. Arts, 12*(2), 173–184.

Stratton, V., & Zalanowski, A. (1999). *Study on music and emotion*. Paper presented at annual meeting of Eastern Psychological Association.

Straussner, S. L. A. (Ed.). (2001). *Ethnocultural factors in substance abuse treatment*. New York: Guilford Press.

Stravynski, A., Gaudette, G., Lesage, A., Arbel, N. et al. (1997). The treatment of sexually dysfunctional men without partners: A controlled study of three behavioural group approaches. *Brit. J. Psychiat., 170,* 338–344.

Stricker, G., & Gold, J. (2003). Integrative approaches to psychotherapy. In A. S. Gurman & S. B. Messer (Eds.), *Essential psychotherapies: Theory and practice* (2nd ed.). New York: Guilford Press.

Stricker, G., & Trierweiler, S. J. (1995). The local clinical scientist. A bridge between science and practice. *Amer. Psychologist, 50*(12), 995–1002.

Strickland, B. R., Hale, W. D., & Anderson, L. K. (1975). Effect of induced mood states on activity and self-reported affect. *J. Cons. Clin. Psychol., 43*(4), 587.

Strickland, C. J. (1997). Suicide among American Indian, Alaskan Native, and Canadian Aboriginal youth: Advancing the research agenda. *Inter. J. Ment. Hlth., 25*(4), 11–32.

Striegel-Moore, R. H., Cachelin, F. M., Dohm, F. A., Pike, K. M., Wilfley, D. E., & Fairburn, C. G. (2001). Comparison of binge eating disorder and bulimia nervosa in a community sample. *Inter. J. Eat. Disorders, 29*(2), 157–165.

Striegel-Moore, R. H., Silberstein, L. R., & Rodin, J. (1993). The social self in bulimia nervosa: Public self-consciousness, social anxiety, and perceived fraudulence. *J. Abnorm. Psychol., 102*(2), 297–303.

Striegel-Moore, R. H., & Smolak, L. (2000). The influence of ethnicity on eating disorders in women. In R. M. Eisler, M. Hersen, et al. (Eds.), *Handbook of gender, culture, and health*. Mahwah, NJ: Erlbaum.

Strier, F. (1999). Whither trial consulting: Issues and projections. *Law Human Behav., 23*(1), 93–115.

Strober, M., Freeman, R., Lampert, C., Diamond, J., & Kaye, W. (2000). Controlled family study of anorexia nervosa and bulimia nervosa: Evidence of shared liability and transmission of partial syndromes. *Amer. J. Psychiat., 157*(3), 393–401.

Strober, M., Freeman, R., Lampert, C., Diamond, J., & Kaye, W. (2001). Males with anorexia nervosa: A controlled study of eating disorders in first-degree relatives. *Inter. J. Eat. Disorders, 29*(3), 264–269.

Strober, M., & Yager, J. (1985). A developmental perspective on the treatment of anorexia nervosa in adolescents. In D. M. Garner & P. E. Garfinkel (Eds.), *Handbook of psychotherapy for anorexia nervosa and bulimia*. New York: Guilford Press.

Stromme, P., & Diseth, T. H. (2000). Prevalence of psychiatric diagnoses in children with mental retardation: Data from a population-based study. *Dev. Med. Child Neurol., 42*(4), 266–270.

Stromme, P., & Magnus, P. (2000). Correlations between socioeconomic status, IQ and aetiology in mental retardation: A population-based study of Norwegian children. *Soc. Psychiat. Psychiatr. Epidemiol., 35*(1), 12–18.

Strümpfel, U., & Goldman, R. (2002). Contacting Gestalt therapy. In D.J. Cain & J. Seeman (Eds.), *Humanistic psychotherapies: Handbook of research and practice* (pp. 189–220). Washington, DC: APA.

Strupp, H. H. (1996). The tripartite model and the Consumer Reports study. *Amer. Psychologist, 51*(10), 1017–1024.

Stuart, G. L., Treat, T. A., & Wade, W. A. (2000). Effectiveness of an empirically based treatment for panic disorder delivered in a service clinic setting: 1-year follow-up. *J. Cons. Clin. Psychol., 68*(3), 506–512.

Stuart, S., & Noyes, R., Jr. (1999). Attachment and interpersonal communication in somatization. *Psychosomatics, 40*(1), 34–43.

Stunkard, A. J. (1975). From explanation to action in psychosomatic medicine: The case of obesity. *Psychosom. Med., 37,* 195–236.

Stunkard, A. J., Sorenson, T. I. A., Hanis, C., Teasdale, T. W., et al. (1986). An adoption study of human obesity. *N. Engl. J. Med., 314*, 193–198.

Sturgeon, V., & Taylor, J. (1980). Report of a five-year follow-up study of mentally disordered sex offenders released from Atascadero State Hospital in 1973. *Criminal Justice* J. Western S. Univ., San Diego, *4*, 31–64.

Sudhalter, V., Cohen, I. L., Silverman, W., & Wolf-Schein, E. G. (1990). Conversational analyses of males with fragile X, Down syndrome, and autism: Comparison of the emergence of deviant language. *Amer. J. Ment. Retard., 94*, 431–441.

Suinn, R. M. (2001). The terrible twos—anger and anxiety. *Amer. Psychologist, 56*(1), 27–36.

Sullivan, H. S. (1953). *The interpersonal theory of psychiatry.* New York: Norton.

Summers, M. (1996, December 9). Mister clean. *People*, pp. 139–140.

Sundbom, E., Binzer, M., & Kullgren, G. (1999). Psychological defense strategies according to the Defense Mechanism Test among patients with severe conversion disorder. *Psychother. Res., 9*(2), 184–198.

Suppes, T., Baldessarini, R. J., Faedda, G. L., & Tohen, M. (1991). Risk of recurrence following discontinuation of lithium treatment in bipolar disorder. *Arch. Gen. Psychiat., 48*(12), 1082–1088.

Svensson, B., Hansson, L., & Nyman, K. (2000). Stability of outcome in a comprehensive, cognitive therapy based treatment programme for long-term mentally ill patients. A 2-year follow-up study. *J. Ment. Hlth. UK, 9*(1), 51–61.

Swanson, J., Holzer, C., Ganju, V., & Jono, R. (1990). Violence and psychiatric disorder in the community: Evidence from the Epidemiological Catchment Area Surveys. *Hosp. Comm. Psychiat., 41*, 761–770.

Swartz, H. A. (1999). Interpersonal psychotherapy. In M. Hersen & A. S. Bellack (Eds.), *Handbook of comparative interventions for adult disorders* (2nd ed.). New York: Wiley.

Swayze, V. W. (1995). Frontal leukotomy and related psychosurgical procedures in the era before antipsychotics (1935–1954): A historical overview. *Amer. J. Psychiat., 152*(4), 505–515.

Sweeney, M. C. (2003). Gender- and culture-sensitive therapies. In J. O. Prochaska & J. C. Norcross, (Eds.), *Systems of psychotherapy: A transtheoretical analysis* (5th ed). Pacific Grove, CA: Brooks/Cole.

Swendsen, J. D., & Mazure, C. M. (2000). Life stress as a risk factor for postpartum depression: Current research and methodology. *Clin. Psychol.: Sci. Prac., 7*(1), 17–31.

Swendsen, J. D., & Merikangas, K. R. (2000). The comorbidity of depression and substance use disorders. *Clin. Psychol. Rev., 20*(2), 173–189.

Swerdlow, J. L. (1995). Quiet miracles of the brain. *Natl. Geogr., 187*(6), 12–13.

Switzer, P. K. (2000). The effects that medical malpractice concerns have on the practice of psychiatry in South Carolina. *Diss. Abstr. Inter.: Sect. B: Sci. Eng., 61*(2-B), 764.

Swora, M. G. (2001). Personhood and disease in Alcoholics Anonymous: A perspective from the anthropology of religious healing. *Ment. Health, Religion Cult., 4*(1), 1–21.

Szasz, T. S. (1963). *The manufacture of madness.* New York: Harper & Row.

Szasz, T. S. (1970). *The manufacture of madness: A comparative study of the Inquisition and the Mental Health Movement.* Syracuse, NY: Syracuse University Press.

Szasz, T. S. (1977). *Psychiatric slavery.* New York: Free Press.

Szasz, T. S. (1991). *The medicalization of sex. J. Human. Psychol., 31*(3), 34–42.

Szasz, T. S. (1997). The healing word: Its past, present, and future. In J. K. Zeig (Ed.), *The evolution of psychotherapy: The third conference.* New York: Brunner/Mazel.

Szasz, T. S. (2000). Second commentary on "Aristotle's function argument." *Philos. Psychiat. Psychol., 7*(1), 3–16.

Szymanski, S., Cannon, T. D., Gallacher, F., Erwin, R. J., & Gur, R. E. (1996). Course of treatment response in first-episode and chronic schizophrenia. *Amer. J. Psychiat., 153*(4), 519–525.

Tacon, A., & Caldera, Y. (2001). Behavior modification. In R. McComb & J. Jacalyn (Eds.), *Eating disorders in women and children: Prevention, stress management, and treatment*(pp. 263–272). Boca Raton, FL: CRC Press.

Taft, C. T., Stern, A. S., King, L. A., & King, D. W. (1999). Modeling physical health and functional health status: The role of combat exposure, posttraumatic stress disorder and personal resource attributes. *J. Traum. Stress, 12*(1), 3–23.

Tanner, L. (2001, April 25). Study: 30% of kids deal with bullying: "Serious problem" shouldn't be accepted as normal, author says. *The Dallas Morning News,* p. 1A.

Tarrier, N., & Haddock, G. (2002). Cognitive-behavioral therapy for schizophrenia: A case formulation approach. In S. G. Hofmann & M. C. Tompson (Eds.), *Treating chronic and severe mental disorders: A handbook of empirically supported interventions* (pp. 69–95). New York: Guilford Press.

Tartaglia, L. A., Dembski, M., Weng, X., Deng, N. et al. (1995). Identification and expression cloning of a leptin receptor, OB-R. *Cell, 83*, 1263–1271.

Tataranni, P. A., Gautier, J. F., Chen, K., Uecker, A., Bandy, D., Salbe, A. D., Pratley, R. E., Lawson, M., Reiman, E. M., & Ravussin, E. (1999). Neuroanatomical correlates of hunger and satiation in humans using positron emission tomography. *Proc. Natl. Acad. Sci. USA, 96*(8), 4569–4574.

Tate, D. C., Reppucci, N. D., & Mulvey, E. P. (1995). Violent juvenile delinquents. *Amer. Psychologist, 50*(9), 777–781.

Taube, C. A. (1990). Funding and expenditures for mental illness. In R. W. Manderscheid & M. A. Sonnenschein (Eds.), *Mental health, United States, 1990.* (DHHS Publication No. ADM 90-1708). Washington, DC: U. S. Department of Health and Human Services.

Tavris, C. (1993). Beware the incest-survivor machine. *New York Times Book Review.*

Taxman, F. S., & Messina, N. P. (2002). Civil commitment: A coerced treatment model. In C. G. Leukefeld & F. Tims (Eds.), et al., *Treatment of drug offenders: Policies and issues* (pp. 283–298). New York: Springer.

Taylor, B., Miller, E., Farrington, C. P., Petropoulos, M. C., Favot-Mayaud, I., Li, J., & Waight, P. A. (1999). Autism and measles, mumps, and rubella vaccine: No epidemiological evidence for a causal association. *Lancet, 353*, 2026–2029.

Taylor, D., & Nicholls, M. (2001). Munchausen's syndrome by proxy—The legal perspective. In G. Adshead & D. Brooke (Eds.), *Munchausen's syndrome by proxy: Current issues in assessment, treatment and research* (pp. 149–158). London: Imperial College Press.

Taylor, E. A., & Stansfeld, S. A. (1984). Children who poison themselves. *Brit. J. Psychiat., 145*, 127–135.

Taylor, G. M., & Ste. Marie, D. M. (2001). Eating disorders symptoms in Canadian female pair and dance figure skaters. *Int. J. Sport Psychol., 32*(1), 21–28.

Taylor, S. E., Kemeny, M. E., Reed, G. M., Bower, J. E., & Gruenewald, T. L. (2000). Psychological resources, positive illusions, and health. *Amer. Psychologist, 55*(1), 99–109.

Telch, C. F., & Agras, W. S. (1993). The effects of a very low calorie diet on binge eating. *Behav. Ther., 24*, 177–193.

Telner, J. I., Lapierre, Y. D., Horn, E., & Browne, M. (1986). Rapid reduction of mania by means of reserpine therapy. *Amer. J. Psychiat., 143*(8), 1058.

Temple, N. (2002). A critical enquiry into the psychoanalytic theories and approaches to psychosomatic conditions. *Inter. J. Psychoanal., 83*(4), 931–934.

Teplin, L. A., Abram, K. M., & McClelland, G. M. (1994). Does psychiatric disorder predict violent crime among released jail detainees? *Amer. Psychologist, 49*(4), 335–342.

Teri, L., & Lewinsohn, P. M. (1986). Individual and group treatment of unipolar depression: Comparison of treatment outcome and identification of predictors of successful treatment outcome. *Behav. Ther., 17*(3), 215–228.

Terry, D., Mayocchi, L., & Hynes, G. (1996). Depressive symptomatology in new mothers: A stress and coping perspective. *J. Abnorm. Psychol., 105*(2), 220–231.

Thase, M. E., Jindal, R., & Howland, R. H. (2002). Biological aspects of depression. In I. H. Gotlib & C. L. Hammen (Eds.), *Handbook of depression* (pp. 192–218). New York: Guilford Press.

Thase, M. E., Trivedi, M. H., & Rush, A. J. (1995). MAOIs in the contemporary treatment of depression. *Neuropsychopharmacology, 12*(3), 185–219.

Theander, S. (1970). Anorexia nervosa. *Acta Psychiatr. Scandin.,* [Suppl.], pp. 1–194.

Thigpen, C. H., & Cleckley, H. M. (1957). *The three faces of Eve.* New York: McGraw-Hill.

Thomas, A. K., & Loftus, E. F. (2002). Creating bizarre false memories through imagination. *Mem. Cog., 30*(3), 423–431.

Thomas, E. (1996, April 15). What the unabomber did to me. *Newsweek,* pp. 40–41.

Thomas, P., Chantoin-Merlet, S., Hazif-Thomas, C., Belmin, J., Montagne, B., Clement, J. P., Lebruchec, M., & Billon, R. (2002). Complaints of informal caregivers providing home care for dementia patients: The Pixel study. *Inter. J. Ger. Psychiat., 17*(11), 1034–1044.

Thompson, A. H., Stuart, H., Bland, R. C., Arboleda-Florez, J., Warner, R., & Dickson, R. A. (2002). Attitudes about schizophrenia from the pilot site of the WPA worldwide campaign against the stigma of schizophrenia. *Soc. Psychiat. Psychiatr. Epidemiol., 37*(10), 475–482.

Thompson, K. M., Crosby, R. D., Wonderlich, S. A., Mitchell, J. E., Redlin, J., Demuth, G., Smyth, J., & Haseltine, B. (2003). Psychopathology and sexual trauma in childhood and adulthood. *J. Traum. Stress., 16*(1), 35–38.

Thompson, M. P., & Kingree, J. B. (1998). Brief report: The frequency and impact of violent trauma among pregnant substance abusers. *Addic. Behav., 23*(2), 257–262.

Thompson, R. A., & Sherman, R. T. (1993). *Helping athletes with eating disorders.* Champaign, IL: Human Kinetics.

Thompson, R. A., & Sherman, R. T. (1999). "Good athlete" traits and characteristics of anorexia nervosa: Are they similar? *Eat. Disord.: J. Treat. Prev., 7*(3), 181–190.

Thompson, R. F. (2000). *The brain: A neuroscience primer.* New York: Worth.

Thulesius, H., & Hakansson, A. (1999). Screening of posttraumatic stress disorder symptoms among Bosnian refugees. *J. Traum. Stress*, 12(1), 167–174.

Tierney, A. J. (2000). Egas Moniz and the origins of psychosurgery: A review commemorating the 50th anniversary of Moniz's Nobel Prize. *J. Hist. Neurosci.*, 9(1), 22–36.

Tiggeman, M., & Wilson-Barrett, E. (1998). Children's figure ratings: Relationship to self-esteem and negative stereotyping. *Inter. J. Eat. Disorders*, 23, 83–88.

Time. (1982, October 25). *Time*.

Time. (1983, September 5). *Time*.

Time. (1998, October 12). Numbers. *Time*.

Time/CNN Poll. (1998). From what sources do teenagers today mainly learn about sex? In R. Stodghill, II. (1999, March 12). Where'd you learn that? *Time*, 151(23).

Time/CNN Poll. (1999, June 7). *Time*, 153(22), 56.

Time Poll. (2002). Kid poll: Young people's views on 9/11 anniversary conducted by *Nickelodeon* and *Time*. Retrieved on Sept. 16, 2002, from www.lexisnexis.com

Timko, C., Moos, R. H., Finney, J. W., & Lesar, M. D. (2000). Long-term outcomes of alcohol use disorders: Comparing untreated individuals with those in Alcoholics Anonymous and formal treatment. *J. Stud. Alc.*, 61(4), 529–540.

Titone, D. A. (2002). Memories bound: The neuroscience of dreams. *Trends Cog. Sci.*, 6(1), 4–5.

Tobin, D. L. (2000). *Coping strategies therapy for bulimia nervosa*. Washington, DC: American Psychological Association.

Tobin, J. P. (2001). Post traumatic stress disorder and the adrenal gland. *Irish J. Psychol. Med.*, 18(1), 27–29.

Tonigan, J. S. (2001). Benefits of Alcoholics Anonymous attendance: Replication of findings between clinical research sites in project MATCH. *Alcohol. Treat Q.*, 19(1), 67–77.

Torgersen, S. (1983). Genetic factors in anxiety disorders. *Arch. Gen. Psychiat.*, 40, 1085–1089.

Torgersen, S. (1983). Genetics of neurosis: The effects of sampling variation upon the twin concordance ratio. *Brit. J. Psychiat.*, 142, 126–132.

Torgersen, S. (1984). Genetic and nosological aspects of schizotypal and borderline personality disorders: A twin study. *Arch. Gen. Psychiat.*, 41, 546–554.

Torgersen, S. (1990). Comorbidity of major depression and anxiety disorders in twin pairs. *Amer. J. Psychiat.*, 147, 1199–1202.

Torgersen, S. (2000). Genetics of patients with borderline personality disorder. *Psychiatr. Clin. N. Amer.*, 23(1), 1–9.

Torrey, E. F. (1991). A viral-anatomical explanation of schizophrenia. *Schizo. Bull.*, 17(1), 15–18.

Torrey, E. F. (1997). *Out of the shadows: Confronting America's mental illness crisis*. New York: Wiley.

Torrey, E. F. (1999, April 16). Interviewed in J. Lang, Local jails dumping grounds for mentally ill: 700,000 acutely ill held yearly. *Detroit News*.

Torrey, E. F. (2001). *Surviving schizophrenia: A manual for families, consumers, and providers* (4th ed.). New York: HarperCollins.

Torrey, E. F., Bowler, A. E., Taylor, E. H., & Gottesman, I. I. (1994). *Schizophrenia and manic-depressive disorder*. New York: Basic Books.

Torrey, E. F., & Knable, M. B. (2002). *Surviving manic depression: A manual on bipolar disorder for patients, families, and providers*. New York: Basic Books.

Treaster, J. B. (1992, September 20). After hurricane, Floridians show symptoms seen in war. *New York Times*.

Treasure, J., & Szmukler, G. I. (1995). Medical complications of chronic anorexia nervosa. In G. I. Szmukler, C. Dare, & J. Treasure (Eds.), *Handbook on eating disorders: Theory, treatment and research*. Chichester, England: Wiley.

Treasure, J., Todd, G., & Szmukler, G. (1995). The inpatient treatment of anorexia nervosa. In G. Szmukler, C. Dare, & J. Treasure (Eds.), *Handbook of eating disorders: Theory, treatment and research*. Chichester, England: Wiley.

Treffert, D. A. (1999). Pervasive developmental disorders. In S. D. Netherton, D. Holmes, & C. E. Walker (Eds.), *Child and adolescent psychological disorders: A comprehensive textbook*. New York: Oxford University Press.

Troiano, R. P., Frongillo, E. A., Sobal, J., & Levitsky, D. A. (1996). The relationship between body weight and mortality: A quantitative analysis of combined information from existing studies. *Inter. J. Obesity*, 20, 63–75.

Trotter, R. J. (1985, November). Geschwind's syndrome: Van Gogh's malady. *Psychol. Today*, p. 46.

True, W. R., & Lyons, M. J. (1999). Genetic risk factors for PTSD: A twin study. In R. Yehuda et al. (Eds.), *Risk factors for posttraumatic stress disorder*. Washington, DC: American Psychiatric Press.

Trull, T. J., Sher, K. J., Minks-Brown, C., Durbin, J., & Burr, R. (2000). Borderline personality disorder and substance use disorders: A review and integration. *Clin. Psychol. Rev.*, 20(2), 235–253.

Trull, T. J., Stepp, S. D., & Durrett, C. A. (2003). Research on borderline personality disorder: An update. *Curr. Opin. Psychiat.*, 16(1), 77–82.

Trumbetta, S. L., & Mueser, K. T. (2001). Social functioning and its relationship to cognitive deficits over the course of schizophrenia. In R. S. E. Keefe & J. P. McEvoy (Eds.), *Negative symptom and cognitive deficit treatment response in schizophrenia* (pp. 33–67). Washington, DC: American Psychiatric Press.

Tryon, G. (1987). Abuse of therapist by patient. *Profess. Psychologist*, 17, 357–363.

Tsai, J. L., & Chentsova-Dutton, Y. (2002). Understanding depression across cultures. In I. H. Gotlib & C. L. Hammen (Eds.), *Handbook of depression* (pp. 467–491). New York: Guilford Press.

Tsai, L. Y. (1999). Psychopharmacology in autism. *Psychosom. Med.*, 61(5), 651–665.

Tsuang, M. (2000). Schizophrenia: Genes and environment. *Biol. Psychiat.*, 47(3), 210–220.

Tsuang, M. T., Bar, J. L., Harley, R. M., & Lyons, M. J. (2001). The Harvard twin study of substance abuse: What we have learned. *Harv. Rev. Psychiat.*, 9(6), 267–279.

Tsuang, M. T., Fleming, J. A., & Simpson, J. C. (1999). Suicide and schizophrenia. In D. G. Jacobs (Ed.), *The Harvard Medical School guide to suicide assessment and intervention*. San Francisco: Jossey-Bass.

Tsuruta, S., Nomura, S., & Yoshino, A. (2003). Neuroleptic dose reduction in stable chronic schizophrenia. *Schizo. Res.*, 59(1), 95–96.

Turgeon, L., & Chartrand, E. (2003). Psychometric properties of the French Canadian version of State-Trait Anxiety Inventory for Children. *Educ. Psychol. Meas.*, 63(1), 174–185.

Turgeon, L., & Chartrand, E. (2003). Reliability and validity of the revised Children's Manifest Anxiety Scale in a French-Canadian sample. *Psychol. Assess.*, 15(3), 378–383.

Turk, C. L., Heimberg, R. G., & Hope, D. A. (2001). Social anxiety disorder. In D. H. Barlow (Ed.), *Clinical handbook of psychological disorders: A step-by-step treatment manual* (3rd ed.). New York: Guilford Press.

Turkat, I. D., Keane, S. P., & Thompson-Pope, S. K. (1990). Social processing errors among paranoid personalities. *J. Psychopathol. Behav. Assess.*, 12(3), 263–269.

Turkington, C., & Harris, J. R. (2001). *The encyclopedia of memory and memory disorders* (2nd ed.). New York: Facts on File.

Turkington, D., Grant, J. B. F., Ferrier, I. N., Rao, N. S. K., Linsley, K. R., & Young, A. H. (2002). A randomized controlled trial of fluvoxamine in prostatodynia, a male somatoform pain disorder. *J. Clin. Psychiat.*, 63(9), 778–781.

Turner, J., Batik, M., Palmer, L. J., Forbes, D., & McDermott, B. M. (2000). Detection and importance of laxative use in adolescents with anorexia nervosa. *J. Amer. Acad. Child Adol. Psychiat.*, 39(3), 378–385.

Turner, S. M., Beidel, D. C., Dancu, C. V., & Keys, D. J. (1986). Psychopathology of social phobia and comparison to avoidant personality disorder. *J. Abnorm. Psychol.*, 95(4), 389–394.

Turton, M. D., O'Shea, D., Gunn, I., Beak, S. A., et al. (1996, January 4). A role for glucagon-like peptide-1 in the central regulation of feeding. *Nature*, 379, 69–72.

Tweed, J. L., Schoenbach, V. J., & George, L. K. (1989). The effects of childhood parental death and divorce on six-month history of anxiety disorders. *Brit. J. Psychiat.*, 154, 823–828.

Tyler, P., & Simmonds, S. (2003). Treatment models for those with severe mental illness and comorbid personality disorder. *Brit. J. Psychiat.*, 182(Suppl. 44), s15–s18.

U.S. Census Bureau. (1990). *Statistical abstract of the United States*. Washington, DC: U.S. Government Printing Office.

U.S. Census Bureau. (1994). *Statistical abstract of the United States*. Washington, DC: U.S. Government Printing Office.

U.S. Census Bureau. (2000). *Statistical abstract of the United States*. Washington, DC: U.S. Government Printing Office.

U.S. Department of Justice. (1995). *Violence against women: Estimates from the redesigned National Crime Victimization Survey*. Annapolis Junction, MD: Bureau of Justice Statistics Clearinghouse.

Uchoa, D. D. (1985). Narcissistic transference? *Rev. Bras. Psicanal.*, 19(1), 87–96.

Ulrich, R. S. (1984). View from a window may influence recovery from surgery. *Science*, 224, 420–421.

Uniform Crime Reports. (1997). *Crime in the United States: 1996 Uniform Crime Reports*. Washington, DC: FBI.

UNINCB (United Nations International Narcotics Control Board) Report. (1996). Cited in J. Roberts, Behavioral disorders are overdiagnosed in U.S. *Brit. Med. J.*, 312, 657.

Uretsky, S. (1999, June 28). Mate in two: Ideas of perfection vary. *HealthScout*.

Ursano, R. J., Boydstun, J. A., & Wheatley, R. D. (1981). Psychiatric illness in U.S. Air Force Vietnam prisoners of war: A five-year follow-up. *Amer. J. Psychiat.*, 138(3), 310–314.

Ursano, R. J., Fullerton, C. S., Epstein, R. S., Crowley, B., Kao, T. C., Vance, K., Craig, K. J., Dougall, A. L., & Baum, A. (1999). Acute and chronic posttraumatic stress disorder in motor vehicle accident victims. *Amer. J. Psychiat.*, 156(4), 589–595.

Ursano, R. J., Fullerton, C. S., Vance, K., & Kao, T. C. (1999). Posttraumatic stress disorder and identification in disaster workers. *Amer. J. Psychiat.*, 156(3), 353–359.

Usall, J., Haro, J. M., Ochoa, S., Marquez, M., & Araya, S. (2002). Influence of gender on social outcome in schizophrenia. *Acta Psychiatr. Scandin.*, 106(5), 337–342.

Utsey, S. O., Payne, Y. A., Jackson, E. S., & Jones, A. M. (2002). Race-related stress, quality of life indicators, and life satisfaction among elderly African Americans. *Cult. Div. Ethnic Minority Psychol.,* 8(3), 224–233.

Vaillant, G. E. (1994). Ego mechanisms of defense and personality psychopathology. *J. Abnorm. Psychol.,* 103(1), 44–50.

Vaillant, G. E., & Milofsky, E. S. (1982). Natural history of male alcoholism: IV. Paths to recovery. *Arch. Gen. Psychiat.,* 39, 127–133.

Valbak, K. (2001). Good outcome for bulimic patients in long-term group analysis: A single-group study. *Eur. Eat. Disord. Rev.,* 9(1), 19–32.

Valdisseri, E. V., Carroll, K. R., & Hartl, A. J. (1986). A study of offenses committed by psychotic inmates in a county jail. *Hosp. Comm. Psychiat.,* 37, 163–165.

Valenstein, E. S. (1986). *Great and desperate cures.* New York: Basic Books.

Valenti-Hein, D. C., Yarnold, P. R., & Mueser, K. T. (1994). Evaluation of the dating skills program for improving heterosocial interactions in people with mental retardation. *Behav. Mod.,* 18(1), 32–46.

Van Bourgondien, M. E., & Schopler, E. (1990). Critical issues in the residential care of people with autism. *J. Autism Dev. Disorders,* 20(3), 391–399.

Van de Castle, R. (1993). Content of dreams. In M. A. Carskadon (Ed.), *Encyclopedia of sleep and dreams.* New York: Macmillan.

Vandereycken, W. (2003). The place of inpatient care in the treatment of anorexia nervosa: Questions to be answered. *Inter. J. Eat. Disorders,* 34(4), 409–422.

van der Hart, O., Brown, P., & Graafland, M. (1999). Trauma-induced dissociative amnesia in World War I combat soldiers. *Austral. New Zeal. J. Psychiat.,* 33(1), 37–46.

van Hout, W. J. P. J., & Emmelkamp, P. M. G. (2002). Exposure in vivo therapy in anxiety disorders: Procedure and efficacy. *Gedragstherapie,* 35(1), 7–23.

Van Praag, H. M. (1983). CSF 5-HIAA and suicide in non-depressed schizophrenics. *Lancet,* 2, 977–978.

Vatz, R., & Weinberg, L. (1993, January 10). Keno krazy? *Washington Post,* p. C5.

Venditti, E., Wing, R., Jakicic, J., Butler, B., & Marcus, M. (1996). Weight cycling, psychological health, and binge eating in obese women. *J. Cons. Clin. Psychol.,* 64(2), 400–405.

Venneri, A., Bartolo, A., McCrimmon, S., & St. Clair, D. (2002). Memory and dating of past events in schizophrenia. *J. Inter. Neuropsychol. Soc.,* 8(6), 861–866.

Verbaten, M. N. (2003). Specific memory deficits in ecstasy users? The results of a meta-analysis. *Human Psychopharmacology: Clinical and Experimental,* 18(4), 281–290.

Verburg, K., Griez, E., Meijer, J., & Pols, H. (1995). Respiratory disorders as a possible predisposing factor for panic disorder. *J. Affect. Disorders,* 33(2), 129–134.

Verfaellie, M., Cermak, L. S., Blackford, S. P., et al. (1990). Strategic and automatic priming of semantic memory in alcoholic Korsakoff patients. *Brain Cognit.,* 13(2), 178–192.

Vernberg, E. M., La Greca, A. M., Silverman, W. K., & Prinstein, M. J. (1996). Prediction of posttraumatic stress symptoms in children after Hurricane Andrew. *J. Abnorm. Psychol.,* 105(2), 237–248.

Vestergaard, P., Emborg, C., Stoving, R. K., Hagen, C., Mosekilde, L., & Brixen, K. (2002). Fractures in patients with anorexia nervosa, bulimic nervosa and other eating disorders—a nationwide register study. *Inter. J. Eat. Disorders,* 32(3), 301–308.

Vetere, A. (2001). Structural family therapy. *Child Psychol. Psychiat. Rev.,* 6(3), 133–139.

Vetter, H. J. (1969). *Language behavior and psychopathology.* Chicago: Rand McNally.

Vetter, P. H., von Pritzbuer, J., Jungmann, K., Kropp, P., & Koller, O. (2001). The validity of the ICD-10 classification of recurrent affective disorders: Do endogenous and psychogenic depressions form a homogenous diagnostic group? *Psychopathology,* 34(1), 36–42.

Vicary, J. R., & Karshin, C. M. (2002). College alcohol abuse: A review of the problems, issues, and prevention approaches. *J. Primary Prev.,* 22(3), 299–331.

Vieira, C. (1993). Nudity in dreams. In M. A. Carskadon (Ed.), *Encyclopedia of sleep and dreams.* New York: Macmillan.

Viguera, A. C., Nonacs, R., Cohen, L. S., Tondo, L., Murray, A., & Baldessarini, R. J. (2000). Risk of recurrence of bipolar disorder in pregnant and nonpregnant women after discontinuing lithium maintenance. *Amer. J. Psychiat.,* 157(2), 179–184.

Vink, T., Hinney, A., van Elburg, A. A., van Goozen, S. H. M., Sandkuijl, L. A., Sinke, R. J., Herpertz-Dahlmann, B. M., Hebebrand, J, Remschmidt, H., van Engeland, H., & Adan, R. A. H. (2001). Association between an agouti-related protein gene polymorphism and anorexia nervosa. *Mol. Psychiat.,* 6(3), 325–328.

Vinson, D. (1994). Therapy for attention-deficit hyperactivity disorder. *Arch. Fam. Med.,* 3, 445–451.

Volkmar, F. R. (2001). Pharmacological interventions in autism: Theoretical and practical issues. *J. Clin. Child Psychol.,* 30(1), 80–87.

Volkow, N. D., & Fowler, J. S. (2000). Addiction, a disease of compulsion and drive: Involvement of the orbitofrontal cortex. *Cerebral Cortex,* 10(3), 318–325.

Volkow, N. D., Fowler, J. S., & Wang, G. J. (1999). Imaging studies on the role of dopamine in cocaine reinforcement and addiction in humans. *J. Psychopharmacol.,* 13(4), 337–345.

Volkow, N. D., Gillespie, H., Tancredi, L., & Hollister, L. (1995). The effects of marijuana in the human brain measured with regional brain glucose metabolism. In A. Biegon & N. D. Volkow (Eds.), *Sites of drug action in the human brain.* Boca Raton, FL: CRC Press.

Volkow, N. D., Wang, G. J., Fowler, J. S., Logan, J., Gatley, S. J., Hitzemann, R., Chen, A. D., Dewey, S. L., & Pappas, N. (1997). Decreased striatal dopaminergic responsiveness in detoxified cocaine-dependent subjects. *Nature,* 386(6627), 830–833.

Volkow, N. D., Wang, G. J., Fowler, J. S., Logan, J., Gatley, S. J., Wong, C., Hiutzemann, R., & Pappas, N. R. (1999). Reinforcing effects of psychostimulants in humans are associated with increases in brain dopamine and occupancy of D_2 receptors. *J. Pharmacol. Exp. Ther.,* 291(1), 409–415.

Von Burg, M., & Hibbard, R. (1995). Munchausen syndrome by proxy: A different kind of child abuse. *Indiana Med.,* 88(5), 378–382.

Wade, T. D., Bulik, C. M., Neale, M., & Kendler, K. S. (2000). Anorexia nervosa and major depression: Shared genetic and environmental risk factors. *Amer. J. Psychiat.,* 157(3), 469–471.

Wagenaar, A. C., Murray, D. M., & Toomey, T. L. (2000). Communities mobilizing for change on alcohol (CMCA): Effects of a randomized trial on arrests and traffic crashes. *Addiction,* 95(2), 209–217.

Waldman, I. D., Rhee, S. H., Levy, F., & Hay, D. A. (2001). Causes of the overlap among symptoms of ADHD, oppositional defiant disorder, and conduct disorder. In F. Levy & D. A. Hay (Eds.), *Attention, genes, and ADHD* (pp. 115–138). New York: Brunner-Routledge.

Walkup, J. T., & Ginsburg, G. S. (2002). Anxiety disorders in children and adolescents. *Inter. Rev. Psychiat.,* 14(2), 85–86.

Walkup, J. T., Labellarte, M. J., & Ginsburg, G. S. (2002). The pharmacological treatment of childhood anxiety disorders. *Intern. Rev. Psychiat.,* 14(2), 135–142.

Wall, T. L., Shea, S. H., Chan, K. K., & Carr, L. G. (2001). A genetic association with the development of alcohol and other substance use behavior in Asian Americans. *J. Abnorm. Psychol.,* 110(1), 173–178.

Wallace, J., Schneider, T., & McGuffin, P. (2002). Genetics of depression. In I. H. Gotlib & C. L. Hammen (Eds.), *Handbook of depression* (pp. 169–191). New York: Guilford Press.

Walsh, B. T., Wilson, G. R., Loeb, K. L., Devlin, M. J., et al. (1997). Medication and psychotherapy in the treatment of bulimia nervosa. *Amer. J. Psychiat.,* 154, 523–531.

Walsh, E., Buckanan, A., & Fahy, T. (2002). Violence and schizophrenia: Examining the evidence. *Brit. J. Psychiat.,* 180(6), 490–495.

Walters, E. E., & Kendler, K. S. (1995). Anorexia nervosa and anorexia-like syndromes in a population based female twin sample. *Amer. J. Psychiat.,* 152, 64–71.

Walters, G. D. (2000). Behavioral self-control training for problem drinkers: A metal-analysis of randomized control studies. *Behav. Ther.,* 31(1), 135–149.

Walters, G. D. (2002). The heritability of alcohol abuse and dependence: A meta-analysis of behavior genetic research. *Amer. J. Drug Alc.. Abuse,* 28(3), 557–584.

Wanck, B. (1984). Two decades of involuntary hospitalization legislation. *Amer. J. Psychiat.,* 41, 33–38.

Wang, H. Y., Markowitz, P., Levinson, D., Undie, A. S., & Friedman, E. (1999). Increased membrane-associated protein kinase C activity and translocation in blood platelets from bipolar affective disorder patients. *J. Psychiatr. Res.,* 33(2), 171–179.

Wang Ping. (2000). *Aching for beauty: Footbinding in China.* Minneapolis, MN: University of Minnesota Press.

Wang, P. S., Demler, O., & Kessler, R. C. (2002). Adequacy of treatment for serious mental illness in the United States. *Amer. J. Pub. Hlth.,* 92(1), 92–98.

Warnock, J. K., Bundren, J. C., & Morris, D. W. (1999). Female hypoactive sexual disorder: Case studies of physiologic androgen replacement. *J. Sex Marital Ther.,* 25(3), 175–182.

Warren, R. (1997). REBT and generalized anxiety disorder. In J. Yankura, W. Dryden, et al. (Eds.), *Using REBT with common psychological problems: A therapist's casebook.* New York: Springer.

Warwick, H. M. C., & Salkovskis, P. M. (2001). Cognitive-behavioral treatment of hypochondriasis. In V. Starcevic & D. R. Lipsitt (Eds.), *Hypochondriasis: Modern perspectives on an ancient malady* (pp. 314–328). New York: Oxford University Press.

Wasserman, I. M., & Stack, S. (2000). The relationship between occupation and suicide among African American males: Ohio, 1989–1991. In

R. W. Maris, S. S. Canetto, et al. (Eds.), *Review of suicidology, 2000*. New York: Guilford Press.

Watson, C. G., Hancock, M., Gearhart, L. P. Mendez, C. M., et al. (1997). A comparative outcome study of frequent, moderate, occasional, and nonattenders of Alcoholics Anonymous. *J. Clin. Psychol.*, 53(3), 209–214.

Watson, J. B. (1930). *Behaviorism* (Rev. ed.). Chicago: University of Chicago Press.

Watson, J. B., & Rayner, R. (1920). Conditioned emotional reaction. *J. Exp. Psychol.*, 3, 1–14.

Watson, S. J., Benson, J. A., Jr., & Joy, J. E. (2000). Marijuana and medicine: Assessing the science base: A summary of the 1999 Institute of Medicine Report. *Arch. Gen. Psychiat.*, 57(6), 547–552.

Watson Wyatt Worldwide. (1995, July 26). Job satisfaction survey. Cited in M. Reinemer, Work happy. *Am. Demogr.*

Watt, T. T. (2002). Marital and cohabiting relationships of adult children of alcoholics: Evidence from the National Survey of Family and Households. *J. Fam. Issues*, 23(2), 246–265.

Waxweiler, R. J., et al. (1995). Monitoring the impact of traumatic brain injury: A review and update. *J. Neurotrauma*, 12(4).

Webster-Stratton, C., & Reid, M. J. (2003). The incredible years parents, teachers, and children training series: A multifaceted treatment approach for young children with conduct problems. In A. E. Kazdin & J. R. Weisz (Eds.), *Evidence-based psychotherapies for children and adolescents*. New York: Guilford Press.

Wechsler, H., et al. (1997). *Survey on college binge drinking.* Reported by Harvard University School of Public Health, Cambridge, MA.

Wechsler, H., & Isaac, N. (1992). "Binge" drinkers at Massachusetts colleges: Prevalence, drinking styles, time trends, and associated problems. *JAMA*, 267, 2929–2931.

Wechsler, H., Dowdell, G. W., Davenport, A., & Castillo, S. (1995). Correlates of college student binge drinking. *Amer. J. Pub. Hlth.*, 85(7), 921–926.

Wechsler, H., Lee, J. E., Kuo, M., & Lee, H. (2000). College binge drinking in the 1990s: A continuing problem: Results of the Harvard School of Public Health 1999 College Alcohol Study. *J. Amer. Coll. Hlth.*, 48(5), 199–210.

Wechsler, H., Lee, J. E., Kuo, M., Seibring, M., Nelson, T. F., & Lee, H. (2002). Trends in alcohol use, related problems and experience of prevention efforts among US college students 1993 to 2001: Results from the 2001 Harvard School of Public Health college alcohol study. *J. Amer. Coll. Hlth.*, 50, 203–217.

Weeks, D., & James, J. (1995). *Eccentrics: A study of sanity and strangeness.* New York: Villard.

Weersing, V. R., & Brent, D. A. (2003). Cognitive-behavioral therapy for adolescent depression: Comparative efficacy, mediation, moderation, and effectiveness. In A. E. Kazdin & J. R. Weisz (Eds.), *Evidence-based psychotherapies for children and adolescents*. New York: Guilford Press.

Wegner, J. T., & Wegner, A. Z. (2001). Cognitive-behavioral therapy and other short-term approaches in the treatment of eating disorders. In B. P. Kinoy (Ed.), *Eating disorders: New directions in treatment and recovery* (2nd ed., pp. 112–126). New York: Columbia University Press.

Wehmeyer, M. L. (1992). Self-determination and the education of students with mental retardation. *Educ. Training Ment. Retard.*, 27(4), 302–314.

Welfel, E. R. (2001) Protecting clients' rights to privacy. In E. R. Welfel & R. E. Ingersoll (Eds.), *The mental health desk reference* (pp. 447–452). New York: Wiley.

Weinberg, M. K., Tronick, E. Z., Beeghly, M., Olson, K. L., Kernan, H., & Riley, J. M. (2001). Subsyndromal depressive symptoms and major depression in postpartum women. *Amer. J. Orthopsychiat.*, 71(1), 87–97.

Weinberger, D. R. (2002). Schizophrenia, the prefrontal cortex, and a mechanism of genetic susceptibility. *Eur. Psychiat.*, 17(Suppl 4), 355–362.

Weiner, H. (1977). *Psychobiology and human disease.* New York: Elsevier.

Weiner, I. B. (2000). Making Rorschach interpretation as good as it can be. *J. Pers. Assess.*, 74(2), 164–174.

Weingarten, S. M., & Cummings, J. L. (2001). Psychosurgery of frontal-subcortical circuits. In D. G. Lichter & J. L. Cummings (Eds.), *Frontal-subcortical circuits in psychiatric and neurological disorders* (pp. 421–435). New York: Guilford Press.

Weishaar, M. E. (2000). Cognitive risk factors in suicide. In R. W. Maris, S. S. Canetto, et al. (Eds.), *Review of suicidology, 2000*. New York: Guilford Press.

Weiss, D. E. (1991). *The great divide.* New York: Poseidon Press/Simon & Schuster.

Weiss, D. S., Marmar, C. R., Schlenger, W. E., & Fairback, J. A., et al. (1992). The prevalence of lifetime and partial posttraumatic stress disorder in Vietnam theater veterans. *J. Traum. Stress*, 5(3), 365–376.

Weiss, P. (2001). Psychological models of etiology of paraphilias. *Cesko. Psychol.*, 45(3), 216–225.

Weissberg, R. P. (2000). Improving the lives of millions of school children. *Amer. Psychologist*, 55, 1360–1372.

Weissman, M. M., Livingston Bruce, M., Leaf, P. J., Florio, L. P., & Holzer, C., III. (1991). Affective disorders. In L. N. Robins & D. A. Regier (Eds.), *Psychiatric disorders in America: The Epidemiologic Catchment Area Study.* New York: Free Press.

Weissman, M. M., & Markowitz, J. C. (2002). Interpersonal psychotherapy for depression. In I. H. Gotlib & C. L. Hammen (Eds.), *Handbook of depression* (pp. 404–421). New York: Guilford Press.

Weissman, M. M., & Olfson, M. (1995). Depression in women: Implications for health care research. *Science*, 269(5225), 799–801.

Weisz, J. R., Southam-Gerow, M. A., Gordis, E. B., & Connor-Smith, J. (2003). Primary and secondary control enhancement training for youth depression: Applying the deployment-focused model of treatment development and testing. In A. E. Kazdin (Ed.), *Evidence-based psychotherapies for children and adolescents* (pp. 165–182). New York: Guilford Press.

Welburn, K. R., Fraser, G. A., Jordan, S. A., Cameron, C., Webb, L. M., & Raine, D. (2003). Discriminating dissociative identity disorder from schizophrenia and feigned dissociation on psychological tests and structured interview. *J. Traum. Dissoc.*, 4(2), 109–130.

Welch, S., & Fairburn, C. (1994). Sexual abuse and bulimia nervosa: Three integrated case control comparisons. 11th National Conference on Eating Disorders (1992, Columbus Ohio). *Amer. J. Psychiat.*, 151, 402–407.

Welch, S., & Fairburn, C. (1996). Childhood sexual and physical abuse as risk factors for the development of bulimia nervosa: A community-based case control study. *Child Abuse Negl.*, 20, 633–642.

Welch, S. S. (2001). A review of the literature on the epidemiology of parasuicide in the general population. *Psychiatr. Serv.*, 52(3), 368–375.

Wellman, H. M., Cross, D., & Watson, J. (2001). Meta-analysis of theory-of-mind development: The truth about false belief. *Child Dev.*, 72, 655–684.

Wellner, A. S. (2001, February 1). Blowin' smoke: New CDC analysis reveals demographics of nicotine addicts. *Amer. Demog.* Retrieved on Sept. 15, 2002, from www.industryclick.com.

Wells, G. L., Lindsay, R. C., & Ferguson, T. J. (1989). Eyewitness accuracy and confidence: Within- versus between-subjects correlations. The role of eyewitness confidence in juror perceptions of credibility: Accuracy, confidence, and juror perceptions in eyewitness identification. *J. Appl. Psychol.*, 74(2), 356–359.

Wells, G. L., & Olsen, E. A. (2003). Eyewitness testimony. *Annu. Rev. Psychol.*, 54, 277–295.

Wells, M. E., & Hinkle, J. S. (1990). Elimination of childhood encopresis: A family systems approach. *J. Ment. Hlth. Couns.*, 12(4), 520–526.

Welsh, C. J., & Liberto, J. (2001). The use of medication for relapse prevention in substance dependence disorders. *J. Psychiatr. Prac.*, 7(1), 15–31.

Werry, J. S. (1996). Pervasive developmental, psychotic, and allied disorders. In L. Hechtman, (Ed.), *Do they grow out of it? Long-term outcomes of childhood disorders.* Washington, DC: American Psychiatric Press.

Werth, J. (1995). Rational suicide reconsidered: AIDS as an impetus for change. Annual Conference of the Association for Death Education & Counseling. *Death Stud.*, 19(1), 65–80.

Werth, J. (1996). *Rational suicide? Implications for mental health professionals.* Washington, DC: Taylor & Francis.

Werth, J. L., Jr. (Ed.) (1999). *Contemporary perspectives on rational suicide.* Philadelphia, PA: Brunner/Mazel.

Werth, J. L., Jr. (2000). Recent developments in the debate over physician-assisted death. In R. W. Maris, S. S. Canetto, et al. (Eds.), *Review of suicidology, 2000*. New York: Guilford Press.

Wertheimer, A. (2001). *A special scar: The experiences of people bereaved by suicide* (2nd ed.). East Sussex, UK: Brunner-Routledge.

West, A. G. (2001). Current approaches to sex-offender risk assessment: A critical review. *Brit. J. Forensic Prac.*, 3(3), 31–41.

Westen, D., Feit, A., & Zittel, C. (1999). Focus chapter: Methodological issues in research using projective methods. In P. C. Kendall, J. N. Butcher, et al. (Eds.), *Handbook of research methods in clinical psychology* (2nd ed.). New York: Wiley.

Westheimer, R. K., & Lopater, S. (2002). *Human sexuality: A psychosocial perspective.* Baltimore: Lippincott Williams & Wilkins.

Weston, S. C., & Siever, L. J. (1993, Spring). Biological correlates of personality disorders. *J. Pers. Disorders*, (Suppl.), pp. 129–148.

Wetherell, J. L., & Gatz, M. (2001). Recruiting anxious older adults for a psychotherapy outcome study. *J. Clin. Geropsychol.*, 7(1), 29–38.

Wettstein, R. M. (1988). Psychiatry and the law. In J. A. Talbott, R. E. Hales, & A. J. Frances (Eds.), *American Psychiatric Press textbook of psychiatry.* Washington, DC: American Psychiatric Press.

Wettstein, R. M. (1999). The right to refuse psychiatric treatment. *Psychiatr. Clin. N. Amer.*, 22(1), 173–182.

Whalen, C. K., & Henker, B. (1998). Attention-deficit/hyperactivity disorder. In T. H. Ollendick & M. Hersen (Eds.), *Handbook of child psychopathology* (3rd ed.). New York: Plenum.

Whaley, A. L. (1998, January). Racism in the provision of mental health services: A social-cognitive analysis. *Amer. J. Orthopsychiat.*, 68(1), 48–59.

Wheeler, J. G., Christensen, A., & Jacobson, N. S. (2001). Couple distress. In D. H. Barlow (Ed.), *Clinical handbook of psychological disorders: A step-by-step treatment manual* (3rd ed.). New York: Guilford Press.

Whipple, E. E., Webster, S. C., & Stratton, C. (1991). The role of parental stress in physically abusive families. *Child Abuse Negl., 15*(3), 279.

Whisman, M. A. (2001). The association between depression and marital dissatisfaction. In S. R. H. Beach (Ed.), *Marital and family processes in depression: A scientific foundation for clinical practice* (pp. 3–24). Washington, DC: American Psychological Association.

Whisman, M. A., & McGarvey, A. L. (1995). Attachment, depressotypic cognitions, and dysphoria. *Cog. Ther. Res., 19*(6), 633–650.

Whitaker, R. (2002). *Mad in America: Bad science, bad medicine, and the enduring mistreatment of the mentally ill.* Cambridge, MA: Perseus.

White, K. S., & Barlow, D. H. (2002). Panic disorder and agoraphobia. In D. H. Barlow (Ed.), *Anxiety and its disorders: The nature and treatment of anxiety and panic* (2nd ed., pp. 328–379). New York: Guilford Press.

Whitehead, W. E., Crowell, M. D., Heller, B. R., Robinson, J. C., et al. (1994). Modeling and reinforcement of the sick role during childhood predicts adult illness behavior. *Psychosom. Med., 56,* 541–550.

Whitehorn, J. C., & Betz, B. J. (1975). *Effective psychotherapy with the schizophrenic patient.* New York: Jason Aronson.

Whiteside, M. (1983, September 12). A bedeviling new hysteria. *Newsweek.*

Whiting, J. W., et al. (1966). I. *Field guide for a study of socialization. Six cultures series.* New York: Wiley.

WHO (World Health Organization). (1992). World health statistics annual. Geneva: Author.

Whorley, L. W. (1996). Cognitive therapy techniques in continuing care planning with substance-dependent patients. *Addic. Behav., 21*(2), 223–231.

Widiger, T. A. (2002). Personality disorders. In M. M. Antony & D. H. Barlow (Eds.), *Handbook of assessment and treatment planning for psychological disorders* (pp. 453–480). New York: Guilford Press.

Widiger, T. A., & Sankis, L. M. (2000). Adult psychopathology: Issues and controversies. *Annu. Rev. Psychol., 51,* 377–404.

Widloecher, D. (2001). The treatment of affects: An interdisciplinary issue. *Psychoanal. Q., 70*(1), 243–264.

Widom, C. S. (1989). The cycle of violence. *Science, 244,* 160–166.

Widom, C. S. (1991, February). Presentation. Washington, DC: American Association for the Advancement of Science.

Widom, C. S. (2001). Child abuse and neglect. In S. O. White (Ed.), *Handbook of youth and justice* (pp. 31–47). New York: Kluwer Academic/Plenum Press.

Wiederman, M. W. (2001). "Don't look now": The role of self-focus in sexual dysfunction. *Fam. J. Counsel. Ther. Couples Fam., 9*(2), 210–214.

Wiens, A. N., Mueller, E. A., & Bryan, J. E. (2001). Assessment strategies. In M. Hersen & V. B. Van Hasselt (Eds.), *Advanced abnormal psychology* (2nd ed., pp. 23–41). New York: Kluwer Academic/Plenum Press.

Wiggins, J. S., & Trobst, K. K. (2002). The interpersonal adjectives scales: Big five version (IASR-B5). In B. deRaad, et al. (Eds.), *Big five assessment.* Ashland, OH: Hogrefe & Huber.

Wilhelm, S., & Neziroglu, F. (2002). Cognitive theory of body dysmorphic disorder. In R. O. Frost & G. Steketee (Eds.), *Cognitive approaches to obsessions and compulsions: Theory, assessment, and treatment* (pp. 203–214). Amsterdam: Pergamon/Elsevier Science.

Wilkes, M. S., Bell, R. A., & Kravitz, R. L. (2000). Direct-to-consumer prescription drug advertising: Trends, impact, and implications. *Hlth. Affairs, 19*(2), 110–128.

Williams, C. C. (1983). The mental foxhole: The Viet Nam veterans' search for meaning. *Amer. J. Orthopsychiat., 53*(1), 4–17.

Williams, J. (2003). Dementia and genetics. In R. Plomin, J. C. DeFries, et al. (Eds.), *Behavioral genetics in the postgenomic era* (pp. 503–527). Washington, DC: American Psychological Association.

Williams, N., & Leiblum, S. L. (2002). Sexual dysfunction. In G. M. Wingood & R. J. DiClemente (Eds.), *Handbook of women's sexual and reproductive health: Issues in women's health* (pp. 303–328). New York: Kluwer Academic/Plenum.

Williams, R. B. (2001). Hostility (and other psychosocial risk factors): Effects on health and the potential for successful behavioral approaches to prevention and treatment. In A. Baum, T. A. Revenson, & J. E. Singer (Eds.), *Handbook of health psychology* (pp. 661–668). Mahwah, NJ: Erlbaum.

Willick, M. S. (2001). Psychoanalysis and schizophrenia: A cautionary tale. *J. Amer. Psychoanal. Assoc., 49*(1), 27–56.

Willick, M. S., Milrod, D., & Karush, R. K. (1998). Psychoanalysis and the psychoses. In M. Furer, E. Nersessian, et al. (Eds.), *Controversies in contemporary psychoanalysis: Lectures from the faculty of the New York Psychoanalytic Institute.* Madison, CT: International Universities Press.

Willis, L. A., Coombs, D. W., Cockerham, W. C., & Frison, S. L. (2002). Ready to die: A postmodern interpretation of the increase of African-American adolescent male suicide. *Soc. Sci. Med., 55*(6), 907–920.

Wills, T. A., McNamara, G., Vaccaro, D., & Hirky, A. E. (1996). Escalated substance use: A longitudinal grouping analysis from early to middle adolescence. *J. Abnorm. Psychol., 105*(2), 166–180.

Wilson, G. T., Becker, C. B., & Heffernan, K. (2003). Eating disorders. In E. J. Mash & R. A. Barkley (Eds.), *Child psychopathology(2nd ed.)* (pp. 687–715). New York: Guilford Press.

Wilson, G. T. (1994). Behavioral treatment of obesity: Thirty years and counting. *Adv. Behav. Res. Ther., 16,* 31–75.

Wilson, G. T., Fairburn, C. C., Agras, W. S., Walsh, B. T., & Kraemer, H. (2002). Cognitive-behavioral therapy for bulimia nervosa: Time course and mechanisms of change. *J. Cons. Clin. Psychol., 70*(2), 267–274.

Wilson, G. T., Heffernan, K., & Black, C. M. D. (1996). Eating disorders. In E. J. Mash & R. A. Barkley (Eds.), *Developmental psychopathology.* New York: Guilford Press.

Wilson, K. A., & Chambless, D. L. (1999). Inflated perceptions of responsibility and obsessive-compulsive symptoms. *Behav. Res. Ther., 37*(4), 325–335.

Wilson, W. M. (1992). The Stanford-Binet: Fourth Edition and Form L-M in assessment of young children with mental retardation. *Ment. Retard., 30*(2), 81–84.

Wincze, J. P., Richards, J., Parsons, J., & Bailey, S. (1996). A comparative survey of therapist sexual misconduct between an American state and an Australian state. *Profess. Psychol.: Res. Pract., 27*(3), 289–294.

Wing, L. (1976). *Early childhood autism.* Oxford, England: Pergamon Press.

Winick, B. J. (1983). Incompetency to stand trial: Developments in the law. In J. Monahan & H. J. Steadman (Eds.), *Mentally disordered offenders.* New York: Plenum Press.

Winick, B. J. (2001). The civil commitment hearing: Applying the law therapeutically. In L. E. Frost & R. J. Bonnie (Eds.), *The evolution of mental health law* (pp. 291–308). Washington, DC: APA.

Winick, B. J. (2002). The expanding scope of preventive law. *Florida Coastal Law Journal 189,* 3.

Wink, P. (1996). Narcissism. In C. G. Costello (Ed.), *Personality characteristics of the personality disordered.* New York: Wiley.

Winslade, W. J., & Ross, J. (1983). *The insanity plea.* New York: Scribner's.

Winston, A. S. (Ed.). (2004). *Defining difference: Race and racism in the history of psychology.* Washington, DC: American Psychological Association.

Winton, M. A. (2000). The medicalization of male sexual dysfunction: An analysis of sex therapy journals. *J. Sex Educ. Ther., 25*(4), 231–239.

Wiseman, C. V., Gray, J. J., Mosimann, J. E., & Ahrens, A. H. (1992). Cultural expectations of thinness in women: An update. *Inter. J. Eat. Disorders, 11*(1), 85–89.

Wisner, K. L., Perel, J. M., Peindl, K. S., Hanusa, B. H., Findling, R. L., & Rapport, D. (2001). Prevention of recurrent postpartum depression: A randomized clinical trial. *J. Clin. Psychiat., 62*(2), 82–86.

Wituk, S. A., Shepherd, M. D., Warren, M., & Meissen, G. (2002). Factors contributing to the survival of self-help groups. *Amer. J. Comm. Psych., 30*(3), 349–366.

Witztum, E., Maragalit, H., & Van-der-Hart, O. (2002). Combat-induced dissociative amnesia: Review and case example of generalized dissociative amnesia. *J. Traum. Stress, 3*(2), 35–55.

Wlazlo, Z., Schroeder-Hartwig, K., Hand, I., Kaiser, G., & Munchau, N. (1990). Exposure in vivo vs. social skills training for social phobia: Long term outcome and differential effects. *Behav. Res. Ther., 28,* 181–193.

Wolberg, L. R. (1967). *The technique of psychotherapy.* New York: Grune & Stratton.

Wolfe, D. A., Edwards, B., Manion, I., & Koverola, C. (1988). Early intervention for parents at risk for child abuse and neglect: A preliminary investigation. *J. Cons. Clin. Psychol., 56,* 40–47.

Wolfe, J. L., & Russianoff, P. (1997). Overcoming self-negation in women. *J. Rat.-Emot. & Cog.-Behav. Ther., 15*(1), 81–92.

Wolfe, S. M., Sasich, L. D., Hope, R.-E., & Public Citizen's Health Research Group. (1999). *Worst pills, best pills. A consumer's guide to avoiding drug-induced death or illness.* New York: Pocket Books.

Wolff, S. (1991). Schizoid personality in childhood and adult life I: The vagaries of diagnostic labeling. *Br. J. Psychiatry, 159,* 615–620.

Wolff, T. (2000). Practitioners' perspectives. In J. Rappaport & E. Seidman (Eds.), *Handbook of community psychology.* New York: Kluwer Academic/Plenum Publishers.

Wolpe, J. (1958). *Psychotherapy by reciprocal inhibition.* Stanford, CA: Stanford University Press.

Wolpe, J. (1969). *The practice of behavior therapy.* Oxford, England: Pergamon Press.

Wolpe, J. (1987). The promotion of scientific psychotherapy: A long voyage. In J. K. Zeig (Ed.), *The evolution of psychotherapy.* New York: Brunner/Mazel.

Wolpe, J. (1990). *The practice of behavior therapy* (4th ed.). Elmsford, NY: Pergamon Press.

Wolpe, J. (1995). Reciprocal inhibition: Major agent of behavior change. In W. T. O'Donohue & L. Krasner (Eds.), *Theories of behavior therapy: Exploring behavior change.* Washington, DC: APA.

Wolpe, J. (1997). From psychoanalytic to behavioral methods in anxiety disorders: A continuing evolution. In J. K. Zeig (Ed.), *The evolution of psychotherapy: The third conference*. New York: Brunner/Mazel.

Wolpe, J. (1997). Thirty years of behavior therapy. *Behav. Ther., 28*(4), 633–635.

Wong, M. L., & Licinio, J. (2001). Research and treatment approaches to depression. *Nature Reviews Neuroscience, 2*(5), 343–351.

Wong, Y., & Huang, Y. (2000). Obesity concerns, weight satisfaction and characteristics of female dieters: A study on female Taiwanese college students. *J. Amer. Coll. Nutr., 18*(2), 194–199.

Wood, J. M., Garb, H. N., Lilienfeld, S. O., & Nezworski, M. T. (2002). Clinical assessment. *Annu. Rev. Psychol., 53*, 519–543.

Woodside, D. B., Bulid, C. M., Halmi, K. A., Fichter, M. M., Kaplan, A., Berrettini, W. H., Strober, M., Treasure, J., Lilenfeld, L., Klump, K., & Kaye, W. H. (2002). Personality, perfectionism, and attitudes towards eating in parent of individuals with eating disorders. *Inter. J. Eat. Disorders, 31*(3), 290–299.

Woodside, M. R., & Legg, B. H. (1990). Patient advocacy: A mental health perspective. *J. Ment. Hlth. Couns., 12*(1), 38–50.

Woody, G. E., McLellan, A. T., Luborsky, L., & O'Brien, C. P. (1998). Psychotherapy with opioid-dependent patients. *Psychiatr. Times, XV*(11).

Wooley, S. C., & Wooley, O. W. (1985). Intensive outpatient and residential treatment for bulimia. In D. M. Garner & P. E. Garfinkel (Eds.), *Handbook of psychotherapy for anorexia nervosa and bulimia*. New York: Guilford Press.

Woolfolk, R. L. (2001). The concept of mental illness: An analysis of four pivotal issues. *J. Mind Behav., 22*(2), 161–178.

World Health Organization. (1948). World Health Organization constitution. In *Basic documents*. Geneva: Author.

Worthington, E. L., Jr., & Sandage, S. J. (2001). Religion and spirituality. *Psychother. Theory Res. Prac., 38*(4), 473–478.

Wozniak, J., Biederman, J., Faraone, S. V., Blier, H., & Monuteaux, M. C. (2001). Heterogeneity of childhood conduct disorder. Further evidence of a subtype of conduct disorder linked to bipolar disorder. *J. Affect. Disorders, 64* (2–3), 121–131.

Wren, B. (2002). "I can accept my child is transsexual but if I ever see him in a dress I'll hit him": Dilemmas in parenting a transgendered adolescent. *Clin. Child Psychol. Psychiat., 7*(3), 377–397.

Wright, J. (1984). EAP: An important supervisory tool. *Supervisory Management, 29*(12), 16–17.

Wright, N. R., & Thompson, C. (2002). Withdrawal from alcohol using monitored alcohol consumption: A case report. *Alcohol Alcoholism, 37*(4), 344–346.

Wu, J., Kramer, G. L., Kram, M., Steciuk, M., Crawford, I. L., & Petty, F. (1999). Serotonin and learned helplessness: A regional study of 5-HT-sub(1A), 5-HT-sub(2A) receptors and the serotonin transport site in rat brain. *J. Psychiatr. Res., 33*(1), 17–22.

Wuerker, A. K., Long, J. D., Haas, G. L., & Bellack, A. S. (2002). Interpersonal control, expressed emotion, and change in symptoms in families of persons with schizophrenia. *Schizo. Res., 58*(2–3), 281–292.

Wunderlich, U., Bronisch, T., & Wittchen, H. U. (1998). Comorbidity patterns in adolescents and young adults with suicide attempts. *Eur. Arch. Psychiat. Clin. Neurosci., 248*(2), 87–95.

Wurtele, S. K., & Schmitt, A. (1992). Child care workers' knowledge about reporting suspected child sexual abuse. *Child Abuse Negl., 16*(3) 385–390.

Wurtman, J. J. (1987). Disorders of food intake: Excessive carbohydrate snack intake among a class of obese people. *Annals of the New York Academy of Sciences, 499*, 197–202.

Yager, J. (1985). The outpatient treatment of bulimia. *Bull. Menninger Clin., 49*(3), 203–226.

Yalom, I. D. (1985). *The theory and practice of group psychotherapy* (3rd ed.). New York: Basic Books.

Yama, M., Fogas, B., Teegarden, L., & Hastings, B. (1993). Childhood sexual abuse and parental alcoholism: Interactive effects in adult women. *Amer. J. Orthopsychiat., 63*(2), 300–305.

Yarmey, A. D. (2004). Eyewitness recall and photo identification: a field experiment. *Psychol. Crime Law, 10*(1), 53–68.

Yen, S., Sr., Shea, M. T., Battle, C. L., Johnson, D. M., Zlotnick, C., Dolan-Sewell, R., Skodol, A. E., Grilo, C. M., Gunderson, J. G., Sanislow, C. A., Zanarini, M. C., Bender, D. S., Rettew, J. B., & McGlashan, T. H. (2002). Traumatic exposure and posttraumatic stress disorder in borderline, schizotypal, avoidant and obsessive-compulsive personality disorders: Findings from the Collaborative Longitudinal Personality Disorders Study. *J. Nerv. Ment. Dis., 190*(8), 510–518.

Yewchuk, C. (1999). Savant syndrome: Intuitive excellence amidst general deficit. *Dev. Disabil. Bull., 27*(1), 58–76.

Yin, S. (2002, May 1). Coming up short. *Amer. Demog.* Retrieved Sept. 15, 2002, from www.industryclick.com

Yoder, K. A., Hoyt, D. R., & Whitbeck, L. B. (1998). Suicidal behavior among homeless and runaway adolescents. *J. Youth Adolescence, 27*(6), 753–771.

Yolken, R. H., Karlsson, H., Yee, F., Johnston-Wilson, N. L., & Torrey, E. F. (2000). Endogenous retroviruses and schizophrenia. *Brain Res., 31*(2–3), 193–199.

Yoshimasu, K., Kiyohara, C., & Ohkuma, K. (2002). Efficacy of day care treatment against readmission in patients with schizophrenia: A comparison between out-patients with and without day care treatment. *Psychiat. Clin. Neurosci., 56*(4), 397–401.

Young, K. S. (1996). Cited in: middle-aged women are more at risk for Internet addiction. *APA Monitor, 27*(10), 10.

Young, K. S. (1996). Psychology of computer use: XL. Addictive use of the Internet: A case that breaks the stereotype. *Psychol. Rep., 79*(3, Pt 1), 899–902.

Young, K. S. (1998). Internet addiction: The emergence of a new clinical disorder. *CyberPsychol. Behav., 1*(3), 237–244.

Young, K. S. (1999). Evaluation and treatment of Internet addiction. In L. VandeCreek & T. L. Jackson (Eds.), *Innovations in clinical practice: A source book* (Vol. 17, pp. 19–31). Sarasota, FL: Professional Resource Press/Professional Resource Exchange.

Young, M., Benjamin, B., & Wallis, C. (1963). Mortality of widowers. *Lancet, 2*, 454–456.

Young, T. J. (1991). Suicide and homicide among Native Americans: Anomie or social learning? *Psychol. Rep., 68*(3, Pt. 2), 1137–1138.

Zaider, T. I., Johnson, J. G., & Cockell, S. J. (2002). Psychiatric disorders associated with the onset and persistence of bulimia nervosa and binge eating disorder during adolescence. *J. Youth Adolescence, 31*(5), 319–329.

Zakrzewski, R. F., & Hector, M. A. (2004). The lived experiences of alcohol addiction: Men of Alcoholics Anonymous. *Issues Ment. Hlth Nurs., 25*(1), 61–77.

Zal, H. M. (1999). Agitation in the elderly. *Psychiatr. Times, XVI*(1).

Zarin, D. A., Pincus, H. A., Peterson, B. D., West, J. C., Suarez, A. P., Marcus, S. C., & McIntyre, J. S. (1998). Characterizing psychiatry with findings from the 1996 national survey of psychiatric practice. *Amer. J. Psychiat., 155*(3), 397–404

Zec, R. F., Zellers, D., Belman, J., Miller, J., Matthews, J., Ferneau-Belman, D., & Robbs, R. (2001). Long-term consequences of severe closed-head injury on episodic memory. *J. Clin. Exp. Neuropsychol., 23*(5), 671–691.

Zec, R. F., Zellers, D., Belman, J., Miller, J., Matthews, J., Ferneau-Belman, D., & Robbs, R. (2002). "Long-term consequences of severe closed-head injury on episodic memory": Erratum. *J. Clin. Exp. Neuropsychol., 24*(1), 130.

Zerbe, K. J. (1990). Through the storm: Psychoanalytic theory in the psychotherapy of the anxiety disorders. *Bull. Menninger Clin., 54*(2), 171–183.

Zevenbergen, A. A., & Ferraro, F. R. (2001). Assessment and treatment of fetal alcohol syndrome in children and adolescents. *J. Dev. Phys. Disabil., 13* (2), 123–136.

Zhao, M., Hao, W., Yang, D., Zhang, Y., & Li, L. (2001). A prospective study of factors related to relapse in heroin addicts. *Chin. J. Clin. Psychol., 9*(2), 81–83, 89.

Zhou, J.-N., Hofman, M. A., Gooren, L. J. G., & Swaab, D. F. (1995). A sex difference in the human brain and its relation to transsexuality. *Nature, 378*, 68–70.

Zigman, W. B., Schupf, N., Sersen, E., & Silverman, W. (1995). Prevalence of dementia in adults with and without Down syndrome. *Amer. J. Ment. Retard., 100*(4), 403–412.

Zilboorg, G., & Henry, G. W. (1941). *A history of medical psychology*. New York: Norton.

Zito, J. M., Safer, D. J., dos Reis, S., Gardner, J. F., Boles, M., & Lynch, F. (2000). Trends in prescribing of psychotropic medications to preschoolers. *JAMA, 283*(8), 1025–1030.

Zivin, J. (2000, April). Understanding clinical trials. *Scientif. Amer.*, p. 69.

Zohar, J., & Pato, M. T. (1991). Diagnostic considerations. In M. T. Pato & J. Zohar (Eds.), *Current treatments of obsessive-compulsive disorder*. Washington, DC: American Psychiatric Press.

Zucker, K. J. (2000). Gender identity disorder. In A. J. Sameroff, M. Lewis et al. (Eds.), *Handbook of developmental psychopathology* (2nd ed., pp. 671–686). New York: Kluwer Academic/Plenum Press.

Zuckerman, M. (1996). Sensation seeking. In C. G. Costello (Ed.), *Personality characteristics of the personality disordered*. New York: Wiley.

Zuravin, S. J., & Fontanella, C. (1999). The relationship between child sexual abuse and major depression among low-income women: A function of growing up experiences? *Child Maltreat.: J. Amer. Profess. Soc. Abuse Child., 4*(1), 3–12.

Zygmunt, A., Olfson, M., Boyer, C. A., & Mechanic, D. (2002). Interventions to improve medication adherence in schizophrenia. *Amer. J. Psychiat., 159*(10), 1653–1664.

name index

subject index

Psychosomatic disorders. *See* Psychophysiological disorders
Psychosurgery, 36–37, 370b
  memory loss after, 484
  right to refuse, 484
Psychotropic drugs, 15. *See also specific types, e.g., Antidepressants*
  development of, 36f
  effectiveness of, 87–90, 89f
  marketing of, 200b
  psychologists' right to prescribe, 486–487
  right to refuse, 485
  studies of, 26b
  types of, 36
Pyromania, 401b

Quasi-experiment, 25
Quetiapine (Seroquel), 375

Race/ethnicity, 57
  alcohol abuse/dependence and, 283
  anxiety and, 97
  body image and, 263, 264–265, 264b–265b
  culture-sensitive therapy and, 58
  depression and, 194, 212
  eating disorders and, 263, 264b–265b
  needs of elderly and, 466–467, 467f
  schizophrenia and, 352
  sex offender statutes and, 478
  suicide and, 232, 233f, 243, 245
Racism, 57
Random assignment, 24
Rape victims. *See also* Sexual abuse
  stress disorders in, 138–139
Rap groups, 146
Rapid eye movement (REM) sleep, 452b
  erection during, 321
Rapid smoking, 290b
Rapprochement movement, 90
Rational-emotive therapy, 102–103, 104, 211
Rationalization, 39t
Rational suicide, 246b
Reaction formation, 39t
  in obsessive-compulsive disorder, 124
Reactive depression, 198
Receptors, for neurotransmitters, 34, 34f
Recessive genes, 442
Refrigerator mother
  autism and, 435
  schizophrenia and, 366–367
Regression, 39t
Relapse-prevention training
  for pedophilia, 342
  for substance abuse, 306–307
Relaxation training, 156–157, 158
  for generalized anxiety disorder, 106–107
  for phobias, 113
Reliability
  of DSM-IV classifications, 84–85, 386–387, 414–415
  of intelligence tests, 438–439
  interrater, 68
  test, 68
Religion, 53–54

REM sleep, 452b
  erection during, 321
Renaissance, psychologic theory and treatment in, 10–11
Repressed childhood memory of child abuse, 179b
Repression, 39t
  in dissociative disorders, 183–184
Repressive coping style, 151
Research. *See* Clinical research
Residential crisis center, 377
Residential programs, for mentally retarded, 443–444
Residential treatment centers, for substance abusers, 310
Resilience, 155
Resistance, 41
Response inventories, 75, 75t
Restricting-type anorexia nervosa, 254, 259f
Retrograde amnesia, 458b
Retrospective analysis, of suicide, 230–231
Reversal design, 27
Reverse anorexia nervosa, 260b
Reward center, 304
Reward-deficiency syndrome, 304
Rewards, in conditioning, 44
Right to refuse treatment, 484–486
Right to treatment, 483–484, 485
Risperidone (Risperdal), 375
Ritalin, for attention-deficit/hyperactivity disorder, 430, 430b–431b
Rituals, 121t, 122. *See also* Obsessive-compulsive disorder
Rivastigmine (Exelon), 463–464
Robinson v. California, 482–483
Rogers, Carl, 51–52, 55
Role disputes, depression and, 213
Role-playing, 53
Roles, societal, 57–58
Role transition, depression and, 213
Role transitions, stress and, 152, 153t
Rome, ancient, psychologic theory and treatment in, 8
Rorschach test, 72, 72f
Rosenthal effect, 25
Rubella, in pregnancy, mental retardation and, 443
Rumination, depression and, 215b
Rush, Benjamin, 11

Sadism, sexual, 343–344
St. Vitus dance, 8
La Salpetriêre, 11
Savants, 436b
Schizoid personality disorder, 387f, 389–391, 399t
Schizophrenia, 351–382
  abnormal brain structure in, 364
  adoption studies of, 361
  alogia in, 357–358
  avolition in, 358
  biochemical abnormalities in, 362–364
  biological views of, 361–366
  catatonia in, 358, 358t, 360
  cinematic depictions of, 356b–357b

  cognitive view of, 367
  community treatment for, 376–380
  course of, 358–359
  definition of, 351
  delusions in, 353–354
  diagnosis of, 359–360
  diagnostic criteria for, 359–360, 360t
  disordered thinking and speech in, 354–355, 357–358, 367
  dopamine hypothesis for, 363–364
  in elderly, 455
  expressed emotion and, 368, 375
  family dysfunction and, 367–368
  flat affect in, 358
  gender and, 351–352
  genetic factors in, 361, 361f, 362
  genetic linkage studies of, 362
  hallucinations in, 355–356
  heightened perceptions in, 355
  inappropriate affect in, 357
  living situations in, 377, 379–380, 379f
  maternal influence in, 366–367
  molecular biology studies of, 362
  paranoid, 360
  personality disorders and, 387–388
  poverty of speech in, 357–358
  prevalence of, 351
  psychodynamic view of, 366–367
  race/ethnicity and, 352
  residual, 360
  social labeling and, 367, 480b
  social withdrawal in, 358
  sociocultural views of, 367–368
  socioeconomic status and, 351, 352f
  substance abuse and, 377
  suicide and, 236–237, 236b
  symptoms of, 353–358
    negative, 357–358
    positive, 353–357
    psychomotor, 358
  treatment of, 368–381
    antipsychotic drugs in, 372–375
    community approach in, 376–380
    institutional, 369–372
    lobotomy in, 370b
    psychotherapy in, 375–376
  twin studies of, 361, 361f
  Type I, 360
  Type II, 360
  undifferentiated, 360
  viruses and, 35, 364–366
Schizophrenia-spectrum disorders, 387–388
Schizophrenogenic mother, 366–367
Schizotypal personality disorder, 387f, 391–393, 399t
School, state, 443
School phobia, 422
School problems
  attention-deficit/hyperactivity disorder and, 428–430, 430b
  learning disorders and, 434t, 439b
School psychologists, 18
School refusal, 422
School violence, 420t
  bullying and, 426b
Scientific method, 19

DSM-IV CLASSIFICATION*

Diagnostic and Statistical Manual of Mental Disorders, Fourth Edition, Washington, DC, American Psychiatric Association, 2000, 1994. Reprinted by permission.

(All categories are on Axis I except those indicated otherwise.)   *NOS= Not otherwise specified*

Disorders Usually First Diagnosed in Infancy, Childhood, or Adolescence

Mental Retardation

Note: These are coded on Axis II.
Mild mental retardation
Moderate mental retardation
Severe mental retardation
Profound mental retardation
Mental retardation, severity unspecified

Learning Disorders

Reading disorder
Mathematics disorder
Disorder of written expression
Learning disorder NOS

Motor Skills Disorder

Developmental coordination disorder

Communication Disorders

Expressive language disorder
Mixed receptive-expressive language disorder
Phonological disorder
Stuttering
Communication disorder NOS

Pervasive Developmental Disorders

Autistic disorder
Rett's disorder
Childhood disintegrative disorder
Asperger's disorder
Pervasive development disorder NOS

Attention-Deficit and Disruptive Behavior Disorders

Attention-deficit/hyperactivity disorder
    Combined type
    Predominantly inattentive type
    Predominantly hyperactive-impulsive type
Attention-deficit/hyperactivity disorder NOS
Conduct disorder
Oppositional defiant disorder
Disruptive behavior disorder NOS

Feeding and Eating Disorders of Infancy or Early Childhood

Pica
Rumination disorder
Feeding disorder of infancy or early childhood

---

* In 2000 the APA published the *DSM-IV Text Revision (DSM-IV-TR)*. That publication updated background information for each disorder (for example, culture and gender trends); it did not change the DSM-IV categories themselves nor their diagnostic criteria (with but a very few exceptions). Thus DSM-IV technically remains the current edition of the DSM, although some authors prefer to cite DSM-IV-TR.

Tic Disorders

Tourette's disorder
Chronic motor or vocal tic disorder
Transient tic disorder
Tic disorder NOS

Elimination Disorders

Encopresis
    With constipation and overflow incontinence
    Without constipation and overflow incontinence
Enuresis (not due to a general medical condition)

Other Disorders of Infancy, Childhood, or Adolescence

Separation anxiety disorder
Selective mutism
Reactive attachment disorder of infancy or early childhood
Stereotypic movement disorder
Disorder of infancy, childhood, or adolescence NOS

Delirium, Dementia, and Amnestic and Other Cognitive Disorders

Delirium

Delirium due to . . . *(indicate the general medical condition)*
Substance intoxication delirium
Substance withdrawal delirium
Delirium due to multiple etiologies
Delirium NOS

Dementia

Dementia of the Alzheimer's type, with early onset
Dementia of the Alzheimer's type, with late onset
Vascular dementia

Dementia Due to Other General Medical Conditions

Dementia due to HIV disease
Dementia due to head trauma
Dementia due to Parkinson's disease
Dementia due to Huntington's disease
Dementia due to Pick's disease
Dementia due to Creutzfeldt-Jakob disease
Dementia due to . . . *(indicate the general medical condition not listed above)*
Substance-induced persisting dementia
Dementia due to multiple etiologies
Dementia NOS

Amnestic Disorders

Amnestic disorders due to . . . *(indicate the general medical condition)*
Substance-induced persisting amnestic disorder
Amnestic disorder NOS

Other Cognitive Disorders

Cognitive disorder NOS

Mental Disorders Due to a General Medical Condition Not Elsewhere Classified

Catatonic disorder due to . . . *(indicate the general medical condition)*
Personality change due to . . . *(indicate the general medical condition)*
Mental disorder NOS due to . . . *(indicate the general medical condition)*

Substance-Related Disorders

[Alcohol; Amphetamine; Caffeine; Cannabis; Cocaine; Hallucinogen; Inhalant; Nicotine; Opioid; Phencyclidine; Sedative, Hypnotic, or Anxiolytic; Polysubstance; Other]

Substance Use Disorders

Substance dependence
Substance abuse

Substance-Induced Disorders

Substance intoxication
Substance withdrawal
Substance intoxication delirium
Substance withdrawal delirium
Substance-induced persisting dementia
Substance-induced persisting amnestic disorder
Substance-induced psychotic disorder
Substance-induced mood disorder
Substance-induced anxiety disorder
Substance-induced sexual dysfunction
Substance-induced sleep disorder
Substance-related disorder NOS

Schizophrenia and Other Psychotic Disorders

Schizophrenia
    Paranoid type
    Disorganized type
    Catatonic type
    Undifferentiated type
    Residual type
Schizophreniform disorder
Schizoaffective disorder
Delusional disorder
Brief psychotic disorder
Shared psychotic disorder
Psychotic disorder due to . . . *(indicate the general medical condition)*
Substance-induced psychotic disorder
Psychotic disorder NOS

Mood Disorders

Depressive Disorders

Major depressive disorder
Dysthymic disorder
Depressive disorder NOS

Bipolar Disorders

Bipolar I disorder
Bipolar II disorder
Cyclothymic disorder
Bipolar disorder NOS
Mood disorder due to . . . *(indicate the general medical condition)*
Substance-induced mood disorder
Mood disorder NOS

Anxiety Disorders

Panic disorder without agoraphobia
Panic disorder with agoraphobia
Agoraphobia without history of panic disorder
Specific phobia